Critical acclaim for

OPERATIONS MANAGEMENT
SECOND EDITION

The revised version of this text adds to the high quality of the original. The book is the first of its kind to invite students at all levels into the operational working of a business. The invitation is provided through introducing the purpose of study alongside the illustrations of real issues. It thus reveals the need for the analysis leading on to the concepts which structure the working of businesses of all types. Readers of the book will at last engage naturally with the operations functions which previously remained outside their interest and influence.

ALASTAIR NICHOLSON
Professor of Operations Management, London Business School

An exciting book which distinguishes itself through the way it combines an outside-in market orientation and bottom-up process perspective. It has never been so easy for me to select a book for undergraduate, MBA, post-experience and in-company courses on operations management and strategy. As far as I am concerned, by far the best text currently available on the subject – theoretically robust, wide range of questions and exercises, really global in its use of examples and cases. The first edition made me jealous, the second one is even better.

DR HARRY BOER
School of Management Studies, University of Twente, The Netherlands

A terrific textbook! It succeeds in presenting an integrated picture whilst comprehensively explaining the many different aspects of operations management. The theory is blended with a range of interesting and stimulating practical applications from around the world.

DR GEOFF BUXEY
School of Management, Deakin University, Australia

With this second edition, this textbook establishes itself as the leading introductory text on operations management. It takes the student along a pedagogically well designed route of the role of operations, design of the system, planning and controlling activities, developing the system and relating operations to the strategies of the organization. It is both conceptually well structured and empirically anchored. It encompasses both manufacturing and services. It is simply the best text I know of for students in economics and business management.

CHRISTER KARLSSON
Professor of Industrial Production, Stockholm School of Economics

OPERATIONS MANAGEMENT

SECOND EDITION

NIGEL SLACK

STUART CHAMBERS

CHRISTINE HARLAND

ALAN HARRISON

ROBERT JOHNSTON

FINANCIAL TIMES
PITMAN PUBLISHING

FINANCIAL TIMES

MANAGEMENT

LONDON · SAN FRANCISCO
KUALA LUMPUR · JOHANNESBURG

*Financial Times Management delivers the knowledge,
skills and understanding that enable students,
managers and organisations to achieve their ambitions,
whatever their needs, wherever they are.*

London Office:
128 Long Acre, London WC2E 9AN
Tel: +44 (0)171 447 2000
Fax: +44 (0)171 240 5771
Website: www.ftmanagement.com

A Division of Financial Times Professional Limited

———————————

First published in Great Britain in 1995
Second edition published in 1998

© Nigel Slack, Stuart Chambers, Christine Harland,
Alan Harrison, Robert Johnston 1995, 1998

The right of Nigel Slack, Stuart Chambers, Christine
Harland, Alan Harrison and Robert Johnston to be identified
as Authors of this Work has been asserted by them in accordance
with the Copyright, Designs and Patents Act 1988.

ISBN 0 273 62688 4

British Library Cataloguing in Publication Data
A CIP catalogue record for this book can be obtained from the British Library

3 5 7 9 10 8 6 4 2

Typeset by Pantek Arts, Maidstone, Kent.
Printed and bound in Great Britain by William Clowes Ltd, Beccles

*The Publishers' policy is to use paper manufactured
from sustainable forests.*

CONTENTS

v

PREFACE

Introduction

Operations management gets as close as we can in business life to the act of creation. It is concerned with *creating* the products and services upon which we all depend. Since this is the very reason for any organization's existence, operations management should be at the heart of its affairs. No student of organizational or business life should, therefore, be without an understanding of the role, objectives and activities of operations management, at the very least. It is, after all, operations managers who hold the key to either satisfying or disappointing the customers upon whom the whole organization depends, a fact which is well understood by most senior managers. For example, one survey of chief executive officers[1] shows 43 per cent of them citing operations as the most important area of employee know-how (followed by sales and marketing at 29 per cent, technology at 17 per cent and finance at 6 per cent). But, as those who read this book shall see, all managers, irrespective of their job title, create products and services for (often internal) customers. In that sense, *all managers are operations managers*.

The aim of this book

The aim of this book is to provide a clear, well structured and interesting treatment of operations management as it applies to a variety of businesses and organizations. The text is intended to provide both a logical path through the activities of operations management and an understanding of their strategic context.

[1] Hall, R. (1992) 'The Strategic Analysis of Intangible Resources', *The Strategic Management Journal*, Vol 13, p 142.

More specifically this text aims to be:

● *Strategic* in its perspective of operations management's contribution to the organization's long-term success. We are unambiguous in treating the operations function as being central to competitiveness.

● *Conceptual* in the way it explains the reasons why operations managers need to take decisions. Although some quantitative techniques are included, their primary aim is to illustrate the underlying principles of operations decisions.

● *Comprehensive* in its coverage of the significant ideas and issues which are relevant to most types of operation.

● *Practical* in that the issues and difficulties in making operations management decisions *in practice* are discussed. Generally, the treatment reflects actual operations practice, illustrated in the case exercises and 'boxes' which explore the approaches taken by actual companies.

● *International* in the examples which are used. Out of over 110 descriptions of operations practice, around a third are from continental Europe, a third from the UK and a third general or from elsewhere in the world.

● *Balanced* in its treatment. This means we treat service operations with the same level of seriousness as manufacturing operations and, where possible, we have included both a service and a manufacturing example to illustrate a point.

Who should use this book?

This book is intended to provide an introduction to operations management for all students who wish to understand the nature and activities of operations management; for example:

● *Undergraduates* on business studies, technical or joint degrees should find it sufficiently structured to provide an understandable route through the subject (no prior knowledge of the area is assumed).

● *MBA students* should find that its practical discussions of operations management activities enhance their own experience.

● *Postgraduate students* on other specialist masters degrees should find that it provides them with a well-grounded and, at times, critical approach to the subject.

Distinctive features

● *Clear structure*
We have chosen to base the structure of this book on the most common model of operations management by distinguishing between design, planning and control. But we have supported the modern view of operations which sees the separation of planning activities from control activities as inappropriate. Most significantly, we have separated out the improvement activities of operations to reflect the importance of continually improving the performance of operations. Furthermore, we both start and finish the book by treating the strategic aspects of the subject.

● *Illustrations based*
Operations management is a subject which should be based on practice, it cannot be taught satisfactorily in a purely theoretical manner. For this reason we have frequently used abstracted examples to illustrate points of theory. The words 'for example' occur often and we make no apology for this. In addition, the boxed examples explain the issues faced by real operations managers in real companies.

● *Personal profiles*
Again, reflecting the practical orientation of our treatment of the subject, we include at the end of each chapter a personal profile. These are verbatim comments (together with some background information) from interviews with practising operations managers in a variety of operations.

● *Summary answers to key questions*
Each chapter is summarized in the form of a list of bullet points. These extract the essential points which answer the key questions posed at the beginning of each chapter.

● *Case exercises*
Every chapter includes a case exercise which is a short case study suitable for class discussion. The cases are usually short enough to serve as illustrations, which can be referred to in class, but have sufficient content to serve as the basis for seminar-style case sessions.

● *Selected further readings*
Every chapter ends with a list of further readings which either take the topics covered in the chapter further, or treat some important issues related to those covered in the chapter.

● *Instructor's Manual*
An Instructor's Manual is available to lecturers adopting this textbook. It includes short commentaries to each chapter which can be used as student handouts, as well as selected OHP masters, which are also available on a PowerPoint disk.

● *Web site*
A range of support materials is available to lecturers and students on the Financial Times Pitman Publishing website at http://www.ftmanagement.com. This site is up-dated regularly.

New for the Second Edition

The first edition was a phenomenal success (for which we thank everyone who helped us make it one!), so we have not made any *radical* changes to structure, coverage or treatment for the second edition. However, we have received some helpful comments which have been incorporated, and there are other changes which are summarized below.

● Some changes reflect our intention to remain topical, for example, the treatment of business processes is extended.

● Some material has been repositioned; for example, the process of operations strategy formulation has been moved into the operations strategy chapter (Chapter 3).

● The key questions in the Part introductions have been developed and now also form the objectives for each chapter and the headings for the chapter summaries.

● Many of the popular boxed examples have been updated, adapted, or are totally new.

● All boxed examples now have discussion questions to help their use in teaching.

● There are 32 full-colour pages which have been used to provide further illustrated examples; these also have discussion questions.

ABOUT THE AUTHORS

Nigel Slack is the A E Higgs Professor of Manufacturing Policy and Strategy at Warwick University. Previously he was Professor of Manufacturing Strategy and Lucas Professor of Manufacturing Systems Engineering at Brunel University, University Lecturer in Management Studies at Oxford University and Fellow in Operations Management at Templeton College, Oxford.

He worked initially as an industrial apprentice in the hand-tool industry and then as a production engineer and production manager in light engineering. He holds a Bachelor's degree in Engineering and Master's and Doctor's degrees in Management. He is also a chartered engineer. He is the author of several publications in the operations management area, including *The Manufacturing Advantage*, published by Mercury Business Books, 1991, and *Making Management Decisions* (with Steve Cooke) now in its second edition, 1991, published by Prentice Hall, and more recently, *Service Superiority* (with Robert Johnston), published in 1993 by EUROMA and *Cases in Operations Management* (with Robert Johnston, Alan Harrison, Stuart Chambers and Christine Harland) second edition published by Financial Times Pitman Publishing in 1997. His research is in the operations and manufacturing flexibility and operations strategy areas.

Stuart Chambers has been a lecturer at Warwick Business School since 1988. He began his career as an undergraduate apprentice at Rolls Royce Aerospace, graduating in mechanical engineering, and then worked in production and general management with companies including Tube Investments and the Marley Tile Company. In his mid-thirties and seeking a career change, he studied for an MBA, and then took up a three-year contract as a researcher in manufacturing strategy. This work enabled him to help

executives develop the analyses, concepts and practical solutions required for them to develop manufacturing strategies. Several of the case studies prepared from this work have been published in an American textbook on manufacturing strategy.

In addition to lecturing on a range of operations courses at the Business School and in industry, Stuart is continuing his research in the manufacturing strategy field. His research interests also include service quality management in leisure and catering businesses. He undertakes consultancy in a diverse range of industries and is co-author of several operations management books.

Christine Harland is Senior Research Fellow in Strategic Purchasing and Supply at the University of Bath. Her specialist area is supply chain management which includes an interest in purchasing and supply management, logistics, materials management and operations planning and control.

Qualified in purchasing and supply, production and inventory control and with a first degree in business, Christine worked in industry as a buyer, production planner, inventory manager and materials manager for manufacturing companies including the Dowty Group and GEC Telecommunications.

Her research and consultancy is in operations strategy and supply chain management which she has undertaken in various industries including automotive, aerospace, electronics, textiles, food, paper, utilities and public sector administration.

Alan Harrison is Exel Fellow in Automotive Logistics at Cranfield School of Management. His industrial career included posts with Procter & Gamble, BL and GEC – where he was head of manufacturing of two product companies. His research interests focus on the application of Japanese methods and he is working with Exel

Logistics on the flow of materials in different operations environments. Alan has written two books – *How to Make Japanese Management Methods Work in the West* (with Kazuo Murata) and *Just-in-Time Manufacturing in Perspective* – and numerous papers and articles. He also lectures and consults with a number of companies, both in the UK and internationally.

Robert Johnston is Reader in Production/ Operations Management at Warwick Business School and a specialist in service operations. Before moving to academia in 1980, he held several line management and senior management posts in a number of service organizations in both the public and private sectors. He continues to maintain close and active links with many large and small organizations through his research, training and consultancy activities. His main research interests are performance measurement, service quality and operations strategy. He is the author or co-author of many books, as well as chapters in other texts, numerous papers and case studies, and three computer-based simulations. He is an Associate Chair of Warwick Business School and editor of the *International Journal of Service Industry Management.*

INSTRUCTOR'S MANUAL

Andy Neely, BEng, PhD, AMIEE, FRSA, is Lecturer in the Department of Engineering and the Judge Institute of Management at the University of Cambridge. He has taught at a variety of institutions, including Cambridge, Nottingham and Leicester Business Schools, and has also worked in the aerospace industry. His research interests are performance measurement and manufacturing strategy.

FOREWORD

by Rupert Gasser

Executive Vice President, Nestlé S.A.

It is always a pleasure, and satisfying to introduce a book which is serious and of high quality. The text by Nigel Slack and his team on *Operations Management* meets both these criteria, certainly as I measure it against the reality of the largest food company in the world – Nestlé.

Nestlé's network of functions is orchestrated and managed across the entire globe, the final objective of which is to get products to the consumer on time, at reasonable cost, giving good value for money. It is not only the size of Nestlé, with business operations in about 500 factories all over the world and its diversity of products, which is impressive, but also its rate of growth. It has doubled its turnover about every decade. There are on average about six factories or distribution centres under construction at any one time. Its R&D operation supplies new products and technology innovation; Marketing, Sales and Distribution operations bring high quality products to consumers of the industrialized world, as well as to villages in the tropical forests of South America and Africa. Optimization of the effectiveness of these functions, in all their complexity, is the responsibility of our Operations Managers. Their key responsibilities are, of course, to help maintain or improve our competitive edge, to apply consistently and systematically the experience and lessons learned each day in the running of the operation, to maximize the return on our assets, to help effectively to introduce new technologies, to integrate and to drive costs out of the supply chains. It is the Operations Manager's direct responsibility to involve and motivate people and to get the best potential out of them. The Operations Manager continuously has to fight waste and, more importantly, ensure that we maintain our consistently high level of quality. We are right at the heart of any large company when we talk about operations, therefore it is crucial for all managers – and all aspiring managers – to understand the importance and the contribution of operations management.

Operations Management reflects this admirably. Its emphasis on the central contribution which Operations Managers play in ensuring competitiveness is exactly the message which all students of management should grasp. Also, its international perspective shows how the subject is relevant to all types of operations in all parts of the world.

Nigel Slack and his team have written a lively and interesting text on what I believe to be a valuable subject. I am convinced that this book will contribute to operations management being taken seriously by all of tomorrow's managers.

RUPERT GASSER
EXECUTIVE VICE PRESIDENT, NESTLÉ S.A.

ACKNOWLEDGEMENTS
FOR THE SECOND EDITION

Again, in preparing the second edition of this book, the authors unashamedly exploited their friends and 'picked the brains' of their colleagues. We express our gratitude to all who helped us in the original and this edition, especially, Professor Sven Åke Hörte of Lulea University of Technology, Colin Armistead of Bournemouth University, David Barnes of Thames Valley University, David Bennett of Aston University, Ruth Boaden of the University of Manchester Institute of Science and Technology, Peter Burcher of Aston University, Geoff Buxey of Deakin University, Philippa Collins of Heriot-Watt University, Henrique Correa of Saõ Paulo University, Doug Davies of University of Technology, Sydney, Job de Haan of Tilburg University, David Evans of Middlesex University, Paul Forrester of Keele University, Ian Graham of Edinburgh University, Alan Harle of Sunderland University, Norma Harrison of Macquarie University, Catherine Hart of Loughborough Business School, Chris Hillam of Sunderland University, Ian Holden of Bristol Business School, Tom Kegan of Bell College of Technology, Hamilton, Peter Long of Sheffield Hallam University, John Maguire of the University of Sutherland, Charles Marais of the University of Pretoria, Harvey Maylor of Cardiff University, Jane McLean of Brighton University, John Meredith Smith of EAP, Oxford, Keith Moreton of Staffordshire University, Adrian Morris of Sunderland University, Andy Neely of Cambridge University, Alastair Nicholson of London Business School, Peter Race of Brunel University, Ian Sadler of Victoria University, Amrik Sohal of Monash University, Alex Skedd of Northumbria Business School, Martin Spring of UMIST, Roy Staughton of University of Bath, R Stratton of Nottingham Trent University, Mike Sweeney of Cranfield University, Dr Nelson Tang of the University of Leicester, Helen Valentine of the University of the West of England, Professor Roland van Dierdonck of DeVlerick School voor Management, University of Ghent, and Dr Dirk Pieter van Donk of the University of Groningen.

Our academic colleagues in the Operations Management Group at Warwick Business School also helped, both by contributing ideas and by creating a lively and stimulating work environment. Our thanks go to Hilary Bates, Simon Croom, Mike Lewis, Mike Shulver, Rhian Silvestro and Paul Walley.

The flesh on the theoretical bones of the book comes courtesy of all our industrial contacts, those managers who kindly agreed to be interviewed as subjects of our personal profiles and those companies who co-operated in providing examples. Special thanks go to Marc Palacio Balmer of Torres Wines, Barbara Fairclough of Jaeger, David Garman of Allied Bakeries, Terry King of CV Clothing, Hans Mayer of Nestlé, Peter Norris of NatWest Bank, Bill Shardlow of Coats Viyella and Dick Van Hoepen of Nestlé.

During the writing of the first edition we were assisted, kept cheerful and encouraged by Fiona Rennie (now of City Bank). We still remember her contributions with affection. Mary Walton is secretary to our group at Warwick Business School. Her continuing efforts at keeping us organized (or as organized as we are capable of being) are always appreciated, but never more so than when we were engaged on 'the book'. Yet again we had the benefit of the very professional team at Financial Times Pitman Publishing. Our appreciation and respects go to all the Financial Times Pitman Publishing staff with our special thanks to Penelope Woolf, Annette McFadyen, Colin Reed, Mike Rogers and Stuart Hay (now at Routledge).

Finally, every word of the first edition, and all the new material in the second edition was word-processed by Angela Slack. She typed and retyped several versions of both manuscripts, made sense of our writing, spelling, eccentric word-processing styles and creative punctuation. It was, again, an heroic effort, which she undertook with (relatively) little complaint. To Angela – our thanks.

HOW TO USE THIS BOOK

All academic textbooks in business management are, to some extent, simplifications of the messy reality which is actual organizational life. Any book has to separate topics, in order to study them, which in reality are closely related. For example, technology choice impacts on job design which in turn impacts on quality control; yet we have treated these topics individually. The first hint therefore in using this book effectively is to *look out for all the links between the individual topics*. Similarly with the sequence of topics, although the chapters follow a logical structure, they need not be studied in this order. With the exceptions of Chapters 1, 4, 10 and 18 which form introductions to each part of the book, every chapter is, more or less, self-contained. Therefore study the chapters in whatever sequence is appropriate to your course or your individual interests. But because each part has an introductory chapter, those students who wish to start with a brief 'overview' of the subject may wish first to study Chapters 1, 4, 10 and 18 and the chapter summaries of selected chapters. The same applies to revision – *study the introductory chapters and summary answers to key questions*.

The book makes full use of the many practical examples and illustrations which can be found in all operations. Many of these were provided by our contacts in companies, but many also come from journals, magazines and newspapers. So if you want to understand the importance of opera-tions management in everyday business life *look for examples and illustrations of operations management decisions and activities in newspapers and magazines*. There are also examples which you can observe every day. Whenever you use a shop, eat a meal in a restaurant, borrow a book from the library or ride on public transport, *consider the operations management issues of all the operations for which you are a customer*.

The case exercises and discussion questions are there to provide an opportunity for you to think further about the ideas discussed in the chapters. Discussion questions should be used to test out your understanding of the specific points and issues discussed in the chapter. *If you cannot answer these you should revisit the relevant parts of the chapter*. The case exercises at the end of each chapter will require some more thought. *Use the questions at the end of each case exercise to guide you through the logic of analysing the issue treated in the case*. When you have done this individually *try to discuss your analysis with other course members*. Most important of all, every time you analyse one of the case exercises (or any other case or example in operations management) start off your analysis with the two fundamental questions:

● how is this organization trying to compete (or satisfy its strategic objectives if a not-for-profit organization)?, and,
● what can the operation do to help the organization compete more effectively?

PLAN OF THE BOOK

PART ONE – INTRODUCTION

Chapter 1 Operations management	**Chapter 2** The strategic role and objectives of operations	**Chapter 3** Operations strategy

PART TWO – DESIGN

Chapter 4 Design in operations management	**Chapter 5** The design of products and services	**Chapter 6** Design of the operations network
Chapter 7 Layout and flow	**Chapter 8** Process technology	**Chapter 9** Job design and work organization

PART THREE – PLANNING AND CONTROL

Chapter 10 The nature of planning and control	**Chapter 11** Capacity planning and control	**Chapter 12** Inventory planning and control
Chapter 13 Supply chain planning and control	**Chapter 14** MRP	**Chapter 15** Just-in-time planning and control

Chapter 16 Project planning and control	**Chapter 17** Quality planning and control

PART FOUR – IMPROVEMENT

Chapter 18 Operations improvement	**Chapter 19** Failure prevention and recovery	**Chapter 20** Total quality management

PART FIVE – THE OPERATIONS CHALLENGE

Chapter 21 The operations challenge

PART ONE

INTRODUCTION

This part of the book introduces the idea of the operations function in different types of organization. It identifies the common set of objectives to which operations managers aspire in order to serve their customers, and it explains how operations strategy influences the activities of operations managers.

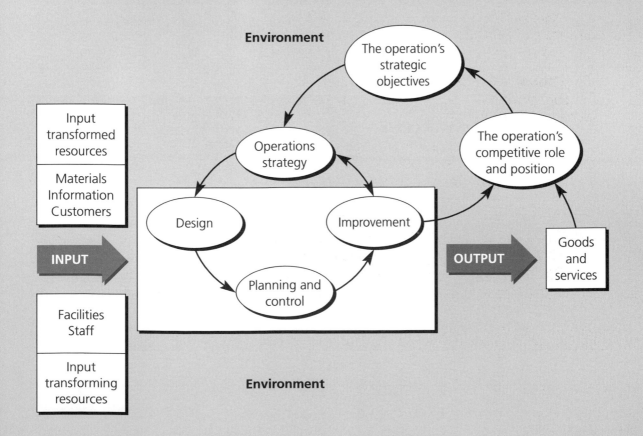

Chapter 1
OPERATIONS MANAGEMENT

- *What is operations management?*
- *What are the similarities between all operations?*
- *How are operations different from each other?*
- *What do operations managers do?*

Chapter 2
THE STRATEGIC ROLE AND OBJECTIVES OF OPERATIONS

- *What role should the operations function play in achieving strategic success?*
- *What are the performance objectives of operations and what are the internal and external benefits which derive from excelling in each of them?*

Chapter 3
OPERATIONS STRATEGY

- *What is an operations strategy?*
- *How does operations strategy fit into a company's overall strategy?*
- *How do we know which performance objectives are the most important?*
- *What are the specific decision areas which are usually included in an operations strategy?*
- *How can an operations strategy be put together?*

OPERATIONS MANAGEMENT

INTRODUCTION

Operations management is about the way organizations produce goods and services. Everything you wear, eat, sit on, use, read or knock about on the sports field comes to you courtesy of the operations managers who organized its production. Every book you borrow from the library, every treatment you receive at the hospital, every service you expect in the shops and every lecture you attend at university – all have been produced. While the people who supervised their 'production' may not always be called operations managers, that is what they really are. And that is what this book is concerned with – the tasks, issues and decisions of those operations managers who have made the services and products on which we all depend. In this introductory chapter we will examine the overall nature of operations management and the activities of operations managers. The model which is developed to explain the subject is shown in Fig. 1.1.

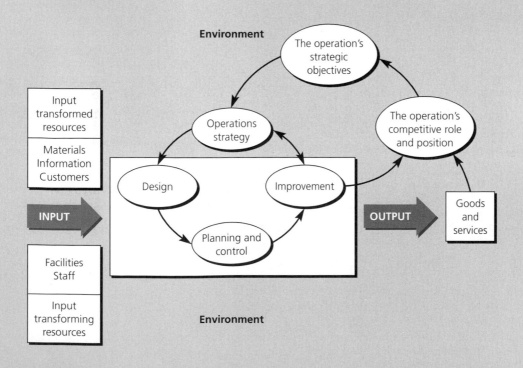

Figure 1.1 A general model of operations management

3

CHAPTER 1: KEY QUESTIONS

- *What is operations management?*
- *What are the similarities between all operations?*
- *How are operations different from each other?*
- *What do operations managers do?*

EFFECTIVE OPERATIONS MANAGEMENT

Operations management is, above all else, a practical subject which deals with real issues. So let us start our examination of the subject with a practical example of an organization which is known for the originality of its operations.

IKEA[1]

IKEA is a furniture retailer with a difference. With around 100 giant stores operating in over 15 countries world-wide it has managed to develop its own special way of selling furniture. IKEA customers typically spend between one-and-a-half and two hours in the store – far longer than in rival furniture retailers. An important reason for this is the way it organizes its stores – all of which are the same in most important respects all around the world. The design and philosophy of its store operations go back to the original business which was started in southern Sweden by Ingvar Kamprad in the 1950s. At that time Mr Kamprad was successfully selling furniture, through a catalogue operation. In response to customer requests to be able to see some of his furniture, he built a showroom in Stockholm, not in the centre of the city where land was expensive, but on the outskirts of town. Instead of buying expensive display stands, he simply set the furniture out more or less as it would be in a domestic setting. Also, instead of moving the furniture from the warehouse to the showroom area, he asked customers to pick the furniture up themselves from the warehouse. This 'anti-service' approach to service, as it has been described, is the foundation of IKEA's stores today.

IKEA's furniture is 'value for money' with a wide range of choice. It is usually designed to be stored and sold as a 'flat pack' but is capable of easy assembly by the customer. The stores are all designed around the same self-service concept – that finding the store, parking, moving through the store itself, and ordering and picking up goods should be simple, smooth and problem-free. At the entrance to each store are large notice-boards which proclaim IKEA's philosophy and provide advice to shoppers who have not used the store before. Catalogues are also available at this point showing illustrations, dimensions and the available range of the store's products. Perhaps most significantly for shoppers with young children, there is also a supervised children's play area, a small cinema, a parent and baby room and toilets. Parents can leave their children in the supervised play area for a limited period of time. Each child is attired in a yellow, numbered top while he or she is in this area and parents are recalled via the loudspeaker system if the child has any problems. Customers may also borrow pushchairs to keep their children with them as they move round the store.

Some parts of the showroom are set out in 'room settings' while others show, for example, all beds together, so that customers can make comparisons. Customers are not approached by staff offering help or advice. The IKEA philosophy is not to 'hassle' customers in this way but rather to let them make up their minds in their own time. If a customer does want advice, there are information points around the showroom where staff, in their bright red uniforms, can help and guide customers, provide measuring rules, paper for sketching and so on. Every piece of furniture carries a ticket which indicates its dimensions, price, materials used, country of origin and the other colours in which it is available. It also has a code number which indicates the location in the warehouse from where it can be collected. The tickets on larger items ask customers to go to the information desks for assistance. After viewing the showroom, customers pass into the 'free-service' area where smaller items are displayed on shelves. These can be picked directly off the display shelves by customers and put into yellow shoulder bags or trolleys. Customers then pass through the self-service warehouse where they can pick up the items they viewed in the showroom. Finally, the customers pay at the check-outs, each of which is constructed with a ramped conveyor belt which moves the customer's purchases up to the check-out staff member and along to the exit area. At the exit area there are information and service points, and often a 'Swedish Shop' with Swedish food-stuffs. A large loading area allows customers to bring their cars from the car park and load their purchases. Any customers who have bought more than their car will carry can rent or buy a roof rack.

Nor is IKEA's innovative approach to its business confined only to the physical layout and design of its stores; it also extends to its management style and philosophy. All employees in the store wear either red or grey sweatshirts which distinguish customer-contact and non-contact staff. ■

Questions

1 How is the IKEA operations design different from that of most furniture retail operations? Use the four dimensions of operations (volume, variety, variation and customer contact) to characterize these differences (*see* pp. 25–32 for further information on these topics).

2 What do you think might be the major problems in running an operation like IKEA?

3 What do you identify as the 'operations function' within IKEA? How is this different from the marketing function? (*See* pp. 7–9 for further information on this topic.)

So why is IKEA able to survive and succeed? It certainly keeps a very tight control of its costs, and it also understands its market and how it can serve the needs of its customers. Furthermore, the products it designs and sells must be regarded by its customers as representing outstanding value for money. At least as important as all these, however, is the way it organizes the delivery of its services within its stores. This is the responsibility of the company's operations management. The staff in the store, the staff who liaise with suppliers, the staff who store and transport goods to the stores and the staff who design, plan, control and constantly improve the way things are done, the buildings, the computers and check-outs, the warehouses and the transportation system – all are engaged in *operations management*. IKEA owes its success, in no small measure, to the effectiveness of its operations management, who provide:

- a smooth customer flow;
- a clean, well-designed environment;
- sufficient goods to satisfy demand;
- sufficient staff to serve customers and stock the warehouse;
- an appropriate quality of service;
- a continuous stream of ideas to improve its, already impressive, operations performance.

Without these, the company, no matter how well it marketed and financed its activities, would not be the success it is.

Now is the point to establish some definitions.

- The *operations function* of the organization is the arrangement of resources which is devoted to the production of its goods and services. Every organization has an operations function because every organization produces some type of goods and/or services. However, not all types of organization will necessarily call the operations function by this name, as we will discuss later.

  Note that we also use the shorter terms 'the operation' or 'operations' and, at times, the 'operations system' interchangeably with the 'operations function'.
- *Operations managers* are the staff of the organization who have particular responsibility for managing some, or all, of the resources which comprise the operations function. Again in some organizations the operations manager could be called by some other name. For example, he or she might be called the 'fleet manager' in a distribution company, or the 'administrative manager' in a hospital, or the 'store manager' in a supermarket.
- *Operations management* is the term which is used for the activities, decisions and responsibilities of operations managers.

As we have seen in the case of IKEA, if the operations function is to be effective it must use its resources efficiently and produce goods and services in a way that satisfies its customers. In addition, it must be creative, innovative and energetic in introducing novel and improved ways of producing goods and services (*see* the box on Swatch, for example). If the operation can do these things it will provide the organization with the means to survive in the long term because it gives the organization a competitive advantage over its commercial rivals. An alternative way of putting this in a not-for-profit organization is that an effective operation gives the means to fulfil the organization's long-term strategic goals.

SWATCH REVOLUTIONIZES WATCH MANUFACTURE[2]

In the early 1980s the Swiss watch industry was nearly dead. Competition from cheap but often high-quality products from Far Eastern manufacturers such as Seiko and Casio had almost obliterated the traditional Swiss industry. Trying to protect their investments, the Swiss banks organized a merger of the two largest companies on the advice of Nicolas Hayek, now Chairman and Chief Executive of Swatch's parent company SMH formed from the merger. He saw the potential of a new plastic-cased watch which was already being developed inside one of the companies. One of its major advantages was that it could be made in high volume at very low cost. The quartz mechanism was built directly into the all-plastic case and the number of components in the watch had been cut to just 51; this was less than half the number in most other watches. Fewer components also meant that the manufacture of the watch could be fully automated. This made Swatches cheap to produce even in Switzerland, which has one of the highest labour costs in the world.

The innovative design, some creative marketing, but above all else the operation's success at producing the watch cheaper than anyone else brought the company significant rewards. In the early 1980s the total market share for all Swiss watches was around 25 per cent; ten years later it had more than doubled. The ability to offer a good watch at a low price had released the potential of the watch to become a fashion accessory – a trend which meant that the company's operations reaped the benefits of high volume but had to cope with an ever-increasing variety of product designs. Through automation and rigid standardization of the internal mechanism of the watch, the company managed this increase in variety without it crippling its costs. It is the success of the company's operations managers in keeping their costs low (direct labour cost is now less than seven per cent of the total cost of production) that has allowed Swatch to succeed. Not that everything the company has done has been successful. Some designs never caught the public imagination and some distribution and marketing mistakes were made, especially in the United States. However, continuing innovation, high quality and low cost makes it much easier to overcome such problems. ∎

Questions

1 What do you think has been the contribution of the marketing function, the product design function and the operations function to the success of Swatch?

2 How do you think Swatch compares with most watch manufacturers? (Again, use the four dimensions of operations to help you do this – *see* page 25 onwards.)

OPERATIONS IN THE ORGANIZATION

The operations function is central to the organization because it produces the goods and services which are its reason for existing, but it is neither the only, nor necessarily the most important, function. All organizations have other functions with their own part to play. Yet organizations do differ in the way they define their functional areas and the boundaries between them. Here we divide the organization into three other *major functions*:

- the marketing function
- the accounting and finance function
- the product/service development function

and *support functions*, which supply and support the operations function, including:

Table 1.1 The activities of functions in some organizations

Typical functional activities	Church	Fast food chain	University	Furniture manufacturer
Marketing	Call on newcomers Proselytize	Advertise on TV Devise promotional materials	Develop brochures Mail out brochures Attend shows	Advertise in magazines Determine pricing policy Sell to stores
Accounting and finance	Count contributions Manage appeals Pay rents Pay bills	Pay suppliers Collect takings Pay staff	Pay faculty and support staff Monitor expenditure Collect fees	Pay staff Pay suppliers Prepare budgets Manage cash
Product/service development	Search for meaning of existence Retranslate scriptures	Design hamburgers, pizzas, etc. Design decor for restaurants	Develop new courses Design research programmes	Design new furniture Co-ordinate with fashionable colours
Operations	Conduct weddings Conduct funerals Conduct services Save souls	Make burgers, pizzas, etc. Serve customers Clear away Maintain equipment	Communicate knowledge Conduct research Administer courses	Make components Assemble furniture
Personnel	Train priests Appraise priestly performance	Train staff Devise remuneration schemes	Train staff Manage contracts Appraise performance	Recruit staff Train staff
Purchasing	Buy consumables Develop vestment supplies	Buy foodstuff Buy plates, cartons, napkins, etc.	Buy equipment Buy consumables	Buy raw materials, wood, etc. Buy fabric
Engineering/ technical	Maintain church buildings, etc.	Develop or purchase equipment, ovens, etc. Install equipment, ovens, etc.	Purchase audiovisual equipment Maintain equipment and facilities	Develop or purchase woodworking machines Maintain machines

Source: Adapted from Heizer and Render[3]

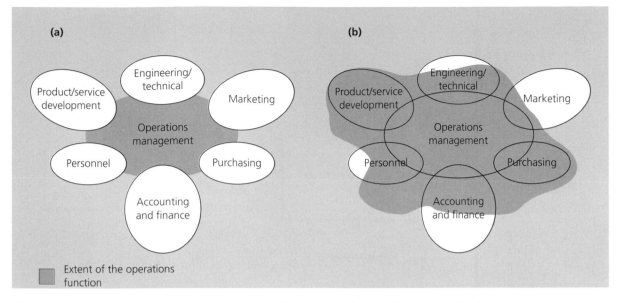

Figure 1.2 **The boundaries of the operations function: (a) a narrow definition, (b) a broad definition**

- the human resources function
- the purchasing function
- the engineering/technical function.

Table 1.1 shows the activities of these functions for a sample of operations.

It is important to stress, however, that functional names, boundaries and responsibilities vary between organizations – a complication which is particularly true of the operations function. This leads to some confusion over where the boundaries of the operations function should be. For example, a narrow definition of the operations function's boundaries would exclude all activities shared with any other functions. At the other extreme, a very broad definition of operations would include all activities which had any connection with the production of goods and services – in practice every activity with the exception of the core marketing/selling and accounting/finance activities. Figure 1.2 illustrates how the functional boundary of operations management would differ with narrow and broad definitions.

In this book we incline towards a relatively broad definition of operations. We treat much of the product/service development activities, most of the engineering/technical and purchasing activities and some of the personnel, marketing, and accounting and finance activities as coming within the sphere of operations management. However, we do not set out to take the place of more detailed texts in these areas.

THE TRANSFORMATION PROCESS MODEL

All operations produce goods or services or a mixture of the two, and they do this by a *process of transformation*. By transformation we mean that they use their *resources* to

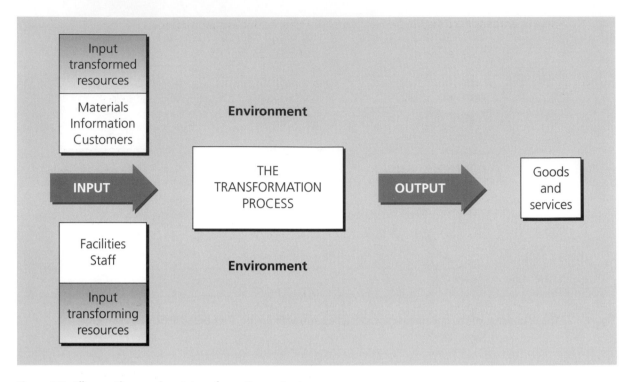

Figure 1.3 All operations are input–transformation–output processes

change the state or condition of something to produce *outputs*. Figure 1.3 shows this general *transformation model* which is used to describe the nature of operations. Put simply, operations take in a set of input resources, use them either to transform something, or to be transformed themselves, into outputs of goods and services.

All operations conform to this general input–transformation–output model. For example, hospitals have inputs of doctors, nurses and other medical staff, administrators, cleaning staff, beds, medical equipment, pharmaceuticals, blood, dressings, and so on. Their purpose is to transform sick patients into healthy patients. The outputs from the operation are treated patients, medical test results, medical research and 'best practice' medical procedures. Table 1.2 shows that one can describe a wide range of operations in this way. However, there are differences between different operations. If you stand far enough away from, say, a hospital or a motor vehicle plant, they might look the same. Each is likely to be a large building into which staff enter and deliveries take place. But move closer and clear differences do start to emerge. For a start, one is a manufacturing operation producing largely physical goods, and one is a service operation which produces changes in the physiological condition, feelings and behaviour of patients. The nature of the processes which each building contains will also be different. The motor vehicle plant contains metal cutting and forming machinery and assembly processes, whereas the hospital contains diagnostic, care and therapeutic processes. Perhaps the most important difference between the two operations, however, is the nature of their inputs. Both have 'staff' and 'facilities' as inputs to the operation but they act upon very different things. The motor vehicle plant uses its staff and facilities to *transform steel, plastic, cloth, tyres and other materials*. They make them into vehicles

Table 1.2 Some operations described in terms of input–transformation–output processes

Operation	Input resources	Transformation process	Outputs

Airline	Aircraft
	Pilots and aircrew
	Groundcrew
	Passengers and freight
		Move passengers and
		  freight around the world
			Transported passengers
			  and freight

Department store	Goods for sale Staff sales Computerized registers Customers	Display goods Give sales advice Sell goods	Customers and goods assembled together
Dentist	Dental surgeons Dental equipment Nurses Patients	Check and treat teeth Give preventative advice	Patients with healthy teeth and gums
Zoo	Zoo keepers Animals Simulated environments Customers	Display animals Educate customers Breed animals	Entertained customers Informed customers Non-extinct species
Printer	Printers and designers Printing presses Paper, ink, etc.	Design Print Bind	Designed and printed material

Police	Police officers
	Computer systems
	Information
	Public (law-abiding
	  and criminals)
		Prevent crime
		Solve crime
		Apprehend criminals
			Lawful society
			Public with feeling of
			  security

Frozen food
  manufacturer
	Fresh food
	Operators
	Food-processing
	  equipment
	Freezers
		Food preparation
		Freeze
			Frozen food

which are eventually delivered to customers. The staff and technology in the hospital, on the other hand, *transform the customers themselves*. The patients form part of the input to the operation – it is they who are being 'processed'. This has important implications for how the operation needs to be managed.

Inputs to the transformation process

The inputs to an operation can be conveniently classified as either:

● *transformed resources* – the resources that are treated, transformed or converted in some way; or
● *transforming resources* – the resources that act upon the transformed resources.

Transformed resources

The transformed resources which operations take in are usually a mixture of:

- materials;
- information; and
- customers.

Often one of these is dominant in an operation. For example, a bank devotes part of its energies to producing printed statements of accounts for its customers. In doing so, it is processing materials and acting as a printer, but no one would claim that a bank and a printer are the same type of operation. The bank also processes customers. It gives them advice regarding their financial affairs, cashes their cheques, deposits their cash, and has direct contact with them. However, most of the bank's activities are concerned with processing information about its customers' financial affairs. As customers, we may be unhappy with badly printed statements and we may be more unhappy if we are not treated appropriately in the bank. If the bank makes errors in our financial transactions, however, we suffer in a far more fundamental way. This is not to say that materials processing or customer processing is unimportant to the bank. On the contrary, it must be good at these things to keep its customers happy. Error-free, fast and efficient *information processing* though is the central objective of the bank.

It is the same with other types of operation. Take, for example, a company which manufactures the high-speed machinery used for packaging food products. Some of the company's operation will be devoted to processing the technical requirements of its customers. The operation will also need to 'process' the customers by visiting their factories, by bringing the customers to the factory to see the progress being made on the equipment, by working with the customers during its installation and finally, by educating the customers in the use of the equipment. Yet although the operation will process both information and people, its main task is *materials processing* to make the equipment itself.

Finally, a hospital will process information in the form of patients' medical records. It will also devote some of its resources to processing materials, for example in the way it produces meals for patients. The main operations task of a hospital, however, is to process customers in a way which satisfies its patients, maximizes their health care and minimizes its costs. It is predominantly a *customer processing* operation.

Table 1.3 gives examples of operations with their dominant transformed resources.

Transforming resources

There are two types which form the 'building blocks' of all operations:

- *facilities* – the buildings, equipment, plant and process technology of the operation;
- *staff* – those who operate, maintain, plan and manage the operation. (Note we use the term 'staff' to describe all the people in the operation, at any level.)

Of course the exact nature of both facilities and staff will differ between operations. To a five-star hotel, its facilities consist mainly of buildings, furniture and fittings. To a nuclear-powered aircraft carrier, its facilities are the nuclear generator, turbines, and sophisticated electronic detection equipment. One operation has relatively 'low-technology' facilities and one 'high-technology' facilities, but both are important to the operation concerned. A five-star hotel would be just as ineffective with worn and broken furniture as an aircraft carrier would be with inoperative electronics.

Table 1.3 Dominant transformed materials of various operations

Predominantly materials processors	Predominantly information processors	Predominantly customer processors
All manufacturing operations	Accountants	Hairdressers
Mining and extraction companies	Bank headquarters	Hotels
Retail operations	Market research company	Hospitals
Warehouses	Financial analysts	Mass rapid transports
Postal services	News service	Theatres
Container shipping line	University research unit	Theme parks
Trucking companies	Archives	Dentists
	Telecoms company	

The nature of staff will also differ between operations. The majority of staff employed in a factory assembling domestic refrigerators do not need a particularly high level of technical skill. In contrast, the majority of staff employed by an accounting company are likely to be highly skilled in their own particular 'technical' skill (accounting). Although the extent and nature of the skills needed by staff will vary, however, they all have a contribution to make to the effectiveness of their operation. An assembly worker who consistently misassembles refrigerators will dissatisfy customers and increase costs just as surely as an accountant who cannot add up. Table 1.4 shows the transforming resources to be found in some operations.

Table 1.4 The facilities and staff transforming resources of three operations

	Ferry company	Paper manufacturer	Radio station
Types of facilities	Ships On-board navigation equipment Dry docks Materials-handling equipment On-shore buildings Computerized reservation systems Warehouses	Pulp-making vats Paper-making machines Reeling equipment Slitting equipment Packing machinery Steam-generating boilers Warehouses	Broadcasting equipment Studios and studio equipment Transmitters Outside broadcast vehicles
Types of staff	Sailors Engineers Catering staff On-board shop assistants Cleaners Maintenance staff Ticketing staff	Operators Chemists and chemical engineers Process plant engineers	Disc jockeys Announcers Technicians

The transformation process

The purpose of the transformation process in operations is closely connected with the nature of its transformed input resources.

Materials processing

Operations which process materials could do so to transform their *physical properties* (such as physical shape, or composition or characteristics). Most manufacturing operations are like this. Other operations which process materials do so to change their *location* (parcel delivery companies, for example). Some, like retail operations, do so to change the *possession* or ownership of the materials. Finally, some materials-processing operations do so primarily to *store* or *accommodate* them, such as a warehouse.

Information processing

Operations which process information could do so to transform their *informational properties* (that is the purpose or form of the information); accountants do this. Some change the *possession* of the information, for example market research companies. Some *store* or *accommodate* the information, for example archives and libraries. Finally, some operations change the *location* of the information, such as telecommunication companies.

Customer processing

Operations which process customers might also transform them in a variety of ways. Some change their *physical properties* in a similar way to materials processors: for example, hairdressers or even cosmetic surgeons. Some customer-processing operations *store* (or more politely) *accommodate* them: hotels, for example. Airlines, mass rapid transport systems and bus companies transform the *location* of their customers. Some are concerned with transforming the *physiological state* of their customers, such as hospitals. Finally, some customer-processing operations are concerned with transforming the *psychological state* of their customers, for example most entertainment services such as music, theatre, television, radio and theme parks. Table 1.5 summarizes these various types of transformation processes.

Outputs from the transformation process

The outputs from (and purpose of) the transformation process are goods and services, which are generally seen as being different, for several reasons.

Tangibility

Goods are usually *tangible:* for example you can physically touch a television set or a newspaper. Services are usually *intangible*. You cannot touch consultancy advice or a haircut (although you can often see or feel the results of these services).

Table 1.5 Different types of transformation processes

	Physical properties	Informational properties	Possession	Location	Storage/ Accommodation	Physiological state	Psychological state
Materials processors	All manufacturing operations Mining and extraction		Retail operations	Postal services Freight distribution Port operations	Warehouses		
Information processors		Bank HQs Accountants Architects	Financial analysts Market research companies Universities Consultants News services	Telecoms company	Library Archives		
Customer processors	Hairdressers Plastic surgeons			Public transport Taxis	Hotels	Hospitals Other health care	Education Psychoanalysts Theatres Theme parks

Storability

Partly because of their tangibility, goods can also be *stored,* at least for a short time after their production. Services, on the other hand, are usually *non-storable:* for example, the service of 'accommodation in an hotel room for tonight' will perish if it is not sold before tonight – accommodation in the same room tomorrow is a different output from the service.

Transportability

Another consequence of tangibility is the ability to *transport* goods. Automobiles, machine tools and video cameras can all be moved. However, if services are intangible, they are *untransportable.* Health services, for example, cannot be exported as such (though the means of producing health services can).

Simultaneity

The other main distinction between goods and services concerns the timing of their production. Goods are nearly always *produced prior* to the customer receiving (or even seeing) them. For example, the CD you just bought was produced well before you bought it. Services, however, are often *produced simultaneously* with their consumption. The service which the shop provided in selling you the CD happened at the same time as you 'consumed' the service by buying it.

Customer contact

The implication of this is that customers have a *low contact* level with the operations which produce goods. Although you probably will have bought and consumed bread for most of your life, you have probably never seen the inside of a bakery. Whereas in services, because they are produced and consumed simultaneously, they must have *high contact* between the customer and the operation.

Quality

Finally, because generally customers do not see the production of goods, they will judge the quality of the operation which produced them on the evidence of the goods themselves. Even if we disagree as to the quality of our new personal computer, we can measure its capabilities in a reasonably objective manner. But in services the customer judges not only the outcome of the service, but also the aspects of the way in which it was produced. For example, in purchasing a new pair of shoes you might be perfectly satisfied that the shoes were in stock and that you were promptly served. Yet if the shop assistant was discourteous, you would not consider the service to be of a high quality. Other customers, on the other hand, might be less sensitive than you in judging the service.

Most operations produce both goods and services

Some operations produce just goods and some produce just services, but most operations produce a mixture of the two. Figure 1.4 shows a number of operations positioned in a spectrum from 'pure' goods producers to 'pure' service producers.

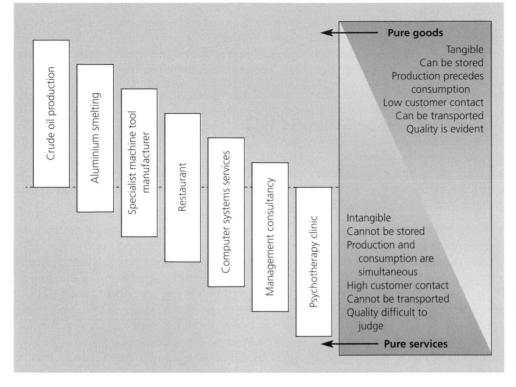

Figure 1.4
The output from most types of operation is a mixture of goods and services

Crude oil producers are concerned almost exclusively with the product which comes from their oil wells. Other 'commodity-like' goods producers, such as aluminium smelters for example, are again largely concerned with the production of products. However, they might also produce some services such as technical advice. Services produced in these circumstances are called *facilitating services*. They are there just to facilitate the sale of the products they support. Machine tool manufacturers are similar insomuch as they too primarily produce goods. To an even greater extent though they also produce facilitating services such as technical advice, applications engineering services and training. The services produced by a restaurant, however, are more than 'facilitating'. They are an essential part of what the customer is paying for. The restaurant is both a manufacturing operation which produces food products and a provider of service in the advice, ambience and service of the food. A computer systems services company will also produce products, for example software products, but primarily it is likely to see itself as providing a service to its customers, with *facilitating goods*. Certainly, a management consultancy, although it produces reports and documents, would see itself as a service provider which uses facilitating goods. Finally, some pure services do not produce products at all. A psychotherapy clinic, for example, provides therapeutic treatment for its customers without any facilitating goods.

The process hierarchy

The transformation process model can also be used within operations. Look inside most operations and they will be made up of several units or departments, which themselves act as smaller versions of the whole operation of which they form a part.

For example, a television programme and video production company has inputs of production, technical and administrative staff, cameras, lighting, sound and recording equipment, studio space, props, video tape, and so on. It transforms these into finished programmes and promotional videos, etc. Within this overall operation, however, there are many smaller operations. For example, there will be, amongst others:

● workshops which manufacture the sets, scenery and props for the productions;
● marketing and sales staff who liaise with potential customers, test out programme ideas and give information and advice to programme makers;
● an engineering maintenance and repair department which cares for, modifies and designs technical equipment;
● production units which organize and shoot the programmes and videos;
● the finance and costing department which estimates the likely cost of future projects and controls operational budgets.

The whole television programme and video production operation could be termed a *macro operation*, while its departments could be termed *micro operations* (*see* Fig. 1.5). These micro operations have inputs, some of which will come from outside the macro operation but many of which will be supplied from other internal micro operations. Each micro operation will also produce outputs of goods and services for the benefit of customers. Again though, some of each micro operation's customers will be other micro operations. This concept of macro and micro operations can be extended further. Within each micro operation there might be sections or groups which also can be considered as operations in their own right. In this way any operations function can be considered as a *hierarchy of operations*.

Internal customer–internal supplier relationships

The terms *internal customer* and *internal supplier* can be used to describe micro operations which take outputs from, and give inputs to, any other micro operations. Thus we could model any operations function as a network of micro operations which are engaged in transforming materials, information, or customers (that is staff) for each other: each micro operation being at the same time both an internal supplier of goods and services and an internal customer for the other micro operation's goods and services.

We cannot treat *internal* customers and suppliers in exactly the same way as we do *external* customers and suppliers, however. External customers and suppliers usually operate in a free market. If an organization believes that in the long run it can get a better deal by purchasing goods and services from another supplier, it will do so. Similarly, the organization would not expect its customers to purchase its own goods and services unless it could in some way offer a better deal than its competitors. Internal customers and suppliers, however, cannot operate like this. They are not in a 'free market' and they usually cannot look outside either to purchase input resources or to sell their output goods and services (although some organizations are moving this way).

Provided we remember that there are differences between internal and external customers, the concept is a very useful one. First, it provides us with a model to analyse the internal activities of an operation. If the macro operation is not working as it should, we can trace the problem back along the internal network of customers and suppliers. Second, it is a useful reminder to all parts of the operation that, by treating their internal customers with the same degree of care that they exercise on their external customers, the effectiveness of the whole operation can be improved. This idea is one of the foundations of total quality management, which we cover in Chapter 20.

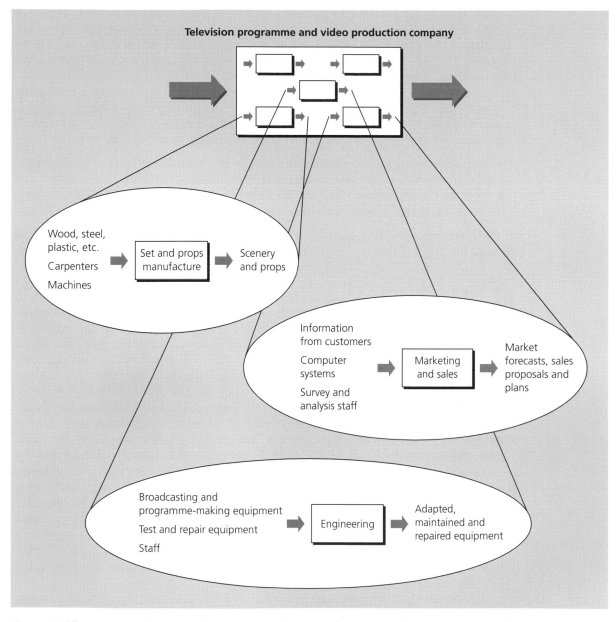

Figure 1.5 **All macro operations are made up of many micro operations**

All parts of the organization are operations

If micro operations act in a similar way to the macro operation, then many of the issues, methods and techniques which we treat in this book have some meaning for each unit, section, group or individual within the organization. For example, the marketing function of an organization can be viewed as a transformation process. It has inputs of market information, staff, computers, and so on. Its staff then transform the information into such outputs as marketing plans, advertising campaigns and sales force organizations. In other words, all functions can be viewed as operations

19

themselves. They are there to provide goods or (more usually) services to the other parts of the organization. Each function will have its 'technical' knowledge. In marketing, this is the expertise in designing and shaping marketing plans; in finance, it is the technical knowledge of financial reporting. Yet each will also have an operations role of producing plans, policies, reports and services.

The implications of this are important. It means that every manager in all parts of an organization is to some extent an operations manager. All managers need to organize their resource inputs effectively so as to produce goods and services. It also means that we must distinguish between two meanings of 'operations':

● *operations as a function*, meaning the part of the organization which produces the goods and services for the organization's external customers;
● *operations as an activity*, meaning any transformation of input resources in order to produce goods and services, for either internal or external customers.

The first meaning of 'operations' is the most commonly used, and the one we shall use in this book. It is always worth remembering the second usage of 'operations', however.

Business processes

Breaking a whole operation down into its constituent micro operations helps to demonstrate that operations management applies to all parts of the organization and helps us to focus on local improvement. But stand back from the macro operation and examine the *connections* between the micro operations. Each micro operation will contribute some part to 'producing' several of the products and services with which the organization attempts to satisfy the needs of its customers. For example, the television programme and video production company, described previously, might satisfy its customers' needs by 'producing' several products and services. Each of these, to different extents, involves the micro operations within the company. So, preparing quotations (estimates of the time and cost involved in potential projects) needs the contributions of the marketing and sales micro operation and the finance and costing micro operation more than the others. Providing technical support (which involves designing systems for, and advising, other media companies) mainly involves the engineering micro operation, but does also need some contribution from the others. Figure 1.6 illustrates the contribution of each micro operation to each product or service. No particular sequence is implied by Fig. 1.6. The contributions of each micro operation will not all occur in the same order. In fact the flow of information, materials or customers between micro operations might be complex, involving delays and recycling.

These collections of contributions from each micro operation which fulfil customer needs are called *business processes*. They address the core purposes of the organization and often cut across conventional organizational boundaries. Reorganizing (or 're-engineering') layouts and organizational responsibilities around these business processes is the philosophy behind business process re-engineering (BPR) which is discussed further in Chapter 18.

Buffering the operation

The turbulent environment in which most organizations do business means that the operations function is having to adjust continually to changing circumstances. Operations are vulnerable to 'environmental' uncertainty in both supply and demand.

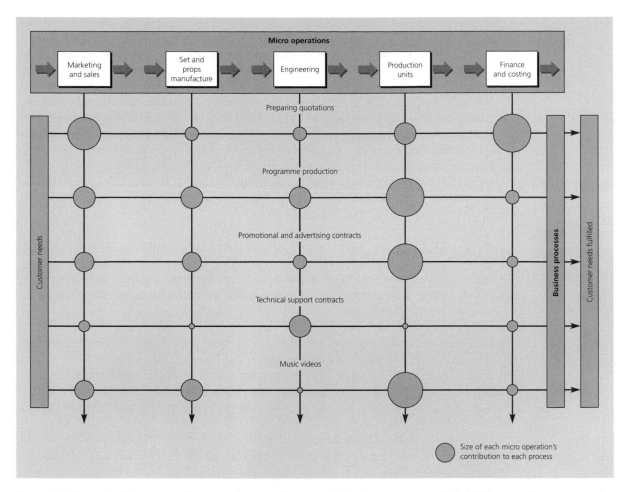

Figure 1.6 Example of how each micro operation contributes to the business processes which fulfill external customer needs

A food-processing operation might not be able to predict exactly when some foods will be harvested. In extreme cases, very bad weather might totally disrupt the supply to a factory for weeks. Demand could also be prone to disruption. Unpredictable changes in the weather, a 'health scare' story in the press, and so on, can all introduce turbulence. One way in which operations managers try to minimize 'environmental' disruption is by *buffering* or insulating the operations function from the external environment. It can be done in two ways:[4]

● *physical buffering* – designing an inventory or stock of resources either at the input side of the transformation process, or at the output side;
● *organizational buffering* – allocating the responsibilities of the various functions in the organization so that the operations function is protected from the external environment by other functions.

Physical buffering

One way of protecting the transformation process of the operation against unpredicted fluctuations in the quality or nature of input resources is to build up a store of the resources. Any interruptions to supply will (initially at least) be absorbed by the store (*see* Fig. 1.7). The operation is storing its input transformed resources before it 'transforms' them. The point here is that operations often do not *need* to store input resources. The reason they do it is that their activities are much more orderly (and therefore usually cheaper) if they can use the 'buffer stocks' to protect themselves.

Similarly, buffering can be applied at the output end of the transformation process. A manufacturer could make its products and put them into a finished goods inventory. Output stocks, however, are not usually relevant to people-processing operations because customers enter the operation as an input. They have usually been processed and the service completed by the time they emerge. Again, operations do not necessarily need to have output stocks; they could react to each customer's request as it was made. Yet if they are able to stock their output, the operation is given much more stability under conditions of demand uncertainty.

Organizational buffering

In many organizations the responsibility for acquiring the inputs to the operation and distributing its outputs to customers is not given to the operations function. For example, the people who staff the operation are recruited and trained by the personnel function; the process technology for the operation is probably selected and commissioned by a technical function; the materials, parts, services and other bought-in resources are acquired through a purchasing function; and the orders from customers which trigger the operation into activity will come through the marketing function. The other functions of the organization are, in effect, forming a barrier or buffer between the uncertainties of the environment and the operations function (*see* Fig. 1.8.)

These relationships have developed partly for stability. Stability is important because it allows the operation to organize itself for maximum efficiency. Organizational buffering, it is also claimed, allows the other functions to specialize in their own particular tasks and leave the operations function to get on with the job of producing goods and services.

Figure 1.7 Physical buffering can be used to protect the operation against environmental uncertainty

Input buffer		Output buffer
E.g. Physical inventories of raw materials and components	**Material processors**	E.g. Physical inventories of finished goods
E.g. Databases in national and local government	**Information processors**	E.g. On-line subscriber services of financial data
E.g. Queues and waiting lists at hospitals	**Customer processors**	Not applicable

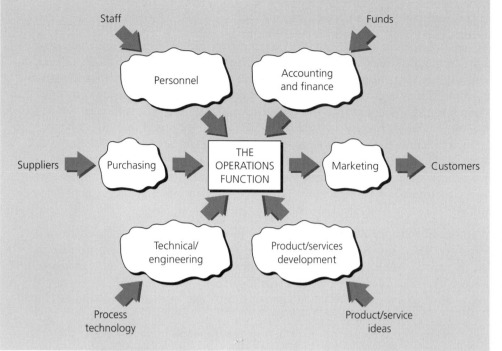

Figure 1.8
The other functions in the organization can buffer the operations core of the organization against environmental uncertainty

The disadvantages of buffering the operation

The whole concept of buffering the operations function is not without its critics, especially in recent years, and partly due to the influence of Japanese operations practice.[5]

A number of objections to buffering can be made:

● The time lag of communicating between the insulating function and the operations function makes change difficult. By the time the insulating function has responded, operations has 'moved on to the next problem'.
● Operations never develops the understanding of the environment (e.g. labour or technological markets) which would help it exploit new developments (not true for companies such as Body Shop (*see* the box overleaf)).
● Operations is never required to take responsibility for its actions. There is always another function to blame and unhelpful conflict may arise between functions.
● Physical buffering often involves tolerating large stocks of input or output resources. These are both expensive (*see* Chapter 12, Inventory planning and control) and prevent the operation improving (*see* Chapter 15, Just-in-time planning and control).
● Physical buffering in customer-processing operations means making the customer wait for service, which in turn could lead to customer dissatisfaction.

For all of these reasons, there has been, in general and in most types of operation, a move towards exposing the operations function to its environment. Operations, in order to cope with this, has needed to develop the necessary flexibility to respond to, and understand, what is really happening with its customers and suppliers.

GREEN OPERATIONS AT BODY SHOP[6]

The Body Shop formulates and manufactures skin- and hair-care products, but perhaps it is best known for its highly successful shops which brim with brightly coloured lotions, soaps, shampoos and oils. It is also renowned for its positive approach to environmentally conscious operations. The company has led the field in green operations by using only minimal and simple packaging, encouraging the recycling and refilling of containers, by not testing products on animals, by using natural materials wherever possible, and by having explicit social policies. Although not without its critics, Body Shop argues that it wanted to prove that it is possible to develop a profitable business and at the same time maintain a respect for the environment, the communities where its operations have an impact, its employees, and its customers. This philosophy affects its operations management policies in a number of ways:

● *Socially responsible purchasing.* At one time wooden foot rollers were purchased from a company in Frankfurt. The company now sources them from a workshop which it set up in an Indian village to provide employment and training for the older children in an orphanage. Ignoring the lower costs, the company paid the same price to the workshop, the revenue being used to help the village to improve its education, health and nutritional standards. Six similar workshops have now been established in India.

● *Using renewable sources.* The company took a lead in encouraging a Nepalese paper factory to switch from clearing the local forest for its raw materials to using renewable sources such as banana skins.

● *Social location.* The company bought an abandoned factory in a deprived area of Glasgow and converted it into a soap factory which now makes over 25 million bars sold throughout the world. As well as bringing much needed employment to the area, a quarter of the profit is returned for community projects.

● *Re-using.* The company provides a refill service in all its shops where empty plastic bottles can be refilled in return for a reduction on the purchase price. Over two million bottles are refilled every year in the UK alone.

● *Recycling waste.* Most synthetic polymers which can be recycled need to be sorted prior to recycling. The company has a standard labelling scheme which identifies the type of plastic used on each of its packages. This makes the sorting process, and therefore recycling, easier. ■

Questions

1 How do you think Body Shop's environmental policy relates to its overall business strategy?

2 What do you think are the dilemmas posed by the decisions described above for the company's operations managers?

TYPES OF OPERATIONS

We have already noted that operations are all similar to each other in the way they all transform input resources into output goods and services. We now examine some of the differences between operations.

There are four particularly important characteristics which can be used to distinguish between different operations:

- the *volume* of their output;
- the *variety* of their output;
- the *variation* in the demand for their output;
- the *degree of customer contact* which is involved in producing the output.

The volume dimension

Let us take a familiar example – the production and sale of the internationally ubiquitous hamburger. The epitome of high-volume hamburger production is McDonald's, which serves over 25 million burgers around the world every day! This is high volume, even when it is divided by its around 21 000 branches world-wide. The volume of burgers produced and served by McDonald's has important implications for the way its operations are organized. Look behind the counter in a high-volume burger bar and the first thing you notice is the *repeatability* of the tasks people are doing. Because tasks are repeated frequently it makes sense to *specialize* the tasks: one person assigned to cooking the burgers, another assembling the buns, another serving, and so on. And when tasks are divided in this way it also allows the *systemization* of the work. In fact large fast-food chains nearly always have standard procedures, set down in a manual, with instructions on how each part of the job should be carried out. Systemization can also lead to higher *capital intensity* of the operation, for example the development of specialized fryers and ovens. The most important implication of high volume, though, is that it gives *low unit costs*; the fixed costs of the operation, such as heating and rent, are spread over a large number of products or services.

Compare a small local cafeteria serving a few 'short order' dishes with the multinational burger chain. The range of items on the menu is likely to be similar to the larger operation, but the volume will be far lower. Here the degree of repetition will be far lower because of the lower volume. Furthermore, the number of staff will be lower (possibly only one person) and, therefore, the amount of the whole job of making and serving the food which each staff member performs will be greater. This may be more rewarding for the staff, but less open to systemization. Fewer burgers cooked also makes it less feasible to invest in specialized equipment. For all of these reasons it follows that the cost per burger served is likely to be higher (even if the price is comparable).

The variety dimension

A taxi company offers a high-variety service. It may confine its services to the transportation of people and their luggage, but it is prepared to pick you up from almost anywhere and drop you almost anywhere. It may even (at a price) take you by a route of your choice. In order to do this it must be relatively *flexible*. It must make sure that

THE HENRY FORD OF OPHTHALMOLOGY[7]

High-volume operations can be found in some surprising places – even surgery. Not all surgery conforms to our preconceptions of the individual 'super-craftsperson', aided by his or her back-up team, performing the whole operation from first incision to final stitch. Many surgical procedures are, in fact, fairly routine. There can be few examples, however, of surgery being made quite as routine as in the Russian clinics of eye surgeon, Svyatoslav Fyodorov.

He has been called the 'Henry Ford of Ophthalmology', and his methods are indeed closer to the automobile assembly plant than the conventional operating theatre. The surgical procedure in which he specializes is a revolutionary treatment for myopia (short-sightedness) called radial keratotomy. In the treatment the curvature of the cornea is corrected surgically – still a controversial procedure among some in the profession, but very successful for Fyodorov. From his Moscow headquarters he controls nine clinics throughout Russia.

The source of his fame is not the treatment as such – other eye surgeons around the world perform similar procedures – but the way he organizes the business of the surgery itself. Eight patients lie on moving tables arranged like the spokes of a wheel around its central axis, only their eyes uncovered. Six surgeons, each with his or her 'station', are positioned around the rim of the wheel so that they can access the patients' eyes. After the surgeons have completed their own particular portion of the whole procedure, the wheel indexes round to take patients to the next stage of their treatment. The surgeons check to make sure that the previous stage of the operation was performed correctly and then go on to perform their own task. Each surgeon's activity is monitored on TV screens overhead and the surgeons talk with each other through miniature microphones and headsets.

The result of this mass production approach to surgery according to Fyodorov is not only far cheaper unit costs (he and his staff are paid for each patient treated, so they are all exceptionally wealthy as a result) but also a better success rate than that obtained in conventional surgery. ■

Questions

1 Compare this approach to eye surgery with a more conventional approach.

2 What do you think are the advantages and disadvantages of this approach to eye surgery?

its drivers have a good knowledge of the area and that the communication between its base and the taxis is effective. The task of keeping track of all its customers' requests and the status of all its taxis can be complex, partly because of the variety of pick-up and drop-off points and routes 'live' at any one time. However, the variety on offer by the service does allow it to match its services closely to its customers' needs. Flexibility, however, does come at a price. The cost per kilometre travelled will be higher for a taxi than for a lower-variety, less-customized form of transport such as a bus service.

There are similarities between a bus service and a taxi service. Both serve, more or less, the same customers with the same needs by providing transport over relatively short distances (say, less than 20 km). Yet in some ways their operations are very dissimilar. This is largely due to the difference in the variety of services they offer.

Whereas the taxi service has in theory an infinite number of routes to offer its customers, the bus service has a few, well-defined routes. The buses travel these routes according to a set schedule, published well in advance and adhered to in a routine manner. If all goes to schedule, little, if any, flexibility is required from the operation. All is *standardized* and *regular*. More significantly, the lack of change and disruption in the day-to-day running of the operation results in relatively low costs compared with using a taxi for the same journey.

The variation dimension

Consider the demand pattern for a successful summer holiday resort hotel. Not surprisingly, more customers want to stay in summer vacation times than in the middle of winter. At the height of 'the season' the hotel could possibly accommodate twice its capacity if it had the space. Off-season demand, however, could be a small fraction of its capacity; it might even consider closing down in very quiet periods. The implication of such a marked variation in demand levels is that the operation *must change its capacity* in some way. It might, for example, hire extra staff for the summer period only. There are other options which an operation might adopt so as to minimize the extent to which it has to change its capacity: for example, if its outputs are storable (as in manufacturing) it could store them in anticipation of future demand. Nevertheless, some kind of *flexibility* in either its output level or the amount of goods it stores will be necessary. But in flexing its activities the hotel must try to predict the level of demand it is likely to receive. If it gets this wrong and adjusts its capacity below the actual demand level, it will lose business. All of these factors have the effect of increasing the hotel's costs. Recruitment costs, overtime costs, and underutilization of its rooms all make for a relatively high cost per guest operation compared with an hotel of a similar standard with level demand.

Conversely, an hotel which is close to both a major road network and a tourist attraction might be patronized by business travellers during the week and by tourists at weekends and holiday periods. Its demand is therefore relatively level. Under these circumstances the hotel can plan its activities well in advance. Staff can be scheduled, food can be bought and rooms can be cleaned in a *routine* and *predictable* manner. This results in a *high utilization* of resources. Not surprisingly, the unit costs of this hotel are likely to be lower than those of the comparable hotel with a highly variable demand pattern. This whole issue of how operations cope with demand fluctuation is treated in Chapter 11.

The customer contact dimension

Earlier it was noted that for some operations the primary transformed resource is their customers. The decision of whether to accept customers into the operation, or keep them away, is a fundamental one, and is very much related to the nature of the service or product itself. This means it is unusual to find a pure high-contact and a pure low-contact version of the same category of operation. Nevertheless, within limits some organizations do have a choice as to how they wish to develop their operations. For example in clothes retailing, an organization could decide to operate as a chain of conventional boutique-type shops. Alternatively, it could decide not to have any shops at all but rather to run a catalogue-based operation.

The shop operation would be a high-contact operation insomuch as the majority of its 'value-adding' activities take place with the customer present. Customers in this type of operation have a relatively *short waiting tolerance*. They will walk out if not served in a reasonable time (unless they are desperate). They might also judge the operation by their perceptions of it rather than always by objective criteria. If they perceive that a member of the operation's staff is discourteous to them, they are likely to be dissatisfied (even if the staff member meant no discourtesy). Given this, high-contact operations require staff with good customer contact skills. Customers could also request goods which clearly would not be sold in such a shop, but because the customers are actually in the operation they can ask what they like! This is called *high received variety*, and will occur even if the variety of service for which the operation is designed is low. This does not make it easy for high-contact operations to achieve high productivity of resources, with the consequence that they tend to be relatively high-cost operations.

Contrast the clothes shop with the catalogue-based operation. The latter is not a pure low-contact operation; it still has to communicate with its customers if it wishes to receive their orders. It will do this either by telephone or (lower contact still) through the mail. For the part of the process which involves the customer talking by telephone with the customer service staff, all the characteristics of the shop will apply. The customers will not want to be kept waiting for the telephone to be answered, the perceptions of different customers can be different even if the service is the same, good customer contact skills (though slightly different) are needed, and received variety is high.

However, the remainder of the process is more 'factory like'. The *time lag* between the order being placed and the items ordered by the customer being retrieved and dispatched does not have to be minutes as in the shop, but can be hours or even days. This allows the tasks of finding the items, packing and dispatching them to be *standardized* by organizing staff, who need *no customer contact skills*, so as to achieve *high staff utilization*. The catalogue-based organization can also centralize its operation on one site, whereas the shop chain, because of its high-contact nature, necessarily needs many sites close to centres of demand. For all these reasons the catalogue operation will have lower costs than the shop chain.

Mixed high- and low-contact operations

The clothes catalogue retail operation described above had both high-contact and low-contact micro operations within the same macro operation. This is typical of many operations and it serves to emphasize the difference which the degree of customer contact makes. Take an airport as an example: some of its activities involve high contact with its customers (ticketing staff dealing with the queues of travellers; the information desk answering people's queries; caterers serving meals and drinks; and passport control and security staff checking documentation and baggage). These staff operate in what is termed a *front-office* environment. That is, they are in the high customer contact micro operations. Other parts of the airport have relatively little if any direct contact with the customers (the baggage handlers; the overnight freight operations staff; the ground crew putting meals on board and refreshing the aircraft; the cleaners preparing them for their next flight; the cooks and the administrators). We rarely see these staff: they perform all the vital low customer contact tasks, and they do so in what is termed the *back-office* part of the operation.

Operations such as airports find it convenient to separate the front-office, high-contact from back-office, low-contact parts of the operation. They do so because they require different skills from their staff, different ways of organizing work, and different operational objectives. Figure 1.9 illustrates this separation.

Figure 1.9
When an operation
has mixed high and
low customer
contact, it is often
separated into
back and front
offices

FORMULE 1 – THE MOST AFFORDABLE HOTEL CHAIN[8]

Providing budget-priced hotel accommodation which is also modern, comfortable, hygienic and of consistent quality seems to be almost a contradiction. Hotels, after all, are outstanding examples of high-contact services – they are both staff intensive and have to cope with the variety demanded by customers, each with a variety of needs and expectations. Is it then impossible to run a highly successful chain of affordable hotels without the crippling costs of high customer contact? Not for Formule 1, a subsidiary of the French Accor group, whose chain of budget hotels stretches throughout Europe and South Africa. They manage to offer outstanding value by adopting two principles not always associated with hotel operations – standardization and an innovative use of technology.

Formule 1 hotels are usually located close to industrial trading estates, by trunk roads, junctions and close to cities, in order to be visible and accessible for prospective customers. The hotels themselves, which are instantly recognizable and made from state-of-the-art volumetric prefabrications, come in five sizes – 50, 64, 73, 80 and 98 rooms. The prefabricated units are arranged in various configurations to suit the characteristics of each individual site. Figure 1.10 shows some configurations. All rooms are nine square metres in area, and are designed to be attractive, functional, comfortable and soundproof. Most important, they are designed to be easy to clean and maintain.

Figure 1.10 Some configurations of Formule 1: premanufactured room units

All have the same fittings including a double bed, an additional bunk-type bed, a wash basin, a storage area, a working table with seat, a wardrobe and a television set.

The reception of a Formule 1 hotel is staffed only from 6.30 am to 10.00 am and from 5.00 pm to 10.00 pm. Outside these times an automatic machine sells rooms to credit card users, providing access to the hotel, dispensing a security code for the room and even printing out a receipt. Technology is also evident in the washrooms. Showers and toilets are automatically cleaned after each use by using nozzles and heating elements to spray the room with a disinfectant solution and dry it before it is used again.

To keep things even simpler, Formule 1 hotels do not include a restaurant as they are usually located near existing restaurants. However, a continental breakfast is available, usually between 6.30 am and 10.00 am, and of course on a 'self-service' basis! ■

Questions

1 What is the role of technology in allowing Formule 1 to keep its costs low?

2 How does the concept of 'standardization' help Formule 1 to keep its costs down?

Figure 1.11 gives some examples of operations at each end of the four dimensions, while Fig. 1.12 summarizes the implications of such positioning. All four dimensions have implications for the cost of creating the products or services. Put simply, high

Figure 1.11 Examples of high and low volume, variety, variation and customer contact

NatWest banks on service

Operators at the Primeline back office operation at Theale in the UK

One of the fastest growing types of product in the banking industry is telephone banking. Many banks around the world have developed a more focused approach to personal customers through new types of accounts, target marketing, personal bankers, longer opening hours and branch refurbishment. More radically, many banks have designed more fundamental changes to their 'non-branch' methods of service delivery. The concept of telephone-based banking services is not new. It was first launched successfully in 1985 by Första Sparbanken in Sweden with a service called Första Direkt. This has become a blue-print for several similar services. One such is the 'Primeline' service offered by NatWest, one of the major UK-based banks. Convenience and quality of service are Primeline's main objectives ...

'You can call us twenty-four hours a day, three hundred and sixty-five days a year. If you want to give us instructions to pay your gas bill on Christmas Day, that's fine. If you want to tell us to transfer money at 2 o'clock in the morning, that's fine too. If you're on the other side of the world in a different time zone you can still call us... Primeline is more than just a convenient telephone banking service. Your own Personal Account Manager will offer you a highly individual approach to both your day-to-day finances and your long-term financial planning.'
(Primeline publicity material).

NatWest has its own operations to support its Primeline product. Personal Account Managers are linked to sophisticated telephone and computer systems where up-to-date account information and customer requests can be dealt with promptly and efficiently.

An individual call centre operation

- *Operations of this type are often called 'call centres'. What do you think the five operations objectives (quality, speed, dependability, flexibility and cost) mean for a call centre operation?*
- *What do you think are the main operations management issues faced by call centre managers?*

→ *Look at Chapters 1 and 2 for guidance*

Van der Lande smoothes the flow

Photo courtesy of Van der Lande

Computers and monitors waiting for final testing and packing

When Packard Bell designed their new assembly centre in Angers, France, they did not want to stock any finished PCs. The key to achieving this came from Van der Lande, the Dutch materials handling equipment specialist. PC manufacture and testing can be complex. It involves a large number of hardware and software components, the specific choice of parts depending on the customers' specification. After assembly the relevant operating and application software is installed and tested for reliability. If a computer is found not to comply fully with the high quality standards, it is automatically transported to the rectification station. After repair the products are re-introduced to the production process. In this way potential loss of material as well as time are reduced to a minimum. Finally, manuals and documentation are added, after which the product is packed and despatched. Throughout the assembly system 'tracking and tracing' technology allows any part of the product to be monitored and steered through the entire production process. This allows any configuration to be produced in any order. All instructions required by each worker in the assembly system are presented on computer terminals which allow operators to view all assembly data and monitor test results as they happen.

Photo courtesy of Van der Lande

Operators have all the information they need at their individual assembly and test stations

- *What kind of flexibility is introduced into the operation by Van der Lande's system?*
- *What advantages does this flexibility give to Packard Bell?*
- *Why are all the monitors switched on in the picture above?*

→ *Look at Chapter 2 for guidance*

Dealing with infinite variety – two examples

The Bombay Tiffin Box Suppliers Association (TBSA) operates a service to transport home-cooked food from workers' homes to office locations in downtown Bombay. Workers from residential districts must ride commuter trains some 30–40 km to work. Typically, they are conservative diners, and are also constrained by strong cultural taboos on food handling by caste, which discourage eating out. TBSA arranges for food to be picked up in the morning in a regulation tin 'tiffin' box, deposited at the office at lunch time, and returned to the home in the afternoon. TBSA takes advantage of public transport to carry the tins, usually using otherwise under-utilized capacity on commuter trains in the mid-morning and afternoon. Different colours and markings are used to indicate to the (sometimes illiterate) TBSA workers the process route for each tin.

Standardized shipping containers

For as long as ships have navigated the seas, ports have had to handle an infinite variety of cargoes with widely different contents, sizes and weights, and, whilst in transit or in storage, protect them from weather and pilferage. Then the transportation industries, in conjunction with the International Standards Organization (ISO), developed a standard shipping container design. Almost overnight the problems of security and weather protection were solved. Anyone wanting to ship goods in volume only had to seal them into a container and they could be signed over to the shipping company. Ports could standardize handling equipment and dispense with warehouses (containers could be stacked in the rain if required). Railways and trucking companies could develop trailers to accommodate the new containers. Such was the success of the new design that very soon specialist containers were developed which still conformed to the ISO standard module sizes. For example, refrigerated containers provide temperature-controlled environments for perishable goods.

- *What are the common features of these two examples?*
- *What other examples of standardization in transport operations can you think of?*

→ *Look at Chapter 1 for guidance*

Standard tiffin boxes being transported from home to office

A focus on jeans

Jeans are now the 'default' clothing option around the world. They are both fashionable and hardwearing. Not surprisingly, the thread which holds them together has to be strong and of high quality. Coats Thread, part of the Coats Viyella Group, is a major manufacturer of jeans thread, supplying product to companies such as Levi-Strauss and Vanity Fair (who manufacture the Lee and Wrangler brands). The manufacture of jeans thread involves spinning the polycotton corespun thread, formulating and mixing the dyes (*see* picture), dyeing the thread in batches (*see* picture), lubricating and winding the thread onto smaller

Photo courtesy of J and P Coats Ltd

Good thread helps to ensure good quality finished products

Photo courtesy of J and P Coats Ltd

Mixing dyes to be 'right first time' is critical for good service

reels and shipping these to the many jeans factories around Europe. For example, there are around 15 different plants making Levis 501s™ in Europe. Up until recently Coats sold product on a country-by-country basis with up to five of its plants each producing jeans thread for customers all over Europe. Now all of Coats' jeans thread for its European markets is made at a single plant, Newton Mearns in Scotland. This has led to significant advantages both for Coats and their customers. The Scottish plant could focus on the manufacturing and marketing skills necessary to sell into this market and their customers had a single point of contact when they wanted to discuss supply issues.

- *What do you think are the main competitive issues in selling thread to jeans manufacturers?*
- *What, therefore, will be the main issues for Coats' operations management?*
- *How do you think focusing all jeans manufacture at one plant helped Coats to compete in this market?*

Photo courtesy of J and P Coats Ltd

Dyeing the thread in batches

➜ *Look at Chapter 3 for guidance*

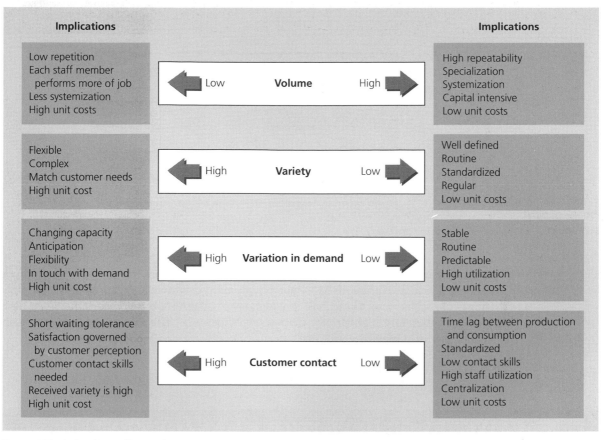

Figure 1.12 A typology of operations

volume, low variety, low variation and low customer contact all help keep processing costs down. Conversely, low volume, high variety, high variation and high customer contact generally carry some kind of cost penalty for the operation. This is why the volume dimension is drawn with its 'low' end at the left, unlike the other dimensions, to keep all the 'low cost' implications on the right.

Operations can position themselves at different points on the dimensions and therefore change the performance of which the operation is capable. For almost any type of industry one can identify operations which inhabit different parts of the four dimensions and therefore implicitly are competing for business in different ways. Figure 1.13 illustrates the different positions on the dimensions of the Formule 1 hotel chain (*see* the box on Formule 1) and a very different type of hotel. An island resort hotel in the Caribbean, for example, provides the same basic service as any other hotel. However, it could very well be of a small, intimate nature with relatively few customers (some hotel resorts of this type cater for only 10 or 20 guests at a time). Its variety of services is almost infinite in the sense that customers can make individual requests in terms of food and entertainment. Variation might be very high, the resort might even close in the off-season. Finally, customer contact, in order to ascertain customers' requirements and provide for them, is likely to be very high. All of which is very different from Formule 1, where volume is high (although not as high as in a large city-centre hotel), variety of

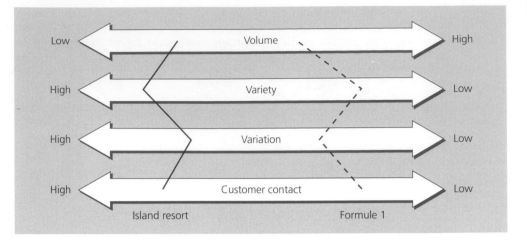

**Figure 1.13
Profiles of two
operations**

service is strictly limited, and business and holiday customers use the hotel at different times which limits variation. Most notably, though, customer contact is kept to a minimum. The island resort hotel has very high levels of service but provides them at a high cost (and therefore high price). Conversely, Formule 1 has arranged its operation in such a way as to minimize its costs.

THE ACTIVITIES OF OPERATIONS MANAGEMENT

Operations managers have some responsibility for all the activities in the organization which contribute to the effective production of goods and services. It is the term 'responsibility' which needs further explanation. Operations managers have:

● *indirect responsibility* for some activities; and
● *direct responsibility* for other activities.

The indirect responsibilities of operations managers

Many of the activities which take place in organizations fall well outside the conventional boundaries of the operations function yet do have an effect on the way it produces its goods and services. For example, the way in which organizations produce their advertising plans is almost always a direct responsibility of the marketing function. Does this mean that operations managers should bear no responsibility for the organization's advertising plans? While the activity is quite clearly in the marketing domain, the effect of the activity could have a significant impact on the operation. It will affect overall demand levels and the exact mix of products and services which customers will want.

In these circumstances the responsibility of operations management is to explore the possible consequences of the advertising plans with the marketing function. It should understand their impact on the operation, make clear to marketing what the operation can and cannot do in response to any change in demand, and work together with marketing to find ways of allowing them to meet, or manage, market needs while also allowing the operation to run efficiently and effectively.

Generally the indirect responsibilities of operations management can be summarized as follows:

● to inform other functions of the opportunities and constraints provided by the operation's capabilities;
● to discuss with other functions how both operations' plans and their own plans might be modified for the benefit of both functions;
● to encourage other functions to suggest ways in which the operations function can improve its 'service' to the rest of the organization.

This approach *of mutual responsibility* for other functions activities is one effect of the *internal customer–internal supplier* concept discussed earlier.

The direct responsibilities of operations management

The exact nature of the operations function's direct responsibilities will, to some extent, depend on the way the organization has chosen to define its operations function. This was discussed previously (*see* Fig. 1.2). There are some general classes of activities, however, which apply to all types of operation no matter how functional boundaries have been drawn. These activities include:

● understanding the operation's strategic objectives;
● developing an operations strategy for the organization;
● designing the operation's products, services and processes;
● planning and controlling the operation;
● improving the performance of the operation.

Understanding the operation's strategic objectives

The first responsibility of any operations management team is to understand what it is trying to achieve. This involves two sets of decisions. The first is to develop a clear vision of what *role* the operation is to play in the organization: that is broadly how the operation should contribute to the organization achieving its long-term goals. The second is to translate the organization's goals into their implications for the operation's *performance objectives*. Performance objectives are the *quality* of its goods and services, the *speed* with which they are delivered to customers, the *dependability* with which the operation keeps its delivery promises, the *flexibility* of the operation to change what it does, and the *cost* of producing its goods and services. All these issues are discussed in Chapter 2.

Developing an operations strategy for the organization

Operations management is a very immediate occupation. It involves hundreds of minute-by-minute decisions through the working week. Because of this, it is vital that operations managers have a set of general principles which can guide decision-making towards the organization's longer term goals. This is an *operations strategy*. It involves being able to place operations strategy in the general strategy hierarchy of the organization, which connects functional and business strategies together. It also involves prioritizing the operation's performance objectives in a way which links them to customer needs and competitor behaviour. Chapter 3 deals with operations strategy.

Designing the operation's products, services and processes

Design in our terms is the activity of determining the physical form, shape and composition of products, services and processes. In operations management it is the set of activities which literally sets the scene for all its other activities.

Direct responsibility for the design of the products and services of the organization might not be part of the operations function in some organizations. However, it is so crucial to the operation's other activities that we consider the design process in general in Chapter 4 and the design of products and services in particular in Chapter 5. But the design activity is also crucial to an area which is always under the direct responsibility of the operations function – the transformation process itself. At the most strategic level, process design means designing the whole network of operations which provide inputs to the operations function and deliver its output to customers. This activity involves consideration of the boundaries of ownership for the operation. These issues are dealt with in Chapter 6. At a more immediate level, operations managers need to design their process layouts and flows of transformed resources through the operation, an issue treated in Chapter 7. The design issues involving the two main 'ingredients' which make up the operation, process technology and staff, are treated in Chapter 8 and Chapter 9 respectively.

Planning and controlling the operation

The design activities should have put all the operation's resources in place, but to work effectively they need to be planned and controlled.

Planning and control is the activity of deciding what the operations resources should be doing, then making sure that they really are doing it. Chapter 10 explains the nature of planning and control activities. At its most aggregated level, planning and control involves managing the capacity of the operation so as to meet fluctuating demand levels, an issue treated in Chapter 11. The planning and control of the flow of the transformed resources through the operation is treated in two parts. Chapter 12 deals with inventory management. Chapter 13 deals with the 'supply chain' management – the flow of goods and services from suppliers to customers. Managing the planning and control of the transformation process itself depends partly on the nature of the operation. Some particular approaches have been developed which are appropriate under different circumstances. For example, materials requirements planning (MRP) controls the timing and quantity of processing in complex operations, and is treated in Chapter 14. The just-in-time (JIT) approach to planning and control is described in Chapter 15, although it is worth noting that many of the philosophies of just-in-time management have influenced several other parts of this book. Chapter 16 treats planning and control in project operations. Finally, Chapter 17 treats the management of the quality of products and services.

Improving the performance of the operation

The strategy of the operation is set, its products, services and processes are designed, and its work is being planned and controlled on an ongoing basis. Yet this is not the end of operations management's direct responsibilities. The continuing responsibility of all operations managers is to improve the performance of their

WHAT OPERATIONS MANAGERS ACTUALLY DO[9]

In all of operations management's direct and indirect activities there is a need to communicate both with internal staff and with external customers, suppliers and the broader community. One survey carried out by Professor Arnoud De Meyer shows how much of a factory manager's time is spent on different activities, and how the importance of each is changing (*see* Table 1.6).

Table 1.6 Breakdown of factory manager's work

Activity	% of time	Degree of change (1 = spending less time, 7 = spending more time)
Direct supervision and support	22	3.5
Consulting with plant staff	16	3.9
Consulting with upper management	12	4.0
Consulting with sales and marketing	10	4.8
Communicating with customers	7	4.8
Communicating with suppliers	7	4.4
Consulting with Research and Development	5	4.7
Dealing with the community	5	4.5
Training (as trainer)	4	4.6
Training (as trainee)	4	4.6

Consulting and communicating with operations staff clearly takes up a large amount of these operations managers' time. But the proportion of their time spent communicating with people outside the operations function and even outside the organization appears to be gaining in importance. This means, says Professor De Meyer, that operations managers are evolving to be more '... *managers of interfaces, as opposed to a caretaker of an isolated manufacturing function*'. ■

Question

1 What implications do these findings have for the future of operations managers' jobs?

operation. Failure to improve at least as fast as competitors (in for-profit organizations) or at the rate of customers' rising expectations (in all organizations) is to condemn the operations function always to fall short of what the organization should expect from it. Chapter 18 describes how the process of improvement can be organized within the operation. The other side of making operations better is stopping them going wrong in the first place. Chapter 19 deals with how failures are prevented in operations, and how the operation can recover when failure does occur. Finally, in this area, there is what is probably the most powerful of all the improvement ideas to influence operations world-wide – total quality management (TQM). This is covered in Chapter 20.

THE MODEL OF OPERATIONS MANAGEMENT

We can now combine two of the ideas we have described to develop the model of operations management which will be used throughout this book. The first idea is the input–transformation–output model and the second is the categorization of operations management's activity areas. Figure 1.14 shows how these two ideas go together. The

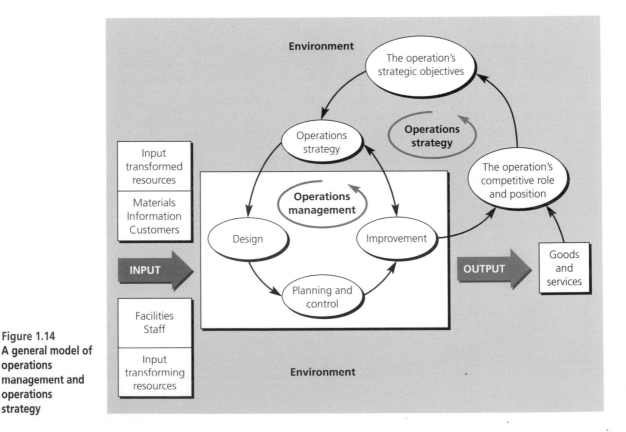

Figure 1.14
A general model of operations management and operations strategy

fundamental purpose of operations management, the transformation of input resources into goods and services, is illustrated by the input–transformation–output diagram. Within the transformation process are the three activity areas which select, locate and organize the transforming resources and which determine the nature and timing of the flow of transformed resources. These are the *design, planning and control* and *improvement* activities. They are shown as being connected in, more or less, the chronological order in which they would happen if a totally new operation was being developed.

The operation's output of products and services is intended to reflect the chosen *competitive role and position of the operation*, which may itself be changed as the performance of the operation improves. The way in which the operation translates its desired competitive role and position into something practical is by expressing it in terms of *strategic objectives*. These impact on *operations strategy*, which, in turn, shapes the design, planning and control, and improvement decisions.

The model now shows two interconnected loops of activities. The bottom one more or less corresponds to what is usually seen as *operations management*, and the top one to what is seen as *operations strategy*. This book concentrates on the former but tries to cover enough of the latter to allow the reader to make strategic sense of the operations manager's job.

Andrew Hawley, United Biscuits

Andrew was sponsored by United Biscuits during his studies for a degree in Business, and his early work experience with the company confirmed his interest in manufacturing operations.

'Where else could you be managing 50 people from the outset, in your early twenties? The satisfaction comes from being responsible for the performance of the plant and staff, seeing immediate results, and above all from beating targets!'

Andrew had various roles in his first five years with the company; initially he was responsible for the day-to-day supervision of a factory, then he became a deputy factory manager of a small specialized plant, before moving to Headquarters, where he is responsible for aspects of operational and strategic planning.

'It is certainly a change being in a team of just six people after helping to manage a factory, and I now face a whole new set of challenges. My hands-on experience of production has been invaluable for my current position. Without it, I wouldn't be able to decide on production systems and procedures three or more years in advance of implementation. The work is very diverse. Sometimes I am working to identify potential problems, so that preventative measures can be implemented, and at other times I am involved in logistics projects aimed at integrating

UB companies all over Europe, which will make enormous savings for the Group.

'Many people have misconceptions about manufacturing and production management; they think that it is just about "doing" and is less stimulating and intellectually demanding than other disciplines. Nothing could be further from the truth in my opinion.

'It has been my job at United Biscuits to ensure that all products leave our plant manufactured to our very demanding specifications. This involves not only responsibility for the process and the people, important though they are, but also for clear communication and involvement with all of the other business functions to ensure that the business unit is run optimally. It is especially important to understand how the production must be involved with the fundamental issues of cost, service, quality and innovation and to be able to create and manage change. Managers in the manufacturing role also have an important part to play in developing the business strategy, notably in co-ordination with the Marketing Department. In a real sense, when you're involved with manufacturing, every other discipline in the company is backing you, because you are the one that is producing exactly what millions of people are buying in the shops every day. This is, after all, what the company is there for in the first place!' ∎

Source: By kind permission of United Biscuits (UK) Limited

SUMMARY ANSWERS TO KEY QUESTIONS

What is operations management?

■ Operations management is the term which is used for the activities, decisions and responsibilities of operations managers who manage the arrangement of resources which are devoted to the production of goods and services within an organization.

■ It is one of the major functions of any business, although it may not be called operations management in some industries.

■ The span of responsibility varies between companies. Some have narrow definitions of the operations function which encompass only the very core direct activities which are concerned with the production of goods and services. Others take a broader definition of the function to include all direct and indirect supporting activities within the organization.

■ Operations management can also be viewed as that part of any function's or manager's responsibility which involves producing the internal goods and services within the organization, as opposed to the strictly technical decisions which they take within their functions.

What are the similarities between all operations?

■ All operations can be modelled as an input–transformation–output process.

■ All have inputs of transforming resources which are usually divided into 'facilities' and 'staff'. All also have transformed resources which are some mixture of materials, information and customers.

■ All operations transform inputs into outputs by acting on some aspect of their physical properties, informational properties, possession, location, storage or accommodation, physiological state or psychological state.

■ All operations produce some mixture of tangible goods or products and less tangible services. Few operations produce only products or only services.

■ All operations can be divided into micro operations which form a network of internal customer–supplier relationships within the operation.

■ All operations can be viewed as a set of business processes which often cut across functionally-based micro operations.

How are operations different from each other?

■ Operations differ in terms of the volume of their outputs, from low volume to high volume. High volume is usually associated with low cost.

■ All operations differ in terms of the variety or range of the output they produce. Low variety is usually associated with low cost.

■ All operations vary in terms of the variation in demand with which they have to cope. Low variation is usually associated with low cost.

■ All operations vary in terms of the degree of customer contact which they have. This is the amount of value-adding activity which takes place with the customer present. Low customer contact is usually associated with low cost.

What do operations managers do?

■ They translate the strategic direction of an organization into operational action.

■ They design the operation. This means not only the design of the products and services themselves, but the systems or processes which produce them.

■ They plan and control the activities of the operation by deciding when and where activities will take place and detecting and responding to any deviations from the plan.

■ They improve the performance of the operation with reference to its strategic objectives, through some combination of major and minor improvement activities.

CASE EXERCISE

A business trip to Brussels

My flight to Stockholm would be late landing. The pilot told us that we were in a 'stack' of planes circling above the snow clouds that were giving Brussels its first taste of winter. Air traffic control had closed the runways for a short period at dawn, and the early morning flights from all around Europe were now being allocated new landing slots along with the long-haul jumbos from the Far East and the US. After a twenty-minute delay, we descended bumpily through the clouds, and landed on a recently cleared runway. Even then there was a further 'hold' on a taxiway; we were told that the de-icing of the apron was being completed so that planes could proceed to their allocated stands and airbridges. All around the airport I could see the scurrying flashing beacons of the snow-clearing vehicles, the catering suppliers' vans, the aviation fuel trucks, the baggage trailers, buses transporting crews and passengers, security police cars, and an assortment of other vehicles all going purposefully about their work. Brussels airport always looks busy, with over 10 million passengers a year, but this morning the complexity and scale of the operations were particularly evident.

Finally, about an hour late, we pulled up to the gate, the engines were turned off, and we disembarked into an icy-cold airbridge, leaving behind a particularly untidy plane strewn with the litter left behind by a full cabin of restless passengers. We passed the team of cleaners and maintenance staff waiting just outside. 'They will have a hard time this morning; more mess to clear and probably less time than usual to do it, as the airline will want a quick turnaround to get back on to schedule,' I commented to my colleagues. We could just hear the sounds of frantic activities going on below the plane: baggage and cargo being unloaded, catering vehicles arriving, fuel being loaded, and technicians checking over the engines and control surfaces – everyone trying to get their work completed quickly and correctly, not least so that they could get back indoors out of the biting cold wind!

From the airbridge we walked past the crowded seating areas, where plane-sized groups were gathering anxiously awaiting the signal from the gate staff to board their much delayed flights. Then on to the moving walkways, conveyed leisurely past other departure lounges, equally overfilled with passengers. Anxious to get ahead of the crowd, we took to a running pace past the rows of cafés, bars and shops, hoping to avoid the usual morning queue for Passport Control. I should have remembered the old saying 'more haste, less speed' because my next journey was to the First Aid room! I had apparently slipped on some spilt coffee that had not been cleaned up in the haste of the morning, and had fallen awkwardly, straining my ankle, and breaking my duty-free brandy. 'At least they would clean the floor after that,' I thought, sadly.

Suitably patched up, I hobbled with my colleagues and joined the long queue for Passport Control, and eventually through to Baggage Reclaim. Even with the excellent new baggage-handling systems in Brussels, the passengers usually get there first, but the accident had changed all that! Scanning the video screens, we found no reference to our flight arrival; the remaining bags from our flight had apparently already been removed from the carousel and stored in an adjacent office. After a simple signing ceremony, we were reunited with our belongings, and hastened (slowly in my case) to the taxi rank. Our hopes of a quick ride to the city were dispelled when we saw the long queue in the icy wind, so we made our way to the station below, where a dedicated 'City Express' train departs every 20 minutes for the Gare de Nord and Gare Centrale. We just missed one!

After a busy and successful day at our Brussels office, a taxi was called, and we were back at the airport in the thick of the evening rush hour. The departures check-in area is the upper floor of a vast new terminal extension, and is very orderly and well equipped. Facing you on entry from the taxi drop-off point is a huge electronic display which lists all departures scheduled for the next few hours, and showing the appropriate check-in desk number for each flight. The speed of the check-in systems has been improved dramatically, so there was no queue at our desk, and the three of us were issued with boarding passes in only a couple of minutes. Our baggage sped away on conveyors down to the new sorting hall two storeys below. Brochures explain that the new terminal extension was designed to make it possible to go from check-in to final boarding in only 20 minutes, which has involved investment in a state-of-the-art automated baggage-handling system. On my last visit, following traffic delays on the way to the airport, I found that this system works, but I doubt that it would if *everyone* arrived only 20 minutes before departure! It is no wonder that they advise checking in one hour before: it also gives passengers much more time to spend money in the duty-free shops, restaurants and bars!

By this time, my injured leg had swollen up and was throbbing painfully. This seemed to be a routine situation for the check-in staff, who arranged for a wheelchair and attendant to take me through Border Control and security checks. While my colleagues travelled down to the departures hall by escalator, I took the slower route by lift, arriving together just outside the duty-free shops where the attendant left them to take care of me. We had some time to spare, so we replenished the brandy, bought some Belgian chocolates, and headed for a café-bar. While Brussels is renowned for its excellent cuisine, we didn't expect to find high standards of food in the quick-service environment of an airport, but we were wrong! The delicious aromas of freshly prepared food attracted our custom, and we weren't disappointed. After a welcome glass of speciality raspberry-flavoured beer to round off the meal, we headed for the airline's executive lounge.

The view across the airfield was not promising! After a bright, crisp day, more snow-laden clouds had arrived, and a chill wind cut across the tarmac. De-icing crews were working on the parked aircraft and others were treating the runways, taking quick action between the aircraft movements. Concerned that we

might be delayed and miss our connecti... checked with the staff at the airline' tion desk. After some phoning. although there could be s arranged to hold connecting gers originated from Brussels. ... and friendly advice made us feel m... ...ase, and they even offered to allow us t... ...ax or phone messages to our destination. They ...uldn't have been more helpful!

Announcements of the minor delays were made over the speaker system, but it wasn't long before we were directed to the departure lounge and were preparing to board. Outside, around the aircraft in the gloom, the baggage trucks were pulling away, and the giant push-off tractor was being connected up to the nose-wheel. Ten minutes later, we were at the end of the runway, ready for take-off.

'Today must have been a very busy one for everyone involved in keeping the airport open,' I thought, 'but perhaps every day has its own challenges in such a complex operation.' ∎

Questions

1 Identify all the micro operations and their activities which are mentioned.

2 Classify them in accordance with the structure in Table 1.5.

3 Which of these micro operations were most affected by the severe weather?

4 Approximately how many different organizations are involved in delivering the goods and services described in this report? What are the implications of this?

DISCUSSION QUESTIONS

(All chapters have discussion questions. Some of them can be answered by reading the chapter. Others will require some general knowledge of business activity and some might require an element of investigation.)

1 The port of Rotterdam is the largest port in the world. It provides a vital link between sea-based transportation of cargo and inland transport into Europe such as rail, road and inland waterways. List the transformation processes which you think the port's operations managers have to run, and identify their inputs and outputs.

2 Describe the operations of the following organizations using the transformation model. Carefully identify the transforming resources, transformed resources, the type of transformation process and the outputs from the transformation process for:
    an international airport
    a supermarket
    a high-volume car plant.

3 What mixture of goods and services are produced by the following operations:
    Airbus Industrie
    The Channel Tunnel
    Marks & Spencer
    Federal Express parcel service
    Volvo motor cars
    Novotel hotels?

4 Why is operations management relevant to managers in other organization functions?

5 Explain the difference between micro and macro operations. Describe some of the micro operations in a university and discuss the relationships between their internal customers and suppliers.

6 Talk with an operations manager from a local organization and find out what they say they do and how they work with the organization's marketing, financial, personnel and purchasing functions.

7 Draw the hierarchy of operations for a small manufacturing company.

8 What are the main differences between internal and external customers?

9 Discuss the advantages and disadvantages of buffering an operation from the environment. Illustrate your answer with an organization of your choice.

10 How do you think a blood transfusion service operation buffers itself against environmental uncertainty?

11 Describe the relative volume, variety, variation and customer contact for the following organizations:
    a theme park
    a bread bakery
    a dentist.

12 Explain the advantages and disadvantages to an operation of reducing its volume, variety and customer contact. How could a university change volume, variety and customer contact in order to reduce its costs?

13 What do you think would be the main design, planning and control, and improvement activities in a large airport such as London's Heathrow airport?

14 Over recent years there has been a resurgence of interest in operations management, in universities but especially in business. Why do you think this is?

NOTES ON CHAPTER

1 Sources: Thornhill, J. (1992) 'Hard Sell on the High Street', The *Financial Times*, May 16. Horovitz, J. and Jurgens Panak, M. (1992) *Total Customer Satisfaction*, Pitman Publishing. Walley, P. and Hart, K. (1993) IKEA (UK) Ltd, Loughborough University Business School.

2 Source: 'Hayek's Watch Works', *World Link*, July 1994.

3 Heizer, J.H. and Render, B. (1988) *Production and Operations Management* (3rd edn), Allyn and Bacon, p 5.

4 A number of authors have commented on the way the operations function is protected from the environment. For example, Thompson, J.D. (1967), *Organizations in Action*, McGraw-Hill, originally commented on organization buffering, while Wild, R. (1977) *Concepts for Operations Management*, John Wiley, extended the ideas to physical buffering.

5 One of the most articulate proponents of how an organization can be more responsive to environmental influence is Richard Schonburger. *See*, for example, *Building a Chain of Customers*, Hutchinson Business Books, 1990.

6 Sources: Franssen, M. (1993) 'Beyond Profits', *Business Quarterly*, Autumn. Hopfenbeck, W. (1992) *The Green Management Revolution*, Prentice Hall.

7 Sources: Pean, P. (1989) 'How to Get Rich on Perestroika', *Fortune*, 8 May, pp 95–6, and 'Vision Factory', *National Geographic*, Nov 1993.

8 Sources: Groupe Accor published accounts 1992, *Formule 1, The Most Affordable Hotel Chain*, company information brochure. Sharon Dannelley (1993) 'Groupe Accor', *Warwick Business School Report*.

9 Source: De Meyer, A. (1993) *Creating the Virtual Factor*, The EFME Conference, London Business School.

SELECTED FURTHER READINGS

Adams, E.E. and Ebert, R.J. (1992) *Production and Operations Management* (5th edn), Prentice Hall.

Albrecht, K. and Bradford, L.J. (1990) *The Service Advantage*, Dow Jones Irwin.

Andrews, C.G. (1982) 'The Critical Importance of Production and Operations Management', *Academy of Management Review*, Vol 7, Jan.

Armistead, C.G. (ed) (1994) *The Future of Services Management*, Kogan Page.

Bowen, D.E., Chase, R.B., Cummings, T.G. and Associates (1990) *Service Management Effectiveness*, Jossey-Bass.

Collier, D.A. (1987) *Service Management: Operating Decisions*, Prentice Hall.

Flaherty, M.T. (1996) *Global Operations Management*, McGraw-Hill.

Gaither, N. (1994) *Production and Operations Management*, Dryden Press.

Gronroos, C. (1990) *Service Management and Marketing*, Lexington Books.

Harris, N.D. (1989) *Service Operations Management*, Cassell.

Hill, T. (1991) *Production/Operations Management* (2nd edn), Prentice Hall.

Johnston, R., Chambers, S., Harland, C., Harrison, A. and Slack, N. (1997) *Cases in Operations Management*, (2nd edn), Pitman Publishing.

Krajewski, L.J. and Ritzman, I.P. (1987) *Operations Management* (3rd edn), Addison-Wesley.

Ould, M.A. (1995) *Business Processes*, John Wiley.

Schonberger, R. (1990) *Building a Chain of Customers*, Hutchinson Business Books.

Voss, C. and Johnston, R. (1996) *Service in Britain: How do we Measure Up?*, Severn Trent.

Wild, R. (1989) *Production and Operations Management* (4th edn), Cassell.

Womack, J.P. and Jones, D.T. (1996) *Lean Thinking: Banish Waste and Create Wealth in your Corporation*, Simon and Schuster.

THE STRATEGIC ROLE AND OBJECTIVES OF OPERATIONS

INTRODUCTION

In Chapter 1 we looked at the activities in which operations managers are involved as well as the many different types of operation which they are managing. But examining what operations managers do does not answer a far more fundamental question: 'What should any company or organization expect from its operation?' Or, to put it another way, 'How does the operations function contribute to the organization's competitiveness or strategic direction?'

If any operation wants to understand its contribution to the organization of which it is a part, it must answer two questions. First, what is the *role* of the operations function – that is, what part is it expected to play within the business? Second, what

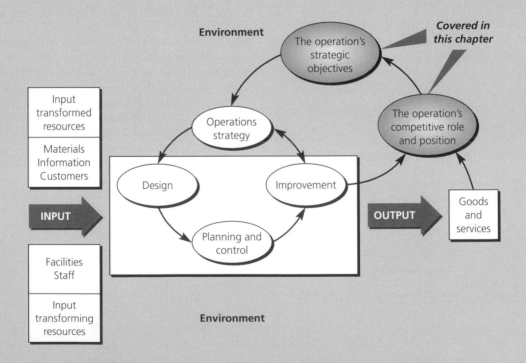

Figure 2.1 This chapter covers the role and strategic objectives of operations management

are the specific *performance objectives* against which the business can assess the contribution of the operation to its strategic aspirations? Both these issues are vitally important to any operation. Without an appreciation of its role within the business, the people who manage the operation can never be sure that they really are contributing to the long-term success of the business. At a more practical level, it is impossible to know whether an operation is succeeding or not if the specific performance objectives against which its success is measured are not clearly spelt out. This chapter deals with both these issues. On our general model of operations management they are represented by the shaded areas of Fig. 2.1.

CHAPTER 2: KEY QUESTIONS

● *What role should the operations function play in achieving strategic success?*

● *What are the performance objectives of operations and what are the internal and external benefits which derive from excelling in each of them?*

THE ROLE OF THE OPERATIONS FUNCTION

By the role of the operations function we mean something beyond its obvious responsibilities and tasks in the company. We mean the underlying rationale of the function – the very reason that the function exists.

Why should any business go to the bother of having an operations function? Most companies and organizations have the option of contracting out the production of their services and goods. They could simply pay some other business to provide what their operations function currently does for them. This then prompts the further question 'What does the operations function have to do in order to justify its continued existence within the business?' This is what we mean by its role. Three roles seem to be particularly important for the operations function:

● as the *implementer* of business strategy;
● as a *support* to business strategy;
● as the *driver* of business strategy.

Implementing business strategy

One role of the operations part of the business is to implement strategy. Most companies will have some kind of strategy but it is the operation which puts it into practice. You cannot after all touch a strategy; you cannot even see it; all you can see is how the operation behaves in practice. For example, if an airline has a strategy of attracting a higher proportion of business-class travellers, it is the operations part of each function which has the task of 'operationalizing' the strategy. Its marketing 'operation' must organize appropriate promotions and pricing activities. The personnel 'operation' needs to train its cabin and ground staff to achieve higher levels of customer service. Most significantly, its operations function will have to supervise the refitting of the aircraft, organize express ticketing, baggage handling and waiting facilities, and design special food, beverages and entertainment for the cabin service. The implication of this role for the operations function is very significant. It means that even the most original and brilliant strategy can be rendered totally ineffective by an inept operations function.

Supporting business strategy

Another role is to support strategy.[1] That is, it must develop its resources to provide the capabilities which are needed to allow the organization to achieve its strategic goals. For example, if a manufacturer of personal computers has decided to compete by being the first in the market with every available new product innovation, then its operations function needs to be capable of coping with the changes which constant innovation will bring. It must develop or purchase processes which are flexible enough to manufacture novel parts and products. It must organize and train its staff to understand the way products are changing and put in place the necessary changes to the operation. It must develop relationships with its suppliers which help them respond quickly when supplying new parts. The better the operation is at doing these things, the more support it is giving to the company's strategy. If the company had adopted a different business strategy its operations function would have needed to adopt different objectives. This idea is developed further in the next chapter.

Driving business strategy

The third role of the operations part of the business is to drive strategy by giving it a long-term competitive edge. Different parts of the business have different effects on a company's ability to prosper. If the finance function does not control cash flow accurately, the business could run out of cash and go out of business almost immediately. Poor financial management can have a serious short-term effect on the business. If the marketing department fails to understand the nature of the company's markets, and how it should set its promotion policies, product positioning, distribution channels and pricing policies, the company will find it difficult to thrive in its markets. Poor marketing management will hamper the company in the medium term. No amount of excellent financial management or clever market positioning, however, can compensate for poor operations performance. Badly made products, sloppy service, slow delivery, broken promises, too little choice of products or services or an operations cost base which is too high will sink any company in the long term. Conversely, any business which makes its products and/or services better, faster, on-time, in greater variety and less expensively than its competition has the best long-term advantage any company could desire. The important point here is that all the things which promote long-term success come directly or indirectly from the operations function. It is the operations part of the business which is the ultimate custodian of competitiveness. Its role is to 'do things better', that is, 'make products better' and 'deliver services better' than other similar operations.

Figure 2.2 summarizes the three roles of the operations function.

Figure 2.2 The three roles of the operations function

TNT – THE WORLD-WIDE TRANSPORTATION GROUP[3]

To illustrate the three roles of the operations function, examine the case of the transportation company, TNT.

TNT Limited is one of the best known of the international transportation groups, principally engaged in freight mail and parcel transportation. It provides regional services in Europe, North and South America and Australasia and also global services which transport freight to almost any destination. The group employs in excess of 53 000 people around the world. TNT's main businesses are general freight, express freight by road and air, and specialist services including bulk cartage, materials handling, car carrying, refrigerated transport, industrial waste disposal, contract distribution and logistics support. The group is also directly involved in passenger and freight airline operations, aircraft leasing, tourism and leisure resort management.

The group's most familiar international face is its TNT Skypack International Express range of services which mail and courier packages, letters and parcels to around 190 countries. The Express Courier service uses a global on-line computer network, linking all parts of its operation for real-time communication of data and immediate access to vital shipment information. The TNT Skytrak information system also services the customer from point of request for collection of a shipment, through driver dispatch, operational routing and tracking, to proof of delivery. The Mailfast's Premium Letter Service offers expedited mailing for businesses by using the mailing network to inject mail direct into destination post offices or to hand deliver in major business centres. The Registered Mail Service offers signed receipt of delivery. The Express Post Service is designed to compete with post-office accelerated services.

▶

The long-term aim of the group is to provide a comprehensive range of transportation services around the world with services to suit a wide variety of customer needs in all major regions of the world. Individually the group's different services compete in different ways. In courier services, price is less important than such factors as variety of service options (next day, overnight, two days, etc.) and dependable delivery. Mailfast focuses on ease of use and quality of service at the collection and delivery stages. Express Post competes on speed of delivery and price. The heavier freight end of the group's range is highly price competitive but customers are willing to sign up for long-term contracts.

The three roles of the operations function in a company such as TNT could be interpreted as follows:

- *Implementing business strategy.* The group as a whole is moving towards being a fully-comprehensive integrated supplier of its services world-wide. Operations must be able to evaluate alternative methods of achieving this and implement whatever investment in aircraft, vehicles, staff and systems is necessary.
- *Supporting business strategy.* Operations must provide dependable delivery for all services with other performance objectives suitable for the nature of competition. Cost especially must be kept low in the heavy freight and Express Post services. Quality of service is particularly important in the courier and Mailfast services. Speed of delivery is vital for the Express Post. The resources devoted to each of these services should be developed to emphasize the key aspects of competitiveness for each service.
- *Driving business strategy.* Operations should move towards providing the capability to exceed competitors' performance and customers' expectations, initially in the more important aspects of competitiveness, and eventually in all aspects of performance. This means providing a more dependable, higher quality, faster, more flexible and cheaper service than any competitor. ∎

Questions

1 How do the various services described above appear to differ from an operations point of view? (Start by identifying the different performance objectives which each service should have.)

2 What do you think are the problems in offering these different services using the same set of operations resources?

JUDGING THE OPERATION'S CONTRIBUTION

The ability of any operation to play these roles within the organization can be judged by considering the organizational aims or aspirations of the operations function. Professors Hayes and Wheelwright of Harvard University,[2] with later contributions from Professor Chase of the University of Southern California,[4] have developed what they call the '*Four-Stage Model*' which can be used to evaluate the competitive role and contribution of the operations function of any type of company. The model traces the progression of the operations function from what is the largely negative role of Stage 1 operations to it becoming the central element of competitive strategy in excellent Stage 4 operations.

Stage 1 Internal neutrality

This is the very poorest level of contribution by the operations function. In a Stage 1 organization the operation is considered a 'necessary evil'. The other functions, if they have anything to say at all about operations, regard it as holding them back from competing effectively. The operations function, they would say, is inward looking and at best reactive. It certainly has very little positive to contribute towards competitive success. It is unlikely even to have developed its resources so as to be appropriate for the company's competitive position. The best that the function can hope for is to be ignored. At least when operations is being ignored it isn't holding the company back in any way. Certainly the rest of the organization would not look to operations as the source of any originality, flair or competitive drive. It is trying to be 'internally neutral', a position it attempts to achieve not by anything positive but by avoiding the bigger mistakes. Even good organizations can be let down by their operations function and the resulting publicity can be damaging (*see* Fig. 2.3).

Stage 2 External neutrality

Hayes and Wheelwright's idea of the first step of breaking out of Stage 1 is for the operations function to begin comparing itself with similar companies or organizations in the outside market. This may not immediately take it to the 'first division' of companies in the market, but at least it is aspiring to reach that position and is measuring itself against its competitors' performance. The operations function is certainly not holding the company back. It may not yet be particularly creative in the way it manages its operations but it is trying to be 'appropriate', by adopting 'best practice' from its competitors. By taking the best ideas and norms of performance from the rest of its industry it is trying to be 'externally neutral'.

Stage 3 Internally supportive

Stage 3 operations have probably reached the 'first division' in their market. They may not be better than their competitors on every aspect of operations performance but they are broadly up with the best. Nevertheless, good as they may be, Stage 3 operations aspire to be clearly and unambiguously the very best in the market. They try to achieve this by gaining a clear view of the company's competitive or strategic goals and then they organize and develop the operations resources to excel in the things in which the company needs to compete effectively. Not only are they developing 'appropriate' resources, they are taking on the role of the 'implementers' of strategy. The operation is trying to be 'internally supportive' by providing a credible operations strategy.

Stage 4 Externally supportive

Until the last few years, Stage 3 was taken as the limit of the operations function's contribution. Yet Hayes and Wheelwright capture the emerging sense of the growing importance of operations management by suggesting a further stage – Stage 4.

Ford recalls Mondeos

Ford is recalling 57,000 of its new Mondeo cars. The company wants owners of Mondeos made from March to June this year to contact their dealers for modifi the handbrake lever. The move comes aft

Engine falls off 747 Freightliner

Being accident investigators have flown

Food firm in court over pasta

Italian pasta sold by the Gateway supermarket chain under its own label and described as "100 per cent n wheat" had been delib

NatWest card error affects up to 60,000 customers

By Alison Smith

Up to 60,000 people have been affected by a mistake in processing by National Westminster Bank, which led to Visa credit d debit card transaction for y 26 being put through its mputer twice.

BT3 slip will cost Barclays millions in compensation

BY PATRICIA TEHAN, BANKING CORRESPONDENT

BARCLAYS Bank faces costs of several million pounds after its stockbroking arm failed to deliver applications from 12,000 private shareholders r BT3 shares in time for n to qualify for shares and clays

thinking that the decision wi overturned", the spokesman said.

Rory Tapner, a d SG Warburg, th co-ordinator

Group 4 frees prisoner awaiting trial

By Jonathan Petre

GROUP 4, the private security firm, admitted yesterday it had wrongly released a man facing burglary charges, even though he insisted he should be returned to custody

Figure 2.3 Even the best organizations can be let down by their operations

Sources: (left to right) *The Sunday Times, Flight International, The Times, Daily Telegraph, Financial Times*

The difference between Stage 3 and Stage 4 is admitted by Hayes and Wheelwright to be subtle, but nevertheless very important. A Stage 4 company is one which sees the operations function as providing the foundation for its future competitive success. Operations looks to the long term. It forecasts likely changes in markets and supply, and it develops operations-based strategies which provide the company with the performance which will be required to compete in future market conditions. In effect, the operations function is becoming central to strategy making. Stage 4 operations are creative and proactive. They are likely to organize their resources in ways which are innovative and capable of adaptation as markets change. Essentially they are trying to be 'one step ahead' of competitors in the way that they create products

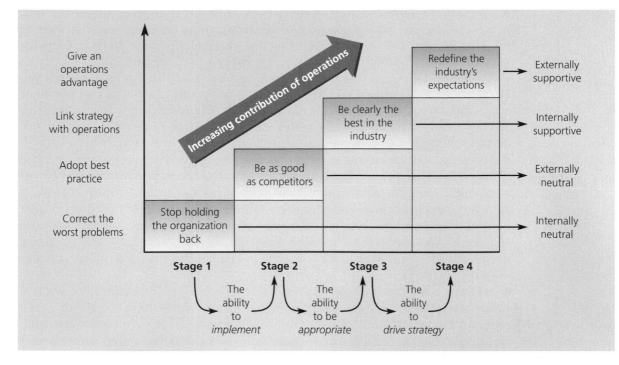

Figure 2.4 The role and the contribution of the operations function

and services and organize their operations – what Hayes and Wheelwright call being 'externally supportive'.

Figure 2.4 brings together the two concepts of the *role* and the *contribution* of the operations function. Moving from Stage 1 to Stage 2 requires operations to overcome its problems of implementing existing strategies. The move from Stage 2 to Stage 3 requires operations actively to develop its resources so that they are appropriate for long-term strategy. Moving up to Stage 4 requires operations to be driving strategy through its contribution to competitive superiority.

THE FIVE PERFORMANCE OBJECTIVES[5]

The operations function contributes to achieving an operations-based advantage through five basic 'performance objectives'. These were used in the TNT example earlier, and can be derived from first principles. Imagine that you are an operations manager in any kind of business – a hospital administrator, for example, or a production manager at a car plant, the operations manager for a city bus company or the manager of a large supermarket. What kind of things are you likely to want to do in order to contribute to competitiveness?

● You would want to *do things right*; that is you would not want to make mistakes. You would want to satisfy your customers by providing error-free goods and services which are 'fit for their purpose'. If the operation succeeds in achieving all this it is giving a *quality advantage* to the company.

51

● You would want to *do things fast*; that is you would want to minimize the time between a customer asking for goods or services and the customer receiving them in full. In doing this you would be increasing the availability of your goods and services to customers and you would be giving the company a *speed advantage*.

● You would want to *do things on time*, so as to keep the delivery promises which you have given to your customers. This might mean being able to estimate a delivery date accurately (or perhaps even accept the customer's required delivery date), communicate this clearly to the customer, and then deliver exactly on time. If the operation can do this, it is giving a *dependability advantage* to its customers.

● You would want to be able to *change what you do*; that is being able to vary or adapt the operation's activities, either because you have to cope with some unexpected circumstances (an individual customer changing his or her mind, or more customers than you expected demanding your services perhaps) or because customers require individual treatment, so the range of goods and services which you produce has to be wide enough to deal with all customer possibilities. Either way, being able to change far enough and fast enough to meet customer requirements gives a *flexibility advantage* to your customers.

● You would want to *do things cheaply*; that is produce goods and services at a cost which enables them to be priced appropriately for the market while still allowing for a return to the organization. Alternatively, if the organization is a not-for-profit organization, doing things cheaply means giving good value to the tax payers or whoever is funding the operation. When the organization is managing to do this, it is giving a *cost advantage* to its customers.

The next part of this chapter examines these five performance objectives in more detail by looking at what they mean for the four different operations previously mentioned: a general hospital, an automobile factory, a city bus company and a supermarket chain.

The quality objective

Quality means 'doing things right', but the things which the operation needs to do right will vary according to the kind of operation (*see* Fig. 2.5). For example, in the hospital, quality could mean making sure that patients get the most appropriate treatment, that the treatment is carried out in a medically correct manner, that patients are kept clearly informed as to what is happening and also are consulted if there are alternative forms of treatment. It would also include such things as ensuring that the hospital is clean, hygienic and tidy and that the staff are well informed and courteous towards patients. In the automobile factory quality means that the car is made to its specifications and is reliable. All parts are assembled correctly and all extras and documents are present and in the right place. Visually the car should look attractive and be blemish- and scratch-free. In a city bus company quality means that the buses are clean, quiet and do not put out unpleasant fumes. It also means that timetables and other published information relating to the bus service are accurate and usable. Finally, it means that the bus staff are courteous and helpful to passengers. For the manager of the supermarket quality means that the goods it sells are in good condition, that the store is clean and tidy, that the decor is attractive and that the staff are helpful and courteous.

**Figure 2.5
Quality means
different things
in different
operations**

Put this way it is not surprising that all operations regard quality as a particularly important objective. In some ways quality is the most visible part of what an operation does. Furthermore, it is something that a customer finds relatively easy to judge about the operation. Is the product or service as it is supposed to be? Is it right or is it wrong? There is something fundamental about quality. Because of this, it is clearly a major influence on customer satisfaction or dissatisfaction. Good quality products and services mean high customer satisfaction and therefore the likelihood that the customer will return (*see* box on Barbour). Conversely, poor quality reduces the chances of a customer coming back for more.

Quality inside the operation

Good quality performance in an operation not only leads to external customer satisfaction; it makes life easier inside the operation as well. Satisfying internal customers can be as important as satisfying external customers.

Quality reduces costs

The fewer mistakes each micro operation or unit makes in the operation, the less time it will need to spend correcting these mistakes and the less confusion and irritation will be spread. For example, if a supermarket's regional warehouse sends the wrong goods to the supermarket it will mean staff time, and therefore cost, being used to sort out the problem.

Quality increases dependability

Increased costs are not the only consequence of poor quality, however. At the supermarket it could also mean that goods run out on the supermarket shelves with a resulting loss of revenue to the operation and irritation to the external customers. Sorting the problem out could also distract the supermarket management from giving its attention to the other parts of the supermarket operation. This in turn could result in further mistakes being made.

The important point here is that the performance objective of quality (like the other performance objectives, as we shall see) has both an external aspect to it which leads to customer satisfaction, and an internal aspect to it which leads to a stable and efficient organization.

THE BEST BRITISH CLOTHING FOR THE WORST BRITISH WEATHER[6]

All success has its price. The price that Barbour, the country clothing manufacturer, has paid for its phenomenal success has been a host of competitors trying to imitate the company's products. The company's response to this has been single minded – to stick close to its original concept of exceptionally high quality.

Based in the north-east of England, J. Barbour and Sons was 100 years old in 1994. It has always made waterproof garments aimed primarily at country and outdoor users. Yet its products have also become fashion garments throughout the world with a corresponding increase in sales. (The company's sales outside the UK increased tenfold in ten years.) The emphasis of the company has always been on maintaining the quality of its products and services. Owners of Barbour jackets are encouraged to send their garments back to the factory when they need repair rather than buy a new one. Retail outlets are selected carefully and expected to provide the company with feedback from their customers. This information is used to improve continuously the company's manufacturing operations. Quality control within the factory is also rigorous. The company's 700 employees (many of whom are second- or third-generation employees) are expected to take responsibility for quality control. Factory wages are high and staff turnover is almost non-existent. To attain its high quality levels, the company insists that each garment produced undergoes 14 separate inspections during its manufacturing process. Not the easiest or cheapest way of making clothing perhaps, but Barbour says it is the best way to preserve a quality reputation through 100 years. ∎

Questions

1 What does 'quality' mean to a company like Barbour?

2 What seems to influence Barbour's quality?

The speed objective

Speed is concerned with how long customers have to wait to receive their products or services (*see* Fig. 2.6). For example, in the hospital it means that patients in the Accident and Emergency department are seen and treated quickly before they suffer any further distress. It also means that the patients with less urgent needs do not have to suffer a long waiting list. For the automobile factory, speed means that the time between a dealer ordering a particular car for one of its customers and the car being delivered from the factory is as short as possible. For the city bus company, speed literally means how fast the operation can get customers from A to B. For the

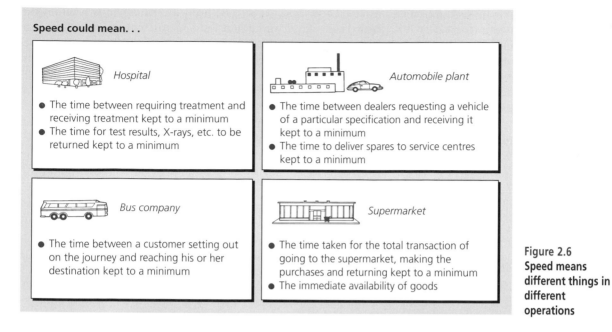

Figure 2.6 Speed means different things in different operations

supermarket manager, speed means how fast customers can get to the store, park their cars, select their purchases, get through the check-out, return to their cars, and arrive back home. In operations like this, speed is also about the availability of goods. If the goods which a customer wants are on the shelf, the customer can have them immediately (that is very fast, in fact instant, service). If the goods are not on the shelf, the likelihood is that the customer will either forego the purchase or, alternatively, go elsewhere and not buy the particular good from that supermarket (that is very slow, in fact infinitely delayed, service).

The main benefit to the operation's (external) customers of speedy delivery of goods and services lies in the way it enhances the operation's offering to the customer. Quite simply, for most goods and services the faster a customer can have the product or service, the more likely he or she is to buy it.

Speed inside the operation

Inside the operation speed is also important. Fast response to external customers is greatly helped by speedy decision making and speedy movement of materials and information inside the operation. Internal speed can have further benefits, however.[7]

Speed reduces inventories

Take, for example, the automobile plant. The steel which is used to make the vehicle's door panels is first delivered to the press shop where it is pressed out into shape. It is then transported to the painting area where it is coated for colour and protection. After this it is moved to the assembly line where it is fitted to the automobile. This is a simple three-stage manufacturing process, but in practice each door panel does not flow smoothly from one stage to the next. If you follow one product through the process its journey can take a surprisingly long time. First, the steel is delivered as part of a far larger batch, containing enough steel to make possibly several hundred products. It might be inspected and then waits to be used. Eventually it is taken to the press area where it is pressed into shape and again waits, along with many other door panels, until transportation to the paint area. It again waits until it can be painted, only to wait once more until it is transported to the assembly line. Yet again it waits by the trackside until it is eventually fitted to the automobile. A relatively short journey along the assembly line then takes it to the point where it leaves the factory as part of the finished product.

The door panel's journey through the factory was far longer than the time needed to actually make and fit the product, and was also composed mainly of waiting time. When hundreds of products are moving through the plant every day, this waiting time results in large stocks (or inventories) of parts and products. If, on the other hand, the waiting can be reduced (say by moving and processing the parts in smaller batches) the parts will move faster through the plant and as a result the amount of inventories between each stage of the process will be reduced. This idea has some very important implications which will be explored in Chapter 15 on just-in-time.

Speed reduces risks

No one really knows what will happen in the future. Yet forecasting tomorrow's events is far less of a risky business than forecasting next year's. The further ahead companies forecast, the more likely they are to get it wrong. This has important implications for the throughput speed of any operation. Consider the automobile plant again. If the total time for the door panel to complete its journey through the plant is six weeks, door panels are being processed through their first operation six weeks before they reach their final destination. The quantity of door panels being processed will be determined by the forecasts for demand six weeks ahead. Almost certainly the plant at any time will be making the wrong number of door panels because the forecast for six weeks ahead will be wrong.

Alternatively, consider the risk of making the wrong number of door panels if, instead of six weeks, they take only one week to move through the plant. Now the door panels being processed through their first stage are intended to meet demand only one week ahead. Under these circumstances it is far more likely that the number and type of door panels being processed are the number and type which eventually will be needed. Thus the faster material moves through the operation, the more likely the operation is to be making what will really be required by its customers.

WHEN SPEED MEANS LIFE OR DEATH[8]

Of all the operations which have to respond quickly to customer demand, few have more need of speed than the emergency services. In responding to road accidents especially, every second is critical. The treatment you receive during the first hour after your accident (what is called the 'golden hour') can determine whether you survive and fully recover or not. Making full use of the golden hour means speeding up three elements of the total time to treatment – the time it takes for the emergency services to find out about the accident, the time it takes them to travel to the scene of the accident, and the time it takes to get the casualty to appropriate treatment.

Alerting the emergency services immediately to an accident occurs in the idea behind Mercedes-Benz's new TeleAid (Telematic Alarm Identification on Demand), offered initially to drivers of their s-class cars in Germany. As soon as the vehicle's air bag is triggered, an on-board micro computer reports through the mobile phone network to a control centre (drivers can also trigger the system manually if not too badly hurt). The on-board satellite facility then allows the vehicle to be precisely located, and the type of vehicle and owner identified (if special medication is needed).

Getting to the accident quickly is the next hurdle. Often the fastest method is by helicopter. For example, in London the Helicopter Emergency Medical Service (HEMS) initially operated from an airfield to the south of the city; later it moved to a specially constructed helipad on the roof of the Royal London Hospital. This relocation halved the average journey time of eight minutes. Now many of the rescues are only a couple of minutes' flying time back to the hospital – an important factor when speed saves lives. Typically, the HEMS attends four or five incidents a day, although eight is not unusual. However, it is not always possible to land the helicopter safely at night (because of possible overhead wires and other hazards) so the team also uses a high-performance Audi Estate (station wagon) to provide a ground-based service. The back of the car is packed with emergency medical equipment, but is not designed to transport the patient – that task is left to the conventional ambulances.

The objective of the Estate is simply to get a single paramedic to the scene *very quickly*. To facilitate fast response, it is usually stationed in the area of high emergency rates, waiting for a call. When not required for accident trauma cases, it attends other types of pre-hospital cases such as heart attacks and premature births. Getting appropriate treatment to an accident victim is also the motivation behind how the helicopter is staffed. Even though the idea of helicopter air ambulances is not new, the HEMS took the concept one stage further, with the deployment on board of two doctors in addition to the paramedic and the pilot. Having so many medical staff on board speeds up the critical emergency work needed to stabilize the patient prior to transfer to the hospital. ∎

Questions

1 Draw a chart which illustrates the stages between an accident occurring and full treatment being made available.

2 What are the key issues (both those mentioned above and any others you can think of) which determine the time taken at each stage?

The dependability objective

Dependability means doing things in time for customers to receive their goods or services when they were promised (*see* Fig. 2.7). A hospital with a high standard of dependability would not cancel operations or any other appointments made with its patients. It would always, for example, deliver the results of tests and X-ray investigations on time and keep to schedule on its immunization programmes. A dependable

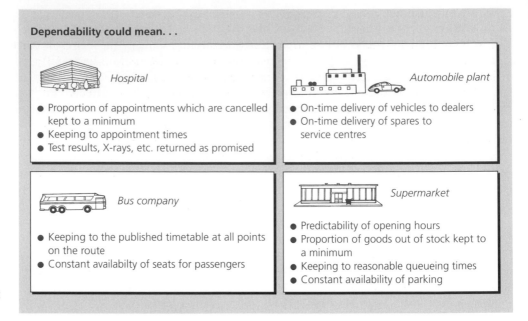

Dependability could mean. . .

Hospital
- Proportion of appointments which are cancelled kept to a minimum
- Keeping to appointment times
- Test results, X-rays, etc. returned as promised

Automobile plant
- On-time delivery of vehicles to dealers
- On-time delivery of spares to service centres

Bus company
- Keeping to the published timetable at all points on the route
- Constant availabilty of seats for passengers

Supermarket
- Predictability of opening hours
- Proportion of goods out of stock kept to a minimum
- Keeping to reasonable queueing times
- Constant availability of parking

**Figure 2.7
Dependability
means different
things in different
operations**

automobile plant will deliver cars and spare parts to the car dealers and service centres exactly as promised. A dependable city bus company will always keep to its published timetable, picking up passengers at every point on the journey precisely on schedule. Furthermore, there will be seats available for the passengers who are there to catch the bus. Each season the company will also publish its revised timetables on the day promised. A dependable supermarket chain has predictable opening hours. It will never run out of stock of any of the items which it has led its customers to expect to be in stock (by advertising or past practice).

Customers might only judge the dependability of an operation after the product or service has been delivered. For example, a customer would probably decide to take a bus across town initially on the criteria of speed and cost. After taking the journey the customer will have some view about the dependability of the service. Initially this will not affect the likelihood that customers will select the service – they have already 'consumed' it. Over time, however, dependability can override all other criteria. No matter how cheap a bus service is, or how fast it is advertised as being, if the service is always late (or unpredictably early) or the buses are always full, then potential passengers will be better off calling a taxi.

Dependability inside the operation

Inside the operation dependability has a similar effect. Internal customers will judge each other's performance partly by how reliable the other micro operations are in delivering material or information on time. Operations where internal dependability is high are more effective than those which are not for a number of reasons.

Dependability saves time

Take, for example, the maintenance and repair centre for the city bus company. The manager will always have a plan of the centre's activities each day for a period ahead.

Probably this plan has been drawn up to keep the centre's facilities as fully utilized as possible while ensuring that the bus fleet always has enough clean and serviced vehicles to match demand at any time. If, one day, the centre runs out of some crucial spare parts which are needed to repair two of the buses which are booked in for servicing that day, the manager of the centre will need to spend time trying to arrange a special delivery of the required parts within the next few days. It is unlikely that the resources which had been reserved to service the buses can be used as productively as they would have been without this disruption. More seriously, the fleet will be short of two buses until they can be repaired. The fleet operations manager will have to spend time rescheduling the services so as to minimize the disruption to customers. On this particular day (and entirely due to the one failure of dependability of supply) a significant part of the operation's time will have been occupied trying to cope with the disruption rather than doing anything directly productive.

Dependability saves money

Most of this ineffective use of time will translate into extra cost in the operation. The spare parts might cost more to be delivered at short notice than by regular delivery. The maintenance staff will expect to be paid even when there is not a bus to work on. Similarly, the fixed costs of the operation, such as heating and rent, will not reduce because the two buses are not being serviced. Out on the road the disruption will also have financial consequences. The rescheduling of buses to routes will probably mean that some routes have inappropriately sized buses and some services could have to be cancelled. This will result in empty bus seats (if too large a bus has to be used) or a loss of revenue (if potential passengers are not transported).

Dependability gives stability

The disruption caused to operations by a lack of dependability goes beyond time and cost. It affects the 'quality' of the operation's time. If everything in an operation is perfectly dependable, and has been for some time, a level of trust will build up between the different parts of the operation. There will be no 'surprises' and everything will be predictable. Under such circumstances each part of the operation can concentrate on improving its own part of the operation without having its attention continually diverted by the lack of dependable service from the other parts of the operation.

The flexibility objective[9]

Flexibility means being able to change the operation in some way. This may mean changing what the operation does, how it is doing it, or when it is doing it. Specifically, customers will need the operation to change so that it can provide four types of requirement:

- *product/service flexibility* – different products and services;
- *mix flexibility* – a wide range or mix of products and services;
- *volume flexibility* – different quantities or volumes of products and services;
- *delivery flexibility* – different delivery times.

Figure 2.8 gives examples of what these different types of flexibility mean to the four operations.

THE *NINE O'CLOCK NEWS* CANNOT BE LATE[10]

Some businesses rely on their operations to be on time, all the time, and every time. The news business is like this. A daily newspaper delivered one day late is practically worthless. The news operation where dependability is perhaps at its most critical, however, is television news. The BBC's *Nine O'Clock News* is expected to start on the second of nine o'clock and last exactly 30 minutes (unless a programming decision is taken to delay it for a sporting event or other exceptional circumstances). The BBC's ability to achieve this level of dependability is made possible by the technology employed in news gathering and editing. For example, until recently a news editor would have scheduled a video-taped report to start its count-down five seconds prior to its broadcast time. The screen would show the numbers as the count-down proceeded and the team would anxiously wait for the visuals to appear to make sure that the correct tape had indeed been loaded. With new technology the tape can be started from a freeze-frame and will roll the instant the command to play is given. The team has faith in the dependability of the process. In addition, technology allows them the flexibility to achieve dependability even when news stories break just before transmission. In the hours before scheduled transmission, journalists and editors prepare an 'inventory' of news items stored electronically. The presenter will prepare his or her commentary on the autocue and each item will be timed to the second. (From experience the team can estimate exactly how long it will take to read any number of words.) If the team needs to make short-term adjustments to the planned schedule of items, the news studio's technology allows the editors to take broadcasts live from journalists at their locations, on satellite 'takes', directly into the programme. Editors can even type news reports directly onto the autocue for the presenter to read as they are typed. Nerve-racking, but it keeps the programme on time. ■

Questions

1 What do each of the five performance objectives mean for an operation such as the BBC's Newsroom which produces the *Nine O'Clock News*?

2 How do these performance objectives influence each other?

Product/Service flexibility

Product/Service flexibility is the operation's ability to introduce new products and services. In the hospital this could mean introducing new surgical techniques or new medical record information. In the automobile plant it means the ability to adapt its manufacturing resources so that it can launch new models. To the city bus company it means that it could introduce new routes or special excursion services, while to the supermarket it means introducing new lines on its shelves, novel promotions or new payment services.

Mix flexibility

Mix flexibility means being able to provide a wide range or mix of products and services. Most operations produce more than one product or service. In addition, most operations do not make their products or services in high enough volumes to dedicate

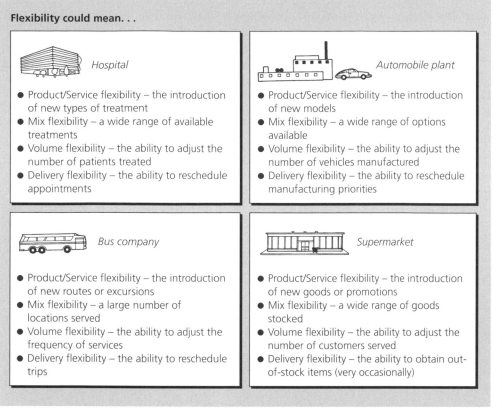

Figure 2.8 Flexibility means different things in different operations

all parts of their activities exclusively to a single product or service. This means that most parts of any operation will have to process more than one type of product or service and so will at times need to change from doing one activity to doing another. For example, some parts of a hospital need to provide a relatively wide range of services. The Accident and Emergency department has to provide immediate treatment for the wide range of complaints from which its patients suffer. The General Surgery department also has a similarly wide range of complaints to treat. The staff, technology and organization of these departments need to be flexible enough to cope with this variety. Other departments in the hospital will require less flexibility because they provide a comparatively narrow range of services. The X-ray department, for example, is expected only to provide radiographic services. In the automobile plant, flexibility is needed to provide all the range of options which customers are able to choose when buying their cars. The city bus company needs to provide a wide enough variety of routes to satisfy demand between its more popular areas of the city. To the supermarket, mix flexibility means being able to stock a wide range of products on its shelves.

Volume flexibility

Volume flexibility is the ability of the operation to change its level of output or activity. All operations will need to change their level of activity because all operations to some extent have to cope with fluctuating demand for their products and services. Of course all operations could theoretically ignore these fluctuations in demand, dispense with all volume flexibility and keep their activity level constant. However, this totally 'inflexible' option can have serious consequences on customer service, operating costs or both. (Chapter 11 on capacity management will deal with this.)

In the hospital the demand for its various services will vary depending on the type of area it serves. For example, a hospital Accident and Emergency unit in a city area which takes in a large number of commuting workers will have to cope with heavy demand during the working and travelling hours of the day but will have relatively quiet evenings, weekends and summer vacation periods. The hospital will need to be flexible enough to provide an appropriate level of service as demand varies throughout the day as well as over the week and the year. In addition, it will need to cope with the occasional unpredictable demand for its services such as when a major road accident occurs. In a similar way, the demand for automobiles will vary throughout the year and the automobile factory will need to adjust its output accordingly. The city bus company will also need to change its activity levels throughout the day as demand varies. In the supermarket, flexibility again means coping with a variety of activity levels as demand varies throughout the day.

Delivery flexibility

Delivery flexibility is the ability to change the timing of the delivery of the service. Usually this means the operation providing goods or services earlier than anticipated, although it may mean delaying delivery.

In the hospital, delivery flexibility means rescheduling a patient's treatment. A maternity ward, for example, needs to have high delivery flexibility (in both senses!) to deal with a patient's premature labour. The automobile plant might occasionally have to rush a particular product through the plant to meet the special needs of a customer (although this might cause expensive disruption to the plant's schedules). The city bus company would be even more unlikely to reschedule its regular services so as to change their delivery times, but might have to do this for its excursion services. Similarly, the supermarket might not generally want to change the regular delivery schedules to its stores but, in exceptional circumstances, to placate a dissatisfied customer, for example, it might bring forward the delivery of an out-of-stock item.

Flexibility inside the operation

Developing a flexible operation can also have advantages to the internal customers within the operation.

Flexibility speeds up response

Being able to give fast service often depends on the operation being flexible. For example, if the hospital has to cope with a sudden influx of patients from a road accident, it clearly needs to deal with injuries quickly. Under such circumstances a flexible hospital which can speedily transfer extra skilled staff and equipment to the Accident and Emergency department will provide the fast service which the patients need.

Flexibility saves time

In many parts of the hospital staff have to treat a wide variety of complaints. Fractures, cuts or drug overdoses do not come in batches. Each patient is an individual with individual needs. The hospital staff cannot take time to 'get into the routine' of treating a particular complaint; they must have the flexibility to adapt quickly. They must also have sufficiently flexible facilities and equipment so that time is not wasted waiting for equipment to be brought to the patient. The time of the hospital's resources is being saved because they are flexible in 'changing over' from one task to the next. (*See* also box on Godiva Chocolatier for an example of how flexibility can save time.)

Flexibility maintains dependability

Internal flexibility can also help to keep the operation on schedule when unexpected events disrupt the operation's plans. For example, if the sudden influx of patients to the hospital also results in emergency surgery being performed, the emergency patients will almost certainly displace other routine operations. The patients who were expecting to undergo their routine operations will have been admitted and probably prepared for their operations. Cancelling their operations is likely to cause them distress and probably considerable inconvenience. A flexible hospital might be able to minimize the disruption by possibly having reserved operating theatres for such an emergency, and being able to bring in medical staff quickly who are 'on call'.

FLEXIBILITY AT GODIVA CHOCOLATIER[11]

The world-famous chocolate maker, Godiva Chocolatier, is situated right in the heart of Brussels, Europe's centre of quality chocolate manufacturing. With an output of only about 1500 tonnes per year, Godiva is a relatively small producer which makes more than 100 different chocolates and packs them in a vast range of cartons and bulk packs to suit its different niche markets. Over the last ten years, the company has invested carefully to achieve improvements in productivity through automation, but at the same time to ensure that flexibility is built in at every stage of production. There are two basic methods of production used at Godiva: *enrobing* and *moulding*.

Enrobed products begin as extruded strips of hard fillings such as marzipan, which are cut into short pieces and passed through a machine which coats them in liquid chocolate. The enrobing department operates by linking together the various pieces of equipment (extruders, guillotines, depositors, enrobers, decorators, etc.) in different sequences and combinations to suit the individual product designs. Sometimes, where the volumes justify the effort involved in repositioning them, this is done by using moveable conveyors to make the link between the machines. Otherwise, the products are transferred around as required in plastic trays, allowing the equipment (and the skilled staff) to be decoupled and thereby to work at different speeds and times. Only small tanks of liquid chocolate (dark, milk and white) are used at the enrobing machines so that changeovers can be fast. Typically it takes only 20 minutes to disconnect the tank and clean out the enrobing machine prior to starting another colour. Because of the wide variety of products made this way, planning is complex, with the sequence of products being critical to productivity, utilization and quality. Normally, it is considered uneconomic and impractical to produce less than 300 kg of a particular colour, but where possible, longer runs of different products with the same chocolate coating are planned, so that the colour change can be carried out at the end of the day's production.

Most *moulded products* are produced on a new and complicated 80 metre long production line, which was designed to handle almost the full range of moulded products. It can mould all three colours with a 20 minute change-over of the liquid chocolate. These are normally done

▶

only at the end of a day's production. Moulds can be changed without stopping the line using a simple operator-assisted mould-changing device. Filling the shells with creams, fondants, etc. is carried out using computer-controlled depositing machines, which give tight control of volume and speed to take account of the physical properties of the fillings. Three of these depositors are available, allowing one or two to be in use while the third is moved aside for cleaning, programming, and setting-up with the next batch of filling. It is possible, therefore, to change product in under one minute, and to use two depositors simultaneously for products where nuts or cherries are to be incorporated in the middle of creams. After demoulding, the chocolates can be routed to an automatic individual wrapping machine, but most are conveyed directly to a new packing robot which picks and places the products on blister packs for bulk sales to shops, or on flat plastic trays for transfer to the assortment packing lines.

The most flexible part of the operation is the *assortment packing* section. Here, the finished chocolates are packed according to the appropriate mix and positions in the various retail cartons. These pass along a conveyor where each individual chocolate is added to the pack by hand. Although it is technically possible for this to be done by a robot, Godiva engineers have found that people are less expensive and can also continuously inspect the quality of every chocolate packed. Many of the staff are also very adept at adding sophisticated and complicated value-added features to the packaging, such as ribbons, bows and labels. ■

Questions

1 Why is flexibility so important to a company like Godiva?

2 What does the company appear to have done to enhance its flexibility?

Source: By kind permission of Godiva SA

The cost objective

Cost is the last objective to be covered, although not because it is the least important. To the companies which compete directly on price, cost will be clearly their major operations objective. The lower the cost of producing their goods and services, the lower can be the price to their customers. Even those companies which compete on things other than price, however, will be interested in keeping their costs low. Every pound, dollar or guilder removed from an operation's cost base is a further pound, dollar or guilder added to its profits. Not surprisingly, low cost is a universally attractive objective.

The ways in which operations management can influence cost will depend largely on where the operation costs are incurred. Put simply, the operation will spend its money on:

● *staff costs* (the money spent on employing people);
● *facilities, technology and equipment costs* (the money spent on buying, caring for, operating and replacing the operation's 'hardware';
● *material costs* (the money spent on the materials consumed or transformed in the operation).

Figure 2.9 shows typical cost breakdowns for the hospital, car plant, supermarket, and bus company.

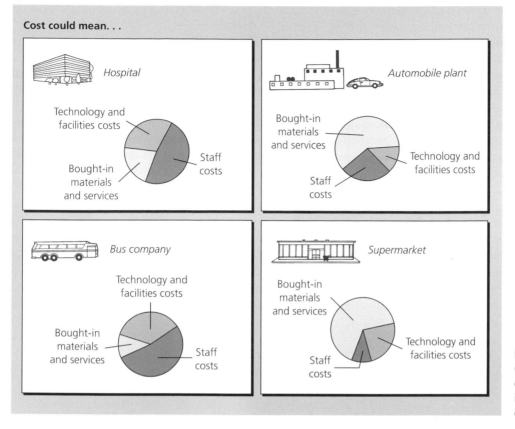

**Figure 2.9
Cost means different things in different operations**

Although comparing the cost structure of different operations is not always straight-forward, and depends on how costs are categorized, some general points can be made.

Many of the hospital's costs are fixed and will change little for small changes in the number of patients it treats. Its facilities such as beds, operating theatres and laboratories are expensive, as are some of its highly skilled staff. Some of the hospital's costs will be payments to outside suppliers of drugs, medical supplies and externally sourced services such as cleaning, but probably not as high a proportion as in the car factory. The car factory's payment for materials and other supplies will by far outweigh all its other costs put together. Conversely, the city bus company will pay very little for its supplies, fuel being one of its main bought-in items. At the other extreme, the supermarket's costs are dominated by the cost of buying its supplies. In spite of its high 'material' costs, however, an individual supermarket can do little if anything to affect the cost of goods it sells. All purchasing decisions will probably be made at company headquarters. The individual supermarket will be more concerned with the utilization of its main asset, the building itself, and its staff.

Cost is affected by the other performance objectives

So far we have described the meaning and effects of quality, speed, dependability and flexibility for the operations function. In doing so, we have distinguished between the value of each performance objective to external customers and, inside the operation, to internal customers. Each of the various performance objectives has several internal effects, but all of them affect cost.

- High-quality operations do not waste time or effort having to re-do things, nor are their internal customers inconvenienced by flawed service.
- Fast operations reduce the level of in-process inventory between micro operations as well as reducing administrative overheads.
- Dependable operations do not spring any unwelcome surprises on their internal customers. They can be relied on to deliver exactly as planned. This eliminates wasteful disruption and allows the other micro operations to operate efficiently.
- Flexible operations adapt to changing circumstances quickly and without disrupting the rest of the operation. Flexible micro operations can also change over between tasks quickly and without wasting time and capacity.

Inside the operation, therefore, one important way to improve cost performance is to improve the performance of the other operations objectives (*see* Fig. 2.10).

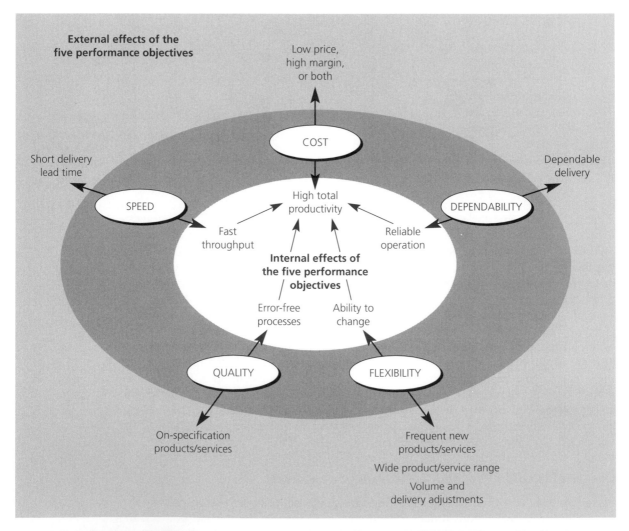

Figure 2.10 Performance objectives have both external and internal effects. Internally, cost is influenced by the other performance objectives

ALDI EINKAUF – EUROPE'S LARGEST RETAILER[12]

They started in Germany and then spread to Denmark, Holland and Belgium. Soon the cut-price retailers were taking larger shares of the market throughout Europe. Cut-price retailers include companies such as Netto (Danish) and Lidl and Schwartz (German), but perhaps the best known is Aldi (also German). Aldi has carefully focused its service concept and delivery system to attract customers in a highly competitive market. It has developed and maintained its own unique style of operation and is continuing to expand in Europe – over the last few years at a rate of 15 per cent per annum – so that it now operates in 12 countries within Europe.

The Aldi operation challenges the norms of retailing. It is deliberately simple, using basic strip lighting in its stores, stocking only a limited range of goods (approximately 5000 in comparison to the 15 000/20 000 stocked by retailers such as Sainsbury's in the UK or Mammouth in France) and using cut-open cases of goods rather than expensive display shelves. The company has formidable buying power (as Europe's largest retailer) and stocks mainly its own brand of goods. Its highly effective distribution channels and low overhead costs also help to keep prices low. Aldi has deliberately followed a 'keep it simple, keep it cheap' concept of service operations, aiming to make life for the customer as easy as possible. Aldi believes that by only accepting cash sales (no cheques or coupons) and by having such a limited range of goods (so that cashiers can remember all of the prices and so work at a higher speed than scanners) they can process customers quickly and reliably. ∎

Question

1 How do companies like Aldi seem to keep their costs down?

Doug Wilson, London Stock Exchange

Doug Wilson is the Operations Manager responsible for the settlement of equity transfers at the London Stock Exchange, which provides a key trading facility to the dominant economies around the world.

The settlement process is handled by the Talisman System, which handles, on average, 32 000 transfers each day. These transfers are confirmation that agents or individuals have requested to buy or sell their shares, and the settlement process transfers ownership of those shares to the new buyer.

The rules, under which the London Stock Exchange operates, oblige it to process, by the end of the following business day, any transactions deposited prior to 1.30 pm – a rigid deadline critical to the operation. The Stock Exchange has no means of controlling or predicting the volumes to be handled each day, and must guarantee to respond to actual levels of market activity. The operations systems must provide total dependability, and the flexibility to increase the capacity to cater for unexpected levels of demand, at very short notice.

Despite the use of the computer system, the operation in Doug's area is very labour intensive, and much of his work is focused on achieving high levels of productivity from the operational staff.

'Our staff are multi-skilled to a certain extent and are trained to carry out a variety of tasks in order to give the operation the flexibility to deal with the high variation in demand. We have to provide extra capacity at short notice, and the department employs a high proportion of part-time staff in order to keep costs to a minimum, while also providing a greater degree of flexibility in terms of staff cover. The Talisman System offers an effective, structured, and yet still flexible operation which is capable of delivering a high quality output within the required time limits. There are spare terminals for the system located at each stage of the process, giving the option to use some of the extra staff, should demand peak.'

The settlement process has to be completed by the end of the following business day and Doug has to ensure that communications are encouraged between sections in the process to inform those functions in the latter part of the system of the volumes to expect.

'This means that although on Day One we are very open to market fluctuations and have to be extremely versatile, those operations carried out on Day Two are given at least 24 hours notice of their resource requirements, and can subsequently organize the necessary number of part-time staff. Unpredictability is part of our business at the Stock Exchange, but we have never failed to deliver and our reputation in the international market depends on maintaining that record.' ∎

Source: By kind permission of the London Stock Exchange

SUMMARY ANSWERS TO KEY QUESTIONS

What role should the operations function play in achieving strategic success?

■ Any operations function has three main roles to play within an organization:
- as an implementer of the organization's strategies;
- as a supporter of the organization's overall strategy;
- as a leader of strategy.

■ The extent to which an operations function fulfils these roles, together with its aspirations, can be used to judge the operations functions' contribution to the organization. Hayes and Wheelwright provide a four-stage model for doing this.

What are the performance objectives of operations and what are the internal and external benefits which derive from excelling in each of them?

■ By 'doing things right' operations seek to influence the quality of the company's goods and services. Externally, quality is an important aspect of customer satisfaction or dissatisfaction. Internally, quality operations both reduce costs and increase dependability.

■ By 'doing things fast' operations seek to influence the speed with which goods and services are delivered. Externally, speed is an important aspect of customer service. Internally, speed both reduces inventories by decreasing internal throughput time and reduces risks by delaying the commitment of resources.

■ By 'doing things on time' operations seek to influence the dependability of the delivery of goods and services. Externally, dependability is an important aspect of customer service. Internally, dependability within operations increases operational reliability, thus saving the time and money that would otherwise be taken up in solving reliability problems and also giving stability to the operation.

■ By 'changing what they do' operations seek to influence the flexibility with which the company produces goods and services. Externally, flexibility can:
- produce new products and services (product/service flexibility);
- produce a wide range or mix of products and services (mix flexibility);
- produce different quantities or volumes of products and services (volume flexibility);
- produce products and services at different times (delivery flexibility).

Internally, flexibility can help speed up response times, save time wasted in change-overs, and maintain dependability.

■ By 'doing things cheaply' operations seek to influence the cost of the company's goods and services. Externally, low costs allow organizations to reduce their price in order to gain higher volumes or alternatively increase their profitability on existing volume levels. Internally, cost performance is helped by good performance in the other performance objectives.

69

CASE EXERCISE

Operations objectives at the Penang Mutiara[13]

There are many luxurious hotels in the South-East Asia region but few can compare with the Penang Mutiara, a 440 room top-of-the-market hotel which nestles in the lush greenery of Malaysia's Indian Ocean Coast. Owned by Pernas–OUE of Malaysia and managed by Singapore Mandarin International Hotels, the hotel's General Manager is Wernie Eisen, a Swiss hotelier who has managed luxury hotels all over the world.

He is under no illusions about the importance of running an effective operation.

'Managing a hotel of this size is an immensely complicated task,' he says. *'Our customers have every right to be demanding. They expect first-class service and that's what we have to give them. If we have any problems with managing this operation, the customer sees them immediately and that's the biggest incentive for us to take operations performance seriously.*

'Our quality of service just has to be impeccable. First of all this means dealing with the basics. For example, our staff must be courteous at all times and yet also friendly towards our guests. And of course they must have the knowledge to be able to answer guests' questions. The building and equipment, in fact all the hardware of the operation, must support the luxury atmosphere which we have created in the hotel. Stylish design and top-class materials not only create the right impression but, if we choose them carefully, they are also durable so the hotel still looks good over the years. Most of all though, quality is about anticipating our guests' needs, thinking ahead so you can identify what will delight or irritate a guest.'

The hotel tries to anticipate guests' needs in a number of ways. For example, if guests have been to the hotel before, staff avoid their having to repeat the information which they gave on the previous visit. Reception staff simply check to see if guests have stayed before, retrieve the information and take them straight to their room without irritating delays. Quality of service also means helping guests sort out their own problems. If the airline loses a guest's luggage *en route* to the hotel, for example, he or she will arrive at the hotel understandably irritated.

'The fact that it is not us who have irritated them is not really the issue. It is our job to make them feel better.'

Speed, in terms of fast response to customers' requests is something else that is important.

'A guest just should not be kept waiting. If a guest has a request, he or she has that request now so it needs to be sorted out now. This is not always easy but we do our best. For example, if every guest in the hotel tonight decided to call room service and request a meal instead of going to the restaurants, our room service department would obviously be grossly overloaded and customers would have to wait an unacceptably long time before the meals were brought up to their rooms. We cope with this by keeping a close watch on how demand for room service is building up. If we think it's going to get above the level where response time to customers would become unacceptably long, we will call in staff from other restaurants in the hotel. Of course, to do this we have to make sure that our staff are multi-skilled. In fact we have a policy of making sure that restaurant staff can always do more than one job. It's this kind of flexibility which allows us to maintain fast response to the customer.'

Likewise, Wernie regards dependability as a fundamental principle of a well-managed hotel.

'We must always keep our promises. For example, rooms must be ready on time and accounts must be ready for presentation when a guest departs; the guests expect a dependable service and anything less than full dependability is a legitimate cause for dissatisfaction.'

It is on the grand occasions, however, when dependability is particularly important in the hotel. When staging a banquet, for example, everything has to be on time. Drinks, food, entertainment have to be available exactly as planned. Any deviation from plan will very soon be noticed by customers.

'It is largely a matter of planning the details and anticipating what could go wrong,' says Wernie. *'Once we've done the planning we can anticipate possible problems and plan how to cope with them, or better still, prevent them from occurring in the first place.'*

Flexibility means a number of things to the hotel. First of all it means that they should be able to meet a guest's requests.

'We never like to say NO!' says Wernie. *'For example, if a guest asks for some Camembert cheese and we don't*

have it in stock, we will make sure that someone goes to the supermarket and tries to get it. If, in spite of our best efforts, we can't get any we will negotiate an alternative solution with the guest. This has an important side effect – it greatly helps us to maintain the motivation of our staff. We are constantly being asked to do the seemingly impossible – yet we do it, and our staff think it's great. We all like to be part of an organization which is capable of achieving the very difficult, if not the impossible.'

Flexibility in the hotel also means the ability to cope with the seasonal fluctuations in demand. They achieve this partly by using temporary part-time staff. In the back-office parts of the hotel this isn't a major problem. In the laundry, for example, it is relatively easy to put on an extra shift in busy periods by increasing staffing levels. However, this is more of a problem in the parts of the hotel that have direct contact with the customer.

'New temporary staff can't be expected to have the same customer contact skills as our more regular staff. Our solution to this is to keep the temporary staff as far in the background as we possibly can and make sure that our skilled, well-trained staff are the ones who usually interact with the customer. So, for example, a waiter who would normally take orders, service the food, and take away the dirty plates would in peak times restrict his or her activities to taking orders and serving the food. The less skilled part of the job, taking away the plates, could be left to temporary staff.'

As far as cost is concerned, around 60 per cent of the hotel's total operating expenses go on food and beverages, so one obvious way of keeping costs down is by making sure that food is not wasted. Energy costs at 6 per cent of total operating costs are also a potential source of saving. However, although cost savings are welcome, the hotel is very careful never to compromise the quality of its service in order to cut costs. Wernie's view is quite clear.

'It is impeccable customer service which gives us our competitive advantage, not price. Good service means that our guests return again and again. At times, around half our guests are people who have been before. The more guests we have, the higher is our utilization of rooms and restaurants, and this is what really keeps cost per guest down and profitability reasonable. So in the end we've come full circle: it's the quality of our service which keeps our volumes high and our costs low.' ■

Questions

1 Describe how you think Wernie will
(a) make sure that the way he manages the hotel is *appropriate* to the way it competes for business;
(b) *implement* any change in strategy;
(c) develop his operation so that *it drives* the long-term strategy of the hotel.

2 What questions might Wernie ask to judge whether his operation is a Stage 1, Stage 2, Stage 3, or Stage 4 operation on Hayes and Wheelwright's scale of excellence?

3 The case describes how quality, speed, dependability, flexibility and cost impact on the hotel's external customers. Explain how each of these performance objectives might have internal benefits.

DISCUSSION QUESTIONS

1 For the following organizations, explain how their operations functions can support business strategy, implement business strategy and drive business strategy:

a fast-food restaurant
a film-processing service
an oil refinery.

2 Explain the seeming paradox of the operations function, which is concerned with day-to-day operational decisions, while having a central role to play in achieving long-term strategic success.

3 Describe how the operations function of a car hire company might perform as it progressed from being a Stage 1 to a Stage 4 operation (using Hayes and Wheelwright's terms).

4 Illustrate the concept of a Stage 4 company by explaining how a Stage 4 operations function within the following organizations could contribute to their long-term competitive success:

a salted snack manufacturer
an airline
a parcel delivery service
an hotel.

5 Discuss what constitutes quality, speed, dependability and flexibility in the following operations:

a university library
a university sports centre
a university restaurant
an operations management course.
(Try asking the managers of these operations!)

6 Describe the different types of flexibility that might be found in each of the following operations:

a university
a factory making tennis racquets
a rail network.

7 For each of the following organizations explain what is meant by, and discuss the relative importance of, quality, speed, dependability and flexibility:

a high-volume car producer
a hairdresser
a package collection and distribution service (e.g. UPS or Federal Express).

8 Many organizations see the role of operations as getting on with the job of making products or serving customers. Discuss the implications of this view of the operations function.

9 Using an example of your own choice, describe how the cost of the operation might be affected by changing the levels of performance of quality, speed, dependability and flexibility.

NOTES ON CHAPTER

1 This idea was first popularized by Wickham Skinner at Harvard University. *See* Skinner, W. (1985) *Manufacturing: The Formidable Competitive Weapon*, John Wiley.

2 Hayes, R.H. and Wheelwright, S.C. (1984) *Restoring our Competitive Edge*, John Wiley.

3 Sources: TNT Group report, 'TNT's Marketing-Led Strategy Changes the Goal Posts', *Business Marketing Digest*, May 1993.

4 Chase, R. and Hayes, R.H. (1991) 'Beefing up Service Firms', *Sloan Management Review*, Fall.

5 The five performance objectives are discussed in far more detail in Slack, N. (1991) *The Manufacturing Advantage*, Mercury Books.

6 Sources: Company literature and *The Economist*, 7 Jan 1994.

7 For a much more detailed discussion of the speed objective *see* Stalk, G. and Hout, T.M. (1990) *Competing Against Time*, Free Press.

8 Sources: 'Angels with an Audi', *The Audi Magazine*, Summer 1994. 'Smart Car will Call Police in a Crash', *The Sunday Times*, 23 Feb 1997.

9 For a further discussion of the flexibility objective *see* Slack, N. (1989) 'Focus on Flexibility' *in* Wild, R. (ed) *International Handbook of Production/Operations Management*, Cassell.

10 Source: Discussions with the News Team at the BBC.

11 Source: Benjamin, M. (1994) 'Chocolate Secrets Unwrapped', *The European*, 1–7 April, and the management of Godiva Chocolatier.
12 Sources: Interviews with Aldi staff, 'Europe's Discount Dogfight', *The Economist*, 8 May 1993.
13 We are grateful to Wernie Eisen and the management of the Penang Mutiara for permission to use this example.

SELECTED FURTHER READINGS

Azzone, G., Bertelé, U. and Masella, C. (1991) 'The Design of Performance Measures for Time Based Companies', *International Journal of Operations and Production Management*, Vol 11, No 3.

Bhattacharya, A.K., Jina, J. and Walton, A.D. (1996) 'Product Market Turbulance and Time Compression: Three Dimensions of an Integrated Approach to Manufacturing Systems Design', *International Journal of Operations and Production Management*, Vol 16, No 9.

Blenkinsop, A. and Burns, N. (1992) 'Performance Measurement Revisited', *International Journal of Operations and Production Management*, Vol 12, No 10.

Chase, R. and Hayes, R.H. (1991) 'Beefing up Operations in Service Firms', *Sloan Management Review*, Fall, pp 15–26.

Chyr, F. (1996) 'The Effect of Varying Set-up Costs', *International Journal of Operations and Production Management*, Vol 16, No 3.

De Meyer, A. and Fedows, K. (1990) 'The Influence of Manufacturing Improvement Programmes on Performance', *International Journal of Operations and Production Management*, Vol 10, No 2.

Feitzinger, E. and Lee, H.L. (1997) 'Mass Customization and Hewlett-Packard: The Power of Postponement', *Harvard Business Review*, Vol 75, No 1.

Gupta, Y.P., Lonial, S.C. and Mangold, W.G. (1991) 'An Examination of the Relationship between Manufacturing Strategy and Marketing Objectives', *International Journal of Operations and Production Management*, Vol 11, No 10.

Hayes, R.H. and Wheelwright, S.C. (1984) *Restoring Our Competitive Edge*, John Wiley, Chap 14.

Hill, T. (1993) *Manufacturing Strategy* (2nd edn), Macmillan.

New, C. (1992) 'World-Class Manufacturing versus Strategic Trade-offs', *International Journal of Operations and Production Management*, Vol 12, No 4.

Pine, B.J. (1993) *Mass Customization*, Harvard Business School Press.

Shaw, W.N., Clarkson, A.H. and Stone, M.A. (1992) 'The Competitive Characteristics of Scottish Manufacturing Companies', *International Journal of Operations and Production Management*, Vol 12, No 6.

Slack, N. (1991) *The Manufacturing Advantage*, Mercury Business Books.

Stalk, G. (1988) 'Time – The Next Source of Competitive Advantage', *Harvard Business Review*, Vol 66, No 4.

Stalk, G. and Webber, A.M. (1993) 'Japan's Dark Side of Time', *Harvard Business Review*, Vol 71, No 4.

OPERATIONS STRATEGY

INTRODUCTION

No organization can plan in detail every aspect of its current or future actions, but all organizations can benefit from some idea of where they are heading and how they could get there. Put another way, all organizations need some strategic direction. It is just the same with the operations function. Once the operations function has understood its role in the business and after it has articulated the performance objectives which define its contribution to strategy, it needs to formulate a set of general principles which will guide its decision making. This is the *operations strategy* of the company. This chapter establishes the concept of 'strategy' and fits operations strategy within the overall strategic decision making in the organization. It also indicates the type of decisions which an operation will have to take in order to establish the content of its operations strategy. Figure 3.1 shows the position of the ideas described in this chapter on the general model of operations management.

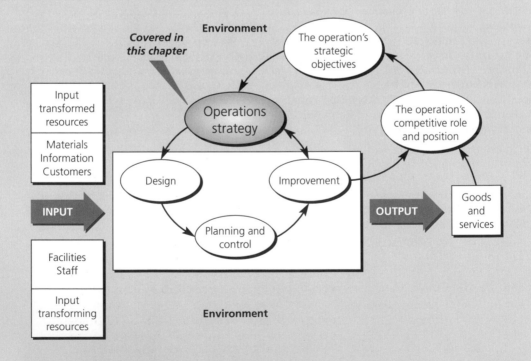

Figure 3.1 This chapter examines operations strategy

CHAPTER 3: KEY QUESTIONS

- *What is an operations strategy?*

- *How does operations strategy fit into a company's overall strategy?*

- *How do we know which performance objectives are the most important?*

- *What are the specific decision areas which are usually included in an operations strategy?*

- *How can an operations strategy be put together?*

WHAT IS STRATEGY?

Before dealing with operations strategy it is necessary to consider what we mean by the term 'strategy'. One thing we assume when an organization articulates its 'strategy' is that it is going to do one set of things rather than another – that it has made decisions which commit the organization to a particular set of actions. Managers make decisions all the time, however, which presumably will commit them to do something but not all of these are strategic decisions.

By the term strategic we usually mean those decisions which:[1]

- are widespread in their effect and so are significant in the part of the organization to which the strategy refers;
- define the position of the organization relative to its environment;
- move the organization closer to its long-term goals.

The strategy hierarchy

The term 'strategy', as we have defined it above, depends partly on what we mean by 'the organization'. If 'the organization' is a large, diversified corporation, its strategy will position it in its global, economic, political and social environment and will consist of decisions about what types of business the group wants to be in, in what parts of the world it wants to operate, what businesses to acquire and what to divest, how to allocate its cash between its various businesses, and so on. Decisions such as these form the *corporate strategy* of the corporation – they guide and manoeuvre the corporation in its global, economic, social and political environment. Each business unit within the corporate group will also need to put together its own *business strategy* which sets out its individual mission and objectives as well as defining how it intends to compete in its markets. This business strategy guides the business in an environment which consists of its customers, markets and competitors, but also includes the corporate group of which it is a part. Similarly, within the business each function will need to consider what part it should play in contributing to the strategic and/or competitive objectives of the business. The operations, marketing, finance, research and development, and other functions will all need to translate the objectives of the business into terms which have meaning for them and consider how best they should organize their resources to support them. In other words each function of the business needs a *functional strategy* which guides its actions within the business. This time the 'environment' of the function includes the business itself.

These three levels of strategy – corporate, business and functional – form a hierarchy. Figure 3.2 illustrates this strategic hierarchy, with some of the decisions at each level and the main influences on the strategic decisions.

In fact the relationship between the levels in the strategy hierarchy is more complex than this. The hierarchy model is a convenient way of thinking about strategy but is not intended to represent the way strategies really are formulated. At the simplest level, the connection between the three levels of strategy might be taken to indicate a 'top-down' relationship. That is, business strategy is devised only within the context of a well-defined corporate strategy, and functional strategies only within a well-defined business strategy. This is neither what does, nor should, happen in reality.

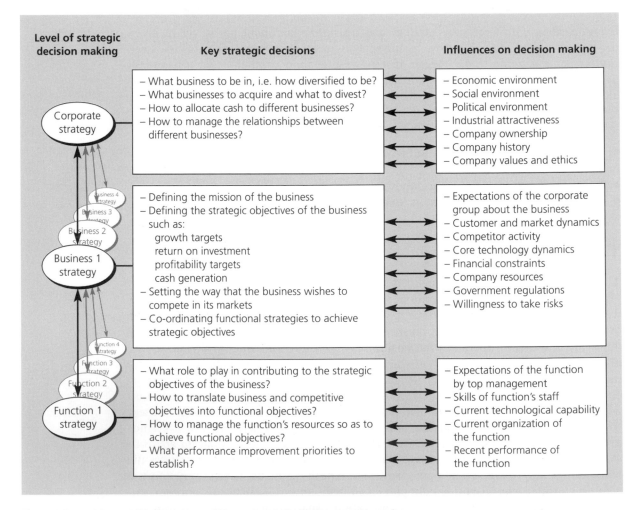

Figure 3.2 Decisions and influences at different levels in the strategy hierarchy

When any group is reviewing its corporate strategy, it will of course be influenced by environmental factors such as market conditions. It will also take into account, however, the circumstances, preferences, and capabilities of the various businesses which form the group. Similarly, the individual businesses, when reviewing their strategies, will consult the individual functions within the business about their constraints and capabilities. The three levels of strategy, in reality, both overlap and influence each other.

OPERATIONS STRATEGY

Accepting the simplifications of the hierarchical model, we can take the hierarchical nature of strategic linkage further into the operation itself. As we discussed in Chapter 1, all of an organization's 'macro' operations are made up of a hierarchy of 'micro' operations. Each micro operation might need to develop its own unit or departmental plans which, in the context of the micro operation, might be termed strategic in that they will guide its decision making within the total (macro) operation.

At the level of the macro operation, operations strategy can be defined as follows:

Operations strategy is the total pattern of decisions and actions which set the role, objectives and activities of the operation so that they contribute to and support the organization's business strategy.[2]

At the level of the micro operation, an operation's plan or strategy can be defined as follows:

(Micro) operations strategy is the total pattern of decisions and actions which set the role, objectives and activities of each part of the operation so that they contribute to and support the operations strategy of the business.

So each unit's operations strategy contributes to the strategic objectives of the next level up. But as well as helping the next level up in the hierarchy to achieve its strategic objectives, operations strategy must take into account the needs of its internal customers and suppliers as we discussed in Chapter 1.

This means that an operations strategy always has two purposes:

● to contribute directly to the strategic objectives of the next level up in the hierarchy; and

● to help other parts of the business make their own contribution to strategy.

The content and process of operations strategy

When companies develop their operations strategies they must consider two separate, but overlapping, sets of questions. Some are concerned with what is known as the *content* of the operations strategy. These are questions which will determine the specific strategies which govern the day-to-day decision making in the operation. The other questions will be concerned with the *process* of how these strategies are actually determined in the organization.

THE CONTENT OF OPERATIONS STRATEGY

Operations strategy *content* is the collection of policies, plans and behaviours which the operation chooses to pursue. To determine the content of its operations strategy an operation needs to do two things:

● Decide on the relative *priority of its performance objectives*. Should it concentrate on being particularly good at quality or speed or dependability or flexibility or keeping cost down or some combination of two or more of them?

● Decide on the overall approach and long-term objectives it wishes to adopt for the *specific decision area strategies* of the operation. There are several ways of categorizing these specific decision areas. Here we use categories which divide operations activities into 'structural' and 'infrastructural' activities.

Priority of performance objectives

Chapter 2 described and illustrated the five performance objectives. But in our discussion nothing was implied about under what circumstances some of the performance objectives might become particularly important to an organization. The relative importance of performance objectives for this, or any other, operation will depend on a number of different influences, and three in particular (*see* Fig. 3.3):

● the specific needs of the company's *customer groups*;
● the activities of the company's *competitors*;
● the stage of the *product life cycle* at which the product or service stands.

Customer influence on performance objectives

Of all the influences on the priority an organization gives to its performance objectives, the most immediate are the organization's customers. Operations seek to satisfy customers through developing their five performance objectives. For example, if customers particularly value low-priced products or services, the operation will put emphasis on its cost performance. If customers insist on error-free products or services, the operation will concentrate on its quality performance. A customer emphasis on fast delivery will make speed important with the operation, while a customer emphasis on reliable delivery will make dependability important. If customers expect very innovative products and services, the operation must provide a high degree of flexibility in order to get its innovations to its customers before its rivals. Similarly, if a wide range of products and services are demanded by customers, the operation will need to be flexible enough to provide the necessary variety without excessive cost.

These factors which define the customer's requirements are called *competitive factors*.[3] Figure 3.4 shows the relationship between some of the more common competitive factors and the operation's performance objectives. This list is not supposed to be exhaustive. In any particular set of circumstances many other factors could be important, from the location of an hotel to the willingness of company executives to

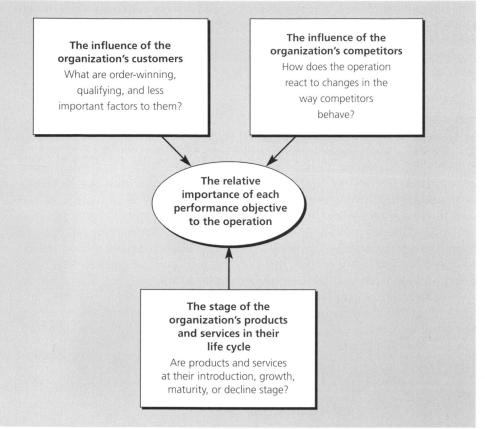

Figure 3.3
The influences on
the relative
importance of
performance
objectives

Figure 3.4
Different
competitive factors
imply different
performance
objectives

play golf with customers. The important point is that the relative priority of each performance objective is influenced by how the organization translates the needs (and potential needs) of its customers into terms which are meaningful within the operation. Some organizations put considerable effort into bringing an 'image' of their customers' needs into the operation. The box on Kwik-Fit illustrates this.

KWIK-FIT CUSTOMERS' NEEDS[5]

In an industry which is not known for the integrity of its companies, Kwik-Fit, the auto repair chain, has carved out a reputation for service which combines low cost with fast and trustworthy service. Founded in 1971, the company has over 3000 employees in more than 600 branches around Europe. The service dilemma of the company is how to satisfy (or even delight) customers who do not want to be in a repair shop at all. Customers have not planned to have a breakdown; they are making a *distress purchase* and can often be suspicious of the company. They may believe that it is in the company's interest to recommend an expensive repair or replacement, even when it is not necessary. Customers want to be able to trust the diagnosis and advice they receive, get served as fast and with as little hassle as possible, have their problem solved and not be charged an excessive amount. Each branch must be conveniently located, visible from a main traffic route, clean, open long and predictable hours, and recognizable as a Kwik-Fit centre.

I AM YOUR CUSTOMER

I am your customer. Satisfy my wants, add personal attention and a friendly touch, and I will become a walking advertisement for your products and services. Ignore my wants, show carelessness, inattention and poor manners, and I will simply cease to exist, as far as you are concerned.

I am sophisticated. Much more so than I was a few years ago. My needs are more complex. I have grown accustomed to better things. I have money to spend. I am an egotist. I am sensitive; I am proud. My ego needs the nourishment of a friendly, personal greeting from you. It is important to me that you appreciate my business. After all, when I buy your products and services, my money is feeding you.

I am a perfectionist. I want the best I can get for the money I spend. When I criticise your products or services – and I will, to anyone who will listen, when I am dissatisfied – then take heed. The source of my discontent lies in something you or the products you sell have failed to do. Find that source and eliminate it or you will lose my business and that of my friends as well.

I am fickle. Other businessmen continually beckon me with offers of 'more' for my money. To keep my business, you must offer something better than they. I am your customer now, but you must prove to me again and again that I have made a wise choice in selecting you, your products and services above all others.

These competitive factors have shaped the company's operations performance objectives. It sums its operations strategy up as '*a quality of service which will give 100 per cent customer satisfaction*' – an objective which is captured by the notices which decorate the walls of Kwik-Fit centres. ■

Questions

1 What do you think are the major operations objectives of a Kwik-Fit centre? (One way of approaching this is to take the five performance objectives – quality, speed, dependability, flexibility and cost – and define what you think they mean for a Kwik-Fit centre.)

2 What do you think are the main structural and infrastructural decision areas which would constitute an operations strategy for Kwik-Fit?

3 You now have a list of performance objectives and a list of decision areas. Which decision areas do you think are particularly important in influencing each performance objective? (For example, you might think that quality will be particularly influenced by workforce and organization strategy.)

Order-winning and qualifying objectives

A particularly useful way of determining the relative importance of competitive factors is to distinguish between what Professor Terry Hill of London Business School calls 'order-winning' and 'qualifying' factors.[4]

Order-winning factors are those things which directly and significantly contribute to winning business. They are regarded by customers as key reasons for purchasing the product or service. They are, therefore, the most important aspects of the way a company defines its competitive stance. Raising performance in an order-winning factor will either result in more business or improve the chances of gaining more business.

Qualifying factors may not be the major competitive determinants of success, but are important in another way. They are those aspects of competitiveness where the operation's performance has to be above a particular level just to be considered by the customer. Below this 'qualifying' level of performance the company probably won't even be considered by many customers. Above the 'qualifying' level, it will be considered, but mainly in terms of its performance in the order-winning factors. Any further improvement in qualifying factors above the qualifying level is unlikely to gain much competitive benefit.

To order-winning and qualifying factors can be added *less important factors* which are those factors which are neither order-winning nor qualifying. They do not influence customers in any significant way. They are worth mentioning here only because they may be of importance in other parts of the operation's activities.

Figure 3.5 shows the difference between order-winning, qualifying and less important factors in terms of their utility or worth to the competitiveness of the organization. The curves illustrate the relative amount of competitiveness (or attractiveness to customers) as the operation's performance at the factor varies. Order-winning factors show a steady and significant increase in their contribution to competitiveness as the operation gets better at providing them. Qualifying objectives only start to make much of a contribution to competitiveness when the operation manages to raise its performance to the qualifying level. Less important objectives have little impact on customers no matter how well the operation performs in them.

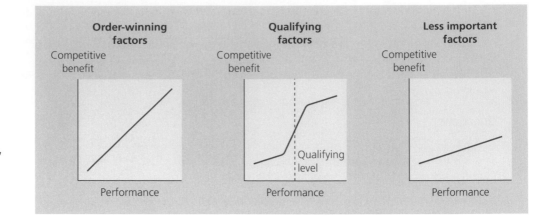

**Figure 3.5
Order-winning,
qualifying and
less important
competitive
factors**

Different customer needs imply different objectives

If, as is likely, an operation produces goods or services for more than one customer group, it will need to determine the order-winning, qualifying and less important competitive factors for each group. For example, Table 3.1 shows how two product groups manufactured by one instrument manufacturer differ in their manufacturing requirements. The first product group is a range of standard electronic medical equipment which is sold 'off the shelf' direct to hospitals and clinics. The second product group is a wider range of electronic measuring devices which are sold to original equipment manufacturers who incorporate them in their own products. These electronic measuring devices often have to be customized to individual customer requirements.[6]

The analysis of the two product groups shown in Table 3.1 shows that they have very different competitive factors. Therefore different performance objectives are required from the manufacturing operation. Such very different competitive needs could possibly require two separate operations – one for each product group – each focused on its own objectives and devoted to providing the things which are important in its particular markets.

Table 3.2 shows a similar analysis but this time in the banking industry.[7] Here the distinction is drawn between the customers who are looking for banking services for their private and domestic needs (current accounts, overdraft facilities, savings accounts, mortgage loans, etc.) and those corporate customers who need banking services for their, often large, organizations. These latter services would include such things as letters of credit, cash transfer services and commercial loans.

It should be remembered, however, that customers' needs are rarely static. They will change with customers' own circumstances and they will respond to whatever products and services are available.

Table 3.1 Different product groups require different performance objectives

	Product group 1	*Product group 2*
Products	Standard electronic medical equipment	Electronic measuring devices
Customers	Hospitals/clinics	Other medical equipment companies
Product specification	Not high tech. but periodic updates	Most types, high performance
Product range	Narrow – four variants	Very wide, some customization
Design changes	Infrequent	Continual
Delivery	Fast – from stock	On-time delivery important
Quality	Means reliability	Means performance
Demand	Predictable	Unpredictable
Volume per product type	High	Medium to low
Profit margins	Low to medium	Medium to very high

Competitive factors		
Order winners	Price Product reliability	Product specification Product range
Qualifiers	Delivery speed Product performance Quality	On-time delivery Delivery speed Price
Less important	Product range	

Internal performance objectives	Cost Quality	Product/service flexibility Mix flexibility Dependability

Table 3.2 Different banking services require different performance objectives

	Retail banking	*Corporate banking*
Products	Personal financial services such as loans and credit cards	Special services for corporate customers
Customers	Individuals	Businesses
Product range	Medium but standardized, little need for special terms	Very wide range, many need to be customized
Design changes	Occasional	Continual
Delivery	Fast decisions	Dependable service
Quality	Means error-free transactions	Means close relationships
Volume per service type	Most services are high volume	Most services are low volume
Profit margins	Most are low to medium, some high	Medium to high

Competitive factors		
Order winners	Price Accessibility Speed	Customization Quality of service Reliability
Qualifiers	Quality Range	Speed Price
Less important		Accessibility

Internal performance objectives	Cost Speed Quality	Flexibility Quality Dependability

Competitor influence on performance objectives

Customers are clearly an important influence on the priority of performance objectives, but they are not the only one. Operations are also influenced by what competitors are doing. If, for example, a home delivery pizza operation competes by guaranteeing a fast delivery to customers in its area, it is concentrating on delivery speed because that is what it believes its customers want. However, if a rival pizza shop offers equally fast delivery together with an extended range of pizza toppings, the operation could become concerned with extending its own range. Its priorities might shift from speed towards developing the flexibility to offer a sufficiently wide range of products to match its competitor.

Not that an organization will always match its competitors' moves. The pizza operation could have responded to its competitor's extended product range by shifting its priorities to some totally different competitive factor. For example, instead of extending its own range it could have chosen to shorten its delivery times even more, so as to capitalize on its experience of fast delivery. Alternatively, it could have chosen an entirely new competitive direction such as cutting its prices. Figure 3.6 (p. 87) illustrates this.

The main point here is that, even without any direct change in the preferences of its customers, an organization could have to change the way it competes and therefore the priority of its performance objectives. Alternatively, an organization might choose to compete in a different way to its rivals in order to distinguish itself from its competitors (*see* the box on Southwest Airlines).

SOUTHWEST AIRLINES UNDERCUTS ITS RIVALS[8]

While most of the western world's airlines are trying to outdo their competitors by providing ever more sophisticated services, including excellent catering and the latest entertainment technology, one company has chosen to return to its core product (transportation), and cut out almost all the extras. Southwest Airlines, based in Dallas, is one of the few airlines in the US which can boast of having been consistently profitable throughout the last two turbulent decades. Its strategy has been to compete on price, with cut-price advance booked fares as much as 50 per cent below those of larger competitors. Indeed some of its larger competitors have been forced to defend their markets by attempting to copy Southwest's formula and price.

The idea of providing air travel in the style of bus travel is certainly not unique, and there have been many failures, particularly in the US. For Southwest, however, the consistency and coherence of the operations strategy have played a big part in its survival and growth to a business that now has a five per cent share of the enormous US market. To compete on price over the long term, operations costs must be the lowest in the market, and that is precisely what the airline's flamboyant founder and owner, Herbie Kelleher, has achieved, often in quite unique ways. Passengers notice the difference even before they enter the plane, as Southwest's numbered boarding passes are plastic and reusable. Passengers are called forward in groups, but once they are in the plane they are free to sit where they wish. There is no attempt to provide the normal meals service, so passengers are just offered a bag of peanuts, a glass of orange

▶

juice, with a narrow choice of drinks available to those that wish to purchase them. Passengers, and even crew, often bring their own food and drinks with them.

Despite the very obvious lack of conventional offerings such as in-flight films and the personal attention of the cabin crew, passengers seem impressed with the whole package, scoring the airline highly in most research surveys. The staff are renowned for their informal yet personable approach, and this is reinforced by their simple 'uniform' of brightly coloured shorts and T-shirts. The company's style and culture are reinforced by the owner, who has been seen on board some flights, for example, wearing an Easter rabbit suit and entertaining the passengers in his own particular way.

The simplicity of the entire service gives Southwest a particularly strong cost advantage on short routes, where the turnaround time at airports becomes critical. Because there are no meals, there is less mess to clear up, and so the cabin is routinely cleaned by the crew. There is also less time needed to prepare the galley, as no meals are carried, and the overhead costs of organizing meals and entertainment is eliminated.

Southwest has shown that it is possible to challenge conventional ways of operating an airline and has provided value to its customers at minimum cost. Its service doesn't suit everyone, but those who do buy a ticket at least get what they want and expect. ■

Questions

1 Southwest Airlines competes primarily on price. List the most important things you believe Southwest has done to keep its costs low so that it can offer a low price.

2 How sensitive do you think an airline operation like Southwest is to variations in the volume of passengers it carries? (That is, if the number of customers carried in a particular time period goes up or down, how much difference do you think it makes to the costs of the operation?; how much difference do you think it makes to the revenue earned by the operation?; and therefore, how will profits change as volume varies?)

The product/service life cycle[9] influence on performance objectives

One way of generalizing the behaviour of both customers and competitors is to link it to the life cycle of the products or services which the operation is producing. From the time it is introduced by a company to the point at which customers are no longer interested in purchasing it, a product or service passes through several distinct stages. The exact form of product/service life cycles will vary, but generally they are shown as the sales volume passing through four stages – *introduction, growth, maturity* and *decline*.

Professor Phillip Kotler, the well-known marketing authority, derives four implications from the product life cycle:[10]

1 Products (or services) have a limited life.
2 Sales of the product (or service) pass through distinct stages, each posing different challenges to the seller (and producer).
3 Profits rise and fall at different stages of the product life cycle.

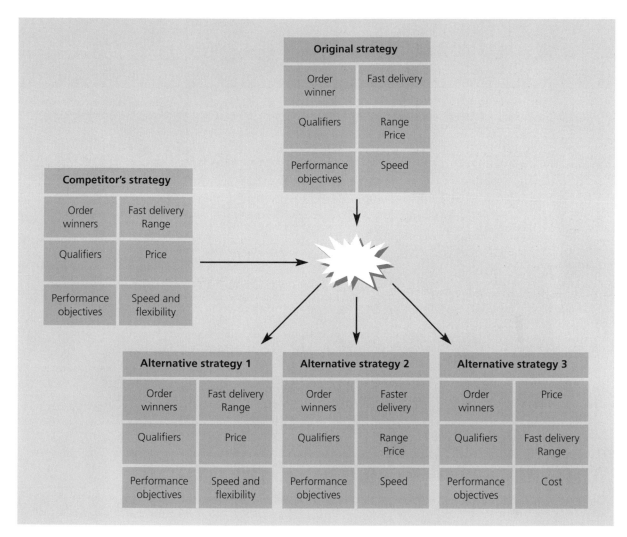

Figure 3.6 Competitor activity can affect the relative importance of performance objectives

4 Products (and services) require different marketing, financial, manufacturing (or operations), purchasing and personnel strategies in each stage of their life cycle.

It is the last point that is particularly important for all operations managers. It implies that the way in which operations should be managed and the objectives they should set themselves will change as the product or service ages in its market. Figure 3.7 shows how product/service and industry characteristics are likely to vary through different stages of the product/service life cycle.

Introduction stage

When a product or service is first introduced, it is likely to be presented to the market on the basis that it is offering something new in terms of its design or performance. If the product or service is really novel, few if any competitors will be offering the same product or service and, because the number of customers is also relatively low and

	Introduction	Growth	Maturity	Decline
	Product/service first introduced to market	Product/service gains market acceptance	Market needs start to be fulfilled	Market needs largely met
Volume	Slow growth in sales	Rapid growth in sales volume	Sales slow down and level off	Sales decline
Customers	Innovators	Early adoptors	Bulk of market	Laggards
Competitors	Few/none	Increasing number	Stable number	Declining number
Variety of product/service designs	Possible high customization or frequent design changes	Increasingly standardized	Emerging dominant types	Possible move to commodity standardization
Likely order winners	Product/service characteristics, performance or novelty	Availability of quality products/services	Low price Dependable supply	Low price
Likely qualifiers	Quality Range	Price Range	Range Quality	Dependable supply
Dominant operations performance objectives	Flexibility Quality	Speed Dependability Quality	Cost Dependability	Cost

Sales volume (y-axis label)

Figure 3.7 The effects of the product/service life cycle on the organization

because their needs are possibly not perfectly understood, the design of the product or service could be subject to frequent change. Given the relatively high uncertainty inherent in these market conditions, the operations management of the company can best contribute to competitiveness by developing the flexibility to cope with changes in the specification of the product or service and possibly also in its output volume. At the same time they will also need to maintain quality levels so as not to undermine the performance of the product/service which is the main basis of competitiveness.

Growth stage

If products or services survive the rigours of their introduction to the market, they will begin to be more widely adopted. Increasing numbers of customers accept the value of the product or service and volume starts to grow – perhaps rapidly. Competitors, seeing the attractiveness of the product or service, start to develop their own versions,

RECYCLING STRATEGY AT VEKA UPVC WINDOWS[11]

Although customers and competitors are the main drivers of strategic change, strategies can be changed as a response to other factors, even when the product is 'mature'. Sometimes there are significant changes in the legislative environment which creates new pressures and opportunities for new enterprises. Germany's tough environmental laws, for example, limit disposal of waste in landfill sites. The final disposal of end-of-life products is severely constrained, encouraging disassembly into component materials which can then be reused. This might sound easy, but most modern products are made up of complex assemblies of different materials. A typical large car, for example, may include up to 20 types of plastic including fibrous composites, several different metals and alloys, natural and man-made cloths, leather, wood, rubber, oils and paints. Complete disassembly of such products is either impractical or excessively expensive in terms of labour and energy. For some less complex products, however, the task is more feasible, and the rewards are more commercially attractive.

UPVC windows have been used in Germany for several decades, and some are now being replaced, either because the wooden subframe is rotting (common in eastern Germany where poor quality materials were used) or because of the superior performance and appearance of the latest products. At one time some 100 000 windows were deposited in landfill sites in Germany, but legislation curtailed this. Veka, the world's largest producer of UPVC windows, recognized the potential impact of this legislation on the entire business, and set about the development and design of a recycling process for discarded windows. The new DM 30 million plant, constructed in Behringen, shreds complete windows into fragments which are then sorted into the reusable component materials of glass, metals, rubber, and UPVC. The latter is used by Veka itself in new products, completing the cycle of materials; less than three per cent of the materials go to waste.

Veka's environmentally friendly operations strategy has not only been a logical response to a changing legislative environment, but has also created a new competitive advantage. Purchasers of new windows could not fail to be impressed with the product and processes which allow valuable materials to be recycled. In addition, Veka has also gained a sustained source of cheap materials, insulating itself from the fluctuating price of new plastic. ■

Questions

1 What have been the major pressures on Veka which caused it to change its operations strategy?

2 What implications for the running of its operations do you think the move to recycling had at Veka?

3 What opportunities for the operation do you think were created by the move to recycling?

both to keep up with the market and to protect their own position within it. In the growing market, different customer groups will probably start to emerge and the design of the product or service could start to standardize. Standardization is actually quite helpful in that it allows the operation to supply the rapidly growing market. Keeping up with demand could prove to be the main preoccupation of organizations which have products or services in this part of the life cycle. Rapid and dependable response to demand will help to keep demand buoyant while ensuring that the company keeps its share of the market as competition starts to increase. The increasing competition also means that the company cannot afford to let its quality levels drop as it ramps up its level of activity.

Maturity stage

After a period of rapid growth, products and services are no longer the novel, or even the 'up-and-coming', forces in the market. They become the 'norm', the 'standard' – they 'mature'. Demand starts to level off because many customers have already been supplied. Some early competitors might even have left the market and the industry has probably settled down to a few larger companies, perhaps with some smaller companies occupying small niches in the market. The designs of the products or services have probably also stabilized to a few standard types. Competition will almost certainly move to emphasize price or value for money, although individual companies might try to prevent this by attempting to differentiate themselves in some way (*see* the box on Veka). This increasingly competitive and price-conscious environment means that operations will be expected to get its costs down, either to maintain profits or to allow price cutting, or both (*see* the box on Air Travel). Because of this shift to price competition, cost and productivity issues, together with dependable supply, are likely to be the operation's main concerns.

AIR TRAVEL TAKES OFF[12]

Air travel has grown substantially over the last 30 years. Although, like any industry, it has had its ups and downs – world politics, wars and economic cycles all affect our tendency to travel – growth in passenger miles travelled is forecast to continue. Increasing volume prompted changes

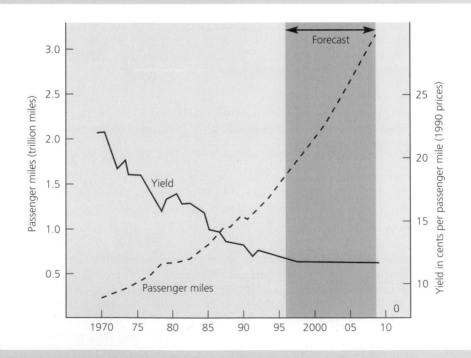

Figure 3.8 Yield (one indicator of price) decreases as air travel (volume) increases

in airline operations process technology, such as the introduction of wide-bodied aircraft. This reduced airline costs even further and has been translated into lower prices. In addition, changes in the industry, most especially deregulation of the market in some parts of the world and the privatization of some airlines, have also kept costs down.

The increasing importance of price-based competition is reflected in Fig. 3.8 which shows the growth in volume (and forecast volume) in the industry and the fall in yields. Yield is the revenue which the airlines make for every mile they carry a passenger. At around 22 cents per passenger mile in 1970, yield has fallen to around 13 cents per passenger mile and is expected to continue to fall away. Because costs have also been declining, this fall in yield reflects an even more significant fall in real prices.

Increasing volumes and increasing price competition have also resulted in a change in the way airlines organize their operations. Especially in the US, airlines have moved to a 'hub-and-spoke' arrangement of routes. This involves aircraft flying between 'hub' airports where passengers connect with flights to other hubs. It is the same principle which is used in mail-sorting offices. Although the system is not always convenient for some passengers, the airlines see it as the only way to 'standardize' their routes, and keep costs down. ■

Questions

1 The use of 'hub-and-spoke' arrangements is mentioned above. Why do you think such a system keeps costs down for airlines?

2 What do you think are the disadvantages of the 'hub-and-spoke' way of organizing routes?

Decline stage

When the product or service has been in the market for some time, the need which it was filling will eventually be largely met. Sales will decline. Competitors are likely to start dropping out of the market, the rate of their drop-out governing, to some extent, the speed of decline of whatever business is left for the remaining companies. The products or services serving the market could possibly fragment. To the companies left with the old products or services there might be a residual market but, if capacity in the industry lags demand, the market will continue to be dominated by price competition. Operations objectives will therefore still be dominated by cost.

The polar representation of performance objectives

A useful way of representing the 'pattern' of performance objectives for a product or service is shown in Fig. 3.9. This is called the *polar representation* because the scales which represent the importance of each performance objective have the same origin. A line describes the importance of each performance objective. The closer the line is to the common origin, the less important is the performance objective. Figure 3.9 illustrates how the two services of corporate and retail banking, described earlier in Table 3.2, might look on a polar representation. The differences between the two services are clearly shown by the diagram.

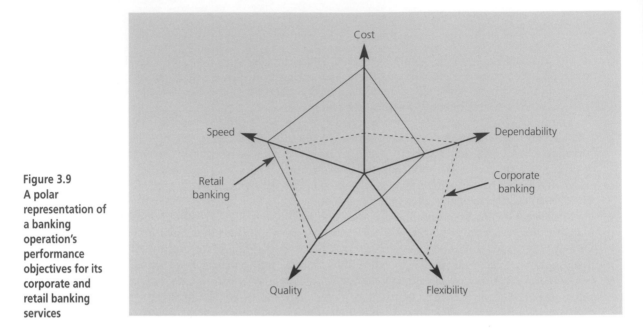

Figure 3.9
A polar representation of a banking operation's performance objectives for its corporate and retail banking services

OPERATIONS STRATEGY DECISION AREAS

As well as determining which are the most significant performance objectives, the other requirement of an operations strategy is that it sets the general direction for each of the operation's major decision areas.[13]

Structural and infrastructural decisions

A common distinction in operations strategy is that which is drawn between those strategic decisions which determine an operation's structure, and those which determine its infrastructure. An operation's structural decisions are those which we have classed as primarily influencing design activities, while infrastructural decisions are those which influence the workforce organization and the planning and control, and improvement activities. This distinction in operations strategy has been compared to that between 'hardware' and 'software' in a computer system.[14] The hardware of a computer sets limits to what it can do. In a similar way, investing in advanced technology and building more or better facilities can raise the potential of any type of operation. Within the limits which are imposed by the hardware of a computer, the software governs how effective the computer actually is in practice. The most powerful computer can only work to its full potential if its software is capable of exploiting its potential. The same principle applies with operations. The best and most costly facilities and technology will only be effective if the operation also has an appropriate infrastructure which governs the way it will work on a day-to-day basis.

Table 3.3 illustrates both structural and infrastructural decision areas, arranged to correspond approximately to the chapter headings used in this book. The table also shows some typical questions which each strategic decision area should be addressing.

Table 3.3 Structural and infrastructural strategic decision areas

Structural strategic decisions	Typical questions which the strategy should help to answer
New product/service development strategy	Should the operation be developing its own novel product or service ideas or following the lead of others? How should the operation decide which products or services to develop and how to manage the development process?
Vertical integration strategy	Should the operation expand by acquiring its suppliers or its customers? If so, what suppliers should it acquire? And if so, what customers should it acquire? What balance of capabilities should it develop along its network of operations?
Facilities strategy	What number of geographically separate sites should the operation have? Where should the operations facilities be located? What activities and capacity should be allocated to each plant?
Technology strategy	What broad types of technology should the operation be using? Should it be at the leading edge of technology or wait until the technology is established? What technology should the operation be developing internally and what should it be buying in?

Infrastructural strategic decisions	Typical questions which the strategy should help to answer
Workforce and organization strategy	What role should the people who staff the operation play in its management? How should responsibility for the activities of the operations function be allocated between different groups in the operation? What skills should be developed in the staff of the operation?
Capacity adjustment strategy	How should the operation forecast and monitor the demand for its products and services? How should the operation adjust its activity levels in response to demand fluctuations?
Supplier development strategy	How should the operation choose its suppliers? How should it develop its relationship with its suppliers? How should it monitor its suppliers' performance?
Inventory strategy	How should the operation decide how much inventory to have and where it is to be located? How should the operation control the size and composition of its inventories?
Planning and control systems strategy	What system should the operation use to plan its activities? How should the operation decide the resources to be allocated to its various activities?
Improvement strategy	How should the operations performance be measured? How should the operation decide whether its performance is satisfactory? How should the operation ensure that its performance is reflected in its improvement priorities? Who should be involved in the improvement process? How fast should the operation expect improvement in performance to be? How should the improvement process be managed?
Failure prevention and recovery strategy	How should the operation maintain its resources so as to prevent failure? How should the operation plan to cope with a failure if one occurs?

Operations strategy influences performance objectives

To some extent all the decisions made in all strategy areas will exert some influence on all the performance objectives of the operation. Some strategies, however, are particularly influential on certain objectives. Table 3.4 highlights those objectives which will be particularly influenced by each strategy (though remember that the important links between strategies and objectives will to some extent depend on the type of operation and the circumstances in which it finds itself).

Table 3.4 Strategies with a particularly significant effect on particular performance objectives

	Quality	Speed	Dependability	Flexibility	Cost
New product/service development strategy	✔				✔
Vertical integration strategy		✔	✔		✔
Facilities strategy		✔	✔	✔	✔
Technology strategy	✔			✔	✔
Workforce and organization strategy	✔			✔	✔
Capacity adjustment strategy		✔		✔	✔
Supplier development strategy	✔		✔		✔
Inventory strategy		✔	✔		✔
Planning and control systems strategy		✔	✔		✔
Improvement strategy	✔	✔	✔	✔	✔
Failure prevention and recovery strategy	✔		✔		✔

THE PROCESS OF OPERATIONS STRATEGY

The 'process' of operations strategy refers to the procedures which are, or can be, used to formulate those operations strategies which the organization should adopt. Several ways of doing this have been suggested. Most consultancy companies have developed their own frameworks, as have several academics. Two well-known procedures are briefly described here to give the flavour of how operations strategies are formulated in practice. These are the *Hill methodology* and the *Platts–Gregory procedure*.

The Hill methodology[15]

One of the first, and certainly most influential, approaches to operations strategy formulation (although once again its development is largely connected with manufacturing operations) is that devised by Professor Terry Hill of London Business School. The so-called 'Hill methodology' is illustrated in Fig. 3.10. Hill's model, which is here adapted to the terminology used in this book, follows the well-tried approach of providing a connection between different levels of strategy making. It is essentially a five-step procedure. Step one involves understanding the long-term corporate objectives of the organization so that the eventual operations strategy can be seen in terms of its contribution to these corporate objectives. Step two involves understanding how the marketing strategy of the organization has been developed to achieve corporate objectives. This step, in effect, identifies the product/service markets which the operations strategy must satisfy as well as identifying the product or service characteristics such as range, mix and volume, which the operation will be required to provide. Step three translates marketing strategy into what we called earlier 'competitive factors'. Hill goes on to divide the factors which win business into order-winners and qualifiers. Step four is what Hill calls 'process choice'. This is similar to the volume/variety analysis which we will treat in the next chapter. Its purpose is to define a set of structural characteristics of the operation which are consistent with each other and appropriate for the way the company wishes to compete. Step five involves a similar process, but this time with the infrastructural features of the operation.

Hill's methodology is not intended to imply a simple sequential movement from step one to step five, although during the formulation process the emphasis does move in this direction. Rather, Hill sees the process as an iterative one, whereby operations managers cycle between an understanding of the long-term strategic requirements of the operation and the specific resource developments which are

Step 1	Step 2	Step 3	Step 4	Step 5
Corporate objectives	Marketing strategy	How do products or services win orders?	Operations strategy	
			Process choice	Infrastructure
• Growth rates • Profitability • Return on net assets • Cash flow • Financial 'gearing'	• Product/service markets and segments • Range of products/ services • Mix of specifications • Volumes • Standardization or customization • Rate of innovation	• Price • Quality • Delivery speed • Delivery dependability • Product/service range • Product/service design • Brand image • Supporting services	• Process technology • Trade-offs embodied in process • Role of inventory • Capacity, size, timing, location	• Functional support • Operations planning and control systems • Work structuring • Payment systems • Organizational structure

Figure 3.10 The Hill methodology of operations strategy formulation
Source: Based on Hill, T. (1993) *Manufacturing Strategy* (2nd edn), Macmillan

required to support strategy. In this iterative process the identification of competitive factors in step three is seen as critical. It is at this stage where any mismatches between what the organization's strategy *requires* and what its operation can *provide*, become evident.

The Platts–Gregory procedure[16]

Another influential process is that developed by Ken Platts and Professor Mike Gregory of Cambridge University. The procedure has three stages. Stage one involves developing an understanding of the market position of the organization. This is done by assessing the opportunities and threats within the competitive environment. More specifically it also involves identifying the factors which are required by the market and compares these to the level of achieved performance (in terms of the operation being able to satisfy the market). This is an important part of the Platts–Gregory procedure and is different in emphasis from the Hill methodology described previously. Whereas the Hill methodology places its main emphasis on an operations strategy being developed from the customers' view of competitive factors, this procedure explicitly makes the comparison between what the market wants and how the operation performs. The procedure uses 'profiles' of market requirements and achieved performance to show up the gaps which the operation strategy must address. Figure 3.11 illustrates the use of these profiles.[17]

Stage two of the procedure involves assessing the capabilities of the operation. Its purpose is to identify current operations practice and assess the extent to which this practice helps to achieve the type of performance which was indicated as being important in stage one.

Stage three concerns the development of new operations strategies. This stage involves reviewing the various options which are available to the organization and selecting those which best satisfy the criteria identified in the two previous stages.

Common elements of operations strategy procedures

The two formulation procedures described here are broadly representative of those available. Yet neither includes all the various points and issues which, taken together, operations strategy formulation procedures address. Typically, many of the formulation processes include the following elements:

● A process which formally links the total organization strategic objectives (usually a business strategy) to resource level objectives.
● The use of competitive factors (called various things such as order winners, critical success factors, etc.) as the translation device between business strategy and operations strategy.
● A step which involves judging the relative importance of the various competitive factors in terms of customers' preference.
● A step which includes assessing current achieved performance, usually as compared against competitor performance levels.
● An emphasis on operations strategy formulation as an iterative process.
● The concept of an 'ideal' or 'green field' operation against which to compare current operations. Very often the question asked is

'If you were starting from scratch on a green-field site, how, ideally, would you design your operation to meet the needs of the market?'

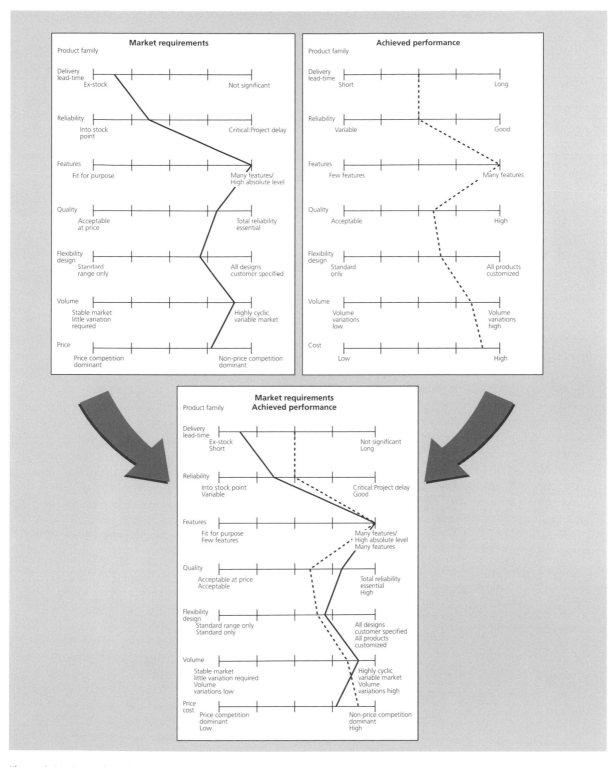

Figure 3.11 Uses of profiling in the Platts–Gregory procedure

This can then be used to identify the differences between current operations and this ideal state.

● A 'gap-based' approach. This is a well-tried approach in all strategy formulation which involves comparing what is required of the operation by the market place against the levels of performance which the operation is currently achieving.

David Garman, Allied Bakeries

David Garman is the Managing Director of Allied Bakeries Ltd, a division of Associated British Foods and the UK market leader in bakery products.

David described his position at Allied Bakeries as someone who leads the development of a shared vision for the management team and one that the company can be committed to.

'The attraction of the job at this level,' he says *'depends on the opportunity to "make a difference" and my priority at present is the development of a strategy to rebuild a sustainable competitive position. The recent competitive environment has accelerated downward pressure on prices and profit margins. This is particularly true in the volume bread sector where there is strong retail price competition and the maturity of the market makes it difficult to achieve sustainable competitive advantage. Against this background it is particularly important for the business to have clear strategic objective priorities, implemented through an interactive and team-based culture, which develops the potential contribution of all employees.'*

David feels that the role of Managing Director encompasses four main areas:

● developing a vision that can shape the company's future objectives and priorities;
● devising a strategy in order to implement that vision;
● creating an appropriate culture within the company which will support implementation of that strategy; and
● monitoring indicators which measure current performance of the business and taking appropriate action to achieve planned results.

The bakery industry could be described as one of the traditional sectors in the food industry and, in different areas, it is both people and capital intensive. For the major manufacturers, it is a multi-site operation and Allied Bakeries has 24 bakeries employing 8000 people. These factors make the management of change particularly challenging.

David has involved each of the bakeries in a major business review, profiling their activities and involving an analysis of performance data along with operational strengths and priorities. This process is linked to the central perspective of two board-level steering groups – one for marketing and the other for operations, the two key areas for forward strategy. This must be linked to the insight provided by customers and a clear understanding of the competitive environment. In this context, David gives a high priority to meeting major customers and receiving feedback, which can influence the development of appropriate competitive strategies.

Although much of his job involves forward thinking, David is keen to stress the importance of current performance.

'Operations strategy is not just about what we do "tomorrow"; there is no point in planning for the future if the current methods and policies are not effective in the short term.

'In today's world, senior executives cannot afford to rely on the command and control style of "vertical management". The supply chain is a horizontal one and this needs to be reflected in an approach whereby departmental barriers are seen as an anachronism and people are encouraged to think laterally in developing positive solutions that will really meet customer requirements and company objectives.' ■

SUMMARY ANSWERS TO KEY QUESTIONS

What is an operations strategy?

■ Operations strategy is the total pattern of decisions and actions which set the role, objectives and activities of the operation so that they contribute to and support the organization's business strategy. This definition refers to the macro operation, but one can also use the term 'operations strategy' when referring to micro operations. Each micro operation could have an 'operations strategy' which identifies how the micro operation is going to contribute to the operations strategy of the whole business.

■ An operations strategy has *content* and *process*. The *content* of an operations strategy deals with the relative importance of the performance objectives to the operation, as well as with giving general guidance to decision-making activities within the operation. The *process* of operations strategy is the procedure which is used within an operation to formulate the operations strategy.

How does operations strategy fit into a company's overall strategy?

■ Strategic decisions can be viewed at a number of levels. *Corporate strategy* sets the objectives for the different businesses which make up a group of businesses. *Business strategy* sets the objectives for each individual business and how it positions itself in its market place. *Functional strategies* set the objectives for each function's contribution to its business strategy. In this sense we use the term operations strategy as a functional strategy which deals with the parts of the organization which create goods and services.

■ It is common to define any level of strategy in a similar way to that in which we defined operations strategy. So the strategy of any organization or part of an organization is the total pattern of decisions and actions which position the organization in its environment.

How do we know which performance objectives are the most important?

■ The relative importance to an operation of performance objectives is influenced by the organization's specific customer groups and their needs, the activities of the organization's competitors, and the stage of its products and services in their life cycle. A particularly important concept here is the distinction between order-winning performance objectives and order-qualifying performance objectives. This distinction is used in some operations strategy formulation processes (for example the Hill methodology).

What are the specific decision areas which are usually included in an operations strategy?

■ Strategic decision areas in operations are usually divided into *structural* and *infrastructural* decisions. Structural decisions are those which define an operation's shape and form. What, in the rest of the book, we call design activities are largely structural decisions. Infrastructural decisions are those which influence the systems and procedures which determine how the operation will work in practice. Workforce organization, planning and control, and improvement activities are infrastructural decisions.

How can an operations strategy be put together?

■ There are many different procedures which are used by companies, consultancies and academics to formulate operations strategies. The two we describe in this chapter are the Hill methodology and the Platts-Gregory procedure. The Hill methodology is based on the idea of making connections between different levels of strategy making, from corporate objectives through marketing strategy, operations objectives and structural and infrastructural decisions. The Platts-Gregory procedure is based on identifying the gaps between, on the one hand, what the market requires from an operation and, on the other, how the operation is performing against market requirements.

CASE EXERCISE

Birmingham Amusement Machines[18]

Birmingham Amusement Machines was a company which manufactured gaming and video-amusement machines. The company sold its products to an operating company which distributed them to bars, country clubs, casinos and pubs. Both companies were started by Bob Greenwood, an engineer who was fascinated by the design of the early mechanical gaming machines. Largely through innovative design, the company had grown to be one of the four largest in the market with a 30 per cent market share.

Four years ago Bob Greenwood sold out to a large industrial group, but he was retained as chief executive of the manufacturing company. The new owners were happy to let Bob indulge his talent for design, especially since the company had entered the video-amusement market. Video-amusement machines did not pay out cash prizes like gaming machines, but allowed the player time on the machine to play a game, usually with a theme drawn from the 'Wild West' or 'Interplanetary Space Warfare'. The company manufactured all parts for the gaming machines and assembled them in its factory. However, many of the components for the video-amusement machines were imported and only assembled into the outer casings in the factories.

Recently, the owners became dissatisfied with the company's performance. The market for its goods was still growing, but the company's profitability had failed to match expectations. The owners decided to install a new chief executive and to fire Bob, who was predictably upset at being replaced:

'It's always been the combination of high technology and fashion that's fascinated me about this industry. You have to be first in the field with every advance in technology, especially now video amusements are a big part of our business, but you also have to keep an eye out for the fashionable trends. On average, we've brought out a new product every four months, for the last five years. You can't run a company like this by putting an accountant as its boss – you need an innovator.'

In fact the owners had installed an accountant to be the head of the company. On his first day, the new boss made a tour of the plant, after which he called the manufacturing manager into his office and began to criticize what he had seen of the production set-up:

'It seems to me that the whole plant is totally disorganized. There's part-finished goods everywhere, and no one seems to know exactly what they're going to do next. I found some parts of the plant clearly overworked, and other parts with nothing to do. I am sure, with a bit of tighter management, you could get your unit production costs down dramatically.'

The production manager was defensive.

'Of course I'd like to get my unit costs down, and of course I could rearrange the whole plant to make it more efficient. The trouble is, the design department are getting me to change products every few months, so I never really have time to let the production system settle down. At the same time, marketing are wanting me to give them instant delivery on new products, almost as soon as I have the drawings from the design office, and they insist on quality being of the highest standard at all times.'

The new boss called in the marketing manager to explain these demands placed on the production system. The marketing manager was equally forthright.

'I couldn't care less about his unit costs. It's not low cost which sells these machines. Look at it this way: in a heavy gambling club one of these machines can pay for itself in less than three months. Under those circumstances, nobody in this industry is competing on price. It's not totally unimportant, but plus or minus 10 per cent isn't going to make much difference to our sales. What sells machines is a new product on the books every few months or so and almost instant delivery – many of the club owners buy on impulse – and an unimpeachable reputation for the highest product reliability.'

After listening to the testimony of his managers, the new boss was a lot less certain on how he should proceed to reshape the business. ∎

Questions

1 What do you think were Bob Greenwood's objectives when he ran the company?

2 List what you think might now be the priority objectives of:

(a) the production manager

(b) the marketing manager

(c) the new boss.

DISCUSSION QUESTIONS

1 Explain the difference between corporate strategy, business strategy and functional strategy.

2 Describe what you think is the business strategy for your university (you might like to have this confirmed). Describe what you think might be the strategies of some of the micro operations, such as library, catering, student union and grounds maintenance. You might like to compare your views with those of the managers of some of these operations.

3 Illustrate how the strategy hierarchy would operate in a 'not-for-profit' organization such as a charity which provides hostel accommodation and other welfare services to the homeless.

4 Explain how an individual branch of a large supermarket chain can:
(a) contribute directly to the strategic aims of the whole company;
(b) help other parts of the company to contribute.

5 Take the example of a prison and describe the specific needs of the different groups of customers (prisoners, society and the victims). For each customer, identify what you think will be the key operations performance objectives and discuss any conflicts between them.

6 Identify what you think might be the order-winning, qualifying and less important objectives for a music store selling records, tapes and compact discs. Discuss how the organization might go about changing its operation by focusing on the less important objectives to give itself an advantage in the market place.

7 Assuming that video cassette recorders (VCRs) are in the maturity stage of their life cycle, how might the main performance objectives of a VCR manufacturer have changed over the life of the product type so far?

8 For organizations providing the following products or services, what do you think would be their order-winning factors and qualifying factors:
estate agency services
school textbooks
basic aluminium extrusions
accountancy services
industrial washing machines?

9 'When a company is introducing a totally novel product or service, it is competing exclusively on the technical specification of the product or service. The operations function therefore has no significant role to play.' Discuss.

10 Many Japanese manufacturers have based their success on products which were regarded as well into their 'mature' stage, such as automobiles and televisions. How did they manage to revitalize the markets for these products and what part did operations management play in this?

11 'A Rolls Royce motor car will always cost more than a Skoda.' Discuss this statement with reference to the trade-off theory of operations objectives.

12 Draw up a list of design, planning and control, and improvement strategies for the following operations:
a TV rental company
a ship repair facility
Disneyland Paris
a national train network.

NOTES ON CHAPTER

1 There are many good books on strategy. For example, *see* Johnson, G. and Scholes, K. (1992) *Exploring Business Strategy* (3rd edn), Prentice Hall.

2 For a thorough review of the literature relating to operations strategy *see* Anderson, J.C., Cleveland, G. and Schroeder, R. (1989) 'Operations Strategy – a Literature Review', *Journal of Operations Management*, Vol 8, No 2. There are also many definitions of operations (or more usually, manufacturing) strategy: for example, Hayes and Wheelwright (*see* Note 14) define it as:

'...a sequence of decisions that, over time, enables a business to achieve a desired manufacturing structure, infrastructure and set of specific capabilities'.

An interesting slant on the topic is given by Professor Abby Ghobadian who defines it as

'...the manner and extent by which the management put the company's manufacturing resources at risk in order to support and achieve its chosen overall objective'.

3   Also called critical success factors by some authors.

4   Hill, T. (1993) *Manufacturing Strategy* (2nd edn), Macmillan.

5   Gabb, A. (1992) 'Making Kwik Fit Fitter', *Management Today*, Mar.

6   Adapted from an example in Slack, N. (1991) *The Manufacturing Advantage*, Mercury Business Books.

7   Adapted from Lim, B.K. (1993) 'Gaining Competitive Advantage from Operations in a Bank', Internal document, University of Warwick.

8   Source: Carnwell, T. (1994) 'Southwest Takes Off with No-Frills Flight Plan', *The European*, 17–23 June.

9   There are many treatments of the product life cycle. *See*, for example, Doyle, P. (1976) 'The Realities of the Product Life Cycle', *Quarterly Review of Marketing*, Summer.

10   Kotler, P. (1991) *Marketing Management*, Prentice Hall International.

11   Gibson, M. (1994) 'Veka Opens Window on Recycling', *The European*, 26 Aug–1 Sept.

12   Source: 'Wrong Altitude', *The Economist*, 6 Mar 1993.

13   Skinner, W. (1985) *Manufacturing: The Formidable Competitive Weapon*, John Wiley.

14   Hayes, R.H. and Wheelwright, S.C. (1984) *Restoring our Competitive Edge*, John Wiley.

15   Hill, T. (1993) *Manufacturing Strategy* (2nd edn), Macmillan.

16   Platts, K.W. and Gregory, M.J. (1990) 'Manufacturing Audit in the Process of Strategy Formulation', *International Journal of Operations and Production Management*, Vol 10, No 9. Also, for a very full explanation of all the steps in this procedure, *see Competitive Manufacturing*, The Department of Trade and Industry and IFS Publications, Kempston, UK (1988).

17   This profiling method is based on New, C.C. (1987) *UK Manufacturing: The Challenge of Transformation*, Cranfield School of Management.

18   Adapted from Cooke, S. and Slack, N. (1991) *Making Management Decisions* (2nd edn), Prentice Hall.

SELECTED FURTHER READINGS

Baden-Fuller, C. and Pitt, M. (1996) *Strategic Innovation*, Routledge.

Berry, W.L. and Hill, T. (1992) 'Linking Systems to Strategy', *International Journal of Operations and Production Management*, Vol 12, No 10.

Croom-Morgan, S. (1994) 'Managing External Resources: Strategic Positioning and Organizational Capability' *in* Platts, K.W., Gregory, M.J. and Neely, A.D. (eds) *Operations Strategy and Performance*, European Operations Management Association, Cambridge University.

Davidow, W.H. and Uttal, B. (1989) 'Service Companies: Focus or Falter', *Harvard Business Review*, Vol 67, No 4.

Hamel, G. and Prahalad, C.K. (1993) 'Strategy as Stretch and Leverage', *Harvard Business Review*, Vol 71, Nos 2 & 3.

Hayes, R.H. and Wheelwright, S.C. (1984) *Restoring our Competitive Edge*, John Wiley, Chap 2.

Hayes, R.H., Wheelwright, S.C. and Clarke, K.B. (1988) *Dynamic Manufacturing*, Free Press, Chaps 1 and 2.

Hayes, R.H. and Pisano, G.P. (1994) 'Beyond World Class: The New Manufacturing Strategy', *Harvard Business Review*, Vol 72, No 1.

Hayes, R.H., Pisano, G.P. and Upton, D.M. (1996) *Strategic Operations*, Free Press.

Hill, T. (1993) *Manufacturing Strategy* (2nd edn), Macmillan, Chaps 2 and 3.

Kinnie, N.J., Staughton, R.V.W. and Davies, E.H. (1992) 'Changing Manufacturing Strategy: Some Approaches and Experiences', *International Journal of Operations and Production Management*, Vol 12, No 7/8.

Lindberg, P. (1990) 'Strategic Manufacturing Management: A Proactive Approach', *International Journal of Operations and Production Management*, Vol 10, No 2.

Lindberg, P. and Trygg, L. (1991) 'Manufacturing Strategy in the Value System', *International Journal of Operations and Production Management*, Vol 11, No 3.

New, C. (1992) 'World Class Manufacturing Versus Strategic Trade-offs', *International Journal of Operations and Production Management*, Vol 12, No 4.

Nicholson, T.A.J. (1991) 'Strategy and the Shop Floor: A One-Way Initiative?', *International Journal of Operations and Production Management*, Vol 11, No 3.

Ould, M.A. (1995) *Business Processes*, John Wiley.

Prahalad, C.K. and Hamel, G. (1990) 'The Core Competence of the Corporation', *Harvard Business Review*, Vol 68, No 3.

Samson, D. (1991) *Manufacturing and Operations Strategy*, Prentice Hall, Chap 1.

Slack, N. (1991) *The Manufacturing Advantage*, Mercury Business Books.

Stobaugh, R. and Telesio, P. (1983) 'Match Manufacturing Policies and Products Strategies', *Harvard Business Review*, Vol 61, No 2.

Sweeney, M.T. (1991) 'Towards a Unified Theory of Strategic Manufacturing Management', *International Journal of Operations and Production Management*, Vol 11, No 8.

Voss, C.A. (1992) *Manufacturing Strategy*, Chapman and Hall, Part 4.

Womack, J.P. and Jones, D.T. (1996) *Lean Thinking: Banish Waste and Create Wealth in your Corporation*, Simon and Schuster.

Woodcock, D.J. (1989) 'Measuring Strategic Control and Improvement in Manufacturing', *International Journal of Operations and Production Management*, Vol 9, No 5.

PART TWO

DESIGN

This part of the book looks at the design of products and services as well as the design of the processes which produce
them. At the most strategic level, process design means
designing the network of operations which get products and
services to the customer. At a more operational level, process
design means the physical arrangement of the operation's
facilities, technology and people.

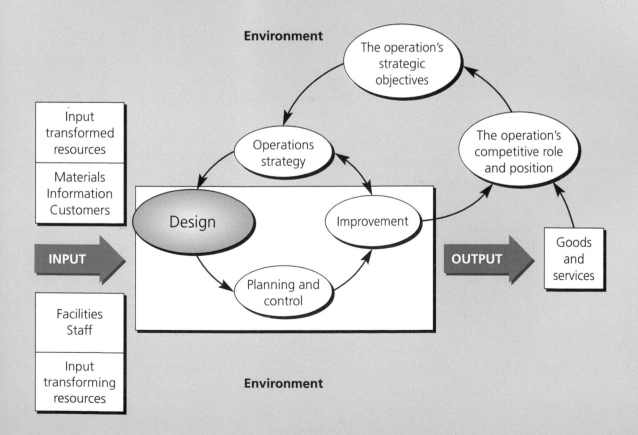

Chapter 4
DESIGN IN OPERATIONS MANAGEMENT

- *What is design in operations management?*
- *What objectives should the design activity have?*
- *How can design decisions be made?*
- *How does the design activity differ in different types of operation?*
- *What are 'process types'?*

Chapter 5
THE DESIGN OF PRODUCTS AND SERVICES

- *Why is good product and service design important?*
- *What are the stages in product and service design?*
- *Why should product and service design and process design be considered interactively?*
- *How should interactive design be managed?*

Chapter 6
DESIGN OF THE OPERATIONS NETWORK

- *Why should an organization take a total supply network perspective?*
- *How much of a network should an operation own?*
- *Where should an operation be located?*
- *How much capacity should an operation plan to have?*

Chapter 7
LAYOUT AND FLOW

- *What are the basic layout types used in operations?*
- *What type of layout should an operation choose?*
- *What is layout design trying to achieve?*
- *How should each basic layout type be designed in detail?*

Chapter 8
PROCESS TECHNOLOGY

- *What is process technology?*
- *What are the significant materials-processing technologies?*
- *What are the significant information-processing technologies?*
- *What are the significant customer-processing technologies?*
- *What are the generic characteristics of process technology?*

Chapter 9
JOB DESIGN AND WORK ORGANIZATION

- *What are the main decisions in job design?*
- *What are the main objectives of job design?*
- *What have been the significant influences on job design practice?*
- *How do the influences on job design differ?*

DESIGN IN OPERATIONS MANAGEMENT

INTRODUCTION

The most widely held image of a designer is of someone who is concerned with the looks of a product – a fashion designer or a motor car designer, for example. The design activity, however, goes far beyond. In fact all operations managers are designers. The purchase of every machine or piece of equipment which is bought is a design decision because it affects the physical shape and nature of the operation. Similarly, every time a machine or piece of equipment is moved, or a method improved, or a member of staff's responsibility changed, the design of the operation is changed. Operations managers also have an important influence on the 'technical' design of the

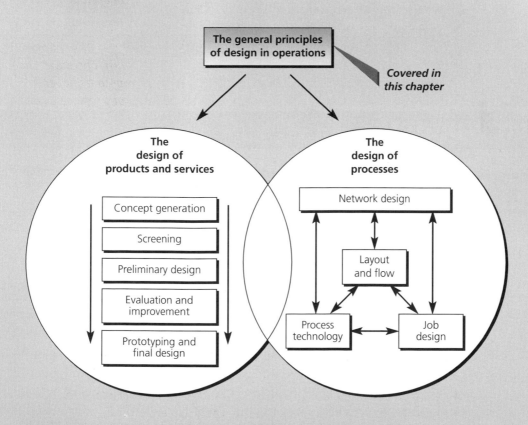

Figure 4.1 The design activities in operations management covered in this part

products and services they produce, by providing much of the information necessary for their design as well as providing the systems which produce them. This is why operations managers cannot afford to be ignorant of the basic principles of design, no matter whether it is a product, service or process which is being designed. This chapter serves as an introduction to Part Two of this book, which treats all the main issues concerned with the design activity in operations management. This includes *both* the design of products and services and the design of the processes which create them. Figure 4.1 shows the issues covered in Part Two and how they relate to each other.

CHAPTER 4: KEY QUESTIONS

- *What is design in operations management?*

- *What objectives should the design activity have?*

- *How can design decisions be made?*

- *How does the design activity differ in different types of operation?*

- *What are 'process types'?*

WHAT IS DESIGN?

There is no universally recognized definition of 'design'. Our view of the meaning of design is neatly captured by this quotation:

'In my definition, design is the conceptual process by which some functional requirement of people, individually or en masse, is satisfied through the use of a product or of a system which derives from the physical translation of the concept. As examples of individual products which satisfy a public or a market need there is the motor car, the television set and the radio, the fridge and the dishwasher, shoes and socks and baby nappies but also the painting, the sculpture, the musical score and the other manifold realized expressionism of the artist, etc.; and as to systems there is the telephone and the railway, the motorway and the supermarket, the orchestra, the provision of utilities (gas, water and electricity), and so on.' (Sir Monty Finneston)[1]

The important points which can be extracted from this description of design are as follows:

- The purpose of the design activity is to *satisfy the needs of customers*.
- The design activity applies to both *products* (or *services*) and *systems* (what we would call *processes*).

- The design activity is itself a *transformation process*.
- Design starts with a *concept* and ends in the translation of that concept into a *specification* of something which can be created.

Each of these aspects of design is worth considering further.

Design means satisfying the needs of customers

The design activity in operations has one overriding objective: to provide the type of products, services and processes which will satisfy the operation's customers (*see* box on the design of the Boeing 777). Product designers will try to achieve aesthetically pleasing designs which meet or exceed customers' expectations. They will also try to design a product which performs well and is reliable during its lifetime. Further, they should design the product so that it can be manufactured easily and quickly, so that errors during manufacture are unlikely and manufacturing costs are minimized. Similarly, service designers try to put together a service which customers will see as at least meeting their expectations. Yet at the same time the service must be within the capabilities of the operation and be delivered at reasonable cost.

The same is true for process designers. The way in which the process which creates the product or service is designed will have a significant impact on the ability of the operation to meet its customers' needs. A process which has been located in the wrong place, or with insufficient capacity, or arranged in a jumbled and confused layout, or given inappropriate technology, or staffed with unskilled people, cannot satisfy customers because it cannot perform efficiently or effectively (*see* box on troublesome technology). Table 4.1 illustrates how each performance objective of an operation is affected by the design of products and services and the design of the process which creates them.

Table 4.1 The impact of product/service and process design on performance objectives

Performance objective	Influence of good product/service design	Influence of good process design
Quality	Can eliminate potential fail points and 'error-prone' aspects of the product or service	Can provide the appropriate resources which are capable of producing the product or service to its design specifications
Speed	Can specify products which can be made quickly (for example, using modular design principles) or services which avoid unnecessary delays	Can move materials, information or customers through each stage of the process without delays
Dependability	Can help to make each stage of the process predictable by requiring standardized, predictable processes	Can provide technology and staff who are themselves dependable
Flexibility	Can allow for variations which allow a range of products or services to be offered to customers	Can provide resources which can be changed quickly so as to create a range of products or services
Cost	Can reduce the costs of each component part which goes into the product or service and also can reduce the cost of putting them together	Can ensure high utilization of resources and therefore efficient and low-cost processes

TROUBLESOME TECHNOLOGY[2]

Failure to understand the needs of customers and work these thoroughly into the design can cause problems which only emerge after the product or service is in use. This can be especially true when designers are motivated solely by the exciting possibilities which a new technology offers. For example, many of the so-called 'intelligent buildings' which incorporated extensive information technology suffered initial teething problems. One building incorpor-ated 'intelligent blinds' on its windows. These were supposed to go up and down in response to the amount of sunlight falling on the windows. The outside lighting was sampled every seven minutes. On a sunny day the blinds were supposed to remain down and when it was cloudy they would stay up to let in more light. Unfortunately, when the sun passed behind a small cloud the blinds could go up and stay there for seven minutes. On intermittently cloudy days the blinds would be forever going up and down, to the considerable annoyance of staff, especially those with computer screens. The problem was eventually 'solved' when staff piled books on the bottom of the blinds until the motors blew up. Another building had conference rooms where the lights were activated by sensors in the ceiling which reacted to movement and heat. The lights went on automatically when people entered the room. Unfortunately this was the only mechanism by which the lights went on and off, so if someone wanted to show slides, everyone in the room had to sit still until the lights went out. ■

Questions

1 Why were each of the systems described in this box regarded as a failure?

2 How would you have ensured that the mistakes made by the designers of these systems could not have occurred?

3 Was it just incompetence that led the designers to install these systems or were they falling into a fairly predictable design trap?

BOEING BRINGS ITS CUSTOMERS ON BOARD[3]

Arguably the most innovative new passenger aircraft to enter service over the last few years was the Boeing 777, a new twin-engined aircraft, in the 300-plus seats category, to compete with established models from McDonnell and Airbus. The existence of established competitor products is important. When Boeing developed the 747 'Jumbo' jet aircraft, it had no direct competitors. The company's customers either wanted the product or they didn't. Not so for the 777; Boeing knew that it must consider its customers' requirements. The company had to take a new course – to understand its customers' needs and then to transform that knowledge into an aircraft that could best meet those needs.

Boeing has always maintained close involvement with its customers, but this project called for a new depth of listening and understanding. Initially, eight large potential customers (including

British Airways, Japan Airlines and Qantas) were invited to participate in creating the design concepts. It soon became clear that the customers did have important requirements, the most vital of which was that the aircraft should be around 25 per cent wider than the 767. In fact Boeing had originally hoped to lengthen the 767 fuselage to give the extra capacity, so avoiding some of the costs involved in a completely new fuselage. The customers also wanted much more flexibility in the configuration of the passenger space. Conventionally, cabin space had been divided up into sections, separated by fixed galleys and toilets at predetermined positions, fixing the ratio of passenger capacities of each class. However, the airlines all indicated that they wanted to be able to configure the cabin to their requirements. Finally, the airlines insisted that the new design should be free of the usual level of minor, but irritating, faults which had bugged the early operations of some of the other aircraft.

Boeing did meet its customers' requirements and even improved upon them in some ways. They achieved this by using design/build teams (a concept similar to the interactive design principle described in Chapter 5), and by a particularly powerful computer-aided design (CAD) system (CAD is described in Chapter 5). Customers were closely involved right from the start of the design. They even came up with some good suggestions. For example, one airline suggested a new layout for the rear galley which allowed an extra twelve seats to be included in the aircraft. ■

Questions

1 What do you think might be the problems in bringing customers together in the way Boeing did?

2 Why do you think that Boeing's customers wanted the flexibility to configure passenger space?

3 What advantages do you think Boeing gained from its use of computer-aided design (CAD)?

Products, services and processes are all designed

In most organizations 'design' is far more likely to be used as referring to the design of the products (or perhaps the services) which are being produced. However, in our terms, the design activity extends also to the processes which create products and services. The design activity, whether applied to products and services or processes, is attempting to achieve the same purpose. It is essentially concerned with determining the overall shape and form of something, and the way in which it is intended to operate.

Product/service design and process design are interrelated

Often we will treat the design of products and services on the one hand, and the design of the processes which make them on the other, as though they were separate activities. Yet in practice they are clearly interrelated. It would be foolish to commit an organization to the detailed design of any product or service without some consideration of how it is to be produced. Small changes in the design of products and services can have profound and expensive implications for the way the operation eventually has to produce them. Similarly, the design of a process can constrain the freedom of product and service designers to operate as they would wish (*see* Fig. 4.2).

This holds good whether the operation is producing products or services. However, the overlap between the two activities is generally greater in operations which produce services. After all, many services involve the customer in being part of the transformation process. The nature and form of the service, as far as the customer sees it, cannot be separated from the process to which the customer is subjected. Of course not all the processes in a service operation will involve the customer. The back-office part of the operation (*see* Chapter 1) will have processes which can be designed, to some extent, separately from the design of the service itself.

The difficulties of overlapping the two activities of product and process design has implications for the way in which the design activity is organized, as will be discussed in Chapter 5. Certainly, when product designers also have to make or use the things which they design, it can concentrate their minds on what is important. For example, in the early days of flight, the engineers who designed the aircraft were also the test pilots who took them out on their first flight. For this reason, if no other, safety was a significant objective in the design activity.

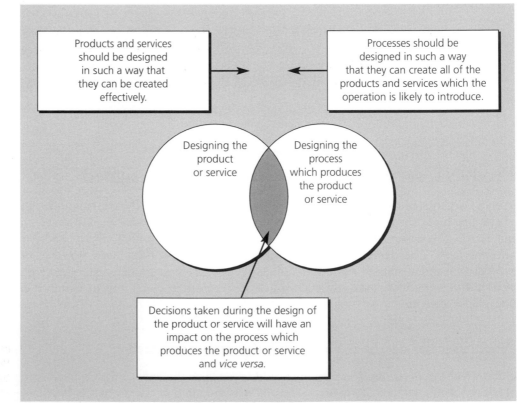

Figure 4.2
The design of products/services and processes are interrelated and should be treated together

The overlap has become important in manufacturing operations

This interrelationship means that the design of products and services and the design of processes should be considered as overlapping activities. In manufacturing especially, considerable effort has recently been put into examining this overlap. There are probably two reasons for this. First is a growing recognition that the design of products has a major effect on the cost of making them. Many of the decisions taken during the design of products (for example, choosing the material from which the product is going to made, or the way in which the various components are fastened together) will all define much of the cost of making it. Figure 4.3 shows how the costs of the design process itself grow quite slowly, especially at the start of the design activity, but the costs to which the design is committing the organization grow very quickly. It makes sense, therefore, to evaluate the various choices which the designer faces in terms of their effect on manufacturing cost as well as the functionality of the product itself. Second, the way overlap between product or service design and process design is managed has a significant effect on the time between having the initial concept for the product or service and eventually getting it to market. This will be discussed further in Chapter 5.

The design activity is itself a transformation process

Producing designs for products, services or the processes which create them is itself a transformation process which conforms to the input–transformation–output model which was described in Chapter 1 and therefore has to be managed. Figure 4.4 illustrates the design activity as an input–transformation–output diagram. The transformed resource inputs will consist mainly of information in the form of market forecasts, market preferences, technical data, and so on. Transforming resource inputs include administrative,

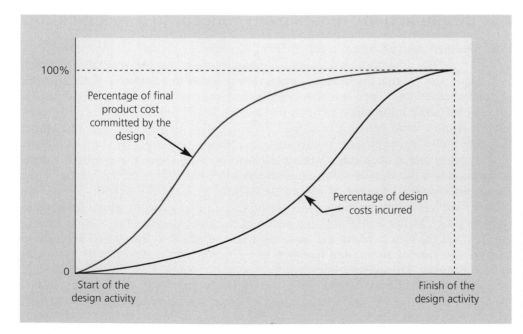

Figure 4.3
Relatively early in the design activity the decisions taken will commit the operation to costs which will be incurred later

113

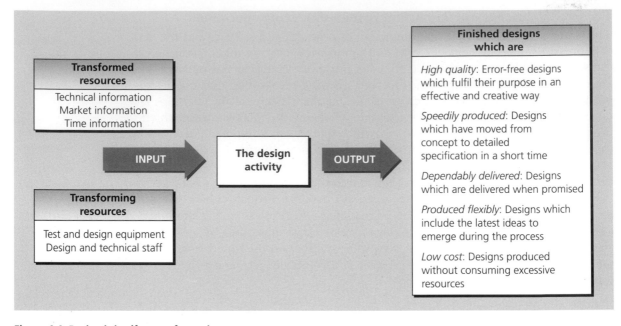

Figure 4.4 Design is itself a transformation process

clerical and technical staff, design equipment such as computer-aided design (CAD) systems (*see* Chapter 5) and perhaps development and testing equipment.

We can describe the objectives of the design activity in the same way as we do any transformation process. All operations satisfy customers by producing their services and goods according to customers' desires for quality, speed, dependability, flexibility and cost. In the same way the design activity attempts to produce designs to the same objectives.

The design activity moves from concept to a specification

Fully specified designs, which totally define every part or activity, do not spring fully formed from the designer's imagination. A design starts as a more general, ill-defined, even vague idea of what might be an appropriate solution to a felt need. Over time this original idea, or 'concept', is refined and made progressively more detailed until it contains sufficient information to be turned into an actual product, service or process. The transition from concept to detailed specification can be divided into stages (Chapter 5 divides the process into six stages). This has two important implications.

The first is that at each stage, when a decision is made about the design, the decision cuts down the number of options which will be available further along in the design activity. For example, if a designer decides to make the outside casing of a camera case in aluminium rather than plastic, this limits decisions which have yet to be made, such as the overall size and shape of the case, the way the body is jointed together and the way in which the outer layer is bonded on to the case. The decision to make the case of aluminium has therefore committed the designer to particular options later on. This means that the uncertainty surrounding the design reduces as the number of alternative designs being considered by the designer decreases. In fact the design activity can be considered as one of progressively reducing the uncertainty regarding a product, service or process (*see* Fig. 4.5).

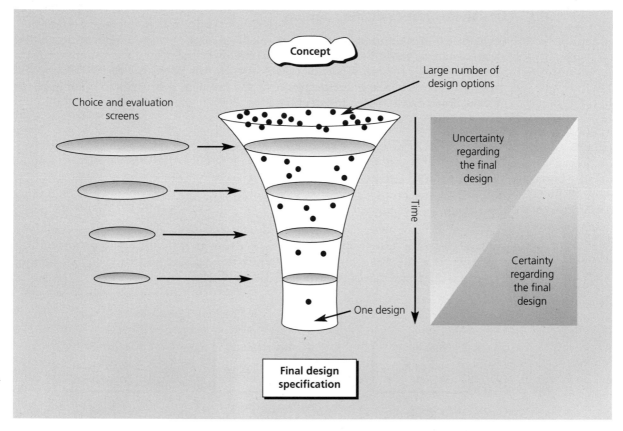

Figure 4.5 **Design involves progressively reducing the number of possibilities until the final design is reached**

The second consequence of the progression from concept to detailed specification concerns the cost of the designers changing their minds on some detail of the design. In most stages of design the cost of changing a decision is bound to incur some sort of rethinking and recalculation of costs. Close to the start of the design activity, before too many fundamental decisions have been made, the costs of change are relatively low. Relatively quickly, however, as the design progresses, the interrelated and cumulative decisions which are made become increasingly expensive to change.

Design involves identifying options

Uncertainty in the design activity is reduced as it progresses from concept to specification by designers choosing between alternative ways of achieving the objectives of the design. At each stage in the design of products, services or processes, until the final stage, designers are faced with *options*. Sometimes the range of options is narrow. It could be yes or no. For example, 'Should we go ahead with redesigning the hotel or not?' At other times the range of options is almost infinite: for example, 'How thick should we make the shielding of a nuclear reactor?' Any thickness between zero to very thick indeed is possible, with different consequences for safety and cost. But whether two or an infinite number of possibilities, the important point is to recognize that there are always options.

Design involves evaluating options

Evaluation in design means assessing the worth or value of each design option, so that a choice can be made between them. This involves assessing each option against a number of *design criteria*. While the criteria used in any particular design exercise will depend on the nature and circumstances of the exercise, it is useful to think in terms of three broad categories of design criteria:[4]

- The *feasibility* of the design option – can we do it?
- The *acceptability* of the design option – do we want to do it?
- The *vulnerability* of each design option – do we want to take the risk?

The feasibility of a design option indicates the degree of difficulty in adopting it and should assess the *investment* in time, effort and money which will be needed. The acceptability of a design option assesses how well it takes the design towards its objectives. It is the *return* or benefit the design gets from choosing the option. The vulnerability of a design option is the extent to which things could go wrong if it is chosen. It is the *risk* which is incurred by the designers in choosing an option. Figure 4.6 illustrates this classification of design criteria.

Figure 4.6
Broad categories of evaluation criteria for assessing design options

Key questions to assess the feasibility of a design option include:

- Do we have the skills (quality of resources) to cope with this option?
- Do we have the organizational capacity (quantity of resources) to cope with this option?
- Do we have the financial resources to cope with this option?

Key questions to assess the acceptability of a design option are:

- Does the option satisfy the performance criteria which the design is trying to achieve? (These will differ for different designs.)
- Does the option give a satisfactory financial return?

Key questions to assess the vulnerability of a design option include:

- Do we understand the full consequences of adopting the option?
- Being pessimistic, what could go wrong if we adopt the option? What would be the consequences of everything going wrong? (This is called the 'downside risk' of an option.)

SIMULATION IN DESIGN

The essence of design is that the designer is making decisions in advance of the real product, service or process being created. This means that the designer is often not totally sure of the consequences of his or her decision. For example, a running shoe designer might make a decision about the construction of the shoe, or an architect about the layout of a public building, based on previous experience and basic theories. To increase their own confidence in their design decision, however, they will probably try to *simulate* how the product and the layout would work in practice. In some ways simulation is one of the most fundamental approaches to decision making. Children play games and 'pretend' so as to extend their experience of novel situations; likewise, managers can gain insights and explore possibilities through the formalized 'pretending' involved in using simulation models. Simulation explores the consequences of decision-making rather than directly advising on the decision itself – it is a *predictive* rather than an *optimizing* technique.

Simulation of some sort or other is one of the most useful tools which a designer can use to explore the consequences of a design decision without having to construct the product, service or process. If some 'model' of the design is made, the designer can experiment and test the 'model' and then use the results to either confirm the original design or adjust it based on the simulated behaviour. The simulation 'model' itself can take many forms. In the case of the running shoe design, the 'model' might be almost identical to the intended product, except that a 'one-off' prototype shoe would have been made rather than one produced on the actual manufacturing system which would be used for the eventual product. The prototype shoe would then be flexed many millions of times to simulate prolonged wear. In the case of the public building, the architect could devise a computer-based 'model' which would simulate the movement of people through the building according to the probability distribution which describes their random arrival and movement. This could then be used to predict where the layout might become overcrowded or where extra space might be reduced.

Simulating processes

Simulation is especially useful in the design of very complex operations processes. For example, a typical use was a computer simulation which was used to redesign a North African shipping port. The model helped the designers to gain an understanding of how the detailed design of the docks and berths for the ships would affect the utilization and turn-round time of the ships depositing and picking up their cargoes at the port. The simulation led to a design which resulted in substantial savings to the World Bank who were involved in the funding of the project.[5]

ENVIRONMENTALLY SENSITIVE DESIGN

With the issues of environmental protection becoming more important, designers are increasingly having to take account of 'green' issues in their work. In many developed countries legislation has already provided some basic standards which restrict the use of toxic materials, limit discharges to air and water, and protect employees and the public from immediate and long-term harm. Most of these constraints affect both the design and operation of *processes* and the design of the products themselves.

VOLVO'S ENVIRONMENTAL PRIORITY STRATEGIES (EPS) SYSTEM[6]

There are many ways in which the life-cycle analysis approach can be used to evaluate environmental data so that it can be used to guide product designers in the use of different materials. One such tool has been developed by Volvo, the Swedish motor manufacturer, in conjunction with the Federation of Swedish Industries and the Swedish Environmental Research Institute. It uses 'environmental indices' calculated for specific materials as follows:

Environmental index = Scope × Distribution × Frequency or Intensity × Durability × Contribution × Remediability

where

Scope = General impression of the environmental impact

Distribution = Extent of affected area

Frequency or intensity = Regularity or intensity of the problem in the affected area

Durability = Permanency of the effects

Contribution = Significance of 1kg of the emission of the substance in relation to the total effect

Remediability = Relative cost to reduce the emission by 1 kg

The 'environmental load unit' (ELU) per kg of any substance can then be calculated as the product of the index and the amount of substance released into the environment. ∎

Questions

1 What do you think are the general problems in trying to quantify the environmental impact of design?

2 What seems to you to be the major weakness of the particular approach presented here?

Interest has focused on some fundamental issues:

- *The sources of materials* used in a product. (Will it damage rain forests? Will it use up scarce minerals? Will it exploit the poor, or use child labour?)
- *Quantities and sources of energy* consumed in the process. (Do plastic beverage bottles use more energy than glass ones? Should waste heat be recovered and used in fish farming?)
- *The amounts and type of waste material* that are created in the manufacturing processes. (Can this waste be recycled efficiently, or must it be burnt or buried in landfill sites? Will the waste have a long-term impact on the environment as it decomposes and escapes?)

- *The life of the product itself.* It is argued that if a product has a useful life of, say, 20 years, it will consume less resources than one that only lasts five years, which must, therefore, be replaced four times in the same period. However, the long-life product may require more initial inputs, and may prove to be inefficient in the latter part of its use, when the latest products use less energy or maintenance to run.
- *The end-of-life of the product.* (Will the redundant product be difficult to dispose of in an environmentally friendly way? Could it be recycled or used as a source of energy? Could it still be useful in third-world conditions? Could it be used to benefit the environment, such as old cars being used to make artificial reefs for sea life?)

Designers are faced with complex trade-offs between these factors, although it is not always easy to obtain all the information that is needed to make the 'best' choices. For example, it is relatively straightforward to design a long-life product, using strong material, over-designed components, ample corrosion protection, and so on. But its production might use more materials and energy and it could create more waste on disposal. To help make more rational decisions in the design process, some industries are experimenting with *Life Cycle Analysis*. This technique analyses all the production inputs, the life-cycle use of the product and its final disposal, in terms of total energy used (and more recently, of all the emitted wastes such as carbon dioxide, sulphurous and nitrous gases, organic solvents, solid waste, etc.). The inputs and wastes are evaluated at *every* stage in its creation, beginning with the extraction or farming of the basic raw materials.

THE VOLUME-VARIETY EFFECT ON DESIGN

Although, so far, we have discussed those aspects of design which apply to all types of operations, there are differences between the design activity in, say, an architects' practice and that in an electricity utility. The most significant factor is the difference between their volume and variety characteristics.

In Chapter 1 we saw how operations can range from producing a very high volume of products or services (for example, a food canning factory) to very low volume (for example, major project consulting engineers). We also saw how operations can range from producing a very low variety of products or services (for example, in an electricity utility) to very high variety (as, for example, in an architects' practice). Usually the two dimensions of volume and variety go together. Low-volume operations often have a high variety of products and services, and high-volume operations often have a narrow variety of products and services. Thus there is a continuum from low volume–high variety through to high volume–low variety, on which we can position operations.

If you have had the opportunity to study operations, even at a superficial level, you may have noticed that different operations, perhaps within the same industry, have adopted different approaches to the design of their products, services and processes. Not all the retail operations you use, for example, are organized in the same way, or even look the same. Even within a single operation, different approaches to designing products, services and processes can be found. Many manufacturing plants will have a large area, organized on a 'mass-production' basis, in which it makes its high-volume 'best selling' products. In another part of the plant it may also have an area where it makes a wide variety of products in much smaller volumes. Both the design of each set of products and the design of the process which makes them are likely to be different. Similarly in a medical service, compare the approach taken during mass medical treatments, such as large-scale immunization programmes, with a transplant operation where the treatment is designed specifically to meet the needs of one person. These differences go well beyond their differing technologies, or the different processing requirements of the products or services. They are explained by the fact that no one way of arranging resources is best for all types of operation in all circumstances. The differences are explained largely by the different *volume–variety positions* of the operations.

Volume and variety influence performance objectives

The volume and variety of an operation's activities are particularly influential in determining the way it thinks about its performance objectives. Figure 4.7 illustrates how the definitions of quality, speed, dependability, flexibility and cost are influenced by the volume–variety position of the operation.

Quality

Quality in a low volume–high variety process, such as an architects' practice, for example, is largely concerned with the final aesthetic appearance of the building and

Volume	Variety	Examples of operation	Performance objectives				
			Quality means...	Speed means...	Dependability means...	Flexibility means...	Cost is...
Low	High		Specification performance	Negotiated waiting time	On-time delivery	Product/ service flexibility	Variable
		Architects' practice					
		Bespoke tailor					
		Fast-food restaurant					
		Document processing					
		Electricity utility					
High	Low		Conformance to standard	Instant delivery	Availability	Volume flexibility	Constant

Figure 4.7 An operation's position on the volume–variety continuum influences the meaning of the operation's performance objectives

the appropriateness of its detailed design. In an exceptionally high volume–low variety process, such as an electricity supply company, quality is exclusively concerned with error-free service – electricity must be constantly available in the correct form (in terms of voltage, frequency, etc.). The meaning of quality has shifted from being concerned primarily with the performance and specification of the product or service towards conformity to a predefined standard, as we move from low volume–high variety operations through to high volume–low variety operations.

Speed

Speed for the architects' practice means negotiating a completion date with each client, based on the client's needs and the architects' estimates of how much work is involved in each project. Speed is taken to its extreme in the electricity utility where speed means literally instant delivery. No electricity company could ask its customers to wait for their 'delivery' of electricity. Speed therefore means an individually negotiated delivery time in low volume–high variety operations, but moves towards meaning 'instant' delivery in some high volume–low variety operations.

Dependability

Dependability in processes such as the architects' practice means keeping to each individually negotiated delivery date. In continuous operations, dependability often means the availability of the service itself. A dependable electricity supply is one which is always there. So dependability has moved from meaning 'on-time delivery' in low volume–high variety operations to 'availability' in high volume–low variety operations.

Flexibility

Flexibility in low volume–high variety processes such as the architects' practice means the ability to design many different kinds of buildings according to its clients' various requirements. With the electricity company's process, the need for product flexibility has disappeared entirely (electricity is electricity, more or less) but the ability to meet almost instantaneous demand changes through volume flexibility is vital if the company is to maintain supply. Flexibility has moved from meaning product flexibility in low volume–high variety operations to volume flexibility in high volume–low variety operations.

Cost

Cost, in terms of the unit cost per product or service, varies with both the volume of output of the operation and the variety of products or services it produces. The variety of products or services in low-volume operations is relatively high, which means that running the operation will be expensive because of the flexible and high skill levels employed. Further, because the volume of output is relatively low, a few products or services are bearing the operation's high cost base. Also, and more significantly for the operation, the cost of each product or service is different. At the other end of the scale, high-volume operations usually produce similar products or services, output is high, so that whatever the base cost of the operation, it is shared among a high number of products or services. Cost per unit of output is therefore usually low for operations such as the electricity utility but, more significantly, the cost of producing one second of electricity is the same as the next second. Cost is relatively constant.

Volume and variety affect the design activity

The volume–variety position of an operation has implications far beyond its performance objectives. It will also influence almost every aspect of the operation's design activities (*see* Table 4.2).

Take again the two operations discussed previously at the extremes of the volume–variety spectrum – the architects' practice and the electricity utility. The architects' high variety means that its services have little standardization. Some elements of the service will be common – all new designs will need a proposal to put before the client, an internal schedule of activities, plans, and so on – but the details of these will vary from job to job. This variety of activities also means that whatever technology the operation possesses (for example, computer-aided design systems) will need to be sufficiently general purpose to cope with all types of job. The flow of information within the operation will depend on the state of the projects being designed, the circumstances of clients and the overall level of activity in the operation. It will certainly not be regular; rather it will flow in an intermittent manner. The individual task skills of the architects themselves are likely to be more valued by the practice than the skill involved in running the operation itself.

The electricity utility, on the other hand, exhibits almost the mirror-image characteristics of the architects' practice. Volume is high, variety is virtually non-existent since electricity is almost a totally standardized product. The generators – its process technology – cannot be used to do much else but make electricity, which it does more or less continuously. No individual craft skills are needed directly to make electricity (although they will be needed to maintain the generators) but the skills of managing the 'electricity generating system', so as to provide continuous supply at the lowest feasible cost, are considerable.

Table 4.2 The impact of the volume–variety position of an operation on different aspects of its design activities

Volume	Variety	Design emphasis in the operation	Product/service standardization	Location	Flow	Process technology	Staff skills
Low	High	Product/service design	Low	Can be decentralized	Intermittent	General purpose	Task
↓	↓	↓	↓	↓	↓	↓	↓
High	Low	Process design	High	Usually centralized	Continuous	Dedicated	System

PROCESS TYPES IN MANUFACTURING AND SERVICES

The position of an operation on the volume–variety continuum, by influencing the nature of its performance objectives and its design activities, also shapes the general approach it takes to managing the transformation process. These 'general approaches' to managing the transformation process are called *process types*. Different terms are used to identify process types in manufacturing and service industries.

In manufacturing, these process types are (in order of increasing volume and decreasing variety):

- project processes
- jobbing processes
- batch processes
- mass processes
- continuous processes.

In service operations there is less consensus on the terms of the process type. The terms we use here are (again in order of increasing volume and decreasing variety):[7]

- professional services
- service shops
- mass services.

Process types in manufacturing

Each process type in manufacturing implies a different way of organizing operations' activities with different volume and variety characteristics (*see* Fig. 4.8).

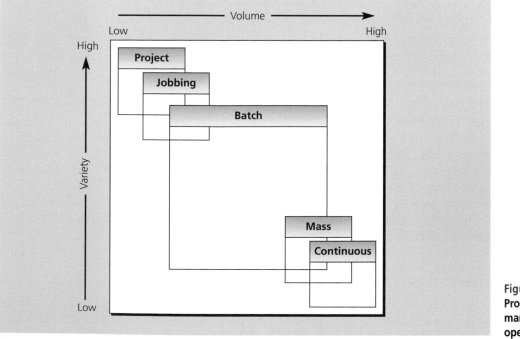

Figure 4.8
Process types in manufacturing operations

Project processes

Project processes are those which deal with discrete, usually highly customized products. Often the timescale of making the product or service is relatively long, as is the interval between the completion of each product or service. So low volume and high variety are characteristics of project processes. The activities involved in making the product can be ill-defined and uncertain, sometimes changing during the production process itself. Examples of project processes include shipbuilding, most construction companies, movie production companies, building the Channel Tunnel, large fabrication operations such as those manufacturing turbo generators, drilling oil wells, and installing a computer system. The essence of project processes is that each job has a well-defined start and finish, the time interval between starting different jobs is relatively long and the transforming resources which make the product will probably have been organized especially for each product.

Jobbing processes

Jobbing processes also deal with very high variety and low volumes. Whereas in project processes each product has resources devoted more or less exclusively to it, in jobbing processes each product has to share the operation's resources with many others. The resources of the operation will process a series of products but, although all the products will require the same kind of attention, each will differ in its exact needs. Examples of jobbing processes include many precision engineers such as specialist toolmakers, furniture restorers, bespoke tailors, and the printer who produces tickets for the local social event. Jobbing processes produce more and usually smaller items than project processes but, like project processes, the degree of repetition is low. Most jobs will probably be 'one-offs'.

Batch processes

Batch processes can often look like jobbing processes, but batch does not have quite the degree of variety associated with jobbing. As the name implies, each time batch processes produce a product they produce more than one. So each part of the operation has periods when it is repeating itself, at least while the 'batch' is being processed. The size of the batch could be just two or three, in which case the batch process would differ little from jobbing, especially if each batch is a totally novel product. Conversely, if the batches are large, and especially if the products are familiar to the operation, batch processes can be fairly repetitive. Because of this, the batch type of process can be found over a wider range of volume and variety levels than other process types. Examples of batch processes include machine tool manufacturing, the production of some special gourmet frozen foods, the manufacture of most of the component parts which go into mass-produced assemblies such as automobiles, and the production of most clothing.

Mass processes

Mass processes are those which produce goods in high volume and relatively narrow variety – narrow, that is, in terms of the fundamentals of the product design. An automobile plant, for example, might produce several thousand variants of car if every option of engine size, colour, extra equipment, etc. is taken into account. Yet essentially it is a mass operation because the different variants of its product do not affect the basic process of production. The activities in the automobile plant, like all mass operations, are essentially repetitive and largely predictable. Examples of mass processes include the automobile plant, most consumer durable manufacturers such as a television plant, most food processes such as a frozen pizza manufacturer, a beer bottling plant and CD production.

Continuous processes

Continuous processes are one step beyond mass processes insomuch as they operate at even higher volume and often have even lower variety. They also usually operate for far longer periods of time. Sometimes they are literally continuous in that their products are inseparable, being produced in an endless flow. They may even be continuous in that the operation must supply the products without a break. Continuous processes are often associated with relatively inflexible, capital-intensive technologies with highly predictable flow. Examples of continuous processes include petrochemical refineries, electricity utilities, steel making, and some paper making.

Process types in service operations

As with manufacturing operations, each process type in service operations implies a different way of organizing the operation to cope with different volume–variety characteristics (*see* Fig. 4.9).

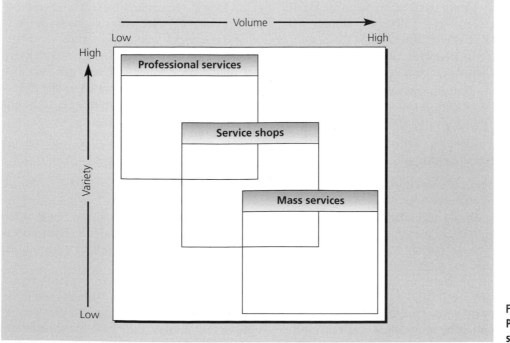

Figure 4.9
Process types in
service operations

Professional services

Professional services are defined as high-contact organizations where customers spend a considerable time in the service process. Such services provide high levels of customization, the service process being highly adaptable in order to meet individual customer needs. A great deal of staff time is spent in the front office and contact staff are given considerable discretion in servicing customers. The amount of time and attention provided for each customer probably means that the ratio of staff to customers is high. Professional services tend to be people-based rather than equipment-based, with emphasis placed on the process (how the service is delivered) rather than the 'product' (what is delivered). Professional services include management consultants, lawyers' practices, architects, doctors' surgeries, auditors, health and safety inspectors and some computer field service operations.

A typical example would be Andersen Consulting, which sells the problem-solving expertise of its skilled staff to tackle clients' problems. Typically, the problem will first be discussed with clients and the boundaries of the project defined. Each 'product' is different. The project manager's role is to create a project team with the appropriate mix of skills to tackle the problem. A high proportion of work takes place at the client's premises, with frequent contact between members of the project team and the client.

At the other extreme are mass services.

Mass services

Mass services have many customer transactions, involving limited contact time and little customization. Such services are often predominantly equipment-based and 'product' oriented, with most value added in the back office and relatively little judgement applied by front-office staff. The mainly non-professional staff are likely to have a closely defined division of labour and to follow set procedures. Mass services include supermarkets, a national rail network, an airport, telecommunications service, library, television station, the police service, and the enquiry desk at a utility.

For example, rail services such as Virgin Trains in the UK or SNCF in France all move a large number of passengers with a variety of rolling stock on an immense infrastructure of railways. Passengers pick a journey from the range offered. The rail company ticket-office staff can advise passengers on the quickest or cheapest way to get from A to B, but they cannot 'customize' the service by putting on a special train for them.

Service shops

Service shops are characterized by levels of customer contact, customization, volumes of customers and staff discretion, which position them between the extremes of professional and mass services. Service is provided via mixes of front- and back-office activities, people and equipment, and of product/process emphasis. Service shops include banks, high street shops, holiday tour operators, car rental companies, schools, most restaurants, hotels and travel agents.

For example, the Multibroadcast rental organization in the UK offers both rental and retail sale of home electronic products. Its range of products is displayed in its front-office outlets, while back-office operations looks after purchasing and administration. The front-office staff are not there solely to take money; they have some technical

Giordano – cheerful as well as cheap

Exterior of a Giordano shop in Hong Kong

The rules of clothes retailing in the fast-growing markets around Hong Kong, Taiwan and Singapore used to be clear. Up-market shops sold high quality products at high prices and gave good service. Cheaper clothes were piled high and sold by sales assistants who were more concerned with taking the cash than smiling at customers. Jimmy Lai, founder of Giordano Holdings, changed all that. Although he originally set up to sell expensive clothes, Mr Lai saw that unpredictable quality and low levels of service offered an opportunity in the casual clothes market. He calculated that giving value and service, together with low prices, would generate a better profit than existing retailers were getting. His methods were radical. Overnight he raised the wages of his sales people by between 30 and 40 per cent, all employees were told they would receive at least 60 hours of training a year and new staff would be allocated a 'big brother' or 'big sister' from among experienced staff to help them develop their service quality skills. Even more startling by the standards of his competitors, Mr Lai brought in a 'no-questions-asked' exchange policy irrespective of how long ago the garment had been purchased. Staff were also trained to talk to customers and seek their opinions on products and the type of service they would like. This information would be immediately fed back to the company's designers for incorporation into their new products (usually limited to a relatively narrow range of 20 or 30 basic styles, but in a wide range of colours). Within a few years of his change in policy Mr Lai had seen dramatic growth in both profits and turnover to a position where Giordano achieved the highest sales per square metre of almost any retailer in Hong Kong.

Interior of a Giordano shop in Hong Kong

- *In what way did Mr Lai change the market position of his Giordano operation?*
- *Why do you think Giordano could still be so profitable even after increasing its wage costs by so much?*
- *What are the advantages in sales staff talking to the customers?*

➔ *Look at Chapters 3 and 20 for guidance*

The virtual reality of design

Photo courtesy of Silicon Graphics

Using a Silicon Graphics Reality Centre for operations design

Virtual reality, sometimes seen solely as a high technology arcade entertainment medium, is quietly establishing itself as a powerful, three-dimensional professional design tool, with applications including architecture, car design, and the planning of delicate surgical operations. It gives designers a much clearer concept of the relative positions of the individual elements than is possible with static, two-dimensional representations. Perhaps even more importantly, it also allows others, in particular the non-technically trained user, to visualize and suggest modifications to the design before any work is done on the physical entity concerned. An architect can allow the client to roam around the virtual building, walking along corridors and entering rooms at will. PERA, the European consultancy, R & D and technology transfer company, uses a 'Virtual Reality Centre' to help its clients visualize the implications of their operations designs. Powered by a Silicon Graphics Onyx Infinite Reality supercomputer, the world's most powerful graphics supercomputer, the Centre offers visualizations of real-time data.

'VR offers significant benefits in industrial applications, from market testing and design, to training and maintenance planning. The Virtual Reality Centre bridges the gap between software vendors and potential users by delivering tailored applications to address specific needs,' says Gary Eves, Business Manager at PERA. For example, Barclaycard, the bank card company, has employed Reality Centre technology to let some of its 2500 staff in Northampton walk through and help design its new offices. Barclaycard staff could view the new building as it would look, with groups of staff encouraged to give feedback on the design of the offices including floor layout and accessibility.

- *What are the advantages of 'visualizing' operations before they are constructed?*
- *PERA's Virtual Reality Centre cost £2 million using the latest Silicon Graphics technology. How do you think it justified such an investment?*

→ *Look at Chapter 4 for guidance*

Teams and lines in the garment industry

Photo courtesy of Terry King, CV Clothing

Line production of underwear and nightwear

Photo courtesy of Terry King, CV Clothing

Cell production of fashion clothes

Job design is a crucial issue in the European garment industry. Most companies have to operate under the twin pressures of seasonal fashion design changes, as well as constant cost pressures. The relatively high wage rates in Europe mean that companies are always under threat from lower wage economies. Devising a job design which answers both of these needs is a continuing challenge for the industry's operations managers. The illustrations (above) show two different approaches. On the left is part of a production line manufacturing ladies' and children's underwear and nightwear. The line has around 30 people including supervisers, a trainer and quality inspectors. The total work content for most products is around 1.5 standard minutes and so products spend only a matter of seconds at each (single person) station. After performing their task, each operator puts the product into 'work-in-progress' stores between each stage. Typically, these will contain around 12 partly finished products. Most workers have been trained only to do their own task, but within the team there would be three or four multi-skilled 'floaters' who can cover for absent operators.

The picture on the right shows a different type of organization. Here a team of five or six operators is making relatively high-fashion ladieswear – more complex products. Batches of garments, once produced, are rarely repeated so operators have to 'learn afresh' each time they start a batch. The operators are organized in a relatively flexible manner, moving within a horseshoe-shaped cell, using the machines which are positioned around the cell. Generally there will be around three times as many machines as there are operators, with operators moving between machines as necessary. Although work-in-progress is present in the cell, it is relatively low – typically one or two garments between each 'station'. Because runs of a single product will be short and therefore the tasks allocated to individual workers will change frequently, operators need to be multi-skilled.

- *What do you think are the advantages and disadvantages of the two types of work organization?*
- *How would product/market differences between types of product produced affect the choice between these two systems?*

→ *Look at Chapters 7 and 9 for guidance*

Dyson appliances sweep ahead

James Dyson with one of his products

James Dyson (pictured above) has revolutionized the vacuum cleaner industry. His approach to the design, manufacture and servicing of domestic appliances has brought him to the point where sales have eclipsed those of his main competitors. It all began when Dyson became frustrated with the performance of his own vacuum cleaner.

'The bag in the cleaner was empty, but the pores were clogged. A similar thing had been happening to the air filter in the spray-finishing room of a company where I had been working. We finally found the solution to the problem – a cyclone tower which removed the particles by centrifugal force.'

He immediately started experimenting with the same idea applied to the domestic vacuum cleaner. Five thousand prototypes later he had a working design which has since won the European Design Prize, where it was praised for its 'uniqueness and functionality'. However, existing vacuum cleaner manufacturers were not as impressed. Two major manufacturers rejected the design outright. So Dyson set up his own factory which now outsells those two rivals by a margin of over two to one. The aesthetics and functionality of the design help to keep sales growing in spite of a higher retail price. He also emphasizes customer service. Dyson will pick up a broken machine from a customer's home, repair it and delivery it back within a few days. He hires mainly young graduates who have 'fresh ideas, enthusiasm and energy'. He is also committed to manufacturing, *'A lot of industrialists who I have spoken to ask us why we are in manufacturing at all. We like to know as much as we can about our product – what works, what doesn't, what can be made better or more efficiently – and the only way to do this is to make it ourselves.'*

- *What do you think makes 'good design' in markets such as the domestic appliances market?*

- *Why do you think the two major vacuum cleaner manufacturers rejected Dyson's ideas?*

- *How do you think Dyson's approaches to product design, service and manufacturing help each other?*

➔ *Look at Chapter 5 for guidance*

The production line at Dyson Appliances Ltd

training and can advise customers during the process of selling the product. Essentially the customer is buying a fairly standardized product but will be influenced by the process of the sale which can be customized in the sense that the individual customer's needs are diagnosed and, within the limits of the operation's product range, met.

The product–process matrix

Making comparisons along a spectrum which goes, for example, from shipbuilding at one extreme to electricity generation at the other, has limited value. No one grumbles that yachts are so much more expensive than electricity. The real point is that in both manufacturing and service operations, because the different process types overlap, organizations often have a choice of what type of process to employ. This choice will have consequences to the operation, especially in terms of its cost and flexibility.

The classic representation of how cost and flexibility vary with process choice comes from Professors Hayes and Wheelwright of Harvard University.[8] They represent process choices on a matrix with the volume–variety as one dimension, and what we have called process types as the other. Figure 4.10 shows their matrix adapted to fit with the terminology used here. Most operations stick to the 'natural' diagonal of the matrix, and few, if any, operations are found in the extreme corners of the matrix. However, because there is some overlap between the various process types, operations might be positioned slightly off the diagonal.

The diagonal of the matrix shown in Fig. 4.10 represents a 'natural' lowest cost position for an operation. Operations which are on the right of the 'natural' diagonal have processes which would normally be associated with lower volumes and higher

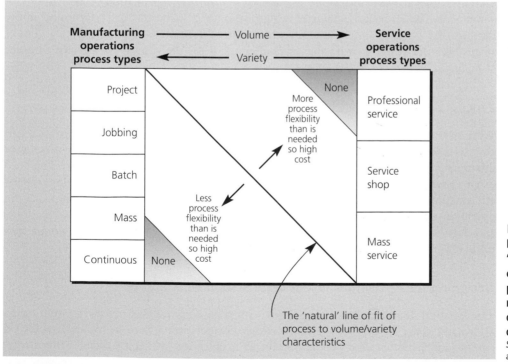

Figure 4.10 Deviating from the 'natural' diagonal on the product–process matrix has consequences for cost and flexibility
Source: Based on Hayes and Wheelwright[8]

variety. This means that their processes are likely to be more flexible than seems to be warranted by their actual volume–variety position. Put another way, they are not taking advantage of their ability to standardize their processes. Because of this, their costs are likely to be higher than they would be with a process which was closer to the diagonal. Conversely, operations who are on the left of the diagonal have adopted processes which would normally be used in a higher volume and lower variety situation. Their processes will therefore be 'over-standardized' and probably too inflexible for their volume–variety position. This lack of flexibility can also lead to high costs because the process will not be able to change from one activity to another as efficiently as a more flexible process.

DESIGN – THE STRUCTURE OF PART TWO

The various aspects of the design activity in operations management are treated in the remaining five chapters of Part Two. All these aspects are shown in Fig. 4.1 at the beginning of this chapter.

The design of products and services is a prerequisite (Chapter 5)

Notwithstanding our emphasis on the desirability of overlapping the design of products and services and the design of the processes which create them, some understanding of the product or service must be the starting point for all design considerations in operations management. This is why we begin our detailed examination of design with the *design of products and services* in Chapter 5. It will look at some of the basic design principles which we have covered in this chapter and apply them to the various stages which form the product/service design activity. These stages take the designer from the original concept for the product or service through to its final detailed specification.

Process design starts with the whole network (Chapter 6)

With an outline of what the products and services should look like, an operation can start to design the processes which will have to create them. At its most strategic level this means considering the whole network of operations which together produce and deliver products and services to the customers. From the perspective of a single operation within the network, design decisions will include how much of the network the operation wants to own (its vertical integration), where to place its sites (its location), and how large to make each site (its capacity). Chapter 6, *Design of the operations network*, covers all these design decisions.

Designing the operations layout defines its flow (Chapter 7)

The location decision is also significant within each individual site in the total operations network. At this level the decisions concerning where to locate machines, equipment, facilities, and people relative to each other, is usually termed the operation's layout. Layout decisions are particularly important because they determine the pattern of flow through the operation. Chapter 7, *Layout and flow*, deals with these decisions.

Technology plays a key role (Chapter 8)

Location of the machines and equipment within the operation will determine the pattern of its flow, but the nature of its technology will determine its capability. Although operations managers do not always need to know all the detailed science which lies behind the technologies they use, it is necessary to understand the implications of using alternative technologies. Chapter 8, *Process technology*, describes some of the more significant technologies which process materials, information and customers.

People make the processes work (Chapter 9)

Even after the products and services have been designed, the network configured, each site's layout determined and the process technology chosen, the operation cannot work until it is staffed. The people in any operation are the catalyst which makes the whole operation come alive. While the subject of this text is not human resources management as such, it is important to understand how the staff in the operation interact with its physical design. Chapter 9, *Job design and work organization*, examines how different approaches to designing people's jobs in operations influence the performance of the operation as a whole.

Peter Grant, Grant and Blunt Business Designs

Grant and Blunt is a company which specializes in the internal design of offices throughout Europe. It develops layouts which optimize the use of space, while improving communication and the productivity within the workforce.

Peter Grant has always been interested in interior design, having enjoyed helping his parents and friends choose paint colours and furniture, even when young. This interest eventually led him to take courses in art and design, and finally to set up the partnership, specializing in office space planning. The business is now located in the idyllic setting of a converted coach house in rural central England. This sleepy setting belies the high-technology business activities going on inside: computer screens and CAD workstations are the tools of this profession. Here is where the skills of aesthetic design are applied to the practical business realities of office design. Peter and his staff take the 'inputs' of customer requirements, building surveys, furniture and decoration databases, and convert them into productive, pleasant and aesthetically pleasing working environments.

'We invariably start off a project by finding out all we can about the client's activities in the office, the departments and numbers of people involved, the organization structures, and their plans for the future. From this we can plot the flow of information and paperwork, so that the most sensible layouts can be determined from the outset, and this process also gives us the chance to get to know some of the key people and to get a feel for the culture of the organization, which can have a big influence on all aspects of the design.

'The first actual design stage is the sketching of "bubble plans" on the floor diagrams of the building. We work with the clients to get a basic idea of the layout of each department, with circles (or bubbles) indicating clusters of people, and showing numbers of employees and the lines of communication between them. We also have to consider how the office space might operate in the future, and because of the increasing likelihood of changes in organization and activity, most clients now choose not to have any cellular (fixed wall) offices for individual employees. Total privacy, when needed, is often only available by using interview rooms. Larger multi-purpose rooms can also be adapted for use as boardrooms one day, and for training lecture theatres the next. Space is expensive, and companies need to get maximum value for their investment, but not all employees like having to share workspace. Some employees may claim that it would affect their work, or simply complain that they have always had their own office. All these problems are delicate, and time-consuming, but must be resolved during this consulting process.

'Once we have produced a fairly detailed plan that has met the client's needs, we can start on the interior design work, concentrating on making the office a pleasant working environment. We usually present our ideas as a range of preliminary sketches, from which the client selects the styles of office they wish us to develop further. This choice is then transferred to the CAD system, where we work on the details. All the furniture designs are provided by the manufacturers as CAD images, so we can easily select what we want, and apply it to our layouts. We can present the final design as a coloured 3D view, so the client has a clear idea of what the final design will look like.

'This is very satisfying and challenging work. We have to be able to understand a company's operations, organization and culture, and then apply our skills and knowledge to create a practical and beautiful working environment. The design process is very iterative; at every stage we must continually involve the customer and make modifications as new information and opinions emerge. I think that it is our relentless attention to detail and careful analysis of clients' needs which have made us so successful.' ■

SUMMARY ANSWERS TO KEY QUESTIONS

What is design in operations management?

■ Design is the activity which shapes the physical form and purpose of both products and services and the processes which produce them. It is an activity which starts with a concept and ends in the translation of that concept into a specification of something which can be created.

■ The overall purpose of the design activity is to meet the needs of customers, whether through the design of the products or services themselves, or through the design of the processes which will produce them.

What objectives should the design activity have?

■ The design activity can be viewed as a transformation process in the same way as any other operation. It therefore can be judged in terms of its quality, speed, dependability, flexibility, and cost.

■ These objectives are more likely to be satisfied if the complementary activities of product or service design and process design are co-ordinated in some way.

■ The design activity must also take account of environmental issues. These include examination of the source and suitability of materials, the sources and quantities of energy consumed, the amount and type of waste material, the life of the product itself, and the end-of-life state of the product.

How can design decisions be made?

■ Design is a multi-stage process which moves from concept through to detailed specification.

■ At each stage it is important to understand the design options and evaluate these in terms of their feasibility, acceptability and vulnerability.

■ As the design activity progresses through its stages, uncertainty regarding the finished design is reduced. This makes it increasingly difficult to change previous decisions.

How does the design activity differ in different types of operation?

■ The key characteristics of an operation which determine the nature of its design activity are the volume and variety of its output.

■ An operation's position on the volume–variety continuum influences many aspects of its design activity, including the emphasis which is placed on either product/service design or process design, the location policy it chooses, the standardization of its products and services, its choice of process technology, the nature of its layout and flow, and the staff skills it requires.

What are 'process types'?

■ Process types are general approaches to managing the transformation process and depend on the volume and variety of an operation's output.

■ In manufacturing, these process types are (in order of increasing volume and decreasing variety) project, jobbing, batch, mass, and continuous processes.

■ In service operations, although there is less consensus on the terminology, the terms often used (again in order of increasing volume and decreasing variety) are professional services, service shops, and mass services.

LHI GmbH

LHI (Lausitz-Hölitz Ing) GmbH is a firm of consulting engineers, based in Germany with offices in the United States and Singapore. It specializes in the design of chemical process plants. Although a relatively small company, it has already established itself as an innovator in the process design field. The company was particularly excited by a new design technique recently developed by one of its young engineers. She claimed that by using this new technique, significant construction cost savings could be achieved on almost any type of plant. The technique had been reviewed by the company's senior engineers and seemed to be theoretically sound, but, as yet, no actual plant had been designed using the technique, and no experimental pilot rig had been constructed for verification tests.

While the senior engineers were deciding whether to sanction the expense of a pilot rig to test the new technique, the company won an order to design a chemical plant in China. Immediately, two design teams started to produce preliminary designs, one using conventional design techniques and the other using the new technique. These designs became known as Design 1 and Design 2, respectively. At the same time, cost estimates were collected to establish the total cost of setting up an experimental pilot rig to test some of the assumptions involved in the new design, Design 2, before final plans would have to be submitted. In fact, the Design 2 team produced two designs – one using the new technique, and one which was a modification of the new design, which could be used if the design did not prove successful.

When all this information had been brought together, the senior engineers were presented with the following financial summary:

Cost of pilot rig test	=	DM800 000
Design 1 (conventional design) Profit to the company	=	DM2 000 000
Design 2 (experimental design) Profit to the company if the design is successful	=	DM4 000 000
Profit to the company if modification is necessary	=	DM500 000

Both designs were relatively straightforward to build, although Design 2 would involve more of the company's engineers to be allocated to the project during its construction. This might limit the company's ability to take on any other major projects. The performance of the plant, whether constructed to Design 1 or Design 2, would almost certainly be identical, but Design 2, if successful, would be finished in about 80 per cent of the time which would be necessary to construct the conventional plant built to Design 1. This could give the company a considerable advantage in winning further orders. However, if the Design 2 was attempted, but needed subsequent modification, the company's reputation might suffer, temporarily.

The senior engineers then discussed the chances of the designs being successful. They were agreed that Design 1, using tried and tested conventional theories, was sure to be successful. They were less sure, however, of the experimental design. The theory looked good, but it hadn't been tried before, so without further information they assessed the chances of the design being successful at around 60 per cent.

Discussion then turned to considering the advisability of building a pilot rig to test the new design. They had built similar rigs before, and knew that they were extremely reliable in indicating whether a design was feasible or not. If they decided to build the test rig, they would still have plenty of time to decide between Design 1 and Design 2. ■

Questions

1 What specific criteria do you think the company should use to evaluate the two designs? (Use the general headings of feasibility, acceptability and vulnerability.)

2 Within the limits of the information you have available, draw up a table of the relative merits of the two designs.

3 Where do you think the company would be positioned on the volume–variety continuum, and what does that indicate about the nature of all aspects of design (not just product design) in the company?

DISCUSSION QUESTIONS

1 Explain how the good design of the products or services and processes of the following operations can support the five performance objectives:
- a washing-machine manufacturer
- a computer-software house specializing in accountancy packages
- a rock concert.

2 Why do you think product design and process design have been separate activities in many manufacturing organizations? Explain why this is changing.

3 Describe the activity of designing a new product or service of your choice in terms of the transformed and transforming resources, the activity and the outputs.

4 Discuss with someone who is involved in designing new products or services the problems involved.

5 The university catering manager is contemplating – adding a take-away burger bar to the portfolio of outlets. Explain how the idea can be assessed.

6 Explain how the 'idea' of design might apply to the design of a 'home-banking' service.

7 Explain the importance of the volume–variety dimension as a way of understanding operations and their approach to design.

8 Describe how the five performance objectives vary between:
- a burger bar and a high-class restaurant
- a high-volume car producer and a classic car restorer
- a corner grocery store and a supermarket.

9 What do you think would be the key design issues to be faced when setting up a hairdressing salon?

10 Explain the relationship between variety and volume and describe why you are unlikely to find many high volume–high variety and low volume–low variety operations.

NOTES ON CHAPTER

1 Sir Monty Finneston (1987) Address to the Department of Education and Science Conference, Loughborough University, UK, quoted *in* Norman, E., Riley J., Urry, S. and Whitacker, M. (1990) *Advanced Design and Technology*, Longman.
2 Source: *The Times,* 16 July 1993.
3 Sources: Wheatley, M. (1993/94) 'Boeing, Boeing', *Business Life,* Dec/Jan.
4 Cooke, S. and Slack, N. (1991) *Making Management Decisions* (2nd edn), Prentice Hall.
5 Most textbooks on financial analysis will describe the return on investment (ROI) criterion. For example, *see* Cooke, S. and Slack, N., *op. cit.*
6 Horkeby, I. (1993) 'Environmentally Compatible Product and Process Development', *NAE Workshop on Corporate Environmental Stewardship*, 10–13 Aug, Woods Hole, Massachusetts, USA.
7 Fitzgerald, L., Johnston, R., Brignall, S., Silvestro, R. and Voss, C. (1991) *Performance Measurement in Service Industries*, CIMA.
8 Hayes, R.H. and Wheelwright, S.C. (1984) *Restoring our Competitive Edge*, John Wiley.

SELECTED FURTHER READINGS

Abernathy, W.J. (1976) 'Production Process Structure and Technological Change', *Design Sciences*, Vol 7, No 4.

Barker, T.B. (1994) *Quality by Experimental Design*, Marcel Dekker, New York.

Baxter, M. (1995) *Product Design*, Chapman and Hall.

Chaharbaghi, K. (1990) 'Using Simulation to Solve Design and Operational Problems', *International Journal of Operations and Production Management*, Vol 10, No 9.

Cooke, S. and Slack, N. (1991) *Making Management Decisions* (2nd edn), Prentice Hall.

Cross, N. (1984) *Developments in Design Methodology*, John Wiley.

Cross, N. (1989) *Engineering Design Methods*, John Wiley.

de Bono, E. (1970) *Lateral Thinking – A Textbook of Creativity*, Ward Lock Educational.

Fox, J. (1993) *Quality Through Design: The Key to Successful Product Delivery*, McGraw-Hill.

Lorenz, C. (1990) *The Design Dimension*, Blackwell.

Love, D. and Barton, J. (1996) 'Evaluation of Design Decisions Through CIM and Simulation', *Integration Manufacturing Systems*, Vol 7, No 4.

Ramaswamy, R. (1996) *Design and Management of Service Processes*, Addison-Wesley Longman.

Shostack, G.L. (1982) 'How to Design a Service', *European Journal of Marketing*, Vol 16, No 1.

Sparke, P. (1986) *An Introduction to Design and Culture in the Twentieth Century*, Allen and Unwin.

Walker, D. and Cross, N. (1983) *An Introduction to Design*, Open University Press.

Walsh, V., Roy, R., Bruce, M. and Potter, S. (1992) *Winning By Design, Technology, Product Design and International Competitiveness*, Blackwell.

Webb, A. (1994) *Managing Innovative Projects*, Chapman and Hall.

THE DESIGN OF PRODUCTS AND SERVICES

INTRODUCTION

Products and services are usually the first thing which customers see of a company, so it is important that they are designed to meet their needs and expectations. Customers might also expect that designs are updated at frequent intervals to reflect fashion, technological advances or their changing needs. So, in addition to the intrinsic merit of its product and service designs, it is also the continual development of designs and the creation of totally new designs which help to shape an organization's competitive position. Operations managers do not always have the direct responsibility for product and service design, but they always have an indirect responsibility to provide the information and advice upon which successful product or service development depends.

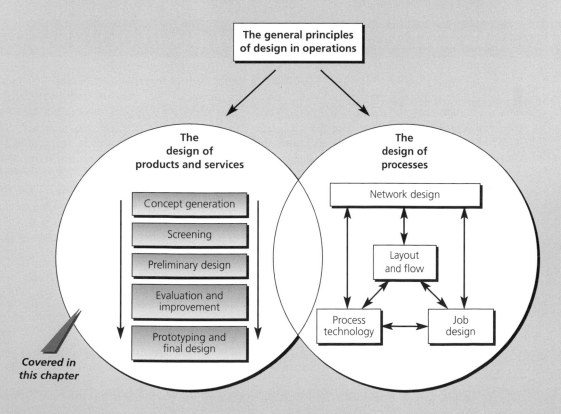

Figure 5.1 The design activities in operations management covered in this chapter

Figure 5.1 shows where this chapter fits into the overall operations design model. Remember though that there is an overlap between product/service design and process design, especially in the design of services. For this reason it is important to include consideration of the process which makes and delivers products and (especially) services.

CHAPTER 5: KEY QUESTIONS

- *Why is good product and service design important?*

- *What are the stages in product and service design?*

- *Why should product and service design and process design be considered interactively?*

- *How should interactive design be managed?*

THE COMPETITIVE ADVANTAGE OF GOOD DESIGN

The objective of designing products and services is to satisfy customers by meeting their actual or anticipated needs and expectations. This, in turn, enhances the competitiveness of the organization. Product and service design, therefore, can be seen as starting and ending with the customer. First, the task of marketing is to gather information from customers (and sometimes non-customers) in order to understand and identify their needs and expectations, and also to look for possible market opportunities. Following this, the task of the product and service designers is to take those needs and expectations, as interpreted by marketing, and create a specification for the product or service. This is a complex task which involves bringing together many different aspects of a company's objectives (*see* box on Braun). The specification is then used as the input to the operation itself which creates and delivers the product or service to its customers (*see* Fig. 5.2).

What is designed in a product or service?

All products and services can be considered as having three aspects:

- *a concept*, which is the set of expected benefits that the customer is buying;
- *a package* of 'component' products and services that provide those benefits defined in the concept;
- *the process* by which the operation produces the package of 'component' products and services.

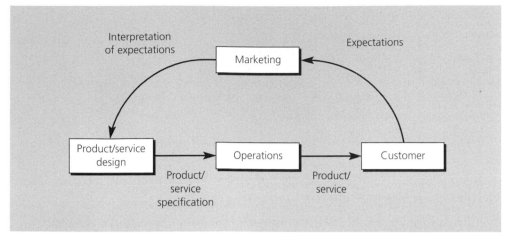

Figure 5.2
The customer–marketing–design feedback loop

DESIGN PRINCIPLES AT BRAUN AG AND THE NEW BRAUN MULTIMIX[1]

Braun, the leading European manufacturer of small appliances, is renowned for the innovative and functional designs of its products (over 60 per cent of the company's sales are of products which were launched within the last five years). The company has 150 of its products in the permanent collection of the Centre Pompidou in Paris and has 40 products on exhibition at the New York Museum of Modern Art. But Braun's design principles go beyond the aesthetic. Its designers follow their 'Ten principles of good design'. We will describe the design of the Braun Multimix, the design brief of which was 'to combine three specialist kitchen appliances (blender, food processor, kitchen machine) in such a way that the new single product performs at least as well in each of the applications as the best equivalent specialized product'.

Braun's ten industrial design principles applied to the Multimix

1 *Usefulness.* The functionality of a product is the central reason for its existence. It was decided to align the motor, gearing and attachments in a single vertical direction (competitive products have horizontal motor and vertical attachments, requiring a complex gearbox). The 'form' of the product then follows its 'function'.

2 *Quality.* Braun designers emphasize four aspects of quality. First, its *versatility* provides a full range of tasks required in cooking: mixing, blending, kneading and chopping. Second, the high mechanical efficiency of the appliance and the seven speed settings provide *high performance* across the range of tasks. Third, many unique *safety features* have been included to prevent contact with moving parts and to prevent accidents. Fourth, the application of *advanced process technology* has enabled many integrated elements to be incorporated in a single moulding. A complex production moulding tool was developed to produce two housings in one injection moulding step.

3 *Ease of use.* Great emphasis was placed on 'human engineering' to ensure that the Multimix is convenient, comfortable to use and easy to clean.

▶

137

4 *Simplicity.* Braun engineers believe in achieving maximum results with minimum means: what is relevant is stressed, what is superfluous is omitted.

5 *Clarity.* Particular emphasis is placed on eliminating the need for complex instructions: the Multimix controls 'speak for themselves'. For example, insertion of the attachments automatically sets the appropriate speed range of the drive.

6 *Order.* All details of a product should have a logical, meaningful place with nothing arbitrary or coincidental.

7 *Naturalness.* Braun designers strive to avoid any forced, contrived, or artificial decorative elements. Braun refers to a principle of 'understatement and modesty'.

8 *Aesthetics.* Although aesthetic quality is not a primary objective of the Braun designers during the development process, it is achieved through attention to detail and the quest for order and naturalness.

9 *Innovation.* Braun is committed to achieving long-lasting appeal in its designs, so innovations are carefully developed and brought together for new appliances such as the Multimix.

10 *Truthfulness.* A principle followed by Braun is that 'only honest design can be good design', so any attempt to play on people's emotions and weaknesses is avoided. ■

Questions

1 Braun is proud of its success in aesthetic design. What benefit do you think this gives the company with the domestic appliance buying public?

2 Braun's ten industrial design principles are applied above to a domestic appliance. How do you think they might change if they were applied to an industrial product such as a machine tool?

3 Pick a service with which you are familiar in an educational operation (such as your university, school or college) and evaluate it against Braun's ten principles. Which of these ten principles do you think were the most useful in making your evaluation?

Customers buy 'concepts'

When customers make a purchase, they are not simply buying a product or service. They are buying a set of expected benefits to meet their needs and expectations. This is known as the concept of the product or service. For example, when customers buy a washing machine, they are purchasing a set of expected benefits which might include:

- an attractive metal box,
- that will fit in a conventional kitchen space,
- and will provide the means of cleaning clothes,
- over a long period of time,
- in the comfort of the customer's own home.

Similarly, a restaurant meal is purchased to provide us with more than the satisfaction of filling our stomachs. The expected benefits of the purchase include:

- an attractive environment,
- in which to consume a well cooked and presented meal,
- in a relaxing atmosphere.

In both cases the set of expected benefits is referred to as the *product* or *service concept* – that is, the overall intention of the product or service as seen from the customer's perspective. The concept is not a statement of the physical bits and pieces that we buy – the box, pumps and drum of the washing machine or the meat and vegetables of the meal – rather it is the way that the customers, and hopefully also the organization, its staff and shareholders, perceive the benefits of the product or service. It follows that, in order to design products or services, operations managers must understand exactly what it is that the customers are buying from them. That is, they must thoroughly understand the concept.

Concepts comprise a package of products and services

Normally the word product implies a tangible physical object, such as a washing machine or a watch, and a service implies a more intangible experience, such as an evening at a restaurant or a night club. In fact, as we discussed in Chapter 1, most, if

IT SEEMED A GOOD IDEA AT THE TIME[2]

Not all concepts, no matter how ingenious, prove successful in the market place. What may seem to be an innovative sure-fire hit on paper can, with hindsight, fail to take account of customers' real needs. Take, for example, the Lawn Ranger, a robotic grass-mowing machine devised by an American company. The product concept was an automatic grass-cutting machine which would need only to be shown the perimeter of an area to be cut and then could be left to complete the task while its owner relaxed. All it needed was an initial 'human-guided' trip around the outside of the lawn. It would then continue to cut round, working its way inwards until it finished the task. The basic technology was indeed ingenious. It included a sensor which could detect the difference between cut and the longer uncut grass as well as sensing potential obstacles in its path. This intriguing concept failed to take account of one important factor, however. People apparently *like* mowing their grass. It would appear that many people who would have been potential customers for this product prefer to cut the grass themselves because they find it therapeutic. ■

Questions

1 How might the concept for the product described above be modified in order to make it more commercially successful?

2 If the cost of including this technology in grass-cutting machines were reduced to a small proportion of the total product cost, how do you think it would affect the product's concept and its commercial success?

not all, operations produce a combination of products *and* services. The restaurant meal includes:

- products such as 'food' and 'drink';
- services such as 'the delivery of the food to the table' and 'the attentions of the waiter or waitress'.

Similarly, the purchase of the washing machine includes:

- the product, that is 'the washing machine itself';
- services such as 'warranties', 'after-sales services' and 'the services of the person selling the machine'.

This means that whatever is being designed, whether it is nominally a 'product' or a 'service', it will usually involve designing a collection of component products and services. This collection of products and services is usually referred to as the *package* that customers buy. Some of the products or services in the package are *core*, that is they are fundamental to the purchase and could not be removed without destroying the nature of the package. Other parts will serve to enhance the core. These are *supporting* goods and services. In the case of the washing machine, the attractive box and guarantees are supporting goods and services. The core good is the machine itself. At the restaurant, the meal itself is the core. Its provision and preparation are important but not absolutely necessary (in some restaurants you might serve and even cook the meal yourself).

By changing the core, or adding or subtracting supporting goods and services, organizations can provide different packages, and in so doing design quite different product or service concepts. For instance, a washing machine could be built to a smaller size, supporting a concept of a machine for the 'smaller kitchen'. Alternatively, it could be provided without after-sales support and guarantees as an 'economical purchase'. The restaurant may just provide you with the food but you may have to collect it yourself – the 'self-service' concept. Alternatively, you may even have to select the raw food yourself and cook it on burners at your own table. It is defining the package of goods and services which starts the design activity of translating the concept into reality.

Products and services have to be created – the process

As explained in Chapter 4, it is quite possible, particularly in the case of manufactured products, to design the product and the process independently of each other. It is possible (although certainly not advised) that 'product engineers' could design the components of a washing machine and then 'process engineers' could decide the best way to fit them all together. This is more difficult in services where the process by which the service is delivered is an integral part of the service itself. For example, it is difficult to distinguish between a service that includes food served at the table and the process of bringing the food to the table. The 'process' is the part of the operation that creates the goods and services, puts them together into the package and delivers them to the customer to fulfil the concept.

The provision of most goods and services requires many different types of processes. For example, the washing machine includes three main types of processes:

- the manufacture and assembly of components;
- the retailing of the machine;
- after-sales support and servicing.

Each process can be broken down further into many sub-processes. The manufacture and assembly of components, for example, will include such sub-processes as body pressing, wiring and stock control.

The restaurant too will have several processes:

- food production;
- beverage dispensing and control;
- front-of-house activities.

Again, each of these may be split into many sub-processes. The front-of-house activities, for example, will include 'meeting', 'seating', 'serving' and 'billing' the customer.

THE STAGES OF DESIGN – FROM CONCEPT TO SPECIFICATION

The outcome of the activity of design is a fully detailed specification of the product or service. The specification will require the collection of information which fully defines the product or service, namely:

- its overall concept (specifying the form, function and overall purpose of the design and the benefits it will provide);
- its package (specifying all the collection of individual products and services which are required to provide and support the concept);
- the process by which the package will be created (specifying how the various individual products and services in the package are to be produced).

To get to this point the design activity must pass through several stages. These form an approximate sequence, although in practice designers will occasionally recycle or backtrack through the stages. We will describe them in the order in which they usually occur, as shown in Fig. 5.3.

The *concept generation* stage starts with an idea for a product or service. These ideas need to be formalized by translating them into a product or service concept. The concepts are then *screened* by different parts of the organization to try to ensure that, in broad terms, they will be a sensible addition to its product/service portfolio. The outcome of these first two stages is an agreed and acceptable product/service concept. The agreed concept has then to be turned into a *preliminary design* of the package and the process. This preliminary design then goes through a stage of *evaluation and improvement* to see if the concept can be served better, more cheaply or more easily. An agreed design can then be subjected to *prototyping and final design*. The outcome of this stage is a fully developed specification of the product or service.

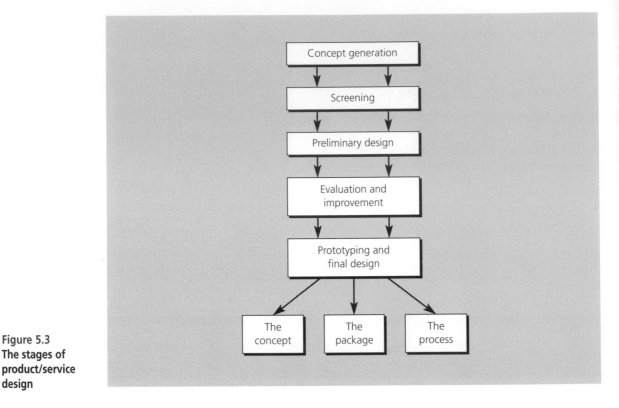

Figure 5.3
The stages of
product/service
design

CONCEPT GENERATION

The ideas for new product or service concepts can come from sources outside the organization, such as customers or competitors, and from sources within the organization, such as staff (for example, from sales staff and front-of-house staff) or from the R&D department (*see* Fig. 5.4).

Ideas from customers

Marketing is responsible for keeping an eye and ear on the market place in order to identify new opportunities and possible products or services that might be appropriate. There are many market research tools for gathering data from customers in a formal and structured way, including questionnaires and interviews. These techniques, however, usually tend to be structured in such a way as only to test out ideas or check products or services against predetermined criteria. Listening to the customer, in a less-structured way, is sometimes seen as a better means of generating new ideas.[3]

Focus groups

One formal but unstructured way of collecting ideas and suggestions from customers is through focus group discussions. A focus group typically comprises seven to ten participants who are unfamiliar with each other but who have been selected because

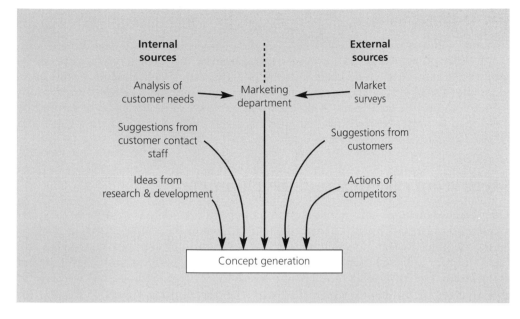

Figure 5.4
Ideas can originate from both inside and outside the organization

they have certain characteristics in common that relate to the particular topic of the focus group.[4] Participants in focus groups are invited to 'discuss' or 'share ideas with others'. The concept researcher tries to create a permissive environment in the focus group that nurtures different perceptions and points of view, without pressurizing participants to vote, plan or reach a consensus. The group discussion is conducted several times with similar types of participants in order to identify trends and patterns in perceptions. Careful and systematic analysis of the discussions provides clues and insights into product or service opportunities.

Listening to customers

Many suggestions and ideas may come from customers on a day-to-day basis. Customers may write to complain about a particular product or service, or make suggestions for its improvement or replacement. Ideas may also come in the form of suggestions to staff during the purchase of the product or delivery of the service. Unfortunately, some staff may not see the passing on of this information as an important role; there may not even be the mechanisms in place to facilitate it. Although some organizations do have implicit mechanisms to capture ideas in a structured and formal way, few have internal mechanisms for passing on good ideas or snippets from customers.

Ideas from competitor activity

Many organizations keep a sharp eye on the activities of their competitors. A new idea translated into a saleable concept, package and process may give a competitor an edge in the market place, even if it is only a temporary one. Competing organizations will then have to decide to follow the actions of the competitor with a similar product or service, or alternatively to come up with a somewhat different idea that may minimize or even reverse the competitor's lead.

Ideas from staff

Just one step away from the customers are the people who have to deal directly with them. The contact worker in a service organization or the sales person in a product-oriented organization could meet customers every day. These staff may have good ideas about what customers like and do not like. They may have gathered suggestions from customers or have ideas of their own as to how products or services could be developed to meet the needs of their customers more effectively, or how a gap could be filled in the product or service range.

Ideas from research and development

One formal function found in many product-based organizations (but as yet few service-based organizations) is Research & Development (R&D). As its name implies, its role is twofold. Research usually means attempting to develop new knowledge and ideas in order to solve a particular problem or to grasp an opportunity. Development is the attempt to try to utilize and operationalize the ideas that come from research. In this chapter we are mainly concerned with the 'development' part of R&D – for example, exploiting new ideas that might be afforded by new materials such as thermoplastics or new technologies such as satellite communications. Different industries rely on R&D for their new product or service ideas to different extents.

Reverse engineering

'Reverse engineering' is taking apart a product to understand how a competing organization has made it. Closely analysing exactly what constitutes a competitor's design and how the product has been produced can help to isolate the key features of the design which are worth emulating. As a result, a company may amend and incorporate the key features in some way. Alternatively, it might apply to use, under licence, the part of the product that seems to be providing the difference. One example is the so-called 'widget' which is incorporated into the bottom of some canned beers. This device releases gas on opening to create a creamy head on the beer, thus giving the texture and appearance of draught beer. It is a design idea which was soon incorporated into many canned beers after its initial introduction.

Some aspects of services may be more difficult to reverse engineer (especially back-office services) as they are less transparent to competitors. However, by consumer testing a service, it may be possible to make educated guesses about how it has been created. Many service organizations employ 'testers' to check out the services provided by competitors. Just as supermarkets regularly check the prices displayed by rival supermarkets, so too do they investigate new services, such as delivery services, cashback options, telephone ordering and packing services to see if they might be suitable for development or reproduction. Even if particular aspects of a competitor's product or service are not reproducible, they can still provide the stimulus for creativity.

From idea to concept

Ideas are not the same as concepts. In fact ideas need to be transformed into concepts so that they can be evaluated and then 'operationalized' by the organization. Concepts

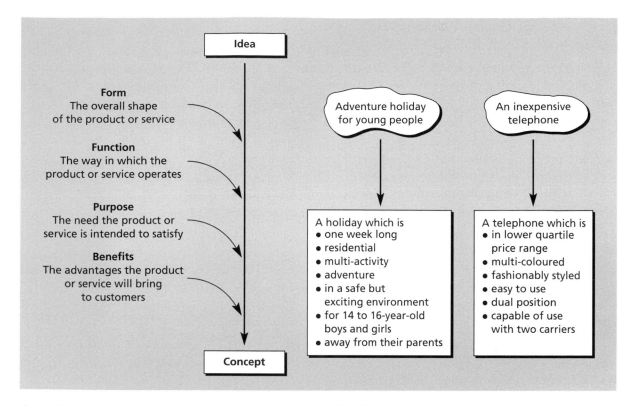

Figure 5.5 Transforming an idea into a concept may involve including details of the form, function, purpose and benefits of the product or service; for example, here for an adventure holiday and a telephone

are different to ideas in that they are clear statements that both encapsulate the idea and also indicate the overall form, function, purpose and benefits of the idea. The concept should be simple to communicate so that everyone in the organization can understand it, make it, and sell it. Figure 5.5 illustrates two examples of how ideas have been enriched to become concepts. The broad idea of an adventure holiday is further defined to include its duration, purpose, residential nature and target market. The inexpensive telephone idea is defined in terms of its price, functionality, and physical appearance.

CONCEPT SCREENING

Not all concepts which are generated will necessarily be capable of further development into products and services. Designers need to be selective as to which concepts they progress to the point of designing the preliminary aspects of their package and processes. The purpose of the concept-screening stage is to take the flow of concepts emerging from the organization and evaluate them for their feasibility, acceptability and 'vulnerability' or risk (*see* Chapter 4). Concepts may have to pass through many different screens, and several functions might be involved (for example, marketing, operations and finance), though they may each use different criteria to screen the proposals (*see* Fig. 5.6).

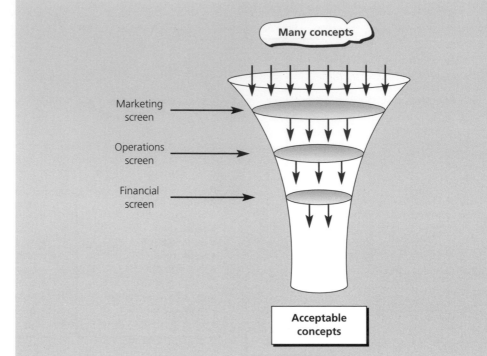

**Figure 5.6
Concept screening
involves
progressively
filtering concepts**

The marketing screen

From its close relationship with customers and knowledge of the marketplace, marketing may be concerned to screen out concepts that it feels:

- will not work in the markets;
- are too similar to, or even too different from, competing products or services;
- would not be able to generate sufficient demand to make it worthwhile;
- will not fit with existing marketing policy.

The operations screen

At this stage the operations function is primarily concerned with the feasibility of the new product/service concepts. It needs to judge whether it can produce the product or provide the service. In particular, it needs to decide whether it has available, or could make available, the following resources:

- the capacity within the operation;
- the skills in its human resources;
- the technology which would be necessary.

In addition, the operations function will need to provide the information which can be used to estimate the likely cost of creating the product or service.

Finance screen

While marketing might be able to provide indications of potential volumes and revenues, and operations provide estimations of the cost of materials, people and technology to make the product or create the service, the finance department will need to put these together to calculate the financial implications of any new product or service, such as:

- capital and investment requirements;
- operating costs;
- profit margins;
- likely pay-back rate.

Example

Figure 5.7, shown overleaf, illustrates how screening might be applied for the telephone example described previously.

Competitor analysis

Products are selected which already occupy roughly the same target market as the proposed new telephone. In this case, five competitor products have been chosen and evaluated against a number of criteria (their handling characteristics, their aesthetic styling, their robustness of construction, and the ease with which they can be fixed in different positions). However, each of these criteria is not of equal importance. In this case, styling is given a weight of four times, and handling two times that of robustness and fixing. Each of the competitor products is evaluated by giving it a score out of ten (where one indicates poor performance and ten indicates exceptionally good performance). An indication of overall product performance can then be obtained by calculating the weighted total for each product (i.e. the score for each criterion multiplied by the weight and then summed across the row). In addition to product performance, the price of each competitor product is also obtained.

Price-performance targeting

The information from the competitor analysis now allows each competitor product to be evaluated on a price–performance graph as illustrated. This not only allows for comparison between competitor products, but more importantly it allows the product designers to identify the target area for the new telephone. In Fig. 5.7 it has been decided to design a product for a £30 'price point' but having performance characteristics superior to anything in the close price range.

Financial analysis

The company is now in a position to check the financial feasibility of the proposed new product. This is done in two ways: first, a 'top-down' or *price minus* approach is used to work backwards from the selling price. Typically, the retailer's margin and distribution margin are taken off the selling price in order to determine the price at which the telephone manufacturer must be able to sell the product, in order to meet

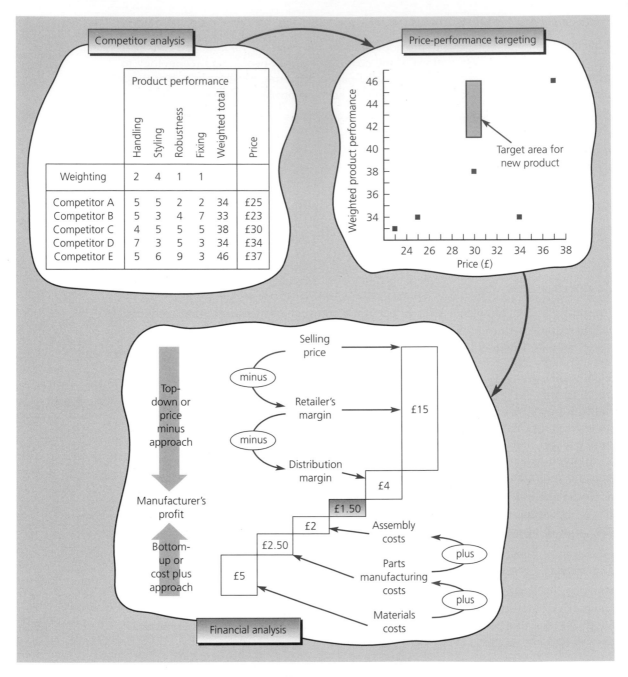

Figure 5.7 Analysis of competitor products or services allows the desired price–performance area to be targeted which, in turn, enables initial financial analysis

the proposed selling price. Subtracting the retailer's margin and the distribution margin from the final selling price indicates that the telephone manufacturing company must be able to sell the product for £30 – £15 – £4 = £11, if the product is to be sold at its price point.

The other approach to costing can then be used by using the 'bottom-up' or *cost plus* approach. This involves starting from zero and adding the manufacturing costs: in this case, materials costs plus parts manufacturing costs plus assembly costs. This indicates that the cost of producing the telephone will be £5 + £2.50 + £2 = £9.50. This leaves a manufacturer's profit of £1.50. The issue for the company then is whether this profit is sufficient to give it a return on its investment in such things as design costs, extra manufacturing equipment and market launch costs. If not, then it must either reconsider its target area on the price–performance graph and/or revisit its assumptions of how it is going to make the product. This may mean changing the design in order to reduce material costs or parts manufacturing costs or assembly costs.

PRELIMINARY DESIGN

Having generated a product or service concept that is acceptable to the various parts of an organization, an organization tackles the next stage which is to create a preliminary design. The objective of this stage is to have a first attempt at:

● specifying the component products and services in the *package*;
● defining the *processes* to create the package.

Specify the components of the package

The first task in this stage of design is to define exactly what will go into the product or service: that is, specifying the components of the package. This will require the collection of information about such things as the *constituent component parts* which make up the product or service package, *the product/service structure*, that is the order in which the component parts of the package have to be put together, and the *bill of materials* (BOM), that is the quantities of each component part required to make up the total package. The BOM, in particular, is a method of defining products or services which is used widely in other areas of operations management's activity (*see*, for example, Chapter 14).

Example 1: Adventure holiday

Each activity on the adventure holiday can be broken down in this way. For example, the materials and equipment needed for each child to undertake the rifle-shooting activity might include:

● a .22 air rifle
● some shot
● a backboard
● a target holder
● some card targets
● some model targets.

The product/service structure is shown in Fig. 5.8. The bill of materials, which incorporates the product/service structure and also includes the quantities which will be required, is shown in Table 5.1.

**Figure 5.8
The product/
activity structure
for rifle shooting**

Table 5.1 Bill of materials for the rifle-shooting activity

Level 0	Level 1	Level 2	Level 3	Quantity
Rifle-shooting activity				
	Rifle			1
	Shot			50
	Target			
		Backboard		1
		Holder		1
		Targets		
			Cards	10
			Models	5

Example 2: Telephone

The components for the telephone may include:

- a handset casing
- a base casing
- an earpiece
- a mouthpiece
- a cord
- an input lead
- electronic circuitry
- a plug.

The product structure shows how these components fit together to make the telephone (*see* Fig. 5.9). The bill of materials, which incorporates the product/service structure and also includes the quantities which will be required, is shown in Table 5.2.

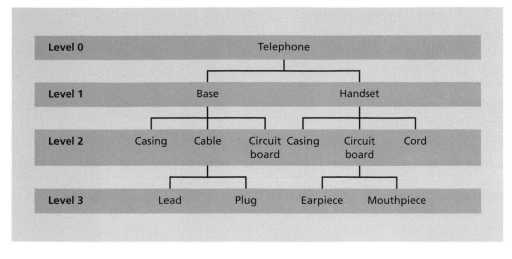

**Figure 5.9
The product
structure of the
telephone**

Table 5.2 Bill of materials for the telephone

Level 0	Level 1	Level 2	Level 3	Quantity
Telephone				
	Base			1
		Casing		1
		Cable		1
			Lead	1
			Plug	1
		Circuit board		1
	Handset			1
		Casing		1
		Circuit board		1
			Earpiece	1
			Mouthpiece	1
		Cord		1

Define the processes to create the package

The product/service structure and bill of materials specify *what* has to be put together; the next stage is to specify *how* the processes will put together the various components to create the final product or service. There are many techniques which can be used for documenting processes (or *blueprinting,* as it is sometimes called). However, all the techniques have two main features:[5]

- they show the *flow* of materials or people or information through the operation;
- they identify the different *activities* that take place during the process.

We shall examine four common types of blueprinting techniques here. These are:

- simple flow charts
- routing sheets
- flow process charts
- the customer-processing framework.

Simple flow charts

Simple flow charts are used to identify the main elements of a process.

They frequently include symbols which originated in computer flow charting and which identify the key decisions in the process and the implications of each decision. Figure 5.10 shows a flow chart which indicates the flow of information in the customer enquiries bureau of an electricity utility company.

Routing sheets

Routing sheets (also known as operations process charts) provide more information about the activities involved in the process, including a description of the activity and the tools or equipment needed. Part of a route sheet for the assembly of the telephone is shown in Fig. 5.11.

Flow process chart

The most commonly used chart for documenting processes in operations management is the flow process chart. This type of chart, as well as documenting the flow and the various activities, uses a number of different symbols to identify the different types of activities (*see* Fig. 5.12).

Flow process charts permit a more detailed design and evaluation of a design. Figure 5.13 shows a flow process chart for one day on an adventure holiday. This charting method is covered in greater detail in Appendix 3 at the end of this book.

Customer-processing framework

The customer-processing framework[6] is a charting method devised specifically for customer flows. It identifies some of the key activities that may occur in 'processing' customers through an operation, including:

- the *selection* – the decision by the customer to choose one of several possible service operations;
- the *point of entry* – the point at which the customer first makes contact with the chosen operation, either physically by entering the system, or remotely by telephone, for example;
- the *response time* – the time a customer has to wait for the system to respond;
- the *point of impact* – the moment at which the service worker starts to deal with the customer;
- the *delivery* – the part of the process which delivers the core service to the customer;
- the *point of departure* – the point at which the customer leaves the service process;
- the *follow up* – the activities of the service staff to check on the customer after the completion of the service.

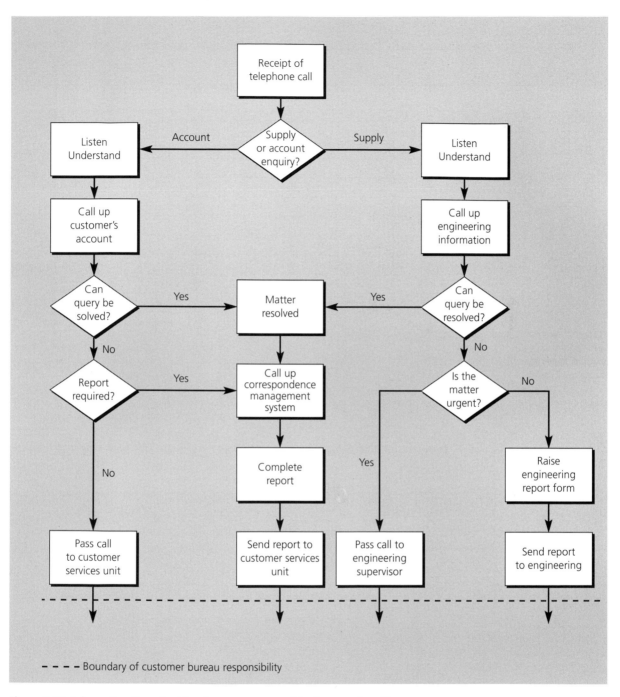

Figure 5.10 Information flow chart for the customer enquiries bureau of a utility company

Figure 5.14 illustrates these key stages in the design of a hospital's Accident and Emergency department. When examined in more detail most service operations comprise several customer-processing sequences which may be in series and/or in parallel with each other. The number of processes and the interrelationships between them are indications of the scale and complexity of the operations task.

Route sheet

Item .... Telephone h1209 .... **Date** .... 1 / 5 / 97 ....

Item No. .... # 1209 (h) .... **Issued by** ....

Operation number	Operation description	Equipment
1	Assemble earpiece and mouthpiece	Jig #24/35A
2	Fix to lower casing	Jig #24/122
3	Insert and fix cord	Wire stripper (type #22)
		and screwholder/driver
4	Assemble upper casing	- -
5	Align and seal	Jig #24/490 and polysege
6	Light and vibration test	Qualitest 12 (main #488)
		and vibration board

**Figure 5.11
Routing sheet for
the telephone**

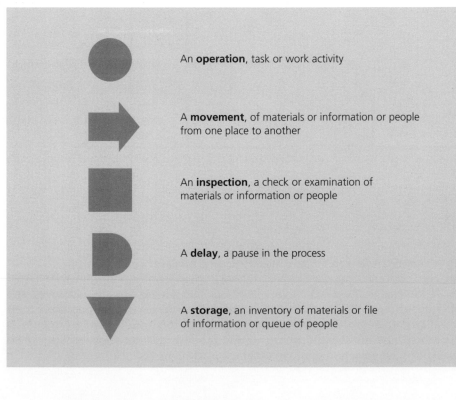

An **operation**, task or work activity

A **movement**, of materials or information or people from one place to another

An **inspection**, a check or examination of materials or information or people

A **delay**, a pause in the process

A **storage**, an inventory of materials or file of information or queue of people

**Figure 5.12
Flow process chart
symbols**

Flow process chart

Activity	A day on the adventure holiday	Location	Perinong

	Description of element	●	➡	D	■	▼
1	Get up					
2	Go to washroom					
3	Wash, brush teeth					
4	Return to bedroom					
5	Dress					
6	Go to dining room					
7	Await serving					
8	Eat					
9	Go to rifle range					
10	Await instructor and equipment					
11	Check equipment					
12	Rifle shooting					
13	Go to dining room					
14	Eat lunch					
15	Go to bedroom					
16	Prepare for sailing					
17	Go to lake					
18	Await instructor					
19	Check equipment					
20	Sailing					
21	Go to bedroom					
22	Change					
23	Go to dining room					
24	Eat					
25	Wait for camp fire					
26	Camp fire					
27	Go to bedroom					
28	Prepare for bed					
29	Go to washroom					
30	Go to bed					
31	Go to toilet					
32	Go to bed again					
33	Sleep					

Figure 5.13 Flow process chart for one day on an adventure holiday

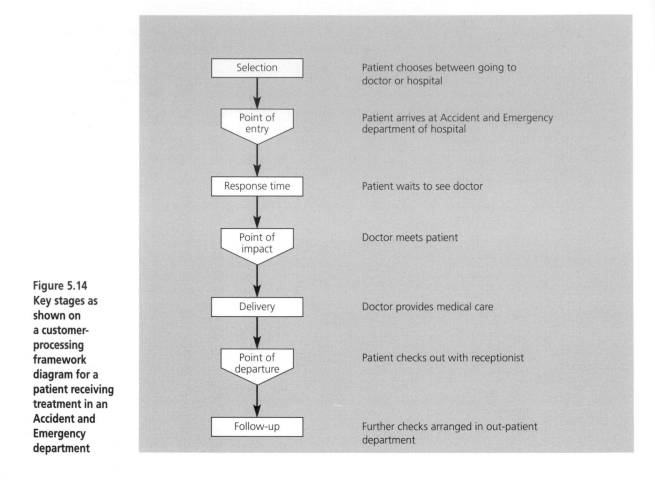

**Figure 5.14
Key stages as
shown on
a customer-
processing
framework
diagram for a
patient receiving
treatment in an
Accident and
Emergency
department**

Selection	Patient chooses between going to doctor or hospital
Point of entry	Patient arrives at Accident and Emergency department of hospital
Response time	Patient waits to see doctor
Point of impact	Doctor meets patient
Delivery	Doctor provides medical care
Point of departure	Patient checks out with receptionist
Follow-up	Further checks arranged in out-patient department

DESIGN EVALUATION AND IMPROVEMENT

The purpose of this stage in the design activity is to take the preliminary design and see if it can be improved before the product or service is tested in the market. There are a number of techniques that can be employed at this stage to evaluate and improve the preliminary design. Here we treat three which have proved particularly useful. They are:

- Quality function deployment (QFD)
- Value engineering (VE)
- Taguchi methods.

HOW ICL USES QFD[8]

In ICL, the computer company, a small team is formed to work on a new product opportunity or enhancement. A typical team consists of two customers, one marketing professional, two engineers, and one manufacturing or service representative. The team, which is kept small, is assisted by a facilitator who provides training in the priority and matrix techniques as required. The team will translate the needs into solutions, using the information to concentrate their efforts on the features which provide most value to customers.

Figure 5.15 Quality function deployment used to investigate the design of an electronic mail product
Source: Courtesy of ICL Training

The example shown in Fig. 5.15 is an extract from a typical study about a product requirement – in this case electronic mail. The customers' needs are shown, as are their opinions about a similar product from a competitor. The various sections of the matrix are explained in the order they are used.

A   The *whats* are verbatim customer-perceived needs, and the *relative priority* of these is recorded (with *accurate* being the highest priority in this case).

B   The customers' perception of how a competitor's mail system might perform is recorded on the right. The triangle is the assessment of ICL's system, and the square of the competitor's. They are better than the competitor for remote access, but worse for fast.

C   The team then uses brain-storming techniques to work out *how* the needs can best be met. Any new ideas which occur are captured for later evaluation. The facilitator helps to ensure that *whats* and *hows* do not get mixed up.

D   The central matrix represents the team's view of the interrelationship between the *whats* and *hows*, based on a value judgement of whether the contribution made by each *how* towards meeting a particular need is strong, medium, weak or none. (For example, the relationship between passwords and secure is strong.) All the relationships are studied, but in many cases there is none.

Figure 5.16 Quality function deployment matrices can be linked with the 'hows' of the upper matrix forming the 'whats' of the lower

E A calculation which combines the customer priority and the interrelationships gives the *absolute importance*. (For example, dial up lines has an importance of 6×9 + 4×3 = 66.) The ranking of the *hows* is given by numerical calculation and gives the *relative importance*. In this case high performance database is the most important.

F The roof of the 'house' captures any information the team has about the correlations (positive) or conflicts (negative) between the *hows*.

Next the *hows*, with target values, are listed in priority order, and are taken forward for future evaluation. In particular, if there is inadequate time or resources to provide all the elements of the solution, a subset can be selected which maximizes customer satisfaction.

The continuing work can also be represented by a House of Quality, where the *hows* from the previous stage become the *whats* of the next (*see* Fig. 5.16). Some experienced users of QFD have up to four houses. If engineering or process trade-offs need to be made at a later stage, the interrelated houses enable the effect on customer perception to be determined. ■

Questions

1 What do you think are the major advantages and disadvantages for a company like ICL in using this type of technique?

2 How might a technique like QFD be used by a company which has a chain of medium-priced hotels largely serving business people? Draw the QFD matrix for what you believe might be an appropriate set of 'whats' and 'hows'.

Quality function deployment

The key purpose of quality function deployment is to try to ensure that the eventual design of a product or service actually meets the needs of its customers. Customers may not have been considered explicitly since the concept generation stage, and therefore it is appropriate to check that what is being proposed for the design of the product or service will meet those needs.

Quality function deployment (QFD) is a technique that was developed in Japan at Mitsubishi's Kobe shipyard and used extensively by Toyota, the motor vehicle manufacturer, and its suppliers. It is also known as the 'House of Quality' (because of its shape) and the 'Voice of the Customer' (because of its purpose). The technique tries to capture *what* the customer needs and *how* it might be achieved.[7]

Value engineering

The purpose of value engineering is to try to reduce costs, and prevent any unnecessary costs, before producing the product or service. Simply put, it tries to eliminate any costs that do not contribute to the value and performance of the product or service. (Value analysis is the name given to the same process when it is concerned with cost reduction after the product or service has been introduced.)

Value-engineering programmes are usually conducted by project teams consisting of designers, purchasing specialists, operations managers and financial analysts. Pareto analysis (*see* Chapters 12 and 18) is often used to identify the parts of the package that are worthy of most attention. The chosen elements of the package are then subject to rigorous scrutiny. The team analyses the function and cost of those elements and tries to find any similar components that could do the same job at lower cost. More specifically, the team would attempt to reduce the number of components; use cheaper materials; and simplify the processes. For example, Motorola, the electronics manufacturer, used value engineering to reduce the production cost of its cellular phone. Initially its cellular phone had about 3200 parts. Three years later, after value engineering its new models, the number of parts had been reduced to 400. In so doing, the time to make the phone had been reduced from 40 hours to less than two.

Value engineering requires innovative and critical thinking, but it is also carried out using a formal procedure. The procedure examines the purpose of the product or service, its basic functions and its secondary functions. Taking the example of the telephone used previously:

- The *purpose* of the telephone is to communicate with another person.
- The *basic functions* are to hear and speak to the other person.
- The *secondary functions* are to connect with the other person's equipment, to key other numbers and to store other people's telephone numbers.

Team members would then propose ways to improve the secondary functions by combining, revising or eliminating them. For example, the earpiece and mouthpiece could be incorporated into the base casing, eliminating the need for a handset, or the circuitry and dial pad could be incorporated into the handset, eliminating the need for a base. All ideas would then be checked for feasibility, acceptability and vulnerability and their contribution to the value and purpose of the product or service.

Cost-to-function analyses

A revealing analysis of any product or service can be gained by examining how much of its cost is spent on its primary and secondary functions. Components of the product or service which seem to be taking up a disproportionate share of the total cost when related to their function would warrant special attention. For example, Fig. 5.17 shows the features of a washing machine and Table 5.3 shows the breakdown of the washing

Table 5.3 The functional breakdown of a washing machine

Function	% of cost	Cumulative % of costs			
Control operations	24.41	24.41	The washing function	A practical machine	A marketable product
Provide or restrain motion	28.48	52.82			
Distribute water	11.09	63.91			
Retain water	8.89	72.80			
Heat water	4.29	77.09			
Provide protection	10.07	87.16			
Position parts	6.67	93.82			
Look attractive	6.18	100.00			

Figure 5.17
Main components
of an automatic
washing machine

machine's functions and the percentage of the total cost of the product which is devoted to achieving each function. In this case, 77.09 per cent of its cost is associated with achieving its basic function.[9] As the machine is an automatic model, much of the cost is devoted to controlling the sequence of its activities. After the functions which provide the washing and controlling function, the remainder of the cost is spent on the functions which make the machine practical in operation and marketable to customers.

Taguchi methods

The main purpose of Taguchi methods, as advocated by Genichi Taguchi,[10] is to test the robustness of a design. The basis of the idea is that the product or service should still perform in extreme conditions. A telephone, for example, should still work even when it has been knocked on to the floor. Although one does not expect customers to knock a telephone to the floor, this does happen, and so the need to build strength into the casing should be considered in its design.

Likewise, a pizza parlour should be able to cope with a sudden rush of customers and an hotel should be able to cope with early arrivals. Product and service designers therefore need to brain-storm to try to identify all the possible situations that might

161

occur and check that the product or service is capable of dealing with those that are deemed to be necessary and cost effective.

In the case of the adventure holiday, for example, the designers need to plan for such contingencies as:

- foul weather – the need for bad weather alternatives;
- equipment failure – the provision of enough equipment to cover for maintenance;
- staff shortages – flexible working to allow cover from one area to another;
- accidents – the ability to deal with an accident without jeopardizing the other children in the group, with easily accessible first-aid equipment, and using facilities and equipment that are easy to clean and unlikely to cause damage to children;
- illnesses – the ability to deal with ill children who are unable to take part in an activity.

The job of the product or service designer is to achieve a design which can cope with all these uncertainties. The major problem designers face is that the number of design factors which they could vary to try to cope with the uncertainties, when taken together, is very large. For example, in designing the telephone casing there could be many thousands of combinations of casing size, casing shape, casing thickness, materials, jointing methods, etc. Performing all the investigations (or experiments as they are called in the Taguchi technique) to try to find a combination of design factors which gives an optimum design can be a lengthy process. The Taguchi procedure is a statistical procedure for carrying out relatively few experiments and yet still being able to determine the best combination of design factors. Here 'best' means the lowest cost and the highest degree of uniformity.

PROTOTYPING AND FINAL DESIGN

The next stage in the design activity is to turn the improved design into a prototype so that it can be tested. It may be too risky to go into full production of the telephone, or the holiday, before testing it out, so it is usually more appropriate to create a prototype.

Product prototypes may include card or clay models and computer simulations, for example. Service prototypes may include computer simulations but also the actual implementation of the service on a pilot basis. Many retailing organizations pilot new products and services in a small number of stores in order to test customers' reaction to them.

Computer-aided design (CAD)

The construction of physical prototypes has been eased as a result of the use of new technologies such as computer-aided design (CAD). CAD entails the use of computer simulations of products where the performance of the product can be tested to a high degree of accuracy without physical testing. Similar computer simulations are also used in the simulation of many services, such as the scheduling of aircraft to landing slots and the training of aircraft pilots. It should be stressed, however, that CAD is not only used in the prototyping stage of design. It is now extensively used in all stages.

CAD systems provide the computer-aided ability to create and modify product drawings. These systems allow conventionally used shapes (called entities) such as points, lines, arcs, circles, and text, to be added to a computer-based representation of the product. Once incorporated into the design, these entities can be copied, moved about, rotated through angles, magnified, or deleted. The system can usually also 'zoom in and out' to reveal different levels of detail. The designs thus created can be saved in the memory of the system and retrieved for later use. This enables a library of standardized drawings of parts and components to be built up. Not only can this dramatically increase the productivity of the process but it also aids the standardization of parts in the design activity. Some CAD systems come already supplied with their own libraries of standard parts.

CAD hardware

CAD systems can be configured in various ways. These range from using large main-frame computers down to single PC-based systems. CAD systems first of all need some kind of input device – these include such things as joysticks, light pens, electronic tablets, a mouse, or even the keyboard itself. The processing unit includes the central processing unit (CPU) and the software. The data storage part of the system usually includes either disk storage or magnetic tape storage. The display unit is usually a graphic terminal while the output device can be either a printer or a plotter.

CAD software

The software used in CAD systems varies in its degree of sophistication and modelling ability. The simplest type models only in two dimensions. This produces plans and elevations of the design in a similar way to a conventional engineering 'blueprint'. More sophisticated systems can model products in three dimensions. This can be done, in very basic form, by 'extruding' the two-dimensional image to give thickness to different parts of the two-dimensional shape. However, this approach is not capable of modelling complex products. It is often known as the two-and-a-half dimension approach. True three-dimensional software is capable of presenting an object accurately in full three-dimensional form. It may do this either by representing the edges and corners of the shape (known as a wire-frame model) or as a full solid model. The advantage of wire-frame modelling is that it demands considerably less computer power because an object is represented only by its outline. However, for complex objects wire-frame models can be confusing.

The advantages of CAD

The most obvious advantage of CAD systems is that their ability to store and retrieve design data quickly, as well as their ability to manipulate design details, can considerably increase the productivity of the design activity. In addition to this, however, because changes can be made rapidly to designs, CAD systems can considerably enhance the flexibility of the design activity, enabling modifications to be made much more rapidly. Further, the use of standardized libraries of shapes and entities can reduce the possibility of errors in the design. Perhaps most significantly, though, CAD can be seen as a prototyping device as well as a drafting device. In effect the designer is modelling the design in order to assess its suitability prior to full production.

THE BENEFITS OF INTERACTIVE DESIGN

Let us return to one of the first points we made in this chapter, namely that in practice it is a mistake to separate the design of products and services from the design of the processes which will produce them. In other words, operations managers should have some involvement from the initial evaluation of the concept right through to the production of the product or service and its introduction to the market. Merging the design of products/services and the processes which create them is sometimes called *interactive design*.

The benefits of interactive design are best described in terms of the elapsed time taken for the whole design activity, from concept through to market introduction. This is often called the design's *time to market* (TTM). The argument in favour of reducing time to market is quite simply that doing so gives increased competitive advantage. For example, if it takes a company five years to develop a product from concept to market, with a given set of resources, it can introduce a new product only once every five years. If its rival can develop products in three years it can introduce its new product, together with its (presumably) improved performance, once every three years. This means that the rival company does not have to make such radical improvements in performance each time it introduces a new product because it is introducing its new products more frequently. In other words, shorter TTM means that companies get more opportunities to improve the performance of their products or services.

In addition, if a company is late in getting its products and services to market compared to its competitors, the effects will be felt on its costs, its revenue and therefore its overall profitability. If the development process takes longer than expected (or even worse, longer than competitors) two effects are likely to show. The first is that the costs of development will increase. Having to use development resources, such as designers, technicians, subcontractors, and so on, for a longer development period usually increases the costs of development. Perhaps more seriously, the late introduction of the product or service will delay the revenue from its sale (and possibly reduce the total revenue substantially if competitors have already got to the market with their own products or services). The net effect of this could be not only a considerable reduction in sales but also reduced profitability – an outcome which could considerably extend the time before the company breaks even on its investment in the new product or service. This is illustrated in Fig. 5.18.

A number of factors have been suggested which can significantly reduce time to market for a product or service, including the following:

- simultaneous development of the various stages in the overall process;
- an early resolution of design conflict and uncertainty;
- an organizational structure which reflects the development project.

Simultaneous development

Earlier in the chapter we described the design process as essentially a set of individual, predetermined stages. Sometimes one stage is completed before the next one commences. This step-by-step, or *sequential*, approach has traditionally been the typical form of product/service development. It has some advantages. It is easy to manage

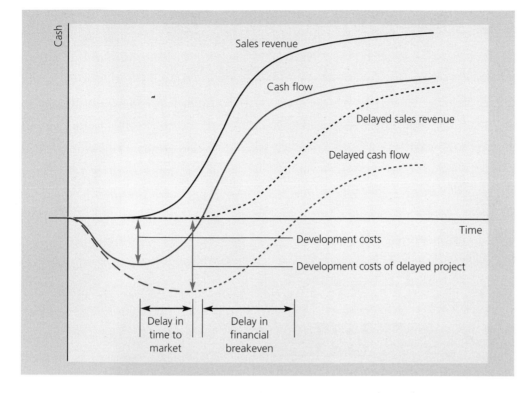

Figure 5.18
Delay in the time to market of new products and services not only reduces and delays revenues, it also increases the costs of development. The combination of both of these effects usually delays the financial breakeven point far more than the delay in the time to market

and control design projects organized in this way, since each stage is clearly defined. In addition, each stage is completed before the next stage is begun so each stage can focus its skills and expertise on a limited set of tasks. The main problem of the sequential approach is that it is both time-consuming and costly. When each stage is separate, with a clearly defined set of tasks, any difficulties encountered during the design at one stage might necessitate the design being halted while responsibility moves back to the previous stage. This sequential approach is shown in Fig. 5.19(a).

Often there is really little need to wait until the absolute finalization of one stage, however, before starting the next. For example, perhaps while generating the concept, the evaluation activity of screening and selection could be started. It would have to be a crude evaluation maybe, but nevertheless it is likely that some concepts could be judged as 'non-starters' relatively early on in the process of idea generation. Similarly, during the screening stage, it is likely that some aspects of the design will become obvious before the phase is finally complete. Therefore, the preliminary work on these parts of the design could be commenced before the end of the final screening and selection process. This principle can be taken right through all the stages of design. In other words, one stage commences before the previous one has finished, so there is *simultaneous* or *concurrent* work on the stages (*see* Fig. 5.19(b)).

We can link this idea with the idea of uncertainty reduction which was discussed in the last chapter. There, we made the point that uncertainty reduces as the design progresses. This also applies to each stage of the design, so uncertainty regarding the concept reduces through the concept generation stage, uncertainty about the preliminary design reduces through that phase, and so on. If this is so then there must be some degree of certainty which the next stage can take as its starting point prior to the end of the previous stage. In other words, designers can be continually reacting to a

165

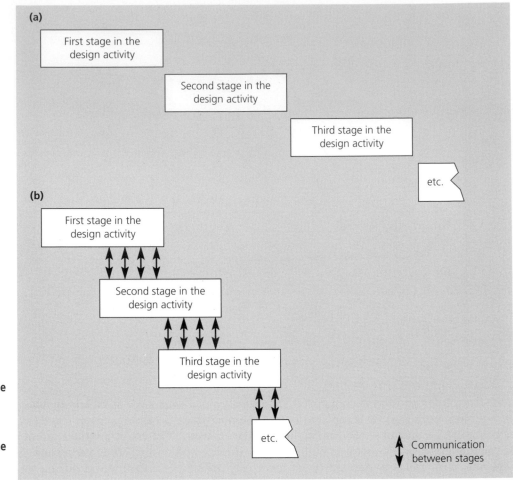

Figure 5.19
(a) Sequential arrangement of the stages in the design activity
(b) simultaneous arrangement of the stages in the design activity

series of decisions and clues which are given to them by the designers working on the preceding stage. However, this can only work if there is effective communication between each pair of stages.

Simultaneous engineering

What we have called simultaneous development is often called simultaneous (or concurrent) engineering in manufacturing operations. Although there is no single universally accepted definition of simultaneous engineering, most organizations' views are reasonably similar. For example, the following quotations give an idea of how the term is understood:

'*Simultaneous engineering means that people who design or manufacture products work under the same targets and the same sense of values to tackle the same problems enthusiastically from the early phases. The targets here are the reduction of lead time, design for manufacturing, product development and development of advanced production technologies. The common measure of value is the satisfaction of customers, which is one of the corporate philosophies of the entire company.*'[11]

'Simultaneous engineering attempts to optimize the design of the product and manufacturing process to achieve reduced lead times and improve quality and cost by the integration of design and manufacturing activities and by maximizing parallelism in working practices.'[12]

'Bureaucratic and cumbersome decision processes in product and service development can stifle technical competence. One of the reasons often cited for why IBM failed to dominate the personal computer market in spite of setting the standard for such products is that they were outmanoeuvred by smaller, more agile and sharper rivals. Often products just arrived on the market too late. Products would arrive a year or so after they would have been a really good idea.'[13]

Early conflict resolution

Characterizing the design activity as a whole series of decisions is a useful way of thinking about design. However, a decision, once made, need not totally and utterly commit the organization. For example, if a design team is designing a new vacuum cleaner, the decision to adopt a particular style and type of electric motor might have seemed sensible at the time the decision was made but might have to be changed later, in the light of new information. It could be that a new electric motor becomes available which is clearly superior to the one initially selected. Under those circumstances the designers might very well want to change their decision.

There are other, more avoidable, reasons for designers changing their minds during the design activity, however. Perhaps one of the initial design decisions was made without sufficient discussion among those in the organization who have a valid contribution to make. It may even be that when the decision was made there was insufficient agreement to formalize it, and the design team decided to carry on without formally making the decision. Yet subsequent decisions might be made as though the decision had been formalized. For example, suppose the company could not agree on the correct size of electric motor to put in its vacuum cleaner. It might well carry on with the rest of the design work while further discussions and investigations take place on what kind of electric motor to incorporate in the design. Yet much of the rest of the product's design is likely to depend on the choice of the electric motor. The plastic housings, the bearings, the sizes of various apertures, and so on, could all be affected by this decision. Failure to resolve these conflicts and/or decisions early on in the process can prolong the degree of uncertainty in the total design activity. In addition, if a decision is made (even implicitly) and then changed later on in the process, the costs of that change can be very large (as was discussed in Chapter 4).

However, if the design team manages to resolve conflict early in the design activity, this will reduce the degree of uncertainty within the project and reduce the extra cost and, most significantly, time associated with either managing this uncertainty or changing decisions already made. Figure 5.20 illustrates two patterns of design changes through the life of the total design, which imply different time-to-market performances.

Project-based organization structures

The total process of developing concepts through to market will almost certainly involve personnel from several different areas of the organization. To continue the vacuum cleaner example, it is likely that the vacuum cleaner company would involve

THE MANIFOLD FOR THE FORD ZETA ENGINE[14]

The development of the 1.6 Zeta engine by Ford was one of its most important design projects for years. Like any engine design, it was a huge and complex task. Indeed, each part of the engine needed to go through all the stages of the 'concept through to market' design activity. Take, for example, the air intake manifold. This plays a particularly important part in the engine because it recirculates exhaust gases from the engine, reburning some of them and therefore reducing the overall emission levels from the engine.

In the Zeta engine the manifold (unusually) is made not from metal but from a glass-reinforced nylon resin. The advantages of using this material include its strength, impact resistance, heat resistance and ease of processing. However, there were many design problems to sort out, including noise and vibration, the dimensional stability of the product and the ability of the material to stand up to the very high temperatures involved.

The design of the engine manifold took almost three years and was organized using all the interactive design principles. First of all, the various stages in the design were compressed and run in parallel (what Ford calls 'concurrent engineering'). Secondly, the various fundamental design problems were sorted out right at the beginning of the process. Third, a design team was put together involving not only various personnel from the Ford Motor Company but also the more significant suppliers. Those involved included design representatives from the Du Pont chemical company who were supplying the material, Dunlop who were to perform the moulding operation, and several specialist suppliers including Dowty who were designing the seals, Elring who were involved in gasket design, Elm Steel who were involved with supplying tubing, and so on.

Design technology also played a large part in the development of this product. For example, Du Pont used computer-aided design (CAD) techniques to study the effects of engine vibration on the manifold. By simulating engine conditions, the various stress levels in the manifold could be estimated. This allowed the team to explore different design solutions without having to devote time and cost to manufacturing too many alternative prototypes – particularly important because the design of the manifold had to fit in with the overall design of the engine itself. Prototype manifolds were needed to supply the main engine design team who were wanting to start engine testing several months before the end of the manifold design process.

By involving its suppliers, by using them to resolve the considerable technical problems early on in the project, and by solving the technical problems in an interactive and simultaneous manner, the team managed to get a highly complex and very novel product designed to fit into the overall engine project more quickly, more cheaply and more dependably than it could otherwise have done. ■

Questions

1 In developing this product Ford put together a team of suppliers. Do you think it would do the same for every single supplier of every part in every product? If not, how should it choose which suppliers, which parts and which products to subject to this sort of treatment?

2 Should Ford have included its suppliers' suppliers as well?

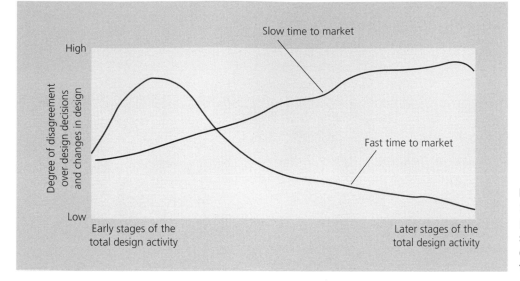

**Figure 5.20
Sorting out
problems early
saves greater
disruption later in
the design activity**

staff from its research and development department, engineering, production management, marketing, and finance. All these different functions will have some part to play in making the decisions which will shape the final design. Yet any design project will also have an existence of its own. It will have a project name, an individual manager or group of staff who are championing the project, a budget and, hopefully, a clear strategic purpose in the organization. The organizational question is which of these two ideas – the various organizational functions which contribute to the design or the design project itself – should dominate the way in which the design activity is managed?

Before answering this it is useful to look at the range of organizational structures which are available – from pure functional to pure project forms. In a pure functional organization all staff associated with the design project are based unambiguously in their functional groups. There is no project-based group at all. They may be working full-time on the project but all communication and liaison is carried out through their functional manager. The project exists because of agreement between these functional managers.

At the other extreme, all the individual members of staff from each function who are involved in the project could be moved out of their functions and perhaps even physically relocated to a 'task force' dedicated solely to the project. The task force could be led by a project manager who might hold all the budget allocated to the design project. Not all members of the task force necessarily have to stay in the team throughout the development period, but a substantial core might see the project through from start to finish. Some members of a design team may even be from other companies, as in the team which developed the inlet manifold for the Ford Zeta engine (*see* box).

In between these two extremes there are various types of 'matrix' organization with varying emphasis on these two aspects of the organization (*see* Fig. 5.21).

Although the 'task force' type of organization, especially for small projects, can sometimes be a little cumbersome, it seems to be generally agreed that, for substantial projects at least, it is more effective at reducing overall time to market.[15]

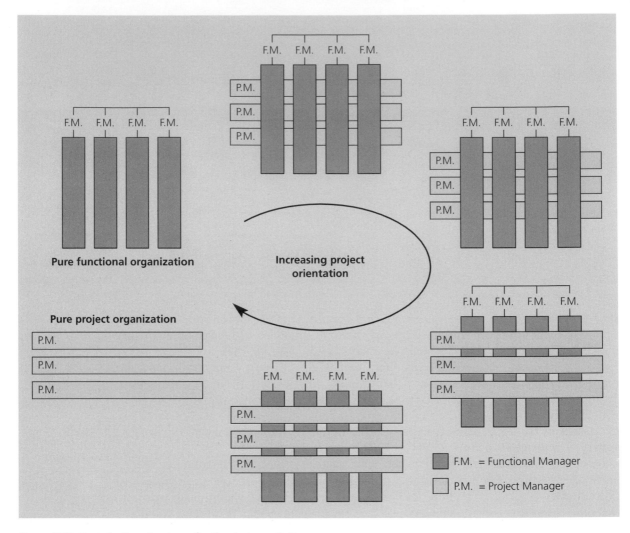

Figure 5.21 Organization structures for the design activity

Debbie Lundberg, Design Executive

Debbie is responsible for a team of over 20 designers who use the latest computer-aided design (CAD) to create the concepts and detailed patterns for new garments.

'Because most of our design work is ultimately prepared for the retailers Marks and Spencer (M&S), yet is contracted by clothing manufacturers, I have to ensure that we work effectively as a three-way partnership, which is a major challenge.

'We used to have specialist designers employed to work on particular types of clothing, such as ladies' wear or children's wear, with a similar separation in the prototype production areas; so machinists specialized as well. Now we have moved to project teams, to share ideas and develop new ranges of products. All our employees are more multi-skilled, which gives us greater flexibility to respond to changes in the mix of work, and it also stimulates the generation of new ideas.'

Debbie's work involves some market research, in conjunction with major customers, but above all she has to keep the team up to date with trends in the fashion industry, fabric technologies, new sources and types of fabric, and ways of illustrating concepts and specific designs prior to manufacturing.

'In the past, perhaps only eight out of 400 designs would be chosen for full-scale production, meaning that vast amounts of design effort and costings were wasted. Nowadays, development times are much shorter than in the past – the customers demand it. But CAD has speeded things up considerably, and gives us the opportunity to come very much closer to what the customer wants first time. Now we would expect only to prepare 50 designs for a show, of which perhaps ten would be chosen.

'The CAD system is being improved all the time, and we are exploring new ways of using it. For example, three-dimensional modelling allows us to show clothes on a 3D body, giving clients a much more realistic impression of the appearance of the garment before we obtain materials and produce a prototype. We can fine-tune any feature as we discuss the design, so finalizing the proposals is quicker than ever before. Although CAD systems started in engineering and graphic design, they are now much more tailored to the specific needs of the textile and garments industry. Not only do they help us conceptualize a product, but they allow us to communicate quickly and effectively with our clients and with the factories. It is also possible to link effectively the CAD system to CAM (computer-aided manufacturing) systems which produce patterns and cut cloth. The business opportunities afforded by this technology are almost beyond belief.' ∎

SUMMARY ANSWERS TO KEY QUESTIONS

Why is good product and service design important?

■ Good product and service design translates customer needs into the shape and form of the product or service and by doing this specifies the required capabilities of the operation. Therefore, product and service design in effect connects the operation itself to its customers.

■ This translation process includes formalizing three particularly important issues for operations managers. These are the concept, package and process implied by the design.

■ Companies like Braun (*see* the box earlier) have found that good aesthetic and functional design enhances their profitability.

What are the stages in product and service design?

■ *Concept generation* transforms an idea for a product or service into a concept which indicates the form, function, purpose and benefits of the idea.

■ *Screening* the concept involves examining its acceptability in broad terms to ensure that it is a sensible addition to the company's product or service portfolio. Market, financial and operations evaluations must all be carried out during the screening process.

■ *Preliminary design* involves the identification of all the component parts of the product or service and the way they fit together. Typical tools used during this phase include activity/product structures, bills of materials, and flow charts.

■ *Design evaluation and improvement* involves re-examining the design to see if it can be done in a better way, more cheaply or more easily. Typical techniques used here include quality function deployment, value engineering and Taguchi methods.

■ *Prototyping and final design* involves providing the final details which allow the product or service to be produced. Computer-aided design (CAD) is often used at this point, although it may also be used elsewhere in the design process. The outcome of this stage is a fully developed specification for the package of products and services, as well as a specification for the processes that will make and deliver them to customers.

Why should product and service design and process design be considered interactively?

■ Looking at them together can improve the quality of both product and service design and process design. Considering the constraints of the operation during product and service design ensures that the final designs are 'producable'. Considering product and service design during process design ensures that processes are developed with the long-term needs of products and services in mind.

■ Interactive design helps fast time to market. This ensures that the company will 'break even' on its investment in the new design earlier than would otherwise have been the case.

How should interactive design be managed?

■ Employ *simultaneous development* where design decisions are taken as early as they can be, without necessarily waiting for a whole design phase to be completed. Such early commitment of design resources must also include effective communication between the phases in the design activity.

■ Ensure early *conflict resolution* which allows contentious decisions to be resolved early in the design process, thereby not allowing them to cause far more delay and confusion if they emerge later in the process.

■ Use a *project-based organisational structure* which can ensure that a focused and coherent team of designers is dedicated to a single design or group of design projects.

CASE EXERCISE

The Royal Mint

A unique manufacturing operation in the UK is the Royal Mint at Llantrisant in South Wales. The Royal Mint is designated as an Executive Agency responsible to the Treasury of HM Government. The Chancellor of the Exchequer is appointed (*ex officio*) as Master of the Mint. Its objective is to provide the Government with coinage at a competitive price. The Royal Mint has the capacity to handle all of the UK business and still be able to bid for contracts from those countries who do not have their own minting operation. It serves over 60 countries in any one year and produces in excess of three billion coins annually. Its manufacturing requirement ranges from high volumes of standard coinage to individual service medals or commemorative coins.

In the UK, the Treasury contracts with the Royal Mint on an annual basis for the likely requirements for coin in the following 12 months, and the Treasury is also responsible for decisions on any changes to the coinage. The last coin that was introduced was the new, smaller 10p coin; this involved an issue of over one billion new coins and the withdrawal of all the old coins from circulation. This represents one of the largest single projects undertaken and a massive logistics exercise to co-ordinate the movement of the coins. The Mint meets every three months with executives from the UK clearing banks to discuss their requirements for currency in the shorter term. These estimates are then updated at weekly planning meetings. The Mint would like to work to a 'just-in-time' schedule, but because of the nature of the product and the implications of the money not being available, they are obliged to keep a predetermined safety stock to cover any shortfalls.

As in any manufacturing operation, the unit cost of the product is a critical factor in measuring performance, and in the case of the Royal Mint, there is a unique cost ceiling, in that their cost base must always be less than the face value of the coins being produced. Therefore, this mass manufacturing process must focus on monitoring its operating costs. The issue of payment for the product is an interesting concept within the 'minting' industry and in the UK. The clearing banks pay the face value of the coins to the Treasury and the annual contract agreement with the Royal Mint is based on the Treasury agreeing to cover a fixed percentage of their fixed costs and the variable cost of each unit then purchased over the year. The Royal Mint can then invoice the Treasury for the currency produced.

The coins are costed in terms of pounds per thousand pieces. Of that cost, approximately 40 to 50 per cent is comprised of the raw material cost, with the next 20 to 40 per cent coming from the production process which transforms that raw metal into a blank coin. The actual stamping of the die on to the coin and the simultaneous milling of the edges is an almost insignificant part of the overall process cost, mainly due to the vast economies of scale at this stage. The efficiency of the stamping process is nominally determined by the life expectancy of the die, and the research at the Mint is involved in initiatives to improve the materials being used in both the coins and dies to extend this period of use. The coining machines used in the manufacturing process are flexible in that they can run to produce any of the UK and most overseas coins without long change-over periods and orders vary from 1000 million coins for a large country to an order of 5000 for a small island. The machines are able to operate at speeds up to 750 coins per minute and therefore the nature of a 5000 coin run is very costly, but all the same still viable.

One issue has been the threat of the intrinsic raw metal cost exceeding the face value of the coin: something which has been most prevalent in those countries facing high inflation and which leads to coinage being withdrawn from circulation by those wishing to capitalize on the returns available from the base material. In the UK, the smaller denominations were reaching that point and the Mint had to change the composition of the 2p and 1p coins to a steel core with an electroplated copper outer layer. This reduced the unit cost of the coin and also added to its expected lifetime because it used a less expensive base metal. This new format of coin represents the biggest change in the manufacturing process of coins to occur over the past few years and the pioneering of the electroplating technique, whereby a mild steel core is electroplated with copper, nickel or brass, resulted in a process which will aid the conservation of materials. The reduction in costs is also being achieved without a noticeable reduction in the recognized value of the coin. Another consequence of the electroplating procedure is that the coins have magnetic properties due to the presence of a mild steel core and this has caused initial problems for vending machine manufacturers. ■

Source: Reproduced by kind permission of the Royal Mint

Questions

1 What is the 'concept' of the Mint's products?
2 Explain the criteria which the Mint will need to take into account when it designs new coinage.
3 How might the concept of simultaneous design be applied in the design of coinage?

DISCUSSION QUESTIONS

1 Describe what you think might be the concept, package and the main processes involved in creating or providing the following:
- a high-performance car
- an airline flight
- a visit to the dentist
- an operations management textbook.

2 Using your knowledge as a customer of a university library, try to generate three new ways in which library services could be provided to you. Discuss the acceptability, feasibility and viability of each.

3 Take apart a simple product, such as a pen or an old cassette. Explain how it might have been put together (reverse engineering) and see if you can improve on its design.

4 Explain the difference between an idea and a concept. A hairdresser is considering opening up on campus. Develop this idea into what you think might be an acceptable, feasible and viable concept.

5 Look carefully at an item of furniture you have and create a product structure and bill of materials for it. Don't forget the nails, different types of screws and glue.

6 Draw an information flow chart describing the decision processes involved in a decision you frequently have to make, such as what to do in an evening. Evaluate the complexity and completeness of the chart.

7 Draw a process flow chart describing your last visit to see the doctor. How do you think the process could be improved?

8 Blueprinting, in one form or another, is a key tool for analysing, designing and developing products and services. Why do you think this is so?

9 Apply quality function deployment to a drawing pin and assess how well it appears to meet your perceived needs.

10 Explain what is meant by 'interactive design' and discuss the benefits for those organizations that employ it.

11 Why is it difficult or inappropriate to separate out the design of a product or service from the process of creating it?

12 Read again the box on Braun's Multimix design at the beginning of this chapter and answer the following questions:

(a) To what extent do the 'Braun Design Principles' appear to incorporate elements of:
- design for manufacture
- standardization
- simultaneous engineering
- quality function deployment?

(b) Which performance objectives are the most important for Braun?

(c) Braun has chosen to undertake most of its manufacturing in Europe, and much of it in Germany. What are the implications of this policy for the design of the company's products?

NOTES ON CHAPTER

1 Source: Presentation speech by Hartmut Stroth, Director of Communication at Braun AG, Mar 1994.

2 Source: Lloyd, C. (1994) 'It Seemed a Good Idea at the Time', *The Sunday Times*, 16 Jan.

3 Peters, T. and Waterman, R. (1982) *In Search of Excellence*, Harper & Row, New York.

4 For more information on focus groups *see*, for example, Krueger, K.A. (1988) *Focus Groups*, Sage Publications.

5 Quinn, J.B. and Gagnon, C.E. (1986) 'Will Services Follow Manufacturing into Decline?', *Harvard Business Review*, Vol 64, No 6, pp 95–103.

6 Johnston, R. (1987) 'A Framework for Developing a Quality Strategy in a Customer Processing Operation', *International Journal of Quality and Reliability Management*, Vol 4, No 4, pp 35–44.

7   For more information on QFD for products and services *see*, for example:

Behara, R.S. and Chase, R.B. (1993) 'Service Quality Deployment: Quality Service by Design' *in* Sarin, R.V. (ed) *Perspectives in Operations Management: Essays in Honor of Elwood S. Buffa*, Kluwer Academic Publisher.

Evans, J.R. and Lindsay, W.M. (1993) *The Management and Control of Quality* (2nd edn), West.

Fitzsimmons, J.A. and Fitzsimmons, M.J. (1994) *Service Management for Competitive Advantage*, McGraw-Hill.

Harrison, A. (1992) *Just-in-Time Manufacturing in Perspective*, Prentice Hall.

Hauser, J.R. and Clausing, D. (1988) 'The House of Quality', *Harvard Business Review*, Vol 66, No 3, pp 63–73.

Meredith, J.R. (1992) *The Management of Operations* (4th edn), John Wiley.

8   Cambridge, M. (1992) 'Quality Function Deployment', *Quality and Corporate Affairs Business Improvement Series*, 92/03 ICL, Dec.

9   This example is used by kind permission of Allan Webb, from Webb, A. (1994) *Managing Innovative Projects*, Chapman and Hall.

10 Taguchi, G. and Clausing, D. (1990) 'Robust Quality', *Harvard Business Review*, Vol 68, No 1, pp 65–75.

11 Yamazoe, T. (1990) 'Simultaneous Engineering: A Nissan Perspective' *in The Proceedings of the First International Conference on Simultaneous Engineering*, London, pp 73–80.

12 Broughton, T. (1990) 'Simultaneous Engineering in Aero Gas Turbine Design and Manufacture' *in The Proceedings of the First International Conference on Simultaneous Engineering*, London, pp 25–36.

13 May, M. (1993) 'Big Blue and The Little Meanies', *The Times*, 29 Jan.

14 Costanzo, L. (1992) 'Working as One', *Engineering*, Nov.

15 Hayes, R.H., Wheelwright, S.C. and Clarke, K.B. (1988) *Dynamic Manufacturing*, The Free Press.

SELECTED FURTHER READINGS

Albrecht, K. and Bradford, L.J. (1990) *The Service Advantage*, Dow Jones Irwin.

Baxter, M. (1995) *Product Design*, Chapman and Hall.

Bitner, M.J. (1992) 'Servicescapes: The Impact of Physical Surroundings on Customers and Employees', *Journal of Marketing*, Vol 56, April, pp 57–71.

Chase, R.B. (1991) 'The Service Factory: A Future Vision', *International Journal of Service Industry Management*, Vol 2, No 3, pp 60–70.

Clausing, D.P. (1994) *Total Quality Development*, ASME Press, New York.

Cohen, L. (1995) *Quality Function Deployment*, Addison-Wesley Longman.

Dean, J.H and Susman, G.I. (1984) 'Organizing for Manufacturable Design', *Harvard Business Review*, Vol 62, No 1, pp 28–36.

Groover, M.P. and Zimmers, E.W. (1984) *CAD/CAM Computer-Aided Design and Manufacturing*, Prentice Hall.

Heskett, J.L., Sasser, W.E. and Hart, C.W.L. (1990) *Service Breakthroughs: Changing the Rules of the Game*, The Free Press.

Kingman-Brundage, J. (1989) 'The ABCs of Service System Blueprinting' *in* Bitner, M.J. and Crosby, L. (eds) *Designing a Winning Service Strategy*, American Marketing Association. Also to be found *in* Lovelock, C.H. (1992) *Managing Services* (2nd edn), Prentice Hall International.

Shostack, G.L. (1984) 'Designing Services that Deliver', *Harvard Business Review*, Vol 62, No 1, pp 133–9.

Shostack, G.L. (1987) 'Service Positioning Through Structural Change', *Journal of Marketing*, Vol 51, Jan, pp 34–43.

Stuart, F.I. and Tax, S.S. (1996) 'Planning for Service Quality: An Integrative Approach', *International Journal of Service Industry Mangement*, Vol 7, No 4.

Thomas, R.J. (1995) *New Product Success Stories*, John Wiley.

Whitney, D.E. (1988) 'Manufacturing by Design', *Harvard Business Review*, Vol 66, No 1, pp 83–91.

DESIGN OF THE OPERATIONS NETWORK

INTRODUCTION

No operation, or part of an operation, exists in isolation. Every operation is part of a larger and interconnected network of other operations. This network will include suppliers and customers. It will also include suppliers' suppliers and customers' customers, and so on. At a strategic level, operations managers are involved in 'designing' the shape and form of the network in which their operation is set. These network design decisions start with setting the strategic objectives for an operation's position in its network. This helps to determine the extent to which an operation chooses to be 'vertically integrated' into the network, the location of each operation within the network, and the capacity of each part of the network. This chapter treats all these strategic design decisions in the context of operations networks (*see* Fig. 6.1).

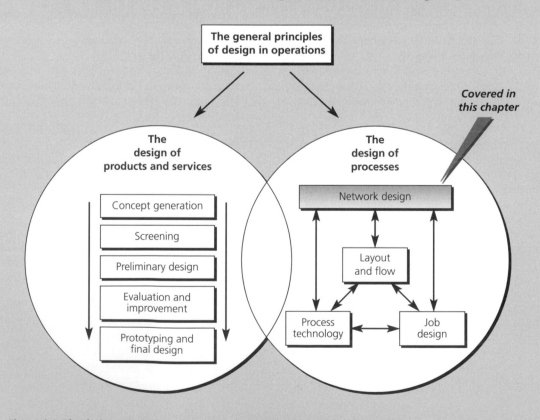

Figure 6.1 **The design activities in operations management covered in this chapter**

THE NETWORK PERSPECTIVE

We begin our treatment of transformation processes design by setting the operation in the context of all the other operations with which it interacts, some of which are its suppliers and some of which are its customers. Materials, parts, assemblies, information, ideas and sometimes people, all flow through the network of customer–supplier relationships formed by all these operations. On its *supply side* an operation has its suppliers of parts, or information, or services. These suppliers themselves have their own suppliers who in turn could also have suppliers, and so on. On the *demand side* the operation has customers. These customers might not be the final consumers of the operation's products or services; they might have their own set of customers.

Figure 6.2 illustrates one such network. On its supply side is a group of operations who directly supply the operation; these are often called 'first-tier' suppliers. They are supplied by 'second-tier' suppliers. However, some operations who are primarily second-tier suppliers in an industry may also supply an operation directly, thus missing out a link in the network. Similarly, on the demand side of the network, 'first-tier' customers are the main customer group for the operation. These in turn supply 'second-tier' customers, although again the operation may at times supply second-tier customers directly. The suppliers and customers who have direct contact with an operation are called its *immediate supply network*, whereas all the operations which form the network of supplier's suppliers and customer's customers, etc., are called the *total supply network*.

Figure 6.3 illustrates the total supply network for a plastic homewares (for example, kitchen bowls, food containers, etc.) manufacturer. On its demand side it is supplied by a plastic stockist and a packaging supplier who, in turn, purchase their own materials from their suppliers. Note that on the demand side the homeware manufacturer supplies some of its basic products to wholesalers who supply retail outlets. However, it also supplies some retailers directly with 'made-to-order' products.

Along with the flow of goods in the network from suppliers to customers, each link in the network will feed back orders and information to its suppliers. When stocks run low, the retailers will place orders with the wholesaler or directly with the manufacturer. The wholesaler will likewise place orders with the manufacturer which will in turn place orders with its suppliers, who will replenish their own stocks from their suppliers. It is a two-way process with goods flowing one way and information flowing the other.

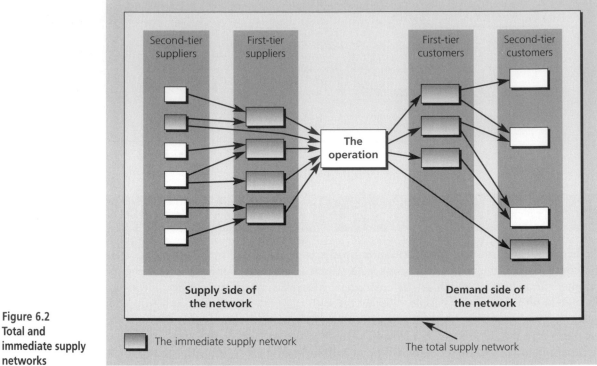

Figure 6.2
Total and
immediate supply
networks

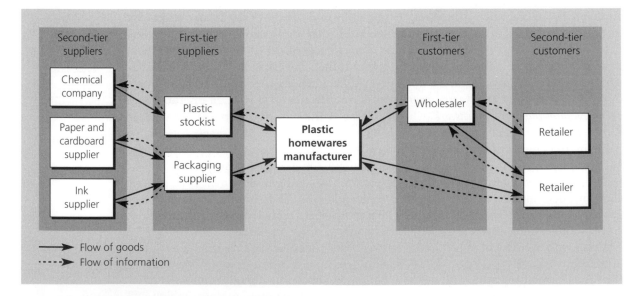

Figure 6.3 Operations network for a plastic homewares manufacturer

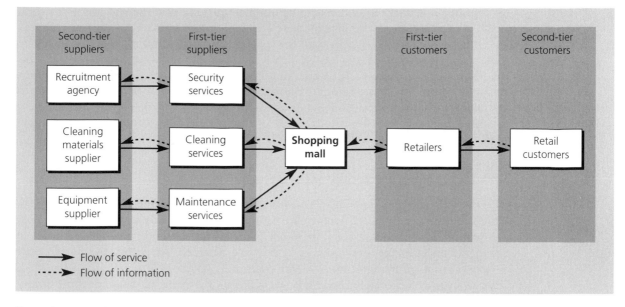

Figure 6.4 Operations network for a shopping mall

It is not only manufacturers who are part of a supply network. Service operations also have suppliers and customers who themselves have their own suppliers and customers. Figure 6.4 shows the supply network for an operation which manages an enclosed shopping mall.

Again there is a flow of information back from customers to suppliers to support the flow of services. This information flow will be slightly different from that in the plastic homewares network described previously. Customers will still place 'orders' with suppliers but on a less frequent basis. For instance, a contract will be negotiated every year between the mall and the security company. Much of the information will be performance monitoring information, such as regularly checking the cleanliness of the premises and feeding back the information to the cleaning company.

Why consider the whole network?

At its most strategic level, the design activity of operations management must include the whole of the network of which an operation is a part. There are three important reasons for this:[1]

- It helps a company to understand how it can compete effectively.
- It helps to identify particularly significant links in the network.
- It helps the company to focus on its long-term position in the network.

Understanding competitiveness

Immediate customers and immediate suppliers, quite understandably, are the main concern to competitively minded companies. Yet sometimes they need to look beyond these immediate contacts and see themselves in the context of the whole network so as to understand why customers and suppliers act as they do. Any operation has only two options if it wants to understand its ultimate customers at the end of the network. First, it can rely on all the intermediate customers and customers' customers, etc., which form the links in the network between the company and its end customers, to transmit the end-customer needs efficiently back up the network. Second, it can take the responsibility on itself for understanding how customer–supplier relationships transmit competitive requirements through the network. Increasingly, organizations are taking the latter course. Relying on one's immediate network is seen as putting too much faith in someone else's judgement of things which are central to an organization's own competitive health.

Identifying significant links in the network

The key to understanding supply networks lies in identifying the parts of the network which contribute to those performance objectives valued by end customers. Any analysis of networks must start, therefore, with an understanding of the elements of competitiveness at the 'downstream' end of the network. After this, the parts of the network which contribute most to end-customer service will need to be identified. This analysis will probably show that every link in the network will contribute something; but not all contributions will be equally significant.

For example, the important end customers for some types of domestic plumbing parts and appliances are the installers and service companies who deal directly with domestic consumers. They are supplied by 'stock holders' whose competitive success relies on a combination of price, range and above all a high availability of supply. That means having all parts in stock and delivering them fast. Suppliers of parts to the stock holders can best contribute to their customers' competitiveness partly by offering a short delivery lead time but mainly through dependable delivery. The key players in this example are the stock holders. Without effective service levels and competitive prices from them, the end customers will not be as likely to buy the products of the parts manufacturer. The best way of winning end-customer business in this case is by giving the stock holder prompt delivery which helps keep costs down while providing high availability of parts.[2]

Focus on long-term issues

There are times when circumstances render parts of a supply network weaker than its adjacent links. A major machine breakdown, for example, or a labour dispute might disrupt an operation. How then should its immediate customers and suppliers react? Should they exploit the weakness as a legitimate move to enhance their own competitive position or should they ignore the opportunity, tolerate the problems, and hope the customer or supplier will eventually recover?[3] A long-term supply network view would be to weigh the relative advantages to be gained from assisting or replacing the weak link.

Design decisions in the network

The network view is useful because it prompts three particularly important design decisions. These are the most strategic of all the design decisions treated in this part of the book, and therefore they are not taken very frequently. It is necessary to understand them at this point, however, because, as well as having a particularly significant impact on the strategy of the organization, they set the context in which all other process design decisions are made. The three decisions are:

1 How much of the network should the operation own? Should it own any of its suppliers or customers? For example, the shopping mall operation might choose to employ its own security staff rather than buy in security services from a specialist company. This decision is called the *vertical integration* decision of the organization.

2 Where should each part of the network owned by the company be located? If the homewares company builds a new factory should it be close to its suppliers or close to its customers, or somewhere in between? How should the shopping mall company choose a particular location for its mall? These decisions are called *operations location* decisions.

3 What physical capacity should each part of the network owned by the company have at any point in time? How large should the homeware factory be? If it expands, should it do so in large capacity steps or small ones? Should it make sure that it always has more capacity then anticipated demand or less? These decisions are called *long-term capacity management* decisions.

In Chapter 13, we will cover the more operational day-to-day issues of managing operations networks. In this chapter we deal with these three related strategic decisions.

THE VERTICAL INTEGRATION OF CAPACITY

Vertical integration is the extent to which an organization owns the network of which it is a part. In its strategic sense, it involves an organization assessing the wisdom of acquiring suppliers or customers. At the level of individual products or services, it means the operation deciding whether to make a particular individual component or to perform a particular service itself, or alternatively buy it in from a supplier.

Professors Hayes and Wheelwright of Harvard Business School[4] define an organization's vertical integration strategy in terms of:

- the *direction* of any expansion;
- the *extent* of the process span required;
- the *balance* among the resulting vertically integrated stages.

The direction of vertical integration

The first vertical integration decision an organization must take concerns the *direction* of any ownership in the network. If the plastic homewares manufacturer illustrated in Fig. 6.3 decides that it should control more of its network, should it expand by buying one of its suppliers (becoming its own plastic materials stockist, for instance) or should it expand by buying one of its customers (a wholesaler or a retailer)? The strategy of expanding on the supply side of the network is sometimes called *backward* or *'upstream' vertical integration,* and expanding on the demand side is sometimes called *forward* or *'downstream' vertical integration.*

Backward vertical integration, by allowing an organization to take control of its suppliers, is often used either to gain cost advantages or to prevent competitors gaining control of important suppliers. This is why backward vertical integration is sometimes considered a strategically *defensive* move. Forward vertical integration, on the other hand, takes an organization closer to its markets and allows more freedom for an organization to make contact directly with its customers. For this reason forward vertical integration is sometimes considered an *offensive* strategic move. Figure 6.5 illustrates backward and forward vertical integration.

The extent of vertical integration

Having established its direction of expansion, an organization must then decide how far it wishes to take the extent of its vertical integration. Some organizations deliberately choose not to integrate far, if at all, from their original part of the network. For example, the shopping mall company illustrated in Fig. 6.4 might decide that it wishes to concentrate solely on the management of its existing properties and the location, financing and building of new properties. It does not want to become a retailer in its own malls nor does it want to employ security, maintenance or cleaning staff. Rather it is content to specialize in what it knows best and 'buy in' all the services which are needed to run the malls.

Alternatively, some organizations choose to become very vertically integrated. Take a large international aluminium company, such as Alcan, for example. Alcan is involved with smelting the minerals which produce aluminium (as well as recycling used aluminium products) to produce its basic ingots of aluminium. It also has operations which take the ingots and roll them into sheet form. Separate Alcan operations then roll the sheet further to produce aluminium foil which can then be made into aluminium containers (for take-away food or home freezing) at yet another Alcan operation. Figure 6.6 illustrates two organizations, one with a narrow 'extent' of vertical integration and one with a wide 'extent' of vertical integration.

Figure 6.5 The direction of vertical integration for an assembly operation

Figure 6.6 The extent of process span of vertical integration for an assembly operation

The balance among stages

The final vertical integration decision is not strictly about the ownership of the network; it concerns the capacity and, to some extent, the operating behaviour of each stage in the network. The *balance* of the part of the network owned by an organization is the amount of the capacity at each stage in the network which is devoted to supplying the next stage. So a totally balanced network relationship is one where one stage produces only for the next stage in the network and totally satisfies its requirements. Less than full balance in the stages allows each stage to sell its output to other companies or to buy in some of its supplies from other companies.

Fully balanced networks have the virtue of simplicity and also allow each stage to focus on the requirements of the next stage along in the network. Having to supply other organizations, perhaps with slightly different requirements, might serve to distract from what is needed by their (owned) primary customer. However, a totally self-sufficient network is sometimes not feasible. For example, within the network of operations which is owned by Alcan are some 'stock-holding' operations; these are the companies which hold stocks of metals in semi-finished form, such as aluminium sheets and extruded bars. They sell partly to the small and medium-sized customers who do not warrant direct deliveries from Alcan's factories. These stock-holding operations could be limited to stocking only Alcan-manufactured products. In fact they are not so limited. A stock-holding company which held the products from only one company would not offer as effective a service to its customers as one which is free to supply a full range of products, including those which Alcan does not manufacture. Figure 6.7 illustrates this.

The effects of vertical integration

The benefits and limitations of vertical integration are complex, and organizations in different circumstances with different objectives are likely to take different decisions. Yet

Figure 6.7 The balance of internal/external trade in a vertically integrated assembly operation

the vertical integration question which all organizations must answer is relatively simple, even if the decision itself is not. 'Do the advantages which vertical integration gives an organization in a particular set of circumstances match the performance objectives which it requires in order to compete more effectively in its markets?' For example, if the main performance objectives for an operation are dependable delivery and meeting short-term changes in customers' delivery requirements, the key question should be 'How does vertical integration enhance dependability and delivery flexibility?'

Answering these questions means judging two sets of opposing factors – those which give the *potential to improve performance*, and those which *work against this potential being realized*.

Vertical integration affects quality

As far as *quality* is concerned, the potential benefits of vertical integration derive from the closeness of the operation to its customers and its suppliers. The origins of any quality problems are usually easier to trace through 'in-house' operations than through outside suppliers, and the subsequent quality problem-solving activity can be concentrated at the most appropriate point in the network. Acting against this is the danger that in-house operations, which are freed from the discipline of a true commercial relationship, will have less incentive to co-operate in quality improvement if there is no real possibility of their losing the business of their captive customers.

Vertical integration affects speed

As far as *delivery speed* is concerned, vertically integrated operations can mean a closer synchronization of schedules which speeds up the throughput of materials and information along the network. In addition, being close to suppliers and customers can help forecasting. This reduces the risk of creating products or services for which demand never materializes. Again these potential advantages can be eroded if guaranteed 'in-house' demand means that the 'in-house' customers get low priority compared with 'proper' outside customers who can take their business elsewhere.

Vertical integration affects dependability

As far as *dependability* is concerned, improved communications along a vertically integrated network which can give better forecasts can also result in more realistic delivery promises. Even when internal hold-ups mean that deliveries will be missed, in-house suppliers might be more likely to give notice of the problem so that it can be communicated to the customer. All of which again assumes that the relationship between vertically integrated links in the network will indeed receive a high priority rather than being overlooked in favour of customers who can trade with competitors if they are not satisfied with the service they receive.

Vertical integration affects flexibility

As far as *new product flexibility* is concerned, vertical integration gives the potential to guide technological developments as well as deny them to competitors. Forward vertical integration gives the potential for products and services to be developed specifically and more precisely to customer needs. The danger is that, if management attention is spread too thinly along a vertically integrated network, opportunities to exploit structural links are missed through dissipation of attention. As far as *volume and delivery flexibility* are concerned, the ownership of suppliers can give the potential to dictate volume changes to match downstream fluctuations, as well as helping to expedite specific orders through the network. Against this there can be a reluctance to inflict volume changes on in-house suppliers and customers. It is sometimes easier to be commercially realistic with independent companies.

Vertical integration affects costs

As far as *cost* is concerned, vertically integrated operations can provide the potential for sharing some costs, research and development or logistics, for example. Over the longer term vertical integration can also allow capacity, and therefore capacity utilization, to be balanced. Perhaps more significantly, if margins are high in supplier operations, it allows integrated companies to capture the profits which would otherwise be lost, and reduce the costs of bought-in parts or services. This assumes that other customers of a newly acquired supplier will be content to continue doing business with it. If they are not, demand could fall and therefore unit costs increase. Even if demand does keep at the same level, there is the question of whether a management now concerned with more separate businesses will be as concerned with keeping costs low as one which is concentrating on keeping its customers.

THE LOCATION OF CAPACITY

After deciding on the overall shape of its operations network through vertical integration decisions, an organization must choose the location of each operation. Location is the geographical positioning of an operation relative to the input resources, other operations or customers with which it interacts. Not all operations can logically justify their location. Some are where they are for historical reasons. Yet even the operations who are 'there because they're there' are implicitly making a decision not to move. Presumably their assumption is that the cost and disruption involved in changing location would outweigh any potential benefits of a new location.

The importance of location

It was reputedly Lord Sieff, the boss of Marks & Spencer, the UK-based retail organization, who said,

'There are three important things in retailing – location, location and location.'

Any retailing operation knows exactly what he meant. Get the location wrong, and it can have a significant impact on profits. In retailing a difference in location of a few metres can make the difference between profit and loss. The location decision is also important in other types of operation. For example, mislocating a fire service station can slow down the average journey time of the fire crews in getting to the fires; locating a factory where there is difficulty attracting labour with appropriate skills will affect the effectiveness of the factory's operations, and so on. In other words, location decisions will usually have an effect on an operation's costs as well as its ability to serve its customers (and therefore its revenues). The other reason why location decisions are important is that, once taken, they are difficult to undo. The costs of moving an operation from one site to another can be hugely expensive and the risks of inconveniencing customers very high. No operation wants to move very often.

Reasons for location decisions

There are two categories of stimuli which cause organizations to make location decisions:

- changes in *demand* for goods and services;
- changes in *supply* of inputs to the operation.

Location decisions prompted by demand changes are often due to increases or decreases in the aggregated volume of demand. For example, increased demand for a clothing manufacturer's products may necessitate more capacity. The company could either expand its existing site or, alternatively, if the site could not accommodate a larger facility, it could choose a larger site in another location. A third option would be to keep its existing plant and find a second location for an additional plant. Two of these options will involve a location decision.

High-contact, customer-processing operations often do not have the choice of expanding on the same site to meet rising demand. For example, if a company which offers a one-hour photo-processing service is so successful that it wants to expand its activities, enlarging its existing site would only bring in marginally more business. The company offers a local, and therefore convenient, service. Part of the way it competes is by having a location close to its customers. Finding a new location for an additional operation is probably its only option for expansion.

Changes in the cost, or availability, of the supply of inputs to the operation is the other reason for making the location decision. For example, a mining or oil company will need

DISNEYLAND PARIS[5]

From the point of view of the Walt Disney Corporation, the decision to invest in Disneyland Paris was one of the most important location decisions it had ever made. In effect the decision was in two parts. First, should Disney open one of its famous and highly successful theme parks in Europe at all? Second, if so, where in Europe should it be located?

The decision to repeat in Europe the formula which had been successful for Disney in California and Florida was influenced partly by its experiences in Japan. Tokyo Disneyland, officially opened in 1983, had been a tremendous success right from the time of its opening. It had caught the Japanese trend towards more leisure spending and appealed to the Japanese taste for American popular culture. It also allowed Japanese customers to sample the Disney experience without the expense and trouble of travelling to the US. In Europe, however, there was already a well-established market in holidays to Florida which took in Disney and other theme parks. For holiday-makers in the UK especially, Florida was only slightly more expensive than travelling to, what was then called, Euro Disney, with the added benefit of better weather. There was also a difference between the Japanese view of the themes of the Disney experience and the European view. Many of the Disney stories are based on European legends. '*Why*', said some critics, '*build a fake castle on a continent full of real castles? Why build a theme park on a continent which is already a theme park?*'

If any doubts troubled Disney it overcame them. Its next decision was where in Europe to build the park. At least two sites were considered – one in Spain and one in France. The advantage of France was that it was a far more central location. The demography of Europe means that by locating its theme park 30 kilometres east of Paris puts it within relatively easy travelling distance of literally millions of potential customers. Spain is geographically less convenient. There was also an existing transport infrastructure in this part of France which was made even better by the French government as an inducement. The French government also offered Disney numerous other financial inducements, from placing low values on the land to granting tax concessions to the company.

Spain, geographically more isolated and reputedly unable to match the French government's inducements, had the critical advantage, however, of better and more predictable weather. What perhaps was not forecast at the time was the initial hostility of the French media to what some regarded as cultural imperialism. The project was called a '*cultural Chernobyl*', and described by one French critic as '*a horror made of cardboard, plastic and appalling colours; a construction of hardened chewing gum and idiotic folklore taken straight out of comic books written for obese Americans*'. Initally there were also, reportedly, some cultural issues in the recruitment and training of staff (or 'cast' as Disney calls them). Not all the European (largely French) staff were as amenable to the strict dress and behaviour codes as were their American equivalents in Disney's US locations. ■

Questions

1 Summarize what you see as the major factors influencing the Walt Disney Corporation's decision to locate near Paris.

2 What difficulties do you think the Disney Corporation must have faced in the early days of running Disneyland Paris?

3 When transferring a service operation of this type between national or regional cultures, how might the design of the operation need to change?

to relocate as the minerals it is extracting become depleted. A manufacturing company might choose to relocate its operations to a part of the world where labour costs are low, because the equivalent resources (people) in its original location have become relatively expensive. Sometimes it is the price of land which prompts a move. For example, a company might choose to move its headquarters office because the value of the land it occupies is considerably more than an alternative, equally good, location. Selling the site and moving could generate considerable funds for the company.

The objectives of the location decision

The aim of the location decision is to achieve an appropriate balance between three related objectives:

● the *spatially variable costs* of the operation (spatially variable means that something changes with geographical location);
● the *service* the operation is able to provide to its customers;
● the *revenue* potential of the operation.

In for-profit organizations the last two objectives are related. The assumption is that the better the service the operation can provide to its customers, the better will be its potential to attract custom and therefore generate revenue. In not-for-profit organizations, revenue potential might not be a relevant objective and so cost and customer service are often taken as the twin objectives of location.

In making decisions about where to locate an operation, operations managers are concerned with minimizing spatially variable costs and maximizing revenue/customer service. Location affects both of these but not equally for all types of operation. For example, with most products customers may not care very much where they were made. Moving the operation which made them is unlikely to affect the operation's revenues significantly. On the other hand, the costs of the operation will probably be very greatly affected by location.

The location decision for any operation is determined by the relative strength of supply-side and demand-side factors. Figure 6.8 illustrates some supply-side and demand-side factors. Not all will apply to every location decision made by all operations, but they give an indication of the factors which usually need to be taken into account when making location decisions.

Supply-side influences

Labour costs

The wage and other costs of employing people with particular skills can vary between different areas in any country, but are likely to be a far more significant factor when international comparisons are made. For example, Fig. 6.9 shows the wage and non-wage costs of employment for a number of countries.[6] Wage costs are fairly self-explanatory; they are the costs to the organization of paying wages directly to individual employees. Non-wage costs are the employment taxes, social security costs, holiday payments and any welfare provision which the organization has to make in order to employ people.

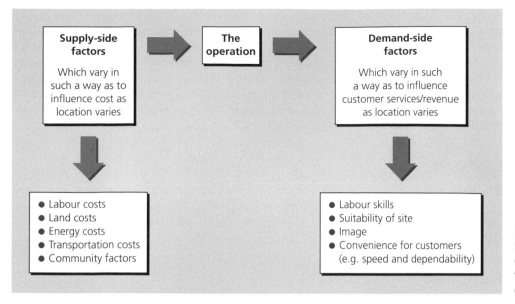

Figure 6.8
Supply-side and demand-side factors in location decisions

* Western only

Figure 6.9
Manufacturing labour costs in selected countries (1995)

The labour costs illustrated in Fig. 6.9 should be read with some caution, however. Two factors can influence them. The first is the productivity of labour. On an international level, this tends to be inversely related to labour costs. That means that generally each person can produce more in a given unit of time in the countries with higher labour costs. This effect goes some way to offset the large international variations in labour costs. The second factor is the rate of exchange of the countries' currencies. Although all costs are quoted in the same currency, exchange rates can swing considerably over time. This in turn changes relative labour costs. Yet in spite of such adjustments to the actual value of relative labour costs, they exert a major influence on the location decision, especially in some industries such as clothing where labour costs as a proportion of total costs are relatively high.

Land costs

The cost of acquiring the site itself is sometimes a relevant factor in choosing a location. Land and rental costs vary between countries and cities. At a more local level, land costs are also important. A retail operation, when choosing 'high street' sites, will pay a particular level of rent only if it believes it can generate a certain level of revenue from the site.

Energy costs

Operations which use large amounts of energy, such as aluminium smelters, can be influenced in their location decisions by the availability of relatively inexpensive energy. This may be direct, as in the availability of hydro-electric generation in an area, for example, or indirect, such as low-cost coal which can be used to generate inexpensive electricity.

Transportation costs

Transportation costs can be considered in two parts:

(a)   the cost of transporting inputs from their source to the site of the operation;
(b)   the cost of transporting goods from the site to customers.

Whereas almost all operations are concerned to some extent with (a), not all operations transport goods to customers, rather customers come to them (for example, hotels), and so are not concerned with (b). Even for operations who do transport their goods to customers (most manufacturers, for example), we consider transportation as a supply-side factor because as location changes transportation costs also change.

Proximity to sources of *supply* dominates the location decision where the cost of transporting input materials is high or difficult. Food processing and other agricultural-based activities, for example, are often carried out close to growing areas. Similarly, forestry and mining operations could only be located very close to their sources of supply. Conversely, transportation to *customers* dominates location decisions where transportation to customers is expensive or difficult. Civil engineering projects, for example, are constructed mainly where they will be needed.

Community factors

Community factors are those influences on an operation's costs which derive from the social, political and economic environment of its site. These include:

- local tax rates
- capital movement restrictions
- government financial assistance

- government planning assistance
- political stability
- local attitudes to 'inward investment'
- language
- local amenities (schools, theatres, shops, etc.)
- availability of support services
- history of labour relations
- labour absenteeism and turnover rates
- environmental restrictions and waste disposal
- planning procedures and restrictions.

Community factors can have a direct impact on the profitability of an organization. Local tax rates, for example, not surprisingly, play an important part in the location decisions of international companies. Others, such as the language spoken in the area, may not seem to have many cost consequences but can, in practice, prove very important (*see* box on Japanese inward investment).

WHY JAPAN INVESTED IN THE UK[7]

The 1990s have seen many hundreds of Japanese companies setting up operations in Europe. Manufacturing companies particularly have recognized the importance of developing a foothold in the huge European market to avoid having to add European Union import duties to the cost of their products. The largest number of these companies have chosen to locate in the UK.

Some large early arrivals, such as Nissan, were attracted to the UK by generous government-funded financial support and tax concessions in regional development areas, most of which were in areas of high unemployment, yet with a tradition of industrial activity. They recognized that although potential employees did not necessarily have the skills needed to make their products, they were willing to be trained, and did not come with any 'bad habits' picked up from similar employment. Later arrivals had much fewer direct financial incentives to come to the UK, but saw the other advantages gained by the early arrivals. In some areas, such as Telford and Milton Keynes, a critical mass of Japanese companies developed, creating a flow of good publicity back to Japan, and encouraging further interest in these locations. This success was reinforced by a growth in support infrastructure, such as Japanese schools, social activities, and even food retailing to help the expatriate families feel at home.

Another important factor was language. Many Japanese manufacturing companies are accustomed to trading and producing in the US, and so the English language is the first foreign language of most business people. Drawings of products and processes, instruction sheets and computer programs were often immediately available for use without further translation for the UK. This meant a lower risk of misunderstandings and mistranslation, smoothing communications between the new plant and head office in Japan.

As Japanese corporations became aware of some of the early successes in the UK, it became apparent that both the quality and cost of labour was an important reason to locate in the UK. While many large indigenous manufacturing companies had been criticizing the educational standard of the workforce, Japanese companies took great care to select employees who were keen to learn, adaptable, willing to work hard, and able to create improvements. Some companies were able to quote exceptionally high levels of productivity and quality

▶

performance in the UK, as an example to their Japanese workforce. Others began to export products from the UK to Japan. At the same time, the total cost of labour in the UK was relatively low, both due to hourly wage rates significantly below those typically paid in some other European Union countries, but also because of low costs directly associated with labour, such as state insurance and sickness benefit. Other significant reasons for a choice of the UK have been the relatively low rate of corporation tax, good communication links with most parts of the world, and a stable political and social system that doesn't create too many surprises.

The development planning process is (as in most advanced economies) cumbersome, but at least it is transparent and difficulties of bribery and protection do not usually arise.

There are also other underlying factors which cannot be discounted. The UK is renowned for its excellent golf courses; spacious housing is available in countryside near industrial development areas; and London is known for its excellent shopping and leisure facilities. The climate, although not the kindest in Europe, is temperate and the rainfall is not unlike that in Japan. ■

Questions

1 Summarize what you see as being the major factors which favoured the UK in attracting inward investment from Japan.

2 Nissan, Toyota and Honda all now have plants in the UK. What factors do you think will influence whether these plants expand or not?

Demand-side influences

Labour skills

The abilities of a local labour force can have an effect on customer reaction to the products or services which the operation produces. For example, 'science parks' are usually located close to universities because they hope to attract companies who are interested in using the skills available at the university. Those companies who located at the Cambridge Science Park in the UK did so because they believed that the intellectual talent and atmosphere of the area would result in their producing better products and services.

The suitability of the site itself

Different sites are likely to have different intrinsic characteristics which can affect an operation's ability to serve customers and generate revenue. For example, the location of a luxury resort hotel which offers up-market holiday accommodation (such as the one described in the case exercise in Chapter 2) is very largely dependent on the intrinsic characteristics of the site. Located next to the beach, surrounded by waving palm trees and overlooking a picturesque bay, the hotel is very attractive to its customers. Move it a few kilometres away into the centre of an industrial estate, and it rapidly loses its attraction.

Image of the location

Some locations are firmly associated in customers' minds with a particular image. Suits from Savile Row (the centre of the up-market bespoke tailoring district in London) may be no better than high-quality suits made elsewhere but, by locating its operation there, a tailor has probably enhanced its reputation and therefore its revenue. The product and fashion design houses of Milan and the financial services in the City of London's 'square mile' also enjoy a reputation shaped partly by that of their location.

Convenience for customers

Of all the demand-side factors this is, for many operations, the most important. Locating a general hospital, for instance, in the middle of the countryside may have many advantages for its staff and even maybe for its costs, but it clearly would be very inconvenient to its customers. Those visiting the hospital would need to travel long distances. Those being attended to in an emergency would have to wait longer than necessary to be brought in for admission. Because of this, general hospitals are located close to centres of demand. Similarly with other public services, location has a significant effect on the ability of the operation to serve its customers effectively. Likewise with restaurants, stores, banks, petrol filling stations and many other high customer contact operations, location determines the effort to which customers have to go in order to use the operation.

Levels of the location decision

The location decision is usually presented at three levels:

- choosing the region/country in which to locate the operation;
- choosing the area of the country or region;
- choosing the specific site within the area.

Choosing the region or country

Increasingly the location decision in many larger companies is taken with the whole world offering possible locations. While it has always been possible to manufacture in one part of the world in order to sell in another, until recently non-manufacturing operations were assumed to be confined to their home market. But no longer; the operational skills (as well as the brand image) of many service operations are transferable across national boundaries. Companies such as Novotel hotels, McDonald's restaurants, Benetton clothing shops and Andersens (the accountants), make location decisions on an international stage. Similarly, information processing operations can now locate outside their immediate home base, thanks to sophisticated telecommunications networks. If a bank sees a cost advantage in locating part of its back-office operation in a part of the world where the 'cost per transaction' is lower, it can do so. The keyboard operators, computer service managers and computer programmers of Stockholm, Frankfurt and London are now often competing directly with those in Delhi, Kuala Lumpur and Seoul.

Choosing an area within the country or region

Once an organization has decided in which country it wishes to locate, it will then need to choose an area of the country. Many of the factors which went into deciding the country will also play a part in deciding the area. Political stability and language might be less of an issue. Land prices, the local labour force, infrastructural development and community factors can play an important part, however.

Choosing a site

The choice of a site within an area is a different type of decision to those taken at the two 'higher' levels. Usually the number of alternatives is far smaller. At any time there may be just one available site, and the decision is whether to take it or not. If not, the search for an acceptable site will continue.

The factors used to accept or reject a site are usually concerned with the characteristics of the specific site and its immediate surroundings. For example, the shape of the site and its soil composition can limit the nature of any buildings erected on the site. The access to any site by road or rail, so that materials and goods can be shipped conveniently in and out of the site, is also likely to be important. Similarly, the availability of utilities, drains and waste-disposal facilities will need to be taken into account. More difficult to judge can be the capability of the site to fit in with future developments in the operation. Room for expansion, for example, might be an issue, so the ability to lease or buy land close by or adjacent to the site could be important.

Location techniques

Although operations managers must exercise considerable judgement in the choice of alternative locations, there are some systematic and quantitative techniques which can help the decision process. We describe two here – the weighted-score method and the centre-of-gravity method.

Weighted-score method

The procedure involves, first of all, identifying the criteria which will be used to evaluate the various locations. Second, it involves establishing the relative importance of each criterion and giving weighting factors to them. Third, it means rating each location according to each criterion. The scale of the score is arbitrary. In our example we shall use 0 to 100, where 0 represents the worst possible score and 100 the best.

Example

An Irish company which prints and makes specialist packaging materials for the pharmaceutical industry has decided to build a new factory somewhere in the Benelux countries so as to provide a speedy service for its customers in continental Europe. In order to choose a site it has decided to evaluate all options against a number of criteria. These criteria are:

- the cost of the site;
- the rate of local property taxation;
- the availability of suitable skills in the local labour force;

- the the site's access to the motorway network;
- the site's access to the airport;
- the potential of the site for future expansion.

After consultation with its property agents the company identifies three sites which seem to be broadly acceptable. These are known as sites A, B and C. The company also investigates each site and draws up the weighted-score table shown in Table 6.1. It is important to remember that the scores shown in Table 6.1 are those which the manager has given as an indication of how each site meets the company's needs specifically. Nothing is necessarily being implied regarding any intrinsic worth of the locations. Likewise, the weightings are an indication of how important the company finds each criterion in the circumstances it finds itself. The 'value' of a site for each criterion is then calculated by multiplying its score by the weightings for each criterion.

Table 6.1 Weighted-score method for the three sites

Criteria	Importance weighting	Scores Sites		
		A	B	C
Cost of the site	4	80	65	60
Local taxes	2	20	50	80
Skills availability	1	80	60	40
Access to motorways	1	50	60	40
Access to airport	1	20	60	70
Potential for expansion	1	75	40	55
Total weighted scores		585	580	605[*]

[*]Preferred option

For location A, its score for the 'cost-of-site' criterion is 80 and the weighting of this criterion is 4, so its value is $80 \times 4 = 320$. All these values are then summed for each site to obtain its total weighted score.

Table 6.1 indicates that location C has the highest total weighted score and therefore would be the preferred choice. It is interesting to note, however, that location C has the lowest score on what is, by the company's own choice, the most important criterion – cost of the site. The high total weighted score which location C achieves in other criteria, however, outweighs this deficiency. If, on examination of this table, a company cannot accept what appears to be an inconsistency, then either the weights which have been given to each criterion, or the scores that have been allocated, do not truly reflect the company's preference.

The centre-of-gravity method

The centre-of-gravity method is used to find a location which minimizes transportation costs. It is based on the idea that all possible locations have a 'value' which is the sum of all transportation costs to and from that location. The best location, the one which minimizes costs, is represented by what in a physical analogy would be the

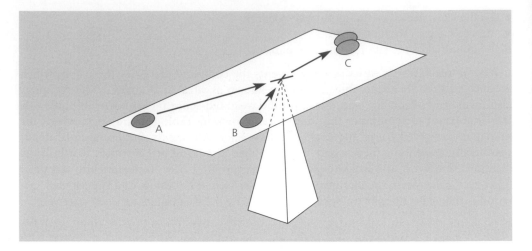

**Figure 6.10
The centre-of-
gravity method**

weighted centre of gravity of all points to and from which goods are transported. So, for example, in Fig. 6.10 two suppliers, each sending 20 tonnes of parts per month to a factory, are located at points A and B. The factory must then assemble these parts and send them to one customer located at point C. Since point C receives twice as many tonnes as points A and B (transportation cost is assumed to be directly related to the tonnes of goods shipped) then it has twice the weighting of points A or B. The lowest transportation cost location for the factory is at the centre of gravity of a (weightless) board where the two suppliers' and one customer's locations are represented to scale and have weights equivalent to the weightings of the number of tonnes they send or receive.

Example

A company which operates four out-of-town garden centres has decided to keep all its stocks of products in a single warehouse. Each garden centre, instead of keeping large stocks of products, will fax its orders to the warehouse staff who will then deliver replenishment stocks to each garden centre as necessary.

The location of each garden centre is shown on the map in Fig. 6.11. A reference grid is superimposed over the map. The centre-of-gravity co-ordinates of the lowest cost location for the warehouse, $\bar{x}$ and $\bar{y}$, are given by the formulae:

$$\bar{x} = \frac{\sum x_i V_i}{\sum V_i}$$

and

$$\bar{y} = \frac{\sum y_i V_i}{\sum V_i}$$

where

x_i = the x co-ordinate of source or destination i

y_i = the y co-ordinate of source or destination i

V_i = the amount to be shipped to or from source or destination i.

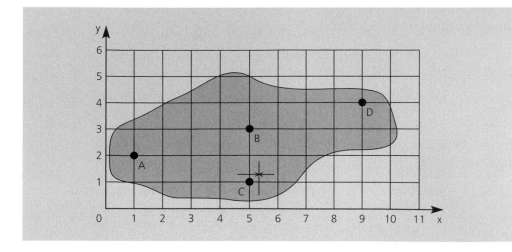

Figure 6.11
Centre-of-gravity location for the garden centre warehouse

Each of the garden centres is of a different size and has different sales volumes. In terms of the number of truck loads of products sold each week, Table 6.2 shows the sales of the four centres.

Table 6.2 The weekly demand levels (in truck loads) at each of the four garden centres

	Sales per week (truck loads)
Garden centre A	5
Garden centre B	10
Garden centre C	12
Garden centre D	8
Total	35

In this case

$$\bar{x} = \frac{(1 \times 5) + (5 \times 10) + (5 \times 12) + (9 \times 8)}{35}$$

$$= 5.34$$

and

$$\bar{y} = \frac{(2 \times 5) + (3 \times 10) + (1 \times 12) + (4 \times 8)}{35}$$

$$= 1.14$$

So the minimum cost location for the warehouse is at point (5.34, 1.14) as shown in Fig. 6.11. That is, at least, theoretically. In practice, the optimum location might also be influenced by other factors such as the transportation network. So if the

FOUR LOCATION DECISIONS[8]

In practice companies are driven by a whole variety of motives when they make their location decisions. Here are four which illustrate a diversity of operations objectives.

In 1994 the Ford Motor Company embarked on one of its most radical reorganizations on a world-wide scale. Part of its plan was to establish five vehicle programme centres (VPCs). Each VPC was to take responsibility for the design of a particular type of vehicle world-wide. The idea of forming these five VPCs was to avoid costly duplication of design and development effort. For example, the Ford Escort launched in the early 1990s had been developed separately for the US and European markets. Although both cars were of almost the same dimensions and aimed at very similar parts of their respective markets, entirely unrelated versions were built in the US and Europe. Ford figured that locating all design and development of each class of vehicle in one place would prevent this kind of waste. The location of its five VPCs was based on which part of its organization had the greater experience and expertise. For example, the European VPC would take world-wide responsibility for the design, development and engineering of all of Ford's small and medium front-wheel-drive cars. North America by contrast had the greater experience in larger cars, trucks, higher displacement engines and automatic transmission.

The Polish government has been engaged in its strategy of returning formerly state-owned industries into private hands. One industry in particular has attracted considerable interest and investment from western companies. The country's car- and truck-making capacity was the focus of attention from such car giants as Fiat, PSA (Peugeot and Citroen), Ford, Volvo, General Motors, Mercedes-Benz, and Volkswagen. The cause of all this interest was only partially due to Poland's lower manufacturing costs (anyway, exports from Poland were sometimes restricted: for example, the European Union allowed only a certain number of models to be imported free of its 30 per cent customs duty). The car companies were playing a longer game. They had in mind the potential growth in the East European market in the medium to long term. When Fiat bought 90 per cent of the former state-held FSM car maker based in Bielsko-Biola in Southern Poland, it was not only investing in the experience and under-utilized resources of the company, it was seeing its investment as a longer-term gateway to other East European markets.

When Hyundai moved its personal computer operations to America its market share had shifted from 5 per cent in the late '80s down to 1.5 per cent in the '90s. It seems, therefore, an unusual decision to move to a country with higher labour and accommodation costs. In fact, Hyundai reckoned that the increased costs were more than offset by savings in time and inventories. When it manufactured in Korea its goods used to take two months to reach the US, after which its sales operations used to hold the stocks for around three months of sales. After the move the amount of stock was reduced to less than a third and responsiveness to market trends was enhanced by being far closer to the market itself. Also, product development time, which had been between 12 and 18 months, was reduced to five months after the move.

In 1994 the domestic appliance manufacturer Hoover (owned by the American Maytag Corporation) closed its French vacuum cleaner manufacturing operation and relocated production to its Scottish plant. The decision was primarily influenced by cost of manufacture. The company had figured that, to remain competitive in its global business, all vacuum cleaner production for Europe should be concentrated on a single plant in order to gain economies of scale. Hoover's workers in Scotland were also paid lower wages than their French counterparts. Furthermore, non-wage costs such as health insurance were a much lower percentage of overall costs in Britain than they were in France. Reportedly, the company also believed that the workforce in its Scottish plant had demonstrated more flexibility in adapting to new working methods, which would help it to keep manufacturing costs down in the future. ∎

Questions

1 For each of these four location decisions, rank what you think are the main factors which influenced the location decision.

2 What do you think the companies described in each of these four location decisions were trying to improve and why?

3 In the decision by the Ford Motor Company to establish vehicle programme centres, do you think the factors influencing the location of design centres are different from those that influence the location of manufacturing operations?

optimum location was at a point with poor access to a suitable road or at some other unsuitable location (in a residential area, or the middle of a lake, for example) then the chosen location will need to be adjusted. The technique does go some way, however, towards providing an indication of the area in which the company should be looking for sites for its warehouse.

LONG-TERM CAPACITY MANAGEMENT

After the vertical integration of the operation's network and the location of its various operations have been decided, the next set of decisions concerns the size or capacity of each part of the network. Here we shall treat capacity in a general long-term sense. The specific issues involved in measuring and adjusting capacity in the medium and short terms are examined in Chapter 11.

The optimum capacity level

Most organizations need to decide on the size (in terms of capacity) of each of their facilities. An air-conditioning unit company, for example, might operate plants each of which has a capacity (at normal product mix) of 800 units per week. At activity levels below this, the average cost of producing each unit will increase because the fixed costs of the factory are being covered by fewer units produced. Figure 6.12 illustrates the theoretical cost curve for the factory. The total production costs of the factory have some elements which are fixed – they will be incurred irrespective of how much,

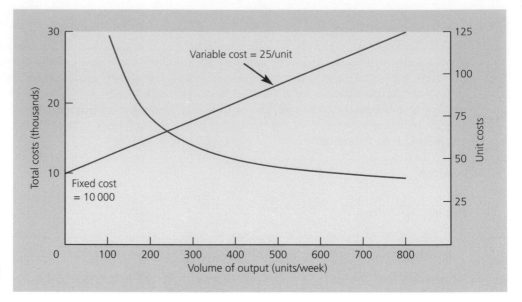

Figure 6.12
Unit cost of output varies as volume of output varies

or little, the factory produces. The slope of the total cost line in Fig. 6.12 represents the variable cost per unit produced – that is, the costs incurred by the factory for each unit it produces. Dividing the total cost at any output level by the output level itself gives the average cost of producing units at that output rate.

The average cost of producing the units seems to reach its lowest point at maximum capacity. However, the actual average cost curve may be different from that shown in Fig. 6.12 for a number of reasons:

● All fixed costs are not incurred at one time as the factory starts to operate. Rather they occur at many points (called fixed cost 'breaks') as volume increases. This makes the theoretically smooth average cost curve more discontinuous.
● Production levels may be increased above the theoretical capacity of the plant, by using prolonged overtime, for example, or temporarily sub-contracting some parts of the work.
● There may be less obvious cost penalties of operating the plant at levels close to or above its nominal capacity. For example, long periods of overtime may reduce productivity levels as well as costing more in extra payments to staff; operating plant for long periods with reduced maintenance time may increase the chances of breakdown, and so on. This usually means that average costs start to increase after a point which will often be lower than the theoretical capacity of the plant.

Figure 6.13 illustrates how the actual (smoothed) average cost curve might look for the 800-unit-a-week plant.

A similar relationship occurs between the average cost curves for plants of increasing size. Figure 6.14 illustrates a series of average cost curves. At first, as the nominal capacity of the plants increases, the lowest cost points reduce. There are two main reasons for this:

● The fixed costs of an operation do not increase proportionately as its capacity increases. An 800-unit plant has less than twice the fixed costs of a 400-unit plant.
● The capital costs of building the plant do not increase proportionately to its capacity. An 800-unit plant costs less to build than twice the cost of a 400-unit plant.

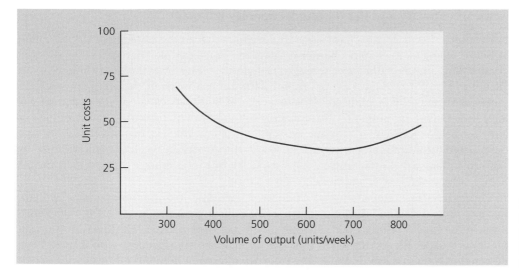

Figure 6.13
Unit costs of output allowing for diseconomies of scale

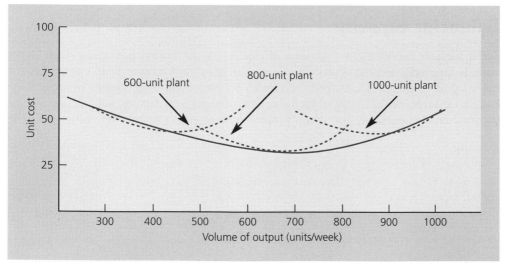

Figure 6.14
Unit cost of output curves for plants of varying capacities

These two factors, taken together, are often referred to as *economies of scale*. However, above a certain size, the lowest cost point may increase. In the illustration in Fig. 6.14 this happens with plants above 800 units capacity. This occurs because of what are called the *diseconomies of scale*, two of which are particularly important:

● Transportation costs can be high for large operations. For example, if a manufacturer supplies the whole of its European market from one major plant in Denmark, all supplies may have to be brought from several countries to the single plant and all products shipped from there throughout Europe.

● Complexity costs increase as size increases. The communications and co-ordination effort necessary to manage an operation tends to increase faster than capacity. Although not seen as a direct cost, this can nevertheless be very significant.

Scale of capacity and the demand–capacity balance

Large units of capacity also have some disadvantages when the capacity of the operation is being changed to match changing demand. For example, suppose that the air-conditioning unit manufacturer forecasts demand increase over the next three years as shown in Fig. 6.15, to level off at around 2400 units a week. If the company seeks to satisfy all demand by building three plants, each of 800 units capacity, the company will have substantial amounts of over-capacity for much of the period when demand is increasing. Over-capacity means low capacity utilization which in turn means higher unit costs (from the average cost curve in Fig. 6.12). If the company builds smaller plants, say 400-unit plants, there will still be over-capacity but to a lesser extent, which means higher capacity utilization and possibly lower costs.

The inherent risks of changing capacity using large increments can also be high. For example, if demand does not reach 2400 units a week but levels off at 2000 units a week, the final 800-unit plant will only be 50 per cent utilized. However, if 400-unit plants are used, the likelihood is that the over-optimistic forecast would have been detected in time to delay or cancel the final plant, leaving demand and capacity in balance (*see* Fig. 6.16).

Balancing capacity

So far we have confined our discussion of capacity to the assumption that a single operation is internally homogeneous. Yet, as we discussed in Chapter 1, all operations are made up of micro operations, and each micro operation will itself have its own capacity. So, for example, the 800-unit capacity air-conditioning unit factory not only assembles the products but probably also manufactures most of the parts from which it is made. If

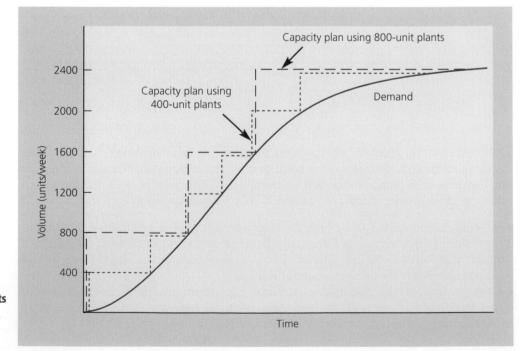

Figure 6.15 The scale of capacity increments affects the utilization of capacity

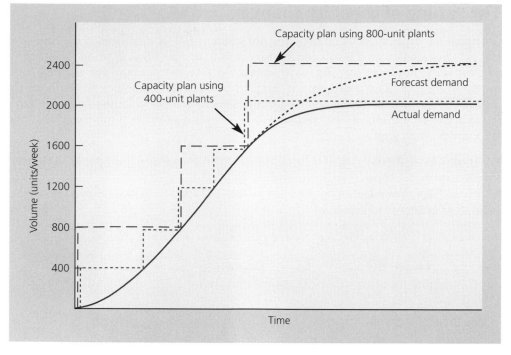

Figure 6.16
Smaller scale capacity increments allow the capacity plan to be adjusted to accommodate changes in demand

so, the capacity of the parts manufacturing section of the factory must be capable of producing parts at a rate sufficient for the assembly department to produce units at a rate of 800 per week, if the output from the whole factory is not to be reduced. Similarly, further down the network of internal operations, the air-conditioning units are moved to the warehouse after assembly, where they are packed in cases, stored and loaded on to trucks as needed. The company's fleet of trucks then distributes them to its customers.

This is a four-stage network of operations. Parts manufacturing feeds assembly which feeds the warehouse which feeds the distribution operation. For the network to operate efficiently, all its stages must have the same capacity. If they have different capacities, the capacity of the network as a whole will be limited to the capacity of its slowest link. This can be visualized as a series of pipes of different diameters, through which liquid is flowing. The throughput rate of the whole system will be limited by the pipe with the smallest diameter. Figure 6.17 illustrates this for the air-conditioning unit manufacturer. In this case the warehouse is what is called the *bottle-neck* in the supply network.

Figure 6.17
When capacity at each stage is not balanced, the capacity of the total system is limited by that of the bottle-neck stage

203

The timing of capacity change

Changing the capacity of an operation is not just a matter of deciding on the best size of a capacity increment. The operation also needs to decide when to bring 'on-stream' new capacity. For example, Fig. 6.18 shows the forecast demand for the new air-conditioning unit. The company has decided to build 400-unit-per-week plants in order to meet the growth in demand for its new product. In deciding *when* the new plants are to be introduced the company must choose a position somewhere between two extreme strategies:

● *Capacity leads demand* – timing the introduction of capacity in such a way that there is always sufficient capacity to meet forecast demand;
● *Capacity lags demand* – timing the introduction of capacity so that demand is always equal to or greater than capacity.

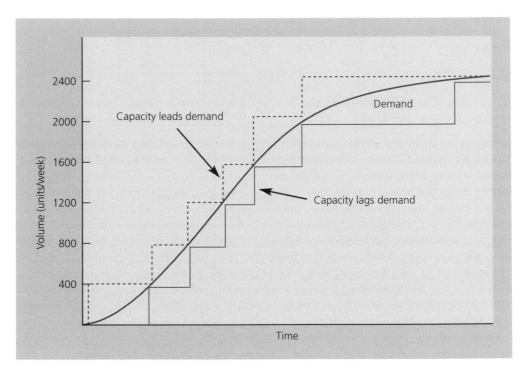

**Figure 6.18
Capacity-leading
and capacity-
lagging strategies**

Figure 6.18 shows these two extreme strategies, although in practice the company is likely to choose a position somewhere between the two extremes. Each strategy has its own advantages and disadvantages. These are shown in Table 6.3. The actual approach taken by any company will depend on how it views these advantages and disadvantages. For example, if the company's access to funds for capital expenditure is limited, it is likely to find the delayed capital expenditure requirement of the capacity-lagging strategy relatively attractive.

Table 6.3 The arguments for and against pure leading and pure lagging strategies of capacity timing

Advantages	Disadvantages
Capacity-leading strategies	
Always sufficient capacity to meet demand, therefore revenue is maximized and customers satisfied.	Utilization of the plants is always relatively low, therefore costs will be high.
Most of the time there is a 'capacity cushion' which can absorb extra demand if forecasts are pessimistic.	Risks of even greater (or even permanent) over-capacity if demand does not reach forecast levels.
Any critical start-up problems with new plants are less likely to affect supply to customers.	Capital spending on plant early.
Capacity-lagging strategies	
Always sufficient demand to keep the plants working at full capacity, therefore unit costs are minimized.	Insufficient capacity to meet demand fully, therefore reduced revenue and dissatisfied customers.
Over-capacity problems are minimized if forecasts are optimistic.	No ability to exploit short-term increases in demand.
Capital spending on the plants is delayed.	Under-supply position even worse if there are start-up problems with the new plants.

'Smoothing' with inventory

The strategy on the continuum between pure leading and pure lagging strategies can be implemented so that no inventories are accumulated. All demand in one period is satisfied (or not) by the activity of the operation in the same period. Indeed, for customer-processing operations there is no alternative to this. An hotel cannot satisfy demand in one year by using rooms which were vacant the previous year. For some materials- and information-processing operations, however, the output from the operation which is not required in one period can be stored for use in the next period. The economies of using inventories are fully explored in Chapter 12. Here we confine ourselves to noting that inventories can be used to obtain both the advantages of capacity leading and lagging.

Figure 6.19 shows how this can be done. Capacity is introduced such that demand can always be met by a combination of production and inventories, and capacity is, with the occasional exception, fully utilized.

This may seem like an ideal state. Demand is always met and so revenue is maximized. Capacity is usually fully utilized and so costs are minimized. There is a price to pay, however, and that is the cost of carrying the inventories. Not only will these have to be funded (*see* Chapter 12) but the risks of obsolescence and deterioration of stock are introduced. Table 6.4 summarizes the advantages and disadvantages of the 'smoothing-with-inventory' strategy.

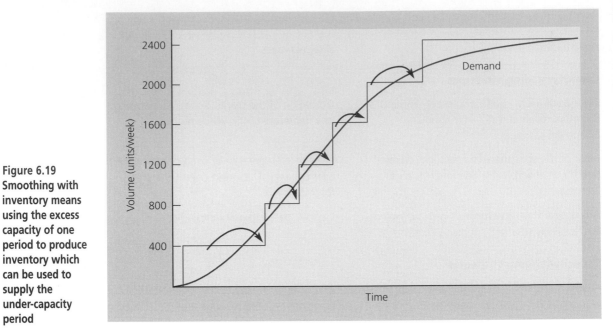

Figure 6.19 Smoothing with inventory means using the excess capacity of one period to produce inventory which can be used to supply the under-capacity period

Table 6.4 The advantages and disadvantages of a smoothing-with-inventory strategy

Advantages	Disadvantages
All demand is satisfied, therefore customers are satisfied and revenue maximized.	The cost of inventories in terms of working capital requirements can be high. This is especially serious at a time when the company requires funds for its capital expansion.
Utilization of capacity is high and therefore costs are low.	Risks of product deterioration and obsolescence.
Very short-term surges in demand can be met from inventories.	

Break-even analysis of capacity expansion

An alternative view of capacity expansion can be gained by examining the cost implications of adding increments of capacity on a break-even basis. Figure 6.20 shows how increasing capacity can move an operation from profitability to loss. Each additional unit of capacity results in a *fixed-cost break*, that is a further lump of expenditure which will have to be incurred before any further activity can be undertaken in the operation.

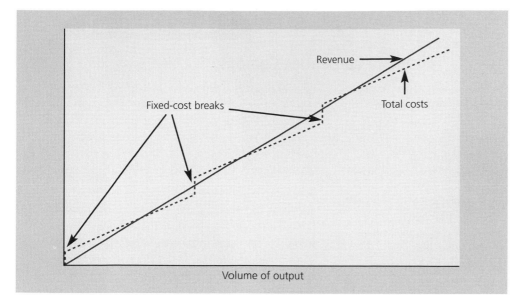

**Figure 6.20
Repeated incurring
of fixed costs can
raise total costs
above revenue**

The operation is therefore unlikely to be profitable at very low levels of output. Eventually, assuming that prices are greater than marginal costs, revenue will exceed total costs. However, the level of profitability at the point where the output level is equal to the capacity of the operation may not be sufficient to absorb all the extra fixed costs of a further increment in capacity. This could make the operation unprofitable in some stages of its expansion.

Normand Carpentier, Camoplast

In a small French-Canadian village in 1959, Joseph Armand Bombardier invented the snowmobile. The commercialization of his invention was highly successful and by 1970 it had become an important industry with more than 200 manufacturers.

In 1982, Bombardier rationalized its operations and decided to sell four of its subsidiaries to two former Bombardier executives, Normand Carpentier and Michel Lasalle. The new company, named Camoplast, was made up of subsidiaries which had previously supplied Bombardier with plastic, fibreglass, rubber components and snowmobile clothing. Says Carpentier:

'By 1989 we had managed to win new customers, reducing our dependability on Bombardier. Rockland was our largest plant and was located 30 kilometres north of Bombardier's main plant in Quebec. By 1989 the plant had diversified and was mixing its own rubber, manufacturing engine rubber mounts, snowmobile tracks and a wide variety of other moulded rubber components. However, we were having difficulties in generating profits for the company. In addition, we were having serious problems negotiating with the provincial trade union and we just couldn't see how the situation could improve. After analysing the situation carefully we decided it was time for a drastic decision.

'We decided to give up all the other rubber markets in which we had been competing and focus solely on the manufacturing of snowmobile tracks. The next step was to choose a new location for our operations. Because we were experiencing quality problems with our snowmobile tracks, it was extremely difficult to evaluate what future capacity requirements would be. We wanted a location close to our head office and close to our existing customer – Bombardier. The two alternatives considered were going either to Ontario, Canada or to a small industrial town in the US near the Canadian border.'

Carpentier was hoping that by focusing all their efforts on the manufacturing of snowmobile tracks, they could eventually leapfrog their competition in terms of quality and manufacturing cost. He also knew that going to the United States would increase the chance of getting orders from the other two most important US-based snowmobile manufacturers due to the 'buy American' campaign.

'Due to the uncertainty of future demand, we wanted to find a small plant. However, it was essential to select a location where it would be possible to expand if we turned out to be successful. Eventually the perfect plant was found in Plattsburg, New York. The location met all of our criteria and more. The 50 000 square feet plant could be expanded and was located in an industrial park with good access, and where massive layoffs had just occurred giving easy access to labour.'

Carpentier's strategy paid off. By focusing on one product only, Camoplast was able to dominate the market and went from a production of 27 000 snowmobile tracks in its first season in its new plant, to more than 200 000 in 1997. Since moving to its new facility, Camoplast has had to expand the plant three times to increase capacity. ∎

SUMMARY ANSWERS TO KEY QUESTIONS

Why should an organization take a total supply network perspective?

■ The main advantage is that it helps any operation to understand how it can compete effectively within the network. This is because a supply network approach requires operations managers to think about their suppliers and their customers *as operations*.

■ Taking a supply network perspective can also help to identify particularly significant links within the network and hence identify long-term strategic changes which will affect the operation.

■ The starting point for all these advantages is taking a broad perspective not only of the immediate supply network (that is the customers and suppliers with which an operation has immediate contact) but also of the total supply network (that is all the significant operations on the supply side and the demand side of an operation).

How much of a network should an operation own?

■ This issue is called the *vertical integration* decision and is defined by the direction of ownership, the extent of ownership and the type of relationships envisaged.

■ The direction of ownership decision refers to whether an organization wants to own the operations on its supply side (backwards integration) or on its demand side (forward integration).

■ The extent of ownership decision relates to how many of the demand-side or supply-side operations the organization wants to own.

■ The nature of the relationship decision relates to whether stages in the network involve exclusive relationships, in which each stage serves only its own in-house customers, or alternatively where each stage is free to trade with parts of the network which are not owned by the organization.

Where should an operation be located?

■ An existing operation will relocate only if the costs and disruption of moving are less than the benefits it believes it will gain from its new location.

■ The stimuli which act on an organization during the location decision can be divided into supply-side and demand-side influences. Supply-side influences are the factors such as labour, land, and utility costs which change as location changes. Demand-side influences include such things as the image of the location, its convenience for customers, and the suitability of the site itself.

■ All of the factors above can be applied (to different degrees) at three levels: the choice of a country or region, the choice of an area within a country or region, the choice of the specific site itself.

How much capacity should an operation plan to have?

■ The amount of capacity an organization will have depends on its view of current and future demand. It is when its view of future demand is different from current demand that this issue becomes important.

■ When an organization has to cope with changing demand, a number of capacity decisions need to be taken. These include choosing the optimum capacity for each site, balancing the various capacity levels of the operation in the network, and timing the changes in the capacity of each part of the network.

■ Important influences on these decisions include the concepts of economy and diseconomy of scale, supply flexibility if demand is different from that forecast, and the profitability and cash-flow implications of capacity timing changes.

CASE EXERCISE

Delta Synthetic Fibres[9]

DSF is a small but technically successful company in the man-made fibre industry. The company is heavily dependent on the sales of Britlene, a product it developed itself, which accounted in 1996 for some 95 per cent of total sales.

Britlene is used mainly in heavy-duty clothing, although small quantities are used to produce industrial goods such as tyre cord and industrial belting. Its main properties are very high wear resistance, thermal and electrical insulation.

In 1996 the company developed a new product, Britlon. Britlon had all the properties of Britlene but was superior in its heat-resistant qualities. It was hoped that this additional property would open up new clothing uses (e.g. a substitute for mineral wool clothing, added to night-wear to improve its inflammability), and new industrial uses in thermal and electrical insulation.

By late 1996 the major technical and engineering problems associated with bulk production of Britlon seemed to have been solved and the company set up a working party to put forward proposals on how the new product should be phased into the company's activities.

The basic production method of Britlene and Britlon is similar to that of most man-made fibres. To make a man-made fibre, an oil-based organic chemical is polymerized (a process of joining several molecules into a long chain) in conditions of intense pressure and heat, often by the addition of a suitable catalyst. This polymerization takes place in large autoclaves (an industrial pressure cooker). The polymer is then extruded (forced through a nozzle like the rose of a garden watering can), rapidly cooled and then either spun onto cones or collected in bales.

The raw materials for Britlene and Britlon are produced at Teeside in the UK.

Britlene facilities

Britlene is produced at three factories in the UK: Teeside, Bradford and Dumfries. The largest site is Teeside with three plants. There is one plant at each of the other two sites.

All five production plants have a design capacity of 5.5 million kg per year of Britlene. However, after allowing for maintenance and an annual shutdown, expected output is 5 million kg per year. Each plant operates on a 24-hours-per-day, seven-days-per-week basis.

Proposed Britlon facilities

Britlon's production process is very similar to that used for Britlene but a totally new type of polymerization unit is needed prior to the extrusion stage.

DSF approached Alpen Engineering Company, an international chemical plant construction company, for help on a large-scale plant design of the new unit. Together they produced and tested an acceptable design.

Acquiring Britlon capacity

There are two ways of acquiring Britlon capacity. DSF could convert a Britlene plant, or it could construct an entirely new plant.

For a conversion, the new polymer unit would need to be constructed first. When complete it would be connected to the extrusion unit which would require minor conversion. At least two years would be needed either to build a new Britlon plant or to convert an old Britlene plant to Britlon production.

The company Chief Executive Officer was quoted as saying:

'*The creation of an entirely new site would increase the complexities of multi-site operation to an unacceptable level. Conversely, the complete closure of one of the three existing sites is, I consider, a waste of the manpower and physical resources that we have invested in that location. I believe expansion could take place at one, two or all of the existing sites.*'

Table 6.5 Forecast sales for Britlene and Britlon (millions of kg per year)

Potential sales	Britlene	Britlon
1996(actual)	24.7	–
1997	22	–
1998	20	–
1999	17	3 (assuming availability)
2000	13	16
2001	11	27
2002	10	29

Only on Teeside is there higher than average general unemployment, but the unemployment rate for skilled and semi-skilled workers is quite low at all sites. Demand for skilled labour on Teeside is from two giant companies, both of whom are expanding in that area; at Dumfries and Bradford there is little or no competition.

Demand

Demand forecasts for the two products are shown in Table 6.5. They show that, although Britlene sales will probably fall rapidly once Britlon is introduced, there is likely to be a residual level of sales of the older product. ■

Questions

1 What order schedule would you propose for conversions and new plant?

2 In which locations would you make these capacity changes?

3 What criteria have you used to make your recommendations?

4 What do you see as the main dangers facing DSF as it changes its capacity over the next five or six years?

DISCUSSION QUESTIONS

1 Talk to an operations manager and then construct a diagram depicting the organization's supply network. How is the performance of suppliers monitored?

2 Why should operations managers be concerned with the whole network? Illustrate your answer using an organization of your own choice.

3 Explain what is meant by vertical integration. Explain how and why upstream and downstream integration might be used by a Mediterranean-based sailing holiday company.

4 Most organizations could, if they wished, choose to reduce the extent of their vertical integration. For the following operations, which activities do you think the organization could sub-contract out if it wished to focus more on its primary activity of serving customers:

a public library
a sports complex
a fast-food restaurant
a bank?

5 Oil companies are some of the most integrated companies in the world. For a large oil company, such as BP or Shell, draw the supply network from raw materials through to the end customers. Which of the activities you have drawn in the network do you think a company like Shell is involved in? Why do you think such companies are so vertically integrated?

6 An aluminium extrusion company, part of a large integrated aluminium company, has traditionally been engaged in extruding aluminium sections for use in the construction of double-glazed windows. However, the fashion in double-glazed windows has recently moved from aluminium towards a combination of aluminium and UPVC (a polymer). Currently all the aluminium which the extrusion company buys in comes from other parts of the integrated company. Do you think the extrusion company should continue to extrude aluminium sections and provide demand for the other parts of the company, in spite of the changes in its own markets? Alternatively, should the company pursue its own interests and begin extruding aluminium/UPVC combined sections, which it would appear the market wants?

7 A research company has decided to set up a new laboratory in Australia to provide analysis services for mineral extraction companies. Table 6.6, overleaf, shows the three locations it is considering and the criteria which it is using to make the decision. If the first two factors are twice as important as the rest, which location do you think is most suitable for the new laboratory?

8 A Hong Kong company specializing in the manufacture of garden furniture has decided to establish a distribution centre in Europe. The possible locations are Birmingham, Amsterdam and Belgrade. Several criteria have been scored out of 100 (see Table 6.7).

Table 6.6 Scoring for three locations (scores out of 100)

Factor	Perth	Sydney	Darwin
Closeness to customers	80	50	90
Closeness to universities	70	90	20
Attractiveness of city	70	90	50
Climate	60	80	60
Schools	70	80	60
Housing costs	60	20	100
Availability of sites	70	50	100

Table 6.7 Scoring for three locations

Factor	Birmingham	Amsterdam	Belgrade
Cost of land	60	50	80
Distribution costs	15	70	60
Expected annual labour turnover	30	30	70
Housing availability	60	20	75
Market access	50	60	55
Expansion possibilities	70	20	80

The Managing Director considers the cost of land and the distribution costs to be three times as important as labour turnover and housing availability, and twice as important as the market access and expansion possibilities. Which location should the company adopt?

9 Join with a colleague and assess the location of two or three competing services; for example, supermarkets, dentists or car repair garages. Undertake your assessment individually then compare your results and identify and try to reconcile the differences in ratings and criteria. Are there any other performance criteria that compensate for any organization's poor location?

10 The Vegocream Corporation has decided to extend its operations from North America to Europe. The company retails its extensive range of vegetable-flavoured ice-creams through its high street outlets, where it caters for sit-down customers as well as take-away business. What decisions do you think the Vegocream company will have to take in planning its locations strategy? Draw up a series of questions which you think might be useful to the company when it decides whether to take up the lease on a particular site when it is offered.

11 Location is always considered of particular importance in retail operations. Why do you think this is so?

12 A company which assembles garden furniture obtains its components from three suppliers. Supplier A provides all the boxes and packaging material; supplier B provides all metal components; supplier C provides all plastic components. Supplier A sends one truck load of the materials per week to the factory and is located at the position (1,1) on a grid reference which covers the local area. Supplier B sends four truck loads of components per week to the factory and is located at point (2,3) on the grid. Supplier C sends three truck loads of components per week to the factory and is located at point (4,3) on the grid. After assembly, all the products are sent to a warehouse which is located at point (5,1) on the grid. Assuming there is little or no waste generated in the process, where should the company locate its factory so as to minimize transportation costs? Assume that transportation costs are directly proportional to the number of truck loads of parts, or finished goods, transported per week.

13 What is meant by capacity? What input and output measures of capacity might be used for the following operations and explain which one is more likely to be used:
    car plant
    bus company
    water company
    chiropodist?

14 The forecast demand for a new product over the next seven periods is as shown in Table 6.8. The company is deciding the timing of its capacity expansion and contraction strategy. If the company has decided to build plants with a capacity of 15 000 units per period, when would you recommend the company commissions, or takes out of commission, its plants, assuming that:

(a) it adopts a capacity-leading strategy; or
(b) it adopts a capacity-lagging strategy?

Table 6.8 Forecast demand

Period	Demand
1	10 000
2	30 000
3	50 000
4	60 000
5	64 000
6	62 000
7	55 000

15 A solicitor, although not as yet working as much as he would like, wishes to treble the size of his practice over the next five years. Explain how this might be achieved and the advantages and disadvantages of leading or lagging demand.

16 Why should the timing of capacity expansion affect the profitability of a company and its cash flow? Do you think the strategy which maximizes profitability also gives the best cash-flow performance?

NOTES ON CHAPTER

1 Jones, C. (1990) 'Cross-boundary Supply Chain Management', *Professional Engineer*, Vol 3, No 5.
2 Slack, N. (1991) *The Manufacturing Advantage*, Mercury Business Books.
3 Jones, C. (1990), *op. cit.*
4 Hayes, R.H. and Wheelwright, S.C. (1994) *Restoring our Competitive Edge*, John Wiley.
5 Sources: 'Unlucky or Unwise?', *The Financial Times*, 13 Nov 1993 and Loveman, G. 'Euro Disney: The First 100 Days', *Harvard Business School Case Study 5-093-013*.
6 Source: The Swedish Employers Confederation.
7 Sources: Pitman, J. (1994) 'Land of the Rising Sun Casts a Long Shadow', *The Times*, 7 Sept 1994, and Garner, R. (1990) 'Why Toyota Chose Derby', *The Financial Times*, 5 June 1990.
8 Sources: 'Ford Revamp Leads Europe in the Driving Seat for Small Cars', *The European*, 29 April 1994. 'Car Giant Makes Poland their Gateway to the East', *The European*, 29 April 1994. 'Gone West', *The Economist*, 11 July 1992.
9 This case is based on an original case 'Doman Synthetic Fibres' by Peter Jones of Sheffield Hallam University, UK.

SELECTED FURTHER READINGS

Bartlett, C. and Ghoshal, S. (1989) *Managing Across Borders*, Harvard Business School Press.
Blackstone, W.H. Jnr (1989) *Capacity Management*, South Western.
Bulow, J.J. (1985) 'Holding Idle Capacity to Deter Entry', *Economic Journal*, Vol 95, Mar.
Craig, C.S. *et al.* (1984) 'Models of the Retail Location Process', *Journal of Retailing*, Vol 60, No 1.
Freidenfelds, J. (1981) *Capacity Expansion*, Elsevier-North Holland.
Fuller, J.B., O'Connor, J. and Rawlinson, R. (1993) 'Tailored Logistics: The Next Advantage', *Harvard Business Review*, Vol 71, No 3.
Ghosh, A. and Craig, C.S. (1983) 'Formulating Retail Location Strategy in a Changing Environment', *Journal of Marketing*, Vol 47, Summer.
Goldhar, J.D. and Jelenek, M. (1983) 'Plan for Economies of Scope', *Harvard Business Review*, Vol 61, No 6.
Hammesfahr, R.D.J., Hope, J.A. and Ardalan, A. (1993) 'Strategic Planning for Production Capacity', *International Journal of Operations and Production Management*, Vol 13, No 5.
Hayes, R.H. and Wheelwright, S.C. (1984) *Restoring our Competitive Edge*, John Wiley.
Heinz, P. (1993) *Mutual Competitive Advantage*, Financial Times/Pitman Publishing.
Jarillo, J.C. (1993) *Strategic Networks: Creating the Borderless Organisation*, Butterworth-Heinemann.
Kanter, R.M. (1991) 'Transcending Business Boundaries, 12 000 World Managers You Change', *Harvard Business Review*, Vol 69, No 3.

Lamming, R. (1993) *Beyond Partnership: Strategies for Innovation and Lean Supply*, Prentice Hall.

Manne, A.S. (1967) *Investments for Capacity Expansion*, George Allen and Unwin.

Poirier, C.C and Reiter, S.E. (1996) *Supply Chain Optimisation*, Berrett-Koehler.

Sasser, W.E. (1976) 'Match Supply and Demand in Service Industries', *Harvard Business Review*, Vol 54, No 6.

Schmenner, R.W. (1976) 'Before You Build a Big Factory', *Harvard Business Review*, Vol 54, No 4.

Schmenner, R.W. (1982) *Making Business Location Decisions*, Prentice Hall.

Sugiura, H. (1990) 'How Honda Localises its Global Strategy', *Sloan Management Review*, Fall.

Voss, C.A. (1989) 'The Managerial Challenges of Integrated Manufacturing', *International Journal of Operations and Production Management*, Vol 9, No 3.

CHAPTER 7

LAYOUT AND FLOW

INTRODUCTION

The layout of an operation is concerned with the physical location of its transforming resources. Put simply, layout is deciding where to put all the facilities, machines, equipment and staff in the operation. Layout is one of the most obvious characteristics of an operation. It is the thing most of us would first notice on entering an operation for the first time, because it determines its 'shape' and appearance. It also determines the way in which the transformed resources – the materials, information and customers – flow through the operation. Relatively small changes in the position of a machine in a factory, or goods in a supermarket, or changing rooms in a sports centre can affect the flow of materials or people through the operation. This, in turn, can affect the costs and general effectiveness of the operation. Figure 7.1 shows the facilities layout activity in the overall model of design in operations.

Figure 7.1 **The design activities in operations management covered in this chapter**

215

THE LAYOUT PROCEDURE

There are some practical reasons why the layout decision is an important one in most operations:

● Layout is often a lengthy and difficult task because of the physical size of the transforming resources being moved.
● The re-layout of an existing operation can disrupt its smooth running, leading to customer dissatisfaction or lost production.
● If the layout (with hindsight) is wrong, it can lead to over-long or confused flow patterns, inventory of materials, customer queues building up in the operation, customers being inconvenienced, long process times, inflexible operations, unpredictable flow and high cost.

In effect there is a double pressure on the layout decision. Changing a layout can be difficult and expensive to execute, so operations managers are reluctant to do it too often. At the same time they have to get it right. The consequences of any misjudgements in an operation's layout will have a considerable, and usually long-term, effect on the operation.

Designing the layout of an operation, like any design activity, must start with an appreciation of the operation's strategic objectives. However, this is only the starting point of what is a multi-stage process which leads to the final physical layout of the operation (*see* Fig. 7.2).

Select the process type

The first decision which will need to be made was described in Chapter 4, namely the choice of *process type*. Largely, it is the volume–variety characteristics of the operation which dictate its process type. There is often some overlap, however, between the process types which can be used for a given volume–variety position. In cases where more than one process type is possible, the relative importance of the operation's performance objectives can influence the decision. Broadly speaking, the more important the cost objective is to the operation, the more likely it is to adopt the process type closer to the high volume–low variety end of the process-type spectrum.

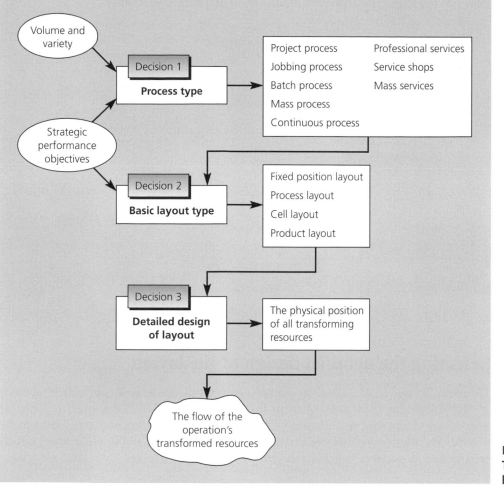

Figure 7.2
The facilities
layout decision

Select the basic layout

After the process type has been selected, the *basic layout* type needs to be selected. The basic layout type is the general form of the arrangement of the facilities in the operation.

Most practical layouts are derived from only four *basic layout types*. They are:

- fixed-position layout
- process layout
- cell layout
- product layout.

The relationship between process type and basic layout type is not totally deterministic. One process type does not necessarily imply one particular basic layout. As Table 7.1 indicates, each process type could adopt a different basic layout type.

Table 7.1 The relationship between process types and basic layout types

Selecting the detailed design of the layout

Although the choice of a basic layout type governs the general way in which facilities are arranged relative to each other, it does not precisely define the exact position of each individual part of the operation. The final stage in the layout activity is to move towards this fully specified design of the layout. There are many techniques which help to do this, some of which are described later in the chapter.

THE BASIC LAYOUT TYPES

Fixed-position layout

Fixed-position layout is in some ways a contradiction in terms since the transformed resources do not move between the transforming resources. Instead of materials, information or customers flowing through an operation, the recipient of the processing is stationary and the equipment, machinery, plant and people who do the processing move as necessary. The reasons for this could be that the product or the recipient of the service is too large to be moved conveniently, or it might be too delicate to move, or perhaps it could object to being moved.

For example:

- *Motorway construction* – The product is too large to move.
- *Open-heart surgery* – Patients are too delicate to move.
- *High-class service restaurant* – Customers would object to being moved to where food is prepared.

- *Shipbuilding* – The product is too large to move.
- *Mainframe computer maintenance* – The product is too big and probably also too delicate to move, and the customer might object to bringing it in for repair.

A construction site is typical of a fixed-position layout in that there is a limited amount of space which must be allocated to the various transforming resources. The main problem in designing this layout will be to allocate areas of the site to the various contractors so that:

- they have adequate space for their needs;
- they can receive and store their deliveries of materials;
- all contractors can have access to the part of the project on which they are working without interfering with each other's movements;
- the total movement of contractors and their vehicles and materials is minimized as far as possible.

In practice, the effectiveness of a fixed-position layout such as this will be tied up with the scheduling of access to the site and the reliability of deliveries. On most sites there is not room to allocate permanent space to every contractor who will, at some time, need access. Only the larger, more important, or longer-term contractors, are likely to warrant permanent space. Other contractors will take up space on a temporary basis. This leaves the layout vulnerable to any disruptions to the planning and control of the project (some of these issues are discussed in detail in Chapter 16). For example, if some materials are delivered early there may not be space for them in their ideal location and they will have to be stored somewhere on the site on a temporary basis. It is not uncommon for materials to be moved several times in this way before they are eventually used. This is why large, complex construction sites often appear chaotic.

Process layout

Process layout is so called because the needs and convenience of the transforming resources which constitute the processes in the operation dominate the layout decision. In process layout, similar processes (or processes with similar needs) are located together. The reason can be that it is convenient for the operation to group them together, or that the utilization of transforming resources is improved. This means that when products, information or customers flow through the operation they will take a route from process to process according to their needs. Different products or customers will have different needs and therefore take different routes through the operation. For this reason the flow pattern in the operation might be very complex.

Examples of process layouts include:

- *Hospital* – Some processes (e.g. X-ray machines and laboratories) are required by several types of patient; some processes (e.g. general wards) can achieve high staff and bed utilization.
- *Machining the parts which go into aircraft engines* – Some processes (e.g. heat treatment) need specialist support (heat and fume extraction); some processes (e.g. machining centres) require the same technical support from specialist setter–operators; some processes (e.g. grinding machines) get high machine utilization as all parts which need grinding pass through a single grinding section.

FIXED-POSITION LAYOUT AT GEC ALSTHOM COMBINED-CYCLE GENERATORS[1]

GEC Alsthom, an Anglo-French joint venture company, is one of the world's largest manufacturers of power generation and traction machinery. A growing area of its business is in the project management, manufacturing and construction of combined-cycle gas-turbine electricity generation stations. A typical project, illustrated in Fig. 7.3, is an enormous undertaking, extending over at least three years. Most of the equipment is made-to-order, very large and heavy, and manufactured to very high specification and conformance.

Almost all aspects of the site construction of a power station involve fixed-position layouts. Components and raw materials, such as concrete and steel, are brought to the point of use and are progressively incorporated into the work. Cranes, building machinery and all the specialist equipment needed for the tasks are brought to site, along with the skilled employees and contractors who each undertake specific tasks on the project.

Once most of this work is completed, the mechanical and electrical items are delivered to the site, according to a carefully prepared schedule. Some of these arrive as complete units, others as modules or kits of parts to be built up on site in their fixed positions. For example, one part of the steam turbine is made and assembled at the factory, again using a fixed-position layout, and then transported in one piece to site. A similar approach is used for the generator stator assembly which is built up on a frame in the factory.

**Combined Cycle Power Plant
VEGA 109F Single Shaft – 350 MW**

Figure 7.3 Products like this one are manufactured in a fixed-position layout
Source: Courtesy of GEC Alsthom Gas Turbines and Diesels

At one time it was normal for the whole turbine/generator to be fully assembled in a fixed position in the factory; it was then dismantled and taken to site for reassembly. This was because many of the parts had to be adjusted to fit together perfectly, and so preassembly was used to ensure that everything was correct before delivery. Now, however, improvements in design and manufacturing technologies have enabled the company to make these large components much more accurately, so that much more assembly can be done once only at the exact position required on site. This has also helped the company respond to market pressures which require much shorter lead times and lower prices. ■

Questions

1 Although the products described in this box are assembled in place using a fixed-position layout, they are not exactly one-offs. The company must have installed many of these type of machines. Do you think the nature of the layout for the installation is the same every time it installs a generator? If not, what factors at each site are likely to influence the layout?

2 Increasingly, parts of these products are assembled in the factory and transported to the site. What advantage do you think this gives the company?

● *Supermarket* – Some processes, such as the area holding tinned vegetables, are convenient to restock if grouped together. Some, such as the area holding frozen vegetables, need the common technology of freezer cabinets. Others, such as the areas holding fresh vegetables, might be together because together they can be made to look attractive to customers (vegetables on market stalls, for example).

Figure 7.4 shows a process layout in a Business School library. The various 'processes' – reference books, enquiry desk, journals, and so on – are located in different parts of the operation. The customer is free to move between the processes depending on his or her requirements. The figure also shows the route taken by one customer on one visit to the library. If the routes taken by all the customers who visited the library were superimposed on the plan, the pattern of the traffic between the various parts of the operation would be revealed. The density of this traffic flow is an important piece of information in the detailed design of this type of layout, as we shall see later in this chapter. The main point to understand at this point is that changing the location of the various processes in the library will change the pattern of flow for the library as a whole.

Cell layout

A cell layout is one where the transformed resources entering the operation are preselected (or preselect themselves) to move to one part of the operation (or cell) in which all the transforming resources, to meet their immediate processing needs, are located. The cell itself may be arranged in either a process or product (*see* next section) layout. After being processed in the cell the transformed resources may go on to another cell. In effect, cell layout is an attempt to bring some order to the complexity of flow which characterizes process layout.

Figure 7.4   An example of a process layout in a library showing the path of just one customer

Examples of cell layouts include:

● *Some computer component manufacture* – The processing and assembly of some types of computer parts may need a special area dedicated to the manufacturing of parts for one particular customer who has special requirements such as particularly high quality levels.

● *'Lunch' products area in a supermarket* – Some customers use the supermarket just to purchase sandwiches, savoury snacks, cool drinks, yoghurt, etc. for their lunch. These products are often located close together so that customers who are just buying lunch do not have to search round the store.

● *Maternity unit in a hospital* – Customers needing maternity attention are a well-defined group who can be treated together and who are unlikely to need the other facilities of the hospital at the same time that they need the maternity unit.

Although the idea of cell layout is often associated with manufacturing operations, the same principle can, and is, used in services. In Fig. 7.5 the ground floor of a department store is shown comprising displays of various types of goods in different parts of the store. In this sense the predominant layout of the store is a process layout. Each display area can be considered a separate process devoted to selling a particular class of good – shoes, clothes, books, and so on. The exception is the sports shop. This area is a

Jaeger excels at service

Photo courtesy of Jaeger

Jaeger store, Seoul, South Korea

The Daily Telegraph and British Telecom Service Quality Award

that details of garment properties or possible problems are sent to branches to maximize the advice provided to customers. Technology is also important. Electronic point-of-sale tills link to mainframe computers to give branches more direct information and stock control. Also a 'special order' system means that if an item is not in the shop, the system tracks available stock, requests it from any other Jaeger shop where available and ensures immediate delivery to the customer's home or nearest branch.

What is it that makes a company special enough to win *The Daily Telegraph* and British Telecom award for Customer Service? For Jaeger, the retailer of quality women's and menswear fashion garments, it is because they believe that *'service is about creating unique person-to-person shopping experiences. It's about adding quality people and quality service to a quality product in a major way. It's about getting personal. And the only means by which this can be truly achieved is to empower those closest to the customer to deliver great service.'*

Putting this into practice includes many initiatives, often suggested by staff. These include 'mystery shopping' using actual customers, 'fast-reaction' systems to solve customers' problems, and branches collecting information on Customer Profile Cards. This information is the central point to generate better service tailored to individual service and stock requirements. This has led to initiatives such as early morning/late night shopping for individual customers, toys and videos for children, home shopping, and home deliveries at weekends. The use of complaint information was also improved and a 'no fuss' returns policy introduced. Any member of staff can go to any length to satisfy customers. Examples include home deliveries on Sundays with birthday gifts, etc., birthday cards for customers, and advising on complementary products or alternatives from competing retailers. Responsive training ensures

Photo courtesy of Jaeger

Using the electronic point-of-sale tills with the 'special order' system

- *Jaeger sells high quality formal and casual clothes. How do you think their operations objectives differ from a mass market casual clothing retail operation?*
- *How does Jaeger's use of its human and technological resources help it to achieve its objectives?*

→ **Look at Chapters 3 and 17 for guidance**

Verenigde Bloemenveiling Aalsmeer (VBA) – (United Flower Auctions), Aalsmeer, Holland

Standard 'trolleys' waiting in the 'sellers' section'

VBA is the largest flower auction operation in the world. It comprises two main parts. The first is the sellers' area known as the 'auction section' where flowers are received, held in cooled storage areas and auctioned. The second is the 'buyers' section' where around 300 buyers, exporters and wholesalers rent space to prepare flowers for shipment. Trucks leave Aalsmeer every working day to destinations (including airports) throughout Europe. On a typical day there are about 10 000 people working at the centre (1800 of whom work directly for VBA), together handling 17 million cut flowers and 2 million plants. This large and complex operation is held together by its information processing technology.

Flowers are extremely perishable, so dealing with them in such large quantities makes the speed, accuracy and dependability of the operation critical. During the evening and overnight, flowers are brought into the operation in standard containers which are subsequently handled in standard wheeled cages (there are over 124 000 of these 'trolleys' in circulation – *see* picture). Each lot of flowers is assigned a reference number, a quality inspection is made by VBA staff, and a description is entered on the 'delivery forms' attached to each trolley. The trolleys are then held in cold storage until they are collected for the auctioning process the following morning.

The auction takes place every week day in five separate halls, specialized by category of flower or plant. The largest flower auction hall has tiered desks for up to 500 buyers, each linked to the auction computer. Each buyer has an uninterrupted view of the flowers (which are automatically conveyed through the auction halls in their trolleys), and of the four auction price 'clocks' behind the auctioneers. Buyers can then choose the clock of their choice at any time using a selection switch. The auctioneer in charge of each clock may give brief information on the quality of a particular lot, relayed to the appropriate bidders' desk speakers, but most of the important information about the flowers is shown automatically on the clocks' displays (*see* picture). Flowers are sold by 'Dutch auction',

An auction hall in the 'buyers' section' showing the auction clocks

Photo courtesy of Bloemenveiling Aalsmeer

whereby the clock, scaled 100 to 1 at its rim, is started by the auctioneer and moves rapidly downwards. The first bidder to press his desk button stops the clock and becomes the buyer of that lot. This type of bidding is particularly suitable for automation because only one bid needs to be recorded for each transaction. All the details are recorded by computer and printed out on a 'distribution voucher' which is attached to the appropriate trolley. The whole bidding process, including the processing of the information, takes only a few seconds. The lots are then distributed on the trolleys to the appropriate packing or loading areas. For each buyer, the VBA computer prints an invoice for all the purchases made, which must be settled daily by bank letter of credit or by cash drawn at one of the four banks adjacent to the cashier's office.

The high levels of computerization and automation of material flow allow VBA to operate with very low costs (about five per cent of turnover), at high speed and dependability. Each

of the 13 clocks handles about 1000 transactions per hour. Almost all business takes place between 7.00 am and 10.00 am so that fresh flowers can be in the shops as early as possible – by lunchtime in Holland, by early afternoon in London, Paris and Berlin, and by early morning the next day in New York.

- *Which of the five operations performance objectives (quality, speed, dependability, flexibility and cost) are the most important for VBA, and why?*
- *How does process technology help this operation to achieve its objectives?*
- *Sketch the flow of flowers in the VBA operation. What do you think are the critical points in this flow?*

→ *Look at Chapters 5 and 8 for guidance*

Yamaha tunes its assembly lines

The grand piano assembly line at Yamaha

The Yamaha Corporation of Japan, founded in 1887, has grown to become the world's largest manufacturer of musical instruments, as well as producing a whole variety of other goods, from semi-conductors and robots through to sporting goods and furniture. In recent years it has developed a reputation for product diversification, an understanding of new markets and, especially, innovative manufacturing methods. For example, it was one of the first piano manufacturers to make up-market grand pianos using assembly line techniques (the picture shows grand pianos being assembled in the same way that motor vehicles are assembled). Traditionally, grand pianos (as opposed to the less expensive and better selling vertical pianos) were made using individual build methods which relied on craft skills. The main advantage of this was that skilled workers could accommodate individual variations in the (often inconsistent) materials from which the piano is made. Each individual piano would be constructed around the idiosyncrasies of the material to make a product unique in its tone and tuning. Not so with Yamaha, who although making some of the highest quality pianos in the world, emphasize consistency and reliability, as well as richness of tone.

- *Grand pianos are clearly 'quality products'. What aspects of quality do you think are important for pianos in general and grand pianos in particular?*
- *Which of these various aspects of quality which you have listed are likely to be affected by Yamaha's strategy of producing its grand pianos on assembly lines?*
- *In the picture a white piano is moving down the assembly line along with the black ones. Do you think this will pose any problems for managing this assembly line?*

→ *Look at Chapters 7 and 17 for guidance*

LAYOUT OF DELHAIZE DE LEEUW SUPERMARKET IN OUDERGHEM, BELGIUM[2]

The Delhaize Group operates over 400 retail outlets in Belgium, of which there are around 100 local Delhaize De Leeuw supermarkets. Delhaize supermarkets compete both by choices of location, which are convenient for frequent shoppers, and by the quality of the products and service. To remain profitable every Delhaize manager must maximize the revenue and contribution per square metre but must also minimize the costs of operating the store, in terms of material handling and check-out productivity, for example.

The Ouderghem supermarket has a somewhat unusual layout, having two entry points and two exit points. In common with most supermarket designs, the check-outs are positioned near the outside wall, but during most of the day only a few are used. Cigarettes, tram tickets, and postage stamps are sold at the check-outs, but not confectionery. Newspapers are sold near the check-out queues, so that customers can catch up with the news while waiting. Check-out operators face into the store, towards the queue, to emphasize the need to work quickly when there is a queue. The store has ten check-outs – a very large number for a store of only 1500 square metres. This is because there is a large peak of sales in the early evening, when people return from work, and long queues at the check-out would be unacceptable.

Delhaize has chosen to use relatively wide aisles between the shelves, to ensure good flows of trolleys, but this has been at the expense of reduced shelf space which would allow a wider range of products to be stocked. The actual location of all the products is a critical management decision, directly affecting the convenience to customers, their level of spontaneous purchases, and the costs of filling the shelves. The overall layout of the supermarket is a typical process layout, with separate, clearly marked self-service areas for packaged food, drinks, fruit and vegetables, and household items. Customer flows are random, both because of the two-entrance arrangement, and because of the frequent but relatively small purchases made by regular customers (in contrast, shoppers at many large hypermarkets are encouraged to flow past most of the displays in a logical and uniform route). The served delicatessen area (which sells products with above-average margins) is positioned centrally so that most shoppers must pass it – to be tempted by its attractive displays to make spontaneous purchases. The displays of fruit and vegetables are located adjacent to the main entrance, as a signal of freshness and wholesomeness, providing an attractive and welcoming point of entry to the store.

At a detailed level, the actual position selected for each product must be decided. High-turnover, 'essential', known-value items (KVIs), such as rice, pasta, sugar and oil are positioned centrally and visibly, so that they are easy to find. Profitable, fast-moving items are displayed at eye level, both to help the customer and to make restocking easier for the employees. Conversely, low-margin and low-turnover items are placed low down. Bulky or heavy products, such as packs of beer, are located near to the storage area to facilitate restocking. Frozen foods are located at the end of aisles, near to the check-outs, so that they can be purchased last. In some supermarkets, these positions are only used for promotions, as customers move slower around the end of aisles and the goods on display can be seen from most directions. ■

Questions

1 What is the basic layout type used by this supermarket?

2 Are the objectives in designing a supermarket layout broadly similar to the objectives in designing a high-variety manufacturing operation? If not, what is the difference?

Figure 7.5 The ground floor plan of a department store showing the sports goods shop-within-a-shop retail 'cell'

shop-within-a-shop area which is devoted to many goods which have a common sporting theme. For example, it will stock sports clothes, sports shoes, sports bags, sports magazines, sports books and videos, sports equipment and gifts and sports energy drinks. Within the 'cell' there are all the 'processes' which are also located elsewhere in the store. They have been located in the 'cell' not because they are similar goods (shoes, books and drinks would not usually be located together) but because they are needed to satisfy the needs of a particular type of customer. The store management calculates that enough customers come to the store to buy 'sports goods', rather than shoes, clothes, books, etc. separately, to devote an area specifically for them. The store is also aware that someone coming to the store with the intention of purchasing some sports shoes might also be persuaded to buy other sports goods if they are placed in the same area.

Product layout

Product layout involves locating the transforming resources entirely for the convenience of the transformed resources. Each product, piece of information or customer follows a prearranged route in which the sequence of activities which are required matches the sequence in which the processes have been located. The transformed resources 'flow' along a 'line' of processes. This is why this type of layout is sometimes called 'flow' or 'line' layout. The flow of products, information or customers in product layout is clear, predictable and therefore relatively easy to control. In fact in some customer-processing service operations, a product layout is adopted partly to help control the flow of customers through the operation. Predominantly though it is the standardized requirements of the product or service which lead to operations choosing product layouts.

Examples of product layout include:

● *Automobile assembly* – Almost all variants of the same model require the same sequence of processes.
● *Mass-immunization programme* – All customers require the same sequence of clerical, medical and counselling activities.
● *Self-service cafeteria* – Generally the sequence of customer requirements (starter, main course, dessert, drink) is common to all customers, but layout also helps control customer flow.

Figure 7.6 shows the sequence of processes in a paper-making operation. Such an operation would use product layout. The flow of materials through the operation is both evident and regular. Gone are the complexities of flow which characterized process layouts, and to a lesser extent cell layout, and although different types of paper are produced in this operation, all types have the same processing requirements. First, the wood chips are combined with chemicals, water and steam in the 'cooking' process to form the 'pulp'. The pulp is then put through a cleaning process before being refined to help the fibres lock together. The mixing process combines the refined pulp with more water, fillers, chemicals and dyes, after which it is spread on a fine flexible wire or plastic mesh. This is shaken from side to side as it moves along to lock the fibres into the sheet of paper and to drain away the water. The press rollers squeeze more water out of the paper and press the fibres closer together. The drying process continues to reduce the water level in the paper before, finally, it is wound on to large reels.[3]

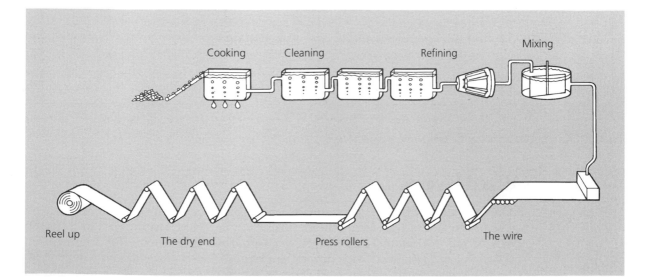

Figure 7.6 The sequence of processes in paper-making; each process will be laid out in the same sequence

It makes sense then to locate these processes in the order that they are required by the product and let materials flow along in a predictable manner. In fact this particular example of product layout is an extreme one in some ways because for the first part of its manufacture the paper is in a semi-liquid form. It would be physically difficult to handle the product in any way other than causing it to 'flow' between processes. Nevertheless, other products which have a common sequence of processes, such as televisions, freezers, air-conditioning units, and so on, are also manufactured using product layouts.

Service operations can also adopt a product layout if the 'processing' needs of customers or information have a common sequence. For example, recruits on joining the armed forces are likely to be 'processed' through an induction programme organized on a product-layout basis. Figure 7.7 shows the layout of an army induction unit. The diagram shows the route taken by one recruit, but all people entering the operation progress through the same sequence of activities – the taking of their personal and medical history, an X-ray test, a blood test, a medical examination, the issuing of a uniform, and finally an induction briefing. These processes are laid out in that sequence because they represent the required sequence of activities.

Figure 7.7 An army induction centre which uses a product layout

Mixed layouts

Many operations either design themselves hybrid layouts which combine elements of some or all of the basic layout types, or use the 'pure' basic layout types in different parts of the operation. For example, a hospital would normally be arranged on process-layout principles – each department representing a particular type of process (the X-ray department, the surgical theatres, the blood-processing laboratory, and so on). Yet within each department quite different layouts are used. The X-ray department is probably arranged in a process layout, the surgical theatres in a fixed-position layout, and the blood-processing laboratory in a product layout.

Another example is shown in Fig. 7.8. Here a restaurant complex is shown with three different types of restaurant and the kitchen which serves them all. The kitchen is arranged in a process, layout with the various processes (food storage, food preparation, cooking processes, etc.) grouped together. Different foods will take different

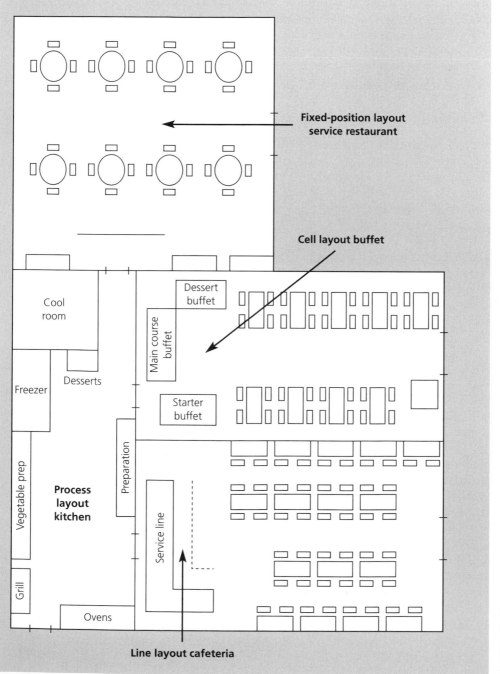

Figure 7.8
A restaurant complex with all four basic layout types

227

routes between the processes, depending on their processing requirements. The traditional service restaurant is arranged in a fixed-position layout. The customers stay at their tables while the food is brought to (and sometimes cooked at) the tables. The buffet restaurant is arranged in a cell-type layout with each buffet area having all the processes (dishes) necessary to serve customers with their starter, main course or dessert. In this case customers who intend to partake of all three courses will need to be processed through all three cells before the completion of the service. Finally, in the cafeteria restaurant all customers take the same route when being served with their meal. They may not take the opportunity to be served with every dish but they move through the same sequence of processes.

CHOCOLATE AND CUSTOMERS FLOW THROUGH CADBURY'S[4]

Flow of chocolate

In the famous Cadbury's chocolate factory at Bournville, on the outskirts of Birmingham, UK, chocolate products are manufactured to a high degree of consistency and efficiency. Production processes are based on a *product layout*. This has allowed Cadbury's engineers to develop and procure machinery to meet the technical and capacity requirements of each stage of the process. Consider, for example, the production of Cadbury's Dairy Milk bars. First, the standard liquid chocolate is prepared from cocoa beans, fresh milk, and sugar using specialized equipment, connected together with pipes and conveyors. These processes operate continuously, day and night, to ensure consistency of both the chocolate itself, and the rate of output. Next, the liquid is pumped through heated pipework to the moulding department, where it is automatically dispensed into a moving line of precision-made plastic moulds which form the chocolate bars and vibrate them to remove any trapped air bubbles. The moulds are continuously conveyed into a large refrigerator, allowing sufficient time for the chocolate to harden. The next stage inverts the moulds and shakes out the moulded bars. These then pass directly to a set of highly automated wrapping and packing machines, from where they go to the warehouse. Because the product is highly standardized (virtually unchanged since its introduction in 1866), the layout has been designed to suit the product, minimizing the costs of materials handling, and allowing ever-increasing levels of automation to be developed.

Flow of customers

In 1990, the company opened a large visitor centre called 'Cadbury World' alongside the factory (linked to a viewing area which looks on to the packaging area described above). Cadbury World is a permanent exhibition devoted entirely to chocolate and the part Cadbury played in its fascinating history. Because most of the attractions are indoors, with limited circulation space, the main exhibition and demonstration areas are designed to allow a smooth flow of customers, where possible avoiding bottle-necks and delays. The design is also a 'product' layout with a single route for all customers, as shown in Fig. 7.9.

Entry to the Exhibition Area is by timed ticket, to ensure a constant flow of input customers, who are free to walk around at their preferred speed, but are constrained to keep to the single track through the sequence of displays. On leaving this section, they are directed up stairs to the Chocolate Packaging Plant, where a guide escorts standard-sized batches of customers to the appropriate positions where they can see the packing processes and a video presentation. The groups are then led down to and around the Demonstration Area, where skilled employees demonstrate small-scale production of hand-made chocolates. Finally, visitors are free to roam unaccompanied through a long winding path of the remaining exhibits.

Cadbury has chosen to use the product layout design for both the production of chocolates and the processing of its visitors. In both cases, volumes are large and variety offered is narrow. Sufficient demand exists for each standard 'product', and the operations objective is to achieve consistent high quality at low cost. Neither operation has much volume flexibility, and both are expensive to change. ▪

Figure 7.9 A sketch of the Cadbury World site

Source: From Johnston et al. (1997) Cases in Operations Management (2nd edn), Pitman Publishing

Questions

1 Both customers and chocolate in the Cadbury's operation do seem to conform to a product-type layout. Does this mean that both operations have the same objectives?

2 Could the line-balancing techniques which are likely to have been used in the chocolate factory also be used in Cadbury World (*see* pp. 253–4 for further information on this topic)? How might they need to be modified?

Volume–variety and layout type

The importance of flow to an operation will depend on its volume and variety characteristics. When volume is very low and variety is relatively high, 'flow' is not a major issue. For example, in telecommunications satellite manufacture, a fixed-position layout is likely to be appropriate because each product is different and because products 'flow' through the operation very infrequently. Under these conditions it is just not worth arranging facilities to minimize the flow of parts through the operation.

With somewhat higher volume and lower variety, the flow of the transformed resources becomes an issue which any layout must address. If the variety is still high, however, an entirely flow-dominated arrangement is difficult because products or customers will have different flow patterns. For example, the library in Fig. 7.4 will arrange its different categories of books and its other services partly to minimize the average distance its customers have to 'flow' through the operation. Because its customers' needs vary, however, the library at best will arrange its layout to satisfy a majority of its customers but perhaps inconvenience a minority. When the variety of products or services reduces to the point where a distinct 'category' with similar requirements becomes evident but variety is still not small, cell layout could become appropriate, as in the sports goods cell in Fig. 7.5. When the variety of products or services is relatively small and volume high, the flow of materials, information or customers can become regularized and a product-based layout is likely to be appropriate, as in an assembly plant.

Examining these examples of the different basic layout types, we can see the different effects of volume and variety (*see* Fig. 7.10). Increasing volume increases the *importance* of flow whereas reducing variety increases the *feasibility* of a layout based on evident and regular flow.

Selecting a layout type

The decision of which layout type to adopt rarely, if ever, involves choosing between all four basic types. The volume–variety characteristics of the operation will, to a large extent, narrow the choice down to one or two options. Yet, as is implied in Fig. 7.10, the spans of volumes and varieties encompassed by each layout type do overlap. The

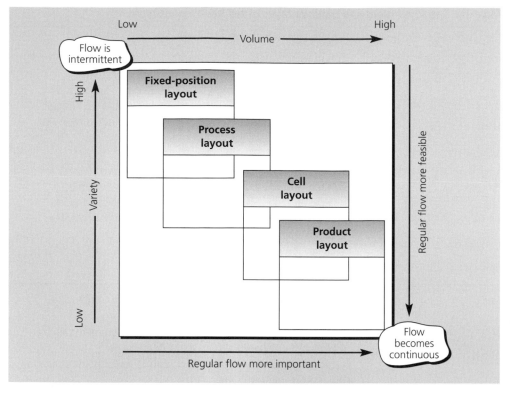

Figure 7.10
The volume–variety process position of an operation influences its layout and in turn the flow of transformed resources

decision as to which layout type to adopt will be influenced by an understanding of their relative advantages and disadvantages.

Table 7.2 shows some of the more significant advantages and disadvantages associated with each layout type. It should be stressed, however, that the type of operation will influence their relative importance. For example, a high-volume television manufacturer may find the low-cost characteristics of a product layout attractive, but an amusement theme park may adopt the same layout type primarily because of the way it 'controls' customer flow. There may also be other ways of achieving flow objectives. The Eurohub terminal at Birmingham Airport switches the direction of flow by using technology to change customer routes.

Of all the characteristics of the various layout types, perhaps the most generally significant are the unit cost implications of layout choice. This is best understood by distinguishing between the fixed and variable cost elements of adopting each layout type. For any particular product or service the fixed costs of physically constructing a fixed-position layout are relatively small compared with any other way of producing the same product or service. However, the variable costs of producing each individual product or service are relatively high compared to the alternative layout types. Fixed costs then tend to increase as one moves from fixed-position, through process and cell, to product layout. Variable costs per product or service tend to decrease, however. The total costs for each layout type will depend on the volume of products or services produced and are shown in Fig. 7.11(a). This seems to show that for any volume there is a lowest-cost basic layout.

Table 7.2 **The advantages and disadvantages of the basic layout types**

	Advantages	Disadvantages
Fixed-position	Very high mix and product flexibility Product or customer not moved or disturbed High variety of tasks for staff	Very high unit costs Scheduling of space and activities can be difficult Can mean much movement of plant and staff
Process	High mix and product flexibility Relatively robust if in the case of disruptions Relatively easy supervision of equipment or plant	Low facilities utilization Can have very high work-in-progress or customer queueing Complex flow can be difficult to control
Cell	Can give a good compromise between cost and flexibility for relatively high-variety operations Fast throughput Group work can result in good motivation	Can be costly to rearrange existing layout Can need more plant and equipment Can give lower plant utilization
Product	Low unit costs for high volume Gives opportunities for specialization of equipment Materials or customer movement is convenient	Can have low mix flexibility Not very robust if disruption Work can be very repetitive

However, in practice, the cost analysis of layout selection is rarely as clear as this. The exact cost of operating the layout is difficult to forecast and will probably depend on many, often difficult to predict, factors. Rather than use lines to represent the cost of layout as volume increases, broad bands, within which the real cost is likely to lie, are probably more appropriate (*see* Fig. 7.11(b)). The discrimination between the different layout types is now far less clear. There are ranges of volume for which any of two or three layout types might provide the lowest operating cost. The less certainty there is over the costs, the broader the cost 'bands' will be, and the less clear the choice will be. The probable costs of adopting a particular layout need to be set in the broader context of advantages and disadvantages in Table 7.2.

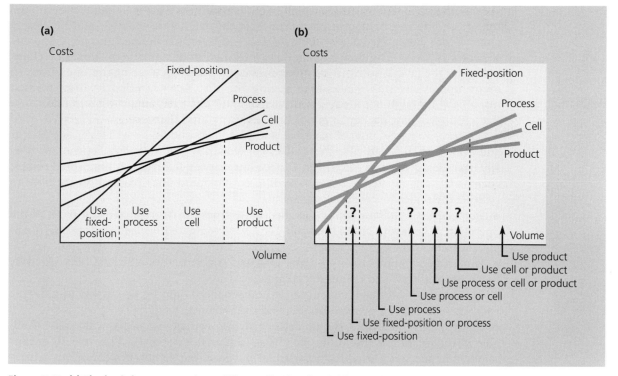

Figure 7.11 (a) The basic layout types have different fixed and variable cost characteristics which seem to determine which one to use, (b) in practice the uncertainty about the exact fixed and variable costs of each layout means the decision can rarely be made on cost alone

DETAILED DESIGN OF THE LAYOUT

Once the basic layout type has been decided the next step is to decide the detailed design of the layout. Detailed design is the act of operationalizing the broad principles which were implicit in the choice of the basic layout type.

The output from the detailed design stage of layout is:

● the precise location of all facilities, plant, equipment and staff which constitute the 'work centres' of the operation;
● the space to be devoted to each work centre;
● the tasks which will be undertaken by each work centre.

What makes a good layout?

Before considering the various methods used in the detailed design of layouts, it is useful to consider the objectives of the activity. To a certain extent the objectives will depend on circumstances, but there are some general objectives which are relevant to all operations:[5]

233

- *Inherent safety* – All processes which might constitute a danger to either staff or customers should not be accessible to the unauthorized. Fire exits should be clearly marked with uninhibited access. Pathways should be clearly defined and not cluttered.
- *Length of flow* – The flow of materials, information or customers should be channelled by the layout so as to be appropriate for the objectives of the operation. In many operations this means minimizing the distance travelled by transformed resources. Although not always, supermarkets, for example, might wish to make sure that customers pass particular goods on their way round the store.
- *Clarity of flow* – All flow of materials and customers should be well signposted, clear and evident to staff and customers alike. For example, manufacturing operations usually have clearly marked gangways. Service operations often rely on signposted routes, such as in hospitals which often have different coloured lines painted on the floor to indicate the routes to various departments.
- *Staff comfort* – Staff should be located away from noisy or unpleasant parts of the operation. The layout should provide for a well-ventilated, well-lit and, where possible, pleasant working environment.
- *Management co-ordination* – Supervision and communication should be assisted by the location of staff and communication devices.
- *Accessibility* – All machines, plant or equipment should be accessible to a degree which is sufficient for proper cleaning and maintenance.
- *Use of space* – All layouts should achieve an appropriate use of the total space available in the operation (including height as well as floor space). This usually means minimizing the space used for a particular purpose, but sometimes can mean achieving an impression of spacious luxury, as in the entrance lobby of a high-class hotel.
- *Long-term flexibility* – Layouts need to be changed periodically as the needs of the operation change. A good layout will have been devised with the possible future needs of the operation in mind. For example, if demand is likely to increase for a product or service, has the layout been designed to accommodate any future expansion?

Detailed design in fixed-position layout

In fixed-position arrangements the location of resources will be determined, not on the basis of the flow of transformed resources, but on the convenience of transforming resources themselves. The objective of the detailed design of fixed-position layouts is to achieve a layout for the operation which allows all the transforming resources to maximize their contribution to the transformation process by allowing them to provide an effective 'service' to the transformed resources. The detailed layout of some fixed-position layouts, such as building sites, can become very complicated, especially if the planned schedule of activities is changed frequently. Imagine the chaos on a construction site if heavy trucks continually (and noisily) drove past the site office, delivery trucks for one contractor had to cross other contractors' areas to get to where they were storing their own materials, and the staff who spent most time at the building itself were located furthest away from it.

Resource location analysis

Resource location analysis is a systematic approach to allocating work centres to locations in stable, fixed-position arrangements. It involves evaluating the effects of locating the various transforming resources (known as resource centres) at all available locations on the site by using criteria associated with the site itself (site criteria) and criteria associated with the interaction of the resources (relative-location criteria).

The procedure in resource location analysis is as follows:

Step 1 Define the site and its available locations.

Step 2 Define the resource centres to be located and their requirements.

Step 3 Formalize the evaluation criteria by considering the site characteristics and the requirements of the resource centres, and by doing so define (a) the site criteria and (b) the relative-location criteria.

Step 4 Calculate the degree of fit between resource centres and available locations using the site criteria.

Step 5 Devise a preliminary allocation of resource centres to locations based on site criteria.

Step 6 Adjust the allocation of resource centres to locations based on the relative-location criteria.

As an example of resource location analysis, we can consider a manufacturer of specialist marine exploration equipment which has devoted part of its plant to the assembly of underwater exploration vehicles using a fixed-position layout. These vehicles are small, submarine-like vessels, used by oil exploration and mineral extraction companies. All the vehicles are made to order and all individual vehicles are different in some way from each other.

Step 1 – Define the site

The assembly area for this product is shown in Fig. 7.12. Two assembly bays have already been located in the centre of the area and a 'free-access' zone has been designated around the bays to avoid the assembly bays becoming cluttered. There are two access points: one to the outside of the plant, the second to the other parts of the plant. The remaining available area is shown divided into 14 locations of approximately equal size. It is these locations which need to be allocated to the resource centres.

Free-access zone

Assembly areas

Figure 7.12
The assembly area of a specialist underwater exploration vehicle

235

Step 2 – Define the needs of resource centres

Many different types of staff together with their equipment and materials will need access to the assembly bays. Six resource centres were judged to need permanent space in the assembly area, however. The locations allocated to the resources should also be together if possible.

● *Structural fabricators.* This group needs four locations to store its materials and set up its own work areas. It is important that these workers are located close to the external access point so that they can receive deliveries of material. It is also necessary to extract the fumes from their welding and painting operations, so a location on an external wall would be convenient.

● *Mechanical fitters.* This group needs three location areas. They receive some material delivered directly to the assembly area but most comes into the area after being preprocessed elsewhere in the factory.

● *Electricians.* This group needs two location areas. Because of the sensitivity of their testing operations, it is advisable that the electricians are located away from the structural fabrication area where noise, fumes and vibration could interfere with the tests.

● *Control engineers.* This group requires two location areas. They need to be relatively close to the access point for the other areas in the plant and, again, should not be close to the structural fabricators.

● *Communication engineers.* This group needs two location areas. Because of customer-driven changes in the communication systems during assembly, this group would like to be close to the planning office to make sure that there is effective communication. They also need to be away from their structural fabrication colleagues.

● *The planning office.* This needs only one location area and houses the operations manager, project managers and a meeting area. It needs to be in a location which affords it good access to the rest of the area and, especially, a good view of the direct delivery of materials to the assembly area. It also needs to be away from any noisy processes.

Step 3 – Formalize evaluation criteria

There are five criteria on which the location of the resources could be evaluated, three concerned with the site itself and two concerned with location relative to other resource centres:

● *Site criteria*
(a) Closeness to external access point
(b) Closeness to internal access point
(c) Closeness to external wall
● *Relative-location criteria*
(a) Closeness to planning office
(b) Distance from structural fabricators

Step 4 – Calculate the degree of fit

This step is carried out in three stages. The first stage is to allocate a 'location score' for how well each of the locations satisfies the site criteria. The simplest way of doing this is to score each location as follows:

Location is ideal   = 3
Location is acceptable = 2
Location is poor   = 1

Table 7.3 Individual location scores for underwater vehicle assembly area

Site criteria	1	2	3	4	5	6	7	8	9	10	11	12	13	14
							Location							
External access	3	3	2	2	1	1	1	1	1	1	2	2	3	3
Internal access	1	1	2	2	3	3	3	3	3	3	2	2	1	1
External wall	3	3	3	3	3	2	2	1	1	1	1	1	1	1

In this example, the operations management team scored the locations as shown in Table 7.3.

The next stage is to allocate a weighting factor to each of the site criteria which corresponds to the perceived importance of the criteria to each of the resources. Table 7.4 shows how the criteria were scored in this example, using the scale as follows:

Very important criterion   = 3
Important criterion   = 2
Fairly important criterion   = 1
Not at all important criterion = 0

Table 7.4 Weightings for importance of each site criterion to the resource centres

Site criteria	Structural fabricators	Mechanical fitters	Electricians	Control engineers	Communications engineers	Planning office
External access	3	1	0	0	0	2
Internal access	1	3	1	1	1	1
External wall	3	0	0	0	0	0

Now the final stage of calculating a 'degree-of-fit' score for each resource being allocated to each location can be carried out. This is done by simply summing the weighting multiplied by the location score for each criterion.

So, for example, the degree of fit allocating the structural fabricators to location 1 is as follows:

  external access weighting × location score for location 1's external access
plus internal access weighting × location score for location 1's internal access
plus external wall weighting   × location score for location 1's external wall

This equals

$(3 \times 3) + (1 \times 1) + (3 \times 3) = 19$

Table 7.5 shows the degree-of-fit resource location scores for each of the resources in all the locations.

Step 5 – Devise preliminary layout

The resource location scores shown in Table 7.5 give an indication not only of the degree of fit between a resource centre and a location (the higher the score, the better

Table 7.5 Resource location scores for the underwater vehicle assembly area

Resource	Location													
centre	1	2	3	4	5	6	7	8	9	10	11	12	13	14
Structural fabricators	19	19	17	17	15	12	12	9	9	9	11	11	13	13
Mechanical fitters	6	6	8	8	10	10	10	10	10	10	8	8	6	6
Electricians	1	1	2	2	3	3	3	3	3	3	2	2	1	1
Control engineers	1	1	2	2	3	3	3	3	3	3	2	2	1	1
Communications engineers	1	1	2	2	3	3	3	3	3	3	2	2	1	1
Planning office	7	7	6	6	5	5	5	5	5	5	6	6	7	7

the fit) but also of how important its location is to each resource centre. The structural fabricators, for example, have high resource location scores which shows that they are particularly sensitive to their location. The resource centres with the higher scores should therefore be allocated locations first. In this example the structural fabricators should be located first, initially to the four locations which give them their highest location scores – locations 1, 2, 3 and 4. After this the mechanical fitters are allocated location, and so on. Figure 7.13(a) shows the preliminary location which results from this process.

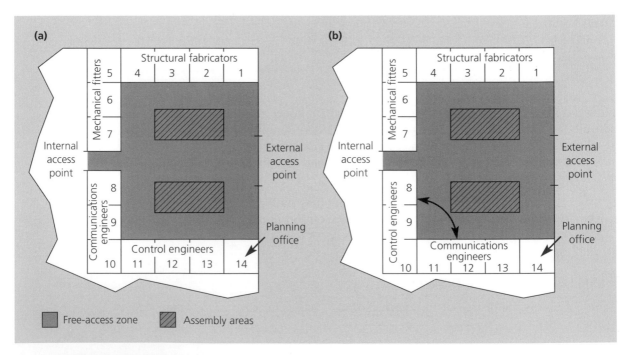

Figure 7.13 (a) Preliminary layout of the assembly area, (b) final layout of the assembly area

Step 6 – Adjust the layout

The final step is to check the preliminary layout against the relative-location criteria. In this example all the resources which needed to avoid the structural fabricators have done so in the preliminary layout. The communications engineers are not adjacent to the planning office, however. Reference to the resource location scores in Table 7.5 shows that the control engineers and the communications engineers could exchange their respective locations without any loss of score. The final layout is shown in Fig. 7.13(b).

Detailed design in process layout

The detailed design of process layouts is marked by the complexity, which is also the main flow characteristic, of this type of layout. Chief among the factors which lead to this complexity is the very large number of different options. For example, in the very simplest case of just two work centres, there are only two ways of arranging these *relative to each other*. But there are six ways of arranging three centres and 120 ways of arranging five centres.

The relationship is a factorial one. For N centres there are factorial N, ($N!$) different ways of arranging the centres, where

$$N! = N \times (N-1) \times (N-2) \times \ldots (1)$$

So for a relatively simple process layout with, say, 20 work centres, there are

$$20! = 2.433 \times 10^{18}$$

ways of arranging the operation.

It is partly because of this *combinatorial complexity* of process layouts that optimal solutions are difficult to achieve in practice. Most process layouts are designed by a combination of intuition, common sense, and systematic trial and error.

The information for process layouts

Before starting the process of detailed design in process layouts there are some essential pieces of information which the designer needs:

● the area required by each work centre;
● the constraints on the shape of the area allocated to each work centre;
● the degree and direction of flow between each work centre (for example, number of journeys, number of loads, or cost of flow per distance travelled);
● the desirability of work centres being close together or close to some fixed point in the layout.

The last two pieces of information are particularly important because both influence directly the consequences of locating work centres relative to each other.

The degree and direction of flow are usually shown on a *flow record chart* like that shown in Fig. 7.14(a) which records in this case the number of loads transported between departments. There are many ways in which this information could be gathered. For example, in some manufacturing operations flow data can be derived from routing information for products and the demand for those products. Where flow is more random, as in a library for example, the information could be collected by observing the routes taken by customers over a typical period of time. If the direction of the flow between work centres makes little difference to the layout, the information can be collapsed as shown in Fig. 7.14(b), an alternative form of which is shown in Fig. 7.14(c).

In some operations there are significant differences in the cost of moving materials or customers between different work centres. For example, in Fig. 7.14(d) the unit cost of transporting a load between the five work centres is shown. Here the unit cost of moving loads from work centre B is slightly higher than that from most other departments. There could be many reasons for this, for example because the products are particularly delicate after being processed at work centre B and need careful handling, or because they need to maintain temperature after being heat treated and before they are processed further. Combining the unit cost and flow data gives the

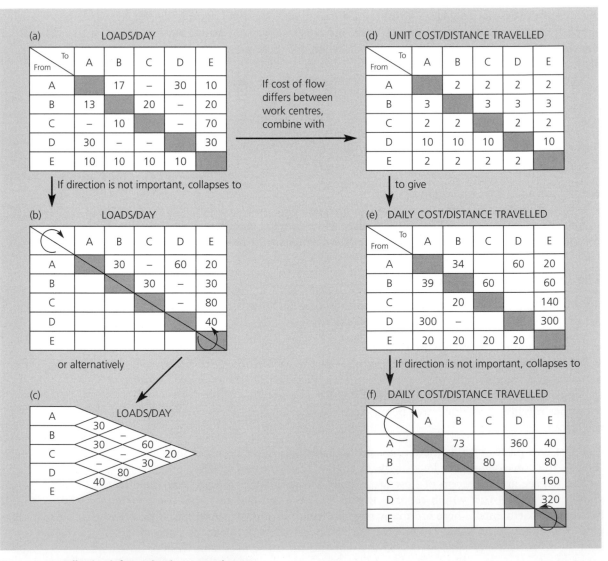

Figure 7.14 Collecting information in process layout

cost per distance travelled data shown in Fig. 7.14(e). This has been collapsed as before into Fig. 7.14(f).

An alternative qualitative method of indicating the relative importance of the relationship between work centres is the *relationship chart*. A relationship chart indicates the desirability of pairs of work centres being close to each other. Figure 7.15 shows the relationship chart for a testing laboratory. It is particularly important that some departments are close together, for example Electronic Testing and Metrology. Other departments must be kept as far as possible from each other, for example Metrology and Impact Testing.

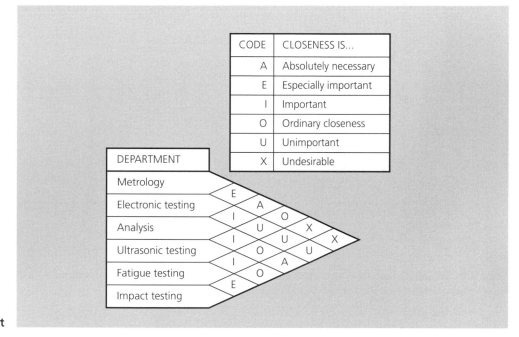

Figure 7.15
A relationship chart

The objectives of process layout

In most examples of process layout, the prime objective is to minimize the costs to the operation which are associated with the flow of transformed resources through the operation. So, for example, a furniture manufacturer would locate work centres in the factory so as to minimize the need to transport components. Similarly, a hospital would locate its departments to minimize the movement of its patients (and perhaps staff). In some operations the emphasis is shifted to maximizing the revenue associated with flow rather than minimizing its cost. Retail operations especially might lay out their operations to this objective (*see*, for example, box on the Delhaize supermarket). Some entertainment operations such as theme parks may also have this objective. Cost minimization is by far the most common objective, however.

At the simplest level an operation might judge the effectiveness of its layout solely on the total distance travelled in the operation. For example, Fig. 7.16(a) shows a simple six-centre process layout with the total number of journeys between centres each day. The effectiveness of the layout, at this simple level, can be calculated from:

Effectiveness of layout $= \Sigma F_{ij} D_{ij}$ for all $i \neq j$.

241

where $\qquad$ F_{ij} = the flow in loads or journeys per period of time from work centre i to work centre j

$\qquad$ D_{ij} = the distance between work centre i and work centre j.

The lower the effectiveness score the better the layout.

In this example the total of the number of journeys multiplied by the distance for each pair of departments where there is some flow is 4450 metres. This measure will indicate whether changes to the layout improve its effectiveness (at least in the narrow terms defined here). For example, if centres C and E are exchanged as in Fig. 7.16(b) the effectiveness measure becomes 3750, showing that the new layout now has reduced the total distance travelled in the operation.

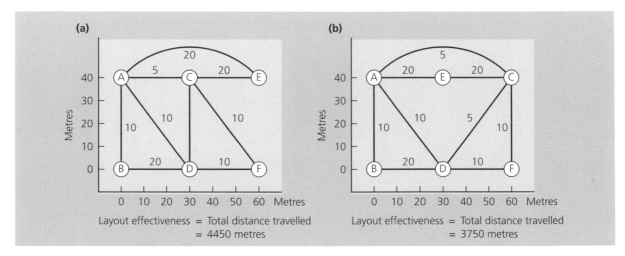

Layout effectiveness = Total distance travelled
= 4450 metres

Layout effectiveness = Total distance travelled
= 3750 metres

Figure 7.16 (a) and (b) The objective of most process layouts is to minimize the cost associated with movement in the operation, sometimes simplified to minimizing the total distance travelled

The calculations above assume that all journeys are the same in that their cost to the operation is the same. In some operations this is not so, however. For example, in the hospital some journeys involving healthy staff and relatively fit patients would have little importance compared with other journeys where very sick patients need to be moved from the operating theatres to intensive-care wards.

In these cases it might be worthwhile to incorporate a cost (or difficulty) element into the measure of layout effectiveness which is being minimized:

Effectiveness of layout $\quad = \quad \Sigma F_{ij} D_{ij} C_{ij}$ for all $i \neq j$

where $\qquad$ C_{ij} = the cost per distance travelled of making a journey between departments i and j.

The general process layout design method

The general approach to determining the location of work centres in a process layout is as follows:

Step 1 Collect information relating to the work centres and the flow between them.
Step 2 Draw up a schematic layout showing the work centres and the flow between them, putting the work centres with the greatest flow closest to each other.

Step 3 Adjust the schematic layout to take into account the constraints of the area into which the layout must fit.

Step 4 Draw the layout showing the actual work centre areas and distances which materials or customers must travel. Calculate the effectiveness measure of the layout either as total distance travelled or as the cost of movement.

Step 5 Check to see if exchanging any two work centres will reduce the total distance travelled or the cost of movement. If so, make the exchange and return to Step 4. If not, make this the final layout.

Example: Rotterdam Educational Group

As an example of a process layout, we can consider Rotterdam Educational Group (REG), a company which commissions, designs and manufactures education packs for distance-learning courses and training. It has leased a new building with an area of 1800 square metres, into which it needs to fit eleven 'departments'. Prior to moving into the new building it has conducted an exercise to find the average number of trips taken by its staff between the eleven departments. Although some trips are a little more significant than others (because of the loads carried by staff) it has been decided that all trips will be treated as being of equal value.

Step 1 – Collect information

The areas required by each department together with the average daily number of trips between departments are shown in the flow chart in Fig. 7.17. In this example the direction of flow is not relevant and very low flow rates (less than five trips per day) have not been included.

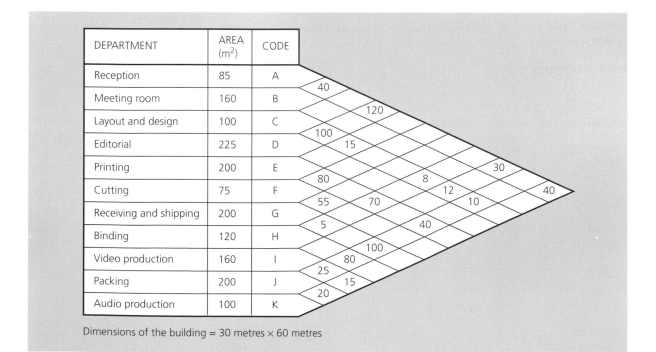

Figure 7.17 **Flow information for Rotterdam Educational Group**

Step 2 – Draw schematic layout

Figure 7.18 shows the first schematic arrangement of departments. The thickest lines represent high flow rates of between 70 and 120 trips per day, the medium lines are used for flow rates of between 20 and 69 trips per day, and the thinnest lines for flow rates between 5 and 19 trips per day. The objective here is to arrange the work centres so that those with the thick lines are closest together. The higher the flow rate, the shorter the line should be.

Step 3 – Adjust the schematic layout

If departments were arranged exactly as shown in Fig. 7.18, the building which housed them would be of an irregular, and therefore high-cost, shape. The layout needs adjusting to take into account the shape of the building. Figure 7.19 shows the departments arranged in a more ordered fashion which corresponds to the dimensions of the building.

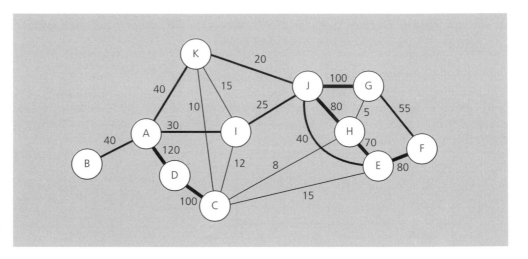

Figure 7.18
Schematic layout placing centres with high traffic levels close to each other

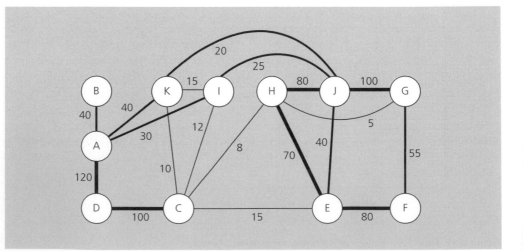

Figure 7.19
Schematic layout adjusted to fit building geometry

244

Step 4 – Draw the layout

Figure 7.20 shows the departments arranged with the actual dimensions of the building and occupying areas which approximate to their required areas. Although the distances between the centroids of departments have changed from Fig. 7.19 to accommodate their physical shape, their relative positions are the same. It is at this stage that a quantitative expression of the cost of movement associated with this relative layout can be calculated.

Step 5 – Check by exchanging

The layout in Fig. 7.20 seems to be reasonably effective but it is usually worthwhile to check for improvement by exchanging pairs of departments to see if any reduction in total flow can be obtained. For example, departments H and J might be exchanged, and the total distance travelled calculated again to see if any reduction has been achieved.

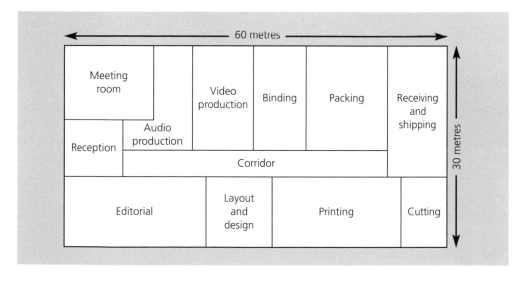

**Figure 7.20
Final layout of building**

Computer-aided process layout design

The combinatorial complexity of process layout has led to the development of several heuristic procedures to aid the design process. Heuristic procedures use what have been described as 'shortcuts in the reasoning process' and 'rules of thumb' in the search for a reasonable solution. They do not search for an optimal solution (though they might find one by chance) but rather attempt to derive a good suboptimal solution.

One such computer-based heuristic procedure is called CRAFT (Computerized Relative Allocation of Facilities Technique).[6] The reasoning behind this procedure is that, whereas it is infeasible to evaluate factorial N ($N!$) different layouts when N is large, it is feasible to start with an initial layout and then evaluate all the different ways of exchanging two work centres.

There are:

$$\frac{N!}{2! \, (N-2)!}$$

possible ways of exchanging two out of N work centres. So for a 20 work centre layout, there are 190 ways of exchanging two work centres.

Three inputs are required for the CRAFT heuristic: a matrix of the flow between departments, a matrix of the cost associated with transportation between each of the departments, and a spatial array showing an initial layout. From these:

● the location of the centroids of each department is calculated; and
● the flow matrix is weighted by the cost matrix, and this weighted flow matrix multiplied by the distances between departments to obtain the total transportation costs of the initial layout; and
● the model then calculates the cost consequence of exchanging every possible pair of departments.

The exchange giving the most improvement is then fixed, and the whole cycle repeated with the updated cost flow matrix. These iterations are repeated until no further improvement is made by exchanging two departments. Figure 7.21 shows the initial layout, which was an input to the model, and the final layout generated by the model.

Detailed design in cell layout

Cells are a compromise between the flexibility of process layout and the simplicity of product layout (treated next). For example, Fig. 7.22 shows how a process layout has been divided into four cells, each of which has the resources to process a 'family' of parts. In doing this the operations management has implicitly taken two interrelated decisions regarding:

● the extent and nature of the cells it has chosen to adopt, and
● which resources to allocate to which cells.

The extent and nature of cells

The extent and nature of cells can best be described by examining the amount of the direct and indirect resources which are located within the cell. Direct resources are those which directly transform material, information or customers. Indirect resources are there to support the direct resources in their transformation activities. Figure 7.23 shows a two-way classification of cells based on the degree of direct and indirect resources included in the cell.

In the bottom-right quadrant is what might be called a 'pure' cell. Its activities are focused on completing the whole of the transformation, and all the direct resources needed to do this are included in the cell. The top-right quadrant represents the logical extension of the cell concept to include all the support and administrative indirect resources needed for the cell to 'stand alone'. These large 'cells' are sometimes referred to as the 'plant-within-a-plant' concept. Similarly, a maternity unit could, if it contains all its support resources, also stand alone. The bottom-left quadrant represents the type of cell where resources are placed together because they are frequently needed in the same part of total transformation. For example, two machines which are always used one after the other could be put together. Similarly, a large library, although it probably has a copy machine area, could also locate a copy

(a)

Location pattern   Iteration 0

```
     1  2  3  4  5  6  7  8  9 10 11 12 13 14 15 16 17 18 19 20
 1   A  A  A  A  A  A  B  B  B  B  C  C  C  C  C  C  C  D  D  D
 2   A                 A  B        B  C                    D     D
 3   A                 A  B        B  C                 C  D     D
 4   A  A  A  A  A  A  B           B  C                 C  D     D
 5   E  E  E  E  E  E  B  B  B  B  C  C  C  C  C  C  C  D  D  D
 6   E                 E  F  F  F  F  F  G  G  G  G  G  G  G  G
 7   E                 E  F        F  G                       G
 8   E  E  E  E  E  E  F  F  F  F  F  G                       G
 9   H  H  H  I  I  I  I  I  I  I  I  G                       G
10   H     H  I                    I  G                       G
11   H     H  I              I  I  I  G  G  G  G  G  G  G  G
12   H     H  I           I  J  J  J  J  J  K  K  K  K  K
13   H     H  I           I  J              J  K              K
14   H  H  H  I  I  I  I  I  I  J  J  J  J  J  K  K  K  K  K
```

Total cost 11711.24   Est cost reduction 0

(b)

Location pattern   Iteration 4

```
     1  2  3  4  5  6  7  8  9 10 11 12 13 14 15 16 17 18 19 20
 1   E  E  E  E  E  E  B  B  B  B  C  C  C  C  C  C  C  J  J  J
 2   E                 E  B        B  C                    J     J
 3   E                 E  B        B  C                 C  J     J
 4   E  E  E  E  E  E  B           B  C                 C  J     J
 5   A  A  A  A  A  A  B  B  B  B  C  C  C  C  C  C  C  J  J  J
 6   A                 A  D  D  D  D  D  G  G  G  G  G  G  G  G
 7   A                 A  D        D  G                       G
 8   A  A  A  A  A  A  D  D  D  D  D  G                       G
 9   K  K  K  I  I  I  I  I  I  I  I  G                       G
10   K     K  I                    I  G                       G
11   K     K  I              I  I  I  G  G  G  G  G  G  G  G
12   K     K  I           I  F  F  F  F  F  H  H  H  H  H  H
13   K     K  I           I  F              F  H              H
14   K  K  K  I  I  I  I  I  I  F  F  F  F  F  H  H  H  H  H  H
```

Total cost 11238.43   Est cost reduction 472.81

Move A to E
Move D to F
Move K to H
Move F to J

Figure 7.21
(a) Initial layout array for the CRAFT heuristic, (b) Final layout after four iterations of the CRAFT heuristic

machine in the reference area for users to make copies if required. Finally, the top-left quadrant represents cells which some would dispute deserve the name. They only have the direct resources to apply to part of the total process, and in this way they might seem to be little different from a conventional work centre or department in a process layout. The difference is that they include all or most of the indirect resources they need. Again, they might theoretically be capable of 'standing alone' outside the rest of the operation. A specialist heat treatment cell in a manufacturing operation might contain all the specialist maintenance and supervisory and technical indirect staff to provide a complete technical and manufacturing service to the rest of the plant. The internal audit section of a bank might also need to contain its own technical and administrative support – this time perhaps to maintain its independence from the rest of the operation which it is auditing.

Figure 7.22 **Cell layout groups processes together which are necessary for a family of products**

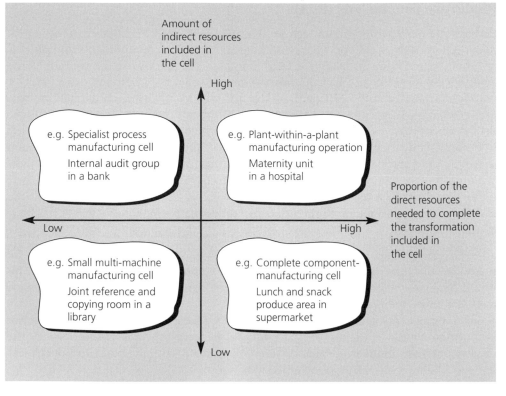

Figure 7.23
Types of cell

Allocating resources to cells

The detailed design of cellular layouts is difficult, partly because the idea of a cell is itself a compromise between process and product layout. With process layout we focus on the location of the various processes in the operation. With product layout (treated next) we focus on the requirements of the 'product' – cell layout needs to consider the needs of both.

Sometimes, in order to simplify the task, it is useful to concentrate on either the process or product aspects of cell layout. If cell designers choose to concentrate on processes, they could use *cluster analysis* to find which processes group naturally together. This involves examining each type of process and asking which other types of processes a product or part using that process is also likely to need. For example, in furniture manufacture, if all the parts which need holes drilling in them also need countersinking, then whatever the cell arrangement which is finally decided, drilling and countersinking machines will need to go together in the same cells. Alternatively, if the operation chooses to concentrate on its products to design its cell formation, they would probably use one of the *parts family coding and classification systems*. These systems use multi-digit codes for each part or product. The codes indicate the characteristics of the product such as shape, size, material and any other factors which define its processing requirements. There are several systems commercially available, for example the Brisch system from the UK, the Opitz system from Germany and MICLASS from the Netherlands.

Production flow analysis (PFA)[7]

Perhaps the most popular approach to allocating tasks and machines to cells is production flow analysis (PFA), which examines both product requirements and process grouping simultaneously. In Fig. 7.24(a) a manufacturing operation has grouped the components it makes into eight families – for example, the components in family 1 require machines 2 and 5. In this state the matrix does not seem to exhibit any natural groupings. If the order of the rows and columns is changed, however, to move the crosses as close as possible to the diagonal of the matrix which goes from top left to bottom right, then a clearer pattern emerges. This is shown in Fig. 7.24(b) and shows that the machines could conveniently be grouped together in three cells, indicated on the diagram as cells A, B and C. Although this procedure is a particularly useful way to allocate machines to cells, the analysis is rarely totally clean. This is the case here where component family 8 needs processing by machine 3 which has been allocated to cell B.

Generally there are three ways of dealing with this, none of them totally satisfactory:

● Another machine the same as machine 3 could be purchased and put in cell A. This would clearly solve the problem but requires investing capital in a new machine which might be under-utilized.

● Send components in family 8 to cell B after they have been processed in cell A (or even in the middle of their processing route if necessary). This solution avoids the need to purchase another machine but it conflicts partly with the basic idea of cell layout – to achieve a simplification of a previously complex flow.

● If there are several components which have this problem it might be necessary to devise a special cell for them (usually called a *remainder cell*) which will almost be like a mini-process layout. Again this does not conform strictly to the simplicity of pure cell layout and also can involve extra capital expenditure. The remainder cell does remove the 'inconvenient' components from the rest of the operation, however, leaving it with a more ordered and predictable flow.

**Figure 7.24
(a) and (b) Using production flow analysis to allocate machines to cells**

Detailed design in product layout

It may seem that there is little detailed design necessary in product layout because it involves arranging the transforming resources of the operation to fit the sequence required by the product or service. However, although the requirements of the product or service do indeed dominate product layout design, there are still many detailed design decisions to be taken. The nature of the design decision also changes a little. In other types of layout the decision is 'where to place what'. In product layout it is concerned more with 'what to place where', insomuch as locations are frequently decided upon and then work tasks are allocated to the location. For example, it may have been decided that four stations are needed to make briefcases on an assembly-line basis. The decision is then which of the tasks that go into making the briefcase should be allocated to which of the four stations.

This design decision is called the '*line-balancing*' decision and is only one (although sometimes the most difficult) of the decisions involved in the detailed design of product layouts. These decisions are as follows:

- What cycle time is needed?
- How many stages are needed?
- How should the task-time variation be dealt with?
- How should the layout be balanced?
- How should the stages be arranged?

The cycle time of product layouts

The cycle time of a product layout is the time between completed products, pieces of information or customers emerging from the operation. Cycle time is a vital factor in the design of product layouts and has a significant influence on most of the other detailed design decisions. It is calculated by considering the likely demand for the products or services over a period and the amount of production time available in that period.

For example, suppose the regional back-office operation of a large bank is designing an operation which will process its mortgage applications. The number of applications to be processed is 160 per week and the time available to process the applications is 40 hours per week.

$$\text{The cycle time for the layout} \; = \; \frac{\text{Time available}}{\text{Number to be processed}}$$

$$\text{In this case, cycle time} \; = \; \frac{40}{160} = \frac{1}{4} \; \text{hours}$$

$$= \; 15 \; \text{minutes}$$

So the bank's layout must be capable of processing a completed application once every 15 minutes.

The number of stages

The next decision in the detailed design of a product layout concerns the number of stages in the layout. In practice this can be anything between one and several hundred, depending partly on the cycle time required and the total quantity of work involved in producing the product or service. This latter piece of information is called the *total work content* of the product or service. The larger the total work content and the smaller the required cycle time, the more stages will be necessary.

For example, suppose the bank calculated that the average total work content of processing a mortgage application is 60 minutes. The number of stages needed to produce a processed application every 15 minutes can be calculated as follows:

$$\text{Number of stages} = \frac{\text{Total work content}}{\text{Required cycle time}}$$

$$= \frac{60 \text{ minutes}}{15 \text{ minutes}}$$

$$= 4 \text{ stages}$$

If this figure had not emerged as a whole number it would have been necessary to round it up to the next largest whole number. It is difficult (although not always impossible) to hire fractions of people to staff the stages.

Task-time variation

Thus far we could imagine a line of four stages, each contributing a quarter of the total work content of processing the mortgage, and passing the documentation on to the next stage every 15 minutes. In practice, of course, the flow would not be so regular. Each station's allocation of work might on average take 15 minutes, but almost certainly the time will vary each time a mortgage application is processed. This is a general characteristic of all repetitive processing (and indeed of all work performed by humans – *see* Appendix 2 at the end of the book) and can be caused by a number of different factors:

● Each product or service being processed along the line might be different – for example different models of automobile going down the same line.
● Products or services, although essentially the same, might require slightly different treatment. For example, in the mortgage-processing example, the time some tasks require will vary depending on the personal circumstances of the person applying for the loan.
● There are usually slight variations in the physical co-ordination and effort on the part of the person performing the task.

This variation can introduce irregularity into the flow along the line, which in turn can lead to both periodic queues at the stages and lost processing time. It may even prove necessary to introduce more resources into the operation to compensate for the loss of efficiency resulting from worktime variation.

Balancing worktime allocation

Perhaps the most problematic of all the detailed design decisions in product layout is that of ensuring the equal allocation of tasks to each stage in the line. This process is called *line balancing*. In the mortgage-processing example we have assumed that the 15 minutes of work content has been allocated equally to the four stations. This is nearly always impossible to achieve in practice and some imbalance in the work allocation between stages results. Inevitably this will raise the effective cycle time of the line. If it becomes greater than the required cycle time, it may be necessary to devote extra resources, in the shape of a further stage, to compensate for the imbalance.

The effectiveness of the line-balancing activity is measured by what is called *balancing loss*. This is the time wasted through the unequal allocation of work as a percentage of the total time invested in processing the product or service. In Fig. 7.25 the work allocations in a four-stage line are illustrated. The total amount of time invested in producing each product or service is four times the cycle time because, for every unit produced, all four stages have been working for the cycle time. When the work is equally allocated between the stages, the total time invested in each product or service produced is 4×2.5 = 10 minutes. However, when work is unequally allocated as illustrated, the time invested is $3.0 \times 4 = 12$ minutes, i.e. 2.0 minutes of time, 16.67 per cent of the total, is wasted.

Balancing techniques[8]

As in the other basic layout types there are a number of techniques available to help in the line-balancing task. Again, in practice, the most useful and most used 'techniques' are the simple heuristic approaches. Foremost among the latter is the *precedence diagram*.

Figure 7.25
Balancing loss is that proportion of the time invested in processing the product or service which is not used productively

253

The precedence diagram is a representation of the ordering of the elements which comprise the total work content of the product or service. Each element is represented by a circle. The circles are connected by arrows which signify the ordering of the elements. Two rules apply when constructing the diagram:

● the circles which represent the elements are drawn as far to the left as possible; and
● none of the arrows which show the precedence of the elements should be vertical.

The precedence diagram, either using circles and arrows or transposed into tabular form, is the most common starting point for most balancing techniques. We do not treat the more complex of these techniques here but it is useful to describe the general approach to balancing product layouts.

This general approach is to allocate elements from the precedence diagram to the first stage, starting from the left, in order of the columns until the work allocated to the stage is as close to, but less than, the cycle time. When that stage is as full of work as is possible without exceeding the cycle time, move on to the next stage, and so on until all the work elements are allocated. The key issue is how to select an element to be allocated to a stage when more than one element could be chosen. Two heuristic rules have been found to be particularly useful in deciding this:

● Simply choose the largest which will 'fit' into the time remaining at the stage.
● Choose the element with the most 'followers': that is the highest number of elements which can only be allocated when that element has been allocated.

Example: Karlstad Kakes

As an example of balancing a product layout, we can consider Karlstad Kakes (KK), a manufacturer of speciality cakes, which has recently obtained a contract to supply a major supermarket chain with a speciality cake in the shape of a space rocket. It has been decided that the volumes required by the supermarket warrant a special production line to perform the finishing, decorating and packing of the cake. This line would have to carry out the elements shown in Fig. 7.26, which also shows the precedence diagram for the total job. The initial order from the supermarket is for 5000 cakes a week and the number of hours worked by the factory is 40 per week. From this:

$$\text{The required cycle time} = \frac{40 \text{ hrs} \times 60 \text{ mins}}{5000}$$

$$= 0.48 \text{ mins}$$

$$\text{The required number of stages} = \frac{1.68 \text{ mins (the total work content)}}{0.48 \text{ mins (the required cycle time)}}$$

$$= 3.5 \text{ stages}$$

This means four stages.

Working from the left on the precedence diagram, elements a and b can be allocated to stage 1. Allocating element c to stage 1 would exceed the cycle time. In fact only element c can be allocated to stage 2 because including element d would again exceed the cycle time. Element d can be allocated to stage 3. Either element e or element f can also be allocated to stage 3, but not both or the cycle time would be exceeded. Following the 'largest element' heuristic rule, element e is chosen. The remaining elements then are allocated to stage 4. Figure 7.27 shows the final allocation and the balancing loss of the line.

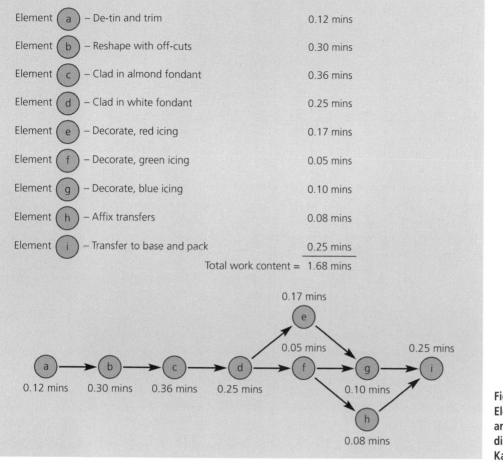

Element (a) – De-tin and trim   0.12 mins

Element (b) – Reshape with off-cuts   0.30 mins

Element (c) – Clad in almond fondant   0.36 mins

Element (d) – Clad in white fondant   0.25 mins

Element (e) – Decorate, red icing   0.17 mins

Element (f) – Decorate, green icing   0.05 mins

Element (g) – Decorate, blue icing   0.10 mins

Element (h) – Affix transfers   0.08 mins

Element (i) – Transfer to base and pack   0.25 mins

Total work content = 1.68 mins

Figure 7.26 Element listing and precedence diagram for Karlstad Kakes

Arranging the stages

Our assumption so far has been that all the stages necessary to fulfil the requirements of the layout will be arranged in a sequential 'single line'. Yet this need not necessarily be so. Return to the mortgage-processing example which requires four stages working on the task to maintain a cycle time of one processed application every 15 minutes. The conventional arrangement of the four stages would be to lay them out in one line, each stage having 15 minutes' worth of work. However, nominally, the same output rate could also be achieved by arranging the four stages as two shorter lines, each of two stages with 30 minutes' worth of work each. Alternatively, following this logic to its ultimate conclusion, the stages could be arranged as four parallel stages, each responsible for the whole work content. Figure 7.28 shows these options.

This may be a simplified example, but it represents a genuine issue. Should the layout be arranged as a single 'long-thin' line, as several 'short-fat' parallel lines, or somewhere in between? (Note that 'long' means the number of stages and 'fat' means the amount of work allocated to each stage.) In any particular situation there are usually technical constraints which limit either how 'long and thin' or 'short and fat' the

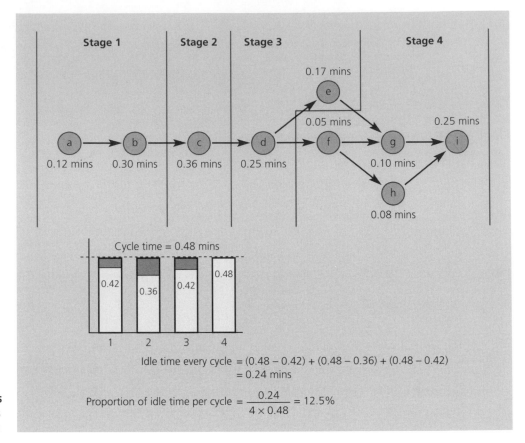

**Figure 7.27
Allocation of
elements to stages
and balancing loss
for Karlstad Kakes**

layout can be, but there is usually a range of possible options within which a choice needs to be made. The advantages of each extreme of the long-thin to short-fat spectrum are very different and help to explain why different arrangements are adopted.

The advantages of the long-thin arrangement
These include:

- *Controlled flow of materials or customers* – which is easy to manage.
- *Simple materials handling* – especially if a product being manufactured is heavy, large or difficult to move.
- *Lower capital requirements*. If a specialist piece of equipment is needed for one element in the job, only one piece of equipment would need to be purchased; on short-fat arrangements every stage would need one.
- *More efficient operation*. If each stage is only performing a small part of the total job, the person at the stage will have a higher proportion of direct productive work as opposed to the non-productive parts of the job, such as picking up tools and materials.

This latter point is particularly important and is fully explained in Chapter 9 when we discuss job design.

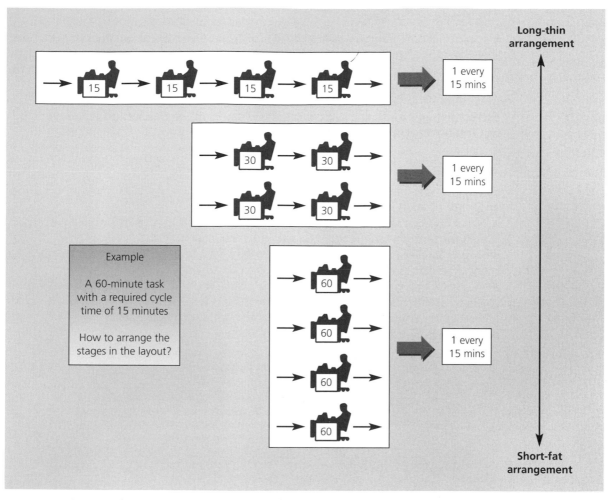

Figure 7.28 The arrangement of stages in product layout can be described on a spectrum from 'long-thin' to 'short-fat'

The advantages of the short-fat arrangement

These include:

- *Higher mix flexibility.* If the layout needs to process several types of product or service, each stage or line could specialize in different types.
- *Higher volume flexibility.* As volume varies, stages can simply be closed down or started up as required; long-thin arrangements would need rebalancing each time the cycle time changed.
- *Higher robustness.* If one stage breaks down or ceases operation in some way, the other parallel stages are unaffected; a long-thin arrangement would cease operating completely.
- *Less monotonous work.* In the mortgage example, the staff in the short-fat arrangement are repeating their tasks only every hour; in the long-thin arrangement it is every 15 minutes.

Again, this latter point is particularly important and is treated further in Chapter 9.

The shape of the line

If it is decided to adopt an arrangement which involves some sequential flow between stages arranged in series, a further decision concerns the shape of the line. Partly inspired by the experience of Japanese manufacturers, many manufacturing operations are adopting the practice of curving line arrangements into U-shaped or 'serpentine' arrangements (*see* Fig. 7.29). U-shapes are usually used for shorter lines and serpentines for longer lines. Richard Schonberger, the expert on Japanese manufacturing, sees several advantages in this:[9]

● *Staffing flexibility and balance.* The U-shape enables one person to tend several work stations – adjacent or across the U – without much walking. This opens up options for balancing work among the people: when demand grows, more labour can be added until every station has an operator.

● *Rework.* When the line bends around itself, it is easy to return bad work to an earlier station for rework without either fuss or much distance travelled.

● *Handling.* From a centre position within the U, a handler (human, vehicle, crane, or robot) can deliver materials and handle tools conveniently.

● *Passage.* Long straight lines interfere with cross travel in the rest of the operation. It is annoying when shelving in a supermarket is too long. People protest when a superhighway cuts a neighbourhood in half. It is the same with flow lines.

● *Teamwork.* A semicircle even looks like a team.

**Figure 7.29
The arrangement of stages – U-shaped arrangements**

Dave Ennis, OKI

Factory layout at OKI (UK)

OKI is a leading Japanese electronics company, specializing in the manufacture of printers and telecommunications equipment. Dave Ennis joined the company just after its decision to go ahead with plans to develop its new factory at Cumbernauld in Scotland. The company had taken over vacant premises, and Dave was one of a team of three responsible for the new facility.

'The initial stages of the new factory project were really exciting. We had the scope to start by creating a picture of what the site should look like, both internally and externally. Inside the factory, we had to decide on an appropriate layout which would give both manufacturing flexibility and the best utilization of the available space. We even built models to help us fully understand what we were committing ourselves to. The design of the premises was heavily influenced by our Japanese colleagues, and so the facility was organized on a cellular basis, which involved the concentration of particular product or processing expertise; each cell was like a self-contained mini factory. This type of design gave us the flexibility to add new cells, if required, for new product developments, and helped to create an identity among the staff, in terms of a feeling of belonging to their cell. We then had to decide what kind of people we were looking for to take on the running of these cells. These people were then to be designated as team leaders and would be responsible for the day-to-day operation of the cell as well as liaising with production control to ensure that a supply of materials was always available when required. The cells were laid out with minimal space allocated for materials, in the knowledge that such a design would encourage the operators to adopt an approach to the ordering of materials which would keep inventory to a minimum. Another key design issue we had to consider was the balance between technology and labour. Our Japanese colleagues were very helpful in being able to offer their advice and experience, and in the end, in order to retain maximum flexibility, the majority of the assembly lines were designed to require a high level of manual labour. By contrast, at the finished product and packing stations, we have automated the process to reduce the need for heavy manual work and reduce the risks of damage.'

Dave commented on the breadth of the decisions made in the layout design.

'Layout is not just concerned with the direct production departments in the factory. For example, the canteen and support facilities have recently been expanded, and we have fitted drinks and food dispensing machines to speed up the service levels at peak times. The location and scope of all of the support facilities were an important part of the original design task, almost as important as the decisions on the process and materials layout.

'The job certainly had a lot of variety and hidden tasks: our first priority was to try to establish an image of OKI, to move away from the old image and association of the former uses of the site. We completely refaced the building and have erected large signs with the company logo, to reinforce the corporate image to anyone coming to visit the factory. OKI is still growing and, thankfully, we still have space within the building into which we can expand. Our product range is increasing, and we are constantly reviewing our layout and always looking ahead to ensure that we are at least giving ourselves room to manoeuvre.' ∎

Source: By kind permission of David Ennis, OKI (UK) Limited

SUMMARY ANSWERS TO KEY QUESTIONS

What are the basic layout types used in operations?

- There are four basic layout types. They are:
  - fixed-position layout
  - process layout
  - cell layout
  - product layout.

What type of layout should an operation choose?

- Partly this is influenced by the nature of the process type, which in turn depends on the volume–variety characteristics of the operation.

- Partly also the decision will depend on the objectives of the operation. Cost and flexibility are particularly affected by the layout decision.

- The fixed and variable costs implied by each layout differ such that, in theory, one particular layout will have the minimum costs for a particular volume level. However, in practice, uncertainty over the real costs involved in layout make it difficult to be precise on which is the minimum-cost layout.

What is layout design trying to achieve?

- In addition to the conventional operations objectives which will be influenced by the layout design, factors of importance include the length and clarity of customer, material or information flow; inherent safety to staff and/or customers; staff comfort; accessibility to staff and customers; the ability to co-ordinate management decisions; the use of space, and long-term flexibility.

How should each basic layout type be designed in detail?

- Obviously this very much depends on the basic layout type chosen.

- In fixed-position layout the materials or people being transformed do not move but the transforming resources move around them. Techniques such as resource location analysis can be used to minimize the costs and/or inconvenience of flow of the transforming resources around the transformed resources.

- In process layout all similar transforming resources are grouped together in the operation. The detailed design task is usually (although not always) to minimize the distance travelled by the transformed resources through the operation. Either manual or computer-based methods can be used to devise the detailed design.

- In cell layout the resources needed for a particular class of product are grouped together in some way. The detailed design task is to group the products or customer types such that convenient cells can be designed around their needs. Techniques such as production flow analysis can be used to allocate products to cells.

- In product layout the transforming resources are located in sequence specifically for the convenience of products or product types. The detailed design of product layouts includes a number of decisions, such as the cycle time to which the design must conform, the number of stages in the operation, the way tasks are allocated to the stages in the line, and the arrangement of the stages in the line. The cycle time of each part of the design, together with the number of stages, is a function of where the design lies on the 'long-thin' to 'short-fat' spectrum of arrangements. This position affects costs, flexibility, robustness and staff attitude to work. The allocation of tasks to stages is called line balancing, which can be performed either manually or through computer-based algorithms.

CASE EXERCISE

Weldon Hand Tools

Weldon Hand Tools, one of the most successful of the European hand tool manufacturers, decided to move into the 'woodworking' tools market. Previously its products had been confined to car maintenance, home decorating, and general hand tools. One of the first products which it decided to manufacture was a general-purpose 'smoothing plane', a tool which smooths and shapes wood. Its product designers devised a suitable design and the company's work measurement engineers estimated the time it would take (in standard minutes – *see* Appendix 2) to perform each element in the assembly process. The marketing department also estimated the likely demand (for the whole European market) for the new product. Its sales forecast is shown in Table 7.6.

Table 7.6 Sales forecast for smoothing plane

Time period	Volume
Year 1	
1st Quarter	98 000 units
2nd Quarter	140 000 units
3rd Quarter	140 000 units
4th Quarter	170 000 units
Year 2	
1st Quarter	140 000 units
2nd Quarter	170 000 units
3rd Quarter	200 000 units
4th Quarter	230 000 units

The marketing department was not totally confident of its forecast, however.

'A substantial proportion of demand is likely to be export sales, which we find difficult to predict. But whatever demand does turn out to be, we will have to react quickly to meet it. The more we enter these parts of the market, the more we are into impulse buying and the more sales we lose if we don't supply.'

This plane was likely to be the first of several similar planes. A further model had already been approved for launch about one year after this, and two or three further models were in the planning stage. All the planes were similar, merely varying in length and width.

Table 7.7 Standard times for each element of assembly task

Fly-press operations	
Assemble poke S/A	0.12 S.M.
(LH poke, RH poke, poke bush)	(standard minutes)
Fit poke S/A to frog	0.10 S.M.
(poke, S/A, poke pin, frog)	
Rivet adjusting lever to frog	0.15 S.M.
(adjust lever, rivet, frog)	
Press adjusting nut screw to frog	0.08 S.M.
(frog, adjusting nut screw)	
TOTAL PRESS OPERATIONS	0.45 S.M.
Bench operations	
Fit adjusting nut to frog	0.15 S.M.
Fit frog screw to frog	0.05 S.M.
FROG S/A COMPLETE	
Fit knob to base	0.15 S.M.
Fit handle to base	0.17 S.M.
Fit frog S/A to base	0.15 S.M.
Assemble blade S/A	0.08 S.M.
Assemble blade S/A, clamp and label to base and adjust	0.20 S.M.
PLANE COMPLETE	
TOTAL FOR PRESS AND ASSEMBLY OPERATIONS	1.40 S.M.
Make up box, wrap plane, pack and stock	0.20 S.M.
TOTAL WORK TIME FOR ASSEMBLY AREA	1.60 S.M.

▶

Designing the manufacturing operation

It has been decided to assemble all planes at one of the company's smaller factory sites where a whole workshop is unused. Within the workshop there is plenty of room for expansion if demand proves higher than forecast. All machining and finishing of parts would be performed at the main factory and the parts shipped to the smaller site where they would be assembled at the available workshop.

An idea of the assembly task can be gained from the partially exploded view of the product (*see* Fig. 7.30). Table 7.7 gives the 'standard time' for each element of the assembly task. Some of the tasks are described as 'fly-press' operations. A fly press is a relatively simple tool, about a metre high, which has two weights mounted on to a screw thread. When the two weights are rotated they give momentum to the downward action of the screw thread which applies a downward force. This force is used for simple bending, riveting or force-fitting operations. A fly press is not an expensive or sophisticated technology.

Figure 7.30 Partially exploded view of the new plane

262

Costs and pricing

The standard costing system at the company involves adding a 150 per cent overhead charge to the direct labour cost of manufacturing the product, and the product would retail for the equivalent of around £25 in Europe where most retailers will sell this type of product for about 70–120 per cent more than they buy it from the manufacturer. ∎

Questions

1 How many staff should the company employ?
2 What type of facilities and technology will the company need to buy in order to assemble this product?
3 Design a layout for the assembly operation (to include the fly-press work) including the tasks to be performed at each part of the system.
4 How would the layout need to be adjusted as demand for this and similar products builds up?

DISCUSSION QUESTIONS

1 Identify the type of layout that might be adopted by the following organizations, explaining the reasoning behind your choice:

a ski resort
a dairy farm
a tree surgeon
a bakery
a bank.

Discuss the implications of variety and volume on flow.

2 Sketch the layout of your local shop, coffee bar or sports hall reception area. Observe the area and draw on to your sketch the movements of people through the area over a sufficient period of time to get over 20 observations. Assess the flow in terms of volume, variety and type of layout.

3 A tractor manufacturer, making a wide range of tractors to customer specification, is considering changing its layout from product to process. Discuss the implications of so doing.

4 Identify the main stages in the construction of a house from laying services and foundations to plastering and decorating. If each of these tasks were to be carried out by different sub-contractors, describe the potential layout problems.

5 (a) Visit a supermarket in your area. Try to get an appointment to talk with the manager to discuss the layout design issues.

(b) Compare the design of your supermarket with that of the Delhaize store described in the box. List and tabulate the main similarities and differences, and try to understand the reasons for these differences.

(c) What do you think, therefore, are the main criteria considered in the design of a supermarket layout?

(d) What competitive or environmental changes may result in the need to change store layouts in the future? Will these apply to all supermarkets, or only certain ones, such as town-centre stores?

6 The flow of materials through eight departments is shown in Table 7.8.

Table 7.8 Flow of materials

	D1	D2	D3	D4	D5	D6	D7	D8
D1	\	30						
D2	10	\	15	20				
D3		5	\	12	2		15	
D4		6		\	10	20		
D5				8	\	8	10	12
D6	3				2	\	30	
D7	3					13	\	2
D8				10	6		15	\

Assuming that the direction of the flow of materials is not important, construct a relationship chart, a schematic layout and a suggested layout, given that each department is the same size and the eight departments should be arranged four along each side of a corridor.

7 The university's students union is going to rearrange the layout of its lounge. It has been noticed that different groups of students use the two bars and four machines in the room in different ways, as shown in Table 7.9. The union would like to group the facilities in twos. Which groupings would you suggest, given that the sandwich bar and drinks bar are at opposite ends of the room and cannot be moved?

Table 7.9 Students' use of union facilities

Facility	Student type					
	1	2	3	4	5	6
Cola machine			X	X		X
Drinks bar		X	X			
Hot-drinks machine	X		X		X	
Cigarette machine		X	X			
Sandwich bar	X				X	
Chocolate machine				X		X

8 Table 7.10 shows 12 work elements that constitute the total work content of an assembly task. Using the information about duration times and precedences in the table, draw a precedence diagram and design an assembly line to produce as near as possible, but no less than, three items per hour. Calculate the balancing loss for the line.

9 Visit an assembly factory and look at the shape of the line. Find out why the line is the shape that it is.

10 A bicycle plant currently has a straight 20-stage assembly line with raw materials coming in at one side of the factory and the finished bikes going out at the other. Assess the implications of moving to a U-shaped line.

Table 7.10 Work content of assembly line

Element number	Duration (mins)	Preceding element(s)
1	4	–
2	7	–
3	5	1
4	6	1,2
5	4	2
6	3	2
7	4	3
8	6	4,5
9	5	5,6
10	4	9
11	6	8,10
12	6	7,11

NOTES ON CHAPTER

1 Source: Discussions with GEC staff.
2 Source: Interviews with company staff.
3 Source: (1991) *Paper and the Environment*, Arjo Wiggins Fine Papers, used with permission.
4 Sources: Interviews with company staff and Johnston, R., Chambers, S., Harland, C., Harrison, A. and Slack, N. (1997) *Cases in Operations Management* (2nd edn), Pitman Publishing.
5 This list kindly supplied by Paul Walley of Warwick University Business School, UK.
6 Armour, G.C. and Buffa, E.S. (1963) 'A Heuristic Algorithm and Simulation Approach to the Relative Location of Facilities', *Management Science*, Vol 9, No 2.
7 Burbidge, J.L. (1978) *The Principles of Production Control* (4th edn), Macdonald and Evans.
8 There are many different methods of balancing. *See*, for example, Kilbridge, K. and Wester, L. (1961) 'A Heuristic Method of Assembly Line Balancing', *Journal of Industrial Engineering*, Vol 57, No 4, or Steyn, P.G. (1977) 'Scheduling Multi-Model Production Lines', *Business Management*, Vol 8, No 1.
9 Schonberger, R. (1990) *Building a Chain of Customers*, Hutchinson Business Books.

SELECTED FURTHER READINGS

Apple, J.M. (1977) *Plant Layout and Materials Handling*, John Wiley.

Francis, R.L. and White, J.A. (1987) *Facility Layout and Location: An Analytical Approach*, Prentice Hall.

Gaither, N., Frazier, B.V. and Wei, J.C. (1990) 'From Job Shops to Manufacturing Cells', *Production and Inventory Management Journal*, Vol 31, No 4.

Green, T.J. and Sadowski, R.P. (1984) 'A Review of Cellular Manufacturing Assumptions and Advantages and Design Techniques', *Journal of Operations Management*, Vol 4, No 2.

Gunther, R.E., Johnson, G.D. and Peterson, R.S. (1983) 'Currently Practiced Formulations of The Assembly Line Balance Problem', *Journal of Operations Management*, Vol 3, No 3.

Hyer, N.L. and Wemmerlov, U. (1984) 'Group Technology and Productivity', *Harvard Business Review*, Vol 62, No 4.

Karlsson, C. (1996) 'Radically New Production Systems', *International Journal of Operations and Production Management*, Vol 16, No 11.

Malas, G.H. (1990) 'Assembly Line Balancing – Let's Remove the Mystery', *Journal of Industrial Engineering*, May.

Miller, J. G. and Vollmann, T.E. (1985) 'The Hidden Factory', *Harvard Business Review*, Vol 63, No 5.

Moore, J.M. (1980) 'Computer Methods in Facilities Layout', *Industrial Engineering*, Sept.

Prickett, P. (1994) 'Cell-based Manufacturing Systems: Design and Implementation', *International Journal of Operations and Production Management*, Vol 14, No 2.

Schuler, R.S., Writzman, L.P. and Davis, V.L. (1981) 'Merging Prescriptive and Behavioural Approaches for Office Layout', *Journal of Operations Management*, Vol 1, No 3.

Shafer, S.M. and Meredith, J.R. (1993) 'An Empirically Based Simulation Study of Functional Versus Cellular Layouts with Operations Overlapping', *International Journal of Operations and Production Management*, Vol 13, No 2.

Shambu, G., Suresh, N.C. and Pegels, C.C. (1996) 'Performance Evaluation of Cellular Manufacturing Systems', *International Journal of Operations and Production Management*, Vol 16, No 8.

Sule, V.E. (1988) *Manufacturing Facilities – Location Planning and Design*, PWS-Kent.

Wu, B. (1994), *Manufacturing System Design and Analysis* (2nd edn), Chapman and Hall.

CHAPTER 8

PROCESS TECHNOLOGY

INTRODUCTION

All operations use some kind of process technology. Whether its process technology is a humble word processor or the most complex and sophisticated of automated factories, the operation will have chosen to use the technology because it hopes to get some kind of advantage from it. Sometimes a process technology helps the operation address a clear market need; at other times the technology becomes available and an operation chooses to adopt it in the expectation that it can exploit its potential in some, as yet unspecified, way. Whatever the motivation, however, all operations managers need to understand what emerging technologies can do, in broad terms how they do it, what advantages the technology can give and what constraints it might impose on the operation. This is the purpose of this chapter. Figure 8.1 shows how the issues which it covers relate to the overall model of design of operations.

Figure 8.1 The design activities in operations management covered in this chapter

WHAT IS PROCESS TECHNOLOGY?

Process technologies are the machines, equipment and devices which help the operation to transform materials and information and customers in order to add value and fulfil the operation's strategic objectives. Fax machines, computers, mobile telephones, mechanical milking machines, robots, body scanners, combine harvesters, aircraft, overhead projectors, optical character recognition scanners, machine tools, and car-wash machines are all examples of process technology. All operations use process technology, even the most labour intensive. It may only be a telephone but it helps to process its transformed resources and, by so doing, it adds value.

Product/service and process technology

It is necessary, although sometimes difficult, to distinguish between product or service technology on one hand and process technology on the other. In manufacturing operations it is a relatively simple matter to separate product from process technology. For example, the technology of a video cassette recorder (VCR) is the way it converts TV signals into a form which can be transferred on to video tape, the way it controls the movement of the tape and the way it reads the information recorded on the tape and converts it into television pictures. On the other hand, the technology of the process which made the VCR is nothing like that. The process technology consists of the machine tools which made the metal components, the machines which mounted the electronic components on to printed circuit boards, the machines which shaped and bent the sheet metal for the casing and the robots which assembled the components.

In some service operations it is far more difficult to distinguish process from product/service technology. For example, large theme park entertainment complexes such as Disney World use flight simulator type technologies in some of their rides. These are large rooms mounted on moveable hydraulic struts which can move the whole room. A combination of wide-screen projection and movement can give a realistic experience of, say, space flight. Using technology in this way is one of the latest in a long history of achievements from what the Disney Corporation calls its 'Imagineers'. Yet is it product/service or process technology? It clearly processes Disney's customers. They literally go in at one side and emerge (the happier for their experience) at the other. It also helps Disney World add value for its customers, which is the purpose of process technology. But the technology is also part of the product. In fact customers go there especially to 'experience' the technology. It is an integral part of what they are paying their entrance fees for. In cases like this, product/service and process technology are, in effect, the same thing.

Notwithstanding the problems of separating product/service and process technology in some operations, we shall in this chapter be examining several technologies which add value in the transformation process.

Life-cycle effects on product/service and process technology

If product/service and process technologies can sensibly be separated in an operation, they will not always receive equal attention. Sometimes developing product technology will be seen as more important than developing process technology and sometimes *vice versa*. One factor which influences this is the stage of the product or service in its life cycle, that is the *maturity* of the product. Figure 8.2 illustrates how the relative rates of product/service and process technology innovation vary as a product matures.[1]

For example, examine how the relative emphasis on product and process technology of personal computers (PCs) has changed since their introduction in the late 1970s. For the first few years after their introduction the product technologies of PCs were their main feature. The fact that a product which was capable of being so conveniently transported could also be so powerful was a major innovation in product technology. These early PCs were often assembled using the most basic production methods. Apple Computer, for example, built its first machines in a garage. That did not matter to customers who were concerned more with what their products could do. As the rate of change in product technology slowed, a little more thought was put into how PCs were to be produced. Increasing volumes made continued use of the 'garage' approach both infeasible and uneconomic. PC manufacturers realized that further market success would depend on investing in automated production technology.

Operations management and process technology

Operations managers are continually involved in the management of process technology. To do so effectively they should be able to:

- articulate how technology could improve the operation's effectiveness;
- be involved in the choice of the technology itself;
- manage the installation and adoption of the technology so that it does not interfere with ongoing operations activities;
- integrate the technology into the rest of the operation;
- monitor continually its performance; and
- upgrade or replace the technology when necessary.

To do this operations managers do not need to be experts in engineering, computing, biology, electronics, or whatever is the core science on which the technology is based. It does mean, however, that they need to know enough about the principles behind the technology to be comfortable in evaluating some technical information, capable of dealing with experts in the technology and confident enough to ask relevant questions, such as:

- What does the technology do which is different to other similar technologies?
- How does it do it? That is, what particular characteristics of the technology are used to perform its function?
- What benefits does using the technology give to the operation?
- What constraints does using the technology place on the operation?

Technology in materials, information and customer processing

The rates of innovation in product/service and process technology shown in Fig. 8.2 are relative only to each other. Taken historically, process technology changes more in some periods than others. Since the 1980s most types of operation have, arguably, seen a noticeable increase in the rate of innovation in their process technology. Radical changes in telecommunications technologies such as information 'super-highways', the totally automated 'factory of the future', and large and/or faster aircraft, are just some of the process technologies which will have a dramatic impact on operations management. Behind almost all of these technological advances is one dominant factor: the availability of commercially available, low-cost microprocessing. The ubiquitous micro chip does not do much that was not achievable 30 years ago, but it can do it several orders of magnitude smaller and cheaper. It is this which is having such an impact in so many process technologies.

In the next section of this chapter we examine some of the process technologies which have particular significance for operations managers. These have been categorized as either materials processing (as in manufacturing operations), information

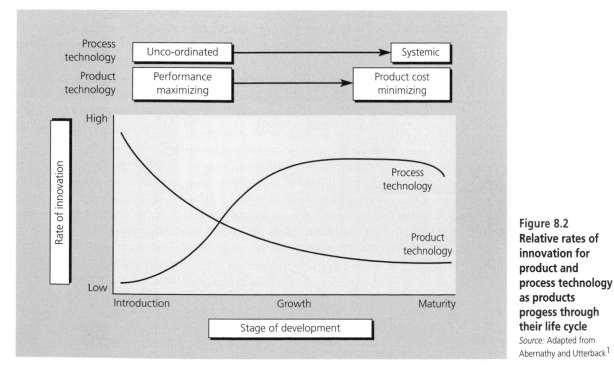

Figure 8.2
Relative rates of innovation for product and process technology as products progess through their life cycle
Source: Adapted from
Abernathy and Utterback[1]

269

processing (as in financial services, for example), and customer processing (as in retail, medical, hotel, transport operations, etc.). This distinction is for convenience only, however. In practice most of the newer technologies are different from what they have replaced because of their information processing capabilities.

MATERIALS-PROCESSING TECHNOLOGY

The way in which metals, plastics, fabric and other materials are processed has generally improved over time. New shaping, forming, cutting, moulding and bending techniques using harder cutting tools, spark erosion and lasers have impacted on many industries. It is not the specific materials-forming technologies with which we are concerned here, however. Rather it is the immediate technological context in which they are used. This includes such issues as the way forming technologies are controlled, how materials are physically moved, and how the manufacturing systems which include the technology are organized.

Numerically controlled machine tools

It was in the 1950s when an American company developed a method of controlling the machine tools which it used to machine helicopter blades. The method involved storing the information which instructed the machine, a numerically controlled (NC) machine, in the form of a punched paper tape. The machine could then read the paper tape which controlled the movements of its tools and the speed of the machine throughout the processing operation. Although most technology of this type is now controlled through its own computer, with instructions stored on disk, the principles are the same. Machines with their own computer are sometimes called computer numerically controlled (CNC) machines. The set of coded instructions and the computers attached to the machine have taken the place of the operator who would previously have controlled the machine by hand. This replacement gives more accuracy, precision and repeatability to the process. It can also give better productivity, partly through the elimination of possible operator error, partly because computer control can work to optimum cutting patterns, and partly because of the substitution of expensive, skilled labour.

NC machining centres

Most early NC machine tools did not actually do much more than the conventional machine tools which they replaced. They did do it better or cheaper, or both, however. The later technologies developed in two ways. First, they increased the degrees of freedom with which their cutting heads moved. Very simple machine tools, such as a drilling machine, might have only one degree of freedom – up and down. Others, such as a lathe, which turns cylindrical shapes, have two – in and out and along the piece being shaped. Machining centres usually have three or more (where the cutting head tilts) degrees of freedom which allow them to shape more complex parts. The second development was the ability of most machining centres to change their own tools. Magazines of different cutting tools are stored within the machine, and when the programme calls for a change of tool the old tool is replaced in the magazine and the new tool put into the cutting head. Together, these two developments greatly increased the variety of different parts which machines could produce, as well as allowing more complex parts to be machined.

Robotics

Robots were first introduced for industrial applications in the early 1960s, since which time their number and versatility have increased steadily. A robot can be defined as:

'...an automatic position-controlled reprogrammable multi-function manipulator having several degrees of freedom capable of handling materials, parts, tools or specialized devices through variable programmed motions for the performance of a variety of tasks... It often has the appearance of one or several arms ending in a wrist. Its control unit uses a memorizing device and sometimes it can use sensing and adaptation appliances that take account of the environment and circumstances. These multi-purpose machines are generally designed to carry out repetitive functions and can be adapted to other functions without permanent alternation of the equipment.' [2]

The movement of robots is controlled in a similar manner to NC machine tools but most robots have many degrees of freedom. Figure 8.3 shows the six standard movements of a robot arm.[3] In terms of their application, robots can be classified as follows:[4]

● *Handling robots.* The work piece is handled by the robot: for example, for material handling, loading and unloading of work pieces for machine tools, casting, pressing, injection moulding, forging, fitting, etc.
● *Process robots.* The tool is gripped by the robot: for example, in various types of metalworking operations (cutting, drilling, grinding, chipping), joining of materials (welding, gluing, wiring), surface treatment (paint spraying, surface coating, polishing), etc.
● *Assembly robots.* Robots are used in the assembly of parts into components and complete products.

More recent robots can also include some limited sensory feedback through vision control and touch control. However, although the sophistication of robotic movement is increasing, their abilities are still more limited than popular images of robot-driven factories suggest. In fact most robots are, in practice, used for mundane operations such as:

● welding
● paint spraying
● stacking pallets
● grinding/deburring
● packing
● loading and unloading machines.

In these tasks the attribute of the robots which is being exploited is their ability to perform repetitive, monotonous and sometimes hazardous tasks for long periods, without variation and without complaining (*see* the box on ABB's robots and the box on Radioactive Robots).

271

Figure 8.3
Robot with six standard movements

Automated guided vehicles (AGVs)

For every activity in a manufacturing process which adds value to the product by physically transferring it, there is usually one which moves or stores the material. Although they are often unavoidable, such activities add no value to the material. Not surprising then that operations managers seek ways of automating them. Automated guided vehicles (AGVs) are one class of technology which does this. AGVs are small, independently powered vehicles which move materials to and from value-adding operations. They are usually guided by cables buried in the floor of the operation and receive instructions from a central computer. Variations on this arrangement include AGVs which have their own on-board computers or optical guidance systems.

In addition to any cost advantages gained by substituting labour with technology, the use of AGVs can help promote just-in-time delivery of parts between stages in the production process (*see* Chapter 15 for a discussion of just-in-time principles). In some industries they are also used as mobile work stations to replace the more traditional conveyor systems. For example, truck engines can be assembled on AGVs, with the AGV moving between assembly stations. The ability to move independently reduces the pacing effect on each stage in the process and allows for variation in the time each stage takes to perform its task. AGVs are sometimes used to move materials in non-manufacturing operations. Warehousing is the obvious example but they are used also in libraries to move books, in offices to move mail and even in hospitals to transport samples.

ABB ROBOTS TAKE OVER SOME OF THE REPETITIVE WORK AT ECCO SHOES AND AT SCANIA TRUCKS[5]

Asea Brown Boveri (ABB) Robotics is a leading manufacturer of industrial robots, whose machines are used in a wide variety of applications, including packing army meal rations, assembling washing machines, and unloading plastic moulding machines. Two very different examples of the application of ABB robots are the final assembly of shoes in Denmark, and the painting of truck axles in Sweden.

Ecco, a Danish shoe company, produces over seven million shoes each year, and has invested in extensive robot facilities in the manufacturing operation, primarily to improve its quality consistency. It has installed over 20 robots since 1984, which work in its factories in Portugal, Denmark and Japan. Initial manufacturing stages are still processed by hand. The soft leather upper is cut and sewn together in the Indian and Indonesian factories before being shipped to the more automated plants for completion. A robot is used to cut a five millimetre track around

Figure 8.4 Robots used in small parts assembly
Source: Courtesy of ABB Robotics

273

the leather upper which is then transferred by a second robot to the sole-forming machine where the leather upper is moulded on to a flexible sole. A third robot is employed to cut away any excess material from the sole, without damaging the upper. Each robot is programmed to operate according to the recognized size and model of shoe being processed. Ecco operations managers believe that the working environment is much improved by using robots for the more physically demanding or boring tasks, as well as giving increased productivity and enhancing quality.

The Swedish truck group Scania decided to build a new painting facility for its axles factory at Falun. The decision to use robotics in the paint shop was based on their ability to meet precise customer requirements for paint type, colour, and specification. The robots are easily and quickly changed over and adaptable to new products. Two operators can run the whole system from a control room, where computer screens depict the movements and settings for each of the robots. The robot first prepares and cleans the parts, then dries off the moisture by blowing compressed air into the cavities and remaining holes, then the parts are primed and finally painted, again all by robots. The axle parts on Scania trucks are shaped differently, which means that the spray guns on the painting system need to be adjusted continually during the process. There is an integrated computer control system which co-ordinates all of these adjustments, controlling the amount of paint being sprayed and thus reducing spillage (both an environmental and cost benefit). Essentially, the main feature of the robots is their flexibility. Scania is confident that it can adapt the systems as necessary to suit its precise needs in the future. The use of robots has also improved the working conditions of the employees, and has assisted in reducing waste and solvent emissions. ■

Questions

1 In Ecco's shoe factories, why are some manufacturing stages performed by hand and some by robots?

2 What are the advantages of using robot technology to paint axles at the Scania plant?

Flexible manufacturing systems

Flexible manufacturing systems (FMS) bring together the technologies we have already described into a coherent system. FMS can be defined as 'a computer-controlled configuration of semi-independent work stations connected by automated material handling and machine loading'.[7] This definition gives an indication of the component parts of FMS:

● NC 'work stations', either machine tools or more sophisticated work centres, which perform the 'machining' operations;
● loading/unloading facilities, often robots which move parts to and from the work stations;
● transport/materials-handling facilities which move the parts between work stations. (These may be AGVs or conveyor systems or, if distances are short, robots.);
● a central computer control system which controls and co-ordinates the activities in the system. This co-ordination could include not only the control of the individual facilities (work stations, robots, AGVs) but also the production-planning sequencing and routing of the parts through the system.

RADIOACTIVE ROBOTS[6]

Decommissioning spent nuclear power stations is an agonizingly slow process which in many countries will take well over 100 years to complete. It is also a delicate and potentially dangerous process for those involved. This is why robots are used where possible to move, dismantle, and manipulate hazardous radioactive material. Robots are also used for controlled-circuit television inspections as well as the pumping and removal of radioactive sludge. For example, at British Nuclear Fuels Limited's Windscale Plant remote-controlled robotic crushers are being used to dismantle the plant's pile chimneys, and in nearby Sellafield a floating robot is draining and dismantling a tank of highly active liquid waste. ■

Question

1 Robots are used in this example because of the hazardous environment in which the tasks take place. What other examples can you think of where the safety of operators is the major motivation for investment in robot technology?

An FMS is more than a single technology as such. It has integrated the single technologies into a system which has the potential to be greater than the sum of its parts. In effect, an FMS is a self-contained 'micro operation' which is capable of manufacturing a whole component from start to finish. Furthermore, the flexibility of each of the individual technologies combine to make an FMS (at least in theory) a supremely versatile manufacturing technology. A sequence of products, each different but within the capability 'envelope' of the system, could be processed in the system in any order and without change-over delays between each product. The 'envelope of capability' concept is important here. Any collection of machines within an FMS must have some finite limits on the size and shape of the materials it can process. The implication of this is that an FMS is best suited to manufacturing applications where the designs of parts are basically similar yet whose batch sizes can be small (perhaps as small as one).

FMS vary considerably in their complexity and size, and the term FMS is often used for technologies which are quite dissimilar. For example, one FMS might be intended to produce a high variety of parts, each in batches of a single piece. Another might be producing a single product in effect for long periods but then changing rapidly to another product. This latter situation is usually accomplished with what is sometimes called a *flexible transfer line* (FTL).

Are FMS really flexible?

The 'flexibility' characteristics of FMS seem to be their main advantage. However, their flexibility advantage may not be what it seems. It is certainly true that, when compared to any previous attempts to automate manufacturing processes, FMS are extremely flexible. Previously, so-called 'hard' automation required the instructions to the machine to be fixed in its hardware. Any change in how the machine was to operate required the machine itself to be physically reconfigured (changing cams, gears and slides, for example). The new manufacturing technologies such as FMS hold their instructions in the form of software which can be changed very easily.

Perhaps this is not the real point, however. FMS may be more flexible than any previous automated manufacturing technologies, but they may not be more flexible than the manufacturing systems which they aim to replace. The fairly high-variety, fairly low-volume operations where FMS seem to be most appropriate would previously have used stand-alone machine tools arranged either in a process or cell layout (*see* Chapter 7 for a description of these layouts). Such a manufacturing system is extremely flexible in terms of the variety of components it can process, certainly more flexible than any FMS. Perhaps this is why most FMS are used for applications where the range of parts is not particularly wide.

The advantages of FMS

One kind of flexibility at which FMS do excel is what we called in Chapter 2 *product flexibility*, that is the ability to introduce changes to product designs. The integrated control and programmable flexibility of FMS make this a relatively straightforward task, especially when compared with the hard automation which was used previously. However, in spite of its flexibility image, most of the benefits reported by companies who have adopted this type of technology come in terms of the other performance objectives.

A survey of 31 firms who have adopted FMS, reported by Professor John Bessant of Brighton University, identifies the following benefits:[8]

1 *Lead time and throughput (factory door-to-door) time reduction.* Here the general experience is that substantial savings can be made in throughput (factory door-to-door) time. Savings of between 60 per cent and 70 per cent were reported.
2 *Inventory savings (especially of work-in-progress).* Another expected consequence of reducing set-up times and integrating process elements is that there is smoother flow of material through the factory with less queueing and build-up of material waiting for machining. For the firms which provided a percentage estimate, the average saving was over 70 per cent.
3 *Increased utilization.* One major problem in batch manufacturing is the relatively low level of utilization of equipment, since so much time is spent waiting for products to be put on machines which are stopped for resetting, maintenance, and so on. The extent of reported improvement over previous methods ranged from 200 per cent to 400 per cent.
4 *Reduced set-up times.* Closely linked to improved utilization is the reduction in set-up times between different batches. Twelve firms reported improvements over previous methods of between 50 per cent and 90 per cent.
5 *Reduced number of machines or operations.* Part of the reduction in set-up times and in throughput times is derived from the physical integration of operations into fewer, more complex machines. In this sample, ten firms provided estimates of the extent of reduction of number of machines, ranging from 45 per cent to 90 per cent.
6 *Increased quality.* Quality improvements cannot be wholly attributed to that technology, since in many firms there is considerable effort being spent to improve quality performance. However, 20 firms reported improved quality as an outcome of their investments, with several others which involved new plant also commenting on the high levels which they were able to achieve. Estimates of this improvement ranged from 20 per cent to 90 per cent.

In addition to the above benefits, a number of others were reported, often on a firm-specific basis. These included:

- space savings
- reduced dependence on sub-contractors
- skill saving
- increased responsiveness to customers (speed and quality of service)
- facilitated more rapid production innovation cycles
- improved prototyping capability.

Comparisons of advanced manufacturing technologies

The progression from conventional machine tools to FMS involves a gradual replacement of manual operations with automated operations. Table 8.1 shows how Professor Chris Voss, of London Business School,[9] characterizes the relationship between the

Table 8.1 **The spectrum of automation in manufacturing**

degree of possible automation and some of the technologies we have described. Note how the steps at the core of the process, involving the shaping or cutting activities, are the first to be automated, after which the more peripheral activities at either end of the whole process are gradually included within the capabilities of the technology.

Volume and variety characteristics

These technologies differ in their flexibility capabilities and economics and will therefore each be appropriate for different parts of the volume–variety continuum. Figure 8.5 positions the technologies on the volume–variety matrix which we introduced in Chapter 4.

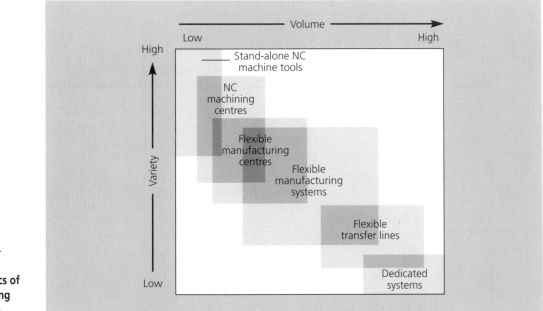

**Figure 8.5
The volume–
variety
characteristics of
manufacturing
technologies**

The positions illustrated in Fig. 8.5 are not intended to be prescriptive, just indicative of what is sensible under current conditions of cost and technological development. Furthermore, the area occupied by FMS technology has increased, and is likely to increase further, as FMS really do become more flexible while retaining the cost advantages of integration and automation.

Computer-integrated manufacturing (CIM)

The integration of the separate developments in manufacturing technology exemplified by FMS can be taken further. FMS integrates those activities which are concerned directly with the transformation process but need not necessarily include the other activities which must have happened prior to the transformation. The products must have been designed, for example, quite possibly using the computer-aided design (CAD) technology described in Chapter 5. Similarly, the production-planning activity must have occurred, otherwise the manufacturing system would not know what to make or when to make it. Behind these activities, other systems in the organization which forecast sales, take orders, set quality standards, plan maintenance, and so on will also be happening.

Most of these 'surrounding' systems will themselves be computer based. It follows then that the potential must exist for these 'surrounding' systems to be integrated with the direct materials-processing technologies such as FMS. This wider integration is known as *computer-integrated manufacturing* (CIM). It can be defined as 'the integration of computer-based monitoring and control of all aspects of the manufacturing process, drawing on a common database and communicating via some form of computer network', although the term CIM is now frequently used to indicate far less ambitious forms of integrated manufacturing.[10]

The hierarchy of integration

Figure 8.6 illustrates how manufacturing technologies can be described as being progressively more integrated states of more basic technologies. The basic technologies which help to design products, control the tools which form materials, transport materials and manage some of the operational aspects of the manufacturing process can come together in stages. The first stage is the integration *between* areas of activity to produce such com-

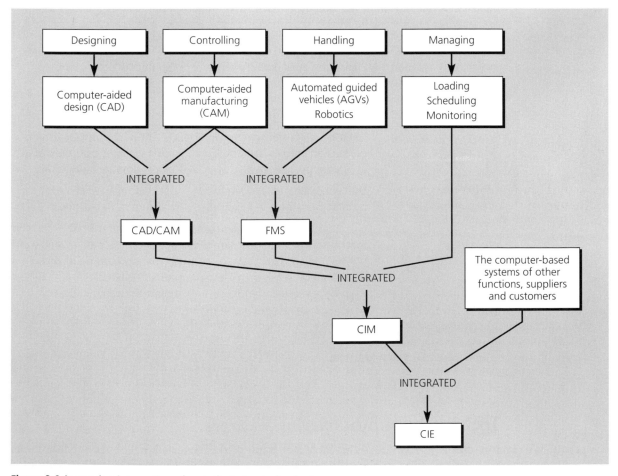

Figure 8.6 Increasing integration of manufacturing technologies

279

bined technologies as CAD/CAM and FMS. Second, the integration of all the internal activities produces the broad definition of CIM. Finally, integration of the organization's CIM activity with other functions and perhaps even suppliers and customers, approaches what has been termed the *computer-integrated enterprise* (CIE).

Human-centred CIM

The desirability of the seemingly inexorable progress towards increasing automation of manufacturing has not gone unchallenged. Some argue that, by taking a purely technical perspective on developing integrated manufacturing systems, process technologies are neglecting the skills of the people who staff them. Rather than design CIM systems to technical criteria and then consider how people are to fit into them, it is argued that a 'parallel design' approach should be adopted. This would allow users of a CIM system to shape its design before the format of the system is finally fixed. This encourages users to integrate their skills and contribution with the technological elements of the system. Table 8.2 illustrates how 'pure' human-centred systems might differ from purely technology-centred systems.

Table 8.2 A comparison of technology-centered and human-centered AMT systems design

Design choice point	Technology-centred systems	Human-centred systems
Allocation of function	Operator carries out only those functions that cannot be automated	Operator allocates functions depending upon particular circumstances and judgement during production
Systems architecture	Centralized control system, with production machines controlled at highest possible level	Decentralized control system, with machines controlled at lowest possible level
Control characteristics of human-machine interface	User actions paced and regulated by directives stored in machine	User discretion and control maximized, the technology does not dictate work methods
Information characteristics	System status data presented only to management; restricted access for shop-floor users	System status data available at all machines; facilitation of cross-functional communication
Allocation of responsibilities	Work controlled by functional specialists	Work controlled by multi-skilled shop-floor users

Source: Adapted from Corbett, J.M. (1992) 'Working at the Interface' in Adler, P.S. and Winograd, T.A. *Usability*, Oxford University Press.

Technology summaries

It is useful to summarize in Table 8.3 some of the materials-processing technologies we have discussed in terms of the four questions which we identified at the beginning of this chapter:

- What does the technology do?
- How does it do it?
- What advantages does it give?
- What constraints does it impose?

Table 8.3 Summary of materials-processing technologies

NC (and CNC) machine tools

What does it do?	Performs the same types of metal cutting and forming operations which have always been done, but with control provided by a computer.
How does it do it?	Preprogrammed instructions are read from a disk, tape or paper tape by a computer which activates the physical controls in the machine tool.
What advantages does it give?	Precision, accuracy, optimum use of cutting tools which maximizes their life, and higher labour productivity.
What constraints does it impose?	Higher capital cost than manual technology. Needs skilled staff to preprogramme the instructions for the controlling computer.

NC machine centres

What does it do?	Performs a relatively wide variety of machining operations within one process activity.
How does it do it?	By computer-controlled movements through several degrees of freedom and the automated changing of cutting tools which are stored within the machine.
What advantages does it give?	More flexibility (range and response – see Chapter 2) than simple NC machine tools, and higher productivity.
What constraints does it impose?	Even higher capital cost than simple NC machine tools and increased complexity of maintenance and programming.

Industrial robots

What does it do?	Moves and manipulates products, parts or tools.
How does it do it?	Through a programmable and computer-controlled (sometimes multi-jointed) arm with an effector end piece which will depend on the task being performed.
What advantages does it give?	Can be used where conditions are hazardous or uncomfortable for humans, or where tasks are highly repetitive. Performs repetitive tasks at lower cost than using humans and gives greater accuracy and repeatability.
What constraints does it impose?	Cannot perform tasks which require delicate sensory feedback or sophisticated judgement.

Automated guided vehicles (AGVs)

What does it do?	Moves materials between operations.
How does it do it?	Independently powered vehicles guided by buried cables and controlled by computer.
What advantages does it give?	Independent movement, flexibility of routing and long-term flexibility of use.
What constraints does it impose?	Capital cost considerably higher than alternative (conveyor) systems.

Table 8.3 continued

Flexible manufacturing systems (FMS)	
What does it do?	Completely manufactures a range of components (occasionally whole simple products) without significant human intervention during the processing.
How does it do it?	By integrating programmable technologies such as machine tools, materials-handling devices and robots through centralized computer control.
What advantages does it give?	Faster throughput times, higher utilization of capital equipment, lower work-in-progress inventories, more consistent quality, higher long-term product flexibility.
What constraints does it impose?	Very high capital costs with uncertain payback, needs programming skills, and can be vulnerable to tool breakage (which can stop the whole system).

Computer-integrated manufacturing (CIM)	
What does it do?	Co-ordinates the whole process of manufacturing and manufactures a part, component or product.
How does it do it?	Connects and integrates the information technology which forms the foundation of design technology (CAD), manufacturing technology (FMC or FMS), materials handling (AGVs or robots) and the immediate management of these activities (scheduling, loading, monitoring).
What advantages does it give?	Fast throughput times, flexibility when compared with other previous 'hard' technologies, the potential for largely unsupervised manufacture.
What constraints does it impose?	Extremely high capital costs, formidable technical problems of communications between the different parts of the system, and some vulnerability to failure and breakdown.

INFORMATION-PROCESSING TECHNOLOGY

Information-processing technologies include any devices which collect, manipulate, store or distribute information. Most of these we class under the general heading of 'computer-based technologies', although it should also include those associated with telecommunications operations. Taken together these technologies include:

● computers – mainframe, mini and personal;
● peripheral devices – storage, printers, readers, etc;
● transmission/receiving devices – satellite dishes, modems, optical cable networks, faxes, telephones;
● software systems and applications.

At the core of these technologies is the computer itself, the most common single type of technology within operations. The presence of computers in nearly all types of operation is largely because of the way the cost of computing power has fallen so dramatically. One of the main problems which operations managers have in coping with information technology is the sheer pace of technical improvement. Usually, organizational and operational issues are the main constraints in applying information technology because managers are unsure how best to use the potential in the technology. The following quotation gives some idea of how fast information technology has changed:

'The rate of progress in information technology has been so great that if comparable advances had been made in the automotive industry, you could buy a Jaguar that would travel at the speed of sound, go 600 miles on a thimble of gas and cost only $2!'[11]

Centralized information processing

All computers used for management purposes (as opposed to process control) were, at one time, large. It was simply the most economical way of buying processing power. The different parts of the organization originally accessed the computer in *batch mode*: that is, each of the separate transactions associated with a particular activity would not be processed as they were originated. Instead they would be collected together or 'batched' until there were sufficient transactions to process together. Alternatively (and more usually) a particular processing activity would be performed at regular intervals. For example, suppose the back office of a bank used a batch access system to process its loan applications. Each time a loan application was received it would be kept until the time allocated to processing loans, and then processed along with all the other loan applications received since the last batch was run. All the documentation and file updating was done at this time.

Decentralized information processing

With the increasing use of computer-based technology and the development of more specifically tailored applications software, centralized computers became viewed as cumbersome for some applications. At the same time the cost and power of mid-range computers reached the point where it was economically feasible for different parts of the operation to have their own dedicated computer. Those 'minicomputers' could be under the direct control of the staff who would use them. Applications software could be designed specifically for their needs and transactions processed when and how they thought appropriate. This is the *distributed processing* concept. The obvious problem with such an arrangement is that, in bringing computing power closer to its users, co-ordinating all the various processing activities is more complex. It is difficult to know what is happening at the various processing centres around the operation. The obvious answer to the problem is for the distributed minicomputers to exchange information. This is an idea which is easy in principle but difficult in practice. The technical problems of achieving total compatibility between essentially stand-alone minicomputer-based systems is sufficiently great to cause considerable operating problems.

Local area networks (LANs)

The need to retain the clear advantages of distributed processing while retaining the control and communication benefits of centralized computing focused attention on the mechanism of communications itself – that is the *network* which connects the distributed processing power. Combine the concept of the network with smaller and cheaper personal computers (PCs) and the concept of the *local area network* (LAN) emerges.

A LAN is a communications network which operates over a limited distance, usually within an operation. Connected to the network are devices such as personal computers, display screens, printers, interfaces and minicomputers. Information (data, text, and sometimes video) is exchanged between the devices along the network. The network itself can be formed from optical fibres, coaxial cable or simple telephone-type wiring, depending on the speed and volume of information which is being exchanged. The most common type of LAN connects the PCs in a work group or several departments and allows all staff to share common access to data files, other devices such as printers, and links to outside networks such as telephone lines. Figure 8.7 illustrates a LAN.

Figure 8.7 A local area network (LAN)

The great advantage of LANs (and their larger cousins, wide area networks (WANs)) is their greater flexibility when compared with other more cumbersome forms of distributed processing. In particular, advantages include the following:[12]

● *Incremental growth*. New devices can be added to the network as they are required or become available.
● *Redundancy*. Robustness can be built into the system by keeping spare machines and duplicate files.
● *Location flexibility*. Work stations and peripherals can be located where needed and relocated with relatively little disruption when necessary.
● *Operational autonomy*. Both the control and the administration of hardware and software can be assigned to those staff who use them.

Telecommunications and information technology

Computer-based technologies in business use have always been based on digital principles, that is converting information into a *binary* form, using 0s and 1s. Telecommunications, on the other hand, were originally based on analogue technology. The digitization of telecommunications transmissions (including digital compression techniques, which allows information to be squeezed into a smaller 'space' so that more can be sent using a given amount of transmission capacity) together with the use of high-capacity optical fibre networks, brought new possibilities. The technologies of computing and telecommunications in effect merged. Digital telecommunication lines could carry both voice and non-voice (text, data, etc.) traffic at the same time, so separate sites of the same organization, or separate operations, could lease lines for their exclusive use. Alternatively, separate operations could use one of the public *integrated services digital networks* (ISDN).

The effect on telecommunications companies of these developments has been far reaching. Figure 8.8 shows the increase in the new types of services they can offer, most of which are the result of digital technologies.

Electronic data interchange

Data exchange networks have had a significant impact in the way information relating to inter-operations trade can be processed. Details of orders placed with suppliers, orders received from customers payments made to suppliers and payments received from customers can all be transmitted through information networks. If suppliers, customers and the banks involved in the financial arrangements have themselves adopted compatible technology, the information can remain in its digital form. This eliminates the need to read paper-based information and key it into their own computers. The use of networks for trading in this way is called *electronic data interchange* (EDI), one of the fastest growing areas of business information processing.

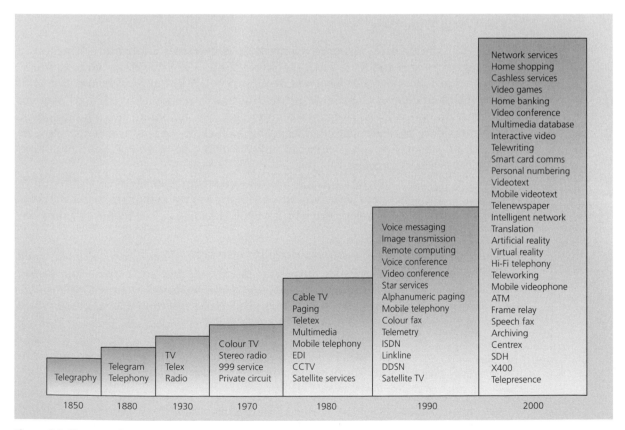

Figure 8.8 The growth in telecommunications services

The networks which carry EDI information are called *value-added network services* (VANs) and are usually run by third parties rather than the traders themselves. VANs providers in Europe, for example, include AT&T's *Easylink*, INS's *Tradanet*, BT's *Edinet*. Customers and suppliers who link into these networks not only need the necessary hardware, but to obtain all the advantages of EDI, they also need internal software and systems which are compatible with those of their trading partners. Figure 8.9 illustrates the way EDI services are being promoted by one UK-based bank.

The Internet

In effect, the Internet is a 'network of networks'. It is used to link computer networks with other computer networks. Its origins lie in the development of local area networks (LANs) in the '70s and '80s (and later, wide area networks or WANs). However, because they used different types of computer, LANs usually found it difficult to talk to each other. Nor did WANs use the same language as LANs. The breakthrough came with the development of a technique called 'packet switching'. This enabled many messages to be sent to different locations at the same time conveniently and allowed individual networks to communicate. In practical terms, though, most of us think of the Internet as the provider of services such as the ability to browse the World Wide Web.

The World Wide Web

Until 1993 the Internet was used primarily by universities and some businesses to exchange messages and files. Then the World Wide Web (WWW or Web) dramatically changed our view. The Web was developed by CERN in Switzerland and MIT in the United States to provide a 'distributed hypermedia/hypertext' system. Information on the Web is organized into pages which contain text and graphics. Elements of the page are identified as links which allow users to transfer to another page of information which in turn has links to other pages, and so on. These links are called *hypertext interfaces*.

As yet, the exact impact of the WWW on operations management is difficult to forecast. Some believe it will be significant, although many authorities see it as something of a 'wild west' frontier town which will need taming before its full potential can be realized.

'Rather than just posting pages on the World Wide Web, for instance, companies may want to move more selectively, clustering themselves into on-line communities where rules prevail and commerce can proceed. Auto parts suppliers, for example, might band together in an exclusive network serving only the auto industry, whereas investment management firms might want to sell their services only where distribution is limited and payment ensured. These sorts of on-line communities will create a very different form of electronic commerce from the one envisioned today by many Internet adherents. The communities will not be open to all; they will increasingly charge customers for their services; and they will not permit information to flow across seamless borders.'[13]

FMS at Yamazaki Mazak

Photo courtesy of Yamazaki Machinery UK Ltd.

FMS installation at Yamazaki Mazak's European plant

The Japanese tool manufacturers, Yamazaki, have, in their European factory, one of the most advanced machine tool manufacturing operations in Europe. Their four FMS systems allow overnight unstaffed production and so allow the company to make the most from its investment. Of course, the Yamazaki products are built by Yamazaki FMS systems (see picture). With a wide range of over 60 products, individual volumes are small. Because of this, the company wanted an operation that would be so flexible it would not matter in which order items were processed. High utilization would be maintained by having very fast set-ups, which would also reduce the need for large batches. The operation can make individual pieces to suit their tight production schedules. This enables the company to offer typical order lead-times of only four weeks, in comparison to competitors' lead-times of eight or more for similar products. All component workpieces are loaded into fixtures mounted on special pallets. The operators prepare enough work to enable the system to run overnight unsupervised. At the centre of the FMS is a host computer which schedules and controls the activity of each machining centre and the materials handling devices. The computer predetermines the pallet locations and, as the machining centres become free, an automatic pick/load device will select the next workpiece from the waiting queue and will place it into the available machine. Each machine is capable of handling almost any of the components so that bottlenecks do not develop at any point in the system. Spare tools used for the machining centres are stored in a central tool bank at the ends of the area and are transported to the required machine by a holding device on a highway which runs above the machining centres. At the end of the shift, the incoming operator can consult the computer for a printout of the tools that may need to be replaced in the tool bank. Many of the materials are delivered from the warehouse to the factory by AGVs, which pick up the items when requested by the central scheduling system.

- *What seem to be the benefits of Yamazaki's investment (over £35m) in its highly automated plant?*
- *What do you think are the main problems with unstaffed overnight operation, and what has Yamazaki done to avoid them?*
- *What type of flexibility does Yamazaki's FMS give them?*

→ *Look at Chapter 8 for guidance*

Quality at Torres Wine

Laser-guided plough

Mechanical harvesting

Back in 1870, Jaime Torres, having been forced to seek his fortune in Cuba when his elder brother inherited the family estates, returned to his native Catalonia. He founded the company which is now Spain's largest independently-owned wine company with a turnover of around 17 million bottles of wine per year, together with around 6 million bottles of brandy. The (still family-owned) company's success is based firmly on the work it has put in to maintain the quality and consistency of its products. This starts with the vineyards themselves. Since the 1960s they have been experimenting with matching grape varieties to the individual microclimates in their estates, planting patterns which preserve water levels in the soil, and using environmentally-friendly cultivation techniques such as the laser-guided plough (*see* picture) which eliminates the need for artificial chemical weed killers. Although much of the harvesting is still done by hand, mechanical harvesting (*see* picture) not only saves time and money, but also allows the fruit to be collected cool during the night and early morning, which further enhances quality. The trailers and tractors which transport the harvested grapes are unloaded into reception hoppers where precision controlled systems, co-ordinated by computer electronics, enable immediate assessment of the quality and ripeness of grapes. The wines ferment in visually striking stainless steel towers (*see* picture). All these vats are equipped with cooling systems to ferment the grape juice at a controlled temperature, thus preserving its natural aromas. The Torres' cellars, where the red wines are aged, extend through two kilometres of cool, dark, underground galleries that house more than

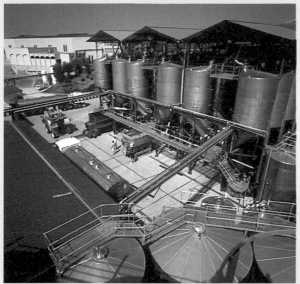

11 000 oak barrels (*see* picture below). The use of new oak barrels for ageing the finest wines requires substantial investment, but it is an essential factor in obtaining the highest quality. The wine is then bottled in the company's on-site modern bottling plant, after which it is bottle-aged in the company's headquarters at nearby Vilafranca.

Fermentation towers

- *What constitutes quality for Torres' products?*
- *Chart the various stages in wine making and identify what influences quality at each stage.*
- *What do you think Torres does, or can do, to pursue environmentally friendly production?*

➔ *Look at Chapters 5 and 17 for guidance*

Cask-ageing cellars

the
"there are three keys to retail success: location, location, location" **solution**

Can a website really rival a storefront on the Ku'damm, Avenue Montaigne or Oxford Street? It can when it's built around IBM's CommercePoint. Our experts can help you open up a real shop on the Internet. One with actual till-ringing sales and millions of affluent potential customers.

People aren't just browsing. They're buying.

We've already helped some of the world's leading companies to make millions by selling their goods and services on the web. Airlines, clothing companies and camera shops are finding new customers at minimal costs.

Virtual shops. Not virtual shoplifters.

IBM Net.Commerce protects you and your customers. We've worked with major credit card organisations to set tough new security standards for payment transactions.

Doesn't opening up on the Internet sound like a smart move? Visit us at www.ibminfo.com/uk4/ or call us on 0800 675 675.

IBM

Solutions for a small planet

In this advertisement, IBM, one of the largest and most experienced information systems providers, questions the relevance of the retail industry's preoccupation with location.

- *Do you think that websites can replace the traditional storefront of retail operations?*
- *What might be the main operations issues for retailers using the Internet for communicating with their customers?*

→ *Look at Chapter 8 for guidance*

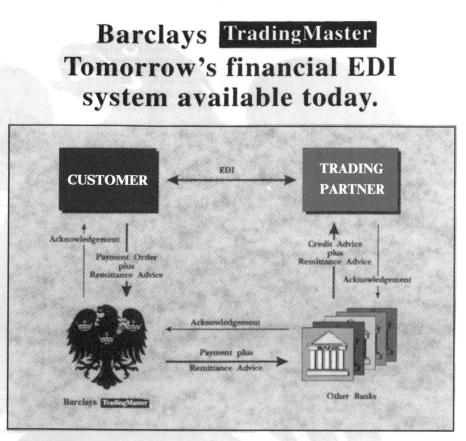

Barclays TradingMaster
Tomorrow's financial EDI system available today.

As the leading UK bank, in the field of EDI, Barclays offers the benefits of "Paperless Trading" to corporate customers, by providing a flexible, effective service, designed to fulfil any financial EDI requirement. Barclays TradingMaster enables complete electronic settlement, accurately and economically, allowing substantial cost savings in your business.

By interfacing to any Value Added Network (VAN) and having compatibility with many EDI software vendors, Barclays TradingMaster couldn't be easier to implement.

Barclays TradingMaster - Business Methodology - in Practice.

For more information on Barclays TradingMaster, contact

Barclays EDI Department

+ + + YOU'RE
BETTER OFF
TALKING TO
BARCLAYS

Figure 8.9
EDI services advertised by a UK clearing bank
Source: By kind permission of Barclays Bank plc

AN OFFICE IN THE SKY[14]

As the technologies of data processing and telecommunications are merging, so too are the services which they support coming together. The individual television screens, now common in aircraft, provide the entertainment which keeps passengers happy on long international flights. Now British Airways has gone one step further in bringing together entertainment technology with information provision and processing. Using a hand-held control device, passengers can access dozens of TV entertainment channels, an up-to-the-minute news service, computer games and a menu of information-processing options. For example, a customer who wants to book a hotel room, reserve a hire car, order flower deliveries or buy duty-free goods, can do so via the screen and control device. Payment for the services or goods ordered is made by swiping a credit card through a slot built into the seat's armrest. Confirmation of the transactions are shown on the screen. The system can also transmit a passenger's own data. A notebook computer can be plugged into the system and a faxed hard copy of the information sent back to the office.

Behind the new service is a communications system which includes the Inmarsat satellite and BA's central booking database in London. The database directs credit card details to the card company and, on authorization, transmits the customer's orders and reservations to the respective companies (*see* Fig. 8.10). The airline views such technology as important in its efforts to provide a superior service.

'*The concept is based on providing customers with a total media centre from their seats. We have the opportunity to provide customers with a whole range of products and services where they will be able to choose what they want to do rather than be fed with entertainment.*' ■

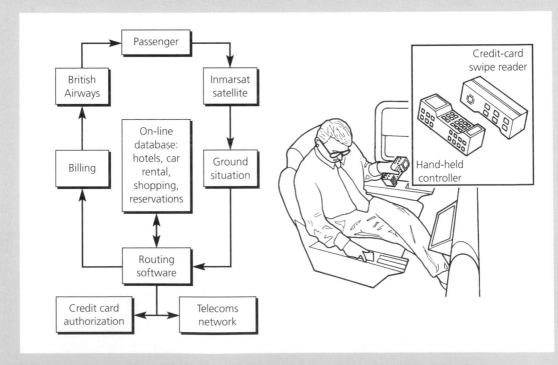

Figure 8.10 Merging telecommunications and information-processing technology in airline service
Source: Ian Moores and *The Sunday Times*, 30 May 1993. Copyright © Times Newspapers Limited 1993

Questions

1 The above describes one particular investment in technology by a major airline. List what you think might be the major process-technology-related decisions which airlines have to take.

2 What effect do each of the technology decisions which you have listed have on the operating profitability of an airline?

3 What advantage do you think the particular technology described above gives to the airline's passengers?

Management information systems (MIS)

Most of our discussion so far has concerned the arrangement of information-processing technologies – what computers and similar devices can do, and how they are connected to each other. Within the configuration of the physical system, however, what is important is the way in which information moves, is changed, is manipulated and presented so that it can be used in managing an organization. These systems are *management information systems* (MIS). Operations managers make considerable use of MIS, especially in their planning and control activities. Systems which are concerned with inventory management, the timing and scheduling of activities, demand forecasting, order processing, quality management, and many other activities are an integral part of many operations managers' working lives, and are referred to in the planning and control chapters of Part 3.

Decision support systems (DSS)

A decision support system is one which provides information with the direct objective of aiding or supporting managerial decision-making. It does this by storing relevant information, processing it, and presenting it in such a way as to be appropriate to the decision being made. In this way, it supports managers by helping them to understand the nature of decisions and their consequences, but it does not actually make the decision itself. Often DSS are used for 'what if' analyses which explore the (often financial) consequences of changing operations practice. For example, suppose a synthetic fibre manufacturer (such as Delta Synthetic Fibres which was discussed as a case example in Chapter 6) is considering adding extra capacity for a new product, as well as converting its existing capacity to manufacture the new product. A typical DSS would have at its disposal the full manufacturing costs associated with making each product at all the company's alternative locations, the costs involved with transporting products to world-wide markets, the costs and lead times involved in the construction and conversion of capacity, and so on. It would then allow managers to enter alternative decisions regarding the location, size and timing of capacity change and show the results in terms of such measures as capacity utilization, inventory levels, profitability and cash flow.

Expert systems (ES)

Expert systems take the idea of DSS one stage further in that they attempt to 'solve' problems that would normally be solved by humans. An ES exhibits (within a specified area) a sufficient degree of expertise to mimic human problem-solving. The key part of an ES is its 'inference engine' which performs the reasoning or formal logic on the rules which have been defined as governing the decision. These rules are called the 'knowledge base' of the ES (which is why ESs are also called knowledge-based systems).

There have been many attempts to utilize the idea of an expert system in operations management. Table 8.4 illustrates some of the decision areas and questions which have been treated. However, although authorities agree that expert systems will become far more important in the future of operations management, not all applications so far have been totally successful. The problems which have been encountered include the following:

● Most expert systems can treat only narrow problems rather than the more realistic issues of integration and conflict between problem areas of the operation.
● Putting even some of an operations manager's expertise into a knowledge base is very expensive in terms of time and processing power.
● Like all information-based systems, it is rendered impotent if the data it is working with is wrong or inaccurate.

Table 8.4 Examples of the application of expert systems in operations management[15]

Decision area	Typical issues	Some current applications
Capacity planning	What is a reasonable size for a facility? What is the workforce size for our operation system?	PEP, CAPLAN
Facility location	Where is the best geographic site to locate the operation?	FADES
Facility layout	How should we arrange equipment in our facility site?	CRAFT, CORELAP, WORKPLACE DESIGNER
Aggregate planning	What should be the output rates and staffing levels for this quarter?	PATRIARCH, CAPLANLITE
Product design	Does the design of the product fit the firm's capability to produce it?	XCON, CDX
Scheduling	Which customers or jobs should receive top priority?	ISIS, MARS
Quality management	How do we best achieve our quality goals? Is the process capable of meeting the specifications?	PL DEFT
Inventory control	How much inventory do we need in our store? How should we control it?	IVAN, LOGIX, RIM
Maintenance	Where do we have a problem in our equipment? What kind of measures should we take to control or remove this problem?	DELTA/CATS

Technology summaries

Again, it is useful to summarize in Table 8.5 the information-processing technologies in terms of our operations questions.

Table 8.5 Summary of information-processing technologies

Centralized information processing

What does it do?	Manipulates and stores information in one centralized processing unit.
How does it do it?	Uses large computers, located centrally and accessed either on a batch system, where a collection of similar transactions queue to be processed, or by teleprocessing, where individual users access the computer through their individual access devices such as keyboards.
What advantages does it give?	The capacity of the central computer can be scheduled efficiently. All information is centralized and therefore able to be controlled.
What constraints does it impose?	Users feel less 'ownership' of the technology (hardware but also, more significantly, applications software). Large 'mainframe' computers can be more expensive per unit of processing power (partly because of their support needs, such as air-conditioned rooms, etc.).

Local area networks (LANs)

What does it do?	Allows decentralized information processors such as personal computers to communicate with each other and with shared devices over a limited distance.
How does it do it?	Through a hard wired network and shared communication protocols.
What advantages does it give?	Flexibility, easy access to other users, shared databases and applications software.
What constraints does it impose?	The cost of installing the network can initially be high.

Integrated services digital networks (ISDN)

What does it do?	Provides a communications network which can carry all types of digital-based information.
How does it do it?	Shared protocols which allow communication and digital compression which packs large amounts of information into a given information 'space'.
What advantages does it give?	Flexible, two-way interactive communication for voice and non-voice information.
What constraints does it impose?	Need to choose commercial network; initial costs can be high.

Electronic data interchange (EDI)

What does it do	Allows companies to exchange information electronically.
How does it do it?	By connecting to a commercially available, value-added network (VAN) which allows customers, suppliers and banks to exchange trading information.
What advantages does it give?	Fast throughput of orders which allows lower inventory levels, a reduction in keying errors and the ability to connect to sales information models and point-of-sale technology.
What constraints does it impose?	The initial cost of connection can be high and computer skills are necessary to integrate EDI into internal systems. This can be especially daunting for small suppliers.

Table 8.5 continued

Internet	
What does it do?	Links LANs and WANs to provide an integrated network.
How does it do it?	Packet switching which allows many messages to be sent simultaneously.
What advantages does it give?	Allows access to the World Wide Web (WWW), the distributed hypermedia/hypertext system. This probably has significant implications for most, if not all, operations management tasks.
What constraints does it impose?	An undisciplined medium with potential for 'information overload'.

Decision support systems (DSS)	
What does it do?	Provides information to assist decision-making.
How does it do it?	Uses data storage, models and presentation formats to structure information and present consequences of decisions.
What advantages does it give?	Speed and sophistication of decision-making.
What constraints does it impose?	Can be expensive to set up and can lead to 'over analysis'. Also dependent on quality of data and models.

Expert systems (ES)	
What does it do?	Makes operational decisions.
How does it do it?	By mimicking human decision-making using data, knowledge bases, and an inference engine.
What advantages does it give?	Takes some routine decision-making out of human hands, saving time and giving consistency.
What constraints does it impose?	Expensive to model human decision-making and can only treat narrow problems.

CUSTOMER-PROCESSING TECHNOLOGY

Traditionally, customer-processing operations have been seen as 'low technology' when compared with materials-processing operations. The assumption is that manufacturing needs machines while services rely on people. To some extent this is understandable: visit most factories and their technology is often very evident. For example, there is no mistaking the significance of a steel producer's process technology to its business. On the other hand, an office or a bank or even a hospital does not seem to be as dominated by process technology. In these type of operations it is the people one would notice before the technology.

Yet even when customer-processing operations do invest less in process technology than their manufacturing counterparts, their competitiveness can be affected just as critically by good or bad process technology decisions. A bank whose automatic teller machines (ATMs) do not work satisfactorily is prevented from competing just as effectively as a steel producer with unreliable rolling mills.

Back- and front-office technology

In Chapter 1 we distinguished between the front-office part of customer-processing operations, which has direct contact with customers, and the back-office part, with which the customers have little or no direct contact. Technology is often present in both the front and back office. Much of back-office technology is concerned with information processing and is of the type previously described. Front-office technology has some kind of contact (direct or indirect) with customers. In some cases, ATMs for example, the technology is there to link customers in the front office with the information-processing power of the back office.

The customer–staff–technology interaction

In materials or information processing, operations managers are concerned with the interaction between staff and technology. In customer-processing operations, however, there is a three-way set of interactions between customers, staff and technology. It is the nature of this interaction which can be used to categorize the various types of customer-processing technology.

Here we distinguish between three types of interaction. The distinction between the categories is not always clear, but they do represent broad approaches to the use of customer-processing technology. They are:

- where there is *no direct interaction* between customers and the technology;
- where there is *passive interaction* between customers and the technology;
- where there is *active interaction* between customers and the technology.

Technology with no direct customer interaction

When the customers of an airline check in at the airport, they choose their seats, give any special requests and receive their boarding passes. To do this the airline staff operate a computer terminal which links into the airline's systems, and a printer which prints boarding passes and baggage tickets. This process technology is vital to the smooth running of the check-in operation. Using it benefits both the airline and the customer. The customer does not directly use the technology, however: the staff member does that on behalf of the customer. The customer may 'navigate'[16] or guide the process but does not 'drive' it. The technology may even be arranged to help customers navigate the process. For example, some airlines have a screen with the seat layout of the aircraft facing the customer, showing which seats are still available. This is an aid to the customer, who has no direct contact as such, however (*see* Fig. 8.11).

Other examples of this kind of technology are the reservations systems in hotels or theatres, the customer-support enquiry lines used by utilities, the package-tracking systems in parcel delivery services, and holiday booking systems in travel agents.

The reason for using this type of technology is usually to produce some combination of better or faster or cheaper services. The hotel or theatre reservation system, for example, facilitates fast response to customers and high utilization of reservation staff. Similarly with the airline check-in technology, customers receive a faster service, with fewer problems, than if the technology were not used.

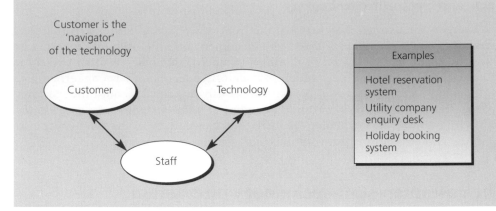

Figure 8.11 Technology with no direct customer interaction

TECHNOLOGY IN MEDICINE[17]

The technological breakthroughs in medical care reported in the press often focus on those dramatic 'miracle cures' which have undoubtedly improved the quality of medical care substantially. Yet a whole collection of changes in medical *process technology* have also had a huge impact on the way health-care operations manage themselves. Here are some examples.

Even in surgery, that ultimate in human skill, robot technology is becoming more common. Whereas the hand of the most experienced surgeon trembles slightly, a robot arm is totally steady. Some applications move instruments around inside the patient under the direction of the surgeon. More radically, robots can now be used to remove soft tissue. For example, the PROBOT technology developed at Guy's Hospital in London has been specially developed for prostate surgery. Guided by an ultrasonic scanner (which, usefully, can see through flesh) the robot can scan the area to be operated on and convert its readings into a three-dimensional image. The human surgeon can then identify the tissue to be removed which is then removed with an electronic probe. The human surgeon, however, is in control throughout the procedure.

It is a routine familiar in hospital wards throughout the world. At more or less the same time each day a doctor progresses from bed to bed doing his or her 'ward rounds' to check up on the progress of each patient. Conventionally, before this happens the doctor would consult the notes of all the patients as a reminder of their recent history and condition. This might take anything from 30 to 60 minutes. In some hospitals, though, this time has been virtually eliminated through the use of radio-connected laptop computers. Doctors just take their laptops to the bedside and access information through the radio receiver. If necessary they can update and change treatment regimes instantly without having to revisit their office. Just as important, the system enables patients to take a hand in their own care. Preferences and opinions can be recorded immediately and added to the central database where they can be accessed by other doctors, physiotherapists, dieticians or social workers.

It is called telemedicine and it is challenging one of the most fundamental assumptions of medical treatment – that medical staff need to be physically present to examine a patient. Connected to his or her patients through a television screen, keyboard and camera, a nurse can talk with a patient and enter their replies into the communications computer as they speak. Using simple electronic instruments the patient can also measure their own pulse rate and take their own temperature while on camera. The proponents of telemedicine claim a number of advantages. The system can make use of decision support diagnostic systems, which give accurate and consistent diagnoses; patients having convenient access to medical advice can make fewer visits to the hospital; and, most significantly, nurses can see up to 15 patients in four hours, whereas visiting them in their home they can see only five or six patients a day. Even when the costs of the technology are taken into account, telemedicine can represent a significant cost saving, especially in rural or remote areas.

The computer screen can also be used to educate and reassure patients without any access to medical staff. For example, multimedia 'MediBooks' are used at St Thomas's hospital in London to help patients understand their own condition. Using large-format, colour-touch screens, patients can be guided through various aspects of their condition on a CD-ROM packed with narrative animations and diagrams. ■

Question

1 From an operations management point of view, what are the major advantages and what are the major problems likely to result from each of the technologies described above?

ELECTRONIC BENEFIT TRANSFER[18]

Even social programmes around the world are being revolutionized through the use of technology. For example, electronic benefit transfer (EBT) is making pension books and welfare cheques obsolete. Countries as diverse as South Africa, Italy, Finland and Namibia are all starting to use cash-dispensing machines to issue state pensions. Pensioners simply use a government-issued card and a personal identity number to obtain their cash. A similar system, shortly to be widespread in the United States, can issue food stamps and other welfare payments to poor families through the card. One such system enables welfare recipients to swipe their cards through a terminal at the retail checkout, enter their PIN number, and the cost of their food is automatically deducted from their entitlement and added to the retailer's account. ■

Question

1 List what you see as being the major advantages and problems as social programmes become more dependent on the type of technology described above.

Hidden technology

In most examples of this type of technology, even when the technology is not obvious to customers, it is not actually hidden from them. Some technologies are invisible or transparent to customers, however. The technology is 'aware' of customers but not the other way round: for example, security monitoring technologies in shopping malls or at national frontier customs areas. The objective of these technologies is for staff to track customers' movements or transactions in an unobtrusive way. Supermarkets, for example, can use bar-code scanner technologies to track the movement of customers around the store and indicate the relationship between customers' propensity to buy particular products. Suppose a retailer wanted to sell soft toys by displaying them next to children's clothes. Bar-code data scanners at the check-out could indicate that these two types of product were purchased by the same customers more often when they were placed next to each other. This would confirm the store's display decision. The same technology could, for example, issue a customer with a discount voucher for a product only if the customer had bought a rival brand. Figure 8.12 illustrates the nature of the relationship in this type of technology. Credit card companies and airlines also use this approach to target their marketing of frequent flier privileges.[19]

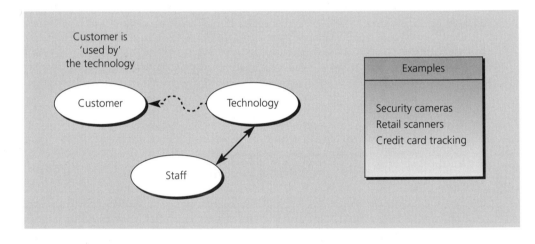

**Figure 8.12
Technology with hidden customer interaction**

Technology with passive customer interaction

A passenger taking a flight is interacting with technology – the aircraft. The technology is neither hidden from the customer nor is it merely a mechanism for helping the airline's staff to serve its customers – customers are in direct physical contact with it. In this case, however, they do not have much influence over the technology. The customer's role is a predominantly passive one. Customers are 'passengers' of the technology; in the case of transportation operations such as the airline, literally passengers. Other transport technologies such as buses, mass rapid transport systems, even moving walkways, also fall into this category. In all these cases the technology 'processes' customers and also *controls* them by constraining their actions in some way, and by doing so helps to reduce the variety in the operation. Figure 8.13 illustrates this class of technology in terms of customers, staff and technology.

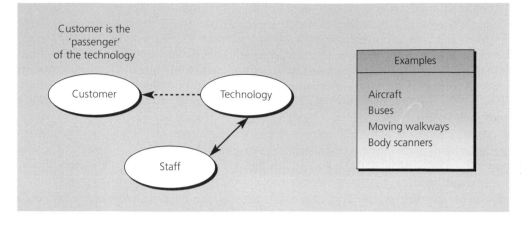

**Figure 8.13
Technology with
passive customer
interaction**

TECHNOLOGY AND THE RETAIL REVOLUTION[20]

Keeping customers out of shops may seem a strange way of enhancing sales but that is what the new generation of cashpoint machines is attempting to do. They are dispensing not only cash but also cinema tickets and airline tickets, car registrations, stamps, and travel cards. But it is not only the variety of products available which has changed, it is the way the service has been enriched. For example, at terminals in Barcelona, Spanish football fans can request a seating plan for the town's famous football stadium and by using the touch screen indicate where they would like to sit. The battle against cashpoint fraud is also progressing. One innovation is 'biometric' ID cashpoints which identify customers' fingerprints instead of cards and identification numbers. A pulse-detection device is also included to discourage criminals from cutting off the fingers of victims in order to gain access!

But not everyone predicts a golden future for automated retail technology. The sociologist Professor Laurie Taylor believes that hi-tech shopping is doomed unless it pays more attention to people's psychological needs.

'People welcome advice,' he says, *'especially when buying such items as clothes, electrical goods and home decoration where they feel they need guidance.'* Retailers must try to bring back conversation into shopping. *'Banishing customers to the remote and impersonal bank teller machines was a huge mistake,'* he says, *'because banks lost all those wonderful human contacts as well as the chance to sell customers life insurance and pensions.'* This may also limit the potential of selling through the Internet. *'The most successful businesses sell books and CDs where people know exactly what they want to buy and the product goes through the letterbox.'* Businesses where customers are less sure about what they want to buy and where products cannot be delivered through the mail may not be the best candidates for technology-based selling. ■

Questions

1 From your own experience, what are the major technologies now being used in high-contact retailing (that is not 'mail order' retailing) in addition to the ones mentioned above?

2 What are the advantages which most of these technologies give?

3 Do you think Professor Laurie Taylor is right in his criticisms of technology in retail operations?

The main concern in the development of these types of technology, whether aircraft or medical robots, is the safety of the customer. By definition, this class of technology is processing customers and is outside of their control. The technology must therefore have the potential to do harm to the customer. This is why aircraft, and most other transport technologies, are governed by strict governmental regulations. Similarly with medical technologies, the pace of progress in robotic surgery, for example, is relatively slow, not because of technological constraints, but because surgeons cannot take risks with their patients' lives.

CUSTOMERS ARE NOT ALWAYS HUMAN[21]

The first milking machines were introduced to grateful farmers over a hundred years ago. Until recently, however, they could not operate without a human hand to attach the devices to the cows. This problem has been overcome by a consortium in the Netherlands which includes the Dutch government and several private firms. They hope that the 'robot milkmaid' will do away with the farmers' early morning ritual of milking. Each machine can milk between 60 and 100 cows a day and 'processes' the cows through a number of stages. Computer-controlled gates activated by transmitters round the cows' necks allow the cows to enter. The machine then checks their health, connects them to the milking machine and feeds them while they are being milked. If illness is detected in any cow, or the machine, for some reason, fails to connect the milking cups to the cow after five attempts, automatic gates divert it into special pens where the farmer can inspect it later. Finally, the machine ushers the cow out of the system. It also cleans the machine periodically and can detect and reject any impure milk. Rather than herding all the cows in a 'batch' to the milking machine twice a day, the system relies on the cows being able to find their own way to the machine. Cows, it would appear, are creatures of habit. Once they

1 Cows enter, two at a time

2 Robot locates udders with scanners and positions milking cups

3 Cows are fed and milked simultaneously

4 Robot nudges cows to exit

Figure 8.14 Cows are also customers

have been shown the way to the machine a few times, they go there of their own volition because they know that it will relieve the discomfort in their udders, which grow heavier as they fill up. The cows may make the journey to the machine three or more times per day (*see* Fig. 8.14).

Farmers also appear to be as much creatures of habit as their cows, however. Mr. Riekes Uneken of Assen, the Dutch farmer who bought the very first robot milking machine, admitted: '*I have a bleeper if things go wrong. But I still like to get up early in the morning. I just like to see what goes on.*' ■

Questions

1 What advantages do you think the technology described above gives?

2 Do you think the cows mind?

3 Why do you think the farmer still goes to watch the process?

Technology with active customer interaction

Having been checked in to his or her flight by staff who were aided by technology, and having been transported by technology in which he or she was a passive user, the airline passenger may choose to use the aircraft's entertainment facilities. This is likely to be an individual screen and headphones which can be used to view movies or listen to audio entertainment. The passenger might even make use of telecommunications-based technology to book hotels or car rental (*see* 'The office in the sky' box). The type of technology the passenger is using here is of the third type – where customers are actively involved in using, or 'driving', the technology. Figure 8.15 illustrates this type of technology. The main interaction is between the customer and the technology, although staff may also occasionally interact with the technology. For example, banking staff occasionally will need to fill an ATM with cash, and vending machine companies need to replenish goods and empty cash from their machines.

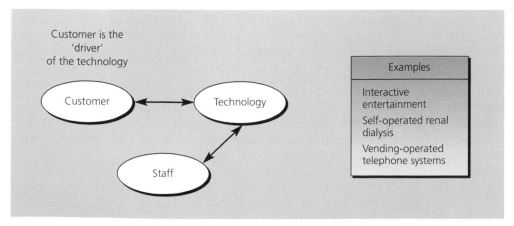

Figure 8.15 Technology with active customer interaction

In complex variants of this category of technology there may be interaction on all three dimensions: customer–technology, technology–staff and staff–customers. Some types of medical technology, for example renal dialysis, are used in this way. Similarly, some on-line software packages may be primarily intended for customers to use (customer–technology interaction) but customers may also require advice from a 'help-line' (customer–staff interaction) and staff may even be able to intervene in the use of the software itself (staff–technology interaction).

Customer training

If customers are to have direct contact with technology, they must have some idea as to how to operate it. Where customers have an active interaction with technology the limitations of customers' understanding of the technology can be the main constraint on its use. For example, even some domestic technology such as video recorders cannot be used to their full potential by most owners. Other 'customer-driven' technologies can face the same problem, with the important addition that if customers cannot use technologies such as ATMs there are serious commercial consequences for a bank's customer service. Staff in manufacturing operations may require several years of training before they are given control of the technology they operate. Service operations rarely have the same opportunity for customer training.

Walley and Amin[22] suggest that the ability of the operation to train its customers in the use of its technology depends on a number of factors.

The complexity of the service

If services are complex to operate, higher levels of training will be needed to ensure correct use of the technology. Alternatively, the need for customer training can be reduced if operational complexity is minimized. In some cases the training is delivered by potential customers watching experienced customers performing the task correctly. For example, the technologies in theme parks and fast-food outlets rely on customers copying the behaviour of others.

Repetition of the service

The frequency with which a technology is used is an important factor in two ways. First, if a service has to invest in customer training for the technology, then the payback for this investment will be greater if the customer uses the technology frequently. The greater the repetition, the more worthwhile the investment becomes. Second, customers may, over time, forget how to use the technology. Regular repetition will reinforce the training. Conversely, if customers do not use the technology for a long period they may require retraining.

Low variety of focus

Training will be easier if the customer is presented with a low variety of tasks. For example, vending machines tend to concentrate on one category of product, so that the sequence of tasks to operate the technology remains consistent.

THE DIMENSIONS OF TECHNOLOGY

So far at least one thing should be clear – process technology comes in many different forms. This makes it difficult to generalize across technologies which are used for such a wide variety of purposes. All operations make choices regarding their technology, however, and there are always alternative ways of configuring any technology. Exploring these alternatives involves thinking on three dimensions:

- the degree of *automation* of the technology;
- the *scale* of the technology;
- the degree of *integration* of the technology.

The degree of automation of the technology

No technology operates totally without human intervention. To some extent they all need human intervention some of the time. It may be minimal – for example, the periodic maintenance interventions in a petrochemical refinery, or occasional reprogramming of a computer control system. Conversely, the staff member who operates the technology may be the entire 'brains' of the process – for example, the operator working a precision lathe or the surgeon using keyhole surgery techniques. Process technology varies in its degree of automation. The ratio of technological to human effort it employs is sometimes called the *capital intensity* of the process technology.

The benefits of automation

Two benefits of increasing the degree of automation in a process technology are usually cited:

- It saves direct labour costs.
- It reduces variability in the operation.

Automation is usually justified on the former, but it is sometimes the latter which is more significant. Nevertheless, it is worth examining what type of labour can be saved through automation in any particular case. Direct labour can often be saved, but that does not mean that the net effect is an overall cost saving. Operations managers need to consider the following points before automating for cost savings alone:

- Can the technology perform the task better or safer than a human? – not just faster (although this can obviously be important) but better in a broader sense. Can the technology make fewer mistakes, change over from one task to the next faster and more reliably, or respond to breakdowns effectively?
- What support activities, such as maintenance or programming, does the technology need in order to function effectively? What will be the effect on indirect costs? – not just the extra people and skills which might be necessary but also the effect of increased complexity of support activities.
- Can the technology cope with new product or service possibilities as effectively as less-automated alternatives? This is a difficult question because no one will know exactly what the operation will need to produce in the future. Nevertheless, it is an important question; automation represents a risk as well as an opportunity.

● What is the potential for human creativity and problem solving to improve the machines' performance? Is it worth getting rid of human potential along with its cost?

Methodology before technology

Automated technologies in many operations have provided the potential for improved performance, but there is a danger. Technology can be seen as a panacea for all the operation's ills, a 'technology fix' which avoids more fundamental problems. If the methods and processes are themselves flawed, technology will just speed up the problems not solve them. Those companies who have attempted the difficult task of separating the benefits which come directly from investment in automated technology from the benefits which come from improved methodology have reported some surprising results. Paradoxically, capital investment often makes it necessary to consider the organization of the operation as a whole, which in turn prompts improvements which are independent of the technology for which it is preparing the way. For example, the following are extracts from surveys of companies who have installed flexible manufacturing systems (FMS):

' ... *on average 40 per cent of the benefits predicted for an FMS are in fact achievable, or have been achieved, before the FMS is delivered. This is because the planning process itself has high-lighted existing custom and practice which ... can be put right without major investment.*'[23]

'*(We) frequently receive estimates that approximately half of the benefits of FMS were derived from managerial and work-based organizational change.*'[24]

' ... *companies who operate FMS, and who have presumably undergone some formal evaluation process, tend to concentrate their efforts more than other manufacturing firms on improving product quality, shortening lead times and set-up times and integrating information and control systems.*'[25]

This does not mean that investing in capital-intensive automated equipment is a waste of time. Rather that there are considerable benefits to be gained from rethinking the overall 'methodology' of the operation, whether or not the investment in technology is subsequently made. Perhaps the right order should be first to improve the methods of the operation and only then to put in automated technology where it is needed.

The scale of the technology

Operations often need to decide between acquiring one large-scale unit of technology or several smaller ones. For example, the duplicating department of a large office complex may decide to invest in a single, very large, fast copier, or alternatively several smaller, slower copiers. An airline may purchase one or two wide-bodied aircraft or a larger number of smaller aircraft. A manufacturer may design its operation around a single large-capacity machine or several smaller machines. No matter what the technology, there is usually some discretion as to how large a piece of plant it is wise to acquire. The economies of the technology itself will influence the decision. Some process technologies, such as intercontinental aircraft, petrochemical refineries, or steel-making plants benefit from scale, and so tend to come in large-capacity increments. Others, like personal computers or ATMs for example, are efficient when operating on a small scale.

The advantages of large-scale technologies are similar to the advantages of large-capacity increments discussed in Chapter 6 and are summarized in Table 8.6.

Table 8.6 Advantages of large-scale and small-scale technologies

Advantages of large-scale technology	Advantages of small-scale technology
Economies of scale can lead to lower cost per product or service delivered	Good mix flexibility – each unit of technology can be engaged on different activities
Lower capital costs per unit of capacity	High robustness against failure
Can incorporate support and control elements in the technology (e.g. 'rest room' facilities in larger buses)	Lower obsolescence risk
Can pool work for better utilization (e.g. batch processing in centralized computer systems)	Can be located closer to where the technology is needed

Many of the advantages of large-scale technologies are connected with the cost advantages they can bring. However, nimbleness and flexibility can be virtues of smaller-scale technology. Mix flexibility (*see* Chapter 2) especially is enhanced. For example, four small machines can between them produce four different products simultaneously (albeit slowly), whereas a single large machine with four times the output can produce one product four times faster. Small-scale technologies are also more robust. Suppose the choice is between three small machines and two larger ones. In the first case, if one machine breaks down a third of the capacity is lost, but in the second, capacity is halved. It is also easier to take advantage of technology improvement with small-scale technology. Buying a small machine just equal to current needs allows the operation to buy the latest technology when demand increases.

The degree of integration of the technology

Integration means the linking together of previously separated activities within a single piece of technology or system. This issue has arisen at points earlier in this chapter. For example, the technological development represented by local area networks (LANs) is largely that of integration. Similarly, the development of advanced manufacturing technologies is the result of microprocessor-based integration.

Integration, synchronization and speed

The benefits of integration come directly from the effects of combining several separate technology units into one simple synchronized whole. First, there is fast throughput of information or of materials. For example, in an FMS there is no inter-machine decision-making over which job has priority. Second, and as a consequence of throughput speed, inventory of materials or information will be lower – it can't accumulate when there are no 'gaps' between activities. Third, flow is simple and predictable. It is easier to keep track of parts when they pass through fewer stages, or information when it is automatically distributed to all parts of an information network.

Integrated technology can be more expensive, however. For example, in manufacturing, even simple materials-handling linkages are costly. Furthermore, the more integrated the technology, the higher the skills can be which are needed to maintain it. When failures do occur, the whole integrated system is likely to go down. In one sense this makes integrated plant more vulnerable. If integration involves linking several production stages which would otherwise be loosely connected in series, this 'disadvantage' of integration can be a useful discipline. If one link in a chain stops then the others should do so anyway. To do otherwise would mean producing for work-in-progress, not for the end customer. This is one of the tenets of just-in-time (JIT) manufacture, which is treated fully in Chapter 15.

Peter Read, British Airways

Selecting aircraft technology

Captain Peter Read's career started as a pilot and he still flies for British Airways. Now, however, he is also the Manager for Aircraft Technology for the company. Part of that role involves evaluating the appropriate technology for use in new aircraft.

'British Airways has several strategic priorities,' explains Peter, 'but in terms of our Operational Division, the safety and security aspect always is, of course, our first and overriding consideration in everything we do. The airline industry is, by nature, very capital intensive and in the selection of an aircraft the team is looking for the opportunities to generate extra revenue where appropriate. For example, if an aircraft can be just five per cent more economical with fuel, then it may mean that we can carry up to 40 more passengers on each long-haul flight. Over just one year, the revenue implications of this would be quite significant.

'We cannot limit our considerations to the airframe and engine specification, however, we also have to look at the in-flight facilities we offer to passengers and the advance of computer-based flight information systems. At present about ten per cent of the aircraft capital cost is allocated to the provision of on-board facilities for the passengers' benefit. These are chosen specifically to suit the intended flight duration and the needs of the passenger during that time. In the past, the focus of design effort was directed more at the likely engine performance and the performance characteristics as a whole. Nowadays, the design team, along with its counterparts at the manufacturers, is spending more and more time trying to improve the facilities available to the passengers at their seats. It is no longer enough to be able to show films on a central screen; we have the technology to be able to build in a screen for each passenger, and with that screen to include satellite television options as well as computer communication facilities. The incorporation of this level of technology bears no relevance to the efficiency and cost of the flight itself, but does have a major bearing on customers' choice of airline.

'The development of "engine communications" systems is also very much at the forefront of our aircraft technology. It has helped reduce our turnaround time on the ground and contain costs on the engineering side by pin-pointing any slight irregularities in any of over 35 different engine parameters. This advanced communications system can transmit details in real time from the aircraft to any ground-based destination, and allows the live data to be compared with expected readings so that the ground crew can be prepared for any necessary maintenance work that may be required when the aircraft lands.

'It is my responsibility to ensure that these various technical developments are pursued in line with the changing needs of our business. You should remember that most of our new aircraft are being ordered up to seven years in advance. This makes decisions on the type and level of technology to be adopted in each area very much strategic issues. Each technology decision may have an enormous impact on our competitiveness in the years to come. It is always a question of striking a balance between all the different design priorities involved. It is getting the choice of our aircraft's specification right which will help BA maintain its leading position in the industry.' ■

Source: By kind permission of Peter Read

SUMMARY ANSWERS TO KEY QUESTIONS

What is process technology?

■ Process technology is the collection of machines, equipment or devices which help operations transform their materials, information or customers.

■ This is different to the technology which is embedded in the product or service itself. However, product technology and process technology issues do overlap, especially in service operations.

■ Operations managers do not need to know the technical details of all technologies but they do need to know: what does it do?, how does it do it?, what advantages does it give?, what constraints does it impose?

What are the significant materials-processing technologies?

■ Technologies which have had a particular impact include numerically controlled machine tools and machining centres, robots, automated guided vehicles, flexible manufacturing systems, and computer-integrated manufacturing systems.

■ Each of these technologies can be seen as implying a different extent of integration between the four basic elements of designing, controlling, handling, and managing materials.

What are the significant information-processing technologies?

■ Significant technologies include centralized and decentralized information processing, incl-

uding local area networks and wide area networks, electronic data interchange, the Internet, and the World Wide Web. Of particular importance are the latter technologies which include the integration of computing and telecommunications technology.

■ Within these information technologies are such developments as management information systems, decision support systems and expert systems.

What are the significant customer-processing technologies?

■ There are no universally agreed classifications of customer-processing technology as there are with materials- and information-processing technology.

■ The way we classify technologies here is through the nature of the interaction between customers, staff and the technology itself. Using this classification, technologies can be classified as those with no direct customer interaction, those with passive customer interaction, and those with active customer interaction.

What are the generic characteristics of process technology?

■ All technologies can be conceptualized on three dimensions: the degree of automation of the technology, the scale of the technology, and the degree of integration of the technology.

CASE EXERCISE

Rochem Ltd

Dr Rhodes was losing his temper.

'It should be a simple enough decision. There are only two alternatives. You are only being asked to choose a machine!'

The Management Committee looked abashed.

Rochem Ltd by 1996 was one of the largest independent companies supplying the food-processing industry. Its initial success had come in the late 1980s with a food preservative, used mainly for meat-based products, and marketed under the name of 'Lerentyl'. Other products were subsequently developed in the food colouring and food container coating fields, so that now Lerentyl accounted for only 25 per cent of total company sales, which in 1996 were slightly over £10 million.

The decision

The problem over which there was such controversy related to the replacement of one of the process units used to manufacture Lerentyl. Only two such units were used, both were 'Chemling' machines. It was the older of the two Chemling units which was giving trouble. High breakdown figures, with erratic quality levels, meant that output level requirements were only just being reached. The problem was: should the company replace the ageing Chemling with a new Chemling, or should it buy the only other plant on the market capable of the required process, the 'AFU' unit? The Chief Chemist's staff had drawn up a comparison of the two units, shown in Table 8.7.

The body considering the problem was the newly formed Management Committee. The committee consisted of the four senior managers in the firm: the Chief Chemist and the Marketing Manager, who had been with the firm since its beginning, together with the Production Manager and the Accountant, both of whom had joined the company only six months before.

What follows is a condensed version of the information presented by each manager to the committee, together with their attitudes to the decision.

The Marketing Manager

By 1996 the market for this type of preservative had reached a size of some £5 million of which Rochem

Table 8.7 A comparison of the two alternative machines

	CHEMLING	AFU
Capital cost	£590 000	£880 000
Processing costs	Fixed: £15 000/mth Variable: £750/kg	Fixed: £40 000/mth Variable: £600/kg
Design capacity	105 kg/mth 98%±0.7% purity	140 kg/mth 99.5%±0.2% purity
Quality	Manual testing	Automatic testing
Maintenance	Adequate but needs servicing	Not known – probably good
After-sales services	Very good	Not known – unlikely to be good
Delivery	Three months	Immediate

Ltd supplied approximately 48 per cent. There had, of late, been significant changes in the market – in particular many of the users of preservatives were now able to buy products similar to Lerentyl. The result had been the evolution of a much more price-sensitive market than had previously been the case. Further market projections were somewhat uncertain. It was clear that the total market would not shrink (in volume terms) and best estimates suggested a market of perhaps £6 million by 2000 (at current prices). However, there were some people in the industry who believed that the present market only represented the tip of the iceberg.

Although the food preservative market had advanced by a series of technical innovations, 'real' changes in the basic product were now few and far between. Lerentyl was sold in either solid powder or liquid form, depending on the particular needs of the customer. Prices tended to be related to the weight of chemical used, however. Thus, for example, in 1996 the average market price was approximately £1050 per kg. There were, of course, wide variations depending on order size, etc.

'At the moment I am mainly interested in getting the right quantity and quality of Lerentyl each month and although Production has never let me down yet, I'm worried that unless we get a reliable new unit quickly, it

soon will. The AFU machine could be on line in a few weeks, giving better quality too. Furthermore, if demand does increase (but I'm not saying it will), the AFU will give us the extra capacity. I will admit that we are not trying to increase our share of the preservative market as yet. We see our priority as establishing our other products first. When that's achieved, we will go back to concentrating on the preservative side of things.'

The Chief Chemist

The Chief Chemist was an old friend of John Rhodes and together they had been largely responsible for every product innovation. At the moment, the major part of his budget was devoted to modifying basic Lerentyl so that it could be used for more acidic food products such as fruit. This was not proving easy and as yet nothing had come of the research, although the Chief Chemist remained optimistic.

'If we succeed in modifying Lerentyl the market opportunities will be doubled overnight and we will need the extra capacity. I know we would be taking a risk by going for the AFU machine, but our company has grown by gambling on our research findings, and we must continue to show faith.'

The Production Manager

The Lerentyl Department was virtually self-contained as a production unit. In fact it was physically separate, being in a building a few yards detached from the rest of the plant. Production requirements for Lerentyl were currently at a steady rate of 190 kg per month. The six technicians who staffed the machines were the only technicians in Rochem who did all their own minor repairs and full quality control. The reason for this was largely historical, since when the firm started, the product was experimental and qualified technicians were needed to operate the plant. Four of the six had been with the firm almost from its beginning.

'It's all right for Dave and Eric (Marketing Manager and Chief Chemist) to talk about a big expansion of Lerentyl sales; they don't have to cope with all the problems if it doesn't happen. The fixed costs of the AFU unit are nearly three times those of the Chemling. Just think what that will do to my budget at low volumes of output. As I understand it, there is absolutely no evidence to show a large upswing in Lerentyl. No, the whole idea (of the AFU plant) is just too risky. Not only is there the risk. I don't think it is generally understood what the consequences of the AFU would mean. We would need twice the variety of spares for a start. But what really worries me is the staff's reaction. As fully qualified technicians they regard themselves as the elite of the firm; so they should, they are paid practically the same as I am! If we get the AFU plant all their most interesting work, like the testing and the maintenance, will disappear or be greatly reduced. They will finish up as highly paid process workers.'

The Accountant

The company had financed nearly all its recent capital investment from its own retained profits, but would be taking out short-term loans in 1997 for the first time for several years.

'At the moment, I don't think it wise to invest extra capital we can't afford in an attempt to give us extra capacity we don't need at the moment. This year will be an expensive one for the company. We are already committed to considerably increased expenditure on promotion of our other products and capital investment in other parts of the firm, and Dr Rhodes is not in favour of excessive funding from outside the firm. I accept that there might eventually be an upsurge in Lerentyl demand but, if it does come, it probably won't be this year and it will be far bigger than the AFU can cope with anyway, so we might as well have three Chemling plants at that time.' ■

Questions

1 How do the two alternative process technologies (Chemling and AFU) differ in terms of their scale and automation? What are the implications of this for Rochem?

2 Remind yourself of the distinction between feasibility, acceptability, and vulnerability, discussed in Chapter 4. Evaluate both technologies using these criteria.

3 What would you recommend the company should do?

DISCUSSION QUESTIONS

1 Identify as many applications of automation as you can in the following operations:
- a hospital
- an airline
- a university
- a chain of hotels
- retail banking
- farming and agriculture.

2 Many universities and colleges around the world are under increasing pressure to reduce the cost per student of their activities. How do you think technology could help operations such as universities to keep their costs down but their quality of education high?

3 In the popular press there have been many stories about the 'fully automated factory', sometimes known as the 'dark factory' because it does not need any human intervention (who would switch the lights on!). What do you think might be some of the major problems in trying to achieve this goal of the fully automated factory? In what kind of manufacturing do you think we are first likely to see the extensive use of full automation?

4 Identify some technologies you use in day-to-day life. Assess the value of them by thinking what it would be like to be without them. Can you identify which ones are product/service technologies and which are process technologies?

5 Assess the differences between a fax machine and a telephone in terms of their operational capabilities.

6 Discuss the relationship between product/service and process technology for a product or service with which you are familiar.

7 Talk to the manager of a plant that has an FMS. Assess the relative volume and variety of products that are produced by the FMS. Does the manager believe that the advantages of FMS (identified by John Bessant) have been attained?

8 'The real advantage of flexible manufacturing systems (FMS) is not in their flexibility at all. Rather it is in the fact that they can process materials cheaper than any previous technology. They really should have been called "low-cost manufacturing systems" rather than "flexible manufacturing systems".' Do you think this statement is right? If so, why do you think that flexible manufacturing systems have been called by that name?

9 The human-centred CIM philosophy aims to retain the advantages of computer-integrated manufacturing while also allowing humans to interact with such systems, so as to fulfil their own job aspirations and needs. Do you think this is just idealism or, alternatively, the only way to achieve the best of the mechanized and human worlds?

10 Explain the differences and relationships between CIE, CIM, FMS and CAD/CAM.

11 Discuss the advantages and disadvantages between centralized and decentralized information processing for air traffic controllers.

12 What benefits could EDI bring to a university?

13 Describe the following technologies that might be found at an airport in terms of the customer–staff–technology interactions:
- X-ray machines for customers at an airport
- airbridges connecting walkways to the aircraft
- air traffic control system
- scanners that check the destination bar codes on luggage
- automatic ticket machines.

14 The vast majority of services offered by retail banks could be provided entirely automatically. Automatic teller machines, automated depositing facilities, interactive screen information links in the branches, and the full range of voice-activated and person-to-person home banking services all raise the possibility of a bank where customers never have face-to-face communication with the staff of the bank. What factors do you think influence retail banks when they are deciding how far to automate their various services?

15 Robot-type technology is starting to play a part in some medical surgical procedures. What would it take before you were willing to subject yourself to a robot doctor?

16 Visit your local or university library and write a report on how technology could be applied to enhance the efficiency and effectiveness of the operation. What do you think might be the biggest problems if the library attempted to operate on an entirely automated basis?

17 Airlines are already discussing with aircraft manufacturers the possibility of the development of an aircraft carrying 600 to 700 passengers. The desire for such large aircraft comes from the increased demand for air travel, especially on some routes. Generally, it is cheaper and faster to run one large aircraft than two half the size. In principle, current technology could allow the development of aircraft which could carry around 1000 passengers. What do you think might limit the use of technology to develop such large aircraft?

18 A high street bank is considering providing a home-banking service using modems and customers' own home-based PCs. What do you think are the main issues that the bank will have to consider in terms of getting customers to use this service?

19 Some Japanese manufacturers prefer to employ simple and unsophisticated technologies rather than large-scale fully integrated technologies. Why do you think this is so?

20 One problem with technology which is open to all members of the public to use, for example cash machines (ATMs), is that they could be open to fraud or misinterpretation. For example, some bank customers have complained that they did not make the transactions at cash machines which have shown up on their accounts. How do you think the technology might be developed to overcome this problem?

NOTES ON CHAPTER

1 Abernathy, W.J. and Utterback, J. (1975) 'A Dynamic Model of Process and Product Innovation', *Omega*, Vol 3, No 6, pp 639–57.

2 Economic Commission for Europe (1985) *Production and Use of Industrial Robots*, UN Economic Commission for Europe, ENC/ENG.ATV/15.

3 From Voss, C.A. (1986) *Managing New Manufacturing Technologies*, Operations Management Association, Monograph 1.

4 Edquist, C. and Jacobsson, S. (1988) *Flexible Automation*, Blackwell.

5 Source: *ABB Robotics Review*, No 2, 1993 and company literature, kindly supplied by ABB.

6 Source: 'When Robots do the Really Dangerous Jobs', *The Times*, 14 Aug 1996.

7 Voss, C.A., *op. cit.*

8 Bessant, J. (1991) *Managing Advanced Manufacturing Technology*, Blackwell.

9 Voss, C.A., *op. cit.*

10 Boaden, R. and Dale, B. (1986) 'What is Computer Integrated Manufacturing?', *International Journal of Operations and Production Management*, Vol 6, No 3.

11 Source: Tobias R.L., Henry Ford II Scholar Award Lecture, Cranfield School of Management, 1992.

12 Gunton, T. (1990) *Inside Information Technology*, Prentice Hall.

13 Spar, D. and Bussgand, J. (1996) 'The Net', *Harvard Business Review*, Vol 74, No 3.

14 Lloyd, C. (1993) 'Office in the Sky Gives a Lift to Business Travel', *The Sunday Times*, 30 May.

15 Adapted from Jayaraman, V. and Srivastara, R. (1996) 'Expert Systems in Production and Operations Management', *International Journal of Operations and Production Management*, Vol 16, No 12.

16 Walley, P. and Amin, V. (1994) 'Automation in a Customer Contact Environment', *International Journal of Operations and Production Management*, Vol 14, No 5, pp 86–100.

17 Sources: 'Know your Ailment Without Taking up the Doctor's Time', *The Times*, 24 Apr 1996. 'Big Sister is Watching You', *The Economist*, 11 Jan 1997. 'How Doctors Improved their Bedside Manners', *The Times*, 11 Sept 1996. 'Robodoc', *The Economist*, 15 June 1996.

18 'Bar Coding the Poor', *The Economist*, 25 Jan 1997.

19 Tansik, D.A. and Smith, W.L. (1993) 'Technology Issues in Services: A Typology and Implications' *in* Johnston, R. and Slack, N. (eds) *Service Superiority*, OMA.

20 'Electronic Shopping Ignores Our Needs', *The Times*, 5 March 1997. 'Revolution Sweeps Through Cashpoints', *The Sunday Times*, 18 Aug 1996.

21 Brown, D. (1993) 'Mechanical Milkman Allows Farmer a Lie In', *The Daily Telegraph*, 11 Sept.
22 Walley, P. and Amin, V., *op. cit.*
23 Bessant, J., *op. cit.*
24 Dempsey, P. (1983) 'New Corporate Perspectives on FMS', *FMS Conference Proceedings*, IFS.
25 Tombak, M. and De Meyer, A. (1986) 'How the Managerial Attitudes of Firms with FMS Differ from Other Manufacturing Firms', *INSEAD Working Paper*, No 86/15.

SELECTED FURTHER READINGS

Abernathy, W.J. (1976) 'Production Process Structure and Technological Change', *Decision Sciences*, Vol 7, No 4.

Adler, T.S. and Winograd, T.A. (1992) *Usability, Turning Technology in Tools*, Oxford University Press.

Avishai, B. (1989) 'A CEO's Common Sense of CIM: An Interview with J.Tracy O'Rourke', *Harvard Business Review*, Vol 67, No 1.

Ayres, R. (1992) 'CIM: A Challenge to Technology Management', *International Journal of Technology Management*, Vol 7, No 2.

Benders, J., DeHaan, J. and Bennett, D. (eds) (1995) *The Symbiosis of Work and Technology*, Taylor and Francis.

Bennett, D., Forrester, P. and Hassard, J. (1992) 'Market-driven Strategies and the Design of Flexible Production Systems: Evidence from the Electronics Industry', *International Journal of Operations and Production Management*, Vol 12, No 2.

Bessant, J. (1991) *Managing Advanced Manufacturing Technology, The Challenge of the Fifth Wave*, NCC, Blackwell.

Collier, D.A. (1985) *Service Management: The Automation of Services*, Reston Publishing.

Delene, L.M. and Lyte, D.M. (1989) 'Interactive Service Operations: The Relationships Among Information, Technology and Exchange Transactions on the Quality of the Customer-Contact Interface', *International Journal of Operations and Production Management*, Vol 9, No 5.

Gerwin, D. (1982) 'Dos and Don'ts of Computerised Manufacturing', *Harvard Business Review*, Vol 60, No 2.

Goldhar, J.D. and Jelinek, M. (1983) 'Plan for Economies of Scope', *Harvard Business Review*, Vol 61, No 6.

Gunton, T. (1990) *Inside Information Technology, A Practical Guide to Management Issues*, Prentice Hall.

Harrison, M. (1990) *Advanced Manufacturing Technology Management*, Pitman Publishing.

Jaikumar, R. (1986) 'Postindustrial Manufacturing', *Harvard Business Review*, Vol 64, No 6.

Kaplan, R.S. (1986) 'Must CIM be Justified by Faith Alone?', *Harvard Business Review*, Vol 64, No 2.

Karlsson, C. (1992) 'Knowledge and Material Flow in Future Industrial Networks', *International Journal of Operations and Production Management*, Vol 12, No 7/8.

Lindburg, P. (1992) 'The Management of Uncertainty in AMT Implementation: The Case of FMS', *International Journal of Operations and Production Management*, Vol 12, No 7/8.

McCutchon, D.M. and Wood, A.R. (1989) 'The Effects of Technical Experience on Robot Implementations', *International Journal of Operations and Production Management*, Vol 9, No 7.

Monroe, J. (1989) 'Strategic Use of Technology', *California Management Review*, Summer.

Rhodes, D. (1989) 'CIM and the Integration of Users, Vendors and Educators', *International Journal of Operations and Production Management*, Vol 9, No 2.

Skinner, W. (1984) 'Operations Technology: Blind Spot in Strategic Management', *Interfaces*, Vol 14, No 1.

Zorkoczy, P. (1993) *Information Technology: An Introduction* (3rd edn), Pitman Publishing.

Job Design and Work Organization

INTRODUCTION

Operations management is often presented as a subject the main focus of which is on technology, systems, procedures and facilities – in other words the non-human parts of the organization. This is not true of course. On the contrary, the manner in which an organization's human resources are managed has a profound impact on the effectiveness of its operations function. In this chapter we look especially at the elements of human resource management which are traditionally seen as being directly within the sphere of operations management. These are the activities which influence the relationship between people, the technology they use, and the work methods employed by the operation. This is usually called job design. Figure 9.1 shows how job design fits into the overall model of design.

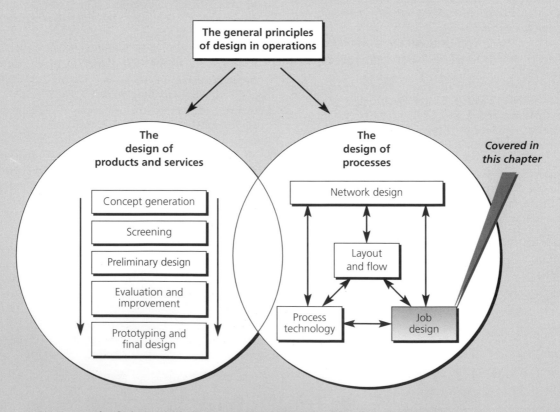

Figure 9.1 The design activities in operations management covered in this chapter

CHAPTER 9: KEY QUESTIONS

- *What are the main decisions in job design?*

- *What are the main objectives of job design?*

- *What have been the significant influences on job design practice?*

- *How do the influences on job design differ?*

THE DESIGN OF JOBS

To say that an organization's human resources are its greatest asset is at best axiomatic and at worst a cliché. Yet for all that it is true, so it is worth reminding ourselves of the importance of human resources, especially in the operations function. It is usually in the operations function where the bulk of its human resources are to be found. It follows that it is operations managers who are most involved in the leadership, development and organization of human resources. In fact the influence of operations management on the organization's staff is not limited to how their jobs are designed. (Nor is the coverage of this book: Chapters 18 and 20, for example, are concerned largely with how the contribution of the operation's staff can be harnessed.) Job design has a particularly pivotal role. Job design defines the way in which people go about their working lives. It positions their expectations of what is required of them, and it influences their perceptions of how they contribute to the organization. It positions their activities in relation to their work colleagues and it channels the flows of communication between different parts of the operation. But of most importance, it helps to develop the culture of the organization – its shared values, beliefs and assumptions. It is for this reason that job design is seen by some as the central aspect of the design of any transformation process.

The elements of job design

Job design is not a single decision. Rather it has a number of separate, yet related elements which, when taken together, define the jobs of the people who work in the operation. Figure 9.2 illustrates some of the elements of job design.

What tasks are to be allocated to each person in the operation?

Producing goods and services on a continuing basis involves a whole range of different tasks which need to be divided between all the people who staff the operation. Different approaches to job design will lead to different task allocations. For example, one company might choose to confine each staff member to repeating the same type of task, so as to encourage simplicity and efficiency. Another company might choose to allocate a wide variety of tasks to each staff member so as to reduce the monotony of his or her job.

313

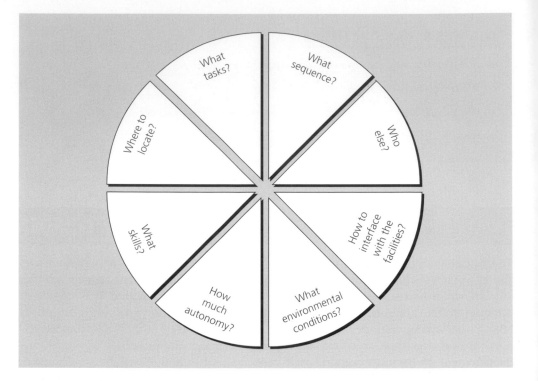

Figure 9.2
The elements of
job design

What sequence of tasks is to be established as the approved manner to do the job?

Sometimes the sequence of tasks is dictated by the design of the product or service. For example, an operator working on an automobile assembly line must put the wheels in place before putting on the wheel nuts. No other sequence would result in a satisfactory product. Sometimes sequence is determined by the desire to avoid mistakes. Next time you pay for goods at a supermarket check-out, note the sequence of taking your cash or card, asking you to sign the authorization form, returning your card, receipt and payment slip, and so on.

Where is the job to be located within the operation?

Some jobs can be performed quite satisfactorily in more than one place. For example, a maintenance worker in a large hospital could be located centrally along with all other maintenance workers. Alternatively, he or she could be assigned responsibility for just one part of the hospital and located in that part.

Who else should be involved in the job?

It may be that instead of allocating a well-defined set of tasks to each person in the operation, a larger set of tasks is allocated to a group of people. The group then might choose, or be guided to, a flexible task-sharing, or a task-rotation, pattern of working. If so, the size of the group and its interactions with other groups and individuals must be decided.

How are the facilities and equipment used in the job to be interfaced with?

Very few jobs do not involve some interaction with tools, equipment, machines or facilities. Inappropriately positioned computer screens, badly designed controls and ill-fitting desks are all failures to consider the interfaces between people and the 'hardware' of their job.

What environmental conditions should be established in the workplace?
The conditions under which jobs are performed can have just as significant an impact on people's effectiveness, comfort and safety as the intrinsic details of the tasks themselves.

How much autonomy is to be included in the job?
There is a difference between allocating tasks to an individual and encouraging autonomy for the way the job is performed. For example, a retail operation might decide that the staff in a section of the shop should be allocated the tasks of reordering stock when it runs low, displaying the goods, organizing their own meal breaks, and so on.

What skills are to be developed in staff?
Different decisions in the elements of job design described here all have implications for the skills and capabilities which people will need to perform their jobs effectively.

The objectives of job design

There are clearly many alternative designs for any given job. For this reason, an understanding of what the job design is supposed to achieve is particularly important. As before, the five performance objectives give us a guide to what is relevant in job design decisions.

1 Quality
The ability of staff to produce high-quality products and services can be affected by job design. This includes avoiding errors in the short term, but also includes designing jobs which encourage staff to improve the job itself in such a way as to make errors less likely.

2 Speed
Sometimes speed of response is the dominant objective to be achieved in job design. For example, the way in which the jobs of emergency service personnel are organized (the range of tasks for which they are trained, the sequence of activities in their approved procedures, the autonomy which they have to decide on appropriate action, and so on) will go a long way to determine their ability to respond promptly to emergencies and perhaps save lives.

3 Dependability
Dependable supply of goods and services is usually influenced, in some way, by job design. For example, in the postal services' working arrangements, multi-skilling, accurate use of sorting equipment through good staff–machine interface design, and even the 'design' of postal staff's clothing, can all aid dependable delivery of letters and parcels.

4 Flexibility
Job design can affect the ability of the operation to change the nature of its activities. New product or service flexibility, mix flexibility, volume flexibility and delivery

flexibility are all dependent to some extent on job design. (*See* Chapter 2 for a full description of these different types of flexibility.) For example, staff who have been trained in several tasks (multi-skilling) may find it easier to cope with a wide variety of models and new product or service introductions.

5 Cost

All the elements of job design described above will have an effect on the productivity, and therefore cost, of the job. Productivity in this context means the ratio of output to labour input: for example, the number of customers served per hour or the number of products made per worker.

In addition, job design will influence two other particularly important objectives.

6 Health and safety

Whatever else a job design achieves, it must not endanger the well-being of the person who does the job, other staff of the operation, the customers who might be present in the operation, or those who use any products made by the operation.

7 *Quality of working life*

The design of any job should take into account its effect on job security, intrinsic interest, variety, opportunities for development, stress level and attitude of the person performing the job.

Approaches to job design practice

There are several approaches which can be taken to job design. Over the years different approaches have been particularly influential at different times. None of these

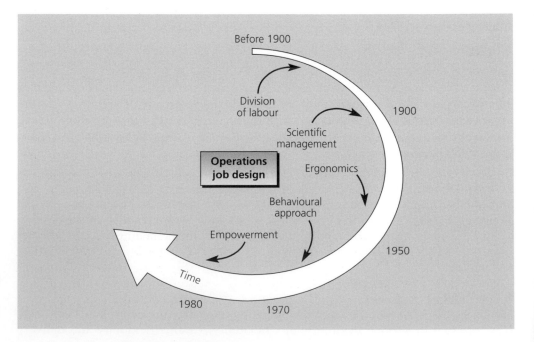

**Figure 9.3
The chronology of
the different
approaches to job
design**

approaches are mutually exclusive as such, but they do represent different philosophies or, at least, emphasize different aspects of job design. This is mainly because they were advanced at different points in the history of operations management. Chronologically, the approaches are as shown in Fig. 9.3, and it is in this order that we will treat them here. It should be stressed, however, that these approaches did not replace each other. The influence of all of them is still evident in the way jobs are designed today. Rather each added a new 'layer' or perspective to the job design activity.

DIVISION OF LABOUR

The division of labour becomes an issue in job design as soon as an operation is large enough to warrant the employment of more than one person. For example, a single tailor will measure clients, select the cloth, cut the cloth, sew the pieces together, fit the clothes to the customer, try to elicit further business, and so on. As soon as business increases such that two or more people are needed to staff the business, the possibility of specialization arises. For example, if volume warrants three people, they could divide the total set of tasks so that one person serves in the shop and measures customers, the second person cuts out the material and the third person sews the clothes.

This idea is called the division of labour – dividing the total task down into smaller parts, each of which is accomplished by a single person. It is an idea which has been evident in job design from the earliest times of organizational activity (arguably back to Greece in the fourth century BC), though it was first formalized as a concept by the economist Adam Smith in his *Wealth of Nations* in 1746.[1] Perhaps the epitome of the division of labour is the assembly line where products move along a single path and are built up by operators continually repeating a single task. This may seem an outdated image yet it is still the predominant model of job design in most mass-produced products, and in some mass-produced services (fast food, for example). This is because, in spite of its drawbacks, there are some real advantages in division-of-labour principles.

It promotes faster learning

It is obviously easier to learn how to do a relatively short and simple task than a long and complex one. This means that new members of staff can be quickly trained and assigned to their tasks when tasks are short and simple.

Automation becomes easier

Dividing a total task into small parts raises the possibility of automating some of those small tasks. Substituting technology for labour is considerably easier for short and simple tasks than for long and complex ones.

Reduced non-productive work

This is probably the most important benefit of division of labour. In large, complex tasks the proportion of time spent picking up tools and materials, putting them down again and generally finding, positioning and searching can be very high indeed. Consider, for example, the unlikely event of one person assembling a whole motor car engine. The task would probably take two or three hours and would involve much bending, searching for parts, positioning, and so on. None of these activities actually

317

contributes directly to making the product. They are there because of the way the job has been designed. If one person really did assemble the whole engine, around half the person's time would be spent on these reaching, positioning, finding tasks (called non-productive elements of work). Now consider how a motor car engine is actually made in practice. The total job is probably divided into 20 or 30 separate stages, each staffed by a person who carries out only a proportion of the total job. Because the individual operatives are concentrating only on one piece of the job, specialist equipment and materials-handling devices can be devised to help them carry out their job more efficiently. Furthermore, there is relatively little finding, positioning and reaching involved in this simplified task. Non-productive work can be considerably reduced, perhaps to under ten per cent. Such improvements in labour efficiency can be very significant in the costs of the operation.

All these benefits contributed to the wide adoption of division of labour principles as industrialization took hold in the developed economies of the early twentieth century. Henry Ford described his use of the principles for the manufacture of the flywheel magneto of the 'Model T' in 1913.

'We had previously assembled the flywheel magneto in the usual method. With one workman doing a complete job he could turn out from 35 to 40 pieces in a nine-hour day, or about 20 minutes to an assembly. What he did alone was then spread into 29 operations; that cut down the assembly time to 13 minutes 10 seconds. Then we raised the height of the line eight inches – this was in 1914 – and cut the time to seven minutes. Further experimenting with the speed that the work should move at cut the time down to five minutes. In short, the result is this; by aid of scientific study one man is now able to do somewhat more than four did only a comparatively few years ago. That line established the efficiency of the method and we now use it everywhere.'[2]

However, it soon became evident that there are also serious drawbacks to highly divided jobs.

1 Monotony

The shorter the task, the more often operators will need to repeat the task. Repeating the same task, for example every 30 seconds, eight hours a day and five days a week, can hardly be called a fulfilling job. As well as any ethical objections to deliberately designing jobs which are unremittingly monotonous, there are other, more obviously practical objections to jobs which induce such boredom. These include the increased likelihood of absenteeism and staff turnover, the increased likelihood of error and even the deliberate sabotage of the job.

2 Physical injury

The continued repetition of a very narrow range of movements can, in extreme cases, lead to physical injury. The over-use of some parts of the body (especially the arms, hands and wrists) can result in pain and a reduction in physical capability. This is sometimes called repetitive strain injury (RSI), and although the extent of physical injury through repetitive work is a cause of some controversy, the fact that repeated work can, under some conditions, cause injury is largely accepted.

3 Low flexibility

Dividing a task up into many small parts often gives the job design a rigidity which is difficult to change under changing circumstances. For example, if an assembly line

Expansion at Café Rouge

Photo courtesy of Café Rouge

Diners enjoy individual service at Café Rouge locations, all of which have a similar layout and appearance

Café Rouge was founded in the UK in 1989 when they opened their first 'French-style café' in Richmond, Greater London. Since then the business has seen phenomenal growth. Jo Cumming, Managing Director of Café Rouge recalls, *'We started with a theme and developed that theme into a service package that would easily fit into any suitable building. We would experiment with café layouts and with menu designs and choices until we had everything as we wanted it. We then documented all of our standard practices so that new locations could quickly learn how to operate. The choice of new sites is a matter of assessing the potential market and considering the structural constraints of any potential properties. Some areas have a better profile of regular restaurant users than others. Also, we needed to locate reasonably close to other restaurants. Our learning curve was quite rapid and now we can recognize whether or not a site will be* *appropriate and have also got the period from moving in to opening up, down to less than two weeks. The restaurant staff are trained in other cafés and the furniture and fittings are all standardized, so it is really just a matter of adding the final touches and we're in and running. We also have to make sure that we can keep up with the rapid pace of expansion. Opening a new site needs both financial and management resources. We put a lot of effort into working out the cash flow and work load implications of each step in our expansion.'*

- What seem to be the main expansion-related issues for Café Rouge?

- Why do they like to locate close to other restaurants?

→ *Look at Chapter 6 for guidance*

Design for work

Digital Equipment Corporation, Finland

The picture shows part of the offices of Digital Equipment Company in Finland, one office which has been designed to facilitate modern office work. Space and facilities are provided for reading reports and contemplating issues, meeting colleagues, accessing information and formal presentations.

In many organizations, workers 'hot desk' – with no fixed desks of their own, they use the desks and computers which are most convenient for them at the time. A parallel development is in the use of 'teleworking' – working from home using a computer with telecommunications link-ups to headquarters. Although not everyone is happy with this form of working, many are. The chart below shows how various factors of working have been affected by teleworking according to one survey. But as Stephen Jupp says, all is not straightforward. '*It is easy to be dazzled by the issues of technology or office space. But these are relatively easy to understand. In practice, it is the people-side of change that is the most important. Understanding the personal, social and management implications of this new way of working will be the key to successful change.*'

After seeing the benefits of flexible technology in manufacturing operations, attention is now turning to the office. Information and communication technologies, and a deeper understanding of what actually goes on in offices, are starting to make an impact on where we work, how we work and what we do with our time. Stephen Jupp of the Home Office Partnership believes that offices in the future may look very different. '*If you want to chat to a colleague about something, where would you prefer to meet? Probably not at a desk or in a meeting room but in a pub or café. But offices don't reflect this idea. They should be providing the most productive work settings for staff to get their work done. So where are the armchairs in our offices? And why doesn't the staff restaurant open all day?*'

- *What do you think might be the advantages and disadvantages of flexible working space such as that shown in the Digital Equipment Company office?*
- *Under what circumstances do you think teleworking would be a good idea?*
- *How might the design of office space depend on the kind of jobs we do?*

➜ *Look at Chapter 8 and 9 for guidance*

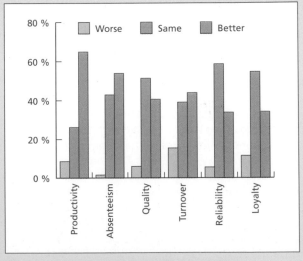

Managers' views of the effects of teleworking

Nissan wins a new model

Engine assembly at Nissan

In the global automobile industry, multinational car manufacturers think very carefully before choosing where to spend the money needed to build new models. Cost factors, local taxes, proximity to markets and expansion opportunities are all issues which influence such decisions. But just as important is each plant's track record of operations improvement. It was (at least, partly) its excellent operations performance that secured Nissan's Sunderland plant in the UK its new model, due to start production in 2000. The Sunderland plant's improvement programme had, over four years, reduced delivery times and the number of reject components from its suppliers significantly from an already low level. It also included a programme to help suppliers enhance their own product development skills. People development activities within the plant embraced improved career development, job rotation to give variety at work and ergonomically-inspired changes to job designs on the shop floor. All this helped push performance up to Japanese averages in many areas – unusual for a European plant. The next initiative (called Next 21) is aiming to bring all of Nissan's European operations up to the best Japanese performance levels.

Final assembly, Nissan Primera

Final assembly, Nissan Micra

- *The improvement initiative which helped to win the Sunderland plant its new model was called NX96, a four-year programme which started in 1992. The new model will not start production until 2000. Why do you think it takes eight years for initiatives like this to come to fruition?*

- *What did Nissan do to help its suppliers? Why do you think it is so important to put time and effort into developing a good supply base?*

- *The pictures show three assembly processes at the Sunderland plant. In all three cases the products are positioned relative to the workers in a different way. Why do you think this is?*

→ *Look at Chapters 9 and 18 for guidance*

Photos courtesy of Nissan Motors UK Ltd

Ergonomics makes work safer at the Royal Mail

Ergonomic trials of the Royal Mail container

Until recently, mail has been collected and transported in strong cloth mailbags, an activity which can be observed at almost any railway station in the world. When the Royal Mail (a part of the UK Post Office) decided to rethink these activities in order to reduce effort and increase productivity, it called in its Ergonomics Design Group, who undertook a study. The handling of mailbags was a particular issue because it often involved staff lifting weights which were heavier than the recommended ergonomic standards. If an item is to be lifted from the floor to chest height, it passes through the 10, 20 and 25 kg zones, so should not be heavier than 10 kg. Furthermore, these recommendations are for tasks that occur

Acceptable forces/weights used in lifting

less than once per minute, and are reduced by up to 80 per cent if they are repeated more than 12 times per minute. Clearly, the existing method of handling mailbags would have to be re-thought. After extensive research, a special 250 kg Royal Mail container was designed.

Trial containers were introduced allowing potential problems to be identified and improvement made. The final design of container (*see* the picture) was introduced only after trials which evaluated its performance under working conditions. As well as providing a safer working method, it allowed significant improvements in labour efficiency because of the greater number of items in each movement.

- *Why do you think it is necessary for organizations like the Royal Mail to have limits on the loads to be lifted as illustrated left?*
- *Initial trials of the new container showed that it was not always easy to handle under all circumstances. How would you go about designing an ergonomic investigation to decide how the containers should be used in practice?*

→ *Look at Chapter 9 for guidance*

has been designed to make one particular product but then has to change to manufacture a quite different product, the whole line will need redesigning. This will probably involve changing every operator's set of tasks, which can be a long and difficult procedure. Compare this with a situation, for example, where each operator manufactures the whole product. Under these circumstances changing from making one product to another one would be a relatively straightforward matter.

4 Poor robustness

Highly divided jobs imply materials (or people, or information) passing between several stages. If one of these stages is not working correctly, for example because some equipment is faulty, the whole operation is affected. On the other hand, if each person is performing the whole of the job, any problems will only affect that one person's output. The rest of the operation will carry on producing as normal.

SCIENTIFIC MANAGEMENT

In the last ten years of the nineteenth century and the first twenty years of the twentieth century, a number of (mainly American) management thinkers developed ideas and principles of job and work design which collectively became known as 'scientific management'. The term 'scientific management' became established in 1911 with the publication of the book of the same name by Fredrick Winslow Taylor (this whole approach to job design is sometimes referred to, pejoratively, as 'Taylorism'). In this work he identified what he saw as the basic tenets of scientific management:[3]

● All aspects of work should be investigated on a scientific basis to establish the laws, rules and formulae governing the best methods of working.
● Such an investigative approach to the study of work is necessary to establish what constitutes a 'fair day's work'.
● Workers should be selected, trained and developed methodically to perform their tasks.
● Managers should act as the planners of the work (analysing jobs and standardizing the best method of doing the job) while workers should be responsible for carrying out the jobs to the standards laid down.
● Co-operation should be achieved between management and workers based on the 'maximum prosperity' of both.

Other contributors to the scientific management movement included Gilbreth, Gantt and Bedaux, all working in the United States. Two separate, but related, fields of study emerged. One, *method study*, concentrates on determining the methods and activities which should be included in jobs. The other, *work measurement*, is concerned with measuring the time which should be taken for performing jobs. Together these two fields are often referred to as *work study* (*see* Fig. 9.4). Work measurement and method study are discussed later in this chapter.

The important thing to remember about scientific management is that it is not particularly 'scientific' as such, although it certainly does take an 'investigative' approach to improving operations. Perhaps a better term for it would be 'systematic management'.

For example, a tale is told of Frank Gilbreth (the founder of method study) addressing a scientific conference with a paper entitled 'The Best Way to Get Dressed in a Morning'. In his presentation he rather bemused the scientific audience by

**Figure 9.4
Work study
comprises method
study and work
measurement**

analysing the 'best' way of buttoning up one's waistcoat in the morning. Among his conclusions was that waistcoats should always be buttoned from the bottom upwards, rather than from the top button downwards. This would enable the man getting dressed to straighten his tie in the same motion. Buttoning from the top downwards would mean that the hands would have to be raised again (a wasted motion) in order to straighten the tie. What his scientific audience felt about these conclusions is not on record, but think of this example if you want to understand scientific management and method study in particular. First of all, he is quite right. Method study and the other techniques of scientific management may often be without any intellectual or scientific validation, but by and large they do seem to work. At least they provide results within the limited objectives which they wish to address. Second, Gilbreth reached his conclusion by a systematic and critical analysis of what motions were necessary to do the job. Again, these are characteristics of scientific management – detailed analysis and painstakingly systematic examination. Third (and possibly most important), the results are relatively trivial. A great deal of effort was put into reaching a conclusion that was unlikely to have any earth-shattering consequences. Indeed one of the criticisms of scientific management, as developed in the early part of the twentieth century, is that it concentrated on relatively limited, and sometimes trivial, objectives. It certainly is not a strategic approach to operations; nor is this the only criticism of scientific management.

Criticisms of scientific management

As early as 1915 criticisms of the scientific management approach were being voiced.[4] In a submission to the United States Commission on Industrial Relations, scientific management is described as:

- being in 'spirit and essence a cunningly devised speeding up and sweating system';
- intensifying the 'modern tendency towards specialization of the work and the task';
- condemning 'the worker to a monotonous routine';
- putting 'into the hands of employers an immense mass of information and methods that may be used unscrupulously to the detriment of workers';
- tending to 'transfer to the management all the traditional knowledge, the judgement and skills of workers';
- greatly intensifying 'unnecessary managerial dictation and discipline';
- tending to 'emphasize quantity of product at the expense of quality'.

Some of this criticism could perhaps be seen in terms of the 'management *versus* organized labour' organizational power struggle which was prevalent at the time. The two themes evident in this early criticism do warrant closer attention, however. The first is that scientific management inevitably results in standardization of highly divided jobs and thus reinforces the negative effects of excessive division of labour previously mentioned. Second, scientific management formalizes the separation of the judgemental, planning and skilled tasks, which are done by 'management', from the routine, standardized and low-skill tasks, which are left for 'operators'. Such a separation, at the very least, deprives the majority of staff of an opportunity to contribute in a meaningful way to their jobs (and, incidentally, deprives the organization of their contribution). Both of these themes in the criticisms of scientific management lead to the same point, that the jobs designed under strict scientific-management principles lead to low motivation among staff, frustration at the lack of control over their work, and alienation from the job.

But before dismissing the whole of the work done by the followers of scientific management it is worth making two points:

- More recent applications of *some* of the principles of scientific management claim to have overcome, at least partly, the objections to it by moving responsibility for the use of its methods and procedures from 'management' to the staff who are being studied. (The box on how scientific management principles were used at the NUMMI plant illustrates this.)
- Some of the methods and techniques of scientific management, as opposed to its philosophy (especially those which come under the general heading of 'method study') can, in practice, prove useful in critically re-examining job designs. It is the practicality of these techniques which possibly explains why they have survived to be influential still in job design almost a century after their inception.

Method study

Method study is the part of scientific management which makes the most direct contribution to job design. It is more of a systematic approach to job design than a set of techniques. It is defined in Fig. 9.4.

NUMMI – NEW UNITED MOTOR MANUFACTURING[5]

In practically all parts of the world, Japanese motor manufacturers are producing their cars to rigorously high standards of quality and cost by using production methods similar to those developed in Japan. One of these Japanese 'implants' is the Toyota plant in Freemont, California, a joint venture between General Motors (GM) and Toyota using a plant which GM had previously closed in 1982. The reasons for GM closing this particular plant were not difficult to understand. Through the '70s and early '80s the quality of products produced in the Freemont plant was extremely poor, even by the relatively low standards of the time. Productivity was among the lowest of any GM plant in the United States, absenteeism was running at around 20 per cent of the workforce, labour relations in the plant were such that it had earned a national reputation for militancy and wild-cat strikes, and alcohol and drug abuse was a problem both inside the plant and out.

Soon after GM had closed the plant, it began discussions with Toyota about the possibility of a joint venture. Agreement was reached in 1983 to produce a Japanese-designed car, sold under the GM name, but manufactured using Toyota's methods of production. The NUMMI plant, as it was now called, was formally opened in 1984. Over the next two years the plant built up production levels, progressively hiring more workers, about 85 per cent of whom had worked in the plant before GM had closed it; several came from the old union hierarchy. The first to be recruited were the team leaders, 450 of whom, together with the entire NUMMI management team, took part in a three-week training programme in Japan. Those trained then played a part in organizing and training the new workers.

The performance of the NUMMI plant could hardly have contrasted more with that of the old GM-run factory. Even though the workforce was largely the same, by the end of 1986 the plant's productivity was more than twice as high as when it was run by GM, and higher than any other GM factory. Indeed, productivity was almost as high as Toyota's Takoaka plant in Japan, in spite of the fact that NUMMI's workforce was new to Toyota's production methods and, on average, ten years older. Quality also improved dramatically. Audits showed that quality levels were almost as high as Takoaka's and certainly higher than any other GM plant. Absenteeism had dropped from over 20 per cent in the old GM-run plant to between three and four per cent. Such improved levels of performance attracted increased investment, both in new manufacturing technology and new products.

Many reasons for the success of the NUMMI plant have been put forward. These include clearer organizational goals, a selective approach to recruiting those employees who had been employed previously in the plant, the move towards single status and dress codes for every-one in the factory, even the pride of working on an intrinsically better designed product. However, what is notable is that the new plant and its management did not abandon the techniques of scientific management which the previous plant's regime had supposedly used. The philosophy of job standardization was still rigorously applied, if anything more rigorously than in the past. Every job in the plant is carefully analysed using method study principles to achieve maximum efficiency and quality. Jobs are timed, using stop watches, and the detail of jobs questioned critically.

Yet there is now a major difference. Whereas, before, the company's industrial engineers were in charge of applying method-study techniques, now it is the operators (or team members as they are called) themselves who perform the analysis of their own jobs. Team members time each other, using stop watches, and analyse the sequence of tasks in each job.

They look for alternative ways of doing the job which improve safety and efficiency and can be sustained at a reasonable pace throughout the day. Each team will then take its improved job proposals and compare them with those developed by the comparable team doing the same job on a different shift. The resulting new job specification is then recorded and becomes the standard work definition for all staff performing that job.

NUMMI's claim is that the standardization of tasks results in less variability in task performance, which has in turn led to several further benefits:

● Safety and work-related stress injuries improve because potentially dangerous or harmful elements have been removed from the job.
● Productivity improves because wasted elements of the job have been eliminated.
● Quality standards improve because potential 'fail points' in the job have been analysed out.
● Flexibility improves and job rotation is easier because standards are clearer and all staff understand the intrinsic structure of their jobs.

One team leader compared the way in which the industrial engineers in the old plant had designed jobs with the way it was done under the NUMMI regime.

'I don't think the industrial engineers were dumb. They were just ignorant. Anyone can watch someone else doing a job and come up with improvement suggestions … and it's even easier to come up with the ideal procedure if you don't even bother to watch the worker at work, but just do it from your office … almost anything can look good that way. Even when we do our own analysis in our teams some of the silliest ideas can slip through before we actually try them out. … there's a lot of things that enter into a good job design … the person actually doing the job is the only one who can see all factors.' ■

Questions

1 What do you see as the main differences between traditional work study as described in the text and the way in which NUMMI operates it?

2 What other aspects of job design seem to be put into practice at NUMMI?

The method-study approach involves systematically following six steps.

1 Select the work to be studied.
2 Record all the relevant facts of the present method.
3 Examine those facts critically and in sequence.
4 Develop the most practical, economic and effective method.
5 Install the new method.
6 Maintain the method by periodically checking it in use.

Step 1 – Selecting the work to be studied

Most operations have many hundreds and possibly thousands of discrete jobs and activities which could be subjected to study. The first stage in method study is to select those jobs to be studied which will give the most return on the investment of the time spent studying them. This means it is unlikely that it will be worth studying activities which, for example, may soon be discontinued or are only performed occasionally. On the other hand, the type of jobs which should be studied as a matter of priority are those which, for example, seem to offer the greatest scope for improvement, or which are causing bottle-necks, delays, or problems in the operation.

Step 2 – Recording the present method

There are many different recording techniques used in method study. Most of them:

- record the sequence of activities in the job;
- record the time interrelationship of the activities in the job; or
- record the path of movement of some part of the job.

Perhaps the most commonly used recording technique in method study is the flow process chart which was discussed in Chapter 5 and is extended in Appendix 3.

Note that we are here recording the present method of doing the job. It may seem strange to devote so much time and effort to recording what is currently happening when after all the objective of method study is to devise a better method. The rationale for this is, first of all, that recording the present method can give a far greater insight into the job itself, and this can lead to new ways of doing it. Second, recording the present method is a good starting point from which to evaluate critically and therefore improve the method. In this last point the assumption is that it is easier to improve the method by starting from the current method and then criticizing it in detail than to start with a 'blank sheet of paper'.

There are other types of process chart which can be used to record the sequence of activities in a job. There are also many other recording techniques used in method study. Appendix 3 describes the more important of these in a little more detail.

Step 3 – Examining the facts

This is probably the most important stage in method study and the idea here is to examine the current method thoroughly and critically. This is often done by using the so-called 'questioning technique'. This technique attempts to expose the reasons behind existing methods in order to detect weaknesses in their rationale and therefore develop alternative methods.

Questions are asked regarding:

- *the purpose of each element*:
    What is done?
    Why is it done?
    What else could be done?
    What should be done?
- *the place in which each element is done*:
    Where is it done?
    Why is it done there?
    Where else could it be done?
    Where should it be done?

This may suggest a combination of certain activities or operations.

- *the sequence in which the elements are done*:
    When is it done?
    Why is it done then?
    When should it be done?

This may suggest a change in the sequence of the operation.

- *the person who does the element*:
    Who does it?
    Why does that person do it?
    Who else could do it?
    Who should do it?

This may suggest a combination and/or change in sequence.

- *the means by which each element is done:*
    How is it done?
    Why is it done in that way?
    How else could it be done?
    How should it be done?

Following this approach may appear somewhat detailed and tedious, yet it is fundamental to the method-study philosophy – everything must be critically examined. Understanding the natural tendency to be less than rigorous at this stage, some organizations use pro forma questionnaires, asking each of these questions and leaving space for formal replies and/or justifications, which the job designer is required to complete.

Step 4 – Developing a new method

The previous critical examination of current methods has by this stage probably indicated some changes and improvements. This stage involves taking these ideas further in an attempt to:

- eliminate parts of the activity altogether;
- combine elements together;
- change the sequence of events so as to improve the efficiency of the job; or
- simplify the activity to reduce the work content.

A useful aid during this process is a checklist such as the 'Revised Principles of Motion Economy'. Table 9.1 illustrates these.

Steps 5 and 6 – Install the new method and regularly maintain it

The method-study approach to the installation of new work practices is, by modern standards, rather naïve. It concentrates largely on 'project managing' the installation process (*see* Chapter 16 for a full description of project management) rather than examining the reactions of the staff whose jobs and methods are being affected. The method-study approach also emphasizes the need to monitor regularly the effectiveness of job designs after they have been installed. However, although this was not intended as some kind of 'continuous improvement' philosophy (rather it was to make sure that conditions had not changed to make the method anything less than optimal for its purpose), it can be used as an opportunity to rethink and improve methods on a continuous basis.

Table 9.1 The principles of motion economy

Using the human body the way it works best	1	Work should be arranged so that a natural rhythm can become automatic.
	2	Consider the symmetry of the body, for example the motions of the arms should be: – simultaneous; and – opposite and symmetrical.
	3	The full capabilities of the human body should be employed. For example: – Neither hand should ever be idle. – Work should be distributed to parts of the body in line with their ability. – The safe 'design limits' of the body should be observed.
	4	Arms and hands as weights are subject to the physical laws and energy should be conserved. For example: – Momentum should work for the body and not against it. – The smooth, continuous arc of ballistic motions is most efficient. – The distance of movements should be minimized.
	5	Tasks should be simplified. For example: – Eye contacts should be few and grouped together. – Unnecessary actions, delays, and idle time should be eliminated. – The degree of required precision and control should be minimized. – The number of individual motions should be minimized along with the number of muscle groups involved.
Arranging the workplace to assist performance	1	There should be a defined place for all tools and materials.
	2	Tools, materials and controls should be located close to the point of use.
	3	Tools, materials and controls should be located to permit the best sequence and path of motions.
	4	The workplace should be fitted both to the tasks and to human capabilities.
Using mechancial devices to reduce human effort	1	Vices and clamps should hold the work precisely where needed.
	2	Guides should assist in positioning the work without close operator attention.
	3	Controls and foot-operated devices can relieve the hands of work.
	4	Mechanical devices can multiply human abilities.
	5	Mechanical systems should be fitted to human use.

Source: Adapted from Barnes, Frank C. (1983) 'Principles of Motion Economy: Revisited, Reviewed, and Restored', *Proceedings of the Southern Management Association Annual Meeting* (Atlanta, GA 1983), p 298.

METHOD STUDY AT INTEL

Although dating from the scientific management period, method study has undergone something of a revival in the last few years. In non-manufacturing operations especially, the method-study approach of systematically challenging methods of work is proving an effective approach to improvement. For example, Fig. 9.5 shows the flow process chart which Intel Corporation, the computer chip company, drew to describe its method of processing expense reports (claims forms).

Flow process chart

Activity	Processing expense reports	Location	Accounts Dept

	Description of element	●	➡	◗	■	▼
1	Report arrives at accounts payable desk	●	➡	◗	■	▼
2	Wait for processing	●	➡	◗	■	▼
3	Check expenses report	●	➡	◗	■	▼
4	Stamp and date report	●	➡	◗	■	▼
5	Send cash to receipt desk	●	➡	◗	■	▼
6	Wait for processing	●	➡	◗	■	▼
7	Check to see if advance payment has been made	●	➡	◗	■	▼
8	Send to accounts receivable desk	●	➡	◗	■	▼
9	Wait for processing	●	➡	◗	■	▼
10	Check employee's past account	●	➡	◗	■	▼
11	Send to accounts payable desk	●	➡	◗	■	▼
12	Attach payment voucher to report	●	➡	◗	■	▼
13	Log report	●	➡	◗	■	▼
14	Check items against company guidelines	●	➡	◗	■	▼
15	Wait for batching	●	➡	◗	■	▼
16	Collect reports into batch	●	➡	◗	■	▼
17	Batch goes to audit desk	●	➡	◗	■	▼
18	Wait for processing	●	➡	◗	■	▼
19	Batch of reports logged	●	➡	◗	■	▼
20	Check payment vouchers	●	➡	◗	■	▼
21	Reports go to batch control	●	➡	◗	■	▼
22	Control number applied to batch	●	➡	◗	■	▼
23	Copies of reports to filing	●	➡	◗	■	▼
24	Reports filed	●	➡	◗	■	▼
25	Copies of payment voucher to keyboard	●	➡	◗	■	▼
26	Cheque	●	➡	◗	■	▼
		●	➡	◗	■	▼

Symbol	Element	No.
●	Operation	7
➡	Transport	8
◗	Delay	5
■	Inspection	5
▼	Storage	1

Figure 9.5 The flow process chart for processing expense reports at Intel ▶

Flow process chart

Activity	Processing expense reports / Description of element	Location	Accounts Dept ● ➡ D ■ ▼
1	Report arrives at accounts payable desk		
2	Stamp and date report		
3	Check expenses report		
4	Attach payment voucher to report		
5	Wait for batching		
6	Collect reports into batch		
7	Batch goes to audit desk		
8	Wait for processing		
9	Check totals of reports and vouchers		
10	Reports go to batch control		
11	Control number applied to batch		
12	Copies of reports to filing		
13	Reports filed		
14	Copies of payment voucher to keyboard		
15	Cheque issued		

Symbol	Element	No.	Total time
●	Operation	5	
➡	Transport	5	
D	Delay	2	
■	Inspection	2	
▼	Storage	1	

Figure 9.6 The flow process chart for processing expense reports at Intel after critical analysis

After critically examining its existing method of processing these reports, the company developed a new method which cut the number of elements from 26 down to 15 (*see* Fig. 9.6). The accounts payable desk's activities were combined with the cash-receipt's activities of checking employees' past expense accounts (elements 8, 10 and 11) which also eliminated elements 5 and 7. After consideration, it was decided to eliminate the activity of checking items against company guidelines, because it seemed '*... more trouble than it was worth*'. Also, logging the batches was deemed unnecessary. All this combination and elimination of activities had the effect of removing several 'delays' from the process. The end result was a much simplified process which reduced the staff time needed to do the job by 28 per cent and considerably speeded up the whole process. ∎

Questions

1 This box describes how Intel used a flow process chart. What was the nature of the improvement it effected by doing this?

2 Do you think it was necessary to draw this chart in order to make the improvement?

3 What do you think are the limitations of using charts like this for improvement?

Work measurement and performance measurement

The other legacy of scientific management is work measurement, which is often used to evaluate alternative job designs. Work measurement is the process of establishing the time that a given task should take when performed by a '*qualified worker*' working at a '*defined level of performance*'. Both concepts are difficult to define exactly and both are somewhat controversial.

There are various ways in which work may be measured using a variety of techniques (*see* Appendix 2). The end result is a standard time (measured in 'standard minutes' or 'standard hours') which includes the time the work 'should' take (when carried out by a qualified worker), plus additional allocations in the form of allowances, where appropriate, to cover relaxation time, contingency time and, perhaps, unoccupied time which increases the overall work cycle, such as waiting for a machine to finish a processing cycle.

Notwithstanding the weak theoretical basis of work measurement, understanding the work-time consequences is clearly an important part of job design. The advantage of structured and systematic work measurement is that it gives a common currency for the evaluation and comparison of all types of work.

Example

Two work teams in the Monrovian Embassy have been allocated the task of processing visa applications. Team A processes applications from Europe, Africa and the Middle East. Team B processes applications from North and South America, Asia and Australasia. Team A has chosen to organize itself in such a way that each of its three team members processes an application from start to finish. The four members of Team B have chosen to split themselves into two sub-teams. Two open the letters and carry out the checks for a criminal record (no one who has been convicted of any crime other than a motoring offence can enter Monrovia), while the other two team members check for financial security (only people with more than Monrovian $1000 may enter the country).

The head of consular affairs is keen to find out if one of these methods of organizing the teams is more efficient than the other. The problem is that the mix of applications differs region by region. Team A typically processes around two Business applications to every one Tourist application. Team B processes around one Business application to every two Tourist applications.

A study revealed the following data:

Average standard time to process a Business visa = 63 standard minutes

Average time to process a Tourist visa   = 55 standard minutes

Average weekly output from Team A is:
85.2   Business visas
39.5   Tourist visas

Average weekly output from Team B is:
53.5   Business visas
100.7   Tourist visas

All team members work a 40-hour week.

The efficiency of each team can be calculated by comparing the actual output in standard minutes and the time worked in minutes.

So Team A processes:

$(85.2 \times 63) + (39.5 \times 55)$ = 7540.1 standard minutes of work

in $3 \times 40 \times 60$ minutes   = 7200 minutes

So its efficiency $= \dfrac{7540.1}{7200} \times 100 = 104.72\%$

Team B processes:

$(53.5 \times 63) + (100.7 \times 55)$ = 8909 standard minutes of work

in $4 \times 40 \times 60$ minutes   = 9600 minutes

So its efficiency $= \dfrac{8909}{9600} \times 100 = 92.8\%$

The initial evidence therefore seems to suggest that the way Team A has organized itself is more efficient.

ERGONOMICS

Ergonomics is concerned primarily with the physiological aspects of job design that is with the human body and how it fits into its surroundings. This involves two aspects. First of all, ergonomics is concerned with how the person interfaces with the physical aspect of his or her workplace, where the 'workplace' includes tables, chairs, desks, machines, computers, and so on. Second, it involves how a person interfaces with environmental conditions in his or her immediate working area. By this we mean the ambient conditions in which the person works, for example the temperature, lighting, noise environment, and so on. Ergonomics is sometimes referred to as 'human factors engineering' or just 'human factors'.

Both of these aspects are linked by two common ideas which permeate the ergonomics approach to job design.

- The first idea is that there must be a fit between people and the jobs they do. To achieve this fit there are only two alternatives. Either the job can be made to fit the people who are doing it, or, alternatively, the people can be made (or perhaps less radically, recruited) to fit the job. Ergonomics addresses the former alternative.
- The second theme which runs through ergonomics is that of data collection. It really does attempt to take a 'scientific' approach to job design insomuch as it collects data to indicate how people react under different job design conditions and tries to find the best set of conditions for comfort and performance.

Ergonomic workplace design

In many operations, new demands, technologies and work methods have refocused attention on the way people interface with the physical parts of their jobs. This is especially noticeable in office and information-related work because of the predominance of computer, keyboard and screen-based 'interfaces'.

Understanding how workplaces affect performance, fatigue, physical strain and injury are all part of the ergonomics approach to job design.

Anthropometric aspects

Many ergonomic improvements are primarily concerned with what are called the anthropometric aspects of the people–workplace interface – that is the aspects related to people's size, shape and other physical abilities, for example strength or left-handedness. The design of an assembly task, for example, should be governed partly by the size and strength of the operators who do the job. The data which ergonomists use when doing this is called *anthropometric data*. Table 9.2 shows an example of anthropometric data.

Table 9.2 An example of anthropometric data – US civilian body dimensions, female/male in cm for ages 20 to 60 years

	Percentiles			Std. dev.
	5th	*50th*	*95th*	
Stature (height)	149.5/161.8	160.5/173.6	171.3/184.4	6.6/6.9
Eye height	138.3/151.1	148.9/162.4	159.3/172.7	6.4/6.6
Shoulder height	121.1/132.3	131.1/142.8	141.9/152.4	6.3/6.1
Elbow height	93.6/100.0	101.2/109.9	108.8/119.0	4.6/5.8
Height, sitting	78.6/84.2	85.0/90.6	90.7/96.7	3.5/3.7
Eye height, sitting	67.5/72.6	73.3/78.6	78.5/84.4	3.3/3.6
Shoulder height, sitting	49.2/52.7	55.7/59.4	61.7/65.8	3.8/4.0
Elbow rest height, sitting	18.1/19.0	23.3/24.3	28.1/29.4	2.9/3.0
Knee height, sitting	45.2/49.3	49.8/54.3	54.4/59.3	2.7/2.9
Back of knee height, sitting	35.5/39.2	39.8/44.2	44.3/48.8	2.6/2.8
Thigh clearance height, sitting	10.6/11.4	13.7/14.4	17.5/17.7	1.8/1.7

Source: Adapted from Kroemer, K.H.E. (1983) 'Engineering Anthropometry: Work Space and Equipment to Fit the User' *in* Osborne, D.J. and Gruneberg, M.M. (eds) *The Physical Environment at Work*, John Wiley.

It is important to understand that, as individuals, we all vary in our size and capabilities. It is therefore not the average capability of people in which ergonomists are particularly interested, but the range of capabilities – usually expressed in percentile terms as in Table 9.2. Figure 9.7 illustrates this idea. This shows the idea of size (in this case height) variation. Only five per cent of the population are smaller than the person on the extreme left (5th percentile), whereas 95 per cent of the population are smaller than the person on the extreme right (95th percentile). When this principle is applied to other dimensions of the body, for example arm length, it can be used to design work areas. Figure 9.7 shows the normal and maximum work areas derived from anthropometric data. It would be inadvisable, for example, to place frequently used components or tools outside the maximum work area derived from the 5th percentile dimensions of human reach.

Neurological aspects

Ergonomics is also concerned with the way in which people's sensory capabilities are engaged when interfacing with their workplaces. These so-called neurological aspects of job design include the sight, feel, sound and perhaps even smell, which the workplace displays in order to give information to an operator, and the way in which an operator can transmit instructions back to the workplace. The part of the 'workplace' in which we are interested is usually some type of process technology or machine, and the interface between the operator and machine involves *displays* of information from the machine to the operator and the manipulation of *controls* by the operator in communicating to the machine. Figure 9.8 illustrates this 'person–machine loop'.

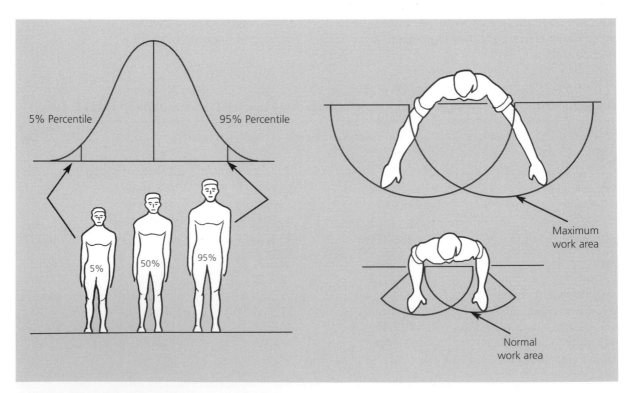

Figure 9.7 The use of anthropometric data in job design

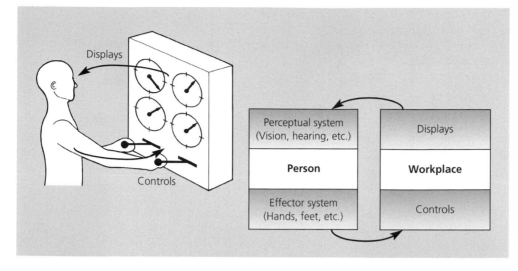

**Figure 9.8
The 'person–
workplace loop'**

A much quoted but illustrative example of how the design of displays can affect the effectiveness with which the operator senses the information displayed by them is shown in Fig. 9.9 overleaf. The seemingly obvious way of laying out a bank of dials would be to arrange them so that the zero mark is at the top. When switched on the dials are all likely to display different levels but often the 'normal' range is marked on the dial. However, detecting a dial which is displaying an 'out of normal' reading still takes some effort by the operator. Alternatively, the dials could be arranged so that their normal ranges are all pointing in the same way when the dials are switched on rather than off. Any deviation from the normal range then is very easily detected.

Ergonomic environmental design

The immediate environment in which jobs take place can influence the way they are performed. Working conditions which are too hot or too cold, insufficiently illuminated or glaringly bright, excessively noisy or irritatingly silent, will all influence the way jobs are carried out. Ergonomics is also concerned with this aspect of job design. Perhaps one point to note is the boost which this aspect of ergonomics received from the introduction of occupational health and safety legislation which controls environmental conditions in workplaces throughout the world. A thorough understanding of this aspect of ergonomics is necessary to work within the guidelines of such legislation.

Working temperature

Predicting the reactions of individuals to working temperature is not straightforward. Individuals vary in the way their performance and comfort vary with temperature. Furthermore, most of us judging 'temperature' will also be influenced by other factors such as humidity and air movement. Nevertheless, some general points regarding working temperatures provide guidance to job designers:[6]

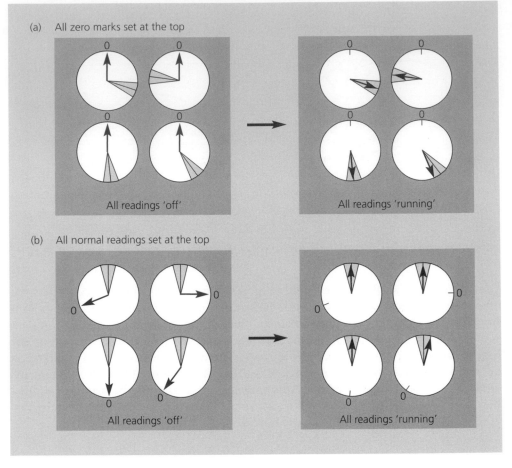

Figure 9.9
Setting all the normal readings at the top makes it easier to detect deviations from the normal readings

● Comfortable temperature range will depend on the type of work being carried out – lighter work requiring higher temperatures than heavier work.

● The effectiveness of people at performing vigilance tasks reduces at temperatures above about 29°C; the equivalent temperature for people performing light manual tasks is a little lower.

● The chances of accidents occurring increase at temperatures which are above or below the comfortable range for the work involved.

Illumination levels

The intensity of lighting required to perform any job satisfactorily will depend on the nature of the job. Some jobs which involve extremely delicate and precise movement, surgery for example, require very high levels of illumination. Other, less delicate, jobs do not require such high levels. Table 9.3 shows the recommended illumination levels (measured in lux) for a range of activities.

Table 9.3 Examples of recommended lighting levels for various activities[7]

Activity	Illuminance (lx)
Normal activities in the home, general lighting	50
Furnace rooms in glass factory	150
General office work	500
Motor vehicle assembly	500
Proofreading	750
Colour matching in paint factory	1 000
Electronic assembly	1 000
Close inspection of knitwear	1 500
Engineering testing inspection using small instruments	3 000
Watchmaking and fine jewellery manufacture	3 000
Surgery, local lighting	10 000–50 000

Noise levels

The damaging effects of excessive noise levels are perhaps easier to understand than some other environmental factors. Noise-induced hearing loss is a well-documented consequence of working environments where noise is not kept below safe limits. The noise levels of various activities are shown in Table 9.4. When reading this list bear in mind that the recommended (and often legal) maximum noise level to which people can be subjected over the working day is 90 decibels (dB) in the UK (although in some parts of the world the legal level is lower than this). Also bear in mind that the decibels unit of noise is based on a logarithmic scale, which means that noise intensity doubles about every 3 dB.

In addition to the damaging effects of high levels of noise, it can also affect work performance at far lower levels – for example on tasks requiring attention and judgement:[8]

● Intermittent and unpredictable noises are more disruptive than steady-state noise at the same level.
● High-frequency noise (above about 2000 Hz) usually produces more interference with performance than low-frequency noise.
● Noise is more likely to affect the error rate (quality) of work rather than the rate of working.

Table 9.4 Noise levels for various activities

Noise	Decibels(dB)
Quiet speech	40
Light traffic at 25 metres	50
Large busy office	60
Busy street, heavy traffic	70
Pneumatic drill at 20 metres	80
Textile factory	90
Circular saw – close work	100
Riveting machine – close work	110
Jet aircraft taking off at 100 metres	120

Ergonomics in the office

As the number of people working in offices (or office-like workplaces) has increased, ergonomic principles have been applied increasingly to this type of work. At the same time, legislation has been moving to cover office technology such as computer screens and keyboards. For example, European Union directives on working with display screen equipment require organizations to:[9]

- assess all work stations to reduce the risks inherent in their use;
- make sure that all work stations meet specific requirements;
- plan work times to all breaks and changes in activity;
- provide information and training for users;
- test the eyesight of users if they request it.

Figure 9.10 illustrates some of the ergonomic factors which should be taken in to account when designing office jobs.

BEHAVIOURAL APPROACHES TO JOB DESIGN

Chronologically, the next major influence on job design practice came in the 1960s and 1970s, although its roots precede that time. This was what one might call (for the want of a better term) the 'behavioural' approach to job design. The ideas and concepts concerning motivation theory contributed to the behavioural approach to job design. It was argued that the jobs which were designed purely on division of labour, scientific management, or even purely ergonomic principles, often alienated the people performing the jobs. What was required was an approach to job design which took into account the desire of individuals to fulfil their needs for self-esteem and personal development. This achieves two important objectives of job design. First, it provides jobs which have an intrinsically higher quality of working life – an ethically desirable end in itself. Second, because of the higher levels of motivation it engenders, it is instrumental in achieving better performance for the operation, both in terms of the quality and the quantity of output.[10]

In fact the behavioural approach does represent a major shift in how job design was seen as a process. Whereas previous approaches to job design assumed a more or less direct connection between the characteristics of the job and people's performance at that job, the behavioural approach to job design implicitly adopted a different model. This assumed an intervening variable of the person's motivation for performing the job. Now the approach to job design would involve two stages: first, exploring how the various characteristics of the job affect people's motivation; second, exploring how individuals' motivation towards the job affects their performance at that job. Generally, it was held that, to reduce alienation and increase personal motivation and commitment, the job should:

- allow people to feel personally responsible for an identifiable and meaningful portion of the work;
- provide a set of tasks which are intrinsically meaningful or worthwhile;
- provide feedback about performance effectiveness.

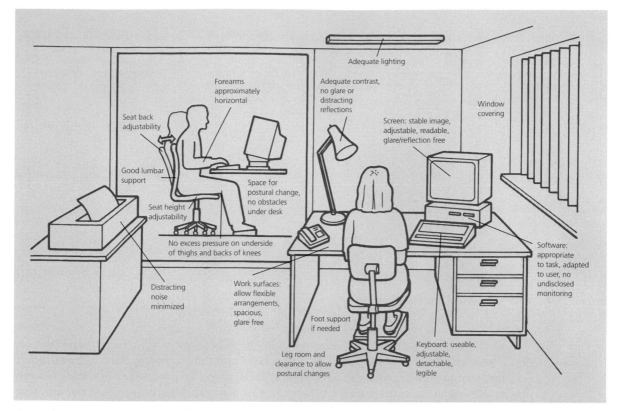

Figure 9.10 Ergonomics in the office environment

Typical of the models which underlie this approach to job design is that by Hackman and Oldham shown in Fig. 9.11.[11] Here a number of 'techniques' of job design are recommended in order to affect particular core 'characteristics' of the job. These core characteristics of the job are held to influence various positive 'mental states' towards the job. In turn these are assumed to give certain performance outcomes.

In Fig. 9.11 some of the 'techniques' (which Hackman and Oldham originally called 'implementing concepts') need a little further explanation:

● Combining tasks means increasing the number of separate elements or activities allocated to individuals.

● Forming natural work units means putting together activities which make a coherent (preferably also a continuing) whole.

● Establishing client relationships means that staff make contact with their internal customers (*see* Chapter 1) directly rather than exclusively through their supervisors.

● Vertical loading means including 'indirect' activities (such as the maintenance, scheduling and general management of the job) in the tasks allocated to the individual.

● Opening feedback channels means ensuring that internal customers not only feed back perceptions of performance directly to staff, but also that they are provided with information regarding their overall performance.

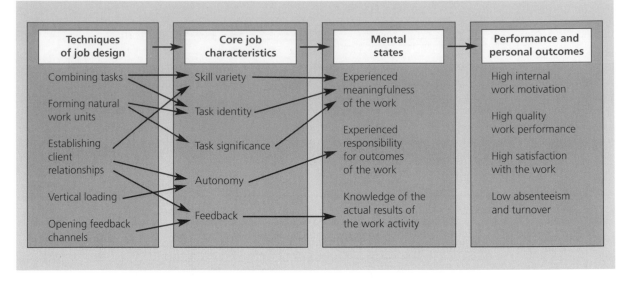

Figure 9.11 A typical 'behavioural' job design model

Hackman and Oldham also indicate how these techniques of job design shape the core characteristics of the resulting job, and further, how the core characteristics influence the 'mental states' of the person doing the job. By 'mental states' they mean the attitude of individuals towards their jobs – specifically, how meaningful they find the job, how much responsibility and control they feel they have over the way the job is done, and how much they understand about the results of their efforts. High levels of all these mental states, it is held, positively influence people's performance at their job in terms of their motivation, quality of work, satisfaction with their work, turnover and absenteeism.

Job rotation

If increasing the number of related tasks in the job is constrained in some way, for example by the technology of the process, one approach may be to rotate jobs. This means moving individuals periodically between different sets of tasks to provide some variety in their activities. When successful, job rotation can increase skill flexibility and make a small contribution to reducing monotony. However, it is not viewed as universally beneficial either by management, because it can disrupt the smooth flow of work, or by the people performing the jobs, because it can interfere with their rhythm of work.

Job enlargement

The most obvious method of achieving at least some of the objectives of behavioural job design is by allocating a larger number of tasks to individuals (what Hackman and Oldham called *combining* tasks). If these extra tasks are broadly of the same type as those in the original job, the change is called *job enlargement*. This may not involve more demanding or fulfilling tasks, but it may provide a more complete and therefore slightly more meaningful job. If nothing else, the person performing an enlarged job will not repeat his or herself as often, which could make the job marginally less monotonous.

So, for example, suppose that the manufacture of a product has traditionally been split up on an assembly-line basis into ten equal and sequential jobs. If that job is then redesigned so as to form two parallel assembly lines of five people, the output from the system as a whole would be maintained but each operator would have twice the number of tasks to perform. This is job enlargement. The operator repeats him or herself less frequently and presumably the variety of tasks is greater although no further responsibility or autonomy is necessarily given to each operator.

Job enrichment

Job enrichment, like job enlargement, increases the number of tasks which are allocated to jobs. However, it means allocating extra tasks which involve more decision-making, greater autonomy and therefore greater control over the job. For example, the extra tasks could include the maintenance of, and adjustments to, any process technology used, the planning and control of activities within the job, or the monitoring of quality levels. The effect is both to reduce repetition in the job and to increase the autonomy and personal development opportunities in the job. So, in the assembly-line example, each operator, as well as being allocated a job which is twice as long as that previously performed, could also be allocated responsibility for carrying out routine maintenance and such tasks as record keeping and managing the supply of materials. As a result, both the autonomy and decision-making responsibility of the job have been increased.

One way of understanding the difference between job enlargement and job enrichment is by thinking of changing jobs on what are sometimes termed horizontal dimensions of job design and vertical dimensions of job design. Figure 9.12 illustrates the difference between horizontal and vertical changes. Broadly, horizontal changes are those which extend the variety of *similar* tasks assigned to a particular job. Vertical job changes are those which add responsibilities, decision-making or autonomy to the job. Job enlargement implies movement only in the horizontal scale, whereas job enrichment certainly implies movement on the vertical scale and perhaps both scales.

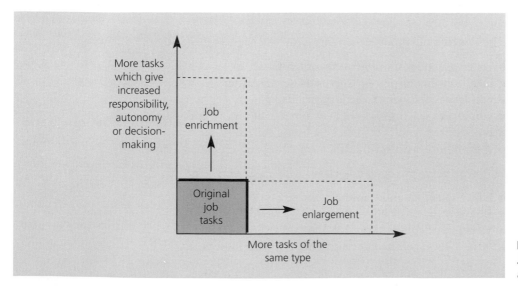

Figure 9.12
Job enlargement and job enrichment

EMPOWERMENT

The last phase in any sequence of developments is always likely to be controversial. We do not have the clarity of hindsight to judge whether a popular idea was either a temporary 'blip' or a genuine trend. With this in mind, the latest trend is (arguably) the move towards the *empowerment* of people in their jobs. Empowerment is an extension of the *autonomy* job characteristic prominent in the behavioural approach to job design.

Empowerment, however, is usually taken to mean more than autonomy. Whereas autonomy means giving staff the *ability* to change how they do their jobs, empowerment means giving staff the *authority* to make changes to the job itself as well as how it is performed. This can be designed into jobs to different degrees: 'suggestion involvement', 'job involvement', or 'high involvement'.[12]

- *Suggestion involvement* is not really empowerment in its true form but does 'empower' staff to contribute their suggestions for how the operation might be improved. However, staff do not have the autonomy to implement changes to their jobs. High-volume operations, such as fast-food restaurants or the NUMMI car plant in the earlier box, may choose not to dilute their highly standardized task methods, yet they do want staff to be involved in how these methods are implemented.
- *Job involvement* goes much further and empowers staff to redesign their jobs. However, again there must be some limits on the way each individual makes changes which could impact on other staff and on the performance of the operations as a whole.
- *High involvement* means including all staff in the strategic direction and performance of the whole organization. This is the most radical type of empowerment and there are few examples. However, the degree to which individual staff of an operation contribute towards, and take responsibility for, overall strategy can be seen as a variable of job design. For example, a professional service such as a group of consulting engineers (who design large engineering projects) might very well move in this direction. It may be partly to motivate all its staff. It may be partly to ensure that the operation can capture everyone's potentially useful ideas.

The benefits of empowerment are generally seen as including the following:

- faster on-line responses to customer needs;
- faster on-line responses to dissatisfied customers;
- employees feel better about their jobs;
- employees will interact with customers with more enthusiasm;
- empowered employees can be a useful source of service;
- it promotes 'word-of-mouth' advertising and customer retention.

However, there are costs associated with empowerment:

- larger selection and training costs;
- slower or inconsistent training;
- violation of equity of service and perceived fair play;
- 'give-aways' and bad decisions made by employees.

Table 9.5 The contingencies of empowerment

Factor	Non-empowerment approach	Empowerment approach
Basic business strategy	Low cost, high volume	Differentiation, customized, personalized
Links with customer	Transaction, short time period	Relationship, long time period
Technology	Routine, simple	Non-routine, complex
Business environment	Predictable, few surprises	Unpredictable, many surprises.
Types of people	Autocratic managers, employees with low growth needs, low social needs, and weak interpersonal skills.	Democratic managers, employees with high growth needs, high social needs and strong interpersonal skills.

Source: Adapted from Bowen, D. and Lawler, E. (1992) 'Empowerment', *Sloan Management Review*, Spring.

A number of key factors will determine whether the benefits outweigh the costs of empowerment. These factors are contained in Table 9.5. The closer an individual job design requirement is to the right of the continuum, the more likely that an empowerment approach should be adopted.

Autonomous work teams

A development in job design which is closely linked with the empowerment concept is that of team-based work organization (sometimes called self-managed work teams). This is where staff, often with overlapping skills, collectively perform a defined task and have a high degree of discretion over how they actually perform the task. The team would typically control such things as task allocation between members, scheduling work, quality measurement and improvement, and sometimes the hiring of staff. Companies such as 3M, Levi Strauss, Alcan, Jaeger, and General Motors have all reported benefits from this type of work organization. These benefits are usually described in terms of higher quality, better job satisfaction, enhanced flexibility and higher productivity.

Yet not all experiments in the use of self-managed teams have been successful. Problems reported where teams have failed to perform include:

- unclear objectives given to teams;
- ambiguity over the limits of team autonomy;
- difficulty in coping with individuals who just do not want to adopt team values and behaviour;
- teams seen just as a 'quick fix' by management rather than thought through;
- teams not integrated with other parts of the operation so reinforcing inter-departmental separation.

CONTROL VERSUS COMMITMENT

It is important to stress again that, although we have presented them in the chronological order of their emergence, the various approaches have not replaced each other. The principles of division of labour are still influential today and take their place along with ideas concerning empowerment and all the other approaches. However, there are clear differences between the approaches, both in the methods and 'techniques' which they adopt to design jobs and, more importantly, in their underlying aims and philosophies. The most obvious difference between approaches is the relative emphasis they place on the need for management to *control* the job, and the desire to engage the *commitment* of the staff performing the job.

Figure 9.13 shows how the balance between control and commitment has moved with the emergence of each approach to job design. Division of labour is totally concerned with controlling the work done by staff. Management control over the job allows it to be reduced, routinized and thereby made more efficient. Scientific management in its original form might also be regarded as concerned exclusively with controlling the way the job is performed. Again, it is argued that control is necessary to find the 'best' method of doing the job. However, the recent developments in method study could be seen as moving the use of scientific management techniques more into the hands of staff, and thereby increasing its concern with staff commitment. Ergonomics, by being concerned with the way staff respond to physical and environmental conditions, can be considered to be, at least partly, attempting to influence their commitment. However, ergonomics is concerned more with staff's physiological responses as much as, if not more than, their psychological responses.

**Figure 9.13
The different approaches to job design: each implies a different balance between control and commitment**

Behavioural approaches to job design focus far more on the commitment of staff to their jobs, and indeed place staff engagement and motivation as the central theme of job design. Finally, empowerment not only highlights the commitment of staff but also transfers to them at least part of the control of their jobs. Paradoxically, this moves the emphasis back to control, but now it is individual or group control rather than 'managerial' control.

Iain Lambeth, Land Rover

Job design at Land Rover

Iain Lambeth joined Land Rover, having completed a degree in production engineering. He is now responsible for facilitating the development of managers, engineers and team leaders in workplace skills, and for the ongoing development of factory floor operatives (known as 'associates' at Land Rover).

Land Rover has been producing its familiar four-wheel drive vehicles since 1948. These vehicles come in three different ranges: the Discovery, the Range Rover, and the Defender (the classic Land Rover). Models of the Defender are sent all over the world, and most are prepared to specific customer requirements. Variety is high: the factory could run for two years without making the same model twice. It is this complexity which dictates that the systems employed have to be flexible enough to handle the variety of options available, yet strict enough to ensure a high level of built-in quality, for which the company is famous. The philosophy at Land Rover is to focus on team working, and the concept of 'internal customers' has been introduced, where each individual associate sees his or her customer as the person within the factory who works at the next stage on in the manufacturing process. The idea of having internal customers is that if each person along the line is satisfied with the product, then there is a high probability that the finished vehicle will be 'right first time'.

Iain has been involved with the training of the associates on each of the production lines, and has helped to introduce the philosophies of team working. Each team on the assembly line, or in the other production areas, now takes responsibility for a group of tasks, and each is concerned with satisfying its own internal customers in terms of the quality of product handed over. As Iain says:

'The concept of ownership is very much behind the whole move to team working. In an effort to generate ideas for improvements, we have turned to those people who have been doing the job; they are the people with the relevant experience and it would

be a waste of resources and potential not to involve them! In the past, the work study engineer and the foreman would have issued an operator with a task sheet, giving details of each job and the expected output schedule. The production track moved at a constant speed and each operator performed a single task on each vehicle. The company used to employ quality inspectors to enforce standards and everyone had to clock in and out. Nowadays, we have encouraged that operator to join a team where complete tasks, including quality control and process improvement, are allocated to the group as a whole. The appointed team leader will then distribute the tasks among the team members, having first decided whether the tasks are more appropriate to individual or group working. These tasks are fairly broad and the team must take a collective responsibility in achieving the outputs required. There are no quality inspectors. Teams are very quickly notified by their internal customers if the job has not been completed to the required standard. Similarly, team members no longer have to clock in and out; they operate on the basis that the peer pressure within the team offers a stronger incentive to be on time. Also the company works on the basis of trusting its staff to be at work on time. In order to maintain the throughput on the lines we designed the groups' tasks so that they had a common identity; for instance, all of the interior trim work is carried out by one group, all of the 'under-the-bonnet' operations are completed by another. The implications of this reorganization are far reaching. Each worker now has more autonomy, and by creating the scope for workers to carry out more than one type of task within their team, we hope to have enriched their working environment.'

Iain's job requires a lot of effort in persuading people that the changes will be worthwhile, and he admits that it is not always easy.

'In the beginning, the idea of redesigning people's jobs was seen as a threat to their job security. But now that teams are becoming established, the results are starting to show through and people do seem more positive.' ∎

Source: By kind permission of Land Rover

SUMMARY ANSWERS TO KEY QUESTIONS

What are the main decisions in job design?

■ Job design involves deciding what tasks to allocate to each person in the organization, and in what sequence to perform them, where to locate the job, who else should be involved in it, how people should interact with their workplace and their immediate work environment, what autonomy to give the staff and what skills to develop in the staff.

What are the main objectives of job design?

■ All job design decisions should attempt to devise jobs which engage the interest of staff, are inherently safe, and give a reasonable quality of working life, as well as the more conventional objectives of operations – quality, speed, dependability, flexibility, and cost.

What have been the significant influences on job design practice?

■ Historically, the first influence was the concept of division of labour. This involves taking a total task and dividing it into separate parts, each of which can be allocated to a different individual to perform. The advantages of this are largely concerned with reducing costs. However, highly divided jobs are monotonous and, in their extreme form, contribute to physical injury.

■ Scientific management took some of the ideas of division of labour but applied them more systematically. The area of work study (divided into method study and work measurement) is most often associated with scientific management. Although scientific management in its original form has fallen out of favour, new forms in which staff themselves perform method study analyses have been successfully applied more recently.

■ Ergonomics is concerned primarily with the physiological aspects of job design. This includes both the study of how the human body fits into its workplace and how humans react to their immediate environment, especially its heating, lighting and noise characteristics.

■ Behavioural models of job design are more concerned with individuals' reactions to, and attitudes to, their job. It is argued that jobs which are designed to fulfil people's need for self-esteem and personal development are more likely to achieve satisfactory work performance.

■ More recently the empowerment principle of job design has concentrated on increasing the autonomy which individuals have to shape the nature of their own jobs.

How do the influences on job design differ?

■ The major difference lies in the relative balance between the two concepts of *control* of the job and the commitment of the staff performing the job. The chronological progression of influences on job design from division of labour through to empowerment are broadly in line with the movement from an emphasis on managerial control to an emphasis on the commitment and engagement of staff.

345

CASE EXERCISE

Secret plans at Penn Savings Bank[13]

During the last few years, almost every retail bank has launched into some sort of major 'customer-care' or 'service-improvement' programme, in an attempt to win or retain business in their intensively competitive market places. Regrettably, a great many of these initiatives have failed to create sustained changes, and have even been known to discredit the judgement of the senior managers.

At Penn Savings Bank in the US, the directors realized that they first had to make customer service part of their philosophy and a key part of their corporate culture, influencing the everyday attitudes and behaviour of all employees. Their initiative developed into an unusual and large-scale project. Customer and employee surveys had indicated that they shared a common view of what was meant by high-quality service; and this included such things as promptness, accuracy, knowledge and basic courtesy. The bank decided that it wanted its service programme to be memorable and fun and they developed the Penn Savings SECRET formula – with each letter in SECRET denoting what was seen as a key behavioural requirement when dealing with the customers – Smiles, Enthusiasm, Caring, Response, Ensured satisfaction and Thanks. The SECRET formula was launched at the Employees' Awards Dinner, and subsequently all staff attended customer-service programmes, covering material relevant to the different areas of their jobs, but always focusing on how better to service the customer, even the internal ones.

After months of preparation, the launch date for the programme arrived and each staff member wore a T-shirt proclaiming 'Customers are Number 1 at Penn Savings Bank' and everyone entering the building was greeted with a polite 'I'm glad that you are here!' The bank management was involved too, at every branch, ensuring that employees gained motivation and encouragement through seeing the commitment to the programme from the top levels of the organization. Throughout the day, branches of the bank received deliveries of mementos such as

pens and balloons, all containing messages of commitment to customers and all adding to the feeling of involvement and sincerity. The initiative continued with the production of business cards for all employees, giving their title as purely 'Customer Service' – the idea being that a business card always states what an individual is responsible for in the organization, and the bank wanted everyone to be aware of their basic responsibility for customer service.

Another unusual enhancement to the programme involved a monthly draw in which two lucky customers from each branch were sent a five dollar note, along with an explanatory letter. This asked them to please bring in the money on their next visit to the branch and, if they received good service, to give the five dollars to their cashier; if the service was unacceptable in any way, to keep it and have lunch on the bank. Within only two weeks, nine employees had received five dollar notes from satisfied customers! The issue of empowerment became more prominent with the management decision to allow any employee in the bank the autonomy to spend up to $50 on the spot to recover a potentially damaging situation with a customer. This added a higher level of responsiveness to the service delivery and also helped to sustain staff morale, by encouraging them to take ownership of a problem as it arose, and to use their initiative to ensure that their customers left the bank feeling comfortable with the final situation. ■

Questions

1 List the key characteristics of Penn Savings Bank's approach to designing the jobs of its staff, as they are portrayed in the case exercise.
2 To what extent are each of these characteristics concerned with control and to what extent with commitment?
3 How generally applicable are the characteristics to other high customer contact operations?
4 How could 'empowerment' be taken further at Penn Savings Bank?

DISCUSSION QUESTIONS

1 Imagine that you and four friends have to prepare and serve a five-course meal for 20 people. Identify and describe the main elements that will be involved in designing the jobs involved.

2 Explain how the design of a job which involves making overhead transparencies for university lecturers might affect the performance of the person doing the job.

3 Explain the difference between division of labour and scientific management.

4 Get together with a few colleagues and undertake a method study of an operation: for example, the loading and unloading of a local car ferry, a small catering operation or a gardening task. What improvements could you make and how acceptable might they be to the operators involved?

5 Draw a process chart for the following tasks:
loading paper into a printer
changing the tyre on a car
making a cup of coffee.

6 Assess the workplace design of your lecture theatre.

7 Explain why some operations managers might be concerned about implementing job rotation, enrichment and enlargement.

8 Explain how empowerment differs from the behavioural approaches.

9 How might empowerment differ between professional and mass-service organizations? Illustrate your answer with references to organizations of your choice.

NOTES ON CHAPTER

1 For a discussion of the origins of the division of labour *see* Wild, R. (1972) *Mass Production Management*, John Wiley.

2 Ford, H. with Crowther, S. (1924) *My Life and Works* (rev. edn), Heinemann.

3 Taylor, F.W. (1947) *Scientific Management* (edn published by Harper and Row, New York).

4 Hoxie, R.F. (1915) *Scientific Management and Labour*, D. Appleton.

5 Source: Adler, P.S. (1933) 'Time and Motion Regained', *Harvard Business Review*, Vol 11, No 1.

6 Kobrick, J.L. and Fine, B.J. (1983) 'Climate and Human Performance' *in* Osborne, D.J. and Gruneberg, M.M. (eds) *The Physical Environment and Work*, John Wiley.

7 *Illuminating Engineering Society*, IES Code for Interior Lighting, 1977.

8 Environmental Protection Agency (US)(1974), 'Information on Levels of Environmental Noise Requisite to Protect Public Health and Welfare with Adequate Margin of Safety' EPA.

9 There are other recommendations similar to those published in the European Union Directive; they broadly agree on what is good practice.

10 Hackman, J.R. and Lawler, E.E. (1971) 'Employee Reaction to Job Characteristics', *Journal of Applied Psychology*, Vol 55, pp 259–86.

11 Hackman, J.R. and Oldham, G. (1975) 'A New Strategy for Job Enrichment', *California Management Review*, Vol 17, No 3.

12 Bowen, D. and Lawler, E. (1992) 'Empowerment', *Sloan Management Review*, Spring.

13 Source: Nangle, J.S. (1990) 'How Penn Savings Keeps the Focus on Service', *Bank Marketing Journal*, Vol 22, No 1.

SELECTED FURTHER READINGS

Bailey, J. (1983) *Job Design and Work Organisation*, Prentice Hall.

Berggren, C. (1992) *The Volvo Experience, Alternatives to Lean Production in the Swedish Auto Industry*, Macmillan.

Carlisle, B. (1983) 'Job Design Implications for Operations Managers', *International Journal of Operations and Production Management*, Vol 3, No 2.

Clegg, C.W. and Corbett, J.M. (1987) 'Research and Development in "Humanising" Advanced Manufacturing Technology' *in* Wall, T.D., Clegg, C.W. and Kemp, N.J. (eds) *The Human Side of Advanced Manufacturing Technology*, John Wiley.

Corlett, N., Wilson, J. and Manencia, F. (eds) (1986) *Ergonomics of Working Posture*, Taylor and Francis.

Cunningham, J.B. and Eberle, T. (1990) 'A Guide to Job Enrichment and Redesign', *Personnel*, Feb.

Fisher, K.K. (1993) *Leading Self-Directed Workteams*, McGraw-Hill.

Hackman, R.J. and Oldham, G. (1980) *Work Redesign*, Addison-Wesley.

Herzberg, F. (1987) 'One More Time: How Do You Motivate Employees?' (with retrospective commentary), *Harvard Business Review*, Vol 65, No 5.

Katzenbach, J.R. and Smith, D.K. (1993) *The Wisdom of Teams: Creating the High Performance Organisation*, Harvard Business School Press.

Knights, D., Willmott, H. and Collison, D. (1985) (eds) *Job Redesign*, Gower.

Main, J. (1982) 'Battling your own Bureaucracy' *in Working Smarter*, by the Editors of *Fortune*, New York, Viking Press, Prentice Hall, pp 88–9.

Malone, T.W. (1997) 'Is Empowerment Just a Fad?', *Sloan Management Review*, Winter.

Osborne, D.J. (1995), *Ergonomics at Work* (3rd edn), John Wiley.

Rubenowitz, S. (1992) 'The Role of Management in Production Units with Autonomous Work Groups', *International Journal of Operations and Production Management*, Vol 12, No 7/8.

Scarborough, H. and Corbet, M. (1992) *Technology and Organisation*, Routledge.

Wild, R. (1975) *Work Organisation*, John Wiley.

PART THREE

PLANNING AND CONTROL

The physical design of an operation should have provided the fixed resources which are capable of satisfying customers' demands. Planning and control is concerned with operating those resources on a day-to-day basis and ensuring availability of materials and other variable resources in order to supply the goods and services which fulfil customers' demands. This part of the book will look at several different aspects of planning and control, including some of the specialist approaches which are used in particular types of operations.

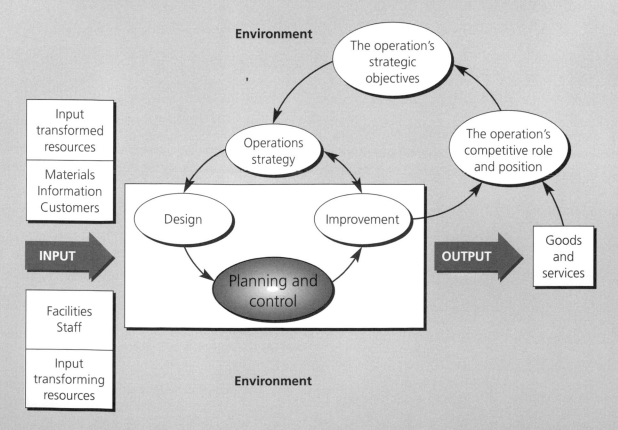

Chapter 10
THE NATURE OF PLANNING AND CONTROL

- *What is planning and control?*
- *What is the difference between planning and control?*
- *Why is planning and control important?*
- *How does the nature of demand affect planning and control?*
- *What is involved in planning and control?*

Chapter 11
CAPACITY PLANNING AND CONTROL

- *What is capacity planning and control?*
- *Why is capacity planning and control important?*
- *How is capacity measured?*
- *What are the ways of coping with demand fluctuation?*
- *How can operations plan their capacity level?*
- *How can operations control their capacity level?*

Chapter 12
INVENTORY PLANNING AND CONTROL

- *What is inventory?*
- *Why is it necessary?*
- *How much inventory should an operation hold?*
- *When should an operation replenish its inventory?*
- *How can inventory be controlled?*

Chapter 13
SUPPLY CHAIN PLANNING AND CONTROL

- *What is the difference between terms such as purchasing, physical distribution, logistics, materials management, and supply chain management?*
- *What is the purpose and objective of purchasing management?*
- *What is the purpose and objective of physical distribution management?*
- *How is the concept of supply chain management different?*

Chapter 14
MRP

- *What is MRP?*
- *What is the process involved in MRP planning and control?*
- *What are the main elements in an MRP system?*
- *What is 'closed loop' MRP?*
- *What is MRP II?*

Chapter 15
JUST-IN-TIME PLANNING AND CONTROL

- *What is JIT and how is it different from traditional operations practice?*
- *What are the main elements of JIT philosophy?*
- *What are the techniques of JIT?*
- *How can JIT be used for planning and control?*
- *Can JIT be used in service operations?*
- *Can JIT and MRP co-exist?*

Chapter 16
PROJECT PLANNING AND CONTROL

- *What is a project and project management?*
- *Why is it important to understand the environment in which a project takes place?*
- *How are specific projects defined?*
- *What is project planning and why is it important?*
- *What techniques can be used for project planning?*
- *What is project control and how is it done?*

Chapter 17
QUALITY PLANNING AND CONTROL

- *How can quality be defined?*
- *How can quality problems be diagnosed?*
- *What steps lead towards conformance to specification?*
- *How can statistical process control help quality planning and control?*
- *How can acceptance sampling help quality planning and control?*

351

THE NATURE OF PLANNING AND CONTROL

INTRODUCTION

Within the constraints imposed by its design, an operation has to be run on an ongoing basis. This is what 'planning and control' is concerned with – managing the ongoing activities of the operation so as to satisfy customer demand. All operations require plans and require controlling, although the formality and detail of the plans and the control may vary. Some operations are more difficult to plan than others. Those where there is a high level of unpredictability can be particularly difficult to plan. Some operations are more difficult to control than others. Those which have high customer contact may be difficult to control because of the immediate nature of their operations and the variability that customers may impose on the operation. This chapter introduces and provides an overview of some of the principles and methods of planning and control. Some of these, such as MRP (materials requirements planning) and JIT (just-in-time), have been developed into more extensive concepts and these are examined in separate chapters. Similarly, there are separate specialist tools to plan and control in project environments and a separate chapter is devoted to this area. In all cases, however, the different aspects of planning and control can be viewed as representing the reconciliation of supply with demand (*see* Fig. 10.1).

Figure 10.1 **Planning and control reconciles the supply of an operation's products and services with the demand for them**

CHAPTER 10: KEY QUESTIONS

- What is planning and control?

- What is the difference between planning and control?

- Why is planning and control important?

- How does the nature of demand affect planning and control?

- What is involved in planning and control?

WHAT IS PLANNING AND CONTROL?

In Chapter 1 we introduced the model of input–transformation–output to represent an 'operation'. The previous part of this book examined the design activities which operations managers must perform on the input–transformation–output system. These design activities determine the form and nature of the system and the resources it contains, but they are not concerned with the day-to-day running of the system. That is the purpose of planning and control – to ensure that the operation runs effectively and efficiently and produces products and services as required by customers. To do this the resources of the operation should be available:

- in the appropriate *quantity*
- at the appropriate *time*, and
- at the appropriate level of *quality*.

Consider, for example, the organization of a rock concert. Ticket holders turn up on the night, take their seats and enjoy the performance. What they don't see is the months, sometimes years, of planning and preparation that went on before the night. One of the first details that requires planning is an agreed date and venue for the concert. This is then the date that all other plans are geared up to. There will need to be a plan that informs every electrician of the work which is required and when to supply the lighting and sound systems. Even before this, someone must plan how many electricians will be required. Someone also has to predict how many people will attend; this determines the amount of support services required such as food facilities. Someone must understand the sequence in which jobs must be done – in flexible layout concert halls the size and position of the stage set may determine where spectator seating can and cannot be positioned. Some locations may have an obscured view. Every floor covering that needs tacking down, every burger bun that needs slicing, every T-shirt display that needs arranging – hundreds of people using millions of pounds' worth of buildings, equipment and technology all need to know what they are to do and when they are to do it. Just as important, however, in the run-up to the concert and during the performance, adjustments to the plans will have to be made to keep the event on track. All this is the planning and control task; however, the rock concert example, as described here, is a one-off project. Planning and control in operations with an ongoing demand for a varied mix and volume of products and services is far more complex.

Reconciling supply with demand

The design activities which we described in the previous chapters were concerned with setting the nature of the resources within the operation. The sum of the design activities set the capabilities of the staff and facilities within the operation. In making these decisions, operations managers try to meet the broad competitive and strategic objectives of quality, speed, dependability, flexibility and cost. In effect, design sets the potential of the operation's performance – the broad limits within which the operation can work. Customers, when considered, are treated *en masse*, as a group creating a demand which must be met in general terms. They are not usually considered as individuals with specific needs.

So we have two entities. On the one hand, we have the resources of the operation which have the capability to *supply* to customers, but as yet have not been given the instructions on how to do so. On the other hand, we have a set of both general and specific *demands* from the actual and potential customers for the operation's products or services. Planning and control activities provide the systems, procedures and decisions which bring these two entities together. This model of planning and control as the reconciling activity between supply and demand is one that we shall use throughout this part of the book. Different aspects of supply and demand, and different circumstances under which supply and demand must be reconciled, will be treated in the various chapters. But in every case the purpose is the same – to make a connection between the two, which will trigger the operation into satisfying its customers.

Constraints on the planning and control task

In any operation the supply of resources is not infinite. The electrical work for the concert could be performed in a few hours if several hundred electricians all arrived and set about the task simultaneously, but this would be more expensive than using a smaller number over a longer time. There might also be a physical constraint on how many electricians are available in the time. Even with an infinite budget, if there are only ten electricians available to do the work within the time period, then that is the limit on the number which can be hired. There will also be constraints imposed by the quality of what is required by the concert promoters. For example, it might be possible, with a relatively small number of electricians and in a relatively short space of time, to set up some kind of basic sound system. However, the requirements of the performers and the promoter and the expectations of the customers will be for a higher standard of sound. Finally, the most evident constraint will be the timing of the concert. In this kind of event it is an absolute requirement that everything must be ready for the planned 'delivery date' of the concert. No concert promoter can put all the effort into advertising such an event only to ask the ticket holders to wait a couple of days because everything isn't finished.

The nature of the rock concert is that of a 'one-off' project. Nevertheless, all the characteristics used to plan and control the 'manufacture' of this product will hold true for other products and services. Similarly, the constraints within which the planning and control activity has to take place will also apply to most types of operation. Generally these are as follows:

- *Cost constraints* – products and services must be produced within an identified cost.
- *Capacity constraints* – products and services must be produced within the designed capacity limits of the operation.[1]

- *Timing constraints* – products and services must be produced within the time when they still have value for the customer.
- *Quality constraints* – products and services must conform to the designed tolerance limits of the product or service.

The difference between planning and control

In this text we have chosen to treat planning and control together. This is because the division between planning and control is not clear, either in theory or in practice. However, there are some general features that help to distinguish between the two.

A *plan* is a formalization of what is intended to happen at some time in the future. A plan does not guarantee that an event will actually happen; it is a *statement of intention* that it will happen. Plans are based on expectations, however, and expectations are only hopes concerning the future. When operations attempt to implement plans, things do not always happen as expected. Customers change their minds about what they want and when they want it. Suppliers may not always deliver on time, machines may fail, staff may be absent through illness. Any of these reasons may mean that the plan cannot be carried out. There are many different variables, any one of which could cause a plan to become unworkable. *Control* is the process of coping with changes in these variables. It may mean plans need to be redrawn in the short term. It may also mean that an 'intervention' will need to be made in the operation to bring it back 'on track': for example, finding a new supplier who can deliver quickly, repairing the machine which failed, or moving staff from another part of the operation to cover for the absentees. Control makes the adjustments which allow the operation to achieve the objectives which the plan set, even when the assumptions which the plan made do not hold true.

We can define a plan as an intention, and control as the driving through of the plan, monitoring what actually happens and making changes as necessary. For example, it may be intended in the plan that the rock concert takes place at a set time. A temperamental performer may try to delay that time; control is immediately exercised by someone persuading the performer to get ready more quickly, while at the same time other people are stepping up the complimentary services of music and entertainment for the waiting audience, concessions are increasing the amount of food and drinks they vend. The control is intended to reduce the potential of customer dissatisfaction that may arise because the plan is not being adhered to, as well as minimizing the disruption to the operation.

The balance of planning and control over time

When the rock concert is being planned as a date in the promoter's diary two years hence, the nature of the planning and control task is largely one of forward planning. As those two years go by, more plans have to be formulated and implemented. The closer the rock concert gets, the more difficult it becomes to change the plans. Once promotional activity has started and ticket sales have been made, it is very difficult to change the date and venue of the concert. As the event date gets very close, replanning of the number of T-shirts for sale is not possible. It is also difficult to arrange for additional lighting at short notice because it has to work with the rest of the lighting set. The implications of changing some plans at short notice are just too disruptive to the whole event to be justifiable. In the short term, control is exercised to cope within the limits of those plans which cannot be changed. Adjustments are made to those parts of the plan which can be changed, but on the day of the concert relatively little replanning is possible. Any deviations from the plan at that point can only be treated by direct intervention in the process. Figure 10.2 shows how the control aspects of planning and control increase in significance closer to the date of the event.

Long-, medium- and short-term planning and control

All operations are similar to the rock concert described above in the sense that the nature of planning and control changes over time. In the very long term, operations managers make plans concerning what they intend to do, what resources they need, and what objectives they hope to achieve. The emphasis is on planning rather than control because there is little to control as such. They will use forecasts of likely demand which are described in aggregated terms. For example, a hospital will make plans for '2000 patients' without necessarily going into the details of the individual needs of those 2000 patients. Similarly, the resources will be planned in an aggregated form. For example, the hospital might plan to have 100 nurses and 20 doctors but

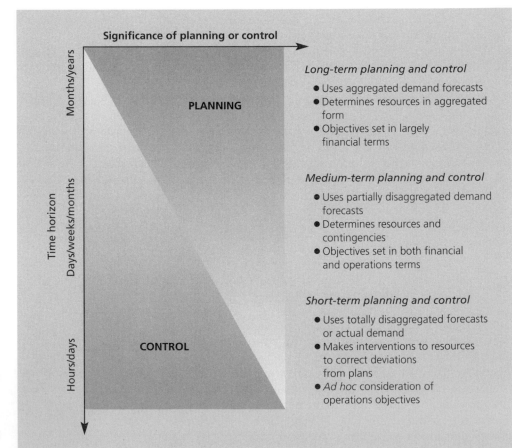

Figure 10.2 The balance between planning and control activities changes in the long, medium and short terms

Significance of planning or control

Time horizon

Months/years

Days/weeks/months

Hours/days

PLANNING

CONTROL

Long-term planning and control
- Uses aggregated demand forecasts
- Determines resources in aggregated form
- Objectives set in largely financial terms

Medium-term planning and control
- Uses partially disaggregated demand forecasts
- Determines resources and contingencies
- Objectives set in both financial and operations terms

Short-term planning and control
- Uses totally disaggregated forecasts or actual demand
- Makes interventions to resources to correct deviations from plans
- *Ad hoc* consideration of operations objectives

again without deciding on the specific attributes of the staff. In carrying out their planning activities the operations managers will be concerned mainly to achieve financial targets. Budgets will be put in place which identify the costs and revenue targets which it is intended to achieve.

Medium-term planning and control is concerned with both planning in more detail (and replanning if necessary). It looks ahead to assess the overall demand which the operation must meet in a partially disaggregated manner. By this time, for example, the hospital must distinguish between different types of demand. The number of patients coming as accident and emergency cases will need to be distinguished from those requiring routine operations. Similarly, resources will be set at a more disaggregated level. For example, different categories of staff will have been identified and broad staffing levels in each category set. Just as important, contingencies will have been put in place which allow for slight deviations from the plans. These contingencies will act as 'reserve' resources and make planning and control easier in the short term.

In short-term planning and control many of the resources will have been set and it will be difficult to make large-scale changes in resourcing. However, short-term interventions are possible if things are not going to plan. By this time demand will be assessed on a totally disaggregated basis. For example, the hospital will be treating all types of surgical procedures as individual activities. More importantly, individual patients will have been identified by name and specific time slots booked for their treatment. In making short-term interventions and changes to plan, operations managers will be attempting to balance the quality, speed, dependability, flexibility, and costs of their operation on an *ad hoc* basis. It is unlikely that they will have the time to carry out detailed calculations of the effects of their short-term planning and control decisions on all these objectives, but a general understanding of priorities will form the background to their decision-making.

THE NATURE OF DEMAND AND SUPPLY

If planning and control is the process of reconciling demand with supply then the nature of the decisions taken to plan and control an operation will depend both on the nature of demand and the nature of supply in that operation. In this next section we examine some differences in demand and supply which can affect the way in which operations managers plan and control their activities.

Uncertainty in supply

Some operations are reasonably predictable and usually run to plan. In these situations, the need for control is minimal. For example, cable TV services provide programmes to a schedule into subscribers' homes via reliable technology. It is rare that the programme schedule, or plan, is not adhered to. Conversely, local village carnivals rarely work to plan. Processions take longer to arrive than expected, some of the acts scheduled in the programme may be delayed *en route*, some traders do not turn up on the day. The event requires a good compère to keep the event rolling along and the crowd amused while they're waiting. The compère and his or her helpers are exercising much of the short-term control which is used to minimize customer dissatisfaction.

OPERATIONS CONTROL AT BRITISH AIRWAYS[2]

British Airways (BA) is the world's largest international airline operator. A BA flight takes off somewhere around the world, on average, every 90 seconds. The difficulties in planning a schedule which involves the world-wide resources of British Airways and ensuring that every flight leaves on time must be one of the most complex planning and control tasks in any operation.

The BA headquarters at Heathrow Airport near London is its busiest hub. It is there that you will find a small, but vitally important department known as Operations Control, which handles the seven days prior to take-off for long-haul flights, and the three days prior to take-off for short-haul flights. Initial flight schedules are produced up to two years in advance, and the route schedules are negotiated at a six-monthly global conference. The planning and scheduling group at BA will then manage the production of a flight timetable, taking account of the longer term implications of allocating certain aircraft types to each route. Any new routes or timings agreed are passed to Operations Control for comment on the practicalities of what is being proposed.

Operations Control inherits this final flight schedule, and can only make minor changes in order to cope with unexpected situations arising during the period prior to take-off. It is responsible for co-ordinating the three main resources required to provide the flight services, which are the schedule, the aircraft and the crew. They also are responsible for managing the knock-on effects of any delays, shortages or disruption to any of these inputs. The Operations Control team is in charge of every flight until it lands, when departments such as Engineering and Station Control can take over. This handover is illustrated in Fig. 10.3.

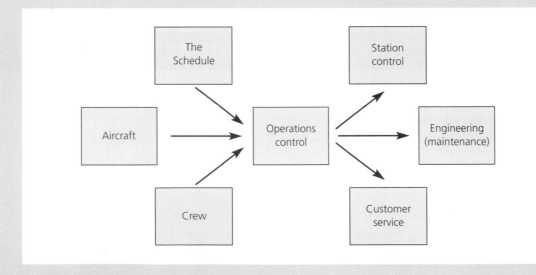

Figure 10.3 British Airways – Operations control centre

The performance of the Operations Control team is evaluated in terms of the *regularity* and subsequent *punctuality* of their flights. Regularity is defined as the percentage of flights actually taking off compared with the number scheduled. Passengers need to have total confidence that their flight will actually operate, and current performance is almost 99 per cent (cancelling a flight is the very last resort for Operations Control). Punctuality is the measure of the timing of the take-offs. BA sets an internal standard whereby a flight is considered late if it does not take off at the time defined in the schedule. Thus a flight can only be early, dead-on-time, or late.

Other component parts of the Operations Control Centre are the Emergency Procedures Information Centre (EPIC) and the Operations Control Intelligence Centre (OCIC) back-up centres. These are unmanned areas, set up to deal with certain types of incident at the 'press of a button'. The staff who would operate the centres are nominated, and are well trained in advance, even down to having simulated exercises on a regular basis. The EPIC centre is activated should BA, or any other contracted airline (there are over 60 subscribers to the service) be involved in an accident or serious incident, and it acts as a contact point for the public, and as a focal point for information regarding those on board. The OCIC centre is used only when a serious global incident, such as war, is affecting the entire BA business. Again, the centre is manned by specially trained staff and headed by a BA board director. The team will then be on 24-hour action stations until the crisis has been resolved. These two crisis centres have become well known, and EPIC is frequently used by other organizations.

The strategy of having independent crisis centres means that the day-to-day business units do not have to cater for every eventuality. They continue to work in the knowledge that an emergency situation will not be their responsibility, and they can thus focus more efficiently on the core operation. ■

Questions

1 What factors in the nature of demand are likely to affect the long-, medium- and short-term planning and control activities at British Airways?

2 How is the supply of transformed and transforming resources likely to affect planning and control?

3 Do you think the way in which the Operations Control team is evaluated is appropriate?

4 How is the planning and control task of the Emergency Procedure Information Centre and Operations Control Intelligence Centre different from the day-to-day operations control activities?

Dependable supply requires availability of all transformed and transforming resources. If any are absent it is unlikely that supply can occur. So, when trying to understand uncertainty in supply, it is important to understand the uncertainty of each input resource which governs supply. This involves asking questions such as: 'What is the likelihood of materials not arriving on time?', 'How often are staffing levels insufficient?', 'How reliable is the information system that provides instructions on what to supply and when to supply it?'

Uncertainty in demand

Demand can also be uncertain, but not in all operations; in some demand is fairly predictable. In a school, for example, once classes are fixed and the term, or semester, has started, a teacher knows how many pupils are in his or her class. When planning how many handouts are required the demand is predictable. Any absentee can have his or her handouts on return, so this variable does not affect demand. However, this is the medium and short term of the total planning and control of the school's operation. Prior to the start of the year, the head teacher may not know exactly how many new pupils will be joining the school and how many existing pupils will leave the area or move to another school. Therefore, in the long term, the head teacher has to predict this demand to determine resources such as staff, books, and computers, for which commitment must be made in advance.

In other operations, demand is unpredictable even in the short term. A fast-food outlet inside a shopping centre does not know how many people will arrive, when they will arrive and what they will order. It is possible to predict certain patterns, such as an increase in demand over the lunch and tea-time periods, but a sudden rain storm that drives shoppers indoors into the centre could significantly increase demand unpredictably in the very short term. Demand for fast-moving consumer goods such as packets of biscuits varies enormously depending on television advertising campaigns – a successful campaign can have an impact the following day which can cause demand to soar to ten times its normal selling pattern. While some extra stocks could be provided to supermarkets in advance of the campaign, the size of the reaction is not easy to predict.

Dependent and independent demand

Some operations can look ahead and make forward provision because they have firm orders from customers into the future. In addition to these orders, the operation may have a reasonably good idea of what other customers will order. Other operations, however, can only make predictions, often based on history, and use this as their best indicator of what the future will hold. They have no absolute certainty on which to depend. In the first case, the operation is said to be driven by *dependent demand* and, in the second case, it is driven by *independent demand*. The difference between the two is easily described by the analogy of driving a car. We drive cars *dependent* on what the road ahead looks like. Driving the car *independently* would be done by having a 'prediction' of the road ahead (based partly by looking in the rear-view mirror). If the road ahead (future demand) is very similar to the road a driver has just travelled on (previous demand), it may be possible to drive for a short time without crashing. Also, if the driver has taken the route many times before and there is no other traffic (competitors) the curves in the road may be predicted. However, if the driver is on a country road with many twists and turns (an uncertain future demand) the operation has a good chance of 'going off the road'.

Dependent demand, then, is demand which is relatively predictable because it is dependent upon some factor which is known. For example, the manager who is in charge of ensuring that there are sufficient tyres in an automobile factory will not treat the demand for tyres as a totally random variable. He or she will not be totally surprised by the exact quantity of tyres which are required by the plant every day. The process of demand forecasting is relatively straightforward. It will consist of examining the manufacturing schedules in the car plant and deriving the demand for tyres from these. If 200 cars are to be manufactured on a particular day, then it is simple to calculate that 1000 tyres will be demanded by the car plant on that day (each car has five tyres). Demand is dependent on a known factor – the number of cars to be manufactured. Because of this, the tyres can be ordered from the tyre manufacturer to a delivery schedule which is closely in line with the demand for tyres from the plant (*see* Fig. 10.4). In fact the demand for every part of the car plant will be derived from the assembly schedule for the finished cars. Manufacturing instructions and purchasing requests will all be dependent upon this figure. Other operations will act in a dependent demand manner because of the nature of the service or product which they provide. For example, a jobbing dressmaker will not buy fabric and patterns and make up dresses in many different sizes just in case someone comes along and wants to buy one. Nor will a high-class restaurant begin to cook food just in case a customer arrives and requests it. In both these cases a combination of *risk* and the *perishability* of the product or service prevents the operation from starting to create the goods or services until it has a firm order.

Dependent demand planning and control concentrates on the consequences of the demand within the operation. Materials requirements planning, which is treated in Chapter 14, is one such dependent demand approach.

Some operations have little choice but to take decisions on how they will supply demand without having any firm forward visibility of customer orders. For example, customers do not have to inform a supermarket when they are arriving and what they will buy. The supermarket takes its planning and control decisions based on its experience and understanding of the market, independent of what may actually happen. They run the risk of being out of stock of items when demand does not match their expectations. For example, the Ace Tyre Company, which operates a drive-in tyre replacement service, will need to manage a stock of tyres. In that sense it is exactly the same task that faced the manager of tyre stocks in the car plant. However, demand is very different for Ace Tyres. It cannot predict either the volume or specific needs of customers. It must make decisions on how many and what type of tyres to stock, based on demand forecasts and in the light of the risks it is prepared to run of being

Figure 10.4 The demand for tyres in a car plant is dependent on the manufacturing schedule of the cars

out of stock. This is the nature of *independent demand planning and control*. It makes 'best guesses' concerning future demand, attempts to put the resources in place which can satisfy this demand, and attempts to respond quickly if actual demand does not match the forecast (*see* Fig. 10.5). Inventory planning and control, treated in Chapter 12, is typical of independent demand planning and control.

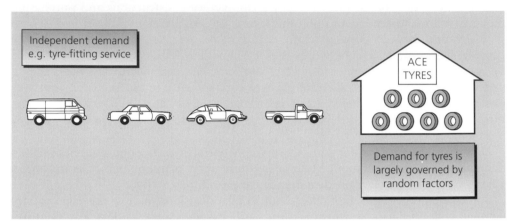

Figure 10.5
The demand for tyres at Ace Tyres is independent of any single determining factor

Responding to demand

Dependent and independent demand concepts are closely related to how the operation chooses to respond to demand. In conditions of dependent demand, an operation will only start the process of producing goods or services when it needs to. Each order triggers the planning and control activities to organize their production. For example, a specialist house builder might only start the process of planning and controlling the construction of a house when requested to do so by the customer. The builder might not even have the resources to start building before the order is received. The material which will be necessary to build the house will be purchased only when the timing and nature of the house are certain. The staff and the construction equipment might also be 'purchased' only when the nature of demand is clear. In a similar way, a specialist conference organizer will start planning for an event only when specifically requested to do so by the clients. A venue will be booked, speakers organized, meals arranged, and the delegates contacted only when the nature of the service is clear. The planning and control necessary for this kind of operation can be called *resource-to-order* planning and control.[3]

Other operations might be sufficiently confident of the nature of demand, if not its volume and timing, to keep 'in stock' most of the resources it requires to satisfy its customers. Certainly it will keep its transforming resources if not its transformed resources. However, it would still make the actual product or service only to a firm customer order. For example, a house builder who has standard designs might choose to build each house only when a customer places a firm order. Because the design of the house is relatively standard, suppliers of materials will have been identified, even if the building operation does not keep the items in stock itself. The equivalent in the conference business would be a conference centre which has its own 'stored' permanent resources (the building, staff, etc.) but only starts planning a conference when it has a firm booking. In both cases the operations would need *make-to-order* planning and control.

Some operations produce goods or services ahead of any firm orders 'to stock'. For example, some builders will construct predesigned standard houses or apartments ahead of any firm demand for them. This will be done either because it is less expensive to do so or because it is difficult to create the goods or services on a one-off basis (it is difficult to make each apartment only when a customer chooses to buy one). If demand is high, customers may place requests for houses before they are started or during their construction. In this case the customer will form a backlog of demand and must wait. The builder is also taking the risk, however, of holding a stock of unsold houses if buyers do not come along before they are finished. In fact it is difficult for small builders to operate this way, but less so for (say) a bottled cola manufacturer or other mass producer. The equivalent in the conference market would be a conference centre which schedules a series of events and conferences, programmed in advance and open to individual customers to book into or even turn up on the day. Cinemas and theatres usually work in this manner. Their performances are produced and supplied irrespective of the level of actual demand. Operations of this type will require *make-to-stock* planning and control.

Figure 10.6 illustrates some of the differences between operations which resource to order at one extreme through to those which make for stock at the other. The former base their planning and control on dependent demand, whereas the latter are independent-demand driven. The nature of the activities is also different. In resource-to-order planning and control the size of each product or service relative to the total capacity of the operation is usually very large. The builder, for example, might only be able to organize one job at any time and the conference organizer organize one conference at any time. In each case the product is occupying all the operation's resources. On the other hand, make-for-stock planning and control is usually concerned with products or services which are small compared to the total capacity of the operation. One house for a major house builder or one bottle of cola

**Figure 10.6
The implications of adopting resource-to-order, make-to-order or make-to-stock planning and control**

for a large drinks bottler accounts for only a small part of their capacity. Similarly, one attendee at a major conference centre is likely to be a small part of the conference centre's total capacity.

P:*D* ratios[4]

Another way of characterizing the graduation between resource-to-order planning and control and make-to-stock planning and control is by contrasting the total length of time customers have to wait between asking for the product or service and receiving it, demand time, *D*, and the total throughput time, *P*. Throughput time is how long the operation takes to obtain the resources, produce and deliver the product or service.

P and *D* times depend on the operation

In a typical make-to-stock operation such as those making consumer durables, demand time, *D*, is the sum of the times for transmitting the order to the company's warehouse or stock point, picking and packing the order and physically transporting it to the customer – the 'deliver' cycle. Behind this visible order cycle, however, lie other cycles. Reduction in the finished goods stock will eventually trigger the decision to manufacture a replenishment batch. This cycle – the 'make' cycle – involves scheduling work to the various stages in the manufacturing process. Physically this involves withdrawing materials and parts from input inventories and processing them through the various stages of the manufacturing route. Behind the 'make' cycle lies the 'purchase' cycle – the time for replenishment of the input stocks – involving transmitting the order to suppliers and awaiting their delivery.

So, for this type of manufacturing, the 'demand' time which the customer sees is very short compared with the total 'throughput' cycle. Contrast this with a resource-to-order operation. Here *D* is the same as *P*. Both include the 'purchase', 'make' and 'delivery' cycles. The make-to-order operation lies in between these two (*see* Fig. 10.7).

Some operations are hybrids. Take, for example, a manufacturer of industrial couplings whose product range is far wider than the range of components it makes because it can configure components in many different ways. Given its wide range of finished products, the company does not hold them as inventories. Instead it makes most of its components 'to stock' and then assembles its products (a relatively short process) 'to order'. This is shown in Fig. 10.8. Not all the company's products are made in this way, however. Some are demanded so infrequently that it makes them entirely to order as 'specials'. Most operations will operate with different *P*:*D* ratios for different classes of product or service.

P:*D* ratios indicate the degree of speculation

In the company previously described, reducing total throughput time *P* will have varying effects on the time the customer has to wait for demand to be filled. For many of its 'specials', *P* and *D* are virtually the same – the customer waits from the material being ordered, through all stages in the production process and for delivery. Speeding up any part of *P* will reduce the customer's waiting time, *D*. On the other hand, the customers purchasing standard 'assemble-to-order' products would only see reduced

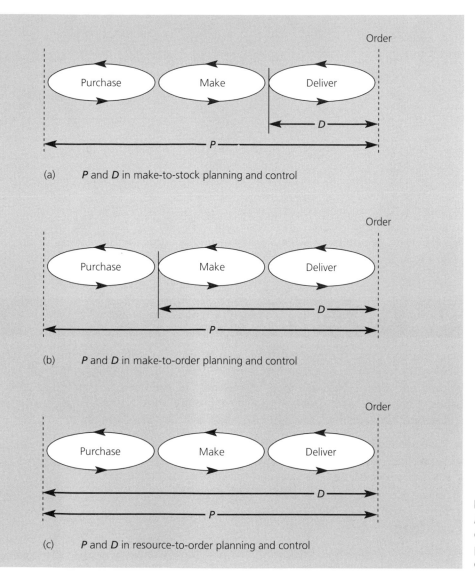

(a) *P* and *D* in make-to-stock planning and control

(b) *P* and *D* in make-to-order planning and control

(c) *P* and *D* in resource-to-order planning and control

Figure 10.7
***P* and *D* for the different types of planning and control**

D time if the 'assemble' and 'deliver' parts of *P* were reduced and savings in times were passed on to the customer.

In Fig. 10.7, *D* is always shown as being smaller than *P*, which is the case for most companies. How much smaller *D* is than *P* is important because it indicates the proportion of the operation's activities which are speculative, that is carried out on the expectation of eventually receiving a firm order for the work. The larger *P* is compared with *D*, the higher the proportion of speculative activity in the operation and the greater the risk the operation carries. The speculative element in the operation is not there only because *P* is greater than *D*, however; it is there because *P* is greater than *D* *and* demand cannot be forecast perfectly. With exact or close to exact forecasts, risk would be non-existent or very low, no matter how much bigger *P* was than *D*. Expressed another way: when *P* and *D* are equal then no matter how

Figure 10.8
P and *D* in make-to-stock, assemble-to-order planning and control

inaccurate the forecasts are, speculation is eliminated because everything is made to a firm order (although bad forecasting will lead to other problems). Reducing the *P:D* ratio becomes, in effect, a way of taking some of the risk out of operations planning and control.

THE PLANNING AND CONTROL TASK

Planning and control requires the reconciliation of supply and demand in terms of *volumes*, in terms of *timing*, and in terms of *quality*. In this chapter we will focus on volume and timing because most of this part of the book is concerned with these issues. Chapter 17 will deal with quality planning and control. To reconcile volume and timing, three distinct, though integrated, activities are performed:

- *loading* – determining the volume that an operation can cope with;
- *sequencing* – determining the priority of tasks to be performed;
- *scheduling* – deciding on a start and finish time for each task.

Loading

Loading is the amount of work that is allocated to a work centre. For example, a machine on the shop floor of a manufacturing business is available, in theory, 168 hours a week. However, this does not necessarily mean that 168 hours of work can be loaded on to that machine. Figure 10.9 shows what erodes this available time. For some periods the machine cannot be worked; for example, it may not be available on statutory holidays and weekends. Therefore, the load put on to the machine must take this into account. Of the time that the machine is available for work, some tasks other than producing output must be performed, which further reduces available time. For example, time may be lost while changing over from making one component to another. In addition, the machine may need cleaning between operations before another can be started. These lost times must also be taken into account when a plan is formed of how much work can be loaded on to the machine. If the machine breaks down, it will not be available. If there is machine reliability data available, this must also be taken into account.

There are two main approaches to loading operations – *finite* and *infinite loading*.

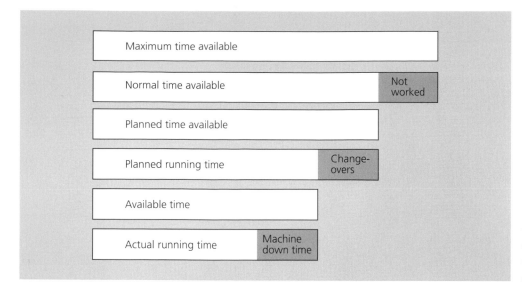

**Figure 10.9
The reduction in
the time available
for loading work
on to a machine**

Finite loading

Finite loading is an approach which only allocates work to a work centre (a person, a machine, or maybe a group of people or machines) up to a set limit. This limit is the estimate of capacity for the work centre (based on the times available for loading). Work over and above this capacity is not accepted. Figure 10.10 shows that the load on the work centre is not allowed to exceed the capacity limit.

Finite loading is particularly relevant for operations where:

● *it is possible to limit the load*. For example, it is possible to run an appointment system for a general medical practice or a hairdresser.
● *it is necessary to limit the load*. For example, for safety reasons a finite number of people and weight of luggage is allowed on aircraft.
● *the cost of limiting the load is not prohibitive*. For example, the cost of maintaining a finite order book at a specialist sports car manufacturer does not adversely affect demand, and may even enhance it.

Infinite loading

Infinite loading is an approach to loading work which does not limit accepting work, but instead tries to cope with it. Figure 10.11 illustrates a loading pattern where capacity constraints have not been used to limit loading.

Infinite loading is relevant for operations where:

● *it is not possible to limit the load*. For example, an accident and emergency department in a hospital should not turn away arrivals needing attention.
● *it is not necessary to limit the load*. For example, fast-food outlets are designed to flex capacity up and down to cope with varying arrival rates of customers. During busy periods, customers accept that they must queue for some time before being served. Unless this is extreme, the customers might not go elsewhere.

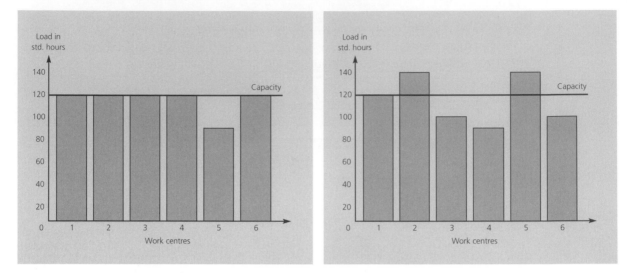

Figure 10.10   Finite loading

Figure 10.11 Infinite loading

● *the cost of limiting the load is prohibitive.* For example, if a retail bank turned away customers at the door because a set amount were inside, customers would feel less than happy with the service.

In complex planning and control activities where there are multiple stages, each with different capacities and with a varying mix arriving at the facilities, such as a machine shop in an engineering company, the constraints imposed by finite loading make loading calculations complex and not worth the considerable computational power which would be needed.

Sequencing

Whether the approach to loading is finite or infinite, when work arrives, decisions must be taken on the *order* that the work will be tackled. This activity is termed *sequencing*.

The priorities given to work in an operation are often set by some predefined set of rules. Some of these rules are summarized below.

Physical constraints

The physical nature of the materials being processed may determine the priority of work. For example, in an operation using paints or dyes, lighter shades will be sequenced before darker shades. On completion of each batch, the colour is slightly darkened for the next batch. This is because darkness of colour can only be added and not removed from the colour mix. Similarly, the physical nature of the equipment used may determine sequence. For example, in the paper industry the cutting equipment is set to the width of paper required. It is easier and faster to move the cutting equipment to an adjacent size (up or down) than it is to reset the machine to a very different size.

Sometimes the mix of work arriving at a part of an operation may determine the priority given to jobs. For example, when fabric is cut to a required size and shape in garment manufacture, the surplus fabric would be wasted if not used for another product. Therefore, jobs that physically fit together may be scheduled together to reduce waste.

Customer priority

Operations will sometimes allow an important or aggrieved customer, or item, to be 'processed' prior to others, irrespective of the order of arrival of the customer or item. This approach is typically used by operations whose customer base is skewed, containing a mass of small customers and a few large, very important customers. Some banks, for example, give priority to important customers. Similarly, in hotels, complaining customers will be treated as a priority because their complaint may have an adverse affect on the perceptions of other customers.

However, sequencing work by customer priority may mean that 'large-volume' customers receive a very high level service, but service to many other customers is eroded. This may lower the average performance of the operation if existing work flows are disrupted for important customers. It can also erode the quality and productivity of the operation, making it less efficient overall.

Due date

Prioritizing by due date means that work is sequenced according to when it is 'due' for delivery, irrespective of the size of each job or the importance of each customer. For example, a support service in an office block, such as a reprographic unit, will often ask when photocopies are required, then sequence the work according to that due date. Due date sequencing usually improves the delivery reliability of an operation and improves average delivery speed. However, it may not provide optimal productivity, as a more efficient sequencing of work may reduce total costs. However, it can be flexible when new, urgent work arrives at the work centre.

LIFO

Last In First Out (LIFO) is a method of sequencing usually selected for practical reasons. For example, unloading an elevator is more convenient on a LIFO basis as there is only one entrance and exit. However, it is not an equitable approach. Patients at hospital clinics may be infuriated if they see medical records added to a pile in the sequence of arriving patients, which means that, if the doctor takes the records from the top of the pile first, patients are served in reverse order of when they arrived. LIFO has a very adverse effect on delivery speed and reliability. The sequence is not determined for reasons of quality, flexibility or cost, therefore none of these performance objectives are well served by this method.

FIFO

Some operations serve customers in exactly the sequence they arrive in, on a First-In-First-Out (FIFO) basis. For example, the UK passport offices receive post and put it in a pile according to the day on which it arrived. They work through the post, opening it in sequence, then processing the passport applications as they come to them. Queues in theme parks may be designed so that one long queue snakes around the lobby area until the row of counters is reached. When customers reach the front of the queue they are served at the next free counter.

In high-contact operations, arrival time may be viewed by customers in the system as a fair way of sequencing, thereby minimizing customer complaints, and enhancing service performance. However, because there is no consideration of urgency or due date, some customers' needs may not be served as well as others. Delivery speed and delivery reliability, therefore, may not be at their highest. It is also difficult to be flexible in a system where this prioritization is visible to customers. If the 'queue' is not physically visible, it may be more possible to exercise some flexibility, allowing some work to queue jump without other customers being aware of it happening.

Longest operation/longest total job time first

Under certain circumstances, operations may feel obliged to sequence their longest jobs first. This has the advantage of occupying the work centres within the operation for long periods. Relatively small jobs progressing through an operation will take up time at each work centre which will need to change over from one job to the next. Especially where staff are under some incentive to keep utilization high, such a sequencing rule might seem attractive. However, although utilization may be high (and therefore cost relatively low) this rule does not take into account delivery speed, delivery reliability or flexibility. Indeed it may work directly against these performance objectives.

Shortest operation/shortest total job time first

Most operations at some stage become cash constrained. In these situations, the sequencing rules may be adjusted to tackle short jobs first. These jobs can then be invoiced and payment received to ease cash-flow problems. Larger jobs that take more time will not enable the business to invoice as quickly. This has an effect of improving delivery performance, if the unit of measurement of delivery is jobs. However, it may adversely affect total productivity and can damage service to larger customers.

Scheduling

Having determined the sequence that work is to be tackled in, some operations require a detailed timetable showing at what time or date jobs should start and when they should end. This is a schedule. Schedules are familiar statements of volume and timing in many consumer environments. For example, a bus schedule shows that more buses are put on routes at more frequent intervals during rush-hour periods. The bus schedule shows the time each bus is due to arrive at each stage of the route. Schedules of work are used in operations where some planning is required to ensure that customer demand is met. Other operations, such as rapid-response service operations where customers arrive in an unplanned way, cannot schedule the operation in a short-term sense. They can only respond at the time demand is placed upon them.

The complexity of scheduling[5]

The scheduling activity is one of the most complex tasks in operations management. First, schedulers must deal with several different types of resource simultaneously. Machines will have different capabilities and capacities; staff will have different skills. More importantly, the number of possible schedules increases rapidly as the number of activities and processes increases. For example, suppose one machine has five different jobs to process. Any of the five jobs could be processed first and following that any one of the remaining four jobs, and so on. This means that there are:

$5 \times 4 \times 3 \times 2 = 120$ different schedules possible.

Or, more generally, for *n* jobs there are *n!* (factorial n) different ways of scheduling the jobs through a single process.

We can now consider what impact there would be if, in the same situation, there was more than one type of machine. If we were trying to minimize the number of set-ups on two machines, there is no reason why the sequence on Machine 1 would be the same as the sequence on Machine 2. If we consider the two sequencing tasks to be independent of each other, for two machines there would be:

$120 \times 120 = 14\ 400$ possible schedules of the two machines and five jobs.

A general formula can be devised to calculate the possible number of schedules in any given situation. This is:

Number of possible schedules $= (n!)^m$
where   *n* is the number of jobs
            m is the number of machines.

If we relate this to a real situation, where there may be 100 jobs going through 30 machines, in a route which takes each individual job through five different machines, then we can see that the scheduling task rapidly becomes very complicated. Within this vast number of schedules there are many acceptable options as to which are appropriate routes and sequences for any set of jobs. Even where a product is manufactured repeatedly there may be a number of different routes which that product could take. However, most of the schedules which are possible in theory will not be workable in practice and these can be rapidly eliminated.

The scheduling task has to be repeated on a very frequent basis to allow for market variations and product mix changes. Remember that even minor product mix changes may cause the capacity constraints within the facility to change very dramatically over a comparatively short period of time, hence bottle-neck operations may move about the factory quite quickly.

Forward and backward scheduling

Forward scheduling involves starting work as soon as it arrives. Backward scheduling involves starting jobs at the last possible moment to prevent them being late. For example, assume that it takes six hours for a contract laundry to wash, dry and press a batch of overalls. If the work is collected at 8.00 am and is due to be picked up at 4.00 pm, there are more than six hours available to do the work. Table 10.1 shows the different start times of each job, depending on whether they are forward or backward scheduled.

Table 10.1 The effects of forward and backward scheduling

Task	Duration	Start time (backwards)	Start time (forwards)
Press	1 hour	3.00 pm	1.00 pm
Dry	2 hours	1.00 pm	11.00 am
Wash	3 hours	10.00 am	8.00 am

Table 10.2 Advantages of forward and backward scheduling

Advantages of forward scheduling	Advantages of backward scheduling
High labour utilization – workers always start work to keep busy	Lower material costs – materials are not used until they have to be, therefore delaying added value until the last moment
Flexible – the time slack in the system allows unexpected work to be loaded	Less exposed to risk in case of schedule change by the customer
	Tends to focus the operation on customer due dates

The choice of backward or forward scheduling depends largely upon the circumstances. Table 10.2 lists some advantages and disadvantages of the two approaches. In theory, both materials requirements planning (MRP) (*see* Chapter 14) and just-in-time (JIT) (*see* Chapter 15) both use backward scheduling, only starting work when it is required. In practice, however, users of materials requirements planning have tended to allow too long for each task to be completed, therefore each task is not started at the last possible time. In comparison, just-in-time is started, as the name suggests, just-in-time.

Scheduling work patterns

Where the dominant resource in an operation is its staff, then the schedule of work times effectively determines the capacity of the operation itself. The main task of scheduling, therefore, is to make sure that sufficient numbers of people are working at any point in time to provide a capacity appropriate for the level of demand at that point in time. Operations such as postal delivery services, telephone operators, policing services, holiday couriers, shop workers, and hospital staff, will all need to schedule the working hours of their staff with demand in mind. This is a direct consequence of these operations having relatively high customer contact (we introduced the idea of high customer contact in Chapter 1). Such operations cannot store their outputs in inventories and so must respond directly to customer demand.

For example, Fig. 10.12 shows the scheduling of shifts for one part of a home-banking enquiry service. This particular department gives advice to customers on home loans and insurance. It advertises a 24-hour service and, indeed, some customers do make use of the enquiry service throughout the night. However, during this period demand is relatively low. It builds up during the morning to peak half-way through the day. There is another small peak in the early evening, but demand then falls away during the later part of the evening. The scheduling task here is to allocate start and finish times to staff such that:

- capacity matches demand;
- the length of each shift is neither excessively long nor too short to be attractive to staff;
- working at unsocial hours is minimized.

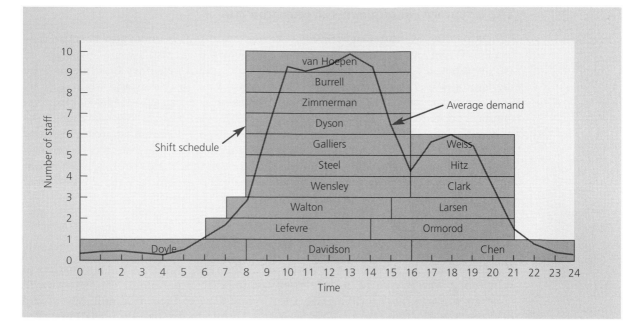

Figure 10.12 Shift scheduling in a home-banking enquiry service

Controlling the operation

Having created a plan for the operation through loading, sequencing and scheduling, each part of the operation has to receive some form of instruction or signal to commence work. There are two main types of signal which can be characterized as 'push' and 'pull' control.

Push and pull control

In a *push system* of control, activities are scheduled by means of a central system, and completed in line with central instructions, such as an MRP system. Each work centre pushes out work without considering whether the succeeding work centre can make use of it. Work centres are co-ordinated by means of the central operations planning and control system. In practice, however, there are many reasons why actual conditions differ from those planned. As a consequence, idle time, inventory and queues often characterize push systems.

In a *pull system* of control the pace and specification of what is done is set by the 'customer' work station, which 'pulls' work from the preceding (supplier) work station. The customer acts as the only 'trigger' for movement. If a request is not passed back from the customer to the supplier, the supplier cannot produce anything or move any materials. A request from a customer not only triggers production at the supplying stage, it will also prompt the supplying stage to request a further delivery from its own suppliers. In this way demand is transmitted back through the stages from the original point of demand by the original customer.

The inventory consequences of push and pull

Understanding the differing principles of push and pull is important because they have different effects in terms of their propensities to accumulate inventory in the operation. Pull systems are far less likely to result in inventory build up and are therefore favoured by JIT operations (*see* Chapter 15). To understand why this is so, consider an analogy. The 'gravity' analogy is illustrated in Fig. 10.13. Here a push system is represented by an operation, each stage of which is on a lower level than the previous stage. When parts are processed by each stage it pushes them down the slope to the next stage. Any delay or problem at that stage will result in the parts accumulating as inventory. In the pull system, parts cannot naturally flow uphill, so they can only progress if the next stage along deliberately pulls them forward. Under these circumstances inventory cannot accumulate as easily.

The tools and techniques of scheduling

We do not have space here to give details of all the various models and approaches to scheduling which have been developed for specific situations. However, we will illustrate the area by describing two approaches. One of these is simple, visual and non-optimizing. The other is also relatively simple but is based on mathematical optimization. Indeed, mathematically optimizing approaches are usually applicable only in relatively simple applications. The complexity of the scheduling task is beyond the reach of most optimizing models. This is why operations scheduling is still more of an art than a science.

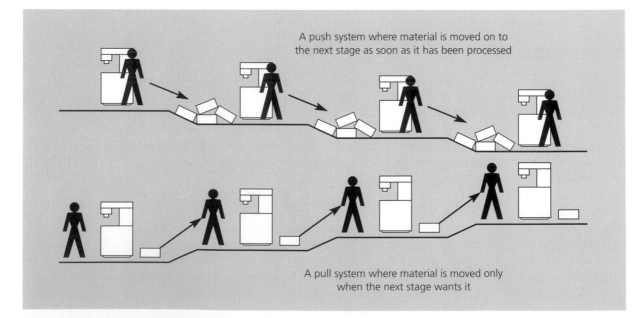

Figure 10.13 Push versus pull: the gravity analogy

Gantt charts

The most commonly used method of scheduling is by use of the Gantt chart. A Gantt chart is a simple device (first devised by H.L. Gantt in 1917) which represents time as a bar, or channel, on a chart. Often the charts themselves are made up of long plastic channels into which coloured pieces of paper can be slotted to indicate what is happening with a job or a work centre. The start and finish times for activities can be indicated on the chart and sometimes the actual progress of the job is also indicated on the same chart. Figures 10.14 and 10.15 illustrate two Gantt charts for a small specialist

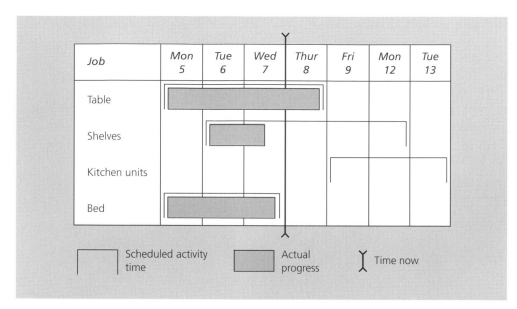

**Figure 10.14
Gantt chart for
job progress**

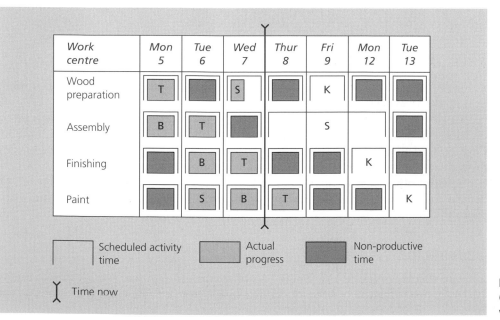

**Figure 10.15
Gantt chart for
work centres**

THE HOSPITAL TRIAGE SYSTEM[6]

One of the most difficult-to-schedule environments in a hospital is the Accident and Emergency department, where patients arrive at random, without any prior warning, throughout the day. It is up to the hospital's reception, and the medical staff, to devise very rapidly a schedule which meets most of the necessary criteria. In particular, patients who arrive having had very serious accidents, or presenting symptoms of a serious illness, need to be attended to urgently. Therefore, the hospital will schedule these cases first. Less urgent cases – perhaps where patients are in some discomfort, but their injuries or illnesses are not life-threatening – will have to wait until the urgent cases are treated. Routine non-urgent cases will have the lowest priority of all. In many circumstances these patients will have to wait for the longest time, which may be many hours, especially if the hospital is busy. Sometimes these non-urgent cases may even be turned away if the hospital is too busy with more important cases.

In situations where hospitals expect sudden influxes of patients, they have developed what is known as a *triage system*, whereby medical staff hurriedly sort through the patients who have arrived to determine which category of urgency each patient fits into. In this way a suitable schedule for the various treatments can be devised in a short period of time. ■

Questions

1 Why do you think that the triage system is effective in controlling operations in Accident and Emergency departments?

2 Are there any dangers in this approach?

---

furniture manufacturer. Figure 10.14 is a *job progress* Gantt chart. This indicates when each job is scheduled to start and finish as well as the degree of completion of the job. Also indicated on the chart is the current time. In this case the table has been completed already, even though it was not scheduled to be completed until the end of the next day.

On the other hand, the shelves are behind schedule. The manufacturer of the kitchen units is not scheduled to start for another day. Figure 10.15 illustrates another Gantt chart which may be used by this company. This time it indicates the activities which are taking place at each work centre. Here we can see that the shelves seem to be held up in the wood preparation work centre.

The advantages of Gantt charts are that they provide a simple visual representation of what should be happening and what actually is happening in the operation. Furthermore, they can be used to 'test out' alternative schedules. Especially when using moveable pieces of paper, it is a simple task to represent alternative schedules (even if it is a far from simple task to find a schedule which fits all the resources satisfactorily). Of course the Gantt chart is in no way an optimizing tool. It merely facilitates the development of alternative schedules by communicating them effectively.

Johnson's Rule[7]

Johnson's Rule applies to the scheduling of *n* jobs through two work centres. Figure 10.16 illustrates the use of Johnson's Rule. In this case a printer has to print and bind

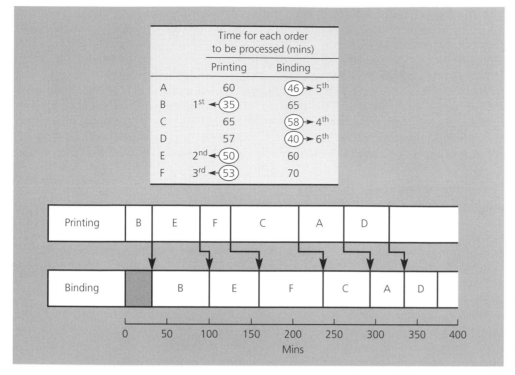

Figure 10.16
The application of Johnson's Rule for scheduling _n_ jobs through two work centres

six jobs. The times for processing each job through the first work centre (printing) and the second work centre (binding) are shown in the figure. The rule is simple. First look for the smallest processing time. If that time is associated with the first work centre (printing in this case) then schedule that job first, or as near first as possible. If the next smallest time is associated with the second work centre then schedule that job last or as near last as possible. Once a job has been scheduled, delete it from the list. Carry on allocating jobs until the list is complete. In this particular case the smallest processing time is 35 minutes for printing job B. Because this is at the first process (printing), job B is assigned first position in the schedule. The next smallest processing time is 40 minutes for binding – job D. Because this is at the second process (binding), it is scheduled last. The next lowest processing time, after jobs B and D have been struck off the list, is 46 minutes for binding job A. Because this is at the second work centre it is scheduled as near last as possible, which in this case is fifth. This process continues until all the jobs have been scheduled. It results in a schedule for the two processes which is also shown in Fig. 10.16.

THE VOLUME–VARIETY EFFECT ON PLANNING AND CONTROL

In Chapter 4 we identified that many of the detailed design decisions in operations management were significantly affected by the volume–variety position of an operation. This is also true of the planning and control activities. Operations which produce a high variety of products or services in relatively low volume will clearly have customers who require a different set of factors and use processes which have a different set of needs to those operations which create standardized products or services in high volume (*see* Table 10.3).

Again, let us take the two operations which were discussed in Chapter 4 which occupy the two extremes of the volume–variety spectrum – an architects' practice and an electricity utility. The architects' high variety means that their services will have little or no standardization. This means that they cannot produce their designs in advance of customers requesting them. Because of this, the time it will take to respond to customers' requests will be relatively slow. Indeed their customers will understand this and expect to be consulted extensively as to their needs. Thus the *P:D* ratio of the

THE WIZARD SYSTEM AT AVIS

It is possible to rent cars at almost every major airport and city centre in the world, and there is invariably intense competition to attract and keep customers. Since the hire companies all offer similar ranges of relatively new vehicles, and the reliability of these cars is taken for granted by most customers, competition is generally on service and/or price. The most critical service factor is the availability of the desired category (size and specification) of car, and the speed with which all the hire contract paperwork can be completed, so that the customer is not unnecessarily delayed. This depends on the effectiveness of the hire company's planning and control system. One of the most important Avis sites in Belgium is the operation at Brussels National Airport at Zaventem, which deals predominantly with business customers, and hires out up to 200 cars on a busy day. Avis's advertisement, targeted at the business market, emphasizes its ability to process customers quickly and efficiently. The objective is to complete the transaction in less than two minutes, and this is facilitated by Avis's well-developed computer system known as WIZARD which handles all reservations, preparation of hire contracts at the service desks, inventory management and invoicing systems. WIZARD is a globally integrated system, with over 15 000 terminals in Avis branches world-wide, allowing international reservations to be made with accuracy and certainty, and helping to maximize the utilization of vehicles throughout the network.

Regular customer surveys and analyses of actual demand patterns are carried out to determine the customers' preferences in terms of type and category of vehicles, providing a guide to the Belgian fleet composition, which is managed from the central 'clearing house' at Machelen. Because each of the Belgian branch offices has access to a pool of cars held at Machelen, their local buffer stock requirements can be minimized. The requirements for the movement of car inventory between branches and between countries is centralized in this way, allowing the branches to concentrate on the task of providing good customer service. Each regular business customer has a unique reference number in WIZARD, allowing reservations to be made and rental contracts to be completed quickly, with only three pieces of information: the customer's number, the type of car required, and the duration of the hire. This type of transaction is usually completed in under two minutes, after which the customer goes directly to the car park and collects the car. ∎

Questions

1 What do you see as the main planning and control tasks of the Wizard system?

2 How would you evaluate the effectiveness of the planning and control activity at Avis?

Table 10.3 The volume–variety effects on planning and control

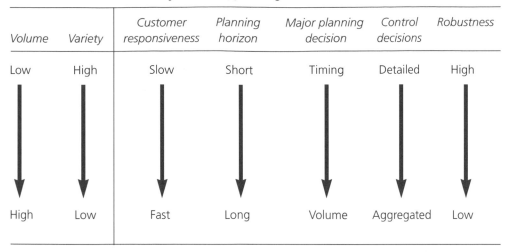

Volume	Variety	Customer responsiveness	Planning horizon	Major planning decision	Control decisions	Robustness
Low	High	Slow	Short	Timing	Detailed	High
↓	↓	↓	↓	↓	↓	↓
High	Low	Fast	Long	Volume	Aggregated	Low

operation will be 1 or very close to 1. The details and requirements of each job will emerge only as each individual building is designed to the client's requirements. This means that planning occurs on a relatively short-term basis. The architects are unlikely to be able to plan several years ahead because they do not know what jobs they will be doing at that time. The individual decisions which are taken in the planning process will usually concern the timing of activities and events: for example, when a design is to be delivered, when building should start, when each individual architect will be needed to work on the design, and so on. Most of the control decisions will be at a relatively detailed level. A small delay in calculating one part of the design could have very significant implications in many other parts of the job. In general, the planning and control of the operation cannot be totally routinized; rather it will need managing on an individual project basis. Finally, the robustness of the operation (that is its vulnerability to serious disruption if one part of the operation breaks down) will be relatively high. There are probably plenty of other things to get on with if an architect is prevented from progressing one part of the job.

The electricity utility, on the other hand, will exhibit very different planning and control characteristics. Volume is high, production continuous, and variety is virtually non-existent. Customers expect extremely fast response to their request for the product. In effect they expect instant 'delivery' whenever they plug in an appliance. The planning horizon in electricity generation can be very long. Major decisions regarding the capacity of power stations are made many years in advance. Even the fluctuations in demand over a typical day can be forecast to a certain extent in advance. Popular television programmes can affect minute-by-minute demand and these are scheduled weeks or months ahead. The weather, which also affects demand, is less prone to being forecast, but can to some extent be predicted. The individual planning decisions made by the electricity utility will centre not around the timing of output, but rather the volume of output. Control decisions will not be concerned with the detailed intricacies of the operation's output because the product is more or less homogeneous. Rather, control will concern aggregated measures of output such as the total kilowatts of electricity generated. Finally, the robustness of the operation is very low insomuch as, if the generator fails, the operation's capability of supplying electricity from that part of the operation also fails (*see* Table 10.3).

Paola Petré, Brussels Airport Terminal Company SA

BATC is the recently privatized operating company responsible for the passenger- and baggage-handling processes at Brussels National Airport at Zavantem, on the outskirts of Europe's busy administrative capital.

Paola studied business administration at the Université Libre de Bruxelles, and then joined a large bank, working in a department responsible for improving operating systems, mainly in back-office administrative processes.

'The broad experience that I gained in the analysis and development of systems and procedures has been invaluable in my career development, and has been a good foundation for my work in operations planning at the airport. My current position as Allocation Controller involves analysis of the utilization of key resources in the terminal; particularly the check-in desks, baggage-handling systems, and the gates or stands where the aircraft park.

'Most of the airlines operating here would prefer to be able to occupy more check-in desks than they really need, and these would stand idle for most of the time except at the peak periods in the morning and evening. As with almost all operations at the airport, space is limited, and with the growth in traffic it is not possible to satisfy all this demand. It is my responsibility to allocate what we have on a fair and equitable basis, based on a thorough understanding and analysis of schedules and passenger numbers for the different types of service. Check-in procedures are very fast for charter flights, and passengers tend to arrive long before departure and are queue (line) tolerant. On the other hand, European scheduled flights are predominantly business people; many arrive at the last moment possible and, if they are not processed quickly, become very upset. Long-haul flights usually involve much larger numbers of passengers, longer check-in times, and much more baggage handling. To complicate the analysis further, until recently, there

were different check-in computer systems for each of the three handlers: American Airlines, Sabena and Belgavia, so allocations became fixed by the system incompatibility. I was closely involved in the planning of the new terminal, which will give us 120 new desks, all using a common computer system, allowing me the flexibility to allocate on a more logical basis. I held many briefing meetings with the handlers to ensure that they "bought-in" to the analysis.

'Each check-in desk has a baggage conveyor that connects it to the new baggage hall below. Each item carries a bar code, and drops into a tray which is then automatically sorted into its correct loading "chute". These are rather like the spiral slides found at funfairs: there are only 132 of them, which might sound a lot, but really is another bottle-neck for me to deal with. The handlers like to keep different classes of baggage separate (First, Club, Business, Economy, and Transfer) and on long-haul, several chutes will be needed to cope with the large volumes of items. Different schedules are needed every day to cope with the changing mix of traffic, so this is a very complex operation to plan. It is vital for me to ensure that the schedule meets the needs of all the users, without wasted capacity, and yet avoid bottle-necks building up that could delay loading of the aircraft. Our top priority is to ensure that the baggage systems resource at Brussels allows the handlers to achieve faster throughput than comparable airports in Europe. This will be one of our "competitive edges" in the quest for more business.

'Another of my responsibilities is to allocate gates and stands for aircraft. During the middle of the day there are lots of empty gates, allowing access for all suitably sized aircraft to link up to air bridges. At peak times, however, it is necessary to schedule tightly the requirements of the airlines, both to ensure that large planes and long-haul flights always get a space, and to be seen to be fair to all the operators, and minimize the use of buses to remote stands. The allocation of the gates is a *similar problem to that of the chutes; demand equals or exceeds capacity, and optimization/prioritization decisions must be made.*

'This has been a fantastic period to work for BATC. I have been closely involved with the planning of the enormous new facility, which has more than doubled capacity, and I have worked with the airlines and handlers to analyse and agree our planning and control systems. Now we can also have the satisfaction of monitoring the improvements we have made in throughput speed and quality. It is fascinating to watch the smooth flow of passengers which is the result of all our years of detailed work in the back office.' ■

Source: By kind permission of Paola Petré

SUMMARY ANSWERS TO KEY QUESTIONS

What is planning and control?

■ Planning and control is the reconciliation of the potential of the operation to supply products and services, and the demands of its customers on the operation. It is the set of day-to-day activities which runs the operation on an ongoing basis

What is the difference between planning and control?

■ A plan is a formalization of what is intended to happen at some time in the future. Control is the process of coping with changes to the plan and the operation to which it relates

■ Although planning and control are theoretically separable, they are usually treated together.

■ The balance between planning and control changes over time. Planning dominates in the long term, and is usually done on an aggregated basis. At the other extreme, in the short term, control usually operates within the resource constraints of the operation but makes interventions into the operation in order to cope with short-term changes in circumstances.

Why is planning and control important?

■ Without consideration of planning and control activities, operations would have no indication of what they were supposed to do or when they were supposed to do it, nor could they cope with deviations from what was expected.

■ If planning and control activities are efficient and effective, they should ensure that products and services are produced
  – in the appropriate quantity;
  – at the appropriate time;
  – at the appropriate level of quality.

How does the nature of demand affect planning and control?

■ The degree of uncertainty in demand affects the balance between planning and control. The greater the uncertainty, the more difficult it is to plan and greater emphasis must be placed on control.

■ This idea of uncertainty is linked with the concepts of dependent and independent demand. Dependent demand is relatively predictable because it is dependent on some known factor. Independent demand is less predictable because it depends on the chances of the market or customer behaviour.

■ The different ways of responding to demand can be characterized by differences in the $P{:}D$ ratio of the operation. The $P{:}D$ ratio is the ratio of total throughput time of goods or services to demand time.

What is involved in planning and control?

■ In planning and controlling the volume and timing of activity in operations, three distinct activities are necessary:

– loading, which dictates the amount of work which is allocated to each part of the operation;

– sequencing, which decides the order in which work is tackled within the operation;

– scheduling, which determines the detailed timetable of activities and when activities are started and finished.

■ Control can be classified as either 'pull' or 'push' control. Pull control is a system whereby demand is triggered by requests from a work centre's (internal) customer. Push control is a centralized system whereby control (and sometimes planning) decisions are issued to work centres which are then required to perform the task and supply the next work station.

■ In manufacturing, 'pull' schedules generally have far lower inventory levels than 'push' schedules.

■ The volume and variety position of an operation has an effect on the nature of its planning and control. Customer responsiveness, the planning horizon, the major planning decisions, the control decision, and the robustness of planning and control are especially affected by volume and variety.

CASE EXERCISE

Two multiplex cinemas
Kinepolis Cinema in Brussels, Belgium and
UCI Cinema in Solihull, Birmingham, UK

Kinepolis Cinema in Brussels, Belgium

Kinepolis is thought to be the largest cinema complex in the world (*see* Fig. 10.17), with 28 screens, a total of 8000 seats, and four showings of each film every day. It dominates the cinema market in the area, attracting around a 60 per cent share of attendances. One of the reasons for its success is that it is equipped with a full range of the latest projection technology (large screens, THX sound, Dolby stereo, Cinema Digital sound, and Imax). Kinepolis is located on the outskirts of Brussels in Bruparck next to the Heizel Stadium and the famous Atomium, a journey of about 15 minutes by car or by the Metro public transport system. Although the majority of customers come by car, there is usually ample parking space either in the cinema's own car park or at the adjacent Bruparck facilities.

All the film performances are scheduled to start at the same times every day: at 4 pm, 6 pm, 8 pm and 10.30 pm. Since the majority of the visitors arrive within 30 minutes of the start of the film, during busy periods queues can often build up considerably at the 18 ticket desks; ten in the large, airport-style foyer, and eight at the rear entrance. Above the desks there are TV monitors which display the menu of the films, classification, and the remaining availability of seats for each. It takes three monitors to provide the whole menu!

Each desk has a networked computer terminal and a ticket printer. For each customer, a screen code is first entered to identify and confirm seat availability of their requested film. Then the number of seats required is entered, and the tickets are printed, but these do not allocate specific seat positions. The operator then takes payment by cash or credit card and issues the tickets. These operations take an average of 19.5 seconds and a further 5 seconds is needed for the the next customer to move forward, and start the cycle again. In this way, the peak capacity is approximately 150 transactions per desk per hour; 2700 per hour using all the desks. Since an average transaction involves the sale of approximately 1.7 tickets, the ticketing process can satisfy an input of 4500 customers per hour, which is sufficient for most normal levels of demand; queueing times rarely exceed five minutes. The ticketing capacity would clearly be under strain if demand approached the full seating capacity of the centre.

UCI Cinema in Solihull, Birmingham, UK

This UCI (United Cinemas International) cinema has been open since 1989, and has eight screens (*see* Fig. 10.18). It was built on a premium site, on a business park close to the busy motorway network at the very centre of England. Almost all the customers come by car, and go to the cinema's own private car park, where there are usually adequate spaces; but there is occasionally considerable congestion at the entry/exit just before the start of popular films.

The cinema incorporates many 'state-of-the-art' features, including the high-quality THX sound system, fully computerized ticketing, and a video games arcade off the main hall. There are two sets of giant TV screens in the entrance hall, giving notice of future attractions. In total the eight screens can seat 1840 people; the sizes (seating) of the screens vary, and thus the cinema management can allocate the more popular films to the larger screens and use the smaller screens for the more minority showings.

The film titles are selected for the cinema by Head Office, but local management has responsibility for the scheduling of the showings on each screen. Contracts from the distributors govern the number of showings each day, but the detailed schedule is at the discretion of the cinema management. The starting times of the eight films at UCI are usually staggered by ten minutes, with the most popular film in each category (e.g. adults only) being scheduled to run first. Because the films are of different durations, and since the manager must try to maximize the utilization of the seating, the scheduling task is complex and critical to the financial performance of the site.

383

Ground floor (0)

Basement (–1)

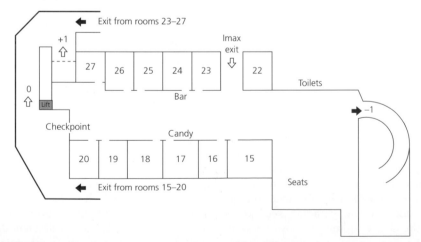

First floor (+1)

Figure 10.17 A plan of the Kinepolis cinema

Figure 10.18 A plan of the UCI cinema

The ticket office staff are continually aware of the remaining capacity of each screen through their terminals. There are up to four ticket desks open at any one time. The target time per overall transaction is 20 seconds, thus the maximum throughput is 12 sales per minute, or 720 per hour. The average number of ticket sales per transaction is 1.8, therefore the maximum seat sales per hour is 1300: easily within maximum expected demand levels. All tickets indicate specific seat positions, and these are allocated on a first-come-first-served basis. A central pre-booking facility is now offered by the UCI group, where customers can call a UK freephone number and order their tickets by credit card, for collection at their local cinema. Although there is a small charge for this service, the view is that the convenience will attract more users to purchase their tickets in this way and thus reduce the numbers queueing to pay for tickets on the night.

UCI's mission statement emphasizes the need to provide clean and tidy premises, cheerful staff, adequate food facilities, and above all, a high-quality film and sound presentation. UCI believes that it provides the best cinema experience outside London. ■

Questions

1 What are the main differences between the two cinemas from the perspectives of the operations managers?

2 What are the advantages and disadvantages of the two different methods of scheduling the films on to the screens? How does each approach affect different types of customers?

3 Group exercise

(a) Find out the running times and classification of eight popular films. Try to schedule these on to the UCI Solihull screens, taking account of what popularity you might expect at different times. You should allow at least 20 minutes for emptying and cleaning, 10 minutes for admitting the next audience, and 15 minutes for advertising, before the start of the film.

(b) Try to make an appointment to visit your local cinema to meet the manager. Compare the operations with those at Kinepolis and UCI, particularly in terms of scheduling.

DISCUSSION QUESTIONS

1 Identify the ways in which planning and control activity could reconcile supply and demand in the following operations:

- an ambulance service
- a medical centre
- a pizza-manufacturing company
- a national rail service
- a psychotherapy clinic
- a bespoke tailor.

2 What is the difference between dependent and independent demand?

3 To what extent is demand dependent or independent in the following types of operation:

- a manufacturer of nuclear-powered submarines
- a specialist catering company
- a fast-food hamburger restaurant
- a specialist packaging manufacturer who supplies a computer manufacturer
- a television production company?

4 How does scheduling affect the five performance objectives of operations management?

5 How might a police force schedule its officers so as to match its capacity to demand?

6 If you were a tutor at a local university, which sequencing rule would you use to determine the order in which you saw your students? What do you think are the advantages and disadvantages of each sequencing rule in this particular situation?

7 A painter of fake masterpieces has been commissioned to paint and frame five different paintings. Each of the paintings requires a different, but ornate, frame. The painter wishes to execute this commission as quickly as possible and has estimated the times for painting and framing the paintings as follows:

Van Gogh painting 2 hours; framing $4\frac{1}{2}$ hours
Monet painting 3 hours; framing $3\frac{1}{2}$ hours
Pollock painting 10 minutes; framing 1 hour
Renoir painting 4 hours; framing 2 hours
Picasso painting $1\frac{1}{2}$ hours; framing $4\frac{1}{2}$ hours

The painter has employed a specialist framer to join him on this enterprise. In what order should the pair tackle the paintings?

8 In the chapter, a description was given of the planning and control of a rock concert. How do you think these planning and control activities would change if the organization promoting the concert gave the same concert every week of the year?

9 Visit a local automotive service centre which carries out servicing and repairs on cars and find out the following:
(a) What is their approach to prioritizing jobs?
(b) What is the typical utilization of some of their equipment?
(c) How do they cope when a job takes longer than they expect?

10 What is the main difference between planning and controlling a hospital where the majority of surgical procedures are routine operations, and planning and controlling a hospital which has a very high level of accident and emergency work?

NOTES ON CHAPTER

1 Some specialist planning and control approaches are designed to organize operations around capacity bottle-necks. *See* the discussion on OPT in Chapter 14.

2 Source: Discussions with company staff.

3 For an interesting discussion of how these categories of planning and control can be modelled *see* Wild, R. (1988) *Production and Operations Management*, Cassell.

4 The concept of *P:D* ratios comes originally from Shingo, S. (1981) 'Study of Toyota Production Systems', Japan Management Association, and was extended by Mather, K. (1988) *Competitive Manufacturing*, Prentice Hall.

5 We are grateful to our colleague Paul Walley for this section.

6 Source: Walley, P. and Slack, N. (1994) MBA Course Notes, Warwick University, UK.

7 Johnson, S.M. (1954) 'Optimal Two-stage and Three-stage Production Schedules', *Naval Logistics Quarterly*, Vol 1, No 1.

SELECTED FURTHER READINGS

Baker, K.R. (1984) *Introduction to Sequencing and Scheduling*, John Wiley.

Browne, J.J. (1979) 'Simplified Scheduling of Routine Work Hours and Day Off', *Industrial Engineering*, Dec.

Conway, R.W. (1965) 'Priority Despatching and Job Lateness in a Job Shop', *Journal of Industrial Engineering*, Vol 16, No 4.

Fry, T.D. and Philipoom, P.R. (1989) 'A Despatching Rule for Allowing Trade-offs Between Inventory and Customer Satisfaction', *International Journal of Operations and Production Management*, Vol 9, No 7.

Goldratt, E.Y. and Cox, J. (1984) *The Goal*, North River Press.

Kanet, J.K. and Hayya, J.C. (1982) 'Priority Despatching with Operation Due Dates in a Job Shop,' *Journal of Operations Management*, Vol 2, No 3.

CAPACITY PLANNING AND CONTROL

INTRODUCTION

Providing the capability to satisfy current and future demand is a fundamental responsibility of operations management. An appropriate balance between capacity and demand can generate high profits and satisfied customers, whereas getting the balance 'wrong' can be potentially disastrous. Yet although planning for, and controlling, capacity is a major responsibility of operations managers, it should also involve other functional managers. There are three reasons for this. The first is that capacity decisions have a company-wide impact. The second is that all the other functions provide vital inputs to the planning process. The third is that each business function will usually have to plan and control the capacity of its own 'micro operations' to match that of the main operations function.

What we have called here *capacity planning and control* is also sometimes referred to as *aggregate planning and control*. This is because, at the 'highest level' of the planning and control process, demand and capacity calculations are usually performed on an aggregated basis which does not discriminate between the different products and services which an operation might produce. The essence of the task is to reconcile, at a general and aggregated level, the supply of capacity with the level of demand which it must satisfy (*see* Fig. 11.1).

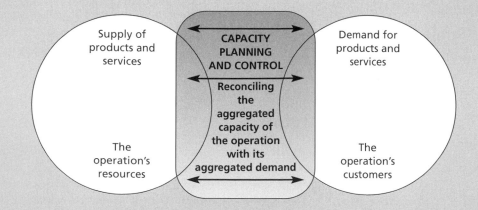

Figure 11.1 A definition of capacity planning and control

> ## CHAPTER 11: KEY QUESTIONS
>
> - *What is capacity planning and control?*
> - *Why is capacity planning and control important?*
> - *How is capacity measured?*
> - *What are the ways of coping with demand fluctuation?*
> - *How can operations plan their capacity level?*
> - *How can operations control their capacity level?*

WHAT IS CAPACITY?

The most common use of the word 'capacity' is in the static, physical sense of the fixed *volume* of a container, or the space in a building. This meaning of the word is also sometimes used by operations managers. For example, a pharmaceutical manufacturer may invest in new 1000-litre capacity reactor vessels, a property company purchases a 500-vehicle capacity city-centre car park, and a 'multiplex' cinema is built with ten screens and a total capacity of 2500 seats. Although these capacity measures describe the *scale* of these operations, they do not reflect the processing capacities of these investments. To do this we must incorporate a *time* dimension appropriate to the use of assets. So the pharmaceutical company will be concerned with the level of output that can be achieved using the 1000-litre reactor vessel. If a batch of standard products can be produced every hour, the planned processing capacity could be as high as 24 000 litres per day. If the reaction takes four hours, and two hours are used for cleaning between batches, the vessel may only produce 4000 litres per day. Similarly, the car park may be fully occupied by office workers during the working day, 'processing' only 500 cars per day. Alternatively it may be used for shoppers staying on average only one hour, and theatregoers occupying spaces for three hours in the evening. The processing capacity would then be up to 5000 cars per day. Thus the definition of the capacity of an operation is the *maximum level of value-added activity over a period of time* that the process can achieve under normal operating conditions.

Capacity constraints

Many organizations operate at below their maximum processing capacity, either because there is insufficient demand completely to 'fill' their capacity, or as a deliberate policy, so that the operation can respond quickly to every new order. Often though, organizations find themselves with some parts of their operation operating below their capacity while other parts are at their capacity 'ceiling'. It is the parts of the operation which are operating at their capacity 'ceiling' which are the *capacity constraint* for the whole operation.

The concept of one micro operation acting as the 'bottle-neck' constraint on capacity was introduced in Chapter 6. Depending on the nature of demand, different parts of an operation might be pushed to their capacity ceiling and act as a constraint on the total operation. For example, a retail superstore might offer a gift-wrapping service which at normal times can cope with all requests for its services without delaying customers unduly. At Christmas, however, the demand for gift wrapping might increase proportionally far more than the overall increase in custom for the store as a whole. Unless extra resources are provided to increase the capacity of this micro operation, it could constrain the capacity of the whole store.

PLANNING AND CONTROLLING CAPACITY

Capacity planning and control is the task of setting the effective capacity of the operation so that it can respond to the demands placed upon it. This usually means deciding how the operation should react to fluctuations in demand. We have faced this issue before in Chapter 6 where we examined long-term changes in demand and the alternative capacity strategies for dealing with the changes. These strategies were concerned with introducing (or deleting) major increments of physical capacity. We called this task *long-term capacity strategy*. In this chapter we are treating the shorter time- scale where capacity decisions are being made largely within the constraints of the physical capacity limits set by the operation's long-term capacity strategy.

Medium- and short-term capacity

Having established long-term capacity, operations managers must decide how to adjust the capacity of the operation in the *medium term*. This usually involves an assessment of the demand forecasts over a period of 2 to 18 months ahead, during which time planned output can be varied, for example, by changing the number of hours the equipment is used. In practice, however, few forecasts are accurate, and most operations also need to respond to changes in demand which occur over a shorter timescale. Hotels and restaurants have unexpected and apparently random changes in demand from night to night, but also know from experience that certain days are on average busier than others. So operations managers also have to make *short-term capacity adjustments*, which enable them to flex output for a short period, either on a predicted basis (for example, bank check-outs are always busy at lunchtimes) or at short notice (for example, a sunny warm day at a theme park).

Aggregate demand and capacity

The important characteristic of capacity planning and control, as we are treating it here, is that it is concerned with setting capacity levels over the medium and short terms in aggregated terms. That is, it is making overall, broad capacity decisions, but is not concerned with all of the detail of the individual products and services offered. Thus aggregate plans assume that the mix of different products and services will remain relatively constant during the planning period. Figure 11.2 shows how four operations might aggregate their capacity and demand levels.

391

**Figure 11.2
Examples of
aggregation in
capacity and
demand
measurement**

The objectives of capacity planning and control

The decisions taken by operations managers in devising their capacity plans will affect several different aspects of performance:

● *Costs* will be affected by the balance between capacity and demand (or output level if that is different). Capacity levels in excess of demand could mean under-utilization of capacity and therefore high unit cost.

● *Revenues* will also be affected by the balance between capacity and demand, but in the opposite way. Capacity levels equal to or higher than demand at any point in time will ensure that all demand is satisfied and no revenue lost.

● *Working capital* will be affected if an operation decides to build up finished goods inventory prior to demand. This might allow demand to be satisfied but the organization will have to fund the inventory until it can be sold.

● *Quality* of goods or services might be affected by a capacity plan which involved large fluctuations in capacity levels, by hiring temporary staff for example. The new staff and the disruption to the routine working of the operation could increase the probability of errors being made.

● *Speed* of response to customer demand could be enhanced, either by the build-up of inventories (allowing customers to be satisfied directly from the inventory rather than having to wait for items to be manufactured) or the deliberate provision of surplus capacity to avoid queueing.

● *Dependability* of supply will also be affected by how close demand levels are to capacity. The closer demand gets to the operation's capacity ceiling, the less able it is to cope with any unexpected disruptions and the less dependable its deliveries of goods and services could be.

● *Flexibility*, especially volume flexibility, will be enhanced by surplus capacity. If demand and capacity are in balance, the operation will not be able to respond to any unexpected increase in demand.

**Figure 11.3
The steps in
capacity planning
and control**

The steps of capacity planning and control

The sequence of capacity planning and control decisions which need to be taken by operations managers is illustrated in Fig. 11.3. Typically, operations managers are faced with a forecast of demand which is unlikely to be either certain or constant. They will also have some idea of their own ability to meet this demand. Nevertheless, before any further decisions are taken they must have quantitative data on both capacity and demand. So the first step will be to *measure the aggregate demand and capacity* levels for the planning period. The second step will be to *identify the alternative capacity plans* which could be adopted in response to the demand fluctuations. The third step will be to *choose the most appropriate capacity plan* for their circumstances.

MEASURING DEMAND AND CAPACITY

Forecasting demand fluctuations

In most organizations, demand forecasting is the responsibility of the sales and/or the marketing departments. However, it is a major input into the capacity planning and control decision which is usually an operations management responsibility. After all, without an estimate of future demand it is not possible to plan effectively for future events, only to react to them. It is therefore important for operations managers to understand the basis and rationale for these demand forecasts. Appendix 1 at the end of the book describes forecasting techniques. As far as capacity planning and control is concerned there are three requirements from a demand forecast.

It is expressed in terms which are useful for capacity planning and control

If forecasts are expressed only in money terms and give no indication of the demands that will be placed on an operation's capacity, they will need to be translated into realistic expectations of demand, expressed in the same units as the capacity (e.g machine hours per year, operatives required, space, etc.).

It is as accurate as possible

In capacity planning and control the accuracy of a forecast is important because, whereas demand can change instantaneously, there is a lag between deciding to change capacity and the change taking effect. Thus many operations managers are faced with a dilemma. In order to attempt to meet demand they must often decide output in advance, based on a forecast which might change before the demand occurs, or worse prove not to reflect actual demand at all.

It gives an indication of relative uncertainty

Decisions to operate extra hours and recruit extra staff are usually based on forecast levels of demand, which could in practice differ considerably from actual demand, leading to unnecessary costs or unsatisfactory customer service. For example, Fig. 11.4 shows the average demand levels of a supermarket throughout one day in terms of the number of customers entering the store. Demand is initially slow but then builds up to a lunchtime rush. After this, demand slows only to build up again for the early evening rush, and finally falls again at the end of trading. The supermarket manager can use this forecast to adjust (say) check-out capacity throughout the day. But although this may be an accurate average demand forecast, no single day will exactly conform to this pattern. Of equal importance is an estimate of how much actual demand could differ from the average. This can be found by examining demand statistics to build up a distribution of demand at each point in the day. The importance of this is that the manager now has an understanding of when it will be important to have reserve staff, perhaps filling shelves on call to staff the check-outs should demand warrant it. Generally, the advantage of probabilistic forecasts such as this is that it allows operations managers to make a judgement between possible plans that would virtually

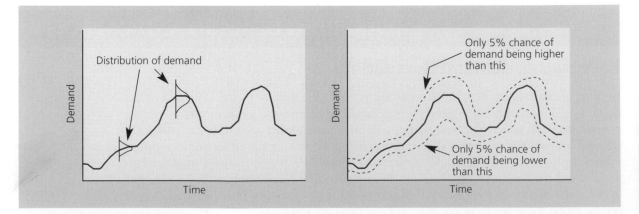

Figure 11.4 Good forecasts are essential for effective capacity planning, but so is an understanding of demand uncertainty because it allows the operation to judge the risks to service level

guarantee the operation's ability to meet actual demand, and plans that minimize costs. Ideally, this judgement should be influenced by the nature of the way the business wins orders: price-sensitive markets may require a risk-avoiding cost minimization plan, that does not always satisfy peak demand, whereas markets that value responsiveness and service quality may justify a more generous provision of operational capacity.

Seasonality of demand

In many organizations capacity planning and control is concerned largely with coping with seasonal demand fluctuations. Almost all products and services have some *seasonality of demand* and some also have *seasonality of supply*, usually where the inputs are seasonal agricultural products – for example, in processing frozen vegetables. These fluctuations in demand, or in supply, may be reasonably forecastable, but some are usually also affected by unexpected variations in the weather, and by changing economic conditions. Figure 11.5 gives some examples of seasonality.

Consider the four organizations previously referred to in Fig. 11.2. Their demand patterns are shown in Fig. 11.6. The woollen knitwear business and the city hotel both have seasonal sales demand patterns, but for different reasons: the woollen knitwear business because of climatic patterns (cold winters, warm summers) and the hotel because of demand from business people, who take vacations from work at Christmas and in the summer. The retail supermarket is a little less seasonal, but is affected by pre-vacation peaks, and reduced sales during vacation periods. The aluminium producer shows virtually no seasonality, but is showing a steady growth in sales over the forecast period.

Weekly and daily demand fluctuations

Seasonality of demand occurs over a year, but similar predictable variations in demand can also occur for some products and services on a shorter cycle. We have already illustrated the daily demand pattern of a supermarket in Fig. 11.4, and it will

Figure 11.5 Many types of operation have to cope with seasonal demand

Figure 11.6 Aggregate demand fluctuations for four organizations

also be subjected to predictable demand fluctuations over a week. Demand might be low on Monday and Tuesday, build up during the latter part of the week and reach a peak on Friday and Saturday. Banks, public offices, telephone sales organizations and electricity utilities all have weekly and daily or even hourly demand patterns which require capacity adjustment. The extent to which an operation will have to cope with very short-term demand fluctuations is partly determined by how long its customers are prepared to wait for their products or services. An operation whose customers are incapable of, or unwilling to, wait will have to plan for very short-term demand fluctuations. Emergency services, for example, will need to understand the hourly variation in the demand for their services and plan capacity accordingly. Similarly, the order-taking department of a catalogue retailer must be able to answer customers' telephone enquiries within a few rings of the telephone. If they cannot, the probability of the customer hanging up increases significantly.

Measuring capacity

The main problem with measuring capacity is the complexity of most operations. Only when the operation is highly standardized and repetitive is capacity easy to define unambiguously. So if a television factory produces only one basic model, the weekly capacity could be described as 2000 Model A televisions. A government office may have the capacity to print and post 500 000 tax forms per week. A fast ride at a theme park might be designed to process batches of 60 people every three minutes – a

Table 11.1 Input and output capacity measures for different operations

Operation	Input measure of capacity	Output measure of capacity
Air-conditioner plant	Machine hours available	**Number of units per week**
Hospital	**Beds available**	Number of patients treated per week
Theatre	**Number of seats**	Number of customers entertained per week
University	**Number of students**	Students graduated per year
Retail store	**Sales floor area**	Number of items sold per day
Airline	**Number of seats available on the sector**	Number of passengers per week
Electricity company	Generator size	**Megawatts of electricity generated**
Brewery	Volume of fermentation tanks	**Litres per week**

(Note: The most commonly used measure is shown in bold.)

capacity to transform 1200 people per hour. In each case, the *output* is the most appropriate measure of capacity because the output from the operation does not vary in its nature. For many operations, however, the definition of capacity is not so obvious. Especially when a much wider range of outputs places varying demands on the process, output measures of capacity are less useful. Here *input* measures are frequently used to define capacity. Almost every type of operation could use a mixture of both input or output measures, but in practice, most choose to use one or the other (*see* Table 11.1).

Capacity depends on activity mix

The hospital measures its capacity in terms of its resources, partly because there is not a clear relationship between the number of beds it has and the number of patients which it treats. If all its patients required relatively minor treatment with only short stays in hospital, it could treat many people per week. Alternatively, if most of its patients require long periods of observation or recuperation it will treat far fewer. Output depends on the mix of activities in which the hospital is engaged and, because most hospitals perform many different types of activities, output is difficult to predict. Certainly it is difficult to compare directly the capacity of hospitals which have very different activities.

Example

Suppose an air-conditioner factory produces three different models of air-conditioner unit: the deluxe, the standard and the economy. The deluxe model can be assembled in 1.5 hours, the standard in 1 hour and the economy in 0.75 hours. The assembly area in the factory has 800 staff hours of assembly time available each week.

If demand for deluxe, standard and economy units is in the ratio 2:3:2, the time needed to assemble 2 + 3 + 2 = 7 units is:

$$(2 \times 1.5) + (3 \times 1) + (2 \times 0.75) \quad = \quad 7.5 \text{ hours}$$

The number of units produced per week is:

$$\frac{800}{7.5} \times 7 = 746.7 \text{ units}$$

If demand changes to a ratio of deluxe, economy, standard units of 1:2:4, the time needed to assemble $1 + 2 + 4 = 7$ units is:

$$(1 \times 1.5) + (2 \times 1) + (4 \times 0.75) = 6.5 \text{ hours}$$

Now the number of units produced per week is:

$$\frac{800}{6.5} \times 7 = 861.5 \text{ units}$$

Design capacity and effective capacity

The theoretical capacity of an operation – the capacity which its technical designers had in mind when they commissioned the operation – cannot always be achieved in practice. For example, a company coating photographic paper will have several coating lines which deposit thin layers of chemicals on to rolls of paper at high speed. Each line will be capable of running at a particular speed. Multiplying the maximum coating speed by the operating time of the plant gives the *theoretical design capacity* of the line. But in reality the line cannot be run continuously at its maximum rate. Different products will have different coating requirements, so the line will need to be stopped while it is changed over. Maintenance will need to be performed on the line which will take out further productive time. Technical scheduling difficulties might mean further lost time. Not all of these losses are the operations manager's fault; they have occurred because of the market and technical demands on the operation. The actual capacity which remains, after such losses are accounted for, is called the *effective capacity* of operation. Not that these causes of reduction in capacity will be the only losses in the operation. Such factors as quality problems, machine breakdowns, absenteeism and other avoidable problems will all take their toll. This means that the *actual output* of the line will be even lower than the effective capacity. The ratio of the output actually achieved by an operation to design capacity, and the ratio of output to effective capacity are called respectively the *utilization* and the *efficiency* of the plant.

$$\text{Utilization} = \frac{\text{Actual output}}{\text{Design capacity}}$$

$$\text{Efficiency} = \frac{\text{Actual output}}{\text{Effective capacity}}$$

Example

Suppose the photographic paper manufacturer has a coating line, the design capacity of which is 200 square metres per minute and the line is operated on a 24-hour day, 7 days per week (168 hours per week) basis.

Design capacity is $200 \times 60 \times 24 \times 7 = 2.016$ million square metres per week. The records for a week's production show the following lost production time:

1 Product change-overs (set-ups)   20 hrs
2 Regular preventative maintenance   16 hrs
3 No work scheduled   8 hrs
4 Quality sampling checks   8 hrs
5 Shift change times   7 hrs
6 Maintenance breakdown   18 hrs
7 Quality failure investigation   20 hrs
8 Coating material stockouts   8 hrs
9 Labour shortages   6 hrs
10 Waiting for paper rolls   6 hrs

During this week the actual output was only 582 000 square metres.

The first five categories of lost production occur as a consequence of reasonably unavoidable, planned occurrences and amount to a total of 59 hours. The last five categories are unplanned, and avoidable, losses and amount to 58 hours.
Measured in hours of production, and illustrated in Fig. 11.7:

Design capacity   = 168 hours per week

Effective capacity   = 168 − 59   = 109 hrs

Actual output   = 168 − 59 − 58   = 51 hrs

$$\text{Utilization} = \frac{\text{Actual output}}{\text{Design capacity}} = \frac{51 \text{ hrs}}{168 \text{ hrs}} = 0.304$$

$$\text{Efficiency} = \frac{\text{Actual output}}{\text{Effective capacity}} = \frac{51 \text{ hrs}}{109 \text{ hrs}} = 0.468$$

Figure 11.7
Utilization and efficiency

Utilization as a measure of operations performance

For many businesses, utilization is used as one of the key measures of the performance of the operation. It is an indication of the proportion of the designed capacity that has been used to produce value-added goods or services. The justification for placing such importance on utilization is usually that any lost production time could have been used to produce more outputs which would generate more profit (this is called the 'opportunity cost' argument). Many organizations require high utilization levels before they will authorize investment in additional capacity. Utilization may be known by different names in different industries. For example:

● the 'room occupancy level' in hotels;
● the 'load factor' for aircraft seats;
● 'uptime' in some factories.

Unfortunately, as a measure of an operation's performance, it can be misleading. Low utilization could result either from low demand, or because the plant is frequently breaking down, or running out of materials. Hence, it is measuring the performance of many parts of the business rather than operations alone. Nor is seeking high utilization always desirable. Particularly in batch-type operations, an emphasis on high utilization can result in the build-up of in-process inventories. This is discussed further in Chapter 15 on just-in-time planning and control. High utilization can also adversely affect the customer if it reduces the speed and volume flexibility of the overall operation. Popular, high utilization ATMs at banks will frequently be accompanied by long queues. High runway utilization at airports during the morning and evening commuter rush results in aircraft 'stacking' which wastes fuel and delays passengers. Occasionally, however, high utilization is seen favourably by customers: live rock music events and dance clubs, for example, are enhanced by a full crowd.

THE ALTERNATIVE CAPACITY PLANS

With an understanding of both demand and capacity, the next step is to consider the alternative methods of responding to demand fluctuations. There are three 'pure' options available for coping with such variation:

● Ignore the fluctuations and keep activity levels constant (*level capacity plan*).
● Adjust capacity to reflect the fluctuations in demand (*chase demand plan*).
● Attempt to change demand to fit capacity availability (*demand management*).

In practice most organizations will use a mixture of all of these 'pure' plans, although often one plan might dominate.

Level capacity plan

In a level capacity plan, the processing capacity is set at a uniform level through-out the planning period, regardless of the fluctuations in forecast demand. This means that the same number of staff operate the same processes and should therefore be capable of producing the same aggregate output in each period. Where non-perishable materials

BRITVIC SOFT DRINKS[1]

The Britvic Soft Drinks canning operation at Rugby, central England, is one of the highest capacity and most automated factories of its type in Europe, supplying the market with a range of Britvic drinks such as Tango, and also canning and distributing Pepsi Cola. The factory is linked by underground conveyor to Continental Can's can-making operation on an adjacent site, which also supplies vast quantities of cans every day to other drinks manufacturers.

The operations manager, Bob Pursley, emphasizes the enormous potential output of the plant.

'We have four state-of-the-art high-speed canning lines, each producing 1500 cans per minute, giving a combined output of 6000 cans per minute. Our theoretical capacity over a 24-hour period, with no change-overs or downtime, would equate to an incredible 8.5 million cans, which would then occupy 1000 square metres of warehouse space to a height of 4.5 metres. These products are bulky and have a limited shelf life. We have only enough space for five days' output, so we need to respond rapidly in production to fluctuation in demand.

'In Northern Europe, the consumption of canned drinks is always seasonal, especially in the UK where the biggest problem is the unpredictability of the weather! A few very hot and sunny days have a dramatic effect on demand and we must respond without delay or we would run out of stock of many of our products within days. The way that we run the factory addresses both seasonality and the shorter-term weather-related fluctuations. The canning lines are normally run 24 hours a day, as adjacent pairs, a system we call 'back-to-back', so that a crew of employees can operate one line (in periods of predicted low demand) or almost instantly two, to meet peak

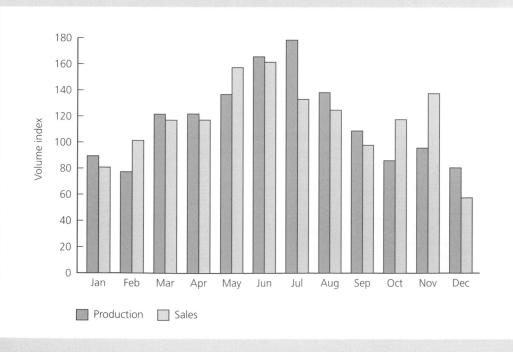

Figure 11.8 Britvic drinks – sales and production (index of 100 = previous year's average sales)

demand. In hot weather, we can also boost production by up to 40 per cent for a period with no change in the numbers of employees. This is achieved by changing from five to seven days a week, thanks to the co-operation of our employees. This arrangement can boost capacity to around 40 million cans a week, but there are obviously limits to the length of time that is possible, as everyone needs a break, eventually. In periods of lower demand, particularly in winter, staff are switched into training and development activities. We don't need the maximum capacity, so we utilize some of the time to train, develop and prepare employees to cope more effectively in the following summer peak. Employees are also encouraged to take some of their annual leave in the winter. Major maintenance projects are planned for completion during these quiet periods and smaller, more routine maintenance in short blocks of time is carried out in the summer to minimize the impact on productive time.'

Figure 11.8 indicates how production volumes and sales at the Britvic plant vary throughout the year. ■

Questions

1 What are the factors which seem to influence the demand fluctuation for this operation?

2 How does the company vary its output levels?

3 The company 'chases demand' rather than using a 'level capacity' strategy or a 'change demand' strategy (*see* pp. 400–8 for further information on these topics). Why do you think this is?

Source: By kind permission of Britvic Soft Drinks Ltd

are processed, but not immediately sold, they can be transferred to finished goods inventory in anticipation of sales at a later time period. Thus this plan is feasible (but not necessarily desirable) for our examples of the woollen knitwear company and the aluminium producer (*see* Fig. 11.9).

Figure 11.9 Level capacity plans which use anticipation inventory to supply future demand

Level capacity plans of this type can achieve the objectives of stable employment patterns, high process utilization, and usually also high productivity with low unit costs. Unfortunately, they can also create considerable inventory which has to be financed and stored. Perhaps the biggest problem, however, is that decisions have to be taken as to what to produce for inventory rather than for immediate sale. Will green woollen sweaters knitted in July still be fashionable in October? Could a particular aluminium alloy in a specific sectional shape still be sold months after it has been produced? Most firms operating this plan, therefore, give priority to only creating inventory where future sales are relatively certain and unlikely to be affected by changes in fashion or design. Clearly, such plans are not suitable for 'perishable' products such as foods, some pharmaceuticals, and for products where fashion changes rapidly and unpredictably (for example, popular music CDs, young people's clothing), or where products are tailor-made against specific customer requirements.

A level capacity plan could also be used by the hotel and supermarket, although this would not be the usual approach of such organizations, because it usually results in a waste of staff resources, reflected in low productivity. Because service cannot be stored as inventory, a level capacity plan would involve running the operation at a uniformly high level of capacity availability. The hotel would employ sufficient staff to service all the rooms, to run a full restaurant, and to staff the reception even in months when demand was expected to be well below capacity. Similarly, the supermarket would plan to staff all the check-outs, warehousing operations, and so on, even in quiet periods (*see* Fig. 11.10).

Very high under-utilization levels can make level capacity plans prohibitively expensive in many service operations, but may be considered appropriate where the opportunity costs of individual lost sales are very high: for example, in the high-margin retailing of jewellery and in (real) estate agents. It is also possible to set the capacity somewhat below the forecast peak demand level in order to reduce the degree of under-utilization. However, in the periods where demand is expected to exceed planned capacity, customer service may deteriorate. Customers may have to queue for long periods or may be 'processed' faster and less sensitively. While this is obviously far from ideal, the benefits to the organization of stability and productivity may outweigh the disadvantages of upsetting some customers.

Figure 11.10 Level capacity plans with under-utilization of capacity

Chase demand plan

The opposite of a level capacity plan is one which attempts to match capacity closely to the varying levels of forecast demand. This is much more difficult to achieve than a level capacity plan, as different numbers of staff, different working hours, and even different amounts of equipment may be necessary in each period. For this reason, pure chase demand plans are unlikely to appeal to operations which manufacture standard, non-perishable products. Also, where manufacturing operations are particularly capital-intensive, the chase demand policy would require a level of physical capacity, all of which would only be used occasionally. It is for this reason that such a plan is less likely to be appropriate for the aluminium producer than for the woollen garment manufacturer (*see* Fig. 11.11). A pure chase demand plan is more usually adopted by operations which cannot store their output, such as customer-processing operations or manufacturers of perishable products. It avoids the wasteful provision of excess staff that occurs with a level capacity plan, and yet should satisfy customer demand throughout the planned period. Where output can be stored, the chase demand policy might be adopted in order to minimize or eliminate finished goods inventory.

Sometimes it is difficult to achieve very large variations in capacity from period to period. If the changes in forecast demand are as large as those in the hotel example (*see* Fig. 11.12), significantly different levels of staffing will be required throughout the year. This would mean employing part-time and temporary staff, requiring permanent employees to work longer hours, or even bringing in contract labour. The operations managers will then have the difficult task of ensuring that quality standards and safety procedures are still adhered to, and that the customer service levels are maintained.

Methods of adjusting capacity

The chase demand approach requires that capacity is adjusted by some means. There are a number of different methods of achieving this, although all may not be feasible for all types of operation. Some of these methods are listed below:

Figure 11.11 Chase demand capacity plans with changes in capacity which reflect demand change

Figure 11.12 Chase demand capacity plans with changes in capacity which reflect demand change

Overtime and idle time

Often the quickest and most convenient method of adjusting capacity is by varying the number of productive hours worked by the staff in the operation. When demand is higher than nominal capacity, the working day may be extended, and when demand is lower than nominal capacity the amount of time spent by staff on productive work can be reduced. In the latter case it may be possible for staff to engage in some other activity such as cleaning or maintenance. This method is only useful if the timing of the extra productive capacity matches that of the demand. For example, there is little to be gained in asking a retail operation's staff to work extra hours in the evening if all the extra demand is occurring during their normal working period. The costs asso-ciated with this method are either the extra payment which is normally necessary to secure the agreement of staff to work overtime, or in the case of idle time, the costs of paying staff who are not engaged in direct productive work. Further, there might be costs associated with the fixed costs of keeping the operation heated, lit and secure over the extra period staff are working. There is also a limit to the amount of extra working time which any workforce can deliver before productivity levels decrease.

Varying the size of the workforce

If capacity is largely governed by workforce size, one way to adjust capacity is to adjust the size of the workforce. This is done by hiring extra staff during periods of high demand and laying them off as demand falls. However, there are cost and ethical implications to be taken into account before adopting such a method. The costs of hiring extra staff include those associated with recruitment, as well as the costs of low productivity while new staff go through the learning curve. The costs of lay-off may include possible severance payments, but might also include the loss of morale in the operation and loss of goodwill in the local labour market. At a micro operation level, one method of coping with peaks in demand in one area of an operation is to build sufficient flexibility into job design and job demarcation so that staff can transfer across from less busy parts of the operation. For example, the French hotel chain Novotel has trained some of its kitchen staff to escort customers from the reception area up to their rooms. The peak times for registering new customers coincide with the least busy times in the kitchen and restaurant areas.

Using part-time staff

A variation on the previous strategy is to recruit staff on a part-time basis, that is for less than the normal working day. This method is extensively used in service operations such as supermarkets and fast-food restaurants but is also used by some manufacturers to staff an evening shift after the normal working day. However, if the fixed costs of employment for each employee, irrespective of how long they work, are high then using this method may not be worthwhile.

Sub-contracting

In periods of high demand an operation might buy capacity from other organizations. This might enable the operation to meet its own demand without the extra expense of investing in capacity which will not be needed after the peak in demand has passed. Again, there are costs associated with this method. The most obvious one is that sub-contracting can be very expensive. The sub-contractor will also want to make sufficient margin out of the business. A sub-contractor may not be as motivated to deliver on time or to the desired levels of quality. Finally, there is the risk that the sub-contractors might themselves decide to enter the same market.

Manage demand

Stable and uniform demand could allow an organization to reduce costs *and* improve service; capacity could be better utilized, and profit potential could be enhanced. Many organizations have recognized these benefits, and attempt to 'manage demand' in various ways. The objective is to transfer customer demand from peak periods to quiet periods. This is usually beyond the immediate responsibility of operations managers, being the responsibility of marketing and/or sales functions. The primary role of the operations manager is, therefore, to identify and evaluate the benefits of demand management, and to ensure that the resulting changes in demand can be satisfactorily met by the operations system. One method of managing demand is to *change demand*; more radical policies may create *alternative products or services* to fill capacity in quiet periods.

Change demand

The most obvious mechanism to change demand is through price. Although this is probably the most widely applied approach in demand management, it is less common for products than services. For example, some city hotels offer low-cost 'city break' vacation packages in the months when fewer business visitors are expected. Skiing and camping holidays are cheapest at the beginning and end of the season and are particularly expensive during school vacations. Discounts are given by photo-processing firms during winter periods, but never around summer holidays. Ice-cream is 'on offer' in many supermarkets during the winter. The objective is invariably to stimulate off-peak demand and to constrain peak demand, in order to smooth demand as much as possible. Organizations can also attempt to increase demand in low periods by appropriate advertising. For example, turkey growers in the UK and the USA make vigorous attempts to promote their products at times other than Christmas and Thanksgiving.

WORKING BY THE YEAR[2]

One method of fluctuating capacity as demand varies throughout the year without many of the costs associated with overtime or hiring temporary staff is called the Annual Hours Work Plan. This involves staff contracting to work a set number of hours per year rather than a set number of hours per week. The advantage of this is that the amount of staff time available to an organization can be varied throughout the year to reflect the real state of demand. For example, Figure 11.13 shows the total number of hours worked by staff in a photo-processing company throughout the year.

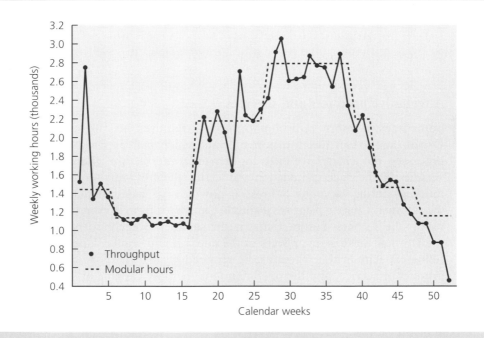

Figure 11.13 The use of annualized hours to reflect seasonal demand at a photo-processing company

Source: From Lynch, P. (1991) 'Making Time for Productivity', *Personnel Management*, March, reproduced with permission

Annual hours plans can also be useful when supply varies throughout the year. For example, a UK cheese factory of Express Foods, like all cheese factories, must cope with processing very different quantities of milk at different times of the year. In spring and during early summer cows produce large quantities of milk, but in late summer and autumn the supply of milk slows to a trickle. Before the introduction of annualized hours, the factory had relied on overtime and hiring temporary workers during the busy season. Now the staff are contracted to work a set number of hours a year with rotas agreed more than a year in advance and after consultation with the union. This means that at the end of July staff broadly know exactly what days and hours they will be working until the September of the next year. If an emergency should arise, the company can call in from a group of 'super crew' who work more flexible hours in return for higher pay but can do any job in the factory.

However, not all experiments with annualized hours have been as successful. Especially when demand is very unpredictable, staff can be asked to come in to work at very short notice. This can cause considerable disruption to social and family life. For example, at ITN, a UK news-broadcasting company, the scheme caused some initial problems. Some journalists and camera crew who went to cover the Gulf War found that they had worked so many hours that they were asked to take the whole of one month off to compensate. Since they had no holiday plans, many would have preferred to work. ■

Question

1 What do you see as being the major advantages and disadvantages both to the company and to the staff of adopting the Annual Hours Work Plan?

Alternative products and services

Sometimes, a more radical approach is required to fill low demand periods. Organizations can develop new outputs which can be produced on the existing processes, but which have different demand patterns throughout the year. Most universities fill their accommodation and lecture theatres with conferences and company meetings during vacations. Ski resorts provide organized mountain activity holidays in the summer. Charter planes that shuttle Canadians from Toronto to Florida in the winter ply the Toronto–Europe routes in the summer. Some garden tractor companies in the US now make snow movers in the autumn and winter. The apparent benefits of filling capacity in this way must be weighed against the risks of damaging the core product or service, and the operation must be fully capable of serving both markets. Some universities have been criticized for providing sub-standard, badly decorated accommodation which met the needs of impecunious undergraduates, but which failed to impress executives at a trade conference.

Mixed plans

Each of the three 'pure' plans is applied only where its advantages strongly outweigh its disadvantages. For many organizations, however, these 'pure' approaches do not match their required combination of competitive and operational objectives. Most operations managers are required simultaneously to reduce costs and inventory, to minimize capital investment, and yet to provide a responsive and customer-oriented approach at all times. For this reason, most organizations choose to follow a mixture of the three approaches. This can be best illustrated by the woollen knitwear company example in Fig. 11.14. Here some of the peak demand has been brought forward by the company offering discounts to selected retail customers (manage demand plan). Capacity has also been adjusted at two points in the year to reflect the broad changes in demand (chase demand plan). Yet the adjustment in capacity is not sufficient to avoid totally the build up of inventories (level capacity plan).

GETTING THE MESSAGE[3]

Companies which traditionally operate in seasonal markets can demonstrate some considerable ingenuity in their attempts to develop counter-seasonal products. One of the most successful industries in this respect has been the greetings card industry. Mother's Day, Father's Day, Hallowe'en, Valentine's Day, and other occasions have all been promoted as times to send (and buy) appropriately designed cards. Now, having run out of occasions to promote, greetings card manufacturers have moved on to 'non-occasion' cards, which can be sent at any time. These have the considerable advantage of being less seasonal, thus making the companies' seasonality less marked.

Hallmark Cards, the market leader in North America, has been the pioneer in developing non-occasion cards. Their cards include those intended to be sent from parent to child with messages such as, 'Would a hug help?' or, 'Sorry I made you feel bad', and 'You're perfectly wonderful – it's your room that's a mess'. Other cards deal with more serious adult themes such as friendship ('You're more than a friend, you're just like family') or even alcoholism ('This is hard to say, but I think you're a much neater person when you're not drinking'). Whatever else these products may be, they are not seasonal! ■

Questions

1 What seem to be the advantages and disadvantages of the strategy adopted by Hallmark Cards?

2 What else could it do to cope with demand fluctuations?

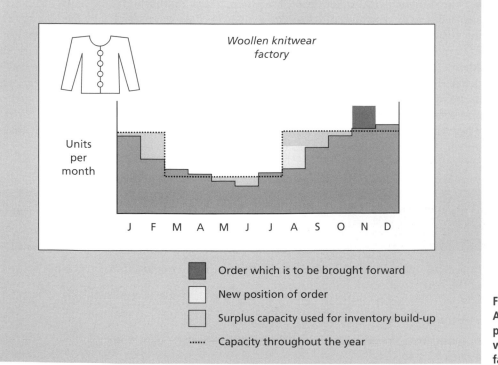

Figure 11.14 A mixed capacity plan for the woollen knitwear factory

409

Yield management

In operations which have relatively fixed capacities, such as airlines and hotels, it is important to use the capacity of the operation for generating revenue to its full potential. One approach used by such operations is called *yield management*.[4] This is really a collecting of methods, some of which we have already discussed, which can be used to ensure that an operation maximizes its potential to generate profit. Yield management is especially useful where:

- capacity is relatively fixed;
- the market can be fairly clearly segmented;
- the service cannot be stored in any way;
- the services are sold in advance;
- the marginal cost of making a sale is relatively low.

Airlines, for example, fit all these criteria. They adopt a collection of methods to try to maximize the yield (i.e. profit) from their capacity. These include the following:

- *Over-booking capacity.* Not every passenger who has booked a place on a flight will actually show up for the flight. If the airline did not fill this seat it would lose the revenue from it. Because of this, airlines regularly book more passengers on to flights than the capacity of the aircraft can cope with. If they over-book by the exact number of passengers who fail to show up, they have maximized their revenue under the circumstances. Of course, if more passengers show up than they expect, the airline will have a number of upset passengers to deal with (although they may be able to offer financial inducements for the passengers to take another flight). If they fail to over-book sufficiently, they will have empty seats. By studying past data on flight demand, airlines try to balance the risks of over-booking and under-booking.
- *Price discounting.* At quiet times, when demand is unlikely to fill capacity, airlines will also sell heavily discounted tickets to agents who then themselves take the risk of finding customers for them. In effect this is using the price mechanism to affect demand.
- *Varying service types.* Discounting and other methods of affecting demand are also adjusted depending on the demand for particular types of service. For example, the relative demand for first-, business-, and economy-class seats varies throughout the year. There is no point discounting tickets in a class for which demand will be high. Yield management also tries to adjust the availability of the different classes of seat to reflect their demand. They will also vary the number of seats available in each class by upgrading or even changing the configuration of airline seats (*see* box in Chapter 4 on the new Boeing 777).

CHOOSING A CAPACITY PLANNING AND CONTROL APPROACH

Before an operation can decide which of the capacity plans to adopt, it must be aware of the consequences of adopting each plan in its own set of circumstances. Two methods are particularly useful in helping to assess the consequences of adopting particular capacity plans:

- cumulative representations of demand and capacity;
- queueing theory.

Cumulative representations

Figure 11.15 shows the forecast aggregated demand for a chocolate factory which makes confectionery products. Demand for its products in the shops is greatest at Christmas. To meet this demand and allow time for the products to work their way through the distribution system, the factory must supply a demand which peaks in September, as shown. One method of assessing whether a particular level of capacity can satisfy the demand would be to calculate the degree of over-capacity below the graph which represents the capacity levels (areas A and C) and the degree of under-capacity above the graph (area B). If the total over-capacity is greater than the total under-capacity for a particular level of capacity, then that capacity could be regarded as adequate to satisfy demand fully, the assumption being that inventory has been accumulated in the periods of over-capacity.

However, there are two problems with this approach. The first is that each month shown in Fig. 11.15 may not have the same amount of productive time. Some months (August, for example) may contain vacation periods which reduce the availability of capacity. The second problem is that a capacity level which seems adequate may only be able to supply products *after* the demand for them has occurred. For example, if the period of under-capacity occured at the beginning of the year, no inventory could have accumulated to meet demand. A far superior way of assessing capacity plans is first to plot demand on a *cumulative* basis. This is shown as the thicker line in Fig. 11.16.

The cumulative representation of demand immediately reveals more information. First, it shows that although total demand peaks in September, because of the restricted number of available productive days, the peak demand per productive day occurs a month earlier in August. Second, it shows that the fluctuation in demand over the year is even greater than it seemed. The ratio of monthly peak demand to monthly lowest demand is 6.5:1, but the ratio of peak to lowest demand per productive day is 10:1. Demand per productive day is more relevant to operations managers because productive days represent the time element of capacity.

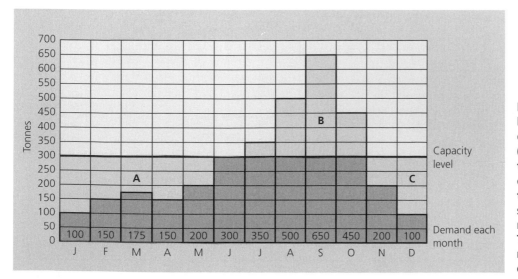

Figure 11.15
If the over-capacity areas (A+C) are greater than the under-capacity area (B) the capacity level seems adequate to meet demand. This may not necessarily be the case, however

411

The most useful consequence of plotting demand on a cumulative basis is that, by plotting capacity on the same graph, the feasibility and consequences of a capacity plan can be assessed. Figure 11.16 also shows a level capacity plan which produces at a rate of 14.03 tonnes per productive day. This meets cumulative demand by the end of the year. It would also pass our earlier test of total over-capacity being the same or greater than under-capacity.

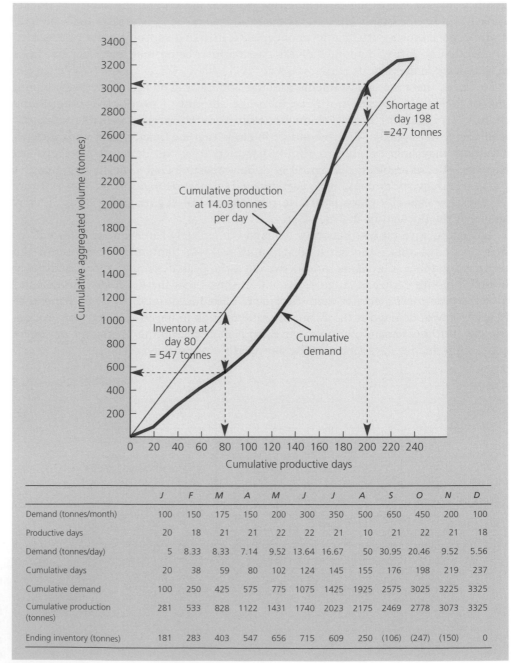

	J	F	M	A	M	J	J	A	S	O	N	D
Demand (tonnes/month)	100	150	175	150	200	300	350	500	650	450	200	100
Productive days	20	18	21	21	22	22	21	10	21	22	21	18
Demand (tonnes/day)	5	8.33	8.33	7.14	9.52	13.64	16.67	50	30.95	20.46	9.52	5.56
Cumulative days	20	38	59	80	102	124	145	155	176	198	219	237
Cumulative demand	100	250	425	575	775	1075	1425	1925	2575	3025	3225	3325
Cumulative production (tonnes)	281	533	828	1122	1431	1740	2023	2175	2469	2778	3073	3325
Ending inventory (tonnes)	181	283	403	547	656	715	609	250	(106)	(247)	(150)	0

Figure 11.16
A level capacity plan which produces shortages in spite of meeting demand at the end of the year

However, if one of the aims of the plan is to supply demand when it occurs, the plan is inadequate. Up to around day 168 the line representing cumulative production is above that representing cumulative demand. This means that at any time during this period more product has been produced by the factory than has been demanded from it. In fact the vertical distance between the two lines is the level of inventory at that point in time. So by day 80, 1122 tonnes have been produced but only 575 tonnes demanded. The surplus of production above demand, or inventory, is therefore 547 tonnes. When the cumulative demand line lies above the cumulative production line, the reverse is true. The vertical distance between the two lines now indicates the shortage, or lack of supply. So by day 198, 3025 tonnes have been demanded but only 2778 tonnes produced. The shortage is therefore 247 tonnes.

For any capacity plan to meet demand as it occurs, its cumulative production line must always lie above the cumulative demand line. This makes it a straightforward task to judge the adequacy of a plan, simply by looking at its cumulative representation. An impression of the inventory implications can also be gained from a cumulative representation by judging the area between the cumulative production and demand curves. This represents the amount of inventory carried over the period. Figure 11.17 illustrates an adequate level capacity plan for the chocolate manufacturer, together with the costs of carrying inventory. It is assumed that inventory costs £2 per tonne per day to keep in storage. The average inventory each month is taken to be the average of the beginning and end-of-month inventory levels, and the inventory carrying cost each month is the product of the average inventory, the inventory cost per day per tonne and the number of days in the month.

Comparing plans on a cumulative basis

Chase demand plans can also be illustrated on a cumulative representation. Rather than the cumulative production line having a constant gradient, it would have a varying gradient representing the production rate at any point in time. If a pure demand chase plan was adopted, the cumulative production line would match the cumulative demand line. The gap between the two lines would be zero and hence inventory would be zero. Although this would eliminate inventory carrying costs, as we discussed earlier, there would be costs associated with changing capacity levels. These *capacity change costs* are sometimes drawn as shown in Fig. 11.18. The cost of a capacity change depends on the degree of change, the direction of the change, and the capacity level from which the change is being made. Usually, the marginal cost of making a capacity change increases the greater the change. For example, if the chocolate manufacturer wishes to increase capacity by five per cent, this can be achieved by requesting its staff to work overtime – a simple, fast and relatively inexpensive option. If the change is 15 per cent, overtime cannot provide sufficient extra capacity and temporary staff will need to be employed – a more expensive solution which also would take more time. Increases in capacity of above 15 per cent might only be achieved by sub-contracting some work out. This would be even more expensive. The cost of the change will also be affected by the point from which the change is being made, as well as the direction of the change. Usually, it is less expensive to change capacity towards what is regarded as the 'normal' capacity level than away from it.

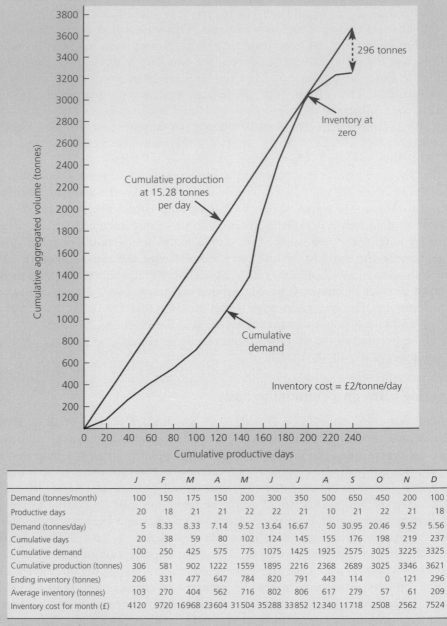

Figure 11.17
A level capacity plan which meets demand at all times during the year

	J	F	M	A	M	J	J	A	S	O	N	D
Demand (tonnes/month)	100	150	175	150	200	300	350	500	650	450	200	100
Productive days	20	18	21	21	22	22	21	10	21	22	21	18
Demand (tonnes/day)	5	8.33	8.33	7.14	9.52	13.64	16.67	50	30.95	20.46	9.52	5.56
Cumulative days	20	38	59	80	102	124	145	155	176	198	219	237
Cumulative demand	100	250	425	575	775	1075	1425	1925	2575	3025	3225	3325
Cumulative production (tonnes)	306	581	902	1222	1559	1895	2216	2368	2689	3025	3346	3621
Ending inventory (tonnes)	206	331	477	647	784	820	791	443	114	0	121	296
Average inventory (tonnes)	103	270	404	562	716	802	806	617	279	57	61	209
Inventory cost for month (£)	4120	9720	16968	23604	31504	35288	33852	12340	11718	2508	2562	7524

Total inventory cost for year = £191 608

Example

Suppose the chocolate manufacturer, which has been operating the level capacity plan as shown in Fig. 11.17, is unhappy with the inventory costs of this approach. It decides to explore two alternative plans, both involving some degree of demand chasing.

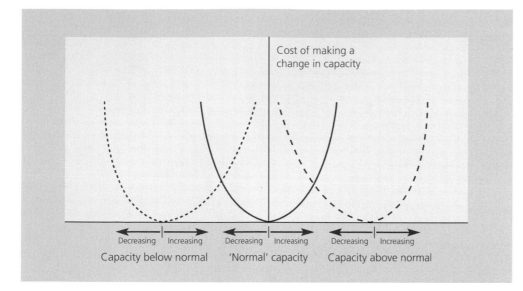

Figure 11.18
The costs of changing capacity will depend on the point from which the change is made, the degree of change and the direction of the change

Plan 1

● Organize and staff the factory for a 'normal' capacity level of 8.7 tonnes per day.
● Produce at 8.7 tonnes per day for the first 124 days of the year, then increase capacity to 29 tonnes per day by heavy use of overtime, hiring temporary staff and some sub-contracting.
● Produce at 29 tonnes per day until day 194, then reduce capacity back to 8.7 tonnes per day for the rest of the year.

The costs of changing capacity by such a large amount (the ratio of peak to normal capacity is 3.33 to 1) are calculated by the company as being:

Cost of changing from 8.7 tonnes/day to 29 tonnes/day = £110 000
Cost of changing from 29 tonnes/day to 8.7 tonnes/day = £60 000

Plan 2

● Organize and staff the factory for a 'normal' capacity level of 12.4 tonnes per day.
● Produce at 12.4 tonnes per day for the first 150 days of the year, then increase capacity to 29 tonnes per day by overtime and hiring some temporary staff.
● Produce at 29 tonnes/day until day 190 then reduce capacity back to 12.4 tonnes per day for the rest of the year.

The costs of changing capacity in this plan are smaller because the degree of change is smaller (a peak to normal capacity ratio of 2.34 to 1), and they are calculated by the company as being:

Cost of changing from 12.4 tonnes/day to 29 tonnes/day = £35 000
Cost of changing from 29 tonnes/day to 12.4 tonnes/day = £15 000

Figure 11.19 illustrates both plans on a cumulative basis. Plan 1, which envisaged two drastic changes in capacity, has high capacity change costs but, because its production levels are close to demand levels, it has low inventory carrying costs. Plan 2 sacrifices some of the inventory cost advantage of Plan 1 but saves more in terms of capacity change costs.

415

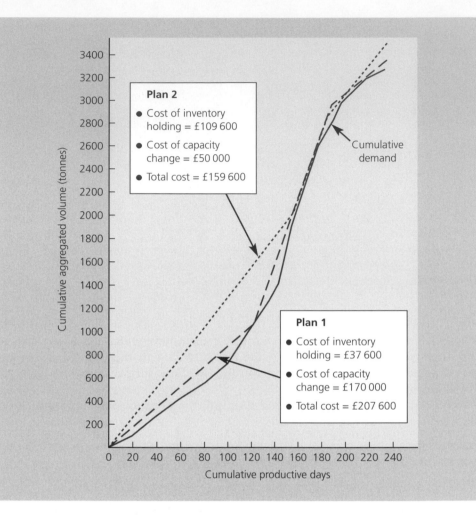

Figure 11.19 Comparing two alternative capacity plans

Queueing theory

Cumulative representations of capacity plans are useful where the operation has the ability to store its finished goods as inventory. For operations which, by their nature, cannot store their output, such as most service operations, capacity planning and control presents a different set of problems.

Although service operations do, of course, make forecasts of their expected average level of demand, they cannot usually predict exactly when each individual customer or order will arrive. A distribution which describes the probability of customers arriving might be known, but not each individual arrival. This makes providing adequate capacity particularly difficult. Furthermore, as well as the arrival of customers being uncertain, the time which each customer will need in the operation might also be uncertain. Figure 11.20 shows the general form of this capacity issue. Customers arrive according to some probability distribution, wait to be processed (unless part of the operation is idle), when they have reached the front of the queue they are processed by one of the *n* parallel 'servers' (their processing time also being described by a probability distribution) after which they leave the operation.

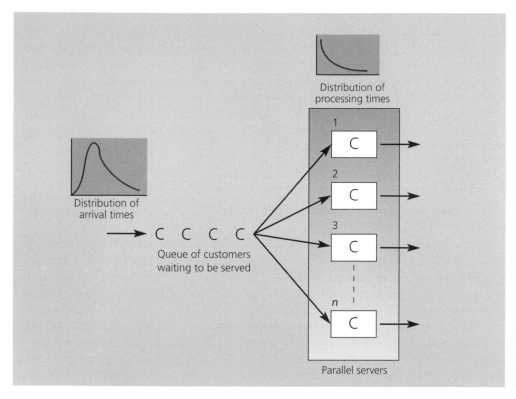

**Figure 11.20
The general form
of the capacity
decision in
queueing systems**

The capacity planning and control problem here is how many parallel servers to have available for service at any point in time. Because of the probabilistic arrival and processing times, only rarely will the arrival of customers match the ability of the operation to cope with them. Sometimes, if several customers arrive in quick succession and require longer-than-average processing times, queues will build up in front of the operation. At other times, when customers arrive less frequently than average and also require shorter-than-average processing times, some of the servers in the system will be idle. So even when the average capacity (processing capability) of the operation matches the average demand (arrival rate) on the system, both queues and idle time will occur. There are many examples of this kind of system. Table 11.2 illustrates some of these.

Table 11.2 Examples of operations which have parallel processors

Operation	Arrivals	Processing capacity
Bank	Customers	Tellers
Supermarket	Shoppers	Check-outs
Hospital clinic	Patients	Doctors
Graphic artist	Commissions	Artists
Custom cake decorators	Orders	Cake decorators
Ambulance service	Emergencies	Ambulances with crews
Telephone switchboard	Calls	Telephonists
Maintenance department	Breakdowns	Maintenance staff

417

If the operation has too few servers (that is, capacity is set at too low a level), queues will build up to a level where customers become dissatisfied with the time they are having to wait, although the utilization level of the servers will be high. If too many servers are in place (that is, capacity is set at too high a level), the time which customers can expect to wait will not be long but the utilization of the servers will be low. This is why the capacity planning and control problem for this type of operation is often presented as a trade-off between customer waiting time and system utilization. What is certainly important in making capacity decisions is being able to predict both of these factors for a given queueing system.

Analytical queueing models

Management scientists have developed formulae which can predict the steady-state behaviour of different types of queueing system. The type of system which we illustrated in Fig. 11.20 is the most useful for capacity management purposes, but it is only one of several types of queueing system. Unfortunately, these formulae can be extremely complicated, especially for all but the most simple assumptions, and are beyond the scope of this book. In fact, computer programs are almost always now used to predict the behaviour of queueing systems. However, Fig. 11.21 shows some curves, derived from queueing formulae, which give the relationship between the mean number of customers in the system (either queueing or being served) and the 'utilization factor' (which indicates the average proportion of their time which the servers spend processing customers) for various values of n, the number of parallel servers.

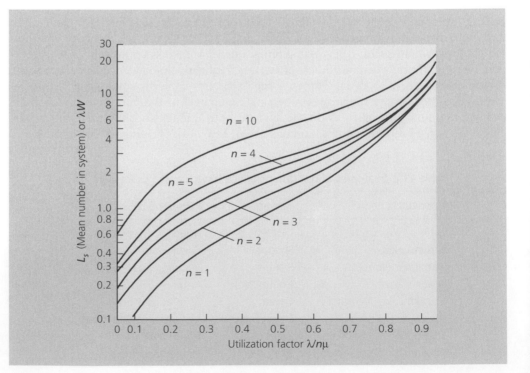

Figure 11.21 Queueing curves for a system with n parallel servers

Source: Adapted from Fitzsimmons, J.A. and Fitzsimmons, M.J. (1994) *Service Management for Competitive Advantage*, McGraw-Hill. Copyright © McGraw-Hill, with permission

MANAGING QUEUES AT MADAME TUSSAUD'S SCENERAMA, AMSTERDAM[5]

A short holiday in Amsterdam would not be complete without a visit to Madame Tussaud's Scenerama, located on four upper floors of the city's most prominent department store in Dam Square. With 600 000 visitors each year, this is the third most popular tourist attraction in Amsterdam, after the flower market and canal trips. On busy days in the summer, the centre can just manage to handle 5000 visitors. On a wet day in January, however, there may only be 300 visitors throughout the whole day. The centre is open for admission, seven days a week, from 10 am to 5.30 pm.

In the streets outside, orderly queues of expectant tourists snake along the pavement, look-ing in at the displays in the store windows. In this public open space, Tussaud's can do little to entertain the visitors, but entrepreneurial buskers and street artists are quick to capitalize on a captive market. On reaching the entrance lobby, individuals, families and groups purchase their admissions tickets. The lobby is in the shape of a large horseshoe, with the ticket sales booth in the centre. On winter days or at quiet spells, there will only be one sales assistant, but on busier days, visitors can pay at either side of the ticket booth, to speed up the process. Having paid, the visitors assemble in the lobby outside the two lifts. While waiting in this area, a photographer wanders around offering to take photos of the visitors standing next to life-sized wax figures of famous people. They may also be entertained by living look-alikes of famous personalities who act as guides to groups of visitors in batches of around 25 customers (the capacity of each of the two lifts which takes visitors up to the facility). The lifts arrive every four minutes and customers simultaneously disembark forming one group of about 50, customers who stay together throughout the Scenerama section. ∎

Questions

1 Generally, what could Madame Tussaud's do to cope with its demand fluctuations?

2 What does the operation do to make queueing relatively painless? What else could it do?

Source: By kind permission of Dr Willem Bijleveld, Director, Madame Tussaud Scenerama B.V., Amsterdam

---

The curves in Fig. 11.21 are calculated on the assumption that customers arrive in a random fashion. That is, the arrival of each customer is independent of that of the other customers. The number of arrivals per unit of time is assumed to be described by a Poisson distribution. Processing times are assumed to be described by a negative exponential distribution. Both these assumptions are made largely for mathematical convenience, but are usually quite appropriate for actual arrival and processing rates in many real systems. The final assumptions are that customers are sufficiently patient to stay in the queue once they have joined it, and are processed on a 'first come, first served' basis.

We shall use the following notation:

λ = mean arrival rate (customer arrivals per hour)
μ = mean service rate per busy server (capacity, in customers per hour)
ρ = traffic intensity (λ/μ)
n = number of servers
L_s = mean number of customers in the system

L_q = mean number of customers in queue = $L_s - \rho$

W_s = mean time customer spends in the system = $\dfrac{L_q}{\lambda} + \dfrac{1}{\mu}$

W_q = mean time customer spends in the queue = $\dfrac{L_q}{\lambda}$

Example

A bank wishes to decide how many enquiry staff to schedule during the busy lunch period. Its investigations have revealed that, during this period, customers arrive at a rate of nine per hour and the enquiries which customers have during this period (checking on accounts, opening new accounts, arranging loans, etc.) take, on average, 15 minutes. The bank manager feels that four staff should be on duty during this period but wants to make sure that customers do not wait more than three minutes on average before they are served.

λ = arrival rate = 9 per hour

μ = service rate = $\dfrac{1}{0.25}$ = 4 per hour

n = 4 servers

Utilization factor = $\dfrac{\lambda}{n\mu}$ = $\dfrac{9}{4 \times 4}$

= 0.5625

From Fig. 11.21, for a utilization factor of 0.5626 and $n = 4$,

L_s = mean number of customers in the system = 2.56
L_q = mean number of customers in the queue = $L_s - \rho$

= $2.56 - \dfrac{9}{4} = 0.31$

W_q = mean queueing time = $\dfrac{L_q}{\lambda}$

= $\dfrac{0.31}{9}$ = 0.0344 hrs

= 2.07 minutes

So the manager can be assured that, with a capacity of four enquiry staff during the lunch period, the average time a customer will wait is less than three minutes.

The dynamics of capacity planning and control

Our emphasis so far has been on the planning aspects of capacity management. In practice, the management of capacity is a far more dynamic process which involves controlling and reacting to *actual* demand and *actual* capacity as it occurs. The capacity control process can be seen as a sequence of partially reactive capacity decision processes as shown in Fig. 11.22. At the beginning of each period, operations management considers its forecasts of demand, its understanding of current capacity and

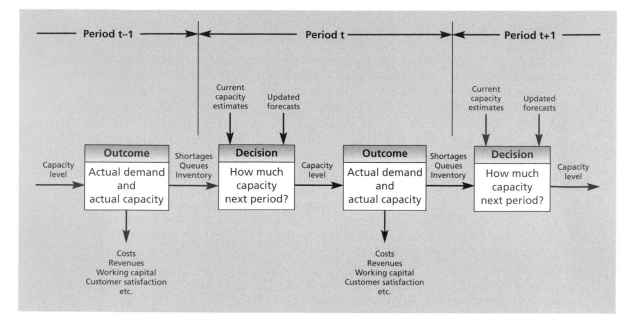

Figure 11.22 Capacity planning and control as a dynamic sequence of decisions

(if appropriate) how much inventory has been carried forward from the previous period. Based on all this information, it makes plans for the following period's capacity. During the next period demand might, or might not, be as forecast and the actual capacity of the operation might, or might not, turn out as planned. But whatever the actual conditions during that period, at the beginning of the next period the same type of decisions must be made, but in the light of the new circumstances.

The outlook matrix[6]

One of the main influences on operations managers, when they are making period-by-period capacity decisions, is their confidence in future demand matching their future capacity. If they are confident that, in the long term, demand is likely to exceed current capacity then, irrespective of the current level of demand, they will be more likely to be tolerant of policies which could lead to short-term over-capacity. Conversely, if long-term demand looks poor, it will be necessary to start implementing policies which will reduce long-term capacity. Overlaying this are the needs of current demand. Even if long-term demand looks poor it might be necessary to increase capacity if there is a short-term requirement. Figure 11.23 gives examples of the type of methods which might be adopted for different combinations of long-term and short-term outlook. Here outlook is defined as:

$$\text{Outlook} = \frac{\text{Forecast demand}}{\text{Forecast capacity}}$$

Three broad states of outlook are identified for both the long and short term. 'Poor' is when the ratio of forecast demand to forecast capacity is less than 1. 'Normal' is when the ratio is approximately equal to 1. 'Good' is when the ratio is greater than 1.

421

THREE-PHASE PRODUCTION AT BOOTS[7]

In the United Kingdom, when your sales rely on the weather, demand forecasting is understandably problematic. An extreme example of this is the manufacture of sun tan cream. A good summer can leave the shelves empty, whereas poor weather could mean a warehouse full of unwanted product. Boots, the UK manufacturer and retailer, which manufactures the Soltan range of sun preparation products, attempts to reduce the uncertainty in its sun tan product factory by phasing its production in three stages. This allows the company to compensate for weather patterns early in the season by increasing or decreasing its production rate in the final phase of production. About 70 per cent of all its sales are made between the beginning of May and the end of August. The peak production time is somewhat earlier (to allow for distribution) and runs between October and April. Because of the lag between manufacture and demand in the shops, Boots has to commit itself to the first two phases. The results of the weather come too late to affect production. However, it can use the third phase to react to sales early in the season. If the weather has been poor, no product may be needed in the third phase, whereas good weather will mean production continuing throughout the summer. Nevertheless, a decision must be made by the end of May. Decisions after that would come too late to affect that year's sales. ■

Questions

1 Why does Boots divide its production of Soltan into three phases?

2 What else could it do to cope with demand fluctuations?

When both long-term and short-term outlook is poor there is relatively little choice but to reduce the capacity of the operation; capacity is not needed now, nor is it likely to be in the future. Staff lay-offs might be the only method of achieving this. When short-term outlook is normal, but long-term outlook is poor, current capacity needs to be maintained though certainly not increased. Under these circumstances the operation is most likely to delay any decisions. Certainly it would not commit investments in capacity which are unlikely to be needed in the future. When short-term outlook is good in spite of long-term outlook being poor, the operation faces a dilemma. It does not want to make any permanent commitments to increase capacity because the extra capacity will not be needed in the future. However, it does need to meet current levels of demand. Under these circumstances the use of overtime or the recruitment of temporary staff might be the least permanent methods of achieving short-term capacity requirements.

When long-term outlook is normal and short-term outlook is poor, capacity needs to be temporarily reduced but not in such a way as to compromise longer-term requirements. The operation here is likely to tolerate a certain amount of unproductive or idle time, or might perhaps reduce the working hours of its staff temporarily. When both long-term and short-term outlook is normal no action is required. However, when short-term outlook is good, capacity will need to be increased but not in any permanent manner. Again, overtime and the use of temporary staff are likely to be appropriate methods.

When the long-term outlook is good there will be a requirement to build up capacity in some way, irrespective of short-term circumstances. So, when the short-term

		Short-term outlook	
	POOR Outlook < 1	NORMAL Outlook = 1	GOOD Outlook > 1
POOR Outlook < 1	Lay-off staff	Delay any action	Overtime Hire temporary staff
NORMAL Outlook = 1	Short-time Idle time	Do nothing	Overtime Hire temporary staff
GOOD Outlook > 1	Make for inventory Short-time	Hire and make for inventory Start to recruit	Hire staff

Long-term outlook

$$\text{Outlook} = \frac{\text{Forecast demand}}{\text{Forecast capacity}}$$

Figure 11.23
The dynamics of capacity planning are governed partly by the combination of long-term and short-term outlook

outlook is poor the operation will not want to do anything which compromises long-term capacity. It may even, if possible, use any short-term surplus capacity to build up inventory. It is also likely to do this when long-term outlook is good and the short-term outlook is normal. Here though it will need to start recruiting extra staff or working overtime if it wants to make products for inventory. Finally, when both long-term and short-term outlook is good, capacity will need to be increased relatively quickly and probably in a permanent manner through hiring extra staff.

Chief Inspector Brian Paddick, London Metropolitan Police

Brian has overall policing responsibility for the Brixton Division, one of London's largest inner-city areas, which employs many hundreds of police officers. Around two-thirds are uniformed; these officers interact directly with the public, and are seen 'on the beat', at the front-office desks of the police stations, and at the scenes of disturbances, crimes, accidents, and so on. The Division is, of course, required to provide its services at all times, so Brian has to ensure that there is sufficient 'officer coverage' in his capacity management plan.

'The level of demand for policing can never be accurately predicted in advance because of the random – and often intangible – nature of demand, but there are actually some significant factors which we can take into account. For example, when it rains there is usually a significantly lower level of street crimes and disturbances, but the frequency of accidents increases, so the mix of our work changes. Thursday, Friday, and Saturday evenings are usually busy, particularly in the summer, because many people in the area spend their free time socializing on the streets. There is potential for small disturbances to escalate and with large numbers of naturally inquisitive people on the scene of an incident, there may be a small minority who will join in, or who will take advantage of the opportunity to commit a separate crime. We also anticipate a peak on Monday mornings, when businesses discover burglaries that have occurred over the weekend.

'In our capacity planning and workforce scheduling, the safety of our officers must be given high priority, so we always try to ensure that there is support and back-up to provide a minimum safety level of staffing. We operate using "core teams" to provide 24-hour cover for the whole Division and "sector teams" for the town centre shopping areas and housing estates. The sector teams are scheduled with different starting times throughout the day, so that we can have maximum capacity when indicated by crime trend analysis. These officers work a five-shift rota that enables us to provide a relatively level capacity coverage on the normal four-shift basis, as well as scheduling other small teams from the fifth shift to coincide with the anticipated peaks. We like

these officers to be very visible to the public, particularly in those areas that are likely to attract crowds; partly as a deterrent, but equally to support the public's need for a feeling of security on the street. The deployment of these teams is highly targeted on specific problems which have been highlighted by detailed crime analysis.

'Frequently our officers are required to attend court, and this is invariably during weekdays, in daytime. Officers attending court deplete our scheduled availability for teams, and so we have to use overtime to provide cover. Sometimes the high level of activity on the Brixton streets on warm summer evenings has led us to call in help from neighbouring police stations to provide the extra needed capacity. Until recently, policy had prevented us from using any part-time staff, but this is now permitted: for example, we now have a part-time Sergeant. She is responsible for the process of submitting papers to the Crown Prosecution. I am sure that the use of part-time staff will give us better scope to cover duties that have relatively predictable levels of fluctuating demand.

'Some special events give us particular capacity management problems. For example, Europe's largest street carnival is held annually in the nearby area of Notting Hill, on a holiday weekend in late August, and this has been attracting ever larger crowds; well over one million spectators attend. It is a very colourful and enjoyable event but from a policing perspective, it is a major task, both for crowd safety and for crime prevention. Our Division is required to provide large numbers of officers to help in this task, so our rota is designed to require everyone to be on duty on the busiest day. The careful planning for this event has brought dividends – the level of serious crime that marred the event in its early years has been almost eliminated, and the huge numbers of spectators seem to be having a safe, happy and crime-free day out. Good policing requires attention to detail, not least in the planning of capacity to match the needs, and it is my responsibility to ensure that we can provide acceptable cover, while not wasting our resources, at all times. This is a difficult balance to achieve, but critically important for us and our customers!' ■

SUMMARY ANSWERS TO KEY QUESTIONS

What is capacity planning and control?

■ It is the way operations organize the level of value-added activity which they can achieve under normal operating conditions over a period of time.

■ We usually distinguish between a long-, medium- and short-term capacity decision. This chapter has dealt with medium- and short-term capacity management where the capacity level of the organization is adjusted within the fixed physical limits which are set by long-term capacity decisions.

■ This is sometimes called aggregate planning and control because it is necessary to aggregate the various types of output from an operation into one composite measure.

Why is capacity planning and control important?

■ Because decisions made in capacity planning and control affect the ability to generate revenues and the extent of working capital required by the organization, as well as the normal operations objectives of quality, speed, dependability, flexibility and cost.

■ Also because almost all operations have some kind of fluctuation in demand (or seasonality) caused by some combination of climatic, festive, behavioural, political, financial, or social factors.

How is capacity measured?

■ Either by the availability of its input resources or by the output which is produced.

■ Which of these measures is used partly depends on how stable is the mix of outputs. If it is difficult to aggregate the different types of output from an operation, input measures are usually preferred.

■ The usage of capacity is measured by the factors 'utilization' and 'efficiency'.

What are the ways of coping with demand fluctuation?

■ Output can be kept level, in effect ignoring demand fluctuations. This will result in under-utilization of capacity where outputs cannot be stored, or the build up of inventories where output can be stored.

■ Output can chase demand by fluctuating the output level through some combination of overtime, varying the size of the workforce, using part-time staff and sub-contracting.

■ Demand can be changed, either by influencing the market through such measures as advertising and promotion, or by developing alternative products with a counter-seasonal demand pattern.

■ Most operations use a mix of all these three 'pure' strategies.

How can operations plan their capacity level?

■ Representing demand and output in the form of cumulative representations allows the feasibility of alternative capacity plans to be assessed.

■ In many operations, especially service operations, queueing theory can indicate the consequences of alternative capacity strategies.

How can operations control their capacity level?

■ By considering the capacity decision as a dynamic decision which periodically updates the decisions and assumptions upon which decisions are based.

■ By considering the major influences on which periodically capacity strategies are adopted. The 'outlook matrix' which compares long-term and short-term outlook for demand (against capacity) is one way of doing this.

Fine Country Fruit Cakes

September 1994 was a year to remember for Jean and Dave Fulbright! Their twin sons, Michael and Alan, then five years old, started school, and in the same month, Dave, a 29-year-old master baker at a large bakery, was made redundant. Jean, who had a part-time secretarial job with a local builder, saw this misfortune to be an unrepeatable opportunity. They had always wanted to work together, and it seemed to be a good chance to set up a small speciality business, based on Dave's skills and financed by his redundancy payments plus a small loan.

Traditionally, small local baking and confectionery businesses produce a wide range of breads, cakes, biscuits, etc., many on a daily basis. This involves a very early start (4 am), high complexity and considerable risk. Dave wanted a 'simpler' business that would involve relatively normal hours of work, for both himself and his wife. Neither wanted to be employers; the business would be run by just the two of them. Dave felt that his greatest satisfaction came from producing high-quality decorated fruit cakes, so together they decided that there was an opportunity to specialize in this product. Using an old family recipe, samples were made and packaged. 'Market research' was confined to taking these samples to various retail outlets in the area; the reaction was so enthusiastic, and the potential margin seemed so high, that by January 1993 they were in business. They rented a small modern factory near home, modestly equipped with weighing and preparation equipment, a large 15 kg food mixer, two small catering ovens, a small coolroom, and sundry utensils. Talking to a friend in Spring 1997, Dave recalled:

'In early 1995 we only made one size: beautiful 2 kg cakes, symmetrically decorated on top with a pattern of almonds, cherries, walnuts and ginger. We sold most to cafés and restaurants; their customers loved portions of them with their teas/coffees. Demand ran at about 150–200 cakes a month, which wasn't enough to make much of a living, but we had time to visit our customers and to try new outlets. Although sales were growing, it gradually became clear that we should be selling a smaller cake to retail shops for family purchasers – one which could be bought as a treat, or as a gift for friends. We introduced the 1kg cake (with the same recipe) in July 1995. We had no problems selling these, and demand soon exceeded all our expectations. The delicatessens in the area

heard about our products and soon sales of the 1kg cake overtook those of the original 2 kg cake. Somehow, however, it's not been so easy running the business since then; we can only just cope every day making the cakes. Jean can go to get the children from school at about 3.30 pm (a neighbour takes them in the morning) but I rarely get back before 7.00 pm in the week; and we usually do our selling and prospecting for new customers on Saturdays. We certainly don't want to start production at weekends; we couldn't cope with that! Anyway, although we're making a reasonable profit now, I feel we could do a better job somehow. There were times last year (1996) when we had overproduced, and we had to sell off some stock at a discount because of its age. Tests have shown that this recipe of rich fruit cakes lasts for up to 12 months, but for best flavour and texture, it should really be eaten within six months. The retailers demand at least three months of this, so I can't keep stock more than three months here at the factory. Anyway, I only have space for about 3000 kg in the coolroom, allowing for stock rotation.'

Jean's view of the business was somewhat different:

'I think we are chasing the wrong markets! The delicatessens demand big discounts and are always expecting us to deliver at short notice, particularly around Easter (March/April) and at Christmas (November/December) when the cakes are apparently popular gifts. I have found that craft shops and visitor centres of local tourist spots (such as castles and historic houses) can also sell our 1kg cakes and, moreover, they don't expect much discount! We were really pleased with the level of orders from these outlets last summer, but we don't hear from them much during the winter. I really should go and take some more samples! I also feel we should open a factory shop where regular users could come and buy directly, but I am sure we would need to provide a bigger range of cakes. We could develop lots of different types in the two sizes – then we would get a lot more repeat business!'

Production

PREPARATION

In order to simplify weighing, mixing, and baking, all production is done in nominal 10 kg batches of one size at a time. Thus a batch is either ten 1 kg cakes or five 2 kg cakes. For each batch, dried fruits (raisins, sultanas, currants, cherries, crystallized ginger, etc.) are weighed and cleaned as necessary,

Table 11.3 Company records of sales 1995/96 and forecast sales for 1997

	1995							1996								1997
		Jan	Feb	Mar	Apr	May	Jun	Jul	Aug	Sep	Oct	Nov	Dec	Total	(Forecast)
1 kg cakes	900	80	200	600	320	120	80	120	80	240	480	800	1 600	4 720	6 000
2 kg cakes	1 950	160	340	300	240	140	160	240	160	180	260	300	400	2 880	3 500
Total (kg)	4 800	400	880	1 200	800	400	400	600	400	600	1 000	1 400	2 400	10 480	13 000

other ingredients are prepared and measured, and a cake mixture is made in the mixer. Tins are greased, and the mixture is weighed into each; the top surface is then decorated with carefully selected specimen dried fruits and nuts, and brushed with a glaze. This complete preparation stage takes almost exactly 30 minutes per batch for Dave and Jean working as a team, for either size of cake. Each batch is prepared just before the oven is ready to accept it, to avoid contamination, and to maintain consistency of method, and hence of texture.

BAKING

The ovens are turned on at 8.00 am and are ready by 8.30 when the first batch is loaded (which only takes a few minutes). A 10 kg batch of cakes fills one oven; baking time is three hours for the 1 kg cakes, four and a half hours for 2 kg cakes. When ready, the cakes are removed from the hot oven, which is ready for a further batch in a quarter of an hour. For convenience, Dave has always baked the 1kg cakes in the oldest oven (Oven 1) to avoid having to carry 10 tins to Oven 2 which is further from the workbench. Each oven normally bakes only two batches per day. Dave thinks that the temperature control on Oven 1 is inaccurate which would be a particular problem for the larger size cakes!

fix it !

PACKING

Cakes are turned out on to racks to cool overnight. The next day, once the first batches are into the oven, the previous day's cakes are then inspected, packed in a film, a decorative ribbon and an outer-wrap, and are then labelled and dated. Packed cakes are then carried to the coolroom and stacked according to size. These processes take two people six minutes per cake (either size). The couple take one hour for lunch from 12.30 to 1.30 (when Oven 2 is ready to unload).

PLANNING

'The only times in 1996 that we changed production were in March, April and November and December when we increased 2kg output only by 50 per cent (one extra batch

per day). I had to bake the 2 kg cakes in Oven 1 and the quality wasn't really so good, but none of our regular customers noticed! Even so, I had to work into the evenings all those months; it was a lot of work. All other months we have kept to the plan of two batches of each size each day (1 kg, followed by 2 kg, 1 kg, 2 kg) which helps us keep to a rhythm.'

SALES

Records were kept of monthly sales of each size during 1996 (Table 11.3). On 1st January 1996 there was an opening stock of 100 of each size of cake. Dave commented:

'I am worried that we won't be able to cope with demand in 1997, and that we will start giving bad service. Perhaps we should drop the idea of selling to the tourist spots, although the margins are very attractive. Clearly, we musn't upset the retailers who give us so much business.' ∎

Questions

1 With the current method of working, what is the monthly and annual capacity of the business? Is the total weight (kg) of product a useful aggregate measure of capacity for this business? How does capacity compare with demand in 1996 and forecast demand in 1997?

2 Why did Dave have to sell stock at reduced prices in 1996? In which months do you think that happened, and explain clearly the reasons. Justify your answer with simple calculations.

3 Jean believes that they should try to get more business from craft shops and tourist centres. What advantages/disadvantages would this market have compared with the existing retail outlets?

4 What are the main differences in operations tasks of running the proposed retail shop? What are the implications of this for the owners?

5 What are the operational implications of making ten varieties of cake, each in two sizes?

DISCUSSION QUESTIONS

1 Explain what is meant by capacity planning and control and describe the implications of a capacity constraint in one of the micro operations of an organization of your own choice.

2 Discuss the implications of having too much or too little capacity for the following operations:

a national train network

a lecture room

a vineyard's grape-pressing equipment.

3 Discuss with an operation's manager the demand trends for the organization's products or services, covering the long, medium and short terms. Find out the periods over which the manager makes or uses forecasts and the problems resulting from any inaccuracies in those forecasts.

4 Identify several ways in which the following organizations might measure their capacity (discuss the relative merits of each and suggest the one you think each organization will use):

a city bus company

a dentist

a lift (elevator) maintenance company

a jobbing plumber.

5 A car battery manufacturer makes four types of car battery: compact, compact-heavy duty, standard and standard-heavy duty. Table 11.4 shows the number of batteries of each type currently produced to order for existing customers and the amount of time each battery spends with the acid-filling machine. The machine is capable of working up to 24 hours a day and needs no adjusting between battery types. The operations manager is under pressure to increase the utilization of the plant. The company has been approached by two new customers to supply batteries. Company A requires someone to supply them with between 80 and 100 batteries per day of various types. Company B requires 10 compact and 70 standard batteries a day, all heavy duty; however, delivery must be assured.

Assuming the acid-filling machine is the only capacity constraint, review the merits of each order.

6 Explain how utilization might be measured in the operations following and discuss the relative merits

Table 11.4 Battery production

	Number produced per day	Time with acid filler (mins)
Compact	80	3
Compact HD	50	5
Standard	90	4
Standard HD	20	6

of using utilization and efficiency as measures of operations performance:

a doctor's surgery

a university lecture

an ice-cream manufacturer.

7 Discuss with an operations manager how capacity is managed. Identify the different plans used and how they are implemented.

8 Which do you think will be the main capacity plans, and how might they be implemented, for the following organizations:

a university

an Accident and Emergency ward at a hospital

a compact disc producer

a taxi service?

(Explain the reasons for your choice.)

9 The management of an hotel on a popular Greek holiday island is concerned that its hotel is full between March and September, is about 80 per cent occupied in February, March and December and about 30 per cent occupied during the other months. Discuss ways in which it might try to move towards 100 per cent occupancy all the year round.

10 A computer bureau's telephone help desk is staffed by ten people throughout the day. It is known that the bureau handles about 15 customers an hour and the average time it takes to deal with a problem is 10 minutes. The operations manager believes that customers will be aggrieved if they have to wait for more than two minutes for their calls to be answered. Comment on the situation.

11 The Speedy Cleaning Company operates a drive-in car valeting service. This comprises a number of cleaning bays where customers can drive in and use special cleaning equipment to valet their cars. On Saturday mornings the arrival rate averages five customers per hour. The arrival rate appears to conform to a Poisson distribution. The average time to clean a car is ten minutes with times being distributed according to a negative exponential distribution. How many bays should the company open to ensure that customers wait no longer than three minutes before being able to enter a bay?

12 The Dagenham Chow-Mein Pizza Company has a demand forecast for the next 12 months which is shown in Table 11.5.

The current workforce of 100 staff can produce 1000 cases of pizzas per month.
(a) Prepare a production plan which keeps the output level. How much warehouse space would the company need for this plan?
(b) Prepare a demand chase plan. What implications would this have for staffing levels, assuming that the maximum amount of overtime would result in production levels of only 10 per cent greater than normal working hours?

Table 11.5 Pizza demand forecast

Months	Demand (cases per month)
January	600
February	800
March	1000
April	1500
May	2000
June	1700
July	1200
August	1100
September	900
October	2500
November	3200
December	900

NOTES ON CHAPTER

1 Source: Interviews with company staff.
2 Sources: Lynch, P. (1991) 'Making Time for Productivity', *Personnel Management*, March, and Pickard, J. (1991) 'Annual Hours: A Year of Living Dangerously', *Personnel Management*, Aug.
3 Source: *The Economist*, 10 Aug 1991.
4 Kimes, S. (1989) 'Yield Management: A Tool for Capacity-constrained Service Firms', *Journal of Operations Management*, Vol 8, No 4.
5 Source: Discussions with company staff.
6 Based on Colley, J.L., Landell, R.D. and Fair, R.R. (1978) *Operations Planning and Control*, Holden Day.
7 Source: Gabb, A. (1991) 'Braving the Elements', *Management Today*, Jan.

SELECTED FURTHER READINGS

Bleuel, W.H. (1975) 'Management Science's Impact on Service Strategy', *Interfaces*, Vol 6, No 1.
Buxey, G. (1993) 'Production Planning and Scheduling for Seasonal Demand', *International Journal of Operations and Production Management*, Vol 13, No 7.
Chaiken, J.M. and Larson, R.C. (1972) 'Methods for Allocating Urban Emergency Units Survey', *Management Science*, Vol 19, No 4.
Coker, J.L. (1985) 'Analysing Production Switching Heuristics for Aggregate Planning Models via an Application', *Production and Inventory Management*, 4th Quarter.
Fitzsimmons, J.A. and Fitzsimmons, M.J. (1994) *Service Management for Competitive Advantage*, McGraw-Hill.
Gallagher, G.R. (1980) 'How to Develop a Realistic Master Schedule', *Management Review*, Apr.
Grassman, W.K. (1988) 'Finding the Right Number of Servers in Real-World Queueing Systems', *Interfaces*, Vol 8, No 2.

Holt, C., Modigliani, C.F. and Simon, H. (1955) 'A Linear Decision Rule for Production and Employment Scheduling', *Management Science*, Vol 2, No 2.

Lee, S.M. and Moore, L.J. (1974) 'A Practical Approach to Production Scheduling', *Production and Inventory Management*, 1st Quarter.

Lee, W.B. and Khumwala, B.M. (1974) 'Simulation Testing of Aggregate Production Planning Models in an Implementation Methodology', *Management Science*, Vol 20, No 6.

Mangiameli, P. and Krajewski, L. (1983) 'The Effects of Work Force Strategies on Manufacturing Operations', *Journal of Operations Management*, Vol 3, No 4.

Mapes, J. (1993) 'The Effect of Capacity Limitations on Safety Stock', *International Journal of Operations and Production Management*, Vol 13, No 10.

Northcraft, G.B. and Chase, R.B. (1985) 'Managing Service Demand at the Point of Delivery', *Academy of Management Review*, Vol 10, Jan.

Rothstein, M. (1985) 'Operations Research and the Airline Overbooking Problem', *Operations Research*, Vol 33, No 1.

Sasser, W.E. (1976) 'Match Supply and Demand in Service Industries', *Harvard Business Review*, Vol 54, No 6.

Vollmann, T.E., Berry, W.L. and Whybark, D.C. (1988) *Manufacturing Planning and Control Systems*, Irwin.

INVENTORY PLANNING AND CONTROL

INTRODUCTION

Operations managers usually have an ambivalent attitude towards inventories. On the one hand, they are costly, tying up sometimes considerable amounts of working capital. They are also risky because items held in stock could deteriorate, become obsolete or just get lost, and, furthermore, they take up valuable space in the operation. On the other hand, they provide some security in a complex and uncertain environment. Knowing that you have the items in stock, should customers or production schedules demand them, is a comforting insurance against the unexpected. Certainly when a customer goes elsewhere because just one item is out of stock, or when a major project is waiting for just one small part, the value of inventories seems indisputable. This is the dilemma of inventory management: in spite of the cost and the other disadvantages associated with holding stocks, they do facilitate the smoothing of supply and demand. In fact they only exist because supply and demand are not in harmony with each other (*see* Fig. 12.1).

Figure 12.1 A definition of inventory planning and control

> ## CHAPTER 12: KEY QUESTIONS
>
> ● *What is inventory?*
>
> ● *Why is it necessary?*
>
> ● *How much inventory should an operation hold?*
>
> ● *When should an operation replenish its inventory?*
>
> ● *How can inventory be controlled?*

WHAT IS INVENTORY?

Inventory, or 'stock' as it is more commonly called in some countries, is defined here as *the stored accumulation of material resources in a transformation system*. Sometimes inventory is also used to describe any stored resource. Thus, a bank would have a 'stock' of staff, a 'stock' of ATMs, even a 'stock' of retail branches. However, although these transforming resources are technically held as 'stocks' insomuch as they are not especially obtained every time a customer makes a request of the bank, they are not what we normally mean by the term 'stock' or 'inventory'. Usually we use the term to refer only to *transformed input resources*. So a manufacturing company will hold stocks of materials, a tax office will hold stocks of information and a theme park will hold stocks of customers (when it is customers which are being processed we normally refer to the 'stocks' of them as 'queues' – it is the same idea, but 'queues' is considered a more courteous term).

In this chapter we will deal particularly with inventories of materials. Inventories of customers are referred to elsewhere in Chapter 11. However, this does not imply that this chapter is only relevant when examining predominantly materials-processing operations such as manufacturing operations. All operations keep physical stocks of materials of some sort.

All operations keep inventories

If you walk around any operation you will see several types of stored material. Table 12.1 gives some examples for several operations. However, there are differences between the examples of inventory given in Table 12.1. Some are relatively trivial to the operation in question: for example, the cleaning materials which are stored in the television factory are far less important than the stocks of steel, plastic and components which it also holds. The value of the cleaning materials held by the factory will be considerably less than the value of its steel, plastic and components. More importantly, the television plant would not stop if it ran out of cleaning materials, whereas if it ran out of any of its component parts, its activities would be severely disrupted. However, cleaning materials would be a far more important item of inventory for an industrial cleaning company, not only because it uses far more of this input, but also because its operation would stop if it ever ran out of them.

There is also a difference between how often the operations stock the items. Some of the examples of inventory are items which are stored just once within the operation. For example, food in an hotel is delivered to the hotel, stored and then used. In other operations, items are stored several times. For example, in a television factory a single piece of material is likely to progress through many different stages. Between each stage it has probably been stored as inventory.

Table 12.1 Examples of inventory held in operations

Operation	Examples of inventory held in operations
Hotel	Food items, drinks, toilet items, cleaning materials
Hospital	Wound dressings, disposable instruments, whole blood, food, drugs, cleaning materials
Retail store	Goods to be sold, wrapping materials
Warehouse	Goods being stored, packaging materials
Automotive parts distributor	Automotive parts in main depot, automotive parts at local distribution points
Television manufacturer	Components, raw materials, part-finished sub-assemblies, finished televisions, cleaning materials
Precious metals refiner	Material (gold, platinum, etc.) waiting to be processed, material partly processed, fully refined material

The value of inventories

Perhaps the most obvious difference between the operations in Table 12.1 is in the value of the inventories which they hold. In some, the value of inventory is relatively small compared to the costs of the total inputs to the operation. In others, it will be far higher, especially where storage is the prime purpose of the operation. For example, the value of the goods held in the warehouse is likely to be very high compared to its day-to-day expenditure on such things as labour, rent and running costs. Sometimes the value of the inventories can be so high that it is not even included in the organization's general financial accounts; this would be true, for example, of the precious metals refiner.

The difference in the value of stocks in various organizations is illustrated in Table 12.2.[1]

Why inventory exists

No matter what is being stored as inventory, or where it is positioned in the operation, it will exist because there is a difference in the timing or rate of supply and demand. If the supply of any item occurred exactly when it was demanded the item would never be stored. A common analogy is the water tank shown in Fig. 12.2. If, over time, the rate of supply of water to the tank differs from the rate at which it is demanded, a tank

433

Table 12.2 Inventory (stocks) and sales in selected companies

Company	Country	Business	Stock	Sales	Stock/Sales
Atlas Copco	Sweden	Construction and mining	SEK 4 425 million	SEK 16 007 million	0.28
British Gas	UK	Natural gas	£593 million	£10 254 million	0.058
Sandoz	Switzerland	Pharmaceuticals	SFr. 3 027 million	SFr. 14 416 million	0.21
Essilor	France	Opthalmics	US$ 281 million	US$ 1 018 million	0.27
BP	UK	Petroleum	£3 379 million	£33 250 million	0.1
Elf	France	Chemicals	FFr. 22 107 million	FFr. 36 288 million	0.61
Reebok	USA	Sportswear	US$ 434 million	US$ 3 022 million	0.14
BMW	Germany	Auto	DM 3 140 million	DM 31 241 million	0.1
Carnaud Metalbox	France	Metal packaging	FFr. 3 534 million	FFr. 24 830 million	0.14
Stena Line	Sweden	Shipping	SEK 152 million	SEK 7 979 million	0.019
Carlsberg	Denmark	Brewing	DKK 1 646 million	DKK 14 957 million	0.11
PSA Peugeot–Citroen	France	Auto	FFr. 27 000 million	FFr. 155 431 million	0.17
Eurocoptor	France	Helicopters	FFr. 10 210 million	FFr. 11 600 million	0.88

of water (inventory) will be needed if supply is to be maintained. (More generally we use the process charting symbols (from Appendix 3) which are also shown in Fig. 12.2.) When the rate of supply exceeds the rate of demand inventory increases; when the rate

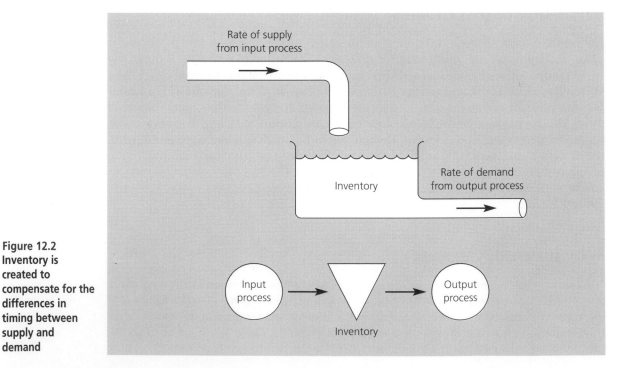

Figure 12.2 Inventory is created to compensate for the differences in timing between supply and demand

of demand exceeds the rate of supply inventory decreases. The obvious point to make is that if an operation can make efforts to match supply and demand rates it will also succeed in reducing its inventory levels. This important point is the basis of the just-in-time approach to inventory which we shall explore in more detail in Chapter 15.

Types of inventory[2]

The various reasons for an imbalance between the rates of supply and demand at different points in any operation lead to the different types of inventory. There are four types of inventory: buffer inventory, cycle inventory, anticipation inventory and pipeline inventory.

Buffer inventory

Buffer inventory is also called safety inventory. Its purpose is to compensate for the uncertainties inherent in supply and demand. For example, a retail operation can never forecast demand perfectly, even when it has a good idea of the most likely demand level. It will order goods from its suppliers such that there is always a certain amount of most items in stock. This minimum level of inventory is there to cover against the possibility that demand will be greater than expected during the time taken to deliver the goods. This is *buffer*, or *safety*, *inventory*. It compensates for the uncertainties in the process of the supply of goods into the store and that of the demand of goods from the store. Similarly, two stages in a production process might produce at exactly the same rate on average, but individual processing times might vary about the average. This variation could be either because of the natural human variation in processing times, or perhaps because of occasional breakdowns or other interruptions to normal processing.

Cycle inventory

Cycle inventory occurs because one or more stages in the operation cannot supply all the items it produces simultaneously. For example, suppose a baker makes three types of bread, each of which is equally popular with its customers. Because of the nature of the mixing and baking process, only one kind of bread can be produced at any time. The baker would have to produce each type of bread in batches (or 'lots' as they are sometimes known) as shown in Fig. 12.3. The batches must be large enough to satisfy the demand for each kind of bread between the times when each batch is ready for sale. So even when demand is steady and predictable, there will always be some inventory to compensate for the irregular supply of each type of bread.

Anticipation inventory

We have already seen how anticipation inventory can be used in Chapter 11. Again, it was used to compensate for differences in the timing of supply and demand. There, rather than make chocolate only when it was needed, it was produced throughout the year ahead of demand and put into inventory until it was needed. *Anticipatory inventory* is most commonly used when demand fluctuations are significant but relatively predictable. It might also be used when supply variations are significant, such as in the canning of seasonal foods.

**Figure 12.3
Cycle inventory in
a bakery**

Pipeline inventory

Pipeline inventory exists because material cannot be transported instantaneously between the point of supply and the point of demand. If a retail store orders a consignment of items from one of its suppliers, the supplier will allocate the stock to the retail store in its own warehouse, pack it, load it on to its truck, transport it to its destination, and unload it into the retailer's inventory. From the time that stock is allocated (and therefore it is unavailable to any other customer) to the time it becomes available for the retail store, it is said to be *in the pipeline*. All stock thus in transit is pipeline inventory.

The position of inventory

Not only are there several reasons for supply–demand imbalance, there could also be several points where such imbalance could exist between different stages in the operation. Figure 12.4 illustrates different levels of complexity of inventory relationships within an operation. Perhaps the simplest level is the single-stage inventory system, such as a retail store, which will have only one stock of goods to manage. An automotive parts distribution operation will have a central depot and various local distribution points which contain inventories. In many manufacturers of standard items there are three types of inventory. The *raw material and components store inventories* (sometimes called input inventories) receive goods from the operation's suppliers; the raw materials and components work their way through the various stages of the production process but spend considerable amounts of time as *work-in-progress* (WIP) before finally reaching the *finished goods inventory*.

A development of this last system is the *multi-echelon* inventory system. This maps the relationship of inventories between the various operations within a supply network (*see* Chapter 6). In Fig. 12.4 there are five interconnected sets of inventory systems. The second-tier supplier's (yarn producer's) inventories will feed the first-tier supplier's (cloth producer's) inventories, who will in turn supply the main operation. The products are distributed to local warehouses from where they are shipped to the final customers. We will discuss the behaviour and management of such multi-echelon systems in the next chapter.

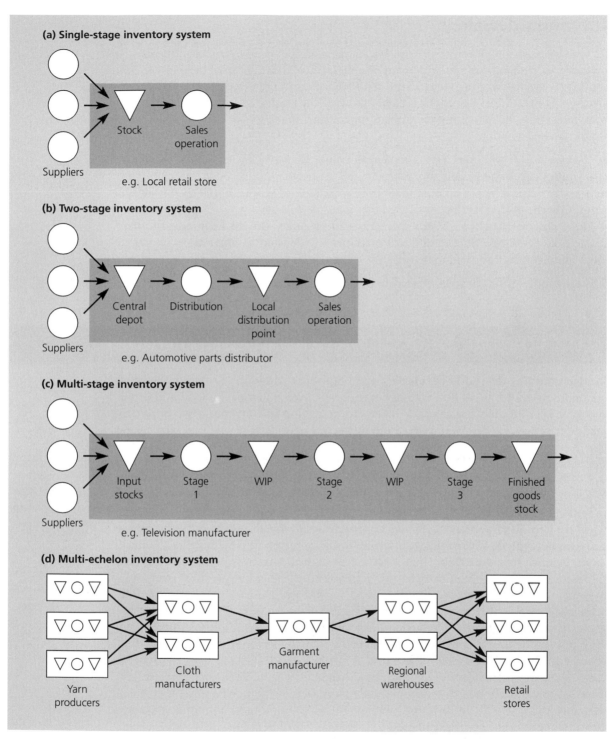

Figure 12.4 (a) Single stage, (b) two-stage, (c) multi-stage inventory systems, and (d) a multi-echelon inventory system

Inventory decisions

At each point in the inventory system operations managers need to manage the day-to-day tasks of running the system. Orders will be received from internal or external customers; these will be dispatched and demand will gradually deplete the inventory. Orders will need to be placed for replenishment of the stocks, deliveries will arrive and require storing. In managing the system, operations managers are involved in three major types of decision:

● *How much to order.* Every time a replenishment order is placed, how big should it be (sometimes called the *volume decision*)?
● *When to order.* At what point in time, or at what level of stock, should the replenishment order be placed (sometimes called the *timing decision*)?
● *How to control the system.* What procedures and routines should be installed to help make these decisions? Should different priorities be allocated to different stock items? How should stock information be stored?

The remainder of this chapter deals with these three major decisions.

THE VOLUME DECISION – HOW MUCH TO ORDER

To illustrate this decision consider a simple domestic situation. Probably the most common inventory we all deal with in our domestic lives is that of the food and provisions we keep in our apartment or house. In managing this inventory we implicitly make decisions on *order quantity*, that is how much to purchase at one time. In making this decision we are balancing two sets of costs: the costs associated with going out to purchase the food items and the costs associated with holding the stocks. One option would be to hold very little or no inventory of food and purchase each item only when it is needed. The advantage of this approach is that we would never have to raise the large amounts of money necessary to make major purchases, spending only when we needed to. However, such an approach would involve going out to purchase provisions three or four times a day. The costs in terms of our time and general inconvenience would probably make this a very unattractive proposition. At the very opposite extreme, we could make one journey to the local superstore every few months and purchase all the provisions we would need until our next visit. The advantage of this is that the time and costs incurred in making the purchase are incurred very infrequently. The major disadvantage is that we would have to pay out a very large amount of money each time the trip was made – money which could otherwise be in the bank and earning interest. A further disadvantage might be that the costs of storing such large quantities of food would also be expensive. We might have to invest in extra cupboard units and a very large freezer. Somewhere between these extremes there will lie an ordering strategy which will minimize the total costs and effort involved in the purchase of food.

Inventory costs

Exactly the same principles apply in commercial order-quantity decisions as in the domestic situation. In making a decision on how much to purchase, operations managers first try to identify the costs which will be affected by their decision. A number of costs are relevant.

1 *Cost of placing the order.* Every time an order is placed to replenish stock a number of transactions are needed which incur costs to the company. These include the clerical tasks of preparing the order and all the documentation associated with it, arranging for the delivery to be made, arranging to pay the supplier for the delivery, and the general costs of keeping all the information which allows us to do this. If we are placing an order on part of our own operation, there are still likely to be the same types of transaction concerned with internal record-keeping, but also there could be a 'change-over' cost incurred by the part of the operation which is to supply the items and caused by the need to change from producing one type of item to another.

2 *Price discount costs.* In many industries suppliers offer discounts on the normal purchase price for large quantities; alternatively they might impose extra costs for small orders.

3 *Stock-out costs.* If we misjudge the order-quantity decision and our inventory runs out of stock there will be costs to us incurred by failing to supply our customers. If the customers are external, they may take their business elsewhere; if internal, stock-outs could lead to idle time at the next process, inefficiencies and eventually again, dissatisfied external customers.

4 *Working capital costs.* Soon after we place a replenishment order, suppliers will demand payment for their goods. Eventually, when we supply our own customers, we in turn will receive payment. However, there will probably be a lag between paying our suppliers and receiving payment from our customers. During this time we will have to fund the costs of however much we have in stock. This is called the *working capital* which we need to run the inventory. The costs associated with it are the interest we pay the bank for borrowing it, or the opportunity costs of not investing it elsewhere.

5 *Storage costs.* These are the costs associated with physically storing the goods. Renting, heating and lighting the warehouse can be expensive, especially when special conditions are required such as low-temperature or high-security storage.

6 *Obsolescence costs.* If we choose an ordering policy which involves very large order quantities, which will mean that stocked items spend a long time stored in inventory, there is a risk that the items might either become obsolete (in the case of a change in fashion, for example) or deteriorate with age (in the case of most foodstuffs, for example).

7 *Production inefficiency costs.* According to just-in-time philosophies high, inventory levels prevent us seeing the full extent of problems within the operation. This argument is fully explored in Chapter 15.

We can divide all these inventory-associated costs into two groups. The first three categories are costs which usually decrease as order size is increased. The other categories of cost usually increase as order size is increased.

Inventory profiles

An inventory profile is a visual representation of the inventory level over time. Figure 12.5 shows a simplified inventory profile for one particular stock item in a

**Figure 12.5
Inventory profiles
chart the variation
in inventory level**

retail operation. Every time an order is placed, Q items are ordered. The replenishment order arrives in one batch instantaneously. Demand for the item is then steady and perfectly predictable at a rate of D units per month. When demand has depleted the stock of the items entirely, another order of Q items instantaneously arrives, and so on. Under these circumstances:

The average inventory $= \dfrac{Q}{2}$ (because the two shaded areas in Fig. 12.5 are equal)

The time interval between deliveries $= \dfrac{Q}{D}$

The frequency of deliveries = the reciprocal of the time interval $= \dfrac{D}{Q}$

The economic order quantity (EOQ) formula

The most common approach to deciding how much of any particular item to order when stock needs replenishing is called the economic order quantity (EOQ) approach. Essentially this approach attempts to find the best balance between the advantages and the disadvantages of holding stock. For example, Fig. 12.6 shows two alternative order-quantity policies for an item. Plan A, represented by the unbroken line, involves ordering in quantities of 400 at a time. Demand in this case is running at

**Figure 12.6
Two alternative
inventory plans
with different
order quantities (Q)**

1000 units per year. Plan B, represented by the dotted line, envisages smaller but more frequent replenishment orders. This time only 100 are ordered at a time with orders being placed four times as often. However, the average inventory for plan B is one quarter of that for plan A.

To find out whether either of these plans, or some other plan, minimizes the total cost of stocking the item, we need some further information, namely the total cost of holding one unit in stock for a period of time (C_h) and the total costs of placing an order (C_o). Generally, holding costs are taken into account by including:

- working capital costs
- storage costs
- obsolescence risk costs.

Order costs are calculated by taking into account:

- cost of placing the order (including transportation of items from suppliers if relevant);
- price discount costs.

In this case the cost of holding stocks is calculated at £1 per item per year and the cost of placing an order is calculated at £20 per order.

We can now calculate total holding costs and ordering costs for any particular ordering plan as follows:

Holding costs $=$ Holding cost/unit $\times$ average inventory

$$= C_h \times \frac{Q}{2}$$

Ordering costs $=$ Ordering cost $\times$ number of orders per period

$$= C_o \times \frac{D}{Q}$$

So, total cost, $C_t \quad = \dfrac{C_h Q}{2} + \dfrac{C_o D}{Q}$

We can now calculate the costs of adopting plans with different order quantities. These are illustrated in Table. 12.3. As we would expect with low values of Q, holding costs are low but the costs of placing orders are high because orders have to be placed very frequently. As Q increases, the holding costs increase but the costs of placing orders decrease. Initially the decrease in ordering costs is greater than the increase in holding costs and the total cost falls. After a point, however, the decrease in ordering costs slows, whereas the increase in holding costs remains constant and the total cost starts to increase. In this case the order quantity, Q, which minimizes the sum of holding and order costs, is 200. This 'optimum' order quantity is called the *economic order quantity (EOQ)*. Graphically, this is illustrated in Fig. 12.7.

A more elegant method of finding the EOQ is to derive its general expression. This can be done using simple differential calculus as follows. From before:

Total cost $=$ Holding cost $+$ Order cost

$$C_t = \frac{C_h Q}{2} + \frac{C_o D}{Q}$$

Table 12.3 Costs of adoption of plans with different order quantities

Demand (*D*) = 1000 units per year Holding costs (*C_h*) = £1 per item per year Order costs (*C_O*) = £20 per order				
Order quantity (*Q*)	Holding costs (0.5*Q* × *C_h*)	+	Order costs ((*D*/*Q*) × *C_O*)	= Total costs
50	25		20 × 20 = 400	425
100	50		10 × 20 = 200	250
150	75		6.7 × 20 = 134	209
200	100		5 × 20 = 100	200*
250	125		4 × 20 = 80	205
300	150		3.3 × 20 = 66	216
350	175		2.9 × 20 = 58	233
400	200		2.5 × 20 = 50	250

* Minimum total cost

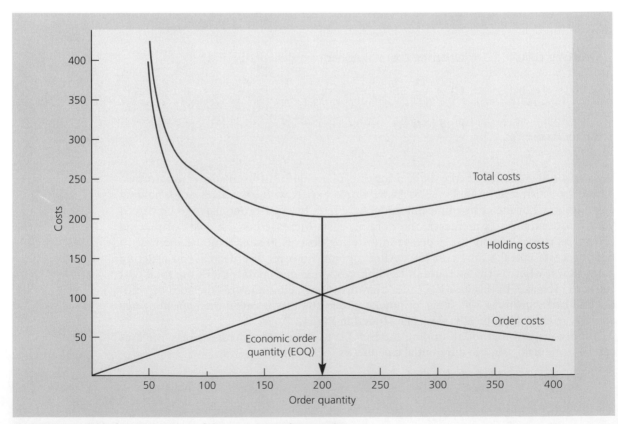

Figure 12.7 Graphical representation of the economic order quantity

The rate of change of total cost is given by the first differential of C_t with respect to Q

$$\frac{\mathrm{d}Ct}{\mathrm{d}Q} = \frac{C_h}{2} - \frac{C_oD}{Q^2}$$

The lowest cost will occur when $\dfrac{\mathrm{d}C_t}{\mathrm{d}Q} = 0$.

That is:

$$0 = \frac{C_h}{2} - \frac{C_oD}{Q_o{}^2}$$

where Q_o = the EOQ

Rearranging this expression gives:

$$Q_o = EOQ = \sqrt{\frac{2C_oD}{C_h}}$$

When using the EOQ:

$$\text{Time between orders} = \frac{EOQ}{D}$$

$$\text{Order frequency} = \frac{D}{EOQ} \text{ per period}$$

Sensitivity of the EOQ

Examination of the graphical representation of the total cost curve in Fig. 12.7 shows that, although there is a single value of Q which minimizes total costs, any relatively small deviation from the EOQ will not increase total costs significantly. In other words, costs will be near-optimum provided a value of Q which is reasonably close to the EOQ is chosen. Put another way, small errors in estimating either holding costs or order costs will not result in a significant deviation from the EOQ. This is a particularly convenient phenomenon because, in practice, both holding and order costs are not easy to estimate accurately.

Example

A building materials stockist obtains its cement from a single supplier. Demand for cement is reasonably constant throughout the year. Last year the company sold 2000 tonnes of cement. It estimates the costs of placing an order at around £25 each time an order is placed, and charges inventory holding at 20 per cent of purchase cost. The company purchases cement at £60 per tonne. How much cement should the company order at a time?

$$EOQ \text{ for cement} = \sqrt{\frac{2C_oD}{C_h}}$$

$$= \sqrt{\frac{2 \times 25 \times 2000}{0.2 \times 60}}$$

443

$$= \sqrt{\frac{100\ 000}{12}}$$

$$= 91.287 \text{ tonnes}$$

After calculating the EOQ the operations manager feels that placing an order for 91.287 tonnes *exactly* seems somewhat over-precise. Why not order a convenient 100 tonnes?

Total cost of ordering plan for Q = 91.287:

$$= \frac{C_h Q}{2} + \frac{C_o D}{Q}$$

$$= \frac{(0.2 \times 60) \times 91.287}{2} + \frac{25 \times 2000}{91.287}$$

$$= \pounds 1095.454$$

Total cost of ordering plan for Q = 100:

$$= \frac{(0.2 \times 60) \times 100}{2} + \frac{25 \times 2000}{100}$$

$$= \pounds 1100$$

The extra cost of ordering 100 tonnes at a time is $\pounds 1100 - \pounds 1095.45 = \pounds 4.55$. The operations manager therefore should feel confident in using the more convenient order quantity.

Gradual replacement – the economic batch quantity (EBQ) model

Although the simple inventory profile shown in Fig. 12.5 made some simplifying assumptions, it is broadly applicable in most situations where each replacement order arrives as a single delivery to the inventory point. In many cases, however, a replenishment order arrives over a time period rather than in one lot. A typical example of this is where an order is placed within the operation for a batch of parts to be produced on a machine. The machine will start to produce the parts and ship them in a more or less continuous stream into the inventory point. During the time that these units are being added to the inventory, demand is continuing to take place. Provided the rate at which parts are being made and put into the inventory (P) is higher than the rate at which demand is depleting the inventory (D) then the size of the inventory will increase. After the batch has been completed the machine will go on to produce some other part and demand will continue to deplete the inventory level. The resulting profile is shown in Fig. 12.8. Such an inventory profile is typical of the inventories supplied by batches or 'lots' of items produced internally. For this reason the minimum-cost order quantity for this profile is called the *economic batch quantity (EBQ)*. It is also sometimes known as the economic manufacturing quantity (EMQ) or the production order quantity (POQ). It is derived as follows:

Maximum stock level $= M$
Slope of inventory build-up $= P - D$

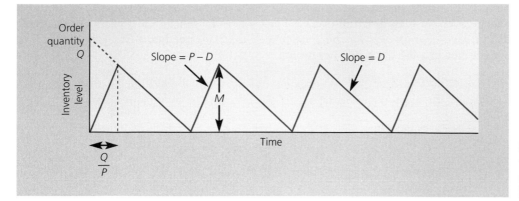

Figure 12.8
Inventory profile
for gradual
replacement of
inventory

Also:

Slope of inventory build-up $= M \div \dfrac{Q}{P}$

$ = \dfrac{MP}{Q}$

So,

$$\dfrac{MP}{Q} = P - D$$

$$M = \dfrac{Q\,(P-D)}{P}$$

$$\text{Average inventory level} = \dfrac{M}{2}$$

$$\phantom{\text{Average inventory level}} = \dfrac{Q\,(P-D)}{2P}$$

As before:

$$\text{Total cost} = \text{Holding cost} + \text{Order cost}$$

$$C_t = \dfrac{C_h Q\,(P-D)}{2P} + \dfrac{C_o D}{Q}$$

$$\dfrac{dC_t}{dQ} = \dfrac{C_h(P-D)}{2P} - \dfrac{C_o D}{Q^2}$$

Again, equating to zero and solving Q gives the minimum-cost order quantity EBQ.

$$EBQ = \sqrt{\dfrac{2C_o D}{C_h(1-(D/P))}}$$

Example

The manager of a bottle-filling plant which bottles soft drinks needs to decide how long a 'run' of each type of drink to ask the lines to process. Demand for each type of drink is reasonably constant at 80 000 per month (a month has 160 production

445

hours). The bottling lines fill at a rate of 3000 bottles per hour but take an hour to change over between different drinks. The cost (of labour and lost production capacity) of each change-over has been calculated at £100 per hour. Stock-holding costs are counted at £0.1 per bottle per month.

$$D = 80\,000 \text{ per month}$$

$$= 500 \text{ per hour}$$

$$EBQ = \sqrt{\frac{2C_oD}{C_h(1-(D/P))}}$$

$$= \sqrt{\frac{2 \times 100 \times 80\,000}{0.1\,(1-(500/3000))}}$$

$$EBQ = 13\,856$$

The staff who operate the lines have devised a method of reducing the change-over time from 1 hour to 30 minutes. How would that change the EBQ?

$$\text{New } C_o = £50$$

$$\text{New } EBQ = \sqrt{\frac{2 \times 50 \times 80\,000}{0.1(1-(500/3000))}}$$

$$= 9798$$

The economic batch quantity with shortages

Another assumption which was made when we derived the basic economic batch quantity formula was that there would never be a time where the inventory level fell to zero for any continuing period. Yet this is not the case in many inventory situations. It could be that customers are willing (though probably not happy) to wait if an item they request is not in stock. In this case, demand continues even though no items are in stock, in effect producing negative inventory. When the replenishment order arrives, the customers who have been waiting are supplied from the replenishment order before it is counted into the stock levels. This results in a profile as shown in Fig. 12.9.

**Figure 12.9
Inventory plans
allowing for
shortages**

Controlling the project and controlling the plant

Part of Black Point's central control room

One of Black Point's eight generator units

The construction of Black Point, Hong Kong's first natural gas-fired station, was a major task for GEC Alsthom, the consortium leader for the project. They had two control issues to face. One was how to control the vast construction project itself so that it would be delivered to the customer, China Light and Power (CLP), on time, on specification and on budget. The other was how to ensure that the plant, when in operation, could be controlled to ensure reliable, safe and efficient operation. Managing such a large project, lasting several years, called for exceptional project management skills. These included coping with the environmental implications of the project (using simulation), managing the other contractors who had responsibility for the various parts of the project (for example, GE, the engineering multinational, took technical

responsibility for co-ordination of the power train, the main power transmission mechanisms) and monitoring progress. Once operating, the power station is controlled using highly automated systems, with a single operator controlling four of the eight generator units during normal operation. The control systems are designed with 'redundancy' built in so that control is maintained even if some parts of the system malfunction. The central control room has been ergonomically designed with the supervisory operator workstations at the centre. Around this central hub are positioned the unit control desks, which communicate with the units. The plant is also provided with computerized facilities to monitor and predict the plant condition, including efficiency, environmental conditions, life expectancy, etc. An on-site plant simulator helps operator training and the development of optimum plant operating procedures.

Black Point power station, Hong Kong

> ■ *What are the main differences between controlling a major project such as the construction of the Black Point power plant, and controlling the automated continuous process when the plant is in full operation?*

→ *Look at Chapters 10 and 16 for guidance*

An Ideal Standard of inventory

Photo courtesy of Ideal Standard

Even at reduced inventory levels, stocks can take up space

Ideal Standard, part of American Standard Inc., are manufacturers of bathroom and sanitary wear. Like many manufacturers of consumer products, they must plan and control their operations so as to best utilize their production resources, as well as give a good standard of customer service. At one time the only way of doing this was thought to be by the use of large finished goods inventories. But since the advent of 'just-in-time' type principles, manufacturers such as Ideal Standard have managed to raise productivity, improve quality and dramatically reduce inventory. The programme which was put in place throughout American Standard Inc. was called 'Demand Flow Manufacturing'. All areas of inventory holding were scrutinized and driven down by reducing batch sizes and making-to-demand rather than making-to-stock. In some parts of the company, stock turns increased threefold and the money tied up in inventories reduced by over 75 per cent; productivity and quality have also improved significantly.

■ *What do you think are the particular difficulties in inventory management at Ideal Standard?*

■ *What are the major changes in attitude necessary in moving from a make-to-stock to a make-to-order philosophy of planning and control?*

→ *Look at Chapter 12 and 15 for guidance*

Planning and control at ICI Chlor-Chemicals

Customer service receiving orders ...

... triggers the plant to schedule production ...

Many businesses depend on their ability to perform a perpetual balancing act between supply and demand. Throw in too many orders and the plant becomes overloaded, with the threat of leaving customers dissatisfied. Manufacture too much product and the plant shifts the other way, tying up money and filling storage space with unsold stock. At ICI Chlor-Chemicals a process known as sales and operations planning (S&OP) works to ensure that the business keeps all the promises it makes to its customers. The S&OP process helps the business to order the raw materials and services it needs with accuracy, while also providing its plants with information as to which products to produce and in what quantity. The process has the power to plot the best plans and schedules for virtually any set of circumstances – planned or unplanned – in a way which will make best use of all the company's resources. By running a financial model, it is possible to find a solution to unforeseen production problems by rescheduling production in a way that keeps customers satisfied and avoids a potentially damaging impact on the

bottom line. By providing accurate estimates of future demand, it helps the procurement process and reduces the amount of both raw materials and products that need to be held in stock. The interface with the S&OP programme is via computer terminals and Local Area Networks (LANs) which allow customer service staff to view the production plans for the coming days and weeks. Every time customer service staff pick up the telephone to take a customer order, details of the relevant production plans are displayed automatically on screen to allow an instant, and informed, response. Receipts of raw materials trigger payments to the supplier, just as despatches of finished product trigger the raising of an invoice to the customer. By providing more people with more information, S&OP helps the company's staff to take better decisions – for the benefit of the business and its customers.

- *What should a good planning and control system be able to do to help a complex operation such as ICI Chlor-Chemicals?*
- *Why is the financial modelling part of S&OP useful?*

➜ *Look at Chapter 14 for guidance*

... and eventual despatch to the customer

Coping with seasonality at Nestlé

Some of Nestlé's popular chocolate products

Packing high-quality chocolate assortments

Any food manufacturer has to learn how to cope with seasonal fluctuations. Nestlé, the Swiss-based multinational, the largest food company in the world, has more experience than most. Either the supply of materials is seasonal (frozen vegetables), or demand is seasonal (ice-cream), or both (dried milk). The manufacture of chocolate products is typical. Demand is driven partly by the weather – chocolate is less popular in summer – and partly by cultural factors – chocolate is a popular gift at Christmas and Easter in many countries. Nestlé plants use a combination of strategies to cope with these demand fluctuations. Some products can be stored in anticipation of seasonal peaks. However, there is a 'shelf-life' limit on storage time if Nestlé's high quality standards are to be maintained. Off-peak sales volumes can also be influenced through the use of 'special offers' and product promotions. Within Nestlé's plants themselves, output rates can be fluctuated, though different ways of doing this may be appropriate at different stages in the process. The manufacture of the chocolate itself is constrained by the capacity limits of the process technology, whereas in the packing of assortments, for example (*see picture*), extra staff can be hired at peak times. All this makes for a sensitive decision-making environment. If Nestlé managers get it wrong, either we run out of our favourite products, or the company is left with surplus stock.

- *What are the main 'trade-offs' which Nestlé managers have to get right in coping with the seasonality of their chocolate products?*
- *What do you think are the differences between managing seasonality for the popular products illustrated above left (known as 'count lines') and the up-market chocolate assortments shown being packed in the right-hand picture?*

→ *Look at Chapter 11 for guidance*

Deriving an expression for the EBQ in a similar manner gives,

$$EBQ = \sqrt{\frac{2DC_o}{C_h}} \sqrt{\frac{C_h + C_s}{C_s}}$$

where C_s = cost per unit of shortage per time period.

Example

Super Soups manufactures specialist gourmet frozen soups for the restaurant trade. All its soups used to sell at a reasonably steady rate of 700 litres per day. Recently the company adopted a policy of reducing the price by £1 per litre for every day a customer had to wait for delivery. Normally orders are delivered on the same day as ordering but if the soup is not in stock, customers have to wait until it is next manufactured. Keeping soup frozen is expensive and the company charges itself for storage at a rate of £0.16 per litre per day. It has also calculated that the cost of changing its production processes to make a different flavour costs £100. The new policy was a success and increased demand for all its soups to 1000 litres per day. What effect should these changes have on its stock-ordering policy?

Previously:

$$D = 700 \text{ litres/day}$$

$$C_o = £100$$

$$C_h = £0.16 \text{ per day}$$

$$EOQ = \sqrt{\frac{2 \times 700 \times 100}{0.16}} = 935 \text{ litres}$$

Now:

$$C_s = £1 \text{ per litre per day}$$

From formula allowing shortages:

$$EOQ = \sqrt{\frac{2 \times 1000 \times 100}{0.16}} \times \sqrt{\frac{0.16 + 1}{1}}$$

$$= 1204$$

The economic order quantity needs to be increased from 935 litres per day to 1204 litres per day.

If customers won't wait – the news-seller problem

A special case of the inventory order-quantity decision refers to the situation where an order quantity of items is purchased for a specific event or time period, after which the items are unlikely to be sold. A simple example of this is the decision taken by a newspaper seller of how many newspapers to stock for the day. If the news-seller should run out of papers, customers will either go elsewhere or decide not to buy a paper that day.

If any newspapers are left over at the end of the day, the value of yesterday's news is zero. Demand for the newspapers varies day by day depending on who happens to be passing, the weather at the time, and the appeal of that day's news. In deciding how many newspapers to carry, the news-seller is in effect balancing the risk and consequence of running out of newspapers against that of having newspapers left over at the end of the day. To a certain extent retailers and manufacturers in the fashion garment business, publishers and popular music CD producers all face the same problem. The method for determining the optimum order quantity is best illustrated through an example.

Example

A concert promoter needs to decide how many concert T-shirts to order emblazoned with the logo of the main act. The profit on each T-shirt sold at the concert is £5 and any unsold T-shirts are returned to the company who supplies them, but at a loss to the promoter of £3 per T-shirt. Demand is uncertain but is estimated to be between 200 and 1000. The probabilities of different demand are as follows:

Demand level	200	400	600	800
Probability	0.2	0.3	0.4	0.1

How many T-shirts should the promoter order? Table 12.4 shows the profit which the promoter would make for different order quantities and different levels of demand.

Table 12.4 Pay-off matrix for T-shirt order quantity (profit or loss in £s)

Demand level	200	400	600	800
Probability	0.2	0.3	0.4	0.1
Promoter orders 200	1000	1000	1000	1000
Promoter orders 400	400	2000	2000	2000
Promoter orders 600	−200	1400	3000	3000
Promoter orders 800	−800	800	2400	4000

We can now calculate the *expected* profit which the promoter will make for each order quantity by weighting the outcomes by their probability of occurring.

If the promoter orders 200 T-shirts:

$$\text{Expected profit} = 1000 \times 0.2 + 1000 \times 0.3 + 1000 \times 0.4 + 1000 \times 0.1$$

$$= £1000$$

If the promoter orders 400 T-shirts:

$$\text{Expected profit} = 400 \times 0.2 + 2000 \times 0.3 + 2000 \times 0.4 + 2000 \times 0.1$$

$$= £1680$$

If the promoter orders 600 T-shirts:

Expected profit $= -200 \times 0.2 + 1400 \times 0.3 + 3000 \times 0.4 + 3000 \times 0.1$

$= £1880$

If the promoter orders 800 T-shirts:

Expected profit $= -800 \times 0.2 + 800 \times 0.3 + 2400 \times 0.4 + 4000 \times 0.1$

$= £1440$

The order quantity which gives the maximum profit is 600 T-shirts, which results in a profit of £1880.

Criticism of the EOQ approach[3]

The approach to determining order quantity which involves optimizing costs of holding stock against costs of ordering stock, typified by the EOQ and EBQ models, has always been subject to criticisms. Originally these concerned the validity of some of the assumptions of the model; more recently they have involved the underlying rationale of the approach itself. We shall examine three classes of criticism concerning:

- the assumptions included in the models;
- the real costs of stock in operations;
- the use of the models as prescriptive devices.

Model assumptions

In order to keep EOQ-type models relatively straightforward, it was necessary to make assumptions concerning such things as the stability of demand, the existence of a fixed and identifiable ordering cost, the cost of stock holding which can be expressed by a linear function, shortage costs which were identifiable, and so on. While none of these assumptions is often strictly true, most of them can approximate to reality. Furthermore, as we have pointed out before, the shape of the total cost curve has a relatively flat optimum point which means that small errors will not significantly affect the total cost of a near-optimum order quantity. However, at times the assumptions do pose severe limitations to the models. For example, the assumption of steady demand (or even demand which conforms to some known probability distribution) is untrue for a wide range of the operation's inventory problems. For example, a book seller might be very happy to adopt an EOQ-type ordering policy for some of its products such as dictionaries and other reference books. However, estimating demand for some books is far more difficult. For some novels the probability distribution which describes likely demand is bi-modal. If the book does not catch the public's imagination it will sell a reasonable number to customers who are familiar with the author; however, if it is well reviewed or other publicity surrounds it, the demand could be many times what it would otherwise be. An EOQ approach has difficulty in coping with such wild fluctuations in demand.

Other questions surround some of the assumptions made on the nature of stock-related costs. For example, placing an order with a supplier as part of a regular and multi-item order might be relatively inexpensive, whereas asking for a special one-off delivery of one item could prove far more costly. Similarly with stock-holding costs, although many companies make a standard percentage charge on the purchase price of stock items, this might not be appropriate over a wide range of stock-holding levels. The marginal costs of increasing stock-holding levels might be merely the cost of the working capital involved. On the other hand, it might necessitate the construction or lease of a whole new stock-holding facility such as a warehouse. Operations managers using an EOQ-type approach must check that the decisions implied by the use of the formulae do not exceed the limits within which the cost assumptions apply.

How costly is stock?

In Chapter 15 we fully explore the just-in-time approach to operations management which holds that inventories generally exert a malign influence in operations. We will postpone exploration of this idea until Chapter 15, but it is useful at this stage to examine the effect on an EOQ approach of regarding stock as being more costly. Increasing the slope of the holding cost line increases the level of total costs of any order quantity, but more significantly, shifts the minimum cost's optimum point substantially to the left, in favour of a lower economic order quantity. In other words, the less sanguine an operation is about holding stock, the more it should move towards smaller, more frequent ordering.

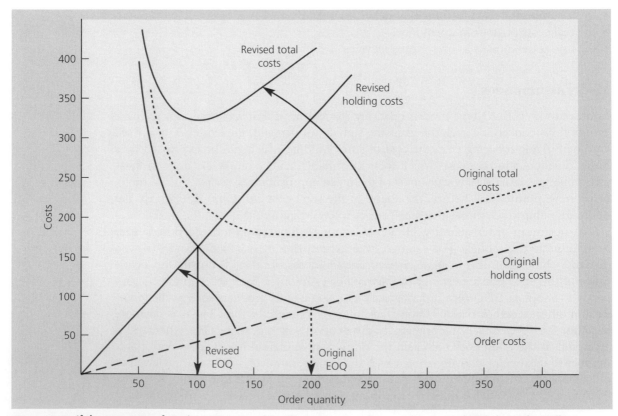

Figure 12.10 If the true costs of stock holding are taken, the economic order quantity, the real EOQ, is much smaller

Using EOQ models as prescriptions

Perhaps the most fundamental criticism of the EOQ approach again comes from the Japanese-inspired JIT philosophies. The emphasis of EOQ is on trying to determine representative costs of ordering and stock holding and then optimizing order decisions in the light of these costs. Implicitly the costs are taken as fixed, in the sense that the task of operations managers is to find out what are the true costs rather than to change them in any way. EOQ is essentially a reactive approach. Some critics would argue that it fails to ask the right question. Rather than asking the EOQ question of 'What is the optimum order quantity?', operations managers should really be asking, 'How can I change the operation in some way so as to reduce the overall level of stocks it is necessary to hold in the operation?'. The EOQ approach may be a reasonable description of stock-holding costs but should not necessarily be taken as a strict prescription over what decisions to take.

For example, many organizations have made considerable efforts to reduce the effective cost of placing an order. Often they have done this by working to reduce change-over times on machines. This means that less time is taken changing over from one product to the other and therefore less operating capacity is lost, which in turn reduces the cost of the change-over. Under these circumstances, the order cost curve in the EOQ formula reduces and, in turn, reduces the effective economic order quantity. Figure 12.10 shows the EOQ formula represented graphically with increased holding costs (see the previous discussion). Figure 12.11 shows also the further effects of reduced order costs, the net effect of which is to shift the value of the EOQ even further to the left.

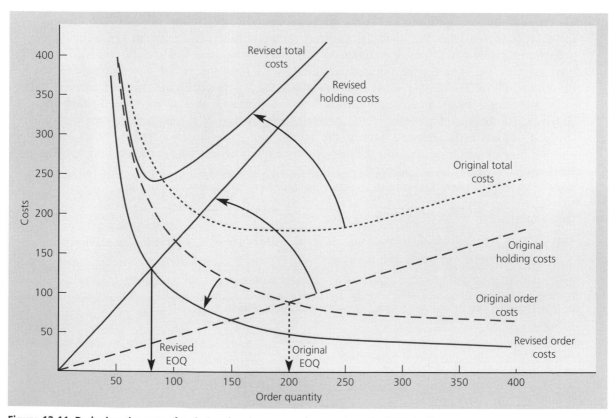

Figure 12.11 Reducing the cost of ordering (or change-over) can reduce the EOQ further

SHOULD WE REORDER? – THE MARKS & SPENCER APPROACH[4]

A special case of the 'how much to order?' decision in inventory control is the 'Should we order any more at all?' decision. Retailers especially need continually to review the stocked lines they keep on the shelves. One company known for its ruthless approach to the restocking decision is Marks & Spencer (M & S), which is one of the most successful large retailers in Europe in terms of the profitability of its operations. M & S has a simple philosophy: if it sells, restock it quickly and avoid stock-outs; if it doesn't sell, get it off the shelves quickly and replace it with something which *will* sell. The M & S approach is purely pragmatic, based on trial-and-error, and very unsentimental. This often means putting a new line on the shelves of a pilot store and watching customer reaction very closely. The store most often used for these trials is the company's Marble Arch store in London – said to have the fastest stock turnover of any store in the world. Sometimes it is possible to make a restocking decision within a few hours – not surprising when the time frame for stock rotation can be as little as a week.

For more routine stock control decisions the company uses an automatic stock-ordering system which it calls ASR (Assisted Stock Replenishment – *see also* box on Marks & Spencer in Chapter 13). This helps always to have the right stock of textile products in the store at the right time. The system, which is now installed in its flagship Marble Arch store, takes into account all goods bought at the till through the electronic point-of-sale (EPOS) system and automatically generates an order to replenish that item. The system anticipates orders for each item based on the previous week's sales and delivers in advance. The current day's sales are continually reviewed and any extra items required are delivered the next day. Orders arrive at the store from the local distribution centre at Neasden in North London. New orders are usually placed before 8.30 am and 85 per cent of these will arrive before close of business that day. The remainder arrives the following morning before opening time. The number of deliveries each day varies between 14 and 24 depending on the level of business.

On the sales floor the main stock control tasks are to ensure that all the clothing rails are fully stocked, that the stock tickets reflect the sales information on display and that everything is neatly and correctly arranged. During the day the area supervisor watches the stock levels and the flow of customers around the displays in case any changes to stock location need to be made. The store has a policy of not bringing stock out on to the floor during opening hours; but in the case of fast-moving items, this can at times be unavoidable. ■

Questions

1 Why is it particularly important for retail operations such as Marks & Spencer to make judgements quickly about how well a product is likely to sell?

2 What do you see as the major advantages of using the electronic point-of-sale (EPOS) system?

3 What kind of inventory policy seems to operate in Marks & Spencer's stores?

THE TIMING DECISION – WHEN TO PLACE AN ORDER

When we assumed that orders arrived instantaneously and demand was steady and predictable, the decision on when to place a replenishment order was self-evident. An order would be placed as soon as the stock level reached zero. This would arrive instantaneously and prevent any stock-out occurring. If replenishment orders do not arrive instantaneously but have a lag between the order being placed and it arriving in the inventory, we can calculate the timing of a replacement order as shown in Fig. 12.12. The lead time for an order to arrive is in this case two weeks, so the re-order point (ROP) is the point at which stock will fall to zero minus the order lead time. Alternatively, we can define the point in terms of the level which the inventory will have reached when a replenishment order needs to be placed. In this case this occurs at a re-order level (ROL) of 200 items.

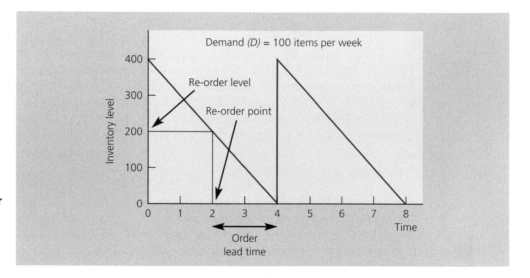

Figure 12.12 Re-order level (ROL) and re-order point (ROP) are derived from the order lead time and demand rate

However, this assumes that both the demand and the order lead time are perfectly predictable. In most cases of course this is not so. Both demand and the order lead time are likely to vary to produce a profile which looks something like Fig. 12.13. In these circumstances it is necessary to make the replenishment order somewhat earlier than would be the case in a purely deterministic situation. This will result in, on average, some stock still being in the inventory when the replenishment order arrives. This is buffer or safety stock (s). The earlier the replenishment order is placed, the higher will be the expected level of safety stock (s) when the replenishment order arrives. But because of the variability both of lead time (t) and demand rate (d), there will sometimes be a higher-than-average level of safety stock and sometimes lower. The main consideration in setting safety stock is not so much the average level of stock when a replenishment order arrives but rather the probability that the stock will not have run out before the replenishment order arrives.

The key statistic in calculating how much safety stock to allow is the probability distribution which shows the *lead-time usage*. The lead-time usage distribution is a combination of the distributions which describe lead-time variation and the demand rate during the lead time. If safety stock is set below the lower limit of this distribution then there will be shortages every single replenishment cycle. If safety stock is set above the upper limit

**Figure 12.13
Safety stock (*s*)
helps to avoid
stock-outs when
demand and/or
order lead time is
uncertain**

of the distribution, there is no chance of stock-outs occurring. Usually, safety stock is set to give a predetermined likelihood that stock-outs will not occur. Figure 12.13 shows that, in this case, the first replenishment order arrived after t_1 resulting in a lead-time usage of d_1. The second replenishment order took longer, t_2, and demand rate was also higher, resulting in a lead-time usage of d_2. The third order cycle shows several possible inventory profiles for different conditions of lead-time usage and demand rate.

Example

A company which imports running shoes for sale in its sports shops can never be certain of how long, after placing an order, the delivery will take. Examination of previous orders reveals that out of ten orders: one took one week, two took two weeks, four took three weeks, two took four weeks and one took five weeks. The rate of demand for the shoes also varies between 110 pairs per week and 140 pairs per week. There is a 0.2 probability of the demand rate being either 110 or 140 pairs per week and a 0.3 chance of demand being either 120 or 130 pairs per week. The company needs to decide when it should place replenishment orders if the probability of a stock-out is to be less than ten per cent.

Both lead time and the demand rate during the lead time will contribute to the lead-time usage. So the distributions which describe each will need to be combined. Figure 12.14 and Table 12.5 show how this can be done. Taking lead time to be either one, two, three, four or five weeks and demand rate to be either 110, 120, 130 or 140 pairs per week, and also assuming the two variables to be independent, the distributions can be combined as shown in Table 12.5. Each element in the matrix shows a possible lead-time usage with the probability of its occurrence. So if the lead time is one week and the demand rate is 110 pairs per week, the actual lead-time usage will be $1 \times 110 = 110$ pairs. Since there is a 0.1 chance of the lead time being one week, and a 0.2 chance of demand rate being 110 pairs per week, the probability of both these events occurring is $0.1 \times 0.2 = 0.02$.

We can now classify the possible lead-time usages into histogram form. For example, summing the probabilities of all the lead-time usages which fall within the

**Figure 12.14
The probability distributions for order lead time and demand rate combine to give the lead-time usage distribution**

Table 12.5 Matrix of lead time and demand rate probabilities

			Lead time probabilities			
		1 *0.1*	*2* *0.2*	*3* *0.4*	*4* *0.2*	*5* *0.1*
110	*0.2*	110 (0.02)	220 (0.04)	330 (0.08)	440 (0.04)	550 (0.02)
120	*0.3*	120 (0.03)	240 (0.06)	360 (0.12)	480 (0.06)	600 (0.03)
130	*0.3*	130 (0.03)	260 (0.06)	390 (0.12)	520 (0.06)	650 (0.03)
140	*0.2*	140 (0.02)	280 (0.04)	420 (0.08)	560 (0.04)	700 (0.02)

Demand rate probabilities

range 100–199 (all the first column) gives a combined probability of 0.1. Repeating this for subsequent intervals results in Table 12.6.

This shows the probability of each possible range of lead-time usage occurring, but it is the cumulative probabilities which are needed to predict the likelihood of stock-out (*see* Table 12.7).

Table 12.6 Combined probabilities

Lead-time usage	100–199	200–299	300–399	400–499	500–599	600–699	700–799
Probability	0.1	0.2	0.32	0.18	0.12	0.06	0.02

Table 12.7 Combined probabilities

Lead-time usage X	100	200	300	400	500	600	700	800
Probability of usage being greater than X	1.0	0.9	0.7	0.38	0.2	0.08	0.02	0

Setting the re-order level at 600 would mean that there is only a 0.08 chance of usage being greater than available inventory during the lead time, i.e. there is a less than ten per cent chance of a stock-out occurring.

Continuous and periodic review

The approach we have described to making the replenishment timing decision is often called the *continuous review approach*. This is because to make the decision in this way operations managers need to review continuously the stock level of each item and then place an order when the stock level reaches its re-order level. The virtue of this approach is that, although the timing of orders may be irregular (depending on the variation in demand rate), the order size (Q) is constant and can be set at the optimum economic order quantity. However, continually checking on inventory levels can be time consuming, especially when there are many stock withdrawals compared to the average level of stock.

An alternative and far simpler approach, but one which sacrifices the use of a fixed (and therefore possibly optimum) order quantity, is called the *periodic review approach*. Here, rather than ordering at a predetermined re-order level, the periodic approach orders at a fixed and regular time interval. So the stock level of an item could be checked, for example, at the end of every month and a replenishment order placed to bring the stock level up to a predetermined level. This level is calculated to cover demand between the replenishment order being placed and the following replenishment order arriving. Figure 12.15 illustrates the parameters for the periodic review approach.

At time T_1 in Fig. 12.15 the inventory manager would examine the stock level and order sufficient to bring the stock level up to some maximum stock level Q_m. However, that order of Q_1 items will not arrive until a further time of t_1 has passed, during which demand continues to deplete the stocks. Again both demand and lead time are uncertain. The Q_1 items will arrive and bring the stock level up to some level lower than Q_m (unless there has been no demand in t_1). Demand then continues until T_2 when again an order Q_2 is placed which is the difference between the current stock at T_2 and Q_m. This order arrives after t_2 by which time demand has depleted the

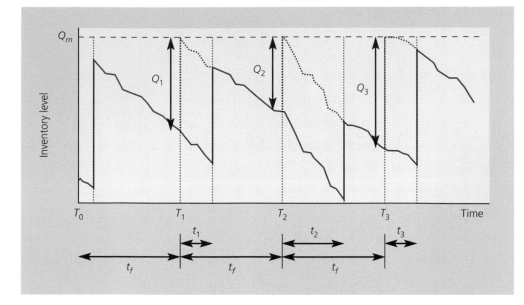

Figure 12.15
A periodic review approach to order timing with probabilistic demand and lead time

stocks further. Thus the replenishment order placed at T_1 must be able to cover for the demand which occurs until T_2 and t_2. Safety stocks will need to be calculated, in a similar manner to before, based on the distribution of usage over this period.

The time interval

The interval between placing orders, t_1, is usually calculated on a deterministic basis, and derived from the EOQ. So, for example, if the demand for an item is 2000 per year, the cost of placing an order £25, and the cost of holding stock £0.5 per item per year:

$$EOQ = \sqrt{\frac{2C_oD}{C_h}} = \sqrt{\frac{2 \times 2000 \times 25}{0.5}} = 447$$

The optimum time interval between orders t_f is therefore:

$$t_f = \frac{EOQ}{D} = \frac{447}{2000} \text{ years}$$

$$= 2.68 \text{ months}$$

It may seem paradoxical to calculate the time interval assuming constant demand when demand is, in fact, uncertain. However, uncertainties both of demand and lead time can be allowed for by setting Q_m to allow for the desired probability of stock-out based on usage during the period t_f + lead time.

Two-bin and three-bin systems

Keeping track of inventory levels is especially important in continuous review approaches to re-ordering. A simple and obvious method of indicating when the re-order point has been reached is necessary, especially if there are a large number of items to be monitored. The two- and three-bin systems illustrated in Fig. 12.16 are such systems. The simple two-bin system involves storing the re-order point quantity

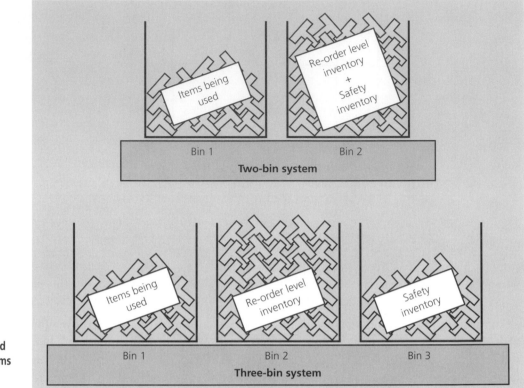

**Figure 12.16
The two-bin and
three-bin systems
of re-ordering**

plus the safety inventory quantity in the second bin and using parts from the first bin. When the first bin empties, that is the signal to order the next re-order quantity. Sometimes the safety inventory is stored in a third bin (the three-bin system), so it is clear when demand is exceeding that which was expected.

Different 'bins' are not always necessary to operate this type of system. For example, a common practice in retail operations is to store the second 'bin' quantity upside-down behind or under the first 'bin' quantity. Orders are then placed when the upside-down items are reached

INVENTORY ANALYSIS AND CONTROL SYSTEMS

The models we have described so far, even the ones which take a probabilistic view of demand and lead time, are still simplified compared to the complexity of real stock management. Coping with many thousands of stocked items, supplied by many hundreds of different suppliers, with possibly tens of thousands of individual customers, makes for a complex and dynamic operations task. In order to control such complexity, operations managers have to do two things. First, they have to discriminate between different stocked items, so that they can apply a degree of control to each item which is appropriate to its importance. Second, they need to invest in an information-processing system which can cope with their particular set of inventory control circumstances.

INVENTORY MANAGEMENT AT FLAME ELECTRICAL[5]

Inventory management in some operations is more than just a part of their responsibility; it is their very reason for being in business. Flame Electrical, South Africa's largest independent supplier and distributor of lamps, is such a business. It stocks over 2900 different types of lamp which vary in value from 25 cents (5p) to over 7000 rand (£1000). The lamps, which are sourced from 14 countries including South Africa, are stored in a 5000 square metre warehouse, and distributed to customers throughout the country.

'In effect our customers are using us to manage their stocks of lighting sources for them,' says Jeff Schaffer, the Managing Director of Flame Electrical. *'They could, if they wanted to, hold their own stock but might not want to devote the time, space, money or effort to doing so. Using us they get the widest range of products to choose from, and an accurate, fast and dependable service.'*

Central to the company's ability to provide the service which its customers expect is its computerized stock management system. The system holds information on all of Flame's customers, the type of lamps they may order, the quality and brand of lamps they prefer, the price to be charged, the internal product codes which Flame uses to identify each item it stocks, and the location of each item in the warehouse. When a customer phones in to order, the computer system immediately accesses all this information, which is confirmed to the customer. This only leaves the quantity of each lamp required by the customer to be keyed in. The system then generates an instruction to the warehouse to pick and dispatch the order. This instruction includes the shelf location of each item. The system even calculates the location of each item in the warehouse which will minimize the movement of stock for warehouse staff.

Orders for the replenishment of stocks in the warehouse are triggered by a re-order point system. The re-order point is set for each stocked item depending on the likely demand for the product during the order lead time (forecast from the equivalent period's orders the previous year), the order lead time for the item (which varies from 24 hours to four months) and the variability of the lead time (from previous experience). The size of the replenishment order depends on the lamp being ordered. Flame prefers most orders to be for a whole number of container loads (the shipping costs for part-container loads being more expensive). However, lower order quantities of small or expensive lamps may be used. The order quantity for each lamp is based on its demand, its value and the cost of transportation from the suppliers. However, all this can be overridden in an emergency. If a customer, such as a hospital, urgently needs a particular lamp which is not in stock, the company will even use a fast courier to fly the item in from overseas – all for the sake of maintaining its reputation for high service levels.

'We have to get the balance right,' says Jeff Schaffer. *'Excellent service is the foundation of our success. But we could not survive if we did not control stocks tightly. After all we are carrying the cost of every lamp in our warehouse until the customer eventually pays for it. If stock levels were too high we just could not operate profitably. It is for that reason that we go as far as to pay incentives to the relevant staff based on how well they keep our working capital and stocks under control.'* ∎

Questions

1 Define what you think the five performance objectives (quality, speed, dependability, flexibility and cost) mean for an operation such as Flame Electrical.

2 What are the most important of these performance objectives for Flame Electrical?

3 What seems to influence the stock replenishment policy of Flame Electrical?

4 How does this differ from conventional economic order quantity theory?

Inventory priorities – the ABC system

In any inventory which contains more than one stocked item, some items will be more important to the organization than others. Some items, for example, might have a very high usage rate, so if they ran out many customers would be disappointed. Other items might be of particularly high value, so excessively high inventory levels would be particularly expensive. One common way of discriminating between different stock items is to rank them by the *value of their usage* (their usage rate multiplied by their individual value). Items with a particularly high value of usage are deemed to warrant careful control, whereas those with low usage values need not be controlled quite so rigorously. Generally, a relatively small proportion of the total items contained in an inventory will account for a large proportion of the total inventory value. This phenomenon is known as the *Pareto law* (after the person who described it), sometimes referred to as the 80/20 rule. It is called this because, typically, 80 per cent of an operation's inventory value is accounted for by only 20 per cent of all stocked item types. The Pareto law is also used elsewhere in operations management (*see*, for example, Chapter 18). Here the relationship can be used to classify the different types of items kept in an inventory by their usage value. This allows inventory managers to concentrate their efforts on controlling the more significant items of stock.

- *Class A items* are those 20 per cent or so of high-value items which account for around 80 per cent of the total stock value.
- *Class B items* are those of medium value, usually the next 30 per cent of items which account for around 10 per cent of the total value.
- *Class C items* are those low-value items which, although comprising around 50 per cent of the total types of items stocked, probably only account for around 10 per cent of the total value of stocked items.

Example

Table 12.8 shows all the parts stored by an electrical wholesaler. The 20 different items stored vary in terms of both their usage per year and cost per item as shown. However, the wholesaler has ranked the stock items by their usage value per year. The total usage value per year is £5 569 000. From this it is possible to calculate the usage value per year of each item as a percentage of the total usage value, and from that a running cumulative total of the usage value as shown. The wholesaler can then plot the cumulative percentage of all stocked items against the cumulative percentage of their value. So, for example, the part with stock number A/703 is the highest value part and accounts for 25.14 per cent of the total inventory value. As a part, however, it is only one-twentieth or five per cent of the total number of items stocked. This item together with the next highest value item (D/012) account for only ten per cent of the total number of items stocked, yet account for 47.37 per cent of the value of the stock, and so on.

This is shown graphically in Fig. 12.17. Here the wholesaler has classified the first four part numbers as class A items and will monitor the usage and ordering of these items very closely. A few improvements in order quantities or safety stocks for these items could bring significant savings. Part numbers C/375 through to A/138 are to be treated as class B items with slightly less effort devoted to their control. All other items are classed as class C items whose stocking policy is reviewed only occasionally.

Table 12.8 Warehouse items ranked by usage value

Stock no.	Usage (items/year)	Cost (£/item)	Usage value (£000/yr)	% of total value	Cumulative % of total value
A/703	700	20.00	1400	25.14	25.14
D/012	450	2.75	1238	22.23	47.37
A/135	1000	0.90	900	16.16	63.53
C/732	95	8.50	808	14.51	78.04
C/375	520	0.54	281	5.05	83.09
A/500	73	2.30	168	3.02	86.11
D/111	520	0.22	114	2.05	88.16
D/231	170	0.65	111	1.99	90.15
E/781	250	0.34	85	1.53	91.68
A/138	250	0.30	75	1.34	93.02
D/175	400	0.14	56	1.01	94.03
E/001	80	0.63	50	0.89	94.92
C/150	230	0.21	48	0.86	95.78
F/030	400	0.12	48	0.86	96.64
D/703	500	0.09	45	0.81	97.45
D/535	50	0.88	44	0.79	98.24
C/541	70	0.57	40	0.71	98.95
A/260	50	0.64	32	0.57	99.52
B/141	50	0.32	16	0.28	99.80
D/021	20	0.50	10	0.20	100.00
Total			5569	100.00	

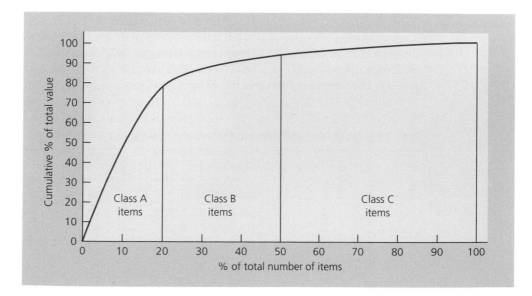

Figure 12.17
Pareto curve for
items in a
warehouse

Although annual usage and value are the two criteria most commonly used to determine a stock classification system, other criteria might also contribute towards classifying each item:

● *Consequence of stock-out.* High priority might be given to those items which would seriously delay or disrupt other operations if they were not in stock.
● *Uncertainty of supply.* Some items, although of low value, might warrant more attention if their supply is erratic or uncertain.
● *High obsolescence or deterioration risk.* Items which lose their value through obsolescence or deterioration might need extra attention and monitoring.

Some more complex stock classification systems might include these criteria by classifying on an A, B, C basis for each. For example, a part might be classed as A/B/A meaning it is an A category item by value, a class B item by consequence of stock-out and a class A item by obsolescence risk.

Measuring inventory

In our example of ABC classifications we used the monetary value of the annual usage of each item as a measure of inventory usage. Monetary value can also be used to measure the absolute level of inventory at any point in time. This would involve taking the number of each item in stock, multiplying it by its value (usually the cost of purchasing the item) and summing the value of all the individual items stored. This is a useful measure of the investment which an operation has in its inventories but gives no indication of how large that investment is relative to the total throughput of the operation. To do this we must compare the total number of items in stock against their rate of usage. There are two ways of doing this. The first is to calculate the amount of time the inventory would last, subject to normal demand, if it were not replenished. This is sometimes called the number of weeks' (days', months', years' etc.) *cover* of the stock. The second method is to calculate how often the stock is used up in a period. This is called the *stock turn* or *turnover of stock* and is the reciprocal of the stock-cover figure mentioned earlier.

Example

A small specialist wine importer holds stocks of three types of wine, Chateau A, Chateau B and Chateau C. Current stock levels are 500 cases of Chateau A, 300 cases of Chateau B, and 200 cases of Chateau C. Table 12.9 shows the number of each held in stock, their cost per item and the demand per year for each.

Table 12.9 Stock, cost and demand for three stocked items

Item	Average number in stock	Cost per item (£)	Annual demand
Chateau A	500	3.00	2000
Chateau B	300	4.00	1500
Chateau C	200	5.00	1000

THE NATIONAL BLOOD SERVICE

In September 1994 a plea was transmitted on the national news in the UK for blood donors to give blood urgently. The empty racks in the blood storage bank on the television screens graphically portrayed the urgency of the request. Momentarily the National Blood Service had lost its continuing battle to balance the supply of blood with demand.

Blood and by-products need to be stored under a variety of conditions. Red blood cells, used for surgical procedures and to correct anaemia, have to be stored at 4°C and have a shelf life of 35 days. Platelets, extracted from donated blood and used to treat leukaemia and bone marrow transplants, have to be stored at 20–24°C and have a shelf life of only five days, during which time they have to be constantly agitated. Frozen fresh plasma is used for liver transplants and for massive transfusion operations. It has to be stored at between –30 and –40°C and has a shelf life of six months. In addition, blood can be categorized by two main systems or groups. The ABO group includes A, B, AB, and O. The rhesus group includes Rh-positive and Rh-negative. In addition there are many less common and more complex types of blood, often relating to ethnic groups. Giving a patient the wrong type of blood can be fatal. However, group O negative can be given to emergency patients before blood tests have been made. Because of this, hospitals like to stock O negative. However, O negative represents only eight per cent of the population whereas 12 per cent of blood issued is of this type.

Demand is affected significantly by accidents. One serious accident involving a cyclist used 750 units of blood, which completely exhausted the available supply (miraculously, he survived). Large-scale accidents usually generate a surge of offers from donors wishing to make immediate donations. There is also a more predictable seasonality to the donating of blood, however, with a low period during the summer vacation period.

Unless blood is controlled carefully, it can easily go past its 'use-by date' and be wasted. For some patients the control of the age of stored blood is critical. For example, new-born babies, the elderly, and patients whose immune systems have been suppressed so that they do not reject transplanted organs, are all prone to infection. Very fresh blood is therefore kept 'on hold' for these patients. ■

Questions

1 What are the factors which constitute inventory holding costs, order costs, and stock-out costs in a National Blood Service?

2 What makes this particular inventory planning and control example so complex?

3 How might the efficiency with which a National Blood Service controls its inventory affect its ability to collect blood?

4 What suggestions do you have which would help this kind of operation to manage its inventory?

$$\text{The total value of stock} = \Sigma(\text{Average stock level} \times \text{cost per item})$$

$$= (500 \times 3) + (300 \times 4) + (200 \times 5)$$

$$= 3700$$

The amount of *stock cover* provided by each item stocked is as follows (assuming 50 sales weeks per year):

$$\text{Chateau A, stock cover} = \frac{\text{Stock}}{\text{Demand}} = \frac{500}{2000} \times 50 = 12.5 \text{ weeks}$$

$$\text{Chateau B, stock cover} = \frac{\text{Stock}}{\text{Demand}} = \frac{300}{1500} \times 50 = 10 \text{ weeks}$$

$$\text{Chateau C, stock cover} = \frac{\text{Stock}}{\text{Demand}} = \frac{200}{1000} \times 50 = 10 \text{ weeks}$$

The *stock turn* for each item is calculated as follows:

$$\text{Chateau A, stock turn} = \frac{\text{Demand}}{\text{Stock}} = \frac{2000}{500} = 4 \text{ times/year}$$

$$\text{Chateau B, stock turn} = \frac{\text{Demand}}{\text{Stock}} = \frac{1500}{300} = 5 \text{ times/year}$$

$$\text{Chateau C, stock turn} = \frac{\text{Demand}}{\text{Stock}} = \frac{1000}{200} = 5 \text{ times/year}$$

To find the average stock cover or stock turn for the total items in the inventory, the individual item measures can be weighted by their demand levels as a proportion of total demand (4500). Thus:

$$\text{Average stock cover} = \left(12.5 \times \frac{2000}{4500} \right) + \left(10 \times \frac{1500}{4500} \right) + \left(10 \times \frac{1000}{4500} \right)$$

$$= 11.11$$

$$\text{Average stock turn} = \left(4 \times \frac{2000}{4500} \right) + \left(5 \times \frac{1500}{4500} \right) + \left(5 \times \frac{1000}{4500} \right)$$

$$= 4.56$$

Inventory information systems

Most inventories of any significant size are managed by computerized systems. The many relatively routine calculations involved in stock control lend themselves to computerized support. This is especially so since data capture has been made more convenient through the use of bar-code readers and the point-of-sale recording of sales transactions. Many commercial systems of stock control are available, although they tend to share certain common functions. These include the following:

Updating stock records

Every time a transaction takes place (such as the sale of an item, or the movement of an item from a warehouse into a truck, or the delivery of an item into a warehouse) the position, status, and possibly value of the stock will have changed. This information needs recording so that operations managers can determine their current inventory status at any time.

Generating orders

The two major decisions we have described previously, namely how much to order and when to order, can both be made by a computerized stock control system. The first decision, setting the value of how much to order (Q), is likely to be taken only at relatively infrequent intervals. The system will hold all the information which goes into the economic order quantity formula but might periodically check to see if demand or order lead times, or any of the other parameters, have changed significantly and recalculate Q accordingly. The decision on when to order, on the other hand, is a far more routine affair which computer systems make according to whatever decision rules operations managers have chosen to adopt: either continuous review or periodic review. Furthermore, the systems can automatically generate whatever documentation is required, or even transmit the re-ordering information electronically through an electronic data interchange (EDI) system. Chapter 8 explained how EDI systems worked.

Generating inventory reports

Inventory control systems can generate regular reports of stock value for the different items stored, which can help management monitor its inventory control performance. Similarly, customer service performance, such as the number of stock-outs or the number of incomplete orders, can be regularly monitored. Some reports may be generated on an exception basis. That is, the report is only generated if some performance measure deviates from acceptable limits.

Forecasting

All inventory decisions are based on forecast future demand. The inventory control system can compare actual demand against forecast and adjust the forecast in the light of actual levels of demand.

Control systems of this type are treated in more detail in Chapter 14.

Ros Kennedy, Boots Plc

Boots the Chemists is the UK's largest retail pharmacy chain and its reputation has been gained primarily from success in that area, although Boots also manufactures a large range of health products and is involved in other retail interests.

Ros Kennedy is a store manager with Boots and is the qualified professional responsible for the day-to-day operation of the in-store pharmacy and also in overall charge of the store itself.

'I have been with Boots since graduating, and started, as all Boots operations managers do, as a pharmacist. I completed my training, working in larger stores supervised by the store manager and have since progressed to the stage where I now manage my own store and am seen in the eyes of the company as a general operations manager. Boots differs from the general high-street retail outlet in that it offers a specialist service, namely the pharmacy, and thus the major requirement of running the store is ensuring that the service is professional and that priority is given to the running of the pharmacy when required. The other facilities and products available in the store are essentially run as secondary operations.

'The retail business is essentially about stocking the right products at the right time and I have to ensure that we use the space to its best end. We monitor the sales carefully and analyse the trends in shopping patterns, both in terms of the timing and content of customer purchases. These figures help us to select the items most likely to sell quickly and also help other stores predict demand more accurately. The store is only very small and the vast proportion is dedicated to front-office operations, namely the shelving and counters. As such, the back office, and the storage area in particular, is very tight so the levels of inventory must be kept to a minimum. It is my responsibility to monitor the pattern of sales of non-pharmaceutical goods and order the items in advance from the local Boots warehouse, to a level that keeps the store in stock, but does not take up valuable space in storage.

'In the pharmacy, the prescriptions and over-the-counter drugs are ordered through a wholesaler and are delivered each day to the shop. That side of the business is very different to the rest of the retailing operation. The priorities are very much about ensuring the quality and accuracy of the service. The pharmacy operates an ABC system, whereby the A items are kept in plentiful supply, B items are kept to a minimum, and the C items have to be ordered on receipt of a prescription for that particular item. The pharmacy operations also have to be tightly controlled in terms of being able to claim back the prescription contributions from the DoH (government department). There are strict procedures and, while always having to deal politely with the customer, any flexibility in the service must still comply with the pharmaceutical legislation if relevant.

'Although the pharmacy and non-pharmacy sides of the business are somewhat different, the basic management task is the same – to make sure that we minimize the number of times we run out of stock and at the same time keep our stock-holding costs and administrative costs under control. This meets our two objectives of satisfying our customers yet being able to operate profitably.' ■

SUMMARY ANSWERS TO KEY QUESTIONS

What is inventory?

■ Inventory, or stock, is the stored accumulation of the transformed resources in an operation.

■ Sometimes the words stock or inventory are also used to describe transforming resources, but the terms *stock control* or *inventory control* are nearly always used in connection with transformed resources.

■ Almost all operations keep some kind of inventory, most usually of materials but also of information and customers (customer inventories are normally called queues).

Why is inventory necessary?

■ Inventory occurs in operations because the timing of supply and the timing of demand do not always match. Inventories are needed, therefore, to smooth the differences between supply and demand.

■ There are four main reasons for keeping inventory. These are:
  – to cope with random or unexpected interruptions in supply or demand (buffer inventory);
  – to cope with an operation's inability to make all products simultaneously (cycle inventory);
  – to cope with planned fluctuations in supply or demand (anticipation inventory);
  – to cope with transportation delays in the supply network (pipeline inventory).

How much inventory should an operation hold?

■ This depends on balancing the costs associated with holding stocks against the costs associated with placing an order. The main stock-holding costs are usually related to working capital, whereas the main order costs are usually associated with the transactions necessary to generate the information to place an order.

■ The most common approach to determining the amount of inventory to order is the economic order quantity (EOQ) formula. The EOQ formula can be adapted to different types of inventory profile using different stock behaviour assumptions.

■ The EOQ approach, however, has been subject to a number of criticisms regarding the true cost of holding stock, the real cost of placing an order, and the use of EOQ models as prescriptive devices.

When should an operation replenish its inventory?

■ Partly this depends on the uncertainty of demand. Orders are usually timed to leave a certain level of average safety stock when the order arrives. The level of safety stock is influenced by the variability of both demand and the lead time of supply. These two variables are usually combined into a lead-time usage distribution.

■ Using re-order level as a trigger for placing replenishment orders necessitates the continual review of inventory levels. This can be time consuming and expensive. An alternative approach is to make replenishment orders of varying size but at fixed time periods.

How can inventory be controlled?

■ The key issue here is how managers discriminate between the levels of control which they apply to different stock items. The most common way of doing this is by what is known as the ABC classification of stock. This uses the Pareto principle to distinguish between the different values of, or significance placed on, types of stock.

■ Inventory is usually managed through sophisticated computer-based information systems which have a number of functions: the updating of stock records, the generation of orders, the generation of inventory status reports and demand forecasts.

CASE EXERCISE

Plastix Plc

Plastix Plc is one of Europe's largest and most profitable manufacturers of plastic household durables. The Swedish factory makes a range of 300 products which are sold to wholesalers and large retailers throughout Europe. The company offers ex-stock delivery of all items, and dispatch within 24 hours of receipt of orders by a reputable international haulier; on this basis, customers expect to receive all their requirements within one week.

Concerned about the declining delivery reliability, increased levels of finished goods inventory, and falling productivity (apparently resulting from 'split-batches' where only part of a planned production batch is produced to overcome immediate shortages), the Managing Director, Laas-Uno Duman, employed consultants to undertake a complete review of operations. On 1 September 1996, a full physical inventory check was taken; a representative sample of 20 products is shown in Table 12.10.

Plastix uses batch-production, injection-moulding processes; typical set-ups (change-overs) take four

Table 12.10 Details of a representative sample of 20 Plastix products

Product reference number*	Description	Unit manufg variable cost (£)	Last 12 mths' sales (000s)	Physical inventory 1 Sept 96 (000s)	Re-order quantity (000s)	Standard moulding rate** (items/hour)
016GH	Storage bin large	1.60	10	0	2	240
033KN	Bread bin + lid	2.40	60	8	2	200
041GH	10 litre bucket	0.50	2200	360	600	300
062GD	Grecian pot	3.00	40	15	5	180
080BR	Bathroom mirror	5.00	5	6	5	260
101KN	1 litre jug	0.60	100	20	10	600
126KN	Pack (10) bag clips	0.30	200	80	50	2000
143BB	Baby bath	2.50	50	1	2	120
169BB	Baby potty	1.50	60	0	2	180
188BQ	Barbecue table	10.80	10	8	5	120
232GD	Garden bird bath	2.00	2	6	2	200
261GH	Broom head	0.80	60	22	8	400
288LY	Pack (10) clothes pegs	1.00	10	17	50	1000
302BQ	Barbecue salad fork	0.20	5	12	2	400
351GH	Storage bin small	1.00	25	2	2	300
382KN	Round mixing bowl	0.50	800	25	80	650
421KN	Pasta jar	2.00	1	3	5	220
444GH	Wall hook	0.05	200	86	50	3000
472GH	Dustbin + lid	6.00	300	3	10	180
506BR	Soap holder	0.80	10	9	20	400

* The reference number uses the following codes for ranges:

BB = Babycare   BQ = Barbecue   BR = Bathroom
GD = Garden   GH = General household   KN = Kitchen
LY = Laundry

** Moulding rate is for the product as described (e.g. includes lids, or pack quantities).

hours, costing approximately £400. Because of current high demand for Plastix products, the backlog of work for planned stock replenishment currently averages eight weeks, and so all factory orders must be planned at least eight weeks in advance. Actual re-order quantities (*see* Table 12.10) are always established by the Estimating Department when each new product is designed and the manufacturing costs are established, based on Marketing's estimates of likely demand. However, in order to minimize the cost of set-ups, and to maximize capacity utilization, all products are now planned for a *minimum* production run of 20 hours, with re-order levels based on the previous 13 weeks' average sales. About 20 per cent of the products (e.g. Barbecue Range and Garden Range) are very seasonal, with peak demand April–August.

Storage bins sell particularly well from October to December. Monthly forecasts of sales value are prepared annually and reviewed quarterly; this analysis is by product range (e.g. Babycare, Gardenware) for budgeting, cash-flow forecasting, and for aggregate capacity planning. The Marketing Manager summarized the current position thus:

'Our coverage of the market has never been so comprehensive; we are able to offer a full range of household plastics in fashionable colours, which appeals to most European tastes. But we will not retain our newly developed markets unless we can give distributors confidence that we will supply all their orders within one week. Unfortunately, at the moment, many receive several deliveries for each order, spread over many weeks. This certainly increases their administrative and handling costs, and our haulage costs. And sometimes the shortfall is only some small, low-value items like clothes pegs!'

The factory operates on three shifts, Monday to Friday: 120 hours per week. Regular overtime, typically 16 hours on a Saturday, has been worked most of the last year. Sunday is never used for production, allowing access to machines for routine and major overhauls. Machines are laid out in groups so that each operator can be kept highly utilized, attending to at least four machines. Although the moulding processes run automatically, the operators are needed to ensure that inputs of raw materials and outputs of products continue to flow without problems. They are encouraged by an output-based bonus scheme which directly rewards the productivity of each operator. All machines are the same size to allow full interchangeability of the tooling, so any product can be made on any machine.

Christian Roos, the Manufacturing Director, gave more details about production:

'Because of the fast output rates of all the moulding machines, it is very easy to produce slightly faulty products at a very fast rate! Typical problems could be damaged or worn tooling causing poor surface finish (marks and scratches); or perhaps slightly bent or twisted products caused by incorrect adjustment of temperatures or pressures. The real problem is that our operators' perception of a fault may be different to that of the inspectors, particularly just after we have had a few customer complaints! The Quality Control Manager, Monique Ryan, reports directly to the MD. Her 14 inspectors (four per shift, two on Saturday mornings) are fully occupied taking random samples from each of our 30 moulding machines, checking them in the laboratory for critical variables and attributes. Recently the reject rate has increased, yet we are also getting higher levels of complaints from the trade ... but that is probably to be expected as our products become more up-market and complicated. Fortunately, all faulty products can be ground up and made into garden pots, so we don't lose any of the expensive material. Monique has recently persuaded the MD to employ another inspector on each shift to try to reduce the quality problems, and I am sure that will help. I am worried, however, that the effect may be to make our delivery problems worse as even more batches are rejected or delayed while problems are rectified. Also further valuable factory and warehouse space is being allocated to Quality Control for their working and storage needs, which I really cannot afford to give up!

'At the moment our warehouse is full, with products stacked on the floor in every available corner, which makes it vulnerable to damage from passing forklifts and from double-handling. We have finally agreed to approve a £1 million warehouse extension to be constructed January–May 1997, which will give good payback as it will replace contract warehousing and associated transport which is costing us about five per cent of the manufacturing costs of the stored capital. The return on investment is well above our current ten per cent cost of capital. There is no viable alternative, because if we run out of space, production will have to stop for a time. Some of our products occupy very large volumes of rack space!

'We all work hard to keep down manufacturing costs. Our Group Central Purchasing Department in Stockholm sources all our raw materials, and because of their purchasing power, we are able to get the lowest prices for all types of plastics. Recently they contracted a Hungarian company to supply polyethylene granules for the Industrial Products Division, and we are able to get this material at a saving of about five per cent. We will have to sample this material carefully, as it is likely to be *more variable than UK-sourced material. Monique, the Quality Control Manager, is a polymer chemist, so she has agreed to do the tests herself every morning to save the cost and time involved in using an outside laboratory.'* ■

Questions

1 Why is Plastix unable to deliver all its products within the target of one week, and what effects might that have on the distributors?

2 What internal problems result from the current planning and control policies? Categorize these broadly into categories of scheduling, capacity management, and inventory management. Do these policies interact?

3 What recommendations would you make to Laas-Uno Duman?

4 How does the company's inventory management impact on its quality performance?

DISCUSSION QUESTIONS

1 Describe and categorize the types of material inventories that might be found in the following organizations:

a theatre
a furniture retailer
a brewery
a city bus company.

2 Talk to an operations manager about the different types of inventory that the organization holds. Find out if there are different ways of planning and controlling some of the different types of inventory.

3 Get hold of the last few years' Annual Report and Accounts for a materials-processing organization of your choice. Calculate the organization's stock–turnover ratio and the proportion of inventory to current assets over the last few years. Try to explain what you think are the reasons for any trends you can identify and discuss the likely advantages and disadvantages for the organization concerned.

4 The Shocking Electricity Company uses 3000 metres of wire every month. The cost of placing an order for the wire has been calculated at £40 and the cost of stocking the wire is 5p per metre per year. In what quantities should the company order the wire? If it adopts an EOQ approach to ordering, what would be its annual inventory cost?

5 A university's printing department uses paper at the rate of 86 packets per day. A pack of paper costs £2 and the annual stock-holding cost is calculated at 10 per cent of the cost of the paper. If it costs £25 every time an order is placed and the department works 250 days in the year, what is the EOQ for the paper? If it takes three days between placing an order and receiving it, what is the re-order point at which an order should be placed?

6 The Pride of Scotland Butchers Limited has a haggis machine which can produce at a rate of 1000 haggises per day. Traditionally the company produces a day's worth of haggises which fully satisfies the demand for one week. The company sells its haggises throughout 50 weeks of the year. Each time the haggis machine is set up to produce a batch of haggises it costs £100. The haggises have to be kept in particularly cool and hygienic conditions and therefore it costs the company £0.5 per haggis per day to store stock. How much money is the company losing by producing 1000 haggises per week in one batch rather than adopting an EBQ policy (make any assumptions you believe reasonable)?

7 A company which has been using the EOQ formula to determine its order quantities has now found that demand has increased by 50 per cent since it last calculated the optimum order quantity. What adjustment will it have to make to its order quantity? What further adjustment will it have to make to its ordering quantity if its stock-holding costs increase by 50 per cent?

470

8 A university MBA programme keeps sweatshirts in stock for its students with the university's logo emblazoned on the front. On average it sells 200 of these sweatshirts every year. There is a fixed postage and packing charge of £5 every time it places an order. The cost of the sweatshirts is £15 and inventory is charged by the university at 30 per cent per year. How many sweatshirts should the university order at a time? The new programme director has responded to complaints from the students that the sweatshirts were out of stock last year by offering to pay £20 into the students' entertainment fund every time there is a stock-out. How would this affect the economic order quantity?

9 An ice-cream seller is required to purchase the ice-creams which are then kept in a cold box at the beginning of a sales day. The seller pays £0.2 for every ice-cream. Ice-creams are sold at £0.5 each but any ice-creams left at the end of the day cannot be returned and go to waste. The ice-cream seller classifies demand as either low, medium or high. Low demand is between 40 and 80 ice-creams, medium demand is between 80 and 120 ice-creams, and high demand is between 120 and 160 ice-creams. The probability of demand being low is 0.2, the probability of demand being medium is 0.5, and the probability of demand being high is 0.3. Approximately how many ice-creams would you advise the ice-cream seller to purchase every morning? If competition forces down the price which the ice-cream seller can charge to £0.4, does this change the decision?

10 A furniture store sells tables which it obtains from a local furniture factory. Each time it places an order on the factory there is a delivery charge and general transaction cost of £60 per order. The stock-holding cost is estimated to be £10 per table per year. Both demand and lead time vary according to the distribution in Table 12.11. Devise a re-order level policy for the furniture store if it is to have less than a five per cent probability of being out of stock each order cycle.

Table 12.11 Lead-time usage of tables

Lead-time usage	Probability
600–650	0.2
650–700	0.2
700–750	0.3
750–800	0.2
800–850	0.05
850–900	0.05

NOTES ON CHAPTER

1 Sources: Company accounts (1992/93).
2 There are several different ways of classifying inventory. This is probably the most straightforward.
3 For further discussion on the limitations of the EOQ *see* Schonberger, R.J. and Knod, E.M. (1994) *Operations Management: Continuous Improvement* (5th edn), Irwin.
4 Sources: *The Economist*, 26 June 1993, and Horovitz J. and Jurgens Panak, M. (1992) *Total Customer Satisfaction*, FT/Pitman Publishing, and discussion with company staff.
5 We thank Jeff Schaffer for his help in supplying the information for this box.

SELECTED FURTHER READINGS

Adkins, A.C. Jr. (1984) 'EOQ in the Real World', *Production and Inventory Management*, Vol 25, No 4.

Austin, L.M. (1977) 'Project EOQ: A Success Story in Implementing Academic Research', *Interfaces*, Vol 7, Aug.

Flores, B.E. and Whybark, D.C. (1987) 'Implementing Multiple Criteria ABC Analysis', *Journal of Operations Management*, Vol 7, No 1.

Fogarty, D.W. and Blackstone, J.H. (1991) *Production and Inventory Management*, South-Western Publishing.

Greene, J.H. (1987) *Production and Inventory Control Handbook* (2nd edn), McGraw-Hill.

Hall, R. (1983) *Zero Inventories*, Dow Jones-Irwin.

Jessop, D. and Morrison, A. (1991) *Storage and Control of Stock*, Pitman Publishing.

Jinchiro, N. and Hall, R. (1983) 'Management Specs for Stockless Production', *Harvard Business Review*, Vol 61, No 3.

Lockyer, K.G. and Wynne, R.M. (1989) 'The Life Profile of Stock as a Control Measure', *International Journal of Operations and Production Management*, Vol 9, No 1.

Mapes, J. (1993) 'The Effect of Capacity Limitations on Safety Stock', *International Journal of Operations and Production Management*, Vol 13, No 10.

Mather, H. (1984) *How to Really Manage Inventories*, McGraw-Hill.

Newell, S., Swan, J. and Clarke, P. (1993) 'The Importance of User Design in the Adoption of New Information Technologies: The Example of Production and Inventory Control Systems', *International Journal of Operations and Production Management*, Vol 13, No 2.

Primrose, P.L. (1992) 'The Value of Inventory Savings', *International Journal of Operations and Production Management*, Vol 12, No 5.

Ronen, D. (1983) 'Inventory Service Measures – A Comparison of Measures', *International Journal of Operations and Production Management*, Vol 3, No 2.

Schonberger, R.J. and Schniederjans, M.J. (1984) 'Reinventing Inventory Control', *Interfaces*, Vol 14, No 3.

Silver, E.A. and Peterson, R. (1985) *Decision Systems for Inventory Management and Production Planning*, John Wiley.

Snyder, R.D. (1993) 'A Computerized System for Forecasting Spare Parts Sales: A Case Study', *International Journal of Operations and Production Management*, Vol 13, No 7.

Tersine, R.J. (1987) *Principles of Inventory and Materials Management* (2nd edn), North Holland.

Williams, K., Williams, J. and Haslam, C. (1989) 'Why Take the Stocks Out? Britain *versus* Japan', *International Journal of Operations and Production Management*, Vol 9, No 8.

CHAPTER 13

SUPPLY CHAIN PLANNING AND CONTROL

INTRODUCTION

Historically operations managers have seen their main responsibility lying within their own operation. However, increasingly they now have to look beyond this traditional internal view to be able to manage their function. As operations become more focused on a tightly defined set of tasks and consequently buy in more of their materials and services from specialist suppliers, the contribution of purchasing and supply to the business increases in importance. At the demand side of the business it is being claimed that up to 25 per cent of total costs can lie in the distribution chain which transports goods and services to customers. This flow of materials and information through a business from the purchasing activity, through the operation and out to customers, by way of a distribution or service delivery activity, is what we described in Chapter 6 as the 'immediate' supply network or supply chain. When operations managers have sought to control this flow they have found that they can obtain speed, dependability, flexibility, cost and quality benefits compared with just managing the flow within the operation itself. Even beyond the immediate supply chain, there are often strategic benefits to be gained from managing the flow between customers' customers and suppliers' suppliers. Inter-company operations management of this nature is now more commonly termed supply chain management. In Chapter 6 we raised the strat-egic and structural issues of designing supply networks. In this chapter we are going to consider the more 'infrastructural' issues of planning and controlling the 'strands' in the supply network. These are called supply 'chains'. Figure 13.1 illustrates the supply–demand linkage treated in this chapter.

Figure 13.1 Supply chain management is concerned with managing the flow of materials and information between the operations which form the strands or 'chains' of a supply network

473

WHAT IS SUPPLY CHAIN PLANNING AND CONTROL?

In Chapter 6 we used the term 'supply network' to refer to all the operations which were linked to provide the supply of goods and services to an operation and the demand for its goods and services through to the end customers. In this chapter we are dealing with the flow of goods and services through this network along individual channels or strands of the network. In large organizations there can be many hundreds of strands of linked operations through which goods and services flow into and out of the operation. These strands are more commonly referred to as *supply chains*. Many of the topics covered in this chapter on supply chain planning and control are relatively new. This means that some of the terms used to describe them are not universally applied. Furthermore, some of the concepts behind the terminology overlap in the sense that they refer to common parts of the total supply network. This is why it is useful first of all to distinguish between the different terms we shall use in this chapter. These are illustrated in Fig. 13.2.

● *Purchasing and supply management* is a well-accepted term in business practice for the function that deals with the operation's interface with its supply markets.

● *Physical distribution management* is again a well-accepted term for managing the operation of supplying immediate customers.

● *Logistics* is an extension of physical distribution management and usually refers to the management of materials and information flow from a business, down through a distribution channel, to end customers (although sometimes the concept is extended to include more of the supply chain, as we will discuss later).

● *Materials management* refers to the management of the flow of materials and information through the immediate supply chain. This has been defined as including purchasing, inventory management, stores management, operations planning and control and physical distribution management.[1]

● *Supply chain management* has been developed into a concept with a much broader span of concern and an holistic approach to managing across company boundaries. It is recognized that there are substantial benefits to be gained from strategically trying to drive a whole chain in the direction of satisfying end customers.[2]

A supply chain as a whole can be viewed as the flow of water in a river: organizations located closer to the original source of supply are described as being 'upstream', whereas those located closer to the end customer are 'downstream'. (However, whether an individual operation is regarded as upstream or downstream depends on

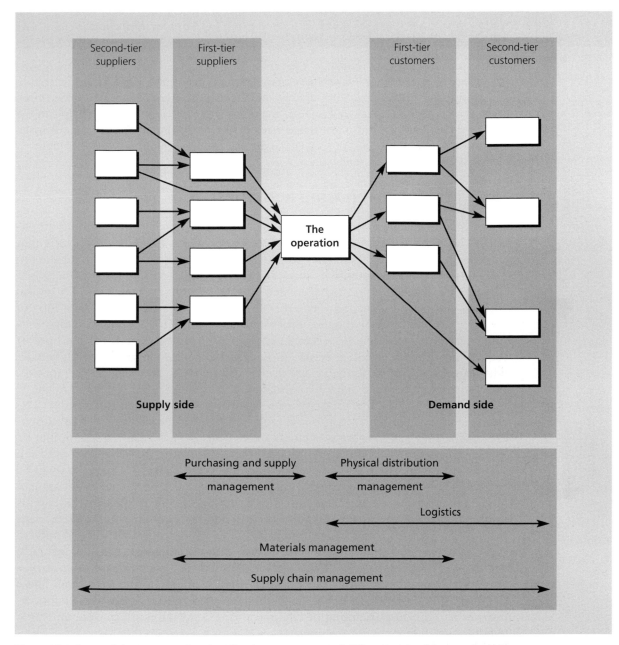

Figure 13.2 Some of the terms used to describe the management of different parts of the supply chain

the exact position of the operation in the stream.) The terms which we have defined above represent an increasing degree of integration – being concerned with the flow of the whole river and its ultimate destination. Purchasing and supply, and physical distribution relate to only one part of the whole supply chain, upstream and downstream respectively. Logistics and materials management take in larger parts of the supply chain, while supply chain management includes the whole chain. In this chapter we will examine these concepts, and the processes and functions associated with them.

PURCHASING AND SUPPLIER DEVELOPMENT

At the supply end of the business, the purchasing function forms contracts with suppliers to buy in materials and services. Some of these materials and services are used in the production of the goods and services sold on to customers (we termed these transformed resources, *see* Chapter 1). Other materials and services are used to help run the business: for example, staff catering services or oil for machinery. These do not make up part of the finished good or service but are still essential purchases for operations.

Operational purchasing activities

Purchasing managers provide a vital link between the operation itself and its suppliers. To be effective they must understand the requirements of all the processes within the operation and also the capabilities of the suppliers (sometimes thousands in numbers) who could potentially provide products and services for the operation. Figure 13.3 shows a simplified sequence of events in the management of a typical supplier–operation interaction which the purchasing function must facilitate. First of all, the operation formally requests products or services. This may happen on a routine basis if the products or services are part of its general needs or as a one-off request for the creation of 'specials'. In the latter case, the operation might consult with purchasing as to the exact nature of the products or services it requires. Purchasing should keep extensive information about potential suppliers and might be able to suggest alternative materials or services for the operation to consider. The purchasing function prepares a formal request which can be sent to potential suppliers so that they can prepare quotations for the business. These requests might be sent to several suppliers if the products or services are either novel or have not been purchased for some time. The various quotations submitted by suppliers will be examined, possibly in conjunction with the operation itself, and, after negotiation, a 'preferred' supplier selected. The next important task for the purchasing function is to prepare a purchase order. The purchase order is important because it often forms the legal basis of the contractual relationship between the operation and its supplier. Again, the purchasing function needs to liaise with the operation over the technical details of the purchase order. When the supplier receives the purchase order it produces and delivers the products or services, usually directly to the operation. These then form the input into the operation's transformation process, but also the operation should inform purchasing of the arrival of the products or services and their condition on delivery.

Traditional objectives of the purchasing function

Most operations buy in a wide variety of materials and services, and typically the volume and value of these purchases are increasing as organizations concentrate on their 'core tasks'. Despite the variety of purchases that a firm makes, there are some underlying objectives of purchasing which are true for all materials and services bought. These have been termed 'the five rights of purchasing':[3]

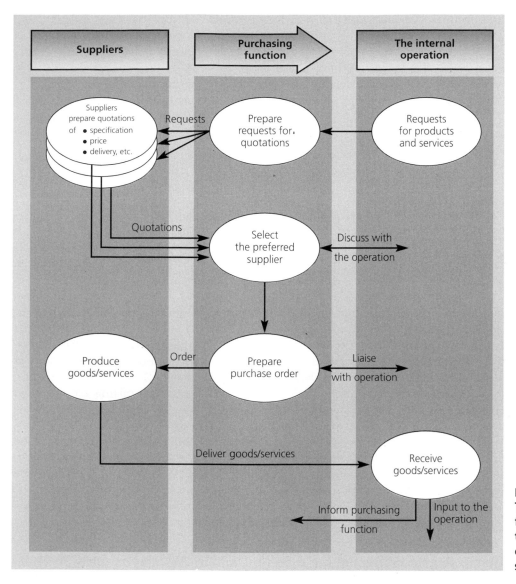

**Figure 13.3
The purchasing
function brings
together the
operation with its
suppliers**

- at the *right price*
- for delivery at the *right time*
- of goods and services to the *right quality*
- in the *right quantity*
- from the *right source*.

Purchasing at the right price

The most obvious benefit of purchasing at the right price is that it can provide an operation with a *cost advantage*. Historically, this objective of purchasing has been emphasized in purchasing theory and practice. Much of the skill of professional purchasing staff was concerned traditionally with negotiation with suppliers to secure the

477

best overall price deal. The performance of purchasing staff was even judged using cost savings as the main measure. The reason for this emphasis on 'the right cost' is understandable because purchasing can have a very significant impact on any operation's costs. This in turn will have an impact on the organization's profits.

To illustrate the impact which price-conscious purchasing can have on profits, consider a simple manufacturing operation with the following financial details:

$$
\begin{aligned}
\text{Total sales} &= £10\ 000\ 000 \\
\text{Purchased services and materials} &= £7\ 000\ 000 \\
\text{Salaries} &= £2\ 000\ 000 \\
\text{Overheads} &= £500\ 000 \\
\text{Therefore, profit} &= £500\ 000
\end{aligned}
$$

Profits could be doubled to £1 million by any of the following:

- increase sales revenue by up to 100 per cent
- decrease salaries by 25 per cent
- decrease overheads by 100 per cent
- decrease purchase costs by 7.1 per cent.

Doubling sales revenue does sometimes occur in very fast-growing markets, but would be regarded by most sales and marketing managers as an exceedingly ambitious target. Decreasing the salaries bill by a quarter is likely to require substantial alternative investment – for example in automation – or reflects a dramatic reduction in medium- to long-term sales. Similarly, reducing overheads by 100 per cent is unlikely to be possible over the short to medium term without compromising the business. However, reducing purchase costs by 7.1 per cent, although a challenging objective, is usually far more of a realistic option than the other actions.

The reason for the dramatic impact which purchase price savings can have on total profitability is that purchase costs are such a large proportion of total costs. Relatively small changes in purchase costs will, therefore, be large compared with profits. The higher purchase costs are as a proportion of total costs, the more profitability can be improved in this way. This is why retail operations such as supermarkets devote such efforts to reducing the costs of their bought-in goods. Figure 13.4 illustrates this.

Purchasing for delivery at the right time and in the right quantity

Purchasing at the right time and in the right quantity can impact on the operation's performance in terms of delivery speed, delivery reliability and flexibility. Chapter 12 on inventory management described how order volumes and times are calculated based on current stock levels and historical demand. Chapter 14 describes how these volume and timing decisions for purchases are determined by looking forward at what will be required to satisfy future demand. However, purchasing must also deal with some characteristics of an operation's supply market which can affect the volume and timing decisions. For example, international purchasing that involves 'deep-sea' transportation may mean that purchases must be made two months earlier than if they were bought locally. This allows the time for the purchases to be transported to the docks, loaded, shipped over, unloaded and transported to their destination. There may also be characteristics of the products or services themselves which determine the timing of the purchase. For example, many food crops have to be purchased and picked at exactly the right time when they become ripe.

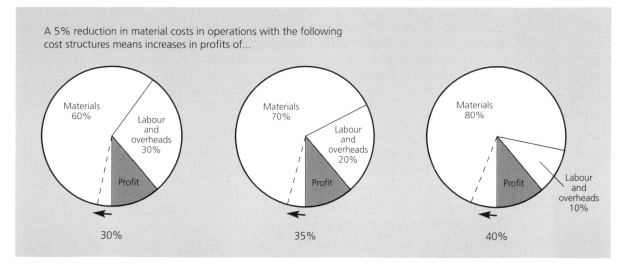

Figure 13.4 The larger the level of material costs as a proportion of total costs, the greater the effect on profitability of a reduction in material costs

But whether the volume and timing of purchases are determined through forecasting ahead, through evaluating economic order quantities or through special product or market characteristics, the purchasing function will be involved: usually by originating the orders which authorize suppliers to supply at the required time and in the required volume. Sometimes the job of ensuring that purchase orders and contracts are adhered to is performed by an 'expediting' function whose responsibility is to track or 'progress' orders with suppliers until the goods and services are delivered. In this situation purchasing staff form the contract with the supplier and the expediter 'chases' it. This chasing function adds no value to the transaction. Indeed, if all suppliers kept to their end of the bargain, it would be redundant. In recent years, suppliers are being encouraged to be more reliable and so the role of expediting in most organizations has been either substantially reduced or removed completely.

Purchasing at the right quality

Buying the right quality of products and services will have a significant effect on whether the operation itself can provide a quality advantage. In addition, quality will also affect delivery speed and reliability. Poor quality components or services can delay delivery of the finished product or service. Similarly, quality failures of bought-in products or services will also increase costs. Traditionally, suppliers were not trusted to provide goods and services of the right quality. When goods were supplied or when services were provided they were inspected to ensure that they conformed to the required specification. More recently, suppliers are being encouraged to ensure that they take responsibility themselves to provide a 'right-first-time' level of quality. Furthermore, they are required to certify to the purchasing company that quality levels have been met. This self-certification is based on a level of trust and confidence which has come about partly because purchasing organizations have invested time, money and effort into helping their suppliers reach the required quality levels. This effort has often been through investment in *supplier quality assurance* programmes.

Supplier quality assurance (SQA) programmes monitor and improve levels of supplier quality, partly by assessing supplier capability in terms of their equipment, systems, procedures and training. Quality-conscious purchasing organizations such as aircraft manufacturers have always invested substantial effort in ensuring that suppliers are capable of meeting the right quality. For many other businesses this is a more recent innovation in their purchasing process. Suppliers can self-certify their capability by having their systems and processes certified as conforming to internationally recognized standards such as ISO 9000 (discussed in Chapter 20). In becoming accredited to a set of recognized standards, purchasers can at least gain confidence that the suppliers' systems are capable of providing them with good quality products and services. However, these standards of accreditation only indicate the *capability* of achieving good quality – they do not *guarantee* good quality of output from suppliers.

Purchasing from the right source

On first examination it might seem important to consider the source of products or services only as far as they influence price, quality and delivery. However, purchasing staff might sometimes choose to buy from a particular source because of the current or future *potential* from that source rather than its immediate and direct benefits. For example, a purchasing department might be comparing two suppliers, A and B. Supplier A has submitted a quotation which is superior on price and delivery and, as far as they can tell, on quality also. However, the purchasing department might suspect that supplier A might be inflexible in terms of changing the terms of the supply arrangement. They might also judge that supplier A does not have the capability to develop new products or services which they might require in the future. Supplier B, on the other hand, although its initial quotation might not match that of supplier A, might be judged to have more potential for improvement, or might possess the core capabilities of meeting future requirements. It might even be that the purchasing department judges supplier B to have a 'better attitude' in terms of its willingness to improve the service which it provides.

Single- and multi-sourcing

The decision of what constitutes the 'right source' also includes, by implication, the decision of whether to source each individual product or service from one or more than one supplier. This is known as *single-sourcing* and *multi-sourcing*. (*See* box on Olivetti for an example of single-sourcing.) Some of the advantages and disadvantages of single- and multi-sourcing are shown in Table 13.1.

It may seem as though companies who multi-source do so exclusively for their own short-term benefit. However, this is not always the case: multi-sourcing can have an altruistic motive or at least one which brings benefits to both supplier and purchaser in the long term. For example, Robert Bosch GmbH, the German automotive components manufacturer and distributor, at one time required that sub-contractors do no more than 20 per cent of their total business with them.[4] This was to prevent suppliers becoming too dependent on them. The purchasing organization could then change volumes up and down without pushing the supplier into bankruptcy. However, despite these perceived advantages, there has been a trend for purchasing functions to reduce their supplier base in terms of numbers of companies supplying any one part or service. For example, Rank Xerox, the copier and document company, reduced its supply base from 5000 suppliers to a little more than 300 over a six-year period.[5] Some Japanese automotive manufacturers involve fewer than 300 suppliers in new product development projects (often their Western equivalents may deal with 1000 to

Table 13.1 Advantages and disadvantages of single- and multi-sourcing

	Single-sourcing	*Multi-sourcing*
Advantages	• Potentially better quality because more SQA possibilities • Strong relationships which are more durable • Greater dependency encourages more commitment and effort • Better communication • Easier to co-operate on new product/service development • More scale economies • Higher confidentiality	• Purchaser can drive price down by competitive tendering • Can switch sources in case of supply failure • Wide sources of knowledge and expertise to tap
Disadvantages	• More vulnerable to disruption if a failure to supply occurs • Individual supplier more affected by volume fluctuations • Supplier might exert upward pressure on prices if no alternative supplier is available	• Difficult to encourage commitment by supplier • Less easy to develop effective SQA • More effort needed to communicate • Suppliers less likely to invest in new processes • More difficult to obtain scale economies

2500).[6] This trend of supply base reduction has come about because of the realization of far greater benefits of developing long-term co-operative relationships with suppliers rather than trading with them at arm's length in an adversarial, hostile way.

Make-or-buy decisions

When an operation decides to purchase products or services from a supplier it is implicitly making the decision not to create those products or services itself. This may not always be a straightforward decision. In some cases the operation may be able to produce parts or services in-house at a lower cost or at a higher quality than can suppliers. Yet in other cases suppliers may be able to specialize in the production of certain parts or services and produce them more cheaply or at higher quality than can the operation itself. It is part of the responsibility of the purchasing function to investigate whether the operation is better served buying in products or services, or choosing to create them itself. This is called the *'make-or-buy' decision.*

Often the major criterion used to decide whether to make or buy is financial. If a company can make a part or service in-house more cheaply than it can buy it, it is likely to do so, unless there are other overriding reasons for not doing so. However, the financial analysis involved is not always straightforward. The decision often needs to be based on the *marginal* cost of producing something in-house. The marginal cost is the *extra* cost which is incurred by the operation in creating the product or service. For example, if an operation already has the equipment and staff in place to make a

OLIVETTI PROVIDES SINGLE–SOURCE SUPPORT[7]

Like most retail banks, Barclays Bank has thousands of separate branch and office headquarters' sites and hundreds of thousands of individual pieces of computer equipment. These range from personal computers and work stations to computer peripherals and photocopiers. All of this equipment needs servicing and repair support. Rather than buy in this support from several companies, Barclays decided to single-source these services from Olivetti, the computer and office equipment company. This simplified the administrative procedures and brought substantial cost savings.

Olivetti claims that single-sourcing services provides significant benefits for its clients. Contractual relationships together with invoicing procedures are rationalized and the quality of service becomes more easily measurable. Consistency-of-service procedures are also easier to achieve. These advantages of single-sourcing have also persuaded many other organizations, such as Swiss Railways and the German network of McDonald's restaurants, to concentrate on one supplier. ∎

Questions

1 What do you think are the main operations objectives for a company such as Olivetti's computer support operation?

2 What do you see as being the major advantages and disadvantages of having a single-source agreement for computer equipment and computer equipment servicing?

KLM CATERING SERVICES[8]

KLM Catering Services is the largest provider of aircraft catering and supply at Schiphol Airport near Amsterdam. The company, which employs 1200 people, every day prepares around 30 000 meals and 'services' 200 flights for KLM and about 35 for other operators. It is now far more than just a food-preparation operation; most of its activities involve organizing all on-board services, equipment, food and drinks, newspapers, towels, earphones, and so on.

KLM Catering Services places considerable emphasis on working in unison with cleaning staff, baggage handlers and maintenance crews to ensure that the aircraft are prepared quickly for departure (fast set-ups). Normally, no more than 40 minutes is allowed for all these activities, so complete preparation and a well-ordered sequence of working is essential. These requirements for speed and total dependability would be difficult enough to achieve in a stable environment, but there is a wide range of uncertainties to be managed. Although KLM Catering Services is advised of the likely numbers of passengers for each flight (forecasts are given 11 days, 4 days and 24 hours in advance), the actual *minimum* number of passengers for each class is only fixed six hours before take-off (though numbers can still be increased after this, due to late sales). The agreed menus are normally fixed for six-month periods, but the actual requirements for each flight depend on the destination, the type of aircraft and the mix of passengers by ticket class. Finally, flight arrivals are sometimes delayed, putting pressure on everyone to reduce the turn-around time, and upsetting work schedules.

An additional problem is that, although KLM uses standardized items (such as food trolleys, cutlery, trays and disposables), other airlines have completely different requirements. The inventory of all this equipment is moved around with the planes. Some gets damaged or lost, and it can easily accumulate at a remote airport. If an aircraft arrives without a full inventory of equipment and other items, the company is obliged to fill the gaps from its local inventory which amounts to over 15 000 different items. ∎

Questions

1 Why would an airline use KLM Catering Services rather than organize its own on-board services?

2 What are the main operations objectives which KLM Catering Services must achieve in order to satisfy its customers?

3 Why is it important for airlines to reduce turn-around time when an aircraft lands?

Source: By kind permission of KLM Catering Services, Schiphol Airport, The Netherlands, ©1994 KLM Royal Dutch Airlines

particular product and there is spare capacity within the part of the operation which could make that product, then the extra, or marginal, cost of making the products in-house will be the variable costs associated with their manufacture. In other cases, an operation might decide on grounds other than cost. An increasingly popular rationale for buying in services, for example, is that they are not 'core' to the operation's main activity. Many companies are increasingly 'out-sourcing' such services as transportation, cleaning, computing, catering and maintenance. Putting these services out to specialists allows an operation to concentrate on what directly wins it business in the market place (*see* box on KLM Catering Services).

PHYSICAL DISTRIBUTION MANAGEMENT

On the demand side of the organization, products and services need to be 'communicated' or moved to the customer. In the case of manufacturing operations, this involves the physical transportation of the goods from the manufacturing operation to the customer. In the case of high customer contact services, the service is created in the presence of the customer. Here we limit ourselves to manufacturing operations that need physically to distribute their products to customers (and implicitly to those transportation operations, such as trucking companies, whose primary concern is physical distribution).

Multi-echelon inventory systems

In Chapter 12 we identified some inventory systems as 'multi-echelon' systems. By this we meant that materials flowing through a system would be stored at different points, including points outside the operation, before reaching the customer. Figure 13.5 illustrates the demand-side part of the multi-echelon system we described in Chapter 12. In this case the garment manufacturer, after manufacturing the products, will store them in its own finished goods warehouse. From there they are transported to regional warehouses whose function is to serve as a distribution point for retail stores. When the retail stores require deliveries of garments they will request them from their local warehouse who will arrange for the transportation of these garments to the retail store. The function of the warehouse is to provide an intermediate stage in the distribution system so that the manufacturer does not have to deal with every single customer. From the customers' point of view it also means that they do not have to deal with a whole range of suppliers.

Warehouses can simplify routes and communications

To understand how warehouses can simplify physical distribution, consider Fig. 13.6. Here a manufacturing operation which has three factories is supplying six customers. In the arrangement in Fig. 13.6(a) each factory supplies each customer. This means in total there are 18 routes (one between each pair of factory and customer). Each factory must have separate lines of communication with all six customers and each customer will need to communicate directly with each of the three factories. Now consider the bottom arrangement in Fig 13.6(b). Two regional warehouses have been imposed between the factories and the customers. The three factories now distribute their products to the two regional warehouses from which their local customers are supplied. The total number of routes has been reduced from 18 to 12. Probably more significantly, each factory now has only to deal directly with two sources for its products instead of the previous six. Similarly, each customer now only has to deal with one supplier (its local warehouse) instead of six, as previously.

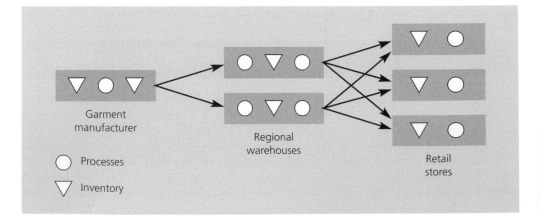

Figure 13.5
Multi-echelon
inventory system

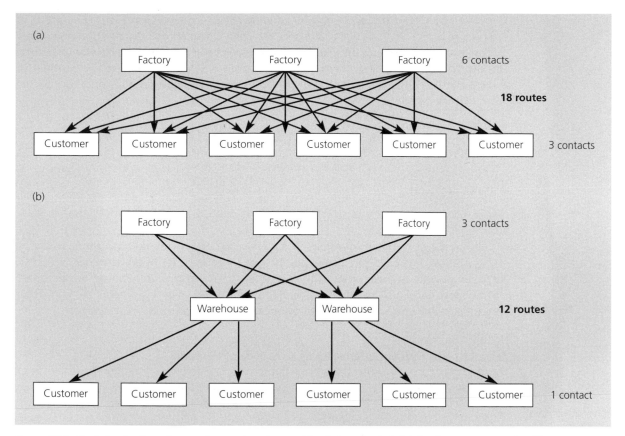

Figure 13.6 The introduction of a warehouse stage in a multi-echelon physical distribution system can simplify routes and communications

The mode of transport in physical distribution

As well as the arrangement of the distribution system, physical distribution managers must decide on which mode of transport is best to distribute their products to their customers. By mode of transport we mean the technology which is used to move goods.

The modes of transport available to the physical distribution manager are:

- road
- rail
- water
- air
- pipeline.

Each of these modes has different characteristics which affect its suitability for the transportation of particular products. For example, air transport is very expensive and limited in the space available (to the size of the aircraft). It is therefore typically used for low-volume, high-value goods which require rapid delivery. Conversely, bulk raw materials such as coal or iron ore lend themselves to carriage by slower, cheaper forms of transport such as water or rail.

Not all modes of transport will be suitable for all types of products. The physical characteristics of the product could limit the choice available to distribution managers. For example, only gases and liquids can be conveniently transported by pipeline; physically large products such as building sections would not fit within the confines of most aircraft. However, the mode of transport is usually chosen with reference to the relative importance of:

- delivery speed
- delivery dependability
- possible quality deterioration
- transportation costs
- route flexibility.

Table 13.2 gives an approximate ranking of each mode of transport under these headings.

The mode of transport chosen will also have an effect on other decisions made by the operation. For example, firms may choose to locate their operations near to ports, airports, railway sidings, or close to junctions of motorways, depending on the mode of transport chosen. At a more day-to-day level, the decision on batch sizes and order quantities will be affected by the carrying capacity of each mode of transport.

Table 13.2 The relative performance of each mode of transport

Operation's performance objective	Mode of transport				
	Road	Rail	Air	Water	Pipeline
Delivery speed	2	3	1	5	4
Delivery dependability	2	3	4	5	1
Quality	2	3	4	5	1
Cost	3	4	5	2	1
Route flexibilty	1	2	3	4	5

Key: 1 = Best performance, 5 = Worst performance

Contract terms

In any supply transaction the buyer and the supplier have to agree on who takes responsibility for the risk and who pays for the transportation. This is a particular specialism in international trade where knowledge of international trade agreements, legislation and documentation are critical to purchasing successfully from other countries. Internationally recognized shipping terms are now in operation which are applied to international transportation by sea or air, as follows:

Ex-works

In an ex-works contract the purchaser accepts full responsibility for arranging transportation from the supplier's location. This involves arranging transportation, insurance and documentation to move the goods to the required port (air or sea), have them loaded on to the mode of transport, transported, unloaded at the destination port, cleared through customs and transported to the purchaser's location. This type of contract may be used if the supplier has little experience of international trade or the purchaser has a transportation network already in place which can group purchases together and ship them in bulk. More recently, purchasers and suppliers have sub-contracted this transportation function to specialists such as Federal Express. (*See* the case exercise at the end of this chapter.)

Free alongside (FAS)

In this arrangement the supplier agrees to deliver to the port specified by the purchaser and is responsible for the transportation and insurance of the goods to that point. However, the purchaser has to arrange and pay for loading on to the vessel and all onward transportation, insurance and documentation.

Free on board (FOB)

Here the supplier pays for and arranges loading on to the outward bound transportation and thereafter the purchaser becomes responsible.

Cost and freight (C&F)

This is a split responsibility arrangement in that the supplier arranges and pays for transportation to an agreed point but the purchaser has to pay insurance from when the goods are loaded on board. The purchaser has to acquire any documentation required by the country of origin. Once the goods have been unloaded at the port of entry, the purchaser is responsible for all ongoing transportation and insurance to its site.

Cost, insurance and freight (CIF)

This is similar to C&F except that here the insurance during transportation is the responsibility of the supplier.

Delivered

This is the opposite of ex-works in that the supplier has total responsibility for the goods, their transportation, insurance and all documentation until they are delivered and accepted by the purchaser.

Figure 13.7 illustrates these differences in contract terms.

Cost and lead time of international supply

In addition to the contract arrangements, international purchasing and supply has a significant impact on the planning and control within the operation. While goods are in transit they are not yielding any benefit to the buyer who may have had to pay with a letter of credit for some or all of the load prior to it departing. If goods are being moved across 'deep sea' over the major oceans, this may take one to three months, depending on the journey and the efficiency of the documentation arrangers. During this time, all the costs of inventory apply: namely the opportunity cost of capital tied up in the inventory, obsolescence, pilferage (a major problem with lower-security forms of transportation), spoilage and the costs of storage, such as refrigeration costs.

Figure 13.7
Responsibilities
and risk with
different contract
terms

The risks of international supply

In addition to the costs of international transportation, there is the risk, albeit a slight one, of the entire load being lost through accident or piracy: the more valuable and more easily saleable the load, the higher this risk becomes. Interestingly, some exporters have different difficulties when transporting to some countries where wooden packing crates, which can be used for making shanty housing, etc., are valued more highly than the goods inside them. Particular care is required where security is poor. It is often preferred practice in these situations to use local freight forwarders who are familiar with the local conditions and can plan accordingly.

INTEGRATED CONCEPTS

So far we have discussed the linkage between a purchaser in one operation and a supplier in another. Purchasing and supplier development considered the flow of information from purchaser to supplier. Physical distribution considered the physical movement of goods from the supplier to the purchaser. Together they form the links in the supply chain. Any supply chain will consist of a sequence of these purchaser–supplier linkages. In this part of the chapter we move on to consider ways in which more than one of these linkages can be considered as an integrated whole.

There are many different ways in which the linkages involved in the flow of materials and services can be integrated or grouped together. Four main concepts will be discussed here. These have focused attention on managing *across* the traditional functional areas of purchasing operations and physical distribution. These are *materials management, merchandising, logistics* and *supply chain management.* This latter concept is by far the most comprehensive, which is why we have used it as the title of this chapter. Nevertheless, it is important to understand the progressively more integrative concepts which lead up to the development of supply chain management.

Materials management

This concept originated from purchasing functions who understood the importance of integrating materials flow and its supporting functions, both throughout the business and out to immediate customers. It includes the functions of purchasing, expediting, inventory management, stores management, production planning and control and physical distribution management.

Materials management was originally seen as a means of reducing 'total costs associated with the acquisition and management of materials'.[9] Different stages in the movement of materials through a multi-echelon system are typically buffered by inventory, as shown in Fig. 13.8. Where materials management is not in place to integrate these different stages, they are often managed by different people, reporting to different senior managers within the organization. For example, a production director or vice-president will probably have responsibility for the factory, a procurement director for purchasing, with a marketing or sales director controlling the physical distribution function. These different functions are managed separately, each with its own targets, each optimizing its own small part of the total materials flow system.

The result of this separate functional management of the materials flow is often high inventory levels. The lead time to move materials through the system is long because of the wasted time while materials are held in inventory. Because of the long lead time, materials have to be purchased much earlier to ensure they are available at the start of

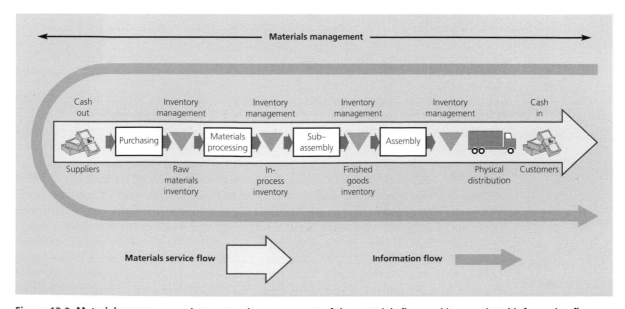

Figure 13.8 Materials management integrates the mangement of the materials flow and its associated information flow

production. This makes the system inflexible to change because commitment to design and volumes is made much earlier. The whole materials movement is difficult to control. It is difficult to keep track of materials because they could be in so many different places, so organizational effort is needed just to track the whereabouts of materials. Materials management means giving responsibilty for the whole materials and information flow to one part of the organization. This allows the co-ordination, reduction and even removal of some intermediate inventories. This speeds up the operation, which reduces lead times, which in turn means less commitment has to be made so far in advance for purchases, thereby reducing the horizon for forecasting in the business. With reduced forecasting, greater accuracy of schedules is possible, bringing about greater planning stability. All of which leads to reduced costs.

Merchandising

In retail operations the purchasing task is frequently combined with the sales and physical distribution task into a role termed *merchandising*. A merchandiser typically has responsibility for organizing sales to retail customers, the layout of the shop floor, inventory management and purchasing. This is because retail purchase operations have to be so closely linked to daily sales to ensure the right mix of goods is available for customers to buy at any time. For example, fashion buyers have to understand what will sell and how garments will look when on display in their retail outlets. In food retailing, buyers specify in detail the packaging in terms of the printing process and materials, to ensure the product looks appealing when displayed in their stores. Daily trends of sales in some retail situations (typically food and fashion) can vary enormously. Replenishment of regularly stocked items has to be very quick to avoid empty shelves or rails. Electronic point-of-sale systems help the planning and control of fast-moving consumer goods; as items are registered as sold at the till, a replenishment signal is returned to the distribution centre to deliver replacements. To facilitate this link many retail operations use bar coding to update the inventory situation and replenish shelves and rails.

Logistics

Logistics orignally related to the movement and co-ordination of troops, armaments and munitions to the required location. When adopted by the business world, it referred to the total flow of finished goods downstream from the plant to the customers. Here the term logistics is being used as analogous to what we called earlier 'physical distribution management'. However, logistics has more recently been extended to include more of the total flow of materials and information. Some authorities adopt a definition of logistics which seems almost identical to that of materials management. There are some differences between materials management and this extended view of logistics, however. Materials management does not concentrate on the physical distribution of finished product, but focuses more on the planning and control of the processes inside an operation (including MRP and JIT, *see* Chapters 14 and 15). Logistics, on the other hand, tends to treat manufacturing as a 'black box', but does provide an emphasis on physical distribution management. These differences, though not great, are present because of the backgrounds of the two groups who originated the concepts. The logisticians tend to come from marketing, the materials managers from operations management, particularly purchasing. Students should be aware of these differences to appreciate the content and focus of discussion of different authors, but should recognize that the common underlying theme is one of benefit through integrated control of the flow of materials and information.

During the last ten years an even broader, more ambitious and strategically significant concept has emerged – *supply chain management*.

Supply chain management

While logisticians have devoted relatively little attention to managing the chain of supply upstream of the purchasing function into suppliers' operations, and materials managers have more or less ignored the management of the flow of finished goods and services downstream through distribution channels, supply chain management views the entire chain as a system to be managed. Supply chain management can be defined as 'managing the entire chain of raw material supply, manufacture, assembly and distribution to the end customer'.

THE LOGISTICS SUPPLY CHAIN AT MARKS & SPENCER[10]

In Chapter 12, a box described part of the Marks & Spencer approach to controlling in-store inventory. Behind each store the company also operates a huge logistics operation. It has to: Marks & Spencer operates over 600 stores throughout the world and employs 62 000 people. Marks & Spencer works with suppliers up to a year in advance of the selling season, discussing styles, designs and colours. These are then consolidated into ranges and eventually contracts are placed for the production of merchandise. Some garments are manufactured pre-season but a significant proportion is now manufactured within the season itself. This gives M&S the ability to control the total volume and flow of production in line with sales. Stock is pulled through the system into distribution centres (DCs), each servicing 30 to 40 stores, which respond to store orders on a daily basis, as was described in Chapter 12.

The system which controls the distribution centres is called the 'User Warehouse System' and was designed and programmed within Marks and Spencer as a special development project over a two-year period at a total cost of £30 million. Through daily transmission of stock availability and on-orders, sales assistants are able to order merchandise from the distribution centre where picking instructions are generated and the merchandise is delivered into the store within 24 hours.

The system has been a great success, with a reduction in storage space, greater transport efficiency and enhanced productivity in stores. The logistics chain alone saw a 20 per cent reduction in the percentage costs to sales, and a substantial number of stockrooms were converted into sales floor space as lower stock levels were achieved. As an additional benefit, goods were moving much faster through the chain and the average period of time from supplier 'call-off' to arriving on the sales floor moved from around two weeks to less than one week.

Marks & Spencer was the first UK retailer to implement EDI (*see* Chapter 8), connecting all of its clothing suppliers. EDI was financially justified purely on the basis of the removal of

▶

paper and the elimination of couriers who took the printed reports from the computer centre to all its suppliers throughout the country. There were many other benefits, however, including speedier operations and improved dependability of service.

After the system took over the transmission of orders to the suppliers, it was further developed to allow the transmission to Marks & Spencer of supplier product availability information which is used to update the central database directly. The system also allows suppliers to declare electronically the availability of their merchandise daily, which then automatically triggers the ordering and allocation process. As part of this paperless interface, Marks & Spencer has also moved to a system of 'positive proof of delivery'. This means the supplier does not issue an invoice but is paid based on the merchandise that is received into Marks & Spencer distribution centres. ∎

Questions

1 How might Marks & Spencer decide how many distribution centres to have?

2 Why is information so important to the smooth operation of Marks & Spencer's logistics system?

Objectives of supply chain management

To focus on satisfying end customers

Because supply chain management includes all stages in the total flow of materials and information, it must eventually include consideration of the final customer. The final customer has the only 'real' currency in the supply chain. When a customer decides to make a purchase, he or she triggers action along the whole chain. All the businesses in the supply chain pass on portions of that end-customer's money to each other, each retaining a margin for the value it has added.

To formulate and implement strategies based on capturing and retaining end-customer business

The key operation in a chain is the strongest business which is in a position to influence and direct the others, so that they work together in the common cause of capturing and retaining the end-customer's business. In retail chains, particularly food retailing, the key operation may be the retail operation which sets the direction for the rest of the chain to follow. Some of the food manufacturers further up the chain may be far bigger companies in terms of world-wide sales, but may still follow the lead taken by the retailer. In automotive manufacture, the key operation is usually the vehicle assembler, even though it is located several links upstream in the supply chain. It sets the standards and often determines the design of the infrastructure, such as the information systems used, which the downstream dealer network complies with. (*See also* Chapter 6 for some strategic design considerations when managing supply chains.)

To manage the chain effectively and efficiently

Taking an holistic approach to managing an entire supply chain opens up many opportunities for analysis and improvement. For example, in a supply chain for inno-

DELL COMPUTERS SHAPES ITS SUPPLY CHAIN[11]

As the personal computer industry matured, and competition increasingly focused on the cost of its products, some companies decided to cut out a tier of their network and sell directly to customers rather than through retail outlets. This move into mail-order selling was prompted originally by the need to trim costs. With most manufacturers buying their components from the same group of suppliers, the potential for cost cutting on the supply side of the network was limited. Furthermore, the nature of customers was changing. The growing number of sophisticated second- or third-time customers no longer needed quite the same degree of technical support from dealers. Cutting them out seemed a good move to Dell Computers, who initially became the most successful of the computer companies to bypass its demand-side supply chain and deal directly with its ultimate customers.

Yet Dell also found that reshaping its supply chain yielded benefits other than lower costs. Its (now direct) contact with customers meant that it could learn more about their needs and preferences ahead of rival manufacturers. Realizing that this new-found potential needed to be exploited, Dell built computer-based information systems which could track every contact with customers, from their first enquiry through to details of every service and repair, thus building a service history for every machine. As well as helping to sell and service computers more effectively in the short term, this information base also let sales and support staff pass better information back to product development teams. ■

Questions

1 Sketch what you think might be the structure of the supply chain for a personal computer manufacturer.

2 How did Dell Computers change this supply chain structure and what advantages did it gain? What else could a personal computer manufacturer do to restructure its supply chain?

---

vative products or services, the time for new products to come to market may be critical. Analysing the chain as a whole to find out where most of the time delays currently occur allows the supply chain manager to focus attention on those 'bottle-neck' businesses in order to shorten time to market. In end-customer markets which are very price competitive, performing a cost and value analysis on the entire supply chain can reveal the sources of cost and the potential cost savings.

Barriers to supply chain management

The concept of strategically co-ordinating supply chains made up of businesses owned and run by different people, each with his or her own business objectives, sounds attractive, if somewhat daunting. In long supply chains, involving many businesses, it is not easy to co-ordinate the whole chain. This is especially true when part of the supply chain serves two sets of end customers.

For example, many manufacturers of automotive components serve two distinctly different groups of end customers. One group (the vehicle market) buys cars which contain their components; the other group (the spares market) buys spare parts for the repair of cars already in service. The latter group of customers is known as the 'aftermarket' for components. These two groups are shown in Fig. 13.9.

The operations management implications of managing supply chains which 'branch' to more than one end customer, such as these, are significant. In this case the competitive factors of importance to vehicle manufacturers are focused heavily towards achievement of quality and price. The volumes required by these customers are high and efforts are made by vehicle manufacturers to stabilize planning and control schedules so as to give some stability to the component manufacturers. This is a very different business to the other branch of the chain: the 'aftermarket'. The demands from here are for a much greater variety of parts, as they have to support vehicles up to 20 years old which are still on the road. Delivery speed is also very important. Repair and service of vehicles usually have to be carried out on the same day and, in most cases, the garage carrying out the repair does not know which parts are required until the vehicle is up on the ramp. Technical support and service from component manufacturers is high on the agenda of businesses in the aftermarket supply chains because they may not have the expertise to solve all of the repair problems they encounter.

This gives the component manufacturers who are trying to manage their supply chains some problems. In effect they have two quite different supply chains which value different competitive factors. The way each link in the two supply chains is managed, the role of inventory, the planning and control priorities and price negotiations will all be different for each chain. Unfortunately, the components for both chains are probably made in the same operation. Unless this is carefully managed, or the operation split between the two chains, this can lead to conflicting objectives.

Figure 13.9 Two main groups of end customers served by an auto components manufacturer

Supply chain dynamics

It was demonstrated in the 1960s by Jay Forrester[12] that certain dynamics exist between firms in supply chains that cause errors, inaccuracies and volatility, and that these increase for operations further upstream in the supply chain. This effect (also known as the Forrester Effect) is analogous to the children's game of Chinese Whispers. The first child whispers a message to the next child who, whether he or she has heard it clearly or not, whispers an interpretation to the next child, and so on. The more children the message passes between, the more distorted it tends to become. When the game finishes and the last child says out loud what the message is, the first child and all the intervening children are amused by the distortion of the original message.

The Forrester Effect is caused not only by errors and distortions. In fact the main cause is a perfectly understandable and rational desire by the different links in the supply chain to manage their production rates and inventory levels sensibly. To demonstrate this, examine the production rate and stock levels for the supply chain shown in Table 13.3. This is a four-stage supply chain where an original equipment manufacturer (OEM) is served by three tiers of suppliers. The demand from the OEM's market has

Table 13.3 Fluctuations of production levels along supply chain in response to small change in end-customer demand

Period	Third-tier supplier		Second-tier supplier		First-tier supplier		Original equipment mfr		Demand
	Prodn.	Stock	Prodn.	Stock	Prodn.	Stock	Prodn.	Stock	
1	100	100 100	100	100 100	100	100 100	100	100 100	100
2	20	100 60	60	100 80	80	100 90	90	100 95	95
3	180	60 120	120	80 100	100	90 95	95	95 95	95
4	60	120 90	90	100 95	95	95 95	95	95 95	95
5	100	90 95	95	95 95	95	95 95	95	95 95	95
6	95	95 95	95	95 95	95	95 95	95	95 95	95

(Note all operations keep one period's inventory.)

been running at a rate of 100 items per period, but in period 2 demand reduces to 95 items per period. All stages in the supply chain work on the principle that they will keep in stock one period's demand. This is a simplification but not a gross one. Many operations gear their inventory levels to their demand rate. The column headed 'stock' for each level of supply shows the starting stock at the beginning of the period and the finish

THE BENETTON SUPPLY CHAIN[13]

One of the best known examples of how an organization can use its supply chain to achieve a competitive advantage is the Benetton Group. Founded by the Benetton family in the 1960s, the company is now one of the largest garment retailers, with stores which bear its name located in almost all parts of the world. Part of the reason for its success has been the way it has organized both the supply side and the demand side of its supply chain.

Although Benetton does manufacture much of its production itself, on its supply side the company relies heavily on 'contractors'. Contractors are companies (many of which are owned, or part-owned, by Benetton employees) who provide service to the Benetton factories by knitting and assembling Benetton's garments. These contractors, in turn, use the services of sub-contractors to perform some of the manufacturing tasks. Benetton's manufacturing operations gain two advantages from this. First, its production costs for woollen items are significantly below some of its competitors because the small supply companies have lower costs themselves. Second, the arrangement allows Benetton to absorb fluctuation in demand by adjusting its supply arrangements, without itself feeling the full effect of demand fluctuations.

On the demand side of the chain Benetton operates through a number of agents, each of whom are responsible for their own geographical area. These agents are responsible for developing the stores in their area. Indeed many of the agents actually own some stores in their area. Products are shipped from Italy to the individual stores where they are often put directly on to the shelves. Benetton stores have always been designed with relatively limited storage space so that the garments (which, typically, are brightly coloured) can be stored in the shop itself, adding colour and ambience to the appearance of the store. Because there is such limited space for inventory in the stores, store owners require that deliveries of garments are fast and dependable. Benetton factories achieve this partly through their famous policy of manufacturing garments, where possible, *in greggio*, or in grey, and then dying them only when demand for particular colours is evident. This is a slightly more expensive process than knitting directly from coloured yarn, but their supply-side economies allow them to absorb the cost of this extra flexibility, which in turn allows them to achieve relatively fast deliveries to the stores. ■

Questions

1 Draw out the Benetton supply chain.

2 What are the major operations objectives of:
   (a) Benetton's retail operations
   (b) the Benetton physical distribution operation
   (c) the Benetton factory and its suppliers?

3 How well do these three interconnecting sets of operations fit together?

stock at the end of the period. At the beginning of period 2, the OEM has 100 units in stock (that being the rate of demand up to period 2). Demand in period 2 is 95 and so the OEM knows that it would need to produce   sufficient items to finish up at the end of the period with 95 in stock (this being the new demand rate). To do this it only need manufacture 90 items, this together with five items taken out of the starting stock will supply demand and leave a finished stock of 95 items. The beginning of period 3 finds the OEM with 95 items in stock. Demand is also 95 items and therefore its production rate to maintain a stock level of 95 will be 95 items per period. The original equipment manufacturer now operates at a steady rate of producing 95 items per period. Note, however, that a change in demand of only five items has produced a fluctuation of ten items in the OEM's production rate.

Now carry this same logic through to the first-tier supplier. At the beginning of period 2 the second-tier supplier has 100 items in stock. The demand which it has to supply in period 2 is derived from the production rate of the OEM. This has dropped down to 90 in period 2. The first-tier supplier, therefore, has to produce sufficient to supply the demand of 90 items (or the equivalent) and leave one month's demand (now 90 items) as its finish stock. A production rate of 80 items per month will achieve this. It will therefore start period 3 with an opening stock of 90 items but the demand from the OEM has now risen to 95 items. It therefore has to produce sufficient to fulfil this demand of 95 items and leave 95 items in stock. To do this it must produce 100 items in period 3. After period 3 the first-tier supplier then resumes a steady state, producing 95 items per month. Note again, however, that the fluctuation has been even greater than that in the original equipment manufacturer's production rate, decreasing to 80 items a period, increasing to 100 items a period, and then achieving a steady rate of 95 items a period.

This logic can be extended right back to the third-tier supplier. If you do this you will notice that the further back up the supply chain an operation is placed, the more drastic are the fluctuations caused by the relatively small change in demand from the final customer. In this simple case, the decision of how much to produce each month was governed by the following relationship:

Total available for sale in any period = Total required in the same period
Starting stock + production rate = Demand + closing stock
Starting stock + production rate = 2 × demand (because closing stock must be equal to demand)
Production rate = 2 × demand − starting stock

This relatively simple exercise does not include any time lag between a demand occurring in one part of the supply chain and it being transmitted to its supplier. In practice there will be such a lag, and this will make the fluctuations even more marked. Furthermore, the way different parts of the supply chain batch their manufacturing quantities can cause distortions which make production volumes fluctuate in upstream suppliers. Table 13.4 shows a simple example.

In Table 13.4 there is reasonably steady end-customer demand at a rate of five items per week. The end customer orders from a local distributor at this rate who, maybe because of custom and practice, places bi-weekly orders with the area distributor – for this part, this is at a rate of ten every two weeks. The area distributor delivers at this bi-weekly rate but, to replenish its stock, places monthly orders back to the manufacturer. In Table 13.4, this involves ordering 50 in the first month, none in the second and 50 in the third month. The manufacturer actually makes them in economic batches of 100 so therefore makes them only occasionally.

Table 13.4 Distortion of batching in the supply chain

Manufacturer	Area distributor	Local distributor	End customer
100	50	10	5
0	0	0	5
0	0	10	5
0	0	0	5
0	0	10	5
0	0	0	5
0	0	10	5
0	0	0	5
0	50	10	5
0	0	0	5
0	0	10	5

TYPES OF RELATIONSHIPS IN SUPPLY CHAINS

One of the main decisions of interest in supply chain management is how much of the supply chain should be owned by each business. This is called the extent of *vertical integration* and was described in Chapter 6. The alternative to vertical integration is some other form of relationship, not necessarily involving ownership. The relationship between the links of the supply chain will be examined in more detail in terms of the flows between the operations involved. These flows may be of transformed resources, such as materials, or of transforming resources, such as people or equipment. The term used to include all the different types of flow is *exchange*.

The different relationship types which we will describe are as follows:

● integrated hierarchy
● semi-hierarchy
● co-contracting
● co-ordinated contracting
● co-ordinated revenue links
● medium-/ long-term trading commitment
● short-term trading commitment.

Integrated hierarchy

What is known as an integrated hierarchy is a fully vertically integrated firm which houses all activities in the supply chain, from raw material source to dispatch to end customer, as well as all its support activities on one site. In an integrated hierarchy there is no inter-company exchange of orders, information and materials because the entire supply chain is 'under one roof'. Examples of such a totally vertically integrated chain are rare. One example is a small vegetarian restaurant where the owners grow their own vegetables in the back garden, pick them, prepare them, cook them and serve them in the restaurant.

Semi-hierarchy

In a semi-hierarchy organization the firms in the supply chain are owned by the same holding company or are part of the same group, but they operate as separate business units. Oil companies who extract, refine, distribute and retail their products are an example of this type of arrangement.

Both integrated hierarchy and semi-hierarchy are examples of vertical integration as in both cases ownership is by the same firm. In a semi-hierarchy, however, there is an exchange process between different organizations where materials, services and money change hands between the separate business units. In addition to material and information exchange, there is likely to be a common set of systems and technologies exchanged between the parties. People may be exchanged between the organizations for particular projects or on a regular basis, depending on the design of the organization structure. The benefits which come from high-volume purchasing may exchange if there is centralized purchasing for the corporation.

Co-contracting

Co-contracting is a term used to describe alliances between organizations which have long-term relationships but which, for various reasons, do not merge but do transfer some equity (ownership), technology, people and information as well as goods and services. Such alliances are evident in the aerospace and automotive industries (for example, Airbus Industrie). These alliances typically do not include the whole supply chain.

A type of co-contracting receiving significant attention is what is called a 'partnership'.[14] This is, '*the sharing of risks and rewards, of technology and innovation leading to a reduction in costs, improvements in delivery and quality and the creation of sustainable competitive advantage*'.

Organizations may enter partnerships for very different reasons. One reason might be to transfer an activity from one organization to the partnership because it can be performed more efficiently by the partners together (or even by one of the other partners alone). Professor Richard Lamming (1993) of Bath University proposed that the West's perception of partnership is based on profitability and cost reduction whereas the partnership philosophy should be based on improving productivity and efficiency.[15]

In partnerships, the supplier is a stakeholder in the customer's organization. Partnership is a long-term process and should not be viewed as an instant cost-saving exercise but rather as an investment where future returns are possible, but only in the medium to long term.[16]

Professor Lamming also proposed a model of customer–supplier relationship which moves beyond simple partnership, which he calls *lean supply*. Whereas in partnership relationships the supplier is still the junior partner, in lean supply both supplier and customer are equal partners. Table 13.5 illustrates some of the characteristics of lean supply.

In both partnership and lean relationships, boundaries may become 'blurred', which can create close connections between the two parties involved. However, the partners do not lose their own legal identity, as happens in merger or acquisition. They also retain their own culture, structure and pursue their own strategies. Inevitably, however, they reduce their freedom of action to some extent by strengthening their ties with the other organizations.

Table 13.5 Lamming's lean supply concept

Factor	Lean supply characteristics
Nature of competition	Global operation; local presence Based upon contribution to product technology Dependent upon alliances/collaboration
How suppliers are selected by customers	Early involvement of established supplier Joint efforts in target costing/value analysis Single and dual sourcing Supplier provides global benefits Re-sourcing as a last resort after attempts to improve
Exchange of information between supplier and customer	True transparency: costs, etc. Two-way: discussion of costs and volumes Technical and commercial information Electronic data interchange Kanban system for production deliveries (*see* Chapter 15)
Management of capacity	Regionally strategic investments discussed Synchronized capacity Flexibility to operate with fluctuations
Delivery practice	True just-in-time with kanban Local, long-distance and international JIT (*see* Chapter 15)
Dealing with price changes	Price reductions based upon cost reductions from order onwards: from joint efforts of supplier and customer
Attitude to quality	Supplier vetting schemes become redundant Mutual agreement on quality targets Continual interaction and kaizen (*see* Chapter 18) Perfect quality as goal

Source: Adapted from Lamming, R. (1993) *Beyond Partnership: Strategies for Innovation and Lean Supply*, Prentice Hall

Co-ordinated contracting

Co-ordinated contracting involves a prime contractor, such as a jobbing builder, who employs a set of sub-contractors, such as carpenters, bricklayers and electricians, with whom a long-standing relationship exists over several contracts. They are used on a contract basis for each specific job, but in between jobs there is no direct exchange of goods and/or services, though some form of 'sleeping' relationship exists. In co-ordinated contracting the contractor usually provides the specification and instructions for the production of goods and services to be exchanged. It may provide materials and will usually take responsibility for the planning and control of all the sub-contractors. The sub-contractors will often provide the necessary tools and equipment required for their trade or profession. As this example indicates, this type of relationship is often found in project-type operations (*see* Chapter 16).

ROTTERDAM FRUIT PORT IN PARTNERSHIP WITH ITS CUSTOMERS[17]

The port of Rotterdam, the largest and busiest in the world, covers nearly 5000 hectares and has over 60 kilometres of dockside berths. Around 32 000 ships use the port each year, handling nearly 300 million tonnes of cargo. As well as being a vital link in the supply chains of countless organizations, the port also provides services to the transportation companies who ship goods through it. It is in this role – as provider of services – where it sees its future as developing 'partnership' arrangements with its major customers. Competition in the port business is fierce. Rotterdam is acutely aware of the intense competition from other large European ports such as Hamburg, Antwerp, Zeebrugge and Bremen. Forming partnerships with its customers is a response to such competitive pressures.

In order to focus on its customers' needs the port has created dedicated areas of distinct competence which can support the needs of particular customers. One of these is the recently developed Fruit Port where most of the port's fruit, fruit juice and vegetable-related businesses are located, sharing the specially developed modern facilities and infrastructures. This development involves 70 hectares of new land, created by filling in redundant harbour basins. The internal logistics of the site have been redesigned to ensure rapid flows of these highly perishable products between vessels, storage facilities, and land-based transport systems. The advantage of concentrating its fruit-related business in one part of the docks is that all the different operations that provide services related to fruit handling can now link together to ensure speed of handling of both produce and paperwork. The fruit port administration, forwarding agents, customs officers, inspection companies, traders, auctioneers at the fruit exchange, the managers of the temperature control warehouses and the distribution companies themselves are 'partners' who, by understanding each other's professional needs, form an effective link in their supply chain. ■

Questions

1 How is the port of Rotterdam trying to influence its relationship with its customers?

2 What do you think are the advantages and disadvantages in developing the Fruit Port?

Co-ordinated revenue links

This category is used primarily for licensing and franchising and is a form of relationship which transfers ownership to other, usually smaller, firms while still retaining a guaranteed income for the licensor or franchiser.

One of the most significant things to pass between parties in this type of relationship is the contract, which often specifies the following:

● property rights to the product or service, which usually remain with the licensor/franchiser;
● the territory within which the licensee or franchisee can operate;
● the product or service specification;
● the process specification to be used within the operation;
● the process of monitoring performance, and any action that could result from poor performance.

This type of relationship is common in many services, especially those with very high customer contact. These operations need many small local sites which can be located for the convenience of their customers. Rather than manage all the sites themselves, the original owners of the service concept will licence out each individual operation to separate owners. Instant-printing operations, fast-food outlets and dry-cleaning operations are often organized on this basis.

Medium- / long-term trading commitment

It is not uncommon for businesses to trade with each other for 20 years or more but never to exchange formal long-term contracts that legally tie them together. However, where this medium- to long-term trading takes place, some commitment beyond each delivery of a different type can be made. One example is what is called a 'blanket order'. This is an agreement for the purchasing organization to buy a total volume over a period of time at a price determined by the total, rather than the individual daily, weekly or monthly purchased quantity. For example, in the purchase of materials and components there may be a delivery schedule specifying how many items are required each week but also a yearly agreement, on which the price is based. In a service environment there may be a service contract, such as for the regular upkeep of gardens as part of a tenancy agreement, specifying the amount of time that should be spent, or the standard to which the gardens should be maintained.

Short-term trading commitment

In situations where there is no interdependence beyond one order, all that is transferred between the parties to the transaction is the order one way and goods or services the other. The agreement is reached after a market search, sometimes competitive tendering and often price negotiation. Once the goods or services are delivered and payment is made, there may be no further trading between the parties.

Short-term relationships may be used when new companies are being considered as more regular suppliers. Many purchases made by all operations are one-off or very irregular. For example, the replacement of all the windows in a company's office block would typically involve this type of competitive-tendering relationship, whereas it might form a longer-term relationship with its supplier of cleaning services.

Some public sector purchasing of goods and services is still based on short-term contracts such as these. This is mainly because of the need to prove that public money is being spent as judiciously as possible. However, this short-term, price-oriented type of relationship can have a downside in terms of ongoing support and reliability. This may mean that a 'least cost' purchase decision actually involves a higher total cost to the purchasing organization over time. For example, a higher education institution purchased a room full of microcomputers on a lowest cost, spot-order basis, only to find that the computer agent who sold them was a small business whose main income was as a bicycle supplier. The ongoing technical support the university received was problematic.

The different types of relationship and the main elements of exchange in the relationship are summarized in Fig. 13.10.

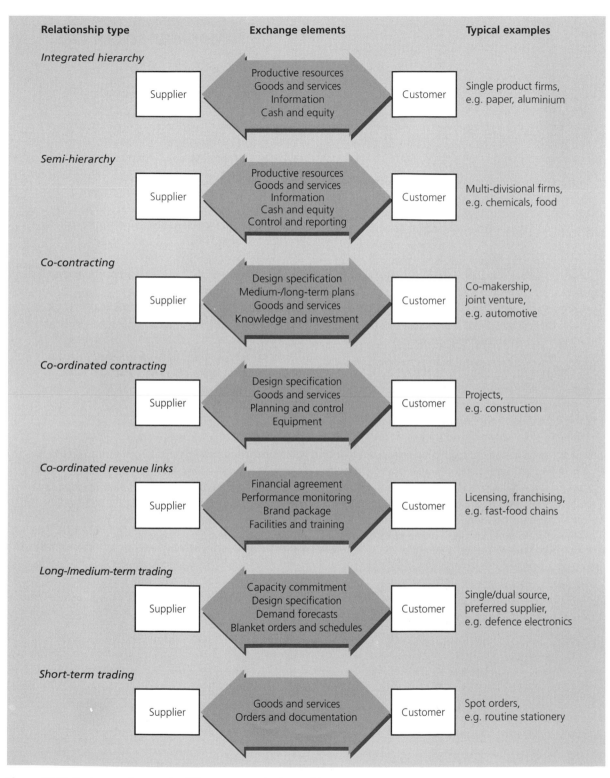

Figure 13.10 Exchange elements in different types of relationships

Julia Dawson, Rover Group

The Rover Group is the UK's largest vehicle manufacturer. Julia Dawson joined the company after graduating in European Business. She is now Logistics Manager, planning component delivery for new models.

'A placement at Fiat in Italy, during my degree course in European Business, convinced me that I wanted to work in manufacturing industry, where there was a clear need for people with a combination of engineering, business and interpersonal skills. Logistics was first explained in the final year of my course. We were shown how it can have a significant effect on the efficiency and success of a business, by improving product flows and by building better customer–supplier relationships, and thereby reducing the levels of raw material and work-in-progress.

'The idea of working in logistics at Rover appealed, and I joined as a graduate on completion of my course. The training in the Logistics Department was very "hands on" and emphasized the need to be able to handle an ever-changing environment. Initially my job involved managing the scheduling, storage, transport, and movement of the Rover Cabriolet hood (soft top) from a supplier in Italy, which is the most expensive single component delivered to the factory. To do the job properly required intimate knowledge of the build strategy and related processes, both of the supplier and of Rover itself. I had to understand the component scheduling methods used in the manufacturing area and to ensure that the suppliers understood and complied with those systems. I had to have a detailed knowledge of component lead times, and of the scheduling of vehicles on the production line. The production plan can be liable to change at short notice and any component delivery planning had to incorporate some flexibility as a key objective.

'Logistics also plays a key role in the planning of new models by ensuring that the supplies will be continuous and cost-effective, involving the development of relationships with the major suppliers allied to the manufacturing strategy within the Rover Group.

'I normally enjoy the job tremendously, but I have to admit that there are obviously some frustrating times when seemingly insignificant details are holding up the negotiation process. On the whole, I find that I am always in the thick of things, and need to be up to date with our current position in order to communicate confidently with suppliers. I also have to liaise with a range of internal customers and suppliers such as manufacturing and facilities engineering to ensure that our plans can be realistically fulfilled. Logistics is about being in the middle – being an effective link in the supply chain …' ∎

SUMMARY ANSWERS TO KEY QUESTIONS

What is the difference between terms such as purchasing, physical distribution, logistics, materials management, and supply chain management?

■ Purchasing is concerned with the supply-side activities of an organization.

■ Physical distribution management is the management of the (often multi-echelon) inventory and transportation systems which link the operation with its customers.

■ Logistics includes the demand-side physical distribution of goods often beyond the immediate customers, through the supply chain to the end customer.

■ Materials management is an integrated concept which includes both purchasing activities and physical distribution activities.

■ Supply chain management is a broader concept which includes the management of the entire supply chain from supplier of raw material to the end customer.

What is the purpose and objective of purchasing management?

■ Purchasing includes the formal preparation of requests to suppliers for a quotation, the evaluation of suppliers, the issuing of formal purchase orders, and the monitoring of delivery.

■ The purchasing function attempts to obtain goods or services

– at the right price
– for delivery at the right time
– in the right quantity
– at the right quality
– from the right source.

■ The effect of savings on the bought-in materials bill in most organizations has a disproportionate effect on their profitability. The greater the proportion of their costs which are devoted to bought-in materials, the greater the saving for a given reduction in bought-in material costs.

What is the purpose and objective of physical distribution management?

■ Physical distribution management decisions include the number and position of warehouses in the system, and the mode of physical transport which needs to be adopted.

■ This area also includes the decision as to which contract terms buyers and suppliers agree. The choice of contract defines the responsibility and risk relating to who pays for transportation. There are internationally recognized terms which define the balance of risks and costs. These include such terms as, ex-works; free alongside; free on board; cost and freight; cost, insurance and freight; and delivered.

How is the concept of supply chain management different?

■ Supply chain management is a more strategic concept which includes the strategic and long-term consideration of supply management issues as well as the shorter term control of flow through the supply chain.

■ The term includes developing an understanding of the dynamic effect (sometimes called the Forrester Effect) which governs the amplification of demand changes as they affect upstream operations within the supply chain.

■ Supply chain management also includes developing appropriate relationships between individual links within the supply chain. These relationship types (which range from integrated hierarchies through to short-term trading commitments) imply different exchange relationships between suppliers and customers.

CASE EXERCISE

Laura Ashley's strategic alliance with Federal Express[18]

Laura Ashley (LA) is a global manufacturer and retailer with its headquarters in a small village in Wales. It must be the benchmark for almost every aspiring entrepreneur's dreams; it has blossomed from Laura and Bernard Ashley's experiments in printing textiles on their kitchen table in 1953, to a business with over 6000 staff and 540 shops in 28 countries. Laura Ashley is famous throughout the world for its unique brand of women's garments, curtain and upholstery fabric and wallpapers, mostly designed with a pastoral, nostalgic and distinctly 'English' style. It uses only natural fabrics including cotton, silk and linen, printed in a wide and constantly evolving range of styles and patterns.

Unfortunately, however, Laura Ashley's spectacular success in product development and design, and in bringing products to market, was not matched in its operations. The company, which had been so profitable throughout the '80s, reported major losses in 1990 and for the following few years. The problem seemed to be that while the business had grown, it had also become very complex, and its logistics operations had failed to adapt, with the resulting symptoms being extremely long lead times for orders, huge inventories, high levels of stock-outs, inventory shortages, and enormous write-offs of obsolete products. The company operated eight major warehouses, contracted eight principal carriers, and ten unconnected management systems. The 1990 and 1991 accounts showed £6.7m and £4.8m exceptional items covering 'restructuring, systems costs, inventory writedowns and other one-time events'. From the external customers' perspective, Laura Ashley's service had deteriorated badly, but the internal customers, both at the factories and at the shops, also suffered from the inadequacies of the system.

In September 1991 Dr Jim Maxmin was appointed Chief Executive, and set about a strategic and operational review aimed at building the brand and restoring the company to profitability. Maxmin's objectives were for LA to become 'strategically led, competitively focused, market oriented, employee driven, and operationally excellent'. He described the existing warehousing, distribution, and delivery operations as 'a disaster, out of control', and formed a global team, headed up by Phil Baker, Special Projects Director in Global Finance, to evaluate options for solving the problems. They were tasked with creating a system

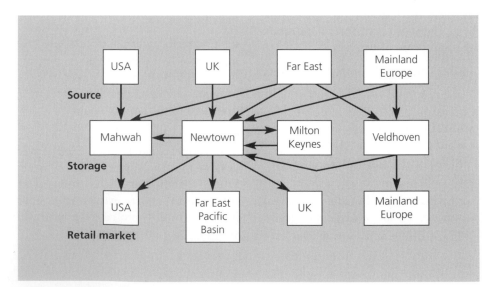

Figure 13.11 Laura Ashley: before

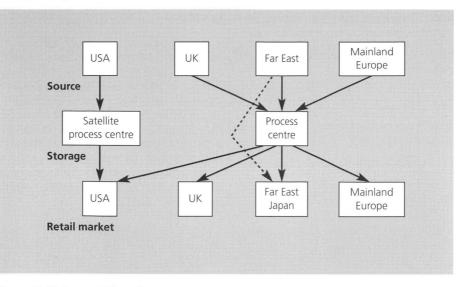

Figure 13.12 Laura Ashley: after

which would increase availability from 80 per cent to 99 per cent, allow all deliveries to be made to stores anywhere in the world within 24 or 48 hours, and reduce inventory by 50 per cent. The existing supply chain held up to 18 months' inventory from product design to point of sale, and inventory turns averaged less than two! During the review, Baker visited an LA store in Germany. A fast-selling item was out of stock, and new supplies would not be available for four months; on his return to Wales, he found that the warehouse had five hundred in unallocated stock.

'Right now, we're the very opposite of service maximization and cost minimization',

he commented. Fig. 13.11 shows LA's logistics structure before the later changes.

After extensive review, the team concluded that the necessary logistic resources and skills could never be developed quickly enough within LA to meet the objectives, and supported Jim Maxmin's proposals for a strategic partnership with Federal Express Business Logistics Service (BLS). Maxmin had previous experience with Federal Express, and the company was already an important supplier of shipping services. The idea of an alliance was very controversial, as many executives felt that it was dangerous to depend on a single supplier, which would be taking over the Welsh warehouses and all of LA's distribution activities world-wide. The strategic alliance

between Federal Express and Laura Ashley commenced in March 1992. It was based on a minimum ten-year term to facilitate an extensive programme of developments, although both parties talked of a 'life-time' partnership. Figure 13.12 shows the new logistics structure.

Several of the warehouses around the world were phased out, and the Welsh facility at Newtown became the 'processing centre', forming the single hub of global distribution, much of it by air on the Federal Express fleet. Consolidating inventory at one site reduced the magnitude of random demand variations experienced at the smaller, local warehouses, so total inventory could be reduced while service level was improved. Direct shipment from the warehouse to the stores eliminated double handling and, surprisingly perhaps, some of the transportation costs involved in the dual shipments. Integration and updating of inventory, point-of-sale and logistics information systems were begun immediately. These and other systems are being continually developed. The specific details of the financial arrangements between the companies have not been made public.

Above all, however, the deal was conceived to provide new opportunities for both partners. Phil Baker summarized his view of the partnership:

'We really can't find any downsides. This is a fantastic opportunity for both companies … The way things had become, there was little else we could have done!'

▶

507

Laura Ashley's goals for its agreement with Federal Express Business Logistics Services were:

● reduce inventory held in the supply chain at any time by 50 per cent;

● cut logistics operating costs by 10–12 per cent, based on like-for-like services;

● eliminate the need to hold out-of-stock lines in stores (currently at 16 per cent);

● develop the capability for a global mail order operation by September 1993;

● integrate and improve all service levels. ∎

Questions

1 What arguments against the agreement might have been made by LA managers and why? How could Maxmin and Baker get their staff to 'buy-in' to this deal, and what approach could have been taken with those who resisted?

2 Do you agree with Phil Baker that there was no alternative to this scheme? If not, what should have been done to transform LA's logistics performance?

3 What risks were taken by Federal Express in reaching this agreement?

4 How could the last objective (integrate and improve all service levels) be evaluated? What performance measures, if any, should be used?

DISCUSSION QUESTIONS

1 If you were the owner of a small, local retail shop, what criteria would you use to select suppliers for the goods which you wish to stock in your shop? Visit three shops which are local to you and ask the owners how they select their suppliers. In what way were their answers different to what you thought they might be?

2 What do you understand by the terms logistics, merchandising, materials management and supply chain management?

3 If you were drawing up a document to be sent out to potential suppliers of a new photocopying machine for your local library, what would you ask them to specify in their quotation?

4 How is vertical integration different from partnership purchasing?

5 A company is considering buying in leaflets to be included with the packaging of its products. Its own in-house printing department could produce the leaflets but not at the same level of quality which a specialist printer could supply. Nevertheless, the in-house printing department is keen to be given the job of printing the leaflets. The cost of printing the leaflets in-house is £10 per 1000 leaflets. This cost includes the cost of the paper and inks (£7), the cost of the energy used by the printing machines (£0.50) and a standard overhead charge calculated according to the time the job would take (£2.50). The in-house printing department has sufficient capacity to print all the leaflets which will be required without any extra staff or machines. The company's purchasing department has several quotations from local printers, the cheapest of which is £8.50 per 1000 leaflets, although the printer made it clear that delivery times would be at least two weeks for each order because they have so much other business currently. How would you advise the company if it asked you whether it should buy in the leaflets or allow its own in-house printing unit to do the job?

6 If you were designing a system to evaluate the performance of a company's purchasing function, what criteria would you use?

7 Why do you think the use of expediters is less common than it once was? Do you think expediters could still play a useful role?

8 How is logistics different from materials management?

9 What do you think should be the main information which is exchanged between the purchasing function and other parts of the organization?

10 Under what circumstances do you think multi-sourcing would be advantageous?

NOTES ON CHAPTER

1 Coyle, R.G. (1982) 'Assessing the Controllability of a Production Raw Material System', *IEEE Transactions*, SMC–12, Vol 6.

2 Harland, C. (1993) Unpublished PhD thesis.

3 Baily, P., Farmer, D., Jessop, D. and Jones, D. (1994) *Purchasing Principles and Management* (7th edn), Pitman Publishing.

4 Sable, C., Herrigel, G., Kazis, R. and Deeg, R. (1987) 'How to Keep Mature Industries Innovative', *Technology Review*, Vol 90, No 3.

5 Morgan, I. (1987) 'The Purchasing Revolution', *McKinsey Quarterly*, Spring.

6 Lamming, R. (1993) *Beyond Partnership: Strategies for Innovation and Lean Supply*, Prentice Hall.

7 Source: Company literature.

8 Source: KLM staff.

9 Lee, L. and Dobler, D.W. (1977) *Purchasing and Materials Management*, McGraw-Hill.

10 Source: Discussion with company staff.

11 Source: 'It's in the Mail', *The Economist*, 2 Mar 1991.

12 Forrester, J.W. (1961) *Industrial Dynamics*, MIT Press.

13 Benetton (A) (1984), Harvard Business School Case Study 6-985-014, and company literature.

14 Lamming, R., *op. cit.*

15 Lamming, R., *op. cit.*

16 Kanter, R.M. (1989) *When Giants Learn to Dance*, Routledge.

17 Source: *Port of Rotterdam News*, 1994.

18 Source: Discussion with company staff.

SELECTED FURTHER READINGS

Bailey, P. and Farmer, D. (1994) *Purchasing Principles and Management* (7th edn), Pitman publishing.

Blumenfeld, D.E., Burns, L.D., Daganzo, C.F., Frick, M.C. and Hall, R.W. (1987) 'Reducing Logistics Costs at General Motors', *Interfaces*, Vol 17, Jan–Feb.

Bund, J.B. (1985) 'Build Customer Relationships That Last', *Harvard Business Review*, Vol 63, No 6.

Burt, D.N. (1984) *Proactive Purchasing*, Prentice Hall.

Burt, D.N. (1989) 'Managing Suppliers Up to Speed', *Harvard Business Review*, Vol 67, No 4.

Burt, D.N. and Soukup, W.R. (1985) 'Purchasing's Role in New Product Development', *Harvard Business Review*, Vol 63, No 5.

Carr, C.H. and Truesdale, T.A. (1992) 'Lessons From Nissan's British Suppliers', *International Journal of Operations and Production Management*, Vol 12, No 2.

Carter, J.R. and Narasimhan, R. (1990) 'Purchasing in the International Market Place: Implications for Operations', *Journal of Purchasing and Materials Management*, Summer.

Chadwick, T. and Rajagopal, S. (1995) *Strategic Supply Management*, Butterworth-Heinemann.

Cousins, P. D. (1992) 'Choosing the Right Partner', *Purchasing and Supply Management Journal*, Mar.

Cousins, P.D. (1992) 'Purchasing: The Professional Approach', *Purchasing and Supply Management Journal*, Sept.

Fisher, M.L. (1997) 'What is the Right Supply Chain for Your Product?', *Harvard Business Review*, Vol 75, No 2.

Fuller, J.B., O'Connor J. and Rawlinson, R. (1993) 'Tailored Logistics: The Next Advantage', *Harvard Business Review*, Vol 71, No 3.

Harrison, A. and Voss, C. (1990) 'Issues in Setting Up JIT Supply', *International Journal of Operations and Production Management*, Vol 10, No 2.

Heinz, P. (1994) *Creating World Class Suppliers: Unlocking Mutual Competitive Advantage*, FT/Pitman Publishing.

Hines, P. and Rich, N. (1997) 'The Seven Value Stream Mapping Tools', *International Journal of Operations and Production Management*, Vol 17, No 1.

Jarillo, J.C. (1993) *Strategic Networks: Creating the Borderless Organisation*, Butterworth-Heinemann.

Lamming, R. (1993) *Beyond Partnership: Strategies for Innovation and Lean Supply*, Prentice Hall.

Lee L. and Dobler D.W. (1977) *Purchasing and Materials Management*, McGraw-Hill.

Macbeth, D.K., Baxter, L.F., Ferguson, N. and Neil, G.C. (1989) 'Not Purchasing but Supply Chain Management', *Purchasing and Supply Management Journal*, Nov.

Poirier, C.C. and Reiter, S.E. (1996) *Supply Chain Optimisation*, Berrett-Koehler.

Rackham, N., Friedman, L. and Ruff, R. (1996) *Getting Partnering Right*, McGraw-Hill.

Ramsay, J. and Wilson, I. (1990) 'Sourcing/Contracting Strategy Selection', *International Journal of Operations and Production Management*, Vol 10, No 8.

Schneider, L.M. (1985) 'A New Era in Transportation Strategy', *Harvard Business Review*, Vol 63, No 2.

Sharman, G. (1984) 'The Rediscovery of Logistics', *Harvard Business Review*, Vol 62, No 5.

Walleigh, R.C. (1986) 'Getting Things Done: What's Your Excuse for Not Using JIT?', *Harvard Business Review*, Vol 64, No 2.

Womack, J.P., Jones, D.T. and Roos, D. (1990) *The Machine that Changed the World*, Rawson Associates.

MRP

INTRODUCTION

It is easy to become confused when trying to understand what MRP is. There are two different but related definitions of MRP – this chapter will define both of these and describe them. Both, however, share the same underlying theme – they help businesses plan and control their resource requirements with the aid of computer-based information systems. MRP can stand for both materials requirements planning or manufacturing resource planning. Over time, the concept of MRP has developed from an operations-management focused concept which helped in planning and controlling materials requirements to become, in recent years, a business system which helps plan all business resource requirements. Typically, MRP is used in manufacturing businesses, although there are some examples of its application in non-manufacturing environments. Figure 14.1 shows the purpose of MRP in reconciling the supply and demand of resources.

Figure 14.1 A definition of MRP

CHAPTER 14: KEY QUESTIONS

- *What is MRP?*

- *What is the process involved in MRP planning and control?*

- *What are the main elements in an MRP system?*

- *What is 'closed loop' MRP?*

- *What is MRP II?*

WHAT IS MRP?

The original MRP dates back to the 1960s, when the letters stood for *materials requirements planning* (now called MRP One or MRP I). MRP I enables a company to calculate how many materials of particular types are required, and at what times they are required. To do this it uses a sales order book which records known future orders and also a forecast of what sales orders the business is reasonably confident might be won. MRP then checks all the ingredients or components which are required to make these future orders and ensures they are ordered in time.

An easy way of thinking about this is to imagine that you have decided to hold a party in two weeks' time and expect about 40 people to attend. As well as some beer, wine and soft drinks, you decide to provide sandwiches and savoury snacks. Prior to shopping, you will probably do some simple calculations, estimating guests' preferences for red or white wine or beer and how much people are likely to drink and eat. You may already have some food and drink in the house which you will use, so you will take that into account when making your shopping list, reducing the list by these items. If any of your planned party food is to be cooked from a recipe, you may have to multiply up the ingredients to cater for 40 people; again you may already have some of these ingredients *in stock*. In addition to calculating *how much* of each item is required, you may also wish to take into account that you will prepare some of the food the week before and freeze it while you will leave the rest to either the day before or the day of the party. Therefore, you will need to decide *when* each item is required so that you can shop in time. In planning for your party you will have been making a series of interrelated decisions about the volume (quantity) and timing of the materials which you need.

MRP is a system that helps companies make *volume* and *timing* calculations similar to these but on a much larger scale, and with a greater degree of complexity. Prior to the 1960s, companies did these types of calculations manually to ensure that they had the right materials available in their business at the right time. However, with the advent of computers and their more widespread use in business from the 1960s onwards, this provided the opportunity to perform these time-consuming, detailed calculations by computer quickly and relatively easily.

During the 1980s and 1990s the system and the concept of materials requirements planning has expanded and been integrated with other parts of the business. This enlarged version of MRP is now known as *manufacturing resource planning*, or

MRP II. MRP II enables companies to examine the engineering and financial implications of future demand on the business, as well as examining the materials requirements implications. Oliver Wight,[1] who with Joseph Orlicky[2] is considered to be the founder of modern MRP, described manufacturing resource planning as a 'total game plan' for a business. Using the party example, the wider implications of future demand can be seen: you may want to rig up a more powerful sound system borrowing a friend's speakers – you have to plan for this to ensure that, at the time of setting up the party, the equipment is available and you know what to do with it. Similarly, the party has financial implications. You may have to agree a temporary extension to your overdraft with your friendly bank manager or temporarily increase your credit card limit. Again, this requires some forward planning in terms of advanced telephone calls, as well as a prior calculation on your part of how much all this is going to cost, and therefore how much extra credit you require. Both these equipment and financial implications may vary if you increase the number of guests from 40 to 80. Similarly, if you postpone the party for a month, these arrangements will change.

Manufacturing businesses may make and sell several thousand different variations of end products to a customer base of several hundred regular customers as well as many hundreds of customers who order only irregularly. Many of these customers are also likely to vary their demand for the products. The implications of this are a bit like throwing 75 parties one week, 40 the next, 53 the following week, all for different groups of guests with different requirements who keep changing their minds about what they want to eat and drink. To make sure that the right food and drink are available at the right party at the right time and that not too much money is spent requires planning and control, not only of materials but also of cash, people and equipment. MRP II helps companies forward plan these types of decisions.

Materials requirements planning is still the heart of any MRP system (I or II) and therefore the majority of this chapter will be concerned with establishing the basic purpose and principles of MRP I.

WHAT IS REQUIRED TO RUN MRP I?

In order to perform the volume and timing calculations of the type just described, materials requirements planning systems (MRP I) typically require an operation to keep certain data records in computer files which, when the MRP I program is run, can be checked and updated. In order to understand the complexities of an MRP system, we must first understand these computer files and records.

Figure 14.2 shows the information required to perform MRP I and some of the outputs from it.

Starting at the top of Fig. 14.2, the first inputs to materials requirements planning are customer orders and forecast demand. The first are firm orders scheduled for some identified date in the future while the second are realistic estimates of the quantity and timing of future orders. MRP performs its calculations based on the combination of these two parts of future demand. All other requirements calculated within the MRP process are derived from, and dependent on, these demands. Because of this, MRP is what we described in Chapter 10 as a *dependent demand system*. As a reminder, dependent demand is demand which is derived from some other decision taken within the operation, whereas independent demand systems are designed to operate where demand is outside the control of the operation.

Figure 14.2
Materials
requirements
planning (MRP I)
schematic

Demand management

Taken together, the management of customer orders and sales forecasts is termed *demand management*. Demand management encompasses a set of processes which interface with the customer market. Depending on the business, these processes may include sales order entry, demand forecasting, order promising, customer service and physical distribution. For example, if you place an order with a mail-order catalogue and ring up a week later to check why your purchase has not arrived, you will frequently be dealt with by a telesales customer service operator. This operator, looking at a computer screen, can access the details of your particular order, and advise why there might have been a hold-up in delivery. In addition he or she may be able to provide you with a delivery promise of when you should receive the item, and inform you what mode of delivery will be used (for example, if a courier will deliver it). The interaction with customers and the resulting requirements from that interaction trigger a chain reaction of operations requirements. To satisfy the customer, the item has to be picked from a warehouse; a stores operator must therefore be provided with the appropriate information to do that. A courier must also be booked for a particular time. This is why it is of vital importance to operations management that demand information is available and communicated effectively so that plans can be made and resources organized.

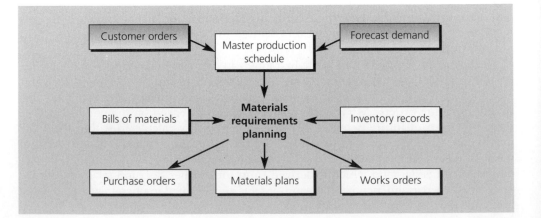

Figure 14.3
The demand
management
inputs to the MRP
process

514

We now need to consider some of the operations implications of managing demand, particularly relating to planning materials requirements. Chapter 11 considered these types of decisions at an aggregate level, but here we deal with the information at a more detailed level, specifically considering known demand, or orders, and forecast demand, as highlighted in Fig. 14.3.

Customer orders

Sales functions in most businesses typically manage a dynamic, changing, order book made up of confirmed orders from customers. This order book may be a paper record in a smaller business but is likely to be a computer file in medium-sized to large operations. Typically this order book would contain information about each customer order. Of particular interest to the MRP I process of calculating materials requirements are the records of exactly what each customer has ordered, how many they have ordered and when they require delivery.

Variation of sales orders

Sales orders usually represent some contractual commitment on behalf of the customer. However, depending on what business a company is in, this may not be as fixed as it may at first seem. Customers can change their minds about what they require, after having placed their orders. They may require a smaller or larger number of a particular item or they may change the date they want their order to be delivered. Because customer service and flexibility are increasingly important competitive factors, having to change requirements is becoming a more common feature in most operations. Indeed, if customers are purchasing industrial goods such as components from a company, it may be that their own customers are the cause of the changing requirements (this aspect of managing the supply chain was discussed in Chapter 13). Considering that each of several hundred customers may make changes to their sales orders, not once, but possibly several times after the order has been placed, it is evident that managing the sales order book is a complex and dynamic process.

Organizations have to make decisions about how much flexibility they will afford to customers and at what stage their customers have to accept liability for the implications of their changes. For example, many cinemas that take credit card bookings will not allow these 'orders' to be changed; the nature of their booking operation is such that this type of flexibility would make their management of capacity and seat allocation process more complicated if changes were allowed. However, cross-channel ferry-crossing operators allow changes in bookings right up to the time of the crossing – passengers arriving early may be allowed on an earlier crossing than they were booked on, if there is space available. These decisions about how much flexibility is allowed to customers have an enormous impact on the operations of the business as a whole and on the calculation of detailed materials and resource requirements.

Not all operations have the same degree of forward 'visibility' in terms of known customer orders. Customers of supermarkets do not have to give advance notice of their arrival or their likely purchases prior to the time they shop. Some train seats can be pre-booked but many, particularly on local services, are purchased by passengers arriving at the station with a desire to travel as soon as possible. Similarly within manufacturing businesses, because competitive environments change so frequently, customers are becoming more reluctant to make firm commitments in advance in the form of detailed orders for specific parts. Furthermore, as delivery speed becomes increasingly important because of just-in-time supply (*see* Chapter 15), when firm orders are received there may be insufficient time to buy the required materials, perform the required manufacturing processes on those materials and then deliver the product to the customer. While many manufacturing businesses are making significant inroads into compressing their response times to customer demand, many have not yet arrived at the state of being able to respond just-in-time when customers place orders. Therefore, for all these reasons, many businesses have to *forecast* their likely future requirements to ensure they have raw materials available to start their own processes once a sales order is received.

The techniques involved in forecasting are discussed in Appendix 1 at the end of the book. Here, however, we will discuss the nature of and implications of forecasting.

Forecast demand

However sophisticated the forecasting process is in any business, using historical data to predict future trends, cycles or seasonality is always difficult. Driving a business using forecasts based on history has been compared to driving a car by looking only at the rear view mirror.[3] In spite of the difficulties, many businesses have no choice but to forecast ahead. To satisfy customers' demands for delivery speed, automotive manufacturers, for example, at the time a customer places an order, have already made estimates of the models, the engines and the colours they think will be sold. When a customer places the order, one of the models in the chosen colour with the right-size engine is already in production and is allocated to him or her. The customer can, at the time of ordering, choose from a wide range of options in terms of trim (such as upholstery and interior colours), audio systems and glass tinting, etc., all of which can be added to the main assembly, effectively giving the impression of customization. The manufacturer has to predict ahead the likely required mix of models and colours to manufacture and the likely mix of options to purchase and have available in inventory.

Combining orders and forecasts

A combination of known orders and forecasted orders is used to represent demand in many businesses. It is important that the forecast which is used for operations planning is not a sales *target,* which might be set optimistically high to give incentives to the sales force. While many businesses use targets, a forecast is something different. It should be the best estimate at any time of what reasonably could be expected to happen.

In Fig. 14.4 one of the most important features of demand management is evident: that is, the further ahead you look into the future, the less certainty there is about demand. Most businesses have knowledge in the short term about demand in terms of individual orders. However, few customers place orders well into the future. Based on history and on market information gained from field sales operatives, a forecast is put together to reflect likely demand. As orders come in, the forecast element of the demand profile should be reduced, giving the impression of the forecast being 'consumed' over time by firm orders.

Different types of operations have different profiles in terms of the mix of known orders and forecast orders. A make-to-order business, such as a jobbing printer, tends

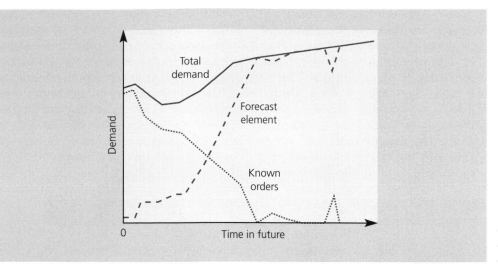

**Figure 14.4
Combining known
orders and forecast
orders**

to have greater visibility of known orders over time than does a make-for-stock business, such as a consumer durables manufacturer. Purchase-to-order businesses do not order most of their raw materials until they receive a confirmed customer order. For example, a jobbing dressmaker would not order fabrics until it was sure that it had been awarded a contract. Other businesses not only cannot risk ordering materials, they also cannot place contracts for labour or equipment. These can be termed 'resource-to-order' businesses. For example, a civil engineering project manager would not order most of the materials for building a bridge until the tender had been won, but also would not be committed to labour and plant hire. At the opposite end of the spectrum, there are some operations who have very little order certainty at the time they take most of their decisions. For example, newspaper publishers distribute newspapers to retail outlets on a sale-or-return basis: that is, real demand is only evident to them after each day's trading has finished and they calculate how many papers were actually sold (*see* Fig. 14.5).

**Figure 14.5
Significance of
forecasting to
different types of
operation**

Many businesses have to operate with a varying combination of known orders and forecasts. For example, the week before Mother's Day, small local florists receive a large volume of orders for bouquets and flower arrangements. At other times of the year, a greater amount of their business is passing trade which is affected by the weather and shopping patterns. Therefore different types of businesses have different degrees of confidence in demand at the time they take operations planning and control decisions, and their confidence may vary over time. From a planning and control perspective, the output from demand management is a prediction ahead over time of what customers will purchase. This information, be it known sales orders, forecast or a combination of both, is the major input to the master production schedule.

OVERCOMING FORECAST PROBLEMS AT RACAL RECORDERS[4]

Racal Recorders manufactures recording systems which are used in many applications, from recording emergency telephone conversations through to recording automobile performance on the test track for later analysis. The technology of these products is sophisticated and the task of controlling their manufacture complex. Racal Recorders is the market leader with a turnover of around £30 million per annum.

One of its major production planning and control problems is how to co-ordinate the production and movement of all the parts which go into its products when virtually all products and systems are configured to meet the requirements of individual customers. An MRP system is needed to translate orders and forecasts into works instructions for purchasing and manufacturing parts, sub-assemblies and finished products. Its main problem was that after running the MRP process, the finished goods were put into stock to await customer orders. Yet the orders when they came never exactly matched what had been manufactured based on the forecast of demand. Some products remained in storage while others had to go back to the workshops to be re-manufactured to form the configurations which customers really did want.

Racal's solution to this was to analyse the common elements within its systems and manufacture 'modules' which could be built up to make whole systems. Forecasts were prepared for the modules which, when manufactured, were kept on the shop floor until orders were firm. On the receipt of a confirmed order, the modules could be assembled to form the finished system as specified by the customer. ■

Questions

1 What exactly seems to be the problem with Racal's forecasting system?

2 What is the advantage, as far as planning and control is concerned, of forecasting demand at a 'modules' level?

Master production schedule

The master production schedule (MPS) is the most important planning and control schedule in a business, and forms the main input to materials requirements planning (*see* Fig. 14.6).

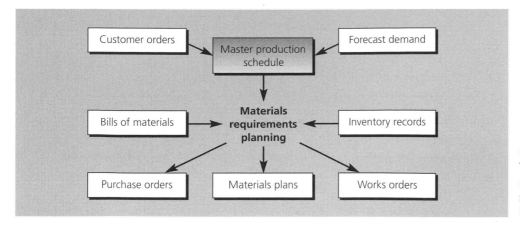

Figure 14.6 The master production schedule in the MRP I schematic

MPS in manufacturing

In manufacturing the MPS contains a statement of the volume and timing of the end products to be made; this schedule drives the whole operation in terms of what is assembled, what is manufactured and what is bought. It is the basis of planning the utilization of labour and equipment and it determines the provisioning of materials and cash.

MPS in services

MPS also can be used in service organizations. For example, in a hospital theatre there is a master schedule which contains a statement of which operations are planned and when. This can be used to provision materials for the operations, such as the sterile instruments, blood and dressings. It also governs the scheduling of staff for operations, including anaesthetists, nurses and surgeons.

Sources of information for the MPS

It is important that all sources of demand are considered when the master production schedule is created. It is often the 'odds and ends' of requirements in a business that disrupt the entire planning system. For example, if a manufacturer of earth excavators plans an exhibition of its products and allows a project team to raid the stores so that it can build two pristine examples to be exhibited, this is likely to leave the factory short of parts. (If it doesn't, then the inventory was excess to requirements and should not have been there anyway.) Similarly, sister companies may be able to 'borrow' parts at short notice for their own purposes. If such practices are allowed, the planning and control system needs to take them into account. Figure 14.7 shows the inputs that may be taken into account in the creation of a master production schedule.

The master production schedule record

Master production schedules are time-phased records of each end product, which contain a statement of demand and currently available stock of each finished item. Using this information, the available inventory is projected ahead in time. When there is insufficient inventory to satisfy forward demand, order quantities are entered on the master schedule line.

Figure 14.7
Inputs into the master production schedule

Table 14.1 is a simplified example of part of a master production schedule for one item. The known sales orders and any forecast are combined to form 'Demand'. This is shown in the first row and can be seen to be gradually increasing. The second row, 'Available', shows how much inventory of this item is expected to be in stock at the end of each weekly period. The opening inventory balance, 'On hand', is shown separately at the bottom of the record. Here, 30 of this part are currently in stock in week 0. The available figure of 20 in the first week is calculated by taking demand of 10 away from the on-hand inventory of 30. The third row is the master production schedule, or MPS; this shows how many finished items need to be completed and available in each week to satisfy demand. As there is adequate inventory already available in weeks 1 and 2, no plans are made to complete more in those weeks. However, in week 3, it is necessary for production to complete ten of these items to satisfy projected demand; if production cannot complete ten at this time, there is the possibility that customers will be put on back order (that is, they will be made to queue).

Table 14.1 Example of a master production schedule

					Week number				
		1	2	3	4	5	6	7	8	9
Demand		10	10	10	10	15	15	15	20	20
Available		20	10	0	0	0	0	0	0	0
MPS		0	0	10	10	15	15	15	20	20
On hand	30									

Chase or level master production schedules

In the example in Table 14.1, the MPS increases as demand increases and aims to keep available inventory at 0 – the master production schedule is 'chasing' demand. As we discussed in Chapter 11 on capacity planning and control, chasing demand involves adjusting the provision of resources, which may not always be desirable. An alternative level MPS for this situation is shown in Table 14.2.

Level scheduling involves averaging the amount required to be completed to smooth out peaks and troughs. Table 14.2 shows how this level schedule generates more inventory than the previous MPS. In this case the average projected inventory of finished items over the nine-week period is 25 per week (that is, more than any one month's demand during this period). In the previous table the average inventory was only 3.

Table 14.2 Example of a 'level' master production schedule

		Week number								
		1	2	3	4	5	6	7	8	9
Demand		10	10	10	10	15	15	15	20	20
Available		31	32	33	34	30	26	22	13	4
MPS		11	11	11	11	11	11	11	11	11
On hand	30									

Available to promise (ATP)

The master production schedule provides the information to the sales function on what can be promised to customers and when delivery can be promised. The sales function can load known sales orders against the master production schedule and keep track of what is *available to promise (ATP)* (see Table 14.3).

The available to promise (ATP) line in the master production schedule shows the maximum in any one week that is still available, against which sales orders can be loaded. If the sales function promises above that figure, it will not be able to keep its promise and the business will be viewed as unreliable by its customers. If sales orders are possible over and above this ATP figure, negotiation should take place with the master production scheduler to see if there is any possibility of satisfying these increased orders by adjusting the MPS. However, this must be run through the MRP process to see the resulting effects on resource requirements.

Examples of poor practice in master scheduling

Unfortunately, many companies accept all sales orders and then try to cope. There are two possibilities here. The first is that the operation fails to cope, cannot manufacture the products, and lets down its customer. The second is that the company somehow always seems to manage. This indicates that its planning system is carrying excess capacity, or slack, in the system, which is not known within the MRP process. Both of these scenarios represent common bad practice in running MRP systems.

Some operations using MRP still (wrongly) treat the master production schedule as a 'target' rather than a plan. There are examples of master schedulers who over-schedule by ten per cent, in the hope that the schedule which they really want to be achieved will be met. The implications of unrealistic master schedules are enormous. If the schedule is over-optimistic by ten per cent, then ten per cent too many materials are provisioned, and ten per cent too much labour is scheduled.

Table 14.3 Example of a level master production schedule including available to promise

		\multicolumn{9}{c}{*Week number*}
		1	*2*	*3*	*4*	*5*	*6*	*7*	*8*	*9*
Demand		10	10	10	10	15	15	15	20	20
Sales orders		10	10	10	8	4				
Available		31	32	33	34	30	26	22	13	4
ATP		31	1	1	3	7	11	11	11	11
MPS		11	11	11	11	11	11	11	11	11
On hand	30									

The bill of materials

The master schedule drives the rest of the MRP process. Having established this top-level schedule, MRP performs calculations to work out the volume and timing of assemblies, sub-assemblies and materials required to meet this master schedule. To explain the process, an example product – a board game called 'Treasure Hunt' – will be used (*see* Fig. 14.8). This fictitious product is a boxed game which involves two to eight players tackling certain quests to find where treasure is buried on a board. To do this, adventure characters use a horse, an air balloon, a cart and other modes of transport to move around the board. Players take turns using two dice to determine their move. A set of instructions is provided with the game.

To be able to manufacture this game, Warwick Operations Games Inc. needs to understand what parts are required to go into each boxed game. If it wishes to use an MRP system to perform this task, it requires computer records of the ingredients or components that go into each item, much the same as a cook requires a list of ingredients required to prepare a dish. These records are called *bills of materials*. The position of the bills of materials in the MRP schematic is shown in Fig. 14.9.

Materials requirements planning programs need to check the components or ingredients for each item that is to be made. In Chapter 5 we discussed design and introduced the idea of product structures. A bill of materials shows which parts and how many of them are required to go into which other parts. It is simplest to think about these as a product structure initially (*see* Fig. 14.10). The product structure in Fig. 14.10 is a simplified structure showing the parts required to make the game. It shows that to make one game you require the components of the game – board, dice, characters and quest cards – a set of rules and the packaging. The packaging comprises a printed cardboard box, and inside the base is an injection-moulded plastic inner tray. Since the game was

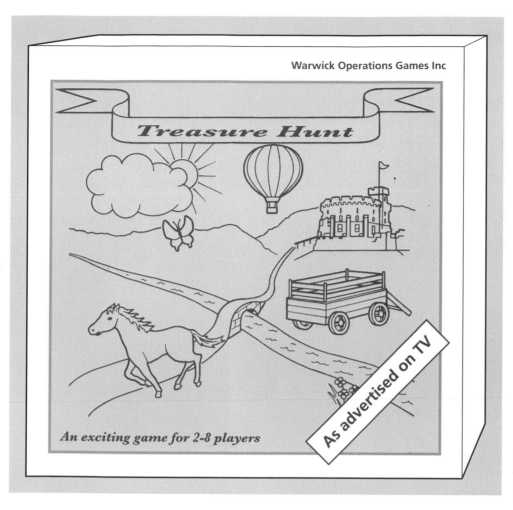

**Figure 14.8
Treasure Hunt
game**

**Figure 14.9
Bills of materials in
the MRP schematic**

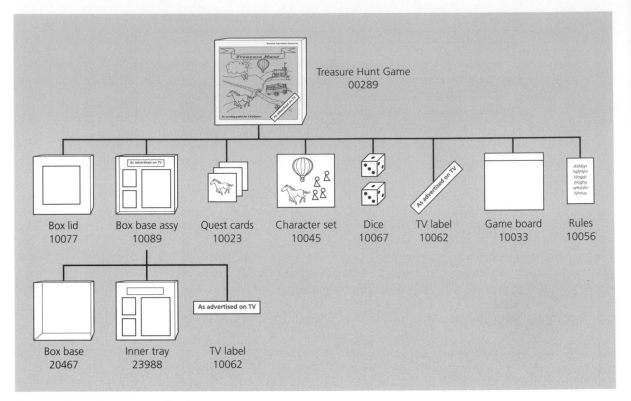

Figure 14.10 Product structure for the Treasure Hunt game

launched, finance was provided for television advertising, so an additional sticker stating 'As advertised on TV' is now stuck on the plastic inner tray and on the front of the complete box.

Levels of assembly

The product structure shows that some parts go into others which, in turn, go into others. In MRP we term these *levels of assembly*. The finished product – the boxed game – is said to be at level 0. The parts and sub-assemblies that go into the boxed game are at level 1, the parts that go into the sub-assemblies are at level 2, and so on.

Features of MRP to note

There are several features of this product structure and of MRP generally that should be noted at this time.

● *Multiples* of some parts are required; this means that MRP has to know the required number of each part to be able to multiply up the requirements.
● The same part (the TV label, part number 10062) may be used in different parts of the product structure. In this example, the label is needed to make the box base assembly and also to complete the Treasure Hunt game. This means that MRP has to cope with this commonality of parts and, at some stage, aggregate the requirements to check how many labels in total are required.

● The product structure stops when it gets down to parts that are not made by this business; for example, another operation makes and supplies the plastic inner trays. This supplier needs to know the product structure for the trays – the weight of plastic granules and the colour of plastic which is required – but the game manufacturer's MRP system treats the plastic tray as a single, bought-in item. This is true even for complex modules or sub-assemblies, such as those bought in by computer manufacturers. Their product structure is not relevant to the in-house MRP, except in terms of the implications on the 'lead time' required to procure them.

The 'shape' of the product structure

The nature of the product structure is closely related to the design of the product. This is reflected in the 'shape' of the product structure. The shape is partly determined by the number of components and parts used at each level – the more used, the wider the shape. Therefore, standardizing components to reduce variety slims the shape of the product structure. Shape is also determined by the amount of the item made in house. If most of the parts are bought in complete, with only assembly occurring in house, such as with the Treasure Hunt game, then the resulting product structure is very shallow, with few levels. However, if all the components are made from raw materials and then assembled all under one roof, the resulting product structure is very deep. There are some recognized typical shapes of product structure – 'A', 'T', 'V' and 'X' (*see* Fig. 14.11).

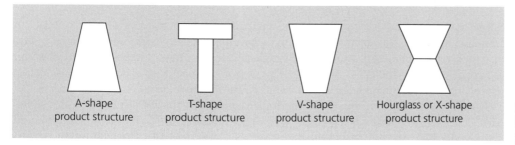

| A-shape product structure | T-shape product structure | V-shape product structure | Hourglass or X-shape product structure |

Figure 14.11
Different shapes of product structure

'A'-shape product structures

The Treasure Hunt game has a shallow 'A' shape in that there is only one finished product into which go a greater number of components. The Henry Ford 'any colour, so long as it's black' approach to automotive manufacture offered a standard product with no customization. This standard product was made from a wide range of materials but resulted in a very small number of finished products. The product structure for this would therefore have been an 'A' shape. The implications of an 'A'-shape structure are that the business only has a limited product range to offer the customer. However, because there is little variety, the volumes of standardized production can give some economies of scale. Such products can also be made for stock, therefore the operation can be planned smoothly, rather than having to chase demand.

'T'-shape product structures

A 'T'-shape product structure is typical of operations that have a small number of raw materials and a relatively standard process but they produce a very wide range of highly customized end products: an example of this is a label manufacturer producing personal name and address labels. Because the final part of the process is highly customized, it must therefore be performed to order. The earlier processes, however, are standard and can provide some economies of scale. The operations difficulties facing a company operating with a 'T' structure often relate to product flow. The part of the operation which makes to order is supplied by a continuous process. This can be difficult to manage because very different styles of operations management are required. The high-volume, low-variety part of the business is aiming for cost reduction and high utilization, whereas the high-variety, customized part of the business is aiming for delivery speed and service performance.

'V'-shape product structures

Similar to a 'T'-shape structure, but with less standardization of process, the 'V'-shape product structure is typical of the petro-chemical industry. Here a small number of raw materials are used to create a wide range of products and by-products, depending on slight changes of mix of the input materials. Operations which have these types of products are driven by customer orders. Because of their reliance on a small number of raw materials, it is critical that these are reliably supplied. Failure of supply of one material can cause disruption of service to much of the customer base.

'X'-shape product structures

Some manufacturers have standardized their designs to consist of a small number of standard modules. For example, kitchen unit manufacturers make standardized bodies to which a wide range of doors and fittings can be attached. These standard modules are represented by the cross of the X. They are combined with a customized selection of features and options, giving a wide range of finished products.

A modern day automotive manufacturer is typical of this 'X'-shape product structure. The same chassis assemblies, transmission assemblies, braking systems and engines are now used on a wide range of vehicles. Owners of a Porsche might be surprised to know that the same engine was used in the VW Scirocco GTX. To some extent the 'X' shape provides the best of both worlds – customization and the impression of making to order at the final assembly stage, combined with the economies and stability of large-volume production in module manufacture. Companies with product structures of this shape tend to master schedule at the intersection of the X, rather than at the level of the ultimate finished product. The intersection represents a manageable number of items to plan and control.

Single-level and indented bills of materials

Referring back to the simple product structure for the board game given earlier, it clearly would not be possible to represent bills of materials in full graphical form. They would simply be too unwieldy. In sophisticated engineering environments, there may be 15 levels of assembly and 5000 different parts within a finished product. MRP systems cope with this by using *single-level bills of materials* and *indented bills of materials*.

In single-level bills of materials, the details of the relationships between parts and sub-assemblies are stored as one single level at a time. For example, the single-level bills for the board game in the example provided previously are shown in Table 14.4. Each single-level bill of materials shows only the parts that immediately go into it.

Table 14.4 Single-level bills for board game

Part number: 00289
Description: Board game
Level: 0

Level	Part number	Description	Quantity
1	10089	Box base assy	1
1	10077	Box lid	1
1	10023	Quest cards set	1
1	10062	TV label	1
1	10045	Character set	1
1	10067	Die	2
1	10033	Game board	1
1	10056	Rules booklet	1

Part number: 10089
Description: Box base assy
Level: 1

Level	Part number	Description	Quantity
2	20467	Box base	1
2	10062	TV label	1
2	23988	Inner tray	1

Most MRP systems store the relationships of parts to particular assemblies in this way but they also usually have the capability of presenting them in the form of an *indented bill of materials* to show several levels at the same time. Table 14.5 shows the whole indented bill of materials for the board game. The term 'indented' refers to the indentation of the level of assembly, shown in the left-hand column.

Table 14.5 Indented bill of materials for board game

Part number: 00289
Description: Board game
Level: 0

Level	Part number	Description	Quantity
0	00289	Board game	1
.1	10077	Box lid	1
.1	10089	Box base assy	1
..2	20467	Box base	1
..2	10062	TV label	1
..2	23988	Inner tray	1
.1	10023	Quest cards set	1
.1	10045	Character set	1
.1	10067	Die	2
.1	10062	TV label	1
.1	10033	Game board	1
.1	10056	Rules booklet	1

STAEDTLER: MANUFACTURING AND THE USE OF MRP[5]

Staedtler is one of the world's premier manufacturers and suppliers of writing instruments with an annual turnover in the region of over DM500 million, and employing almost 4000 people. The Staedtler range extends from standard, high-volume, consumer products such as pens, pencils, crayons and erasers, to highly specialized items designed for specific technical applications and for professional users. As the range has expanded, Staedtler has found that it can achieve very high-quality production by careful selection of raw materials, and by using the latest precision manufacturing techniques. The technologies employed include wood and graphite processing, injection moulding and extrusion of plastics, and the fine engineering of metals. Modern automated assembly machines allow the low-cost, mass-production of volume products such as ball-point pens.

In managing the production of its complex range of over 6000 products, Staedtler has been aided by the use of a well-tried MRP system. Whereas some items, such as standard pencils, have a bill of materials with only a few levels, some of the more involved products require a breakdown of up to seven levels.

An example of a typical Staedtler bill of materials is shown in Table 14.6. This illustrates the different levels of production involved in manufacturing a '110-HB Tradition Pencil in Dozen Box' (level 0). The top level on the bill (shown as .1) gives all the items involved in the final packaging, including the finished pencil itself – coded FTRAD. The next levels in the bill are all required in the production of pencils themselves, with level 2 being the materials required to label the pencils with the Staedtler name and the paint for the dipping to give the traditional 'dipped end' on the end of the pencil. At level 3 are the lacquers and paints required to coat the

Table 14.6 The bill of materials for Staedtler's 'Tradition Pencil in Dozen Box'

Indented explosion		Sales unit	Parent/Sales number	Parent description
		GS	110-HB	Tradition pencil in dozen box

Production level	Component quantity	Component unit	Component number	Component description
.1	12.000000	PC	V12TI	Tradition inners
.1	0.000600	PC	V12TF	Tradition shrinkwrap
.1	0.050000	PC	V12C	Tradition carton
.1	1.000000	GS	FTRAD	Pre-packing tradition pencils
..2	0.007000	KG	DLW	White dip lacquer
..2	0.020000	KG	DLB	Black dip lacquer
..2	0.023000	PC	GFT	Tradition gold foil
..2	1.000000	GS	PTRAD	Pre-finishing tradition pencils
...3	0.100000	KG	PLR	Red polishing lacquer
...3	0.030000	KG	SLB	Black stripe lacquer
...3	1.000000	GS	RTRAD	Pre-polishing tradition pencils
....4	0.050000	PC	CCP2	Wood slats – CCP
....4	0.000600	KG	RASKG	Wood glue
....4	1.000000	GS	STRAD	Tradition pencil slips

Units: PC = Suppliers' unit
        KG = Kilogram
        GS = Gross of pencils

Source: Reproduced by kind permission of Staedtler (UK) Ltd

basic pencil, and finally level 4 details the raw materials, slats of wood, pencil lead slips, and glue which are used in the initial production of the pencil.

The bills of materials for every end product are stored on the MRP system, as well as routing and standard times for the products through each manufacturing and assembly process. An inventory file is kept for every end item, at every level. The master production schedule is initially analysed to ensure that the weekly loadings on each work centre are realistic, and then the full MRP output is created, which schedules all the production requirements at each level. Once a production order has been completed and booked back on to the system, the inventory levels of all items mentioned on the bill of materials are deducted accordingly. ∎

Questions

1 Draw the product structure implied by Table 14.6.

2 What do you think might be the major difficulties that a company like Staedtler faces in using MRP for its planning and control?

Planning bills of materials

Because each end product has its own, often large and detailed, bill of materials, it can become unwieldy to use these detailed bills for planning in the medium to long term. Instead, a smaller number of bills that represent an average product are used. For example, a particular model of car might have two-, three-, four- or five-door choices available. When planning across all models of cars made, the master production scheduler may use a 'super-bill' – a type of planning bill of materials – which lists the average numbers of components across a family of products. The average number of doors may be 3.5; obviously, no car of any model is made with 3.5 doors. However, the purpose of the planning bill is to allow longer term forward planning to give a rough idea of how many doors (and other items) may be required in the future.

Inventory records

The bill of materials file therefore provides MRP with the base data on the ingredients or structure of products. Rather than simply take these ingredients and multiply them up in line with demand to determine the total materials requirements, MRP recognizes that some of the required items may already be in stock. This stock may be in the form of finished goods, work-in-progress or raw materials. It is necessary, starting at level 0 of each bill, to check how much inventory is available of each finished product, sub-assembly and component, then to calculate what is termed the 'net' requirements – the extra requirements needed to supplement the inventory so that demand can be met. To do this, MRP requires that inventory records are kept (*see* Fig. 14.12).

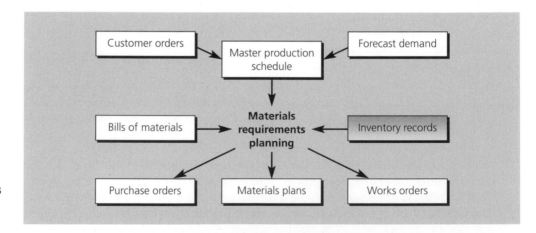

**Figure 14.12
Inventory records
in the MRP
schematic**

There are three main files kept in MRP systems that help to manage inventory. These are:

- the item master file
- the transaction file
- the location file.

The item master file

The key to all inventory records is usually a part number. Each part used in a manufacturing business has to be recognizable by one standard identification so that there is no confusion between people buying and supplying the part or using the part in the manufacturing process. Most manufacturers therefore assign a number to each part. Part numbers might be totally numeric or may be an alphanumeric combination of letters and numbers. Some companies have found it convenient to use mnemonics which help users to recognize which part is represented by a particular part number. Complex cross-checking numbering systems are often adopted to prevent an error being caused through, say, transposing two digits; credit card numbers use this type of cross-checking.

In addition to a part number, the item master file contains all the stable data on a part; this is often a computer screen of fields including the part description, the unit of measure (flour may be recorded in tonnes, washers in 1000s and engines in single discrete units) and a standard cost. Interestingly, the lead time to buy or make the part is often treated as fixed data by virtue of the fact that it is located in the item master file. Many firms fail to monitor adequately the lead time of an item. This may vary between suppliers and change at different times of the year and according to supply market conditions. Instead, many companies still err on the side of caution, entering the maximum lead time that is likely ever to occur. This means that the gap between real lead times and planned lead times in many manufacturing businesses can be quite large.

The transaction file

In order to take inventory levels into account, MRP needs to know the level of inventory of each part. The transaction file keeps a record of receipts into stock, issues from stock and a running balance. In the past, these transactions were entered on to the computer overnight or at periodic intervals; this caused problems in that the information was always lagging behind reality. MRP systems today run their inventory in real time. This means the transaction file is updated at the time a receipt or issue occurs. This has implications for the number of computer terminals required by the operation, their location and the number of people trained to use them. The benefits of real-time processing, however, far outweigh any increased cost of equipment and training.

The location file

The stores, or inventory points in the operation, need to be managed. Some stores operate a fixed location system so that a particular part can always be found at a particular location. However, companies that operate with a wide and changing range of inventory items find this system inefficient. Instead they operate a random location system where parts are located in the nearest available place. A random location system requires careful control as the same item may be kept in several different locations at any one time. In addition to being more efficient on space utilization, a random location system can make it easier to ensure that stock physically 'turns over' by making a first-in-first-out principle easy to implement. When the computer generates picking lists instructing store operators (mechanical or human) to pick items from stock, it can ensure that the oldest stock is picked by sending the picker to the longest-standing location for an item.

Accuracy of the inventory files

As with the management of bills of materials, it is critical to an MRP system that inventory records are accurate and up to date. Mistakes do occur and inventory is pilfered or perishes, so inventory records will never reflect exactly what is physically in stock in a business. Because of this, *perpetual physical inventory* (PPI) checking is performed in many companies.

PPI involves checking that the physical inventory level and location of a part matches the computer record. Where a difference is confirmed, the computer record is updated to reflect reality. This is a bit like painting the Forth Bridge in that, no sooner is the job finished, than it is time to start again at the beginning. Before the PPI process was well established in companies, stock was only checked annually to comply with end-of-year accounting procedures. This meant that, particularly towards the end of the year, there were frequent examples of stores pickers finding empty stores containers while the computer was instructing them to pick items for production. The implications of inaccuracy of inventory records are shortages which lead to the rescheduling of production, with resulting inefficiencies and, possibly, failure to satisfy a customer order.

MRP CALCULATIONS

So far we have examined all the information which is needed for operations to start the planning process. Although this information is a necessary prerequisite to MRP, it is not the 'heart' of the procedure. At its core, MRP is a systematic process of taking this planning information and calculating the volume and timing requirements which will satisfy demand. This next part of the chapter examines the way these calculations are performed, starting with what is probably the most important step, the *netting process*.

The MRP netting process

Figure 14.13 shows simplistically the process that MRP performs to calculate the *volumes* of materials required. MRP takes the master production schedule (the planned production schedule for each end item) and 'explodes', or examines the implications of, this schedule through the single-level bill of materials, checking how many sub-assemblies and parts are required. Before moving down the product structure to the next level, MRP checks how many of the required parts are already available in stock. It then generates 'works orders', or requests, for the net requirements of items that are made in-house. These net requirements then form the schedule which is exploded through the single-level bill of materials at the next level down. Again, available inventory of those items is checked; works orders are generated for the net requirements that are made in-house, as are purchase orders for the net requirements of items that are bought from suppliers. This process continues until the bottom of the product structure is reached.

Figure 14.14 uses our example of the board game to describe this part of the MRP process. Just considering the volume requirements at this moment, a top-level requirement for ten board games does not automatically generate a works order to build ten.

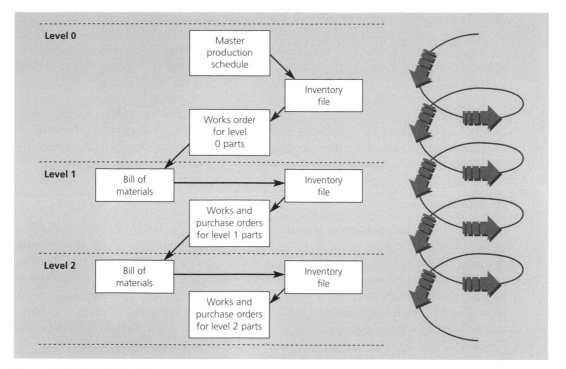

Figure 14.13 The MRP netting process

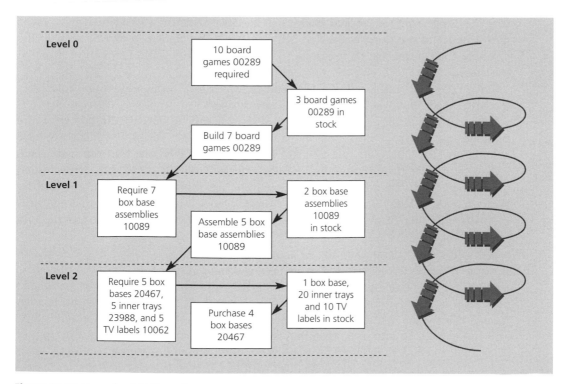

Figure 14.14 Example of MRP netting process

First the available inventory is checked. Because three board games are in stock, a works order to build seven board games is issued. MRP then checks the top, single-level bill for the board game and finds, among other parts, that one box base assembly (10089) is required per board game. MRP then checks how many box base assemblies are in stock and, finding two, generates a works order for the net requirement of five. Next the single-level bill of materials for the box base assembly is checked. This shows that one box base (20467), one inner tray (23988) and one TV label (10062) are required for each box base assembly. Again, the inventory is checked and, as there is one box base in stock, an order to purchase four more is generated. As there are more than enough TV labels and inner trays in stock, there is no need to raise a replenishment instruction.

Back-scheduling

In addition to calculating the volume of materials required, MRP also considers *when* each of these parts is required: that is the timing and scheduling of materials. It does this by a process called *back-scheduling* which takes into account the *lead time* at each level of assembly. Again, using the example of the board game, assume that ten board games are required to be finished by a notional planning day we will term day 35. To determine when we need to start work on all the parts that make up the game, we need to know how much time to allow for each part of the process. These times are called lead times and are stored in MRP files for each part (*see* Table 14.7).

Now examine the Gantt chart shown in Fig. 14.15 which includes the lead time information. If it takes two days to carry out the final assembly, the sub-assemblies must be complete and available on the shop floor at the beginning of day 33. In this way the programme is worked backwards to determine the tasks which have to be performed and the purchase orders which have to be placed. It can be seen in the example that to deliver the required board games on time, the inner trays must be purchased now.

Given the lead times in Table 14.7 and the inventory levels shown in Table 14.8, the MRP records shown in Fig. 14.16 can be derived.

The gross requirements of each part at level 1 can be derived directly from the planned order release of the whole game. So at day 33, seven box lids, box base assemblies, TV labels, etc. are needed. Back scheduling by the lead times for each level-1 item gives their planned order release time. Similarly, the level-2 items which are needed to produce the box base assembly are subject to the same procedure. Note that the TV label is both a level-1 and a level-2 item and has gross requirements originating from the planned order releases of both the game and the box base assembly.

In reality, some items can only be acquired in minimum-sized batches. Because of the time taken and costs involved to set up a machine, it may be seen to be efficient to run it for a reasonable size of batch. Similarly, some purchased items are bought in pack sizes or in order quantities of a size large enough to gain a volume discount, even though this means that more are bought than are needed. Another reason why some operations make or buy more than they immediately need is to give them a margin of safety in the event of unplanned variations in either demand or supply. All these issues of batch sizes and safety stocks were dealt with in Chapter 12.

Figure 14.15 Back-scheduling of requirements in MRP: back-scheduled Gantt chart for board game manufacture

Table 14.7 Back-scheduling of requirements in MRP

Part no.	Description	Lead time (in days)
00289	Board game	2
10077	Box lid	8
10089	Box base assy	4
20467	Box base	12
23988	Inner tray	29
10062	TV label	8
10023	Quest cards set	3
10045	Character set	3
10067	Die	5
10033	Game board	25
10056	Rules booklet	3

Table 14.8 Inventory of parts for board game

Part no.	Description	Inventory
00289	Board game	3
10077	Box lid	4
10089	Box base assy	2
20467	Box base	1
23988	Inner tray	20
10062	TV label	10
10023	Quest cards set	0
10045	Character set	0
10067	Die	0
10033	Game board	0
10056	Rules booklet	0

Treasure Hunt Game

Part number: 00289	1	2	3	4	5	6	7	8	9	10	11	12	13	14	15	16	17	18	19	20	21	22	23	24	25	26	27	28	29	30	31	32	33	34	35
Requirements (gross)																																			10
Scheduled receipts																																			
On hand inventory 3	3	3	3	3	3	3	3	3	3	3	3	3	3	3	3	3	3	3	3	3	3	3	3	3	3	3	3	3	3	3	3	3	3	0	
Planned order release																																	7		

Box lid

Part number: 10077	1	2	3	4	5	6	7	8	9	10	11	12	13	14	15	16	17	18	19	20	21	22	23	24	25	26	27	28	29	30	31	32	33	34	35
Requirements (gross)																																	7		
Scheduled receipts																																			
On hand inventory 4	4	4	4	4	4	4	4	4	4	4	4	4	4	4	4	4	4	4	4	4	4	4	4	4	4	4	4	4	4	4	4	4	0	0	0
Planned order release																												5							

Box base assembly

Part number: 10089	1	2	3	4	5	6	7	8	9	10	11	12	13	14	15	16	17	18	19	20	21	22	23	24	25	26	27	28	29	30	31	32	33	34	35
Requirements (gross)																																	7		
Scheduled receipts																																			
On hand inventory 2	2	2	2	2	2	2	2	2	2	2	2	2	2	2	2	2	2	2	2	2	2	2	2	2	2	2	2	2	2	2	2	2	0	0	0
Planned order release																												5							

Box base

Part number: 20457	1	2	3	4	5	6	7	8	9	10	11	12	13	14	15	16	17	18	19	20	21	22	23	24	25	26	27	28	29	30	31	32	33	34	35
Requirements (gross)																													5						
Scheduled receipts																																			
On hand inventory 1	1	1	1	1	1	1	1	1	1	1	1	1	1	1	1	1	1	1	1	1	1	1	1	1	1	1	1	1	0	0	0	0	0	0	0
Planned order release																	4																		

Inner tray

Part number: 23988	1	2	3	4	5	6	7	8	9	10	11	12	13	14	15	16	17	18	19	20	21	22	23	24	25	26	27	28	29	30	31	32	33	34	35
Requirements (gross)																													5						
Scheduled receipts																																			
On hand inventory 20	20	20	20	20	20	20	20	20	20	20	20	20	20	20	20	20	20	20	20	20	20	20	20	20	20	20	20	20	15	15	15	15	15	15	15
Planned order release																																			

TV label

Part number: 10062	1	2	3	4	5	6	7	8	9	10	11	12	13	14	15	16	17	18	19	20	21	22	23	24	25	26	27	28	29	30	31	32	33	34	35
Requirements (gross)																													5					7		
Scheduled receipts																																			
On hand inventory 10	10	10	10	10	10	10	10	10	10	10	10	10	10	10	10	10	10	10	10	10	10	10	10	10	10	10	10	10	5	5	5	5	0	0	0
Planned order release																												2							

Quest cards set

Part number: 10023	1	2	3	4	5	6	7	8	9	10	11	12	13	14	15	16	17	18	19	20	21	22	23	24	25	26	27	28	29	30	31	32	33	34	35
Requirements (gross)																																	7		
Scheduled receipts																																			
On hand inventory 4	4	4	4	4	4	4	4	4	4	4	4	4	4	4	4	4	4	4	4	4	4	4	4	4	4	4	4	4	4	4	4	4	0	0	0
Planned order release																												3							

Character set

Part number: 10045	1	2	3	4	5	6	7	8	9	10	11	12	13	14	15	16	17	18	19	20	21	22	23	24	25	26	27	28	29	30	31	32	33	34	35
Requirements (gross)																																	7		
Scheduled receipts																																			
On hand inventory 0	0	0	0	0	0	0	0	0	0	0	0	0	0	0	0	0	0	0	0	0	0	0	0	0	0	0	0	0	0	0	0	0	0	0	0
Planned order release																													7						

Die

Part number: 10067	1	2	3	4	5	6	7	8	9	10	11	12	13	14	15	16	17	18	19	20	21	22	23	24	25	26	27	28	29	30	31	32	33	34	35
Requirements (gross)																																	14		
Scheduled receipts																																			
On hand inventory 0	0	0	0	0	0	0	0	0	0	0	0	0	0	0	0	0	0	0	0	0	0	0	0	0	0	0	0	0	0	0	0	0	0	0	0
Planned order release																													14						

Game board

Part number: 10033	1	2	3	4	5	6	7	8	9	10	11	12	13	14	15	16	17	18	19	20	21	22	23	24	25	26	27	28	29	30	31	32	33	34	35
Requirements (gross)																																	7		
Scheduled receipts																																			
On hand inventory 0	0	0	0	0	0	0	0	0	0	0	0	0	0	0	0	0	0	0	0	0	0	0	0	0	0	0	0	0	0	0	0	0	0	0	0
Planned order release					7																														

Rules booklet

Part number: 10023	1	2	3	4	5	6	7	8	9	10	11	12	13	14	15	16	17	18	19	20	21	22	23	24	25	26	27	28	29	30	31	32	33	34	35
Requirements (gross)																																	7		
Scheduled receipts																																			
On hand inventory 0	0	0	0	0	0	0	0	0	0	0	0	0	0	0	0	0	0	0	0	0	0	0	0	0	0	0	0	0	0	0	0	0	0	0	0
Planned order release																													7						

Figure 14.16 Extract of the MRP records for the board game

Closed-loop MRP

When MRP was originally used in manufacturing, materials plans were launched at the beginning of the week, then a complete replanning exercise took place the following week, launching a new set of plans. This process was repeated weekly but there was no feedback loop to say whether a plan was achievable and whether it had actually been achieved. MRP systems which started to include feedback loops became known as 'closed-loop MRP' systems.

Closing the planning loop in MRP systems involves checking production plans against available resources. Therefore, capacity is checked throughout the process and, if the proposed plans are not achievable at any level, they are revised (*see* Fig. 14.17). All but the simplest MRP systems are now closed-loop systems. They use three planning routines to check production plans against the operation's resources:

- resource requirements plans
- rough-cut capacity plans
- capacity requirements plans.

Figure 14.17
Closed-loop MRP

Resource requirements plans (RRP)

Resource requirements plans are static level plans which involve looking forward in the long term to predict the requirements for large structural parts of the operation, such as the numbers of, locations of and sizes of new plants. Because they are attempts at facilitating the long-term production plan by making arrangements to have the required resources available, they are sometimes termed 'infinite capacity plans', as they assume an almost infinite ability to step up production if demand warrants it.

Rough-cut capacity plans (RCCP)

In the medium to short term, master production schedules have to use capacity which is available. The feedback loop at this level checks the MPS against known capacity bottle-necks and key resources only. If the MPS is not achievable, it should be adjusted. So, unlike the RRP, rough-cut capacity plans are 'finite capacity plans' because they have to operate within certain constraints.

Capacity requirements plans (CRP)

On a day-to-day basis, works orders intended to be issued from the MRP will often have a variable effect on the loading of particular machines or individual workers. Capacity requirements plans (CRP) project this load ahead. They are 'infinite capacity plans' insomuch as they do not take the capacity constraints of each machine or work area into account. If this load is lumpy it may be smoothed by replanning to a finite capacity or by allocating temporary resources to the area.

The closed-loop system of MRP can be further developed to drive very short-term plans, as is shown in Fig. 14.18.

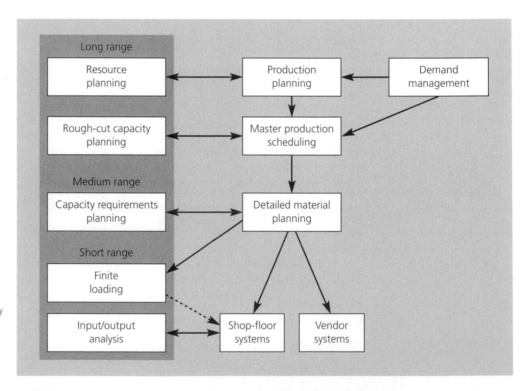

**Figure 14.18
Closed-loop MRP**
Source: Vollmann, T.E., Berry W.L. and Whybark, D.C. (1992) *Manufacturing Planning and Control Systems* (3rd edn), Irwin, p 122

Manufacturing resource planning (MRP II)

MRP I was essentially aimed at the planning and control of production and inventory in manufacturing businesses. However, the concepts have been extended to other areas of the business. This extended concept was termed MRP II by Oliver Wight, one of the founders of MRP. Wight[6] defined MRP II as:

'a game plan for planning and monitoring all the resources of a manufacturing company: manufacturing, marketing, finance and engineering. Technically it involves using the closed-loop MRP system to generate the financial figures.'

Without MRP II integrated systems, separate databases are held by different functions. For example, a product structure or bill of materials is held in engineering and also in materials management. If engineering changes are made to the design of products, both databases have to be updated. It is difficult to keep both databases entirely identical and discrepancies between them cause problems, which often are not apparent until a member of staff is supplied with the wrong parts to manufacture the product. Similarly, cost information from finance and accounting, which is used to perform management accounting tasks such as variance analysis against standard costs, needs to be reconciled with changes made elsewhere in the operation, such as changes in inventory holding or process methods.

MRP II is based on one integrated system containing a database which is accessed and used by the whole company according to individual functional requirements. However, despite its dependence on the information technologies which allow such integration, MRP II still depends on people-based decision-making. In other words, the closing of the loop in MRP systems is still largely down to people taking decisions and corrective action on a minute-by-minute basis.

OPTIMIZED PRODUCTION TECHNOLOGY (OPT)

Other concepts and systems have been developed which also recognize the importance of planning to known capacity constraints, rather than overloading part of the production system and failing to meet the plan. Perhaps the best known is the Theory of Constraints (TOC) which has been developed to focus attention on the capacity constraints or bottle-neck parts of the operation. By identifying the location of constraints, working to remove them, then looking for the next constraint, an operation is always focusing on the part that critically determines the pace of output.

The approach which uses this idea is called *optimized production technology* (OPT). Its development and the marketing of it as a proprietary software product was originated by Eliyahu Goldratt.[7]

OPT is a computer-based technique and tool which helps to schedule production systems to the pace dictated by the most heavily loaded resources, i.e. bottle-necks. If the rate of activity in any part of the system exceeds that of the bottle-neck, then items are being produced that cannot be used. If the rate of working falls below the pace at the bottle-neck, then the entire system is under-utilized.

There are principles underlying optimized production technology which demonstrate this focus on bottle-necks:

OPT principles

1 Balance flow, not capacity.
2 The level of utilization of a non bottle-neck is determined by some other constraint in the system, not by its own capacity.
3 Utilization and activation of a resource are not the same.
4 An hour lost at a bottle-neck is an hour lost for ever out of the entire system.

5 An hour saved at a non bottle-neck is a mirage.

6 Bottle-necks govern both throughput and inventory in the system.

7 The transfer batch may not, and many times should not, equal the process batch.

8 The process batch should be variable, not fixed.

9 Lead times are the result of a schedule and cannot be predetermined.

10 Schedules should be established by looking at all constraints simultaneously.

OPT should not be viewed as a replacement to MRP; nor is it impossible to run both together. However, the philosophical underpinnings of OPT outlined above do show that it could conflict with the way that many businesses run their MRP systems in practice. While MRP as a concept does not prescribe fixed lead times or fixed batch sizes, many operations run MRP with these elements fixed for simplicity. However, demand, supply, and the process within a manufacturing operation all present unplanned variations on a dynamic basis; therefore, bottle-necks are dynamic, changing their location and their severity. For this reason, lead times are rarely constant over time. Similarly, if bottle-necks determine schedules, batch sizes may alter throughout the plant depending on whether a work centre is a bottle-neck or not.

OPT uses the terminology of 'drum, buffer, rope' to explain its planning and control approach. Using OPT, the bottle-neck work centre becomes a '*drum*', beating the pace for the rest of the factory. This 'drum beat' determines the schedules in non bottle-neck areas, pulling through work (the *rope*) in line with the bottle-neck capacity, not the capacity of the work centre. A bottle-neck should never be allowed to be working at less than full capacity; therefore, inventory *buffers* should be placed before it to ensure it never runs out of work.

Some of the arguments for using OPT in MRP environments are that it helps to focus on critical constraints and that it reduces the need for very detailed planning of non bottle-neck areas, therefore cutting down computational time in MRP.

David Alcock, Elida Gibbs

Elida Gibbs, part of Unilever, the multinational household goods producer, manufactures personal products such as shampoo, deodorants, toothpaste, creams and lotions. David Alcock is the Operations and Stock Manager at the Elida Gibbs plant in Leeds (UK) which produces products both for the UK and for export. David's job includes interpreting sales forecasts and converting them into a feasible production plan for the factory. To do this he also has to ensure that the supply chain which supplies all the materials to make the products can support the proposed plan.

'We have a hugely complex business here,' says David. 'Not only do we have a wide range of goods, but many of them are sold in foreign markets which require their own unique set of labelling and packaging materials. Also our main customers, the supermarket chains, are demanding ever faster response times and more frequent deliveries. It all makes for a difficult planning problem. We use an MRP system to help us cope with the complexity. It keeps the product information in terms of bills of materials and basic product structures. The sales forecasts are entered into the system by the brand planning team at head office. Partly based on those forecasts we then have to add to that an independent manufacturing requirement in order to maintain an adequate level of safety stock. Once the total finished goods requirement has been entered into the MRP system, the production and raw materials requirements are generated automatically from the bill of materials. We have to check that our suppliers will be able to deliver the quantities required within the appropriate timescales. If they can't we have to do some replanning.

'The forecast level of sales varies throughout the year. For example, we sell a very high volume of deodorants during the summer months, whereas the more exclusive creams and lotions sell in the pre-Christmas rush. But a forecast is just that and actual sales will always deviate from the forecast. Our safety stock helps us cope with this and we also try to work ahead with our suppliers and educate them in the likely pattern of orders so that they can respond quickly to any fluctuations in our demand.

'We recently launched a new range of shampoos and conditioners supported by a massive TV advertising campaign and the nationwide distribution of samples. Although the initial sales forecasts were considered to be optimistic, the product proved even more popular than we expected and we had continually to revise forecasts upwards. This was when we fully benefited from having the MRP system. It allowed us to do on-line "what if" analyses, so that we could check to make sure that alternative production plans were feasible in terms of material supplies, machine capacity, and resource availability. In the case of the new shampoo range, the revised forecasts seemed to mean that we were constrained in every direction. We had new packaging suppliers who were really having to pull out all the stops to satisfy our orders. We had capacity limitations in the factory. And of course we had the continuing requirement to make our other products. We were continually having to juggle the requirements, using the MRP system to assess which option would make best use of our facilities and the materials available, and cause the least disruption to our excellent customer service record.

'However, I'm pleased to say that we managed to achieve all the production targets set by our sales team and the product is now settling in to a more regular order pattern. Without the MRP system we wouldn't have been able to cope as effectively, or to work as well with the other parts of the business in overcoming the crisis. We are just waiting for the next launch now!' ■

SUMMARY ANSWERS TO KEY QUESTIONS

What is MRP?

■ MRP stands for materials requirements planning which is a dependent demand system which calculates materials requirements and production plans to satisfy known and forecast sales orders.

■ MRP helps make volume and timing calculations based on an idea of what will be necessary to supply demand in the future.

What is the process involved in MRP planning and control?

■ MRP works from a master production schedule which summarizes the volume and timing of end products or services.

■ The master production schedule is a slightly more detailed version of the aggregated capacity plans which were discussed in Chapter 11.

■ Using the logic of the product or services bill of materials (BOM) and the inventory records of the operation, the production schedule is 'exploded' to determine how many sub-assemblies and parts are required, and when they are required in order to achieve the master production schedule.

■ This process of exploding the master production schedule is called the MRP netting process. It is carried out throughout the different levels of the product structure.

■ Within this process, 'back-scheduling' takes into account the lead time required to obtain parts at each level of the assembly.

What are the main elements of an MRP system?

■ A demand management system must interface with customers in order to set the requirements for the master production schedule.

■ The master production schedule is the central reference source for what the system is supposed to produce and when.

■ Bills of materials and product structure information, together with lead times, enable the netting process to take place.

■ Inventory records contain data which allows the MRP system to understand where stock is located, how many parts are in stock, and what issue and receipt transactions have occurred against any parts.

■ The output from the materials requirements planning system is purchase orders, materials plans, and works orders which trigger the purchasing or manufacture of parts.

What is 'closed loop' MRP?

Closed-loop MRP systems contain feedback loops which ensure that checks are made against capacity to see if plans are feasible.

What is MRP II?

MRP II systems are a development of MRP. They integrate many processes that are related to MRP, but which are located outside the operation's function.

■ Without MRP II, separate databases would be held for different functions.

■ A system which performs roughly the same function as MRP II is optimized production technology (OPT). It is based on the theory of constraints which has been developed to focus attention on capacity bottle-necks in the operation.

Psycho Sports Ltd

Peter Townsend knew that he would have to make some decisions pretty soon. His sports goods manufacturing business, Psycho Sports, had grown so rapidly over the last two years that he would soon have to install some systematic procedures and routines to manage the business. His biggest problem was in manufacturing control. He had started making specialist high-quality table tennis bats but now made a wide range of sports products including tennis balls, darts and protective equipment for various games. Furthermore, his customers, once limited to specialist sports shops, now included some of the major sports retail chains.

'We really do have to get control of our manufacturing. I keep getting told that we need what seems to be called an MRP system. I wasn't sure what this meant and so I have bought a specialist production control book from our local bookshop and read all about MRP principles. I must admit, these academics seem to delight in making simple things complicated. And there is so much jargon associated with the technique, I feel more confused now than I did before.

'Perhaps the best way forward is for me to take a very simple example from my own production unit and see whether I can work things out manually. If I can follow the process through on paper then I will be far better equipped to decide what kind of computer-based system we should get, if any!'

Peter decided to take as his example one of his new products: a table tennis bat marketed under the name of the 'high-resolution' bat, but known within the manufacturing unit more prosaically as Part Number 5654. Figure 14.19 shows the product structure for table tennis bat Part Number 5654.

As can be seen from Fig. 14.19, the table tennis bat is made up of two main assemblies: a handle assembly and a face assembly. In order to assemble the two main assemblies together to form the finished bat, various fixings are required, such as nails, connectors, etc.

The gross requirements for this particular bat are shown below. The bat is not due to be launched until Week 13 (it is now Week 1), and sales forecasts have been made for the first 23 weeks of sales:

Weeks 13–21 inclusive, 100 per week
Weeks 22–29 inclusive, 150 per week
Weeks 30–35 inclusive, 200 per week.

Peter also managed to obtain information on the current inventory levels of each of the parts which made up the finished bat, together with cost data and lead

Figure 14.19 Product structure for bat 5654

Table 14.9 Inventory, cost and lead time information for parts

Part no.	Description	Inventory	EQ	LT	Std. cost
5645	Bat	0	500	2	12.00
0499	Handle assy	0	400	3	4.00
7754	Shaft	15	1000	5	1.00
0955	Connector	350	5000	4	0.02
9110	Nail	120	5000	4	0.01
8744	Rivet	3540	5000	4	0.01
0772	Face assy	0	250	4	5.00
1821	Handle	0	500	4	2.00
6511	Rubber face	0	2000	10	0.50
2547	Wooden inner	10	300	7	1.50
8561	Foam panel	0	1000	8	0.50

LT = Lead time for ordering (in weeks), EQ = Economic quantity for ordering, Std. cost = Standard cost in £.

times. He was surprised, however, how long it took him to obtain this information.

'It has taken me nearly two days to get hold of all the information I need. Different people held it, nowhere was it conveniently put together, and sometimes it was not even written down. To get the inventory data I actually had to go down to the stores and count how many parts were in the boxes.'

The data Peter collected was as shown in Table 14.9.

Peter set himself six exercises which he knew he would have to master if he was to understand fully the basics of MRP.

Exercise 1
Draw up:
(a) the single-level bill of materials for each level of assembly;
(b) a complete indented bill of materials for all levels of assembly.

Exercise 2
(a) Create the materials requirements planning records for each part and sub-assembly in the bat.
(b) List any problems that the completed MRP records identify.
(c) What alternatives are there that the company could take to solve any problems? What are their relative merits?

Exercise 3
Based on the first two exercises, create another set of MRP records, this time allowing one week's safety lead time for each item: that is, ensuring the items are in stock the week prior to when they are required.

Exercise 4
Over the time period of the exercise, what effect would the imposition of a safety lead time have on average inventory value?

Exercise 5
If we decided that our first task was to reduce inventory costs by 15 per cent, what action would we recommend? What are the implications of our action?

Exercise 6
How might production in our business be smoothed? ■

Questions

1 Why did Peter have such problems getting to the relevant information?

2 Perform all the exercises which Peter set for himself. Do you think he should now fully understand MRP?

DISCUSSION QUESTIONS

1 What is the difference between MRPI and MRPII?

2 A manufacturer of electronic defence equipment uses an MRP system to control its production. At any time it has regular orders for its standard products as well as specific orders for its specially adapted products. Occasionally also, one-off orders of standard products are received from foreign customers. Part of the company's competitive strategy is to offer a service which includes a full repair, spare-parts supply, and remanufacturing service to its customers. What elements will constitute the sources of demand which it must feed into its MRP system?

3 A company makes two types of mirror. The super-mirror has a golden frame, whereas the basic mirror has a plain black frame. Both mirrors are the same size. As well as the frame, the standard mirror piece and a backing piece is needed to manufacture each product. Both these last two items are exactly the same for both products. The lead time to manufacture either product is two weeks, while the lead time for the frame material is one week, for the mirror material (cut to size) is three weeks, and for the backs, again cut to size, is two weeks. Each mirror needs two-and-a-half metres of frame material. Neither product will be needed for ten weeks when there will be an order to be filled for 200 of each type of mirror. In 11 weeks a further 100 of these standard mirrors will be needed and in 12 weeks 300 of the gold-framed mirrors will be needed. The next order will be in Week 14 when, again, 200 of each mirror will be needed. Currently, there is no inventory of any of the materials on hand. Using MRP procedures derive a schedule which will meet the demand.

4 Draw up a product structure and indented bill of materials for a product described as follows. The main product A consists of one sub-assembly B and two sub-assemblies C. Sub-assembly B consists of one part D and two part Es. Sub-assembly C consists of one part E, one part F and two part Gs.

5 What different methods are there for a company to decide on how many of its parts to order at any time? What are the advantages and disadvantages of ordering whatever is required every single period?

6 What is meant by a closed-loop MRP system?

7 A company manufactures product A which is made up of one unit of B and half a unit of C. Each unit of B is made up of one unit of D, two units of E, and one unit of F. Each unit of C needs half a unit of G and three units of H. The lead times to manufacture all these components are as follows:

A	2 weeks	E	3 weeks
B	1 week	F	1 week
C	2 weeks	G	2 weeks
D	2 weeks	H	1 week

All these parts have 20 units in stock. It is required to make 100 units of A for delivery in seven weeks' time.

(a) Draw up a product structure and indented bill of materials for the product.
(b) Draw up a gross materials requirements plan for the manufacturer of the product.
(c) Construct a net materials requirements plan for the manufacturer of the product.

NOTES ON CHAPTER

1 Wight, O. (1984) *Manufacturing Resource Planning: MRPII*, Oliver Wight Ltd.
2 Orlicky, J. (1975) *Materials Requirements Planning*, McGraw-Hill.
3 Kotler, P. (1991) *Marketing Management*, Prentice Hall.
4 Source: 'A Matter of Life and Death', *Manufacturing Today* (1993). Published by MSPL, an ICL company which installed Racal Recorders' MRPII system.
5 Source: Discussions with company staff at Staedtler.
6 Wight, O. (1984), *op. cit.*
7 Goldratt, E.M. and Cox, J. (1986) *The Goal*, North River Press.

SELECTED FURTHER READINGS

Berry, W.L. (1972) 'Lots Sizing Procedures for Requirements Planning Systems: A Framework for Analysis', *Production and Inventory Management*, Vol 13, 2nd Quarter.

Berry, W.L. and Mabert, V.A. (1992) 'ITEC: An Integrated Manufacturing Instructional Exercise', *International Journal of Operations and Production Management*, Vol 12, No 6.

Burns, O.M., Turnipseed, D. and Riggs, W.E. (1991) 'Critical Success Factors in Manufacturing Resource Planning Implementation', *International Journal of Operations and Production Management*, Vol 11, No 4.

Buxey, G. (1993) 'Production Planning and Scheduling for Seasonal Demand', *International Journal of Operations and Production Management*, Vol 13, No 7.

Jacobi, M.A. (1994) 'How to Unlock the Benefits of MRP II and Just-in-Time', *Hospital Maternity Management Quarterly*, Vol 15, No 4.

Luscombe, M. (1993) *MRP II: Integrating the Business*, Butterworth-Heinemann.

Miller, J.G. and Sprague, L.G. (1975) 'Behind the Growth in Materials Requirements Planning', *Harvard Business Review*, Vol 53, No 5.

Orlicky, J. (1975) *Material Requirements Planning*, McGraw-Hill.

Porter, K., Little, D., Kenworthy, J. and Jarvis, P. (1996) 'Finite Capacity Scheduling Tools: Observations of Installations Offer Some Lessons', *Integrated Manufacturing Systems*, Vol 7, No 4.

Primrose, P.L. (1990) 'Selecting and Evaluating Cost Effective MRP and MRP II', *International Journal of Operations and Production Management*, Vol 10, No 1.

Shah, S. (1991) 'Optimum Order Cycles in MRP Form a Geometric Progression', *International Journal of Operations and Production Management*, Vol 11, No 5.

Steinberg, E.E., Khumawala, B. and Scamell, R. (1982) 'Requirements Planning Systems in the Health Care Environment', *Journal of Operations Management*, Vol 2, No 4.

Vollmann, T.E., Berry, L. and Whybark, D.C. (1989) *Manufacturing Planning and Control Systems* (3rd edn), Irwin.

White, E.M., Anderson, J.C., Schroeder, R.G. and Tupy, S.E. (1982) 'A Study of the MRP Implementation Process', *Journal of Operations Management*, Vol 2, No 3.

Wight, O. (1982) *The Executive's Guide to Successful MRP II*, Prentice Hall.

Wight, O. (1984) *Manufacturing Resource Planning: MRP II*, Oliver Wight Ltd.

Wilson, F., Desmond, J. and Roberts, H. (1994) 'Success and Failure of MRP II Implementation', *British Journal of Management*, Vol 5.

JUST-IN-TIME PLANNING AND CONTROL

INTRODUCTION

Chapter 14 described MRP, one commonly used approach to operations planning and control. This chapter examines a more recent approach which tackles the same issue and the full implications of which are still being discovered by operations managers. This approach goes under the rather narrow name of 'just-in-time' (JIT). In this chapter, we will examine just-in-time (JIT) both as a philosophy and as a method of operations planning and control. This means that, for much of the chapter, we will take a relatively focused view of JIT, concentrating on its planning and control aspects, although in practice it has much wider implications for improving operations performance. In fact many of the wider implications of JIT underlie much of the material presented in this book. The JIT principles which were a radical departure from traditional operations practice have now themselves become the accepted wisdom in operations management. In effect the chapter addresses the question: 'What is JIT, and how does it impact on operations planning and control?' Put another way, 'What are the implications of arranging for the delivery of goods (and sometimes services) literally "just-in-time" for them to be used by their internal or external customers?' Figure 15.1 illustrates the concept of JIT planning and control.

Figure 15.1 Just-in-time planning and control aims to meet demand instantaneously, with perfect quality and no waste

---

CHAPTER 15: KEY QUESTIONS

- *What is JIT and how is it different from traditional operations practice?*
- *What are the main elements of JIT philosophy?*
- *What are the techniques of JIT?*
- *How can JIT be used for planning and control?*
- *Can JIT be used in service operations?*
- *Can JIT and MRP co-exist?*

WHAT IS JUST-IN-TIME?

At its most basic, JIT can be taken literally – JIT means producing goods and services exactly when they are needed – not before they are needed so that they wait as inventory, nor after they are needed so that it is the customers who have to wait. In addition to this 'time-based' element of JIT we can add the requirements of quality and efficiency. A definition of JIT can then be taken as follows:

> *JIT aims to meet demand instantaneously, with perfect quality and no waste.*[1]

Alternatively, for those who prefer a fuller definition:

> *Just-in-time (JIT) is a disciplined approach to improving overall productivity and eliminating waste. It provides for the cost-effective production and delivery of only the necessary quantity of parts at the right quality, at the right time and place, while using a minimum amount of facilities, equipment, materials and human resources. JIT is dependent on the balance between the supplier's flexibility and the user's flexibility. It is accomplished through the application of elements which require total employee involvement and teamwork. A key philosophy of JIT is simplification.*[2]

Remember though that the first definition is a statement of *aims,* it does not imply that, by adopting a JIT approach to organizing operations, these aims will be achieved immediately. Rather, it describes a state which a JIT approach helps to work towards. No definition of JIT fully conveys its full implications for operations practice, however. This is why so many different phrases and terms exist to describe JIT-type approaches. For example:

- continuous flow manufacture
- high value-added manufacture
- stockless production
- war on waste
- fast-throughput manufacturing
- lean manufacturing
- short cycle time manufacturing.

The best way to understand how a JIT approach differs from more traditional approaches to manufacturing is to contrast the two simple manufacturing systems in Fig. 15.2. The traditional approach assumes that each stage in the manufacturing process will place the parts it produces in an inventory which 'buffers' that stage from the next one downstream in the total process. The next stage down will then (eventually) take the parts from the inventory, process them, and pass them through to the next buffer inventory. These buffers are not there accidentally; they are there to insulate each stage from its neighbours. The buffers make each stage relatively independent so that if, for example, stage A stops producing for some reason (say a machine breakdown or parts shortage), stage B can continue working, at least for a time. Stage C can continue working for even longer because it has the contents of two buffers to get through before it runs out of work. The larger is the buffer inventory, the greater is the degree of insulation between the stages, and therefore the less is the disruption caused when a problem occurs. This insulation has to be paid for in terms of inventory (working capital) and slow throughput times (slow customer response) but it does allow each stage to operate in an uninterrupted, and therefore efficient, manner.

The main argument against this traditional approach lies in the very conditions it seeks to promote, namely the insulation of the stages from one another. When a problem occurs at one stage, the problem will not immediately be apparent elsewhere in the system. The responsibility for solving the problem will be centred largely on the staff within that stage, and the consequences of the problem will be prevented from spreading to the whole system. However, contrast this position with that illustrated in the bottom system in Fig. 15.2, which is an extreme form of JIT. Here parts are produced and then passed directly to the next stage 'just-in-time' for them to be processed. Problems at any stage have a very different effect in such a system. For example, now if stage A stops production, stage B will notice immediately and stage C very soon after. Stage A's problem is now quickly exposed to all the system and all the system is affected by the problem. One result of this is that the responsibility for

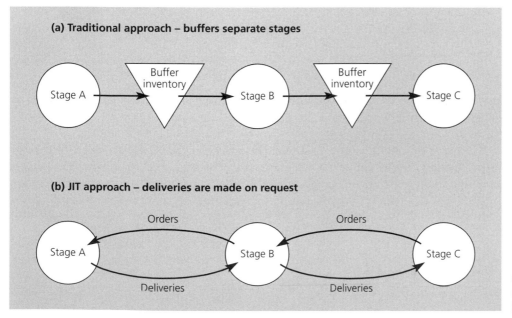

Figure 15.2
(a) Traditional and (b) JIT flow between stages

549

solving the problem is no longer confined to the staff at stage A but is now shared by everyone. This considerably improves the chances of the problem being solved, if only because it is now too important to be ignored. In other words, by preventing inventory from accumulating between stages, the operation has increased the chances of the intrinsic efficiency of the plant being improved.

Although simplified, this highlights the differences between a traditional and a JIT approach. Although they both seek to encourage high efficiency in the operation, they take different routes to doing so. Traditional approaches seek to encourage efficiency by protecting each part of the operation from disruption. Long, uninterrupted production runs are its ideal state. The JIT approach takes the opposite view. Exposure of the system (although not suddenly, as in our simplified example) to problems can both make them more evident and change the 'motivation structure' of the whole system towards solving the problems. JIT sees inventory as a 'blanket of obscurity' which lies over the production system and prevents problems being noticed. The idea of obscuring effects of inventory is often illustrated diagrammatically, as in Fig. 15.3. The many problems of the operation are shown as rocks in a river bed which cannot be seen because of the depth of the water. The water in this analogy represents the inventory in the operation. Yet, even though the rocks cannot be seen, they slow the progress of the river's flow and cause turbulence. Gradually reducing the depth of the water (inventory) exposes the worst of the problems which can be resolved, after which the water is lowered further, exposing more problems, and so on.

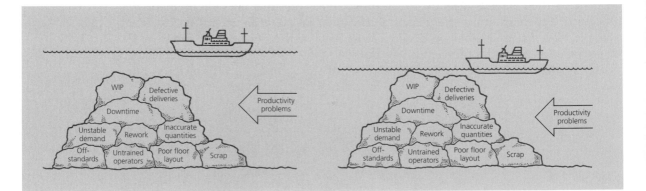

Figure 15.3 Reducing the level of inventory (water) allows operations management (the ship) to see the problems in the operation (the rocks) and work to reduce them

The same argument can be used to characterize the relationship between the stages of production on a larger scale, where each stage is a 'macro' operation. Here stages A, B and C could be a supplier operation, a manufacturer and a customer's operation respectively. At this level the two approaches are traditional 'mass-production' operations and the JIT operation.

What JIT requires

Ideally, JIT requires a high standard in all an operation's performance objectives:

● *Quality* must be high because disruption in production due to quality errors will slow down the throughput of materials, reduce the internal dependability of supply, and possibly cause inventory to build up if errors slow the production rate.

● *Speed,* in terms of fast throughput of materials, is essential if customer demand is to be met directly from production rather than from inventory.

● *Dependability* is a prerequisite for fast throughput, or put the opposite way, it is difficult to achieve fast throughput if the supply of parts or the reliability of equipment is not dependable.

● *Flexibility* is especially important in order to achieve small batch sizes and therefore fast throughput and short delivery lead times. We are referring here primarily to the mix and volume flexibilities described in Chapter 2.

● As a result of excellence in the above performance objectives, *cost* is reduced.

Ultimately the target cost is the sum of the raw materials and the value-adding activities only.

JIT and capacity utilization

Even in advanced JIT, operations achieving high standards in all performance objectives do demand some sacrifice. In JIT the main sacrifice is capacity utilization. Return to the production system shown in Fig. 15.2. When production stoppages occur in the traditional system, the buffers allow each stage to continue working and thus achieve high capacity utilization. The high utilization does not necessarily make the system as a whole produce more parts. Often the extra production goes into the large buffer inventories. In the JIT system, any stoppage will affect the rest of the system, causing stoppages throughout the operation. This will necessarily lead to lower capacity utilization, at least in the short term. However, JIT proponents would argue that there is no point in producing output just for its own sake. Unless the output is useful and causes the operation as a whole to produce saleable products, there is no point in producing it anyway. In fact producing just to keep utilization high is not only pointless, it is counter-productive because the extra inventory produced merely serves to make improvements less likely. For a given level of demand, capacity requirements are often lower under JIT conditions. Figure 15.4 illustrates the two approaches to capacity utilization.

JIT – a philosophy and a set of techniques

To understand JIT it must be viewed on two levels. At its most general, JIT is often called a *philosophy* of manufacturing: that is, JIT gives a clear view which can be used to guide the actions of operations managers in many different activities and many different contexts. At the same time, JIT is a collection of several *tools and techniques* which promote the operational conditions which support its philosophy. Some of these tools and techniques are well known outside the JIT sphere and relate to activities covered in other chapters of this book. Other techniques relate specifically to the way production is planned and controlled under a JIT regime. This chapter summarizes JIT philosophy, draws together some of the techniques described elsewhere, and treats in more detail the planning and control aspects of JIT (*see* Fig. 15.5).

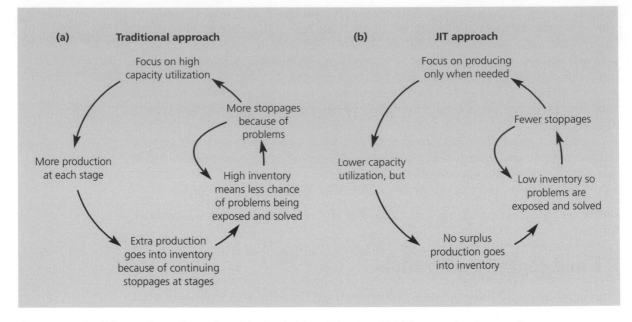

Figure 15.4 The different views of capacity utilization in (a) traditional and (b) JIT approaches to operations

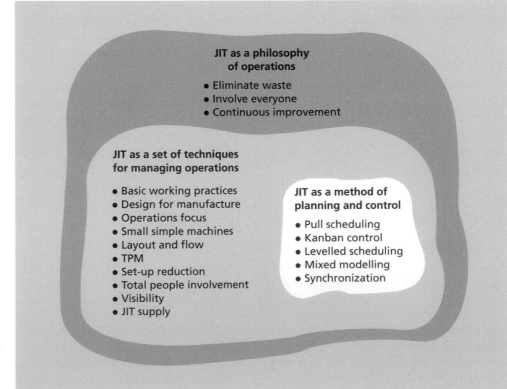

Figure 15.5
JIT is a philosophy,
a set of techniques
and a method of
planning and
control

THE PHILOSOPHY OF JUST-IN-TIME

Just-in-time philosophy and Japanese practice

JIT is the Western embodiment of a philosophy and series of techniques developed by the Japanese. The philosophy is founded on doing the simple things well, on gradually doing them better and on squeezing out waste every step of the way. Leading the development of JIT in Japan has been the Toyota Motor Company (*see* box on Toyota later in this chapter). Toyota's strategy in Japan has been progressively to interface manufacturing more closely with its customers and its suppliers. It has done this by developing a set of practices which has largely shaped what we now call JIT. Indeed some would argue that the origins of JIT lie within Toyota's reaction to the 'oil shock' of rising oil prices in the early 1970s.[3] The need for improved manufacturing efficiencies which this provoked spurred Toyota to accelerate its JIT ideas which were already forming. These developments by Toyota, and other Japanese manufacturers, were undoubtedly encouraged by the national cultural and economic circumstances. Japan's attitude towards waste ('make every grain of rice count'), together with its position as a crowded and virtually naturally resourceless country, were ideal conditions in which to devise a manufacturing philosophy which emphasizes low waste and high added value. An alternative explanation of JIT's origins looks back to Japan's shipbuilding industry.[4] In the late 1950s and early 1960s over-capacity among Japan's steel makers meant that shipbuilders could demand deliveries of steel precisely when they wanted them. Because of this, the shipbuilders improved production methods so that they could reduce their steel inventories from about one month's worth to three days' worth. As the advantages of low stock-holding became apparent, the idea spread to other parts of Japanese industry.

The high dependency theory

One explanation of the JIT approach to operations management is called the high dependency theory.[5] It derives partly from the logic which we used earlier to describe the benefits of low buffer inventories. With high inventories insulating each stage in the production process, the dependency of the stages on one another was low. Take away the inventory and their mutual dependency increases. This is not the only example of high dependency in JIT (and Japanese practice generally). The JIT practice of empowering 'shop-floor' staff makes the organization dependent on their actions. The use of the internal customer concept (mentioned in Chapter 1 but explained further in Chapter 20) formalizes the dependence between all parts of the operation. The use of Total Productive Maintenance (TPM) (explained in Chapter 19) and the JIT-influenced supplier development policies (from Chapter 13) are also examples of dependency. Professors Nick Oliver and Barry Wilkinson sum up the dependency theory in this way:

'Japanese systems of production, particularly JIT and total quality control, heighten the dependency of the organization on its agencies, or 'constituents', especially employees and supplying companies. This means ... that the ability of the organization's constituents to exert leverage in their own interests is increased. The obvious implication is that it is imperative that such organizations take steps to counterbalance this by averting the possibility of such power being used ... In the light of the vulnerability of Japanese production systems to

disruption and in the light of the high dependencies of the organization on its constituents, we suggest that such a system will only work successfully in a situation where organizations have either actively taken the appropriate measures to guard against disruption, or where social, economic and political conditions automatically provide safeguards.'[6]

The JIT philosophy of operations

Three key issues define the core of JIT philosophy.[7] They are the elimination of waste, the involvement of staff in the operation, and the drive for continuous improvement. We will look at each briefly in turn.

Eliminate waste

Waste can be defined as any activity which does not add value. For example, when Cummins Engineering, the engine manufacturer, began its JIT work, it carried out a study of how long it took for a number of products to work through the factory.[8] The study showed that, at best, an engine was only being worked on for 15 per cent of the time it was in the factory. At worst, this fell to 9 per cent, which meant that for 91 per cent of its time, the operation was adding cost to the engine, not adding value. Although already a relatively efficient manufacturer in Western terms, the results alerted Cummins to the enormous waste which still lay dormant in its operations, and which no performance measure then in use had exposed. Cummins shifted its objectives to reducing the wasteful activities and to enriching the value-added ones.[9]

Identifying waste is the first step towards eliminating it. Toyota identified seven wastes, which have been found to apply in many different types of operations – both service and production – and form the core of JIT philosophy.

Over-production

Producing more than is immediately needed by the next process in the operation is the greatest source of waste according to Toyota. Over-production inhibits the flow of products and services by creating inventories and slowing down the detection of defects.

Waiting time

Most operations are aware of waiting time as a source of waste. Machine efficiency and labour efficiency are two popular measures which are widely used to measure machine and labour waiting time respectively. Less obvious is the amount of waiting time of materials, disguised by operators who are kept busy producing WIP which is not needed at the time.

Transport

Although transport clearly does not add value to the product, operations often built it into their process as a 'given'. Moving materials around the plant together with the double and triple handling of WIP from various storage points can become standard practice. For example, Raleigh Industries, the bicycle manufacturer, found at the start of its improvement programme that a cycle frame travelled a total flow distance of 6.5 miles. Layout changes which brought processes closer together, improvements in transport methods and workplace organization all became important in the reduction of waste.

Process

The process itself may be a source of waste. Some operations may only exist because of poor component design, or poor maintenance, and so could be eliminated. Some processes are incapable of making parts to the correct specification. Other processes are themselves waste. In one factory operators had to bend the offcuts from the guillotine so that they would fit into a pallet. The pallet was redesigned so that it could take long strips, thus eliminating the need for the operation.[10]

Inventory

Under a JIT philosophy all inventory becomes a target for elimination. In JIT terms, one can distinguish the excellent company from the average one by the amount of inventory it carries. However, it is only by tackling the causes of inventory that it can be reduced.

Motion

An operator may look busy because he or she is looking for a missing box of parts, or going to the supervisor's office to collect another job card. The value added is actually non-existent. Simplification of work by improving jigs and fixtures is a rich source of reduction in the waste of motion.

Defective goods

Quality waste is often very significant in operations, even if actual measures of quality are limited. Scrap figures indicate the material and maybe part of the labour cost involved in poor quality. Disruption to the production control system, expediting actions, and the failure to deliver as promised are less visible, however. Total costs of quality are much greater than traditionally has been considered, and it is therefore more important to attack the causes of such costs. This is discussed further in Chapter 20.

The involvement of everyone

JIT philosophy is often put forward as a 'total' system. Its aim is to provide guidelines which embrace everyone and every process in the organization. An organization's culture is seen as being important in supporting these objectives through an emphasis on involving all of the organization's staff. This new culture is sometimes seen as synonymous with 'total quality', and is discussed in detail in Chapter 20. In fact JIT and Total Quality have many aspects in common, and they are sometimes referred to together as 'JIT/TQM'.

This JIT approach to people management has also been called the 'respect-for-humans' system. It encourages (and often requires) team-based problem solving, job enrichment (by including maintenance and set-up tasks in operators' jobs), job rotation and multi-skilling. The intention is to encourage a high degree of personal responsibility, engagement and 'ownership' of the job. However, not all commentators see JIT-influenced people-management practices as entirely positive. Kamata wrote an autobiographical description of life as an employee at a Toyota plant called *Japan in the Passing Lane*. His account speaks of '... the inhumanity and the unquestioning adherence ...' of working under such a system.[11] Similar criticisms have been voiced by some trade union representatives.

Continuous improvement

JIT objectives are often expressed as ideals, such as our previous definition ...'to meet demand instantaneously with perfect quality and no waste'. While any organization's performance may be far removed from such ideals, a fundamental belief of JIT is that it is possible to get closer to them over time. Without such beliefs to drive progress, JIT proponents claim improvement is more likely to be transitory than continuous. This is why the concept of continuous improvement is such an important part of JIT philosophy. If the aims of JIT are set in terms of ideals which individual organizations may never fully achieve, then the emphasis must be on the way in which an organization moves closer to the ideal state. The Japanese word for continuous improvement is *kaizen,* and it is a key part of JIT philosophy. It is explained fully in Chapter 18.

JIT TECHNIQUES

The 'engine room' of JIT is a collection of tools and techniques which are the means for cutting out waste. There are many techniques which could be termed 'JIT techniques' and they follow on naturally and logically from the overall JIT philosophy.

Basic working practices

'Basic working practices' form the basic preparation of the organization and its staff and are fundamental to implementing JIT.[12]

1 *Discipline*. Work standards which are critical for the safety of company members and the environment, and for the quality of the product, must be followed by everyone all the time.

2 *Flexibility*. It should be possible to expand responsibilities to the extent of people's capabilities. This applies as equally to managers as it does to shop-floor personnel. Barriers to flexibility, such as grading structures and restrictive practices, should be removed.

3 *Equality*. Unfair and divisive personnel policies should be discarded. Many traditional organizations have divisive 'perks' for different grades of personnel: staff car parks and dining rooms, for example. Japanese companies, even outside Japan, are taking the egalitarian message further – to company uniforms, consistent pay structures which do not differentiate between full-time staff and hourly-rated staff, and open-plan offices. Even a manager's tie can be regarded as a potential barrier to communication.

4 *Autonomy*. Another principle is to delegate increasing responsibility to people involved in direct activities of the business, so that management's task becomes one of supporting the shop floor. Such autonomy is manifest in a JIT operation in activities such as the following:

● *Line stop authority*: if a quality problem arises, an assembly line operative has the authority to stop the line.

● *Materials scheduling*: parts are made to well-known rules (for example, do not produce more unless the customer needs more). Many routine aspects of materials scheduling can thereby be delegated away from the central production control system.

● *Data gathering*: data relevant to shop-floor performance monitoring is gathered and used by shop-floor personnel.

● *Problem solving*: shop-floor personnel get first chance at solving problems which affect the work they do. Only if they need help from experts should that help be sought and provided.

5 *Development of personnel*. Over time, the aim is to create more company members who can support the rigours of being competitive. This ensures a richer mix of people working on improvement activities than in the average company. Partly, this is achieved by long-term personal development of company members.

6 *Quality of working life (QWL)*. Many JIT concepts fall into this category. For example:

● involvement in decision making
● security of employment
● enjoyment
● working area facilities.

7 *Creativity*. This is one of the indispensable elements of motivation. Most of us enjoy not just doing the job successfully, but also improving it for the next time.

In practice, it is difficult to achieve all the 'basic working practices' at the same time. There are trade-offs between discipline, autonomy and creativity, for example. It is best to consider these basic working practices as goals to be achieved.

Design for manufacture

Studies in automotive and aerospace companies have shown that design determines 70 to 80 per cent of production costs.[13] Design improvements can dramatically reduce product cost through changes in the number of components and sub-assemblies, and better use of materials and processing techniques. Often improvements of this magnitude would not be remotely possible by manufacturing efficiency improvements alone.

Operations focus

The concept behind operations focus is that simplicity, repetition, and experience breed competence.[14] Focus within manufacturing is:

● learning to focus each plant on limited, manageable sets of products, technologies, volumes, and markets;
● learning to structure basic manufacturing policies and supporting services so that they focus on one explicit manufacturing task instead of many implicit, inconsistent, conflicting tasks.

Small simple machines

The principle behind this technique is that several small machines are used instead of one large machine. Also 'home-grown', inexpensive equipment can be used to modify general-purpose machines so that they perform more reliably, are easy to maintain, and produce better quality over time. This demands that in-house engineering skills are available, and can be utilized to modify the machines so that new models can be introduced inexpensively. Small machines are also easily moved, so that layout flexibility is enhanced, and the risks of making errors in investment decisions are reduced because small machines usually need lower investment.

Layout and flow

Layout techniques can be used to promote the smooth flow of materials, of data, of people in the operation. Flow is an important concept in JIT. Long process routes around a factory provide opportunities for inventory build-up, add no value to the products, and slow down the throughput time of products, all of which are contrary to JIT principles. Considerations for layout and flow were described in Chapter 7. The principles of layout which JIT particularly recommends are:

- placing work stations close together so that inventory cannot build up;
- placing work stations so that the whole set of work stations which make a particular part are in sight of each other, making flow transparent to all parts of the line;
- using U-shaped lines so that staff can move between work stations to balance capacity;
- adopting cell-based layout (*see* Chapter 7).

Total productive maintenance (TPM)

TPM aims to eliminate the variability in operations processes which is caused by the effect of unplanned breakdowns. This is achieved by involving everyone in the search for maintenance improvements. Process owners are encouraged to assume ownership of their machines and to undertake routine maintenance and simple repair tasks. By so doing, maintenance specialists can then be freed to develop higher order skills for improved maintenance systems. TPM is treated in more detail in Chapter 19.

Set-up reduction (SUR)

Set-up time is defined as the time taken to change over the process from the previous batch to the first good piece of the next batch. Compare the time it takes you to change the tyre on your car with the time taken by a Formula 1 team. In SUR, set-up times can be reduced by a variety of methods such as cutting out time taken to search for tools and equipment, the pre-preparation of tasks which delay change-overs, and the constant practice of set-up routines. Often relatively simple mechanical changes can reduce set-up times considerably. Figure 15.6 illustrates some simple changes in the mechanics of fixing tools and jigs to machines which can reduce set-up times.

The other common approach to SUR is to convert work which was previously performed while the machine was stopped (called internal work) to be performed while the machine is running (called external work). There are three major methods of achieving the transfer of internal set-up work to external work.[15]

1 Pre-set tools so that a complete unit is fixed to the machine instead of having to be built up while the machine is stopped. Preferably, all adjustment should be carried out externally, so that the internal set-up is an assembly operation only.

(a) Pear-shaped holes (Dahma holes) mean fewer turns to release and tighten.

(b) U-washers also need fewer turns to release and tighten.

(c) Cutaway threads are easier to release and tighten.

(d) Standardize the size of fixings.

(e) Reduce the number of bolts used.

**Figure 15.6
Methods of
reducing the time
taken to fix tools
and jigs to a
machine**
Source: Reproduced from
Harrison, A. (1992) *Just-in-
time Manufacturing in
Perspective*, by permission
of Prentice Hall International

559

2 Attach the different tools or dyes to a standard fixture or jig. Again, this enables the internal set-up to consist of a simple and standardized assembly operation.

3 Make the loading and unloading of new tools and dyes easy. Using improved material-handling devices, such as roller conveyor ball-mounted surface tables, can greatly help.

SUR is the means by which Cummins Engineering first convinced itself of the power of JIT. Set-up time on the head face drill (a CNC machine tool on the block line) was 17 minutes. The operator team reduced this time to just eight seconds, and spent less than £100 in doing so. Within a few months all set-up times on the block line were down to less than five minutes. Batch sizes were cut from about 80 (two weeks' production) to one.[16]

FLEXIBILITY HELPS JIT AT L'ORÉAL[17]

L'Oréal cosmetics is now the world's largest toiletries and cosmetics group, with a presence in over 140 different countries. In the UK the 45 000 square metre purpose-built facility in mid-Wales produces 1300 product types in a spotlessly clean environment which is akin to a pharmaceutical plant in terms of hygiene, safety and quality. The plant has 55 production lines and 45 different production processes, and the manufacturing systems employed are of a flexibility that allows them to run each of the 1300 product types every two months. That means over 150 different products each week. But the plant was not always as flexible as this. It has been forced to enhance its flexibility by the requirement to ship over 80 million items each year. The sheer logistics involved in purchasing, producing, storing and distributing the volume and variety of goods has led to its current focus on introducing JIT principles into the manufacturing process.

To help achieve its drive for flexibility and for just-in-time production, L'Oréal organized the site into three production centres, each autonomous and focused within technical families of products. Their processes and production lines are then further focused within product sub-divisions. Responsible for all the activities within his area, from pre-weighing to dispatch, is the Production Centre Manager, and his role also encompasses staff development, training and motivation. Within the focused production centres, improvement groups have been working on improving shop-floor flexibility, quality and efficiency. One of the projects reduced the set-up times on the line which produces hair colourants from 2.5 hours to only eight minutes. These new change-over times mean that the company can now justify even smaller batches, and may give the company the flexibility to meet market needs just-in-time. Prior to the change in set-up time, batch size was 30 000 units; now batches as small as 2000 to 3000 units can be produced cost-effectively. ■

Questions

1 What did L'Oréal do to help it organize the process of set-up reduction?

2 What do you think L'Oréal gained from doing each of these things?

3 If we could halve all change-over times in the factory, what effect would this have on inventory?

Total people involvement

Total people involvement[18] can be seen as an extension of 'basic working practices'. However, it sees staff taking on much more responsibility to use their abilities to the benefit of the company as a whole. They are trained, capable and motivated to take full responsibility for all aspects of the work they do. In turn, they are trusted to carry out these responsibilities with autonomy for their own work area. Staff are expected to participate in such activities as the following:

- the selection of new recruits;
- dealing directly with suppliers over schedules, quality issues and delivery information;
- the self-measurement of performance and improvement trends;
- spending improvement budgets (SP Tyres reputedly allocates 25 per cent of capital budgets to be spent by operators[19]);
- planning and reviewing work done each day through communication meetings;
- dealing directly with customer problems and requirements.

Visibility

Problems, quality projects and operations checklists are made visible by displaying them so that they can be easily seen and understood by all staff. Visibility measures include:

- displayed performance measures in the work place;
- coloured lights indicating stoppages;
- displayed SPC control charts (*see* Chapter 17);
- visible improvement techniques and checklists;
- a separate area displaying samples of own company products and competitors' products together with samples of good and defective products;
- visual control systems such as kanbans;
- open-plan work-place layouts.

JIT supply

Just-in-time supply epitomizes the popular meaning of the term 'JIT', and conjures up the vision of parts arriving at the assembly process 'just-in-time'. Indeed, a misinterpretation of this view was first seized upon by some non-Japanese manufacturers, who often forced their suppliers to deliver just-in-time while contributing little or nothing to improved logistics themselves. JIT supply is in fact a very rich area for improvement activity. In Chapter 13 we described 'partnerships', 'lean' relationships and 'integrated concepts' which are all based on JIT supply principles.

JIT planning and control techniques

Also classed as JIT techniques are those which deal specifically with the planning and control of operations. These techniques are treated under a separate heading because they relate directly to the planning and control theme of this part of the book.

The techniques and approaches described are as follows:

- kanban control
- levelled scheduling
- mixed modelling
- synchronization.

JUST-IN-TIME PLANNING AND CONTROL

One of the sources of waste identified earlier was that caused by inventory timing. Poor inventory timing (parts arrive too early or too late) causes unpredictability in an operation. Inventory timing is governed by the two schools of thought which were described in Chapter 10 – 'push' planning and control, and 'pull' planning and control. JIT planning and control is based on the principle of a 'pull system', while the MRP approach to planning and control, which was described in the previous chapter, is a 'push system'.

Kanban control

The term *kanban* was sometimes used as being equivalent to 'JIT planning and control' (which it is not) or even to the whole of JIT (which it most certainly is not). However, kanban control is one method of operationalizing a pull-based planning and control system. Kanban is the Japanese for card or signal. It is sometimes called the 'invisible conveyor' which controls the transfer of materials between the stages of an operation. In its simplest form, it is a card used by a customer stage to instruct its supplier stage to send more materials. Kanbans can also take other forms. In some Japanese companies they are solid plastic markers or even coloured ping-pong balls, the different colours representing different parts. There are also different types of kanban.

- *The move or conveyance kanban.* A move kanban is used to signal to a previous stage that material can be withdrawn from inventory and transferred to a specific destination. This type of kanban would normally have details of the particular part's name and number, the place where it should be taken from, and the destination to where it is being delivered.
- *The production kanban.* A production kanban is a signal to a production process that it can start producing a part or item to be placed in an inventory. The information contained on this type of kanban usually includes the particular part's name and number, a description of the process itself, the materials required for the production of the part, and the destination to which the part or parts need to be sent when they are produced.
- *The vendor kanban.* Vendor kanbans are used to signal to a supplier to send material or parts to a stage. In this way it is similar to a move kanban but it is usually used with external suppliers.

Whichever kind of kanban is being used, the principle is always the same; that is, that the receipt of a kanban triggers the movement, production or supply of one unit or a standard container of units. If two kanbans are received it triggers the movement, production or supply of two units or standard containers of units, and so on. The kanbans are the *only* means by which movement, or production or supply can be authorized. This is true even when the kanban is not a card or object. Some companies use 'kanban squares'. These are marked spaces on the shop floor or bench which are drawn to fit one or more work pieces or containers. The existence of an empty square triggers production at the stage which supplies the square. Full squares mean that the preceding process must stop. Other variants include container-as-kanban (where the empty container acts as an instruction), verbal (simply shouting 'send some more'!), and colour-coded tokens (e.g. red = top priority, orange = moderate, green = normal).

There are two procedures which can govern the use of kanbans. These are known as the single-card system and the dual-card system. The single-card system is most often used because it is by far the simplest system to operate. It uses only move kanbans (or vendor kanbans when receiving supply of material from an outside source). The dual-card system uses both move and production kanbans.

The single-card system

Figure 15.7 shows the operation of a single-card kanban system. At each stage (only two stages are shown, stage A and stage B) there is a work centre and an area for holding inventory. All production and inventory is contained in standard containers, all of which contain exactly the same number of parts. When stage B requires some more parts to work on, it withdraws a standard container from the output stock point of stage A. After work centre B has used the parts in the container, it places the move kanban in a holding area and sends the empty container to the work centre at stage A. The arrival of the empty containers at stage A's work centre is the signal for production to take place at work centre A. The move kanban is taken from the holding box back to the output stock point of stage A. This acts as authorization for the collection of a further full container to be moved from the output stock of stage A through to the work centre at stage B. Two closed loops effectively control the flow of materials between the stages. The move kanban loop (illustrated by the thin arrows) keeps

Figure 15.7 **The operation of the single-card kanban system of pull control**

materials circulating between the stages, and the container loop (illustrated by the thicker arrows), connects the work centres with the stock point between them and circulates the containers, full from A to B and empty back from B to A.

The sequence of actions and the flow of kanbans may at first seem complicated. However, in practice their use provides a straightforward and transparent method of calling for material only when it is needed and limiting the inventory which accumulates between stages. The number of kanbans which are put into the loops between the stages or between the stock points and the work centres equals the number of containers in the system and therefore the inventory which can accumulate. Taking a kanban out of the loop has the effect of reducing the inventory. In summary, the rules which govern the use of kanbans are as follows:

- Each container must have a kanban card, indicating part number and description, user and maker locations, and quantity.
- The parts are always pulled by the succeeding process (the customer or user).
- No parts are started without a kanban card.
- All containers contain exactly their stated number of parts.
- No defective parts may be sent to the succeeding process.
- The maker (supplier section) can only produce enough parts to make up what has been withdrawn.
- The number of kanbans should be reduced.
- The time period should be made shorter (months to weeks to days to hours).

These simple rules can be used to plan and control many other operations tasks. For example, spare parts benefit from the visibility and discipline that a kanban brings. Instead, for example, of electric motors lying in an unsorted heap in a corner of a maintenance department, kanban control would allow working parts to be stored in exact locations in exact quantities. When one is required for a repair, the kanban card could be used to place a replenishment order.

Levelled scheduling

Heijunka is the Japanese word for overall levelling of the production schedule so that mix and volume are even over time. For example, instead of producing 500 parts in one batch which would cover the needs for the next three months, levelled scheduling would require the operation to make only one piece per hour regularly. The principle of levelled scheduling is straightforward but the requirements to put it into practice are quite severe, although the benefits resulting from it can be substantial. The move from conventional to levelled scheduling is illustrated in Fig. 15.8. Conventionally, if a mix of products were required in a time period (usually a month), a batch size would be calculated for each product and the batches produced in some sequence. Figure 15.8 (a) shows three products which are produced in a 20-day time period in a production unit.

> Quantity of product A required = 3000
> Quantity of product B required = 1000
> Quantity of product C required = 1000
>
> Batch size of product A = 600
> Batch size of product B = 200
> Batch size of product C = 200

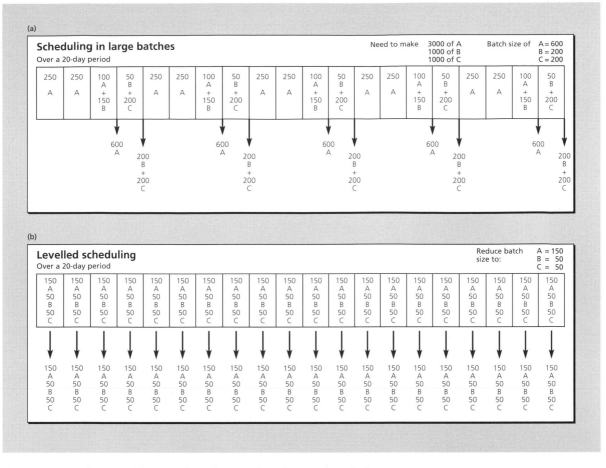

Figure 15.8 Levelled scheduling equalizes the mix of products made each day

Starting at day 1 the unit commences producing product A. During day 3 the batch of 600 As is finished and dispatched to the next stage. The batch of Bs is started but is not finished until day 4. The remainder of day 4 is spent making the batch of Cs and both batches are dispatched at the end of that day. The cycle then repeats itself. The consequence of using large batches is first that relatively large amounts of inventory accumulate within and between the units, and second that most days are different from one another in terms of what they are expected to produce (in more complex circumstances no two days would be the same).

Now suppose that the flexibility of the unit could be increased to the point where the batch sizes for the products were reduced to a quarter of their previous levels without loss of capacity (*see* Fig. 15.8 (b)).

Batch size of product A = 150
Batch size of product B = 50
Batch size of product C = 50

A batch of each product can now be completed in a single day, at the end of which the three batches are dispatched to their next stage. Smaller batches of inventory are moving between each stage, which will reduce the overall level of work-in-progress in the operation. Just as significant, however, is the effect on the regularity and rhythm of production at the unit. Now every day in the month is the same in terms of what needs to be produced. This makes planning and control of each stage in the operation much easier. For example, if on day 1 of the month the daily batch of As were finished by 11.00 am, and all the batches were successfully completed in the day, the next day the unit knows that if it again has completed all the As by 11.00 am, it is on schedule. When every day is different, the simple question, 'Are we on schedule to complete our production today?' requires some investigation before it can be answered. However, when every day is the same, everyone in the unit can tell whether production is on target by looking at the clock. Control becomes visible and transparent to all and the advantages of regular, daily schedules can be passed to upstream suppliers.

Mixed modelling

The principle of levelled scheduling can be taken further to give a repeated mix of parts. Suppose that the machines in the production unit can be made so flexible that they achieve the JIT ideal of a batch size of one. The sequence of individual products emerging from the unit could be reduced progressively as illustrated in Figure 15.9. This would produce a steady stream of each product flowing continuously from the unit.

However, the sequence of products does not always fall as conveniently as in Fig. 15.9. The unit production times for each product are not usually identical and the ratios of required volumes are less convenient.

Example

Suppose the number of products required in the 20-day period are:

Product A = 1920
Product B = 1200
Product C = 960

**Figure 15.9
Levelled scheduling and mixed modelling: mixed modelling becomes possible as the batch size approaches one**

Assuming an eight-hour day, the cycle time for each product – that is, the interval between the production of each of the same type of product (*see* Chapter 7 for a full explanation of cycle time) – is as follows:

$$\text{Product A, cycle time} = \frac{20 \times 8 \times 60}{1920} = 5 \text{ mins}$$

$$\text{Product B, cycle time} = \frac{20 \times 8 \times 60}{1200} = 18 \text{ mins}$$

$$\text{Product C, cycle time} = \frac{20 \times 8 \times 60}{960} = 10 \text{ mins}$$

So, the production unit must produce:

1 unit of A every 5 minutes
1 unit of B every 8 minutes
1 unit of C every 10 minutes

Put another way, by finding the common factor of 5, 8 and 10:

8 units of A every 40 minutes
5 units of B every 40 minutes
4 units of C every 40 minutes

This means that a sequence, which mixes eight units of A, five of B and four of C, and repeats itself every 40 minutes, will produce the required output. There will be many different ways of sequencing the products to achieve this mix. For example:

... BACABACABACABACAB ... repeated ... repeated

This sequence repeats itself every 40 minutes and produces the correct mix of products to satisfy the monthly requirements.

TOYOTA PRODUCTION SYSTEM

Toyota's version of JIT, which it calls the Toyota Production System (TPS), has been the driving force behind its advance into what has been called a 'truly great manufacturing company'. The 'two pillars' of TPS are (and have always been):

● *Just-in-time*: the rapid and co-ordinated movement of parts throughout the production system and supply chain to meet customer demand. JIT is operationalized by means of *heijunka* (levelling and smoothing the flow of materials), *kanban* (signalling to the preceding process that more parts are needed) and *nagare* (laying out processes to achieve smoother flow of parts throughout the production process).
● *Jidoka*: humanizing the interface between operator and machine. Toyota philosophy is that the machine is there to serve the operator's purpose, while the operator should be free to exercise his/her judgement. Jidoka is operationalized by means of *fail-safeing* (*see* Chapter 19)

▶

or machine jidoka, *line-stop authority* or human jidoka, and *visual control* – at-a-glance status of production processes and visibility of process standards.

To Toyota the key control tool is its kanban system. The kanban is seen as serving three purposes:

● It is an instruction for the preceding process to send more.
● It is a visual control tool to show up areas of over-production and lack of synchronization.
● It is a tool for *kaizen* (continuous improvement). Toyota's rules state that 'the number of kanbans should be reduced over time'.

Toyota uses two of the basic types of kanban to support JIT pull scheduling: the 'production' kanban and the 'move' kanban. The production kanban authorizes the preceding process to make more parts. This kanban comes in two variants: the multi-process kanban for complex activities such as machining, and the single-process kanban for simple activities such as press work and casting. The move kanban shows the timing and quantity of parts involved when a process owner picks up a new supply of parts from a preceding process. This kanban also comes in two variants: internal (for internal suppliers) and external (for external suppliers).

Examples of the use of production and move kanbans are shown in Fig. 15.10. The two-kanban system provides tight control, not only over production but also over movement.

Figure 15.10 Move kanbans and production kanbans at Toyota

Kanbans replace works orders and routing cards with a simple, visual control system which enables routine material control to be delegated to process owners.

The number of parts per container is governed by factors such as part size and commonality between processes. Toyota believes that it is usually best that the number is divisible by 8 to facilitate hourly synchronization. This also means that the number of parts per container should be standardized where possible. The number of containers (hence the number of kanbans) is influenced by demand per hour, the lead time for the part and the number of parts per container. This is increased by a factor to allow for disruptions like breakdowns and absenteeism. The number of kanbans should of course never be fixed, but subject to *kaizen*.

Major sub-assemblies like engines are not controlled by kanban. There are numerous different end options for such major sub-assemblies, and inventory would simply be generated if separate kanbans were used for each one. Engines are therefore controlled by a different method. They are sequenced by *assembly line broadcasting*. In this approach, the exact customer requirements for a vehicle are broken down to major components and communicated ('broadcast') to the relevant production section. The procedure, therefore, is to sequence control major sub-assemblies, and to use kanbans for components and smaller sub-assemblies. ■

Questions

1 List all the different techniques and practices which Toyota adopts. Which of these would you call just-in-time philosophies and which are just-in-time techniques?

2 How are operations objectives (quality, speed, dependability, flexibility, cost) influenced by the practices which Toyota adopts?

Synchronization

Many companies make a wide variety of parts and products, not all of them with sufficient regularity to warrant the full levelled scheduling treatment. Synchronization means the pacing of output at each stage in the production process to ensure the same flow characteristics for each part or product as it progresses through each stage. To do this, parts need to be classified according to the frequency with which they are demanded. One method of doing this distinguishes between *runners, repeaters*, and *strangers*.[20]

● *Runners* are products or parts which are produced frequently, such as every week.
● *Repeaters* are products or parts which are produced regularly, but at longer time intervals.
● *Strangers* are products or parts which are produced at irregular and possibly unpredictable time intervals.

There are advantages in trying to reduce the variability of timing intervals for producing runners and repeaters. The aim is to synchronize processes concerned with parts and sub-assemblies for such products so that they appear to take place on a 'drumbeat' pulse which governs material movements. It might even be better to slow down faster operations than to have them produce more than can be handled in the same time by the next process. In this way output is made regular and predictable.

JIT IN SERVICE OPERATIONS

Many of the principles and techniques of just-in-time, although they have been described in the context of manufacturing operations, are also applicable to service settings. In fact some of the philosophical underpinning to just-in-time can also be seen as having its equivalent in the service sector. Take, for example, our argument concerning the role of inventory in manufacturing systems. The comparison between manufacturing systems which held large stocks of inventory between stages and those which did not, centred on the effect which inventory had on improvement and problem solving. Exactly the same argument could be applied when, instead of queues of material (inventory), an operation has to deal with queues of customers. Table 15.1 shows how certain aspects of inventory are analogous to certain aspects of queues.

In this part of the chapter we describe two service organizations which have benefited from applying some of the principles of just-in-time. The first is the Little Chef restaurant chain and the second is a hospital. You might also like to read the case exercise at the end of this chapter which gives a further example of just-in-time in a hospital setting.

Table 15.1 Inventory and queues have similar characteristics

	Inventory (Queues of material)	Queues (Queues of people)
Cost	Ties up capital	Waste time
Space	Needs warehouse	Need waiting areas
Quality	Defects are hidden	Give negative impression
Decoupling	Makes stages independent	Promote division of labour and specialization
Utilization	Stages kept busy by work-in-progress	Servers kept busy by waiting customers
Co-ordination	Avoids having to synchronize flow	Avoid having to match supply and demand

Source: Adapted from Fitzsimmons, J.A. (1990) 'Making Continual Improvement: A Competitive Strategy for Service Firms' in Bowen, D.E., Chase, R.B., Cummings, T.G. and Associates, *Service Management Effectiveness*, Jossey-Bass

Little Chef

Most drivers in the UK are familiar with the Little Chef roadside restaurant chain, which has over 350 sites located on busy roads around the UK. Success has come through offering consistency and reliability of service throughout its network.

Of Little Chef's 35 million customers a year, most are on journeys of over two hours. Week-day users are mostly business travellers, while leisure travellers take over at weekends and during school holidays. All restaurants trade from 7.00 am to 10.00 pm, 364 days a year and offer an all-day menu, supplemented by part-day menus and various seasonal promotions. Customers receive a table service of cooked-to-order meals. Target times are 30 minutes for a starter plus main course with an extra ten minutes for a dessert. Each restaurant is run as a profit centre with an average management team of four staff. With a simple, standardized service package, many aspects of JIT-style operations can be seen in the Little Chef operation. Here we review operations planning and control issues at a typical Little Chef restaurant which is located at Towcester East (in the central part of the UK).

Operations planning

Figure 15.11 shows that demand levels fluctuate by season, by day of the week and throughout the day. To achieve a high standard of customer service, it is necessary to forecast demand as accurately as possible, and then to provide for sufficient resources (staff, food, etc.) to meet that demand. In practice, an all-year-round core of regular staff is maintained, supplemented by seasonal staff at peak periods. Staff planning is undertaken at three levels:

● *The quarterly manpower plan.* The main input to this plan is the forecast number of customers for each of the 12 weeks of the forecast period. The forecast is based on a mix of historical data and trends, adjusted by the personal view of the manager.
● *The weekly forecast.* The sales forecast from the quarterly plan is updated and broken down into daily sales. The forecast 'covers' (number of customers) and the average spend per head (a key productivity measure) are multiplied together to give forecast sales. Actual figures are added to this document as the week progresses. The document therefore starts as a planning tool, becomes a monitoring tool, and is later used again as a planning tool for the same week next year.
● *The daily plans.* The duty manager draws up a shift planner to plan the allocation of duties between staff. This is a working tool, and is updated during the day.

All materials (food, cleaning items and crockery) are supplied from a single supplier. This helps to ensure that goods are up to a consistent standard. Each restaurant has three deliveries a week, typically Monday, Wednesday and Friday, with orders being placed the same morning. A weekly stock-take provides consumption of each item. The manager uses a locally determined re-order level combined with forecast daily sales to compute material orders. Most foods are delivered and stored frozen. Only salads and cured meats arrive date coded, usually with four to five days' shelf life after delivery. Bread and milk are delivered daily by local suppliers. Stock-holding amounts to about seven days at any one time.

Operations control

Each restaurant has a 'menu manual', which specifies the ingredients, cooking procedures and presentation standards for every item on the menu. Orders are added to the cook's order pad, including the time when the waitress took the order. Orders are marked once cooking has started, and marked again when cooking has finished. The cooking process is simple, and does not require special qualifications. Most restaurants have a 'cook skills sharer', who has undergone special training in order to teach others to cook. The cooking equipment is also simple – griddles, fryers and pre-programmed microwave ovens. Similarly, a housekeeping board is maintained as both a planning and control tool, enabling 'at a glance' an assessment of jobs which need to be done. Standard cleaning products and methods are used throughout the company,

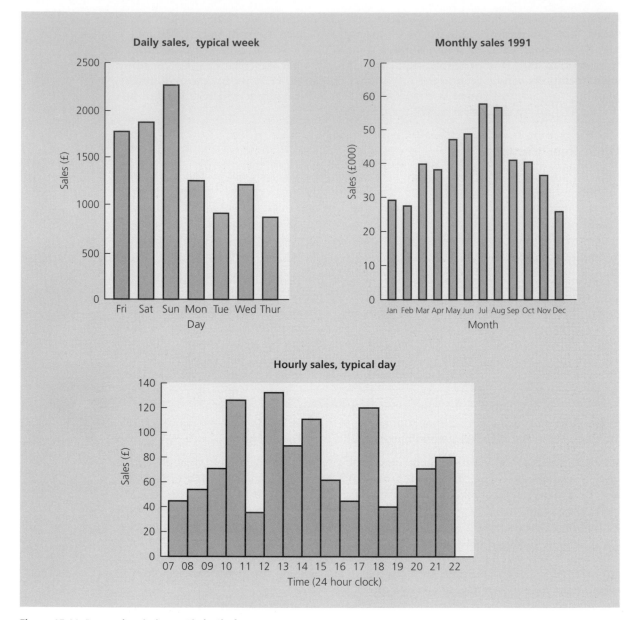

Figure 15.11 Demand variation at Little Chef restaurant at Towcester East

and each cleaning task is broken down into 'how, what, when' elements. To help ensure that standards are maintained across the network, quality audits are conducted every three months by the local training officer.

Tasks fall into eight categories; there is usually enough flexibility to react on a daily basis to changing needs, however. The categories are:

- reception/cashier
- cooking/production
- beverage production

- sweet/salad production
- serving to tables
- relaying tables
- washing up
- cleaning/toilet checks.

Staff are cross-trained for greater flexibility. Fifty per cent of staff can cook, for example. At busy times, each function is staffed, but at quieter times, one person may perform more than one task. To support staff flexibility, Little Chef provides a computer-based training package which provides details of all tasks to be performed, tests understanding and records training. Facility flexibility is assisted by moveable tables and chairs so that parties of varying sizes can be accommodated.

Although different from a manufacturing company, some of the principles which apply in the Little Chef case are similar to those used in a JIT manufacturer:

- *Limited product range* – this helps to simplify the materials control task. The operation only produces 'runners' and 'repeaters'.
- *Simple products* – which only require basic production equipment.
- *Pull scheduling* – known customer orders are used to pull meals from the kitchen to the restaurant according to actual demand. There are no buffer stocks. The signal to make more is the order from the waitress. The routine is simple but strict: order one, make one, supply one in response to specific customer demand.
- *A batch size of one* – orders are not held up (or batched) until a sufficient number have been accumulated, nor are they produced in advance; they are made on receipt of the order.
- *Flexibility* – a standard time for serving a customer is aimed for irrespective of the demand level. This is done by flexing the number of staff on duty.
- *JIT supply* – replenishment stocks are ordered on a short (daily) cycle from Little Chef's sole supplier.
- *Visibility* – recipes, preparation methods, pictures of ideal finished products and cleaning checklists are all examples of how key data can be made visible to all staff, both for control and audit purposes.

Temple University Hospital, Pennsylvania

The Temple University Hospital in Pennsylvania in the USA is a 500-bed, acute-care, university-affiliated teaching hospital. The array of services provided covers 11 surgical areas, including cardio-thoracic, neurology, and orthopaedics. It uses the latest surgical technology and carries out 11 000 procedures per year in a new building housing 14 operating rooms. A layout for this building is shown in Fig. 15.12.

Before changing its methods, Temple Hospital held high inventories of materials. Eleven charge nurses staffed the 14 operating rooms (ORs), each nurse dedicated to a surgical speciality. Their prime task was to ensure that the materials which were needed for operations by the physicians were always available. Physicians used different supply sources for the same operation, and each nurse had an individual system for controlling materials. Case carts which hold the materials ready for the operations were located along the rear corridor of the building. Stocks of materials were held in cabinets and storage rooms in the operating rooms and elsewhere. A further buffer stock was held in a central store, which is not shown in the figure. Cabinets and storage rooms

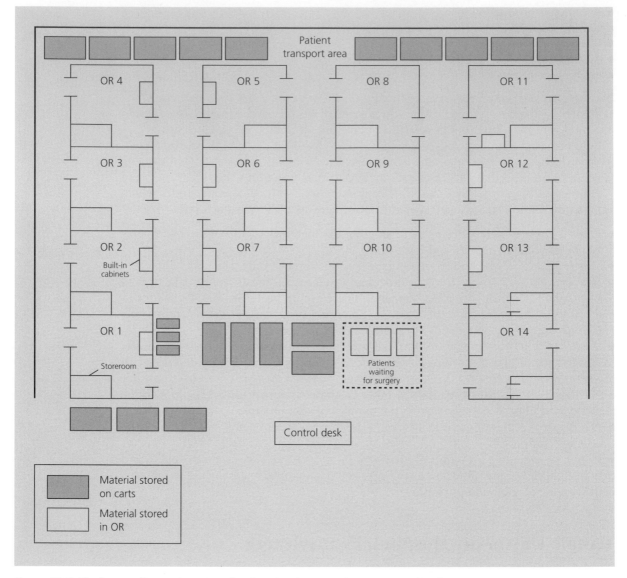

Figure 15.12 The layout of operating rooms (ORs) at Temple Hospital prior to use of exchange-cart and case-cart systems

were kept full. The goal for charge nurses was to provide a 100 per cent service to the physicians. It was important never to run out of anything which might be needed. As a result, numerous parts were kept as 'squirrel stocks', including expensive items like artificial joints. The material inventory was estimated at $750 000, of which $80 000 was estimated to be obsolete. In effect the hospital was a good example of a 'just-in-case' stock policy.

In the USA, the government pays for the treatment of about 40 per cent of patients through the Medical Aid (Medicaid) system. In order to control costs, 460 'Diagnostic-Related Groups' (DRGs) were defined. DRGs limit the amount that a hospital can charge for a defined operation, and lead to hospitals being paid on a 'cost-to-deliver' basis. The DRG specifies standard materials which must be used in the operation in order to encourage tighter control. In effect, DRGs define the bill of materials for a given operation. Once hospitals had accepted the concept of DRGs, the insurance companies followed suit. This encouraged the standardization of methods by the physicians themselves. It also provided an attractive opportunity. If surgery could be predicted in advance, a master schedule could be defined and material requirements could be forecast.

The planning and control breakthrough at Temple was to recognize the value of the operating room controller, who had hitherto been an under-utilized resource. He or she was in a position to schedule operations up to two weeks ahead, which was well above the lead time for most materials (average three days). It was possible, therefore, to arrive at a master schedule, and to input this into the material procurement system. This enabled operation-specific materials to be scheduled by means of DRGs.

The materials management system at Temple University Hospital was implemented at three levels as follows:

- *An exchange-cart system*. This is used for general-purpose materials such as bandages and sutures. These are supplied on a 'pull' basis by Central Supply & Distribution (CSD), which maintains stocks on a real-time computer system. Bar coding and computer terminals at the receiving areas are used to check receipt of carts. Availability of these materials is assured by flow of a few fully stocked exchange carts from CSD to the operating rooms several times a day. The carts themselves act as a kanban between CSD and the theatres.
- *A case-cart system*. This is used for materials associated with specific surgical procedures. By scheduling operations through the planning and control system, the relevant materials are called up for the given procedure and surgeon. Purchasing personnel order materials called up for all operations. CSD personnel then make up case carts containing all such intermediate-value materials. These are delivered on a JIT basis to the operating rooms.
- *The high-value speciality item*. The bill of materials has been designed to identify special delivery requirements for these parts. Suppliers bypass the normal delivery to CSD, and instead deliver directly to the given operating room, also on a JIT basis.

The implementation of the new low-stock JIT system required that surgeons needed to be convinced that the system's reliability would be at least as good as the previous method. Communication between material suppliers and the operating areas needed to be such that there was confidence to operate with low stocks. After implementation it was accepted that the JIT system had actually *improved* communication links. Eliminating buffer stocks had the effect of forcing improved integration between the surgeons, the nurses, CSD, purchasing and finance.

JIT AND MRP

The wide acceptance of the JIT principles and techniques outlined in this chapter came in the 1980s, after many manufacturing operations had made use of the MRP-based systems which were described in Chapter 14. Furthermore, the operating philosophies of MRP and JIT do seem to be fundamentally opposed. JIT encourages a 'pull' system of planning and control, whereas MRP is a 'push' system. JIT has aims which are wider than the operations planning and control activity, whereas MRP is essentially a planning and control 'calculation mechanism'. Yet the two approaches can reinforce each other in the same operation, provided their respective advantages are preserved. This part of this chapter will address two important questions for operations managers:

● How can JIT and MRP be combined in the same operation?
● How do we choose whether to use an MRP-based or a JIT-based or a combined approach to planning and control?

Before treating these two questions, however, it is necessary to summarize the characteristics of each approach.

Key characteristics of MRP

● Although designed as a pull system (the master schedule provides the pull signal which drives the system), the way MRP is actually used internally is as a push system. Inventory is driven through each process in response to detailed, time-phased plans, calculated by part number.
● MRP uses orders derived from the master schedule as the unit of control. Therefore, achievement against schedule is a key control monitor.
● MRP systems usually need a complex, centralized computer-based organization to support the necessary hardware, software and systems. This can make the needs of the customer appear remote to staff whose responsibilities lie two or three levels down the organization structure.
● MRP is highly dependent on the accuracy of data derived from bills of materials, stock records, and so on.
● MRP systems assume a fixed operations environment, with fixed lead times which are used to calculate when materials should arrive at the next operation. However, loading conditions and other factors mean that lead times are in reality far from fixed. MRP systems find it extremely difficult to cope with variable lead times.
● MRP records take a long time to update. In theory, each transaction requires a full update of data records. In practice, it is more usual to batch the changes into weekly (or monthly) updates. Even sophisticated MRP systems, which allow net change features to be updated daily, are relatively insensitive to hour-by-hour changes.

Key characteristics of JIT

● The flow between each stage in the manufacturing process is 'pulled' by demand from the previous stage.
● The control of the pull between stages is accomplished by using simple cards, tokens, or empty squares to trigger movements and production. This results in simple, visual and transparent control.
● Decision-making for operations control is largely decentralized: tactical decisions do not rely on computer-based information processing.
● JIT scheduling is 'rate-based' (calculated in terms of output of a part per unit of time) rather than volume-based (the absolute number of parts to be made in a given day or week).
● JIT assumes (and encourages) resource flexibility and minimized lead times.
● JIT planning and control concepts are only one part of a wider and explicit JIT philosophy of operations.

JIT and MRP similarities and differences

Examining key characteristics of each approach to planning and control provides an indication of how they can be used together. MRP seeks to meet projected customer demand by directing that parts and sub-assemblies are only produced as needed to meet that demand. As we noted in Chapter 14, MRP back-schedules demand for parts and sub-assemblies by using the bill of materials to calculate how many are needed and when they must be made. This is how MRP connects customer demand with the internal and external supply network. The irony is that JIT planning and control has similar objectives. Pull scheduling aims to connect the new network of internal and external supply processes by means of invisible conveyors so that parts only move in response to co-ordinated and synchronized signals derived from end-customer demand.

Given the similarities in objectives, what are the differences? MRP is driven by the master production schedule, which identifies *future* end-item demand. It models a fixed lead-time environment, using the power of the computer to calculate how many of, and when, each part should be made. Its output is in the form of time-phased requirements plans that are centrally calculated and co-ordinated. But while MRP is based on ideals that are analogous to pull scheduling (only ordering parts to be made as needed), the way it is used is quite different. Parts are made in response to central instructions, regardless of whether the next process can take them or actually needs them at the time. Day-to-day disturbances, such as quality problems and inaccurate stock records, undermine MRP authority and make the plans unworkable at shop-floor level. While MRP is excellent at planning, it is weak at control.

On the other hand, JIT-style pull scheduling aims to meet demand instantaneously. This aim is achieved through simple, paperless control systems based on kanban. But in practice, as described in Chapter 10, the actual throughput time of which the system is capable must be recognized. If the total throughput time (P) is less than the demand lead time (D), then JIT systems should be capable of meeting that demand. But if the $P{:}D$ ratio is greater than 1, some speculative production will be needed. And if demand is suddenly far greater than expected for certain products, the JIT system may be unable to cope. Pull scheduling is a *reactive* concept that works best when independent demand has been levelled and dependent demand synchronized. While JIT may be good at control, it is weak on planning.

Finally, MRP is better at dealing with *complexity*, as measured by numbers of parts and finished products. It can handle detailed parts requirements, even for products that are made infrequently and in low volumes ('strangers'). JIT pull scheduling is less capable of responding instantaneously to changes in demand as the part count, options and colours increase. Therefore, JIT production systems favour designs based on simpler product structures with high parts commonality. Such disciplines challenge needless complexity, so that more parts may be brought under pull-scheduling control.

Putting the relative advantages and disadvantages of JIT and MRP together suggests how the two approaches can be blended. Two blends are briefly described in the following sections.

Separate systems for different products

Using the runners, repeaters, strangers terminology described earlier, pull scheduling using kanban can be used for 'runners' and 'repeaters'. MRP planning is used for supplier scheduling as described below. MRP control is then only necessary for strangers, for which works orders are issued to identify what must be done at each stage, and then the work itself is monitored to push materials through manufacturing stages.[21] The advantage of this is that by increasing responsiveness and reducing inventories it makes it worthwhile to increase their number by design simplification.

As an example of the application of this approach, Professor Bill Berry describes a company where product structure analysis provided an understanding of how MRP and JIT could co-exist.[22] A fork-lift truck manufacturer had always looked on itself as a jobbing system, with 240 000 possible end product options of which 20 000 were currently offered for sale, and 8 000 were master scheduled. The product range was divided up into five families, and detailed analysis of the bill of materials for each member of the product range in each family showed that, in the worst case, 50 per cent of the part numbers were common. (Strict rules were applied: in order to be classified as 'common', a part number had to be used in all family members.) The opportunity arose of using pull scheduling for the common parts without using time-phased MRP records. So common parts (runners and repeaters), both made in and bought out, could be controlled by rate-based weekly requirements. Irregularly made parts (strangers), on the other hand, would continue to be governed by time-based, weekly MRP. Figure 15.13 shows how the bill of materials could be redrawn in two parts: a common parts planned bill for runners and repeaters and an options record for strangers. Further opportunities are then opened up to downsize the MRP system and to run it more frequently and more accurately, to control options more closely, and to rethink product designs to increase common parts.

MRP for overall control and JIT for internal control

MRP planning of supplier materials aims to ensure that sufficient parts are in the pipeline to enable them to be called up 'just-in-time'.[23] Figure 15.14 illustrates a simplified version of what may be achieved by the use of pull scheduling in manufacture

**Figure 15.13
Using kanbans for
higher volume
parts and MRP for
lower volume parts**

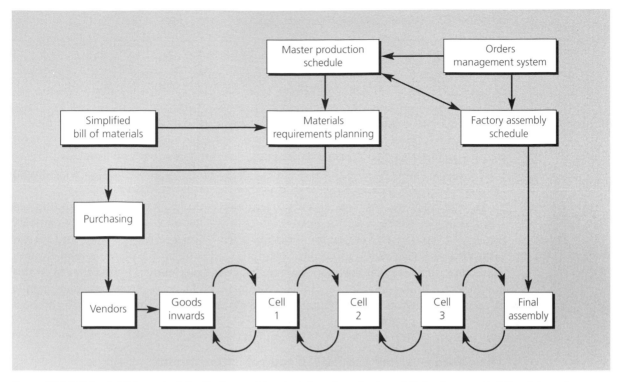

Figure 15.14 Using MRP to control the final assembly schedule and purchasing while kanbans control flow internally

supported by MRP materials procurement. The master production schedule (*see* Chapter 14) is broken down by means of MRP for supplier schedules (forecast future demand). Actual materials requirements for supplies are signalled by means of kanban to facilitate JIT delivery. Within the factory, all materials movements are governed by kanban loops between operations. The 'drum beat' for the factory is set by the factory assembly schedule.

A number of advantages over conventional MRP are claimed by combining the two systems in this way:

- There is no need for internal interstage works orders.
- In-process inventory need only be monitored between cells rather than for each activity.
- The bill of materials has fewer levels than in a conventional MRP system.
- Process-route information is simplified.
- Work-centre planning and control is simplified.
- Lead times and WIP are reduced.

When to use JIT, MRP and combined systems

Again it is the advantages and disadvantages of JIT and MRP which guide when to use 'pure' versions of the two, or one of the combined options. There are two ways of looking at this: one uses the system's ability to handle complexity as the main determinant of the decision, the other combines the volume and variety characteristics of the operation and the level of control required in order to make the choice.

The complexity determinant

Figure 15.15 distinguishes between the complexity of product structures and the complexity of the flow-path routings through which they must pass.[24] Simple product structures which have routings with high repeatability are prime candidates for pull control. JIT can easily cope with their relatively straightforward requirements. As structures and routings become more complex, so the power of the computer is needed in order to break down product structures and so to assign orders to suppliers.

In many environments, it is possible to use pull scheduling for the control of most internal materials. Again, prime candidates for pull control are materials which are used regularly each week or each month. Their number can be increased by design standardization, as indicated by the direction of the arrow in Fig. 15.15.

As structures and routings become even more complex, and parts usages become more irregular, so the opportunities for using pull scheduling decrease. Very complex structures require networking methods like PERT (program evaluation and review technique – *see* Chapter 16 on project planning and control) for planning and control. Such structures provide few opportunities for pull scheduling. However, even in this environment, a possible use for JIT is to limit the build-up of inventory, for example by means of kanban squares painted on the floor, so work cannot move to the next operation until a square is free.

The volume–variety and level of control determinants

Figure 15.16 again uses a matrix to determine the relative suitability of planning and control approaches. This time the dimensions are the type of production process and the level for which the control system is being designed.[25]

The *type of production* uses the volume–variety characteristics we have used before. Taken together they indicate the complexity of manufacturing. Variation in processing lead times, the number of alternative product routes, the complexity of product structures, and the variety of product types, can all be related to volume and variety.

The *level of control* indicates which set of production control tasks are being considered. High-level control involves broadly co-ordinating the flow of materials to the various parts of the plant, as well as giving an indication of what level of output they will be expected to achieve in future periods. Medium-level control is the detailed allocation of production orders to each part of the plant. Low-level control is the detailed monitoring and readjustment of day-to-day shop-floor activities.

Two of the areas in Fig. 15.16 need some explanation. Area A indicates that, in some high-volume automated-type manufacturing, the shop-floor level of control may be incorporated into the technology itself. For example, the integrated technologies of some food-processing plants automatically transfer materials from one part of the plant to another. It usually requires intervention on the part of operations management to prevent transfer occurring. Area B represents the detailed shop-floor scheduling and control in very complex, high-variety customized manufacture. Here it is the nature of each individual job which dominates the production control task. Specialized techniques such as network planning (PERT for example – *see* the next chapter) are usually needed.

Figure 15.15
Complexity as a determinant of an appropriate planning and control system
Source: from Voss, C.A. and Harrison, A.[24]

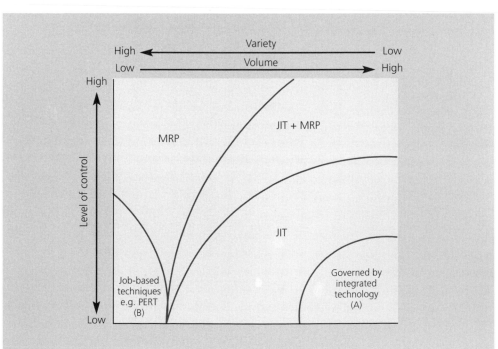

Figure 15.16
Volume–variety and the level of control as determinants of the appropriate planning and control system

Steve Millward, Rainford Group

Steve Millward is Manufacturing Director for the Rainford Group in Coventry, a company which has experienced rapid growth. One of Steve's key tasks, in the short term, is to manage that growth, by deciding on new policies and structures to give increased focus and control. Just-in-time manufacturing is one of these new policies.

The mainstream business for Rainford in Coventry is the supply of mobile telecommunications 'base station' structures to cellular communications companies. The markets themselves are booming, but Rainford has also decided to expand its core business by vertical integration and is moving into operations such as installation, testing and maintenance. Steve has worked with his management team to formulate their policy on the future direction of the business, and their priorities for improving the performance of the business so as to keep up with the rapid growth.

'We have recognized that we need to refocus in order to cope with the growth in both the volume and variety of our business,' he says *'and the key strategic issues and action points are based on restructuring the operation away from its present functional format, into a more product-oriented structure. We want to create smaller business units and cells, so we can manage on a more individual basis, focusing on the objectives in each particular sector of our market. As the business expands and the restructuring starts to take place, we are also going to use the opportunity to revise our manufacturing control systems. In some cells, we see the most appropriate means of controlling production as just-in-time control. The business is very regular in terms of the orders placed on the cells and is not particularly complex in terms of the number of variants required. To move the manufacturing operation to a JIT system, we are going to rearrange the layout in the assembly areas so that the product flows along a defined assembly path, with a provision for kanban boxes between each operating station. It will mean that one stage in the process will not progress a product until the next stage really does need it. This will effectively control the level of work-in-progress on the line, ensuring that the line will work at the pace of the slowest section. It will produce goods only when they are actually needed. We will also be using a levelled schedule in order to keep the production rates of each model steady and to provide some predictability in the cells. The analysis required to design the operation for JIT control involves balancing the level of activity at each station, so as not to create any bottle-necks. This load balancing can be done by increasing the number of people at some cells while increasing the number of tasks to be completed at others. Another issue of JIT involves the availability of the raw materials and parts for the operation. These will be stored in racks alongside the line, for easy access. The size of the racking and the components required for each area are still to be decided, but deliveries to the line will also be on a just-in-time basis.*

'It will be a big culture change, moving to a just-in-time type operation, not least in the area of quality inspection. At present, we have a dedicated team of quality inspectors, yet the JIT philosophy clearly states that quality should be built into the process, encouraging each operator to be responsible for the quality of his or her own work. Each member of the team will have to be able to identify any defects in the product as well as finding the solution to be identified and implemented. These issues are very much related to the development of integrated teams and the acceptance of a culture whereby questions are encouraged and ideas taken on board. We recognize that this will take time and that very much depends on the nature and attitude of the management in supporting and driving the process.

'It is very exciting looking at the issues in moving in this direction and we can see clear benefits in terms of control, but the changing from a batch and functional structure to a product group – cell layout with just-in-time delivery capability – is proving to be a bigger part of the challenge than we anticipated!' ■

SUMMARY ANSWERS TO KEY QUESTIONS

What is JIT and how is it different from traditional operations practice?

■ JIT (just-in-time) is an approach to operations which tries to meet demand instantaneously with perfect quality and no waste.

■ It is an approach which differs from traditional operations practices insomuch as it stresses waste elimination and fast throughput, both of which contribute to low inventories.

■ The ability to deliver just-in-time not only saves working capital (through reducing inventory levels) but also has a significant impact on the ability of an operation to improve its intrinsic efficiency.

What are the main elements of JIT philosophy?

■ As a philosophy, JIT can be summarized as concerning three overlapping elements. These are:

– the elimination of waste in all its forms (This is best visualized as the time wasted as materials, information or customers move through the system.);
– the inclusion of all staff of the operation in its improvement (In this way it is similar to some of the ideas described in Chapter 9.);
– the idea that all improvement should be on a continuous basis (This is explored in greater depth in Chapter 18.).

■ A common feature of JIT philosophy is the progressive removal of (surplus) resources so as to enable the operation to learn how to manage without these resources.

What are the techniques of JIT?

■ The techniques which are usually associated with JIT (not specifically concerned with planning and control, see next point) are:

– developing 'basic working practices' which support waste elimination and continuous improvement;

– design for manufacture;
– focused operations which reduce complexity;
– using simple, small machines which are robust and flexible;.
– rearranging layout and flow to enhance simplicity of flow;
– employing total productive maintenance (see Chapter 19) to encourage reliability;
– reducing set-up and change-over times to enhance flexibility;
– involving all staff in the improvement of the operation;
– making any problems visible to all staff;
– extending the above principles to suppliers.

How can JIT be used for planning and control?

■ Many JIT techniques directly concern planning and control. They are:

– pull scheduling
– kanban control
– levelled scheduling
– mixed-model scheduling
– synchronization of flow.

Can JIT be used in service operations?

■ Many of the above techniques are directly applicable in service operations although some translation occasionally is required.

Can JIT and MRP co-exist?

■ Although they may seem to be different approaches to planning and control, they can be combined in several ways to form a hybrid system.

■ The way in which they can be combined depends on the complexity of product structures, the complexity of product routing, the volume–variety characteristics of the operation and the level of control required.

Just-in-time at Jimmy's[26]

St. James's Hospital, affectionately known as 'Jimmy's', is Europe's largest teaching hospital. It employs around 4500 people to support the 90 000 in-patient treatments per year and over 450 000 total admissions. Under increasing pressure to reduce costs, to contain inventory and to improve service, the Supplies Department has recently undertaken a major analysis of its activities, helped by the consultancy division of Lucas Industries, the UK-based manufacturing company.

The initial review highlighted that Jimmy's had approximately 1500 suppliers of 15 000 different products at a total cost of £15 million. Traditionally, the Supplies Department ordered what the doctors asked for, with many cases of similar items supplied by six or more firms. Under a cross-functional task force, comprising both medical and supply staff, a major programme of supplier and product rationalization was undertaken, which also revealed many sources of waste. For example, the team found that wards used as many as 20 different types of gloves, some of which were expensive surgeons' gloves costing around £1 per pair, yet in almost all cases these could be replaced by fewer and cheaper (20 pence) alternatives. Similarly, anaesthetic items which were previously bought from six suppliers, were single-sourced. The savings in purchasing costs, inventory costs, and general administration were enormous in themselves, but the higher order volumes also helped the hospital negotiate for lower prices. Suppliers are also much more willing to deliver frequently in smaller quantities when they know that they are the sole supplier. Peter Beeston, the Supplies Manager, said,

'We've been driven by suppliers for years ... they would insist that we could only purchase in thousands, that we would have to wait weeks, or that they would only deliver on Wednesdays! Now, our selected suppliers know that if they perform well, we will assure them of a long-term commitment. I prefer to buy 80 per cent of our requirements from 20 or 30 suppliers, whereas previously, it involved over a hundred.'

The streamlining of the admissions process also proved fertile ground for improvement along JIT principles. For example, in the Urology Department, one third of patients for non-urgent surgery found their appointments were being cancelled. One reason for this was that in the time between the consultant saying that an operation was required and the patient arriving at the operating theatre, there were 59 changes in responsibility for the process. The hospital reorganized the process to form a 'cell' of four people who were given complete responsibility for admissions to Urology. The cell was located next to the ward and made responsible for all record keeping, planning all operations, ensuring that beds were available as needed, and telling the patient when to arrive. As a result the 59 handovers are now down to 13 and the process is faster, cheaper and more reliable.

Jimmy's also introduced a simple kanban system for some of its local inventory. In Ward Nine's store-room, for example, there are just two boxes of 10 mm syringes on the shelf. When the first is empty, the other is moved forward and the Ward Sister then orders another. The next stage will be to simplify the reordering: empty boxes will be posted outside the store, where codes will be periodically read by the Supplies Department, using a mobile data recorder.

The hospital's management are convinced of the benefits of their changes.

'Value for money, not cost cutting, is what this is all about. We are standardizing on buying quality products and now also have more influence on the buying decision ... from being previously functionally oriented with a number of buyers, we now concentrate on materials management for complete product ranges. The project has been an unmitigated success and although we are only just starting to see the benefits, I would expect savings in cost and in excess inventory to spiral! The report on Sterile Wound Care Packs shows the potential that our team has identified.

'The "old" pack consisted of:

— four pairs of plastic forceps
— cotton wool balls
— a plastic pot

which were used with or without additional gloves. This pack cost approximately 60 pence excluding the gloves. The 'new' pack consists of:

— a plastic pot
— swabs, etc.
— one pair of latex gloves only.

This pack costs approximately 33 pence including gloves. Total target saving is approximately £20 000.' ∎

Questions

1 List the elements in St. James's new approach which could be seen as deriving from JIT principles of manufacturing.

2 What further ideas from JIT manufacturing do you think could be applied in a hospital setting such as St. James's?

DISCUSSION QUESTIONS

1 Explain your views on whether you think that JIT is a philosophy, a strategy or a selection of techniques.

2 Why does continuous improvement require a long-term view of the business? Discuss what is meant by an 'enabling company culture' in which continuous improvement can flourish.

3 How do make-to-order businesses avoid waste?

4 Why are work-in-progress and lead time related? How does this relationship affect a building society on a Saturday morning?

5 If you were aiming to develop your company into a JIT company, what would you look for in your suppliers?

6 Simplicity is often a theme associated with JIT companies. How does Little Chef incorporate this theme into its management of operations?

7 What are the deficiencies of the Economic Order Quantity (EOQ) from a JIT point of view?

8 Explain how mixed modelling is used to develop a detailed operations schedule. How does this differ from a master schedule?

9 How can new technology be used to supply kanbans in a JIT operation?

10 Explain how JIT techniques can be used to support volume and mix flexibility in operations management.

11 Why is Jidoka (line-stop authority) described as a 'cornerstone of the Toyota Production System'?

12 Referring to the Temple Hospital case described in the text, explain the advantages of ordering materials at 'three different levels'. How did this lead to more accurate material provisioning to the physicians while stocks were actually reduced?

13 Explain the key differences between a 'traditional' approach and a JIT approach to manufacturing. Do these differences occur in service organizations?

14 Discuss the advantages and disadvantages of working just-in-time.

15 The elimination of waste is a core philosophy of JIT. What is meant by 'waste' and explain the origins and intentions of this approach?

16 Discuss the benefits of set-up time reduction on each of the five operations performance objectives: cost, flexibility, quality, dependability and speed.

17 Explain the difference between 'push' and 'pull' planning and control. Why might different organizations choose such approaches?

18 Discuss how kanbans might be applied, and the form they might take, in a fast-food restaurant.

19 A manufacturer of printed circuit boards (PCBs) is currently producing them at a rate of one every three minutes from a four-part container. The overall efficiency of the system has been estimated to be 90 per cent and the existing set-up times are 180 minutes per day. The management would like to develop a JIT system but with no more than three kanbans. To what level will set-up times need to be reduced to achieve this?

20 Discuss the benefits of reducing batch quantities.

21 What do you think might be the advantages and disadvantages of employing 'jidoka' in service organizations. Illustrate your answer using an organization of your choice.

NOTES ON CHAPTER

1 Bicheno, J. (1991) *Implementing Just-in-time*, IFS.
2 Voss, C.A. (1987) *in* Voss, C.A. (ed) *Just-in-time Manufacture*, IFS/Springer-Verlag.
3 Voss, C.A., *op. cit.*
4 Schonberger, R. (1982) *Japanese Manufacturing Techniques*, The Free Press.
5 Oliver, N. and Wilkinson, B. (1988) *The Japanization of British Industry*, Basil Blackwell.
6 Oliver, N. and Wilkinson, B., *op. cit.*
7 Harrison, A. (1992) *Just-in-time Manufacturing in Perspective*, Prentice Hall.
8 Lee, D.C. (1987) 'Set-up Time Reduction: Making JIT Work' *in* Voss, C.A. (ed), *Just-in-time Manufacture*, IFS/Springer-Verlag.
9 Quoted in Harrison, A., *op. cit.*
10 Quoted in Harrison, A., *op. cit.*
11 Kamata, S. (1983) *Japan in the Passing Lane: An Insider's Account of Life in a Japanese Auto Factory*, Allen and Unwin.
12 Harrison, A., *op. cit.*
13 Whitney, D.E. (1990) 'Manufacturing by Design', *Harvard Business Review*, Vol 68, No 4.
14 Skinner, W. (1978) *Manufacturing in the Corporate Strategy*, John Wiley.
15 Yamashina, H. 'Reducing Set-up Times Makes your Company Flexible and More Competitive', unpublished, quoted in Harrison A., *op. cit.*
16 Harrison, A., *op. cit.*
17 Source: 'Behind the Face of Beauty – Manufacturing Flexibility for the Mass Market', *Europlus*, Jan 1994.
18 Hall, R. (1987) *Attaining Manufacturing Excellence*, Dow Jones/Irwin.
19 Harrison, A., *op. cit.*
20 Parnaby, J. (1988) 'A Systems Approach to the Implementation of JIT Methodologies in Lucas Industries', *International Journal of Production Research*, Vol 26, No 3.
21 Parnaby, J., *op. cit.*
22 Berry, W.L., Talon, W.J. and Bol, W.J. (1988) *Production Structure Analysis for the Master Scheduling of Assemble-to-Order Products*, Working paper at the Centre for Manufacturing Excellence, Kenan Flagar School of Business, University of North Carolina.
23 Parnaby, J., *op. cit.*
24 Voss, C.A. and Harrison, A. (1987) 'Strategies for Implementing JIT' *in* Voss, C.A. (ed) *Just-in-time Manufacture*, IFS/Springer-Verlag.
25 Slack, N. (1991) *The Manufacturing Advantage*, Mercury Books.
26 Sources: *The Independent on Sunday*, 4 July 1993, *Update*, Issue 18, Aug 1993.

SELECTED FURTHER READINGS

Andersen Consulting (1992) *The Lean Enterprise Benchmarking Report*, Andersen Consulting/Cardiff Business School/Cambridge University.

Bennett, D.J. and Rajput, S.K. (1989) 'Design and Implementation of Production Systems for High Variety Electronics Assembly', *International Journal of Operations and Production Management*, Vol 9, No 5.

Bicheno, J. (1991) *Implementing JIT*, IFS Publications.

Cheng, T.C.E. and Podolsky, S. (1996) *Just-in-time Manfacturing* (2nd edn), Chapman and Hall.

Fiedler, K., Galletly, J.E. and Bicheno, J. (1993) 'Expert Advice for JIT Implementation', *International Journal of Operations and Production Management*, Vol 13, No 6.

Goyal, S.K. and Deshmukh, S.G. (1992) 'A Critique of the Literature on Just-in-time Manufacturing', *International Journal of Operations and Production Management*, Vol 12, No 1.

Harrison, A. and Voss, C. (1990) 'Issues in Setting up JIT Supply', *International Journal of Operations and Production Management*, Vol 10, No 2.

Harrison, A.S. (1992) *Just-in-Time Manufacturing in Perspective*, Prentice Hall.

Henricks, J.A (1994) 'Performance Measures for a JIT Manufacturer', *Industrial Engineering*, Vol 26, No 1.

Jordan, H.H. (1988) 'Inventory Management in the JIT Age', *Production and Inventory Management Journal*, Vol 29, No 13.

Kidd, P.T. (1994) *Agile Manufacturing: Forging New Frontiers*, Addison-Wesley.

Marisako, S. (1992) *Prices, Quality and Trust*, Cambridge University Press.

Murata, K. with Harrison, A.S. (1991) *How to Make Japanese Management Methods Work in the West*, Gower.

Oliver N. and Wilkinson, B. (1992) *The Japanization of British Industry* (2nd edn), Basil Blackwell.

Oliver, N. (1990) 'Human Factors in the Implementation of Just-in-time Production', *International Journal of Operations and Production Management*, Vol 10, No 4.

Schniederjans, M.J. (1993) *Topics in Just-in-Time Management*, Allyn & Bacon.

Schonberger, R.J. (1982) *Japanese Manufacturing Techniques: Nine Hidden Lessons in Simplicity*, The Free Press.

Schonberger, R.J. (1986) *World Class Manufacturing: The Lessons of Simplicity Applied*, The Free Press.

Schonberger, R.J (1996) *World Class Manufacturing: The Next Decade*, The Free Press.

Schonberger, R.J. and Schniederjans, M.J. (1983) 'Reinventing Inventory Control', *Interfaces*, Vol 13, No 3.

Sohal, A.S., Keller, A.Z. and Fouad, R.H. (1988) 'A Review of Literature Relating to JIT', *International Journal of Operations and Production Management*, Vol 8, No 3.

Sohal, A.S., Ramsey, L. and Samson, D. (1993) 'JIT Manufacturing Industry: Analysis and a Method for Implementation', *International Journal of Operations and Production Management*, Vol 13, No 7.

Vollmann, T., Berry, W.L. and Whybarck, D.C. (1992) *Manufacturing Planning and Control Systems* (3rd edn), Irwin.

Womack, J.P., Jones, D.T. and Roos, D. (1990) *The Machine that Changed the World*, Rawson Associates.

Womack, J.P. and Jones, D.T. (1996) *Lean Thinking: Banish Waste and Create Wealth in Your Corporation*, Simon and Schuster.

PROJECT PLANNING AND CONTROL

INTRODUCTION

This chapter is concerned with the planning and control of operations which occupy the low volume–high variety end of the continuum which we introduced in Chapter 4. These 'project' operations are engaged in complex, often large-scale, activities with a defined beginning and end. The pioneers of planning and controlling project operations were the engineers and planners who worked on complex defence and construction projects. More recently, the methods they developed have been applied to projects as diverse as new product launches, education projects in the Third World and theatrical productions. Project planning and control is important because all managers will, at some point, get involved with managing projects. Many of these projects may be relatively small – a Human Resources manager planning a training course, for example. Some will be far larger, for example where the manager is part of a project team – such as an accountant providing cost information for a new marketing promotion. Whether large or small, however, the planning and control aspects of managing projects follow similar principles *(see* Fig. 16.1).

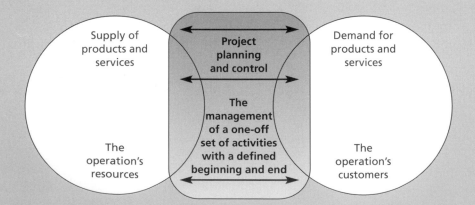

Figure 16.1 **A definition of project planning and control**

> ### CHAPTER 16: KEY QUESTIONS
>
> - *What is a project and project management?*
> - *Why is it important to understand the environment in which a project takes place?*
> - *How are specific projects defined?*
> - *What is project planning and why is it important?*
> - *What techniques can be used for project planning?*
> - *What is project control and how is it done?*

WHAT IS A PROJECT?

A project is a set of activities which has a defined start point and a defined end state, pursues a defined goal and uses a defined set of resources. Although many small-scale operations management endeavours conform to this definition of a project, we will devote the majority of this chapter to examining the management of larger-scale projects. The assumption of 'large projects' when we discuss project management provides us with the opportunity to explore some of the special characteristics which come with large-scale activities. Large-scale (and therefore complex) undertakings consume a relatively large amount of resources, take a long time to complete and typically involve interactions between different parts of an organization. To plan and control a project, managers need to devise a model which both describes the project's complexity and extends it forward in time to make sure that the project will achieve its goals. The model of the project (its plan) can then be used to check progress as the real project proceeds (control of the project).

The first project to be managed in a way which we would today recognize as project management was the Manhattan project which created the first atom bomb. However, the enterprises undertaken by the ancient civilizations were of a scale and complexity (even if the resources which they used were less constrained) to imply some form of organization. It is difficult to imagine the construction of the great pyramids of Egypt being achieved without an ordered, and systematic planning and control effort. Today projects come in many and various forms, including the following:

- the Apollo moon programme
- an AIDS information campaign
- producing a television programme
- constructing the Channel Tunnel
- designing the Airbus
- putting on a one-week course in project management
- relocating a factory
- refurbishing an hotel
- installing a new information system
- cleaning up after an oil tanker spillage.

The elements of a project

To a greater or lesser extent all these projects have some elements in common. These common elements form the characteristics which will help us to understand the nature of projects and therefore project planning and control.

- *An objective.* A definable end result, output, or product, which is typically defined in terms of the cost, the quality and timing of the output from the project activities.
- *Complexity.* Many different tasks are required to be undertaken to achieve a project's objectives. The relationship between all these tasks can be complex, especially when the number of separate tasks in the project is large.
- *Uniqueness.* A project is usually a 'one-off', not a repetitive undertaking. Even 'repeat' projects, such as the construction of another chemical plant to the same specification, will have distinctive differences in terms of resources used and the actual environment in which the project takes place.
- *Uncertainty.* All projects are planned before they are executed and therefore carry an element of risk. A 'blue sky' research project carries the risk that expensive, high technology resources will be committed with no worthwhile outcome.
- *Temporary nature.* Projects have a defined beginning and end, so a temporary concentration of resources is needed to carry out the undertaking. Once their contribution to the project objectives has been completed, the resources are usually redeployed.
- *Life cycle.* The resource needs for a project change during the course of its life cycle. The typical pattern of resource needs for a project follow a predictable path. From a planning and control perspective, it is therefore necessary to divide up the life cycle of a project into *project phases*.

These elements serve to distinguish projects from other types of operation. They also serve to distinguish *projects* from *programmes*. A *programme,* such as a continuous improvement programme (*see* Chapter 18), has no defined end point. Rather it is an ongoing process of change. Projects, such as the Apollo 12 mission, may be individual sub-sections of an overall programme (the Lunar Apollo Programme in this case). Programme management overlays and integrates the individual projects.

Although the management of projects is associated with operations of the low volume–high variety type, this does not mean that only these types of operation will be concerned with projects. High-volume and continuous production operations, such as a bulk chemical producer, will be a customer for projects. The chemical company's new plant will be constructed as a 'one-off' project, the plant will be maintained according to a project plan, its staff will be trained by services organized on a project basis, and so on. However, the operations which create these projects for the bulk chemical producer are likely to be of the low volume–high variety type (a construction company, maintenance contractors and the training department respectively). It is necessary, therefore, for managers in all types of operation to understand the nature of project planning and control. Even if their prime operations rationale is not to create projects, they are likely to be either customers for them or suppliers to them at some time.

A typology of projects

Selecting two of the above elements of projects, Fig. 16.2 illustrates a typology for projects according to their *complexity* – in terms of size, value and the number of people involved in the project – and their *uncertainty* of achieving the project objectives of cost, time and quality.

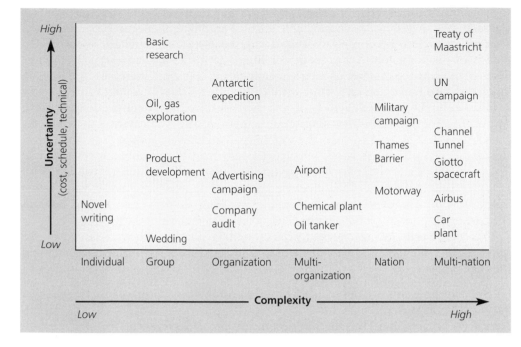

**Figure 16.2
A typology of
projects**
Source: Adapted from
Nicholas, J. M. (1990)
*Managing Business and
Engineering Projects:
Concepts and
Implementations*,
Prentice Hall

The typology helps to give a rational presentation of the vast range of undertakings where project management principles can be applied.[1] It also gives a clue to the nature of the projects and the difficulties of managing them. Uncertainty particularly affects project planning, and complexity particularly affects project control.

Projects with *high uncertainty* are likely to be especially difficult to define and set realistic objectives for. If the exact details of a project are subject to change during the course of its execution, the planning process is particularly difficult. Resources may be committed, times may be agreed, but if the objectives of the project change or if the environmental conditions change, or if some activity is delayed, then all the plans which were made prior to the changes will need to be redrawn. When uncertainty is high the whole project planning process needs to be sufficiently flexible to cope with the consequences of change. For example, the implementation of a political treaty in the European Union is subject to the ratification of all the member governments. Politics being an uncertain business, any of the member countries might either fail to ratify the treaty or attempt to renegotiate it. The central planners at EU headquarters must therefore have contingency plans in place which indicate how they might have to change the 'project' to cope with any political changes. Table 16.1 illustrates the effects of uncertainty on project planning.

Table 16.1 The effects of uncertainty on project planning

Aspect of project planning	Uncertainty	
	High	Low
Planning objectives	Evolving	Determined
Extent of planning	Ill defined	Clear
Outline of plan	Fuzzy	Defined

Projects with *high levels of complexity* need not necessarily be difficult to plan, although they might involve considerable effort; controlling them can be problematic, however. As projects become more detailed with many separate activities, resources and groups of people involved, the scope for things to go wrong increases alarmingly. Furthermore, as the number of separate activities in a project increases, the ways in which they can impact on each other increases exponentially. This increases the effort involved in monitoring each activity. It also increases the chances of overlooking some part of the project which is deviating from the plan. Most significantly, it increases the 'knock-on' effect of any problem. For example, in a relatively simple project with few activities (even if they are large) which are performed by organizationally separate resources, any delay or other problem can be reasonably well contained; it will not affect the other parts of the project. However, in a project with many separate activities with a high degree of dependency between them and involving shared resources, any delay in one part of the project will transmit its consequences to the rest of the project.

The (only partly joking) 'laws of project management' which were issued by the American Production and Inventory Control Society give a flavour of uncertain and complex projects:

1 No major project is ever installed on time, within budget, or with the same staff that started it. Yours will not be the first.

2 Projects progress quickly until they become 90 per cent complete, then they remain at 90 per cent complete for ever.

3 One advantage of fuzzy project objectives is that they let you avoid the embarrassment of estimating the corresponding costs.

4 When things are going well, something will go wrong.

– When things just cannot get any worse, they will.

– When things appear to be going better, you have overlooked something.

5 If the project content is allowed to change freely, the rate of change will exceed the rate of progress.

6 No system is ever completely debugged. Attempts to debug a system inevitably introduce new bugs that are even harder to find.

7 A carelessly planned project will take three times longer to complete than expected; a carefully planned project will take only twice as long.

8 Project teams detest progress reporting because it vividly manifests their lack of progress.

SUCCESSFUL PROJECT MANAGEMENT

There are some points of commonality in project success and failure, which allow us to identify some general points which seem to minimize the chances of a project failing to meet its objectives. The following factors are particulary important:[2]

● *Clearly defined goals*: including the general project philosophy or general mission of the project, and a commitment to those goals on the part of the project team members.

● *Competent project manager*: a skilled project leader who has the necessary interpersonal, technical, and administrative skills.

● *Top-management support*: top-management commitment for the project that has been communicated to all concerned parties.

- *Competent project team members*: the selection and training of project team members, who between them have the skills necessary to support the project.
- *Sufficient resource allocation*: resources, in the form of money, personnel, logistics, etc., which are available for the project in the required quantity.
- *Adequate communications channels*: sufficient information is available on project objectives, status, changes, organizational conditions, and client's needs.
- *Control mechanisms*: the mechanisms which are in place to monitor actual events and recognize deviations from plan.
- *Feedback capabilities*: all parties concerned with the project are able to review the project's status, and make suggestions and corrections.
- *Responsiveness to clients*: all potential users of the project are concerned with and are kept up to date on the project's status.
- *Trouble-shooting mechanisms*: a system or set of procedures which can tackle problems when they arise, can trace them back to their root cause and resolve them.
- *Project staff continuity*: the continued involvement of key project personnel through its life. Frequent turnover of staff can dissipate the team's acquired learning.

Project managers

In order to co-ordinate the efforts of many people in different parts of the organization (and often outside it as well), all projects need a project manager. Put simply, the role of the project manager is to achieve the project objectives. They do this by planning and controlling the project from initiation to conclusion, trying to bring order to complexity and reducing the level of uncertainty. Many of a project manager's activities are concerned with managing human resources. The people working in the project team need a clear understanding of their roles in the (usually temporary) organization. They must take responsibility for effective communication. Controlling an uncertain project environment requires the rapid exchange of relevant information with the project stakeholders, both within and outside the organization. They also need to procure all the resources for the project. People, equipment and other resources must be identified and allocated to the various tasks. Finally, they are concerned with controlling uncertainty by forecasting, planning for, and resolving problems. Undertaking these tasks successfully makes the management of a project a particularly challenging operations management activity. Five characteristics in particular are seen as important in an effective project manager:[4]

- background and experience which are consistent with the needs of the project;
- leadership and strategic expertise, in order to maintain an understanding of the overall project and its environment, while at the same time working on the details of the project;
- technical expertise in the area of the project in order to make sound technical decisions;
- interpersonal competence and the people skills to take on such roles as project champion, motivator, communicator, facilitator and politician;
- proven managerial ability in terms of a track record of getting things done.

PROJECT FAILURE AT THE LONDON AMBULANCE SERVICE[3]

An ambulance service deals in life and death. Its fast and accurate response to emergency calls and its paramedic skills can dictate the survival of any of us when we are at our most vulnerable.

On 26 October 1992 the ambulance service in the UK's capital city was thrown into utter disarray. The computer system which logged emergency calls to the service, traced and dispatched ambulances and monitored the status of each emergency had malfunctioned under the strain of trying to cope with only a slightly higher than average number of emergency calls. On a normal day the service could expect to deal with around 2300 calls. On that day the number had risen to 2900 but it broke the system. Calls were left unanswered, whole banks of logged calls were wiped off the system and the service's target response time of 14 minutes extended into the distance. The whole of the service was paralysed. The failure had caused incalculable pain, suffering, and perhaps death, and the root cause of it was bad project management.

The three-person team of inquiry which later investigated the failure put the blame directly on the recently installed computer system. The project management team which had designed, commissioned and installed the system had, according to the inquiry team, '... *made virtually every mistake in the book*'.

- The project was always a 'high-uncertainty' investment in a new technology. This was never fully appreciated. It was an over-ambitious project which had an unrealistic total project time of two years. Five years might have been a better estimate.
- Procurement rules for buying in services concentrated on quantitative criteria to the detriment of qualitative criteria.
- The budget for the project of £1.5 million was too low. Around £4 million would have been more realistic.
- The whole culture of the project revolved around a fear of failure and, despite early signs of problems, the management team had pressed on.
- The project manager's qualifications and motivation were questioned.
- One part of the software development was sub-contracted to a small software house who had little experience of handling projects of this complexity or scope.
- The installation team at the contract company had failed to meet the initial programme schedule of January '92 and, under pressure to stay on track, had installed and tested the system on a piece meal basis throughout the year.
- There was insufficient ownership of the system by its developers and mistrust by its users.
- There was insufficient training of the staff who eventually had to use the system. ∎

Questions

1 What do you think should have been the major objectives for the project of installing the new system?

2 Review the criticisms of the enquiry team and identify which part of the total project management activity they refer to.

THE PROJECT PLANNING AND CONTROL PROCESS

Figure 16.3 proposes a project management model which is used as a framework for this chapter. The model categorizes project management activities into five stages, four of which are relevant to project planning and control.

Stage 1 Understanding the project environment – internal and external factors which may influence the project.

Stage 2 Defining the project – setting the objectives, scope and strategy for the project.

Stage 3 Project planning – deciding how the project will be executed.

Stage 4 Technical execution – performing the technical aspects of the project.

Stage 5 Project control – ensuring that the project is carried out according to plan.

We shall examine project planning and control under the headings of stages 1, 2, 3, and 5 – the project environment, project definition, project planning and project control. (Stage 4, the technical execution of the project, is determined by the specific technicalities of individual projects.) However, it is important to understand that the stages are not a simple sequential chain of steps; it is essentially an *iterative* process. Problems or changes which become evident in the control stage may require replanning and may even cause modifications to the original project definition.

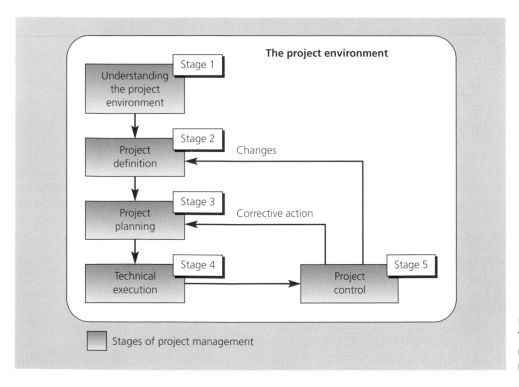

Figure 16.3
The project management model

Stage 1 – Understanding the project environment

The project environment comprises all the factors which may affect the project during its life. It determines the setting and circumstances in which the project is executed. Examples of factors which may affect the environment are shown in Fig. 16.4.

Understanding the importance of the environment in which a project will be undertaken is essential for two reasons. First, the environment influences the way a project is executed. For example, the scale, timing and nature of any other projects being carried out by an organization could affect the plans which are drawn up for a new project. Second, the environment of the project is the main determinant of the uncertainty which will be inherent in it. For example, the state of a supplier's financial security will influence a project management's willingness to use them.

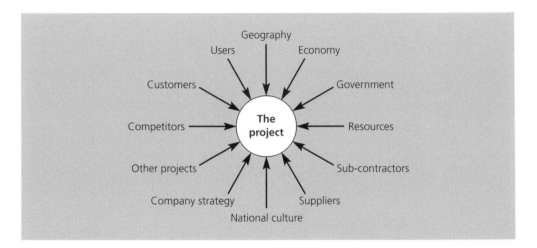

Figure 16.4
The project environment consists of all the factors which can affect the project

Example: An overseas education agency

The governments of many countries have agencies which organize the distribution of overseas aid by managing specific development projects in partnership with the host government. Such projects might include the building of schools, the design and development of a teacher education scheme, and the organization of a primary health education programme. Many environmental factors will affect the individual projects undertaken by an agency. The following are examples:

● *Geography*. Land-locked countries such as Afghanistan can be subject to serious shipment delays through neighbouring countries, which can extend activity times.
● *Finance*. Fluctuating commodity prices may impact on the ability of host governments to meet their resource commitments to a project.
● *Politics*. The political stance taken by the host government and the possibility of internal political dissent can influence the scale and timing of the project.
● *Local laws*. Local laws can vary considerably and influence the resources needed for a project. For example, in francophone African countries, local labour law allows employees to take three days' absence when a close relative dies. With large families, this can cause serious losses of staff availability which must be allowed for at the planning stage.

● *National culture.* Developing an understanding of host country cultures is crucial to success in overseas projects. Even when a single language is being used by project managers, there can be differences in the meaning of words or phrases. People in some cultures may not be comfortable giving a direct response to some questions, so while a project manager from one country might say that 'work has not started', a project manager from another might say that the 'work is not yet complete'. The subtle difference in meaning could lead to costly misinterpretation.

● *Users.* The full needs and expectations of users are not always apparent to outside agencies. For example, water wells built with World Bank patronage in the Ivory Coast were built in a forest area which is held sacred by local people – they remain unused.

Stage 2 – Project definition

Before starting the complex task of planning and executing a project, it is necessary to be as clear as possible about what is going to be done. This is not always straightforward. Some projects are simpler to define than others. Projects where all the major tasks have been done before – such as the construction of a repeat coal-fired power station, where methods and equipment have already been proven – can be defined reasonably well in advance. Completely new projects – such as a major one-off aerospace project like the Giotto satellite construction and launch (*see* box, pp. 611–12) – will be much more difficult to define. Three different elements are needed to define a project:

● *its objectives*: the end state which project management is trying to achieve;
● *its scope*: the exact range of the responsibilities taken on by project management;
● *its strategy*: how project management is going to meet its objectives.

Project objectives

A project's objectives provide the overall direction for the project and help staff to focus on the rationale of the project and its expected results. Paradoxically, objective setting requires the project manager to start at the end of the project: that is to decide what end state must be achieved before the project could be deemed a success. Objectives help to provide a definition of the end point which can be used to monitor progress and to identify when success has been achieved. Yet the judgement on the success of a project can depend on who is asked. For example, a project to design and install a new production planning and control information system in a factory might be regarded as successful by the customer who commissioned the project (the Information Systems Department) but less so by the people who use the new system (the production controllers). This is why it is useful to phrase the objectives of a project in *user terms*.

The hierarchy of objectives

The objectives of each part of the project must be related to its overall objective or goal. The goal to '... place an American on the moon this decade and to return him safely to earth ...' dictated the objectives of all the projects which contributed to achieving it. Within those projects (each of them major in their own right) the objectives of each sub-project will have been related to the project's objectives, and so on. In other words, any project can be disaggregated into a set of sub-projects whose objectives form an hierarchy.

Objectives must be clear

Good objectives are those which are clear, measurable and, preferably, quantifiable. If they are not clear it is difficult to assess whether the project has been successful. One method of clarifying objectives which has been found helpful is to break down project objectives into three categories – the purpose, the end results, and the success criteria. For example, a project which is expressed in general terms as 'improve process X' could be broken down into:

- *Purpose* – to prevent production from failing to meet output targets as forecast.
- *End result* – a report which identifies the causes of lost production, and which recommends how the target output can be met.
- *Success criteria* – the report should be completed by 30 June. The recommendation should enable output to reach at least 70 tonnes per year. Cost of the recommendations should not exceed £100 000.

Performance objectives in project management

Projects, like any other operations, can be judged in terms of the five performance objectives we outlined in Chapter 2 – quality, speed, dependability, flexibility and cost. However, the convention in project management is slightly different. First, flexibility is regarded as a 'given' in most projects which, by definition, are to some extent one-offs. Second, speed and dependability are compressed to one composite objective – 'time'. This results in what are known as the 'three objectives of project management' – cost, time and quality.

- *Cost.* Although money is a 'flexible' resource within the project, the project's overall cost is set at the outset. A key project management task is to control resources so that the planned cost is not exceeded.
- *Time.* Time is a totally inflexible resource: once a day has passed, nothing can bring it back. Although activities can be shortened, the time to complete a project can only be changed through a redefinition of its objectives.
- *Quality.* The output from a project undertaking must be fit for its intended purpose; that is, it must work as it is supposed to. (The various aspects of quality will be explored fully in Chapter 17.)

The relative importance of each objective will differ for different projects. Some aerospace projects, such as the development of a new aircraft, which impact on passenger safety, will place a very high emphasis on quality objectives. With other projects, for example, in a research project that is being funded by a fixed government grant, cost might predominate. Other projects emphasize time, for example the organization of an open-air music festival has to happen on a particular date if the project is to meet its objectives. In each of these projects, although one objective might be particularly important, the other objectives can never be totally forgotten. Figure 16.5 shows the 'project objectives triangle' with these three types of project marked.[5]

Project scope

The second part of a project's definition is the project scope. The scope of a project identifies its work content and its products or outcomes. It is essentially a boundary-setting exercise which attempts to define the dividing line between what each part of the project will do and what it won't do. This helps clarify the responsibilities of all the parties who are involved in the project. Defining scope is particularly important for

Figure 16.5
The project
objectives triangle

managing contractors because of the commercial and legal aspects of an outside contractor's relationship with the organization which is managing the project. A contractor's *scope of supply* will identify the boundaries within which the work must be done.

In general, defining the scope of a project or work package is helped by defining the following:

- *The parts of the organization which are affected*: for example, 'designing and installing an automated guided vehicle system in the warehouse up to the receiving bay'.
- *The time period involved*: for example, 'installation to begin no earlier than 15 January and to be completed no later than 2 March'.
- *The business processes involved*: for example, 'to interface with the current order retrieval system and stock location system'.
- *The resources to be used*: for example, 'to provide own power supply and limit the number of staff working on the installation to five at any one time'.
- *The contractor's responsibilities*: for example, 'to include all ancillary power and information supply systems, full maintenance schedules and initial training'.

The project specification

The scope of the project is formalized in the *project specification*, which is the written, pictorial and graphical information used to define the output, and the accompanying terms and conditions. Although written before the project starts, changes may have to be made to the scope which was originally specified. Better ways of doing things are often recognized only after work has begun. This is illustrated by the larger feedback loop in Fig. 16.3. There are two broad categories of change which need to be considered: internal and external changes. *Internal changes* result from decisions by the project management to do things differently from the original specification. For example, a chemical plant construction company might decide to change the type of storage vessel originally specified because a superior one was not available at the time the project specification was agreed. *External changes* occur when a customer has decided to change the specification. For example in a defence project, a European air force may need to change the specification of the communication equipment in an aircraft if the agreed standards change within NATO. The difference between these two types of change in a commercial project can be very important. Often the company managing the project can demand payment for external changes, but not for internal changes.

Project strategy

The third part of a project's definition is the project strategy. The project strategy defines, in a general rather than specific way, how the organization is going to achieve its project objectives and meet the related measures of performance. It does this in two ways. First, the project strategy should define the *phases* of the project. Phases break the project down into time-based sections. The phases may be very simple, for example the beginning, the middle and the end phases, or more detailed. Although there may be considerable overlap and iteration between phases, they are a valuable way of conceiving the project and simplifying the process of project definition. In the case of a software development project, the phases might be as follows:

- *Specification phase*: where customer requirements are specified, and a systems specification is drawn up.
- *Design phase*: where systems design and sub-system specifications are determined.
- *Implementation phase*: where modules are specified.
- *Module-testing phase*: where each module is tested separately.
- *Integration-testing phase*: where sub-systems and finally the complete system are tested.
- *Delivery phase:* where the system is handed over to the customer.

Second, the project strategy should set milestones. Milestones are important events during the project's life at which specific reviews of time, cost and quality are made. They are the significant points in the project which indicate whether it is on schedule. At this stage the actual dates for each milestone are not necessarily determined – that will probably come later in the planning stage. It is useful, however, to at least identify the significant milestones, either to define the boundary between phases or to help in discussions with the customer.

For example, the milestones which are defined for the production of a television commercial campaign might be as follows:

Milestone 1	Overall concept agreed with client
Milestone 2	Story-board outline prepared and agreed
Milestone 3	Shooting fully planned and organized
Milestone 4	First portfolio presented to client
Milestone 5	Final cut agreed with client.

Stage 3 – Project planning

The planning process fulfils four distinct purposes:

- It determines the cost and duration of the project. This enables major decisions to be made – such as the decision whether to go ahead with the project at the start.
- It determines the level of resources which will be needed.
- It helps to allocate work and to monitor progress. Planning must include the identification of who is responsible for what.
- It helps to assess the impact of any changes to the project.

Planning is not a one-off process. It may be repeated several times during the project's life as circumstances change. Nor is replanning a sign of project failure or mismanagement. In uncertain projects especially, it is a normal occurrence. In fact later stage plans typically mean that more information is available, and that the project is becoming less uncertain. The process of project planning involves five steps (*see* Fig. 16.6). Each of these processes is now described, followed by an illustration of its application to a simple 'project'.

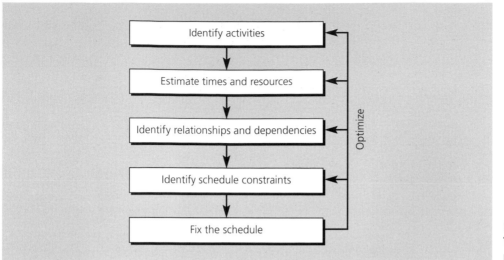

Figure 16.6
The process of
project planning

Identify activities – the work breakdown structure

Most projects are too complex to be planned and controlled effectively unless they are first broken down into manageable portions. This is achieved by structuring the project into a 'family tree', along similar lines to the bill of materials (Chapter 14). But unlike the bill of materials, which specifies items, this specifies the major tasks or sub-projects. These in turn are divided up into smaller tasks until a defined, manageable series of tasks called a *work package* is arrived at. Each work package can be allocated its own objectives in terms of time, cost and quality. The output from this is called the *work breakdown structure* (WBS). The WBS brings clarity and definition to the project planning process. It shows 'how the jigsaw fits together'.[6] It also provides a framework for building up information for reporting purposes.

Example project
As a simple example to illustrate the application of each stage of the planning process, let us examine the following domestic project.

The project definition is:

● *purpose:* to make breakfast in bed;
● *end result:* breakfast in bed of boiled egg, toast and orange juice;
● *success criteria:* plan uses minimum staff resources and time, and product is high quality (egg freshly boiled, warm toast, etc.);
● *scope:* project starts in kitchen at 6.00 am, and finishes in bedroom; needs one operator and normal kitchen equipment.

The work breakdown structure is based on the above definition and can be constructed as shown in Fig. 16.7

Estimate times and resources

The next stage in planning is to identify the time and resource requirements of the work packages. Without some idea of how long each part of a project will take and

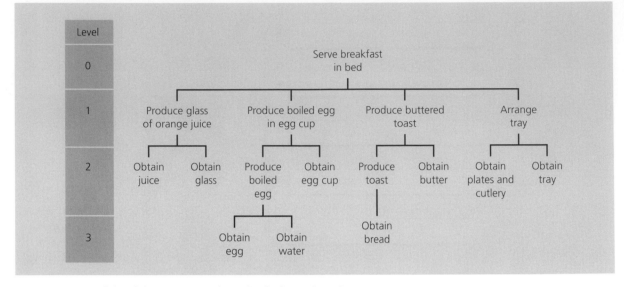

Figure 16.7 A work breakdown structure for a simple domestic project

how many resources it will need, it is impossible to define what should be happening at any time during the execution of the project. Estimates are just that, however – a systematic best guess, not a perfect forecast of reality. Estimates may never be perfect but they can be made with some idea of how accurate they might be. The more effort is put into making an estimate, the better it should be. To some extent, therefore, the accuracy of a forecast reflects the willingness of project managers to spend time and money on obtaining it. This will depend on what use is going to be made of the estimate. The degree of accuracy of an estimate is strongly related to the stage of the project's life when it is used. At the start of a project when a rough 'ball park' estimate is needed, the actual figure only has an 'illustrative' value, whereas during the detailed execution of the project, final 'definitive' estimates are needed for control on a day-to-day basis.

Example project

Returning to our very simple example 'breakfast-in-bed' project, the activities were identified and times estimated as in Table 16.2.

While some of the estimates may appear generous, they take into account the time of day and the state of the operator.

Probabilistic estimates

The amount of uncertainty in a project has a major bearing on the level of confidence which can be placed on an estimate. The impact of uncertainty on estimating times leads some project managers to use a probability curve to describe the estimate. In practice, this is usually a positively skewed distribution, as in Fig. 16.8. The greater the risk, the greater the range of the distribution. The natural tendency of some people is to produce *optimistic* estimates, but these will have a relatively low probability of being correct because they represent the time which would be taken if *everything* went well. *Most likely* estimates have the highest probability of proving correct. Finally,

Table 16.2 Time and resources estimates for a 'breakfast-in-bed' project

Activity	Effort (person-min)	Duration (min)
Butter toast	1	1
Pour orange juice	1	1
Boil egg	0	4
Slice bread	1	1
Fill pan with water	1	1
Bring water to boil	0	3
Toast bread	0	2
Take loaded tray to bedroom	1	1
Fetch tray, plates, cutlery	1	1

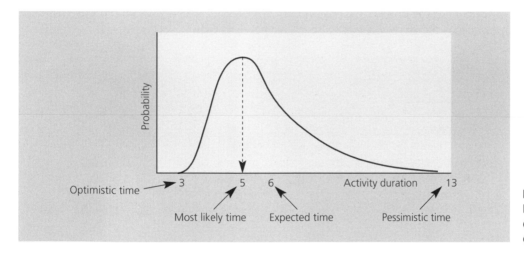

Figure 16.8 Probability distribution of time estimates

pessimistic estimates assume that almost everything which could go wrong does go wrong. Because of the skewed nature of the distribution, the expected time for the activity will not be the same as the most likely time.

Identify relationships and dependencies

All the activities which are identified as comprising a project will have some relationship with one another which will depend on the logic of the project. Some activities will, by necessity, need to be executed in a particular order. For example, in the construction of a house, the foundations must be prepared before the walls are built, which in turn must be completed before the roof is put in place. These activities have a *dependent* or *series* relationship. Other activities do not have any such dependence on each other. The rear garden of the house could probably be prepared totally independently of the garage being built. These two activities have an *independent* or *parallel* relationship.

603

Example project

Table 16.2 identified the activities for the breakfast preparation project. The list shows that some of the activities must necessarily follow others. For example, 'boil egg' cannot be carried out until 'fill pan with water' and 'bring water to boil' have been completed. Further logical analysis of the activities in the list shows that there are two major 'chains', where activities must be carried out in a definite sequence:

> Slice bread – Toast bread – Butter toast
> Fill pan with water – Bring water to boil – Boil egg

Both of these sequences must be completed before the activity 'take loaded tray to bedroom'. The remaining activities ('pour orange juice' and 'fetch tray, plates, cutlery') can be done at any time provided that they are completed before 'take loaded tray to bedroom'. An initial project plan might be as shown in Fig. 16.9. Here, the activities have been represented as blocks of time in proportion to their estimated durations. From this, we can see that the 'project' can be completed in nine minutes. Some of the activities have spare time (called float) indicated by the dotted line. The sequence 'Fill pan – Boil water – Boil egg – Bedroom' has no float, and is called the *critical path* of the project. By implication, any activity which runs late in this sequence would cause the whole project to be delayed accordingly.

**Figure 16.9
Initial project plan
for a simple project**
Source: Courtesy of Neil Anderson, DCE

Identify schedule constraints

Once estimates have been made of the time and effort involved in each activity, and their dependencies identified, it is possible to compare project requirements with the available resources. The finite nature of critical resources – such as special skills – means that they should be taken into account in the planning process. This often has the effect of highlighting the need for more detailed replanning. There are essentially two fundamental approaches:[7]

- *Resource constrained.* Only the available resource levels are used in resource scheduling, and are never exceeded. As a result, the project completion may slip. Resource-limited scheduling is used, for example, when a project company has its own highly specialized assembly and test facilities.
- *Time constrained.* The overriding priority is to complete the project within a given time. Once normally available resources have been used up, alternative ('threshold') resources are scheduled.

Example project

Returning to the breakfast-in-bed project, we can now consider the resource implications of the plan in Fig. 16.9. Each of the four activities scheduled at the start (pour orange, cut bread, fill pan, fetch tray) consume staff resources. Charting the required resources will give a resource profile as in Fig. 16.10. There is clearly a resource-loading problem, because the project definition states that only one person is available. This is not an insuperable difficulty, however, because there is sufficient float to move some of the activities. A plan with levelled resources can be produced which is shown in Fig. 16.11. All that has been necessary is to delay the toast preparation by one minute, and to use the elapsed time during the toasting and water-boiling processes to pour orange and fetch the tray.

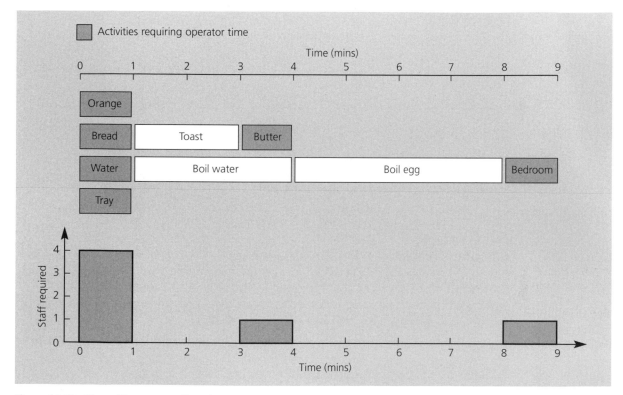

Figure 16.10 Plan with resource allocation

Fix the schedule

Project planners should ideally have a number of alternatives to choose from. The one which best fits project objectives can then be chosen or developed. For example, it may be appropriate to examine both resource-limited and time-limited options. However, it is not always possible to examine several alternative schedules. Especially in very large or very uncertain projects, as the computation could be prohibitive. However, modern computer-based project management software is making the search for the best schedule more feasible.

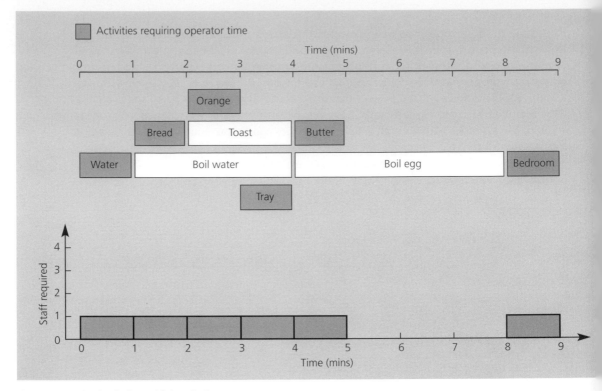

Figure 16.11 Revised plan with levelled resources

Example project

A further improvement to the plan can yet be made. Looking again at the project definition, the success criteria state that the product should be 'high quality'. In the plan shown in Fig. 16.11, although the egg is freshly boiled, the toast might be cold. An 'optimized' plan which would provide hot toast would be to prepare the toast during the 'boil egg' activity. This plan is shown in Fig. 16.12.

Stage 5 – Project control

The stages in project planning and control have so far all taken place before the actual project takes place. This stage deals with the management activities which take place during the execution of the project. Project control is the essential link between planning and doing.

The process of project control involves three sets of decisions:

● how to *monitor* the project in order to check on its progress;
● how to *assess the performance* of the project by comparing monitored observations of the project with the project plan;
● how to *intervene* in the project in order to make the changes which will bring it back to plan.

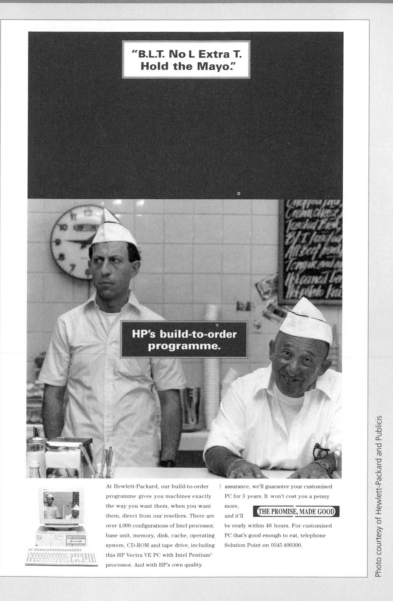

"B.L.T. No L Extra T. Hold the Mayo."

HP's build-to-order programme.

At Hewlett-Packard, our build-to-order programme gives you machines exactly the way you want them, when you want them, direct from our resellers. There are over 4,000 configurations of Intel processor, base unit, memory, disk, cache, operating system, CD-ROM and tape drive, including this HP Vectra VE PC with Intel Pentium® processor. And with HP's own quality assurance, we'll guarantee your customised PC for 3 years. It won't cost you a penny more, and it'll be ready within 48 hours. For customised PC that's good enough to eat, telephone Solution Point on 0345 400300.

THE PROMISE, MADE GOOD

Photo courtesy of Hewlett-Packard and Publicis

In this advertisement for Hewlett-Packard computers, an analogy is made between the way we ask for variations on standard products and when we buy a meal (in this case a BLT – bacon, lettuce and tomato sandwich) and the way we cannot always do the same for more complex products.

- *Why is this type of customization important for competitiveness?*
- *Why does offering customers product variety in products such as motor cars and computers create problems for the operation which makes them?*
- *What do you think H-P might have done to help it overcome the problems posed by product variety?*

➔ *Look at Chapter 2 for guidance*

The Channel Tunnel

During the construction of the Channel Tunnel

The £15 billion Channel Tunnel project was the largest construction project ever undertaken in Europe and the biggest single investment in transport anywhere in the world. The project, which was funded by the private sector, made provision for a 55-year concession for the owners to design, build and run the operation. The Eurotunnel Group (technically two holding companies, one French and one in the UK) awarded the contract to design and build the tunnel to TML (Trans-Manche Link), a consortium of ten French and British construction companies. For the project managers it was a formidable undertaking. The sheer scale of the project was daunting in itself. The volume of rubble removed from the tunnel was three times greater than that of the Cheops Pyramid in Egypt. It increased the size of Britain by 90 acres, equivalent to 68 football fields. Two main railway tunnels, split by a service/access tunnel, each 7.6 metres in diameter, run 40 metres below the sea bed. In total there are in excess of 150 kilometres of tunnel. The whole project was never going to be a straight-forward management task. During the early negotiations, political uncertainty surrounded the commitment of both governments, and in the planning phase geological issues had to be investigated by a complex series of tests. Even the financing of the project was complex. It required investment by over 200 banks and finance houses, as well as over half a million shareholders. Furthermore, the technical problems posed by both the drilling itself and, more importantly, in the commissioning of the tracks and systems within the tunnel, needed to be overcome. Yet in spite of some delays and cost over-runs, the project ranks as one of the most impressive of the twentieth century.

- *What factors made the Channel Tunnel a particularly complex project and how might these have been dealt with?*
- *What factors contributed to 'uncertainty' in the project and how might these factors have been dealt with?*

➜ *Look at Chapter 16 for guidance*

Process control at Walkers

Photo courtesy of Walkers Ltd

A team leader records process control data at Walkers Snack Foods

Walkers Snack Foods Limited, part of the worldwide Pepsico Company, operates in a highly competitive sector of the fast-moving consumer goods (FMCG) market. With increasingly discriminating customers, they need the competitive edge of high quality manufacturing to help them retain customer satisfaction. This means that they must keep close control of all their manufacturing processes, a task which is especially difficult when success of your products means booming sales and therefore continually increasing production volumes. Walkers use a version of statistical process control, which they call 'control point management' (CPM) to maintain and improve their quality levels. The picture shows a team leader in the company's Doritos plant completing control chart sheets. The control points in the manufacturing process where process variables are measured are all specified for each production line. If any measurements fall outside the control limits, procedures in the form of decision trees help to guide the production technicians in bringing the process back within standard.

- *What do you think are the characteristics of product quality for Walkers products which influence overall customer satisfaction? (Sample a packet and discuss this with friends!)*
- *Why is it important that direct production staff, as opposed to managers or engineers, collect and analyse process data?*
- *What purpose do the 'corrective' decision trees serve in controlling the process?*

→ *Look at Chapter 17 for guidance*

Virtual project management

Photo courtesy of CADCENTRE

CADCENTRE's Visuality group visualization system enables project teams to check and validate design proposals using interactive computer models

The oil industry has always placed high value on project management. Cost and time over-runs in the construction of off-shore facilities or on-shore refineries can mean the difference between profit and loss in the early years of most capital projects. The operating companies themselves are increasingly stepping back from hands-on engineering activities to focus more on their core business. They are relying on project management experts who can integrate services extending from design and fabrication to maintenance and asset management. The working practices of these project management collaborators are also changing. Advanced computer-aided systems are helping to facilitate a new approach to major project design and management.

The picture above shows examples of this. Here, project teams are viewing computer models of an off-shore structure using CADCENTRE plant design software and visualization system. This allows them to check out not only the original design but any modifications that have to be made during construction. More detailed CAD images can be used for more specific analysis.

- *Why do you think a realistic picture of a completed project helps the process of project management?*
- *Why are such visualizations becoming more important?*

→ *Look at Chapter 16 for guidance*

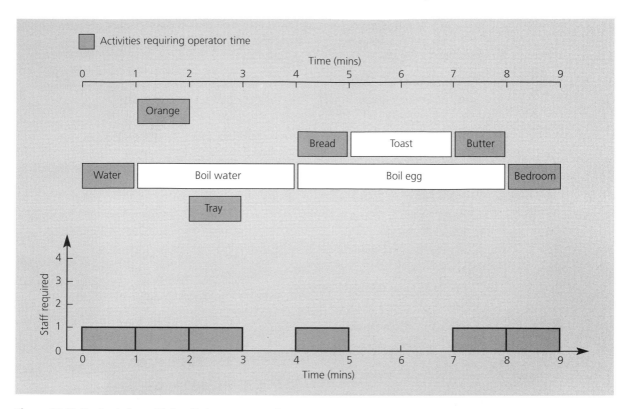

Figure 16.12 Revised plan with levelled resources and warm toast

Project monitoring

Project managers have first to decide what they should be looking for as the project progresses. The project objectives triangle in Fig. 16.5 helps in this matter. If the main objectives of project management are cost, quality and time, then that is what should be monitored. Usually a variety of measures are monitored, some of which relate directly to one of the performance objectives and some of which indicate problems with two or all three of them. Table 16.3 illustrates some typical monitored measures and the main performance objectives which they affect.

Note how some monitored measures in Table 16.3 affect mainly cost, some mainly time, but when something affects the quality of the project there are also time and cost implications. This is because quality problems in project planning and control usually have to be solved in a limited amount of time.

Assessing project performance

The monitored measures of project performance at any point in time need to be assessed so that project management can make a judgement concerning overall performance. Again this is done for all three project performance objectives: cost, quality and time. Most detailed effort often goes into assessing cost and time, however. Quality problems will show up (as we noted earlier) as cost and time problems eventually.

Table 16.3 Monitored measures and their effect on project performance objectives

Monitored measure	Main performance objectives affected
Costs exceeding budget	Cost
Cash running low	Cost
Supplier price changes	Cost
Excessive overtime	Cost
Changes in project scope	Quality, Time, Cost
Technical performance poor	Quality, Time, Cost
Inspection failures	Quality, Time, Cost
Errors in information	Quality, Time, Cost
Waiting for resource delays	Time, Cost
Supplier delays	Time, Cost
Customer changes delivery date	Time, Cost
Activities not started on time	Time
Activities not finished on time	Time
Missed milestones	Time

A typical planned cost profile of a project through its life is shown in Fig. 16.13. At the beginning of a project some activities can be started, but most activities will be dependent on others finishing. As more activities finish, therefore, even more can be started. Finally, only a few activities remain to be completed. This pattern of a slow start followed by a faster pace with an eventual tail-off of activity holds true for almost all projects, which is why the rate of total expenditure follows an S-shaped pattern as shown in Fig. 16.13, even when the cost curves for the individual activities are linear. For any particular project a planned cost or expenditure curve can be drawn in this way, derived from the activity schedule. It is against this curve that actual costs can be compared in order to check whether the project's costs are being incurred to plan. Figure 16.14 shows the planned and actual cost figures compared in this way. It shows that the project is incurring costs, on a cumulative basis, ahead of what was planned.

Earned-value control

The 'earned-value' method of project control assesses performance of the project by combining cost and time together. Rather than measure the progress of the project in days, it measures it in the value of the work done. A project which has a total value of £100 000, therefore, would be half complete when the value of the activities which have actually been completed is £50 000. Figure 16.15 shows the progress of a project measured on an earned-value basis. It shows actual cost incurred against work completed. Because the work done is measured in monetary units, the line which represents the project plan will be at 45 degrees. That means that when £10 000 worth of work has been completed the expenditure should have actually been £10 000, and so on. It actually shows that, at the end of three periods, this project has completed

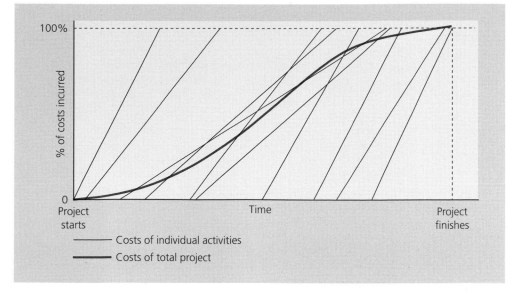

Figure 16.13
Typical S-shaped cost curve for the total project

£50 000 worth of work when it should have completed £60 000 worth. Furthermore, the actual cost it has incurred is £65 000. These three figures each have terms to describe them:

● *The budgeted cost of work scheduled* (BCWS) is the amount of work which should have been completed by a particular time (£60 000 in our example).
● *The budgeted cost of work performed* (BCWP) is the actual amount of work which has been completed by a particular time (£50 000 in our example).
● *The actual cost of work performed* (ACWP) is the actual expenditure which has been spent on doing the work completed by a particular time (£65 000 in our example).

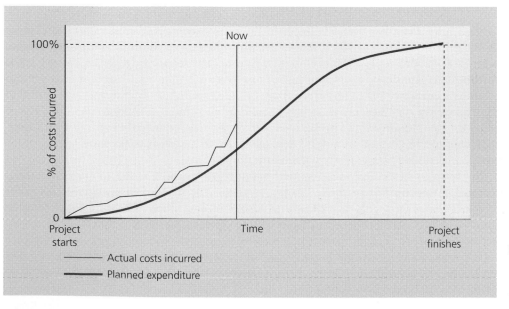

Figure 16.14
Comparing planned with actual expenditure

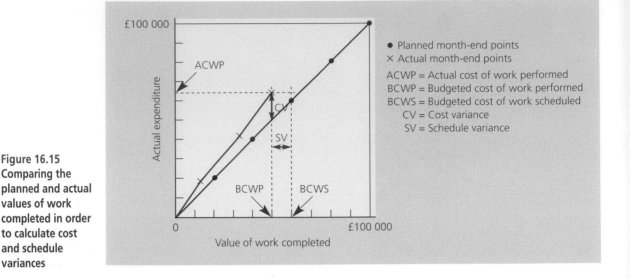

Figure 16.15 Comparing the planned and actual values of work completed in order to calculate cost and schedule variances

From these three figures two *variances*, which indicate the deviation from plan, can be derived.

Schedule variance (SV) = BCWP – BCWS

In our example: SV = £50 000 – £60 000
= – £10 000

Cost variance (CV) = BCWP – ACWP

In our example: CV = £50 000 – £65 000
= – £15 000

Intervening to change the project

Once a judgement has been made concerning the current performance of a project, a decision is needed as to whether project managers need to intervene in the project activity. If the project is obviously out of control in the sense that its costs, quality levels or times are significantly different from those planned, then some kind of intervention is almost certainly likely to be required. The exact nature of the intervention will depend on the technical characteristics of the project, but it is likely to need the advice of all the people who would be affected. Given the interconnected nature of projects – a change to one part of the project will have knock-on effects elsewhere – this means that interventions often require wide consultation.

Sometimes intervention is needed even if the project looks to be proceeding according to plan. For example, Fig. 16.16 shows the schedule and cost variances for a project, together with the 'allowable range' of variance. These are the tolerance limits between which the variance can move without it indicating that there is necessarily a problem. The project appears to be on target. When the project managers look forward and project activities and cost into the future, however, they see that problems are very likely to arise. In this case it is the *trend* of performance which is being used to trigger intervention.

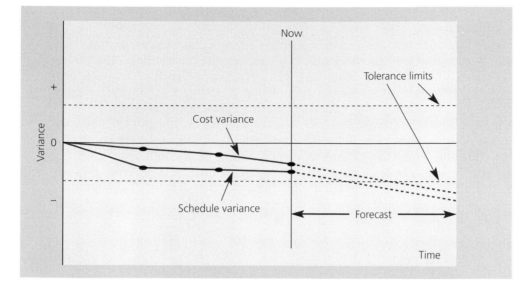

Figure 16.16
Plotting cost and schedule variance over time and forecasting from the trend

ONCE IN A LIFETIME[8]

The opportunity to carry out some projects comes just once in a lifetime. Such projects cannot be late. The Giotto project was of this type. Giotto was the name given to the spacecraft designed to intercept Halley's Comet when it was 100 million miles away from Earth on the 2 July 1985. The project was funded and managed by the European Space Agency (ESA) and contracted out in the main part to British Aerospace. The accepted payload consisted of ten experiments which were designed to establish, in more detail than ever before, the exact characteristics and composition of the comet. If the project missed the launch date significantly the whole project would have been judged a massive waste of millions of ECUs.

The ten experiments on board were contributed by various groups in 11 different member countries. Although this enhanced the international image of the project, it also added to the complexity of a project which was dominated by a demanding and inflexible completion requirement. Leading up to the delivery of the spacecraft, the project moved through four phases which were termed (1) concept, (2) sub-system definition and bids, (3) project definition and formal bid for delivery and (4) procurement and assembly. During the project, emphasis was placed by all parties on co-operation between the management team from the ESA and its international partners. The cost management involved initial capital proposals and then a reassessment of the costs after the first two phases of the project. All the activities which made up the programme of work were planned in fine detail and all planning information placed on a central computer system which was visible to all involved. Any modifications were dealt with very quickly. The policy was never to have more than three or four outstanding modifications over any three-week period, so as to reduce the amount of uncertainty in the project. This relied on the team paying particular attention to ensuring visible and efficient client contact or relationships. The team made considerable use of network planning methods such as PERT (*see* later section) which were particularly useful in keeping all information on the current state of, and the future plans for, the project fully visible.

▶

Like many large scientific organizations, the European Space Agency has an intricate hierarchy of standards and approval procedures, all of which are time consuming. The project could never have been completed to schedule if the agency had not adopted a 'fast-track' procedure for getting approval through its various committees. It screened, in principle, aspects of technical compliance, feasibility and the financial resources backing any proposal.

The spacecraft was eventually shipped, on time, to the launch site on 29 April 1985 for trials and the final countdown to launch on 30 June 1985. The project itself was very successful, intercepting the comet as planned and contributing enormously to scientific knowledge and analysis of such phenomena. The final cost of developing and constructing the craft did overshoot its budget by about 10 per cent, which at the time was a relatively small amount for a project of this type. Good project planning and control, a clear project definition and disciplined project management had all played their part. ■

Questions

1 How would you classify this project on the complexity–uncertainty matrix?

2 How would you define the environment of this project?

3 How do you think the project management team balanced its objectives in this project?

NETWORK PLANNING

The process of project planning and control, which we have described in this chapter, is greatly aided by the use of techniques which help project managers to handle its complexity and time-based nature. The simplest of these techniques is the Gantt chart (or bar chart) which we introduced in Chapter 10. This spawned later techniques, most of which go under the collective name of *network analysis*. It is these which are now used, almost universally, to help plan and control all significant projects but which can also prove helpful in smaller ventures. The two network analysis methods we will examine are the *critical path method* (CPM) or *analysis* (CPA) and *program evaluation and review technique* (PERT).

Example

An example of a Gantt chart used to plan a project is shown in Fig. 16.17. The chart is being used to plan and monitor the implementation of a new logistics operation. The new operation will involve the purchase of a fleet of trucks, the design of new routes and the building of a new distribution centre and associated handling equipment. The following major activities are planned:

1 *Design logistics solution*. Approximately three months' duration, given good data and direction from customer. (Key task is getting information from people who are not directly involved with the project.)

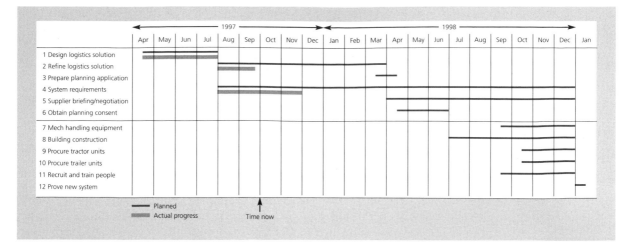

Figure 16.17 Implementing new logistics operation: Gantt chart
Source: Courtesy of Dan Ellerton, Exel Logistics

2 *Refine logistics solution.* An ongoing process which must be kept on track once an outline has been selected. (It must be completed before suppliers can be briefed.)

3 *Prepare planning application.* Needs four weeks. (Building specification must be ready first.)

4 *System requirements.* An ongoing process of integrating information systems. (All systems are available, but they must be integrated into overall project objectives.)

5 *Supplier briefing/negotiation.* New procedures need to be explained on an ongoing basis to all suppliers by the central co-ordination team.

6 *Obtain planning consent.* Statutory time is eight weeks, but experience suggests that 12 weeks is the norm.

7 *Mechanical handling equipment.* Lead time is currently 12 weeks for standard equipment, up to 16 weeks for specialist. (Have assumed standard. This activity includes design and layout of racking.)

8 *Building construction.* This would be six months for a 100 000 square foot building. (Weather can have a major impact.)

9 *Tractor procurement.* Currently 10 to 12 weeks' lead time.

10 *Trailer procurement.* Eight weeks standard to 12 weeks for special requirements.

11 *Recruit and train.* Need to start recruitment of 100 staff three months before start-up. (Training to start two weeks before start-up.)

12 *Prove new system.* Two weeks are needed for system trials, proving and final training.

The length of the bar for each activity is directly proportional to the calendar time, and so indicates the relative duration of each activity. Progress against each activity is shown by the lower strips. The arrow which shows 'time now' indicates that all activities to the left should by now have been completed. Gantt charts are the simplest way to exhibit an overall project plan, because they have excellent visual impact and are easy to understand. They are also useful for communicating project plans and status to senior managers as well as for day-to-day project control. However, Gantt charts are limited in the number of activities which they can handle before they become too 'busy'.

Critical path method (CPM)

As project complexity increases, so it becomes necessary to identify the relationships between activities. It becomes increasingly important to show the logical sequence in which activities must take place. The two fundamental relationships which we described earlier were:

- *activities in series:* where activity A must be completed before activity B can start;
- *activities in parallel:* where activity B can proceed while activity A is still proceeding.

Critical path method (CPM) models the project by clarifying the relationships between activities diagrammatically. The first way we can illustrate this is by using arrows to represent each activity in a project. For example, examine the simple project in Fig. 16.18 which involves the decoration of an apartment. Six activities are identified together with their relationships. The first, activity a, 'remove furniture', does not require any of the other activities to be completed before it can be started. However, activity b, 'prepare bedroom', cannot be started until activity a, 'remove furniture', has been completed. The same applies to activity d, 'prepare the kitchen'. Similarly activity c, 'paint bedroom', cannot be started until activity b has been completed. Nor can activity e, 'paint the kitchen', be started until the kitchen has been prepared. Only when both the bedroom and the kitchen have been painted can the apartment be furnished again. The logic of these relationships is shown as an arrow diagram, where each activity is represented by an arrow (the length of the arrows are not proportional to the duration of the activities).

This arrow diagram can be developed into a network diagram as shown in Fig. 16.19. At the tail (start) and head (finish) of each *activity* (represented by an arrow) is a circle which represents an *event*. Events are moments in time which occur at the start or finish of an activity. They have no duration and are of a definite recognizable nature. Networks of this type are composed only of activities and events.

The rules for drawing this type of network diagram are fairly straightforward.

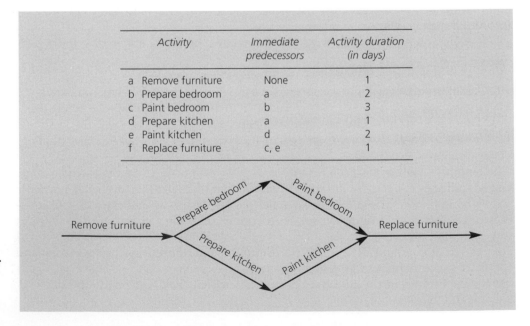

Activity	Immediate predecessors	Activity duration (in days)
a Remove furniture	None	1
b Prepare bedroom	a	2
c Paint bedroom	b	3
d Prepare kitchen	a	1
e Paint kitchen	d	2
f Replace furniture	c, e	1

Figure 16.18 The activities, relationships, durations and arrow diagram for the project 'decorate apartment'

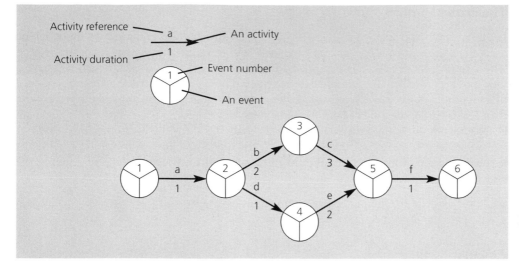

Figure 16.19
A network diagram for the project 'decorate apartment'

Rule 1 An event cannot be reached until all activities leading to it are complete. Event 5 in Fig. 16.19 is not reached until activities c and e are complete.

Rule 2 No activity can start until its tail event is reached. In Fig. 16.19 activity f cannot start until event 5 is reached.

Rule 3 No two activities can have the same head and tail events. In Fig. 16.20 activities x and y cannot be drawn as first shown; they must be drawn using a *dummy activity*.

Dummy activities have no duration and are usually shown as a dotted line arrow. They are used either for clarity of drawing or to keep the logic of the diagram consistent with that of the project.

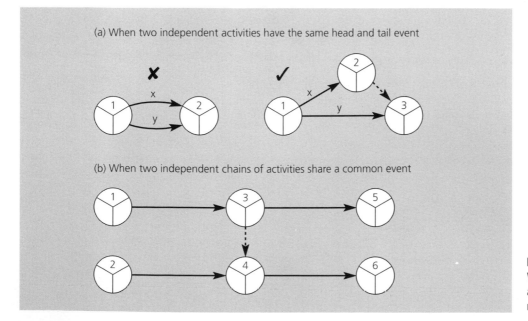

Figure 16.20
When dummy activities are necessary

The critical path

In all network diagrams where the activities have some parallel relationships there will be more than one sequence of activities which will lead from the start to the end of the project. These sequences of activities are called *paths* through the network. Each path will have a total duration which is the sum of all its activities. The path which has the longest sequence of activities is called the *critical path* of the network (note that it is possible to have more than one critical path if they share the same joint longest time). It is called the critical path because any delay in any of the activities on this path will delay the whole project.

In Fig. 16.19, therefore, the critical path through the network is a, b, c, f, which is seven days long. This is the minimum duration of the whole project. By drawing the network diagram we can:

● identify which are the particularly important activities, and
● calculate the duration of the whole project.

Calculating float

Earlier in the chapter we described the flexibility to change the timings of activities, which is inherent in various parts of a project, as *float*. We can use the network diagram to calculate this for each activity. The procedure is relatively simple.

1 Calculate the earliest and latest event times for each event. The earliest event time (EET) of an event is the very earliest the event could possibly occur if all preceding activities are completed as early as possible. The latest event time (LET) for an event is the latest time that the event could possibly take place without delaying the whole project.
2 Calculate the 'time window' within which an activity must take place. This is the time between the EET of its tail event and the LET of its head event.
3 Compare the actual duration of the activity with the time window within which it must take place. The difference between them is the float which the activity has.

Consider again the simple network example. The critical path is the sequence of activities a, b, c, f. We can calculate the EET and LET for each event as shown in Fig. 16.21. If activity a starts at time 0, the earliest it can finish is 1 because it is a one-day activity. If activity b is started immediately, it will finish at day 3 (EET of tail event + duration, 1 + 2). Activity c can then start at day 3 and because it is of three days' duration it will finish at day 6. Activity e also has event number 5 as its head event so we must also calculate the EET of activity e's tail event. This is determined by activity d. If activity d starts at day 1 (the earliest it can) it will finish at day 2. So the EET of event number 4 is day 2. If activity e is started immediately, it will then finish at day 4. Event

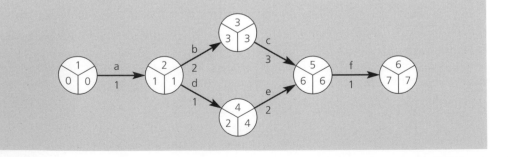

**Figure 16.21
A network diagram
for the project
'decorate
apartment' with
earliest and latest
event times**

number 5 cannot occur, however, until both e and c have finished, which will not be until day 6 (*see* rule 1 above). Activity f can then start and will finish at day 7.

The LETs can be calculated by using the reverse logic. If event number 6 *must* occur no later than day 7, the LET for event number 5 is day 6. Any later than this and the whole project will be delayed. Working back, if activity c must finish by day 6 it cannot start later than day 3, and if activity b must finish by day 3 it must start by day 1. Similarly, if activity e is to finish by day 6 it must start no later than day 4, and if activity d is to finish by day 4 it must start no later than day 3. Now we have two activities with event number 2 as their tail event, one of which needs to start by day 1 at the latest, the other by day 3 at the latest. The LET for event number 2, therefore, must be the smaller of the two. If it was delayed past this point, activity b, and therefore the whole project, would be delayed.

Activity on node networks

The network we have described so far uses arrows to represent activities and circles at the junctions or nodes of the arrows to represent events. This method is called the *activity on arrow* (AoA) method. An alternative method of drawing networks is the *activity on node* (AoN) method. In the AoN representation activities are drawn as boxes and arrows are used to define the relationships between them. There are three advantages to the AoN method:

● It is often easier to move from the basic logic of a project's relationships to a network diagram using AoN rather than using the AoA method.
● AoN diagrams do not need dummy activities to maintain the logic of relationships.
● Most of the computer packages which are used in project planning and control use an AoN format.

An AoN network of the 'apartment decorating' project is shown in Fig. 16.22.

Figure 16.22 Activity on node network diagram for project 'decorate apartment'

Example

Returning to the 'new logistics' operation described previously, an AoN network diagram is shown in Fig. 16.23. In this example (as in most realistic examples) relationships are not always clear cut. For example, 'Refine logistics' has been shown as impacting only on 'Supplier negotiation'. In practice, it would also impact on 'System requirements', and probably also on the design issues in activities 7 through 11. Such relationships could be shown on a lower-level network, which goes into more detail on such issues. The activity on System requirements is a sub-project in itself, and would require its own bar charts and logic diagrams for planning and monitoring.

Figure 16.23 New logistics operation: logic diagram

Time analysis

Figure 16.24 provides a full AoN network for the simple logic diagram in Fig. 16.23. Activity numbers and abbreviated descriptions are as before.

The *earliest start times* for each activity are found by working from left to right across the network. Each start event can begin at *t*=0. At a 'merge' event (where two or more activities come together, as at event 12), use the latest completion date of the various activities which lead into it. Earliest finish times of a 'burst' activity (such as activity 6, where five succeeding activities literally 'burst' out) are carried forward to form the earliest start dates of the succeeding activities (7 through 11).

The *latest start times* for each activity are found by working back from right to left across the network. The earliest start time for the final event on the network is often used as the latest start time for that event as well. At a 'merge' event (such as event 6), use the earliest completion date of the various activities.

First, we carry out a *forward pass* of the network (i.e. proceed from left to right). Activity 1 is given a start date of week 0. The earliest finish is then week 17, because the duration is 17 weeks. The earliest start date for activity 2 must then also be week 17. Activity 5 starts at 17 + 34, the duration for activity 2. Activity 4 is in parallel with activity 2, and can start at the same time. The rest of the forward pass is straightforward until we reach activity 12. Here, seven activities merge, so we must use the highest earliest finish of the activities which lead into it as the earliest start time for activity 12. This is 91 (the earliest finish time for activity 4). Since the duration of activity 12 is two weeks, the earliest finish time for the whole network is 93 weeks.

Now we can carry out a *backward pass* by assuming that the latest finish time is also 93 weeks (the bottom right-hand box on activity 12). This means that there is no

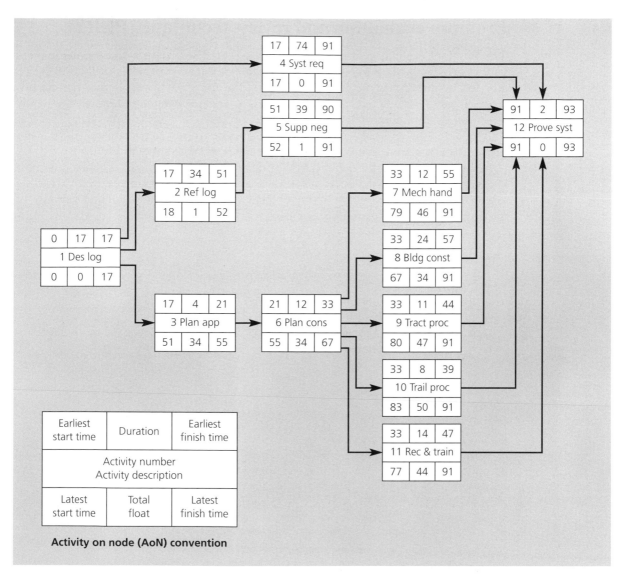

Figure 16.24 New logistics operation: precedence network

'float', i.e. the difference between the earliest and latest start dates for this activity is zero. Hence, the latest start time is also week 91. This gets downdated into activities 7 through 11, which have week 91 as the latest finish time. The difference between week 91 and the various earliest finish times for these activities means that there is float on each one, that is that they can start much later than indicated by the earliest start dates. On the backward pass, activity 6 forms a merge event for activities 7 through 11. Take the lowest latest start time from these activities, i.e. week 67, as the latest finish time for activity 6. If all goes well, and the analysis is correct, there should also be zero float for activity 1. The *critical path* for the network is then the line which joins the activities with minimum float, i.e. activities 1, 4 and 12.

Program evaluation and review technique (PERT)

The program evaluation and review technique, or PERT as it is universally known, had its origins in planning and controlling major defence projects in the US Navy. The first reported success was the completion of the Polaris missile programme two years ahead of schedule in 1958. PERT had its most spectacular gains in the highly uncertain environment of space and defence projects. The technique recognizes that activity durations and costs in project management are not deterministic (fixed), and that probability theory can be applied to estimates, as was shown in Fig. 16.8.

In this type of network each activity duration is estimated on an optimistic, a most likely and a pessimistic basis, as shown in Fig. 16.25. If it is assumed that these time estimates are consistent with a beta probability distribution, the mean and variance of the distribution can be estimated as follows:

$$t_e = \frac{t_o + 4t_l + t_p}{6}$$

where

t_e = the expected time for the activity
t_o = the optimistic time for the activity
t_l = the most likely time for the activity
t_p = the pessimistic time for the activity

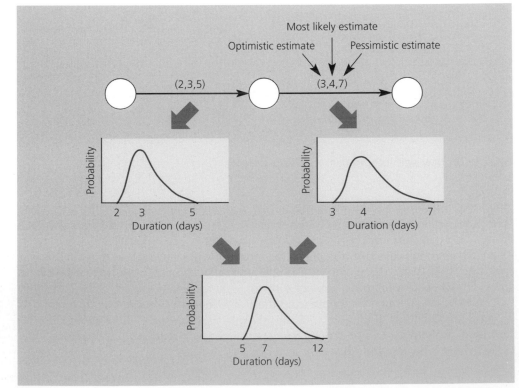

Figure 16.25 Probabilistic time estimates can be summed to give a probabilistic estimate for the whole project

The variance of the distribution (V) can be calculated as follows:

$$V = \frac{(t_p - t_o)^2}{6^2} = \frac{(t_p - t_o)^2}{36}$$

The time distribution of any path through a network will have a mean which is the sum of the means of the activities which make up the path, and a variance which is a sum of their variances. In Fig. 16.25:

The mean of the first activity $= \dfrac{2 + (4 \times 3) + 5}{6} = 3.17$

The variance of the first activity $= \dfrac{(5 - 2)^2}{36} = 0.25$

The mean of the second activity $= \dfrac{3 + (4 \times 4) + 7}{6} = 4.33$

The variance of the second activity $= \dfrac{(7 - 3)^2}{36} = 0.44$

The mean of the network distribution $= 3.17 + 4.33 = 7.5$

The variance of the network distribution $= 0.25 + 0.44 = 0.69$

It is generally assumed that the distribution for the whole path will be normally distributed.

The advantage of this extra information is that we can examine the 'riskiness' of each path through a network as well as its duration. For example, Fig. 16.26 shows a simple two-path network. The top path is the critical one, the distribution of its

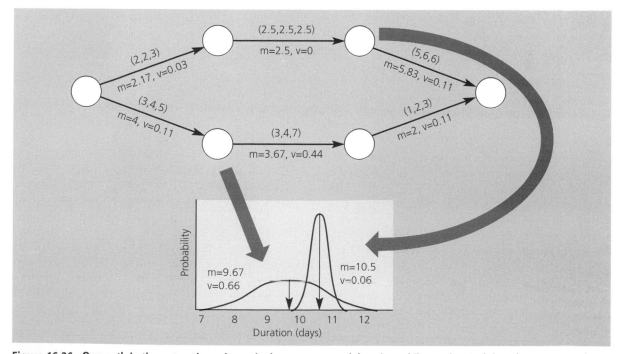

Figure 16.26 One path in the network can have the longest expected duration while another path has the greater variance

621

duration is 10.5 with a variance of 0.06 (therefore a standard deviation of 0.245). The distribution of the non-critical path has a mean of 9.67 and a variance of 0.66 (therefore a standard deviation of 0.812). The implication of this is that there is a chance that the non-critical path could in reality be critical. Although we will not discuss the probability calculations here, it is possible to determine the probability of any sub-critical path turning out to be critical when the project actually takes place. However, on a practical level, even if the probability calculations are judged not to be worth the effort involved, it is useful to be able to make an approximate assessment of the riskiness of each part of a network.

Introducing resource constraints

The logic which governs network relationships is primarily derived from the technical details of the project as we have described. However, the availability of resources may impose its own constraints which can materially affect the relationships between activities. Figure 16.27 shows a simple two-path network with details of both the duration of each activity and the number of staff required to perform each activity. The total resource schedule is also shown. The three activities on the critical path, a, c, and e, have been programmed into the resource schedule first. The remaining activities all have some float and therefore have flexibility as to when they are performed.

The resource schedule in Fig. 16.27 has the non-critical activities starting as soon as is possible. This results in a resource profile which varies from seven staff down to three. Even if seven staff are available, the project manager might want to even out the loading

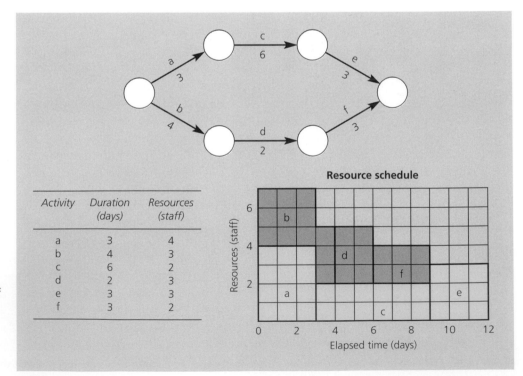

Figure 16.27 Resource profile of a network assuming that all activities are started as soon as possible

Activity	Duration (days)	Resources (staff)
a	3	4
b	4	3
c	6	2
d	2	3
e	3	3
f	3	2

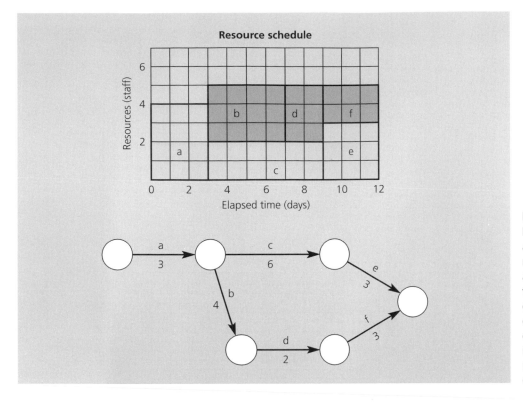

Figure 16.28
Resource profile of a network with non-critical activities delayed to fit resource constraints; in this case this effectively changes the network logic to make all activities critical

for organizational convenience. If the total number of staff available is less than seven, however, the project will need rescheduling. Suppose only five staff are available. It is still possible to complete the project in the same time, as shown in Fig. 16.28. Activity b has been delayed until after activity a has finished. This results in a resource profile which varies only between four and five staff and is within the resourcing limit of five staff.

However, in order to achieve this it is necessary to *require* activity b to start only when activity a is completed. This is a logic constraint which, if it were included in the network, would change it as shown in Fig. 16.28. In this network all activities are critical, as indeed one can see from the resource schedule.

Crashing networks

Crashing networks is the process of reducing time spans on critical path activities so that the project is completed in less time. Usually, crashing activities incurs extra cost. This can be as a result of:

- overtime working;
- additional resources, such as manpower;
- sub-contracting.

Figure 16.29 shows an example of crashing a simple network. For each activity the duration and normal cost are specified together with the (reduced) duration and (increased) cost of crashing them. Not all activities are capable of being crashed; here activity e cannot be crashed. The critical path is the sequence of activities a, b, c, e. If

623

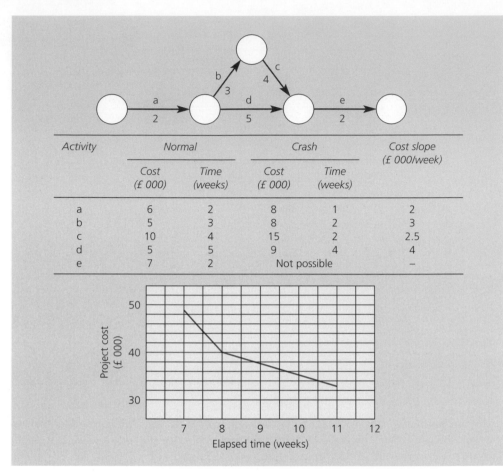

Activity	Normal		Crash		Cost slope (£ 000/week)
	Cost (£ 000)	Time (weeks)	Cost (£ 000)	Time (weeks)	
a	6	2	8	1	2
b	5	3	8	2	3
c	10	4	15	2	2.5
d	5	5	9	4	4
e	7	2	Not possible		–

**Figure 16.29
Crashing activities
to shorten project
time becomes
progessively more
expensive**

the total project time is to be reduced, one of the activities on the critical path must be crashed. In order to decide which activity to crash, the 'cost slope' of each is calculated. This is the cost per time period of reducing durations. The most cost-effective way of shortening the whole project then is to crash the activity on the critical path which has the lowest cost slope. This is activity a, the crashing of which will cost an extra £2000 and will shorten the project by one week. After this, activity c can be crashed, saving a further two weeks and costing an extra £5000. At this point all the activities have become critical and further time savings can only be achieved by crashing two activities in parallel.

The shape of the time-cost curve in Fig. 16.29 is entirely typical. Initial savings come relatively inexpensively if the activities with the lowest cost slope are chosen. Later in the crashing sequence the more expensive activities need to be crashed and eventually two or more paths become jointly critical. Inevitably by that point, savings in time can only come from crashing two or more activities on parallel paths.

Mike Ross, Project Management Services

Mike Ross, Managing Director of Project Management Services, founded the company to provide project management expertise to the automotive industry world-wide. During his career as an engineer in the UK car industry he has been responsible for many different developments, both of new vehicles and 'model year face-lifts'. Manufacturers often use specialist contractors to provide part of the engineering capability which they require to ensure fast product introduction. With large numbers of contractors involved, it is critical that new products are developed in a cohesive manner. Strong project management is essential.

'South East Asia is emerging as the fastest growing automotive market, and we are very active there. For example, we've assisted one company to engineer its first completely new car. Our client lacked the technical and organizational skills to tackle a project of that scale. The only experience it had was in assembling kits. But this did not deter it from wanting to develop the car, build a new factory, and source most of the parts locally, all in 36 months or less! One of our roles is to inject a sense of reality at the planning stage of the project. In particular we need to alert clients to the external factors which could influence the outcome of the project. For example, we make it our business to understand the supply and lead time constraints of key components. There are often very few suppliers of some advanced technologies such as engine management systems, headlight systems, air-conditioning equipment, and it may be very difficult to obtain suitable designs and supplies of these for a new vehicle. We also help the clients to evaluate the business risks involved in long projects, and the impact of changing legislation around the world, such as the tightening of exhaust emissions and safety regulations.

'Our professional project managers have to be able to select and use appropriate tools and techniques to plan and control the tasks. For small projects, such as the introduction of a new alloy wheel, we find that simple Gantt charts are usually adequate for the work. Larger complex projects such as complete new vehicles demand the use of computer-based techniques such as CPA.

'But the biggest challenge is the human side of project management. In my experience getting the right blend of people in the team greatly enhances the chance of success – it's all about people, and the technical, communication, and business skills that they bring to the team. The stronger they are, the less need there is for formal organization.

'However, project review must always be done formally. The critical path is the focus of our attention at all times, and the teams at every level must be kept up to date about their part in the whole picture. The project manager must pay attention to every detail, taking both the "helicopter" and the "microscope" view!

'It is fascinating to see how different organizations, in different cultures, and in different business situations tackle projects which are broadly very similar. The common features are that each requires engineering excellence at the lowest cost and as fast as possible, but there the similarities end!' ■

SUMMARY ANSWERS TO KEY QUESTIONS

What is a project and project management?

■ A project is a set of activities which has a defined start point and a defined end state, that pursues a defined goal and uses a defined set of resources.

■ All projects can be characterized by their degree of complexity and the inherent uncertainty in the project.

■ Project management is the process of managing the activities within a project by planning the work, executing it, and co-ordinating the contribution of the staff and organizations who have an interest in the project.

■ Project management has five stages, four of which are relevant to project planning and control. These are:
Stage 1 – understanding the project environments;
Stage 2 – defining the project;
Stage 3 – planning the project;
Stage 4 – technical execution of the project (not part of project planning and control);
Stage 5 – project control.

Why is it important to understand the environment in which a project takes place?

■ It is important for two reasons. First, the environment influences the way a project is carried out. Second, the nature of the environment in which a project takes place is the main determinant of the uncertainty surrounding it.

How are specific projects defined?

■ Projects can be defined in terms of:
– their objectives: the end state which project management is trying to achieve;
– their scope: the exact range of the responsibilities taken on by project management;
– their strategy: how project management is going to meet the project objectives.

What is project planning and why is it important?

■ Project planning involves five stages.
– Identifying the activities within a project;
– Estimating times and resources for the activities;
– Identifying the relationship and dependencies between the activities;
– Identifying the schedule constraints;
– Fixing the schedule.

■ Project planning is particularly important where complexity of the project is high. The interrelationship between activities, resources and times in most projects, especially complex ones, is such that unless they are carefully planned, resources can become seriously overloaded at times during the project.

What techniques can be used for project planning?

■ Network planning and Gantt charts are the most common techniques. The former (using either the activity-on-arrow or activity-on-node format) is particularly useful for assessing the total duration of a project and the degree of flexibility or float of the individual activities within the project.

■ The most common method of network planning is called the critical path method (CPM).

■ The logic inherent in a network diagram can be changed by resource constraints.

■ Network planning models can also be used to assess the total cost of shortening a project where individual activities are shortened.

What is project control and how is it done?

■ The process of project control involves three sets of decisions: how to monitor the project in order to check its progress, how to assess the performance of the project by comparing monitored observations to the project plan, and how to intervene in the project in order to make the changes which will bring it back to plan.

■ Earned-value control assesses the performance of the project by combining cost and time together. It involves plotting the actual expenditure on the project against the value of the work completed, both in the form of what was planned and what is actually happening. Both cost and schedule variances can then be detected.

Lemming Television

Lemming Television (LTV) is a television production company which specializes in making outside broadcast (OB) 'specials' for a variety of television networks. It was recently commissioned to make a series of 'summer roadshow' programmes which would be shot at locations around Europe during the spring and early summer and broadcast by the customer (a satellite broadcasting network) during the summer. The programmes would involve circus acts, displays, events and computer-graphic displays to entertain the crowds and popular entertainment acts and interviews which would be interspersed with contestant games. Managing the preparation for the series was the responsibility of the show's producer, Flo Brown. Flo, who had recently graduated with distinction from her MBA course, knew that she would need to keep a tight grip on the arrangements for the roadshow series. The shooting would start at the end of May and the final show would be recorded at the end of July. The shows would be broadcast between early July and late August, so any delay either in recording the material or in editing the programmes would cause considerable complications.

The company had known that it would be commissioned to make the programmes since December, but Flo had only been allocated the job in early February! Her first act was to list the various jobs which would have to be done before shooting could start. She then discussed each job with the part of the company which would carry it out, to try to understand what decisions would need to be made before they could start on their jobs. The jobs which needed to be done prior to the start of the shooting are listed below together with some details.

The producer's responsibilities (as well as managing the whole project) included:

- *Scheduling the venues:* would take about two weeks to finalize and could be started straight away.
- *Defining the design concept:* would need discussions with the chief designer and would take about four weeks of considering alternative designs before finalizing the concept, but could be started straight away.
- *Specifying computer-graphic displays:* again in consultation with the chief designer, it would take about a week but could not be started until all the detailed planning had been finalized.

The design department's responsibility was:

- *Producing artwork for printed materials:* would take about three weeks but could be started only after completion of the detailed planning.

The programme planning department's responsibilities were:

- *Booking the venues:* a one-week job which could be started as soon as the venues had been decided by Flo.
- *Detailed planning:* the preparation of detailed plans and schedules, a two-week task which could be started once the design concept had been finalized and the venues booked.
- *Printing the brochures:* an outside printer could be given this job as soon as the artwork for the printed materials had been prepared by the design department. The printer usually quoted a four-week delivery from receipt of the artwork.
- *Printing the display posters:* again depended on the preparation of the artwork but could be delivered within two weeks of the artwork being ready.
- *Ordering the roadshow vehicles:* several trailer trucks and ancillary vehicles were needed which could be ordered on completion of the detailed planning, delivery of the vehicles would take about six weeks.
- *Writing the graphic display software:* contracted out to a software house, it would take about four weeks but could only be started after the computer graphics had been specified by the producer and chief designer.
- *Final testing and rehearsals:* the programme planning department were finally responsible for getting the 'whole act together' immediately prior to shooting. Testing and rehearsals could only start once the brochures had been printed, the vehicles fully fitted out and customized and the promotion staff trained. Final tests and rehearsals should take around a week but, if things went wrong at any stage, could take longer.

The workshop's responsibility was:

- *Customizing and fitting out the vehicles:* after the vehicles are delivered and the artwork agreed and the computer-graphics software finished, the vehicles could be fitted out and customized for the shows, this would normally take around two weeks.

▶

The personnel department was responsible for:

● *Recruiting the promotion (promo) staff:* these were the staff (often 'resting' actors) who staffed the exhibits and entertained the crowds; they could be recruited as soon as the detailed planning was completed. Usually it took two weeks to recruit all the promo staff.

● *Training the promo staff:* once all promo staff had been recruited they would need training – a one-week task. ■

Questions

1 Can Flo get the project together in time to start shooting on schedule?

2 Which are the jobs which she will have to manage particularly closely?

3 What general advice would you give her which would help her to manage this project?

1 Would professional services, such as a management consultancy project, benefit from the application of project management principles in the same way as would the manufacturer of a turbine generator set for a power station?

2 (a) Why is the concept of earliest and latest start times of value in project planning?
(b) Draw up cumulative time–cost curves for the new logistics operation shown in Fig. 16.17 and developed later in the chapter. Assume the total costs for each activity are as follows:

Activity 1	£34 000	Activity 7	£120 000
Activity 2	£68 000	Activity 8	£480 000
Activity 3	£12 000	Activity 9	£1.1m
Activity 4	£370 000	Activity 10	£400 000
Activity 5	£39 000	Activity 11	£42 000
Activity 6	nil cost	Activity 12	£20 000

Money is consumed in a linear manner over time: that is if one week has elapsed in a four-week activity, then one quarter of the cost has been incurred.
(c) Show cumulative cost curves assuming that:
all work starts at the earliest start times;
all work starts at the latest start times.

3 Why is the critical path a helpful concept in project planning and control?

4 (a) If the network shown in Fig. 16.24 had to be crashed to achieve a completion at week 80, which activities would need to have reduced durations?
(b) What would be the implications for activity 4?
(c) What would the cumulative time–cost curve now look like?

5 Identify possible differences between internal and external project performance reports.

6 Evaluate the job of the project manager.
(a) Does project management tend to make people value short-term expediency in order to get the job done?

(b) Why does the project manager tend to resist changes?
(c) Is project management good training for general management?

7 Identify a number of projects with which you have been involved, for example 'project work' as part of the university course, moving house, preparing a large meal, organizing a foreign trip for several people, etc. Assess each of them in terms of their project elements and the complexity–uncertainty typology.

8 Using the list of projects identified in question 7, assess the success of each of them. Did any fail or not succeed as well as planned and what do you think were the reasons for this? Compare your findings with the project management success factors.

9 Discuss the problems of managing a large-scale famine relief project.

10 Identify the key project planning phases for a major rock concert.

11 What criteria might you use to monitor a theatrical production?

12 The activities, their durations and precedences for designing, writing and installing a bespoke computer database are shown overleaf in Table 16.4. Draw a Gantt chart for the operation and calculate the fastest time in which the operation might be completed.

13 Construct a network diagram which satisfies the following relationships:
A, B and C are the first activities of the project and can start simultaneously.
A and B precede D.
B precedes E, F and H.
F and C precede G.
E and H precede I and J.
C, D, F and J precede K.
K precedes L.
I, G and L are the terminal activities of the project.

Table 16.4 Bespoke computer database activities

Activity	Duration (weeks)	Activities that must be completed before it can start
1 Contract negotiation	1	–
2 Discussions with main users	2	1
3 Review of current documentation	5	1
4 Review of current systems	6	2
5 Systems analysis (a)	4	3, 4
6 Systems analysis (b)	7	5
7 Programming	12	5
8 Testing (prelim)	2	7
9 Existing system review report	1	3, 4
10 System proposal report	2	5, 9
11 Documentation preparation	19	5, 8
12 Implementation	7	7, 11
13 System test	3	12
14 Debugging	4	12
15 Manual preparation	5	11

14 A catering manager has been asked to organize a banquet for 100 guests. Table 16.5 shows the key activities, their durations and precedences. Identify the critical activities and prepare a Gantt chart showing all the activities and the float available for the non-critical activities.

Table 16.5 Banquet activities

Activity	Duration (mins)	Preceding activities
A Prepare ingredients	30	–
B Clear/clean room	20	–
C Prepare room and lay tables	20	B
D Prepare dressings and cold dishes	20	A
E Prepare meat, to oven	30	A
F Meet and seat guests	50	C,D,E
G Plate, dress and serve starter	70	C,D,E
H Cook vegetables	30	C,E
I Plate up puddings	20	C,E
J Clear starter, serve main course	15	G,H
K Clear main, serve pudding and coffee	15	J
L Clear tables	20	K

Table 16.6 Project activities

Activity	Duration (weeks)			Preceding activities
	Optimistic	Most likely	Pessimistic	
A	1	2	3	–
B	3	5	11	A
C	5	7	9	A
D	5	7	12	B
E	1	2	3	C
F	7	9	11	C
G	2	3	4	D, E

15 Given the information in Table 16.6:
(a) What is the shortest time in which the project can be completed?
(b) What are the critical activities?
(c) What is the standard deviation of the critical path?
(d) What is the probability that the project will be completed in 20 weeks?

16 The chief surveyor of a firm that moves earth in preparation for the construction of roads has identified the activities, their durations and the number of mechanical diggers required for each stage of an operation to prepare a difficult stretch of motorway (see Table 16.7). The surveyor needs to know the minimum number of mechanical diggers required during the project.

Table 16.7 Road construction activites

Activity	Duration (days)	Preceding activities	No. of mechanical diggers required
A	5	–	3
B	10	–	5
C	1	–	4
D	8	B	2
E	10	B	3
F	9	B	1
G	3	A, D	5
H	7	A, D	4
I	4	F	9
J	3	F	7
K	5	C, J	1
L	8	H, E, I, K	2
M	4	C, J	10

NOTES ON CHAPTER

1 Based on an idea by Nicholas, J.M. (1990) *Managing Business and Engineering Projects: Concepts and Implementation*, Prentice Hall.

2 Based on Pinto, J.K. and Slevin, D.P. (1987) 'Critical Success Factors in Successful Project Implementation', *IEEE Transactions on Engineering Management*, Vol 34, No 1.

3 Source: *Computer Weekly*, Mar 1993.

4 Weiss, J.W. and Wysocki, R.K. (1992) *Five-Phase Project Management: A Practical Planning and Implementation Guide*, Addison-Wesley.

5 Barnes, M. (1985) 'Project Management Framework', *International Project Management Yearbook*, Butterworth Scientific.

6 Lock, D. (1996) *Project Management* (6th edn), Gower.

7 Lock, D. *op. cit.*

8 Sources: ESA press releases.

SELECTED FURTHER READINGS

Baker, B.N. and Wileman, D.L. (1981) 'A Summary of Major Research Findings Regarding the Human Element in Project Management', *IEEE Engineering Management Review*, Vol 9, No 3.

Boddy, D. and Buchanan, D. (1992) *Take the Lead: Interpersonal Skills for Project Managers*, Prentice Hall.

Burke, R. (1993) *Project Management Planning and Control* (2nd edn), John Wiley.

Davis, E.W. (1973) 'Project Scheduling Under Resource Constraints – A Historical Review', *AIEE Transactions*, Vol 5, No 4.

Gilbreath, R.D. (1986) *Winning at Project Management*, John Wiley.

Harrison, F.L. (1981) *Advanced Project Management*, Gower.

Icmeli, O., Erenguc, S.S. and Zappe, C.J. (1993) 'Project Scheduling Problems: A Survey', *International Journal of Operations and Production Management*, Vol 13, No 11.

Littlefield, T.K. and Randolph, P.H. (1991) 'PERT Duration Times: Mathematical or MBO', *Interfaces*, Vol 21, No 6.

Lockyer, K. and Gordon, J. (1996) *Project Management and Project Network Techniques* (6th edn), Pitman Publishing.

Maylor, H. (1996) *Project Management*, Pitman Publishing.

Meredith, J.R. and Mantel, S. (1995) *Project Management: A Managerial Approach* (3rd edn), John Wiley.

Moder, J.J., Phillips, C.R. and Davis, E.W. (1983) *Project Management with CPM/PERT and Precedence Diagramming*, Van Nostrand Reinhold.

Morris, P.W. and Hough, G.H. (1987) '*The Anatomy of Major Projects*', John Wiley.

Nicholas, J.M. (1990) *Managing Business and Engineering Projects: Concepts and Implementation*, Prentice Hall.

Obeng, E. (1993) *All Change: The Project Leaders' Secret Handbook*, Pitman Publishing.

O'Neal, K. (1987) 'Project Management Computer Software Buyers Guide', *Industrial Engineering*, Vol 9, No 1.

Randolph, W.A. and Posner, B.Z. (1988) 'What Every Project Manager Needs to Know About Project Management', *Sloan Management Review*, Vol 29, No 4.

Reinertson, D.G. and Smith, P.G. (1991) *Developing Products in Half the Time*, Van Nostrand Reinhold.

QUALITY PLANNING AND CONTROL

INTRODUCTION

Quality is the only one of the five 'operations performance criteria' to have its own dedicated chapter in this book (or two chapters if you include total quality management which is covered in Chapter 20). There are two reasons for this. First, in many organizations there is a separate and identifiable part of the operations function which is devoted exclusively to the management of quality. It is necessary, therefore, to examine the issues which concern staff in this area. Second, it is a current and key concern of many organizations. Business newspapers and management journals are dominated by articles on quality. It would appear that we have undergone a 'quality revolution'. Certainly there is a growing realization that high-quality goods and services can give an organization a considerable competitive edge. Good quality reduces costs of rework, scrap and returns and, most importantly, good quality generates satisfied customers. Some operations managers believe that, in the long run, quality is the most important single factor affecting an organization's performance relative to its competitors. Figure 17.1 illustrates the supply–demand relationship covered in this chapter.

Figure 17.1 Quality planning and control is concerned with the systems and procedures which govern the quality of the products and services supplied by the operation

---

CHAPTER 17: KEY QUESTIONS

- *How can quality be defined?*

- *How can quality problems be diagnosed?*

- *What steps lead towards conformance to specification?*

- *How can statistical process control help quality planning and control?*

- *How can acceptance sampling help quality planning and control?*

WHAT IS QUALITY AND WHY IS IT SO IMPORTANT?

It is worth revisiting some of the arguments which were presented in Chapter 2 regarding the benefits of high quality. This will explain why quality is seen as being so important by most operations. Figure 17.2 illustrates the various ways in which quality improvements can affect other aspects of operations performance.[1] Both contributors to profitability can be improved by higher quality. Revenues can be increased by better sales and enhanced prices in the market. At the same time, costs can be brought down by improved efficiencies, productivity and the use of capital.

If quality is indeed so important to any organization's performance then a key task of the operations function must be to ensure that it provides quality goods and services to its internal and external customers. This is not necessarily straightforward. For example, there is no clear or agreed definition of what 'quality' means.

Professor David Garvin[2] has categorized many of the various definitions into 'five approaches' to quality: *the transcendent approach, the manufacturing-based approach, the user-based approach, the product-based approach* and *the value-based approach.*

The transcendent approach

The transcendent approach views quality as synonymous with *innate excellence*. A 'quality' car is a Rolls Royce. A 'quality' flight is one provided by Singapore Airlines. A 'quality' watch is a Rolex. Using this approach, quality is being defined as the absolute – the best possible, in terms of the product's or service's *specification*.

The manufacturing-based approach

The manufacturing-based approach is concerned with making products or providing services that are *free of errors* and that conform precisely to their design specification. A car which is less expensive than a Rolls Royce, or a Swatch watch or an economy flight, although not necessarily the 'best' available, is defined as a 'quality' product provided it has been built or delivered precisely to its design specification.

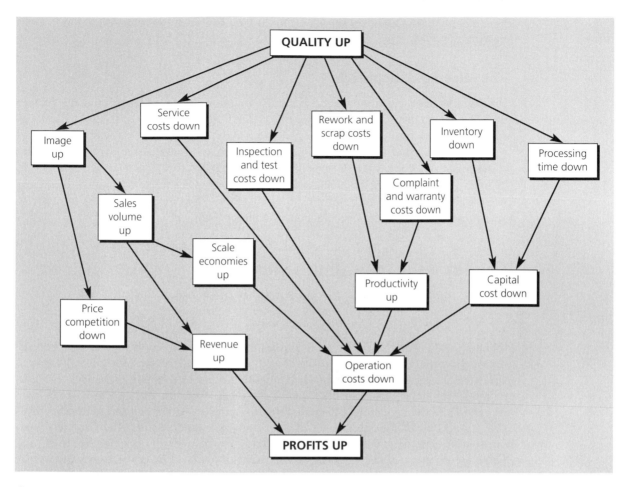

Figure 17.2 Higher quality has a beneficial effect on both revenues and costs
Source: Based on Gummesson, E. (1993)

The user-based approach

The user-based approach is about making sure that the product or service is *fit for its purpose*. This definition demonstrates concern not only for its adherence to specification but also with the appropriateness of that specification for the customer. A watch that is manufactured precisely to its design specification yet falls to pieces after two days is clearly not 'fit for its purpose'. The cabin service on a night-time flight from Sydney to Stockholm may be designed to provide passengers with drinks every 15 minutes, meals every four hours and frequent announcements about the position of the plane. This quality specification may not be appropriate, however, for the customer whose main need is a good sleep.

The product-based approach

The product-based approach views quality as a precise and *measurable set of characteristics* that is required to satisfy the customer. A watch, for example, may be designed to run, without the need for servicing, for at least five years while keeping time correct to within five seconds.

The value-based approach

Finally, the value-based approach takes the manufacturing definition a stage further and defines quality in terms of *cost and price*. This approach contends that quality should be perceived in relation to price. A customer may well be willing to accept something of a lower specification quality, if the price is low. A simple and inexpensive watch may give good value by performing quite satisfactorily for a reasonable period of time. A passenger may be willing to fly from Singapore to Amsterdam with a four-hour wait in Bangkok and endure cramped seating and mediocre meals in order to save hundreds of guilders over the cost of a direct flight.

Quality – the operation's view

Here we try to reconcile some of these different views in our definition of quality:

Quality is consistent conformance to customers' expectations.

The use of the word 'conformance' implies that there is a need to meet a clear specification (the manufacturing approach); ensuring a product or service conforms to specification is a key operations task. 'Consistent' implies that conformance to specification is not an *ad hoc* event but that the materials, facilities and processes have been designed and then controlled to ensure that the product or service meets the specification using a set of measurable product or service characteristics (the product-based approach). The use of 'customers' expectations' attempts to combine the user- and value-based approaches.[3] It recognizes that the product or service must meet the expectations of customers, which may indeed be influenced by price.

The use of the word 'expectations' in this definition, rather than needs or wants, is important. 'Wants' would imply that anything the customer desires should be provided by the organization. 'Needs' implies only the meeting of a basic requirement. Take the example of a car. Our *need* might be for a mobile box that gets us from A to B. We might *want* a car that has the looks and acceleration of a sports car, with the carrying capacity of an estate, the ruggedness of a cross-country vehicle, and which comes to us at no cost. Our *expectation*, however, is that which we believe to be likely. We know that it is difficult to get sports performance with a large carrying capacity, and certainly not at zero cost.

Quality – the customer's view

One problem with basing our definition of quality on customer expectations is that individual customers' expectations may be different. Past experiences, individual knowledge and history will all shape their expectations. Furthermore, customers, on receiving the product or service, may each *perceive* it in different ways. One person may perceive a long-haul flight as an exciting part of a holiday; the person on the next seat may see it as a necessary chore to get to a business meeting. One person may perceive a car as a status symbol; another may see it merely as an expensive means of getting from home to work. Quality needs to be understood from a customer's point of view because, to the customer, the quality of a particular product or service is whatever he or she perceives it to be. If the passengers on a skiing charter flight perceive it to be of good quality, despite long queues at check-in or cramped seating and poor meals, then the flight really *is* of good perceived quality. If customers believe that expensive German cars are of good quality despite short service intervals, expensive parts and poor fuel consumption, then the car really *is* of high perceived quality.[4]

Furthermore, in some situations, customers may be unable to judge the 'technical' operational specification of the service or product. They may then use surrogate measures as a basis for their perception of quality.[5] For example, after a visit to a dentist it might be difficult for a customer to judge the technical quality of the repair of a tooth except insofar as it does not give any more trouble. The customer may in reality judge, and therefore perceive, the quality of the repair in terms of such things as the dress and demeanour of the dentist and technician, the information that was provided, or the way in which it was provided.

Reconciling the operation's and the customer's views of quality

The operation's view of quality is concerned with trying to meet customers' *expectations*. The customer's view of quality is what he or she *perceives* the product or service to be. To create a unified view, quality can be defined as the degree of fit between customers' expectations and their perception of the product or service.[6] Using this idea allows us to see the customers' view of quality (and, therefore, satisfaction) with the product or service as the result of the customers comparing their expectations of the product or service with their perception of how it performs.

If the product or service experience was better than expected then the customer is satisfied and quality is perceived to be high. If the product or service was less than his or her expectations then quality is low and the customer may be dissatisfied. If the product or service matches expectations then the perceived quality of the product or service is seen to be acceptable. These relationships are summarized in Fig. 17.3.

Both customers' expectations and perceptions are influenced by a number of factors, some of which cannot be controlled by the operation and some of which, to a certain extent, can be managed. Figure 17.4 shows some of the factors that will influence the gap between expectations and perceptions. This model of customer-perceived quality can help us understand how operations can manage quality and identifies some of the problems in so doing.

The bottom part of the diagram represents the operation's 'domain' of quality and the top part the customer's 'domain'. These two domains meet in the actual product or service, which is provided by the organization and experienced by the customer. Within the operation's domain, management is responsible for designing the product or service and providing a specification of the quality to which the product or service has to be created. The specification of a car, for example, might include the surface finish of the body, its physical dimensions, reliability, and so on. Within the customer's domain, his or her expectations are shaped by such factors as previous experiences with the particular product or service, the marketing image provided by the organization and word-of-mouth information from other users. These expectations are

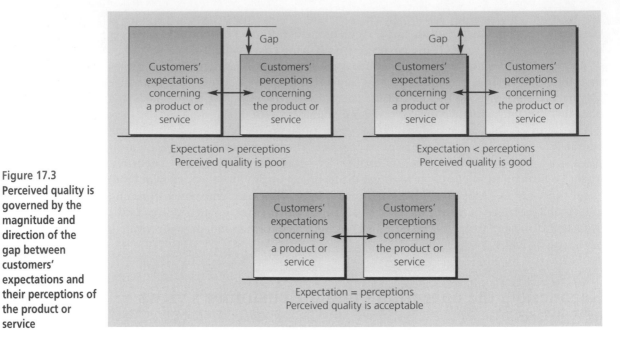

Figure 17.3
Perceived quality is governed by the magnitude and direction of the gap between customers' expectations and their perceptions of the product or service

internalized as a set of quality characteristics. A customer's expectations about the car, for example, may include its appearance, performance, luggage space, fuel consumption, leg room, and so on.

Diagnosing quality problems[7]

The purpose of describing perceived quality as we have done in Fig. 17.4 is so that we can use it to diagnose quality problems. If the perceived quality gap is such that customers' perceptions of the product or service fail to match their expectations of it, then the reason (or reasons) must lie in other gaps elsewhere in the model. Four other gaps could explain a perceived quality gap between customers' perceptions and expectations (*see* Fig. 17.5).

Gap 1 The customer's specification–operation's specification gap

Perceived quality could be poor because there may be a mismatch between the organization's own internal quality specification and the specification which is expected by the customer. For example, a car may be designed to need servicing every 10 000 kilometres but the customer may expect 15 000 kilometre service intervals. An airline may have a policy of charging for drinks during the flight whereas the customer's expectation may be that the drinks would be free.

Gap 2 The concept–specification gap

Perceived quality could be poor because there is a mismatch between the product or service concept (*see* Chapter 5) and the way the organization has specified the

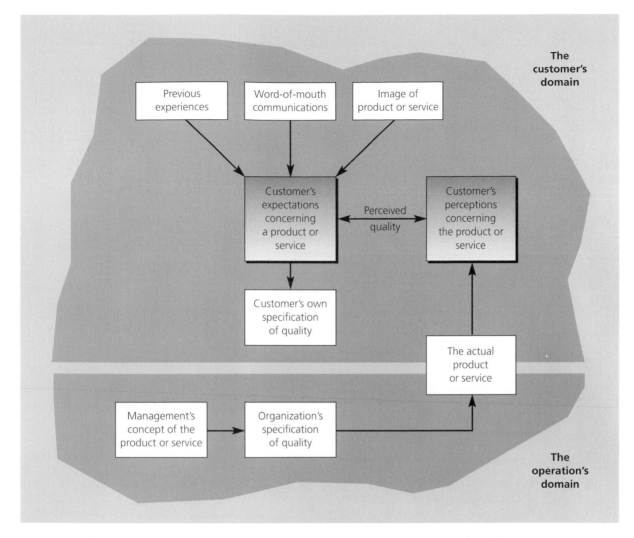

Figure 17.4 The customers' domain and the operation's domain in determining the perceived quality
Source: Adaped from Parasuraman, A. *et al.* (1985) 'A Conceptual Model of Service Quality and Implications for Future Research', *Journal of Marketing*, Vol 49, Fall.

quality of the product or service internally. For example, the concept of a car might have been for an inexpensive, energy-efficient means of transportation, but the inclusion of a catalytic converter may have both added to its cost and made it less energy efficient.

Gap 3 The quality specification–actual quality gap

Perceived quality could be poor because there is a mismatch between the actual quality of the service or product provided by the operation and its internal quality specification. This may be the result, for example, of an inappropriate or unachievable specification, or of poorly trained or inexperienced personnel, or because effective control systems are not in place to ensure the provision of defined levels of quality. For example, the internal quality specification for a car may be that the gap between

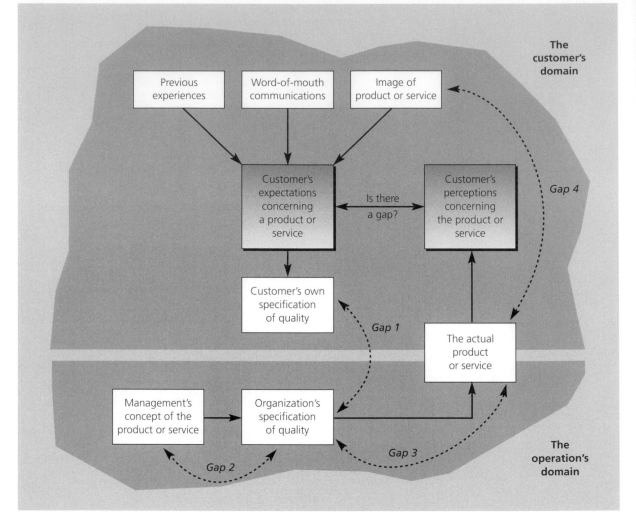

Figure 17.5 A gap between customers' expectations and their perception of a product or service could be explained by one or more gaps elsewhere in the model

its doors and body, when closed, must not exceed 7 mm. However, because of inadequate equipment, the gap in reality is 9 mm. A further example is where, despite an airline's policy of charging for drinks, some flight crews might provide free drinks, adding unexpected costs to the airline and influencing customers' expectations for the next flight when they may be disappointed.

Gap 4 The actual quality–communicated image gap

Perceived quality could also be poor because there is a gap between the organization's external communications or market image and the actual quality of the service or product delivered to the customer. This may be the result of either the marketing function setting unachievable expectations in the minds of customers or operations not providing the level of quality expected by the customer. For example, an advert-

Table 17.1 The organizational responsibility for closing quality gaps

Gap	Action required to ensure high perceived quality	Main organizational responsibility
Gap 1	Ensure that there is consistency between the internal quality specification of the product or service and the expectations of customers	Marketing Operations Product/service development
Gap 2	Ensure that the internal specification of the product or service meets its intended concept or design	Marketing Operations Product/service development
Gap 3	Ensure that the actual product or service conforms to its internally specified quality level	Operations
Gap 4	Ensure that the promises made to customers concerning the product or service can in reality be delivered by the operation	Marketing

ising campaign for an airline might show a cabin attendant offering to replace a customer's shirt on which food or drink has been spilt, whereas such a service may not in fact be available should this happen.

The organizational responsibility for closing the gaps

The existence of any one of these gaps is likely to result in a mismatch between expectations and perceptions and result in poor perceived quality. It is therefore important that managers take action to prevent quality gaps. Table 17.1 shows the actions which will be required to close each of the gaps and indicates the parts of the organization who bear the main responsibility for doing so.

Closing gaps 1 and 2 is the joint responsibility of marketing, operations and product/service development. (These issues were discussed in Chapter 5.) Gap 4 is a key task for marketing which is responsible for communicating with the market. The task for which operations bears most responsibility is to ensure that the product or service conforms to its required specification (gap 3) – in other words, to make sure that gap 3 does not exist. This gap is called the 'conformance to specification' gap and the remainder of this chapter discusses how operations managers can try to ensure conformance to specification.

CONFORMANCE TO SPECIFICATION

Conformance to specification means producing a product or providing a service to its design specification. During the design of any product or service, its overall concept, purpose, package of components and the connection between the components will have been specified (*see* Chapter 5). The model used to describe this activity in Chapter 5 was shown in Fig. 5.2. We can extend this model to include the activities of ensuring that products and services are indeed made to conform with their specifications. This is the quality planning and control activity (*see* Fig. 17.6). Quality planning and control can be divided into six sequential steps:

Step 1   Define the quality characteristics of the product or service.
Step 2   Decide how to measure each quality characteristic.
Step 3   Set quality standards for each quality characteristic.
Step 4   Control quality against those standards.
Step 5   Find and correct causes of poor quality.
Step 6   Continue to make improvements.

This chapter will deal with steps 1 to 4. Steps 5 and 6 are dealt with in Chapters 18, 19 and 20.

Step 1 – Define the quality characteristics

Much of what defines the 'quality' of a product or service will have been specified, at least implicitly, in its design. But not all the design details of a product or service are useful in controlling the quality of its production. For example, the design of a television may specify that its outer cabinet is made with a particular veneer and that each electronic component must have particular characteristics. Each television is not checked, however, to make sure that the cabinet is indeed made from that particular veneer or that each component has its specified characteristics. Rather it is the *consequences* of the design specification which are examined – the appearance of the cabinet and the clarity of the picture, for example.

These consequences for quality planning and control of the design are called the *quality characteristics* of the product or service. Table 17.2 shows a list of the quality characteristics which are generally useful for planning and controlling the quality of both products and services. The terms in Table 17.2 need a little further explanation.

Figure 17.6
The product/service design cycle including quality planning and control

Table 17.2 Quality characteristics for a motor car and an air journey

Quality characteristic	Car	Air journey
Functionality	Speed, acceleration, fuel consumption, ride quality, road-holding, etc.	Safety and duration of journey, on-board meals and drinks, car and hotel booking services
Appearance	Aesthetics, shape, finish, door gaps, etc.	Decor and cleanliness of aircraft, lounges and crew
Reliability	Mean time to failure	Keeping to the published flight times
Durability	Useful life (with repair)	Keeping up with trends in the industry
Recovery	Ease of repair	Resolution of service failures
Contact	Knowledge and courtesy of sales staff	Knowledge, courtesy and sensitivity of airline staff

PUTTING ITS MONEY WHERE ITS MOUTH IS[8]

In the retail banking world the costs of poor quality are going up and at least some of these costs are self-inflicted. But now some banks are offering to pay cash to wronged customers for every mistake they make. Centrebank, the telephone-banking service of the Bank of Scotland, is one bank which is putting its money where its mouth is. It pays at least £10 to customers if the bank makes a mistake.

'We believe we have a good level of service already,' says the bank, 'We are not saying that we want to make mistakes, but we want to show customers that we are determined to offer good service.'

One of the first quality schemes of this type originated at the Colorado National Bank of Denver. It used the slogan of 'putting its money where its mouth is' or PIMWIMI for short. Its strategy was straightforward: if 'quality' was actually guaranteed to customers, then the customer relationship would be strengthened. The programme had three main principles:

● The responsiveness, accuracy and courtesy of the service delivery would be guaranteed.
● Systems would be monitored for customer friendliness and front-line staff would be empowered to influence situations in which service quality could be improved.
● It would be easy for customers to express their opinions of the service, in order to gain feedback on progress.

Customers should not wait more than three minutes in a teller line, more than five minutes in Personal Banking, Personal Finance or Customer Assistance, and they should be received in a friendly manner, greeted by name and receive next-day turnaround on enquiries and personal loan applications, while expecting no less than 100 per cent accuracy throughout.

▶

The scheme called for the bank to:

'give a note from the President in the form of a $5 bill, every time a customer had cause for complaint, either due to system failure or staff behaviour'.

No problem was ever too small to be considered worthy of the $5 compensation – if it merited a moan or a mention of disappointment, then $5 was a small price to pay, to recover that customer's favour. The level of payoff remained at zero, however, well into the scheme. ■

Questions

1 What conditions do you think have to be obtained within an operation before a scheme of this type could be introduced?

2 What advantages do you think this kind of scheme gives, both from the customer's point of view and from the operation's point of view?

3 What problems could it lead to?

Functionality means how well the product or service does the job for which it is intended. This includes its performance and features. *Appearance* refers to the sensory characteristics of the product or service: its aesthetic appeal, look, feel, sound and smell. *Reliability* is the consistency of the product's or service's performance over time, or the average time for which it performs within its tolerated band of performance. *Durability* means the total useful life of the product or service, assuming occasional repair or modification. *Recovery* means the ease with which problems with the product or service can be rectified or resolved. *Contact* refers to the nature of the person-to-person contact which might take place. For example, it could include the courtesy, empathy, sensitivity and knowledge of contact staff.

Step 2 – Decide how to measure each characteristic

For any particular product or service these characteristics must be defined in such a way as to enable them to be measured and then controlled. This involves taking a very general quality characteristic such as the 'appearance' of a car and breaking it down, as far as one can, into its constituent elements. For example, 'appearance' is difficult to measure as such, but 'colour match', 'surface finish', and 'number of visible scratches' are all capable of being described in a more objective manner. They may even be quantifiable. If so, the organization can measure changes in quality levels over time.

The process of disaggregating quality characteristics into their measurable subcomponents, however, can result in the characteristics losing some of their meaning. For example, a quantified list of colour match, the 'roughness' or 'smoothness' of the surface finish and the number of visible scratches does not convey everything about the appearance of a product. Customers will react to more factors than these: the shape and character of the car, for example, the amount of chrome, and so on. Many of the factors lost by disaggregating 'appearance' into its measurable parts, are those which are embedded in the design of the car rather than the way it is produced.

Some of the quality characteristics of a product or service cannot themselves be measured at all. The 'courtesy' of airline staff, for example, has no objective quantified measure. Yet operations with high customer contact, such as airlines, place a great deal of importance on the need to ensure courtesy in their staff. In cases like this the operation will have to attempt to measure customer *perceptions* of courtesy.

Variables and attributes

The measures used by operations to describe quality characteristics are of two types: *variables* and *attributes*. Variable measures are those that can be measured on a continuously variable scale (for example length, diameter, weight or time). Attributes are those which are assessed by judgement and are dichotomous, i.e. have two states (for example right or wrong, works or does not work, looks OK or not OK). Table 17.3 categorizes some of the measures which might be used for the quality characteristics of the car and the airline journey.

Table 17.3 Variable and attribute measures for quality characteristics

Quality characteristic	Car		Airline journey	
	Variable	*Attribute*	*Variable*	*Attribute*
Functionality	Acceleration and braking characteristics from test bed	Is the ride quality satisfactory?	Number of journeys which actually arrived at the destination (i.e. didn't crash!)	Was the food acceptable?
Appearance	Number of blemishes visible on car	Is the colour to specification?	Number of seats not cleaned satisfactorily	Is the crew dressed smartly?
Reliability	Average time between faults	Is the reliability satisfactory?	Proportion of journeys which arrived on time	Were there any complaints?
Durability	Life of the car	Is the useful life as predicted?	Number of times service innovations lagged competitors	Generally, is the airline updating its services in a satisfactory manner?
Recovery	Time from fault discovered to fault repaired	Is the serviceability of the car acceptable?	Proportion of service failures resolved satisfactorily	Do customers feel that staff deal satisfactorily with complaints?
Contact	Level of help provided by sales staff (1 to 5 scale)	Did customers feel well served? (Yes or no)	The extent to which customers feel well treated by staff (1 to 5 scale)	Did customers feel that the staff were helpful? (Yes or no)

Step 3 – Set quality standards

When operations managers have identified how any quality characteristic can be measured they need a quality standard against which it can be checked, otherwise they will not know whether it indicates good or bad performance. For example, suppose that, on average, one passenger out of every 10 000 complains about the food. Should the airline regard that as good because it seems that 9999 passengers out of 10 000 are satisfied? Or should it regard it as bad because, if one passenger complains, there must be others who, although dissatisfied, did not bother to complain? Or, if that level of complaint is broadly similar to other airlines, should it regard its quality as just about satisfactory? While it might seem to be appropriate to have an absolute standard – that is perfection – and indeed strive for it, to use perfection as an operational standard could be both demoralizing and expensive. Most manufactured products and delivered services are not 'perfect'. No car will last for ever. No airline could guarantee that there will always be seats available on its aircraft.

If a car is meant to survive for a reasonable length of time, the critical question for operations is how long is reasonable? If cabin attendants have to respond to requests, how long may they take before it is unacceptable? How quickly should a car accelerate from 0 to 100 kph? What should be the mean time between failures for a product? What should be the acceptable noise level in an aircraft? The quality standard is that level of quality which defines the boundary between acceptable and unacceptable. Such standards may well be constrained by operational factors such as the state of technology in the factory, and the cost limits of making the product. At the same time, however, they need to be appropriate to the expectations of customers. The quality standard for the reliability of a watch might be ten maintenance-free years, for the availability of airline seats might be that seats it should be available 95 per cent of the time, and so on.

Step 4 – Control quality against those standards

After setting up appropriate standards that are capable of being met by the operation and that will meet customers' expectations, the operation will then need to check that the products or services conform to those standards. In all operations there may well be times when products or services are produced which do not conform to those standards. When making manufactured goods, tools may wear or there may be variation in the materials used. Similarly in service operations there may be technical breakdown and variability in staff behaviour. Chapter 19 deals with the question of what operations can do when things do go wrong. Here we concern ourselves with how operations can try to ensure that it does things right, first time, every time. As far as operations managers are concerned this involves three decisions:

1 Where in the operation should they check that it is conforming to standards?
2 Should they check every product or service or take a sample?
3 How should the checks be performed?

Where should the checks take place?

The key task for operations managers is to identify the critical control points at which the service, products or processes need to be checked to ensure that the product or services will conform to specification. There are three main places where checks may be carried out: at the start of the process, during the process and after the process.

At *the start of the process* the incoming transformed resources could be inspected to make sure that they are to the correct specification. For example, a car manufacturer may wish to check that the car headlights which are supplied to its production line are of the right specification. An airline might check that incoming food is satisfactory. A night club may wish to check that its incoming guests are dressed appropriately. A university will wish to screen applicants to try to ensure that they have a high chance of getting through the programme.

During the process checks may take place at any stage, or indeed all stages, but there are a number of particularly critical points in the process where inspection might be important (Polaroid, described in the box overleaf, is a good example of this). These are:[9]

- before a particularly costly part of the process;
- before a series of processes during which checking might be difficult;
- immediately after part of the process with a high defective rate or a fail point;
- before a part of the process that might conceal previous defects or problems;
- before a 'point of no return', after which rectification and recovery might be impossible;
- before potential damage or distress might be caused;
- before a change in functional responsibility.

Checks may also take place *after the process* itself to ensure that the product or service conforms to its specification or that customers are satisfied with the service they have received.

Check every product and service or take a sample?

Having decided the points at which the goods or services will be checked, the next decision is how many of the products or services to check. While it might seem ideal to check every single product being produced or every service being delivered, there are many good reasons why this might not be sensible.

- It might be dangerous to inspect the whole item or every constituent part. A doctor, for example, checks just a small sample of blood rather than taking all of a patient's blood because this would be life-threatening. The characteristics of this sample are taken to represent those of the rest of the patient's blood.
- The checking of every single product or every customer might destroy the product or interfere with the service. It would be inappropriate for a light bulb manufacturer to check the length of life of every single light bulb leaving the factory, as this would entail the destructive testing of each bulb. Likewise, it would not be appropriate for a head waiter to check whether his or her customers are enjoying the meal or having a good time every 30 seconds.
- Checking every product or service can be both time consuming and costly. For example, it just might not be feasible to check every single item from a high-volume plastic moulding machine or to check the feelings of every single bus commuter in a major city every day.

POLAROID DEFEATS THE DARK[10]

Many companies have some stages of production which, for some reason, it is more important to get right than others. The Polaroid factory at Dumbarton in Scotland is the largest film manufacturing plant in Europe, specializing in the production of instant film cartridges. In its process one of the most critical stages has to take place in the dark. Quality checks are important at all stages in the process but especially during the light-sensitive stage of the process.

'We have to be careful that the light-sensitive stage is reliable and that the quality of product we will get from that stage is predictable. Once the line is set up and running, there is a high level of disruption and downtime if we have to stop the line and open up the dark room. For small problems such as alignment, we can adjust the process and scrap only the small amount of the product which is produced in the meantime. In more drastic circumstances, we will stop the process and accept the loss of the product currently in progress by opening the "dark stage".'

The critical nature of the 'dark stage' has focused the company's efforts on making sure that it is as error-free as possible. Error rates for this stage in the process are now small both in absolute terms and as a proportion of the total quality problems in the plant. This has been achieved through improving the design of the process technology, working closely with suppliers, matching key components prior to running the line, and by providing back-up facilities. ■

Questions

1 Why is quality particularly important for a product such as Polaroid's film?

2 Why is an understanding of the process behaviour of film manufacture particularly important for Polaroid?

The use of 100 per cent checking, moreover, does not guarantee that all defects or problems will be identified, for a number of reasons:

● Making the checks may be inherently difficult. For example, although a doctor may undertake all the correct testing procedures to check for a particular disease, he or she may not necessarily be certain to diagnose it.

● Staff may become fatigued over a period of time, when inspecting repetitive items where it is easy to make mistakes. (For example, try counting the number of 'e's on this page. Count them again and see if you get the same score!)

● Quality measures may be unclear and staff making the checks may not know precisely what to look for. For example, how can an interviewer, making offers for university places, really tell whether a student will actually have the right attitude to group work or will be diligent?

● Wrong information may be given. For example, although all the customers in a restaurant may tell the head waiter, when asked, that 'everything is all right', they may actually have serious reservations about the food or their treatment.

Type I and Type II errors

Using a sample to make a decision about the quality of products or services, although requiring less time than 100 per cent checking, does have its own inherent problems. Like any decision activity, we may get the decision wrong. Take the example of a pedestrian waiting to cross a street. He or she has two main decisions: whether to continue waiting or to cross. If there is a satisfactory break in the traffic and the pedestrian crosses then a correct decision has been made. Similarly, if that person continues to wait because the traffic is too dense then he or she has again made a correct decision. There are two types of incorrect decisions or errors, however. One incorrect decision would be if he or she decides to cross when there is not an adequate break in the traffic, resulting in an accident – this is referred to as a *Type I error*. Another incorrect decision would occur if he or she decides not to cross even though there was an adequate gap in the traffic – this is called a *Type II error*. In crossing the road, therefore, there are four outcomes which are summarized in Table 17.4.

Type I errors are those which occur when a decision was made to do something and the situation did not warrant it. Type II errors are those which occur when nothing was done, yet a decision to do something should have been taken as the situation did indeed warrant it. For example, if a school's inspector checks the work of a sample of 20 out of 1000 pupils and all 20 of the pupils in the sample have failed, the inspector might draw the conclusion that all the pupils have failed. In fact the sample just happened to contain 20 out of the 50 students who had failed the course. The inspector, by assuming a high fail rate would be making a Type I error. Alternatively, if the inspector checked 20 pieces of work all of which were of a high standard, he or she might conclude that all the pupils' work was good despite having been given, or having chosen, the only pieces of good work in the whole school. This would be a Type II error. Although these situations are not likely, they are possible. Therefore any sampling procedure has to be aware of these risks.

How should the checks be performed?

In practice most operations will use some form of sampling to check the quality of their products or services. The decision then is what kind of sample procedure to adopt. There are two different methods in common use for checking the quality of a sample product or service so as to make inferences about all the output from an operation. Both methods take into account the statistical risks involved in sampling.

The first, and by far the best known, is the procedure called *statistical process control* (SPC). SPC is concerned with sampling the process during the production of the goods or the delivery of service. Based on this sample, decisions are made as to whether the process is 'in control', that is operating as it should be. The second

Table 17.4 Type I and Type II errors for a pedestrian crossing the road

	Road conditions	
Decision	Unsafe	Safe
Cross	Type I error	Correct decision
Wait	Correct decision	Type II error

SURGICAL STATISTICS[11]

Understanding the nature of Type I and Type II errors is an essential part of any surgeon's quality planning. Take the well-known appendectomy operation, for example. This is the removal of the appendix when it becomes infected or inflamed. Removal is necessary because of the risk of the appendix bursting and causing peritonitis, a potentially fatal poisoning of the blood. The surgical procedure itself is a relatively simple operation with expected good results but there is always a small risk associated with any invasive surgery needing a general anaesthetic. In addition, like any surgical procedure, it is expensive. The cost the USA's approximately quarter-of-a-million appendectomies averages out to around $4500 per operation. Unfortunately, appendicitis is difficult to diagnose accurately. Using standard X-ray procedures a definite diagnosis can only be obtained about ten per cent of the time. But now a new technique, developed in the Massachusetts General Hospital in Boston, claims to be able to identify 100 per cent of true appendicitis cases before surgery is carried out. The new technique (Focused Appendix Computed Tomography) uses spiral X-ray images together with a special dye. It scans only the relevant part of the body, so exposure to radiation is not as major an issue as with conventional X-ray techniques. The technique can also help in providing an alternative diagnosis when an appendectomy is not needed. Most significant, the potential cost savings are very great. The test itself costs less than $250 which means that one single avoided surgery pays for around 20 tests. ■

Questions

1 How does this new test change the likelihood of Type I and Type II errors?

2 Why is this important?

method is called *acceptance sampling* and is more concerned with whether to regard an incoming or outgoing batch of materials or customers as acceptable or not. The rest of this chapter is concerned with these two quality planning and control methods.

STATISTICAL PROCESS CONTROL (SPC)

Statistical process control (SPC) is concerned with checking a product or service during its creation. If there is reason to believe that there is a problem with the process, then it can be stopped (where this is possible and appropriate) and the problem can be identified and rectified. For example, an international airport regularly may ask a sample of customers if the cleanliness of its restaurants is satisfactory. If an unacceptable number of customers in one sample is found to be unhappy, airport managers may have to consider improving the procedures in place for cleaning tables. Similarly, a car manufacturer periodically will check whether a sample of door panels conforms to its standards so as to know whether the machinery which produces them is performing correctly. Again, if a sample suggests that there may be problems, then the machines may have to be stopped and the process checked.

Control charts

The significant value of SPC, however, is not just to make checks of a single sample but to monitor the results of many samples over a period of time. It does this by using *control charts*, to see if the process looks as though it is performing as it should, or alternatively if it is going out of control. If the process does seem to be going out of control, then steps can be taken *before* there is a problem.

Most operations chart their quality performance in some way. Figure 17.7, or something like it, could be found in almost any operation. The chart could, for example, represent the percentage of customers in a sample of 1000, each month, dissatisfied with the restaurant's cleanliness. While the amount of dissatisfaction may be acceptably small, management should be concerned that it has steadily been increasing over time and may wish to investigate why this is so. In this case, the control chart is plotting an attribute measure of quality (satisfied or not).

Alternatively, the chart could just as easily represent the average impact resistance of samples of door panels selected each week (a variable measure). Again there is evidence of a clear trend. This time, though, the quality measure seems to be getting better. Yet this chart could be equally as disturbing to the car manufacturers, however, as the airport's survey results were to the airport management. If the impact resistance is moving above the 'necessary' level, it could indicate that too much material is being used in the process. Certainly, if the reasons for the upward trend are unknown, the management of the operation should want to investigate the causes.

Looking for trends is an important use of control charts. If the trend suggests the process is getting steadily worse, then it will be worth investigating the process. If the trend is steadily improving, it may still be worthy of investigation to try to identify what is happening that is making the process better. This information might then be

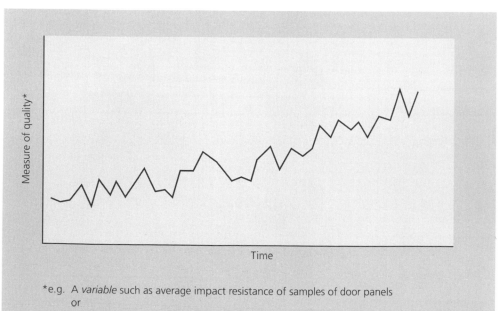

*e.g. A *variable* such as average impact resistance of samples of door panels
or
An *attribute* such as percentage of customer sample who are dissatisfied with cleanliness

**Figure 17.7
Charting trends in
quality measures**

651

shared with other parts of the organization, or, on the other hand, the process might be stopped as the cause could be adding unnecessary expense to the operation.

Variation in process quality

Common causes

The processes charted in Fig. 17.7 showed an upwards trend. The trend was neither steady nor smooth, however. It varied, sometimes up, sometimes down. All processes vary to some extent. No machine will give precisely the same result each time it is used. All materials vary a little. The staff in the operation differ marginally in the way they perform each time they perform a task. Even the environment in which the processing takes place will vary. Given this, it is not surprising that the measure of quality (whether attribute or variable) will also vary. Variations which derive from these *common causes* can never be entirely eliminated (although they can be reduced).

For example, if a machine is filling boxes with rice, it will not place *exactly* the same weight of rice in every box it fills; there will be some variation around an average weight. When the filling machine is in a stable condition (that is, no exceptional factors are influencing its behaviour) each box could be weighed and a histogram of the weights could be built up. Figure 17.8 shows how the histogram might develop. The first boxes weighed could lie anywhere within the natural variation of the process but are more likely to be close to the average weight (*see* Fig. 17.8 (a)). As more boxes are weighed they clearly show the tendency to be close to the process average (*see* Fig. 17.8 (b) and (c)). After many boxes have been weighed they form a smoother distribution (Fig. 17.8

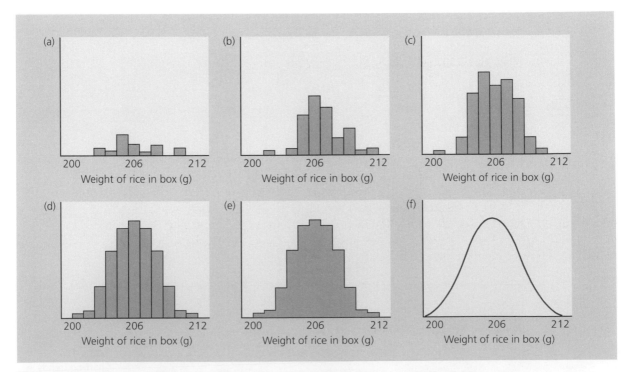

Figure 17.8 The natural variation in the filling process can be described by a normal distribution

(d)) which can be drawn as a histogram (Fig. 17.8 (e)) which will approximate to the underlying process variation distribution (Fig. 17.8 (f)).

Usually this type of variation can be described by a normal distribution with 99.7 per cent of the variation lying within ± 3 standard deviations.

In this case the weight of rice in the boxes is described by a distribution with a mean of 206 grams and a standard deviation of 2 grams. The obvious question for any operations manager would be 'is this variation in the process performance acceptable?' The answer will depend on the acceptable range of weights which can be tolerated by the operation. This range is called the *tolerance range*, or *specification range*. If the weight of rice in the box is too small then the organization might infringe labelling regulations; if it is too large, the organization is 'giving away' too much of its product for free. If, in this case, the specification range is 198 grams to 214 grams, the natural variation of the filling process (the process average ± 3 standard deviations) lies well within the specification.

$$\text{Specification range} = 214 - 198 = 16 \text{ g}$$
$$\text{Natural variation of process} = 6 \times \text{standard deviation}$$
$$= 6 \times 2 = 12 \text{ g}$$

Process capability

The *capability* of the process is a measure of the acceptability of the variation of the process. The simplest measure of capability (C_p) is given by the ratio of the specification range to the 'natural' variation of the process (i.e. ± 3 standard deviations).

$$C_p = \frac{\text{UTL} - \text{LTL}}{6s}$$

where UTL = the upper tolerance limit
LTL = the lower tolerance limit
s = the standard deviation of the process variability.

In the case of the filling process:

$$C_p = \frac{214 - 198}{6 \times 2} = \frac{16}{12} = 1.333$$

Generally, if the C_p of a process is greater than one it is taken to indicate that the process is 'capable', and a C_p of less than one indicates that the process is not 'capable', assuming that the distribution is normal. (*See* Fig. 17.9 (a), (b) and (c).)

The simple C_p measure assumes that the average of the process variation is at the mid-point of the specification range. Often the process average is off-set from the specification range, however (*see* Fig. 17.9 (d)). In such cases, *one-sided* capability indices are required to understand the capability of the process.

$$\text{Upper one-sided index } C_{pu} = \frac{\text{UTL} - \text{X}}{3s}$$

$$\text{Lower one-sided index } C_{pl} = \frac{\text{X} - \text{LTL}}{3s}$$

where X = the process average.

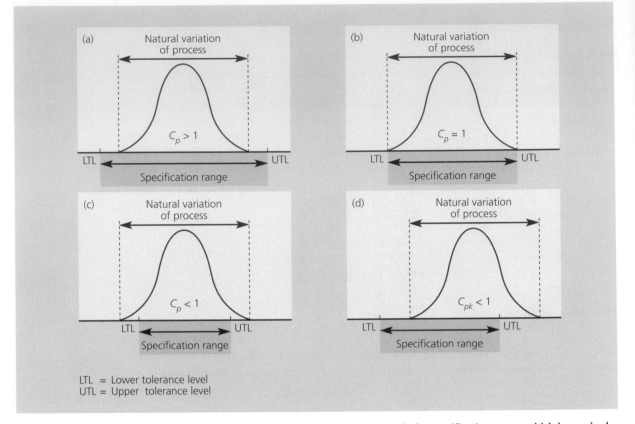

Figure 17.9 Process capability compares the natural variation of the process with the specification range which is required

Sometimes only the lower of the two one-sided indices for a process is used to indicate its capability (C_{pk}).

$$C_{pk} = \min \ (C_{pu}, \ C_{pl})$$

For example, if the natural variation of the filling process changed to have a process average of 210 grams but the standard deviation of the process remained at 2 grams:

$$C_{pu} = \frac{214 - 210}{3 \times 2} = \frac{4}{6} = 0.666$$

$$C_{pl} = \frac{210 - 198}{3 \times 2} = \frac{12}{6} = 2.0$$

$$C_{pk} = \min \ (0.666, 2.0)$$
$$= 0.666$$

Assignable causes of variation

Not all variation in processes is the result of common causes, however. There may be something wrong with the process which is assignable to a particular and preventable

MOTOROLA'S SIX-SIGMA QUALITY[12]

It is not often that the technical details of process capability become synonymous with a company's total quality programme, but that is what has happened for Motorola. Motorola is one of the world's largest industrial corporations making electronic components, semiconductors and communication systems, among other things. It employs over 100 000 people throughout the world at in excess of 50 sites. All the people in all the sites and many outside the company have now heard of Motorola's six-sigma quality objectives.

The foundations for six-sigma quality were laid some years ago when the company decided on its aim of 'total customer satisfaction'. According to Motorola this is only achieved when the product is delivered when promised, with no defects, the product does not experience any early-life failures, and the product does not fail excessively in service. To achieve this, Motorola initially focused on removing manufacturing defects. It soon came to realize, however, that many problems were caused by latent defects: that is, defects hidden within the design of its products. They may not show initially but eventually will cause failures in the field. The only way to eliminate these defects was to make sure that its design specifications were tight and its processes very capable indeed.

Motorola's six-sigma quality concept means that the natural variation of its processes (±3 standard deviations) should be half their specification range. In other words, the specification range of any part of a product should be ±6 times the standard deviation of the process. The Greek letter sigma (σ) is often used to indicate the standard deviation of a process, hence the six-sigma label. A process capability (C_p) of 1 is represented by 'three sigma' quality. This implies a defect rate of 2.7 defects per 1000. Six-sigma quality is considerably more ambitious. It implies a defect rate of only 3.4 defects per *million*. ∎

Questions

1 What process capability is implied by Motorola's six-sigma target?

2 Do you think it is worth trying to achieve such high levels of conformance?

cause. Machinery may have worn or have been set up badly. An untrained member of staff may not be following the prescribed procedure for the process. The causes of such variation are called *assignable causes*. The question for operations management is whether the results from any particular sample, when plotted on the control chart, simply represent the variation due to common causes or due to some specific and correctable, *assignable* cause. Figure 17.10, for example, shows the control chart for the average impact resistance of samples of door panels taken over time. Like any process the results vary, but the last three points seem to be lower than usual. The question is whether this is natural variation or the symptom of some more serious cause. Is the variation the result of common causes or does it indicate assignable causes in the process?

To help make this decision, *control limits* can be added to the control chart which indicate the expected extent of 'common-cause' variation. If any points lie outside these control limits then the process can be deemed out of control in the sense that variation is likely to be due to assignable causes. These control limits could be set intuitively by examining past variation during a period when the process was thought

**Figure 17.10
Control chart for
the impact
resistance of door
panels**

to be free of any variation which could be due to assignable causes. For example, if
the monthly survey of airport customers usually includes between three and four per
cent of customers who are dissatisfied with the cleanliness of the airport's restaurants,
an upper control limit could be set at four per cent complaints per month. If the
actual proportion is ever four per cent or more then the situation is investigated.

Control limits can be set in a more statistically revealing manner, however, based
on the probability that the mean of a particular sample will differ by more than a set
amount from the mean of the population from which it is taken. For example, if the
process which tests door panels had been measured to determine the normal distribution which represents its common-cause variation, then control limits can be based on
this distribution. Figure 17.11 shows the same control chart as Fig. 17.10 with the
addition of control limits put at ±3 standard deviations (of the population of sample

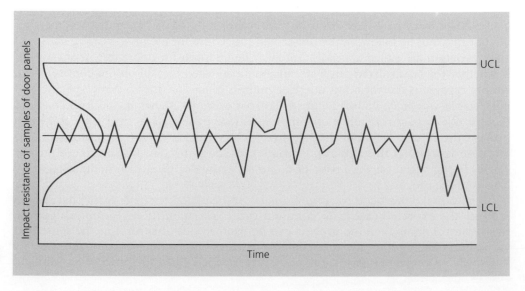

**Figure 17.11
Control chart for
the impact
resistance of door
panels with control
limits added**

means) away from the mean of sample averages. It shows that the probability of the final point on the chart being influenced by an assignable cause is very high indeed. When the process is exhibiting behaviour which is outside its normal 'common-cause' range, it is said to be 'out of control'.

From this evidence alone, however, we cannot be absolutely certain that the process is out of control. There is a small but finite chance that the (seemingly out of limits) point is just one of the rare but natural results at the tail of the distribution which describes perfectly normal behaviour. Stopping the process under these circumstances would represent a Type I error because the process is actually in control. Alternatively, ignoring a result which in reality is due to an assignable cause is a Type II error (*see* Table 17.5).

Table 17.5 Type I and Type II errors in SPC

Decision	Actual process state	
	In control	Out of control
Stop process	Type I error	Correct decision
Leave alone	Correct decision	Type II error

Control limits are usually set at three standard deviations either side of the population mean. This would mean that there is only a 0.3 per cent chance of any sample mean falling outside these limits by chance causes (that is, a chance of a Type I error of 0.3%). The control limits may be set at any distance from the population mean, but the closer the limits are to the population mean, the higher the likelihood of investigating and trying to rectify a process which is actually problem-free. If the control limits are set at two standard deviations, the chance of a Type I error increases to about 5 per cent. If the limits are set at one standard deviation then the chance of a Type I error increases to 32 per cent. When the control limits are placed at ± 3 standard deviations away from the mean of the distribution which describes 'normal' variation in the process, they are called the *upper control limit* (UCL) and *lower control limit* (LCL).

Control charts for attributes

Attributes have only two states – 'right' or 'wrong', for example – so the statistic calculated is the proportion of wrongs (p) in a sample. (This statistic follows a binomial distribution.) Control charts using p are called 'p-charts'.

In calculating the limits, the population mean ($\bar{p}$) – the actual, normal or expected proportion of 'defectives' or wrongs to rights – may not be known. Who knows, for example, the actual number of city commuters that are dissatisfied with their journey time? In such cases the population mean can be estimated from the average of the proportion of 'defectives', ($\bar{p}$) from m samples each of n items, where m should be at least 30 and n should be at least 100:

$$\bar{p} = \frac{p^1 + p^2 + p^3 \dots p^n}{m}$$

One standard deviation can then be estimated from:

$$\sqrt{\frac{\bar{p}\,(1-\bar{p})}{n}}$$

The upper and lower control limits can then be set as:

UCL = $\bar{p}$ + 3 standard deviations

LCL = $\bar{p}$ − 3 standard deviations

Of course, the LCL cannot be negative, so when it is calculated to be so it should be rounded up to zero.

Example

A credit card company deals with many hundreds of thousands of transactions every week. One of its measures of the quality of service it gives its customers is the dependability with which it mails customers' monthly accounts. The quality standard it sets itself is that accounts should be mailed within two days of the 'nominal post date' which is specified to the customer. Every week the company samples 1000 customer accounts and records the percentage which were not mailed within the standard time. When the process is working normally only two per cent of accounts are mailed outside the specified period, that is two per cent are 'defective'.

Control limits for the process can be calculated as follows:

Mean proportion defective, $\bar{p}$ = 0.02

Sample size n = 1000

Standard deviation $s = \sqrt{\dfrac{\bar{p}\,(1-\bar{p})}{n}}$

$= \sqrt{\dfrac{0.02\,(0.98)}{1000}}$

= 0.0044

With the control limits at $\bar{p} \pm 3s$:

Upper control limit (UCL) = 0.02 + 3(0.0044) = 0.0332

= 3.32%

and Lower control limit (LCL) = 0.02 − 3(0.0044) = 0.0068

= 0.68%

Figure 17.12 shows the company's control chart for this measure of quality over the last few weeks, together with the calculated control limits. It also shows that the process is in control.

Sometimes it is more convenient to plot the actual number of defects (c) rather than the proportion (or percentage) of defectives, on what is known as a c-chart. This is very similar to the p-chart but the sample size must be constant and the process mean and control limits are calculated using the following formulae:

Process mean $\bar{c} = \dfrac{c_1 + c_2 + c_3 \ldots c_m}{m}$

Control limits $= \bar{c} \pm 3\sqrt{c}$

**Figure 17.12
Control chart for
the percentage of
customer accounts
which are mailed
outside their
two-day period**

where c = number of defects
       m = number of samples

Control chart for variables

The most commonly used type of control chart employed to control variables is the $\overline{X}$-R *chart*. In fact this is really two charts in one. One chart is used to control the sample average or mean ($\overline{X}$). The other is used to control the variation within the sample by measuring the range (R). The range is used because it is simpler to calculate than the standard deviation of the sample.

The means ($\overline{X}$) chart can pick up changes in the average output from the process being charted. Changes in the means chart would suggest that the process is drifting generally away from its supposed process average, although the variability inherent in the process may not have changed (*see* Fig. 17.13).

The range (R) chart plots the range of each sample, that is the difference between the largest and the smallest measurement in the samples. Monitoring sample range gives an indication of whether the variability of the process is changing, even when the process average remains constant (*see* Fig. 17.13).

Control limits for variables control chart

As with attributes control charts, a statistical description of how the process operates under normal conditions (when there are no assignable causes) can be used to calculate control limits. The first task in calculating the control limits is to estimate the grand average or population mean ($\overline{\overline{X}}$) and average range ($\overline{R}$) using m samples each of sample size n.

The population mean is estimated from the average of a large number (m) of sample means:

$$\overline{\overline{X}} = \frac{\overline{X}_1 + \overline{X}_2 + \dots \overline{X}_m}{m}$$

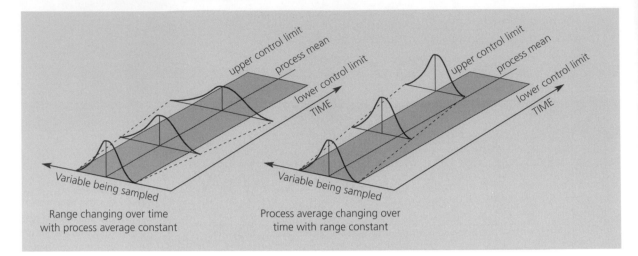

Figure 17.13 The process mean or the process range (or both) can change over time

The average range is estimated from the ranges of the large number of samples:

$$\bar{R} = \frac{R_1 + R_2 + \dots R_m}{m}$$

The control limits for the sample means chart are:

$$\text{Upper control limit (UCL)} = \bar{\bar{X}} + A_2\bar{R}$$

$$\text{Lower control limit (LCL)} = \bar{\bar{X}} - A_2\bar{R}$$

The control limits for the range charts are:

$$\text{Upper control limit (UCL)} = D_4\bar{R}$$

$$\text{Lower control limit (LCL)} = D_3\bar{R}$$

The factors A_2, D_3 and D_4 vary with sample size and are shown in Table 17.6.

The LCL for the means chart may be negative (for example, temperature or profit may be less than zero) but it may not be negative for a range chart (or the smallest measurement in the sample would be larger than the largest). If the calculation indicates a negative LCL for a range chart then the LCL should be set to zero.

Example

GAM (Groupe As Maquillage) is a contract cosmetics company, based in France but with plants around Europe, which manufactures and packs cosmetics and perfumes for other companies. One of its plants, in Ireland, operates a filling line which automatically fills plastic bottles with skin cream and seals the bottles with a screw-top cap. The tightness with which the screw-top cap is fixed is an important part of the quality of the filling line process. If the cap is screwed on too tightly there is a danger

Table 17.6 Factors for the calculation of control limits

Sample size n	A_2	D_3	D_4
2	1.880	0	3.267
3	1.023	0	2.575
4	0.729	0	2.282
5	0.577	0	2.115
6	0.483	0	2.004
7	0.419	0.076	1.924
8	0.373	0.136	1.864
9	0.337	0.184	1.816
10	0.308	0.223	1.777
12	0.266	0.284	1.716
14	0.235	0.329	1.671
16	0.212	0.364	1.636
18	0.194	0.392	1.608
20	0.180	0.414	1.586
22	0.167	0.434	1.566
24	0.157	0.452	1.548

that it will crack, if screwed on too loosely it might come loose when packed. Either outcome could cause leakage of the product in its journey between the factory and the customer. The Irish plant had received some complaints of product leakage which it suspected was caused by inconsistent fixing of the screw-top caps on its filling line.

The 'tightness' of the screw tops could be measured by a simple test device which recorded the amount of turning force (torque) which was required to unfasten the tops. The company decided to take samples of the bottles coming out of the filling-line process, test them for their unfastening torque and plot the results on a control chart. Several samples of four bottles were taken during a period when the process was regarded as being in control. The following data were calculated from this exercise:

The grand average of all samples $\bar{\bar{X}}$ = 812 g/cm³

The average range of the sample $\bar{R}$ = 6 g/cm³

Control limits for the means ($\bar{X}$) chart were calculated as follows:

$$\begin{aligned} \text{UCL} &= \bar{\bar{X}} + A_2\,\bar{R} \\ &= 812 + (A_2 \times 6) \end{aligned}$$

From Table 17.6, we know, for a sample size of four, $A_2 = 0.729$. Thus:

$$\begin{aligned} \text{UCL} &= 812 + (0.729 \times 6) \\ &= 816.37 \end{aligned}$$

$$\begin{aligned} \text{LCL} &= \bar{\bar{X}} - (A_2\bar{R}) \\ &= 812 - (0.729 \times 6) \\ &= 807.63 \end{aligned}$$

Control limits for the range chart (R) were calculated as follows:

$$
\begin{aligned}
\text{UCL} \quad &= \quad D_4 \times \overline{R} \\
&= \quad 2.282 \times 6 \\
&= \quad 13.69 \\[8pt]
\text{LCL} \quad &= \quad D_3 \overline{R} \\
&= \quad 0 \times 6 \\
&= \quad 0
\end{aligned}
$$

After calculating these averages and limits for the control chart, the company regularly took samples of four bottles during production, recorded the measurements and plotted them as shown in Fig. 17.14.

The control chart revealed that only with difficulty could the process average be kept in control. Occasional operator interventions were required. Also the process range was moving towards (and once breaking) the upper control limit. The process seemed to be becoming more variable. After investigation it was discovered that, because of faulty maintenance of the line, skin cream was occasionally contaminating the torque head (the part of the line which fitted the cap). This resulted in erratic tightening of the caps.

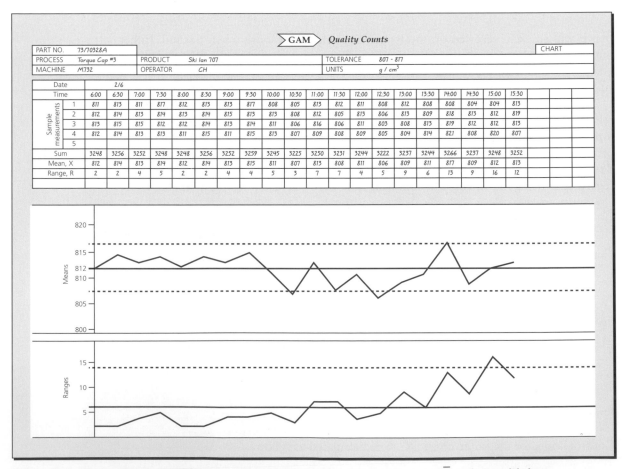

Figure 17.14 The completed control form for GAM's torque machine showing the mean ($\overline{X}$) and range (R) charts

MEASURING QUALITY AT ZANUSSI[13]

Zanussi Elettrodomestici SpA, part of the giant Swedish Electrolux company, is the biggest European producer of domestic appliances. Its Quality Assurance and Control staff act as co-ordinators of improvement actions, including problem-solving sessions, 'kaizen' meetings (*see* Chapter 19) and training programmes for all the employees. They are also responsible for the procedures and the measurement of quality performance.

Internally, quality at Zanussi is measured by 'indicators of non-conformance', where defects are classified into four types:

'Critical' (C)   – defects dangerous for the user.
'Primary' (P)   – defects causing product failure.
'Secondary' (S) – defects that permit the product to work.
'Tertiary' (T)   – aesthetic defects.

So, for example, the indicators of non-conformance for a washing machine would be as follows:

- the Safety Index (SI) is $1000 \times C/N$, where C is the number of critical defects after six working cycles of the product, and N is the number of products tested;
- the Quality Index (QI) is $1000 \times P/N$, where P is the number of primary defects after one working cycle of the product, and N is the number of products tested;
- the Confidence Index (CI) is similar to the preceding index but the defects P are counted after six working cycles;
- the Reliability Index (RI) is similar to the preceding index but the defects P are counted after 60 working cycles;
- the Mean Quality Index (MQI), taken daily, is defined as:
  $1000 \times (P + 0.5 \times S + 0.1 \times T)/N$; with P referred to only one working cycle.

The processes are controlled by recording these measures on X and R control charts.

In addition, scrap and rework are measured together with the number of rejected finished products (before and after sales) and after-sales service costs. Measures of *perceived quality and customer satisfaction* are particularly important to any producer of consumer products. At Zanussi the main indicators are the 'call rate' (calculated by model, component causing failure, production line) and the 'fidelity index' (brand re-buying percentage). The company also makes sure that quality performance results are communicated to everybody through an internal journal (*The Quality Letter*) and through huge coloured tables, set up near each product line. ■

Questions

1 What are the main elements of Zanussi's quality measurement system?

2 What do you think are the advantages and disadvantages of systems such as the ones Zanussi uses?

Interpreting control charts

Plots on a control chart which fall outside control limits are an obvious reason for believing that the process might be out of control, and therefore investigating the process. This is not the only clue which could be revealed by a control chart, however. Figure 17.15 shows some other patterns which could be interpreted as behaviour sufficiently unusual to warrant investigation.

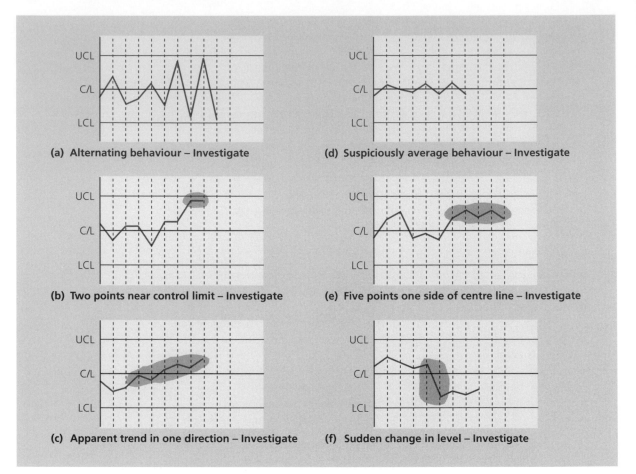

Figure 17.15 In addition to points falling outside the control limits, other unlikely sequences of points should be investigated

ACCEPTANCE SAMPLING

Process control is usually the preferred method of controlling quality because quality is being 'built-in' to the process rather than being inspected afterwards. However, sometimes it may be necessary to inspect batches of products or services either before or after a process. The purpose of acceptance sampling is to decide whether, on the basis of a sample, to accept or reject the whole batch. Examples of when batches are judged on the basis of a sample include incoming component parts from a supplier, or a batch of finished products, or a large number of examination scripts from an internal examiner, or a batch of coded questionnaires from a market research company.

Acceptance sampling is usually carried out on attributes rather than variables. It uses the proportion of wrongs to rights, or defectives to acceptables. For example, one defective item per thousand might be acceptable for incoming components or finished products; a ten per cent failure rate might be normal for a particular examination.

Table 17.7 The risks inherent in acceptance sampling

	The batch actually is	
Decision	*OK*	*Not OK*
Reject batch	Type I error	Correct decision
Accept batch	Correct decision	Type II error

Again in acceptance sampling, like process control, it is important to understand the risks inherent in using a sample to make a judgement about a far larger batch. Table 17.7 illustrates the risks of acceptance sampling in the form of Type I and Type II errors.

In acceptance sampling the Type I risk is often referred to as the producer's risk because it is the risk that the operation rejects a batch that is actually of good quality. The Type II risk is usually called the consumer's risk because it is the risk of accepting a batch that is actually poor and sending it to the consumer of the product or service.

Sampling plans

Acceptance sampling involves a sample being taken from a batch and a decision to accept or reject the batch being made by comparing the number of 'defects' found in the sample to a predetermined acceptable number. The sampling plan which describes this procedure is defined by two factors, n and c, where:

n = the sample size
c = the acceptance number of defects in the sample.

If x = number of defects actually found in the sample, a decision is made based on the following simple decision rule:

If $x \leq c$ then accept the whole batch.
If $x > c$ then reject the whole batch.

Unlike control charts it is not necessary for organizations to create their own acceptance plans. A set of tables called the Dodge-Romig Sampling Inspection Tables provides values for n and c for a given set of risks. The ability of this plan to discriminate between good batches and bad ones is based upon the binomial distribution and is described by an operating characteristic (OC) curve. The OC curve for a sampling plan shows the probability of accepting a batch as the actual percentage of defects varies. An ideal operating characteristic curve would look like the solid line in Fig. 17.16.

In this example the level of defects which is regarded as acceptable is 0.4 per cent and the sampling plan is perfect at discriminating between acceptable and unacceptable batches. The probability of accepting a batch whose actual level of defects is less than 0.4 per cent is 100 per cent and there is no chance of ever accepting a batch whose actual level of defects is more than 0.4 per cent. However, in practice, no procedure based on sampling, and therefore carrying risk, could ever deliver such an ideal curve. Only 100 per cent inspection using a perfect inspector could do so.

Any use of sampling will have to accept the existence of Type I and Type II errors. In Fig. 17.16 the dotted line shows a sampling plan for sampling 250 items ($n=250$)

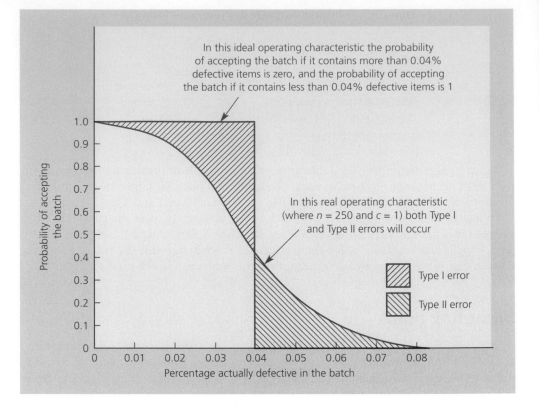

In this ideal operating characteristic the probability of accepting the batch if it contains more than 0.04% defective items is zero, and the probability of accepting the batch if it contains less than 0.04% defective items is 1

In this real operating characteristic (where $n = 250$ and $c = 1$) both Type I and Type II errors will occur

Type I error

Type II error

Figure 17.16
Ideal and real operating characteristics

and rejecting the batch if there is more than one defect ($c=1$) in the sample. A batch is acceptable if it contains 0.4 per cent or less defects (1/250 = 0.04 per cent).

What is not known is the actual percentage of defective items in any one batch, and because the procedure relies on a sample, there will always be a probability of rejecting a good batch because the number of defects in the sample is two or more despite the batch in fact being acceptable (Type I risk shown by the top shaded area). There is also a probability that in spite of accepting a batch (because the number of defects it contains is zero or one) the actual number of defects in the whole batch might be greater than 0.04 per cent (Type II risk shown in the lower shaded area of Fig. 17.16). If the sizes of these risks are felt to be too great, the sample size can be increased which will move the shape of the curve towards the ideal. However, this implies increased time and cost in inspecting the batch.

Creating an acceptance sampling plan

To create an appropriate sampling plan (that is, to decide the values of n and c) the levels of four factors need to be specified. These have been identified on the operating characteristic curve in Fig. 17.17. These four factors are then fed into the Dodge–Romig tables to give the respective values for c and n. (Using these tables is beyond the scope of this book.) The four factors are Type I error, Type II error, acceptable quality level (AQL) and lot tolerance percentage defective (LTPD).

● *Type I error.* The usual value used for producer's risk (Type I error) is often set with a probability of 0.05. This means that management is willing to take a five per cent

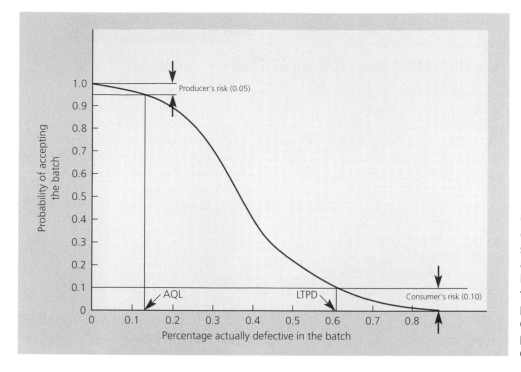

Figure 17.17
Operating
characteristic
showing
acceptable quality
level (AQL), lot
tolerance
percentage
defective (LTPD),
producer's risk and
consumer's risk

chance that a batch of good quality will be rejected when it is actually acceptable. This also implies that there is a 95 per cent chance that a good quality batch will be accepted.

● *Type II error*. The value for the consumer's risk (Type II error) is often set with a probability of 0.1. This means that management is willing to risk at most a ten per cent chance that a poor quality batch will be accepted, implying that there is a 90 per cent chance that a poor quality batch will actually be rejected.

● *AQL*. The acceptable quality level is the actual percentage of defects in a batch which the organization is willing to reject mistakenly (by chance) five per cent of the time (assuming a 0.05 Type I error) when the batch is actually acceptable.

● *LTPD*. The lot tolerance percentage defective is the actual percentage of defects in a batch that management is willing to accept mistakenly ten per cent of the time (assuming a 0.1 Type II error).

Criticisms of acceptance sampling

A frequently made criticism of acceptance sampling is that it assumes that some amount of defects and failure is acceptable to the organization, or its customers. By accepting the inevitability of failure and poor quality, it is argued, the operation will become 'lazy' at trying to eliminate the causes of bad quality. Rather than see quality as primarily something to be improved, acceptance sampling views it as being almost 'predetermined' by the characteristics of the process. The main task is to measure output and understand the risks involved, not to get to the root causes of poor quality. More recent approaches to quality management (such as TQM, *see* Chapter 20) suggest that 'right first time every time' is the only acceptable approach and that organizations should strive to produce zero defective items rather than some 'acceptable quality level'.

Zak Limbada, Pretoria Portland Cement Company

After its country's first democratic elections, South Africa's cement industry found itself at the centre of the new government's house-building efforts. A typical 60 square metre house requires six tonnes of cement with, on average, another two tonnes required to provide roads and services. The Pretoria Portland Cement Company is the largest cement producer in the whole of Africa and provides 45 per cent of South Africa's requirements from its seven factories. Zak Limbada is a Production Superintendent at one of the plants. His job is to ensure the efficient and effective manufacture of the various cement products at the plant (but product quality is among his main concerns).

'Quality and consistency of quality is particularly important in cement manufacture because of the downstream implications in its application. Any deviations from the specified characteristics of the cement could affect its strength in use. This is why we put so much effort into quality control. First, the basic raw materials, limestone and iron ore, are milled to a powder form. This is where the factory's quality control starts. Samples of the milled output are automatically taken every hour. The samples are examined with an X-ray fluorescence spectrometer and the results fed into a process-control computer which automatically makes adjustments to the feeders which control the flow of input materials to the process. In this way we control the exact characteristics of the milled output.

'The next stage is the blending process where rotary distributors ensure that a consistent mixture of the milled materials is transferred to a storage silo. After blending, the material is sampled two hourly and fed to a kiln 148 metres long at a rate of 86 tonnes per hour and heated to 1400°C so that the lime and silica combine. The product from this process is called clinker. Quality checks here are made on an hourly basis. The clinker is now ready for the final milling process called 'cement milling'. Gypsum is added and the material crushed to a very fine powder. It is the fineness of this grinding process together with the chemical composition of the cement which determines the final strength of the cement. The best way to test for quality at this stage is to sample the output every hour for surface area and actually make a cube or prism of the daily composite of cement. This can be crushed in order to test its strength. The cement powder is then bagged and palletized, ready for sale to the market.'

The process which Zak manages is highly capital intensive. A typical factory costs R500 million (£100 million) to build and employs around 250 people. He sees people as the key factor in achieving a quality product, however.

'Although many of the quality improvements over the last few years have been made by improving the level of technology we use in the plant, it is our operating staff who release the potential of the technology. Vigilant staff can ensure good quality. Perfect vigilance means perfect quality. We rely on our staff to detect problems so that when necessary the "experts" can be called in to adjust the process. We work hard at equipping and motivating our staff to know how to make that judgement. Training can provide the skill but maintaining motivation in a fairly monotonous process is more of a challenge. We do this by communication and empowerment. Staff are responsible for quality testing and recording results on control charts. The statistical control limits on the charts trigger process adjustments. We also have what we call "green areas". These are special rooms, in the plant, where we meet every day to discuss quality and other work-related issues. We explain how production went yesterday, what problems were encountered, and through collective wisdom and input agree what we should do about them. It is a general forum for making sure that everyone knows what is going on, and that no quality problems are overlooked. More importantly, it demonstrates that everybody in the plant is involved in quality management. This is the key to the point. The paradox is that the advances in our process technology have made us even more dependent on our people.' ■

SUMMARY ANSWERS TO KEY QUESTIONS

How can quality be defined?

■ In several ways. Among the approaches are the transcendent approach which views quality as meaning 'innate excellence', the manufacturing-based approach which views quality as being 'free of errors', the user-based approach which views quality as 'fit for purpose', the product-based approach which views quality as a 'measurable set of characteristics' and the value-based approach which views quality as a balance between 'cost and price'.

■ The definition of quality used in this book combines all these approaches to define quality as 'consistent conformance to customers' expectations'.

How can quality problems be diagnosed?

■ At a broad level, quality is best modelled as the gap between customers' expectations concerning the product or service and their perceptions concerning the product or service.

■ Modelling quality this way will allow the development of a diagnostic tool which is based around the perception–expectation gap. If such a gap exists it is likely to be caused by one or more of the gaps between factors which influence expectations and perceptions.

■ There are four main gaps:
– the gap between a customer's specification and the operation's specification;
– the gap between the product or service concept and the way the organization has specified it;
– the gap between the way quality has been specified and the actual delivered quality;
– the gap between the actual delivered quality and the way the product or service has been described to the customer.

■ It is the third gap (between the specification of quality and the actual quality delivered) which is of particular concern to operations managers.

What steps lead towards conformance to specification?

■ Six steps, which are:
– define quality characteristics;
– decide how to measure each of the quality characteristics;

– set quality standards for each characteristic;
– control quality against these standards;
– find and correct the causes of poor quality;
– continue to make improvement.

■ Most quality planning and control involves sampling the operations performance in some way. Sampling can give rise to erroneous judgements which are classed as either Type I or Type II errors. Type I errors involve making corrections where none are needed. Type II errors involve not making corrections where they are in fact needed.

How can statistical process control help quality planning and control?

■ Statistical process control (SPC) involves using control charts to track the performance of one or more quality characteristics in the operation. The power of control charting lies in its ability to set control limits derived from the statistics of the natural variation of processes. These control limits are often set at ± 3 standard deviations of the natural variation of the process samples.

■ Control charts can be used for either attributes or variables. An attribute is a quality characteristic which has two states (for example, right or wrong). A variable is one which can be measured on a continuously variable scale.

■ Process control charts allow operations managers to distinguish between the 'normal' variation inherent in any process and the variations which could be caused by the process going out of control.

How can acceptance sampling help quality planning and control?

■ Acceptance sampling helps managers to understand the risks they are taking when they make decisions about a whole batch of products on the basis of a sample taken from that batch. The risks of any particular sampling plan are shown on its operating characteristic (OC) curve.

■ Some of the assumptions within acceptance sampling (most notably that a certain level of defects is 'acceptable') are not looked on favourably by proponents of total quality management (see Chapter 20).

669

Handles and Hinges (H&H) Ltd

H&H was established in Birmingham, England, in 1984 by two young entrepreneurs, Dave Philips and Chris Agnew, both experienced in the hardware trade. The business specialized in the 'designer' market for polished metal (brass or stainless-steel) door handles, cupboard knobs, furniture fittings (mostly used in shop/office furniture) and hinges. By 1996, sales had grown to about £5 million per year. This success was based on H&H's reputation for high quality, unique designs of both traditional and modern products, many of which were selected and specified by architects for large and prestigious projects such as new office developments in London's Docklands. Dave, the Chief Executive Officer, with responsibility for sales, believed that most orders from construction companies were placed with H&H because they assumed they had no other choice once the H&H products had been specified. Larger companies would sometimes suggest to the architect that similar products were available at less than half the price. This advice was invariably ignored as the architect would be attracted by H&H's designs and quality, and would be reluctant to risk 'spoiling' multi-million-pound projects for the sake of saving a few thousand pounds. Dave outlines the characteristics of the changing market place.

'Because of the recession in the construction industry, particularly in office building, we have, since 1990, expanded our direct sales to large UK hardware retail companies, which now account for about 40 per cent of our sales value, but only about 15 per cent of our gross profit. This segment is much more price-sensitive, so we must be able to manufacture good-quality, simple, standard products at low costs comparable to those of our competitors. Some of the reduced costs have been achieved by using thinner and cheaper materials similar to those used in our competitors' products. We have just received our first consignment of brass sheet from Poland with a saving of over ten per cent in this case. We also had to re-organize to reduce our processing costs. Chris has done a great job of changing all production to modern batch methods (see Fig. 17.18). However, I am concerned that we are often late delivering to our UK retail customers, and this makes it difficult to keep good relationships, and to get repeat orders. Fast delivery of relatively small quantities is required in the 'retail segment'. Whereas the construction/contractors market allows very long production lead times, and dependable delivery is crucial to avoid completion delays, for which we have been held financially accountable on some occasions!

'When customers complain about delivery or about faulty products, we try to compensate them in some way to keep their business – for example, by credit notes or discounts on the next order. Our representatives each spend about one day a week dealing with the consequences of late deliveries, but on the positive side, a meeting with a client is an opportunity to get the next order. The hardware retail companies often require very quick delivery, which is often only achieved by switching production to the item which is required first.

'Really, I am more concerned about reports of quality problems; an increasing number of construction companies have complained to us about dented or scratched handles, but our production department assures us that they left the factory in good condition and must have been damaged on site; which is to be expected on a large construction site. The Quality Control Manager says, however, he cannot give an absolute guarantee that they were all OK, because we only do sampling of final production; if more than a few in a sample are found at final inspection to be sub-standard, the whole batch is rejected, reinspected, sorted and reworked. Using express courier transport and overtime in the factory, rework usually can be done in about a week, but invariably the contractors complain to the architect, perhaps because they dislike being told who to buy from. This can lead to lots of correspondence and meetings between H&H, the contractor and the architect, when we could be doing other things. This problem seems to have got worse in the last two years; often it's also difficult to agree if the product is sub-standard. It is frequently just a question of how shiny (or matt) the polish and lacquer finish is; at other times there are scratches in areas that really can't been seen in use. Often the customers are too fussy, anyway.'

Discussions with Chris (the Manufacturing Director) put a different perspective on the problem.

'The sales catalogue shows pictures of our products prepared for photography; special effects are used to give a bright polished finish but we actually use a matt finish. The samples used by Sales are specially made by experienced craftsmen to eliminate any scratching or minor

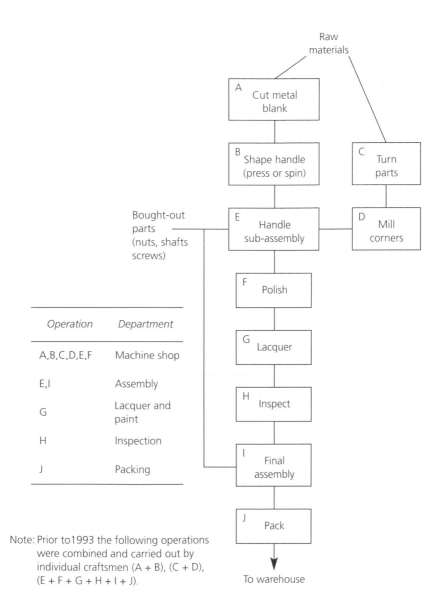

Raw materials

| A | Cut metal blank |

| B | Shape handle (press or spin) | | C | Turn parts |

Bought-out parts (nuts, shafts screws)

| E | Handle sub-assembly | | D | Mill corners |

| F | Polish |

| G | Lacquer |

| H | Inspect |

| I | Final assembly |

| J | Pack |

To warehouse

Operation	Department
A,B,C,D,E,F	Machine shop
E,I	Assembly
G	Lacquer and paint
H	Inspection
J	Packing

Note: Prior to 1993 the following operations were combined and carried out by individual craftsmen (A + B), (C + D), (E + F + G + H + I + J).

Figure 17.18 Typical production processes for batches of handles

faults; of course, we cannot always repeat that standard with the modern batch production methods.

'We were aware that the reorganization of production methods could lead to quality problems, so I introduced statistical control, a subject I studied extensively in a quantitative methods course at the local college. Our inspectors now take random samples of batches of com- *ponents and measure important dimensions such as the diameter or length of brass handles, the thickness of the incoming materials, etc. Batches which fail are either rejected or reworked, and all material where we have identified any fault at all is returned to the supplier, and our buyers routinely threaten to place orders elsewhere. I instructed the supervisors to inspect press tooling just*

671

before the start of each production batch to ensure that there are no surface faults, so I think it is unlikely that the dents and blemishes are caused in production. I must make a point of checking that this is happening. Anyway, our final inspection sampling has been changed to give an acceptable quality level (AQL) of two per cent whereas until recently it was only five per cent. We have had to increase the number of final inspectors by four at a cost of £15 000 each per annum, but all the management team agrees that with quality products we must be confident of the final quality before packing. We trained some of our best assemblers in SPC and made them full-time inspectors; the combination of their technical and statistical skills ensures that we have the right people for this job. We could not rely on our operators to do any dimensional checks; hardly any of them know how to measure using a metric rule, let alone a micrometer or vernier gauge. It is best to keep them concentrating on achieving correct output targets. I believe that most quality problems here must be caused by occasional operator carelessness.

'The batch method of production has given us much more control over operations. No longer do we have to rely on hard-to-recruit craftsmen who did everything slowly and unpredictably. Now we make the most of economic batches at each stage, benefiting from the economies of scale of longer runs and cheaper unskilled labour. With incentive bonuses based on effective performance against agreed standard times, all our people are working faster to achieve the company's goal of higher productivity. There is no doubt that our operations are now more productive than they've ever been. With high quality and low costs, we are now set for a major assault on the competition. We expect our profits to rise dramatically from the currently inadequate one per cent return on sales.' ■

Questions

1 How does the company compete in its market place, and what is the role of 'quality' in its competitive strategy?

2 Do you think that the company's use of statistical quality control is sensible?

3 Apply the gap model of quality diagnostics (Fig. 17.5) to the company.

DISCUSSION QUESTIONS

1 Describe and explain the differences between needs, wants and expectations that a customer might have for:

a tourist-class flight to America
a talking doll
an operations management course.

2 Define the quality characteristics for the following products and services and suggest ways in which each characteristic could be measured. Identify whether the characteristics are attributes or variables:

a restaurant meal
a washing machine
a taxi service.

3 Discuss the advantages and disadvantages of 100 per cent inspection. Comment on the appropriateness of 100 per cent inspection, and how it might be carried out, in the following examples:

– the temperature of a restaurant meal
– the appropriateness of a student for a first-class honours degree
– the punctuality of a fleet of city buses
– the results to be obtained from a packet of garden seeds.

4 Explain why, when 100 per cent inspection takes place, errors in the product or service may still get through to the customer. Illustrate your answer with a product and service of your own choice. What might be done to try to minimize such errors occurring?

5 A factory uses two machines to slice plastic extrusions. The specification range for the output of machine 1 is 16.7 to 17.3 cm and is 22 to 26 cm for machine 2. The outputs of the machines are normally distributed around 17 and 24 cm respectively with standard deviations of 1.7 and 2.1 cm. The normal variation in the two machines is known to be 0.5 and 1.9 cm. The operations manager has the budget to upgrade one of the two machines this year. Which one would you recommend is replaced on the basis of its ability to do the job?

6 A manufacturer of printed circuit boards (PCBs) is concerned that the process is becoming out of control. The usual proportion of defective boards is six per cent which is thought to be better than the industry average. The manager has taken one sample a day for the last ten days, with 100 boards in each sample. The results are shown below. Draw a control chart and comment on the process.

Sample no.   1 2 3 4   5 6 7   8 9 10
No. of defects 3 0 1 4 10 0 6 12 5   7

7 The regional manager of a national train network is considering giving guarantees to customers about the reliability of the trains arriving at the principal station in the region. The arrival times of 20 trains were checked each day over a period of several weeks when there were no known unusual circumstances. It was found that the trains were, on average, three minutes later than their scheduled time of arrival. The average range was 12 minutes. What advice would you give the manager?

8 Describe the advantages of using control charts to monitor processes. Discuss how appropriate they might be for the following activities:
– complaint monitoring for a package holiday company
– monitoring of marks for operations management examinations
– engine failure in aircraft
– supermarket check-out queues.

9 Once a day a company that specializes in ride-on lawn mowers undertakes a thorough check of a small sample of its products. There are five main checks covering the machine's appearance (measured in terms of the number of blemishes in the metalwork), its reliability (mean time between failures in hours), top speed (mph), fuel consumption (mpg) and noise levels (dB). Table 17.8 provides the UCLs, LCLs and averages for each factor and the results of the last ten checks. Comment on whether or not you think any parts of the process need investigating and explain your reasons.

10 Explain what is meant by acceptance sampling. Compare this approach to quality control with the total quality management (TQM) approach explained in Chapter 20.

Table 17.8 Lawn mower sample checks

Factor	Appearance	Reliability	Speed	Fuel	Noise
UCL	5	190	10.5	45	3.4
Average	2	150	9	38	2.8
LCL	0	110	7.5	31	2.2
Sample					
1	2	112	8.6	41	3.0
2	1	161	8.4	38	2.9
3	2	120	8.7	43	2.6
4	2	182	8.8	35	2.8
5	1	115	9.0	32	2.9
6	2	173	9.6	41	2.7
7	4	143	9.1	34	3.0
8	4	180	9.2	33	2.3
9	4	119	9.8	33	2.3
10	4	175	9.5	32	2.5

NOTES ON CHAPTER

1 Based on Gummesson, E. (1993) 'Service Productivity, Service Quality and Profitability', *Proceedings of the 8th International Conference of the Operations Management Association*, Warwick, UK.

2 Garvin, D. (1984) 'What Does "Product Quality" Really Mean?', *Sloan Management Review*, Fall.

3 Gummesson, E. *op.cit.*

4 Parasuraman, A., Zeithaml, V.A. and Berry, L.L. (1985) 'A Conceptual Model of Service Quality and Implications for Future Research', *Journal of Marketing*, Vol 49, Fall, pp 41–50 and Gummesson, E. (1987) 'Lip Service: A Neglected Area in Services Marketing', *Journal of Services Marketing*, Vol 1, No 1, pp 19–23.

5 Haywood-Farmer, J. and Nollet, J. (1991) *Services Plus: Effective Service Management*, Morin.

6 Berry, L.L. and Parasuraman, A. (1991) *Marketing Services: Competing Through Quality*, The Free Press.

7 Based on Parasuraman, A., *op. cit.*

8 Sources: 'Centrebank Says Sorry with Cash', *The Times*, 19 June 1994 and Browing, D.D. (1989) 'Put your Money Where your Mouth is', *Bank Marketing*, Vol 21, No 9.

9 Based on Wild, R. (1989) *Production and Operations Management*, Cassell.

10 Source: Discussion with company staff.

11 Source: 'Scan Avoids Needless Appendectomy', *The Sunday Times*, 23 Feb 1997.

12 Source: Discussions with company staff and company press releases.

13 Source: De Toni A., Nassimbeni, G. and Tanchia, S. (1995) 'An instrument for Quality Performance Measurement', *International Journal of Production Economics*, Vol 38, pp 199–207.

SELECTED FURTHER READINGS

Bounds, G., Yorks, L., Adams, M. and Ranney, G. (1994) *Beyond Quality Management: Towards the Emerging Paradigm*, McGraw-Hill.

Dale, B.G. and Shaw, P. (1991) 'Statistical Process Control: An Examination of Some Common Queries', *International Journal of Production Economics*, Vol 22, No 1.

Dale, B.G. (ed) (1994) *Managing Quality* (2nd edn), Prentice Hall.

Dale, B.G. and Oakland, J.S. (1994) *Quality Improvement Through Standards* (2nd edn), Stanley Thornes.

Dodge, H.F. and Romig, G.H. (1959) *Sampling Inspection Tables – Single and Double Sampling* (2nd edn), John Wiley.

Duncan, A.J. (1974) *Quality Control and Industrial Statistics*, Irwin.

Evans, J.R. and Lindsay, W.M. (1993) *The Management and Control of Quality* (2nd edn), West.

Garrity, S.M. (1993) *Basic Quality Improvement*, Prentice Hall International.

Garvin, D.A. (1988) *Managing Quality*, The Free Press.

Gupta, V.K. and Sagar, R. (1993) 'Total Quality Control Using PCs in an Engineering Company', *International Journal of Production Research*, Vol 31, No 1.

Kehoe, D.F. (1996) *The Fundamentals of Quality Management*, Chapman and Hall.

Montgomery, D.C. (1985) *Introduction to Statistical Quality Control*, John Wiley.

Montgomery, D.C. (1991) *Introduction to Statistical Quality Control* (2nd edn), John Wiley.

Mortimer, J. (ed) (1988) *Statistical Process Control – an ISF Executive Briefing*, IFS/Springer-Verlag.

Oakland, J.S. and Followell, R.F. (1990) *Statistical Process Control – A Practical Guide* (2nd edn), Heinemann.

Oakland, J.S. (1993) *Total Quality Management* (2nd edn), Butterworth-Heinemann.

Owen, M. (1993) *SPC and Business Improvement*, IFS.

Swenseth, S.R., Muralidhr, K. and Wilson, R.L. (1993) 'Planning for Continual Improvement in a Just-in-time Environment', *International Journal of Operations and Production Management*, Vol 13, No 6.

Zeithaml, V.A., Parasuraman, A. and Berry, L.L. (1990) *Delivering Quality Service: Balancing Customer Perceptions and Expectations*, The Free Press.

PART FOUR

IMPROVEMENT

Even the best operation will need to improve because the operation's competitors will also be improving. This part of the book looks at how managers can make their operation perform better, how they can stop it failing, and how they can bring their improvement activities together.

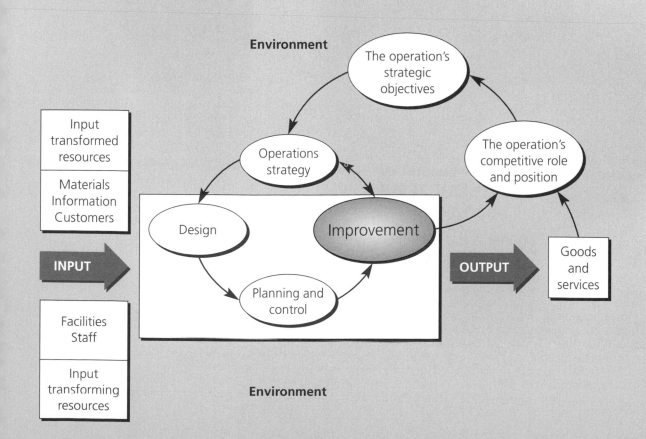

Chapter 18
OPERATIONS IMPROVEMENT

- *How can operations measure their performance in terms of the five performance objectives?*
- *How can operations managers prioritize improvement of performance objectives?*
- *What are the broad approaches to managing the rate of improvement?*
- *Where does business process re-engineering (BPR) fit into the improvement activity?*
- *What are the techniques of improvement?*

Chapter 19
FAILURE PREVENTION AND RECOVERY

- *Why do operations fail?*
- *How is failure measured?*
- *How can failure and potential failure be detected and analysed?*
- *How can operations improve their reliability?*
- *How should operations recover when failure does occur?*

Chapter 20
TOTAL QUALITY MANAGEMENT

- *Where did the idea of total quality management (TQM) come from?*
- *What are the main differences between traditional quality management and TQM?*
- *What is the role of ISO 9000 in TQM?*
- *What are the main implementation issues in TQM initiatives?*
- *How do quality awards and models contribute towards TQM?*

OPERATIONS IMPROVEMENT

INTRODUCTION

Even when an operation is designed and its activities planned and controlled, the operations manager's task is not finished. All operations, no matter how well managed, are capable of improvement. In fact in recent years the emphasis has shifted markedly towards making improvement one of the main responsibilities of operations managers. In this part of the book we choose to treat improvement activities in three stages. The first, in this chapter, looks at the approaches and techniques which can be adopted to improve the operation. The second, in Chapter 19, looks at improvement from another perspective, that is how operations can prevent failure and how they can recover when they do suffer a failure. Finally, in Chapter 20, we look at how improvement activities can be supported through the total quality management (TQM) approach. These three stages are interrelated as shown in Fig. 18.1.

Figure 18.1 Model of operations improvement showing the issues covered in this chapter

CHAPTER 18: KEY QUESTIONS

● *How can operations measure their performance in terms of the five performance objectives?*

● *How can operations managers prioritize improvement of performance objectives?*

● *What are the broad approaches to managing the rate of improvement?*

● *Where does business process re-engineering (BPR) fit into the improvement activity?*

● *What are the techniques of improvement?*

MEASURING AND IMPROVING PERFORMANCE

Before operations managers can devise their approach to the improvement of their operations, they need to know how good they are already. The urgency, direction and priorities of improvement will be determined partly by whether the current performance of an operation is judged to be good, bad or indifferent. All operations therefore need some kind of *performance measurement* as a prerequisite for improvement.

Performance measurement

Performance measurement is the process of *quantifying action*, where measurement means the process of quantification and the performance of the operation is assumed to derive from actions taken by its management.[1] Performance here is defined as the degree to which an operation fulfils the five performance objectives at any point in time, in order to satisfy its customers.

The polar diagrams (which we introduced in Chapter 3) in Fig. 18.2 illustrate this concept. The five performance objectives which we have used throughout this book can be regarded as the dimensions of overall performance which satisfy customers. The market's needs and expectations of each performance objective will vary (as we also discussed in Chapter 3). The extent to which an operation meets its market's needs will also vary, possibly only meeting them in some dimensions. In addition, market requirements and the operation's performance could also change over time. In Fig. 18.2 the operation is originally almost meeting the requirements of the market as far as quality and flexibility are concerned, but is under-performing on its speed, dependability and cost. After some time has elapsed the operation has improved its speed and cost to match market requirements but its flexibility no longer matches market requirements, not because it has deteriorated in an absolute sense but because the requirements of the market have changed.

Performance measures

The five performance objectives – quality, speed, dependability, flexibility and cost – are really composites of many smaller measures. For example, an operation's cost is derived

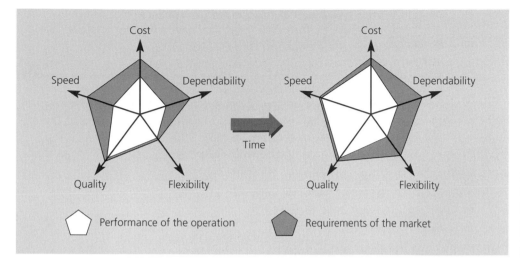

**Figure 18.2
Customers' needs
and the operation's
performance might
both change over
time**

from many factors which could include the purchasing efficiency of the operation, the efficiency with which it converts materials, the productivity of its staff, the ratio of direct to indirect staff, and so on. All of these factors individually give a partial view of the operation's cost performance, and many of them overlap in terms of the information they include. Each of them does give a perspective on the cost performance of an operation, however, which could be useful either to identify areas for improvement or to monitor the extent of improvement. If an organization regards its 'cost' performance as unsatisfactory, therefore, disaggregating it into 'purchasing efficiency', 'operations efficiency', 'staff productivity', etc. might explain the root cause of the poor performance.

Table 18.1 shows some of the partial measures which can be used to judge an operation's performance.

Performance standards

After an operation has measured its performance by using a 'bundle' of partial measures, it needs to make a judgement as to whether its performance is good, bad, or indifferent. There are several ways it can do this, each of which involves comparing the current achieved level of performance with some kind of standard. Four kinds of standard are commonly used.

Historical standards

Historical standards would mean comparing current performance against previous performance. For example, if an organization was delivering products to its customers four weeks after the customer initially requested them, its performance would be judged to be quite good if last year it was taking six weeks to deliver. Historical performance standards are effective when judging whether an operation is getting better or worse over time, but they give no indication as to whether performance should be regarded as satisfactory.

Target performance standards

Target performance standards are those which are set arbitrarily to reflect some level of performance which is regarded as appropriate or reasonable. For example, if, under

Table 18.1 Some typical partial measures of performance

Performance objective	Some typical measures
Quality	Number of defects per unit
	Level of customer complaints
	Scrap level
	Warranty claims
	Mean time between failures
	Customer satisfaction score
Speed	Customer query time
	Order lead time
	Frequency of delivery
	Actual *versus* theoretical throughput time
	Cycle time
Dependability	Percentage of orders delivered late
	Average lateness of orders
	Proportion of products in stock
	Mean deviation from promised arrival
	Schedule adherence
Flexibility	Time needed to develop new products/services
	Range of products/services
	Machine change-over time
	Average batch size
	Time to increase activity rate
	Average capacity/maximum capacity
	Time to change schedules
Cost	Minimum delivery time/average delivery time
	Variance against budget
	Utilization of resources
	Labour productivity
	Added value
	Efficiency
	Cost per operation hour

the circumstances, it is regarded as reasonable for the previously mentioned operation to deliver within four weeks then the performance of an operation which actually did deliver in four weeks would be regarded as acceptable. The budgets which most large organizations prepare are examples of target performance standards.

Competitor performance standards

Competitor performance standards compare the achieved performance of the operation with that which is being achieved by one or more of the organization's competitors. For example, if the operation is delivering within four weeks but most of its competitors can deliver within three weeks then its performance would not be regarded as very good. The advantage of competitor-based performance standards is that they relate an operation's performance directly to its competitive ability in the market place. In terms of strategic performance improvement, competitive standards are the most useful. For some operations in the not-for-profit sector this type of performance standard needs to be modified. Comparison against competitors might not even be possible. A police department, for example, would find it difficult to identify its 'competitors' but could compare its performance to that of similar police departments elsewhere.

Absolute performance standards

An absolute performance standard is one which is taken to its theoretical limits. For example, the quality standard of 'zero defects' or the inventory standard of 'zero inventories' are both absolute standards. These standards are perhaps never achievable in practice but they do allow an operation to calibrate itself against a theoretical limit. In the previous example, the product which was in fact delivered in four weeks to the customer might take only four hours to be made within the factory and delivered to the customer. In practice the operation will probably never achieve a four-hour delivery time, but the standard has illustrated how much the operation could theoretically improve.

Benchmarking

One approach which some companies use to compare their operations with those of other companies, or other parts of its own company, is called *benchmarking*. Originally the term 'benchmark' derives from land surveying where a mark, cut in the rock, would act as a reference point. In 1979 the Xerox Corporation, the document and copying company, used the term 'competitive benchmarking' to describe a process:

'used by the manufacturing function to revitalize itself by comparing the features, assemblies and components of its products with those of competitors'.[2]

(*See* box on Rank Xerox's benchmarking process.) Since that time the term benchmarking has widened its meaning in a number of ways.[3]

● It is no longer restricted only to the manufacturing operations but is also seen as being applicable to other functional areas such as purchasing and marketing.
● It is no longer confined only to manufacturing organizations but has been used in services such as hospitals and banks.
● It is no longer practised only by experts and consultants but can involve all staff in the organization.
● The term 'competitive' has been widened to mean more than just the direct comparison with competitors. It is now taken to mean benchmarking to gain competitive advantage (perhaps by comparison with, and learning from, non-competitive organizations).

Types of benchmarking

There are many different types of benchmarking (which are not necessarily mutually exclusive), some of which are listed below:

● *Internal benchmarking* is a comparison between operations or parts of operations which are within the same total organization. For example, a large motor vehicle manufacturer with several factories might choose to benchmark each factory against the others.
● *External benchmarking* is a comparison between an operation and other operations which are part of a different organization.

XEROX BENCHMARKING[4]

Possibly the best-known pioneer of benchmarking in Europe is Rank Xerox, the document and imaging company, who created the original market for copiers. The virtual monopoly the company had in its sector almost became its undoing, however. Spurred by the threat from

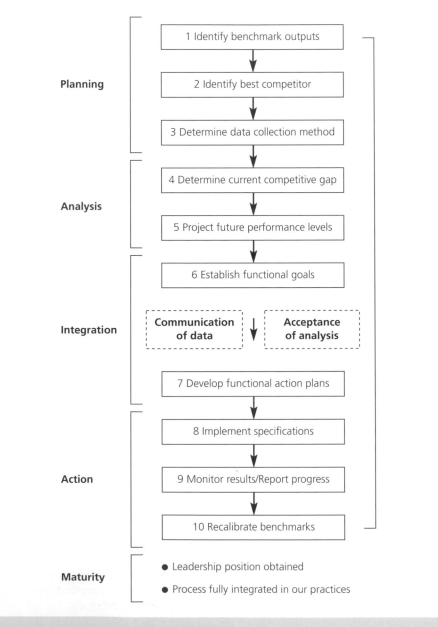

Figure 18.3 Xerox's benchmarking process

the emerging Japanese copier companies, an in-depth study within the company recognized that fundamental changes were needed. To understand how it should change, the company decided to evaluate itself externally – a process which became known as competitive benchmarking. The results of this study shocked the company. Its Japanese rivals were selling machines for about what it cost Xerox to make them. Nor could this be explained by differences in quality. The study found that, when compared with its Japanese rivals, the company had nine times more suppliers, was rejecting ten times as many machines on the production line and taking twice as long to get products to market. Benchmarking also showed that productivity would need to grow 18 per cent per year over five years if it was to catch up with its rivals.

Rank Xerox sees benchmarking as helping it achieve two objectives. At a strategic level it helps set standards of performance, while at an operational level it helps the company understand the best practices and operations methods which can help it achieve its performance objectives. The benchmarking process developed by Rank Xerox has five phases (*see* Fig. 18.3).

Its experience of using this approach has led Xerox to a number of conclusions:

● The first phase, planning, is crucial to the success of the whole process. A good plan will identify a realistic objective for the benchmarking study, which is achievable and clearly aligned with business priorities.

● A prerequisite for benchmarking success is to understand thoroughly your own processes. Without this it is difficult to compare your processes against those of other companies.

● Look at what is already available. A lot of information is already in the public domain. Published accounts, journals, conferences and professional associations all can provide information which is useful for benchmarking purposes.

● Be sensitive in asking for information from other companies. The golden rule is 'Don't ask any questions that we would not like to be asked ourselves'. ■

Questions

1 What kind of information did Xerox discover in its benchmarking study?

2 Of the five performance objectives (quality, speed, dependability, flexibility, cost) which do you think are the most difficult to discover about your competitors' performance?

● *Non-competitive benchmarking* is benchmarking against external organizations which do not compete directly in the same markets.

● *Competitive benchmarking* is a comparison directly between competitors in the same, or similar, markets.

● *Performance benchmarking* is a comparison between the levels of achieved performance in different operations. For example, an operation might compare its own performance in terms of some or all of our performance objectives – quality, speed, dependability, flexibility and cost – against other organizations' performance in the same dimensions.

● *Practice benchmarking* is a comparison between an organization's operations practices, or way of doing things, and those adopted by another operation. For example, a large retail store might compare its systems and procedures for controlling stock levels with those used by another department store. The objective is usually to see whether anything can be learned from the practices adopted by other organizations, which could then be transferred to the organization's own operational practices.

The objectives of benchmarking

Benchmarking is partly concerned with being able to judge how well an operation is doing. It can be seen, therefore, as one approach to setting realistic performance standards. It is also concerned with searching out new ideas and practices which might be able to be copied or adapted. For example, a bank might learn some things from a supermarket about how it could cope with demand fluctuations during the day. The success of benchmarking, however, is largely due to more than its ability to set performance standards and enable organizations to copy one another. Benchmarking is essentially about stimulating creativity and providing a stimulus which enables operations better to understand how they should be serving their customers. Many organizations find that it is the process itself of looking at different parts of their own company or looking at external companies which allows them to understand the connection between the external market needs which an operation is trying to satisfy and the internal operations practices it is using to try to satisfy them. In other words, benchmarking can help to reinforce the idea of the direct contribution which an operation has to the competitiveness of its organization.

IMPROVEMENT PRIORITIES[5]

In Chapter 3 we identified two major influences on the way in which operations decide to which performance objectives they need to pay particular attention. These two influences were:

● the needs and preferences of customers; and
● the performance and activities of competitors.

The consideration of customers' needs has particular significance in shaping the objectives of all operations. The fundamental purpose of operations is to create goods and services in such a way as to meet the needs of their customers. What customers find important, therefore, the operation should also regard as important. If customers for a particular product or service prefer low prices to wide range, then the operation should devote more energy to reducing its costs than increasing the flexibility which enables it to provide a range of products or services. The needs and preferences of customers shape the *importance* of operations objectives within the operation.

The role of competitors is different to that of customers. Competitors are the points of comparison against which the operation can judge its performance. From a competitive viewpoint, as operations improve their performance, the improvement which matters most is that which takes the operation past the performance levels achieved by its competitors. The role of competitors then is in determining achieved *performance*.

Both importance and performance have to be brought together before any judgement can be made as to the relative priorities for improvement. Just because something is particularly important to its customers does not mean that an operation should

FOLLOWING THE BENCHMARKING RULES

Some of the most successful examples of benchmarking have occurred when a number of companies co-operate in exchanging information about themselves. However, the potential for misunderstanding, mis-reporting, or downright misinformation is high. Most organizations are understandably cautious about releasing information that will be of benefit to potential competitors without an equal pay-off. In order to impose some 'rules' into the process of identifying and learning from best practice, it is important for companies mutually to agree common 'protocols' relating to how companies should behave when exchanging information. The following protocol is that recommended by the American-based Productivity and Quality Centre, and gives a flavour of some of the issues which can help the mutual exchange of information.

1 Know and abide by the Benchmarking Code of Conduct.
2 Have basic knowledge of benchmarking and follow a benchmarking process.
3 Prior to initiating contact with potential benchmarking partners, determine what to benchmark, identify key performance variables to study, recognize superior performing companies, and complete a rigorous self-assessment.
4 Develop a questionnaire and interview guide, and share these in advance if requested.
5 Possess the authority to share and be willing to share information with benchmarking partners.
6 Work through a specified host and mutually agree on scheduling and meeting arrangements.

When the benchmarking process proceeds to a face-to-face visit, the following behaviours are encouraged:

- Provide meeting agenda in advance.
- Be professional, honest, courteous and prompt.
- Introduce all attendees and explain why they are present.
- Adhere to the agenda.
- Use language that is universal, not one's own jargon.
- Be sure that neither party is sharing proprietary information unless prior approval has been obtained by both parties from the proper authority.
- Share information about your own process, and, if asked, consider sharing study results.
- Offer to facilitate a future reciprocal visit.
- Conclude meetings and visits on schedule.
- Thank your benchmarking partner for sharing their process. ■

Questions

1 Much of the benchmarking protocol seems concerned with the planning that takes place before companies talk to each other directly. Why do you think this is so important?

2 Why do you think each of the face-to-face visit 'behaviours' is important?

necessarily give it immediate priority for improvement. It may be that the operation is already considerably better than its competitors at serving customers in this respect. Similarly, just because an operation is not very good at something when compared with its competitors' performance, it does not necessarily mean that it should be immediately improved. Customers may not particularly value this aspect of performance. Both importance and performance need to be viewed together to judge the prioritization of objectives.

Judging importance to customers

In Chapter 3 we introduced the idea of *order-winning, qualifying* and *less important competitive factors*.

Order-winning competitive factors are those which directly win business for the operation. *Qualifying competitive factors* are those which may not win extra business if the operation improves its performance, but can certainly lose business if performance falls below a particular point, known as the qualifying level. *Less important competitive factors*, as their name implies, are those which are relatively unimportant compared with the others.

In fact, to judge the relative importance of its competitive factors, an operation will usually need to use a slightly more discriminating scale. One way to do this is to take our three broad categories of competitive factors – order winning, qualifying and less important – and to divide each category into three further points representing strong, medium and weak positions. Figure 18.4 illustrates such a scale.

We will illustrate this and subsequent steps in the improvement prioritization procedure by following an example through each step.

Example: EXL Laboratories

EXL Laboratories is a subsidiary of a large defence electronics organization which carries out research and development contracts and technical problem-solving work for a wide range of companies. Although a large number of its customers are companies within the same group, it operates as a profit centre and charges full commercial rates for the investigations it undertakes. It is particularly keen to improve the level of

Order winner	Strong	1	Provides a crucial advantage
	Medium	2	Provides an important advantage
	Weak	3	Provides a useful advantage
Qualifier	Strong	4	Needs to be up to good industry standard
	Medium	5	Needs to be up to median industry standard
	Weak	6	Needs to be within close range of the rest of the industry
Less important	Strong	7	Not usually of importance but could become more so
	Medium	8	Very rarely considered by customers
	Weak	9	Never considered by customers

**Figure 18.4
A nine-point scale
of importance**

service which it gives to its customers. As the first stage of this improvement process it has had discussions with all of its most important customers and, based on these discussions, it has devised a list of the most important aspects of its service.

- *The quality of its technical solutions.* This means the perceived appropriateness of the results of its research and development projects.
- *The quality of its communications with customers.* This means the frequency and usefulness of the information which it gives to customers while it is carrying out the investigations.
- *The quality of post-project documentation.* This means the appropriateness and usefulness of the instructions and documentations which it hands over to customers, together with the final results of the investigation.
- *The delivery speed of its investigations.* This means the time between a customer requesting an investigation to be carried out and the final results of the investigation being delivered.
- *The delivery dependability of the investigations.* This means the ability of the laboratory to estimate the final project completion date accurately and deliver to that date.
- *The delivery flexibility with which it conducts the investigation.* This means the ability of the laboratory to speed up or slow down the investigation so as to deliver it to a revised delivery date.
- *The specification flexibility of the investigation.* This means the ability of the laboratory to change its investigation to cope with revised requirements from the customer.
- *The price of the investigation.* This means the total amount of money charged to the customer for carrying out the investigation.

Again, based on its discussions with customers, EXL manages to assign a score to each of these factors on the 1 to 9 scale, where 1 means that the factor is extremely important to customers and 9 means that it has no importance (*see again* Fig. 18.4).

Figure 18.5 shows how the managers of the laboratory rated the factors. This represents the 'profile of importance' of the various factors as far as the customer is concerned (as perceived by EXL's managers).

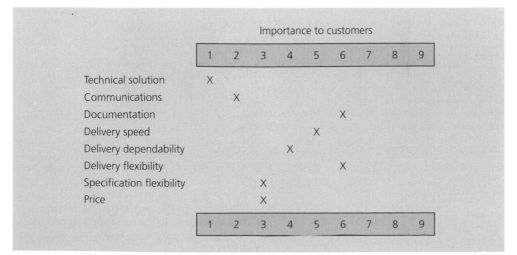

Figure 18.5 Rating 'importance to customers' on the nine-point scale

Judging performance against competitors

At its simplest, a competitive performance standard would consist merely of judging whether the achieved performance of an operation is better than, the same, or worse than that of its competitors. However, in much the same way as the nine-point importance scale was derived, we can derive a more discriminating nine-point performance scale, as shown in Fig. 18.6.

Figure 18.6
A nine-point scale of performance

Better than competitors	Strong	1	Considerably better than competitors
	Medium	2	Clearly better than competitors
	Weak	3	Marginally better than competitors
Same as competitors	Strong	4	Sometimes marginally better than competitors
	Medium	5	About the same as most competitors
	Weak	6	Slightly lower than the average of most competitors
Worse than competitors	Strong	7	Usually marginally worse than most competitors
	Medium	8	Usually worse than competitors
	Weak	9	Consistently worse than competitors

Example – EXL Laboratories (continued)

The management of EXL turned their attention to judging the laboratories' performance using the same factors as they had identified as being of relevance to their customers. Although they could not exactly judge how good all their competitors were

Figure 18.7
Rating 'performance against competitors' on the nine-point scale

Performance against competitors

	1	2	3	4	5	6	7	8	9
Technical solution		X							
Communications								X	
Documentation		X							
Delivery speed						X			
Delivery dependability					X				
Delivery flexibility					X				
Specification flexibility				X					
Cost							X		

on every aspect of performance, they could make some initial estimates. These are shown in Fig. 18.7.

The importance–performance matrix

The priority for improvement which each competitive factor should be given can be assessed from a comparison of their importance and performance. This can be shown on an importance–performance matrix which, as its name implies, positions each competitive factor according to its scores or ratings on these criteria. Figure 18.8 shows an importance–performance matrix divided into zones of improvement priority. The first zone boundary is the 'lower bound of acceptability' shown as line AB in Fig. 18.8. This is the boundary between acceptable and unacceptable performance. When a competitive factor is rated as relatively unimportant (8 or 9 on the importance scale), this boundary will in practice be low. Most operations are prepared to tolerate performance levels which are 'in the same ball-park' as their competitors (even at the bottom end of the rating) for unimportant competitive factors. They only become concerned when performance levels are clearly below those of their competitors.

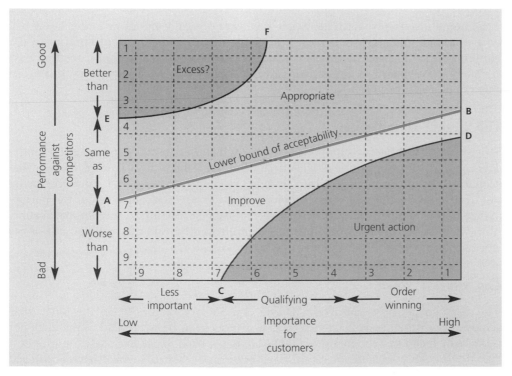

Figure 18.8 Priority zones in the importance–performance matrix

Conversely, when judging competitive factors which are rated highly (1 or 2 on the importance scale) they will be markedly less sanguine at poor or mediocre levels of performance. Minimum levels of acceptability for these competitive factors will usually be at the lower end of the 'better than competitors' class. Below this minimum bound of acceptability (AB) there is clearly a need for improvement; above this line there is no immediate urgency for any improvement. However, not all competitive factors falling below the minimum line will be seen as having the same degree of improvement priority. A boundary approximately represented by line CD represents a distinction between an urgent priority zone and a less urgent improvement zone. Similarly, above the line AB, not all competitive factors are regarded as having the same priority. The line EF can be seen as the approximate boundary between performance levels which are regarded as 'good' or 'appropriate' on one hand and those regarded as 'too good' or 'excess' on the other. Segregating the matrix in this way results in four zones which imply very different priorities.

The 'appropriate' zone

This zone is bounded on its lower edge by the 'lower bound of acceptability', that is the level of performance which the company, in the medium term, would not wish the operation to fall below. Moving performance up to, or above, this boundary is likely to be the first-stage objective for any improvement programme. Competitive factors which fall in this area should be considered satisfactory, at least in the short to medium term. In the long term, however, most organizations will wish to edge performance towards the upper boundary of the zone.

The 'improve' zone

Any competitive factor which lies below the lower bound of the 'appropriate' zone will be a candidate for improvement. Those lying either just below the bound or in the bottom left-hand corner of the matrix (where performance is poor but it matters less) are likely to be viewed as non-urgent cases. Certainly they need improving, but probably not as a first priority.

The 'urgent-action' zone

More critical will be any competitive factor which lies in the 'urgent-action' zone. These are aspects of operations performance where achievement is so far below what it ought to be, given its importance to the customer, that business is probably being lost directly as a result. Short-term objectives must be, therefore, to raise the performance of any competitive factors lying in this zone at least up to the 'improve' zone. In the medium term they would need to be improved beyond the lower bound of the 'appropriate' zone.

The 'excess?' zone

The question mark is important. If any competitive factors lie in this area their achieved performance is far better than would seem to be warranted. This does not necessarily mean that too many resources are being used to achieve such a level, but it may do. It is only sensible, therefore, to check if any resources which have been used to achieve such a performance could be diverted to a more needy factor – anything which falls in the 'urgent-action' area, for example.

Example – EXL Laboratories (continued)

EXL Laboratories plotted the importance and performance ratings it had given to each of its competitive factors on an importance–performance matrix. This is shown in Fig. 18.9. It shows that the most important aspect of competitiveness – the ability

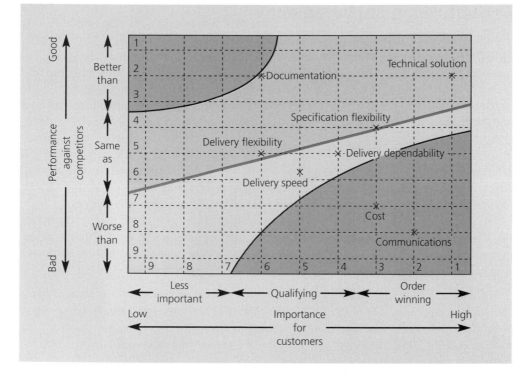

**Figure 18.9
The importance–
performance
matrix for EXL
Laboratories**

to deliver sound technical solutions to its customers – falls comfortably within the appropriate zone. Specification flexibility and delivery flexibility are also in the appropriate zone, although only just. Both delivery speed and delivery dependability seem to be in need of improvement as each is below the minimum level of acceptability for their respective importance positions. However, two competitive factors, communications and cost/price, are clearly in need of immediate improvement. If the managers' estimates of their importance and performance ratings are realistic, both could be losing business for the laboratory. These two factors should therefore be assigned the most urgent priority for improvement. The matrix also indicates that the company's documentation could almost be regarded as 'too good'.

The matrix may not reveal any total surprises. The competitive factors in the 'urgent-action' zone may be known to be in need of improvement already. However, the exercise is useful for two reasons:

● It helps to discriminate between many factors which may be in need of improvement.
● The exercise gives purpose and structure to the debate on improvement priorities.

APPROACHES TO IMPROVEMENT

Once the priority of improvement has been determined, an operation must consider the approach or strategy it wishes to take to the improvement process. Two particular strategies represent different, and to some extent opposing, philosophies. These two strategies are *breakthrough improvement* and *continuous improvement*.

Breakthrough improvement

Breakthrough improvement (or 'innovation'-based improvement as it is sometimes called) assumes that the main vehicle of improvement is major and dramatic change in the way the operation works. The introduction of a new, more efficient machine in a factory, or the total redesign of a computer-based hotel reservation system, or the introduction of a new and better degree programme at a university, are all examples of breakthrough improvement. The impact of these improvements is relatively sudden, abrupt and represents a step change in practice (and hopefully performance). Such improvements are rarely inexpensive, usually calling for high investment of capital, often disrupting the ongoing workings of the operation, and frequently involving changes in the product/service or process technology. The bold line in Fig. 18.10 illustrates the pattern of performance with several breakthrough improvements.

One criticism of the breakthrough approach to improvement is that such major improvements are, in practice, difficult to realize quickly and impossible to realize instantly as is implied by Fig. 18.10. The following experience reported by Professor Arnoud De Meyer is typical:[6]

'I was once involved in the start-up of a major green-field site petrochemical plant. That is obviously a major step. The first time that the plant was 'switched on' it ran for a fraction of a second. With much hard work, energy and dedication, the engineers and the workforce succeeded, after about six months, in reaching 99 per cent capacity utilization. Once the start-up period was over, however, dedication and energy went back to normal levels and capacity utilization slipped slightly.'

The improvement pattern illustrated by the broken line in Fig. 18.10 is regarded by some as being more representative of what really occurs when operations rely on pure breakthrough improvement.

**Figure 18.10
The intended and actual pattern of performance improvement with breakthrough improvement**

Continuous improvement

Continuous improvement, as the name implies, adopts an approach to improving performance which assumes more and smaller incremental improvement steps. For example, modifying the way a product is fixed to a machine to reduce change-over time, or simplifying the question sequence when taking a hotel reservation, or rescheduling the assignment completion dates on a university course so as to smooth the students' workload, are all examples of incremental improvements. While there is no guarantee that such small steps towards better performance will be followed by other steps, the whole philosophy of continuous improvement attempts to ensure that they will be. Continuous improvement is not concerned with promoting small improvements *per se*. It does see small improvements, however, as having one significant advantage over large ones – they can be followed relatively painlessly by other small improvements (*see* Fig. 18.11).

Continuous improvement is also known as *kaizen*. Kaizen is a Japanese word, the definition of which is given by Masaaki Imai[7] (who has been one of the main proponents of continuous improvement) as follows:

'Kaizen means improvement. Moreover, it means improvement in personal life, home life, social life and work life. When applied to the work place, kaizen means continuing improvement involving everyone – managers and workers alike.'

In continuous improvement it is not the *rate* of improvement which is important, it is the *momentum* of improvement. It does not matter if successive improvements are small; what does matter is that every month (or week, or quarter, or whatever period is appropriate) some kind of improvement has actually taken place.

The differences between breakthrough and continuous improvement

Breakthrough improvement places a high value on creative solutions. It encourages free thinking and individualism. It is a radical philosophy insomuch as it fosters an approach to improvement which does not accept many constraints on what is possible. 'Starting with a clean sheet of paper', 'going back to first principles', and

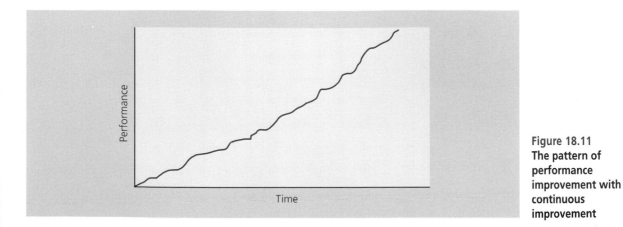

Figure 18.11
The pattern of performance improvement with continuous improvement

693

Table 18.2 Some features of breakthrough and continuous improvement (based on Imai[8])

	Breakthrough improvement	*Continuous improvement*
Effect	Short-term but dramatic	Long-term and long-lasting but undramatic
Pace	Big steps	Small steps
Time frame	Intermittent and non-incremental	Continuous and incremental
Change	Abrupt and volatile	Gradual and constant
Involvement	Select a few 'champions'	Everybody
Approach	Individualism, individual ideas and efforts	Collectivism, group efforts, systems approach
Stimulus	Technological breakthroughs, new inventions, new theories	Conventional know-how and state of the art
Risks	Concentrated – 'all eggs in one basket'	Spread – many projects simultaneously
Practical requirements	Requires large investment but little effort to maintain it	Requires little investment but great effort to maintain it
Effort orientation	Technology	People
Evaluation criteria	Results for profit	Process and efforts for better results

'completely rethinking the system' are all typical breakthrough improvement principles. Continuous improvement, on the other hand, is less ambitious, at least in the short term. It stresses adaptability, teamwork and attention to detail. It is not radical; rather it builds upon the wealth of accumulated experience within the operation itself, often relying primarily on the people who operate the system to improve it. One analogy which helps to understand the difference between breakthrough and continuous improvement is that of the sprint and the marathon. Breakthrough improvement is a series of explosive and impressive sprints. Continuous improvement, like marathon running, does not require the expertise and prowess required for sprinting; but it does require that the runner (or operations manager) keeps on going. Table 18.2 lists some of the differences between the two approaches.

**Figure 18.12
The pattern of performance improvement with continuous improvement superimposed on to breakthrough improvement**

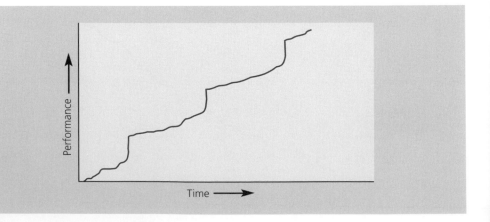

Notwithstanding the fundamental differences between the two approaches, it is possible to combine the two, albeit at different times. Large and dramatic improvements can be implemented as and when they seem to promise significant improvement steps, but between such occasions the operation can continue making its quiet and less spectacular kaizen improvements (*see* Fig. 18.12).

The PDCA cycle

The concept of continuous improvement implies a literally never-ending process of repeatedly questioning and requestioning the detailed workings of an operation. The repeated and cyclical nature of continuous improvement is best summarized by what is called the PDCA cycle (or Deming wheel – named after the famous quality 'guru', W.E. Deming (*see* Chapter 20)). The PDCA cycle is the sequence of activities which are undertaken on a cyclical basis to improve activities (*see* Fig. 18.13).

The cycle starts with the P (for plan) stage, which involves an examination of the current method or the problem area being studied. This involves collecting and analysing data so as to formulate a plan of action which is intended to improve performance. (The next section of this chapter explains some of the techniques which can be used to collect and analyse data in this stage.) Once a plan for improvement has been agreed, the next step is the D (for do) stage. This is the implementation stage during which the plan is tried out in the operation. This stage may itself involve a mini-PDCA cycle as the problems of implementation are resolved. Next comes the C (for check) stage where the new implemented solution is evaluated to see whether it has resulted in the expected performance improvement. Finally, at least for this cycle, comes the A (for act) stage. During this stage the change is consolidated or standard-

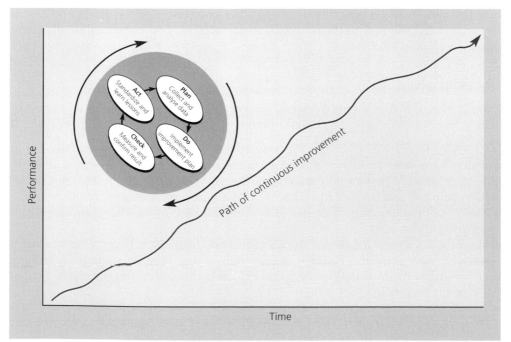

**Figure 18.13
The PDCA cycle
is the basis of
continuous
improvement**

ized if it has been successful. Alternatively, if the change has not been successful, the lessons learned from the 'trial' are formalized before the cycle starts again.

It is the last point about the PDCA cycle which is the most important – the cycle starts again. It is only by accepting that in a continuous improvement philosophy the PDCA cycle quite literally never stops that improvement becomes part of every person's job.

The business process re-engineering approach

Typical of the radical breakthrough way of tackling improvement is the 'business process re-engineering' (BPR) approach. BPR is a blend of a number of ideas which have been current in operations management for some time. Just-in-time concepts, process flow charting, critical examination in method study, operations network management and customer-focused operations all contribute to the BPR concept. It was the potential of information technologies to enable the fundamental redesign of processes, however, which acted as the catalyst in bringing these ideas together. BPR has been defined as:

> 'the fundamental rethinking and radical redesign of business processes to achieve dramatic improvements in critical, contemporary measures of performance, such as cost, quality, service and speed.'[9]

Process *versus* functions

Underlying the BPR approach is the belief that operations should be organized around the total process which adds value for customers, rather than the functions or activities which perform the various stages of the value-adding activity. We have already pointed out the difference between a conventional micro operation organized around a specialist function, and a business process (Fig. 1.6 in Chapter 1 illustrated this idea). The core of BPR is a redefinition of the micro organizations within a total operation, to reflect the business processes which satisfy customer needs. Figure 18.14 shows this idea.

The principles of BPR

Even if BPR is not an entirely original idea, it can be seen as a useful collection of principles which embody the breakthrough approach. The main principles of BPR have been summarized as follows.[10]

● Rethink business processes in a cross-functional manner which organizes work around the natural flow of information (or materials or customers). This means organizing around outcomes of a process rather than the tasks which go into it.
● Strive for dramatic improvements in the performance by radically rethinking and redesigning the process.
● Have those who use the output from a process perform the process. Check to see if all internal customers can be their own supplier rather than depending on another function in the business to supply them (which takes longer and separates out the stages in the process).
● Put decision points where the work is performed. Do not separate those who do the work from those who control and manage the work. Control and action are just one more type of supplier–customer relationship which can be merged.

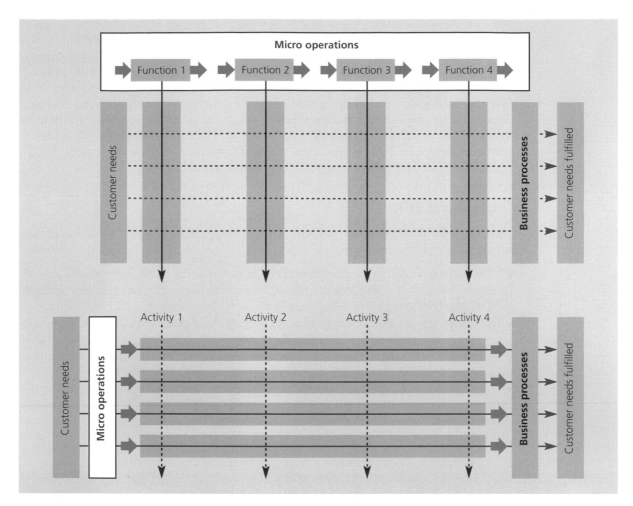

Figure 18.14 BPR advocates reorganizing (re-engineering) micro operations to reflect the natural customer-focused business processes

Example[11]

We can illustrate this idea of reorganizing (or re-engineering) around business processes through the following simple example. Figure 18.15(a) shows the traditional organization of a trading company which purchases consumer goods from several suppliers, stores them, and sells them on to retail outlets. At the heart of the operation is the warehouse which receives the goods, stores them, and packs and dispatches them when they are required by customers. Orders for more stock are placed by Purchasing which also takes charge of materials planning and stock control. Purchasing buys the goods based on a forecast which is prepared by Marketing, which takes advice from the Sales department which is processing customers' orders. When a customer does place an order, it is the Sales department's job to instruct the warehouse to pack and dispatch the order and tell the Finance department to invoice the customer for the goods. So, traditionally, five departments (each a micro operation) have between them organized the flow of materials and information within the total operation. But at each interface between the departments there is the possibility of errors and miscommunication arising. Furthermore, *who is responsible for looking after the customer's needs?* Currently, three separate departments all have dealings with the customer. Similarly, *who is responsible for liaising with suppliers?* This time two departments have contact with suppliers.

Eventually the company reorganized around two essential business processes. The first process (called purchasing operations) dealt with everything concerning relationships with suppliers. It was this process's focused and unambiguous responsibility to develop good working relationships with suppliers. The other business process (called customer service operations) had total responsibility for satisfying customers' needs. This included speaking 'with one voice' to the customer.

Criticisms of BPR

The whole BPR approach is not without its critics. Three criticisms in particular appear to have some validity:

● BPR is often treated as the latest management fad by some managers and as a cure-all for every problem. It is like, say the critics, attempting major surgery on every ailment, even those which would cure themselves naturally with some simple physiotherapy.
● BPR is merely an excuse for getting rid of staff. Companies which wish to 'downsize' (that is reduce numbers of staff within an operation) are using BPR as an excuse. This puts the short-term interests of the shareholders of the company above either their longer-term interests or the interests of the company's employees.
● A combination of radical redesign together with downsizing can mean that the essential core of experience is lost from the operation. This leaves it vulnerable to any environmental changes since it no longer has the knowledge and experience of how to cope with unexpected changes.

THE TECHNIQUES OF IMPROVEMENT[12]

All the techniques described in this book can be regarded as 'improvement' techniques insomuch as they attempt to improve some aspect of the performance of an operation. Some techniques are particularly useful for improving operations generally. For example, statistical process control (SPC) in Chapter 17 and failure mode and effect analysis (FMEA) in Chapter 19 could be used for almost any type of improvement project. In the remainder of this chapter we select some techniques which either have not been described elsewhere or need to be reintroduced in their role of helping operations improvement particularly. For example, flow charts were used in Chapter 5 as a design technique; later we will use essentially the same technique to generate improvements to existing operations.

Input–output analysis

A prerequisite for understanding any improvement opportunity is to understand the context in which the operation is set. This is the purpose of input–output analysis, which has three steps:

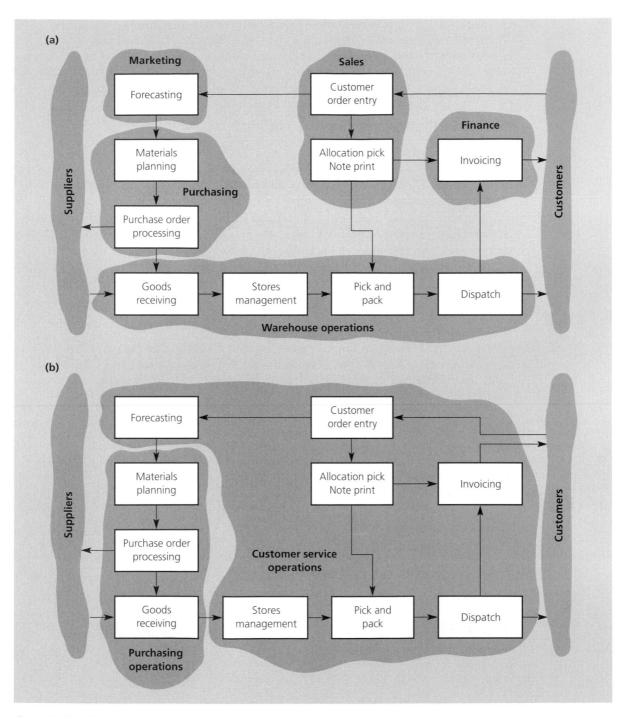

Figure 18.15 (a) Before and (b) after re-engineering a consumer goods trading company

1 identifying the inputs and outputs from the process;

2 identifying the source of the inputs and the destination of the outputs;

3 clarifying the requirements of the internal customers who are served by the outputs from the process, and clarifying what requirements the process has for the internal suppliers who provide inputs to the process.

Example: Kaston Pyral Services Ltd

Kaston Pyral Services Ltd (KPS) is the field service division of Kaston Pyral International, which manufactures and installs gas-fired heating systems. In the same group is KP Manufacturing, which makes the systems and spare parts, and KP Contracts, which installs the systems. The south-eastern region in the UK is the largest region in KPS. It serves a mixture of customers, large commercial office blocks, industrial buildings, schools, colleges and civic buildings. KPS was feeling under pressure from independent, often small, third-party service organizations who were undercutting KPS's prices. Partly as a response to this, KPS's south-eastern Regional Manager decided to initiate an improvement programme. He decided on a team approach which would include himself, all five service engineers in the unit, the accountant/administrator for the unit and occasionally a trainer from KP Group Personnel Department.

Figure 18.16 shows an input–output diagram for KPS. The purpose is to reach an agreed understanding of the operational function of whichever part of the organization the problem is set in. It is not intended that input–output diagrams give any answers as such. They do, however, provide a useful 'way in' to improvement.

Requirements	Suppliers	Input		Output	Customer	Requirements
• Accuracy • Comprehensiveness • Advance notice	• Manufacturers	• Information on systems		• Preventative maintenance	• Commercial	• Cost • Dependability • Response speed • Advice
• Accuracy • Comprehensiveness	• KP Contracts • Customers • Service engineers	• Information on customers	THE KPS SOUTH-EAST REGION FIELD SERVICE UNIT	• Emergency servicing	• Industrial	• Flexibility • Response speed • Cost • Advice
• Accuracy • Comprehensiveness	• Customers • Service engineers	• Customer requests		• Advice on use of system	• Civic	• Cost • Advice • Response speed • Dependability
• Response speed • Reliable delivery • Quality	• Manufacturers • KPS workshop	• Spare parts				
• Availability • Cost	• Various	• Consumables		• Advice on design	• KP Manufacturing	• Analysis • Co-ordination
• Responsiveness • Reliability • Flexibility • Skill	• KP Contracts	• KP Contract engineers		• Advice on installation	• KP Contracts	• Analysis

Figure 18.16 Full input–output diagram showing the suppliers and requirements of all inputs and the customers and requirements for all ouputs

Flow charts

Input–output diagrams give a useful overview of the process context of improvement opportunities. A more detailed technique is the flow chart. Flow charts give a detailed understanding of parts of the process where some sort of flow occurs. They were briefly described in Chapter 5 in the context of new product and service design, but they have a far wider applicability. They record stages in the passage of information, products, labour or customers – in fact, anything which flows through the operation. They do this by requiring the decision makers to identify each stage in the flow process as either:

- an *action* of some sort – recorded in a rectangular box; or
- a *question/decision* – recorded in a diamond-shaped box.

The purpose of this is to ensure that all the different stages in the flow processes are included in the improvement process, and that these stages are in some kind of logical sequence. The act of recording each stage in the process quickly shows up poorly organized flows. The technique can also clarify improvement opportunities and shed further light on the internal mechanics or workings of an operation. Finally, and probably most importantly, flow charts highlight problem areas where no procedure exists to cope with a particular set of circumstances.

Example: Kaston Pyral Services Ltd (continued)

As part of its improvement programme the team at KPS is concerned that customers are not being served well when they phone in with minor queries over the operation of their heating systems. These queries are not usually concerned with serious problems, but often concern minor irritations which can be equally damaging to the customers' perception of KPS's service.

Figure 18.17 overleaf shows the flow diagram for this type of customer query.

The team found the chart illuminating. The procedure had never been formally laid out in this way before, and it showed up three areas where information was not being recorded. These are the three points marked with question marks on the flow chart in Fig. 18.17. As a result of this investigation, it was decided to log all customer queries so that analysis could reveal further information on the nature of customer problems.

Scatter diagrams

Scatter diagrams are a quick and simple method of identifying whether there seems to be a connection between two sets of data: for example, the time at which you set off for work every morning and how long the journey to work takes. Plotting each journey on a graph which has departure time on one axis and journey time on the other could give an indication of whether departure time and journey time are related, and if so, how. Figure 18.18 shows the graph for one person's journeys. It would seem to show: (a) that there is a relationship between the two sets of data; (b) that the longest journeys were when departures were between 8.15 am and 8.22 am; and (c) that the journey is least predictable when departure is between 8.15 am and 8.30 am.

Scatter diagrams can be treated in a far more sophisticated manner by quantifying how strong is the relationship between the sets of data. But however sophisticated the

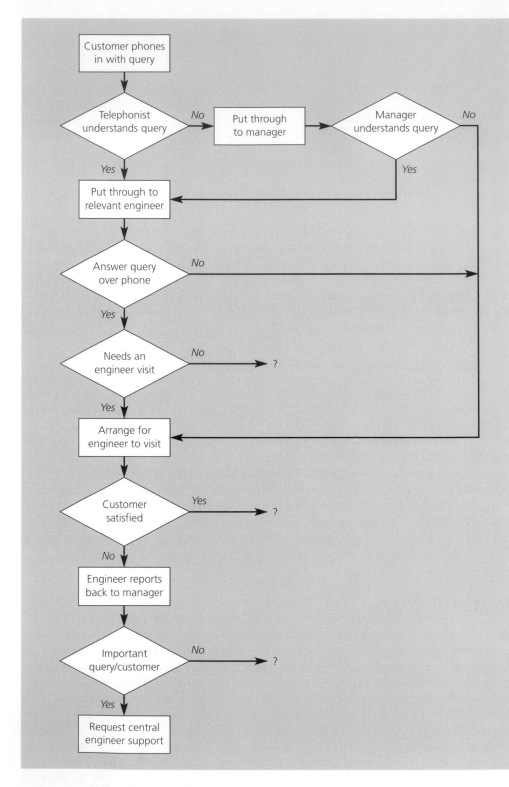

**Figure 18.17
Flow chart for
customer query**

**Figure 18.18
Scatter diagram for
travel time against
departure time**

approach, this type of graph only identifies the existence of a relationship, not necessarily the existence of a cause–effect relationship. If the scatter diagram shows a very strong connection between the sets of data, it is important evidence of a cause–effect relationship, but not proof positive. It could be coincidence!

Example: Kaston Pyral Services Ltd (continued)

The KPS improvement team had completed its first customer satisfaction survey. The survey asked customers to score the service they received from KPS in several ways. For example, it asked customers to score services on a scale of one to ten on promptness, friendliness, level of advice, etc. Scores were then summed to give a 'total satisfaction score' for each customer – the higher the score, the greater the satisfaction.

The spread of satisfaction scores puzzled the team, and they considered what factors might be causing such differences in the way their customers viewed them. Two factors were put forward to explain the differences:

● the number of times in the past year the customer had received a preventive maintenance visit; and
● the number of times the customer had called for emergency service.

All this data was collected and plotted on scatter diagrams as shown in Fig. 18.19. Fig. 18.19(a) shows that there seems to be a clear relationship between a customer's satisfaction score and the number of times the customer was visited for regular servicing. The scatter diagram in Fig. 18.19(b) is less clear. Although all customers who had very high satisfaction scores had made very few emergency calls, so had some customers with low satisfaction scores. As a result of this analysis, the team decided to survey customers' views on its emergency service.

Cause–effect diagrams

Cause–effect diagrams are a particularly effective method of helping to search for the root causes of problems. They do this by asking the what, when, where, how and why questions as before, but this time adding some possible 'answers' in an explicit way.

Figure 18.19 Scatter diagrams for customer satisfaction *versus* (a) number of preventive maintenance calls and (b) number of emergency service calls

They can also be used to identify areas where further data is needed. Cause–effect diagrams (which are also known as 'fish-bone' and 'Ishikawa' diagrams) have become extensively used in improvement programmes. Figure 18.20 shows the general form of the cause–effect diagram.

The procedure for drawing a cause–effect diagram is as follows:

Step 1 State the problem in the 'effect' box.
Step 2 Identify the main categories for possible causes of the problem. Although any categorization can be used for the main branches of the diagram, there are five categories which are commonly used: machinery; manpower; materials; methods and procedures; money.
Step 3 Use systematic fact finding and group discussion to generate possible causes under these categories. Anything which may result in the effect which is being considered should be put down as a potential cause.
Step 4 Record all potential causes on the diagram under each category, and discuss each item in order to combine and clarify causes.

Figure 18.20 Cause–effect diagram

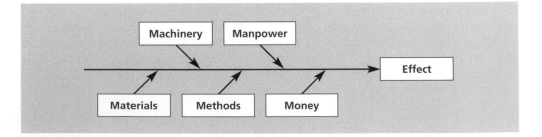

Some tips on using cause–effect diagrams

● Use separate diagrams for each problem. Do not confuse the issue by combining problems on a single diagram.

● Make sure diagrams are visible to everyone involved. Use large sheets of paper with plenty of space between items.

● Do not overload diagrams. Use separate diagrams for each major category on the cause–effect master diagram if necessary.

● Always be prepared to rework, take apart, refine and change categories.

● Take care not to use vague statements such as 'possible lack of'. Rather describe what is actually happening that demonstrates the issues: for example, 'people are not filling out forms properly'.

● Circle causes which seem to be particularly significant.

PROBLEM IDENTIFICATION AT HEWLETT-PACKARD[13]

Hewlett-Packard is proud of its reputation for high-quality products and services. Because of this it was especially concerned with the problems that it was having with its customers returning defective toner cartridges. About 2000 of these were being returned every month. The UK team suspected that not all the returns were actually the result of a faulty product, which is why the team decided to investigate the problem. The cause–effect diagram which they generated is shown in Fig. 18.21.

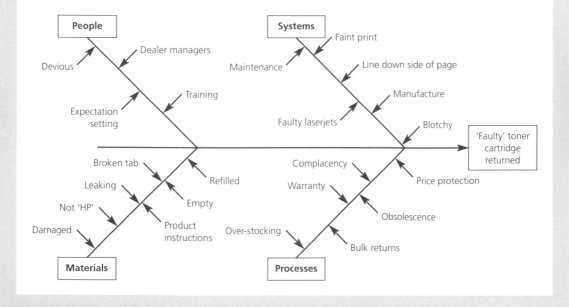

Figure 18.21 Cause–effect diagram for Hewlett-Packard's toner analysis

Three major problems were identified. First, some users were not as familiar as they should have been with the correct method of loading the cartridge into the printer, or in being able to solve their own minor printing problems. Second, some of the dealers were also unaware of how to sort out minor problems. Third, there was clearly some abuse of Hewlett-Packard's 'no-questions-asked' returns policy. Empty toner cartridges were being sent to unauthorized refilling companies who would sell the refilled cartridges at reduced prices. Some cartridges were being refilled up to five times and were understandably wearing out. Furthermore, the toner in the refilled cartridges was not up to Hewlett-Packard's high quality standards. The team went on to use the PDCA sequence of problem solving and made suggestions which tightened up on their returns policy as well as improving the way in which customers were instructed on how to use the products. The results were impressive. Complaints in almost all areas shrank to a fraction of what they had been previously. ■

Questions

1 Take one branch of the decision tree shown in Fig. 18.21 (for example the Materials branch) and expand on the possible reasons which are shown for the cartridge being returned.

2 What is your opinion of the alleged abuse of the 'no-questions-asked' returns policy adopted by Hewlett-Packard?

Example: Kaston Pyral Services Ltd (continued)

The improvement team at KPS was working on a particular area which was proving a problem. Whenever service engineers were called out to perform emergency servicing for a customer, they took with them the spares and equipment which they thought would be necessary to repair the system. Although engineers could never be sure exactly what materials and equipment they would need for a job, they could guess what was likely to be needed and take a range of spares and equipment which would cover most eventualities. Too often, however, the engineers would find that they needed a spare or piece of equipment which they had not brought with them, and therefore they would have to return to the depot in order to collect it. Worse than that, very occasionally the required spare part would not be in stock, and so the customer would have to wait until it was brought from another part of the country. The cause–effect diagram for this particular problem, as drawn by the team, is shown in Fig. 18.22

Pareto diagrams

In any improvement process, it is worthwhile distinguishing what is important and what is less so. The purpose of the Pareto analysis, which was introduced in Chapter 12, is to distinguish between the 'vital few' issues and the 'trivial many'. It is a relatively straightforward technique which involves arranging items of information on the types of problem or causes of problem into their order of importance. This can then be used to highlight areas where further decision-making will be useful.

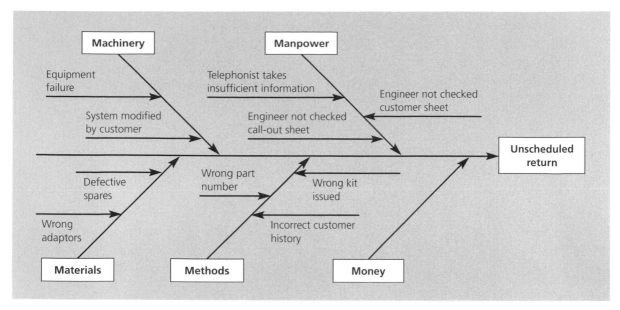

Figure 18.22 Cause–effect diagram of unscheduled returns at KPS

Pareto analysis is based on the frequently occurring phenomenon of relatively few causes explaining the majority of effects. For example, most revenue for any company is likely to come from relatively few of the company's customers. Similarly, relatively few of a doctor's patients will probably occupy most of his time.

Example: Kaston Pyral Services Ltd (continued)

The KPS improvement team which was investigating unscheduled returns from emergency servicing (the issue which was described in the cause–effect diagram in Fig. 18.22) examined all occasions over the previous 12 months on which an unscheduled return had been made. They categorized the reasons for unscheduled returns as follows:

1 The wrong part had been taken to a job because, although the information which the engineer received was sound, he or she had incorrectly predicted the nature of the fault.
2 The wrong part had been taken to the job because there was insufficient information given when the call was taken.
3 The wrong part had been taken to the job because the system had been modified in some way not recorded on KPS's records.
4 The wrong part had been taken to the job because the part had been incorrectly issued to the engineer by stores.
5 No part had been taken because the relevant part was out of stock.
6 The wrong equipment had been taken for whatever reason.
7 Any other reason.

The relative frequency of occurrence of these causes is shown in Fig. 18.23. About a third of all unscheduled returns were due to the first category, and more than half the returns were accounted for by the first and second categories together. It was decided that the problem could best be tackled by concentrating on how to get more information to the engineers which would enable them to predict the causes of failure accurately.

Figure 18.23 Pareto diagram for causes of unscheduled returns

CUSTOMER SERVICE AT GROUPE ACCOR[14]

For over ten years, Accor, the French hotel and restaurant group, has been developing self-managed improvement groups within its hotels. At one hotel reception desk, staff were concerned about the amount of time the desk was left unattended. To investigate this the staff began keeping track of the reasons they were spending time away from the desk and how long each absence kept them away. Everyone knew that reception desk staff often had to leave their post to help or give service to a guest. However, no one could agree what was the main cause of absence. Collecting the information was itself not easy because the staff had to keep records without affecting customer service. After three months the data was presented in the form of a Pareto diagram, which is shown in Fig. 18.24. According to this, reception staff spent an average of 20 minutes away from their desk each shift. It came as a surprise to reception staff and hotel management that making photocopies for guests was the main reason for absence. Fortunately, this was easily remedied by moving the photocopier to a room adjacent to the reception area, enabling staff to keep a check on the reception desk while they were making copies. ■

Questions

1 Do you think it was wise to spend so much time on examining this particular issue? Isn't it a trivial issue?

2 Should the Pareto diagram (Fig. 18.24) be used to reflect improvement priorities? In other words, was the group correct to put priority on avoiding absence through photocopying, and should its next priority be to look at absence because of the telefax service?

Figure 18.24   Pareto diagram of staff time away from the reception desk

Why–why analysis

We finish on another simple but effective technique for helping to understand the reasons for problems occurring. The technique starts by stating the problem and asking *why* that problem has occurred. Once the major reasons for the problem occurring have been identified, each of the major reasons is taken in turn and again the question is asked *why* those reasons have occurred, and so on. This procedure is continued until either a cause seems sufficiently self-contained to be addressed by itself or no more answers to the question 'Why?' can be generated.

Example: Kaston Pyral Services Ltd (continued)

Figure 18.25 illustrates the general structure of the why–why analysis for the KPS example discussed previously. In this example the major cause of unscheduled returns was the incorrect prediction of reasons for the customer's system failure. This is stated as the problem in the why–why analysis. The question is then asked, why was the failure wrongly predicted? Three answers are proposed: first, that the engineers were not trained correctly; second, that they had insufficient knowledge of the particular product installed in the customer's location; and third, that they had insufficient knowledge of the customer's particular system with its modifications. Each of these three reasons is taken in turn, and the questions are asked, why is there a lack of training, why is there a lack of product knowledge, and why is there a lack of customer knowledge? And so on.

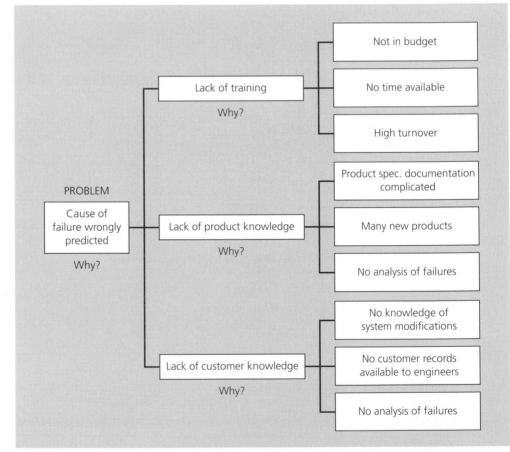

Figure 18.25
Why–why analysis

Stella Dorsett, Cookson Precious Metals

Cookson Precious Metals is an advanced materials technology company with operations all around the world. Stella Dorsett joined the company as a systems developer. Her job was to analyse operations and look for improvements that could be made through changes to the system.

'I wanted to take the opportunity of applying the techniques that I had learned in software development to the manufacture of jewellery. The company was looking to expand the role of information technology in the business, by integrating it more into the operations function. My first assignment involved me in the installation of a new accounting system that took into consideration the real cost "drivers" in the operation itself, and which would be more appropriate for the methods the company used in sales, credit control and other support functions. In order to be effective in setting up this new system, I had to understand the business, and be involved in the development of long-term operations strategies. The emphasis was always on whether or not we could add value by improving the process.

'This first assignment gave me a clear understanding of the operation and of the priorities involved. This helped me in my next task, which was managing a team to look at modernizing and improving the production processes themselves. The principles and techniques employed in looking at operations improvement are really very similar, regardless of the specific area being considered. In this case the requirement was to control batch production in relation to the capacity of each machine in the process. We needed to find a way of monitoring the flow of goods through production

and identifying the potential bottle-necks which might be reducing the capacity and therefore the efficiency of the process. Once we had identified the bottle-necks we needed to find ways of removing them to allow the batches to flow smoothly through the operation.

'Having made recommendations to the local management team, we were then assigned to the next stage, which was to get involved with a small manufacturing unit to test out the ideas and to see what improvements we could make. The trials involved the detailed monitoring and assessing of the flow of materials, in an effort to highlight the problem areas. Overall we created a 20 per cent increase in output, which demonstrated that there was potential in the project, and a full-scale initiative was given 'approval'.

'Once we had approval, we extended our work to the whole of the factory. Even on this larger scale the methods of data analysis which we had developed worked well. The initial results were excellent (undoubtedly because the areas first identified for analysis were those that could deliver the greatest improvements). Although the whole production department benefited from the start, we did find that after the initial "step" improvement, further progress was considerably harder to achieve.

'Looking back, it has been my experience in operations improvements that has given me the opportunity to relate the theories behind processes to a real factory environment. Operations improvement continues to be my main responsibility. It is intellectually challenging and very rewarding in terms of job satisfaction.' ■

SUMMARY ANSWERS TO KEY QUESTIONS

How can operations measure their performance in terms of the five performance objectives?

■ It is unlikely that for any operation a single measure of performance will adequately reflect the whole of a performance objective. Usually operations have to collect a whole bundle of partial measures of performance.

■ Each partial measure then has to be compared against some performance standard. There are four types of performance standard commonly used:

– historical standards, which compare performance now against performance sometime in the past;
– target performance standards, which compare current performance against some desired level of performance;
– competitor performance standards, which compare current performance against competitors' performance;
– absolute performance standards, which compare current performance against its theoretically perfect state.

■ The process of benchmarking is often used as a means of obtaining competitor performance standards.

How can operations managers prioritize improvement of performance objectives?

■ Improvement priorities can be determined by bringing together the relative importance of each performance objective or competitive factor as judged by customers, with the performance which the operation achieves as compared against its competitors.

■ The operation's judgement about both importance and performance can be consolidated on an 'importance–performance matrix'. Different areas on this matrix represent different relative degrees of priority.

What are the broad approaches to managing the rate of improvement?

■ An organization's approach to improving its operation can be characterized as lying somewhere between the two extremes of 'pure' breakthrough improvement and 'pure' continuous improvement.

■ Breakthrough improvement, which is sometimes called innovation-based improvement, sees improvement as occurring in a few, infrequent but major and dramatic changes. Although such changes can be abrupt and volatile, they often incorporate radical new concepts or technologies which can shift the performance of the operation significantly.

■ Continuous improvement assumes a series of never-ending, but smaller, incremental improvement steps. This type of improvement is sometimes called kaizen improvement. It is gradual and constant, often using collective group-based problem-solving. It does not focus on radical change but rather attempts to develop a built-in momentum of improvement.

■ It is claimed that compromises between these two types of improvement philosophy are possible. Organizations can improve by having occasional radical breakthroughs but utilizing a more incremental approach in between these major changes.

Where does business process re-engineering (BPR) fit into the improvement activity?

■ BPR is a typical example of the radical approach to improvement. It attempts to redesign operations along customer-focused processes rather than on the traditional functional basis.

■ BPR has been responsible for some radical improvements in operations performance but it has also been criticized. The main criticisms are that it pays little attention to the rights of staff who are the victims of the 'downsizing' which often accompanies BPR, and that the radical nature of the changes can strip out valuable experience from the operation.

What are the techniques of improvement?

■ Many of the techniques described throughout this book could be considered improvement techniques, for example statistical process control (SPC).

■ Techniques often seen as 'improvement techniques' are:

– input–output analysis, which attempts to clarify the nature of transformation in processes;

– flow charts, which attempt to describe the nature of information flow and decision-making within operations;

– scatter diagrams, which attempt to identify relationships and influences within processes;

– cause–effect diagrams, which structure the brainstorming which can help to reveal the root causes of problems;

–Pareto diagrams, which attempt to sort out the 'important few' causes from the 'trivial many' causes.

Raydale Conference Centre

'Well, I suppose it's a mixed review: there are some things where we come out really well; on the other hand there are clearly areas where we need to improve.'

Alan Ray was speaking after the publication of an article in the *Conference Centre Journal*. Alan was the owner and General Manager of Raydale Conference Centre. He had bought the centre, which used to be a country house hotel, just over two years before and was broadly pleased with the business he had attracted so far. The centre had managed to establish a presence in the fast growing and profitable conference market. His customers (usually large companies) would book some or all of his facilities for their sales conferences, training events and meetings. These events could be anything from one-day's duration through to two weeks'. Raydale Conference Centre, together with three others in the area, had been reviewed by the *Conference Centre Journal*, a summary of whose findings is shown in Table 18.3.

Alan was more worried by some findings than others.

'Not everything is of equal importance, of course. In our part of the business probably the two things that customers value particularly are courtesy of staff, where we score very well, and the flexibility to accommodate their special needs, where we score very badly. I think there are two reasons for this. First of all, our conference rooms are relatively small and we have difficulty in accommodating very large groups. The other reason is, quite frankly, that some of our staff are not used to coping with the unexpected problems. Price is only slightly less important to

our customers but we seem to score reasonably. What worries me more is that I know that our costs tend to be higher than those of our competitors. Given the level of business which we are doing, our profits are less than those being achieved by our competitors. Less important than price comes a middle-range of factors which, although not of prime importance to customers, will certainly irritate them if we are not up to standard. Room decor, room availability, the quality of our food and document errors all come into this category. I am particularly cross about the way they have reviewed document errors. I suppose they talked to our customers and must have got one where we had made mistakes with their invoices or something. I'm sure a wider survey would have revealed us to be no worse than our rivals. Quite frankly, I am unconcerned about our performance in terms of the size of our menu or our ability to give special off-peak price discounts. In our type of market neither of those factors rate particularly highly with any customers.' ■

Questions

1 On what competitive factors would you advise Alan to concentrate if he wished to improve the competitive performance of his operation?

2 Do you think he is right to feel aggrieved by his operation's poor showing on the document errors factor?

3 Is he right to be unconcerned about the size of menu (that is the range of different dishes offered on his standard menu) and his policy of not offering off-peak price discounts?

Table 18.3 Reviews of conference centres

Factor	Raydale	Miston	Hexley	Stannington
Price	Average	High	Average	Low
Size of menu	Excellent	Good	Good	Poor
Quality of food	Good	Excellent	Good	Acceptable
Quality of room	Very good	Good	Good	Good
Courtesy of staff	Very good	Good	Good	Poor
Flexibility to accommodate special needs	Poor	Very good	Good	Good
Documentation errors	Occasional	None	Very few	None
Special off-peak price discounts	No	Yes	Yes	Yes
Room availability	Good	Very good	Poor	Poor

DISCUSSION QUESTIONS

1 A university library wishes to start a performance measurement programme which will enable it to judge the effectiveness with which it organizes its operations. The library loans books to students on both long-term and short-term loans, keeps an extensive stock of journals, will send off for specialist publications to specialist libraries and has an extensive on-line database facility. What measures of performance do you think it would be appropriate to use in this kind of operation and what type of performance standards should the library adopt?

2 Assess the overall performance of an operation that is familiar to you using a polar diagram. Overlap the operation's performance with what you perceive to be the customers' needs and discuss any differences.

3 Using the five performance measures, list ways in which the performance of a university lecturer could be assessed.

4 Discuss with an operations manager how the performance of the operation is measured. Identify a range of measures and find out whether the targets used are based on historical, target performance, competitor performance or absolute performance standards.

5 List some of the micro operations of a humanitarian organization such as the International Red Cross, the Samaritans or United Nations High Commission for Refugees (UNHCR) and discuss the benefits of it benchmarking its operations. Which operations or micro operations might it be appropriate to benchmark against?

6 A university engineering department has chosen to benchmark itself against other university departments as the first step in an operations improvement process. What kinds of benchmarking do you think might be appropriate for the department and on what performance objectives do you think it should be focusing?

7 Identify the order winners, qualifiers and less important criteria for an organization of your own choice. Ask a colleague to assess the same organization and compare and discuss your results.

8 Choose an organization and compare it with a competing organization in terms of whether it is better than, the same as, or worse than the competitor. Ask a colleague to undertake the same evaluation and compare and discuss your results.

9 A bank is conducting a survey of all the customer complaints which it has received in its personal loan department. This department deals with the authorization of loans requested by the bank's customers, processes all the information concerning the loans and then sends documents to the customers. Table 18.4 classifies the type of complaints made by customers together with their frequency of occurrence.

Table 18.4 Customer complaints

Type of complaint	Frequency of occurrence
Authorization signature omitted	4%
Loan amount omitted	17%
Loan detail errors	12%
Arithmetic error	9%
One or more documents omitted	31%
Inappropriate documents included	2%
Payment details omitted	21%
Others	2%

Draw a Pareto diagram which describes the relative frequency of occurrence of different types of errors. Draw a cause–effect diagram which contains possible reasons for the most important category of error.

10 Explain the differences between breakthrough improvement and continuous improvement. Discuss the advantages and disadvantages of each.

11 List and describe ten modifications that could be made to your course. What breakthrough improvements could be made?

12 Apply the PDCA cycle to your method of preparing for lectures. Describe each part of the cycle and assess the outcome.

13 Briefly explain what is meant by business process re-engineering. Why do you think that BPR is seen as a radical and somewhat formidable approach to improvement by many managers, including many operations managers?

14 Develop cause–effect diagrams for the following types of problem:
– customers waiting too long for their calls to be answered when phoning to order from a mail-order catalogue store;
– poor food in the company restaurant;
– poor lecturing from teaching staff at a university;
– customer complaints that the free plastic toy in their breakfast cereal packet is missing;
– staff having to wait excessively long periods to gain access to the photocopier.

15 Construct a flow chart which identifies the different stages in a customer's complaint being processed in a large retail store. The chart should make sure the complaint is dealt with satisfactorily and the organization learns from this complaint to make sure it never happens again.

16 A computer systems field repair company is considering its operations strategy for its 'quickfit' service. This is a simple service which aims to respond to customer requests in less than two hours and repair or replace the defective part of the system within half-an-hour of the service engineer arriving at the customer's site. A survey of customers and competitors has given the results shown in Table 18.5.
(a) Demonstrate how the company could identify its improvement priorities for this service.
(b) How would you go about improving the company's performance at delivering this service?

Table 18.5 'Quickfit' performance

Performance objective	Importance to customers	Performance against main competitors
On-time arrival	Very important	Better than most competitors
Repair/replace in half-hour	Very important	Same as competitors
Helpfulness of service	Important	Same as competitors
Range of equipment covered by service	Very important	Narrower than most competitors
Helpfulness of HQ staff when making initial contact	Only moderately important	Very much better than competitors

---

NOTES ON CHAPTER

1 Based on Neely, A. (1993) *Performance Measurement System Design – Theory and Practice*, Manufacturing Engineering Group, Cambridge University, April.
2 Camp, C. (1989) 'Benchmarking: The Search for Best Practices Which Lead to Superior Performance – Parts 1 to 5', *Quality Progress*, Jan–May.
3 Pickering, I.M. and Chambers, S. (1991) 'Competitive Benchmarking: Progress and Future Developments', *Computer Integrated Manufacturing Systems*, Vol 4, No 2.
4 Sources: Rogers, B. (1991) 'Benchmarking as a Tool in Rank Xerox's Quality Management Strategies', *Quality Link*, Nov–Dec, and Cross, R. and Leonard, P. (1994) 'Benchmarking: A Strategic and Tactical Perspective' *in* Dale, B. (ed) *Managing Quality* (2nd edn), Prentice Hall.
5 Based on Slack, N. (1994) 'The Importance–Performance Matrix as a Determinant of Improvement Priorities', *International Journal of Operations and Production Management*, Vol 14, No 5, pp 59–75.
6 De Meyer, A. (1992) *Creating Product Value*, FT/Pitman Publishing.
7 Imai, M. (1986) *Kaizen – The Key to Japan's Competitive Success*, McGraw-Hill.

8 Imai, M., *op. cit.*

9 Hammer, M. and Champy, J. (1993) *Re-engineering the Corporation*, Nicholas Brealey Publishing.

10 Hammer, M. (1990) 'Re-engineering Work: Don't Automate, Obliterate', *Harvard Business Review*, Vol 68, No 4.

11 Based on an example in Kruse, G. (1995) 'Fundamental Innovation', *Manufacturing Engineer*, Feb.

12 All of this section of this chapter is adapted from Cooke, S. and Slack, N., (1991) *Making Management Decisions* (2nd edn), Prentice Hall.

13 Kowalski, E. and Walley, P. (1993) 'Employee Receptivity to Total Quality', *International Journal of Quality and Reliability Management*, Vol 10, No 1.

14 Source: Orly, C. (1988) 'Quality Circles in France', *The Carnell HRA Quarterly*, Nov.

SELECTED FURTHER READINGS

Armistead, C. and Roland, P. (1996) *Managing Business Processes: BPR and Beyond*, John Wiley.

Codling, S. (1992) *Best Practice Benchmarking*, Industrial Newsletter.

Dale, B.G. (ed.) (1994) *Managing Quality* (2nd edn), Prentice Hall.

DeToni, A. and Tonchia, S. (1996) 'Lean Organisation, Management by Process and Performance Measurement', *International Journal of Operations and Production Management*, Vol 16, No 2.

Evans, J.R. and Lindsay, W.M. (1993) *The Management and Control of Quality*, West.

Fitzgerald, L., Johnston, R., Brignall, S., Sylvestro, R. and Voss, C. (1991) *Performance Measurement in Service Businesses*, The Chartered Institute of Management Accountants.

Flood, R.L. (1993) *Beyond TQM*, John Wiley.

Leibfried, K.H.J. and McNair, C.J. (1992) *Benchmarking: A Tool for Continuous Improvement*, HarperCollins.

Neely, A.D., Mills, J.F., Gregory, M.J., Richards, A.H. and Platts, K.W. (1995) *Performance Measurement System Design*, University of Cambridge Manufacturing Engineering Group.

Oakland, J.S. (1993) *Total Quality Management* (2nd edn), Butterworth-Heinemann.

CHAPTER 19

FAILURE PREVENTION AND RECOVERY

INTRODUCTION

Although no operation should be indifferent to failure, in some operations it is vital that products and services do not fail – aeroplanes in flight or electricity supplies to hospitals, for example. Other products and services should always be there when needed, such as car seat belts, the police service and other emergency services. In these situations dependability is not just desirable, it is essential. In less critical situations having dependable products and services is a way organizations can gain a competitive advantage. For example, Japanese companies made great gains in market share in automobiles and electrical goods through their reputation for high product reliability.

Operations managers, who are almost always concerned with improving the dependability of their operations and the products and services which they produce, try to have strategies in place which attempt to minimize the likelihood of failure and learn from failure when it does occur. They also need to recognize, however, that failures will occur, in spite of all attempts to prevent them. What is then important is that they have plans in place which help them recover from the failures when they do occur. Figure 19.1 shows how this chapter fits into the operation's improvement activities.

Figure 19.1 Model of operations improvement showing the issues covered in this chapter

SYSTEM FAILURE

There is always a chance that in making a product or providing a service things might go wrong. Accepting that failure will occur is not the same thing as ignoring it, however. Nor does it imply that operations cannot or should not attempt to minimize failure. Yet not all failures are equally serious. Some failures are incidental and may not be noticed. In the finale of a concert performance a violinist may play a wrong note and the effect is unlikely to have any great impact. If he or she is giving a solo performance, however, then the error may sour the whole performance. The concert, like all systems, may be more tolerant of some types and some levels of failure than others. For example, if the cigarette lighter in a car or the pen used by a police officer to write a statement fails, the effect may be irritating but not necessarily serious. Conversely, the failure of one component of a system may jeopardize the whole system. For example, leaking hydraulics in a car or a prisoner not informed of his or her rights can put the whole of the process at risk.

Organizations therefore need to discriminate between failures and pay particular attention to those which are critical either in their own right or because they may jeopardize the rest of the operation. To do this we need to understand why something fails and be able to measure the impact of the failure.

Why things fail

Failure in an operation can occur for many different reasons. Machines can break down, customers might make unexpected demands which the operation cannot meet, staff may make simple errors, materials from suppliers could be faulty, and so on. Failures can be grouped as follows:

● those which have their source inside the operation, because its overall design was faulty, or because its facilities (machines, equipment and buildings) or staff fail;
● those which are caused by faults in the material or information inputs to the operation;
● those which are caused by the actions of customers.

Design failures

In its design stage an operation might look fine on paper; only when it has to cope with real circumstances might inadequacies become evident. Some design failures occur because a characteristic of demand was overlooked or miscalculated. A production line might have been installed in a factory which in practice cannot cope with the demands placed upon it, or a theatre front-of-house layout might cause confused and jumbled customer flow at peak times. In both examples there was no unexpected demand placed on the operations; it was straightforward errors in translating the requirements of demand into an adequate design. Other design-related failures occur because the circumstances under which the operation has to work are not as expected. For example, a biscuit production line might have been installed assuming a certain pack size but then the market demands a larger pack size which causes the machine to jam occasionally. The theatre's lighting controls might have been designed for simple lighting sequences, but because it now takes bookings for shows with complex lighting needs, the control system overloads and fails. In both cases the demands placed on the operation were unexpected at the point of design but they are still design failures (*see* box on the Socrates system below). Adequate design includes identifying the range of circumstances under which the operation has to work, and designing accordingly.

FAILED PHILOSOPHER[1]

Sleek, fast and smooth, the TGV trains of France's SNCF rail network look more like aircraft than the traditional train. They provide a service which speeds passengers throughout Europe at speeds in excess of 175 mph. Inside, too, the trains show the influence of air travel. Seats are wide and comfortable with space for leg-stretching relaxation. Descriptions in the French press described the TGV as being like 'an airbus on rails'. SNCF also decided to emulate the airlines by buying a high-tech seat reservation and ticketing system which they named after the Greek philosopher Socrates. That was when their problems began. Design flaws in the booking systems software, combined with inadequate training of SNCF staff, caused chaos for months after the system was introduced. Socrates refused to believe in the existence of some places. Suddenly it refused to issue tickets for Rouen or Barcelona, insisting that neither city existed. It also failed at times to recognize the existence of several of the trains which ran between Paris and Lyon. As a result, the trains made the trip with only four passengers on board. However, these straightforward system design errors have been compounded by over-complexity of some parts of the system: the automatic ticket-vending machines often stand unused by passengers because they have given up trying to understand how to use them. The graffiti outside the Gare de Lyon station reads 'One hour from Lille to Paris ... one hour to buy a ticket!' Although the problems were eventually sorted out, the reputation of what was essentially a fast and efficient operation took longer to recover. ■

Questions

1 This box contrasts two micro operations which affect overall quality from a customer's point of view. What are these two micro operations and what other micro operation might affect the customer's overall perception of quality?

2 Why did the ticket-issuing and reservations system cause such chaos?

Facilities failures

All the facilities (that is the machines, equipment, buildings and fittings) of an operation are liable to break down. The 'breakdown' may only be partial, for example a worn or marked carpet in a hotel, or a machine which can only work at half its normal rate. Alternatively, it can be what we normally regard as a 'failure' – a total and sudden cessation of operation. Either way, it is the effects of a breakdown which are important. Some breakdowns can bring a large part of the operation to a halt. For example, a computer failure in a supermarket chain could paralyse several large stores until it is repaired. Other failures might only have a significant impact if they occur at the same time as other failures. For example, *see* box on air crashes.

TWO MILLION TO ONE[2]

As the number of people travelling by air has grown, the chances of suffering a fatal accident have fallen substantially. Air crashes still do happen, however. Predominantly, the reason for this is not mechanical failure but human failure such as pilot fatigue. Boeing, which dominates the commercial airline business, has calculated that over 60 per cent of all the accidents which have occurred in the past ten years had flight crew behaviour as their 'dominant cause'. In other words, the accidents probably would not have happened had there not been some error by the aircraft's crew.

The chances of an accident are still very small, however. One kind of accident which is known as 'controlled flight into terrain', where the aircraft appears to be under control and yet still flies into the ground, has a chance of happening only *once in two million flights*. For this type of failure to occur a whole chain of minor failures must happen. First, the pilot at the controls has to be flying at the wrong altitude – there is only one chance in a thousand of this. Second, the co-pilot would have to fail to cross-check the altitude – only one chance in a hundred of this. The air traffic controllers would have to miss the fact that the plane was at the wrong altitude (which is not strictly part of their job) – a one-in-ten chance. Finally, the pilot would have to ignore the ground proximity warning alarm in the aircraft (which can be prone to give false alarms) – a one-in-two chance.

Small though the chances of failure are, aircraft manufacturers and airlines are busy working on procedures which make it difficult for aircrew to make any of the mistakes which contribute to fatal crashes. For example, if the chances of the co-pilot failing to check the altitude are reduced to one in two hundred, and the chances of the pilot ignoring the ground proximity alarm are reduced to one in five, then the chances of this type of accident occurring fall dramatically to one in ten million. ■

Questions

1 What are your views on the quoted probabilities of each failure described above occurring?

2 How would you try to prevent these failures occurring?

3 If the probability of each failure occurring could be reduced by a half, what would be the effect on the likelihood of this type of crash occurring?

Staff failures

People failures come in two types: *errors* and *violations*. 'Errors' are mistakes in judgement; with hindsight, a person should have done something different. For example, if the manager of a sports shop fails to anticipate an increased demand for footballs during the World Cup, the shop will run out of stock. This is an error of judgement. 'Violations' are acts which are clearly contrary to defined operating procedure. For example, if a machine operator fails to clean and lubricate his or her machine in the prescribed manner, it is eventually likely to fail. The operator has 'violated' a set procedure.

Supplier failures

Any failure in the delivery or quality of goods and services into an operation can cause failure within the operation. The failure of the band to turn up at a concert will cause the whole event to 'fail'. Similarly, if the band does show but proves to be of dubious talent, the concert could also be regarded as a failure. The more an operation relies on suppliers of materials or services, the more it is liable to failure which is caused by missing or sub-standard inputs.

Customer failures

Not all failures are (directly) caused by the operation or its suppliers. Customers can misuse the products and services which the operation has created. For example, a washing machine might have been manufactured in an efficient and fail-free manner, yet the customer who buys it could overload it or misuse it in some other way which causes it to fail. The customer is not 'always right'. Customers' inattention, incompetence or lack of common sense can be the cause of failure. However, merely complaining about customers is unlikely to reduce the chances of this type of failure occurring. Most organizations will accept that they have a responsibility to educate and train customers and to design their products and services so as to minimize the chances of failure. For example, the sequence of questions at automatic teller machines is designed by banks in such a way as to make their operation as 'fail-free' as possible.

Failure as an opportunity

Notwithstanding our categorization of failure, the origin of all failures is some kind of human failure. A machine failure might have been caused by someone's poor design or maintenance, a delivery failure by someone's errors in managing the supply schedules, and a customer mistake by someone's failure to provide adequate instructions. Failures are rarely the result of random chance; their root cause is usually human failure. The implications of this are, first, that failure can, to some extent, be controlled and, second, that organizations can learn from failure and modify their behaviour accordingly. The realization of this has led to what is sometimes called the *failure as an opportunity* concept. Rather than identifying a 'culprit' who is to be held responsible and blamed for the failure, failures are regarded as an opportunity to examine why they occurred, and to put in place procedures which eliminate or reduce the probability of them recurring. This is treated further, later in this chapter, when we examine 'failure planning'.

Measuring failure

There are three main ways of measuring failure:

- *failure rates* – how often a failure occurs;
- *reliability* – the chances of a failure occurring;
- *availability* – the amount of available useful operating time.

'Failure rate' and 'reliability' are different ways of measuring the same thing – the propensity of an operation, or part of an operation, to fail. Availability is one measure of the consequences of failure in the operation.

Failure rate

Failure rate (FR) is calculated as the number of failures over a period of time. For example, the security of an airport can be measured by the number of security breaches per year, and the failure rate of an engine can be measured in terms of the number of failures divided by its operating time. Failure rate can be measured either as a percentage of the total number of products tested or as the number of failures over time:

$$FR = \frac{\text{number of failures}}{\text{total number of products tested}} \times 100$$

or

$$FR = \frac{\text{number of failures}}{\text{operating time}}$$

Example

A batch of 50 electronic components is tested for 2000 hours. Four of the components fail during the test as follows:

Failure 1	occurred at 1200 hours
Failure 2	occurred at 1450 hours
Failure 3	occurred at 1720 hours
Failure 4	occurred at 1905 hours

$$\text{Failure rate (as a percentage)} = \frac{\text{number of failures}}{\text{number tested}} \times 100 = \frac{4}{50} \times 100 = 8\%$$

The total time of the test $= 50 \times 2000 = 100\ 000$ component hours

But

one component was not operating 2000 – 1200 = 800 hours
one component was not operating 2000 – 1450 = 550 hours
one component was not operating 2000 – 1720 = 280 hours
one component was not operating 2000 – 1905 = 95 hours

Thus:

Total non-operating time $= 1725$ hours

$$\text{Operating time} = \text{total time} - \text{non-operating time}$$
$$= 100\,000 - 1725 \quad = 98\,275 \text{ hours}$$

$$\text{Failure rate (in time)} = \frac{\text{number of failures}}{\text{operating time}} = \frac{4}{98\,275}$$

$$= 0.000041$$

Failure over time – the 'bath-tub' curve

Failure, for most parts of an operation, is a function of time. At different stages during the life of anything the probability of it failing will be different. The probability of, for example, an electric lamp failing is relatively high when it is first plugged in. Any small defect in the material from which the filament is made or in the way the lamp was assembled could cause the lamp to fail. If the lamp survives this initial stage, it could still fail at any point, but the longer it survives, the more likely its failure becomes. Most physical parts an operation behave in a similar manner.

The curve which describes failure probability of this type is called the *bath-tub curve*. It comprises three distinct stages:

● the 'infant-mortality' or 'early-life' stage where early failures occur caused by defective parts or improper use;
● the 'normal-life' stage when the failure rate is usually low and reasonably constant, and caused by normal random factors;
● the 'wear-out' stage when the failure rate increases as the part approaches the end of its working life and failure is caused by the ageing and deterioration of parts.

Figure 19.2 illustrates two bath-tub curves with slightly different characteristics. Curve A shows a part of the operation which has a high initial infant-mortality failure but then a long, low-failure, normal life followed by the gradually increasing likelihood of failure as it approaches wear-out. Curve B has roughly the same relative infant-mortality, normal-life and wear-out stages. It differs markedly, however, in the predictability with which failure occurs. Curve A shows a part with very predictable

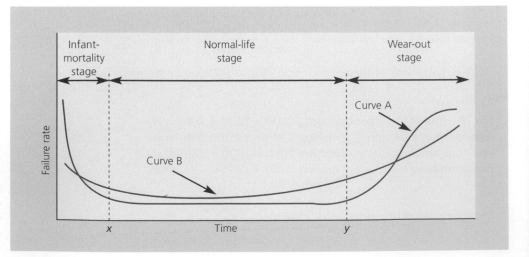

Figure 19.2 Bath-tub curves for two parts of an operation. Curve A represents a part with relatively predictable failure and curve B represents a part with a more random failure pattern

failure characteristics. If it survives infant mortality (that is past time x) it is very likely to survive at least until wear-out starts (at time y). However, after time y its chances of survival rapidly diminish. Curve B, on the other hand, shows a part which is far less predictable. The distinction between the three stages is less clear with infant-mortality failure subsiding only slowly and a gradually increasing chance of wear-out failure.

Facilities with failure curves similar to that shown in curve B are far more difficult to maintain in a planned manner, as will be discussed later.

The failure of operations which rely more on human resources than technology, such as some services, can follow a somewhat different curve. They may be less susceptible to component wear-out but more so to staff complacency as the service, without review and regeneration, may become tedious and repetitive. In such a case there is an initial stage of failure reduction, equivalent to the infant-mortality stage, as problems in the service are ironed out. This may be followed by a long period of increasing failure (*see* Fig. 19.3).

Reliability

Reliability measures the ability of a system, product or service to perform as expected over time.

The importance of any particular failure is determined partly by the effect it has on the performance of the whole operation or system. This in turn depends on the way in which the parts of the system which are liable to failure are related. If components in a system are all interdependent, a failure in any individual component will cause the whole system to fail. For example, if an interdependent system has n components each with their own reliability $R_1, R_2 \cdots R_n$, the reliability of the whole system, R_s, is given by

$$R_s = R_1 \times R_2 \times R_2 \times \cdots R_n$$

where

R_1 = reliability of component 1
R_2 = reliability of component 2
etc.

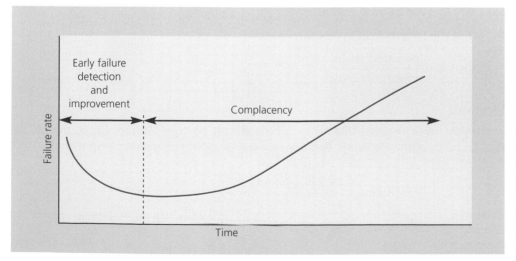

Figure 19.3
Service operations, after an early stage of failure detection and improvement, may suffer from steadily rising failure rates caused by increasing complacency

Example

An automated pizza-making machine in a food manufacturer's factory has five major components, with individual reliabilities (the probability of the component not failing) as follows:

Dough mixer	Reliability = 0.95
Dough roller and cutter	Reliability = 0.99
Tomato paste applicator	Reliability = 0.97
Cheese applicator	Reliability = 0.90
Oven	Reliability = 0.98

If one of these parts of the production system fails, the whole system will stop working. Thus the reliability of the whole system is:

$$R_s = 0.95 \times 0.99 \times 0.97 \times 0.90 \times 0.98$$
$$= 0.805$$

The number of components

In the example above, the reliability of the whole system was only 0.8, even though the reliability of the individual components was significantly higher. If the system had been made up of more components, then its reliability would have been even lower. The more interdependent components a system has, the lower its reliability will be. Figure 19.4 shows the reduction in system reliability as the number of components in the system increases. For a system composed of components which each have an individual reliability of 0.99, with 10 components the system reliability has shrunk to 0.9, with 50 components it is below 0.8, with 100 components it is below 0.4, and with 400 components it is down below 0.05. In other words, with a system of 400 components (not unusual in a large automated operation), even if the reliability of each individual component is 99 per cent, the whole system will be working for less than five per cent of its time.

Mean time between failures

An alternative (and common) measure of failure is the *mean time between failures* (MTBF) of a component or system.

MTBF is the reciprocal of failure rate (in time). Thus:

$$\text{MTBF} = \frac{\text{operating hours}}{\text{number of failures}}$$

Example

In the previous example which was concerned with electronic components, the failure rate (in time) of the electronic components was 0.000041. For that component:

$$\text{MTBF} = \frac{1}{0.000041} = 24\,390.24 \text{ hours}$$

That is, a failure can be expected once every 24 390.24 hours on average.

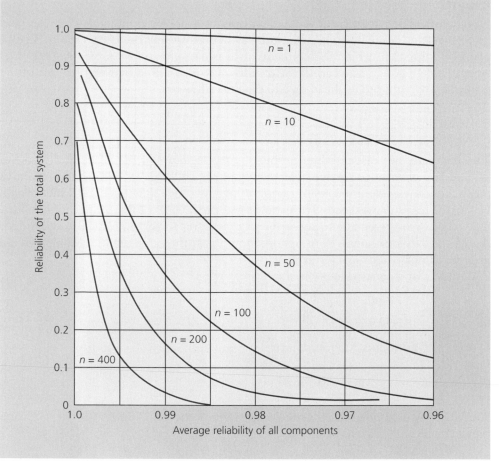

Figure 19.4
The effect of the number of components in a system (n) on the reliability of the total system

Availability

Availability is the degree to which the operation is ready to work. An operation is not available if it has either failed or is being repaired following failure.

There are several different ways of measuring availability depending on how many of the reasons for not operating are included. Lack of availability because of planned maintenance or change-overs could be included, for example. However, when 'availability' is being used to indicate the operating time excluding the consequence of failure, it is calculated as follows:

$$\text{Availability (A)} = \frac{\text{MTBF}}{\text{MTBF} + \text{MTTR}}$$

where

MTBF = the mean time between failures of the operation
MTTR = the mean time to repair, which is the average time taken to repair the operation, from the time it fails to the time it is operational again.

Example

A company, which designs and produces display posters for exhibitions and sales promotion events, competes largely on the basis of its speedy delivery. One particular piece of equipment which the company uses is causing some problems. This is its large platform colour laser printer. Currently, the mean time between failures of the printer is 70 hours and its mean time to repair is six hours.

$$\text{Availability} = \frac{70}{70 + 6} = 0.92$$

The company has discussed its problem with the supplier of the printer who has offered two alternative service deals. One option would be to buy some preventive maintenance (*see* later for a full description of preventive maintenance) which would be carried out each weekend. This would raise the MTBF of the printer to 90 hours. The other option would be to subscribe to a faster repair service which would reduce the MTTR to four hours. Both options would cost the same amount. Which would give the company the higher availability?

With MTBF increased to 90 hours:

$$\text{Availability} = \frac{90}{90 + 6} = 0.938$$

With MTTR reduced to four hours:

$$\text{Availability} = \frac{70}{70 + 4} = 0.946$$

Availability would be greater if the company took the deal which offered the faster repair time.

Failure prevention and recovery

In practical terms, operations managers have three sets of activities which relate to failure. The first is concerned with understanding what failures are occurring in the

Figure 19.5
The three tasks of failure prevention and recovery

operation and why they are occurring. Once the nature of any failures is understood, an operations manager's second task is to examine ways of either reducing the chances of failure or minimizing the consequences of failure. The third task is to devise plans and procedures which help the operation to recover from failures when they do occur. The first of these tasks is, in effect, a prerequisite for the other two (*see* Fig. 19.5). The remainder of this chapter deals with these three tasks.

FAILURE DETECTION AND ANALYSIS

Given that failures will occur, operations managers must first have mechanisms in place which ensure that they are aware that a failure has occurred and, second, have procedures in place which analyse the failure to find out its root cause.

Mechanisms to detect failure

Organizations sometimes may not be aware that the system has failed and thereby lose the opportunity both to put things right for the customer, and to learn from the experience. Customers dissatisfied with the food or the service at a restaurant are very likely to 'vote with their feet' and tell all their friends about the poor experience rather than complain to the management at the time. When customers do complain about a product or a service, the situation may be dealt with on the spot but the system may not be changed to prevent such problems occurring again. This may be due to staff fearing that drawing attention to a problem might be seen to be a sign of weakness or lack of ability, or because there are inadequate failure identification systems, or a lack of managerial support or interest in making improvements.

Many mechanisms are available to seek out failures in a proactive way:

- *In-process checks*. Employees check that the service is acceptable during the process itself. This is often undertaken in restaurants, for example 'Is everything alright with your meal, madam?'
- *Machine diagnostic checks*. A machine is tested by putting it through a prescribed sequence of activities designed to expose any failures or potential failures. Computer servicing procedures often include this type of check.
- *Point-of-departure interviews*. At the end of a service, staff may formally or informally check that the service has been satisfactory and try to solicit problems as well as compliments.
- *Phone surveys*. These can be used to solicit opinions about products or services. Television rental companies, for example, may check on the installation and servicing of equipment in this way.
- *Focus groups*. These are groups of customers who are asked together to focus on some aspects of a product or service. These can be used to discover either specific problems or more general attitudes towards the product or service.
- *Complaint cards or feedback sheets*. These are used by many organizations to solicit views about the products and services. The problem here is that very few people tend to complete them. It may be possible, however, to identify the respondents and so follow up on any individual problem.

● *Questionnaires*. These may generate a slightly higher response than complaint cards. They may only generate general information, however, from which it is difficult to identify specific individual complaints.

Failure analysis

One of the critical activities for an organization when failure has occurred is to understand why the failure occurred. This activity is called *failure analysis*. There are many different techniques and approaches which are used to uncover the root cause of failures. Some of these were described in the final part of the previous chapter. Some others are briefly described in this section.

Accident investigation

Large-scale national disasters like oil tanker spillages and aeroplane accidents are usually investigated by accident investigators specifically trained in the detailed analysis of the causes of the accident. Although the techniques they use have usually been developed to be appropriate for the particular type of accident being investigated, the common role of the accident investigators is to make recommendations to minimize or even eradicate the likelihood of any such failures occurring again.

Product liability

Many organizations (either by choice or more often because of a legal requirement) adopt 'product liability'. This ensures that all their products are traceable. Any failures can be traced back to the process which produced them, the components from which they were produced, or the suppliers who provided them. This means that any fault can be rectified and also that, if necessary, all other similar products can be recalled for checking. This is sometimes seen when car and electrical components or food items are recalled.

Complaint analysis

Complaints, just like errors, will always arise. They are increasingly seen to be a cheap and easily available source of information about errors. Complaints, and indeed compliments, need to be taken seriously as they are likely to represent only the 'tip of the iceberg' of customer attitudes. In some service operations it is believed that for every person who complains there are another 20 who have not. Two key advantages of complaints are that they come unsolicited and also they are often very timely pieces of information that can pin-point problems quickly within an organization. Complaint analysis also involves tracking the actual number of complaints over time, which can in itself be indicative of developing problems. The prime function of complaint analysis involves analysing the 'content' of the complaints to understand better the nature of the problem as it is perceived by the customer.

Critical incident analysis

Critical incident analysis simply requires customers to identify the elements of products or services that they found either particularly satisfying or not particularly satisfying. They are asked to write down incidents which gave them cause for dissatisfaction or satisfaction. The transcript of this anecdotal evidence is then analysed in detail for factors, traits and causes of the satisfaction and dissatisfaction. These causes can then be categorized and linked to possible causes of failure. It is a popular way of collecting information, especially in service operations. Critical incident technique (CIT) has been defined as 'essentially a procedure for gathering certain important facts concerning behaviour in defined situations'.[3] This technique has been applied to many different service industries, including hotels, banks and airlines.

Failure mode and effect analysis

The objective of failure mode and effect analysis (FMEA) is to identify the product or service features that are critical to various types of failure. It is a means of identifying failures before they happen by providing a 'checklist' procedure which is built round three key questions.

For each possible cause of failure:

- What is the likelihood that failure will occur?
- What would the consequence of the failure be?
- How likely is such a failure to be detected before it affects the customer?

Based on a quantitative evaluation of these three questions, a *risk priority number* (RPN) is calculated for each potential cause of failure. Corrective actions, aimed at preventing failure, are then applied to those causes whose RPN indicates that they warrant priority.

It is essentially a seven-step process:

Step 1 Identify all the component parts of the product or service.
Step 2 List all the possible ways in which the components could fail (the failure modes).
Step 3 Identify the possible effects of the failures (down time, safety, repair requirements, effects on customers).
Step 4 Identify all the possible causes of failure for each failure mode.
Step 5 Assess the probability of failure, the severity of the effects of failure and the likelihood of detection. (Table 19.1 illustrates rating scales which can be used to quantify these three factors.)
Step 6 Calculate the RPN by multiplying all three ratings together.
Step 7 Instigate corrective action which will minimize failure on failure modes which show a high RPN.

Example

Part of an FMEA exercise at a transportation company has identified three failure modes associated with the failure of 'goods arriving damaged' at the point of delivery:

- Goods not secured (failure mode 1)
- Goods incorrectly secured (failure mode 2)
- Goods incorrectly loaded (failure mode 3).

The improvement group which is investigating the failures allocates scores for the probability of the failure mode occurring, the severity of each failure mode, and the likelihood that they will be detected, as follows:

Table 19.1 Rating scales for FMEA

A. Occurrence of failure

Description	Rating	Possible failure occurrence
Remote probability of occurrence It would be unreasonable to expect failure to occur	1	0
Low probability of occurrence Generally associated with activities similar	2	1:20 000
to previous ones with a relatively low number of failures	3	1:10 000
Moderate probability of occurrence Generally associated with activities similar	4	1:2000
to previous ones which have resulted in occasional failures	5	1:1000
	6	1:200
High probability of occurrence Generally associated with activities similar	7	1:100
to ones which have traditionally caused problems	8	1:20
Very high probability of occurrence Near certainty that major failures will	9	1:10
occur	10	1:2

Probability of occurrence
    Failure mode 1   5
    Failure mode 2   8
    Failure mode 3   7

Severity of failure
    Failure mode 1   6
    Failure mode 2   4
    Failure mode 3   4

Probability of detection
    Failure mode 1   2
    Failure mode 2   6
    Failure mode 3   7

Table 19.1 continued

B. Severity of failure

Description	Rating
Minor severity	
A very minor failure which would have no noticeable effect on system performance	1
Low severity	
A minor failure causing only slight customer annoyance	2
	3
Moderate severity	
A failure which would cause some customer dissatisfaction, discomfort or annoyance, or would cause noticeable deterioration in performance	4
	5
	6
High severity	
A failure which would engender a high degree of customer dissatisfaction	7
	8
Very high severity	
A failure which would affect safety	9
Catastrophic	
A failure which may cause damage to property, serious injury or death	10

C. Detection of failure

Description	Rating	Probability of detection
Remote probability that the defect will reach the customer. (It is unlikely that such a defect would pass through inspection, test or assembly)	1	0 to 15%
Low probability that the defect will reach the customer	2	6 to 15%
	3	16 to 25%
Moderate probability that the defect will reach the customer	4	26 to 35%
	5	36 to 45%
	6	46 to 55%
High probability that the defect will reach the customer	7	56 to 65%
	8	66 to 75%
Very high probability that the defect will reach the customer	9	76 to 85%
	10	86 to 100%

The RPN of each failure mode is calculated.

Failure mode 1 (goods not secured)	$5 \times 6 \times 2 =$	60
Failure mode 2 (goods incorrectly secured)	$8 \times 4 \times 5 =$	160
Failure mode 3 (goods incorrectly loaded)	$7 \times 4 \times 7 =$	196

Priority is therefore given to failure mode 3 (goods incorrectly loaded) when attempting to eliminate the failure.

Fault-tree analysis

This is a logical procedure that starts with a failure or a potential failure and works backwards to identify all the possible causes and therefore the origins of that failure. The *fault tree* is made up of branches connected by two types of nodes: *AND nodes* and *OR nodes*. The branches below an AND node all need to occur for the event above the node to occur. Only one of the branches below an OR node needs to occur for the event above the node to occur.

CARLSBERG TETLEY'S PRODUCT RECALL[4]

Very few crises happen at convenient times. Carlsberg Tetley learnt of its crisis late one Friday afternoon, with a public holiday the following Monday and on the eve of the Chairman's holiday. Something appeared to have gone wrong with the 'widget' in one of its cans of beer (a widget is the device in the bottom of a can which gives some canned beer its creamy characteristic). One customer had taken a drink from a can of beer and found a piece of plastic in his mouth. He had complained to an environmental health official who had then taken it up with the company. The company's pre-planned crisis management procedure immediately swung into action. A crisis control group of 12 members, with experts on insurance, legal affairs, quality control, and public relations, took control. This group always has everyone's telephone number, so any relevant person in the company can be contacted. It also has a control room at one of the company's sites with fax and telephone lines always available for the sole use of the crisis team. Over the weekend the team investigated the problem and by the following Tuesday had issued a press release, set up a hot-line and taken out national advertising to announce the recall decision. Even though the problem had originated in only one of its six brands, the company decided to recall all of them – a total of one million cans. The hot-line received 500 calls during its first week of operation and all production using the suspect widget was halted. Linda Bain, the company spokeswoman, explained, '*We were very happy with our recall procedure and the effectiveness of the control group. It all went according to plan. In terms of public relations, the coverage we got from the media was positive, factual and up-front, and indicated the company had been as honest and truthful as it possibly could*'. ■

Questions

1 What seem to be the essential elements of this successful recovery from failure?

2 How do the advantages and disadvantages of deciding whether or not to recall products in a case such as this depend on the likelihood of another potential failure being out there in the market?

3 Relate this issue to the concept of Type I and Type II errors dealt with in Chapter 17.

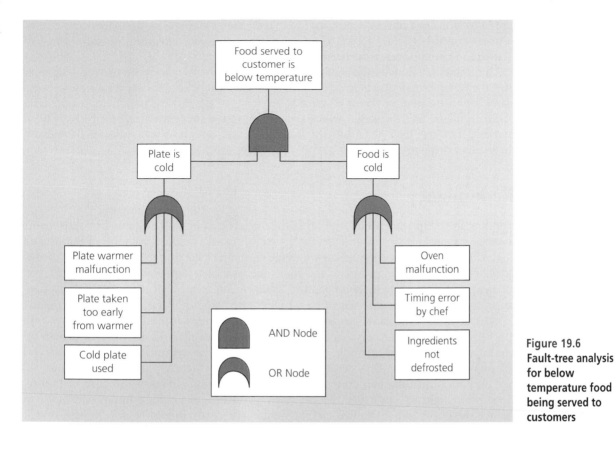

Figure 19.6
Fault-tree analysis for below temperature food being served to customers

Figure 19.6 shows a simple tree identifying the possible reasons for a hot dish being served cold in a restaurant.

IMPROVING THE OPERATION'S RELIABILITY

Once a thorough understanding of the causes and effects of failure has been established, the next responsibility of operations managers is to try to prevent the failures occurring in the first place. They can do this in a number of ways:

- designing out the fail points in the operation;
- building redundancy into the operation;
- 'fail-safeing' some of the activities in the operation;
- maintenance of the physical facilities in the operation.

We will examine each of these, but especially the maintenance of physical facilities (equipment, machines and buildings) which is an important activity in all operations.

Designing out fail points

Chapter 5 on product/service design and Chapter 17 on quality planning and control were concerned with identifying and then controlling product and service characteristics to try to prevent failures occurring. In particular, Chapter 17 described the use of process control charting to try to detect when a process was going out of control so that action could be taken before failures occurred.

All the process flow design methods described in Chapter 5 can be used to 'engineer out' the potential fail points in operations. For example, Fig. 19.7 shows a flow process chart for an automobile repair process. The stages in the process which are particularly prone to failure and the stages which are critical to the success of the service have been marked. This will have been done by the staff of this operation metaphorically 'walking themselves through' the process and discussing each stage in turn.

Redundancy

Building in redundancy to an operation means having back-up systems or components in case of failure. It can be an expensive solution to reduce the likelihood of failure and is generally used when the breakdown could have a critical impact. Redundancy means doubling or even tripling some of the components in a system so that these 'redundant' elements can come into action when one component fails. Nuclear power stations, hospitals and other public buildings have auxiliary or back-up electricity generators ready to operate in case the main electricity supply should fail. Some organizations also have 'back-up' staff held in reserve in case someone does not turn up for work or is held up on one job and is unable to move to the next. This is done by railways, theme parks and hospitals, for example. Spacecraft have several back-up computers on board that will not only monitor the main computer but will also act as a back-up in case of failure. Rear brake lighting sets built into the back of buses and lorries contain two bulbs to reduce the likelihood of showing no red light at the rear. Human bodies contain two of some organs – kidneys and eyes, for example – both of which are used in 'normal operation' but the body can cope with a failure in one of them.

The reliability of a component together with its back-up is given by the sum of the reliability of the original component and the likelihood that the back-up component will both be needed *and* be working.

$$R_{a+b} \quad = R_a + (R_b \times P \text{ (failure)})$$

where

R_{a+b} = reliability of component a with its back-up component b
R_a = reliability of a alone
R_b = reliability of back-up component b
P (failure) = the probability that component a will fail and therefore component b will be needed

Example

The food manufacturer in the earlier worked example has decided that the cheese depositor in the pizza-making machine is so unreliable that it needs a second cheese depositor to be fitted to the machine which will come into action if the first cheese depositor fails.

The two cheese depositors (each with reliability = 0.9) working together will have a reliability of:

$$0.9 + (0.9 \times (1 - 0.9)) = 0.99$$

The reliability of the whole machine is now:

$$0.95 \times 0.99 \times 0.97 \times 0.99 \times 0.98 = 0.885$$

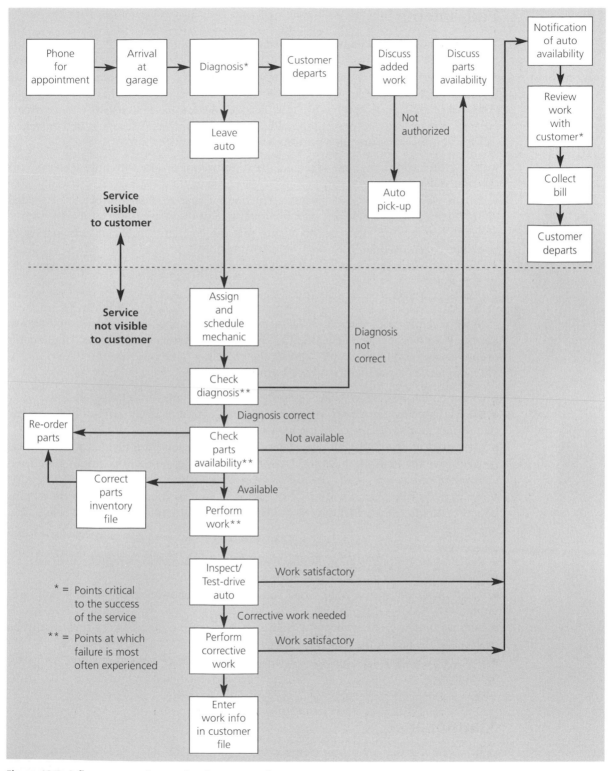

Figure 19.7 A flow process diagram for the auto repair process

Fail-safeing

The concept of fail-safeing has emerged since the introduction of Japanese methods of operations improvement. Called *poka-yoke* in Japan (from *yokeru* (to prevent) and *poka* (inadvertent errors)), the idea is based on the principle that human mistakes are to some extent inevitable. What is important is to prevent them becoming defects. Poka-yokes are simple (preferably inexpensive) devices or systems which are incorporated into a process to prevent inadvertent operator mistakes resulting in a defect.

Typical poka-yokes are such devices as:

- limit switches on machines which allow the machine to operate only if the part is positioned correctly;
- gauges placed on machines through which a part has to pass in order to be loaded on to, or taken off, the machine – an incorrect size or orientation stops the process;
- digital counters on machines to ensure that the correct number of cuts, passes or holes have been machined;
- checklists which have to be filled in, either in preparation for, or on completion of, an activity;
- light beams which activate an alarm if a part is positioned incorrectly.

More recently, the principle of fail-safeing has been applied to service operations. Service poka-yokes can be classified as those which 'fail-safe the server' (the creator of the service) and those which 'fail-safe the customer' (the receiver of the service).[5]

Examples of fail-safeing the server include:

- colour coding cash register keys to prevent incorrect entry in retail operations;
- the McDonald's french-fry scoop which picks up the right quantity of fries in the right orientation to be placed in the pack;
- trays used in hospitals with indentations shaped to each item needed for a surgical procedure – any item not back in place at the end of the procedure might have been left in the patient;
- the paper strips placed round clean towels in hotels, the removal of which helps housekeepers to tell whether a towel has been used and therefore needs replacing.

Examples of fail-safeing the customer include:

- the locks on aircraft lavatory doors, which must be turned to switch the light on;
- beepers on ATMs to ensure that customers remove their cards;
- height bars on amusement rides to ensure that customers do not exceed size limitations;
- outlines drawn on the walls of a child-care centre to indicate where toys should be replaced at the end of the play period;
- tray stands strategically placed in fast-food restaurants to remind customers to clear their tables.

Maintenance

Maintenance is the term used to cover the way in which organizations try to avoid failure by taking care of their physical facilities. It is an important part of most operations' activities, especially those whose physical facilities play a central role in creating

KEEP LEFT[6]

For over half an hour the pilot of an Airbus A320 jet with nearly 200 people on board fought to control his aircraft which did not seem to be responding to the controls. The aircraft would not turn left no matter what the pilot tried. Eventually he managed to make a high-speed emergency landing at the second attempt. Fortunately no one was hurt but the pilot was not pleased to find out that the cause of the near-disaster was that engineers had forgotten to reactivate four of the five spoilers on the right wing. Spoilers are the panels that help the plane to roll and hence turn. The official air accident investigation report on the incident blamed 'a complex chain of human errors', not only by the engineers but also by the pilots who had failed to notice the problem before take-off. The A320 is a 'fly-by-wire' aircraft where computer-controlled electrical impulses activate the hydraulically powered spoilers and surfaces which control the movement of the plane. When the aircraft went for repair to a damaged flap the engineers had put the spoilers into 'maintenance mode' to block them off from the controls so that they could be worked on independently. They had then forgotten to reactivate them when the plane was needed urgently to replace another aircraft. According to the official report, the engineers were not guilty of, '*simple acts of neglect or ignorance. Their approach implied that they believed there were benefits to the organization if they could successfully circumvent problems to deliver the aircraft on time. With the introduction of aircraft such as the A320 it is no longer possible for maintenance staff to have enough information about the aircraft and its systems to understand adequately the consequences of any deviation. The avoidance of future unnecessary accidents with high-technology aircraft depends on an attitude of total compliance within the industry. If a check has previously been carried out numerous times without any fault being present, it is human nature to anticipate no fault when next the check is carried out.*' ∎

Questions

1 Why should fly-by-wire aircraft pose a more complex maintenance problem than conventional aircraft which have a physical link between the control and the flaps?

2 If you were the accident investigator what questions would you want to ask in order to understand why this failure occurred?

their goods and services. In operations such as power stations, hotels, airlines and petrochemical refineries maintenance activities will account for a significant proportion of operations management's time, attention and resources.

The benefits of maintenance

Before examining the various approaches to maintenance, it is worth considering why operations bother to care for their facilities in a systematic manner.

● *Enhanced safety*. Well-maintained facilities are less likely to behave in an unpredictable or non-standard way, or fail outright, all of which could pose a hazard to staff.
● *Increased reliability*. This leads to less time lost while facilities are repaired, less disruption to the normal activities of the operation, and less variation in output rates.

- *Higher quality*. Badly maintained equipment is more likely to perform below standard and cause quality errors.
- *Lower operating costs*. Many pieces of process technology run more efficiently when regularly serviced: motor vehicles, for example.
- *Longer life span*. Regular care can prolong the effective life of facilities by reducing the problems in operation whose cumulative effect causes deterioration.
- *Higher end value*. Well-maintained facilities are generally easier to dispose of into the second-hand market.

The three basic approaches to maintenance

In practice an organization's maintenance activities will consist of some combination of the three basic approaches to the care of its physical facilities. These are *run to breakdown* (RTB), *preventive maintenance* (PM) and *condition-based maintenance* (CBM).

Run to breakdown (RTB)

As its name implies, this approach involves allowing the facilities to continue operating until they fail. Maintenance work is performed only after failure has taken place. For example, the televisions, bathroom equipment and telephones in a hotel's guest rooms will probably only be repaired when they fail. The hotel will keep some spare parts and the staff available to make any repairs when needed. Failure in these circumstances is neither catastrophic (although perhaps irritating to the guest) nor so frequent as to make regular checking of the facilities appropriate.

Preventive maintenance (PM)

Preventive maintenance attempts to eliminate or reduce the chances of failure by servicing (cleaning, lubricating, replacing and checking) the facilities at pre-planned intervals. For example, the engines of passenger aircraft are checked, cleaned and calibrated according to a regular schedule after a set number of flying hours. Taking aircraft away from their regular duties for preventive maintenance is clearly an expensive option for any airline. The consequences of failure while in service are considerably more serious, however. The principle is also applied to facilities with less catastrophic consequences of failure. The regular cleaning and lubricating of machines, even the periodic painting of a building, could be considered preventive maintenance.

Condition-based maintenance (CBM)

Condition-based maintenance attempts to perform maintenance only when the facilities require it. For example, continuous process equipment, such as that used in coating photographic paper, is run for long periods in order to achieve the high utilization necessary for cost-effective production. Stopping the machine to change, say, a bearing when it is not strictly necessary to do so would take it out of action for long periods and reduce its utilization. Here condition-based maintenance might involve continuously monitoring the vibrations, for example, or some other characteristic of the line. The results of this monitoring would then be used to decide whether the line should be stopped and the bearings replaced. Table 19.2 illustrates some of the characteristics which could be monitored to determine whether any maintenance intervention is required.

Table 19.2 **Examples of the characteristics monitored and procedures for monitoring in condition-based maintenance**

Characteristic	Monitoring procedure
Vibration (for example, bearings)	Quality and condition of a machine tool can be measured by vibration characteristics. Vibrations are measured near bearing positions and analysed by a computer program.
Composition (for example, the oil in a press machine)	Instead of replacing oil in presses every 2000 operating hours, samples are analysed regularly. Oil is tested chemically, spectrographically, and for particle contamination; an additional benefit is that oil impurities due to impending part failures can be detected.
Dimensions (for example, the thickness of assembly conveyor chains)	Thickness of chain elements is monitored. The elements of the conveyor are replaced only as necessary.
Temperature (for example, electric motors)	Constant load and operation leads to constant temperature; regular monitoring of the temperature leads to predictions about condition.
Quality of output (for example of manufactured products)	Dimensions of output parts can be an indication of machine condition. SPC can be linked to CBM (*see* Chapter 17).

Source: Adapted from Harrison, A. (1992) *Just-in-time Manufacturing in Perspective*, Prentice Hall

Mixed maintenance strategies

Each approach to maintaining facilities is appropriate for different circumstances. RTB is often used where repair is relatively straightforward (so the consequence of failure is small), where regular maintenance is very costly (making PM expensive), or where failure is not at all predictable (so there is no advantage in PM because failure is just as likely to occur after repair as before). PM is used where the cost of unplanned failure is high (because of disruption to normal operations) and where failure is not totally random (so the maintenance time can be scheduled before failure becomes very likely). CBM is used where the maintenance activity is expensive, either because of the cost of providing the maintenance itself, or because of the disruption which the maintenance activity causes to the operation.

Most operations adopt a mixture of these approaches because different elements of their facilities have different characteristics. Even a motor car uses all three approaches (*see* Fig. 19.8). Some parts of the car are normally replaced only when they fail: light bulbs and fuses, for example. A wise motorist might carry spares and some cars have warning systems to tell the driver when a light bulb has failed, so the failure can be identified and repaired immediately. More fundamental parts of the car should not be run to breakdown, however. The engine oil would be subject to preventive maintenance at the car's regular service. At the service other parts of the car would also be checked and replaced as necessary. Finally, most drivers would also monitor the condition of the car. Some monitoring would be done informally, by listening to the engine noise when driving. Other monitoring might be done regularly, such as measuring the amount of tread on the tyre.

**Figure 19.8
A mixture of maintenance approaches is often used – in a motor car, for example**

Use preventive maintenance

Use run-to-breakdown maintenance

Use condition-based monitoring maintenance

Breakdown *versus* preventive maintenance

Most operations plan their maintenance to include a level of regular preventive maintenance which gives a reasonably low but finite chance of breakdown. Usually the more frequent the preventive maintenance episodes, the less are the chances of a breakdown. The balance between preventive and breakdown maintenance is set to minimize the total cost of breakdown. Infrequent preventive maintenance will cost little to provide but will result in a high likelihood (and therefore cost) of breakdown maintenance. Conversely, very frequent preventive maintenance will be expensive to provide but will reduce the cost of having to provide breakdown maintenance (*see* Fig. 19.9(a)). The total cost of maintenance appears to minimize at an 'optimum' level of preventive maintenance.

This representation of maintenance-related costs, however, although conceptually elegant, may not reflect reality. The cost of providing preventive maintenance may not increase quite so steeply as indicated in Fig. 19.9(a). The curve assumes that it is carried out by a separate set of people (skilled maintenance staff) whose time is scheduled and accounted for separately from the 'operators' of the facilities. Furthermore, every time preventive maintenance takes place, the facilities cannot be used productively. This is why the slope of the curve increases, because the maintenance episodes start to interfere with the normal working of the operation. In many operations, however, at least some of the preventive maintenance can be performed by the operators themselves (which reduces the cost of providing it) and at times which are convenient for the operation (which minimizes the disruption to the operation). The cost of breakdowns could also be higher than is indicated in Fig. 19.9(a). Here the argument is similar to that which we used in Chapter 2 to describe dependability and in Chapter 12 to determine optimum stock levels (and will again in the next chapter when discussing the costs of quality). Unplanned breakdowns may do more than necessitate a repair and stop the operation; they can take away stability from the operation which prevents it being able to improve itself.

Put these two ideas together and the minimizing total curve and maintenance cost curve look more like Fig. 19.9(b). The emphasis is shifted more towards the use of preventive maintenance than run-to-breakdown maintenance.

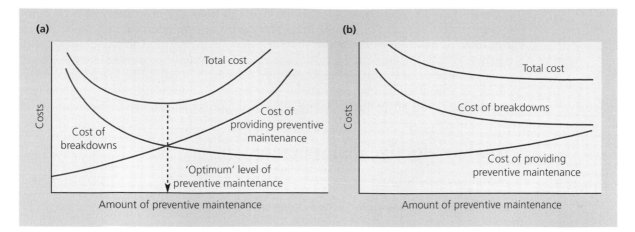

Figure 19.9 **Two views of maintenance costs: (a) One model of the costs associated with preventive maintenance shows an optimum level of maintenance effort; (b) If routine preventive maintenance tasks are carried out by operators and if the real cost of breakdowns is considered, the 'optimum' level of preventive maintenance shifts toward higher levels**

Failure distributions

The shape of the failure probability distribution of a facility will also have an effect on the benefits of preventive maintenance. Fig. 19.10 shows two probability curves for two machines, A and B. For machine A, the probability that it will break down before time x is relatively low. This machine will almost always break down between times x and y. If preventive maintenance was timed to occur just before point x it could reduce the chances of breakdown substantially. Machine B, on the other hand, has a relatively high

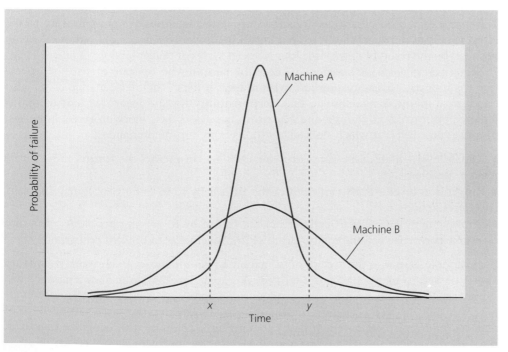

Figure 19.10
Failure curves for
two machines, A
and B

743

probability of breaking down at any time, although again the probability of breakdown increases after time x. This means that applying preventive maintenance at point x (or any other time) cannot bring the dramatic reduction in breakdowns possible with machine A. The implication of this is that preventive maintenance is more likely to lead to benefits when periods of high breakdown are reasonably predictable. When breakdown occurs in a relatively random manner there is less to gain from preventive maintenance because it has little effect on the chance of the machine breaking down in the future.

Total productive maintenance

Total productive maintenance (TPM) is defined as:

'*...the productive maintenance carried out by all employees through small group activities*'

where productive maintenance is:

'*...maintenance management which recognizes the importance of reliability, maintenance and economic efficiency in plant design*'.[7]

In Japan, where TPM originated, it is seen as a natural extension in the evolution from run-to-breakdown to preventive maintenance. TPM adopts some of the team-working and empowerment principles discussed in Chapter 9, as well as a continuous improvement approach to failure prevention as discussed in Chapter 18. It also sees maintenance as an organization-wide issue, to which staff can contribute in some way. It is analogous to the total quality management approach discussed in Chapter 20.

The five goals of TPM

TPM aims to establish good maintenance practice in operations through the pursuit of 'the five goals of TPM':[8]

1 *Improve equipment effectiveness*. Examine how the facilities are contributing to the effectiveness of the operation by examining all the losses which occur. Loss of effectiveness can be the result of down-time losses, speed losses or defect losses.

2 *Achieve autonomous maintenance*. Allow the people who operate or use the operation's equipment to take responsibility for at least some of the maintenance tasks. Also encourage maintenance staff to take responsibility for the improvement of maintenance performance. Murata and Harrison, based on their work at Yuasa batteries, propose three levels at which staff take responsibility for maintenance:[9]

● Repair level – Staff carry out instructions but do not predict the future, they simply react to problems.

● Prevention level – Staff can predict the future by foreseeing problems, and take corrective action.

● Improvement level – Staff can predict the future by foreseeing problems; they not only take corrective action but also propose improvements to prevent recurrence.

For example, suppose the screws on a machine become loose. Each week it jams up and is passed to maintenance to be fixed. A 'repair-level' maintenance engineer will simply repair it and hand it back to production. A 'prevention-level' maintenance engineer will spot the weekly pattern to the problem, and tighten the screws in advance of their loosening. An 'improvement-level' maintenance engineer will recognize that there is a design problem and modify the machine so that the problem cannot recur.

In many ways the striking difference between Japanese maintenance practice and that in other parts of the world is the emphasis put by the Japanese on caring for equipment as though it were a personal prized possession. Why, it is argued, should any of us accept standards of care and cleanliness in a factory that are different from what we would expect in our own homes? This argument can be taken literally. For example, the Nishio Pump factory of Aishin Seiki in Japan has been nicknamed the 'parlour' factory. In Japan one does not wear shoes in anyone's home. They would be left at the door before you entered. Within the Japanese home the zashiki or 'parlour' is the guest room where Japanese families would entertain. It is a matter of pride to the family that it is kept immaculately clean. The Nishio Pump factory is called a parlour factory because it is almost as clean as the parlour of any Japanese home. Although the factory is engaged in normally dirty processes such as cutting metal and assembling parts together, it is spotlessly clean. There are no scrap parts lying about on the floor. There is not even metal-cutting waste on the floor, no oil splatters, no dust; the floor is clean and sparkling.

This may seem like taking things to extremes but the company would argue that it is the state of mind which is important. If the factory is clean and tidy, it encourages everyone to care for equipment as they would their own possessions in their own homes. Staff, it is argued, are more productive and less liable to make mistakes in a clean and orderly environment. Good housekeeping in the factory also allows staff to notice and correct process problems more quickly. Certainly at Aishin Seiki it seems to have been effective. Breakdowns, once running at more than 700 per month, now very rarely occur at all. Quality levels are even more impressive: only 11 defects in every one million pumps produced. ■

Question

1 Do you really think it is worth the effort of being so clean in what is intrinsically a dirty environment?

3 *Plan maintenance.* Have a fully worked out approach to all maintenance activities. This should include the level of preventive maintenance which is required for each piece of equipment, the standards for condition-based maintenance and the respective responsibilities of operating staff and maintenance staff. Table 19.3 illustrates the respective roles of operating and maintenance staff.

Table 19.3 The roles and responsibilities of operating staff and maintenance staff in TPM

	Maintenance staff	*Operating staff*
Roles	To develop ... • preventive actions • breakdown services	To take on ... • ownership of facilities • care of facilities
Responsibilities	Train operators Devise maintenance practice Problem solving Assess operating practice	Correct operation Routine preventive maintenance Routine condition-based maintenance Problem detection

4 *Train all staff in relevant maintenance skills.* The responsibilities listed in Table 19.3 require that both maintenance and operating staff have all the skills to carry out their roles. TPM places a heavy emphasis on appropriate and continuous training.

5 *Achieve early equipment management.* This goal is directed at going some way to avoiding maintenance altogether by 'maintenance prevention' (MP). MP involves considering failure causes and the maintainability of equipment during its design stage, its manufacture, its installation and its commissioning.

Reliability-centred maintenance

One of the criticisms of the total productive maintenance (TPM) approach is that it tends to recommend preventive maintenance (PM) at times when PM would be inappropriate. We have already seen in Fig. 19.10 that the pattern of failure for a particular part of a process will influence how effective a PM approach can be. Reliability-centred maintenance (RCM) uses the pattern of failure for each type of failure mode of a part of a system to dictate the approach to its maintenance. For example, take the process illustrated in Fig. 19.11. This is a simple shredding process which prepares vegetables prior to freezing. The most significant part of the process which requires the most maintenance attention is the cutter sub-assembly. However, there are several modes of failure which could lead to the cutters requiring attention. Sometimes they require changing simply because they have worn out through usage,

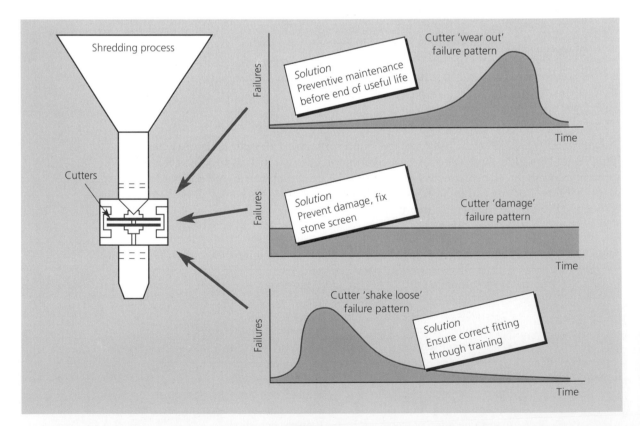

Figure 19.11 One part in one process can have several different failure modes, each of which requires a different approach

sometimes they have been damaged by small stones entering the process, sometimes they have shaken loose because they were not fitted correctly. The failure patterns for these three failure modes are very different, as illustrated in Fig. 19.11. Certainly, 'wear out' can be managed by timing preventive maintenance intervals just prior to the increased likelihood of failure. But this approach would not help prevent stone damage which could happen at any time with equal likelihood. The approach here would be to prevent stones getting to the cutters in the first place, perhaps through fixing a screen. The failure pattern for the cutters shaking loose is different again. If the cutters have been incorrectly fitted, it would become evident soon after the fitting. Again, preventive maintenance is unlikely to help here, rather effort should be put into ensuring that the cutters are always correctly fitted, perhaps by organizing more appropriate training of staff.

The approach of RCM is sometimes summarized as, 'If we cannot stop it from happening, we had better stop it from mattering'. In other words, if maintenance cannot either predict or even prevent failure, and the failure has important consequences, then efforts need to be directed at reducing the impact of the failure.

RECOVERY

In parallel with considering how to prevent failures occurring, operations managers need to decide what they will do when failures do occur. This activity is called *recovery* from failure. All types of operation can benefit from well-planned recovery. For example, a construction company whose mechanical digger breaks down can have plans in place to arrange a replacement from a hire company. The breakdown might be disruptive but not as much as it might have been if the operations manager had not worked out what to do.

Recovery procedures will also shape customers' perceptions of failure. Even where the customer sees a failure it may not necessarily lead to dissatisfaction. Indeed, in many situations, customers may well accept that things do go wrong.[11] If a broken-down car is ten years old and badly in need of a service, or if there is a metre of snow on the train lines, or if the restaurant is particularly popular, we may accept that the product or service does not work or is not available. It is not necessarily the failure itself that leads to dissatisfaction but often the organization's response to the breakdown. The crucial point is that while mistakes may be inevitable, dissatisfied customers are not.

A failure may even be turned into a positive experience. If you are due to catch an aeroplane flight at midnight in a remote airport and are told that it is delayed by five hours, this is a potentially dissatisfying situation. Suppose, however, that then you are told that the aircraft was delayed taking off from its previous destination by a cyclone and that arrangements have been made for you to be taken to a local hotel for a complimentary meal with a room provided for a shower and rest, and that a telephone will be made available so that you can deal with any knock-on effects at the next destination. You might then feel that you have been dealt with well and even recommend that airline to others because you were so well looked after. A good recovery can turn angry, frustrated customers into loyal ones. An effective response to failure may have a high pay-off in terms of the long-term success of the organization. It can also send positive signals to customers and employees about the company's policy to encourage corrective action and to achieve high customer satisfaction.

Professor Colin Armistead of Bournemouth University and Graham Clark of Cranfield University give details of the Technical Assistance Research Programme Inc. (TARP) investigations into customer satisfaction and customer loyalty in relation to service organizations in the USA.[12] TARP used four service scenarios and examined the willingness of customers to use an organization's services again. The four scenarios quoted are:

1 The service is delivered to meet the customers' expectations and there is full satisfaction.
2 There are faults in the service delivery but the customer does not complain about them.
3 There are faults in the service delivery and the customer complains but he/she has been fobbed off or mollified. There is no real satisfaction with the service provider.
4 There are faults in the service delivery and the customer complains and feels fully satisfied with the resulting action taken by the service providers.

The research showed that the decision on whether to repurchase from an organization in future may be greatly influenced by the approach taken to the resolution of complaints. Customers who are fully satisfied and do not experience any problems (1) are the most loyal, followed by complaining customers whose complaints are resolved successfully (4). Customers who experience problems but don't complain (2) are in third place and last of all come customers who do complain but are left with their problems unresolved and feelings of dissatisfaction (3).

Recovery in service operations

Recovery has been developed particularly in operating services. The word 'recovery' was said to have originated from British Airways' 'Putting the Customer First Campaign'.[13] Donald Porter, the consultant involved with BA, stated:

'It had never occurred to us before in any concrete way. "Recovery" was the term we coined to describe a very frequently repeated concern. If something goes wrong, as it often does, will anybody make special efforts to get it right? Will somebody go out of his or her way to make amends to the customer? Does anyone make an effort to offset the negative impact of a screw-up?'

It has also been suggested that service recovery does not just mean 'return to a normal state' but to a state of enhanced perception.

'All breakdowns require the deliverer to jump through a few hoops to get the customer back to neutral. More hoops are required for victims to recover.'[14]

Service operations managers need to recognize that all customers have recovery expectations that they want organizations to meet. Recovery needs to be a planned process. Organizations, therefore, need to design appropriate responses to failure, linked to the cost and the inconvenience caused by the failure to the customer, that will meet the needs and expectations of the customer. Such recovery processes need to be carried out either by empowered front-line staff or by trained personnel who are available to deal with recovery in a way which does not interfere with day-to-day service activities (*see* the discussion of 'Empowerment' in Chapter 9).

Failure planning

Identifying how organizations can recover from failure is of particular interest to service operations because they can turn failures around to minimize the effect on customers or even to turn failure into a positive experience. It is also of interest to other industries, however, especially those where the consequences of failure are particularly severe. Bulk chemical manufacturers and nuclear processors, for example, spend considerable resources in deciding how they will cope with failures. The activity of devising the procedures which allow the operation to recover from failure is called *failure planning*.

Failure planning is often represented by stage models showing the steps to be followed in the event of failure. These stage models all follow a similar pattern. One is represented in Fig. 19.12. We shall follow it through from the point where failure is recognized.

Discover

The first thing any manager needs to do when faced with a failure is to discover its exact nature. Three important pieces of information are needed. First of all, what exactly has happened, second, who will be affected by the failure, and, third, why did the failure occur? This last point is not intended to be a detailed inquest into the causes of failure (that comes later) but it is often necessary to know something of the causes of failure in case it is necessary to determine what action to take.

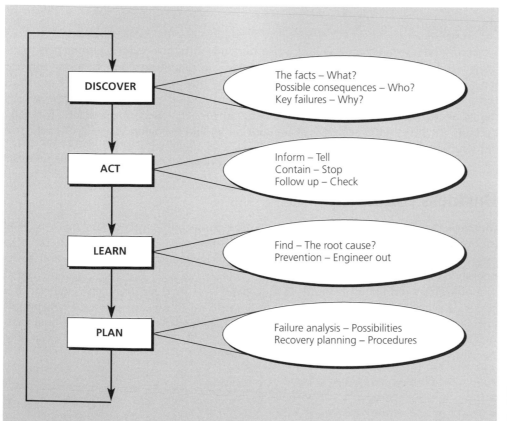

Figure 19.12
The stages in failure planning

Act

The discover stage could only take minutes or even seconds, depending on the severity of the failure. Especially if the failure is a severe one with important consequences we need to move on to doing something about the failure quickly. This means carrying out three actions, the first two of which could be carried out in reverse order, depending on the urgency of the situation. First, tell the significant people involved what you are proposing to do about the failure. In service operations this is especially important where the customers need to be kept informed both for their peace of mind and to demonstrate that something is being done. In all operations, however, it is important to communicate what action is going to happen so that everyone can set their own recovery plans in motion. Second, the effects of the failure need to be contained in order to stop the consequences spreading and causing further failures. The precise containment actions will depend on the nature of the failure. Third, there needs to be some kind of follow-up to make sure that the containment actions really have contained the failure.

Learn

As discussed earlier in this chapter, the benefits of failure in providing learning opportunities should not be underestimated. In failure planning, learning involves revisiting the failure to find out its root cause and then engineering out the causes of the failure so that it will not happen again.

Plan

Learning the lessons from a failure is not the end of the procedure. Operations managers need formally to incorporate the lessons into their future reactions to failures. This is often done by working through 'in theory' how they would react to failures in the future. Specifically, this involves first identifying all the possible failures which might occur (in a similar way to the FMEA approach). Second, it means formally defining the procedures which the organization should follow in the case of each type of identified failure.

Business continuity

Many of the ideas behind failure, failure prevention and recovery are incorporated in the growing field of *business continuity*. Business continuity aims to help operations avoid and recover from disasters while keeping the business going. As operations become increasingly integrated (and increasingly dependent on integrated technologies such as information technologies), critical failures can result from a series of related and unrelated events and combine to disrupt totally a company's business. These events (sometimes called *disasters*) are identified as the critical malfunctions which have the potential to interrupt normal business activity and even stop the entire company. Typically, such disasters are:

- floods, lightning, temperature extremes
- fire
- power or telecommunications failure

- corporate crime, theft, fraud, sabotage
- computer system failure
- bomb blast, bomb scare or other security alert
- key personnel leave, become ill or die
- key supplier ceases trading
- contamination of product or processes
- health and safety infringement.

The procedures adopted by business continuity experts are very similar to those described in this chapter:

- *Identify and assess risks* to determine how vulnerable the business is to various risks and to take steps to minimize or eliminate the risks.
- *Identify core business processes* to prioritize those business processes which are particularly important to the business and if interrupted would have to be brought back to full operation quickly.
- *Quantify recovery times* to make sure staff understand priorities (for example, get customer ordering system back into operation before the internal e-mail).
- *Determine resources needed* to make sure that resources will be available when needed.
- *Communicate* to make sure that everyone in the operation knows what to do if disaster strikes.

Duncan Hine, Royal Mail

Duncan Hine is Engineering Director with the Royal Mail in the UK. He describes the use of total productive maintenance as about getting the best from their mail-processing equipment.

'The development of TPM started some years ago in Japan. The American success with techniques such as preventive maintenance was then combined with the Japanese organization and discipline to produce a new way of working. This new approach resulted in a focus on performance and quality, which has always been at the root of the Japanese growth and success.'

Duncan believes that it was assumed in many industries that operators were no longer needed when the automation equipment was introduced.

'Nothing could be further from the truth. Far from reducing skills, the demands of higher quality and productivity require more from each operator. One of the core tenets of TPM is that every individual is highly trained, involved and motivated.'

The training and motivation is partly achieved at Royal Mail by dedicating operators to specific pieces of equipment and allowing them to assist engineering staff in cleaning and maintaining it. This helps develop a deeper understanding of shortcomings and encourages improvement.

'I have set up a small team at the Royal Mail to look at TPM and how it can help us to improve effectiveness. We have held many workshops in our operating divisions, with over 400 people attending, and we have managed to identify many of the special circumstances peculiar to the Royal Mail. These ideas have been collected together and we have concentrated on those which are more practical and have developed methods for incorporating them into the daily procedures on the processing lines. This has meant discussing the ideas as a group and planning the implementation to suit the local environment.

'Another aspect of TPM which we have considered is the buying of new machinery. We have tried to ensure that it will be easier to maintain, easier to clean and thus easier to operate all round. We have sometimes to make a case for increased expenditure to make sure that new machinery will do this – even when it is only in the long term that we will see the benefits. TPM has helped many companies achieve improved performance. It is my job to see that we become one of its leading practitioners in the UK.' ■

SUMMARY ANSWERS TO KEY QUESTIONS

Why do operations fail?

■ There are three major reasons why operations fail. The first is that the goods or services which are supplied to the operation are themselves faulty. The second is that something is happening within the operation, either because there is an overall failure in its design, or because one or more of the physical facilities break down, or because there is human error. The third is that the customers themselves may cause failure through their incompetent handling of goods or services. Even so, this is the responsibility of the management of the operation.

■ Remember though, not all failures are equally serious and attention is usually directed at those which have the most impact on the operation or its customers.

How is failure measured?

■ There are three ways of measuring failure. 'Failure rates' indicate how often a failure is likely to occur. 'Reliability' measures the chances of a failure occurring. 'Availability' is the amount of available and useful operating time left after taking account of failures.

■ Failure over time is often represented as a failure curve. The most common form of this is the so-called 'bath-tub curve' which shows the chances of failure being greater at the beginning and end of the life of a system or part of a system.

How can failure and potential failure be detected and analysed?

■ Failure detection and analysis involves putting mechanisms into place which sense that some kind of failure has occurred, and then analysing the failure to try to understand its root causes.

■ Failure detection mechanisms include in-process checks, machine diagnostic checks, point-of-departure interviews, phone surveys, focus groups, complaint cards or feedback sheets, and questionnaires.

■ Failure analysis mechanisms include accident investigation, product liability, complaint analysis, critical incident analysis, and failure mode and effect analysis (FMEA).

How can operations improve their reliability?

■ There are four major methods of improving reliability:

– designing out the fail points in the operation;
– building redundancy into the operation;
– 'fail-safeing' some of the activities of the operation;
– maintenance of the physical facilities in the operation;

■ Maintenance is the most common way operations attempt to improve their reliability.

■ There are three broad approaches to maintenance. The first is running all facilities until they break down and then repairing them, the second is regularly maintaining the facilities even if they have not broken down, and the third is to monitor facilities closely to try to predict when breakdown might occur.

■ Two specific approaches to maintenance have been particularly influential. These are total productive maintenance (TPM) and reliability-centred maintenance (RCM).

How should operations recover when failure does occur?

■ Recovery can be enhanced by a systematic approach to discovering what has happened to cause failure, acting to inform, contain, and follow up the consequences of failure, learning to find the root cause of the failure and preventing it taking place again, and planning to avoid the failure occurring in the future.

■ The idea of 'business continuity' planning is probably the most common form of recovery planning.

CASE EXERCISE 1

Better late and happy than just late

Fiona Rennie sat and enjoyed her coffee at Warsaw airport. Returning home to the UK after a week of energetic academic research, she was pondering her latest project – how service businesses have to be more aware of their customers' needs and, in order to compete, must be able to offer a high level of customer service, especially if the intended delivery package has been compromised in some way.

She knew that airlines, especially, had well-developed recovery procedures. In the case of failure the airline could activate various levels of preconceived and *ad hoc* customer care.

Warsaw airport was busy with passengers waiting to board the afternoon British Airways flight to London Heathrow, the anticipation growing as they passed through the scanners and walked down the aisle on to the aircraft. Safely in their seats, the 200 travellers were soon dismayed to hear from the captain that there was a slight mechanical problem and that their take-off would be delayed by approximately half an hour. This delay did not merit having to disembark and complimentary drinks were soon on the way round.

Inevitably, the half-hour delay soon blossomed into a bigger problem and an apologetic captain announced that he felt that passengers would be better placed, waiting for the repair to be completed, back in the departure lounge and please could they take all of their hand baggage off the plane with them. A few grumbles and mutters about connections at Heathrow and other missed appointments – but generally the mood was fairly genial and the airline staff went out of their way to try to accommodate passenger queries. One representative escorted a worried passenger off to the airline office to allow her to phone home and advise her family of the late departure. She had spent all of her Polish 'holiday money' and couldn't use the standard phones in the departure area. After an hour in the departure lounge and with no definitive answer available on the estimated take-off time, the airline moved into the next stage of its 'customer-placating programme' by providing meal vouchers for everyone and directing them to the airport restaurant. As the mood quietened and passengers began to question further just how long they were going to have to wait, the airline announced the departure time – some four hours behind schedule.

The flight itself went according to plan and the cabin crew walked up and down the aisles answering, where possible, queries on connecting flights and subsequent travel arrangements.

On arrival (finally) at Heathrow, the captain, who had been very apologetic throughout the whole process, bade the passengers farewell, expressing his concerns at the late arrival and hoping that it hadn't inconvenienced them too greatly. For some, though, the four-hour delay meant considerable problems in trying to reach their onward destinations that evening and the airline sales desk was soon busy with anxious passengers looking for help. Several were to be put up in a local hotel, courtesy of the airline, leaving them to re-commence their travels, fresh, the next morning. Others did not have so far to go and to stay overnight in the UK's capital city would actually mean more inconvenience the following day. Unperturbed, the airline's Customer Service Manager quickly took it upon himself to arrange chauffeur-driven transport for these people, ensuring that the inconvenience caused by the delay was effectively minimized. The priority wasn't necessarily to deal with each customer as quickly as possible, but to ensure that each person was given a solution that suited his or her needs. No awkward questions asked – only 'How can I help you?' What can I possibly do to ensure that given the choice you will fly again with our airline?

Fiona was certainly impressed, and although very late back, glad to be safely home as planned. ■

Questions

1 Is Fiona a particularly tolerant person or was she right to be impressed by the way British Airways reacted?
2 Draw up a 'failure plan' for delays of this type. How could it help the airline to improve its recovery procedures further?
3 When are failure and recovery particularly important to an operation?

The Chernobyl failure[15]

At 1.24 in the early hours of Saturday morning on the 26 April 1986, the worst accident in the history of commercial nuclear power generation occurred. Two explosions in quick succession blew off the 1000-tonne concrete sealing cap of the Chernobyl–4 nuclear reactor. Molten core fragments showered down on the immediate area and fission products were released into the atmosphere. The accident cost probably hundreds of lives and contaminated vast areas of land in the Ukraine.

Many reasons probably contributed to the disaster. Certainly the design of the reactor was not new – around 30 years old at the time of the accident – and had been conceived before the days of sophisticated computer-controlled safety systems. Because of this, the reactor's emergency-handling procedures relied heavily on the skill of the operators. This type of reactor also had a tendency to run 'out of control' when operated at low power. For this reason, the operating procedures for the reactor strictly prohibited it being operated below 20 per cent of its maximum power. It was mainly a combination of circumstance and human error which caused the failure, however. Ironically, the events which led up to the disaster were designed to make the reactor safer. Tests, devised by a specialist team of engineers, were being carried out to evaluate whether the emergency core cooling system (ECCS) could be operated during the 'free-wheeling' run-down of the turbine generator, should an off-site power failure occur. Although this safety device had been tested before, it had not worked satisfactorily and new tests of the modified device were to be carried out with the reactor operating at reduced power throughout the test period. The tests were scheduled for the afternoon of Friday, 25 April 1986 and the plant power reduction began at 1.00 pm. However, just after 2.00 pm, when the reactor was operating at about half its full power, the Kiev controller requested that the reactor should continue supplying the grid with electricity. In fact it was not released from the grid until 11.10 that night. The reactor was due to be shut down for its annual maintenance on the following Tuesday and the Kiev controller's request had in effect shrunk the 'window of opportunity' available for the tests.

The following is a chronological account of the hours up to the disaster, together with an analysis by James Reason, which was published in the *Bulletin of the British Psychological Society* the following year. Significant operator actions are italicized. These are of two kinds: *errors* (indicated by an '*E*') and *procedural violations* (marked with a '*V*').

25 April 1986

1.00 pm Power reduction started with the intention of achieving 25 per cent power for test conditions.

2.00 pm ECCS disconnected from primary circuit. (This was part of the test plan.)

2.05 pm Kiev controller asked the unit to continue supplying grid. *The ECCS was not reconnected (V).* (This particular violation is not thought to have contributed materially to the disaster; but it is indicative of a lax attitude on the part of the operators toward the observance of safety procedures.)

11.10 pm The unit was released from the grid and continued power reduction to achieve the 25 per cent power level planned for the test programme.

26 April 1986

12.28 am *Operator seriously undershot the intended power setting (E).* The power dipped to a dangerous one per cent. (The operator had switched off the 'auto-pilot' and had tried to achieve the desired level by manual control.)

1.00 am After a long struggle, the reactor power was finally stabilized at seven per cent – well below the intended level and well into the low-power danger zone. *At this point, the experiment should have been abandoned, but it was not (E).* This was the most serious mistake (as opposed to violation): it meant that all subsequent activity would be conducted within the reactor's zone of maximum instability. This was apparently not appreciated by the operators.

1.03 am *All eight pumps were started (V).* The safety regulations limited the maximum number of pumps in use at any one time to six. This showed a profound misunderstanding of the physics of the reactor. The consequence was that the increased water flow (and reduced steam fraction) absorbed more neutrons, causing more control rods to be withdrawn to sustain even this low level of power.

1.19 am *The feedwater flow was increased threefold (V).* The operators appear to have been attempting to cope with a falling steam-drum pressure and water level. The result of their actions, however, was to further reduce the amount of steam passing through the core, causing yet more control rods to be withdrawn. *They also overrode the steam-drum automatic shut-down (V).* The effect of this was to strip the reactor of one of its automatic safety systems.

1.22 am The shift supervisor requested printout to establish how many control rods were actually in the core. The printout indicated only six to eight rods remaining. It was strictly forbidden to operate the reactor with fewer than 12 rods. *Yet the shift supervisor decided to continue with the tests (V).* This was a fatal decision: the reactor was thereafter without 'brakes'.

1.23 am *The steam line valves to No. 8 turbine generator were closed (V).* The purpose of this was to establish the conditions necessary for repeated testing, but its consequence was to disconnect the automatic safety trips. This was perhaps the most serious violation of all.

1.24 am An attempt was made to 'scram' the reactor by driving in the emergency shut-off rods, but they jammed within the now warped tubes.

1.24 am Two explosions occurred in quick succession. The reactor roof was blown off and 30 fires started in the vicinity.

1.30 am Duty firemen were called out. Other units were summoned from Pripyat and Chernobyl.

5.00 am Exterior fires had been extinguished, but the graphite fire in the core continued for several days.

The subsequent investigation into the disaster highlighted a number of significant points which contributed to it.

● The test programme was poorly worked out and the section on safety measures was inadequate. Because the ECCS was shut off during the test period, the safety of the reactor was in effect substantially reduced.

● The test plan was put into effect before being approved by the design group who were responsible for the reactor.

● The operators and the technicians who were running the experiment had different and non-overlapping skills.

● The operators, although highly skilled, had probably been told that getting the test completed before the shut-down would enhance their reputation. They were proud of their ability to handle the reactor even in unusual conditions and were aware of the rapidly reducing window of opportunity within which they had to complete the test. They had also probably 'lost any feeling for the hazards involved' in operating the reactor.

● The technicians who had designed the test were electrical engineers from Moscow. Their objective was to solve a complex technical problem. In spite of having designed the test procedures, they probably would not know much about the operation of the nuclear power station itself.

● Again in the words of James Reason:

'Together, they made a dangerous mixture: a group of single-minded but non-nuclear engineers directing a team of dedicated but over-confident operators. Each group probably assumed that the other knew what it was doing. And both parties had little or no understanding of the dangers they were courting, or of the system they were abusing.' ■

Questions

1 What were the root causes which contributed to the ultimate failure?
2 How could failure planning have helped prevent the disaster?

1 Briefly describe a time when a product you bought or a service you received failed. Identify all the different reasons why this happened and assess which you think was the most likely.

2 In what ways could customers 'fail' in their use of a bank? How might the bank's management use this information to improve its operations?

3 What do you think will be the best ways of measuring failure for:

- a university course
- a lift (elevator)
- a security service
- a home pregnancy-testing kit
- a car.

4 A 24-hour ATM machine outside a bank was closed down between the following times during a seven-day period:

11.00 am Monday – 2.00 pm Monday
1.00 am Tuesday – 10.30 am Tuesday
4.00 pm Tuesday – 10.00 am Wednesday
3.00 pm Friday – 10.00 am Saturday

Calculate the ATM's failure rate (in time), the mean time between failures and its availability.

5 A manufacturer has four machines which are used in sequence: stripping, steaming, buffing and polishing. The reliabilities of the individual machines are 95 per cent, 78 per cent, 45 per cent and 56 per cent respectively. This year the Managing Director has agreed to buy one new machine to replace one of

Table 19.4 Machine failure rates

Possible replacement machines	Known failure rates
Superstripper	1/10
Stripper XXXX	7/30
Steadysteam	1/20
The Steam Machine	3/40
Buffer Mark2	1/10
Buffalot	4/25
Buffalotmore	3/25
Polishoff	6/70
Superfinish*	1/5
Finishkwik*	1/6

*Note the Superfinish and Finishkwik machines will replace both the buffing and polishing machines.

the old ones. The failure rates of the possible replacement machines are shown in Table 19.4. Which one would you recommend should be chosen to maximize the reliability of the whole process?

6 A catering company that provides catering services in people's homes for dinner parties, etc. has encountered a number of problems. From their past activities the managers have identified how many times these problems have occurred and have rated them for importance and the likelihood of detection by the customer, as shown in Table 19.5. The managers wish to try to improve their reputation for a quality service. Which area would you recommend them giving most attention to first?

Table 19.5 Catering problems

Problems encountered	Times problem occurred	Severity of failure	Probability of customer finding out
Insufficient food	1/800	5	50%
Host/hostess wants to be involved	1/25	1	10%
Food damaged in transit	1/3	7	20%
Food kept at wrong temperatures	1/30	9	70%
Breaking customers' equipment	1/90	7	90%

7 Flow chart a service process you have recently encountered, identifying what you consider to be the key fail points. Assess any poka-yokes in evidence and explain how you might design poka-yokes to overcome the fail points you have identified.

8 Describe the difference between 'run-to-breakdown', 'condition-based maintenance' and 'preventive-maintenance' approaches to maintenance. Provide examples from your own experience to illustrate your answer.

9 Talk to an operations manager in a car repair garage or a catering operation, for example, and find out the different ways in which the organization maintains its equipment. Assess the organization's approach to maintenance.

10 Describe a recent equipment, product or service failure that involved you. Did the organization make any attempt to recover from the situation? If so, how? If not, what steps might have been taken to bring about a recovery?

NOTES ON CHAPTER

1 Sources: Ridding, J.(1994) 'Recession and Blunders Derail SNCF', *The Financial Times*, 28 Jan, and Jenkins, I. (1993) 'Socrates Derails French Travellers', *The Sunday Times*, 29 Aug.

2 Source: 'Air Crashes, But Surely ...', *The Economist*, 4 June, 1994.

3 Flanagan, J. (1954) 'The Critical Incident Technique', *Psychological Bulletin*, Vol 51, No 4.

4 Source: 'How to Cope in a Crisis', *The Times*, 24 Aug 1995.

5 Chase, R.B. and Stewart, D.M. (1994) 'Make Your Service Fail-safe', *Sloan Management Review*, Spring, Vol 35, No 3.

6 Source: 'Mistake by Engineers left Holiday Airbus Unable to Turn Left', *The Times*, 25 Jan 1995.

7 Nakajima, S. (1988) *Total Productive Maintenance*, Productivity Press.

8 Nakajima, S., *op. cit.*

9 Murata, K. and Harrison, A. (1991) *How To Make Japanese Management Methods Work In The West*, Gower.

10 Examples based on Nakajima, S., *op. cit.*, and Koelsch, J.R. (1991) 'Where's the Grease?', *Manufacturing Engineering*, Vol 107, No 3.

11 For a full discussion of this idea *see* Hart, C.W.L., Heskett, J.L. and Sasser, W.E. (1990) 'The Profitable Art of Service Recovery', *Harvard Business Review*, Vol 68, No 4.

12 Armistead, C.G. and Clark, G. (1992) *Customer Service and Support*, the FT/Pitman Publishing.

13 Zemke, R. and Schaaf, R. (1990) *The Service Edge: 101 Companies that Profit from Customer Care*, Plume Books.

14 Zemke, R. and Bell, C.R. (1991) *Service Wisdom: Creating and Maintaining the Customer Service Edge*, Lakewood Books.

15 Based on information from Read, P.P. (1994) *Ablaze: The Story of Chernobyl*, Secker and Warburg, and Reason, J. (1987) 'The Chernobyl Errors', *Bulletin of the British Psychological Society*, Vol 4, pp 201–6.

SELECTED FURTHER READINGS

Albrecht, K. and Bradford, L.J. (1990) *The Service Advantage*, Dow Jones Irwin.

Condra, L.W. (1993) *Reliability Improvement with Design of Experiments*, Marcel Dekker, New York.

Dale, B.G. (ed) (1994) *Managing Quality* (2nd edn), Prentice Hall.

Dhillon, B.S. and Reiche, H. (1985) *Reliability and Maintainability Management*, Van Nostrand Reinhold.

Evans, J.R. and Lindsay, W.M. (1993) *The Management and Control of Quality* (2nd edn), West.

Geraghty, T. (1996) 'Beyond TPM', *Manufacturing Engineer*, Aug.

Harrison A. (1992) *Just-in-time Manufacturing in Perspective*, Prentice Hall.

Hayes, R.H. and Clark, K.B. (1986) 'Why Some Factories are More Productive Than Others', *Harvard Business Review*, Vol 64, No 5.

Heskett, J.L., Sasser, W.E. and Hart, C.W.L. (1990) *Service Breakthroughs: Changing the Rules of the Game*, The Free Press.

HMSO (1995) *An Introduction and a Guide to Business Continuity Management*, HMSO.

Moubray, J. (1991) *Reliability-centred Maintenance*, Butterworth-Heinemann.

Nakajima, S. (1988) *Total Productive Maintenance*, Productivity Press.

Raouf, A., Ali, Z. and Duffuaa, S.O. (1993) 'Evaluating a Computerized Maintenance Management System', *International Journal of Operations and Production Research*, Vol 13, No 3.

Sherwin, D.J. (1990) 'Inspect or Monitor', *Engineering Costs and Production Economics*, Jan.

Total Productive Maintenance, Proceedings of the First International Conference 1992, Published by Industrial Newsletters.

Wilkinson, J.J. (1968) 'How to Manage Maintenance', *Harvard Business Review*, Vol 46, No 2.

CHAPTER 20

TOTAL QUALITY
MANAGEMENT

INTRODUCTION

Total quality management (TQM) is arguably the most significant of the new ideas which have swept across the operations management scene over the last few years. There can be few, if any, managers in any developed economy anywhere in the world who have not heard of TQM. It certainly has had an impact on most industries which goes beyond its recent fashionability. There are two reasons for this: first, the ideas of TQM have a great intuitive attraction for many people – most of us want to be 'high quality'. Second, a TQM approach to improvement can result in, sometimes dramatic, increases in operational effectiveness. In this book we have separated the treatment of general quality planning and control (in Chapter 17) from TQM because TQM is concerned with more than quality alone. It is concerned with the improvement of *all* aspects of operations performance and particularly how improvement should be managed.

This chapter looks at TQM both as a philosophy of improvement and also as an organizational process which can be used to manage the improvement effort (*see* Fig. 20.1).

Figure 20.1 **Model of operations improvement showing the issues covered in this chapter**

THE ORIGINS OF TQM

The notion of total quality management was introduced by Feigenbaum in 1957. More recently, it has been developed through a number of widely recognized approaches put forward by several 'quality gurus' such as Deming, Juran, Ishikawa, Taguchi and Crosby. Therefore, to understand the origins of TQM, it is important to understand the contributions from these quality pioneers.

The quality gurus

Armand Feigenbaum

Armand Feigenbaum was a doctoral student at the Massachusetts Institute of Technology in the 1950s when he completed the first edition of his book *Total Quality Control*. He defines TQM as:

'an effective system for integrating the quality development, quality maintenance and quality improvement efforts of the various groups in an organization so as to enable production and service at the most economical levels which allow for full customer satisfaction'.[1]

Despite his early writings in America, it was the Japanese who first made the concept work on a wide scale and subsequently popularized the approach and the term TQM.

W.E. Deming

W. Edwards Deming, considered in Japan to be the father of quality control, asserted that quality starts with top management and is a strategic activity.[2] It is claimed that much of the success in terms of quality in Japanese industry was the result of his lectures to Japanese companies in the 1950s.[3] Deming's basic philosophy is that quality and productivity increase as 'process variability' (the unpredictability of the process) decreases. In his *14 points for quality improvement*, he emphasizes the need for statistical control methods, participation, education, openness and purposeful improvement.

1 Create constancy of purpose.
2 Adopt new philosophy.
3 Cease dependence on inspection.
4 End awarding business on price.
5 Improve constantly the system of production and service.
6 Institute training on the job.
7 Institute leadership.
8 Drive out fear.
9 Break down barriers between departments.
10 Eliminate slogans and exhortations.
11 Eliminate quotas or work standards.
12 Give people pride in their job.
13 Institute education and a self-improvement programme.
14 Put everyone to work to accomplish it.

J.M. Juran

Joseph M. Juran was also a key educator of the Japanese in quality management. He tried to get organizations to move away from the traditional manufacturing-based view of quality as 'conformance to specification' to a more user-based approach, for which he coined the phrase 'fitness for use'. He pointed out that a dangerous product could conform to specification but would not be fit to use. Like Deming, Juran was concerned about management activities and the responsibility for quality, but he was also concerned about the impact of individual workers and involved himself to some extent with the motivation and involvement of the workforce in quality improvement activities.[4]

K. Ishikawa

Kaoru Ishikawa, basing his work on that of Deming, Juran and Feigenbaum, has been credited with originating the concept of quality circles and cause-and-effect diagrams (*see* Chapter 18). Ishikawa[5] claimed that there had been a period of over-emphasis on statistical quality control (in Japan), and as a result people disliked quality control. They saw it as something unpleasant because they were given complex and difficult tools rather than simple ones. Furthermore, the resulting standardization of products and processes and the creation of rigid specification of standards became a burden that not only made change difficult but made people feel bound by regulations. Ishikawa saw worker participation as the key to the successful implementation of TQM. Quality circles, he believed, were an important vehicle to achieve this.

G. Taguchi

Genichi Taguchi (*see also* Chapter 5) was the director of the Japanese Academy of Quality and was concerned with engineering-in quality through the optimization of product design combined with statistical methods of quality control. He encouraged interactive team meetings between workers and managers to criticize and develop product design. Taguchi's definition of quality uses the concept of the loss which is imparted by the product or service to society from the time it is created. His quality loss function (QLF) includes such factors as warranty costs, customer complaints and loss of customer goodwill.[6]

P.B. Crosby

Phillip B. Crosby[7] is best known for his work on the cost of quality. He suggested that many organizations do not know how much they spend on quality, either in putting it right or getting it wrong. He claimed that organizations that have measured their costs say that they equate them to about 30 per cent of sales. (Juran estimated that total quality costs in manufacturing average ten per cent of sales turnover and Feigenbaum suggested the idea of a 'hidden plant' in every organization that uses, to no benefit, one tenth of productive capacity.) Crosby tried to highlight the costs and benefits of implementing quality programmes through his book *Quality is Free* in which he provided a *zero defects* programme which he believed would reduce the total cost of quality. This is summarized in his absolutes of quality management:[8]

1 Quality is conformance to requirements.
2 Prevention not appraisal.
3 The performance standard must be 'zero defects'.
4 Measure the 'price of non-conformance' (PONC).
5 There is no such thing as a quality problem.

Although not an exhaustive catalogue of those who have contributed to TQM thinking, the above list does give the flavour of how TQM developed. Even from these brief summaries of their work, it is evident that each 'guru' stressed a different set of issues from which emerged the TQM approach to operations improvement. Table 20.1 summarizes the strengths and weaknesses of each guru's approach.

WHAT IS TQM?

TQM can be viewed as a logical extension of the way in which quality-related practice has progressed (*see* Fig. 20.2). Originally quality was achieved by inspection – screening out defects before they were noticed by customers. The quality control (QC) concept developed a more systematic approach to not only detecting, but also treating quality problems. Quality assurance (QA) widened the responsibility for quality to include functions other than direct operations. It also made increasing use of more sophisticated statistical quality techniques. TQM included much of what went before but developed its own distinctive themes. We will use some of these themes to describe how TQM represents a clear shift from traditional approaches to quality.

On the face of it, it would appear that the quality 'gurus' provide different solutions to bringing about improvement in organizations. However, it has been suggested that 'they are all talking the same "language" but they use different dialects'.[9] In fact TQM is best thought of as a philosophy of how to approach quality management. It is a way of thinking and working in operations which lays particular stress on the following:

- meeting the needs and expectations of customers;
- covering all parts of the organization;
- including every person in the organization;
- examining all costs which are related to quality, especially failure costs;
- getting things 'right first time', i.e. designing-in quality rather than inspecting it in;
- developing the systems and procedures which support quality and improvement;
- developing a continuous process of improvement (this was treated in Chapter 18).

We shall treat each of these issues in turn.

Table 20.1 The relative strengths and weaknesses of some of the quality gurus[10]

Quality 'guru'	Strengths of approach	Weaknesses of approach
Feigenbaum	• Provides a total approach to quality control • Places the emphasis on the importance of management • Includes socio-technical systems thinking • Participation by all staff is promoted	• Does not discriminate between different kinds of quality context • Does not bring together the different management theories into one coherent whole
Deming	• Provides a systematic and functional logic which identifies stages in quality improvement • Stresses that management comes before technology • Leadership and motivation are recognized as important • Emphasizes role of statistical and quantitative methods • Recognizes the different contexts of Japan and North America	• Action plan and methodological principles are sometimes vague • The approach to leadership and motivation is seen by some as idiosyncratic • Does not treat situations which are political or coercive
Juran	• Emphasizes the need to move away from quality hype and slogans • Stresses the role of the customer both internal and external • Management involvement and commitment are stressed	• Does not relate to other work on leadership and motivation • Seen by some as undervaluing the contribution of the worker by rejecting bottom-up initiatives • Seen as being stronger on control systems than the human dimension in organizations
Ishikawa	• Strong emphasis on the importance of people and participation in the problem-solving process • A blend of statistical and people-oriented techniques • Introduces the idea of quality control circles	• Some of his problem-solving methods seen as simplistic • Does not deal adequately with moving quality circles from ideas to action
Taguchi	• Approach pulls quality back to the design stage • Recognizes quality as a societal issue as well as an organizational one • Methods are developed for practising engineers rather than theoretical statisticians • Strong on process control	• Difficult to apply where performance is difficult to measure (e.g. in the service sector) • Quality is seen as primarily controlled by specialists rather than managers and workers • Regarded as generally weak on motivation and people management issues
Crosby	• Provides clear methods which are easy to follow • Worker participation is recognized as important • Strong on explaining the realities of quality and motivating people to start the quality process	• Seen by some as implying that workers are to blame for quality problems • Seen by some as emphasizing slogans and platitudes rather than recognizing genuine difficulties • Zero defects sometimes seen as risk avoidance • Insufficient stress given to statistical methods

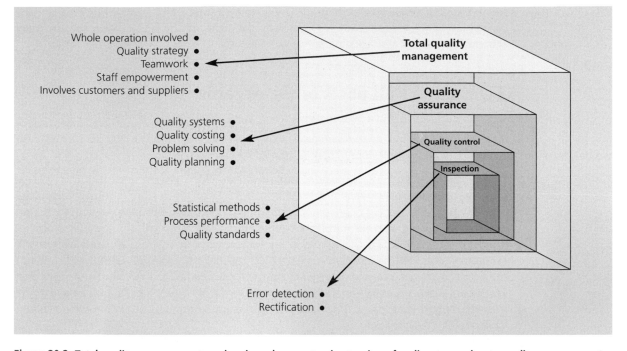

Whole operation involved •
Quality strategy •
Teamwork •
Staff empowerment •
Involves customers and suppliers •

Total quality management

Quality systems •
Quality costing •
Problem solving •
Quality planning •

Quality assurance

Quality control

Inspection

Statistical methods •
Process performance •
Quality standards •

Error detection •
Rectification •

Figure 20.2 Total quality management can be viewed as a natural extension of earlier approaches to quality management

TQM meets the needs and expectations of the customers

In Chapter 17 we defined quality as 'consistent conformance to customers' expectations'. Yet there is little point in putting a quality system in place – calculating costs, training and motivating people, and so on – unless it meets the requirements of the customers. In most organizations, defining customer expectations is a key task for marketing. Marketing, however, must also understand the ability of the operation so that it does not promise something that cannot be delivered. Chapter 17 explained a number of ways in which organizations can find out what customer expectations are. However, in the TQM approach, meeting the expectations of customers means more than this; it means seeing things *from a customer's point of view*. This involves the whole organization in understanding the central importance of customers to its success and even to its survival. Customers are seen not as being *external* to the organization but the most important *part* of it. Customers are also seen as human beings, rather than statistics, with individual needs and expectations and deserving of attentive and courteous treatment.

TQM puts the customer at the forefront of decision making. It requires that the implications for the customer are considered at all stages in corporate decision making and that decisions are made and systems created that will not detract from the customer's experience. Not all companies succeed. For example, one UK brewery used to distribute its beer to bars and public houses (its customers) according to a delivery schedule that suited the brewery. The schedule was designed to be as efficient as possible, minimizing the distance travelled by the delivery vehicles and maximizing the number of deliveries made. This thinking was fine for the brewery but did not take into account the needs of its customers. In fact it could make life very difficult for them. One customer was located in the centre of a major city and had its busiest time on Friday lunch-time. However, this was the time of the week when the brewery scheduled its deliveries, causing severe disruption.

TQM covers all parts of the organization

'For an organization to be truly effective, every single part of it, each department, each activity, and each person and each level, must work properly together, because every person and every activity affects and in turn is affected by others.'[11]

One of the most powerful aspects to emerge from TQM is the concept of the internal customer and supplier. This is a recognition that everyone is a customer within the organization and consumes goods or services provided by other internal suppliers, and everyone is also an internal supplier of goods and services for other internal customers. The implication of this is that errors in the service provided within an organization will eventually affect the product or service which reaches the external customer. So one of the best ways to ensure that external customers are satisfied is to establish the idea that every part of the organization contributes to external customer satisfaction by satisfying its own internal customers. This idea was introduced in Chapter 1 when we discussed the hierarchy of operations.

TQM utilizes this concept by stressing that each 'micro operation' has a responsibility to manage these internal customer–supplier relationships. They do this primarily by defining as clearly as possible what their own and their customers' *requirements* are. In effect this means defining what constitutes 'error-free' service – the quality, speed, dependability and flexibility required by internal customers. The exercise replicates what should be going on for the whole operation and its external customers (*see* Fig. 20.3).

As well as helping to embed the quality imperative in every part of the operation, the internal-customer concept is useful because it impacts on the 'upstream' parts of the internal supply network. These parts of the organization, especially those who provide internal services, can be the origin of errors which do not always become evident until later in the process. Errors may show up further down the physical process route and have to be traced back to their source. In manufacturing operations the Product Design Department is a good example of this. If an error is made in the basic concept of a product, the error is relatively inexpensive to correct – maybe a little time

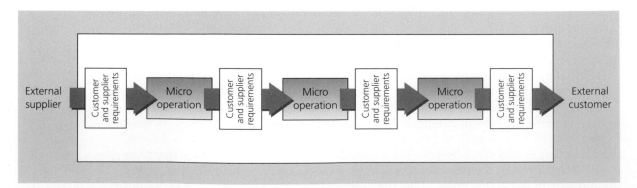

Figure 20.3 The internal customer–supplier relationship between micro operations

Ulster Carpets using the EQA model

A group leader briefs her team as part of the quality process

Ulster Carpet Mills Limited, finalist for the European Quality Award, has doubled its share of the quality carpet sector in recent years and now holds over ten per cent of the world market for its products. By encouraging continuous improvement through self-assessment against the business excellence award model, EQA has created the necessary drive for customer focus. The company's total quality process has graduated from 'total customer satisfaction', to 'total customer delight', to its present form – 'bridging the gap', which is effectively a 'where we are' and 'where we should be' yardstick for the company. Developments in the warehouse are typical. The role of the manager/supervisor has been replaced by the nomination of a group leader who acts in a 'leading role', working within the team. The picture above shows a group leader with her team, each of whom is trained to carry out his/her main job plus five others on a rotating work rota. Fixed hours are

a thing of the past, as is overtime. At peak times, such as the run-up to Christmas, the team works the required hours (be it until 10 pm at night) to despatch orders, and at off-peak times, when work is completed to the satisfaction of the group leader, the team can leave. New technology now means that despatch labels and address labels are computer-generated and the carpets are bar-coded which reduces the possibility of human error. Each process within the warehouse has been analysed and re-engineered to answer the question, 'Do the processes meet the needs?' The company sees the use of the EQA model as a means of evaluation, as well as raising internal awareness of the measures necessary to meet external needs. '*The warehouse is illustrative of what is currently happening within each department of Ulster Carpet Mills. It is the European Quality Model which provides the framework to assess the "enablers" and "results" with fresh eyes, and to identify the challenges of the way forward in relation to our customer,*' says Daniel McLarnon, head of quality.

Loading carpet looms at Ulster Carpets

- *What is implied by the progression of the company's three initiatives from 'total customer satisfaction' to 'total customer delight' to 'bridging the gap'?*
- *What 'enablers' are mentioned in this example, and how might they affect 'results'?*

➜ **Look at Chapter 20 for guidance**

Coming second helps Oslo baggage handlers

Passengers' luggage is loaded off the aircraft by conveyor belt onto individual automated carts

For the last 20 years the airports of the world have used what are known as 'tug cart and conveyor belt' systems to move baggage on and off aircraft and around the airport. Denver International Airport (DIA) was going to be the pioneer in a new type of system where bags would be individually handled on automated carts or 'destination coded vehicles'. But at DIA it all went wrong. The system proved unreliable and difficult to make work properly. Instead of the original $185 million, the eventual cost was over $300 million for only a partially operating system. The airport, which was due to open in 1993, was delayed three times and eventually a further $70 million had to be spent installing a conventional conveyor belt system. This high publicized failure caused Oslo's Gardermoen Airport to think twice before adopting its own new baggage handling technology. However, Oslo learned from Denver's mistakes. Their own system, the Dutch manufactured Bagtrax system, is up to four times quicker than the conventional belt system, requires less maintenance and is cheaper to operate. But unlike Denver's system, it is less complicated and less prone to breakdown. In effect, it allows the airport to tailor baggage delivery to requirements. A single bag can be sent to a single destination without having to start up a whole conventional belt system.

Carts tip to deliver the luggage to the appropriate collection points

- *Why do you think being second or third to use a new technology is sometimes better than pioneering it?*
- *What do you think are the advantages and disadvantages of this automated technology over the conventional manual systems?*

→ *Look at Chapter 8 for guidance*

Eurocamp Travel

Photo courtesy of Eurocamp Ltd

Happy campers at Eurocamp

Eurocamp Travel, which provides family camping holidays, has a reputation for the high quality of its equipment and services, and has become market leader in this rapidly-growing holiday sector. In recent years, sales offices have been opened in The Netherlands and Germany, and Eurocamp's geographic coverage has been extended from its original French sites to include sites throughout Europe. As the business has become larger and more complex, the demands placed on the office systems have also become greater, reinforcing the need for functional specialization of staff, yet requiring more interdepartmental understanding and co-operation. When it became clear that Eurocamp's service package could be copied by competitors eager to attract premium customers, the company decided to reinforce quality at every stage in their process. This was, they believed, the main criterion that already differentiated Eurocamp, and this was also potentially the most difficult for lower priced competitors to follow. A consultant was brought in to facilitate a major quality improvement programme. This was conceived as a 'top-down' approach, whereby important projects were identified and tackled by trained teams. But it soon became apparent that these early projects were not achieving the anticipated sustainable improvements. It also became clear that the failure was largely the

result of only involving senior managers, who could not devote the time required to projects, and did not fully understand the processes concerned. Those employees who did have a very detailed understanding of the processes had been excluded from problem definition, evaluation, and implementation of changes. So, the company launched their quality management system (QMS) initiative. Each department established a quality steering committee which comprised at least one director, a trained facilitator, and volunteers from every grade of employee. The emphasis at this stage was on the identification and improvement of internal processes with further emphasis on satisfying the internal customer. Early success demonstrated the validity of this approach and generated a high level of enthusiasm throughout the company.

■ *What are the differences between the first 'top-down' attempt, and the second attempt at establishing a quality initiative?*

■ *What do you think are the main advantages and problems with the more participative approach?*

➜ *Look at Chapter 20 for guidance*

Recycled St Regis

Photo courtesy of St Regis Paper

Recycled raw materials are processed and pumped through a piping system ...

... to the paper-making machines

Photo courtesy of St Regis Paper

The trend towards materials recycling in many countries can have a significant impact on the way in which some products are manufactured. Perhaps the industry which has had to adjust the most is paper-making. St Regis Paper is one of the largest manufacturers of recycled paper in Europe, producing almost a million tonnes of finished product a year. Its mill in Kemsley, in the UK, is one of the most modern, efficient and environmentally-friendly plants in Europe. Two paper machines running at speeds of up to 900 metres per minute each make 250 000 tonnes a year of high quality brown 'liner grades' (used to make corrugated boxes).

The raw material is 100 per cent recycled paper, which is treated in a state-of-the-art stock preparation plant. This process cleans and sorts the individual paper fibres. When this material is used on the paper machines it produces a product which is practically indistinguishable from conventional paper made from wood pulp.

- *What production problems would you anticipate from using waste papers*
  - *in the stock preparation plant?*
  - *in the paper-making process?*
- *In what ways would you expect recycled products to differ from their conventional counterparts? What steps could you take in the production process to minimize these differences?*
- *Given that a paper machine is likely to make several products, each at different grammages (i.e. weight per unit area), would you regard paper-making as a continuous or a batch process? What difficulties would you anticipate in the scheduling and production processes, and what is the effect on stock preparation likely to be?*
- *What key production issues would you anticipate which are associated with the speed at which paper runs through a paper machine (bearing in mind that the paper is very wet at the beginning of the process)?*

➜ *Look at Chapter 21 for guidance*

HEWLETT-PACKARD'S INTERNAL CUSTOMER CHECKLIST[12]

The computer industry has always been in the forefront of developing and utilizing quality concepts. Quality failures of hardware, software or service are immediately obvious to customers and seriously damaging to their trust in the supplier. Hewlett-Packard, the world-wide information systems company, is no exception. It was one of the first companies to make a success of the internal-customer concept in its operations. One part of the way it used the concept was a short, but effective, checklist 'pocket guide' which came out of its South Queensferry plant in Scotland. The Pocket Guide which it developed was distributed throughout the company. It suggests each part of the organization should ask itself seven questions, which it regards as fundamental to the operation:

- Who are my customers?
- What do they need?
- What is my product or service?
- What are my customers' expectations and measures?
- Does my product or service meet their expectations?
- What is the process for providing my product or service?
- What action is required to improve the process?

H-P then went on to devise a problem-solving methodology, based on its seven questions, the stages for which are as follows:

- Select the quality issue.
- Write an issue statement.
- Identify the process.
- Draw a flow chart.
- Select a process performance measure.
- Conduct a cause-and-effect analysis.
- Collect and analyse the data.
- Identify the major causes of the quality issue.
- Plan for improvements.
- Take the corrective action.
- Collect and analyse the data again.
- Are the objectives met?
- If yes, document and standardize the changes. ■

Questions

1 What do you see as the limitations of the set of questions which comprises Hewlett-Packard's internal customer checklist?

2 Do you think anything is missing from the problem-solving methodology described above?

3 What seems to be the implied problem-solving methodology described above? How does it compare with the Plan-Do-Check-Act (PDCA) process described in Chapter 18?

reresearching or rethinking some issues will be required. If the error is not discovered until the detailed design stage, it can be as much as ten times more expensive to correct it because of the many other decisions that will have been based on the original error. By the time of prototype manufacture, the cost of rethinking and recommissioning designs for the product could easily have escalated to a hundred times of the cost had the error been discovered at concept stage. By pilot production stage, investment in process technologies, job designs, marketing plans, etc. could be up to a thousand

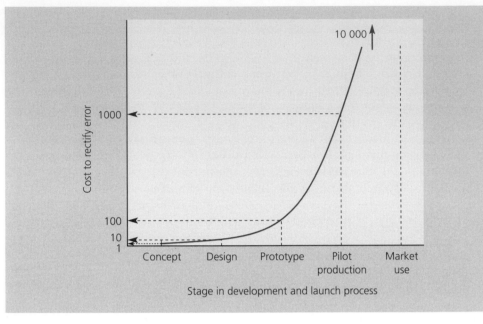

Figure 20.4
The cost of rectifying errors becomes increasingly expensive the longer the errors remain uncorrected in the development and launch process

times more expensive to change. Errors discovered in the market can be phenomenally expensive. The cost illustrated in Fig. 20.4 of 10 000 times the original cost could even be an underestimate (for example, *see* the box on Carlsberg Tetley's product recall in Chapter 19).

Service-level agreements

Some organizations bring a degree of formality to the internal customer concept by encouraging (or requiring) different parts of the operation to agree 'service-level agreements' (SLAs) with each other. SLAs are formal definitions of the dimensions of service and the relationship between two parts of an organization. The type of issues which would be covered by such an agreement could include response times, the range of services, dependability of service supply, and so on. Boundaries of responsibility and appropriate performance measures could also be agreed.

For example, an SLA between an information systems support unit and a research unit in the laboratories of a large company could define such performance measures as:

● the types of information network services which may be provided as 'standard';
● the range of special information services which may be available at different periods of the day;
● the minimum 'up time', i.e. the proportion of time the system will be available at different periods of the day;
● the maximum response time and average response time to get the system fully operational should it fail;
● the maximum response time to provide 'special' services, and so on.

Every person in the organization contributes to quality

TQM is sometimes referred to as 'quality at source'. This notion stresses the impact that each individual staff member has on quality, as well as the idea that it is each person's personal responsibility to get quality right. Some staff can affect quality directly. The staff who physically make products, and the staff who, face-to-face, serve customers, all have the capability to make mistakes which will be immediately obvious to customers (although the effects will be noticed much sooner in high customer contact service operations). Other staff who may be less directly involved in producing goods and services can also generate problems, however – the keyboard operator who mis-keys data, the product designer who fails to investigate thoroughly the conditions under which products will be used in practice. Any person could set in motion a chain of events which customers will eventually see as poor quality products and services.

It follows then that, if everyone has the ability to impair quality, they also have the ability to improve quality – if only by 'not making mistakes'. It is partly because of this that TQM philosophies place considerable emphasis on the contribution which the individual staff of the organization can make to quality. In TQM, however, the contribution of all individuals in the organization is expected to go beyond understanding their contribution and a commitment to 'not make mistakes'. Individuals are expected to bring something positive to the way they perform their jobs. Everyone is capable of improving the way in which they do their own jobs and practically everyone is capable of helping others in the organization to improve theirs. Therefore, neglecting this potential in staff is neglecting a powerful source of improvement. The principles of 'empowerment' (*see* Chapter 9) are frequently cited as supporting this aspect of TQM.

The shift in attitude which is needed to view employees as the most valuable intellectual and creative resource which the organization possesses can still prove difficult for some organizations. When TQM practices first began to migrate from Japan in the late 1970s, the ideas seemed even more radical. Some Japanese industrialists even thought (mistakenly) that companies in Western economies would never manage to change. Take, for example, a statement by Konosuke Matsushito which attracted considerable publicity.

'We are going to win and the industrial West is going to lose out – there is nothing much you can do about it, because the reasons for your failure are within yourselves. For you, the essence of management is getting the ideas out of the heads of bosses into the hands of labour. For us, the core of management is precisely the art of mobilizing and pulling together the intellectual resources of all employees in the service of the firm. Only by drawing on the combined brainpower of all its employees can a firm face up to the turbulence and constraints of today's environment.*

'That is why our large companies give their employees three to four times more training than yours. This is why they foster within the firm such intensive exchange and communication. This is why they seek constantly everybody's suggestions and why they demand from the educational system increasing numbers of graduates as well as bright and well-educated generalists, because these people are the lifeblood of industry.'[13]

All of this has implications for the style of management employed within the organization generally. It is difficult to imagine the basic principles of total quality management fitting comfortably with any management style other than a relatively participative one.

All costs of quality are considered

Few, if any, operations managers would doubt that quality management is a good thing and needs to be done. The benefits have been discussed in Chapters 2 and 17. However, there is a price to pay. The costs of controlling quality may not be small, whether the responsibility lies with each individual or a dedicated quality control department. It is therefore necessary to examine all the costs and benefits associated with quality (in fact 'cost of quality' is usually taken to refer to both costs and benefits of quality). These costs of quality are usually categorized as *prevention costs*, *appraisal costs*, *internal failure costs* and *external failure costs*.

Prevention costs

Prevention costs are those costs incurred in trying to prevent problems, failures and errors from occurring in the first place. They include such things as:

● identifying potential problems and putting the process right before poor quality occurs;
● designing and improving the design of products and services and processes to reduce quality problems;
● training and development of personnel in the best way to perform their jobs;
● process control through SPC.

Appraisal costs

Appraisal costs are those costs associated with controlling quality to check to see if problems or errors have occurred during and after the creation of the product or service. They might include such things as:

● the setting up of statistical acceptance sampling plans;
● the time and effort required to inspect inputs, processes and outputs;
● obtaining processing inspection and test data;
● investigating quality problems and providing quality reports;
● conducting customer surveys and quality audits.

Internal failure costs

Internal failure costs are failure costs associated with errors which are dealt with inside the operation. These costs might include such things as:

● the cost of scrapped parts and material;
● reworked parts and materials;
● the lost production time as a result of coping with errors;
● lack of concentration due to time spent trouble-shooting rather than improvement.

External failure costs

External failure costs are those which are associated with an error going out of the operation to a customer. These costs include such things as:

● loss of customer goodwill affecting future business;
● aggrieved customers who may take up time;

● litigation (or payments to avoid litigation);
● guarantee and warranty costs;
● the cost to the company of providing excessive capability (too much coffee in the pack or too much information to a client).

The relationship between quality costs

In traditional quality management it was assumed that failure costs will reduce as the money spent on appraisal and prevention increases. Furthermore, it was assumed that there is an *optimum* amount of quality effort to be applied in any situation, which minimizes the total costs of quality. The argument is that there must be a point beyond which diminishing returns set in – that is, the cost of improving quality gets larger than the benefits which it brings. Figure 20.5(a) sums up this idea. As quality effort is

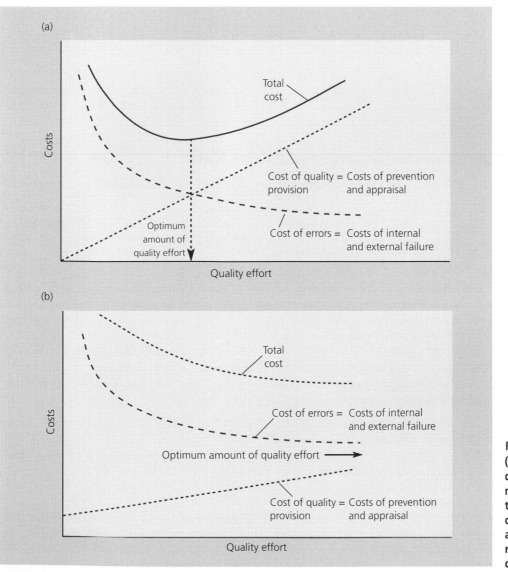

**Figure 20.5
(a) The traditional cost of quality model, and (b) the traditional cost of quality model with adjustments to reflect TQM criticisms**

DELIBERATE DEFECTIVES

A story which illustrates the difference in attitude between a TQM and a non-TQM company has become almost a legend among TQM proponents. It concerns a plant in Ontario, Canada, of IBM, the computer company. It ordered a batch of components from a Japanese manufacturer and specified that the batch should have an acceptable quality level (AQL) of three defective parts per thousand. When the parts arrived in Ontario they were accompanied by a letter which expressed the supplier's bewilderment at being asked to supply defective parts as well as good ones. The letter also explained that they had found it difficult to make parts which were defective, but had indeed managed it. These three defective parts per thousand had been included and were wrapped separately for the convenience of the customer. ■

Question

1 How does this short story illustrate the essence of TQM?

increased, the costs of providing the effort – through extra quality controllers, inspection procedures, and so on – increases proportionally. At the same time, however, the cost of errors, faulty products, and so on, decreases because there are fewer of them.

Criticisms of the traditional quality cost model

A 'pure' TQM approach would be to assert that this logic is flawed in a number of important respects.

1 This compromise position implies that failure and poor quality is acceptable. It recognizes that the 'optimum' point is one where there will be errors and failures. TQM challenges the whole concept of the acceptable quality level (AQL) which was outlined in Chapter 17. Why, it is argued, should any operation accept the *inevitability* of errors? Some occupations seem to be able to accept a zero-defect standard (even if they do not always achieve it). No one accepts that it is inevitable that pilots will crash a certain proportion of their aircraft, or that nurses will drop a certain proportion of the babies which they deliver.

2 It assumes that the costs are known and measurable. Obtaining precise costs of quality is not straightforward, however. Putting realistic figures to the quality cost categories of prevention, appraisal and failure is not a straightforward matter. One study exposes a number of difficulties, including the following:[14]

● It is not easy to separate quality-related costs from those which are an integral part of the manufacturing operation anyway.
● The categorization of costs into prevention, appraisal and failure is more meaningful to quality managers than operations managers.
● Costs of activities which are part-time activities of indirect staff are particularly difficult to derive.
● Accounting systems are not designed to yield quality-related costs and different accounting practices can distort the results in different ways.
● The significance of warranty costs is difficult to gauge because they relate to earlier manufacture.

3 Failure costs in the traditional model are greatly underestimated. In practice, the failure cost is usually taken to include the cost of 'reworking' defective products, 're-serving' customers, the cost of scrapping parts and materials, and the loss of goodwill or even warranty costs if the defective part gets out to the customer. All these are important, but one of the most important costs is that associated with the disruption which errors cause. The real cost of not having quality should include all the management time wasted in organizing rework and rectification. Even more important, it should take into account the loss of concentration, and the erosion of confidence between parts of the operation. If we include these, even though they are difficult costs to measure, it becomes clear that error costs can be considerably higher than traditionally thought.

4 It implies that prevention costs, the costs of getting towards zero defects, are inevitably high. The TQM approach, by stressing the importance of quality to every individual, makes quality an integral part of everyone's work. The traditional assumption is that more quality is achieved primarily by using more inspectors. For example, it is assumed that doubling the effort put into quality means, if not doubling the resources devoted to it, certainly a considerable increase in costs. This need not necessarily be so, however. At the very heart of TQM is the idea that each of us has a responsibility for his or her own quality and is capable of 'doing it right'. This may incur some costs – training, gauges, anything which helps to prevent errors occurring in the first place – but not such a steeply inclined cost curve as the 'optimum-quality' theory.

5 The 'optimum-quality level' approach, by accepting compromise, does little to challenge operations managers and staff to find ways of improving quality.

Put these corrections into the optimum-quality effort calculation and the picture looks very different (*see* Fig. 20.5(b)). If there is an 'optimum', it is a lot further to the right, in the direction of putting more effort (but not necessarily cost) into quality. We used a similar argument to this when describing the 'optimum' degree of preventive maintenance in Chapter 19.

The TQM quality cost model

TQM rejects the optimum-quality level concept and strives to reduce all known and unknown failure costs by preventing errors and failure taking place. Rather than looking for 'optimum' levels of quality effort it is more usual for TQM proponents to stress the relative balance between different types of quality cost. Of the four cost categories, two – costs of prevention and costs of appraisal – are open to managerial influence, while the other two – internal costs of failure and external costs of failure – show the consequences of changes in the first two. Of the two categories open to direct managerial influence, rather than placing most emphasis on appraisal (so that 'bad products and service don't get through to the customer') TQM emphasizes prevention (to stop errors happening in the first place).

What seems to happen is that when more effort is put into defect prevention it has a significant, positive effect on internal failure costs, followed by reductions both in external failure costs and, once confidence has been firmly established, in appraisal costs. Eventually even prevention costs can be stepped down in absolute terms, though prevention remains a significant cost in relative terms. Figure 20.6 illustrates this idea. Initially total quality costs may rise as investment in some aspects of prevention – mainly training – is increased. However, some reduction in total costs can quickly follow.

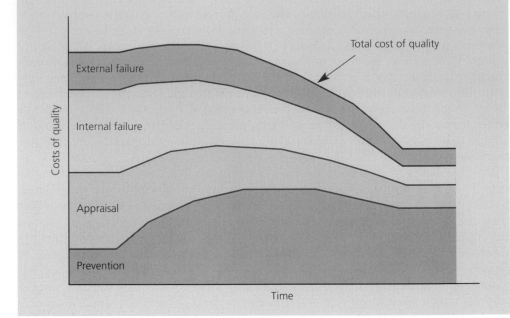

Figure 20.6
Increasing the effort into preventing errors occurring in the first place brings a more than equivalent reduction in other cost categories

Getting things 'right first time'

Accepting the relationships between categories of quality cost as illustrated in Fig. 20.6 has a particularly important implication for how quality is managed. It shifts the emphasis from *reactive* (waiting for something to happen) to *proactive* (doing something before anything happens). This change in the view of quality costs has come about with a movement from an inspect-in (appraisal-driven) approach, to a design-in (getting it right first time) approach.

Quality systems and procedures

Improving quality is not something that happens simply by getting everyone in an organization to 'think quality'. Very often people are prevented from making improvements by the organization's systems and procedures. Indeed, there is a belief that direct operators can only correct, at the moment, 15 per cent of quality problems; the other 85 per cent are management's responsibility because they are due to 'the system' or the lack of one.

A quality system is defined as:

'the organizational structure, responsibilities, procedures, processes and resources for implementing quality management.'[15]

According to Professor Barrie Dale of the University of Manchester Institute of Science and Technology:

'The quality system should define and cover all facets of an organization's operation, from identifying and meeting the needs and requirements of customers, design, planning,

purchasing, manufacturing, packaging, storage, delivery and service, together with all relevant activities carried out within these functions. It deals with organization, responsibilities, procedures and processes. Put simply, a quality system is good management practice.'[16]

The documentation which is used in a quality system can be defined at three levels:

Level 1 *Company quality manual.* This is the fundamental document and provides a concise summary of the quality management policy and quality system along with the company objectives and its organization.

Level 2 *Procedures manual.* Describes the system functions, structure and responsibilities in each department.

Level 3 *Work instructions, specifications and detailed methods for performing work activities.*

There can also be a database (Level 4) which contains all other reference documents (forms, standards, drawings, reference information, etc.).

The ISO 9000 quality system

The ISO 9000 series is a set of world-wide standards that establishes requirements for companies' quality management systems. ISO 9000 is being used world-wide to provide a framework for quality assurance. Most countries have their own quality system standards which are equivalent (usually identical) to the ISO 9000 series. Australia has AS3900, Belgium NBN X50, Denmark DS/EN 29000, Malaysia MS985, Netherlands NEN-9000, South Africa SABS 0157, Sweden SS-ISO 9000, the UK BS5750, and Germany DIN ISO 9000.

ISO 9000 registration requires a third-party assessment of a company's quality standards and procedures and regular audits are made to ensure that the systems do not deteriorate.

The ISO series provides detailed recommendations for setting up quality systems.

ISO 9000 Deals with ... 'quality management and quality assurance standards and guidelines for selection and use'.

ISO 9001 Deals with ... 'quality systems model for quality assurance in design/development, production, installation and servicing'.

ISO 9002 Deals with ... 'quality systems model for quality assurance in production and installation'.

ISO 9003 Deals with ... 'quality systems model for quality assurance in final inspection and test'.

ISO 9004 Deals with ... 'quality management and quality system elements: guidelines'.

The purpose of ISO 9000 is to provide an assurance to the purchasers of products or services that they have been produced in such a way that they meet their requirements. The best way to do this, it is argued, is to define the procedures, standards, and characteristics of the management control system which governs the operation. Such a system will then help to ensure that quality is 'built into' the operation's transformation processes. This is why ISO 9000 is seen as providing benefits both to the organizations adopting it (because it gives them detailed guidance on how to design their control procedures) and especially to customers (who have the assurance of knowing that the products and services they purchase are produced by an operation working to a defined standard). However, the adoption of ISO 9000 is not seen as beneficial by all authorities, and has been subject to some criticism. The following are just some of the advantages and disadvantages associated with ISO 9000:[17]

Advantages

● Many operations do find that it provides a useful discipline to stick to 'sensible' procedures.

● Many operations have benefited in terms of error reduction, reduced customer complaints and reduced costs of quality.

● The ISO 9000 audit (when an organization is inspected to see if it warrants the award of the ISO, or local country, accreditation) is generally accepted and takes the place of other audits such as customer audits.

● Adopting ISO 9000 procedures can identify existing procedures which are not necessary and can be eliminated.

● Gaining the certificate demonstrates to actual and potential customers that the company takes quality seriously; it therefore has a marketing benefit.

Disadvantages

● The emphasis on standards and procedures encourages 'management by manual' and over-systematized decision making.

● Choosing which of the various ISO 9000 series of standards to apply for is not always easy.

● The standards are too much geared to the engineering industries and some of the terms used are unfamiliar in other industries.

● The whole process of writing procedures, training staff and conducting internal audits is expensive and time consuming.

● Similarly, the time and cost of achieving and maintaining ISO 9000 registration is excessive.

● There is little encouragement or guidance in ISO 9000 on such important issues as continuous improvement and statistical quality control.

ISO 9000 AT UNICHEMA CHEMIE BV[18]

The original motive for companies to gain ISO 9000 certification is often pressure from customers. This was certainly one of the reasons at Unichema Chemie BV, the Netherlands chemical company. Yet once gained, it found that there were many other benefits apart from the effect it had on its customers' perceptions of the company.

For example, the company had been puzzled by the number of complaints which it received about delivery delays and errors. These always seemed to be higher in the summer, especially in July and August. This being the holiday season, the overall level of business was lower and so complaints should also have been lower. It found that the reason was that many of Unichema's staff, who were taking their holidays in the summer, were also taking their knowledge of the operation with them. The staff who were covering for them back at the plant, although they were competent at the fundamentals of the job, did not know how to cope with anything out of the ordinary. Once the company's procedures were fully documented and put down on paper (a requirement of ISO certification), people standing in for others had a far better set of guidelines which would help them cope with unusual situations. They were not having continually to improvise. However, the company is aware of some of the dangers of being too procedures-driven.

'Procedures are a support, they are not sacred,' says Mr Jan Löwik, the General Manager of Unichema, *'The whole thing about certification is that you put on paper what you are doing and then do what you put on paper. If a procedure doesn't work, however, do not, as we used to do, throw it in the corner and do it your own way. You modify the procedure instead by writing in how you think it should be done. The people who know best how to do it are my people in the plant. It is their system: they own it, they maintain it and they change it whenever they need to on a continuous basis. If you don't do that it becomes rigid; it becomes a strait-jacket. That is the big danger, and I see it happening in many companies. If the system is too rigid it becomes limiting and leads to bureaucratic behaviour. It should be dynamic.'* ■

Questions

1 What did ISO 9000 do for the 'reserves of stored knowledge' at Unichema?

2 How does the company avoid too much bureaucracy in running ISO 9000?

IMPLEMENTING TQM IMPROVEMENT PROGRAMMES

Not all of the TQM initiatives which are launched by organizations, often with high expectations, will go on to fulfil their potential of having a major impact on performance improvement. *The Economist* magazine, reporting on some companies' disillusionment with their TQM experiences, quoted from several surveys.[19] For example:

'Of 500 US manufacturing and service companies, only a third felt their TQ programmes had significant impact on their competitiveness.'

'Only a fifth of the 100 British firms surveyed believed their quality programmes had achieved tangible results.'

'Of those quality programmes that have been in place for more than two years, two thirds simply grind to a halt because of their failure to produce hoped-for results.'

There are two broad types of failure which affect TQM implementation:

● the TQM initiative is not introduced and implemented effectively; and
● after the TQM has been introduced successfully its effectiveness fades over time.

TQM implementation

A number of factors appear to influence the eventual success of performance improvement programmes such as TQM. These are as follows:

A quality strategy

Without thinking through the overall purpose and long-term goals of a TQM programme it is difficult for any organization to know where it is going. A quality strategy is necessary to provide the goals and guidelines which help to keep the TQM programme heading in a direction which is appropriate for the organization's other strategic aims. Specifically, the quality strategy should have something to say about:

● the competitive priorities of the organization, and how the TQM programme is expected to contribute to achieving increased competitiveness;
● the roles and responsibilities of the various parts of the organization in the quality improvement;
● the resources which will be available for quality improvement;
● the general approach to, and philosophy of, quality improvement in the organization.

Top-management support

The full understanding, support and leadership of an organization's top management emerges as a crucial factor in almost all the studies of TQM implementation. For example, Table 20.2 shows one such study.

The importance of top-management support goes far beyond the allocation of resources to the programme; it sets the priorities for the whole organization. If the organization's senior managers do not understand and show commitment to the programme, it is only understandable that others will ask why they should do so. By 'top-management support' TQM proponents usually mean that senior personnel must:

● understand and believe in the link between 'doing things right' and the company's overall business;
● understand the practicalities of quality and be able to get over the principles and techniques (for example, statistical process control) to the rest of the organization;
● be able to participate in the total problem-solving process to eliminate errors;
● formulate and maintain a clear idea of what quality means for the organization.

Table 20.2 Quality barriers ranked in order of 'very significant' replies[20]

Top-management commitment	92%
Too narrow an understanding of quality	38%
Horizontal boundaries: functions and specialisms	31%
Vested interests	29%
Organizational politics	28%
Cynicism	28%
Organizational structure	27%
Customer expectations	26%
Speed of corporate action	24%

A steering group

The task of a steering group is to plan the implementation of the programme. It could be argued that it also has a second task, that is to make sure that, even if it does not work itself totally out of a job, its role diminishes over time. The first of these tasks involves planning the overall direction of the programme in terms of what it should achieve as it gathers pace. It also involves deciding where to start the programme and who initially to involve. Further, the group is responsible for monitoring the programme and making sure that all the learning and experience, which is accumulated as the programme progresses, is not lost. The second task is achieved, at least partly, by establishing self-supporting improvement groups.

Group-based improvement

No one can really know a process quite like the people who operate it. The staff who work in the operation are often the ones who know best, for example, how to stop the machines malfunctioning, or who can predict that most adjustments will be needed after a product change. People inside the system have access to the informal as well as the formal information networks. However, working as individuals, staff cannot pool their experience nor learn from one another. This is why successful TQM programmes are almost always based on teams.

The nature and composition of the team will depend on the circumstances. *Quality circles* are much used in Japan but have encountered mixed success in the west. A very different type of team is the '*task force*', or what some US companies call a 'tiger team'. Compared with quality circles, this type of group is far more management directed and focused. Most quality improvement teams are between these two extremes (*see* Fig. 20.7).

Figure 20.7 Different types of improvement group have different characteristics

Success is recognized

Any TQM implementation needs to consider how it should respond to the efforts of the improvement teams. If quality improvement is so important, then success should be marked in some way. Recognizing success formally stresses the importance of the quality improvement process as well as rewarding effort and initiative. Participating in the development process itself (a part of their job which most managers take for granted) is also sometimes seen as rewarding by many in the organization. For example, a company making lighting products in Europe has several manufacturing sites. At one site an improvement team had developed a new cell layout with in-process gauging devices and quality charting methods. The company's management had decided to launch a similar series of quality improvement initiatives at one of its other sites. The improvement group of seven operatives together with their supervisor, production management and quality supervisor were asked to give a presentation at the other site. To quote one of the operators:

'We had a rehearsal a few days before we went and we were all nervous – remember we aren't used to doing this kind of thing. But we took photographs of the cell and generally got our act together before the visit. The presentation took place in the works canteen, and I think that we were all daunted by the sea of faces, but it seemed to go well. When they started asking us questions, it was surprising how interested they were in our answers; no one has taken that much notice of me before! At the end they all applauded! That was the best reward of all.'

UNIPART INDUSTRIES IMPLEMENTS A RECOVERY[21]

At one time, the manufacturing division of Unipart, which makes such products as exhaust systems and fuel tanks, was by far the worst performer in the group. Its reputation with customers was one of poor quality, unreliable delivery, and uncompetitive prices. When its largest customer, Rover, told the company that it had 13 weeks to improve its quality or it would switch to alternative suppliers, it became clear that rapid and sustained improvement would be needed. Initially, Unipart decided to inspect-out defective components, saturating the shop floor with an army of inspectors. Although quality improved, the cost of this was unsustainable; yet this action did make it clear both within the company and outside that it meant business. The company then quickly moved on to more fundamental changes. Process layout was reorganized onto a cell basis; multi-skilled flexible teams were introduced; the number of management layers was cut from seven to three; performance results were displayed to all staff; and a type of quality circle known as a 'contribution circle' was introduced.

Not all of these changes were well received, however. The company had sent a group of operators to Japan for six weeks to learn how to operate some new machinery prior to the same equipment being installed in its Oxford factory. The team discovered that the Japanese had a completely different approach to their work. They stressed quality and waste reduction. When they returned, the team were enthusiastic. An unexpected chain of events then began to unfold. The operators who had been sent to Japan by the company were ostracized by the rest of the workforce and accused of being 'management lackeys'. Feelings ran so high that some even had their tyres slashed in the car park.

When the new plant was installed in a dedicated section of the factory and operated by the Japanese-trained team, Unipart's management were surprised to find that the quality and productivity were not as good as that which had been achieved in Japan. Alarmed by these unexpected developments, management were prepared to 'get in there and sort it out'. The operators complained, however, that they were being 'checked up on' and not trusted. As for the adverse treatment from their colleagues, they would resolve that themselves. The managers then made the difficult decision not to get involved. They pulled out all inspection staff and supervisors and left the new plant solely in the hands of its operators. The production rate and quality started to improve and the fears of the rest of the workforce began to be seen as unfounded.

The members of the new section were not paid on their output, but received a salary for the job. Nor did they appear to have to work excessively hard or have to 'clock' in or out. There were no company songs or pre-shift exercises; in fact they seemed very happy with their work and, if anything, management seemed to leave them alone to get on with the job. After a while, other workers began to see some of the advantages of the new approach and attitudes began to move in favour of the new ways.

Eventually, the company introduced single status for all employees, the end of clocking in and out, team working, and salaries linked to individual performances. Far more controversially, the company also announced that it would no longer recognize trade unions as representing its 4000 workers. ■

Questions

1 Why did Unipart initially use inspection as a method of improving quality? Isn't this directly opposed to the idea of TQM?

2 What do you think was the thinking behind the way Unipart implemented its new processes and system?

Training is the heart of quality improvement

It is no coincidence that so many successful programmes have a training manager as one of their prime movers. TQM is, partly at least, an attitudinal change, so the development task is fundamental to it. There are techniques for staff to learn as well, of course, but the purpose of the techniques is solely to work towards the basic objective – the elimination of errors.

TQM loses its effectiveness

Even TQM programmes which are successfully implemented are not necessarily guaranteed to continue to bring long-term improvement. They may lose their impetus over time. This phenomenon has been variously described as *quality disillusionment*[22] and *quality droop*.[23] Figure 20.8 illustrates this loss of effectiveness.

Various researchers and consultants who have experienced quality disillusionment have put forward prescriptions which are intended to reduce the risk of it occurring.

**Figure 20.8
The pattern of
some TQM
programmes which
run out of
enthusiasm**

Typically, these prescriptions include the following:[24]

● Do not define 'quality' in TQM narrowly; it includes all aspects of performance (what we have called the performance objectives of operations management).

● Make all quality improvement relate to the performance objectives of the operation. TQM is not an end in itself; it is a means of improving performance.

● TQM is not a substitute for the responsibilities of normal managerial leadership. Ineffective managers are not made better simply by adopting TQM.

● TQM is not a 'bolt-on' attachment to the company – an activity which is separate from the other activities of the organization. It should be integrated with and indistinguishable from everyday activities.

● Avoid the hype. TQM has a considerable intuitive attraction for many. It is sometimes tempting to exploit the motivational 'pull' of TQM through slogans and exhortations rather than thoroughly thought-out plans.

● Adapt TQM to the circumstances of the organization. Different organizations will have different needs depending on their circumstances. This means that different aspects of TQM might become more or less important.

Criticisms of TQM

Some companies and academics see far more fundamental flaws in the TQM philosophy than are implied by the list of implementation issues described above. The first set of criticisms is centred on the 'quality bureaucracy' which many firms find they need to manage a large-scale TQM initiative. Some companies who were in the vanguard of the TQM movement, such as Hewlett-Packard, admit that at one time they pushed quality for its own sake, and have shifted too much responsibility down to the shop floor. The second criticism is that TQM is incompatible with more radical improvement approaches such as business process re-engineering (BPR), (*see* Chapter 18). Note that one of Deming's original 14 points (*see* the beginning of the chapter) concerned 'driving out fear'. In other words, staff security is important to the acceptance of change. Yet radical BPR is often accompanied by equally radical 'downsizing' of the organization. It is difficult to reconcile such job losses with the job security necessary for true TQM. The third criticism is that TQM, notwithstanding its implications of empowerment and liberal attitude toward shop-floor staff, is merely a further example of management exploiting workers. By its critics, TQM has been defined as 'management by stress'. Or, even more radically, 'TQM is like putting a vacuum cleaner next to a worker's brain and sucking out ideas. They don't want to rent your knowledge anymore, they want to own it – in the end that makes you totally replaceable.'

QUALITY AWARDS

The importance of TQM has been recognized as an important integrator of many aspects of operations improvement, to the extent that various bodies have sought to stimulate quality improvement through establishing quality awards. The three best-known awards are The Deming Prize, The Malcolm Baldrige National Quality Award and the European Quality Award.

The Deming Prize

The Deming Prize was instituted by the Union of Japanese Scientists and Engineers in 1951 and is awarded to those companies, initially in Japan, but more recently opened to overseas companies, which have successfully applied 'company-wide quality control' based upon statistical quality control. There are ten major assessment categories: policy and objectives, organization and its operation, education and its extension, assembling and disseminating of information, analysis, standardization, control, quality assurance, effects and future plans. The applicants are required to submit a detailed description of quality practices. This is a significant activity in itself and many companies claim a great deal of benefit from having done so. A shortlist is then created and site visits are made by inspectors to the organizations on the shortlist. The site visits include company presentations, in-depth questioning by examiners, top-management meetings and the opportunity for examiners to see any parts of the plant and question any worker.

The Malcolm Baldrige National Quality Award

In the early 1980s the American Productivity and Quality Center recommended that an annual prize, similar to the Deming Prize, should be awarded in America. The award was named after the Secretary of Commerce, Malcolm Baldrige, who was killed in an accident shortly before the legislation for the award became law in 1987.

The purpose of the awards was to stimulate American companies to improve quality and productivity, to recognize achievements, to establish criteria for a wider quality effort and to provide guidance on quality improvement. The main examination categories are: leadership, information and analysis, strategic quality planning, human resource utilization, quality assurance of products and services, quality results and customer satisfaction. The process, like that of the Deming Prize, includes a detailed application and site visits.

European Quality Award

In 1988 14 leading Western European companies formed the European Foundation for Quality Management (EFQM). By July 1993 there were more than 300 members from most Western European countries and most business sectors. An important objective of the EFQM is to recognize quality achievement. Because of this, in 1992, it launched the European Quality Award (EQA). The European Quality Award is awarded to the most successful exponent of total quality management in Western Europe each year. European quality prizes are awarded to a number of companies that demonstrate excellence in the management of quality as their fundamental process for continuous improvement. To receive a prize, companies must demonstrate that their approach to total quality management has contributed significantly to satisfying the expectations of customers, employees and others with an interest in the company for the past few years. Prize-winning companies are intended to be a model of excellence through quality, against which all companies can measure their own quality achievements and their own drive for continuous improvement.

The EQA model is based on the idea that customer satisfaction, people (employee) satisfaction and impact on society are achieved through leadership, driving policy and strategy, people management, resources and processes, leading ultimately to excellence in business results. These ideas are incorporated in the EQA model (*see* Fig. 20.9). The nine elements shown in the model can be classified as either 'results' or 'enablers'. Results are concerned with what the company has achieved and is achieving, whereas enablers are concerned with how results are being achieved. The relative values which are ascribed to the nine criteria within the model are shown as percentages.

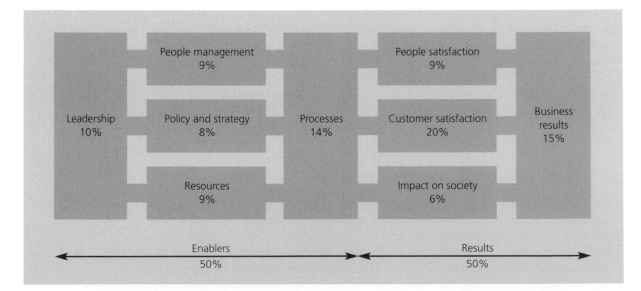

Figure 20.9 The European Quality Award model

The nine elements of the model are defined by the EFQM as follows:

1 *Leadership:* how the executive team and all other managers inspire and drive total quality as the company's fundamental process for continuous improvement.
2 *Policy and strategy:* how the company's policy and strategy reflects the concept of total quality and how the principles of total quality are used in the determination, deployment, review and improvement of policy and strategy.
3 *People management:* how the company releases the full potential of its people to improve its business continuously.
4 *Resources:* how the company's resources are effectively deployed in support of policy and strategy.
5 *Processes:* how processes are identified, reviewed and, if necessary, revised to ensure continuous improvement of the company's business.
6 *Customer satisfaction:* what the perception of the company's external customers is of its products and services.
7 *People satisfaction:* what the company's employees' feelings are about the company.
8 *Impact on society*: what the perception of the company is among the community at large. This includes views of the company's approach to quality of life, the environment and to the preservation of global resources.
9 *Business results:* what the company is achieving in relation to its planned business performance.

Self-assessment

Increasingly, the frameworks behind awards such as the European Quality Award are being used by operations for self-assessment purposes. The European Foundation for Quality Management (EFQM) defines self-assessment as '*a comprehensive, systematic, and regular review of an organization's activities and results referenced against a model of business excellence*', in its case the model shown in Fig. 20.9. The main advantage of using such models for self-assessment seems to be that companies find it easier to understand some of the more philosophical concepts of TQM when they are translated into specific areas, questions and percentages. Self-assessment also allows organizations to measure their progress in changing their organization and in achieving the benefits of TQM. The scoring procedure involved in the awards provides a reasonably objective measurement system around which the organization can understand and discuss its own practices.

Martin Kruger, Honeywell

TQM at Honeywell

Martin Kruger is Director of Quality at Honeywell, which manufactures supply and service control systems and components for industries as varied as commercial buildings, oil refining, avionics and domestic heating.

'At Honeywell the successful adoption of our TQM philosophy over the years has been primarily as a result of persistence, determination, and the development of all our employees' skills. My role as Quality Director has always been to encourage line staff to take full personal responsibility for the quality of the output which they give to their immediate customer – that may be an internal or external customer. Emphasis has been put on giving people new skills, introducing them to fresh tools and techniques and cajoling those same people into applying them in everyday work.'

Nobody attends one of Martin's TQM training events without being tasked to do something with the newly acquired skill or knowledge. Managers and supervisors are required to take on the role of coach, becoming active supporters of change. Although Martin is Director of Quality he has just one person working for him, the TQM administrator.

'I act as the internal conscience for the senior management, spending time coaching them in how to be effective leaders of the TQM culture change. It is also my responsibility to bring the latest thinking on continuous improvement into the company, having first critically evaluated its applicability to Honeywell. One approach to TQM is to reduce everything to a saving in cash or a reduced cost of quality. However, at Honeywell the emphasis is more on our belief that the needs of the customer must come first. There is no area of the company's operation which is immune from this belief. We also believe that the visibility of TQM should begin with the CEO and cascade progressively through the management ranks.'

Martin's personal commitment is to work with anyone at any level in the company to ensure that TQM has a direct meaningful impact where the job is done. Only by giving relevance to personal responsibilities can any real culture change be permanent and TQM be made effective. And how is the success of a long-term TQM process measured? For Honeywell, success is reflected in customer satisfaction, customer recognition (for example receipt of Supplier of the Year awards), staff participation levels and improved process efficiencies. Honeywell now also uses the European Quality Award model as a self-assessment tool, finding that this supports the long-term aim of integrating continuous quality improvement with business.

'After all,' says Martin, *'the only worthwhile measure of our TQM efforts is the success of our business.'* ∎

Source: By kind permission of Martin Kruger, Honeywell Control Systems Ltd

SUMMARY ANSWERS TO KEY QUESTIONS

Where did the idea of total quality management (TQM) come from?

■ Although the origins of TQM go back to the 1940s and '50s, the term was first formally used in 1957 by Feigenbaum. Many authorities have contributed to the development of the idea, however. These authorities include Feigenbaum, Deming, Juran, Ishikawa, Taguchi, and Crosby.

■ The emphasis placed on various aspects of TQM varies among these authorities but the general thrust of their arguments is similar.

■ TQM can be seen as being an extension of the traditional approach to quality – inspection-based quality control being replaced by the concept of quality assurance which in turn has been superseded by TQM.

What are the main differences between traditional quality management and TQM?

■ TQM puts customers at the forefront of quality decision making. Customers' needs and expectations are always considered first in measuring achieved quality.

■ TQM takes an organization-wide perspective. It holds that all parts of the organization have the potential to make a positive contribution to quality. Central to this idea is the concept of the internal customer–supplier chain.

■ TQM places considerable emphasis on the role and responsibilities of every member of staff within an organization to influence quality. It often encourages the idea of empowering individuals to improve their own part of the operation.

■ The implied cost models of TQM are very different from those used in the traditional approach to quality. Traditionally, the emphasis was placed on finding an optimum amount of quality effort which minimized the costs associated with quality. By contrast, TQM emphasizes the balance between different types of quality cost. It argues that increasing the amount of cost and effort placed on prevention will give a more-than-equivalent reduction in other costs. This idea is often summarized in the phrase 'right first time'.

■ TQM also places a heavy emphasis on the ideas of problem solving and continuous improvement dealt with in Chapter 18.

What is the role of ISO 9000 in TQM?

■ ISO 9000 and associated standards are concerned with the systems and procedures which support quality. These are intended to assure purchasers of products and services that they have been produced in a way which meets customer requirements.

■ ISO 9000 has received some criticism as being over-bureaucratic and inflexible.

What are the main implementation issues in TQM initiatives?

■ A number of factors appear to be influential in ensuring the success of TQM. These are:

– the existence of a fully worked-out quality strategy;
– top-management's support;
– a steering group to guide the initiative;
– group-based improvements;
– an adequate recognition and rewards scheme;
– an emphasis on appropriate training.

How do quality awards and models contribute towards TQM?

■ By providing a focused structure for organizations to assess their own quality management and improvement efforts.

■ A number of organizations have attempted to encourage TQM by the awarding of prizes and certificates. The best known of these are the Deming Prize, the Malcolm Baldrige National Quality Award and, in Europe, the European Quality Award (EQA).

■ The EQA is based on a nine-point model which distinguishes between the 'enablers' of quality and the 'results' of quality. This is often now used as a self-certification model.

The Waterlander Hotel[25]

The previous evening's banquet for Plastix International had been a complete disaster, and Walter Hollestelle, the hotel General Manager, was still recovering from the series of telephone conversations of that morning.

First with the Vice-President of Global Marketing, Plastix International Plc:

'I had hoped that by having our annual sales conference at your renowned hotel in Amsterdam, we would be treated to an even better level of service than last year, when we were at Rotterdam; but we were to be deeply disappointed. After all the problems you have caused us over the last two days, from faulty video projection to shortages of cups at coffee breaks, I had hoped that at least the final conference dinner would run smoothly, but you let us down badly. The cocktail reception was a farce: the choice of non-alcoholic drinks that we specially ordered didn't appear until the last minute, and as the President's wife is teetotal, you can imagine the embarrassment that caused! A spilt tray of snacks was not cleared up quickly and several guests got food all over their shoes and dresses. And why did the reception drag on for so long?

'When we were finally asked into the dining room, it clearly wasn't properly prepared. Some of the tables (including ours) were without flowers, which upset my wife, who had been involved with the selection of arrangements. Even the flowers that were there were the wrong variety and looked as if they had been on the tables since yesterday.

'The meal was the worst I have ever seen! I never expect banquet food to be as good as à la carte, but this was awful! The starter was dried up and chewy, and the sweet soufflés were flat and rubbery. And we couldn't believe that anyone could mess up a simple entrée. We were served the cutlets and potatoes, but the sauce and vegetables didn't appear until I'd nearly finished mine.

'And what happened to the microphones on the top table? The photographer didn't turn up either, which is perhaps a blessing, as the tables weren't cleared completely after the sweet, and I'm sure that everyone would have looked in a bad mood after all the mess-up! I can tell you straight – we won't be paying all your exorbitant charges for this banquet and I expect a written apology for all the upset we have been caused. The President must think I am an idiot to have chosen this hotel, and I think he has a point ...'

Next, with the Manager of Aalsmeer Electronics:

'... I was told that the public address system had to be set up by 7.00 pm. We often do jobs of this type, and two hours is more than enough, so we allowed an extra half-hour and started at 4.30 pm. Your staff wouldn't let us get to the tables to wire them, and we had to wait until they cleared them off for us ...'

Then, with his own Hotel Services Manager:

'... it has always been agreed that we must wait until the cutlery has been laid before we set out the flowers, and yesterday we simply weren't given enough time to see to all the tables. As for the types of flowers, we were never told that the client wanted red and pink arrangements. I would have recommended other colours anyway, as reds would not look good against the dining room decor. Unfortunately, the electricians moved our arrangements out of the way against a heating outlet, so by the time we got to them, the flowers looked a bit beyond their best condition. I suppose that's what happens if you allow contractors to interfere with our operation.'

And, with the Conference Manager:

'We were never told that the client wanted to use the video equipment, which was scheduled for repairs next weekend. Had I known, we could have hired in another projector, but we never got the conference checklist back from the client. If we had got that, it would also have indicated that there were an extra ten delegates here just for the morning to make some sort of presentation to the conference. These problems are all down to the client: if they don't follow our system, it's their fault if things go wrong.'

From the Head Chef:

'... I always get a detailed schedule from the head waiter. I get the fish, the sauces, the vegetables and the desserts ready according to that schedule – if things run as late as they did last night, you can expect a few problems. Cooking is an art. All the chefs know how to cook to perfection every time, but if we can't serve the food when it's ready, it will be messed up. I can tell you that if you think the customer was angry, you should have come into the kitchen. Some of the conference delegates were rude to the waiters, who came back into the kitchen and told the chefs. All the staff were really upset and Pierre, our sauce chef, refused to start on the cutlet sauce until the fish course was cleared.'

From the Head Waiter:

'... we weren't told that the electricians would have to wire the tables. They worked setting up the loudspeakers and amplifiers while we were setting the table cloths and laying the place settings. Their foreman then told us that the tables would have to be cleared for them, so you can imagine the problems that caused. I think we did very well to put everything right in under half an hour.'

Finally, with the photographer:

'... we were booked for 10.00 pm and the Conference Manager told us that, according to the customer, we would only be needed for half an hour during the speeches. When we arrived they were still in the middle of the meal, and so I waited a bit, but we had another booking at the Concert Hall at the end of a performance at 11.00 pm, so I had to rush off. If we'd known earlier I could have arranged for a partner to come along ...' ■

Questions

1 Why did things go wrong at the banquet?
2 How could a TQM approach to the hotel's operations help to prevent such disasters occurring in the future?
3 How could ISO 9000 help the hotel?

DISCUSSION QUESTIONS

1 Find out more about one of the 'quality gurus'. Describe his background, his approach to quality and his key contributions to the subject.

2 Talk to an operations manager about TQM. Try to assess what TQM means for that organization and the benefits and problems that have resulted.

3 Identify some of the micro operations that might be found in a high-class restaurant operation. Describe some of the things that might go wrong in each of them and assess the impact of them on the final, external customer.

4 A university is considering creating service-level agreements for its lecturing staff. Explain what is meant by a service-level agreement and suggest some performance measures that might be used.

5 What resistance might there be in an organization to Matsushito's assertion that 'the core of management is precisely the art of mobilizing and pulling together the intellectual resources of all employees in the service of the firm'?

6 Identify the main costs of quality for the following organizations:
   a university library
   a washing-machine manufacturer
   a nuclear electricity generating plant
   a church.

7 Discuss the differences between the 'traditional' and the TQM views on the cost of quality.

8 Get hold of a copy of ISO 9000 or an equivalent and assess its potential impact on quality.

9 Ask an operations manager to describe *how* quality has been improved in the organization over the last few years. Compare and contrast your findings with the section in this chapter on TQM implementation.

10 Discuss the advantages and disadvantages for an organization considering applying to be assessed for a major quality award.

NOTES ON CHAPTER

1 Feigenbaum, A.V. (1986) *Total Quality Control*, McGraw-Hill.

2 Deming, W.E. (1982) *Quality, Productivity and Competitive Position*, MIT Center for Advanced Engineering Study.
Deming, W.E. (1986) *Out of Crisis*, MIT Center for Advanced Engineering Study.

3 Oakland, J.S. (1993) *Total Quality Management* (2nd edn), Butterworth-Heinemann.

4 Juran, J.M. (1989) *Juran on Leadership for Quality, and Executive Handbook*, The Free Press.
Juran, J.M. and Gryna, F.M. (1980) *Quality Planning and Analysis*, McGraw-Hill.
Juran, J.M., Gryna, F.M. and Bingham, R.S. (eds) (1988) *Quality Control Handbook* (4th edn), McGraw-Hill.

5 Ishikawa, K. (1972) *Guide to Quality Control*, Asian Productivity Organization.
Ishikawa, K. (1985) *What is Total Quality Control? – The Japanese Way*, Prentice Hall.

6 Taguchi, G. and Clausing, D. (1990) 'Robust Quality', *Harvard Business Review*, Vol 68, No 1, pp 65–75.

7 Crosby, P.B. (1979) *Quality is Free*, McGraw-Hill.

8 Crosby, P.B., *op. cit.*

9 Oakland, J.S. (1993) *op. cit.*

10 Based on the analysis by Flood, R.L. (1993) *Beyond TQM*, John Wiley.

11 Muhlemann, A., Oakland, J. and Lockyer, K. (1992) *Production and Operations Management* (6th edn), Pitman Publishing.

12 Source: Rees, J. and Rigby, P. (1988) 'Total Quality Control – The Hewlett-Packard Way' *in* Chase, R.L. (ed) (1988) *Total Quality Management*, IFS.

13 Matsushito, K. (1985) 'Why the West will Lose', *Industrial Participation*, Spring.

14 Source: Plunkett, J.J. and Dale, B.S. (1987) 'A Review of the Literature in Quality-Related Costs', *The International Journal of Quality and Reliability Management*, Vol 4, No 1.

15 International Standards Organization, ISO 8402, 1986.

16 Dale, B.G. (1994) 'Quality Management Systems' *in* Dale B.G. (ed) *Managing Quality*, Prentice Hall.

17 Dale, B.G., *op. cit.*

18 'Waging War on Waste' (1994) *European Quality*, Vol 1, No 2.

19 Quoted *in* Smith, S., Tranfield, D., Foster, M. and Whittle, S. (1994) 'Strategies for Managing the TQ Agenda', *International Journal of Operations and Production Management*, Vol 14, No 1.

20 Binney, G. (1992) 'Making Quality Work: Lessons from Europe's Leading Companies', The Economist Intelligence Unit, *Special Report*, No P655.

21 Mason, C. (1994) 'Unipart Industries', *Internal Warwick Business School Report*.

22 Oakland, J.S. (1993) *op. cit.*

23 Slack, N. (1991) *The Manufacturing Advantage*, Mercury Business Books.

24 Slack, N., *op. cit.*

25 Based on an idea originally used by Professor Keith Lockyer.

SELECTED FURTHER READINGS

Albrecht, K. and Bradford, L.J. (1990) *The Service Advantage*, Dow Jones Irwin.

Armistead, C.G. (ed) (1994) *The Future of Services Management*, Kogan Page.

Berry, L.L. and Parasuraman, A. (1991) *Marketing Services: Competing Through Quality*, The Free Press.

Boaden, R.J., Dale, B.G. and Polding, E. (1991) 'A State-of-the-Art Survey of Total Quality Management in the Construction Industry', *A Research Report to the European Construction Institute*, Loughborough.

Bounds, G., Yorks, L., Adams, M. and Ranney, G. (1994) *Beyond Total Quality Management: Towards the Emerging Paradigm*, McGraw-Hill.

Brown, S.W., Gummesson, E., Edvardsson, B. and Gustavsson, B. (eds) (1991) *Service Quality: Multidisciplinary and Multinational Perspectives*, Lexington Books.

Crosby, P.B. (1979) *Quality is Free*, McGraw-Hill.

Dale, B.G. (1994) *Managing Quality* (2nd edn), Prentice Hall.

Dale, B.G. and van der Wiele, T. (1993) *Total Quality Management Directory*, The University Press, Rotterdam.

Deming, W.E. (1986) *Out of the Crisis*, MIT Press.

Feigenbaum, A.V. (1986) *Total Quality Control*, McGraw-Hill.

Garvin, D.A. (1983) 'Quality on the Line', *Harvard Business Review*, Vol 61, No 5, pp 65–75.

Garvin, D.A. (1984) 'What Does "Product Quality" Really Mean?', *Sloan Management Review*, Fall, pp 25–43.

Garvin, D.A. (1987) 'Competing on the Eight Dimensions of Quality', *Harvard Business Review*, Vol 65, No 6, pp 101–9.

Garvin, D.A. (1988) *Managing Quality: The Strategic and Competitive Edge*, The Free Press.

Garvin, D.A. (1991) 'How the Baldrige Award Really Works', *Harvard Business Review*, Vol 69, No 6.

Ghobadian, A. and Gallear, D. (1997) 'TQM and Organisation Size', *International Journal of Operations and Production Management*, Vol 17, No 2.

Harari, O. (1993) 'Ten Reasons Why TQM Doesn't Work', *Management Review*, Jan.

Kehoe, D.F. (1996) *The Fundamentals of Quality Management*, Chapman and Hall.

Kordupleski, R., Rust, R.T. and Zahorik, A.J. (1993) 'Why Improving Quality Doesn't Improve Quality', *Californian Management Review*, Vol 35, Spring.

Leonard-Barton, D. (1992) 'The Factory as a Learning Laboratory', *Sloan Management Review*, Vol 34, No 1.

Lockyer, K.G., Oakland, J.S and Duprey, C.H. (1982) 'Quality Control in British Manufacturing Industry', *Quality Assurance*, Vol 8, No 2.

McGoldrick, G. (1994) *The Complete Quality Manual: A Blueprint for Producing your own Quality Manual*, FT/Pitman Publishing.

Oakland, J.S.(1992) *Total Quality Management* (2nd edn), Heinemann.

Øvretveit, J. (1992) *Health Service Quality*, Blackwell.

Schonberger, R.J. (1994) 'Human Resource Management Lessons from a Decade of TQM and Re-engineering', *California Management Review*, Summer.

Taguchi, G. (1986) *Introduction to Quality Engineering: Designing Quality into Products and Process*, Asian Productivity Organization.

Teboul, J. (1991) *Managing Quality Dynamics*, Prentice Hall.

Whitford, B. and Bird, R. (1996) *The Pursuit of Quality*, Prentice Hall.

PART FIVE

THE OPERATIONS CHALLENGE

The ultimate test for any operations manager is whether he or she can develop an operation which meets the challenges which lie ahead for the organization. This final part of the book identifies a number of key challenges which all operations managers will eventually face.

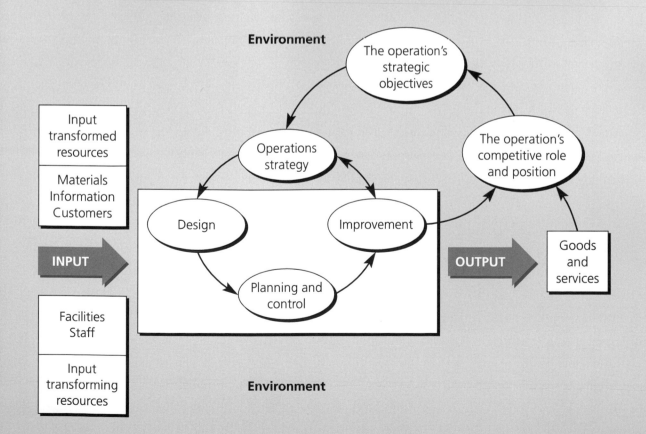

Chapter 21
THE OPERATIONS CHALLENGE

- *Why should organizations have an operations strategy?*
- *How does ethics come into operations strategy?*
- *What are the main international issues faced by organizations formulating their operations strategies?*
- *How can operations strategies be creative?*
- *What influences the successful implementation of operations strategies?*

THE OPERATIONS CHALLENGE

INTRODUCTION

In the preceding 20 chapters we have outlined the nature, purpose and decisions of operations management, and we are now in a position to pull together some of the threads which have run through our treatment of the subject. We have chosen to do this in two ways. First, we return to the strategic view of operations and discuss some general issues concerning operations strategy. Second, we identify some of the challenges which face all operations managers in their continuing attempts to cut through the complexity which characterizes most operations and develop their own operations strategies appropriate for the modern world. Of course this list of strategic 'challenges' could be very long, but we have identified four in particular for attention – the moral imperative to develop *ethical* operations strategies, the necessity to consider the *international* dimension of operation strategies, the need for *creativity* in devising operations strategies and finally the ultimate challenge of *implementing* the chosen strategies. Figure 21.1 illustrates these issues.

Figure 21.1 Issues covered in this chapter

> **CHAPTER 21: KEY QUESTIONS**
>
> - *Why should organizations have an operations strategy?*
> - *How does ethics come into operations strategy?*
> - *What are the main international issues faced by organizations formulating their operations strategies?*
> - *How can operations strategies be creative?*
> - *What influences the successful implementation of operations strategies?*

THE STRATEGY CHALLENGE

Why should operations go to the bother of putting a strategy together? It requires considerable effort and time. All the operation's senior management need to be involved for at least part of their time over a period which has been variously estimated at between four and 18 months.[1] The obvious answer is that an effective operations strategy helps the organization to compete more effectively. There is some empirical evidence to support this. For example, one study of 184 Swedish companies (all manufacturing) concluded that the companies which had formulated an operations strategy which was consistent with their business strategy achieved higher business performance than those without an operations strategy.[2] This is because a formal operations strategy helps to ensure that the policies adopted in the operations function fit together in a coherent manner. With a common purpose and a set of priorities, internal conflicts can be exposed and debated. For example, an organization's technology strategy, amongst other things, shapes the integration between different parts of its processes. Its planning and control strategy has to work within the constraints imposed by the technology. A shared strategy allows not only both areas to measure their own decisions against the common purpose, but also allows the implications of each other's strategy areas to be explored. In this way, a formally constructed operations strategy gives the basic structure which ensures that the many individual decisions taken around the organization all point in the same direction.

Yet many operations managers find the process of strategy formulation more than just worthwhile, it can also be invigorating for those who undertake the task. It provides direction, purpose, and an opportunity to be creative in what is a complex task. Certainly, without direction, purpose, or creativity, success is reduced to a matter of chance. However, the major benefit of strategy formulation is even more far reaching. A credible operations strategy reinforces the centrality of competitiveness in the culture of the organization. It does this by concentrating on the linkages between overall company strategy, operations objectives, the various operations decisions, and the individual resources of the operation.

Difficulties in formulating operations strategy

Even a cursory study of the previous 20 chapters of this book should have made the point that operations management is a complex business, so trying to make strategic sense of any operation will always be a difficult task. Four particular difficulties affect most attempts at the formulation process. The first is the dispersal problem. Operations managers are central to the strategy formulation process, yet they, more than most, are likely to be geographically dispersed among the company's sites. As one operations director of a food-processing company put it,

'My marketing colleague has her senior people all within a few steps of her office. By contrast, my senior people are spread around Europe. The effort of getting them together is not something we can go through every week.'

Second, operations managers operate in 'real time'. They can only allow their attention to drift from the running of the operation for relatively short periods. This responsibility for the day-to-day running of the operation means that they operate under a 'need to deliver' from which only the most important strategic pressures can divert them. Third, the inertia of operational resources imposes a certain amount of conservatism on whoever manages them. With the majority of the organization's resources under their control, no operations manager will, or can, change operational direction without very good reason. Understandable though such caution might be, it does, at times, retard imaginative strategic change. Finally, the cumulative effect of all these pressures has taken its toll over the years. Operations managers often are just not used to thinking, acting or influencing the organization in any strategic manner.

Generic operations strategies

'Generic operations strategies' are common approaches to organizing the operations function which have been observed to be adopted by different types of organization. So, if the operations strategies of many different organizations were reviewed (as they have been in some research studies) it becomes evident that the strategies of the individual organizations can be clustered into groups within which the strategies are similar, or possess common elements. So, for example, the Hayes and Wheelwright four-stage model which we described in Chapter 2 could be considered to be a generic operations strategy classification. All operations could be placed in one of the four categories which they identified.

A somewhat broader categorization is provided by Professor Mike Sweeney of Cranfield University.[3] This is shown in Fig. 21.2. He categorizes operations (more strictly, manufacturing operations) in two dimensions. The first dimension concerns the approach the company takes to process design. Some organizations take a traditional approach to designing their processes, which does not include many of the innovations in technology, layout, job design, organization, and so on, which we have described elsewhere in this book. Others have developed a more enhanced approach to process design which includes such innovations as business process re-engineering, cellular manufacture, JIT organization, etc. The other dimension relates to the approach which the organization takes towards providing service to its customers. Some organizations provide a level of service which might be termed the 'basic' level of which the system is capable. Others have developed an 'enhanced' level of service provision which develops

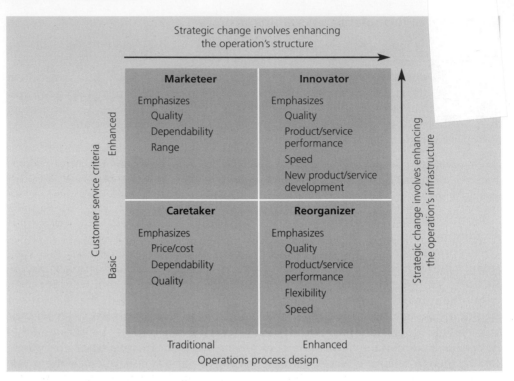

**Figure 21.2
Sweeney's generic
strategies**

the performance of the operation beyond its basic potential. The resulting four-way classification results in generic operations strategies which are termed caretaker, marketeer, reorganizer, and innovator strategies.

The caretaker strategy

This strategy is often employed when an organization believes that there is little competitive advantage to be gained by differentiating itself from its competitors. The operations function is expected to provide as efficient and reliable a service to the rest of the organization as possible without much investment, change or disruption. Operations managers are expected to make sure things do not go wrong, rather than provide much in the way of innovation or creativity.

The marketeer strategy

Marketeer strategies are often used by organizations which experience increased competition and respond by enhancing or extending the level of customer service which they offer. This might include such things as broadening the range of their products or services, increasing quality levels or giving delivery guarantees. No fundamental change has been made to the physical design and organization of the operation itself, but it is expected to respond to marketing-led changes in competitive stance. The operations function tries to do this by developing its infrastructural resources such as planning and control systems, working practices, or quality management methods.

The reorganizer strategy

This strategy implies a change in the way an organization designs and manages its processes. This could mean investment in new technology and (more significantly) a different way of organizing its methods of producing goods and services. Companies adopting JIT and cellular manufacturing principles are typical of organizations adopting this strategy. The new processes often give the enhanced flexibility which allows the operation to respond quickly and effectively to changes in marketing strategy.

The innovator strategy

The innovator strategy is a combination of the marketeer and the reorganizer strategies. Not only has the organization adopted an enhanced approach to designing its operations, it also expects enhanced customer service from its operations function. In other words, it has enhanced not only its structure but also its infrastructure. Usually this means a very high degree of integration between product or service design, operations, and marketing in order not only to be flexible in the short term in response to competitive pressure, but also to introduce new products and services faster and more effectively than competitors.

Sweeney recommends organizations to move, over time, towards innovator strategies. The path taken towards achieving an innovator strategy, however, is also important. Those organizations adopting either a caretaker or a marketeer strategy are recommended first to enhance their operations structure to achieve a reorganizer strategy, after which they can undertake the more difficult infrastructural changes towards an innovator strategy.

Judging the effectiveness of operations strategy

An effective operations strategy should clarify the links between overall competitive strategy and the development of the company's operations resources. It should be able to answer the important 'so what?' questions. For example,

'We intend to compete through aggressive pricing – so what does that imply for the way we develop process technology?' Or 'We have customers with different requirements for different product groups – so what does that imply for the way in which we set performance targets?' Or 'We operate in a turbulent market with frequent product changes – so what does that mean for the way we organize the production, service design–operations interface?'

More specifically, an operations strategy should be:

● *Appropriate.* If the formulation process is to connect operations to the organization's concept of competitiveness then above all it must provide appropriate improvements. In other words, the strategy should guide operations change in a direction which, on balance, is the most likely to provide the performance which best supports the company's competitive strategy.

● *Comprehensive.* An operations strategy cannot define every minor operational decision but it does have to indicate how all parts of the operations function are expected to perform. No part of the operations function is without influence on performance, therefore no part should be left without guidance.

● *Coherent.* Including all parts of the operation in the strategy is a necessary but not sufficient condition for effectiveness. The policies recommended for each part of the function must all point roughly in the same direction. Potential conflicts between the various areas will need addressing directly.

● *Consistent over time.* Although no organization benefits from an overly rigid strategy, the lead time of operations improvement means that consistency must be maintained over a reasonable time period. Failing to provide consistency confuses the organization, but worse it leads to cynicism ...

'*last year was the year of quality, this year it's flexibility, what will be in fashion next year?*'

● *Credible*. A strategy which is not regarded as achievable by the organization will not be supported. Its subsequent failure could merely reinforce the perceived futility of the whole process, therefore strategic change should be seen as feasible.

STRATEGIES MUST BE ETHICAL

The concept of ethical decision making permeates operations management. There are ethical implications in almost every decision area described in this book. Table 21.1 identifies just some of these ethical considerations.

Table 21.1 Some ethical considerations of operations management decisions

Decision area	Some ethical issues
Product/service design	● Customer safety ● Recyclability of materials ● Energy consumption
Network design	● Employment implications of location ● Employment implications of plant closure ● Employment implications of vertical integration ● Environmental impact of location
Layout of facilities	● Staff safety ● Disabled access ● Energy efficiency
Process technology	● Staff safety ● Waste and product disposal ● Noise pollution ● Fume and emission pollution ● Repetitive/alienating work ● Energy efficiency
Job design	● Staff safety ● Workplace stress ● Repetitive/alienating work ● Unsocial working hours ● Customer safety (in high contact operations)
Planning and control (including MRP, JIT and project planning and control)	● What priority to give customers waiting to be served ● Materials utilization and wastage ● Unsocial staff working hours ● Workplace stress ● Restrictive organizational cultures
Capacity planning and control	● 'Hire and fire' employment policies ● Working hours fluctuations ● Unsocial working hours ● Service cover in emergencies ● Relationships with sub-contractors ● 'Dumping' of products below cost

Table 21.1 continued

Decision area	Some ethical issues
Inventory planning and control	• Price manipulation in restricted markets • Energy management • Warehouse safety • Obsolescence and wastage
Supply chain planning and control	• Honesty in supplier relationships • Transparency of cost data • Non-exploitation of developing country suppliers • Prompt payment to suppliers • Minimizing energy consumption in distribution • Using recycled materials
Quality planning and control and TQM	• Customer safety • Staff safety • Workplace stress • Scrap and wastage of materials
Failure prevention and recovery	• Environmental impact of process failures • Customer safety • Staff safety

For our purposes, ethics can be considered as the framework of moral behaviour which determines whether we judge a particular decision as being either right or wrong.[4] In operations management, as in other areas of management, ethical judgements are not straightforward. What might be unremarkable in one country's or company's ethical framework could be regarded as highly dubious in another's. Nevertheless, there is an emerging agenda of ethical issues to which at the very least all operations managers should be sensitive. The first step in this sensitization process is to identify the groups to whom an ethical duty is due. These groups can be categorized as: the organization's customers, its staff, the suppliers who provide it with materials and services, the community in which the environment operates and the shareholders and owners who invest their capital in the business.

Customers' welfare is directly affected by many of the decisions made by operations managers. The first and most obvious effect is that their safety might be compromised by poor operations management decisions. If a product is badly assembled or if the equipment used in a service (such as a rail transport system) is not maintained, customers can come to harm. But customer safety is influenced by more than good manufacturing or maintenance practice, it could also be affected by the degree to which an operation discloses the details of its activities. When should an airline admit that it has received bomb threats? Should all the components or ingredients in a product be fully disclosed? For example, one company used very small amounts of grated peanuts in a pie topping in order to make it look brown and attractive. The company failed however to disclose this ingredient on the package. Subsequently one of its customers, who was allergic to peanuts, died through eating what she regarded as a safe product. At a less serious level, the ethical framework of operations decisions can affect the equity and fairness with which customers are treated. For example, should a bank discriminate between different customers in order to give priority to those from whom they can make more profit?

Staff are constantly exposed to the ethical framework of the organization throughout their working lives. Organizations have a duty to their staff to prevent their exposure to hazards at work. This means more than preventing catastrophic physical injuries, it means that organizations must take into account the longer-term threat to staff health from, say, repetitive strain injury (RSI) due to short-cycle, repetitive work motions. A more subtle ethical duty to staff is the operations responsibility to avoid undue workplace stress. Stress could be caused through not providing employees with the information which allows them to understand the rationale and consequences of operations decisions, or expecting staff to take decisions for which they are not equipped, either because they do not have the information that they need or the training to make the decision. Again though, many staff-related ethical decisions are not straightforward. Should an operation be totally honest with its staff regarding future employment changes when doing so might provoke a labour dispute, or signal the company's intentions to its competitors?

Suppliers are always a source of an ethical dilemma for the operation. Is it legitimate to put suppliers under pressure not to trade with other organizations, either to ensure that you get focused service from them, or to deny competitors this source of supply? Also, do you have any right to impose your own ethical standards on your suppliers, for example, because you would not wish to exploit workers in developing countries? How much effort should you put in to making sure that your suppliers are operating as you would? More significantly, would you be prepared to pay a higher price for their product or service if it meant them abandoning what you regard as unethical practice? The recent increase in the transparency expected from suppliers also poses ethical dilemmas. If you are expecting your supplier to be totally honest and transparent in opening up their costing calculations to you, should you be equally transparent in revealing to them your own internal costings?

The *community* also has a right to expect its organizations to adopt a responsible attitude. At its most obvious level, organizations have a direct impact on levels of environmental pollution in the community. All manufacturing processes have waste emissions of some sort. What, then, should be the balance between an operation's responsibility to minimize its pollution-causing activities on the one hand, and the cost of doing this on the other? Most countries have legislation which sets minimum standards for such decisions, but should an organization try to achieve a better standard if it is technically possible to do so? The ethical dilemma is similar for a company's products after they have been sold. To what extent should an organization ensure that its products are easily disposed of, or recycled, or perhaps even made so durable that they do not need replacing for a long time? Clearly this last option could have a negative effect on a company's revenues. The responsibility to the community means more than pollution and recycling. It also means sharing responsibility for other groups and organizations within the community such as schools, hospitals, groups representing special interests, and so on. To what extent should an operation fund or take part in projects with these groups within the community?

Finally, *shareholders* and owners are also due some ethical duties, even though it may be obvious to state them. They are entitled to a reasonable return on their investments, although what constitutes 'reasonable', and whether the return should be judged in the short term or long term, are both open to interpretation.

Company values

Some decisions take on greater ethical implications in particular operations. For example, deciding on staffing levels in a television manufacturing operation is largely a matter of economics, whereas in a hospital staffing levels can have life and death implications. Of course, staffing-level decisions are also a matter of economics in the hospital, that is exactly what makes the staffing-level decision difficult for the operations managers in the hospital. Indeed, very few of the ethical dilemmas described above are straightforward, but no operation can afford to ignore them. Those organizations which understand the importance of the ethical dimension to operations decisions tend to take a proactive approach to their own ethical stance. This involves deciding the principles upon which

ENVIRONMENTAL POLICY AT 3M[6]

Although the need for organizations to have an environmental policy has become increasingly evident in the last few years, some progressive companies have been aware of their ethical, environmental responsibilities to the community for many years. Back in 1974, 3M published an official corporate environmental policy. This policy articulated the principles by which 3M aimed to solve any environmental pollution it might cause as well as addressing conservation problems. It also set itself measurable environmental goals. These have been updated regularly, so for example, 3M's goal is to reduce emissions to air, land and water by the year 2000 to ten per cent of its 1987 levels. One of the company's early programmes was called Pollution Prevention Pays (3P). Its aim was to reduce, or even eliminate, the sources of pollution for which 3M was responsible through its processes or products. In its first 14 years of operation this programme cut 3M's pollution in half. However, although its original programmes are still in place (albeit updated) the company's approach to pollution control has changed. In the early period of the 3P policy the company controlled pollution largely through 'end-of-line' control. In other words, its basic processes remained largely unchanged but any emissions and pollution were captured and controlled before they could damage the environment. This approach usually requires capital expenditure on the technology which captures, cleans and disposes of emissions. 3M found that a cheaper and fundamentally more sound approach to its environmental management was to focus on *prevention* rather than containment. The concept is to stop all pollution at source, through prevention measures. The 3P programme now seeks to prevent pollution at source, as follows:

● Product reformulation – using different raw materials to reduce the polluting effect of products.
● Process modifications – physically changing the technology of manufacturing processes to reduce the creation of by-products and pollutants.
● Equipment redesign – changing the design of tools and equipment so that they operate more effectively under the specific manufacturing conditions where they are used.
● Resource recovery – the recycling of waste and by-products, either for sale to other organizations or for use in 3M products. ■

Questions

1 How does 3M's 3P policy differ from operations management as we have defined it in this book?

2 Do you have any suggestions for improving the 3P programme?

they will make ethically-sensitive decisions by developing an explicit set of principles which allow organizations to avoid ethically ambiguous activities and gradually build up an ethical framework which becomes accepted within the organizational culture of the operation. Typically such organizations adopt an explicit and public set of values. Table 21.2 shows the mission statement for East Midlands Electricity, a regionally based electricity company in the UK. The mission statement consists of a long-term statement of the company's vision and various 'statements of strategy'. Some of these statements of strategy have quite clear ethical undertones, for example 'adopting and promoting safety and safe working practices in all our activities'. However, the core values which the company sees itself as promoting are identified separately.[5]

Table 21.2 The mission statement of East Midlands Electricity company

The company's mission statement comprises its vision, strategy and values.

The Vision

Simply, to be the best electricity company in the UK.

Strategy

The company's strategies are the means by which we will strive to achieve our vision. The statements of strategy which follow do not appear in any particular order of priority. They should be read as a co-ordinated and coherent whole, as a group of strategies which, taken together, will enable us to achieve our vision.

- Progressive improvement in financial performance and rigorous control of costs.
- Setting and delivering exceptionally high standards of customer service.
- Further development of both the regulated and non-regulated businesses in ways which will contribute to profitable growth.
- Developing and exploiting the synergies between our various businesses.
- Strengthening the image of East Midlands Electricity as a national company with a strong regional base.
- Devolving responsibility and decision-making to the people closest to the issues and achieving the highest standards in each task we perform.
- Vigorous and effective marketing of all our products and services.
- Adopting and promoting safety and safe working practices in all our activities.

- Demonstrating our concern for the community and the environment.
- Employing a highly skilled flexible workforce matched to the needs of the businesses. Training and developing staff to fulfil those needs with due recognition of their own ambition and potential.
- Seeking continuous improvement in all that we do through the total quality process. Continuously learning from our own experiences and from the experiences of others.
- Seeking quality goods and services from our suppliers on a competitive basis while fostering long-term, mutually supportive relationships with them.

Company Values

The company operates by a set of values and ethics which include:

- Adherence not only to the letter but also to the spirit of the law and accepted standards of behaviour.
- Integrity and honesty in all our dealings.
- Respect for the individual.
- Innovation, the seeking and acceptance of change, and the prompt adoption of relevant new techniques.
- The expectation of high performance standards from all its employees and a willingness to recognize and reward achievement.
- Courtesy, concern and quality in personal presentation, language and appearance.
- Concern for the environment.

STRATEGIES MUST BE INTERNATIONAL

Few organizations can afford to limit their operations strategies to within their national boundaries. Only the smallest organizations do not buy any of their supplies from abroad, or do not sell any of their products and services abroad, or should not be, at least, considering doing so. For operations managers the 'environment' within which they make their decisions is, increasingly, a global one. This is especially true for large multinational organizations, who have four types of strategic operations decisions to make:

1 Where should their operations facilities be located?
2 How should their operations network be managed across national boundaries?
3 Should operations in different countries be allowed to develop their own way of doing business?
4 Should an operations practice which has been successful in one part of the world be transferred to another?

International location

The location decision has been discussed in general terms in Chapter 6 as part of the design of the overall network. Networks of operations can spread across several geographic regions. Large global companies such as Mercedes-Benz, the vehicle manufacturer, or Kodak, the photographic materials company, have operations all over the world. However, not all organizations will choose to design their international networks to the same pattern. Different configurations of operations will be appropriate for different organizations. Four configuration strategies have been identified in the location behaviour of international companies.[7]

Strategy 1 – Home country configuration

The simplest strategy for an organization trading around the world is not to locate plants outside its home country and to export its products to foreign markets. In effect any organization adopting this strategy is avoiding the necessity of locating any part of the network over which it has direct control outside its own home country. The reason for adopting this strategy might be, for example, that the technology employed in the product is so novel that it needs to be manufactured close to its Research and Development headquarters. Alternatively, the home location of the company might be part of the attraction of a product such as high fashion garments from Paris.

Strategy 2 – Regional configuration

An alternative strategy is to divide the company's international markets into a small number of regions: for example, the European region, the Pacific region, the American region. Any company adopting this strategy might then try to make each region as self-contained as possible. So, for example, the European region's market would be served by an operation, or operations, in the European region. This can only be achieved if each region has the full range of operations capabilities needed to make the full range of products marketed in the region. Companies adopting this strategy usually do so because their (often industrial) customers demand speedy delivery and prompt after-sales service. If products or services were created outside the region it would be difficult to provide such a level of service, although regional warehouses and service centres could go some way to achieving the required customer service.

Strategy 3 – Global co-ordinated configuration

The converse of the regional strategy, for companies with world-wide locations, is termed the global co-ordinated configuration. Here the various operations concentrate on a narrow set of activities and products and then distribute their products to the markets around the world. So, for instance, a company might take advantage of low labour costs in one region and allocate products with a high labour content to its operations in that region. Another region might have a well-developed technical support infrastructure and so is allocated products which have higher technological requirements. This strategy, therefore, seeks to exploit the particular advantages of each site or region, but by doing so it does place a co-ordination requirement on the headquarters of the company. All product allocations, operations capacities and movement of products need to be planned centrally.

Strategy 4 – Combined regional and global co-ordinated configuration

The regional strategy has the advantage of organizational simplicity and clarity, the global co-ordinated strategy of well-exploited regional advantages. Firms often attempt to seek the advantages of both by adopting a compromise between them. Under such a strategy, regions might be reasonably autonomous but certain products could still be moved between regions to take advantage of particular regional circumstances. This is the strategy which many companies such as Mercedes-Benz and Kodak adopt in practice. Many of their products are made in more than one location around the world but each regional market is served by more than the plants in that region. Figure 21.3 illustrates in diagrammatic form the broad shape of each of the four configurations.

Managing across national boundaries

Once the international network of facilities has been configured, there comes the, in some ways more difficult, task of managing the network on a day-to-day basis. This is not always easy. Operations managers in different plants, located in different parts of the world are likely to face different problems and probably speak different languages. How then can a company exploit the particular advantages of having geographically disparate sites while at the same time getting them to work together in a co-ordinated manner? How does the company prevent the national interests of one part of the network overriding the good of the whole network while encouraging constructive internal competition within the network?

Kodak, for example, maintains a global operations performance measurement system which allows all Kodak plants to assess their own performance against other Kodak plants around the world. So if one plant was dissatisfied with its own performance in (say) delivery reliability, it could consult the international database to find

Figure 21.3 **Four broad types of international operations network configurations**

the Kodak plants who were performing particularly well in this area and then seek advice from them. The plants which have the best performance in each performance measure (called 'Kodak class' plants) are expected to be co-operative in terms of help-ing other Kodak plants to emulate their own success. Of course, such a system is not without its costs. The amount of effort and co-ordination which goes into running the performance database and the expertise necessary to interpret it in a sensible manner is available only to relatively large and sophisticated organizations. The ability to com-pare plants around the world can be a major asset for multinational companies. It enables them continually to keep abreast of good operations practice and it prevents their individual plants from becoming either parochial or complacent. For example, the Volvo Car Corporation, which in the early 1990s had three major car assembly plants in Sweden, was able to judge the performance of its Swedish plants by compar-ing them with its plant in Ghent in Belgium. Although the product mix in the four plants was slightly different, comparisons of productivity, quality and logistics could be made. (In fact the superior operations performance in the Ghent factory caused a radical rethink of the way Volvo organized its car manufacture in Sweden.)

It is the ability of multinationals to compare the performance of plants in different parts of the world that helps them develop a global and multi-cultural perspective. Multi-culturalism is the goal to which many multinational firms aspire. It means that the company sees itself as being a part of all the communities in which it is involved rather than as being primarily associated with its original country of origin. Asea Brown Boveri (ABB), the Swedish–Swiss electrical engineering company, is one such example. The company has a board of eight directors from four different nationalities and an executive committee of eight senior managers from five different countries who run its day-to-day business. With a headquarters in Zurich, English is its corporate language while its financial results are reported in US dollars. It also moves its business around the world in response to global changes. In the first half of 1994 its workforce in the Asian region increased by 8500 while its workforce in Western Europe decreased by 4000. Partly this was a response to high labour costs in its European operations but also it was because of forecast market growth in Asia.[8]

Different regions – different practices

Different parts of the world, because of their differing cultures, economic conditions, history, market needs, demography, and so on, are likely to develop different operations practices. The most obvious example is the way just-in-time and 'lean manufacturing' practice grew up in Japan in the aftermath of the Second World War (*see* Chapter 15). The question, therefore, which multinationals have to face is,

'Should we allow our facilities in different parts of the world to develop their own operations strategies to suit their own conditions, or should we encourage a uniformity of practice which reflects our corporate values?'

For example, linking this back to our discussion of ethics in the earlier part of this chapter, should an organization which originates in a culture where any kind of gift or bribe is highly unethical, prevent its operations from giving small gifts to potential suppliers or customers in a country where this is culturally acceptable? Similarly, should an organization which has built up a strong world-wide brand image allow this to be adapted in different regions? For example, McDonald's, the fast-food chain, developed a rigorous and highly standardized way of organizing its operations which was one of the main reasons for its world-wide success. Yet, eventually it had to allow a certain amount of discretion to local managers to adapt for local tastes (for example, serving Teriyaki burgers in Japan, or serving wine in Lyons).

The prevailing conditions in any part of the world can often lead to organizations developing their operations in a creative way so as to adapt and survive. Just-in-time manufacture (again) can be seen as Japanese manufacturing industry's response to its shortage of natural raw materials. Similarly, the Scandinavian emphasis on liberal work attitudes and high levels of welfare support contributed to its manufacturing companies developing working conditions and job designs which could retain staff in such a social environment.

Transferring operations practices

Different parts of the world, because of their different conditions, develop their own approach to operations management. So, can the practices which grew up under one set of conditions transfer successfully to parts of the world where conditions might be very different? Again, Japanese manufacturing industry provides us with an example. When just-in-time manufacturing began to be noticed by the rest of the world, it was common to hear the view expressed that although it was fine for Japan it would never work 'over here'. North American and European cultures especially were considered to be unsuitable for Japanese methods of manufacture. With hindsight this view was flawed in two ways. First, it failed to distinguish between the 'technical' aspects of just-in-time (such as kanban control, or set-up time reduction) which were relatively easily transferable, and the way in which just-in-time was implemented by harnessing certain 'cultural' factors of Japanese life (such as the emphasis on consensus decision-making). Although just-in-time manufacture has now spread throughout the world, it is not always applied in exactly the same way in North America or the UK, for example, as it is in Japan. Some of the technical aspects may be identical but the way it is put into practice has often been tailored to suit national culture. Secondly, it is an over-simplification to assume that all countries within one region of the world have the same work culture. The cultural contexts of the UK, France and Sweden, for example, are sufficiently different to make it difficult to generalize about the acceptability of just-in-time manufacturing methods in a 'European' culture.

Yet sometimes an operational practice which is wildly successful in one part of the world does not transfer easily. For example, the Federal Express Corporation in America practically invented the overnight express delivery service. Its 'hub-and-spoke' operations structure in the United States enables it to guarantee overnight delivery from any part of the country to any other part by routing all packages through a single hub in Memphis, Tennessee. Influenced partly by the moves towards greater European integration, Federal Express attempted to duplicate its US operation in Europe. However, to some extent Europe is far from being a single integrated economic entity in the same way as is the US. Differences in language, currency, culture, tax rates, and so on, posed problems which were not experienced in the US. After some years of struggling to develop the overnight express business it gave up the struggle and closed this part of its business.

Long-term transfers of operations practice

In the long term one can trace the movement and development of operations management practice as it responds to conditions in one part of the world and then is adopted by other parts. Let us return to the example of just-in-time or 'lean' manufacturing. In fact lean manufacturing is just one stage in what might be an ongoing process of development. Figure 21.4 illustrates this for the case of automobile assembly. Automobiles were originally made by craft-based processes. Each car would be built individually (as horse-drawn coaches had been prior to the development of the internal combustion engine). This was also true in the early years of automobile manufacture in the United States. It was only when demand grew to the point that warranted the development of mass production methods by Henry Ford and others, that the 'standard' way of producing motor cars moved to the assembly-line-based mass production system. So effective was this method of manufacture that it spread from the USA to Europe and later to Japan. As we have already mentioned, the conditions and culture of Japan led to the further development of manufacturing with the adoption of just-in-time methods and continual improvement on to the basic framework of mass production. Again the appropriateness of this new method of manufacturing to late 20th century conditions led to its transferring back both to the USA and to Europe. However, in some parts of Europe some elements of the original craft-based production had survived, either in the luxury end of the motor car business, or where some of the negative factors of mass production were less acceptable. Most notably, Scandinavian manufacturers, both of motor cars and trucks, had adopted what has been termed a 'dock' system of manufacture (which we described in Chapter 7 as a 'short fat' layout). There are now some attempts to combine the economic efficiency of lean manufacturing with the more acceptable social ideals of dock manufacturing. This has been termed 'reflective manufacturing'.

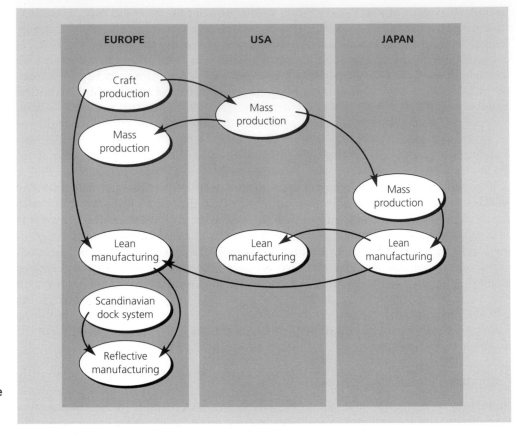

**Figure 21.4
The transfer of
operations practice
in the automotive
industry**

STRATEGIES MUST BE CREATIVE

The operations strategy formulation procedures which we described earlier in this chapter provide a structure and a logical process which help operations managers to move in a sensible direction. However, they will not provide the single best strategic solution. They tell operations managers how to go about developing a strategy; they do not tell them what to do. Different sets of operations managers faced with exactly the same set of circumstances will probably come out with very different strategic solutions. Some might follow fairly conventional and orthodox routes (which may well provide adequate solutions), whereas others might be more imaginative and creative in coming up with their own original strategic solutions, or at least developing ones which embody some original idea. Many successful operations are successful because they thought of an original way of creating their products and services. Federal Express, the parcel delivery company which we described earlier in this chapter, is a good example of this. It was the first to use the 'hub and spoke' principle, whereby all parcels are routed through a central hub, to provide overnight parcel delivery. It is now an 'obvious' solution which is used throughout the world. But it only became obvious after Federal Express thought of it.

The issue which marks the boundary between orthodox and pedestrian operations strategies on one hand and original, creative and imaginative strategies on the other, is that of how operations managers view the relationship between performance objectives. One way of characterizing this relationship is called the trade-off paradigm. We shall describe this and put forward the hypothesis that only by overcoming the trade-off paradigm will operations strategies be sufficiently creative to provide a significant competitive advantage.

Do performance objectives trade off?

One of the important questions which any operation has to decide is the relative priority of its performance objectives. To do this it must consider the possibility that one way in which it can improve its performance in one objective is to sacrifice some performance in another. Put another way, it must consider trading-off one aspect of performance with another. This idea is called the *trade-off paradigm* of operations, and, taken to its extreme, it implies that improvement in one aspect of an operation's performance can only be gained at the expense of performance in another. 'There is no such thing as a free lunch' could be taken as a summary of the trade-off theory (*see* Fig. 21.5).

Probably the best-known summary of the trade-off idea comes from Professor Wickham Skinner, the most influential of the originators of the strategic approach to operations. He said:

'*... most managers will readily admit that there are compromises or trade-offs to be made in designing an airplane or truck. In the case of an airplane, trade-offs would involve matters such as cruising speed, take-off and landing distances, initial cost, maintenance, fuel consumption, passenger comfort and cargo or passenger capacity. For instance, no one today can design a 500 passenger plane that can land on an aircraft carrier and also break the sound barrier. Much the same thing is true in manufacturing.*'[9]

Yet this trade-off model of performance objectives has been challenged – mainly by companies who have managed to give 'the best of both worlds' to their customers. Perhaps the most dramatic example is how the supposed 'trade-off' between quality and cost was challenged and overcome by many types of operation. At one time, a

Figure 21.5
The trade-off paradigm

811

high-quality, reliable and error-free automobile was inevitably an expensive automobile. Now, with few exceptions, we expect even budget-priced automobiles to be reliable and almost free of any defects.

It is mainly the attitude of operations managers which has changed. Taking their lead from pioneering Japanese manufacturers, most manufacturers found that not only could they reduce the number of defects on their vehicles without necessarily incurring extra costs, but they could actually reduce costs by reducing errors in manufacture. They changed their view of quality from one of 'screening the bad products out' to one of 'stopping the mistakes being made in the first place'. Put in terms of the 'lever' model in Fig. 21.5, there are two ways to improve the position of one end of the lever. One is to depress the other end – in other words improving one aspect of performance at the expense of another. But the other way is to raise the pivot of the lever. This would raise one end of the lever without depressing the other end. Alternatively, it could raise both ends. The 'pivot' in a real operation is the set of constraints which prevents both aspects of performance being improved simultaneously. Sometimes the constraints are technical, sometimes attitudinal. But the 'pivot' is stopping one aspect of performance improving without it reducing the performance of another. It should therefore be the prime target for any improvement process and the basis for developing creative strategic solutions in the operation. Figure 21.6 illustrates this.

The approach which has been generally adopted in this book is that, although there are some situations where (especially in the short term) trade-offs between performance objectives have to be made, one of the main jobs of operations managers is to change whatever in the operation is causing one performance objective to deteriorate as the other improves. In fact the 'pivot' of the trade-off is the main target of continuous improvement in operations.

Reducing the trade-off

Even what seem to be inevitable trade-offs can be reduced to some extent. For example, one of the decisions that any supermarket manager has to make is how many check-out positions to open at any time. If too many check-outs are opened

Figure 21.6 Challenging the trade-off paradigm by 'raising the pivot'

then there will be times when the check-out staff do not have any customers to serve and will be idle. The customers, however, will have excellent service in terms of little or no waiting time. Conversely, if too few check-outs are opened the staff will be working all the time but customers will have to wait in long queues. There seems to be a direct trade-off between staff utilization (and therefore cost) and customer waiting time (speed of service). Yet even the supermarket manager deciding how many check-outs to open can go some way to affecting the trade-off between customer waiting time and staff utilization. The manager might, for example, allocate a number of 'core' staff to operate the check-outs but also arrange for those other staff who are performing other jobs in the supermarket to be trained and 'on-call' should demand suddenly increase. If the manager on duty sees a build-up of customers at the check-outs, these other staff could quickly be used to staff check-outs. By devising a flexible system of staff allocation, the manager can both improve customer service and keep staff utilization high. Chapter 11 examined other ways of dealing with demand fluctuations.

Blocks to creativity

Although creativity in operations strategy is seen to be a desirable condition, one can, without too much effort, identify a variety of factors which either block creativity or create a climate in which there is little encouragement for staff to demonstrate their creative abilities. These blocks to creativity range from the way in which staff jobs are structured to the way in which we, as individuals, all respond to each other's ideas. The factors which inhibit creativity include the following:

● developing operations control systems which emphasize efficiency over creativity;
● dividing jobs into those who are expected to be creative and those who are not;
● expecting certain functions in the organization (such as research and development or marketing) to be creative while other functions (such as operations and finance) are not expected to be creative;
● expecting only staff above a certain organizational level to contribute new ideas;
● not recognizing or rewarding those staff who do generate creative solutions to operations strategy.

Socialization into non-creativity

Many staff, especially in large organizations, do not often take part in decision-making activities where they are called upon to exercise some degree of discretion. They are often engaged in carrying out activities that depend on decisions which have already been made by other staff elsewhere in the organization. Even when they do exercise choice it may be with little or no discretion. The alternative courses of action between which they choose may have already been identified and the decision process may merely consist of following a pre-set rule. Under these circumstances individual staff may become *socialized* into an attitude towards their work in which creativity plays little or no part. They just do not see their jobs as being, in any way, creative. This makes the task of harnessing the potential of all staff in the creative process particularly difficult for operations managers. They must themselves then be creative in encouraging creativity (*see* the box on Adtec).

CREATIVITY AT ADTEC[10]

The inspiration for creativity-inducing processes can come from some unusual sources. Adtec, based in Gothenberg, Sweden, develops and markets environmental cleaning systems mainly for the engineering, pharmaceutical, chemical and printing industries. Its clients include such well-known names as Volvo, Lockheed, and 3M.

The company has some very definite views on creativity. In the words of one of the company's founders,

'Labour is the greatest enemy of thinking, so we separate the individual from the work.'

The inspiration for this idea came from the book *Jonathon Livingston Seagull* by Richard Bach. In this book a flock of gulls spend all their lives using their wings only to glide on air currents in an endless search for food. This continual labour prevents them being able to imagine any other kind of life. Their never-ending concentration on survival prevents them using their natural creativity. The hero of the story rejects the conventional wisdom of the flock and continually improves his flying performance by setting goals and raising them each time they are achieved. He devotes time for improvement as distinct from day-to-day survival.

This idea is translated at Adtec into their Wings (Working In New Goal Setting) programme. Wings projects recognize that staff need time away from their daily work tasks in order to stimulate their creativity. Staff have 'Wings hours' – two hours a week where they can work on projects outside their normal jobs. When one project finishes, another one immediately starts, thus encouraging the idea of continuous improvement. Wings time is scheduled by staff at regular meetings. Once set, Wings hours are sacrosanct. No one can demand that they be given up in order to deal with some routine problem, except on the express order of the managing director. The Wings projects themselves must be well planned with a clear focus and a definite time schedule. Each staff member has a mentor to help him or her with the project. The mentor is usually an internal customer of the staff member. At the end of the project a written report or presentation must be given in which the improvements made by the project are identified. For example, one member of staff used his Wings time to develop a system which computerized some purchasing routines. The result was that the gap between estimated purchasing costs and actual costs reduced from 5 per cent down to 0.5 per cent. ■

Questions

1 What do you think are the advantages of Adtec's Wings programme?

2 Do you think that such a programme is all that is required to encourage creativity in organizations? If not, what else is necessary?

STRATEGIES MUST BE IMPLEMENTED

Too often operations strategies fail at the implementation stage. A strategy may set the direction of the operation but implementation defines how it gets there, which is a more difficult task. Operations managers need to start the task by addressing their implementation agenda – the list of general questions, the answers to which set the basic plan for implementation. The questions are:

- When to start?
- Where to start?
- How fast to proceed?
- How to co-ordinate the implementation programme?

When to start?

There is probably only one absolute rule here, which is not to start until all the issues on the implementation agenda have been addressed. Starting off without a reasonably clear idea of how the strategy is to be implemented is a sure way to reduce the chances of success. The implementation agenda, in effect, charts how progress is supposed to be made. Nevertheless, some start times are better than others. Implementation should ideally be started when one can be sure of resourcing it adequately (for example, when the operation's engineers and managers can devote enough time to the project). Similarly, it would not be wise to start when the operation's capacity is seriously overstretched – all efforts will be on short-term output, not the implementation. So operations should start only after the last big push or project has settled down rather than when any major structural change (a new site, product or service launch or process introduction, for example) is imminent.

Where to start?

There are two schools of thought here. The first recommends starting where the operation will get most direct benefit, by being rational and putting effort and resources where the likely return, in terms of improved performance, will be maximized. This could be either where performance is so poor that relatively small improvement gives a disproportionate benefit, or where the potential for dramatic improvement is high. The second favours starting where the operations managers believe there is the best chance of succeeding, preferably in a relatively calm backwater of the operation where any problems will not set back the whole strategy. By doing this, managers can start small and build up experience, learn as they go, keep mistakes small scale and, above all, maintain credibility in the organization. By the time the really important parts of the operation are being tackled, the implementation team will have both the authority and the experience, if not to guarantee success, to make it far more likely. Both approaches are perfectly legitimate, although the second has much to commend it when the improvement programme is inherently risky or when the implementation team has little experience of the type of change being made.

How fast to go?

Managing the speed of improvement means understanding (and often combining) the two modes of improvement – breakthrough improvement and continuous improvement – which are described in Chapter 18.

How to co-ordinate the programme?

An operations strategy implementation is like any other project in that it needs managing using the principles which are described in Chapter 16. The organizational environment in which the programme will have to fight for attention and resources needs to be predicted. Operations managers must answer questions such as, what conditions will the programme have to cope with during its implementation? For example, are there product/service modifications or new product/service launches planned for the period? If so, how will they interfere with the programme? Are there organizational or system changes planned by any other functions which could affect the programme?

The resources which will be needed to staff the programme also need planning. Operations managers need to make sure that everyone with a part to play knows exactly what is required from them and approximately when this is likely to be. Milestones of progress in each area of the programme need to be set, so that feasibility can be judged at the planning stage and progress can be judged throughout the life of the programme.

Successful implementation – the key elements

In the several studies of operations strategy implementation, both successful and unsuccessful, a number of key elements recur regularly, either as important prerequisites of success or as omissions which seriously harmed implementation success.[11]

Top-management support

This always comes out as being important, especially at times of 'breakthrough' improvement where the 'champion' role requires top management to allocate and co-ordinate resources. Continuous improvement requires a different kind of support, emphasizing a long-term continuing expectation of improvement.

Business driven

All operations strategy change is only a means to an end – improved competitiveness. The organization's overall competitive imperatives must be clearly linked to every part of the operations strategy programme throughout its life.

Strategy drives technology

Not the other way round. Competitiveness should drive operations strategy, so in turn, operations strategy determines the way technology is developed.

Change strategies are integrated

Successful operations strategy programmes involve change over several fronts, technological, organizational, cultural. Only considering one aspect is too limiting a view. Integrating improvement strategies so that they support each other gets the operation 'firing on all cylinders'.

Invest in people as well as technology

Some organizations are reluctant to invest in their human resources even a fraction of the cash they do in technology. Yet changes in methods, organization or technology must be supported by changes in attitude by all employees – especially the managerial structure. Technological 'retooling' must be accompanied by 'social retooling'.

Manage technology as well as people

Conversely, organizations often seem reluctant to 'manage' technology after the investment decision has been made. Technology needs integrating into the operation on strictly managerial criteria.

Everybody on board

Any effective operations strategy must be understood and supported throughout the organization, particularly by the management structure. Without this, changes are implemented into 'unreformed' traditional structures, attitudes and work practices.

Clear, explicit objectives

If staff know what is expected of them, it is easier to succeed. An obvious point maybe, but since operations strategy usually involves cross-functional change, the need for explicit communication of overall purpose becomes vital.

Time-framed project management

Keeping control is a prerequisite for maintaining support. Objective setting, schedules, resource plans, and milestones are as important here as for any other project.

SUMMARY ANSWERS TO KEY QUESTIONS

Why should organizations have an operations strategy?

■ Because the evidence seems to show that an effective operations strategy helps organizations to compete more effectively. It does this by helping policies to be more coherent, helping to prioritize internal conflict, and giving structure to the internal debate on which direction to choose.

■ However, there are a number of difficulties in formulating successful operations strategies:
– Operations managers tend to be geographically dispersed.
– Operations managers operate in 'real time' and so need to manage the operation.
– Operations resources are difficult to change.
– Operations managers are not in the habit of contributing to strategic change.

■ Operations strategies can be classified into categories of generic strategies. One such category distinguishes between caretaker strategies, marketeer strategies, reorganizer strategies, and innovator strategies.

How do ethics come into operations strategy?

■ Practically all decisions made by operations managers have some kind of ethical dimension. These ethical considerations affect one or more of the following groups:
– the operation's customers;
– the operation's staff;
– the operation's suppliers;
– the community in which the operation exists;
– the operation's shareholders and owners.

■ Some companies make their ethical stance explicit through a statement of mission and values.

What are the main international issues faced by organizations formulating their operations strategies?

■ The first is how to configure their resources throughout the world. There are four basic configurations:
– home country configuration;
– regional configuration;
– global co-ordinated configuration;
– combined regional and global co-ordinated configuration.

■ International operations need to address the problems of managing their operations across national boundaries. An issue here is how to balance competition and co-operation.

■ Different regions in the world often develop different operations practices depending upon their economic, social and political circumstances. However, some of these practices developed in one part of the world can be transferred (often in a modified form) to other parts of the world.

How can operations strategies be creative?

■ One of the main concepts which helps to explain creativity in operations is that of the 'trade-off'. Originally, theories of operations suggested that operations managers needed merely to manage the extent of trade-offs between performance objectives. More recently, theories suggest that overcoming the long-term effects of trade-offs is a useful way of ensuring creativity in organizations.

What influences the successful implementation of operations strategies?

■ Partly, ensuring that any change is accompanied by a worked-through 'implementation agenda'. This will deal with such basic questions as:

– when to start an implementation?
– where to start an implementation?
– how fast to proceed?
– how to co-ordinate the implementation programme?

■ In addition, studies tend to show that successful implementations have top-management support, are business driven, make technology decisions driven by the strategy itself, have changes which are integrated, invest in people as well as technology, and manage technology as well as people.

Banco Evora do Sul

'You can never tell what is going to happen after deregulation. We certainly do not want a Scandinavian-type situation here. Yet some of Portugal's largest banks have responded to deregulation by some very aggressive lending policies, and all this despite signs that the economy is starting to slow down.'

Alexandere Vaz Pinto, Chairman of the Bankers' Association in Portugal, was commenting on the frenetic activity in the retail banking sector which had built up in his country. He was likening it to the unhealthy loan boom which had occurred after the deregulation of the Scandinavian banking industry. Some banks had been more adventurous than others. Assets at Banco Portugues do Atlantico (BPA) and Banco Commercial Portugues (BCP), two of the largest, recently leapt by 29.4 per cent and 37.5 per cent respectively. This rapid increase in banking activity had been building up since the mid-1980s when banking regulations had been relaxed. Furthermore, several of Portugal's biggest banks had been privatized.

One of those to be privatized was the Banco Evora do Sul (BES). Although not one of the more aggressive lenders, it had nevertheless made quite an impact on the market.

'We must make up for lost time. For years we have been weakened by the state meddling in our affairs. Now we need to get close to our customers and compete on service and innovation. We are already developing a network of alliances with financial institutions throughout Europe, as well as exploring the options for cross-selling our financial services in Portugal.' (Customer Services Manager at BES.)

The development of retail banking services

BES had always been strong in retail banking, especially in the provision of small loans to private customers, for example for the purchase of cars and domestic equipment. It had also invested in both information technology and in refurbishing its branches. So it was generally regarded as being the most innovative in the retail banking area in Portugal. For example, most large branches had interactive computing facilities which allowed customers to model their own mortgages or loan repayments. Also 80 per cent of branches had been refurbished in the previous two years. This investment in computing facilities and in bricks and mortar had, the Bank felt, brought it closer to its customers. Yet it knew it was not alone in following this direction. Its competitor banks were pursuing more or less the same strategy. For example, in the last year Portuguese banks opened over 500 new branches. Even so, with roughly one branch for every 4000 people, Portugal was still less heavily banked than most other European countries.

To pay for all this investment BES knew it needed to increase its revenues, partly by improving the market share of its loan products.

The personal loan product

BES had decided to form a special working group to look at the potential of its personal loan product. This product, known as 'Besloan' was not very dissimilar to its rivals' products. It was a relatively standardized product on which loans were advanced for relatively small sums (up to the equivalent of around US$50 000) and for which all banks charged more or less the same interest rate.

Because of its standardization, the product could be operated relatively profitably. For example, it did not require any special senior management involvement to authorize loans. When the customer had filled in an application form, it was sent to the regional office where a decision was taken at a relatively low level by utilizing a simple 'scoring' process. Also the procedures for issuing the loans and collection of repayments were well-tried and standardized. In fact it consumed relatively little overhead in the bank.

The task party decided to trawl through the bank for any information it could gather on how the loan product was viewed by customers and how other banks operated their equivalent products.

One of the first facts that emerged was that an independent academic study had revealed that Portugal's banks varied somewhat in the proportion of their current account customers who also held personal loans with the same bank. This 'current account penetration' figure varied between 9 per cent and 15 per cent with an average for the larger banks of 12.5 per cent. BES's current account penetration varied between regions but averaged 10.7 per cent.

The working group consolidated the information it had gathered thus far. Exhibit 1 shows a summary of the main points to emerge from a retail banking seminar held in London which two of the working group members had attended. Probably the most important pieces of information though were the results of two surveys carried out by two different parts of the bank two years before. The first was a customer survey which had been carried out by the Bank's Marketing Department. In fact the Department has been conducting this survey regularly for a period of about five years. This is included in Exhibit 2.

The Working Group also unearthed a survey of the Bank's competitors which had been carried out almost simultaneously with the customer survey but independently of it. This had been carried out by the Business Development part of the bank as part of a larger study and unfortunately was not fully compatible with the Customer Survey in so much as it examined personal loans on slightly different criteria. This information is contained in Exhibit 3.

The problem which faced the working group was how to make sense of this information, at least up to the point where they could determine the strategy for the 'Besloan' product.

'It is a matter of getting our strategy right in the way we serve customers in our branches. Personal loans are particularly profitable for us since customers do not seem to realize how much interest they are paying. Nevertheless, we need to keep our costs down in order to maintain our profitability, yet at the same time we must improve our quality of service. But where do we start, that is the dilemma.' (BES Customer Service Manager.) ∎

Exhibit 1 Excerpts from Retail Banking Services Seminar – April 1994

Retail banking sector
- The threat from foreign-owned banks which seemed imminent two or three years ago has probably diminished in the short term but could still be important in the longer term.
- Alliances between main European banks could be aimed at providing 'European-wide' business, travel and vacation cover with 'look-alike services' in the next five to six years.
- All main banks believe that quality of service is likely to be an important differentiator in the near future.

Retail products
- Most banks recognize their errors in 'product proliferation' over the last ten years.
- The absolute number of products will grow little (if at all) in the next five years.
- Innovation is likely to become important, both in product replacement and at the 'general branch service' level.
- Clearer boundaries are likely to be set between standard and non-standard products.
- More guidance is likely to be given to branch management on the rules for customizing selected products.

- There is still considerable evidence that all banks have problems with their staff's product familiarity.

Retail operation and organization
- Location of branches – in some countries (notably the UK) there will be a combination of rationalization (i.e. in the number of branches, probably fewer) and relocation of some branches to more prominent 'high street' locations. In other countries (such as Portugal) branch expansion is likely to continue.
- The quality of service is still a problem for all banks in spite of service initiatives.
- Moves towards 'open environment', high contact design of branches will continue.
- There will be less 'back-office' activity at branches for several reasons:
  - a move towards separating-out back-office activity into separate regional/national administration centres;
  - the increased sophistication of distributed information access systems, primarily for customer-related information;
  - more computer-based expert systems to give guidance for routine decisions;
  - the possible outsourcing (subcontracting) of back-office functions to specialist companies.

Exhibit 2 Customer Survey No 90/32

Date: 30 June 1994

SUMMARY

Subject – Factors influencing customers'[1] choice of product	Score[2]	Spread[3]	Relative to last survey[4]
C/A inertia[5]	4.3	0.3	−0.4
Price	3.9	0.7	+0.1
Advertising	4.0	0.2	same
Trust in 'honesty' of advice	4.7	0.1	+0.2
Trust in technical competence	3.1	0.3	−0.1
Response time	4.5	0.3	same
Response reliability	3.6	0.5	+0.1
Property factors[6]	2.8	0.1	same
Quality of previous service	3.7	0.6	+0.3
Branch advice	4.6	0.5	+0.3
Branch 'atmosphere'[7]	3.6	0.1	+0.1
Branch queueing	3.7	0.2	same
Location convenience	4.0	0.1	−0.2

This data has been modified and codified, it should not be taken as in any way representing policy.

Notes to Exhibit 2

1 The survey includes far more factors than are shown here. Some factors listed are composites.
2 A five-point scale where 1 = very unimportant and 5 = very important is used as standard.
3 Spread is an indication of the degree of consensus expressed by customers surveyed.
4 Compared with previous survey (14 months previously) a positive sign means that the factor's importance rating has increased, a negative means that it is less important.
5 Current account inertia – the propensity of customers to take automatically a personal loan at the bank where they hold their current account.
6 Property factors – decor and layout of branch.
7 Composite of several factors relating to 'friendliness' and quality of customer contact.

Exhibit 3 Survey of Competitors[1]

Date: 4 June 1994

SUMMARY

Product–Personal loan

Factors	BES	Bank No 2	Bank No 3	Bank No 4	Bank No 5
Image retention[2]	3.2	4.2	3.7	3.0	2.9
Image gap[3]	3.0	3.5	3.0	3.1	3.0
Branch expertise[4]	4.5	4.0	4.3	3.8	3.0
Branch attractiveness	4.1	3.3	3.5	3.9	3.9
Contact skills	4.2	4.0	3.9	4.3	3.8
Availability of info	4.0	4.2	4.0	4.0	4.2
Form design	3.3	4.2	3.8	3.5	3.0
Document errors					
• set up	2.5	3.1	3.3	3.2	4.0
• operation	3.8	3.5	3.3	3.9	3.8
Response time					
• for advice	3.0	2.9	2.8	3.3	3.5
• for decision	2.5	3.0	2.8	3.0	3.2
Response reliability	3.0	3.5	3.7	3.6	3.6
Location site score	4.1	4.2	4.1	4.0	4.7
Opening hours	4.0	4.0	3.5	3.5	4.7

▶

Notes to Exhibit 3
1 Conducted by sampling competitors' and own branches without prior notice. Also uses data from publicly published surveys. 1 = very poor, 5 = very good.
2 Degree to which advertising 'image' is retained by customers.
3 Gap between customers' reported experiences and product image as advertised. 1 = large gap, 5 = small gap.
4 Estimate of quality banking expertise available at branch level.

Questions

1 Describe the retail operation of BES (especially relating to the Besloan product) from an operations management perspective. Do this by identifying the issues which the bank's managers would be concerned with under the chapter headings used in this book.

2 How would you advise the bank to formulate its operations strategy?
3 What could the bank do to improve its competitiveness?
4 What ethical considerations do you think are important for a retail bank like BES?
5 How relevant is the 'internationalization of operations' to retail banks?

1 If a busy operations manager said to you, *'Why should I spend time and effort on putting an operations strategy together? I already have enough to do as it is. If I devote any time to such luxuries I would fail to satisfy our customers' immediate needs. This would put us out of business and no operations strategy is going to help us then!'* How would you make a case to the operations manager which convinced him that operations strategy formulation was worthwhile?

2 What do you think the difficulties in operations strategy formulation might be in:
(a) a small manufacturer of cellular telephone communication stations whose business is growing at a rate of over 100 per cent a year?
(b) an international luxury hotel group with hotels around the world?

3 Do you think that operations which have an 'innovator' generic operations strategy will always outperform those which adopt a 'caretaker' operations strategy?

4 Visit a local service operation, such as a theatre, a library, a fast-food outlet, a retail store, or a public transportation company, and by interviewing management (where possible) and by observation perform a brief operations strategy review.

5 What purpose do you think the concept of a 'green field' operation has in developing an operations strategy for an existing organization which cannot afford to move to a new site?

6 List all the operations management decisions which you think will have an impact on the following:

the safety of the operation's staff
the safety of the operation's customers
environmental pollution
energy efficiency.

7 A wholefood co-operative has decided to offer a ten per cent discount to senior citizens on Mondays. It has decided to do this because it wishes to aid this section of society, while at the same time moving demand from busy Saturday mornings to quiet Mondays. Do you think such a move compromises the implicit ethical stance of such an operation?

8 If organizations were charged directly through the tax system for all the direct or indirect pollution for which they are responsible, what effect do you think this would have on the daily working lives of operations managers?

9 Draw up a statement of values which you think would be appropriate for a university.

10 Choose any organization with which you are familiar (either as a member of staff or as a customer) and list the operations trade-offs which may be assumed by the management of the operation. For each of these trade-offs identify ways in which the performance of both factors may be improved.

11 A university wishes to implement a strategy which involves the systematic counselling of all its students twice a year on their progress and general study skills. What options should the university's operations managers be considering when putting together their implementation agenda?

NOTES ON CHAPTER

1 *See* for example Voss, C. (1990) 'The Process of Manufacturing Strategy Implementation', *Proceedings of the OMA Conference*, Warwick University, or Gunn, T.A. (1987) *Manufacturing Strategy for Competitive Advantage*, Ballinger, Cambridge, Mass.

2 Tunalv, C. (1992) 'Manufacturing Strategy – Plans and Business Performance', *International Journal of Operations and Production Management*, Vol 12, No 3.

3 Sweeney, M.T. (1991) 'Towards a Unified Theory of Manufacturing Management', *International Journal of Operations and Production Management*, Vol 11, No 8.

4 Thompson, A. and Strickland, A.J. (1992) *Strategic Management, Concepts and Cases* (6th edn), Irwin.

5 From Stocks, N., Davies, R. and Bland, J. (1993) 'Sparked by Initiative', *Managing Service Quality*, May.

6 Sources: Company information and Hopfenbeck, W. (1992) *The Green Management Revolution: Lessons in Environmental Excellence*, Prentice Hall.

7 Du Bois, F.C. and Oliff, M.D. (1992) 'International Manufacturing Configuration and Competitive Priorities' *in* Voss, C.A. *Manufacturing Strategy: Process and Content*, Chapman and Hall.

8 Sources: Narborough, C. (1994) 'Switch to Low-cost Countries Aids ABB', *The Times*, 18 Aug, and 'The Discrete Charm of the Multinational', *The Economist*, 30 July 1994.

9 Skinner, W. (1969) 'Manufacturing the Missing Link in Corporate Strategy', *Harvard Business Review*, Vol 47, No 3.

10 Source: Johansson, C. (1994) 'Self-investment', *European Quality*, Vol 1, No 4.

11 Based on Tranfield, D. and Smith, S. (1987) 'A Strategic Methodology for Implementing Technical Change in Manufacturing', *BAM Conference*.

SELECTED FURTHER READINGS

Adam, E.E. and Swamidass, P.M. (1989) 'Assessing Operations Management from a Strategic Perspective', *Journal of Management*, Vol 15, No 2.

Adams, J.L. (1988) *The Care and Feeding of Ideas*, Penguin.

Anderson, J.C., Cleveland, G. and Schroeder, R.G. (1989) 'Operations Strategy: A Literature Review', *Journal of Operations Management*, Vol 8, No 2.

Bach, R. (1972) *Jonathon Livingston Seagull*, Turnstone Press.

Bennett, D. and Forrester, P. (1993) *Market Focussed Production Systems*, Prentice Hall.

De Bono, E. (1982) *Lateral Thinking for Management*, Penguin.

Fine, C.H. and Hax, A.C. (1985) 'Manufacturing Strategy: A Methodology and an Illustration', *Interfaces*, Vol 15, No 6.

Flaherty, M.T. (1996) *Global Operations Management*, McGraw-Hill.

Guth, W.D. and Tagruri, R. (1965) 'Personal Values and Corporate Strategy', *Harvard Business Review*, Vol 43, No 5.

Harrison, M. (1993) *Operations Management Strategy*, Pitman Publishing.

Hayes, R.H. and Wheelwright, S.C. (1984) *Restoring Our Competitive Edge*, John Wiley.

Hayes, R.H., Wheelwright, S.C. and Clark, K.B. (1988) *Dynamic Manufacturing*, The Free Press.

Hill, T. (1993) *Manufacturing Strategy* (2nd edn), Macmillan.

Mather, H. (1988) *Competitive Manufacturing*, Prentice Hall International.

Mintzberg, H. (1978) 'Patterns in Strategy Formulation', *Management Science*, Vol 24, No 9.

Murchison, C. and Baird, J. (1996) 'An Introduction to Green Product Development for SMEs', *Engineering Management Journal*, Dec.

Platts, K.W. and Gregory, M.J. (1990) 'Manufacturing Audit in the Process of Strategy Formulation', *International Journal of Operations and Production Management*, Vol 10, No 9.

Roth, A.V. and Giffi, C.A. (1991) 'Manufacturing's Secret Arsenal for the 1990s', *Duke University Working Paper*.

Skinner, W. (1985) *Manufacturing: The Formidable Competitive Weapon*, John Wiley.

Slack, N. (1991) *The Manufacturing Advantage*, Mercury Books.

Stonebreaker, P.W. and Leong, G.K. (1994) *Operations Strategy: Focussing Competitive Excellence*, Allyn and Bacon, Boston.

Swamidass, P.M. and Newell, W.T. (1987) 'Manufacturing Strategy, Environmental Uncertainty, and Performance: A Path Analytic Model', *Management Science*, Vol 33, No 4.

Thompson, A.A. and Strickland, A.J. (1992) *Strategic Management: Concepts and cases* (6th edn), Irwin.

Vancil, R.F. (1986) 'Strategy Formulation in Complex Organisations', *Sloan Management Review*, Vol 17, No 2.

Voss, C.A. (1992) *Manufacturing Strategy*, Chapman and Hall.

Womack, J.P. and Jones, D.T. (1996) *Lean Thinking: Banish Waste and Create Wealth in Your Corporation*, Simon and Schuster.

APPENDIX 1
FORECASTING THE VOLUME OF DEMAND

Any model which describes some aspect of the behaviour of any system or phenomenonon can be used to predict its future behaviour. Here, however, we are specifically concerned with some of the more common models or techniques which are used largely for the prediction of demand levels. Demand is the main determinant of volume, and volume has significant impact on design in operations.

There are several ways in which forecasting models and techniques can be classified. One classification divides techniques into:

- subjective and objective, and
- non-causal and causal.

Subjective forecasting techniques are those which involve judgement and intuition from one or more individuals, whose approach to the forecasting task is unlikely to be explicit, but will be based on experience.

Objective techniques are those which have specified and systematic procedures. This means that results produced by these methods are reproducible no matter who uses them.

Non-causal techniques are those which use the past values of a variable to predict its future values. They assume that the underlying causes of events, which have pertained in the past, will continue to shape events in exactly the same way in the future.

Causal techniques attempt to make predictions on the basis of causal relationship. If the cause–effect relationship between variables can be modelled, then predictions of the factors which influence whatever we are trying to forecast will enable a forecast to be made. The assumption of such methods is that these causal variables can be measured and projected more accurately than actual demand itself.

Some of the more common forecasting methods which we shall briefly describe are classified in Fig. A1.1.

Time series analysis

Time series techniques examine the pattern of past behaviour of a phenomenon over time, and use the analysis to forecast the phenomenon's future behaviour. For example, suppose a company is attempting to predict the future sales of a product. The past three years' sales, quarter by quarter, are shown in Fig. A1.2(a). This series of past sales may be analysed to indicate future sales. For instance, underlying the series might be a linear upward trend in sales. If this is taken out of the data, as in Fig. A1.2(b), we are left with a cyclical seasonal variation. The mean deviation of each quarter from the trend line can now be taken out, to give the average seasonality deviation. What remains is the random variation about the trends and seasonality lines, Fig. A1.2(c). Future sales may now be predicted as lying within a band about a projection of the trend, plus the seasonality. The width of the band will be a function of the degree of random variation.

Forecasting unassignable variations

The random variations which remain after taking out trend and seasonal effects are without any known or assignable cause. This does not mean

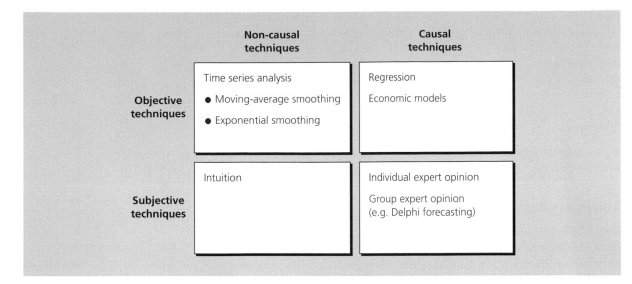

Figure A1.1 Some common forecasting techniques

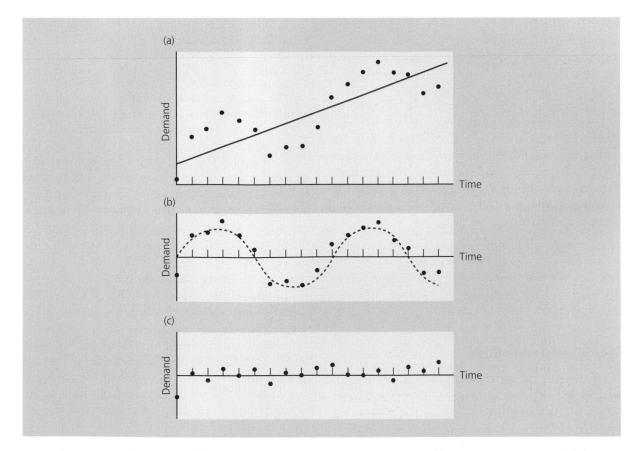

Figure A1.2 Time series analysis with (a) trend, (b) seasonality and (c) random variation

that they do not have a cause, however, just that we do not know what it is. Nevertheless, some attempt can be made to forecast it, if only on the basis that future events will, in some way, be based on past events. We will examine two of the more common approaches to forecasting which are based on projecting forward from past behaviour. These are:

- moving-average forecasting;
- exponentially smoothed forecasting.

Moving-average forecasting

The moving-average approach to forecasting takes the previous n periods' actual demand figures, calculates the average demand over the n periods, and uses this average as a forecast for the next period's demand. Any data older than the n periods plays no part in the next period's forecast. The value of n can be set at any level, but is usually in the range 4 to 7.

Example – Eurospeed parcels

Table A1.1 shows the weekly demand for Eurospeed, a European-wide parcel delivery company. It measures demand, on a weekly basis, in terms of the number of parcels which it is given to deliver (irrespective of the size of each parcel). Each week, the next week's demand is forecast by taking the moving average of the previous four weeks' actual demand. Thus if the forecast demand for week t is F_t and the actual demand for week t is A_t, then:

$$F_t = \frac{A_{t-1} + A_{t-2} + A_{t-3} + A_{t-4}}{4}$$

For example, the forecast for week 35:

$$F_{35} = (72.5 + 66.7 + 68.3 + 67.0)/4$$
$$= 68.8$$

Exponential smoothing

There are two significant drawbacks to the moving-average approach to forecasting. First, in its basic form, it gives equal weight to all the previous n periods which are used in the calculations (although this can be overcome by assigning different weights to each of the n periods). Second,

Table A1.1 Moving-average forecast calculated over a four-week period

Week	Actual demand (thousands)	Forecast
20	63.3	
21	62.5	
22	67.8	
23	66.0	
24	67.2	64.9
25	69.9	65.9
26	65.6	67.7
27	71.1	66.3
28	68.8	67.3
29	68.4	68.9
30	70.3	68.5
31	72.5	69.7
32	66.7	70.0
33	68.3	69.5
34	67.0	69.5
35		68.6

and more important, it does not use data from beyond the n periods over which the moving average is calculated. Both these problems are overcome by *exponential smoothing*, which is also somewhat easier to calculate.

The exponential-smoothing approach forecasts demand in the next period by taking into account the actual demand in the current period and the forecast which was previously made for the current period. It does so according to the formula:

$$F_t = \alpha A_{t-1} + (1 - x) F_{t-1}$$

where α = the smoothing constant.

The smoothing constant α is, in effect, the weight which is given to the last (and therefore assumed to be most important) piece of information available to the forecaster. However, the other expression in the formula includes the forecast for the current period which included the previous period's actual demand, and so on. In this way all previous data has a (diminishing) effect on the next forecast.

Table A1.2 shows the data for Eurospeed's parcels forecasts using this exponential-smoothing method, where $\alpha = 0.2$. For example, the forecast for week 35 is:

$$F_{35} = 0.2 \times 67.0 + 0.8 \times 68.3 = 68.04$$

The value of α governs the balance between the *responsiveness* of the forecasts to changes in demand, and the *stability* of the forecasts. The closer α is to 0 the more forecasts will be dampened by previous forecasts (not very sensitive but stable). Figure A1.3 shows the Eurospeed volume data plotted for a four-week moving average, exponential smoothing with $\alpha = 0.2$ and exponential smoothing with $\alpha = 0.3$.

Regression models

Regression models use statistical techniques to determine the 'best fit' expression which describes the relationship between the variable being forecast and other variables. For example, suppose an ice-cream company is trying to forecast its future sales. After examining previous demand, it figures that the main influence on demand at the factory is the average temperature of the previous week. To understand this relationship, the company plots

Table A1.2 Exponentially smoothed forecast calculated with smoothing constant $\alpha = 0.2$

Week (t)	Actual demand (thousands) (A)	Forecast ($F_t = \alpha A_{t-1} + (1-\alpha) F_{t-1}$) ($\alpha = 0.2$)
20	63.3	60.00
21	62.5	60.66
22	67.8	60.03
23	66.0	61.58
24	67.2	62.83
25	69.9	63.70
26	65.6	64.94
27	71.1	65.07
28	68.8	66.28
29	68.4	66.78
30	70.3	67.12
31	72.5	67.75
32	66.7	68.70
33	68.3	68.30
34	67.0	68.30
35		68.04

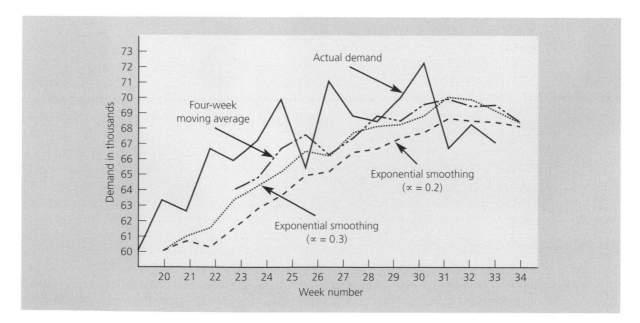

Figure A1.3 A comparison of a moving-average forecast and exponential smoothing with the smoothing constant $\alpha = 0.2$ and 0.3

demand against the previous week's temperatures. This is shown in Fig. A1.4. Using this graph, the company can make a reasonable prediction of demand, once the average temperature is known, provided that the other conditions prevailing in the market are reasonably stable. If they are not, then these other factors which have an influence on demand will need to be included in the regression model, which becomes increasingly complex.

Econometric models

At very high levels of demand forecasting – examining growth rates for a whole industry sector for example – complex regression approaches are called *econometric modelling*. Econometric models consist of a set of regression equations which describe complex cause–effect relationships. These equations are solved simultaneously, which allows a more realistic representation of the relationships within the decision. However, the cost of developing such models is usually very high.

Individual expert judgement

Some events which we may wish to forecast cannot be expressed in a manner which allows the use of quantitative objective models. The rate of technological change in an industry, for example, might be particularly important to a company forecasting demand for its products which are bought as 'add-ons' to other manufacturers' products. The rate of technical change is not a factor which can be predicted by any objective method. Under such circumstances, decision makers have to rely on the opinions of people who, through their experience of similar situations or familiarity with the current problem, are deemed to be 'experts'.

Sometimes, using expert judgement is partially a substitute for some more rigorous but expensive method. For example, a company wishing to predict how its sales will stand up to a well–publicized rival product, due to be launched shortly, may ask all its sales people for their opinions. The sales people will probably base their opinions partly on their perceptions of and 'feel' for the market, and

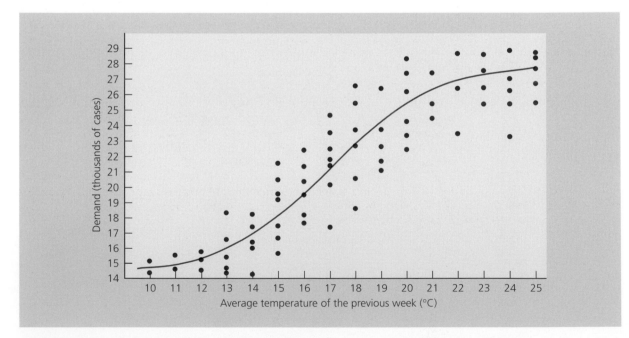

Figure A1.4 Regression line showing the relationship between the previous week's average temperature and demand

partly on the comments made to them by the customers with whom they are in everyday contact. This latter element of expert judgement could well be performed with greater accuracy by a customer survey. However, a customer survey would be more costly, would take time, and might inadvertently publicize the rival product.

Delphi group forecasts

This technique is one of several used to bring together the opinions and forecasts of a group of experts. It has been defined as 'a method of structuring a group or communication process, so that the process is effective in allowing a group of individuals, as a whole, to deal with a complex problem'.[1] The technique seeks to obtain a group opinion through an anonymous process of controlled iterative feedback. The usual method is for a panel of experts (who are not allowed to communicate about the problem) to be interrogated through questionnaires. The information from the group is then collected together, summarized, aggregated and presented anonymously as feedback to the group. Each member of the group can then compare his or her own prediction with the group 'average'. The individual may then modify (or not as the case may be) his or her first-round prediction, and the process is repeated. Eventually it becomes clear whether a consensus is emerging from the group.

The performance of forecasting models

Forecasting models are widely used in management decision-making, and indeed most decisions require a forecast of some kind, yet the performance of this type of model is far from impressive. Hogarth and Makridakis[2], in a comprehensive review of the applied management and finance literature, show that the record of forecasters using both judgement and sophisticated mathematical methods is not good. What they do suggest, however, is that certain forecasting techniques perform better under certain circumstances. In short-term forecasting there is:

'... considerable inertia in most economic and natural phenomena. Thus the present states of any variables are predictive of the short-term future (i.e. three months or less). Rather simple mechanistic methods, such as those used in time series forecasts, can often make accurate short-term forecasts and even outperform more theoretically elegant and elaborate approaches used in econometric forecasting.'[3]

Long-term forecasting methods, although difficult to judge because of the time lapse between the forecast and the event, do seem to be more amenable to an objective causal approach. In a comparative study of long-term market forecasting methods, Armstrong and Grohman[4] conclude that econometric methods offer more accurate long-range forecasts than do expert opinion or time series analysis, and that the superiority of objective causal methods improves as the time horizon increases.

Notes

1 Linstone, H.A. and Turoof, M. (1975) *The Delphi Method: Techniques and Applications*, Addison-Wesley.
2 Hogarth, R.M. and Makridakis, S. (1981) 'Forecasting and Planning: An Evaluation', *Management Science*, Vol 27, pp 115–38.
3 Hogarth, R.M. and Makridakis, S., *op. cit.*
4 Armstrong, J.S. and Grohman, M.C. (1972) 'A Comparative Study of Methods for Long-Range Market Forecasting', *Management Science*, Vol 19, No 2, pp 211–21.

APPENDIX 2
TIME ESTIMATION–WORK MEASUREMENT

Time estimation

One of the most important pieces of information in the design activity of any organization is how long particular tasks will take to complete. Some estimate of a task's duration is an essential prerequisite for many key design decisions. The following list identifies some applications for time data.

Designing products, services and processes (Chapter 5)

● Evaluating alternative product designs which have different methods of assembling or manufacturing products.
● Evaluating alternative ways of designing the serving of customers in high customer contact services.

Designing the operations network (Chapter 6)

● Evaluating transportation times in location decisions.
● Evaluating whether to perform a task in-house.
● Evaluating the amount of capacity which will be needed in the operation.

Layout and flow (Chapter 7)

● Evaluating the times to perform tasks at each stage of a process.
● Evaluating alternative routings through an operation.
● Balancing the work allocated to each stage of an operation (identifying bottle-necks).

Process technology (Chapter 8)

● Evaluating alternative types of technologies.
● Evaluating alternative sizes of machines and equipment.

Job design (Chapter 9)

● Evaluating alternative work methods.
● Evaluating safety allowances.
● Evaluating remuneration schemes and 'allowed-time' schemes.
● Evaluating the performance of individuals, or groups of staff.

It is because of this wide variety of uses for time estimates that all organizations need to make some kind of estimate of the length of time which will be needed for each of the tasks which are performed. In order to get such an estimate all organizations have three options:

● they can guess;
● they can assume that the time which *is* taken to do a job is in fact the *correct time* to do it;
● they can use a measuring technique which is systematic and has reasonably predictable limits of accuracy.

It is the latter approach which we will examine in this Appendix. It involves applying systematic techniques to tasks and work-time estimation, and it is known as *work measurement*.

Work measurement

'Work measurement is the application of techniques designed to establish the time for a qualified worker to carry out a specified job at a defined level of performance.'

This statement of what work measurement sets out to achieve poses three important questions:

- What is a qualified worker?
- What is a specified job?
- What is a defined level of performance?

None of these questions can be defined with much degree of precision, but generally it is agreed that, a *specified job* is one for which specifications have been established to define most aspects of the job. For example:

- the quality standard required;
- the method to be followed by the person performing the job;
- the equipment and materials to be used;
- the working conditions under which the job is performed.

A *qualified worker* is one who is accepted as having the necessary physical attributes, intelligence, skill, education and knowledge to perform the task to satisfactory standards of safety, quality and quantity.

The term *performance* means a rate of working or alternatively a rate of output expressed as an average of the working day or shift. In fact, traditionally, there are two basic conceptions of what the level of performance should be:

- that it should be set at the level of performance which can be reasonably expected under 'motivation' conditions; and
- that it should be set at the level of performance which can be reasonably expected under 'non-motivation' conditions.

The various bodies round the world who recommended standards of practice for work measurement recommend that performance should be pitched at the 'motivation' level. The term used to describe this level of performance is *standard performance*, and is defined as:

'the rate of output which qualified workers will achieve without over-exertion as an average over the working day provided they are motivated to apply themselves to their work.'

Basic times

Terminology is important in work measurement. The terms which are used for time estimates of various types arc all different, and using the wrong term can lead to confusion. When a *qualified worker* is working on a *specified job* at *standard performance*, the time he or she takes to perform the job is called the *basic time* for the job.

Basic times are useful because they are the 'building blocks' of time estimation. With the basic times for a range of different tasks, an operations manager can construct a time estimate for any longer activity which is made up of the tasks. For example, suppose an operations manager of a company which erects temporary buildings needs to estimate the time which should be taken to erect a particular building. The time could be estimated by adding together the basic times for each part of the total job. This is the idea behind 'synthetic' time estimating which will be explained later.

Standard times

The *standard time* for a job is an extension of the basic time and has a different use. Whereas the basic time for a job is a piece of information which can be used as the first step in estimating the time to perform a job under a wide range of conditions, standard time refers to the time *allowed* for the job under specific circumstances. This is because standard time includes *allowances* which reflect the rest and relaxation which is to be allowed because of the conditions under which the job is performed.

So the standard time for each element consists principally of two parts (although in some cases extra allowances may be applicable):

- *Basic time:* the time taken by a qualified worker, doing a specified job at standard performance.
- *Relaxation allowance:* the allowances which are added to the basic time to allow for rest, relaxation and personal needs.

Most of the techniques of work measurement involve the breaking down of the job to be studied into *elements*. For each of these elements, separate *standard times* are then determined. The standard time of the job as a whole is then the sum of all the standard times of its constituent elements (*see* Fig. A2.1).

Example

Suppose a task has four elements, each of which warrants a different allowance as shown in Table A2.1.

This is shown digramatically in Fig. A2.2.

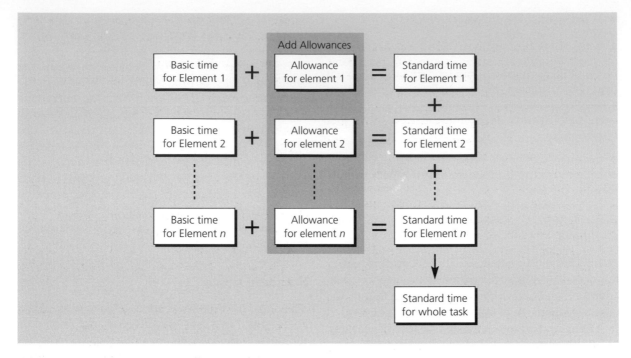

Figure A2.1 The standard time for a whole job is made up of the basic times for all its elements with the addition of the allowances for each element

Table A2.1 Time elements of task

Element	Basic time (mins)	Relaxation allowance (%)	(mins)	Standard time (mins)
a	0.67	18	0.12	0.79
b	0.43	14	0.06	0.49
c	0.85	12	0.10	0.95
d	0.30	17	0.05	0.35
Total	2.25		0.33	2.58

Figure A2.2 Standard time calculation for the example

The advantages of standard time

The standard time for any task is not necessarily the time which will be taken actually to perform it in reality. That is not a disadvantage, however, provided the operations managers who work with the information know how it has been derived. In fact the 'basic time', which is the time which a 'qualified worker, working at standard performance' would take is often a more useful piece of information at the micro level of design. Nevertheless, the standard time for a task, because it is both *normalized* to the performance of someone working at standard performance and also contains the *allowances* which staff should be taking, can be particularly useful.

The standard time for a task is, in effect, an estimate of the total amount of *work* which is needed to perform the task. It enables all types of work to be expressed in terms of a common unit – the 'standard minute' or 'standard hour' (SM or SH). For different tasks the proportion of the standard minute or hour spent actually working and the proportion spent resting will vary, but the two parts together always add up to the common unit. Figure A2.3 illustrates this idea.

Allowances

There are several allowances which may be applied to the basic time, depending on the circumstances. The main one is *relaxation allowance*. Special allowances may also be applied such as:

- contingency allowances
- interfaces or synchronization allowances
- introductory allowances
- unusual condition allowances
- unoccupied time allowances.

Relaxation allowance is defined as:

'... an addition to the basic time intended to provide the worker with the opportunity to recover from the physiological and psychological effects of carrying out specified work under specified conditions and to allow attention to personal needs. The amount of the allowance will depend on the nature of the job.'

The way in which relaxation allowance is calculated, and the exact allowances given for each of the factors which determine the extent of the allowance, varies considerably between different organizations. Table A2.2 illustrates the allowance table used by one company which manufactures domestic appliances. The table shows the percentage allowance to be applied to each element of the job. All allowances are additive and a personal needs allowance of ten per cent is added to all elements.

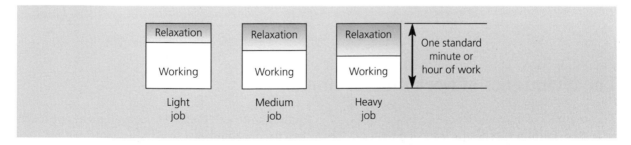

Figure A2.3 Using the standard time approach to work measurement the standard unit of work remains the same, only the proportions of relaxation and working time vary

Table A2.2 An allowances table used by a domestic appliance manufacturer

Allowance factors	Example	Allowance (%)
Energy needed		
Negligible	none	0
Very light	0–3 kg	3
Light	3–10 kg	5
Medium	10–20 kg	10
Heavy	20–30 kg	15
Very heavy	Above 30 kg	15–30
Posture required		
Normal	Sitting	0
Erect	Standing	2
Continuously erect	Standing for long periods	3
Lying	On side, face or back	4
Difficult	Crouching, etc.	4–10
Visual fatigue		
Nearly continuous attention		2
Continuous attention with varying focus		3
Continuous attention with fixed focus		5
Temperature		
Very low	Below 0°C	over 10
Low	0–12°C	0–10
Normal	12–23°C	0
High	23–30°C	0–10
Very high	Above 30°C	over 10
Atmospheric conditions		
Good	Well ventilated	0
Fair	Stuffy/smelly	2
Poor	Dusty/needs filter	2–7
Bad	Needs respirator	7–12

The techniques of work measurement

The method of moving from the basic times for each element of a task to the standard time for the whole task is more or less the same no matter how the basic time is derived. The basic time itself can be measured or estimated by a number of tech-niques, however. The work measurement approach uses five techniques:

1 Time study
2 Synthesis from elemental data

3 Predetermined motion-time systems
4 Analytical estimating
5 Activity sampling

A brief description of each technique follows.

Time study

'A work measurement technique for recording the times and rate of working for the elements of a specified job, carried out under specified conditions, and for analysing the data so as to obtain the time necessary for the carrying out of the job at a defined level of performance.'

The times for the job are recorded using one or more stopwatches on the shop floor which is why time study has met, and still does encounter, opposition. The use of direct timing can be seen as intrusive. Nevertheless, even though time study is now used far less for generating standards which are used in payment schemes (the major source of the technique's unpopularity), it is still used extensively. The technique takes three steps to deriving the basic time for the elements of the job:

● Observing and measuring the time taken to perform each element of the job through several cycles of the job, while at the same time rating the performance of the person doing the job.
● Adjusting, or 'normalizing', each observed time in the light of the rating of performance observed while the element was being timed.
● Averaging the adjusted times to derive the basic time for the element.

Step 1 – observing, measuring and rating

After analysing the job to be studied in order to divide the whole job into its constituent elements, the job is observed through several cycles. Each time an element is performed it is timed using a stopwatch. There are procedures for using one or more stopwatches which allow the observer to time consecutive elements while minimizing observation error. Simultaneously with the observation of time, a rating of the perceived performance of the person doing the job is recorded.

The *rating* of observed times is probably the most controversial part of time study. It is defined as:

'the process of assessing the worker's rate of working relative to the observer's concept of the rate corre-

sponding to standard performance. The observer may take into account, separately or in combination, one or more factors necessary to carrying out the job, such as speed of movement, effort, dexterity, consistency, etc.'

At the most charitable it is a subjective, and at times arbitrary, procedure. Rating does perform a necessary function, however. All individuals have different skills, motivations, and standards of what constitutes a reasonable pace of working. Unless the observer is to measure a large number of people, all performing the same job, then there is little alternative but to 'normalize' the observed times. This normalization adjustment is intended to bring the time to that which a qualified worker, working at standard performance, would have taken.

There are several ways of recording the observer's rating. The most common is on a scale which uses a rating of 100 to represent standard performance. If an observer rates a particular observation of the time to perform an element at 100, the time observed is the actual time which anyone working at standard performance would take. If the rating was lower than 100, a person working at standard performance would have taken less time, and if the rating was higher than 100, the person working at standard performance would have taken more time.

Figure A2.4 shows the results of a simple study. Ten observations of a four-element task were taken and each observed time rated.

Step 2 – adjusting the observed times

The adjustment to normalize the observed time is:

$$\frac{\text{observed rating}}{\text{standard rating}}$$

where standard rating is 100 on the common rating scale we are using here.

For example, if:

The observed time = 130 mins
The observed rating = 90

$$\text{The basic time} = 1.30 \times \frac{90}{100} = 1.17 \text{ mins}$$

Figure A2.5 shows the data from the previous study but with the observed times adjusted to derive individual basic times.

Job _Pack 20 x pt # 73/2A_ .....   Location _Packing Dept._ ....   Observer _FWT_ ....

Element		Observation										Average basic time	Allowances	Element standard time
		1	2	3	4	5	6	7	8	9	10			
Make box	Observed time	0.71	0.71	0.71	0.69	0.75	0.68	0.70	0.72	0.70	0.68			
	Rating	90	90	90	90	80	90	90	90	90	90			
	Basic time													
Pack x 20	Observed time	1.30	1.32	1.25	1.33	1.33	1.28	1.32	1.32	1.30	1.30			
	Rating	90	90	100	90	90	90	90	90	90	90			
	Basic time													
Seal and secure	Observed time	0.53	0.55	0.55	0.56	0.53	0.53	0.60	0.55	0.49	0.51			
	Rating	90	90	90	90	90	90	85	90	100	100			
	Basic time													
Assemble outer,	Observed time	1.12	1.21	1.20	1.25	1.41	1.27	1.11	1.15	1.20	1.23			
fix and label	Rating	100	90	90	90	90	90	100	100	90	90			
	Basic time													

Raw standard time ☐

Allowances for total job ☐ % ☐

Standard time for job ☐ SM

Figure A2.4 Time study on a packing task – raw data

Step 3 – Average the basic times

In spite of the adjustments made to the observed times through the rating mechanism, each separately calculated basic time will not be the same. This is not necessarily a function of inaccurate rating, or even the vagueness of the rating procedure itself; it is a natural phenomenon of the time taken to perform tasks. Any human activity cannot be repeated in *exactly* the same time on every occasion. There will be some 'natural' variation in the time taken which is caused by minor variations in the speed or manner in which the job is performed. Usually this variation is positively skewed (*see* Fig. A2.6).

The positive skewing of the variation is intuitively explained by the fact that while there is a theoretical lower limit to the time necessary to perform any task, a time faster than which it is feasible to go, there is theoretically no upper limit to how long a task can take.

Figure A2.7 shows how the data from the study described previously can be further manipulated to give average basic times for each element in the job. These are the basic times which are used to derive the standard time for the job. Figure A2.7 also shows how the standard time is calculated by including the allowances (low in this example) for each element.

Synthesis from elemental data

'A work measurement technique for building up the time for a job at a defined level of performance by totalling element times obtained previously from the studies in other jobs containing the elements concerned or from synthetic data.'

Job _Pack 20 x pt. # 73/2A_ . . . . . . Location _Packing Dept._ . . . . Observer _FWT_ . . . .

Element		Observation										Average basic time	Allowances	Element standard time
		1	2	3	4	5	6	7	8	9	10			
Make box	Observed time	0.71	0.71	0.71	0.69	0.75	0.68	0.70	0.72	0.70	0.68			
	Rating	90	90	90	90	80	90	90	90	90	90			
	Basic time	0.64	0.64	0.63	0.62	0.60	0.61	0.63	0.65	0.63	0.61			
Pack x 20	Observed time	1.30	1.32	1.25	1.33	1.33	1.28	1.32	1.32	1.30	1.30			
	Rating	90	90	100	90	90	90	90	90	90	90			
	Basic time	1.17	1.19	1.25	1.20	1.20	1.15	1.19	1.19	1.17	1.17			
Seal and secure	Observed time	0.53	0.55	0.55	0.56	0.53	0.53	0.60	0.55	0.49	0.51			
	Rating	90	90	90	90	90	90	85	90	100	100			
	Basic time	0.48	0.50	0.50	0.50	0.48	0.48	0.51	0.50	0.49	0.51			
Assemble outer,	Observed time	1.12	1.21	1.20	1.25	1.41	1.27	1.11	1.15	1.20	1.23			
fix and label	Rating	100	90	90	90	90	90	100	100	90	90			
	Basic time	1.12	1.09	1.08	1.13	1.27	1.14	1.11	1.15	1.08	1.21			

Raw standard time

Allowances for total job   %

Standard time for job   SM

Figure A2.5 Time study of a packing task with basic times calculated at each observation

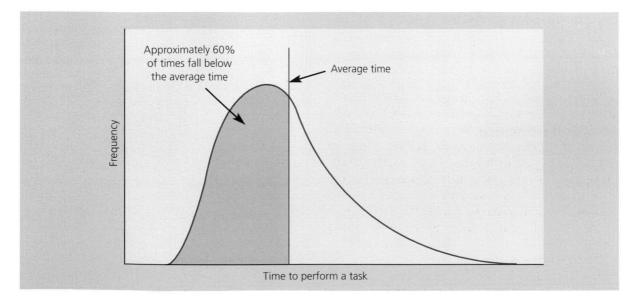

Figure A2.6 The distribution of the time taken to perform most human-influenced tasks is positively skewed

Job _Pack 20 x pt # 73/2A_   Location _Packing Dept._   Observer _FWT_

Element		Observation										Average basic time	Allowances	Element standard time
		1	2	3	4	5	6	7	8	9	10			
Make box	Observed time	0.71	0.71	0.71	0.69	0.75	0.68	0.70	0.72	0.70	0.68			
	Rating	90	90	90	90	80	90	90	90	90	90			
	Basic time	0.64	0.64	0.63	0.62	0.60	0.61	0.63	0.65	0.63	0.61	0.626	10%	0.689
Pack x 20	Observed time	1.30	1.32	1.25	1.33	1.33	1.28	1.32	1.32	1.30	1.30			
	Rating	90	90	100	90	90	90	90	90	90	90			
	Basic time	1.17	1.19	1.25	1.20	1.20	1.15	1.19	1.19	1.17	1.17	1.168	12%	1.308
Seal and secure	Observed time	0.53	0.55	0.55	0.56	0.53	0.53	0.60	0.55	0.49	0.51			
	Rating	90	90	90	90	90	90	85	90	100	100			
	Basic time	0.48	0.50	0.50	0.50	0.48	0.48	0.51	0.50	0.49	0.51	0.495	10%	0.545
Assemble outer,	Observed time	1.12	1.21	1.20	1.25	1.41	1.27	1.11	1.15	1.20	1.23			
fix and label	Rating	100	90	90	90	90	90	100	100	90	90			
	Basic time	1.12	1.09	1.08	1.13	1.27	1.14	1.11	1.15	1.08	1.21	1.138	12%	1.275

Raw standard time	3.817
Allowances for total job	5%
Standard time for job	4.01 SM

Figure A2.7 Time study of a packing task – standard time for the whole task calculated

Predetermined motion-time systems (PMTS)

'A work measurement technique whereby times established for basic human motions (classified according to the nature of the motion and the conditions under which it is made) are used to build up the time for a job at a defined level of performance.'

Analytical estimating

'A work measurement technique, being a development of estimating whereby the time required to carry out the elements of a job at a defined level of performance is estimated from knowledge and experience of the elements concerned.'

Activity sampling

'A technique in which a large number of instantaneous observations are made over a period of time of a group of machines, processes or workers. Each observation records what is happening at that instant and the percentage of observations recorded for a particular activity or delay is a measure of the percentage of time during which that activity or delay occurs.'

APPENDIX 3
THE RECORDING TECHNIQUES OF METHOD STUDY

In Chapter 9 a flow process chart was used as an illustration of one of the many techniques of work study which can be used to record the present method of doing a job. The flow process chart was chosen because it is probably the best known and most used of these techniques. Nevertheless, there are others which deserve at least a mention. Most of these techniques can be used for several purposes but tend to focus on one particular purpose – namely recording the sequence of tasks, recording the time relationships between different parts of a job, and recording the movement of staff, information or materials within the job.

Those techniques which focus primarily on determining the sequence of tasks include:

- outline process charts
- flow process charts
- two-handed process charts.

Those which concentrate primarily on the time relationships between parts of a job include:

- multiple-activity charts
- simo charts.

Those which concentrate on the movement of elements within the job include:

- memo-motion analysis
- micro-motion analysis
- flow diagrams.

Process charts

The flow process chart described in Chapter 9 used the five symbols to describe the sequence of tasks as either operations, inspections, transportations, delays or storages. In fact there are three types of process chart – outline process charts, flow process charts, and two-handed process charts. The symbols may have marginally different meanings, depending on which of these charts is being used. Process charts can be applied to the flow of materials or information through a job, or alternatively can be used to chart the sequence of activities done by the member of staff. Table A3.1 gives the meanings of each symbol for each kind of process chart.

For example, a job might need both a material (or information) flow process chart and a staff flow process chart to describe it completely. Figure A3.1 gives an example of this for the job of adjusting and packing a test meter where each meter is adjusted to a customer's particular requirements.

Outline process charts

Sometimes as a precursor to a full flow process chart, a job might be described by means of an outline process chart. An outline process chart adopts the same principles as the flow process chart but uses only the operation and inspection symbols and often aggregates several small tasks into one overall operation. Figure A3.2 shows an outline process chart for the assembling and packing operation described previously.

Two-handed process chart

The two-handed process chart again adopts the same principles but this time on a more micro

Table A3.1 The symbols used in process charts

Symbol	Outline process chart	Flow process chart (for staff)	Flow process chart (for materials)	Two-handed process chart
●	Operation	Operation	Operation	Operation
➡	Not used	Transportation	Transportation	Transportation
◗	Not used	Delay	Delay	Delay
■	Inspection	Inspection	Inspection	Not used
▼	Not used	Not used	Storage	Hold

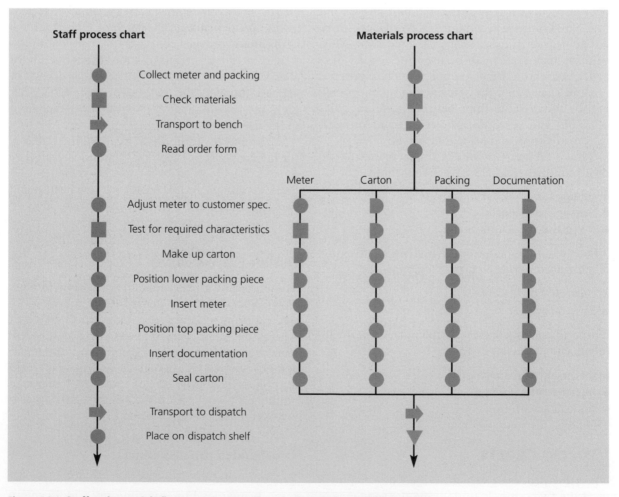

Figure A3.1 **Staff and materials flow process charts for an adjustment and packing task**

Figure A3.2 **Outline process chart for adjustment and packing task**

scale. The sequence of motion of each hand is charted using the same symbols as before. There are slight changes to the meaning of the symbols, however. The delay symbol is used to indicate that the hand is waiting to carry out its next task. The storage symbol is used to indicate that the hand is holding on to a piece of material or a document. Usually two-handed process charts are shown on a pre-formatted diagram similar to that shown in Fig. A3.3. Here a particular assembly job is described by recording the activities of each hand during the total job. The advantage of using a pre-formatted diagram such as this is that the analysis also gives an indication of the relationship of the activities performed by each hand.

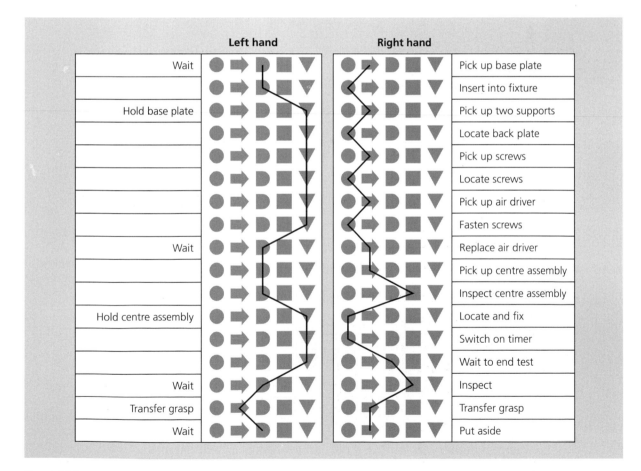

Figure A3.3 **Two-handed process chart**

Time relationship techniques

This idea of describing the time relationship between parts of the job is carried further with techniques such as multiple-activity charts and micro-motion analysis.

Multiple-activity charts

Often jobs involve either more than one member of staff and/or machines. It is sometimes necessary to record and understand the interrelationships between these different resources in the job. To do this, multiple-activity charts are used to record activities against the same time scale, placing the 'time map' for each resource against each other to make comparison easy. For example, Fig. A3.4 shows a multiple-activity chart for two people changing and adjusting a machine used to slit paper reels into smaller reels.

The simo chart

The principles behind the multiple-activity chart and the two-handed process chart may be combined in a simo chart. Whereas the two-handed process chart has a separate line for each element in the job, the simo chart is drawn on a time-based scale. This allows the job designer to see the relative time taken by each part of the job. Figure A3.5 shows a simo chart for the same job that was described in Fig. A3.3.

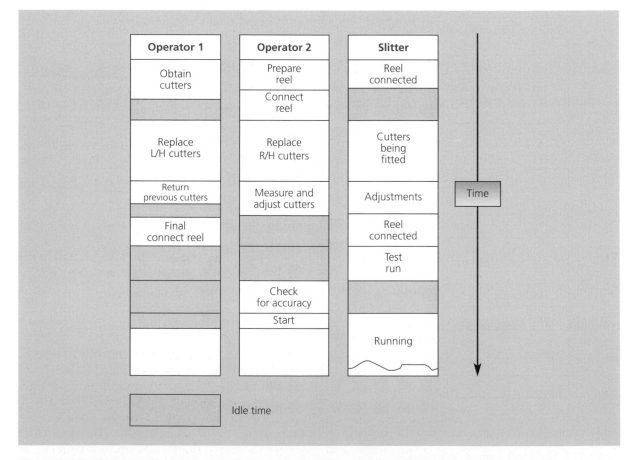

Figure A3.4 Multiple-activity chart for a two-person crew changing a slitting machine

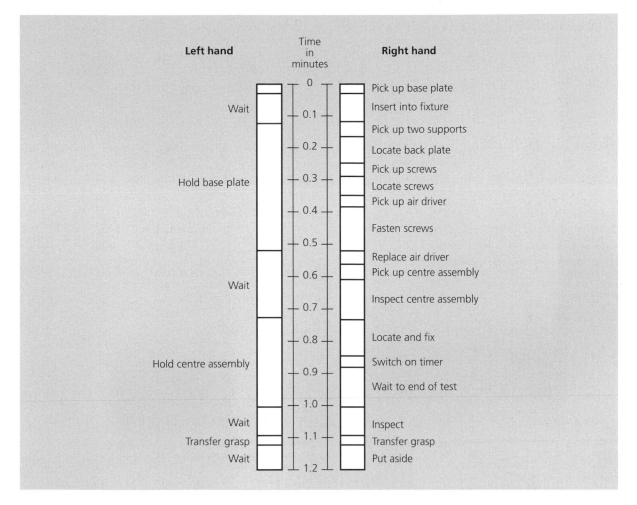

Figure A3.5 Simo chart

Path of movement techniques

In some jobs the path of movement of materials, information or staff is the major concern of the job designer. Work study provides a number of techniques which can be used to track the movement of resources.

Memo-motion video recording

One of the most convenient ways to record the path of movement of any aspect of a job is to record long periods of the job using video cameras. A speeded up play-back of the recording can then compress hours of activity into a few minutes. More importantly, the path of movement within the job can be recorded on charts or plans of the area of work.

Micro-motion analysis

The same principle can be used in the opposite way. For the examination of every detail of fast work (for example, the hand movements in a complicated routine assembly task) video recording of the task can be slowed down to allow the job designer to trace the exact path of movement of the hands during the job. Again, this path can be superimposed on a diagram or picture of the workplace.

INDEX